APICS Strategic Management of Resources References Sourcebook

Excerpts taken from:

Operations and Process Management: Principles and Practice for Strategic Impact, Second Edition
by Nigel Slack, Stuart Chambers, Robert Johnston, and Alan Betts

Financial and Managerial Accounting, Second Edition
by Charles T. Horngren, Walter T. Harrison, and M. Suzanne Oliver

Custom Publishing

New York   Boston   San Francisco
London   Toronto   Sydney   Tokyo   Singapore   Madrid
Mexico City   Munich   Paris   Cape Town   Hong Kong   Montreal

Pearson
Custom Publishing
is a division of

PEARSON

www.pearsonhighered.com

ISBN 10: 0-558-37464-6
ISBN 13: 978-0-558-37464-8

Contents

Preface

Acknowledgments

Part I OPERATIONS & PROCESS MANAGEMENT

Part II FINANCIAL & MANAGERIAL ACCOUNTING

Part III CRAFTING & EXECUTING STRATEGY

Part IV OPERATIONS & SUPPLY MANAGEMENT

Part V ARTICLES – HBR

Part VI GREENER MGMT INT'L

Preface

The APICS Certified in Production and Inventory Management program reference compilation text: *Strategic Management of Resources (SMR) References Sourcebook*, was created to effectively present a varied amount of resource information in a convenient, accessible format for instructors, developers, and exam candidates. Though published texts form the basis of this reference anthology, there was also a desire to provide relevant published materials in all topic areas.

APICS wished to minimize the number of individual reference materials for the SMR module and was extremely pleased to have the professional assistance of Pearson Custom Publishing to help pull it all together. The finished product is a compilation of four major reference books plus all required technical papers in one complete text.

It is the hope of APICS and the SMR Exam Committee that users of this text find this format both easy to use and comprehensive. We expect that studying for the SMR exam or teaching the concepts and principles contained in the SMR module will be facilitated by this single-resource approach. We appreciate your feedback and comments.
Thank you very much.

David Rivers
David Rivers; SMR Chair 2008–2010

Strategic Management of Resources Committee
Stephen N. Chapman, Ph.D., CFPIM
Craig M. Gustin, Ph.D., CFPIM, CIRM, CSCP
Frank Montabon, Ph.D., CPIM, CIRM, CSCP
Rebecca A. Morgan, CFPIM
Andrew Stephen Nourse, CPIM
David Rivers, CFPIM, CIRM, CSCP

About APICS The Association for Operations Management

APICS The Association for Operations Management is the global leader and premier source of the body of knowledge in operations management, including production, inventory, supply chain, materials management, purchasing, and logistics. Since 1957, individuals and companies have relied on APICS for its superior training, internationally recognized certifications, comprehensive resources, and worldwide network of accomplished industry professionals. For more information about APICS, visit www.apics.org

APICS Certified in Production and Inventory Management Program (CPIM)

The APICS CPIM program takes an in-depth look at the production and inventory activities within the internal operations of a company.   The APICS CPIM courseware provides an intense review of certification topics including essential terminology, concepts, and strategies related to demand management, master scheduling, quality control, and continuous improvement. For more information about the APICS CPIM program, visit www.apics.org/cpim.

Acknowledgments

Grateful acknowledgment is made to the following sources for permission to reprint material copyrighted or controlled by them:

Excerpts reprinted from *Crafting and Executing Strategy: The Quest for Competitive Advantage: Concepts and Cases*, Sixteenth Edition, by Arthur Thompson, A.J. Strickland III, and John Gamble (2007), The McGraw-Hill Companies.

Excerpts reprinted from *Operations & Supply Management*, Twelfth Edition, by F. Robert Jacobs, Richard B. Chase, and Nicholas J. Aquilano (2008), The McGraw-Hill Companies.

"Strategy and Society: The Link between Competitive Advantage and Corporate Social Responsibility," by Michael E. Porter and Mark R. Kramer, reprinted from *Harvard Business Review* (December 2006), Harvard Business School Publishing.

"The Contradictions that Drive Toyota's Success," by Hirotaka Takeuchi, Emi Osono, and Norihiko Shimizu, reprinted from *Harvard Business Review* (June 2008), Harvard Business School Publishing.

"The Secrets to Successful Strategy Execution," by Gary L. Neilson, Karla L. Martin, and Elizabeth E. Powers, reprinted from *Harvard Business Review* (June 2008), Harvard Business School Publishing.

"Leading Change: Why Transformation Efforts Fail," by John Kotter, reprinted from *Harvard Business Review* (2007), Harvard Business School Publishing.

"EMS and Sustainable Development: A Model and Comparative Studies of Integration," by Ulku Oktem et al., reprinted from *Greener Management International, ABI/INFORM Global* (summer 2004), Greenleaf Publishing.

"Current Operational Practices of U.S. Small & Medium-Sized Enterprises in Europe," by Edmund Prater and Soumen Ghosh, reprinted from *Journal of Small Business Management* (2005), Blackwell Publishing, Ltd.

"Lean Accounting & Finance," by Orest Fiume and Jean Cunningham, reprinted from *Target* 18, no. 4 (2002).

Part I

Taken from *Operations and Process Management: Principles and Practice for Strategic Impact,* Second Edition by Nigel Slack, Stuart Chambers, Robert Johnston and Alan Betts

Introduction

Operations and process management is about how organizations produce goods and services. Everything you wear, eat, use or read comes to you courtesy of the operations managers who organized its production, as does every bank transaction, hospital visit and hotel stay. The people who produced them may not always be called operations managers, but that is what they really are. Within the operations function of any enterprise, operations managers look after the processes that produce products and services. But managers in other functions, such as Marketing, Sales and Finance, *also* manage processes. These processes often supply internal 'customers' with services such as marketing plans, sales forecasts, budgets, and so on. In fact

Source: Flying Colours/Digital Vision/Getty

parts of all organizations are made up of processes. That is what this book is about – the tasks, issues and decisions that are necessary to manage processes effectively, both within the operations function and in other parts of the business where effective process management is equally important. This is an introductory chapter, so we will examine some of the basic principles of operations and process management. The model that is developed to explain the subject is shown in Figure 1.1.

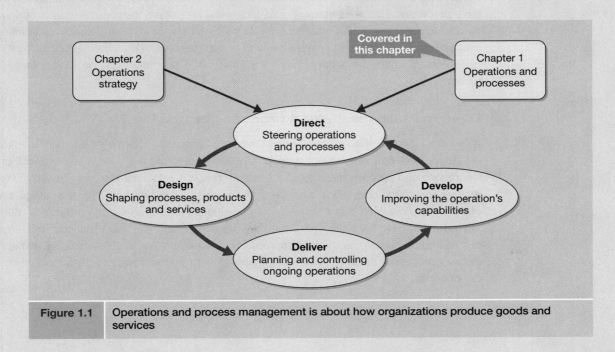

Figure 1.1   Operations and process management is about how organizations produce goods and services

Executive summary

VIDEO
further detail

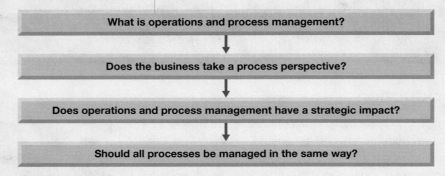

Decision logic chain for operations and processes

Each chapter is structured around a set of diagnostic questions. These questions suggest what you should ask in order to gain an understanding of the important issues of a topic, and as a result, improve your decision making. An executive summary, addressing these questions, is provided below.

What is operations and process management?

The operations function is the part of the organization that produces products or services. Every organization has an operations function because every organization produces some mixture of products and services. 'Operations' is not always called by that name, but whatever its name, it is always concerned with managing the core purpose of the business – producing some mix of products and services. Processes also produce products and services, but on a smaller scale. They are the component parts of operations. But other functions also have processes that need managing. In fact *every* part of *any* business is concerned with managing processes. All managers have something to learn from studying operations and process management, because the subject encompasses the management of all types of operation, no matter in what sector or industry, and all processes, no matter in which function.

Does the business take a process perspective?

A 'process perspective' means understanding businesses in terms of all their individual processes. It is only one way of modelling organizations, but it is a particularly useful one. Operations and process management uses the process perspective to analyze businesses at three levels: the operations function of the business, the higher and more strategic level of the supply network, and a lower, more operational, level of individual processes. Within the business, processes are only what they are defined as being. The boundaries of each process can be drawn as thought appropriate. Sometimes this involves radically reshaping the way processes are organized, for example to form end-to-end processes that fulfil customer needs.

Does operations and process management have a strategic impact?

Operations and process management can make or break a business. When they are well managed, operations and processes can contribute to the strategic impact of the business in four ways: cost, revenue, investment and capabilities. Because the operations function has responsibility for much of a business's cost base, its first imperative is to keep costs under control. But also, through the way it provides service and quality, it should be looking to enhance the business's ability to generate revenue. Also, because operations are often the source of much investment, it should be aiming to get the best possible return on that investment. Finally, the operations function should be laying down the capabilities that will form the long-term basis for future competitiveness.

Should all processes be managed in the same way?

Not necessarily. Processes differ, particularly in what are known as the four Vs: volume, variety, variation and visibility. High volume processes can exploit economies of scale and be systematized. High variety processes require enough inbuilt flexibility to cope with the wide variety of activities expected of them. High variation processes must be able to change their output levels to cope with highly variable and/or unpredictable levels of demand. High visibility processes add value while the customer is 'present' in some way and therefore must be able to manage customers' perceptions of their activities. Generally high volume together with low variety, variation and visibility facilitate low cost processes, while low volume together with high levels of variety, variation and visibility all increase process costs. Yet in spite of these differences, operations managers use a common set of decisions and activities to manage them. These activities can be clustered under four groupings: directing the overall strategy of the operation, designing the operation's products, services and processes, planning and controlling process delivery, and developing process performance.

What is operations and process management?

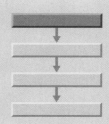

Operations and process management is the activity of managing the resources and processes that produce products and services. The core body of knowledge for the subject comes from 'operations management', which examines how the 'operations function' of a business produces products and services for external customers. We also use the shorter terms 'the operation' or 'operations' interchangeably with the 'operations function'. In some organizations an operations manager could be called by some other name, for example a 'fleet manager' in a logistics company, an 'administrative manager' in a hospital, or a 'store manager' in a supermarket.

All businesses have 'operations', because all businesses produce products, services, or some mixture of both. If you think that you don't have an operations function, you are wrong. If you think that your operations function is not important, you are also wrong. Look at the six businesses illustrated in Figure 1.2.

> **Operations principle**
> All organizations have 'operations' that produce some mix of products and services.

There are two financial service companies, two manufacturing companies and two hotels. All of them have *operations functions* that produce the things that their customers are willing to pay for. Hotels produce accommodation services, financial services invest, store, move or sell us money and investment opportunities, and manufacturing businesses physically change the shape and the nature of materials to produce products. These businesses are from different sectors (banking, hospitality, manufacturing, etc.), but the main differences between their operations activities are not necessarily what one expects. There are often bigger differences *within* economic sectors than *between* them. All the three operations in the left-hand column of the figure provide value-for-money products and services and compete largely on cost. The three in the right-hand column provide more 'up-market' products and services that are more expensive to produce and compete on some combination of

> **Operations principle**
> The economic sector of an operation is less important in determining how it should be managed than its intrinsic characteristics.

high specification and customization. The implication of this is important. It means that the surface appearance of a business and its economic sector are less important to the way its operations should be managed than its intrinsic characteristics, such as the volume of its output, the variety of different products and services it needs to produce, and, above all, how it is trying to compete in its market.

Operations *and process* management

Within the operations shown in Figure 1.2, resources such as people, computer systems, buildings and equipment will be organized into several individual 'processes'. A 'process' is an arrangement of resources that transforms inputs into outputs that satisfy (internal or external) customer needs. So, amongst other processes, banking operations contain account management processes, hotel operations contain room cleaning

Financial services

An account management centre at a large retail bank

Investment banks advise large clients on aspects of their financial strategy

Furniture manufacturing

Mass production of kitchen units

Craft production of reproduction 'antique' furniture

Hotels

Value-for-money hotel

Lobby of an international luxury hotel

Figure 1.2	All types of business have 'operations' because all businesses produce some mix of products and services. And the differences in the operations within a category of business are often greater than the differences between businesses

processes, furniture manufacturing operations contain assembly processes, and so on. The difference between *operations* and *processes* is one of scale, and therefore complexity. Both transform inputs into outputs, but processes are the smaller version. They are the component parts of operations, so the total operations function is made up of individual processes. But, within any business, the production of products and services is not confined to the operations function. For example, the marketing function 'produces' marketing plans and sales forecasts, the accounting function 'produces' budgets, the human resources function 'produces' development and recruitment plans, and so on. In fact *every* part of *any* business is concerned with managing processes. And operations and process management is the term we use to encompass the management of all types of operation, no matter in what sector or industry, and all processes, no matter in which function of the business. The general truth is that processes are everywhere, and all types of manager have something to learn from studying operations and process management.

From 'production', to 'operations', to 'operations and process' management

Figure 1.3 illustrates how the scope of this subject has expanded. Originally, operations management was seen as very much associated with the manufacturing sector. In fact it would have been called 'production' or 'manufacturing' management, and was concerned exclusively with the core business of producing physical products. Starting in the 1970s and 1980s, the term *operations management* became more common. It was used to reflect two trends. First, and most importantly, it was used to imply that many of the ideas, approaches and techniques traditionally used in the manufacturing sector could be equally applicable in the production of services. The second use of the term was to expand the scope of 'production' in manufacturing companies to include not just the core processes that directly produce products, but also the non-core production-related processes that contribute to the production and delivery of products. This would include such processes as purchasing, physical distribution, after-sales service, and so on. More recently the term *operations and process management* (or sometimes just process management) has been used to denote the shift in the scope of the subject to include the whole organization. It is a far wider term than operations management because it applies to all parts of the organization. This is very much how we treat the subject in this book. That is why it is called 'Operations and *Process* Management'. It includes the examination of the operations function in both manufacturing and service sectors and also the management of processes in non-operations functions.

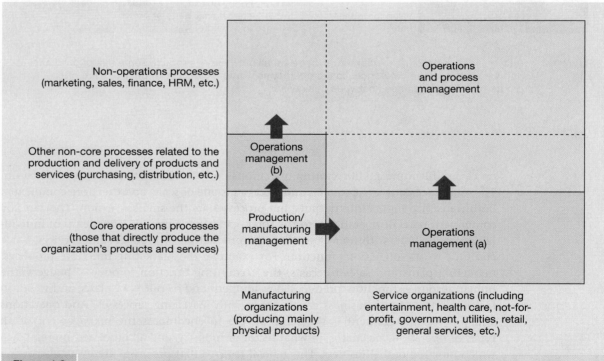

| Figure 1.3 | Operations management has expanded from treating only the core production processes in manufacturing organizations to include service organizations, non-core operations processes, and processes in other functions such as marketing, finance and HRM |

Towards the beginning of all chapters we present two examples of individual businesses, or types of business, that illustrate the topic being examined in the chapter. Here we look at two businesses – one service company and one manufacturing company – which have succeeded partly because of their creative approach to operations and process management.

Example | ## IKEA[1]

Love it or hate it, IKEA is the most successful furniture retailer ever. With 276 stores in 36 countries, most of them in Europe, the USA, Canada, Asia and Australia, they have managed to develop their own special way of selling furniture. Their stores' layout means customers often spend two hours in the store – far longer than in rival furniture retailers. IKEA's philosophy goes back to the original

Source: Vario Images GmbH & Co./Alamy

business, started in the 1950s in Sweden by Ingvar Kamprad. He built a showroom on the outskirts of Stockholm where land was cheap and simply set out the furniture as it would be in a domestic setting. Also, instead of moving the furniture from the warehouse to the showroom area, he asked customers to pickup the furniture from the warehouse themselves – still the basis of IKEA's process today.

Source: Jim Lai/AFP/Getty

The stores are all designed to facilitate the smooth flow of customers, from parking, moving through the store itself, to ordering and picking up goods. At the entrance to each store large notice-boards provide advice to shoppers who have not used the store before. There is a supervised children's play area, a small cinema, a parent and baby room and toilets. Parents can leave their children in the supervised play area for a time and are recalled via the loudspeaker system if the child has any problems. IKEA 'allows customers to make up their minds in their own time' but 'information points' have staff who can help. All furniture carries a ticket with a code number which indicates its location in the warehouse. (For larger items customers go to the information desks for assistance.) There is also an area where smaller items are displayed and can be picked directly. Customers then pass through the warehouse where they collect the items viewed in the showroom. Finally, customers pay at the checkouts, where a ramped conveyor belt moves purchases up to the checkout staff. The exit area has service points and a loading area that allows customers to bring their cars from the car park and load their purchases.

But success brings its own problems and some customers became increasingly frustrated with overcrowding and long waiting times. In response IKEA in the UK launched a £150,000,000 programme in 2006 to 'design out' the bottlenecks. The changes include:

- clearly marked in-store short cuts allowing customers who want to visit just one area to avoid having to go through all the preceding areas
- express checkout tills for customers with a bag only rather than a trolley
- extra 'help staff' at key points to assist customers
- redesign of the car parks, making them easier to navigate
- dropping the ban on taking trolleys out to the car parks for loading (originally implemented to stop vehicles being damaged)
- a new warehouse system to stop popular product lines running out during the day
- more children's play areas.

IKEA spokeswoman Nicki Craddock said: *'We know people love our products but hate our shopping experience. We are being told that by customers every day, so we can't afford not to make changes. We realized a lot of people took offence at being herded like sheep on the long route around stores. Now if you know what you are looking for and just want to get in, grab it and get out, you can.'*

Source: © Tristar Photos/Alamy

Example

Operations at Virgin Atlantic[2]

The airline business is particularly difficult to get right. Few businesses can cause more customer frustration and few businesses can lose their owners so much money. This is because running an airline, and also running the infrastructure on which the airlines depend, is a hugely complex business, where the difference between success and failure really is how you manage your operations on a day-by-day basis. In this difficult business environment one of the most

successful airlines, and one whose reputation has grown because of the way it manages its operations, is Virgin Atlantic. Part of Sir Richard Branson's Virgin group, Virgin Atlantic Airways was founded in 1984 and is owned 51 per cent by the Virgin Group and 49 per cent by Singapore Airlines. Now, the airline flies over 5,000,000 passengers each year to 30 destinations worldwide with a fleet of 38 aircraft and almost 10,000 employees.

In many ways, Virgin Atlantic can be seen as being representative of the whole Virgin story – a small newcomer taking on the giant and complacent establishment while introducing better services and lower costs for passengers, yet also building a reputation for quality and innovative service development. The company's mission statement is 'to grow a profitable airline, that people love to fly and where people love to work', and a commitment to service excellence that is reflected in the many awards it has won.

Virgin Atlantic's reputation includes a history of service innovation. It spent £100,000,000 installing its revolutionary new Upper Class suite that provides the longest and most comfortable flat bed and seat in airline history. It was also the first airline to offer business class passengers individual TVs back in 1989. It now has one of the most advanced in-flight entertainment systems of any airline with over 300 hours of video content, 14 channels of audio, over 50 CDs, audio books, and computer games on demand. The new Upper Class wing recently launched at London's Heathrow airport has a dedicated security channel exclusively for the use of Virgin Atlantic customers, enabling business passengers to speed through the terminal, moving from limousine to lounge in minutes.

Virgin Atlantic emphasizes the practical steps it is taking to make its business as sustainable as possible, using the slogan 'we recycle exhaustively, especially our profits'. This refers to the pledge given by the company's chairman, Sir Richard Branson, to invest profits over the next 10 years from the Virgin transport companies into projects to tackle climate change. '*We must rapidly wean ourselves off our dependence on coal and fossil fuels,*' Sir Richard said. '*The funds will be invested in schemes to develop new renewable energy technologies, through an investment unit called Virgin Fuels.*' Friends of the Earth welcomed Sir Richard's announcement, but the environmental pressure group also warned that the continued rapid growth in air travel could not be maintained 'without causing climatic disaster'.

What do these two examples have in common?

All the operations managers in IKEA and Virgin Atlantic will be concerned with the same basic task – managing the processes that produce their products and services. And many, if not most, of the managers in each company who are called by some other title will also be concerned with managing their own processes that contribute to the success of their business. Although there will be differences between each company's operations and processes, such as the type of services they provide, the resources they use, and so on, the managers in each company will be making the same *type* of decisions, even if *what* they actually decide is different. The fact that both companies are successful because of their innovative and effective operations also implies further commonality. First, it means that they both understand the importance of taking a 'process perspective' in understanding their supply networks, running their operations, and managing all their individual processes. Without this they could not have sustained their strategic impact in the face of stiff market competition. Second, both businesses will expect their operations to make a contribution to their overall competitive strategy. And third, in achieving a strategic impact, both will have come to understand the importance of managing *all* their individual processes throughout the business so that they too can all contribute to the business's success.

Does the business take a process perspective?

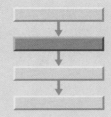

If a business takes a process perspective, it understands that all parts of the business can be seen as processes, and that all processes can be managed using operations management principles. But it is also important to understand that a process perspective is not the only way of describing businesses, or any type of organization. One could represent an organization as a conventional 'organizational structure' that shows the reporting relationships between various departments or groups of resources. But even a little experience in any organization shows that rarely, if ever, does this fully represent the organization. Alternatively one could describe an organization through the way it makes decisions – how it balances conflicting criteria, weighs up risks, decides on actions and learns from its mistakes. Or one could describe the organization's culture – its shared values, ideology, pattern of thinking and day-to-day rituals, or its power relationships – how it is governed, seeks consensus (or at least reconciliation), and so on. Or one can represent the organization as a collection of processes, interconnecting and (hopefully) all contributing to fulfilling its strategic aims. This is the perspective that we emphasize throughout this book. As we define it here, the process perspective analyzes businesses as a collection of interrelated processes. Many of these processes will be within the operations function, and will contribute directly to the production of its products and services. Other processes will be in the other functions of the business, but will still need managing using similar principles to those within the operations function. None of these individual perspectives gives a total picture of real organizations, but nor are they necessarily mutually exclusive. A process perspective does not preclude understanding the influence of power relationships on how processes work, and so on. Each perspective adds something to our ability to understand and therefore more effectively manage a business.

> **Operations principle**
> There are many valid approaches to describing organizations. The process perspective is a particularly important one.

We use the process perspective here, not because it is the only useful and informative way of understanding businesses, but because it is the perspective that directly links the way we manage resources in a business with its strategic impact. Without effective process management, the best strategic plan can never become reality. The most appealing promises made to clients or customers will never be fulfilled. Also the process perspective has traditionally been undervalued. The subject of operations and process management has only recently come to be seen as universally applicable and, more importantly, universally valuable.

So, operations and process management is relevant to all parts of the business

If processes exist everywhere in the organization, operations and process management will be a common responsibility of all managers irrespective of which function they are in. Each function will have its 'technical' knowledge, of course. In Marketing this includes the market expertise needed for designing and shaping marketing plans; in Finance it includes the technical knowledge of financial reporting conventions. Yet each will also have an *operations* role that entails using its processes to produce plans, policies, reports and services. For example, the marketing function has processes with inputs of market information, staff, computers, and so on. Its staff transform the information into outputs such as marketing plans, advertising campaigns and sales force organizations. In this sense all functions are operations with their own collection of processes.

> **Operations principle**
> All parts of the business manage processes so all parts of the business have an operations role and need to understand operations management.

The implications of this are very important. Because every manager in all parts of an organization is, to some extent, an operations manager, they should all want to give good service to their customers, and they will all want to do this efficiently. So, operations management must be relevant for all functions, units and groups within the organization. And the concepts, approaches and techniques of operations management can help to improve any process in any part of the organization.

The 'input–transformation–output' model

> **Operations principle**
> All processes have inputs of transforming and transformed resources that they use to create products and services.

Central to understanding the processes perspective is the idea that all processes transform *inputs* into *outputs*. Figure 1.4 shows the *general transformation process model* that is used to describe the nature of processes. Put simply, processes take in a set of input resources, some of which are transformed into outputs of products and/or services and some of which do the transforming.

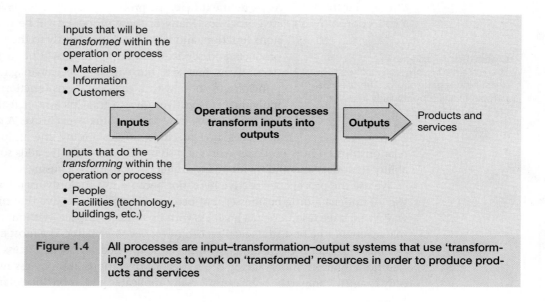

Inputs that will be *transformed* within the operation or process
- Materials
- Information
- Customers

Inputs → **Operations and processes transform inputs into outputs** → **Outputs** → Products and services

Inputs that do the *transforming* within the operation or process
- People
- Facilities (technology, buildings, etc.)

Figure 1.4 All processes are input–transformation–output systems that use 'transforming' resources to work on 'transformed' resources in order to produce products and services

Process inputs

Transformed resource inputs are the resources that are changed in some way within a process. They are usually materials, information or customers. For example, one process in a bank prints statements of accounts for its customers. In doing so, it is processing materials. In the bank's branches, customers are processed by giving them advice regarding their financial affairs, cashing their cheques, etc. However, behind the scenes, most of the bank's processes are concerned with processing information about its customers' financial affairs. In fact, for the bank's operations function as a whole, its information transforming processes are probably the most important. As customers, we may be unhappy with badly printed statements and we may even be unhappy if we are not treated appropriately in the bank. But if the bank makes errors in our financial transactions, we suffer in a far more fundamental way.

There are two types of *transforming* resource that form the 'building blocks' of all processes. They are *facilities* – the buildings, equipment, plant and process technology of the operation – and *people* – who operate, maintain, plan and manage the operation.

The exact nature of both facilities and people will differ between processes. In a five-star hotel, the facilities consist mainly of buildings, furniture and fittings. In a nuclear-powered aircraft carrier, the facilities are the nuclear generator, turbines and sophisticated electronic detection equipment. Although one operation is relatively 'low-technology' and the other 'high-technology', their processes all require effective, well-maintained facilities. People also differ between processes. Most staff employed in a domestic appliance assembly process may not need a very high level of technical skill, whereas most staff employed by an accounting firm in an audit process are highly skilled in their own particular 'technical' skill (accounting). Yet although skills vary, all staff have a contribution to make to the effectiveness of their operation. An assembly worker who consistently misassembles refrigerators will dissatisfy customers and increase costs just as surely as an accountant who cannot add up.

Process outputs

All processes produce products and services, and although products and services are different, the distinction can be subtle. Perhaps the most obvious difference is in their respective tangibility. Products are usually tangible (you can physically touch a television set or a newspaper) whereas services are usually intangible (you cannot touch consultancy advice or a haircut, although you may be able to see or feel the results). Also, services may have a shorter stored life. Products can usually be stored for a time – some food products for only a few days, and some buildings for hundreds of years. But the life of a service is often much shorter. For example, the service of 'accommodation in a hotel room for tonight' will 'perish' if it is not sold before tonight – accommodation in the same room tomorrow is a different service.

The three levels of analysis

Operations and process management uses the process perspective to analyze businesses at three levels. The most obvious level is that of the business itself, or more specifically the operations function of the business. The other functions of the business could also be treated at this level, but that would be beyond the scope of this book. And, while analyzing

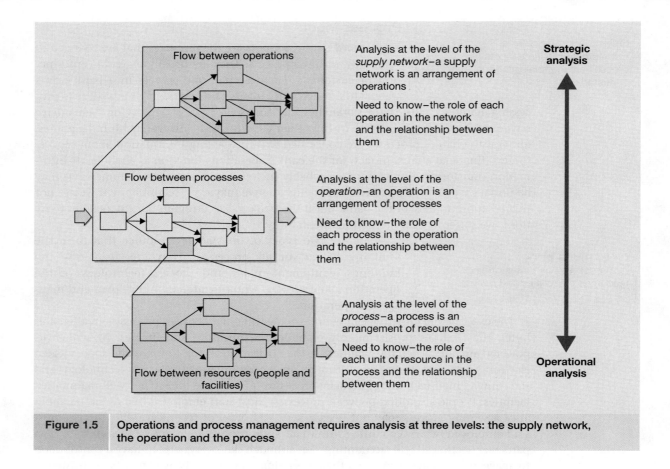

Figure 1.5 Operations and process management requires analysis at three levels: the supply network, the operation and the process

Operations principle
A process perspective can be used at three levels: the level of the operation itself, the level of the supply network and the level of individual processes.

the business at the level of the operation is important, for a more comprehensive assessment we also need to analyze the contribution of operations and process management at a higher and more strategic level (the level of its supply network) and at a lower, more operational level (the level of the individual processes). These three levels of operations analysis are shown in Figure 1.5.

The process perspective at the level of the operation

The operations part of a business is itself an input–transformation–output system, which transforms various inputs to produce (usually) a range of different products and services. Table 1.1 shows some operations described in terms of their main inputs, the purpose of their operations, and their outputs. Note how some of the inputs to the operation are transformed in some way while other inputs do the transforming. For example, an airline's aircraft, pilots, air crew and ground crew are brought into the operation in order to act on passengers and cargo and change (transform) their location. Note also how in some operations customers themselves are inputs. (The airline, department store and police department are all like this.) This illustrates an important distinction between operations whose customers receive their outputs without seeing inside the operation, and those whose customers are inputs to the operation and therefore have some visibility of the operation's processes. Managing high-visibility operations where the customer is inside the operation

Table 1.1	Some operations described in terms of their inputs, purpose and outputs		
Type of operation	What are the operation's inputs?*	What does the operation do?	What are the operation's outputs?
Airline	Aircraft Pilots and air crew Ground crew *Passengers* *Cargo*	Move passengers and freight around the world	Transported passengers and freight
Department store	*Goods for sale* Staff sales Computerized registers *Customers*	Display goods Give sales advice Sell goods	Customers and goods 'assembled' together
Police department	Police officers Computer systems *Information* *Public (law-abiding and criminal)*	Prevent crime Solve crime Apprehend criminals	Lawful society Public with feeling of security
Frozen food manufacturer	*Fresh food* Operators Food-processing equipment Freezers	Food preparation Freeze	Frozen food

*Input resources that are transformed are printed in *italics*.

usually involves a different set of requirements and skills from those whose customers never see inside the operation. (We will discuss this issue of visibility later in this chapter.)

Most operations produce both products and services

Some operations produce just products and others just services, but most operations produce a mixture of the two. Figure 1.6 shows a number of operations positioned in a spectrum from almost 'pure' goods producers to almost 'pure' service producers. Crude oil producers are concerned almost exclusively with the product that comes from their oil wells. So are aluminium smelters, but they might also produce some services such as technical advice. To an even greater extent, machine tool manufacturers produce services such as technical advice and applications engineering services as well as products. The services produced by restaurants are an essential part of what the customer is paying for. They both manufacture food and provide service. A computer systems services company may produce software 'products', but more so, it is providing an advice and customization service to its customers. A management consultancy, although producing reports and documents, would see itself largely as a service provider. Finally, some pure services do not produce products at all. A psychotherapy clinic, for example, provides therapeutic treatment for its customers without any physical product.

> **Operations principle**
> Most operations produce a mixture of tangible products and intangible services.

Services and products are merging

Increasingly the distinction between services and products is both difficult to define and not particularly useful. Even the official statistics compiled by governments have difficulty in separating products and services. Software sold on a disk is classified as a product.

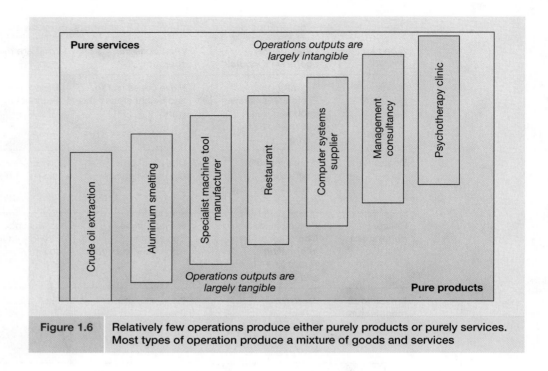

Figure 1.6   Relatively few operations produce either purely products or purely services. Most types of operation produce a mixture of goods and services

FURTHER EXAMPLE

The same software sold over the Internet is a service. Some authorities see the essential purpose of all businesses, and therefore all operations, as being to 'serve customers'. Therefore, they argue, all operations are service providers who may (or may not) produce products as a means of serving their customers. Our approach in this book is close to this. We treat operations and process management as being important for all organizations. Whether they see themselves as manufacturers or service providers is very much a secondary issue.

The process perspective at the level of the supply network

Any operation can be viewed as part of a greater network of operations. It will have operations that supply it with the products and services it needs to make its own products and services. And unless it deals directly with the end consumer, it will supply customers who themselves may go on to supply their own customers. Moreover, any operation could have several suppliers and/or several customers and may be in competition with other operations producing similar services to those it produces itself. This collection of operations is called the supply network.

There are three important issues to understand about any operation's supply network. First, it can be complex. Operations may have a large number of customers and suppliers who themselves have large numbers of customers and suppliers. Also, the relationships between operations in the supply network can be subtle. One operation may be in direct competition with another in some markets while at the same time acting as collaborators or suppliers to each other in others. Second, theoretically the boundaries of any operation's supply chain can be very wide indeed. They could go back to the operation that digs raw material out of the ground and go forward to the ultimate reuse and/or disposal of a product. Sometimes it is necessary to do this (for example, when considering the environmental sustainability of products), but generally some kind of boundary to the network needs to be set so that more attention can be given to the most immediate operations in the network. Third, supply networks are always changing. Not only do operations sometimes lose customers and win others, or change their suppliers, they also may acquire operations that once were their customers or suppliers, or sell parts of their business, so converting them into customers or suppliers.

Thinking about operations management in a supply network context is a particularly important issue for most businesses. The overarching question for any operations manager is 'Does my operation make a contribution to the supply network as a whole?'. In other words, are we a good customer to our suppliers in the sense that the long-term cost of supply to us is reduced because we are easy to do business with? Are we good suppliers to our customers in the sense that, because of our understanding of the supply network as a whole, we understand their needs and have developed the capability to satisfy them? Because of the importance of the supply network perspective, we deal with it twice more in this book: at a strategic level in Chapter 3 where we discuss the overall design of the supply network, and at a more operational level in Chapter 7 where we examine the role of the supply chain in the delivery of products and services.

The process perspective at the level of the individual process

Because processes are smaller versions of operations, they have customers and suppliers in the same way as whole operations. So we can view any operation as a network of individual processes that interact with each other, with each process being, at the same time, an internal supplier and an internal customer for other processes. This 'internal customer' concept provides a model to analyze the internal activities of an operation. If the whole operation is not working as it should, we may be able to trace the problem back along this internal network of customers and suppliers. It can also be a useful reminder to all parts of the operation that, by treating their internal customers with the same degree of care that they exercise on their external customers, the effectiveness of the whole operation can be improved.

Many of the examples used in our treatment of operations and process management are 'operations processes' in that they are part of the operations function. But some are

Table 1.2	Some examples of processes in non-operations functions		
Organizational function	Some of its processes	Outputs from its process	Customer(s) for its outputs
Marketing and sales	Planning process Forecasting process	Marketing plans Sales forecasts	Senior management Sales staff, planners, operations
	Order taking process	Confirmed orders	Operations, finance
Finance and accounting	Budgeting process Capital approval processes Invoicing processes	Budget Capital request evaluations Invoices	Everyone Senior management, requestees External customers
Human resources management	Payroll processes Recruitment processes Training processes	Salary statements New hires Trained employees	Employees All other processes All other processes
Information technology	Systems review process Help desk process System implementation project processes	System evaluation Advice Implemented working systems and aftercare	All other processes All other processes All other processes

'non-operations processes' and are part of some other function. And it is worth empha-sizing again that these processes also need managing, using the same principles. Table 1.2 illustrates just some of the processes that are contained within some of the more com-mon non-operations functions, the outputs from these processes and their 'customers'.

'End-to-end' business processes

There is one particularly important thing to understand about processes – we can define them in any way we want. The boundaries between processes, the activities that they perform, and the resources that they use are all there because they have been designed in that way. It is common in organizations to find processes defined by the type of activity they engage in, for example invoicing processes, product design processes, sales processes, warehousing processes, assembly processes, painting processes, etc. This can be convenient because it groups similar resources together. But it is only one way of drawing the boundaries between processes. Theoretically, in large organizations there must be almost an infinite number of ways that activities and resources could be collected together as distinct processes. One way of redefining the boundaries and responsibilities of processes is to consider the 'end-to-end' set of activities that satisfies defined customer needs. Think about the various ways in which a business satisfies its customers. Many different activities and resources will probably contribute to 'producing' each of its products and services. Some authorities recommend grouping the activities and resources together in an end-to-end manner to satisfy each defined customer need. This approach is closely identified with the 'business process engineering' (or re-engineering) move-ment (examined in Chapter 13). It calls for a radical rethink of process design that will probably involve taking activities and resources out of different functions and placing them together to meet customer needs. Remember, though, that designing processes around end-to-end customer needs is only one way (although often the sensible one) of designing processes.

> **Operations principle**
> Processes are defined by how the organization chooses to draw process boundaries.

FURTHER EXAMPLE

Example | The Programme and Video Division (PVD)

A broadcasting company has several divisions including various television and radio channels (entertainment and news), a 'general services' division that includes a specialist design workshop, and the 'Programme and Video Division' (PVD) that makes programmes and videos for a number of clients including the television and radio channels that are part of the same company. The original ideas for these programmes and videos usually come from the clients who commission them, al-though PVD itself does share in the creative input. The business is described at the three levels of analysis in Figure 1.7.

At the level of the operation
The division produces products in the form of tapes, discs and media files, but its real 'product' is the creativity and 'artistry' captured in the programmes. 'We provide a service,' says the division's boss, 'that interprets the client's needs (and sometimes their ideas), and transforms them into appealing and appropriate shows. We can do this because of the skills, experience and creativity of our staff, and our state-of-the-art technology.'

At the level of the supply network
The division has positioned itself to specialize in certain types of product, including children's pro-grammes, wildlife programmes and music videos. 'We did this so that we could develop a high level of expertise in a few relatively high margin areas. It also reduces our dependence on our own broadcasting channels. Having specialized in this way we are better positioned to partner and do

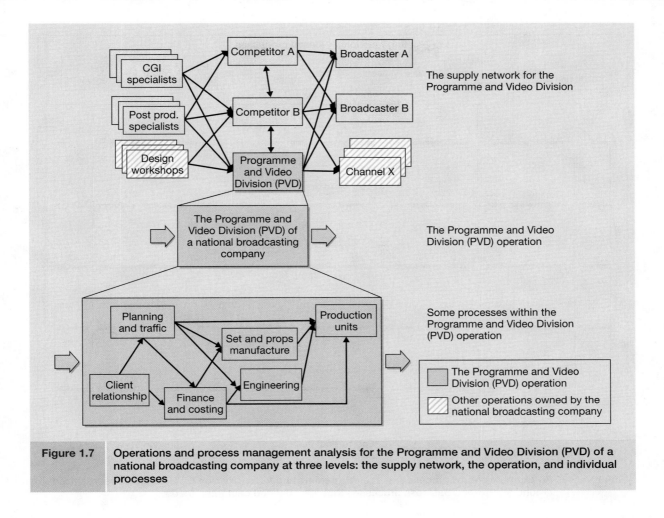

Figure 1.7   Operations and process management analysis for the Programme and Video Division (PVD) of a national broadcasting company at three levels: the supply network, the operation, and individual processes

work for other programme makers who are our competitors in some other markets. Specialization has also allowed us to outsource some activities such as computer graphic imaging (CGI) and post-production that are no longer worth keeping in-house. However, our design workshop became so successful that they were "spun out" as a division in their own right and now work for other companies as well as ourselves.'

At the level of individual processes
Many smaller processes contribute directly or indirectly to the production of programmes and videos, including the following:

- The planning and traffic department that acts as the operations management for the whole operation, drawing up schedules, allocating resources and 'project managing' each job through to completion
- Workshops that manufacture some of the sets, scenery and props for the productions
- Client liaison staff who liaise with potential customers, test out programme ideas and give information and advice to programme makers
- An engineering department that cares for, modifies and designs technical equipment
- Production units that organize and shoot the programmes and videos
- The finance and costing department that estimates the likely cost of future projects, controls operational budgets, pays bills and invoices customers.

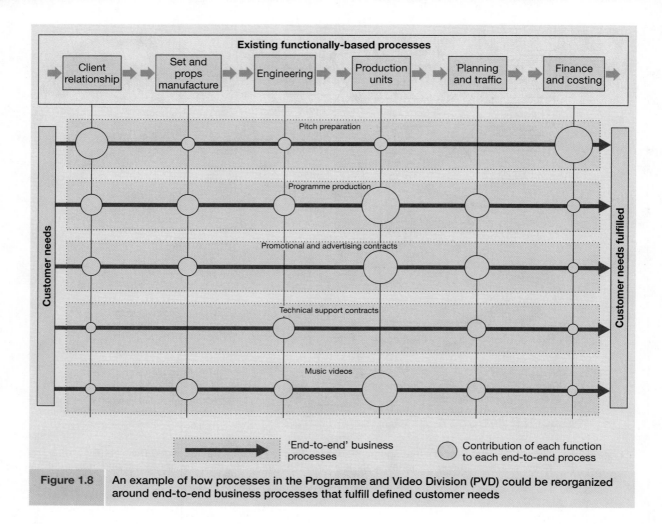

Figure 1.8   An example of how processes in the Programme and Video Division (PVD) could be reorganized around end-to-end business processes that fulfill defined customer needs

Creating end-to-end processes

PVD produces various products and services that fulfill customer needs. Each of these, to different extents, involves several of the existing departments within the company. For example, preparing a 'pitch' (a sales presentation that includes estimates of the time and cost involved in potential projects) needs contributions mainly from Client Relations and the Finance and Costing departments, but also needs smaller contributions from other departments. Figure 1.8 illustrates the contribution of each department to each product or service. (No particular sequence is implied by Figure 1.8.) The contributions of each department may not all occur in the same order. Currently, all the division's processes are clustered into conventional departments defined by the type of activity they perform: engineering, client relationship, etc. A radical redesign of the operation could involve regrouping activities and resources into five 'business' processes that fulfill each of the five defined customer needs. This is shown diagrammatically by the dotted lines in Figure 1.8. It would involve the physical movement of resources (people and facilities) out of the current functional processes into the new end-to-end business processes. This is an example of how processes can be designed in ways that do not necessarily reflect conventional functional groupings.

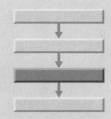

Does operations and process management have a strategic impact?

One of the biggest mistakes a business can make is to confuse 'operations' with 'operational'. Operational is the opposite of strategic; it means detailed, localized, short-term, day-to-day. Operations are the resources that produce products and services.[3] Operations can be treated at an operational *and a strategic* level. We shall examine some views of operations strategy in the next chapter. For now, we treat a fundamental question for any operation – does the way we manage operations and processes have a strategic impact? If a business does not fully appreciate the strategic impact that effective operations and process management can have, at the very least it is missing an opportunity. The IKEA and Virgin Atlantic examples earlier in this chapter are just two of many businesses that have harnessed their operations to create strategic impact.

Operations and process management can make or break a business. Although for most businesses, the operations function represents the bulk of its assets and the majority of its people, the true value of the operation is more than 'bulk'. It can 'make' the business in the sense that it gives the ability to compete through both the short-term ability to respond to customers and the long-term capabilities that will keep it ahead of its competitors. But if an operations function cannot produce its products and services effectively, it could 'break' the business by handicapping its performance no matter how it positions and sells itself in its markets.

Cost, revenue, investment and capability

The strategic importance of operations and process management is being increasingly recognized. It attracts far more attention than it did a few years ago and, according to some reports, accounts for the largest share of all the money spent by businesses on consultancy advice.[4] Partly this may be because the area has been neglected in the past. But it also denotes an acceptance that it can have both short-term and long-term impact. This can be seen in the impact that operations and process management can have on the costs, revenues, investment and capabilities of businesses.

- It can reduce the **costs** of producing products and services by being efficient. The more productive the operation is at transforming inputs into outputs, the lower will be the cost of producing a unit of output. Cost is never totally unimportant for any business, but generally the higher the cost of a product or service when compared with the price it commands in the market, the more important cost reduction will be as an operations objective. Even so, cost reduction is almost always treated as an important contribution that operations can make to the success of any business.
- It can increase **revenue** by increasing customer satisfaction through quality, service and innovation. Existing customers are more likely to be retained and new customers are more likely to be attracted to products and services if they are error-free and appropriately designed, if the operation is fast and responsive in meeting their needs and keeping its delivery promises, and if the operation can be flexible, both in customizing its products and services and in introducing new ones. It is operations that directly

influence the quality, speed, dependability and flexibility of the business, all of which have a major impact on a company's ability to maximize its revenue.

- It can ensure **effective investment** (called *capital employed*) to produce its products and services. Eventually all businesses in the commercial world are judged by the return that they produce for their investors. This is a function of profit (the difference between costs and revenues) and the amount of money invested in the business's operations resources. We have already established that effective and efficient operations can reduce costs and increase revenue, but what is sometimes overlooked is their role in reducing the investment required per unit of output. Operations and process management does this by increasing the effective capacity of the operation and by being innovative in how it uses its physical resources.

> **Operations principle**
> All operations should be expected to contribute to their business by controlling costs, increasing revenue, making investment more effective and growing long-term capabilities.

- It can **build capabilities** that will form the basis for *future* innovation by building a solid base of operations skills and knowledge within the business. Every time an operation produces a product or a service, it has the opportunity to accumulate knowledge about how that product or service is best produced. This accumulation of knowledge should be used as a basis for learning and improvement. If so, in the long term, capabilities can be built that will allow the operation to respond to future market challenges. Conversely, if an operations function is simply seen as the mechanical and routine fulfilment of customer requests, then it is difficult to build the knowledge base that will allow future innovation.

FURTHER EXAMPLE

Example   The Programme and Video Division (PVD) continued

The PVD, described earlier, should be able to identify all four ways in which its operations and processes can have a strategic impact. The division is expected to generate reasonable returns by controlling its costs and being able to command relatively high fees. *'Sure, we need to keep our costs down. We always review our budgets for bought-in materials and services. Just as important, we measure the efficiency of all our processes, and we expect annual improvements in process efficiency to compensate for any increases in input costs.* (Reducing costs) *Our services are in demand by customers because we are good to work with,'* says the division's Managing Director. *'We have the technical resources to do a really great job and we always give good service. Projects are completed on time and within budget. More importantly, our clients know that we can work with them to ensure a high level of programme creativity. That is why we can command reasonably high prices.'* (Increasing revenue) The division also has to justify its annual spend on equipment to its main board. *'We try and keep up to date with the new technology that can really make an impact on our programme making, but we always have to demonstrate how it will improve profitability.* (Effective investment) *We also try to adapt new technology and integrate it into our creative processes in some way so that gives us some kind of advantage over our competitors.'* (Build capabilities)

Operations management in not-for-profit organizations

Terms such as *competitive advantage, markets* and *business* that are used in this book are usually associated with companies in the for-profit sector. Yet operations management is also relevant to organizations whose purpose is not primarily to earn profits. Managing operations in an animal welfare charity, hospital, research organization or government department is essentially the same as in commercial organizations. However, the strategic objectives of not-for-profit organizations may be more complex and involve a mixture of political, economic, social and/or environmental objectives. Consequently, there may be a greater chance of operations decisions being made under conditions of conflicting objectives. So, for example, it is the operations staff in a children's welfare department who have to face the conflict between the cost of providing extra social workers and the risk of a child not receiving adequate protection.

FURTHER EXAMPLE

Should all processes be managed in the same way?

All processes differ in some way, so, to some extent, all processes need to be managed differently. Some of the differences between processes are 'technical' in the sense that different products and services require different skills and technologies to produce them. However, processes also differ in terms of the nature of demand for their products or services. Four characteristics of demand in particular have a significant effect on how processes need to be managed:

> **Operations principle**
> The way in which processes need to be managed is influenced by volume, variety, variation and visibility.

- The volume of the products and services produced
- The variety of the different products and services produced
- The variation in the demand for products and services
- The degree of visibility that customers have of the production of products and services.

The 'four Vs' of processes

Volume

Processes with a high volume of output will have a high degree of repeatability, and because tasks are repeated frequently it often makes sense for staff to specialize in the tasks they perform. This allows the systemization of activities, where standard procedures may be codified and set down in a manual with instructions on how each part of the job should be performed. Also, because tasks are systemized and repeated, it is often worth developing specialized technology that gives higher processing efficiencies. By contrast, low-volume processes with less repetition cannot specialize to the same degree. Staff are likely to perform a wide range of tasks, and while this may be more rewarding, it is less open to systemization. Nor is it likely that efficient, high-throughput technology could be used. The implications of this are that high-volume processes have more opportunities to produce products or services at low unit cost. So, for example, the volume and standardization of large fast-food restaurant chains such as McDonald's or KFC enables them to produce with greater efficiency than a small, local cafeteria or diner.

Variety

Processes that produce a high variety of products and services must engage in a wide range of different activities, changing relatively frequently between each activity. They must also contain a wide range of skills and technology sufficiently 'general purpose' to cope with the range of activities and sufficiently flexible to change between them. A high level of variety may also imply a relatively wide range of inputs to the process and the additional complexity of matching customer requirements to appropriate products or services. So, high-variety processes are invariably more complex and costly than low-variety ones. For example, a taxi company is usually prepared to pick up and drive customers almost anywhere (at a price); they may even take you by the route of your choice. There are an infinite number of potential routes (products) that it offers. But its cost per kilometre travelled will be higher than for a less customized form of transport such as a bus service.

Variation

Processes are generally easier to manage when they only have to cope with predictably constant demand. Resources can be geared to a level that is just capable of meeting demand. All activities can be planned in advance. By contrast, when demand is variable and/or unpredictable, resources will have to be adjusted over time. Worse still, when demand is unpredictable, extra resources will have to be designed into the process to provide a 'capacity cushion' that can absorb unexpected demand. So, for example, processes that manufacture high-fashion garments will have to cope with the general seasonality of the garment market together with the uncertainty of whether particular styles may or may not prove popular. Operations that make conventional business suits are likely to have less fluctuation in demand over time, and be less prone to unexpected fluctuations. Because processes with lower variation do not need any extra safety capacity and can be planned in advance, they generally have lower costs than those with higher variation.

Visibility

Process visibility is a slightly more difficult concept to envisage. It indicates how much of the processes are 'experienced' directly by customers, or how much the process is 'exposed' to its customers. Generally processes that act directly on customers (such as retail or health-care processes) will have more of their activities visible to their customers than those that act on materials and information. However, even material and information-transforming processes may provide a degree of visibility to the customers. For example, parcel distribution operations provide Internet-based 'track and trace' facilities to enable their customers to have visibility of where their packages are at any time. Low-visibility processes, if they communicate with their customers at all, do so using less immediate channels such as the telephone or the Internet. Much of the process can be more 'factory-like'. The time lag between customer request and response could be measured in days rather than the near-immediate response expected from high-visibility processes. This lag allows the activities in a low-visibility process to be performed when it is convenient to the operation, so achieving high utilization. Also, because the customer interface needs managing, staff in high-visibility processes need customer contact skills that shape the customer's perception of process performance. For all these reasons high-visibility processes tend to have higher costs than low-visibility processes.

Many operations have both high- and low-visibility processes. This serves to emphasize the difference that the degree of visibility makes. For example, in an airport some of its processes are relatively visible to its customers (check-in desks, information desks, restaurants, passport control, security staff, etc.). These staff operate in a high-visibility 'front-office' environment. Other processes in the airport have relatively little, if any, customer visibility (baggage handling, overnight freight operations, loading meals on to the aircraft, cleaning, etc.). We rarely see these processes but they perform the vital but low-visibility tasks in the 'back-office' part of the operation.

The implications of the four Vs of processes

All four dimensions have implications for processing costs. Put simply, high volume, low variety, low variation and low visibility all help to keep processing costs down. Conversely, low volume, high variety, high variation and high customer contact generally carry some kind of cost penalty for the process. This is why the volume dimension is drawn with its 'low' end at the left, unlike the other dimensions, to keep all the 'low cost' implications on the right. Figure 1.9 summarizes the implications of such positioning.

FURTHER EXAMPLE

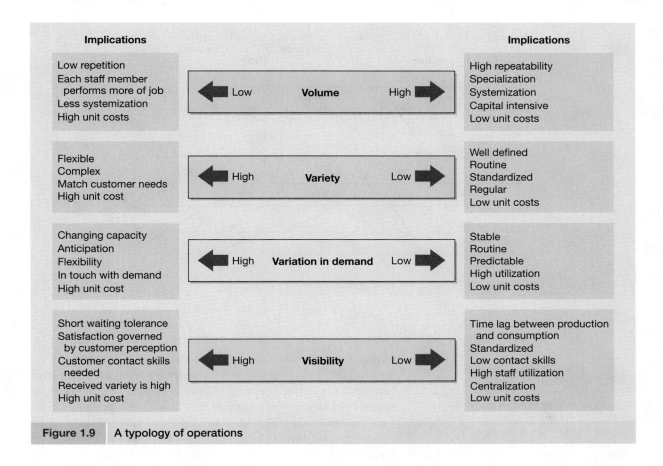

Figure 1.9　A typology of operations

Charting processes using the four Vs

In almost any operation, processes can be identified that have different positions on the four dimensions, and which therefore have different objectives and will need managing in different ways. To a large extent the position of a process on the four dimensions is determined by the demand of the market it is serving. However, most processes have some discretion in moving themselves on the dimensions. Look at the different positions on the visibility dimension that retail banks have adopted. At one time, using branch tellers was the only way customers could contact a bank. Now access to the bank's services could be through (in decreasing order of visibility) a personal banker who visits your home or office, a conversation with a branch manager, the teller at the window, telephone contact through a call centre, Internet banking services or an ATM cash machine. These other processes offer services that have been developed by banks to serve different market needs.

Figure 1.10 illustrates the different positions on the four Vs for some retail banking processes. Note that the personal banking/advice service is positioned at the high-cost end of the four Vs. For this reason such services are often offered only to relatively wealthy customers that represent high profit opportunities for the bank. Note also that the more recent developments in retail banking such as call centres, Internet banking and ATMs all represent a shift towards the low-cost end of the four Vs. New processes that exploit new technologies can often have a profound impact on the implications of each dimension. For example, Internet banking, when compared with an ATM cash machine, offers a far higher variety of options for customers, but because the process is automated through its information technology, the cost of offering this variety is less than at a conventional branch or even a call centre.

PRACTICE NOTE

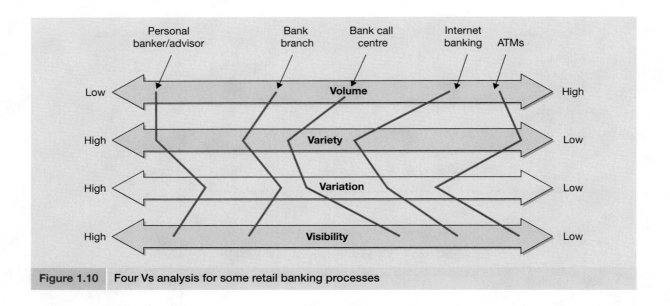

Figure 1.10   Four Vs analysis for some retail banking processes

A model of operations and process management

Managing operations and processes involves a whole range of separate decisions that will determine their overall purpose, structure and operating practices. These decisions can be grouped together in various ways. Look at other books on operations management and you will find many different ways of structuring operations decisions and therefore the subject as a whole. Here we have chosen to classify activities into four broad groups, relating to four broad activities. Although there are some overlaps between these four categories, they more or less follow a sequence that corresponds to the life cycle of operations and processes.

- **Directing** the overall strategy of the operation. A general understanding of operations and processes and their strategic purpose, together with an appreciation of how strategic purpose is translated into reality (direct), is a prerequisite to the detailed design of operations and process.
- **Designing** the operation's products, services and processes. Design is the activity of determining the physical form, shape and composition of operations and processes together with the products and services that they produce.
- Planning and control process **delivery**. After being designed, the delivery of products and services from suppliers and through the total operation to customers must be planned and controlled.
- **Developing** process performance. Increasingly it is recognized that operations and process managers cannot simply routinely deliver products and services in the same way that they have always done. They have a responsibility to develop the capabilities of their processes to improve process performance.

We can now combine two ideas to develop the model of operations and process management that will be used throughout this book. The first is the idea that *operations* and the *processes* that make up both the operations and other business functions are transformation systems that take in inputs and use process resources to transform them into outputs. The second idea is that the resources both in an organization's operations as a

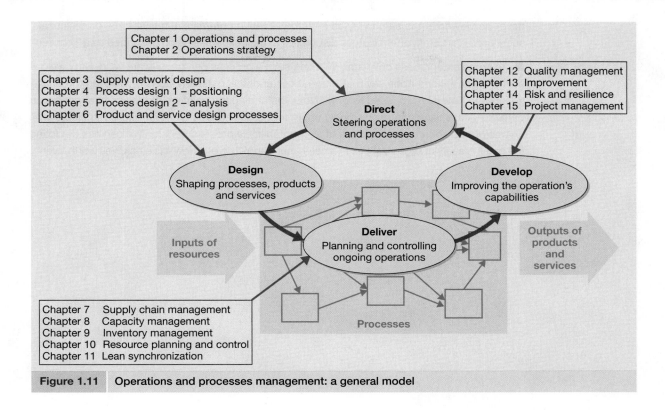

Chapter 1 Operations and processes
Chapter 2 Operations strategy

Chapter 3 Supply network design
Chapter 4 Process design 1 – positioning
Chapter 5 Process design 2 – analysis
Chapter 6 Product and service design processes

Chapter 12 Quality management
Chapter 13 Improvement
Chapter 14 Risk and resilience
Chapter 15 Project management

Direct
Steering operations
and processes

Design
Shaping processes, products
and services

Develop
Improving the operation's
capabilities

Inputs of
resources

Deliver
Planning and controlling
ongoing operations

Outputs of
products
and
services

Processes

Chapter 7 Supply chain management
Chapter 8 Capacity management
Chapter 9 Inventory management
Chapter 10 Resource planning and control
Chapter 11 Lean synchronization

Figure 1.11   Operations and processes management: a general model

whole and in its individual processes need to be managed in terms of how they are *direct-ed*, how they are *designed*, how *delivery* is planned and controlled, and how they are *developed* and improved. Figure 1.11 shows how these two ideas go together. This book will use this model to examine the more important decisions that should be of interest to all managers of operations and processes.

Critical commentary

Each chapter contains a short critical commentary on the main ideas covered in the chapter. Its purpose is not to undermine the issues discussed in the chapter, but to emphasize that, although we present a relatively orthodox view of operations, there are other perspectives.

■ The central idea in this introductory chapter is that all organizations have operations (and other functions) that have processes that produce products and services, and that all these processes are essentially similar. However, some believe that by even trying to characterize organizations in this way (perhaps even by calling them 'processes') one loses or distorts their nature and depersonalizes or takes the 'humanity' out of the way in which we think of the organization. This point is often raised in not-for-profit organizations, especially by 'professional' staff. For example the head of one European 'Medical Association' (a doctors' Trade Union) criticized hospital authorities for expecting a 'sausage factory service based on productivity targets'. No matter how similar they appear on paper, it is argued, a hospital can never be viewed in the same way as a factory. Even in commercial businesses, professionals, such as creative staff, often express discomfort at their expertise being described as a 'process'.

■ To some extent these criticisms of taking such a process perspective are valid. How we describe organizations does say much about our underlying assumptions of what an 'organization' is and how it is supposed to work. Notwithstanding the point we made earlier about how a purely process view can misleadingly imply that organizations are neat and controllable with unambiguous boundaries and lines of accountability, a process perspective can risk depicting the messy reality of organizations in a naive manner. Yet, in our view it is a risk well worth taking.

Summary checklist

This checklist comprises questions that can be usefully applied to any type of operations and reflect the major diagnostic questions used within the chapter.

☐ Is the operations function of the business clearly defined?

☐ Do operations managers realize that they are operations managers even if they are called by some other title?

☐ Do the non-operations functions within the business realize that they manage processes?

☐ Does everyone understand the inputs, activities and outputs of the processes of which they are part?

☐ Is the balance between products and services produced by the operations function well understood?

☐ Are future changes that may occur in the balance between products and services produced by the operation understood?

☐ What contribution is operations making towards reducing the cost of products and services?

☐ What contribution is operations making towards increasing the revenue from products and services?

☐ What contribution is operations making towards better use of capital employed?

☐ How is operations developing its capability for future innovation?

☐ Does the operation understand its position in the overall supply network?

☐ Does the operation contribute to the overall supply network?

☐ Are the individual processes that comprise the operations function defined and understood?

☐ Are individual processes aware of the internal customer and supplier concept?

☐ Do they use the internal customer and supplier concept to increase their contribution to the business as a whole?

☐ Do they use the ideas and principles of operations management to improve the performance of their processes?

☐ Has the concept of end-to-end business processes been examined and considered?

☐ Are the differences (in terms of volume, variety, variation and visibility) between processes understood?

☐ Are the volume, variety, variation and visibility characteristics of processes reflected in the way they are managed?

Case study AAF Rotterdam

'Our growth over the last two or three years has just been amazing. We have clients all over Europe and although many of the jobs we are now doing are more challenging they are far more interesting. We are also now making a good operating profit, even if almost all of it is being swallowed up to fund our growth. Our biggest problem is now adapting ourselves in a way that is appropriate for a larger company. We aren't just a group of friends having a good time any more; we need to become a profession-al business.' The speaker was Marco Van Hopen, one of the three directors of AAF, a theatrical services company, based just outside Rotterdam in The Netherlands. He had founded the company with two friends in 1999 when they decided to make a busi-ness out of their interest in theatrical and stage design. *'It's the combination of skill and adrenalin that I like,'* said Marco. *'Because most events are live there is no chance for a second take; all the equipment must work first time, on time, and every time. Also, there has recently been a dramatic increase in the sophistication of the technology we use, such as programmable automated lighting units.'*

Source: Martin Leeuwner, betsy@wedolife.com

Background

From the original three founders of the company, AAF had now grown to employ 16 full-time employees together with over 20 freelance crew, who were hired as and when necessary. In the previous year the company's revenue had been slightly over €3,000,000 and its operating profit slightly under €200,000. It was located on an industrial estate that provided good access to the main European road network. The majority of the company's 2000 square metre building was devoted to a combined storage area and workshop. Also within the site were the administrative and technical offices and a design studio.

The company had started by hiring and selling stage equipment (mainly lighting, sound and staging equipment) to clients that ranged from small local theatrical groups through to very large production and conference compa-nies. Then it had moved into offering 'production services' that included designing, constructing and installing entire sets, particularly for conferences but also for shows and theatrical events. The majority of the company's 'produc-tion services' clients were production companies that contracted AAF as a 'second-tier' supplier on behalf of the main client, that was usually a corporation putting on its own event (for example, a sales conference). The events organized for the main client could be anywhere in the world, although AAF confined itself to European locations. As Marco Van Hopen says, *'We have succeeded in differ-entiating ourselves through offering a complete "design, build and install" service that is creative, dependable and sufficiently flexible to incorporate last-minute changes. The key skill is to articulate client requirements and trans-late these into a workable set design. This means working closely with clients. It also requires a sound technical understanding of equipment capabilities. Most important, every project is different, that's what makes it so exciting.'*

Although both parts of the business were growing, it was the production services business that was growing particularly quickly. In the previous year around 60 per cent of the company's revenue had come from hiring and selling equipment, with the remainder coming from pro-duction services. However, production services were far more profitable. *'The large production jobs may be 40 per cent of our revenue but last year they accounted for almost 80 per cent of our profits. Some people ask me why we don't focus on production services, but we will never get out of hiring and sales. Partly this is because we have over €1,000,000 invested in the equipment, partly it is because it provides us with a steady and relatively predictable stream of income, but mostly it is because we need access to the latest equipment in order to win production services contracts. However, in the near future our own production services work could be the biggest "customer" for our hire and sales business.'* (Van Hopen)

The workshop and store

The combined workshop and storage area was seen as the heart of the company's operations. Equipment was stored on high-level racks in predetermined locations. A team of eight technicians prepared hire equipment for customers and delivered it to customer sites (about 80 per cent of all orders were delivered, the rest being collected from the AAF site by customers themselves). About 30 per cent of customers, usually the smaller ones, also required the equipment to be installed. The technicians also checked the equipment on return from the customer and carried out any repairs or maintenance that was required. As the equipment had become more sophisticated, the job of preparing, installing and maintaining hire equipment had also become far more technically demanding. These technicians used the workshop area, adjacent to the storage area, to calibrate equipment, pre-program lighting sequences and carry out any repairs. The workshop, which had recently been re-equipped with new wood- and metal-working equipment, was also used to construct the sets used for production services' clients. Two employees worked almost full-time on this, but equipment technicians could also be used for set construction if it was required. If workshop facilities were needed by both equipment hire and production services at the same time, usually production services were given priority, an arrangement that was not always to the liking of the equipment hire technicians.

Design studio

The design studio used computer-aided design equipment and simulations that could predict the effects of different lighting configurations. Although Marco Van Hopen was involved in the design process for many jobs, the company now also employed one full-time and one part-time designer: *'We often bring clients to the design studio to test various ideas on them using our simulation and projection facilities. It is a great way to get clients to visualize the set design and "bring them into" the design process.'*

Administrative and crew offices

The administration office received orders from hire and sales customers as well as providing the first point of contact for production services' clients. Three full-time employees organized the company's operations, sched-uled work for the workshop and crew, sent out invoices and generally managed the business. In addition two part-time account assistants were employed to do cost estimates for the more complex 'production services' jobs. Adjacent to the administrative office was the 'crew office', an area for the production crew to plan the logistics required to ensure efficient installation of sets. *'The crew office is the nerve centre of all the project management that goes into a good service. It is a focal point for designers, workshop people and crew to come together.'* (Van Hopen)

Problems

Although excited by the recent growth of the company and its future prospects, Van Hopen was also concerned that the company should be able to improve its profitability: *'There's no point in growing and doing exciting things if we can't also make money out of it. I realize that, by its nature, growth is expensive. However, I think maybe that we have let our costs slip out of control. We need to be able to get more out of what we already have, and the best way to do this is to get ourselves organized. The main problem is that our activities are getting less predictable. The hire and sales business is basically routine, and although some of our clients can be late in placing their orders, it is largely predictable. Not only do we have a wide range of equipment, we also have excellent relationships with other sound and lighting companies, so that, if we can only partially fulfill a customer's order, we can hire any other equipment we need from our competitors. This may reduce our profits slightly, but we keep the client happy. The irony is that we don't seem to be able to achieve similar levels of flexibility within our own company. This is important now that production services are growing quickly. We have fewer production services contracts (48 last year, compared with almost 3000 hire contracts) but they are complex and you cannot always predict exactly what you will need to complete them. We have succeeded in growing the production services business partly because of the quality of our designs where we put a lot of time and effort into working closely with the client before we submit a final design, but also because we have built up a reputation for dependability. Clients trust us to be totally reliable. This means that sometimes our crews have to be flexible and sometimes work through the night in order to get things ready on time. But we are paying for this flexibility in terms of excessive hours worked. What we perhaps should consider is improving the agility with which we move people out of the store and workshop area and on to fulfilling production services contracts when necessary. I don't know how it would work yet, I just feel that by working together more we could increase our ability to take on more work without increasing our cost base.'*

QUESTIONS

1 Do you think Marco Van Hopen understands the importance of operations to his business?

2 What contribution does he seem to expect from his operations?

3 Sketch out how you see the supply network for AAF and AAF's position within it.

4 What are the major processes within AAF, and how do they relate to each other?

5 Evaluate Van Hopen's idea of increasing the flexibility with which the different parts of the company work with each other.

Active case study   EleXon Computers

ACTIVE CASE

Since its inception 17 years ago, EleXon computers has grown and diversified from a small unit assembling and selling computers primarily within the UK into a much larger international company serving a much wider and more diverse market. Despite its growth, the underlying organization of the company has not changed. The inadequacy of existent systems and processes has become increasingly obvious and increasingly a source of tension within and between departments.

● How would you re-organize the operations and processes to satisfy their differing perspectives and demands?

Please refer to the Active case on the CD accompanying this book to listen to the frustrations of each department.

Applying the principles

HINTS

Some of these exercises can be answered by reading the chapter. Others will require some general knowledge of business activity and some might require an element of investigation. All have hints on how they can be answered on the CD accompanying this book.

1 Quentin Cakes makes about 20,000 cakes per year in two sizes, both based on the same recipe. Sales peak at Christmas time when demand is about 50 per cent higher than in the quieter summer period. The customers (the stores that stock the company's products) order their cakes in advance through a simple Internet-based ordering system. Knowing that there is some surplus capacity, one of the customers has approached the company with two potential new orders.

(a) The *Custom Cake* option – this would involve making cakes in different sizes where consumers could specify a message or greeting to be 'iced' on top of the cake. The consumer would give the inscription to the store which would e-mail it through to the factory. The customer thought that demand would be around 1000 cakes per year, mostly at celebration times such as St Valentine's Day and Christmas.

(b) The *Individual Cake* option – this option involves Quentin Cakes introducing a new line of very small cakes intended for individual consumption. Demand for this individual-sized cake was forecast to be around 4000 per year, with demand likely to be more evenly distributed throughout the year than its existing products.

The total revenue from both options is likely to be roughly the same and the company has the capacity to adopt only one of the two ideas. But which one should it be?

2 Described as having *'revolutionized the concept of sandwich making and eating'*, Prêt A Manger opened its first shop in the mid-1980s, in London. Now it has over 130 shops in the UK, New York, Hong Kong and Tokyo. The company says that its secret is to focus continually on quality, in all its activities. *'Many food retailers focus on extending the shelf life of their food, but that's of no interest to us. We maintain our edge by selling food that simply can't be beaten for freshness. At the end of the day, we give whatever we haven't sold to charity to help feed those who would otherwise go hungry.'* The first Prêt A Manger shop had its own kitchen where fresh ingredients were delivered first thing every morning, and food was prepared throughout the day. Every Prêt shop since has followed this model. The team members serving on the tills at lunchtime will have been making sandwiches in the kitchen that morning. The company rejected the idea of a huge centralized sandwich factory even though it could significantly reduce costs. Prêt also owns and manages all its shops directly so that it can ensure consistently high standards. *'We are determined never to forget that our hardworking people make all the difference. They are our heart and soul. When they care, our business is sound. If they cease to care, our business goes down the drain. We work hard at building great teams. We take our reward schemes and career opportunities very seriously. We don't work nights (generally), we wear jeans, we party!'*

- Do you think Prêt A Manger fully understands the importance of its operations management?
- What evidence is there for this?
- What kind of operations management activities at Prêt A Manger might come under the four headings of direct, design, deliver and develop?

3 Visit a furniture store (other than IKEA). Observe how the shop operates – for example, where customers go, how staff interact with them, how big it is, how the shop has chosen to use its space, what variety of products it offers, and so on. Talk with the staff and managers if you can. Think about how the shop that you have visited is different from IKEA. Then consider the question:

- What implications do the differences between IKEA and the shop you visited have for their operations management?

4 Write down five services that you have 'consumed' in the last week. Try to make these as varied as possible. Examples could include public transport, a bank, any shop or supermarket, attendance at an education course, a cinema, a restaurant, etc. For each of these services, ask yourself the following questions.

- Did the service meet your expectations? If so, what did the management of the service have to do well in order to satisfy your expectations? If not, where did they fail? Why might they have failed?
- If you were in charge of managing the delivery of these services, what would you do to improve the service?
- If they wanted to, how could the service be delivered at a lower cost so that the service could reduce its prices?
- How do you think that the service copes when something goes wrong (such as a piece of technology breaking down)?
- Which other organizations might supply the service with products and services? (In other words, they are your 'supplier', but who are *their* suppliers?)
- How do you think the service copes with fluctuation of demand over the day, week, month or year?

These questions are just some of the issues which the operations managers in these services have to deal with. Think about the other issues they will have to manage in order to deliver the service effectively.

5 Find a copy of a financial newspaper (*Financial Times, The Wall Street Journal, The Economist*, etc.) and identify one company that is described in the paper that day.

- What do you think would be the main operations issues for that company?

Notes on chapter

1 'Ikea plans to end "stressful shopping"' (2006), *London Evening Standard*, 24 April.
2 Source: Virgin Atlantic website.
3 Slack, N. and Lewis, M.A. (2002), *Operations Strategy,* Financial Times Prentice Hall, Harlow, UK.
4 Source: *The Economist,* 22 March 1997.

Taking it further

Chase, R.B., Aquilano, N.J. and Jacobs, F.R. (2001) *Production and Operations Management: Manufacturing and services* (9th edn), Unwin/McGraw-Hill. There are many good general textbooks on operations management. This was one of the first and is still one of the best, though written very much for an American audience.

Hammer, M. and Stanton, S. (1999) *How Process Enterprises Really Work,* Harvard Business Review, November–December. Hammer is one of the gurus of process design. This paper is typical of his approach.

Heizer, J. and Render, B. (1999) *Operations Management* (5th edn), Prentice Hall, New Jersey. Another good US-authored general text on the subject.

Johnston, R., Chambers, S., Harland, C., Harrison, A. and Slack, N. (2003) *Cases in Operations Management* (3rd edn), Financial Times Prentice Hall, Harlow, UK. Many great examples of real operations management issues. Not surprisingly, based around a similar structure as this book.

Johnston, R. and Clark, E. (2005) *Service Operations Management,* Financial Times Prentice Hall, Harlow, UK. What can we say! A great treatment of service operations from the same stable as this textbook.

Keen, P.G.W. (1997) *The Process Edge: Creating value where it counts,* Harvard Business School Press. Operations management as 'process' management.

Slack, N. and Lewis, M. (eds) (2005) *The Blackwell Encyclopedic Dictionary of Operations Management* (2nd edn), Blackwell Business, Oxford. For those who like technical descriptions and definitions.

Useful websites

www.opsman.org Definitions, links and opinions on operations and process management.

www.iomnet.org The Institute of Operations Management site. One of the main professional bodies for the subject.

www.poms.org A US academic society for production and operations management. Academic, but some useful material, including a link to an encyclopaedia of operations management terms.

www.sussex.ac.uk/users/dt31/TOMI One of the longest-established portals for the subject. Useful for academics and students alike.

www.ft.com Useful for researching topics and companies.

FURTHER RESOURCES

For further resources including examples, animated diagrams, self-test questions, Excel spreadsheets, active case studies and video materials please explore the CD accompanying this book.

OPERATIONS STRATEGY

Introduction

In the long term, the major (and some would say only) objective for operations and processes is to provide a business with some form of strategic advantage. That is why the management of a business's processes and operations and its intended overall strategy must be logically connected. Without this connection, operations and processes will be without a coherent direction and they may finish up making internal decisions that either do not reflect the business's strategy, or conflict with each other, or both. So a clear operations strategy is vital. And, although operations and process management is largely 'operational', it also has a strategic dimension that is vital if operations is to fulfil its potential to contribute to competitiveness. Figure 2.1 shows the position of the ideas described in this chapter in the general model of operations management.

Source: Denis Scott/Corbis

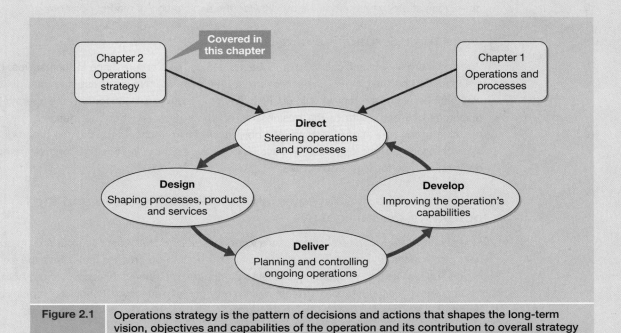

| Figure 2.1 | Operations strategy is the pattern of decisions and actions that shapes the long-term vision, objectives and capabilities of the operation and its contribution to overall strategy |

Executive summary

VIDEO
further detail

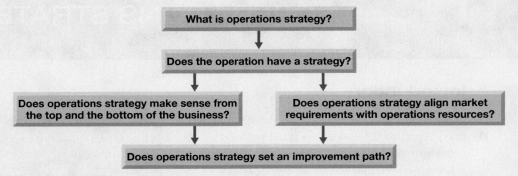

Decision logic chain for operations strategy

Each chapter is structured around a set of diagnostic questions. These questions suggest what you should ask in order to gain an understanding of the important issues of a topic, and as a result, improve your decision making. An executive summary, addressing these questions, is provided below.

What is operations strategy?

Operations strategy is the pattern of decisions and actions that shapes the long-term vision, objectives and capabilities of the operation and its contribution to overall strategy. It is the way in which operations resources are developed over the long term to create sustainable competitive advantage for the business. Increasingly, many businesses are seeing their operations strategy as one of the best ways to differentiate themselves from competitors. Even in those companies that are marketing led (such as fast-moving consumer goods), an effective operations strategy can add value by allowing the exploitation of market positioning.

Does the operation have a strategy?

Strategies are always difficult to identify because they have no presence in themselves, but are identified by the pattern of decisions that they generate. Nevertheless one can identify what an operations strategy should do. First, it should provide a vision for how the operation's resources can contribute to the business as a whole. Second, it should define the exact meaning of the operation's performance objectives. Third, it should identify the broad decisions that will help the operation achieve its objectives. Finally, it should reconcile strategic decision with performance objectives.

Does operations strategy make sense from the top and the bottom of the business?

Operations strategy can be seen both as a top-down process that reflects corporate and business strategy through to a functional level, and as a bottom-up process that allows the experience and learning at an operational level to contribute to strategic thinking. Without both of these perspectives, operations strategy will be only partially effective. It should communicate both top to bottom *and* bottom to top throughout the hierarchical levels of the business.

Does operations strategy align market requirements with operations resources?

The most important short-term objective of operations strategy is to ensure that operations resources can satisfy market requirements. But this is not the only objective. In the longer term, operations strategy must build the capabilities within its resources that will allow the business to provide something to the market that its competitors find difficult to imitate or match. These two objectives are called the market requirements perspective and the operations resource capability perspective. The latter is very much influenced by the resource-based view (RBV) of the firm. The objective of operations strategy can be seen as achieving 'fit' between these two perspectives.

Does operations strategy set an improvement path?

The purpose of operations strategy is to improve the business's performance relative to that of its competitors in the long term. It therefore must provide an indication of how this improvement is to take place. This is best addressed by considering the trade-offs between performance objectives in terms of the 'efficient frontier' model. This describes operations strategy as a combination of repositioning performance along an existing efficient frontier, and increasing overall operations effectiveness by overcoming trade-offs to expand the efficient frontier.

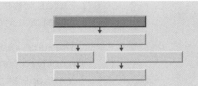

DIAGNOSTIC QUESTION

What is operations strategy?

Operations strategy is the pattern of decisions and actions that shapes the long-term vision, objectives and capabilities of the operation and its contribution to the overall strategy of the business.[1] The term 'operations strategy' sounds at first like a contradiction. How can 'operations', a subject that is generally concerned with the day-to-day creation and delivery of goods and services, be strategic? 'Strategy' is usually regarded as the opposite of those day-to-day routine activities. But, as we indicated in the previous chapter, *'operations'* is not the same as *'operational'*. 'Operations' are the resources that create products and services. 'Operational' is the opposite of strategic, meaning day-to-day and detailed.

Perhaps more significantly, many of the businesses that seem to be especially competitively successful, and that appear to be sustaining their success into the longer term, have a clear and often inventive operations strategy. Just look at some of the high-profile companies quoted in this book, or that feature in the business press. From Tesco to Wal-Mart, from Ryanair to TNT, it is not just that their operations strategy provides these companies with adequate support; it is their operations strategy that is the pivotal reason for their competitive superiority. Yet not all businesses compete so directly through their operations. Some are more marketing led. Consumer product companies like Coca-Cola or Heinz are more marketing driven. But even these types of business need a strong operations strategy. Their brand position may be shaped in the consumer's mind by their promotional activities, but it would soon erode if they could not deliver products on time, or if their quality was sub-standard, or if they could not introduce new products in response to market trends. With this type of business, operations strategy may not be the pre-eminent factor in driving their strategy, but it is still important, and without it their marketing efforts would come to almost nothing.

Look at these two examples of businesses with operations strategies that are clear and explicit and have contributed to their competitive success.

Example

Flextronics[2]

Well-known brand names such as Nokia and Dell are increasingly using electronic manufacturing services (EMS) companies which specialize in providing the outsourced design, engineering, manufacturing and logistics operations for the big brand names. Among the biggest of these is Flextronics, a global company based in Singapore that offers the broadest worldwide EMS capabilities, from design to end-to-end vertically integrated global supply chain services. Operating in

One of Flextronics' industrial parks

Source: Flextronics International Ltd

30 countries, with a workforce that includes approximately 3600 design engineers and revenue of over US$30 billion, Flextronics recently took over Solectron, one of its main rivals.

Flextronics' operations strategy must balance its customers' need for low costs (electronic goods are often sold in a fiercely competitive market) with the need for responsive and flexible service (electronics markets can also be volatile). The company achieves this through a number of strategies. First, it has an extensive network of design, manufacturing and logistics facilities in the world's major electronics markets, giving it significant scale and the flexibility to move activities to any of its locations to fulfil customer requirements. The majority of its manufacturing capacity is located in low-cost regions such as Brazil, China, Hungary, India, Malaysia, Mexico and Poland. Second, it has organized its operations into seven market-focused organizations, such as computing, consumer digital, industrial, medical, and so on. Third, Flextronics offers vertical integration capabilities that simplify the global product development and supply processes and provide meaningful time and cost savings. This moves a product from its initial design through volume production, test, distribution and into post-sales service and support.

Finally, Flextronics has developed integrated Industrial Parks to exploit fully the advantages of its global, large-scale, high-volume capabilities. Positioned in low-cost regions, yet close to all major world markets, Flextronics Industrial Parks can significantly reduce the cost of production. Locations include Gdansk in Poland, Zalaegerszeg and Sárvár in Hungary, Guadalajara in Mexico, Sorocaba in Brazil, Chennai in India and Shanghai in China. Flextronics' own suppliers are encouraged to locate within these Parks, from which products can be produced on site and shipped directly to customers, greatly reducing freight costs of incoming components and outgoing products. Products not produced on site can be obtained from Flextronics' network of regional manufacturing facilities located near the Industrial Parks. Using this strategy, Flextronics says it can provide cost-effective delivery of finished products within 1-2 days of orders. Reducing the lag-time on incoming and outgoing shipping in this way gives customers flexibility and responsiveness, which in turn helps the company to meet consumer demands, as well as decreasing time-to-market.

Example　TNT[3]

Headquartered in the Netherlands, TNT serves more than 200 countries and employs more than 161,500 people, around half of whom work for Royal TNT Post (the Dutch postal service, for which TNT has the concession) and half for the rest of the TNT group. In total, it is an €11 billion business that provides business customers and consumers worldwide with an *'extensive range of services for their mail and express delivery needs'*. TNT states its mission as *'to exceed its customers' expectations in the transfer of their goods and documents around the world. TNT delivers value to its clients by providing the most reliable and efficient solutions through delivery networks'*.

At its most basic, TNT is in the business of transferring goods and documents around the world, tailoring its services to its customers' requirements, and focusing on the speed of its total deliveries and the dependability of its pick-up and delivery times. It is TNT's business to deliver its customers 'business' swiftly, safely, in good condition, at the right time and at the right place. It does this by picking up, transporting, sorting, handling, storing and delivering documents, packets, parcels and freight. In doing so, it uses a combination of physical operations processes such as depots and trucks, electronic technology and processes such as billing and track-and-trace systems, and commercial processes such as financial and customer-care processes.

TNT calls its strategy 'Focus on Networks', meaning simply that the group will focus on what TNT regards as its core strength – providing delivery services by expertly managing delivery networks. In practice TNT's portfolio of networks has different speed characteristics, ranging from *same*-day to *some* day, and different weight characteristics, ranging from letters to heavy parcels and pallets. TNT's Express business focuses on transferring documents, parcels and pallets that require time- or day-certain delivery, while TNT's Mail business focuses on transferring documents with day-uncertain delivery. (However, in practice, in the Netherlands almost 100 per cent of deliveries are next day.)

TNT's networks are also in different phases of development. In Europe, TNT is steadily building on its existing Express and Mail networks organically, as well as through selected acquisitions.

TNT's most mature business is its Mail network in the Netherlands, where its main objective is to maintain its market leadership in a declining market with increasing competition. By contrast, TNT's Express networks in Asia, such as those in India, China and South-east Asia, and other emerging markets such as Brazil, are very different and are among the least mature networks in its portfolio. In these regions TNT has the opportunity to shape the markets as they develop, grow its networks and attempt to achieve market leadership.

What do Flextronics and TNT have in common?

Neither of these companies suffered from any lack of clarity regarding what they wanted to do in the market. They are clear about what they are offering their customers (and they document it explicitly on their websites). They are also both equally clear in spelling out their operations strategy. Flextronics is willing to relocate whole operations in its commitment to responsive but low-cost customer service. TNT focuses on responsiveness and customer service by developing its networks. Without a 'top-down' strategic clarity it is difficult to achieve clarity in the way individual processes should be managed. But both these companies are also known for the way they have developed their operational-level processes to the extent that their learned expertise contributes to strategy in a 'bottom-up' manner. Also in both these cases the requirements of their markets are clearly reflected in their operations' performance objectives (responsiveness and cost for Flextronics, and dependable but responsive levels of customer service for TNT). Similarly, both businesses have defined the way in which they achieve these objectives by strategically directing their operations resources (through the type of trucks, aircraft and sorting facilities that TNT buys and through their location and supply-chain decisions in the case of Flextronics). In other words, both have reconciled their market requirements with their operations resource capabilities. These are the issues that we shall address in this chapter.

DIAGNOSTIC QUESTION

Does the operation have a strategy?

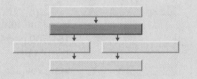

There are some problems in asking this apparently simple question. In most operations management decisions you can see what you are dealing with. You can touch inventory, talk to people, program machines, and so on. But strategy is different. You cannot see a strategy, feel it or touch it. Also, whereas the effects of most operations management decisions become evident relatively fast, it may be years before an operations strategy decision can be judged to be a success or not. Moreover any 'strategy' is always more than a single decision. Operations strategy will be revealed in the total *pattern* of decisions that a business takes in developing its operations in the long term. Nevertheless, the question is an obvious starting point and one that must be addressed by all operations.

So, what should an operations strategy do? First, it should articulate a vision of how the business's operations and processes can contribute to its overall strategy. This is something

> **Operations principle**
> Operations strategy should articulate a 'vision' for the operations function's contribution to overall strategy.

beyond the individual collection of decisions that will actually constitute the strategy. Second, it should translate market requirements into a message that will have some meaning within its operations. This means describing what customers want in terms of a clear and prioritized set of operations *performance objectives*. Third, it should identify the broad decisions that will shape the operation's capabilities, and allow their long-term development so that they will provide the basis for the business's sustainable advantage. Finally, it should explain how its intended market requirements and its strategic operations decisions are to be reconciled.

An operations strategy should articulate a vision for the operations function's contribution

The 'vision' for an operation is a clear statement of how operations intend to contribute value for the business. It is not a statement of what the operation wants to *achieve* (those are its objectives), but rather an idea of what it must *become* and what contribution it should make. A common approach to summarizing operations contribution is the Hayes and Wheelwright Four-Stage Model.[4] The model traces the progression of the operations function from what is the largely negative role of 'stage 1' operations to becoming the central element of competitive strategy in excellent 'stage 4' operations. Figure 2.2 illustrates the four steps involved in moving from stage 1 to stage 4.

Stage 1: Internal neutrality

This is the very poorest level of contribution by the operations function. The other functions regard it as holding them back from competing effectively. The operations function is inward-looking and at best reactive, with very little positive to contribute towards competitive success. Its goal is to be ignored. At least then it isn't holding the company back in any way. Certainly the rest of the organization would not look to operations as the source of any originality, flair or competitive drive. Its vision is to be 'internally neutral', a position it attempts to achieve not by anything positive but by avoiding the bigger mistakes.

Stage 2: External neutrality

The first step of breaking out of stage 1 is for the operations function to begin comparing itself with similar companies or organizations in the outside market. This may not immediately take it to the 'first division' of companies in the market, but at least it is measuring itself against its competitors' performance and trying to be 'appropriate', by adopting 'best practice' from them. Its vision is to become 'up to speed' or 'externally

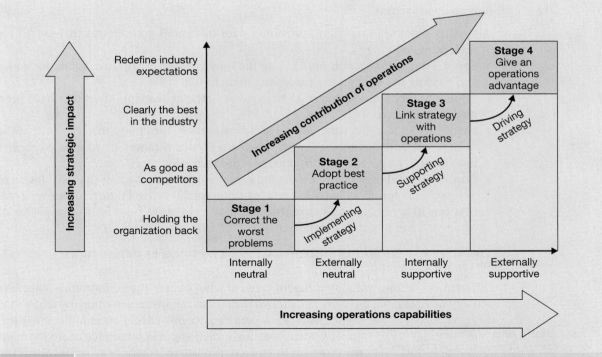

Figure 2.2 Hayes and Wheelwright's Four-Stage Model of operations contribution sees operations as moving from implementation of strategy, through to supporting strategy, and finally driving strategy

neutral' with similar businesses in its industry by adopting 'best practice' ideas and norms of performance from others.

Stage 3: Internally supportive

Stage 3 operations have probably reached the 'first division' in their market. They may not be better than their competitors on every aspect of operations performance but they are broadly up with the best. Yet, the vision of stage 3 operations is to be clearly and unambiguously the very best in the market. They may try to achieve this by gaining a clear view of the company's competitive or strategic goals and developing 'appropriate' operations resources to excel in the areas in which the company needs to compete effectively. The operation is trying to be 'internally supportive' by providing a credible operations strategy.

Stage 4: Externally supportive

Stage 3 used to be taken as the limit of the operations function's contribution. Yet the model captures the growing importance of operations management by suggesting a further stage – stage 4. The difference between stages 3 and 4 is subtle, but important. A stage 4 company is one where the vision for the operations function is to provide *the* foundation for competitive success. Operations looks to the long term. It forecasts likely changes in markets and supply, and, over time, it develops the operations-based capabilities that will be required to compete in future market conditions. The operations function is becoming central to strategy-making. Stage 4 operations are creative and proactive. They are innovative and capable of adaptation as markets change. Essentially they are trying to be 'one step ahead' of competitors in the way that they create products and services and organize their operations – what the model terms being 'externally supportive'.

PRACTICE NOTE

An operations strategy should define operations performance objectives

Operations adds value for customers and contributes to competitiveness by being able to satisfy the requirements of its customers. There are five aspects of operations performance, all of which to a greater or lesser extent will affect customer satisfaction and business competitiveness.

- **Quality** – doing things right, providing error-free goods and services that are 'fit for their purpose'.
- **Speed** – doing things fast, minimizing the time between a customer asking for goods and services and the customer receiving them in full.
- **Dependability** – doing things on time, keeping the delivery promises that have been made to customers.
- **Flexibility** – changing what you do or how you do it, the ability to vary or adapt the operation's activities to cope with unexpected circumstances or to give customers individual treatment, or to introduce new products or services.
- **Cost** – doing things cheaply, producing goods and services at a cost that enables them to be priced appropriately for the market while still allowing a return to the organization (or, in a not-for-profit organization, that gives good value to the taxpayers or whoever is funding the operation).

The exact meaning of performance objectives is different in different operations

Different operations will have different views of what each of the performance objectives actually means. Table 2.1 looks at how two operations, an insurance company and a steel plant, define each performance objective. For example, the insurance company sees quality as being at least as much about the manner in which its customers relate to its service as it does about the absence of technical errors. The steel plant, on the other hand, while not ignoring quality of service, emphasizes primarily

> **Operations principle**
> Operations performance objectives can be grouped together as quality, speed, dependability, flexibility and cost.

Table 2.1   Aspects of each performance objective for two operations

Insurance company	Performance objectives	Steel plant
Aspects of each performance objective include . . .		Aspects of each performance objective include . . .
• Professionalism of staff • Friendliness of staff • Accuracy of information • Ability to change details in future	**Quality**	• Percentage of products conforming to their specification • Absolute specification of products • Usefulness of technical advice
• Time for call centre to respond • Prompt advice response • Fast quotation decisions • Fast response to claims	**Speed**	• Lead-time from enquiry to quotation • Lead-time from order to delivery • Lead-time for technical advice
• Reliability of original promise date • Customers kept informed	**Dependability**	• Percentage of deliveries 'on-time, in-full' • Customers kept informed of delivery dates
• Customization of terms of insurance cover • Ability to cope with changes in circumstances, such as level of demand • Ability to handle wide variety of risks	**Flexibility**	• Range of sizes, gauges, coatings, etc. possible • Rate of new product introduction • Ability to change quantity, composition and timing of an order
• Premium charged • Arrangement charges • 'No-claims' deals • 'Excess' charges	**Cost**	• Price of products • Price of technical advice • Discounts available • Payment terms

product-related technical issues. Although they are selecting from the same pool of factors that together constitute the generic performance objective, they emphasize different elements.

Sometimes operations may choose to re-bundle elements using slightly different headings. For example, it is not uncommon in some service operations to refer to 'quality of service' as representing all the competitive factors we have listed under quality *and* speed *and* dependability (and sometimes aspects of flexibility). For example, information network operations use the term 'Quality of Service' (QoS) to describe their goal of providing guarantees on the ability of a network to deliver predictable results. This is often specified as including uptime (dependability), bandwidth provision (dependability and flexibility), latency or delay (speed of throughput) and error rate (quality). In practice, the issue is not so much one of universal definition but rather consistency within an operation or a group of operations. At the very least it is important that individual companies are clear in their own minds how each performance objective is to be defined.

Operations principle
The interpretation of the five performance objectives will differ between different operations.

The relative priority of performance objectives differs between businesses

Not every operation will apply the same priorities to its performance objectives. Businesses that compete in different ways should want different things from their operations functions. In fact, there should be a clear, logical connection between the competitive stance of a business and its operations objectives. So, a business that competes primarily on low prices and 'value for money' should be placing emphasis on operations objectives such as cost, productivity and efficiency, one that competes on a high degree of customization of its services or products should be placing an emphasis on flexibility, and so on. Many successful companies understand the

Operations principle
The relative importance of the five performance objectives depends on how the business competes in its market.

importance of making this connection between their message to customers and the operations performance objectives that they emphasize, for example:[5]

> 'Our management principle is the commitment to quality and reliability . . . to deliver safe and innovative products and services . . . and to improve the quality and reliability of our businesses.' (Komatsu)

> 'The management team will . . . develop high-quality, strongly differentiated consumer brands and service standards . . . use the benefits of the global nature and scale economies of the business to operate a highly efficient support infrastructure . . . [with] high quality and service standards which deliver an excellent guest experience . . .' (InterContinental Hotels Group)

> 'A level of quality, durability and value that's truly superior in the market place . . . the principle that what is best for the customer is also best for the company . . . [our] customers have learnt to expect a high level of service at all times – from initiating the order, to receiving help and advice, to speedy shipping and further follow-up where necessary . . . [our] employees "go that extra mile".' (Lands' End)

An operations strategy should identify the broad decisions that will help the operation achieve its objectives

Few businesses have the resources to pursue every single action that might improve their operations performance. So an operations strategy should indicate broadly how the operation might best achieve its performance objectives. For example, a business might specify that it will attempt to reduce its costs by aggressive outsourcing of its non-core business processes and by investing in more efficient technology. Or, it may declare that it intends to offer a more customized set of products or services through adopting a modular approach to its product or service design. The balance here is between a strategy that is overly restrictive in specifying how performance objectives are to be achieved, and one that is so open that it gives little guidance as to what ideas should be pursued.

There are several categorizations of operations strategy decisions. Any of them are valid if they capture the key decisions. Here we categorize operations strategy decisions in the same way we categorize operations management decisions, as applying to the activities of design, delivery and development. Table 2.2 illustrates some of the broad operations strategy decisions that fall within each category.

An operations strategy should reconcile strategic decisions to objectives

Operations principle
An operation's strategy should articulate the relationship between operations objectives and the means of achieving them.

PRACTICE NOTE

FURTHER EXAMPLE

We can now bring together two sets of ideas and, in doing so, we also bring together the two perspectives of (a) market requirements and (b) operations resources to form the two dimensions of a matrix. This *operations strategy* matrix is shown in Figure 2.3. It describes operations strategy as the intersection of a company's performance objectives and the strategic decisions that it makes. In fact there are several intersections between each performance objective and each decision area (however one wishes to define them). If a business thinks that it has an operations strategy, then it should have a coherent explanation for each of the cells in the matrix. That is, it should be able to explain and reconcile the intended links between each performance objective and each decision area. The process of reconciliation takes place between *what* is required from the operations function (performance objectives) and *how* the operation tries to achieve this through the set of choices made (and the capabilities that have been developed) in each decision area.

Table 2.2	Some strategic decisions that may need to be addressed in an operations strategy
Strategic decisions concerned with the *design* of operations and processes	• How should the operation decide which products or services to develop and how to manage the development process? • Should the operation develop its products or services in-house or outsource the designs? • Should the operation outsource some of its activities, or take more activities in-house? • Should the operation expand by acquiring its suppliers or its customers? If so, which ones should it acquire? • How many geographically separate sites should the operation have? • Where should operations sites be located? • What activities and capacity should be allocated to each site? • What broad types of technology should the operation be using? • How should the operation be developing its people? • What role should the people who staff the operation play in its management?
Strategic decisions concerned with planning and controlling the *delivery* of products and services	• How should the operation forecast and monitor the demand for its products and services? • How should the operation adjust its activity levels in response to demand fluctuations? • How should the operation monitor and develop its relationship with its suppliers? • How much inventory should the operation have and where should it be located? • What approach and system should the operation use to plan its activities?
Strategic decisions concerned with the *development* of operations performance	• How should the operation's performance be measured and reported? • How should the operation ensure that its performance is reflected in its improvement priorities? • Who should be involved in the improvement process? • How fast should improvement in performance be? • How should the improvement process be managed? • How should the operation maintain its resources so as to prevent failure? • How should the operation ensure continuity if a failure occurs?

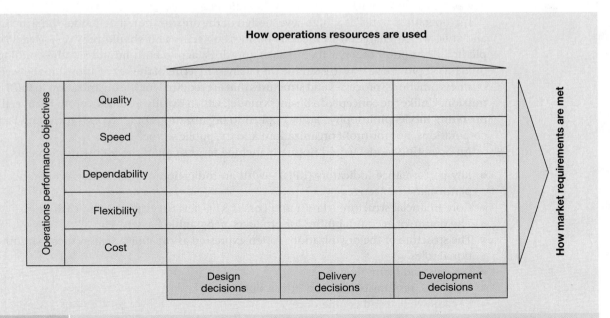

Figure 2.3 The operations strategy matrix defines operations strategy by the intersections of performance objectives and operations decisions

The concepts of the 'business model' and the 'operating model'

Two concepts have emerged over the last few years which are relevant to operations strategy (or at least the terms are new, one could argue that the ideas are far older). These are the concepts of the 'business model' and the 'operating model'.

Put simply, a 'business model' is the plan that is implemented by a company to generate revenue and make a profit. It includes the various parts and organizational functions of the business, as well as the revenues it generates and the expenses it incurs. In other words, what a company does and how it makes money from doing it. More formally, it is 'a conceptual tool that contains a big set of elements and their relationships and allows [the expression of] the business logic of a specific firm. It is a description of the value a company offers to one or several segments of customers and of the architecture of the firm and its network of partners for creating, marketing and delivering this value and relationship capital, to generate profitable and sustainable revenue streams.[6]

One synthesis of literature[7] shows that business models have a number of common elements.

1. The *value proposition* of what is offered to the market.
2. The *target customer segments* addressed by the value proposition.
3. The communication and *distribution channels* to reach customers and offer the value proposition.
4. The *relationships* established with customers.
5. The *core capabilities* needed to make the business model possible.
6. The *configuration of activities* to implement the business model.
7. The *partners* and their motivations for coming together to make a business model happen.
8. The *revenue streams* generated by the business model constituting the revenue model.
9. The *cost structure* resulting from the business model.

One can see that this idea of the business model is broadly analogous to the idea of a 'business strategy' but implies more of an emphasis on *how* to achieve an intended strategy as well as exactly *what* that strategy should be.

An 'operating model' is a 'high-level design of the organization that defines the structure and style which enables it to meet its business objectives'. It should provide a clear, 'big picture' description of what the organization does, across both business and technology domains. It provides a way to examine the business in terms of the key relationships between business functions, processes and structures that are required for the organization to fulfil its mission. Unlike the concept of a business model, which usually assumes a profit motive, the operating model philosophy can be applied to organizations of all types – including large corporations, not-for-profit organizations and the public sector.[8]

An operating model would normally include most or all of the following elements.

- Key performance indicators (KPIs) – with an indication of the relative importance of performance objectives.
- Core financial structure – Profit and Loss (P&L), new investments and cash flow.
- The nature of accountabilities for products, geographies, assets, etc.
- The structure of the organization – often expressed as capability areas rather than functional roles.
- Systems and technologies.
- Processes, responsibilities and interactions.
- Key knowledge and competence.

Note two important characteristics of an operating model. First, it does not respect conventional functional boundaries as such. In some ways the concept of the operating model

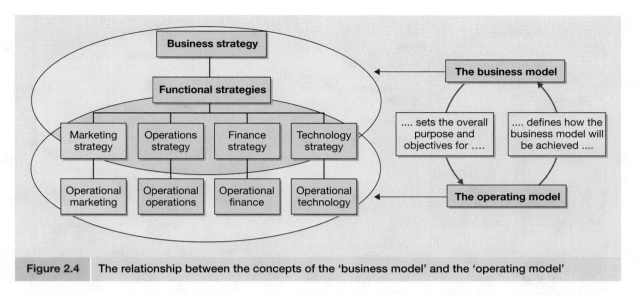

Figure 2.4 The relationship between the concepts of the 'business model' and the 'operating model'

reflects the idea that we proposed in Chapter 1, namely that all managers are operations managers and all functions can be considered as operations because they comprise processes that deliver some kind of service. An operating model is like an operations strategy, but applied across all functions and domains of the organization. Second, there are clear overlaps between the 'business model' and the 'operating model', the main difference being that an operating model focuses more on how an overall business strategy is to be achieved. Operating models have an element of implied change or transformation of the organization's resources and processes. Often the term 'target operating model' is used to describe the way the organization should operate in the future if it is going to achieve its objectives and make a success of its business model. Figure 2.4 illustrates the relationship between business and operating models.

DIAGNOSTIC QUESTION

Does operations strategy make sense from the top and the bottom of the business?

The traditional view of operations strategy is that it is one of several *functional strategies* that are governed by decisions taken at the top of the organizational tree. In this view operations strategy, together with marketing, human resources and other functional strategies, take their lead exclusively from the needs of the business as a whole. This is often called a 'top-down' perspective on operations strategy. An alternative view is that operations strategies emerge over time from the operational level, as the business learns from the day-to-day experience of running processes (both operations and other processes). This is known as the 'emergent' or 'bottom-up' perspective on operations strategy. An operations strategy should reflect both of these perspectives. Any functional strategy, especially operations strategy, cannot afford to be in conflict with the business's overall strategy. Yet at the same time, any operation will be strongly influenced by its day-to-day experiences. Not only will operational issues set practical constraints on strategic direction, but more significantly, day-to-day experiences can be exploited to provide an important contribution to strategic thinking. The left-hand side of Figure 2.5 illustrates this.

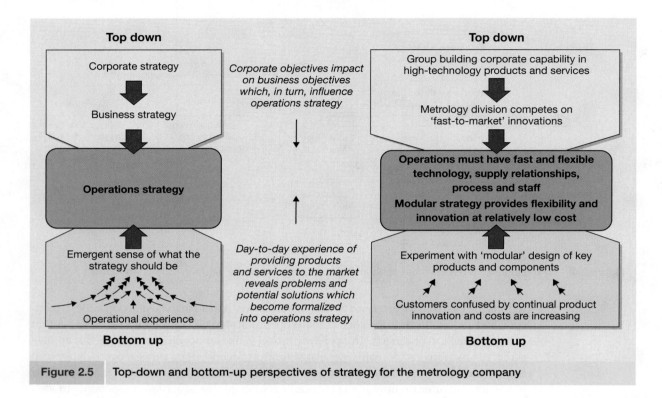

Figure 2.5 Top-down and bottom-up perspectives of strategy for the metrology company

Top-down–operations strategy should reflect the needs of the whole business

A top-down perspective often identifies three levels of strategy: corporate, business and functional. A corporate strategy should position the corporation in its global, economic, political and social environment. This will consist of decisions about what types of business the group wants to be in, what parts of the world it wants to operate in, how to allocate its cash between its various businesses, and so on. Each business unit within the corporate group will also need to put together its own business strategy that sets out its individual mission and objectives. This business strategy guides the business in relation to its customers, markets and competitors, and also defines its role within the corporate group of which it is a part. Similarly, within the business, functional strategies need to consider what part each function should play in contributing to the strategic objectives of the business. The operations, marketing, product/service development and other functions will all need to consider how best they should organize themselves to support the business's objectives.

> **Operations principle**
> Operations strategies should reflect top-down corporate and/or business objectives.

Bottom-up–operations strategy should reflect operational reality

Although it is a convenient way of thinking about strategy, the top-down hierarchical model does not represent the way strategies are always formulated in practice. When any group is reviewing its corporate strategy, it will also take into account the circumstances, experiences and capabilities of the various businesses that form the group. Similarly, businesses, when reviewing their strategies, will consult the individual functions within the business about their constraints and capabilities. They may also incorporate the ideas that come from each function's day-to-day experience. In fact many strategic ideas emerge over time from operational experience rather than being originated exclusively at a senior level. Sometimes companies move in a particular strategic direction because the ongoing experience of providing products and services to customers at an operational level convinces them that it is the right thing to do. There may be no formal high-level decision making that examines alternative strategic options and chooses the one that provides the best way forward. Instead, a general consensus emerges from the operational experience. The 'high-level' strategic decision making, if it occurs at all, may simply confirm the consensus and provide the resources to make it happen effectively. This is sometimes called the concept of emergent strategies.[9] It sees strategies as often being formed in a relatively unstructured and fragmented manner to reflect the fact that the future is at least partially unknown and unpredictable.

> **Operations principle**
> Operations strategy should reflect bottom-up experience of operational reality.

This view of operations strategy reflects how things often happen, but at first glance it seems less useful in providing a guide for specific decision making. Yet while emergent strategies are less easy to categorize, the principle governing a bottom-up perspective is clear: an operation's objectives and actions should be shaped at least partly by the knowledge it gains from its day-to-day activities. The key virtues required for shaping strategy from the bottom up are an ability to learn from experience and a philosophy of continual and incremental improvement.

Example | **Flexibility in innovation**

A metrology systems company develops integrated systems for large international clients in several industries. It is part of a group that includes several high-tech companies. It competes through a strategy of technical excellence and innovation together with an ability to advise and customize its systems to clients' needs. As part of this strategy it attempts to be the first in the market with every available technical innovation. From a top-down perspective, its operations function, therefore, needs to be capable of coping with the changes that constant innovation will bring. It must develop processes that are flexible enough to develop and assemble novel components and systems. It must organize and train its staff to understand the way technology is developing so that they can put in place the necessary changes to the operation. It must develop relationships with its suppliers that will help them to respond quickly when supplying new components. Everything about the operation, its processes, staff and its systems and procedures, must, in the short term, do nothing to inhibit, and in the long term actively develop, the company's competitive strategy of innovation.

However, over time, as its operations strategy develops, the business discovered that continual product and system innovation was having the effect of dramatically increasing its costs. And, although it did not compete on low prices, its rising costs were impacting profitability. Also there was some evidence that continual changes were confusing some customers. Partially in response to customer requests, the company's system designers started to work out a way of 'modularizing' their system and product designs. This allowed one part of the system to be updated for those customers who valued the functionality the innovation could bring, without interfering with the overall design of the main body of the system. Over time, this approach became standard design practice within the company. Customers appreciated the extra customization, and modularization reduced operations costs. Note that this strategy emerged from the company's experience. No top-level board decision was ever taken to confirm this practice, but nevertheless it emerged as the way in which the company organizes its design activity. The right-hand side of Figure 2.5 illustrates these top-down and bottom-up influences for the business.

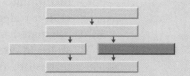

Does operations strategy align market requirements with operations resources?

Any operations strategy should reflect the intended market position of the business. Companies compete in different ways: some compete primarily on cost, others on the excellence of their products or services, others on high levels of customer service, and so on. The operations function must respond to this by providing the ability to perform in a manner that is appropriate for the intended market position. This is a market perspective on operations strategy. But operations strategy must do more than simply meet the short-term needs of the market (important though this is). The processes and resources within operations also need to be developed in the long term to provide the business with a set of competencies or capabilities (we use the two words interchangeably). Capabilities in this context are the 'know-how' that is embedded within the business's resources and processes. These capabilities may be built up over time as the result of the experiences of the operation, or they may be bought in or acquired. If they are refined and integrated they can form the basis of the business's ability to offer unique and 'difficult to imitate' products and services to its customers. This idea of the basis of long-term competitive capabilities deriving from the operation's resources and processes is called the resource perspective on operations strategy.[10]

Operations strategy should reflect market requirements

A particularly useful way of determining the relative importance of competitive factors is to distinguish between what Professor Terry Hill has termed 'order-winners' and 'qualifiers'.[11] Figure 2.6 shows the difference between order-winning and qualifying objectives in terms of their utility, or worth, to the competitiveness of the organization. The curves illustrate the relative amount of competitiveness (or attractiveness to customers) as the operation's performance varies.

> **Operations principle**
> Operations strategy should reflect the requirements of the business's markets.

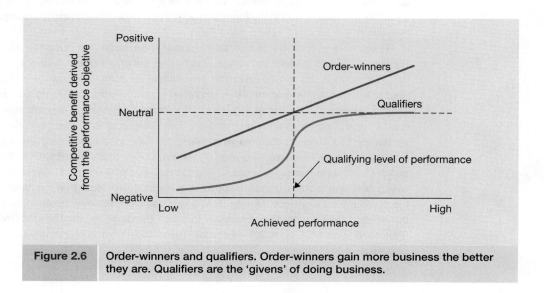

| **Figure 2.6** | Order-winners and qualifiers. Order-winners gain more business the better they are. Qualifiers are the 'givens' of doing business. |

- **Order-winners** are those things that directly and significantly contribute to winning business. They are regarded by customers as key reasons for purchasing the product or service. Raising performance in an order-winner will either result in more business or improve the chances of gaining more business. Order-winners show a steady and significant increase in their contribution to competitiveness as the operation gets better at providing them.

- **Qualifiers** may not be the major competitive determinants of success, but are important in another way. They are those aspects of competitiveness where the operation's performance has to be above a particular level just to be considered by the customer. Performance below this 'qualifying' level of performance may disqualify the operation from being considered by customers. But any further improvement above the qualifying level is unlikely to gain the company much competitive benefit. Qualifiers are those things that are generally expected by customers. Being great at them is unlikely to excite customers, but being bad at them can disadvantage the competitive position of the operation.

Different customer needs imply different objectives

> **Operations principle**
> Different customer needs imply different priorities of performance objectives.

If, as is likely, an operation produces goods or services for more than one customer group, it will need to determine the order-winners and qualifiers for each group. For example, Table 2.3 shows two 'product' groups in the banking industry. Here the distinction is drawn between the customers who are looking for

Table 2.3	Different banking services require different performance objectives	
	Retail banking	*Corporate banking*
Products	Personal financial services such as loans and credit cards	Special services for corporate customers
Customers	Individuals	Businesses
Product range	Medium but standardized, little need for special terms	Very wide range, many need to be customized
Design changes	Occasional	Continual
Delivery	Fast decisions	Dependable service
Quality	Means error-free transactions	Means close relationships
Volume per service type	Most service are high volume	Most services are low volume
Profit margins	Most are low to medium, some high	Medium to high
Order-winners	Price Accessibility Speed	Customization Quality of service Reliability
Qualifiers	Quality Range	Speed Price
Performance objectives emphasized within the processes that produce each service	Cost Speed Quality	Flexibility Quality Dependability

FURTHER EXAMPLE

banking services for their private and domestic needs and the corporate customers who need banking services for their (often large) businesses.

The product/service life cycle influence on performance objectives

One way of generalizing the market requirements that operations need to fulfil is to link them to the life cycle of the products or services that the operation is producing. The exact form of product/service life cycles will vary, but generally they are shown as the sales volume passing through four stages – introduction, growth, maturity and decline. The important implication of this for operations management is that products and services will require operations strategies in each stage of their life cycle (see Figure 2.7).

● **Introduction stage**. When a product or service is first introduced, it is likely to be offering something new in terms of its design or performance. Few competitors will be offering the same product or service, and because the needs of customers are not perfectly understood, the design of the product or service could frequently change. Given the market uncertainty, the operations management of the company needs

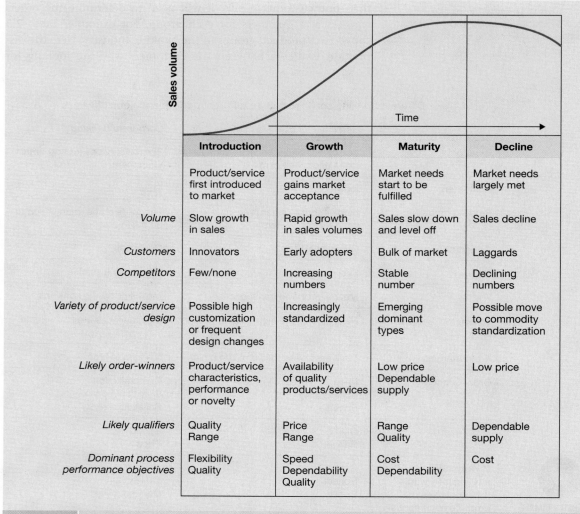

	Introduction	Growth	Maturity	Decline
	Product/service first introduced to market	Product/service gains market acceptance	Market needs start to be fulfilled	Market needs largely met
Volume	Slow growth in sales	Rapid growth in sales volumes	Sales slow down and level off	Sales decline
Customers	Innovators	Early adopters	Bulk of market	Laggards
Competitors	Few/none	Increasing numbers	Stable number	Declining numbers
Variety of product/service design	Possible high customization or frequent design changes	Increasingly standardized	Emerging dominant types	Possible move to commodity standardization
Likely order-winners	Product/service characteristics, performance or novelty	Availability of quality products/services	Low price Dependable supply	Low price
Likely qualifiers	Quality Range	Price Range	Range Quality	Dependable supply
Dominant process performance objectives	Flexibility Quality	Speed Dependability Quality	Cost Dependability	Cost

Figure 2.7   The effects of the product/service life cycle on the operation and its process performance objectives

to develop the flexibility to cope with these changes and the quality to maintain product/service performance.

- **Growth stage**. As the volume of products or services grows, competitors start to develop their own products and services. In the growing market, standardized designs emerge. Standardization is helpful in that it allows the operation to supply the rapidly growing market. Keeping up with demand could prove to be the main operations preoccupation. Rapid and dependable response to demand will help to keep demand buoyant while ensuring that the company keeps its share of the market as competition starts to increase. Also, increasing competition means that quality levels must be maintained.

- **Maturity stage**. Eventually demand starts to level off. Some early competitors will have left the market and the industry will probably be dominated by a few larger companies. The designs of the products or services will be standardized and competition will probably emphasize price or value for money, although individual companies might try to prevent this by attempting to differentiate themselves in some way. So operations will be expected to get the costs down in order to maintain profits or to allow price cutting, or both. Because of this, cost and productivity issues, together with dependable supply, are likely to be the operation's main concerns.

- **Decline stage**. After time, sales will decline and competitors will start dropping out of the market. To the companies left there might be a residual market, but if capacity in the industry lags demand, the market will continue to be dominated by price competition. Operations objectives will therefore still be dominated by cost.

Operations strategy should build operations capabilities

Building operations capabilities means understanding the existing resources and processes within the operation, starting with the simple questions, what do we have, and what can we do? However, trying to understand an operation by listing its resources alone is like trying to understand an automobile by listing its component parts. To understand an automobile we need to describe how the component parts form its internal mechanisms. Within the operation, the equivalents of these mechanisms are its *processes*. Yet, even a technical explanation of an automobile's mechanisms does not convey its style or 'personality'. Something more is needed to describe these. In the same way, an operation is not just the sum of its processes. It also has *intangible* resources. An operation's intangible resources include such things as:

> **Operations principle**
> The long-term objective of operation strategy is to build operations-based capabilities.

- its relationship with suppliers and the reputation it has with its customers
- its knowledge of and experience in handling its process technologies
- the way its staff can work together in new product and service development
- the way it integrates all its processes into a mutually supporting whole.

These intangible resources may not be as evident within an operation, but they are important and often have real value. And both tangible and intangible resources and processes shape its capabilities. The central issue for operations management, therefore, is to ensure that its pattern of strategic decisions really does develop appropriate capabilities.

The resource-based view

The idea that building operations capabilities should be an important objective of operations strategy is closely linked with the popularity of an approach to business strategy called the resource-based view (RBV) of the firm.[12] This holds that businesses with an 'above average' strategic performance are likely to have gained their sustainable competitive advantage because of their core competencies (or capabilities). This means that the way an organization inherits, or acquires, or develops its operations resources will, over the long term, have a significant impact on its strategic success. The RBV differs in its approach from the more traditional view of strategy which sees companies as seeking to protect their competitive advantage through their control of the market, for example by creating *barriers to entry* through product differentiation, or making it difficult for customers to switch to competitors, or controlling access to distribution channels (a major barrier to entry in petrol retailing, for example, where oil companies own their own retail stations). By contrast, the RBV sees firms being able to protect their competitive advantage through *barriers to imitation,* that is by building up 'difficult-to-imitate' resources. Certain of these resources are particularly important, and can be classified as 'strategic' if they exhibit the following properties:

- *They are scarce.* Scarce resources, such as specialized production facilities, experienced engineers, proprietary software, etc., can underpin competitive advantage.
- *They are imperfectly mobile.* Some resources are difficult to move out of a firm. For example, resources that were developed in-house, or are based on the experience of the company's staff, or are interconnected with the other resources in the firm, cannot be traded easily.
- *They are imperfectly imitable and imperfectly substitutable.* It is not enough only to have resources that are unique and immobile. If a competitor can copy these resources, or replace them with alternative resources, then their value will quickly deteriorate. The more the resources are connected with process knowledge embedded deep within the firm, the more difficult they are for competitors to understand and to copy.

FURTHER EXAMPLE

Reconciling market requirements and operations resource capabilities

The market requirements and the operations resource perspectives on operations strategy represent two sides of a strategic equation that all operations managers have to reconcile. On one hand, the operation must be able to meet the requirements of the market. On the other hand, it also needs to develop operations capabilities that make it able to do the things that customers find valuable but competitors find difficult to imitate. And ideally, there should be a reasonable degree of alignment or 'fit' between the requirements of the market and the capabilities of operations resources. Figure 2.8 illustrates the concept of fit diagrammatically. The vertical dimension represents the nature of market requirements

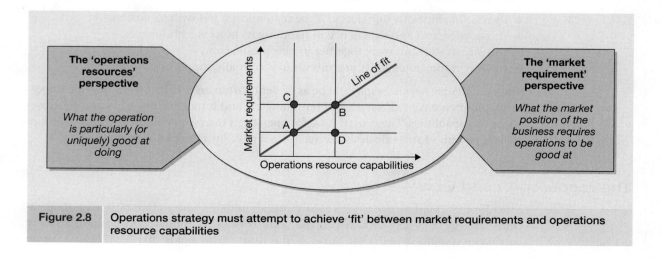

Figure 2.8   Operations strategy must attempt to achieve 'fit' between market requirements and operations resource capabilities

either because they reflect the intrinsic needs of customers or because their expectations have been shaped by the firm's marketing activity. This includes such factors as the strength of the brand or reputation, the degree of differentiation, and the extent of market promises. Movement along the dimension indicates a broadly enhanced level of market 'performance'. The horizontal scale represents the nature of the firm's operations resources and processes. This includes such things as the performance of the operation in terms of its ability to achieve competitive objectives, the efficiency with which it uses its resources, and the ability of the firm's resources to underpin its business processes. Movement along the dimension broadly indicates an enhanced level of 'operations capability'.

If market requirements and operations capability of an operation are aligned, it would diagrammatically be positioned on the 'line of fit' in Figure 2.8. 'Fit' is to achieve an approximate balance between 'market requirements' and 'operations capability'. So when fit is achieved, firms' customers do not need, or expect, levels of operations capability that cannot be supplied. Nor does the operation have strengths either that are inappropriate for market needs or that remain unexploited in the market.[13]

An operation that has position A in Figure 2.8 has achieved 'fit' in so much as its operations capabilities are aligned with its market requirements, yet both are at a relatively low level. In other words, the market does not want much from the business, which is just as well because its operation is not capable of achieving much. An operation with position B has also achieved 'fit', but at a higher level. Other things being equal, this will be a more profitable position than position A. Positions C and D are out of alignment. Position C denotes an operation that does not have sufficient operations capability to satisfy what the market wants. Position D indicates an operation that has more operations capability than it is able to exploit in its markets. Generally, operations at C and D would wish to improve their operations capability (C) or reposition themselves in their market (D) in order to get back into a position of fit.

DIAGNOSTIC QUESTION

Does operations strategy set an improvement path?

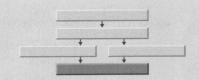

An operations strategy is the starting point for operations improvement. It sets the direction in which the operation will change over time. It is implicit that the business will want operations to change for the better. Therefore, unless an operations strategy gives some idea as to how improvement will happen, it is not fulfilling its main purpose. This is best thought about in terms of how performance objectives, both in themselves and relative to each other, will change over time. To do this, we need to understand the concept of, and the arguments concerning, the trade-offs between performance objectives.

An operations strategy should guide the trade-offs between performance objectives

An operations strategy should address the relative priority of operations performance objectives ('for us, speed of response is more important than cost efficiency, quality is more important than variety', and so on). To do this it must consider the possibility of improving its performance in one objective by sacrificing performance in another. So, for example, an operation might wish to improve its cost efficiencies by reducing the variety of products or services that it offers to its customers. Taken to its extreme, this 'trade-off' principle implies that improvement in one performance objective can *only* be gained at the expense of another. 'There is no such thing as a free lunch' could be taken as a summary of this approach to managing. Probably the best-known summary of the trade-off idea comes from Professor Wickham Skinner, the most influential of the originators of the strategic approach to operations, who said:[14]

> . . . *most managers will readily admit that there are compromises or trade-offs to be made in designing an airplane or truck. In the case of an airplane, trade-offs would involve matters such as cruising speed, take-off and landing distances, initial cost, maintenance, fuel consumption, passenger comfort and cargo or passenger capacity. For instance, no one today can design a 500-passenger plane that can land on an aircraft carrier and also break the sound barrier. Much the same thing is true in . . . [operations].*

But there is another view of the trade-offs between performance objectives. This sees the very idea of trade-offs as the enemy of operations improvement, and regards the acceptance that one type of performance can be achieved only at the expense of another as both limiting and unambitious. For any real improvement of total performance, it holds, the effect of trade-offs must be overcome in some way. In fact, overcoming trade-offs must be seen as the central objective of strategic operations improvement.

These two approaches to managing trade-offs result in two approaches to operations improvement. The first emphasizes 'repositioning' performance objectives by trading off improvements in some objectives for a reduction in performance in other. The other emphasizes increasing the 'effectiveness' of the operation by overcoming trade-offs so that improvements in one or more aspects of performance can be achieved without any reduction in the performance of others. Most businesses at some time or other will adopt both approaches. This is best illustrated through the concept of the 'efficient frontier' of operations performance.

FURTHER EXAMPLE

Trade-offs and the efficient frontier

Figure 2.9(a) shows the relative performance of several companies in the same industry in terms of their cost efficiency and the variety of products or services that they offer to their customers. Presumably all the operations would ideally like to be able to offer very high variety while still having very high levels of cost efficiency. However, the increased complexity that a high variety of product or service offerings brings will generally reduce the operation's ability to operate efficiently. Conversely, one way of improving cost efficiency is to severely limit the variety on offer to customers. The spread of results

in Figure 2.9(a) is typical of an exercise such as this. Operations A, B, C and D have all chosen a different balance between variety and cost efficiency. But none is dominated by any other operation in the sense that another operation necessarily has 'superior' performance. Operation X, however, has an inferior performance because operation A is able to offer higher variety at the same level of cost efficiency and operation C offers the same variety but with better cost efficiency. The convex line on which operations A, B, C and D lie is known as the 'efficient frontier'. They may choose to position themselves differently (presumably because of different market strategies) but they cannot be criticized for being ineffective. Of course any of these operations that lie on the efficient frontier may come to believe that the balance they have chosen between variety and cost efficiency is inappropriate. In these circumstances they may choose to reposition themselves at some other point along the efficient frontier. By contrast, operation X has also chosen to balance variety

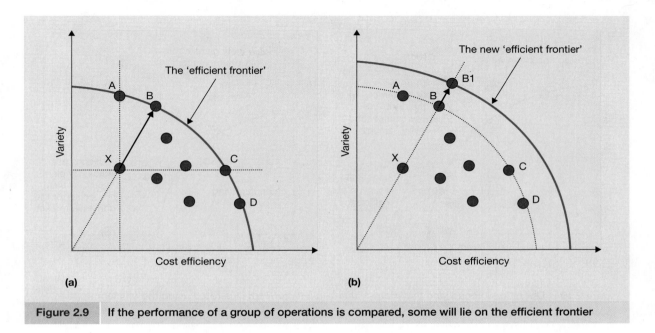

Figure 2.9 If the performance of a group of operations is compared, some will lie on the efficient frontier

and cost efficiency in a particular way but is not doing so effectively. Operation B has the same ratio between the two performance objectives but is achieving them more effectively. Operation X will generally have a strategy that emphasizes increasing its effectiveness before considering any repositioning.

However, a strategy that emphasizes increasing effectiveness is not confined to those operations that are dominated, such as operation X. Those with a position on the efficient frontier will generally also want to improve their operations effectiveness by overcoming the trade-off that is implicit in the efficient frontier curve. For example, suppose operation B in Figure 2.9(b) is the metrology systems company described earlier in this chapter. By adopting a modular product design strategy it improved both its variety and its cost efficiency simultaneously (and moved to position B1). What has happened is that operation B has adopted a particular operations practice (modular design) that has pushed out the efficient frontier. This distinction between positioning on the efficient frontier and increasing operations effectiveness to reach the frontier is an important one. Any operations strategy must make clear the extent to which it is expecting the operation to reposition itself in terms of its performance objectives and the extent to which it is expecting the operation to improve its effectiveness.

Improving operations effectiveness by using trade-offs

Improving the effectiveness of an operation by pushing out the efficient frontier requires different approaches depending on the original position of the operation on the frontier.[15] For example, in Figure 2.10 operation P has an original position that offers a high level of variety at the expense of low cost efficiency. It has probably reached this position by adopting a series of operations practices that enables it to offer the variety even if these practices are intrinsically expensive. For example, it may have invested in general-purpose technology and recruited employees with a wide range of skills. Improving variety even further may mean adopting even more extreme operations practices that emphasize variety. For example, it may reorganize its processes so that each of its larger customers has a dedicated set of resources that understands the specific requirements of that customer and can organize itself to totally customize every product and service it produces. This will

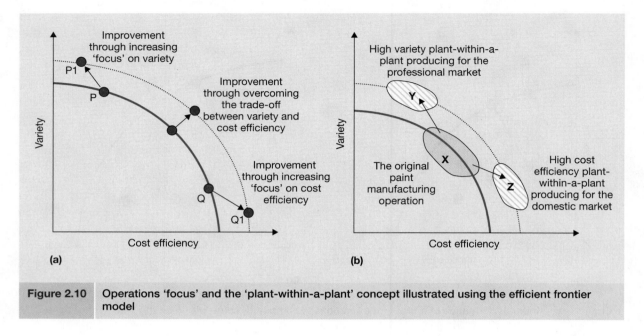

Figure 2.10 Operations 'focus' and the 'plant-within-a-plant' concept illustrated using the efficient frontier model

probably mean a further sacrifice of cost efficiency, but it allows an ever greater variety of products or services to be produced (P1). Similarly, operation Q may increase the effectiveness of its cost efficiency, by becoming even less able to offer any kind of variety (Q1). For both operations P and Q effectiveness is being improved through increasing the focus of the operation on one (or a very narrow set of) performance objective and accepting an even further reduction in other aspects of performance.

The same principle of focus also applies to organizational units smaller than a whole operation. For example, individual processes may choose to position themselves on a highly focused set of performance objectives that matches the market requirements of their own customers. So, for example, a business that manufactures paint for interior decoration may serve two quite distinct markets. Some of its products are intended for domestic customers who are price sensitive but demand only a limited variety of colours and sizes. The other market is professional interior decorators who demand a very wide variety of colours and sizes but are less price sensitive. The business may choose to move from a position where all types of paint are made on the same processes (position X in Figure 2.10(b)) to one where it has two separate sets of processes (Y and Z): one that makes paint only for the domestic market and the other that makes paint only for the professional market. In effect, the business has segmented its operations processes to match the segmentation of the market. This is sometimes called the 'plant-within-a-plant' concept.

Improving operations effectiveness by overcoming trade-offs

This concept of highly focused operations is not universally seen as appropriate. Many companies attempt to give 'the best of both worlds' to their customers. At one time, for example, a high-quality, reliable and error-free automobile was inevitably an expensive automobile. Now, with few exceptions, we expect even budget-priced automobiles to be reliable and almost free of any defects. Auto manufacturers found that not only could they reduce the number of defects on their vehicles without necessarily incurring extra costs, but they could actually reduce costs by reducing errors in manufacture. If auto manufacturers had adopted

Operations principle
An operation's strategic improvement path can be described in terms of repositioning and/or overcoming its performance trade-offs.

a purely focused-based approach to improvement over the years, we might now only be able to purchase either very cheap, low-quality automobiles or very expensive, high-quality automobiles. So a permanent expansion of the efficient frontier is best achieved by over-coming trade-offs through improvements in operations practice.

Even trade-offs that seem to be inevitable can be reduced to some extent. For example, one of the decisions that any supermarket manager has to make is how many checkout positions to open at any time. If too many checkouts are opened then there will be times when the checkout staff do not have any customers to serve and will be idle. The customers, however, will have excellent service in terms of little or no waiting time. Conversely, if too few checkouts are opened, the staff will be working all the time but customers will have to wait in long queues. There seems to be a direct trade-off between staff utilization (and there-fore cost) and customer waiting time (speed of service). Yet even the supermarket manager deciding how many checkouts to open can go some way to affecting the trade-off between customer waiting time and staff utilization. The manager might, for example, allocate a number of 'core' staff to operate the checkouts but also arrange for those other staff who are performing other jobs in the supermarket to be trained and 'on-call' should demand sud-denly increase. If the manager on duty sees a build-up of customers at the checkouts, these other staff could quickly be used to staff checkouts. By devising a flexible system of staff allocation, the manager can both improve customer service and keep staff utilization high.

Critical commentary

Each chapter contains a short critical commentary on the main ideas covered in the chapter. Its purpose is not to undermine the issues discussed in the chapter, but to emphasize that, although we present a relatively orthodox view of operation, there are other perspectives.

■ The ideas that operations strategy could ever become the driver of a business's overall strategy, and the associated concept of the resource-based view of the firm, are both prob-lematic to some theorists. Business strategy, and functional strategies, were for many years seen as, first, market driven and second, planned in a systematic and deliberative manner. So, it became almost axiomatic to see strategy as starting from a full understanding of mar-ket positioning. In fact, the main source of sustainable competitive advantage was seen as unambiguously associated with how a business positioned itself in its markets. Get the mar-ket proposition right and customers would respond by giving you business. Get it wrong and they would go to the competitors with a better offering. Strategy was seen as aligning the whole organization to the market position that could achieve long-term profitable differentia-tion when compared with competitors. Functional strategies were simply a more detailed interpretation of this overall imperative. Furthermore, strategy must be something that could be planned and directed. If managers could not influence strategy, then how could business be anything other than a lottery?

■ The idea that sustainable competitive advantage could come from the capabilities of one's resources was a clear threat to the established position. Furthermore, the idea that strategies emerged, sometimes haphazardly and unpredictably, over time rather than were deliberate decisions taken by senior managers was also seemingly counter-intuitive. Yet there is now considerable research evidence to support both of these, once outrageous, propositions. The position we have taken in this chapter is one of blending some aspects of the traditional view with the more recent ideas. Nevertheless, it is important to understand that there are still dif-ferent views on the very nature of strategic management.

Summary checklist

This checklist comprises questions that can be usefully applied to any type of operations and reflect the major diagnostic questions used within the chapter.

DOWNLOADABLE

☐ Does the operation have a fully articulated operations strategy?

☐ Does it include a vision for the role and contribution of the operations function?

☐ What position on the Hayes and Wheelwright stage 1 to 4 model are your operations?

☐ Are the operation's performance objectives fully articulated?

☐ Are the main strategic decisions that shape operations resources fully identified?

☐ Are the logical links established between what the market requires (in terms of performance objectives) and what capabilities operations possesses (in terms of the major strategic decision areas)?

☐ What is the balance between top-down direction and bottom-up learning in formulating operations strategy?

☐ Is there a recognized process for both top-down and bottom-up communication on strategic issues?

☐ Are performance objectives understood in terms of whether they are order-winners or qualifiers?

☐ Do different parts of the operation (probably producing different products or services) have their own relative priority of performance objectives that reflect their possibly different competitive positions?

☐ Is the idea of operations-based capabilities fully understood?

☐ What capabilities does the operation currently possess?

☐ Are these operations and/or resources scarce, imperfectly mobile, imperfectly imitable or imperfectly substitutable?

☐ If none of the above, are they really useful in terms of their strategic impact?

☐ Where would you put the operation in terms of Figure 2.8 that describes the broad fit between market requirements and operations resource capabilities?

☐ Have the key trade-offs for the operation been identified?

☐ What combination of repositioning in order to change the nature of trade-offs, and overcoming the trade-offs themselves, is going to be used to improve overall operations performance?

Case study   Dresding Wilson

'The last four years have been characterized by many challenges, many opportunities grasped, many lessons learnt and many reasons to feel confident of our continued success.' (Press release from Dresding Wilson, January 2004) In fact, the quote had been lifted directly from the opening address that Dr. Laura Dresding had given to the Dresding Wilson senior management conference a month earlier. What had not made it into the press release were her following comments. *'OK, so we have also made many mistakes. But that is part of growing up, and grown up is what we should start considering ourselves. We need to get more professional in everything that we do. We have entered markets that either are, or will become, more and more competitive. This means that we will need to shift the way we do things. We have grown by "letting many flowers bloom". That is fine when you are a small and ambitious player in an emerging market. Now we must get more integrated in the way we move forward and we must focus ruthlessly on the needs of our customers. Whatever customers find important is what we should find important.'*

Company history

The company, originally called Dresding Medical, was founded in 1991 by Dr. Laura Dresding, a clinician who had also acted as a clinical advisor to several medical equipment companies. It supplied cardiovascular and heart-function monitoring devices, most of which it manufactured in a relatively small factory/laboratory in Bracknell in the south of England. Within three years it had dropped other manufacturers' products to concentrate on sales of its own expanding product range. Originally owning 100 per cent of the company, by 2004 Dr. Dresding's share had dropped to 60 per cent, the rest being owned by three venture capital companies. One of the company's earliest decisions was to remain highly vertically integrated. *'We don't have any objection in principle to outsourcing; in fact we are now outsourcing around 30 per cent of our total production. But we do most of our own work simply because it ensures our control over quality. It has also helped us to convince our customers and the industry standards authorities of our commitment to quality.'* (James Key, MD, Manufacturing Division) Sales, at first relatively

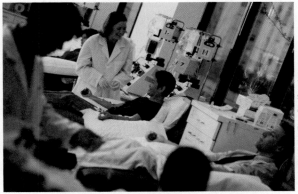

Source: Keith Brofsky/PhotoDisc/Getty Images

slow, started to expand significantly during the mid-1990s, and in 1995 the company bought a Danish medical equipment company that produced neurological stimulators. Although the market for neurological products was growing relatively slowly, the Danish plant was also used to produce components for Dresding's own range of products.

The Technology Development Division

Since 1993, Dresding had also been offering technology consulting advice as well as taking on some development work for other original equipment manufacturers (OEMs). In late 1997 it was decided to split off this activity and form a separate 'Technology solutions' division both to develop new in-house products and to develop and license 'technology solutions' to other OEMs. The new division was moved to a separate building on the Bracknell site and Bob Anderson, then the company's chief engineer, was made its first director. In his words, *'At that time we only had 12 full development engineers and five technicians, together with two development engineers in the Danish plant. But although we were small we were a tightly knit team and highly motivated to make a success of the new division. Within nine months we had issued our first technology licence and within 18 months we had grown our revenues by 350 per cent. We quickly discovered that we were in the service business. By 1998 we had over 20 key clients and had started developing several new initiatives for in-house use.'*

The most significant development to come out of the technology division in 1998 was the 'Insight' monitoring system. This was a method of allowing centralized patient monitoring and surveillance in specific care areas. The system allowed hospitals to avoid transferring patients to high-cost intensive care units and facilitated a better patient-to-medical-staff ratio. It also enabled comprehensive vital signs surveillance both at the bedside and at a central monitoring station. *'We were tremendously excited by the development because it posed a number of challenges, most notably the integration of software development, diagnostic software, new on-patient modules and wireless communication systems. We launched in early 1999 and immediately we were overwhelmed by clients expressing interest. With hindsight, that was where we made our biggest mistake. We expanded too fast, took on too many new staff, did not sufficiently test some of the subcomponents of the system, especially in the areas that were new to us such as diagnostic software. Worst of all, we made promises to the market without being able to fulfil them. In the end it took us two years to get over the problems and convince the market that we really did have a system that they could trust. If it was not for the intrinsic merit of the system, we could have been in real trouble. As it was, we came out of it stronger and with a better grip on our development procedures.'* (Bob Anderson, MD, Technology Division)

The 'Dresding Assurance' initiative

Meanwhile the rest of the company had been developing with less drama. In 1997 a new plant in Winchester, also in the south of England, had been opened and a two-year programme to further embed quality procedures in the company's three manufacturing units (Denmark, Bracknell and Winchester) had been started. *'Our idea was twofold. First we wanted to learn as much as we could from the experiences (and mistakes) of other businesses by examining how they approached quality. Second, we wanted to establish an absolutely impeccable set of standards and build a reputation that we could use in the marketplace. We organized a series of factory tours for all our managers and team leaders in all three plants and visited non-competitor businesses in our own and similar industries. This was a fantastic exercise, it stimulated debate but it also bonded the management teams from all three locations. On the basis of what we had learnt, over a two-year period we got ourselves the highest level of certification from all the major assurance and quality institutions in all our major markets, including, vitally, the FDA in America and several US military certifications.'* (James Key, MD, Manufacturing Division)

By the end of 1999 the company felt sufficiently confident to launch 'Dresding Assurance', a brand-building initiative that emphasized the quality of its products, in all major markets. The initiative was generally successful, no more so than in the Asian markets where sales growth increased almost 70 per cent between 1999 and 2000. In fact, by the end of 1999 Dresding had to open a technical support facility in Singapore. One year later the Singapore technical support office was upgraded to become the 'Singapore development centre' within the technical division of the company.

The financial year 2000/01 saw the fastest growth in the company's revenues. This was partly because of very healthy sales growth from the manufacturing division, and partly because the technology division had overcome some of its problems of two years earlier. However, notwithstanding the revenue growth, the company's profitability shrank by almost 40 per cent in the same year. This was largely because of increased manufacturing costs. *'Although we were running a tight ship in manufacturing, we were offering an increasingly wide range of products and systems that had increased the complexity of our manufacturing processes. To try and overcome this we decided to adopt the same approach that we had used in improving our quality systems. We visited high-variety manufacturers, this time usually in unrelated industries. We were trying to pick up hints on how to use modular design principles and flexible manufacturing cells to reduce the effective cost of variety. Again, it proved a great experience. Adopting more flexible manufacturing cells gave immediate benefits, but redesigning products took far longer.'* (James Key, MD, Manufacturing Division)

The Medical Services Division and the Ryder Wilson merger

In September 2002 the company made its biggest acquisition to date when it took control of Ryder Wilson, a US manufacturer of monitoring systems that also had a clinical management activity. *'Suddenly we had a "Medical service division" that was a significant player in the market. It was at this point that we decided to rename the company Dresding Wilson and position ourselves clearly as an innovation-based provider of technical solutions to the medical equipment and direct health-care industries, with three mutually supportive and integrated divisions.'* (Ruth Zimmerman, MD, Medical Service Division)

Recent developments

'The integration of the Ryder Wilson manufacturing facility went very smoothly. Their manufacturing facility and ours were both world class so we were not coping with

ongoing problems at the time of the merger. We had similar manufacturing policies and were reading the industry in the same way – a market that is demanding more customization and constant reassurance over quality. Ryder Wilson also had a great reputation. They were slightly less innovative but this is not too much of a disadvantage.'
(James Key, MD, Manufacturing Division)

'Our focus has shifted from being primarily a product innovator to being a systems innovator. This is partly because there are fewer "breakthroughs" in product technology compared with when we started the division in 1996. Licence revenue from OEMs has levelled off, but the importance of our support role, especially to the service division, is likely to grow. An interesting part of this role is an increasing involvement with educating customers regarding the technical possibilities and choices that they face as well as training customers' in-house technicians. I can see consultancy and customer training becoming a significant part of our revenue in the next few years.' (Bob Anderson, MD, Technology Division)

'The service and management division is not yet two years old and we are still the baby of the business, but we have by far the greatest potential for growth. Hospitals and clinics all over the world are moving towards outsourcing a greater proportion of their activities. Deploying our undoubted technical expertise should allow us to capitalize on opportunities for designing, installing and running monitoring units. However, I have to admit that we have had some problems. I guess the merger with Ryder Wilson created a lot of publicity just at the time when outsourcing, monitoring and surveillance activities were all hot topics in hospital management. We found ourselves not only designing and installing systems, but also arranging leasing agreements and providing agency staff and

training programmes where we had little or no experience. At the same time we were coping with a certain amount of reorganization after the merger. The result was a number of customers who were not too pleased with us and one lawsuit from a Californian clinic (now settled). We are fixing our problems, but there have been some hard lessons, especially in terms of understanding the risks involved in becoming service providers in this kind of market. We are also competing with existing in-house teams as well as other clinical service companies. Unless we can significantly undercut the cost of service provided by the resident teams, we cannot win the business. Of course our technology helps us to provide a low-cost service, but we can't afford to make any mistakes in how we deliver service. The challenge is to integrate the various service processes that we have, much in the same way as we have integrated the physical systems within our products.'
(Ruth Zimmerman, MD, Medical Service Division)

QUESTIONS

1 What are the significant strategic events in the history of the company from its foundation to the present day?

2 What do you see as the operations strategies for each of the three divisions of the company?

3 How has each division's operations resource capability developed in relation to the requirements of its market over time?

4 What do you see as the strengths and weaknesses of the company's approach to developing its operations strategy?

5 What challenges does the move to becoming a 'service provider' pose for the company?

Active case study   Long Ridge Gliding Club

ACTIVE CASE

Long Ridge Gliding Club is based in the UK on the crest of a ridge overlooking spectacular scenery. The club services two broad types of customer: club members and casual flyers who come for one-off trial flights, holiday courses and corporate events. However, complaints from all types of customer are increasing and the chairman faces a decision.

● Based on your judgement of their operations strategy and performance, how would you advise the chairman?

Please refer to the Active case on the CD accompanying this book to find out more about the club, its services and what seems to be going wrong.

Applying the principles

HINTS

Some of these exercises can be answered by reading the chapter. Others will require some general knowledge of business activity and some might require an element of investigation. All have hints on how they can be answered on the CD accompanying this book.

1   The environmental services department of a city has two recycling services – newspaper collection (NC) and general recycling (GR). The NC service is a door-to-door collection service which, at a fixed time every week, collects old newspapers that householders have placed in reusable plastic bags at their gate. An empty bag is left for the householders to use for the next collection. The value of the newspapers collected is relatively small and the service is offered mainly for reasons of environmental responsibility. By contrast the GR service is more commercial. Companies and private individuals can request a collection of materials to be disposed of, using either the telephone or the Internet. The GR service guarantees to collect the material within 24 hours unless the customer prefers to specify a more convenient time. Any kind of material can be collected and a charge is made depending on the volume of material. This service makes a small profit because the revenue both from customer charges and from some of the more valuable recycled materials exceeds the operation's running costs.

● How would you describe the differences between the performance objectives of the two services?

2   *'It is about four years now since we specialized in the small to medium firms market. Before that we also used to provide legal services for anyone who walked in the door. So now we have built up our legal skills in many areas of corporate and business law. However, within the firm, I think we could focus our activities even more. There seem to be two types of assignment that we are given. About 40 per cent of our work is relatively routine. Typically these assignments are to do with things like property purchase and debt collection. Both these activities involve a relatively standard set of steps which can be automated or carried out by staff without full legal qualifications. Of course, a fully qualified lawyer is needed to make some decisions; however, most work is fairly routine. Customers expect us to be relatively inexpensive and fast in delivering the service. Nor do they expect us to make simple errors in our documentation; in fact if we did this too often we would lose business. Fortunately our customers know that they are buying a standard service and don't expect it to be customized in any way. The problem here is that specialist agencies have been emerging over the last few years and they are starting to undercut us on price. Yet I still feel that we can operate profitably in this market and anyway, we still need these capabilities to serve our other clients. The other 60 per cent of our work is for clients who require far more specialist services, such as assignments involving company merger deals or major company restructuring. These assignments are complex, large, take longer, and require significant legal skill and judgement. It is vital that clients respect and trust the advice we give them across a wide range of legal specialisms. Of course they assume that we will not be slow or unreliable in preparing advice, but mainly it's trust in our legal judgement which is important to the client. This is popular work with our lawyers. It is both interesting and very profitable.*

'The help I need from you is in deciding whether to create two separate parts to our business: one to deal with routine services and the other to deal with specialist services. What I may do is appoint a senior "Operations Partner" to manage each part of the business, but if I do, what aspects of operations performance should they be aiming to excel at?' (Managing Partner, Branton Legal Services)

3   What do you think will be the key tasks for TNT to ensure that the top-down, bottom-up market requirements and operations resources perspectives of operations strategy are met?

4   Search the Internet site of Intel, the best-known microchip manufacturer, and identify what appear to be the main elements in its operations strategy.

5   McDonald's has come to epitomize the 'fast-food' industry. When the company started in the 1950s it was the first to establish itself in the market. Now there are hundreds of 'fast-food' brands in the market competing in different ways. Some of the differences between these fast-food chains are obvious. For example, some specialize in chicken products, others in pizza, and so on. However, some differences are less obvious. Originally, McDonald's competed on low price, fast service and a totally standardized service offering. It also offered a very narrow range of items on its menu. Visit a McDonald's restaurant and deduce what you believe to be its most important performance objectives. Then try to identify two other chains which appear to compete in a slightly different way. Then try to identify how these differences in the relative importance of competitive objectives must influence the structural and infrastructural decisions of each chain's operations strategy.

Notes on chapter

1 For a more thorough explanation, see Slack, N. and Lewis, M. (2008) *Operations Strategy* (2nd edn), Financial Times Prentice Hall, Harlow, UK.

2 Source: company website (www.flextronics.com), and press releases.

3 All material sourced from official TNT websites.

4 Hayes, R.H. and Wheelwright, S.C. (1984) *Restoring our Competitive Edge,* John Wiley.

5 All quotes taken from each company's website.

6 Osterwalder, A., Pigneur, Y. and Tucci, C. (2005) 'Clarifying business models: origins, present and future of the concept', *CAIS,* Vol. 15, pp. 751–5.

7 Osterwalder, A. (2005) 'What is a business model?', http://business-model-design.blogspot.com/2005/11/what-is-business-model.html

8 Based on the definitions developed by consultants Cap Gemini.

9 Mintzberg, H. and Waters, J.A. (1995) 'Of strategies: deliberate and emergent', *Strategic Management Journal,* July/Sept.

10 For a full explanation of this concept, see Slack and Lewis, *op. cit.*

11 Hill, T. (1993) *Manufacturing Strategy* (2nd edn), Macmillan.

12 There is a vast literature which describes the resource-based view of the firm. For example, see Barney, J. (1991) 'The resource-based model of the firm: origins, implications and prospect', *Journal of Management,* Vol. 17, No. 1; or Teece, D.J. and Pisano, G. (1994) 'The dynamic capabilities of firms: an introduction', *Industrial and Corporate Change,* Vol. 3, No. 3.

13 See Slack and Lewis, *op. cit.*

14 A point made initially by Skinner. Skinner, W. (1985) *Manufacturing: The formidable competitive weapon,* John Wiley.

15 Hayes, R.H. and G.P. Pisano (1996) 'Manufacturing strategy at the intersection of two paradigm shifts', *Production and Operations Management,* Vol. 5, No. 1.

Taking it further

There are many good books on strategy. For example, see **Johnson, G. and Scholes, K.** (1998) *Exploring Business Strategy* (4th edn), Prentice Hall; also see **deWit, B. and Meyer, R.** (1998) *Strategy: Process, content, and context,* International Thomson Business Press.

Hamel, G. and Prahalad, C.K. (1993) 'Strategy as stretch and leverage', *Harvard Business Review,* Vol. 71, Nos 2 & 3. This article is typical of some of the (relatively) recent ideas influencing operations strategy.

Hayes, R.H. and Pisano, G.P. (1994) 'Beyond world class: the new manufacturing strategy', *Harvard Business Review,* Vol. 72, No. 1. Same as above.

Hayes, R.H. and Wheelwright, S.C. (1984) *Restoring our Competitive Edge,* John Wiley. This book is all about manufacturing rather than operations generally. However, it was one of the first books on the subject and had a big impact.

Hayes, R.H., Wheelwright, S.C. and Clark, K.B. (1988) *Dynamic Manufacturing,* Free Press, New York. The successor volume to the Hayes and Wheelwright book above. The same comments apply.

Hill, T. (1993) *Manufacturing Strategy* (2nd edn), Macmillan. The first non-US author to have a real impact in the area. As was common at the time, the book concentrates on manufacturing alone.

Prahalad, C.K. and Hamel, G. (1990) 'The core competence of the corporation', *Harvard Business Review,* Vol. 68, No. 3. An easy explanation of the resource-based view of strategy.

Slack, N. and Lewis, M. (2008) *Operations Strategy* (2nd edn), Financial Times Prentice Hall. What can we say – just brilliant!

Useful websites

www.opsman.org Definitions, links and opinion on operations and process management.

www.aom.pac.edu/bps/ General strategy site of the American Academy of Management.

www.cranfield.ac.uk/som Look for the 'Best factory awards' link. Manufacturing, but interesting.

www.worldbank.org Global issues. Useful for international operations strategy research.

www.weforum.org Global issues, including some operations strategy ones.

www.ft.com Great for industry and company examples.

FURTHER
RESOURCES

For further resources including examples, animated diagrams, self-test questions, Excel spreadsheets, active case studies and video materials please explore the CD accompanying this book.

⊢3 SUPPLY NETWORK DESIGN

Introduction

Every business or organization is part of a larger and interconnected network of other businesses and organizations. This is the supply network. It includes suppliers and customers, suppliers' suppliers and customers' customers, and so on. At a strategic level, operations managers are involved in influencing the nature or 'design' of the network, and the role of their operation in it. This chapter treats some of these strategic design decisions in the context of supply networks. It forms the context for 'supply chain management', the more operational aspects managing the individual 'trends' or chains through the supply network. We shall discuss supply chain management in Chapter 7. Because many supply network decisions require an estimate of future demand, this chapter includes a supplement on forecasting. (See Figure 3.1.)

Source: Illustration Works/Getty Images

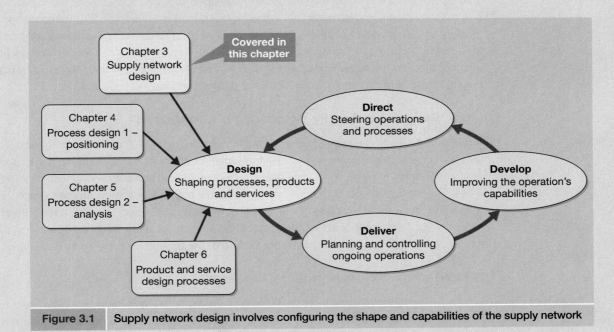

| Figure 3.1 | Supply network design involves configuring the shape and capabilities of the supply network |

Executive summary

VIDEO
further detail

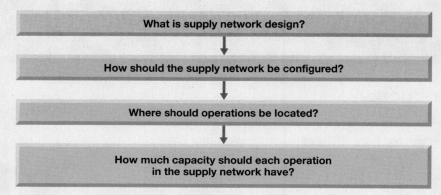

Decision logic chain for supply network design

Each chapter is structured around a set of diagnostic questions. These questions suggest what you should ask in order to gain an understanding of the important issues of a topic, and as a result, improve your decision making. An executive summary, addressing these questions, is provided below.

What is supply network design?

Supply network design involves configuring the shape and capabilities of the supply network. The supply network includes the chains of suppliers providing inputs to the operation, the chain of customers who receive outputs from the operation, and sometimes other operations that may at times compete and other times co-operate. It is a complex task that differs from 'design' in its conventional sense, because one does not necessarily own the assets being 'designed'. It consists of three interrelated activities – shaping the network (including how much of the network to own), influencing the location of operations in the network, and planning the long-term capacity strategy for each part of the network.

How should the supply network be configured?

A number of trends are reshaping networks in many industries. These include reducing the number of individual suppliers, the disintermediation of some parts of the network, and a greater tolerance of other operations being both competitors and complementors at different times. The vertical integration, outsourcing, or 'do or buy' decision also shapes supply networks. The decision to own less of the supply network (to outsource) has also been a trend in recent years. The extent of outsourcing should depend on the effect it has on operations performance and the long-term strategic positioning of the business's capabilities.

Where should operations be located?

Location means the geographical positioning of an operation. It is important because it can affect costs, revenues, customer service and capital investment. Many businesses never consider relocation, but even those that see no immediate need to relocate may find benefits from relocation. Those businesses that actively investigate relocation often do so because of either changes in demand or changes in supply. The process of evaluating alternative locations involves identifying alternative location options, usually reduced to a list of representative locations, and evaluating each option against a set of (hopefully) rational criteria, usually involving consideration of capital requirements, market factors, cost factors, future flexibility, and risk.

How much capacity should each operation in the supply network have?

This will depend on demand at any point in time. Capacity will need to be changed in the long term, as long-term demand changes, either in advance of demand changes (capacity leading) or after demand changes (capacity lagging). Nevertheless, the concept of economy of scale will always be important. Economies of scale derive from both capital and operating efficiencies that derive from large-scale processes. However, after a certain level of capacity, most operations start to suffer diseconomies of scale. The economy of scale curves for operations of different size, put together, give an idea of the optimal capacity size for a particular type of operation. However, this is only an indication. In reality, economy of scale will depend on factors that include risk and strategic positioning.

DIAGNOSTIC QUESTION

DIAGNOSTIC QUESTION

What is supply network design?

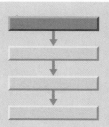

Supply network design involves configuring the shape and capabilities of one's own and other operations with which the business interacts. These include all suppliers and their suppliers, and all customers and their customers. It may also include other businesses that could be competitors under some circumstances. It is the most strategic of all the design activities and in many ways is not the same type of activity as smaller-scale design. In process design, decisions can be made with a high degree of confidence that they will be enacted as intended. In supply network design not only is the task intrinsically more complex, but there is a further crucial difference: most of the network that is being 'designed' may not be under the direct control of the 'designers'. Suppliers, customers and others in the network are independent operations. They will naturally pursue what they see as their own best interests, which may not coincide with one's own. The 'design' in supply network design is being used to mean 'influencing' and 'negotiating' rather than design in its conventional sense. However, design is a useful perspective on the tasks involved in the strategic configuration of supply networks because it conveys the idea of understanding the individual components in the network, their characteristics, and the relationships between them.

Terminology is important when describing supply networks. On the 'supply side' of the 'focal' operation (the operation from whose perspective the network is being drawn) is a group of operations that directly supplies the operation; these are often called first-tier suppliers. They are supplies by second-tier suppliers. However, some second-tier suppliers may also supply an operation directly, thus missing out a link in the network. Similarly, on the demand side of the network, 'first-tier' customers are the main customer group for the operation. These in turn supply 'second-tier' customers, although again the operation may at times supply second-tier customers directly. The suppliers and customers who have direct contact with an operation are called its immediate supply network. Figure 3.2 illustrates this.

Flow through the network

Materials, parts, information, ideas and sometimes people all flow through the network of customer–supplier relationships formed by all these operations. Also along with the forward flow of transformed resources (materials, information and customers) in the network, each customer–supplier linkage will feed back orders and information. For example, when stocks run low, retailers place orders with distributors who likewise place orders with the manufacturer, who will in turn place orders with its suppliers, who will replenish their own stocks from their own suppliers. So flow is a two-way process with items flowing one way and information flowing the other.

It is not only manufacturers who are part of a supply network. The flow of physical materials may be easier to visualize, but service operations also have suppliers and customers who themselves have their own suppliers and customers. One way to visualize the supply networks of some service operations is to consider the downstream flow of information that passes between operations. Most financial service supply networks can be

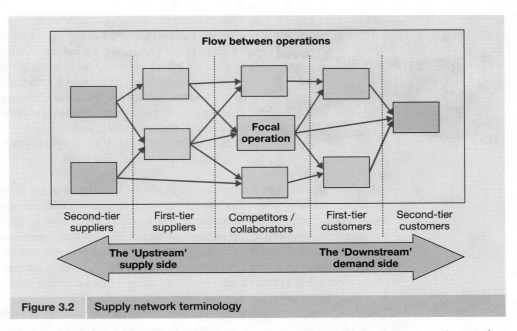

Figure 3.2 | **Supply network terminology**

thought about like this. However, not all service supply networks deal primarily in information. For example, property companies that own and/or run shopping malls have suppliers who provided security services, cleaning services, maintenance services, and so on. These first-tier suppliers will themselves receive service from recruitment agencies, consultants, etc. First-tier customers of the shopping mall are the retailers who lease retail space within the mall, who themselves serve retail customers. This is a supply network like any other. What is being exchanged between operations is the quality, speed, dependability, flexibility and cost of the services each operation supplies to its customers. In other words, there is a flow of 'operations performance' through the network. And although visualizing the flow of 'performance' through supply networks is an abstract approach to visualizing supply networks, it is a unifying concept. Broadly speaking, all types of supply network exist to facilitate the flow of 'operations performance'.

Note that this chapter deals exclusively with decision at the level of the supply network rather than at the level of 'the operation' or 'the process'. Yet networks of processes exist within operations, and networks of resources exist within processes. The issues of network configuration, location and capacity at these more operational levels are discussed in Chapters 4 and 5 (for layout and flow) and Chapter 8 (for capacity management).

Here are two examples of organizations that have made clear 'design' decisions concerning their supply networks.

Example | **Dell[1]**

When he was a student at the University of Texas at Austin, Michael Dell's sideline of buying unused stock of PCs from local dealers, adding components and re-selling the now higher-specification machines to local businesses was so successful that he quit university and founded a computer company which was to revolutionize the industry's supply network management. But his fledgling company was just too small to make its own components. Better, Dell figured to learn how to manage a network of committed specialist component manufacturers and take the best of what was available in the market. He says his commitment to outsourcing was always done for the most positive of reasons. '*We focus on how we can co-ordinate our activities to create the most value for customers.*'

Yet the company still faced a cost disadvantage against its far bigger competitors, so it decided to sell its computers direct to its customers, bypassing retailers. This allowed the company to cut out

Source: Toshfumi Kitamura/Getty Images

the retailer's (often considerable) margin, which in turn allowed Dell to offer lower prices. Dell also realized that cutting out the link in the supply network between the company and the customer provided it with significant learning opportunities by offering the chance to get to know its customers' needs far more intimately. This allowed it to forecast based on the thousands of customer contact calls every hour. It also allowed the company to talk with customers about what they really wanted from their machines. Most importantly it allowed Dell to learn how to run its supply chain so that products could move through the supply chain to the end customer in a fast and efficient manner, reducing Dell's level of inventory and giving it a significant cost advantage.

However, what is right at one time may become a liability later on. Two decades later Dell's growth started to slow down. The irony of this was that what had been the company's main advantages, its direct sales model using the Internet and its market power to squeeze price reductions from suppliers, were starting to be seen as disadvantages. Although the market had changed, Dell's operating model had not. Some commentators questioned Dell's size. How could a $56 billion company remain lean, sharp and alert? Other commentators pointed out that Dell's rivals had also now learned to run efficient supply chains ('Getting a 20-year competitive advantage from your knowledge of how to run supply chains isn't too bad').

However, one of the main factors was seen as the shift in the nature of the market itself. Sales of PCs to business users had become largely a commodity business with wafer-thin margins, and this part of the market was growing slowly compared with the sale of computers to individuals. Selling computers to individuals provided slightly better margins than the corporate market, but they increasingly wanted up-to-date computers with a high design value, and most significantly they wanted to see, touch and feel the products before buying them. This was clearly a problem for a company like Dell which had spent 20 years investing in its telephone and, later, Internet-based sales channels. What all commentators agreed on was that in the fast-moving and cut-throat computer business, where market requirements could change overnight, operations resources must constantly develop appropriate new capabilities.

Michael Dell said the company could regain its spot as the world's number one PC maker by switching its focus to consumers and the developing world. He also conceded that the company had missed out on the boom in supplying computers to home users – who make up just 15 per cent of its revenues – because it was focused on supplying businesses. *'Let's say you wanted to buy a Dell computer in a store nine months ago – you'd have searched a long time and not found one. Now we have over 10,000 stores that sell our products.'* He rejected the idea that design was not important to his company, although he accepted that it had not been a top priority when all the focus was on business customers. *'As we've gone to the consumer we've been paying quite a bit more attention to design, fashion, colours, textures and materials.'*

<table><tr><td>Example</td><td></td></tr></table>

The BBC outsources its Technology Division[2]

The British Broadcasting Corporation (BBC) is one of the world's best-known and most respected broadcasting organizations. The public face of the BBC is its broadcast output listened to and

Source: Monty Rakusen/Digital Vision/Getty

watched by millions all over the world. But behind the scenes it depends on its ability to create, manage and distribute broadcast 'content'. A pivotal part of this capability is BBC Technology, a division of the corporation that provides technology services, not just for the BBC, but also for other broadcasters, platform owners, content owners and government organizations. So, when John Varney, Chief Technology Officer at the BBC, announced that it would 'outsource' much of its technology infrastructure to a subsidiary of Germany's Siemens Company in a massive £2 billion 10-year deal, he caused some surprise among his global broadcasting peers. *'It's a revolutionary deal for this industry,'* said Mitchell Linden, head of what used to be the BBC Technology North America unit in San Francisco. *'Now everyone is intensely curious. We have US broadcasters, media companies and multimedia suppliers like Apple all wanting to find out what we did, why we did it and what we are going to do in the future.'*

What the BBC did is significant. Encouraged by pressure from the British government to cut costs and divest, it conducted an internal strategic review of the Corporation's technology requirements that identified potential annual savings for the BBC of around £30,000,000 if its technology services were outsourced. After evaluating possible candidates, it signed the Technology Framework Contract, which gives Siemens' Business Services full responsibility for maintaining and developing the BBC's UK Information technology (IT) infrastructure – including networks, servers, desktops, telephones, broadcasting systems, channel platforms and distribution, support for 53 overseas news bureaux, and its website. But the £30,000,000 annual cost savings isn't the only reason for outsourcing to Siemens, says John Varney. Because Siemens, with revenues of over £20 billion globally, is one of the world's largest IT and business services providers, it will be able to help move away from tape storage towards making programmes digitally on desktop PCs, something Varney believes will *'revolutionize the use of technology in making and distributing programmes'*. This would make the company's content accessible on everything from the Web to mobile phones, a challenge that faces everyone in the broadcasting industry.

According to Adrian Corcoran, managing director of BBC Technology, *'This is exciting news for our staff and our customers. Being part of a large, global organization gives us the resources, opportunities and investment that just weren't available as part of the BBC, whose focus quite rightly is content, not technology investment.'* But not everyone was happy with the deal. Some BBC staff affiliated with the Broadcasting Entertainment Cinematograph and Theatre Union (BECTU) disputed the BBC's claim that the deal would save £30,000,000 per year and voted in favour of industrial action in reaction to the agreement. *'This isn't just the BBC selling off one of its Crown Jewels, it's a case of handing its central nervous system over to the private sector,'* said Gerry Morrissey, Assistant General Secretary of the union.

What do these two examples have in common?

Both these examples involve operations deciding to position themselves in some (but not all) parts of their supply network. Dell revolutionized its sector by dealing directly with the public and gained an advantage over its rivals that lasted for decades. The BBC, a public corporation, chose to give responsibility for running its technology division to a private company. In doing so it was making implicit decisions about what the core objective of the BBC should be. It was a broadcasting organization, not a technology organization. Also, both examples are not without controversy. Indeed, deciding on where you want to be in the supply network often means that there will be gainers and losers. The trade unions representing BBC staff suspected that what promised to be a good deal for the BBC (and the tax payers who fund it) was not necessarily such a good deal for the staff who worked in the operation. A slightly different sort of risk is illustrated in the example of Dell. Here, the supply network strategy that had helped the company for 20 years started to become something of a liability when the market, and competitor activity, changed. Both of these examples illustrate the first of the three strategic decisions of supply networks that are covered in this chapter.

- How should the network be shaped? Both in terms of ordering the relationships between operations in the network, and in terms of how much of the network the operation should own.
- Where should each part of the network owned by the company be located?
- What capacity should each part of the network owned by the company have at any point in time?

Note that all three of these decisions rely on assumptions regarding the level of future demand. The supplement to this chapter explores forecasting in more detail. In Chapter 7, we will cover the more operational day-to-day issues of managing operations networks.

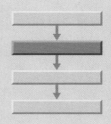

How should the supply network be configured?

An operation may want to use its influence to manage network behaviour by reconfiguring the network so as to change the scope of the activities performed in each operation and the nature of the relationships between them. The most common example of network reconfiguration has come in the attempts made over the last few years by many companies to reduce the number of suppliers with whom they have direct contact. The complexity of dealing with many hundreds of suppliers may both be expensive for an operation and (sometimes more important) prevent the operation from developing close relationships with suppliers. It is not easy to be close to hundreds of different suppliers. This has led many companies to reconfigure their supply-side network to make it simpler and more orderly. It has also meant that some suppliers have become increasingly important to their customers.

> **Operations principle**
> Reducing the number of suppliers can reduce transaction costs and enrich supplier relationships.

For example, take the front part of a car, the bit with the bumper, radiator grill, fog lights, side-lights, badge and so on.[3] At one time each of these components came from different specialist suppliers. Now the whole of this 'module' may come from one 'system supplier'. Traditional car makers are getting smaller and are relying on systems suppliers such as TRW in the US, Bosch in Germany, and Magna in Canada to provide them with whole chunks of car. Some of these system suppliers are global players that rival the car makers themselves in scope and reach. Cost pressures have forced car makers to let their suppliers take more responsibility for engineering and pre-assembly. This also means that they work with fewer suppliers. For example, Ford Europe's old Escort model took parts from around 700 direct suppliers, while the replacement Focus model used only 210. Future models may have fewer than 100 direct suppliers. This can also make joint development easier. For example, Volvo paired up with one supplier (Autoliv) to develop safety systems incorporating side air bags. In return, Volvo got exclusive rights to use the systems for the first year. A smaller number of system suppliers also makes it easier to update components. While a car maker may not find it economic to change its seating systems more than once every seven or eight years, a specialist supplier could have several alternative types of seat in parallel development at any one time.

Disintermediation

Another trend in some supply networks is that of companies within a network bypassing customers or suppliers to make contact directly with customers' customers or suppliers' suppliers. 'Cutting out the middle men' in this way is called *disintermediation*. An obvious example of this is the way the Internet has allowed some suppliers to 'disintermediate' traditional retailers in supplying goods and services to consumers. So, for example, many services in the travel industry that used to be sold through retail outlets (travel agents) are now also available direct from the suppliers. The option of purchasing the individual components of a vacation through the websites of the airline, hotel, car-hire company, etc. is now easier for consumers. Of course, they may still wish to purchase an 'assembled' product from retail travel agents which can have the advantage of convenience. Nevertheless the process of disintermediation has developed new linkages in the supply network.

FURTHER EXAMPLE

Coopetition

One approach to thinking about supply networks is called the 'value net' for a company. It sees any business as being surrounded by four types of players: suppliers, customers, competitors and complementors. Complementors enable one's products or services to be valued more by customers because they can also have the complementor's products or services, as opposed to having yours alone. Competitors are the opposite: they make customers value your product or service less when they can have their product or service, rather than yours alone. Competitors can also be complementors and vice versa. For example, adjacent restaurants may see themselves as competitors for customers' business. A customer standing outside and wanting a meal will choose between the two of them. Yet in another way they are complementors. Would that customer have come to this part of town unless there was more than one restaurant to choose from? Restaurants, theatres, art galleries, tourist attractions generally, all cluster together in a form of co-operation to increase the total size of their joint market. It is important to distinguish between the way companies co-operate in increasing the total size of a market and the way in which they then compete for a share of that market.

Customers and suppliers have 'symmetric' roles. Historically, insufficient emphasis has been put on the role of the supplier. Harnessing the value of suppliers is just as important as listening to the needs of customers. Destroying value in a supplier in order to create it in a customer does not increase the value of the network as a whole. For example, pressurizing suppliers because customers are pressurizing you will not add long-term value. In the long term it creates value for the total network to find ways of increasing value for suppliers as well as customers. All the players in the network, whether they be customers, suppliers, competitors or complementors, can be both friends and enemies at different times. This is not 'unusual' or 'aberrant' behaviour. It is the way things are. The term used to capture this idea is 'coopetition'.[4]

Insource or outsource? Do or buy? The vertical integration decision

No single business does everything that is required to produce its products and services. Bakers do not grow wheat or even mill it into flour. Banks do not usually do their own credit checking – they retain the services of specialist credit-checking agencies that have the specialized information systems and expertise to do it better. This process is called outsourcing and has become an important issue for most businesses. This is because, although most companies have always outsourced some of their activities, a larger proportion of direct activities are now being bought from suppliers. Also many indirect processes are now being outsourced. This is often referred to as business process outsourcing (BPO). Financial service companies in particular are starting to outsource some of their more routine back-office processes. In a similar way many processes within the Human Resource function, from simply payroll services through to more complex training and development processes, are being outsourced to specialist companies. The processes may still be physically located where they were before, but the staff and technology are managed by the outsourcing service provider. The reason for doing this is often primarily to reduce cost. However, there can sometimes also be significant gains in the quality and flexibility of service offered. *'People talk a lot about looking beyond cost cutting when it comes to outsourcing companies' human resource functions,'* says Jim Madden, CEO of Exult, the California-based specialist outsourcing company. *'I don't believe any company will sign up for this (outsourcing) without cost reduction being part of it, but for the clients whose human resource functions we manage, such as BP, and Bank of America, it is not just about saving money.'*

The outsourcing debate is just part of a far larger issue which will shape the fundamental nature of any business. Namely, what should the scope of the business be? In other words, what should it do itself and what should it buy in? This is often referred to

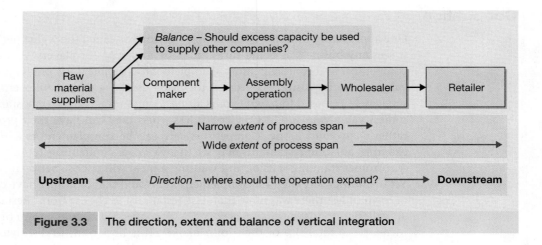

Figure 3.3 The direction, extent and balance of vertical integration

as the 'do or buy decision' when individual components or activities are being considered, or 'vertical integration' when it is the ownership of whole operations that is being decided. Vertical integration is the extent to which an organization owns the network of which it is a part. It usually involves an organization assessing the wisdom of acquiring suppliers or customers. Vertical integration can be defined in terms of three factors (Figure 3.3):[5]

- **Direction**. Should an operation expand by buying one of its suppliers or by buying one of its customers? The strategy of expanding on the supply side of the network is sometimes called backward or upstream vertical integration, and expanding on the demand side is sometimes called forward or downstream vertical integration.
- **Extent**. How far should an operation take the extent of its vertical integration? Some organizations deliberately choose not to integrate far, if at all, from their original part of the network. Alternatively, some organizations choose to become very vertically integrated.
- **Balance among stages**. This is not strictly about the ownership of the network, but rather the exclusivity of the relationship between operations. A totally balanced network relationship is one where one operation produces only for the next stage in the network and totally satisfies its requirements. Less than full balance allows each operation to sell its output to other companies or to buy in some of its supplies from other companies. Fully balanced networks have the virtue of simplicity and also allow each operation to focus on the requirements of the next stage along in the network. Having to supply other organizations, perhaps with slightly different requirements, might serve to distract from what is needed by their (owned) primary customer. However, a totally self-sufficient network is sometimes not feasible, nor is it necessarily desirable.

How any business positions itself in its supply network is a function of what it sees as its particular areas of expertise and where it feels it can be most profitable. However, these two factors do not always coincide. Where a business has expertise may not always be the most profitable part of the supply network. This can be a driver of vertical integration. For example, Ghana's largest cocoa bean co-operative, Kuapa Kokoo, owns 45 per cent of Divine, a chocolate company that produces in Germany. This is because although chocolate sales globally are around $75 billion a year, traditionally the growers of cocoa (from which chocolate is made) have received only around $4 billion a year from the sale of cocoa beans. By taking a share of Divine, Kuapa Kokoo can capture a little more of the revenue further down the supply network.[6]

Making the outsourcing/vertical integration decision

Whether it is referred to as do or buy, vertical integration or no vertical integration, in-house or outsourced supply, the choice facing operations is rarely simple. Organizations in different circumstances with different objectives are likely to take different decisions. Yet the question itself is relatively simple, even if the decision itself is not: 'Does inhouse or outsourced supply in a particular set of circumstances give the appropriate performance objectives that it requires to compete more effectively in its markets?' For example, if the main performance objectives for an operation are dependable delivery and meeting short-term changes in customers' delivery requirements, the key question should be: 'How does in-house or outsourcing give better dependability and deliver flexible performance?'

> **Operations principle**
> Assessing the advisability of outsourcing should include how it impacts on relevant performance objectives.

This means judging two sets of opposing factors – those that give the potential to improve performance, and those that work against this potential being realized. Table 3.1 summarizes some arguments for in-house supply and outsourcing in terms of each performance objective.

Deciding whether to outsource

Although the effect of outsourcing on the operation's performance objective is important, there are other factors that companies take into account when deciding whether outsourcing an activity is a sensible option. For example, if an activity has long-term strategic importance to a company, it is unlikely to outsource it. A retailer might choose to keep the design and development of its website in-house even though specialists could perform the activity at less cost, because it plans to move into Web-based retailing at some point in the future. Nor would a company usually outsource an activity where it had specialized skills or knowledge. For example, a company making laser printers may have built up specialized knowledge in the production of sophisticated laser drives. This capability may allow it to introduce product or process innovations in the future. It would be foolish to 'give away' such capability. After these two more strategic factors have been considered, the company's operations performance can be taken into account. Obviously, if its operations performance is already superior to that of any potential supplier, it would be unlikely to outsource the activity. But also, even if its performance was currently below that of potential suppliers, it may not outsource the activity if it feels that it could significantly improve its performance. Figure 3.4 illustrates this decision logic.

> **Operations principle**
> Assessing the advisability of outsourcing should include consideration of the strategic importance of the activity and the operation's relative performance.

FURTHER EXAMPLE

Outsourcing and offshoring

Two supply network strategies that are often confused are those of outsourcing and offshoring. Outsourcing means deciding to buy-in products or services rather than perform the activities in-house. Offshoring means obtaining products and services from operations that are based outside one's own country. Of course, one may both outsource and offshore, as illustrated in Figure 3.5. Offshoring is very closely related to outsourcing and the motives for each may be similar. Offshoring to a lower-cost region of the world is usually done to reduce an operation's overall costs, as is outsourcing to a supplier which has greater expertise or scale or both.[7]

Table 3.1	How in-house and outsourced supply may affect an operation's performance objectives	
Performance objective	'Do it yourself': in-house supply	'Buy it in': outsourced supply
Quality	The origins of any quality problems are usually easier to trace in-house and improvement can be more immediate, but there can be some risk of complacency.	Supplier may have specialized knowledge and more experience, also may be motivated through market pressures, but communication of quality problems more difficult.
Speed	Can mean closer synchronization of schedules which speeds up the throughput of materials and information, but if the operation also has external customers, internal customers may receive low priority.	Speed of response can be built into the supply contract where commercial pressures will encourage good performance, but there may be significant transport/delivery delays.
Dependability	Easier communications internally can help dependable delivery, which also may help when internal customers need to be informed of potential delays, but as with speed, if the operation also has external customers, internal customers may receive low priority.	Late delivery penalties in the supply contract can encourage good delivery performance, but distance and organizational barriers may inhibit communication.
Flexibility	Closeness to the real needs of a business can alert the in-house operation that some kind of change is required in its operations, but the ability to respond may be limited by the scale and scope of internal operations.	Outsource suppliers are likely to be larger and have wider capabilities than in-house suppliers. This gives them more ability to respond to changes, but they can only respond when asked to do so by the customer and they may have to balance the conflicting needs of different customers.
Cost	In-house operations give the potential for sharing some costs such as research and development, or logistics. More significantly, in-house operations do not have to make the margin required by outside suppliers, so the business can capture the profits that would otherwise be given to the supplier, but relatively low volumes may mean that it is difficult to gain economies of scale or the benefits of process innovation.	Probably the main reason why outsourcing is so popular. Outsourced companies can achieve economies of scale and they are motivated to reduce their own costs because it directly impacts on their profits, but extra costs of communication and co-ordination with an external supplier need to be taken into account.

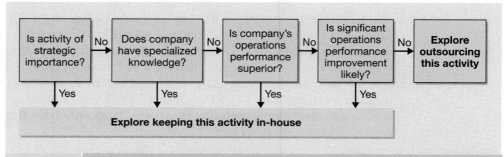

| Figure 3.4 | The decision logic of outsourcing |

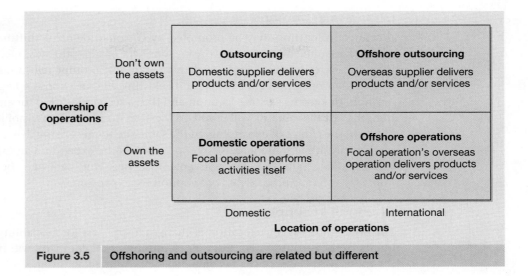

		Domestic	International
Ownership of operations	Don't own the assets	**Outsourcing** Domestic supplier delivers products and/or services	**Offshore outsourcing** Overseas supplier delivers products and/or services
	Own the assets	**Domestic operations** Focal operation performs activities itself	**Offshore operations** Focal operation's overseas operation delivers products and/or services
		\multicolumn{2}{c}{**Location of operations**}	

Figure 3.5   Offshoring and outsourcing are related but different

DIAGNOSTIC QUESTION

Where should operations be located?

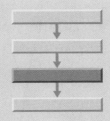

Location is the geographical positioning of an operation. It can be an important decision because it usually has an effect on an operation's costs as well as its ability to serve its customers (and therefore its revenues). So getting location wrong can have a significant impact on profits. In retailing, a difference in location of a few metres can make the difference between profit and loss. Mislocating a fire service station can slow down the average journey time of the fire crews in getting to the fires. Locating a factory where there is difficulty attracting labour with appropriate skills may damage the effectiveness of the factory's operations, and so on. The other reason why location decisions are important is that, once taken, they are difficult to undo. The costs of moving an operation from one site to another can be hugely expensive and the risks of inconveniencing customers very high. No operation wants to move very often.

Why relocate?

> **Operations principle**
> An operation should only change its location if the benefits of moving outweigh the costs of operating in the new location plus the costs of the move itself.

Not all operations can logically justify their location. Some are where they are for historical reasons. Yet even the operations that are 'there because they're there' are implicitly making a decision not to move. Presumably their assumption is that the cost and disruption involved in changing location would outweigh any potential benefits of a new location. Two stimuli often cause organizations to make location decisions: changes in demand for goods and services, and changes in supply of inputs to the operation.

Changes in demand

A change in location may be prompted by customer demand shifting. For example, as garment manufacture moved to Asia, suppliers of zips, threads, etc. started to follow them. Changes in the volume of demand can also prompt relocation. To meet higher demand, an operation could expand its existing site, or choose a larger site in another location, or keep its existing location and find a second location for an additional operation; the last two options will involve a location decision. High-visibility operations may not have the choice of expanding on the same site to meet rising demand. A dry-cleaning service may attract only marginally more business by expanding an existing site because it offers a local, and therefore convenient, service. Finding a new location for an additional operation is probably its only option for expansion.

Changes in supply

The other stimulus for relocation is changes in the cost, or availability, of the supply of inputs to the operation. For example, a mining or oil company will need to relocate as the minerals it is extracting become depleted. A manufacturing company might choose to relocate its operations to a part of the world where labour costs are low, because the equivalent resources (people) in its original location have become relatively expensive. Sometimes a business might choose to relocate to release funds if the value of the land it occupies is worth more than an alternative, equally good, location.

Evaluating potential changes in location

Evaluating possible locations is almost always a complex task because the number of location options, the criteria against which they could be evaluated, and the comparative rarity of a single location that clearly dominates all others, make the decision strategically sensitive. Furthermore, the decision often involves high levels of uncertainty. Neither the relocation activity itself nor the operating characteristics of the new site could be as assumed when the decision was originally made. Because of this, it is useful to be systematic in terms of (a) identifying alternative options, and (b) evaluating each option against a set of rational criteria.

Identify alternative location options

The first relocation option to consider is not to relocate at all. Sometimes relocation is inevitable, but often staying put is a viable option. Even if seeking a new location seems the obvious way forward, it is worth evaluating the 'do nothing' option, if only to provide a 'base case' against which to compare other options. But in addition to the 'do nothing' option there should be a number of alternative location options. It is a mistake to consider only one location, but seeking out possible locations can be a time-consuming activity. Increasingly, for larger companies, the whole world offers possible locations. While it has always been possible to manufacture in one part of the world in order to sell in another, until recently non-manufacturing operations were assumed to be confined to their home market. But no longer: the operational skills (as well as the brand image) of many service operations are transferable across national boundaries. Hotels, fast food, retailers and professional services all make location decisions on an international stage. Similarly, information-processing operations can now locate outside their immediate home base, thanks to virtually seamless telecommunications networks. If a financial services, or any other, business sees a cost advantage in locating part of its back-office operations in a part of the world where the 'cost per transaction' is lower, it can do so.

The implication of the globalization of the location decision is to increase both the number of options and the degree of uncertainty in their relative merits. The sheer number of possibilities makes the location decision impossible to 'optimize'. Unless every single option is explored, no one best choice is possible. Rather, the process of identifying location options usually involves selecting a limited number of sites that represent different attributes. For example, a distribution centre, while always needing to be close to transport links, could be located in any of several regions and could be either close to population centres or in a more rural location. The options may be chosen to reflect a range of both these factors. However, this assumes that the 'supply' of location options is relatively large, which is not always the case. For example, in many retail location decisions, there are a limited number of High Street locations that become available at any point in time. Often, a retailer will wait until a feasible location becomes available and then decide whether to either take up that option or wait and take the chance that a better location becomes available soon. In effect, the location decision here is a sequence of 'take or wait' decisions. Nevertheless, in making the decision to take or wait, a similar set of criteria to the more common location problem may be appropriate.

Set location evaluation criteria

Although the criteria against which alternative locations can be evaluated will depend on circumstances, the following five broad categories are typical.

Capital requirements The capital or leasing cost of a site is usually a significant factor. This will probably be a function of the location of the site and its characteristics. For example, the shape of the site and its soil composition can limit the nature of any buildings erected there. Access to the site is also likely to be important, as are the availability of utilities, etc. In addition the cost of the move itself may depend on which site is eventually chosen.

Market factors Location can affect how the market, either in general or as individual customers, perceives an operation. Locating a general hospital in the middle of the countryside may have many advantages for its staff, but it clearly would be very inconvenient for its customers. Likewise, restaurants, stores, banks, petrol filling stations and many other high visibility operations must all evaluate how alternative locations will determine their image and the level of service they can give. The same arguments apply to labour markets. Location may affect the attractiveness of the operation in terms of staff recruitment and retention. For example, 'science parks' are usually located close to universities because they hope to attract companies that are interested in using the skills available at the university. But not all locations necessarily have appropriate skills available immediately. Staff at a remote call centre in the western islands of Scotland, used to a calm and tranquil life, were stunned by the aggressive nature of many callers to the call centre, and some were reduced to tears by bullying customers. They had to be given assertiveness training by the call centre management.

Cost factors Two major categories of cost are affected by location. The first is the cost of producing products or services. For example, labour costs can vary between different areas in any country, but are likely to be a far more significant factor when international comparisons are made, when they can exert a major influence on the location decision, especially in some industries such as clothing, where labour costs as a proportion of total costs are relatively high. Other cost factors, known as community factors, derive from the social, political and economic environment of its site. These include such factors as local tax rates, capital movement restrictions, government financial assistance, political stability, local attitudes to 'inward investment', language, local amenities (schools, theatres, shops, etc.), the availability of support services, the history of labour relations and behaviour, environmental restrictions and planning procedures. The second category of costs relates to both the cost of transporting inputs from their source to the location of the operation and the cost of transporting products and services from

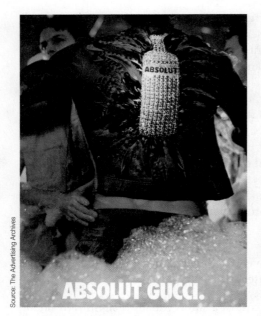

Source: The Advertising Archives

The Swedish company Vin & Spirit was bought by Pernod Ricard, which immediately gave assurances that the company's most important product, Absolut Vodka, would continue to be made in Sweden. 'Making such a quintessential Swedish product as Absolut Vodka anywhere other than Sweden would seriously harm the brand,' said one commentator.

PRACTICE NOTE

the location to customers. Whereas almost all operations are concerned to some extent with the former, not all operations are concerned with the latter, either because customers come to them (for example, hotels), or because their services can be 'transported' at virtually no cost (for example, some technology help desks). For supply networks that process physical items, however, transportation costs can be very significant.

Future flexibility Because operations rarely change their location, any new location must be capable of being acceptable, not only under current circumstances but also under possible future circumstances. The problem is that no one knows exactly what the future holds. Nevertheless, especially in uncertain environments, any evaluation of alternative locations should include some kind of scenario planning that considers the robustness of each in coping with a range of possible futures. Two types of the flexibility of any location could be evaluated. The most common is to consider the potential of the location for expansion to cope with increased activity levels. The second is the ability to adapt to changes in input or output factors. For example, suppliers or customers may themselves relocate in the future. If so, could the location still operate economically?

Risk factors Closely related to the concept of future flexibility is the idea of evaluating the risk factors associated with possible locations. Again, the risk criteria can be divided into 'transition risk' and 'long-term risk'. Transition risk is simply the risk that something goes wrong during the relocation process. Some possible locations might be intrinsically more difficult to move to than others. For example, moving to an already congested location could pose higher risks to being able to move as planned than moving to a more accessible location. Long-term risks could again include damaging changes in input factors such as exchange rates or labour costs, but can also include more fundamental security risks to staff or property.

DIAGNOSTIC QUESTION

How much capacity should each operation in the supply network have?

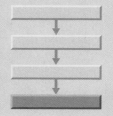

The design of supply networks also includes defining the capacity of each operation in the network. Unless the capacity of individual operations reflects the needs of the network as a whole, it will either limit flow through the network or be the cause of capacity underutilization, both of which will in the long term reduce the effectiveness of the network as a whole. Here we shall treat capacity in a general long-term sense. Shorter-term aspects of capacity management are treated in Chapter 8. But whether over the short or long term, demand forecasts are one of the main inputs to capacity management, which is why forecasting is treated in the supplement to this chapter.

The optimum capacity level

Most organizations need to decide on the size (in terms of capacity) of each of their facilities. A chain of truck service centres, for example, might operate centres that have various capacities. The effective cost of running each centre will depend on the average service bay occupancy. Low occupancy because of few customers will result in a high cost per customer served because the fixed costs of the operation are being shared between few customers. As demand, and therefore service bay occupancy, increases the cost per customer will reduce. However, operating at very high levels of capacity utilization (occupancy levels close to capacity) can mean longer customer waiting times and reduced customer service. This effect is described in more detail in Chapter 5. There may also be less obvious cost penalties of operating centres at levels close to their nominal capacity. For example, long periods of overtime may reduce productivity levels as well as costing more in extra payments to staff; utilizing bays at very high utilization levels reduces maintenance and cleaning time that may increase breakdowns, reduce effective life, and so on. This usually means that average costs start to increase after a point that will often be lower than the theoretical capacity of the operation.

The blue curves in Figure 3.6 show this effect for the service centres of 5-, 10- and 15-bay capacity. As the nominal capacity of the centres increases, the lowest cost point at first reduces. This is because the fixed costs of any operation do not increase proportionately as its capacity increases. A 10-bay centre has less than twice the fixed costs of a 5-bay centre. Also the capital costs of constructing the operations do not increase proportionately to their capacity. A 10-bay centre costs less to build than twice the cost of a 5-bay centre. These two factors, taken together, are often referred to as economies of scale. However, above a certain size, the lowest cost point may increase. This occurs because of what are called diseconomies of scale, two of which are particularly important. First, complexity costs increase as size increases. The communications and co-ordination effort necessary to manage an operation tends to increase faster than capacity. Although not seen as a direct cost, this can nevertheless be very significant. Second, a larger centre is more likely to be partially underutilized because demand within a fixed location will be limited. The equivalent in operations that process physical items is transportation costs. For example, if a manufacturer supplies the whole of its European market from one

> **Operations principle**
> All types of operation exhibit economy of scale effects where operating costs reduce as the scale of capacity increases.

> **Operations principle**
> Diseconomies of scale increase operating costs above a certain level of capacity resulting in a minimum cost level of capacity.

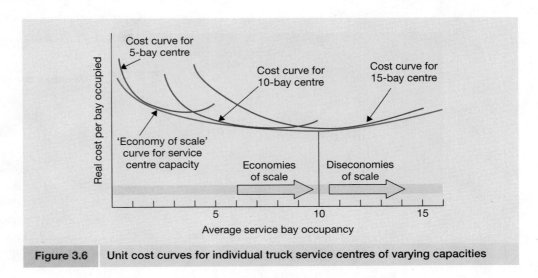

| **Figure 3.6** | Unit cost curves for individual truck service centres of varying capacities |

major plant in Denmark, all supplies may have to be brought in from several countries to the single plant and all products shipped from there throughout Europe.

Being small may have advantages

Although large-scale capacity operations will usually have a cost advantage over smaller units, there are also potentially significant advantages that can be exploited by small-scale operations. One research study showed that small-scale operations can provide significant advantages in the following four areas.[8]

● They allow businesses to locate near to 'hot spots' that can tap into local knowledge networks. Often larger companies centralize their research and development efforts, losing touch with where innovative ideas are generated.
● Responding rapidly to regional customer needs and trends by basing more and smaller units of capacity close to local markets.
● Taking advantage of the potential for human resource development by allowing staff a greater degree of local autonomy. Larger-scale operations often have longer career paths with fewer opportunities for 'taking charge'.
● Exploring radically new technologies by acting in the same way as a smaller, more entrepreneurial rival. Larger, more centralized development activities are often more bureaucratic than smaller-scale agile centres of development.

Scale of capacity and the demand–capacity balance

Large units of capacity also have some disadvantages when the capacity of the operation is being changed to match changing demand. For example, suppose that a manufacturer forecasts demand to increase over the next three years, as shown in Figure 3.7, levelling off at around 2400 units a week. If the company seeks to satisfy all demand by building three plants as demand builds up, each of 800 units capacity, the company will have substantial amounts of overcapacity for much of the period when demand is increasing. Overcapacity means low capacity utilization, which in turn means higher unit costs. If the company builds smaller plants, say 400-unit plants, there will still be overcapacity but to a lesser extent, which means higher capacity utilization and possibly lower costs.

> **Operations principle**
> Changing capacity in large units of capacity reduces the chance of achieving demand – capacity balance.

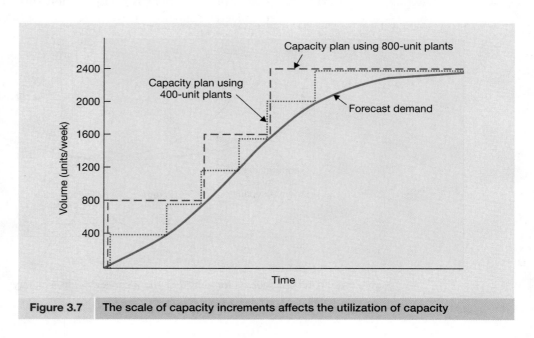

Figure 3.7   The scale of capacity increments affects the utilization of capacity

The timing of capacity change

Changing the capacity of an operation is not just a matter of deciding on the best size of a capacity increment. The operation also needs to decide when to bring new capacity 'on stream'. Continuing the above example, Figure 3.8 shows the forecast demand for the new manufacturing operation. The company has decided to build 400-unit-per-week plants in order to meet the growth in demand for its new product. In deciding when the new plants are to be introduced, the company must choose a position somewhere between two extreme strategies:

> **Operations principle**
> Capacity leading strategies increase opportunities to meet demand.

- Capacity leads demand – timing the introduction of capacity in such a way that there is always sufficient capacity to meet forecast demand.
- Capacity lags demand – timing the introduction of capacity so that demand is always equal to or greater than capacity.

Figure 3.8 shows these two extreme strategies, although in practice the company is likely to choose a position somewhere between the two. Each strategy has its own advantages and disadvantages. These are shown in Table 3.2. The actual approach taken by any company will depend on how it views these advantages and disadvantages. For example, if the company's access to funds for capital expenditure is limited, it is likely to find the delayed capital expenditure requirement of the capacity-lagging strategy relatively attractive.

> **Operations principle**
> Capacity-lagging strategies increase capacity utilization.

'Smoothing' with inventory

> **Operations principle**
> Using inventory to overcome demand – capacity imbalance tends to increase working capital requirements.

The strategy on the continuum between pure leading and pure lagging strategies can be implemented so that no inventories are accumulated. All demand in one period is satisfied (or not) by the activity of the operation in the same period. Indeed, for customer-processing operations there is no alternative to this. A hotel cannot satisfy demand in one year by using rooms which

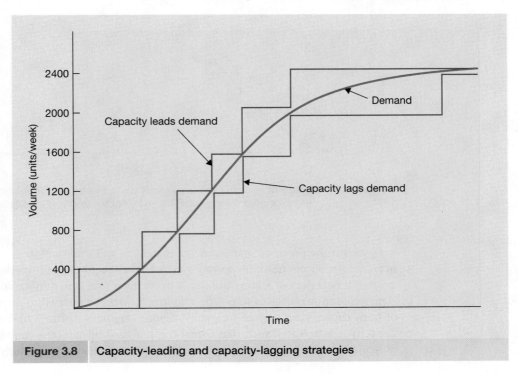

Figure 3.8   Capacity-leading and capacity-lagging strategies

Table 3.2	The arguments for and against pure leading and pure lagging strategies of capacity timing

Advantages	Disadvantages
Capacity-leading strategies	
Always sufficient capacity to meet demand, therefore revenue is maximized and customers are satisfied	Utilization of the plants is always relatively low, therefore costs will be high
Most of the time there is a 'capacity cushion' which can absorb extra demand levels if forecasts are pessimistic	Risk of even greater (or even permanent) over-capacity if demand does not reach forecast levels
Any critical start-up problems with new plants are less likely to affect supply to customers	Capital spending on plant early
Capacity-lagging strategies	
Always sufficient demand to keep the plants working at full capacity, therefore unit costs are minimized	Insufficient capacity to meet demand fully, therefore reduced revenue and dissatisfied customers
Overcapacity problems are minimized if forecasts are optimistic	No ability to exploit short-term increases in demand
Capital spending on the plants is delayed	Under-supply position even worse if there are start-up problems with the new plants

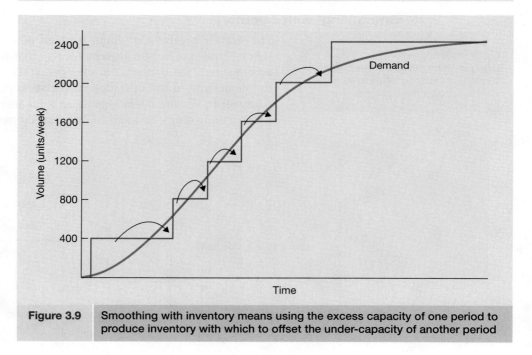

Figure 3.9	Smoothing with inventory means using the excess capacity of one period to produce inventory with which to offset the under-capacity of another period

were vacant the previous year. For some materials- and information-processing operations, however, the output from the operation which is not required in one period can be stored for use in the next period. The economies of using inventories are fully explored in Chapter 10. Here we confine ourselves to noting that inventories can be used to obtain the advantages of both capacity leading and capacity lagging. Figure 3.9 shows how this can be done. Capacity is introduced such that demand can always be met by a combination of production and inventories, and capacity is, with the occasional exception, fully utilized.

This may seem like an ideal state. Demand is always met and so revenue is maximized. Capacity is usually fully utilized and so costs are minimized. There is a price to pay, however, and that is the cost of carrying the inventories. Not only will these have to be funded but the risks of obsolescence and deterioration of stock are introduced (see Chapter 9). Table 3.3 summarizes the advantages and disadvantages of the 'smoothing-with-inventory' strategy.

Break-even analysis of capacity expansion

Excel

PRACTICE NOTE

An alternative view of capacity expansion can be gained by examining the cost implications of adding increments of capacity on a break-even basis. Figure 3.10 shows how increasing capacity can move an operation from profitability to loss. Each additional unit of capacity results in a fixed-cost break, which is a further lump of expenditure that will have to be incurred before any further activity can be undertaken in the operation.

The operation is therefore unlikely to be profitable at very low levels of output. Eventually, assuming that prices are greater than marginal costs, revenue will exceed total costs. However, the level of profitability at the point where the output level is equal to the capacity of the operation may not be sufficient to absorb all the extra fixed costs of a further increment in capacity. This could make the operation unprofitable in some stages of its expansion.

Table 3.3	The advantages and disadvantages of a smoothing-with-inventory strategy
Advantages	*Disadvantages*
All demand is satisfied, therefore customers are satisfied and revenue is maximized	The cost of inventories in terms of working capital requirements can be high. This is especially serious at a time when the company requires funds for its capital expansion
Utilization of capacity is high and therefore costs are low	Risk of product deterioration and obsolescence
Very short-term surges in demand can be met from inventories	

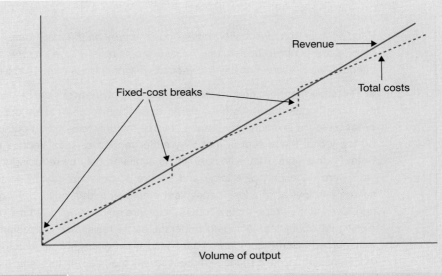

Figure 3.10 Incurring fixed costs repeatedly can raise total costs above revenue over some ranges of output

Worked example

A specialist graphics company is investing in new systems that will enable it to make high-quality images for its clients. Demand for these images is forecast to be around 100,000 images in year 1 and 220,000 images in year 2. The maximum capacity of each system is 100,000 images per year. They have a fixed cost of €200,000 per year and a variable cost of processing of €1 per image. The company believes it will be able to charge an average of €4 per image. What profit is it likely to make in the first and second years?

$$\text{Year 1 demand} = 100,000 \text{ images; therefore company will need one machine}$$
$$\text{Cost of producing images} = \text{fixed cost for one machine} + (\text{variable cost} \times 100,000)$$
$$= €200,000 + (€1 \times 100,000)$$
$$= €300,000$$
$$\text{Revenue} = \text{demand} \times \text{price}$$
$$= 100,000 \times €4$$
$$= €400,000$$
$$\text{Therefore profit} = €400,000 - €300,000$$
$$= €100,000$$
$$\text{Year 2 demand} = 220,000 \text{ units; therefore company will need three machines}$$
$$\text{Cost of producing images} = \text{fixed cost for three machines} + (\text{variable cost} \times 220,000)$$
$$= (3 \times €200,000) + (€1 \times 220,000)$$
$$= €820,000$$
$$\text{Revenue} = \text{demand} \times \text{price}$$
$$= 220,000 \times €4$$
$$= €880,000$$
$$\text{Therefore profit} = €880,000 - €820,000$$
$$= €60,000$$

Note: the profit in the second year will be lower because of the extra fixed costs associated with the investment in the two extra machines.

Critical commentary

Each chapter contains a short critical commentary on the main ideas covered in the chapter. Its purpose is not to undermine the issues discussed in the chapter, but to emphasize that, although we present a relatively orthodox view of operation, there are other perspectives.

■ Probably the most controversial issue in supply network design is that of outsourcing. In many instances there has been fierce opposition to companies outsourcing some of their processes. Trade unions often point out that the only reason that outsourcing companies can do the job at lower cost is that they either reduce salaries, reduce working conditions, or both. Furthermore, they say, flexibility is achieved only by reducing job security. Employees who were once part of a large and secure corporation could find themselves as far less secure employees of a less benevolent employer with a philosophy of permanent cost cutting. Even some proponents of outsourcing are quick to point out the problems. There can be significant obstacles, including understandable resistance from staff who find themselves 'outsourced'. Some companies have also been guilty of 'outsourcing a problem'. In other words, having failed to manage a process well themselves, they ship it out rather than face up to why the process was problematic in the first place. There is also evidence that, although long-term costs can be brought down when a process is outsourced, there may be an initial period when costs rise as both sides learn how to manage the new arrangement.

Summary checklist

DOWNLOADABLE

This checklist comprises questions that can be usefully applied to any type of operations and reflect the major diagnostic questions used within the chapter.

☐ Is the operation fully aware of all its first- and second-tier suppliers' and customers' capabilities and requirements?

☐ Are capabilities of suppliers and requirements of customers understood in terms of all aspects of operations performance?

☐ Does the operation have a view on how it would like to see its supply network develop over time?

☐ Have the benefits of reducing the number of individual suppliers been explored?

☐ Are any parts of the supply network likely to become disintermediated, and have the implications of this been considered?

☐ Does the operation have an approach to how it treats others in the supply network who might be both complementors and competitors?

☐ Is the vertical integration/outsourcing issue always under review for possible benefits?

☐ Is outsourcing (or bringing back in-house) evaluated in terms of all the operation's performance objectives?

☐ Is there a rational set of criteria used for deciding whether to outsource?

☐ Is the relocation decision ever considered?

☐ Have factors such as changes in demand or supply that may prompt a relocation been considered?

☐ If considering a relocation, are alternative locations always evaluated against each other and against a 'do nothing' option?

☐ Are sufficient location options being considered?

☐ Do location evaluation criteria include capital, market, cost, flexibility and risk factors?

☐ Is the optimum economy of scale for the different types of operation with the business periodically assessed?

☐ Are the various strategies for timing changes in capacity always evaluated in terms of their advantages and disadvantages?

☐ Are the fixed-cost breaks of capacity increase understood, and are they taken into account when increasing or decreasing capacity?

Case study Disneyland Resort Paris (abridged)[9]

In August 2006, the company behind Disneyland Resort Paris reported a 13 per cent rise in revenues, saying that it was making encouraging progress with new rides aimed at getting more visitors. '*I am pleased with year-to-date revenues and especially with third quarter's, as well as with the success of the opening of Buzz Lightyear Laser Blast, the first step of our multi-year investment programme. These results reflect the group's strategy of increasing growth through innovative marketing and sales efforts as well as a multi-year investment programme. This performance is encouraging as we enter into the important summer months,*' said Chairman and Chief Executive Karl L. Holz. Revenue for the quarter ending 30 June rose to €286.6 million ($362 million) from €254 million a year earlier. The results helped to boost overall profits at Disney Company and the company's stock price soared.

Yet it hadn't always been like that. The 14-year history of Disneyland Paris had more ups and downs than any of its rollercoasters. The company had hauled itself back from what some commentators had claimed was the brink of bankruptcy in 2005. In fact, from 12 April 1992, when Euro Disney opened, through to this more optimistic report, the resort had been subject simultaneously to wildly optimistic forecasts and widespread criticism and ridicule. An essay on one critical Internet site (called 'An Ugly American in Paris') summarized the whole venture in this way: '*When Disney decided to expand its hugely successful theme park operations to Europe, it brought American management styles, American cultural tastes, American labor practices, and American marketing pizzazz to Europe. Then, when the French stayed away in droves, it accused them of cultural snobbery.*'

The 'Magic' of Disney

Since its founding in 1923, The Walt Disney Company had striven to remain faithful in its commitment to '*producing unparalleled entertainment experiences based on its rich legacy of quality, creative content and exceptional storytelling*'. It did this through four major business divisions: Studio Entertainment, Parks and Resorts, Consumer Products, and Media Networks. Each segment consisted of integrated businesses that worked together to '*maximize exposure and growth worldwide*'.

In the Parks and Resorts division, according to the company's description, customers could experience the

Source: Picture Partners/Alamy

'*magic of Disney's beloved characters*'. It was founded in 1952, when Walt Disney formed what is now known as Walt Disney Imagineering to build Disneyland in Anaheim, California. By 2006, Walt Disney Parks and Resorts operated or licensed 11 theme parks at five Disney destinations around the world. They were Disneyland Resort, California, Walt Disney World Resort, Florida, Tokyo Disney Resort, Disneyland Resort Paris, and the latest park, Hong Kong Disneyland. In addition, the division operated 35 resort hotels, two luxury cruise ships and a wide variety of other entertainment offerings. But in the history of the Walt Disney Company, perhaps none of its ventures had proved to be as challenging as its Paris resort.

Service delivery at Disney resorts and parks

The core values of the Disney Company and, arguably, the reason for its success originated in the views and personality of Walt Disney, the company's founder. He had what some called an obsessive focus on creating images, products and experiences for customers that epitomized fun, imagination and service. Through the 'magic' of legendary fairytale and story characters, customers could escape the cares of the real world. Different areas of each Disney Park are themed, often around various 'lands' such as Frontierland, Fantasyland, Tomorrowland and Adventureland. Each land contains attractions and rides, most of which are designed to be acceptable to a wide range of ages. Very few rides are 'scary' when compared with those in many other entertainment parks. The architectural styles, décor, food, souvenirs and cast costumes are all designed to reflect the theme of the 'land', as are the films and shows.

Although there were some regional differences, all the theme parks followed the same basic setup. Over the years, Disney had built up a reputation for imaginative rides. Its 'imagineers' had years of experience in using 'auto animatronics' to help recreate and reinforce the essence of the theme. The terminology used by the company reinforced its philosophy of consistent entertainment. Employees, even those working 'back stage', were called 'cast members'. They did not wear uniforms but 'costumes', and rather than being given a job they were 'cast in a role'. All park visitors were called 'guests'.

Disney employees were generally relatively young, often of school or college age. Most were paid hourly on tasks that could be repetitive even though they usually involved constant contact with customers. Yet employees were still expected to maintain a high level of courtesy and work performance. All cast members were expected to conform to strict dress and grooming standards. Applicants to become cast members were screened for qualities such as how well they responded to questions, how well they listened to their peers, how they smiled and used body language, and whether they had an 'appropriate attitude'.

All Disney parks had gained a reputation for their obsession with delivering a high level of service and experience through attention to operations detail. To ensure that their strict service standards were met they had developed a number of specific operations policies.

- All parks employed effective queue-management techniques such as providing information and entertainment for visitors.
- Visitors (guests) were seen as having a role within the park. They were not merely spectators or passengers on the rides, they were considered to be participants in a play. Their needs and desires were analyzed and met through frequent interactions with staff (cast members). In this way they could be drawn into the illusion that they were actually part of the fantasy.
- Disney's stated goal was to exceed its customers' expectations every day.
- Service delivery was mapped and continuously refined in the light of customer feedback.

- The staff induction programme emphasized the company's quality-assurance procedures and service standards. These were based on the four principles of safety, courtesy, show and efficiency.
- Parks were kept fanatically clean.
- The same Disney character never appeared twice within sight – how could there be two Mickeys?
- Staff were taught that customer perceptions were the key to customer delight but also were extremely fragile. Negative perceptions can be established after only one negative experience.
- Disney University was the company's in-house development and learning facility with departments in each of the company's sites. The University trained Disney's employees in strict service standards as well as providing the skills to operate new rides as they were developed.
- Staff recognition programmes attempted to identify outstanding service delivery performance as well as *'energy, enthusiasm, commitment and pride'*.
- All parks contained phones connected to a central question hot-line for employees to find the answer to any question posed by customers.

Tokyo Disneyland

Tokyo Disneyland, opened in 1982, was owned and operated by the Oriental Land Company. Disney had designed the park and advised on how it should be run and it was considered a great success. Japanese customers revealed a significant appetite for American themes and brands, and already had a good knowledge of Disney characters. Feedback was extremely positive, with visitors commenting on the cleanliness of the park and the courtesy and efficiency of staff members. Visitors also appreciated the Disney souvenirs because giving gifts is deeply embedded in the Japanese culture. The success of the Tokyo Park was explained by one American living in Japan. *'Young Japanese are very clean-cut. They respond well to Disney's clean-cut image, and I am sure they had no trouble filling positions. Also, young Japanese are generally comfortable wearing uniforms, obeying their bosses, and being part of a team. These are part of the Disney formula. Also, Tokyo is very crowded and Japanese here are used to crowds and waiting in line. They are very patient. And above all, Japanese are always very polite to strangers.'*

Disneyland Paris

By 2006 Disneyland Paris consisted of three parks: the Disney village, Disneyland Paris itself and the Disney Studio Park. The Village was comprised of stores and restaurants, the Disneyland Paris was the main theme park and Disney Studio Park had a more general movie-making theme. At the time of the European park's opening more than 2,000,000 Europeans visited the US Disney parks, accounting for 5 per cent of the total visitors. The company's brand was strong and it had over half a century of translating the Disney brand into reality. The name 'Disney' had become synonymous with wholesome family entertainment that combined childhood innocence with high-tech 'Imagineering'.

Alternative locations

Initially, as well as France, Germany, Britain, Italy and Spain were all considered as possible locations, though Germany, Britain and Italy were soon discarded from the list of potential sites. The decision soon came to a straight contest between the Alicante area of Spain, which had a similar climate to Florida for a large part of the year, and the Marne-la-Vallée area just outside Paris. Certainly, winning the contest to host the new park was important for all the potential host countries – the new park promised to generate more than 30,000 jobs.

The major advantage of locating in Spain was the weather. However, the eventual decision to locate near Paris was thought to have been driven by a number of factors that weighed more heavily with Disney executives. These included the following:

● There was a site available just outside Paris which was both large enough and flat enough to accommodate the park.
● The proposed location put the park within a two-hour drive for 17,000,000 people, a four-hour drive for 68,000,000 people, a six-hour drive for 110,000,000 people and a two-hour flight for a further 310,000,000 or so.
● The site also had potentially good transport links. The Euro Tunnel that was to connect England with France was due to open in 1994. In addition, the French autoroutes network and the high-speed TGV network could both be extended to connect the site with the rest of Europe.
● Paris was already a highly attractive vacation destination and France generally attracted around 50,000,000 tourists each year.
● Europeans generally take significantly more holidays each year than Americans (five weeks of vacation as opposed to two or three weeks).
● Market research indicated that 85 per cent of people in France would welcome a Disney park in their country.
● Both national and local government in France were prepared to give significant financial incentives (as were the Spanish authorities), including an offer to invest in local infrastructure, reduce the rate of value-added tax on goods sold in the park, provide subsidized loans and value the land artificially low to help reduce taxes. Moreover, the French government was prepared to expropriate land from local farmers to smooth the planning and construction process.

Early concerns that the park would not have the same sunny, happy feel in a climate cooler than Florida were allayed by the spectacular success of Disneyland Tokyo in a location with a similar climate to Paris.

Construction was starting on the 2000-hectare site in August 1988. But from the announcement that the park would be built in France, it was subject to a wave of criticism. One critic called the project a *'cultural Chernobyl'* because of how it might affect French cultural values. Another described it as *'a horror made of cardboard, plastic, and appalling colours; a construction of hardened chewing-gum and idiot folk lore taken straight out of comic books written for obese Americans'*. However, as some commentators noted, the cultural arguments and anti-Americanism of the French intellectual elite did not seem to reflect the behaviour of most French people, who *'eat at McDonald's, wear Gap clothing, and flock to American movies'*.

Designing Disneyland Resort Paris

Phase 1 of the Euro Disney Park was designed to have 29 rides and attractions, a championship golf course together with many restaurants, shops, live shows and parades as well as six hotels. Although the park was designed to fit in with Disney's traditional appearance and values, a number of changes were made to accommodate what were thought to be the preferences of European visitors. For example, market research indicated that Europeans would respond to a 'wild west' image of America. Therefore, both rides and hotel designs were made to emphasize this theme. Disney was also keen to diffuse criticism, especially from French left-wing intellectuals and politicians, that the design of the park would be too 'Americanized' and would become a vehicle for American 'cultural imperialism'. To counter charges of American imperialism, Disney gave the park a flavour that stressed the European heritage of many of the Disney characters and increased the sense of beauty and fantasy. It was, after all, competing against Paris's exuberant architecture and sights. For example, Discoveryland featured storylines from Jules Verne, the French author. Snow White (and her dwarfs) was located in a Bavarian village. Cinderella was located in a French inn. Even Peter Pan was made to appear more 'English Edwardian' than in the original US designs.

Because of concerns about the popularity of American 'fast food', Euro Disney introduced more variety into its restaurants and snack bars, featuring foods from around the world. In a bold publicity move, Disney invited a number of top Paris chefs to visit and taste the food. Some anxiety was also expressed concerning the different 'eating behaviour' between Americans and Europeans.

Whereas Americans preferred to 'graze', eating snacks and fast meals throughout the day, Europeans generally preferred to sit down and eat at traditional meal times. This would have a very significant impact on peak demand levels in dining facilities. A further concern was that in Europe (especially French) visitors would be intolerant of long queues. To overcome this, extra diversions such as films and entertainments were planned for visitors as they waited in line for a ride.

Before the opening of the park, Euro Disney had to recruit and train between 12,000 and 14,000 permanent and around 5000 temporary staff. All these new employees were required to undergo extensive training to prepare them to achieve Disney's high standard of customer service as well as to understand operational routines and safety procedures. Originally, the company's objective was to hire 45 per cent of its employees from France, 30 per cent from other European countries and 15 per cent from outside of Europe. However, this proved difficult and when the park opened around 70 per cent of employees were French. Most cast members were paid around 15 per cent above the French minimum wage.

An information centre was opened in December 1990 to show the public what Disney was constructing. The 'casting centre' was opened on 1 September 1991 to recruit the 'cast members' needed to staff the park's attractions. But the hiring process did not go smoothly. In particular, Disney's grooming requirements that insisted on a 'neat' dress code, a ban on facial hair, set standards for hair and finger nails, and an insistence on 'appropriate undergarments' proved controversial. Both the French press and trade unions strongly objected to the grooming requirements, claiming they were excessive and much stricter than was generally held to be reasonable in France. Nevertheless, the company refused to modify its grooming standards. Accommodating staff also proved to be a problem when the large influx of employees swamped the available housing in the area. Disney had to build its own apartments as well as rent rooms in local homes just to accommodate its employees. Nevertheless, notwithstanding all the difficulties, Disney did succeed in recruiting and training all its cast members before the opening.

The park opens

The park opened to employees for testing during late March 1992, during which time the main sponsors and their families were invited to visit the new park, but the opening was not helped by strikes on the commuter trains leading to the park, staff unrest, threatened security problems (a terrorist bomb had exploded the night before the opening) and protests in surrounding villages which demonstrated against the noise and disruption from the park. The opening day crowds, expected to be 500,000, failed to materialize and at close of the first day only 50,000 people had passed through the gates.

Disney had expected the French to make up a larger proportion of visiting guests than they did in the early days. The poor turnout may have been partly due to protests from French locals who feared their culture would be damaged by Euro Disney. Also all Disney parks had traditionally been alcohol-free and to begin with Euro Disney was no different. However, this was extremely unpopular, particularly with French visitors who like to have a glass of wine or beer with their food. Whatever the cause, the low initial attendance was very disappointing for the Disney Company.

It was reported that in the first nine weeks of operation, approximately 1000 employees left Euro Disney, about one half of them 'voluntarily'. The reasons cited varied. Some blamed the hectic pace of work and the long hours that Disney expected. Others mentioned the 'chaotic' conditions in the first few weeks of the park opening. Even Disney conceded that conditions had been tough immediately after the park opened. Some leavers blamed Disney's apparent difficulty in understanding 'how Europeans work'. *'We can't just be told what to do, we ask questions and don't all think the same.'* Some visitors who had experience of the American parks commented that the standards of service were noticeably below what would be acceptable in America. There were reports that some cast members were failing to meet Disney's normal service standard. *'Even on opening weekend some clearly couldn't care less. My overwhelming impression . . . was that they were out of their depth. There is much more to being a cast member than endlessly saying "Bonjour". Apart from having a detailed knowledge of the site, Euro Disney staff have the anxiety of not knowing in what language they are going to be addressed. Many were struggling.'*

It was also noticeable that different nationalities exhibited different types of behaviour when visiting the park. Some nationalities always used the waste bins while others were more likely to drop litter on the floor. Most noticeable were differences in queuing behaviour. Northern Europeans tend to be disciplined and content to wait for rides in an orderly manner. By contrast some Southern European visitors *'seem to have made an Olympic event out of getting to the ticket taker first'.* Nevertheless, not all reactions were negative. European newspapers quoted plenty of positive reaction from visitors, especially children. Euro Disney was so different from the existing European theme parks, with immediately recognizable characters and a wide variety of attractions. Families who could not afford to travel to the United States could now interact with Disney characters and 'sample the experience at far less cost'.

The next 15 years

By August 1992 estimates of annual attendance figures were being drastically cut from 11,000,000 to just over 9,000,000. Euro Disney's misfortunes were further compounded in late 1992 when a European recession caused property prices to drop sharply and interest payments on its large start-up loans forced the company to admit serious financial difficulties. Also the cheap dollar resulted in more people taking their holidays in Florida at Walt Disney World. While at the first anniversary of the Paris park's opening, in April 1993, Sleeping Beauty's Castle was decorated as a giant birthday cake to celebrate the occasion, further problems were approaching. After criticism for having too few rides, the rollercoaster Indiana Jones and the Temple of Peril was opened in July. This was the first Disney rollercoaster that included a 360-degree loop, but just a few weeks after opening emergency brakes locked on during a ride, causing some guest injuries. The ride was temporarily shut down for investigation. Also in 1993 the proposed Euro Disney phase 2 was shelved due to financial problems, which meant Disney MGM Studios Europe and 13,000 hotel rooms would not be built to the original 1995 deadline agreed upon by the Walt Disney Company. However, Discovery Mountain, one of the planned phase 2 attractions, did get approval.

By the start of 1994 rumours were circulating that the park was on the verge of bankruptcy. Emergency crisis talks were held between the banks and backers, with things coming to a head during March when Disney offered the banks an ultimatum. It would provide sufficient capital for the park to continue to operate until the end of the month, but unless the banks agreed to restructure the park's $1 billion debt, the Walt Disney company would close the park and walk away from the whole European venture, leaving the banks with a bankrupt theme park and a massive expanse of virtually worthless real estate. Michael Eisner, Disney's CEO, announced that Disney was planning to pull the plug on the venture at the end of March 1994 unless the banks were prepared to restructure the loans. The banks agreed to Disney's demands.

In May 1994 the connection between London and Marne-la-Vallée was completed, along with a TGV link, providing a connection between several major European cities. By August the park was starting to find its feet at last, and all of its hotels were fully booked during the peak holiday season. Also, in October, the park's name was officially changed from Euro Disney to 'Disneyland Paris' in order to 'show that the resort now was named much more like its counterparts in California and Tokyo'. The end-of-year figures for 1994 showed encouraging signs despite a 10 per cent fall in attendance caused by the bad publicity over the earlier financial problems.

For the next few years new rides continued to be introduced. 1995 saw the opening of the new rollercoaster, 'Space Mountain de la Terre à la Lune', and Disneyland Paris announced its first annual operating profit in November that year, helped by the opening of Space Mountain in June. In 1997 the five-year celebrations included parties, a new parade with Quasimodo and all the characters from the latest Disney blockbusting classic 'The Hunchback of Notre Dame', the *'YEAR TO BE HERE'* marketing campaign, the resort's first Halloween celebration and a new Christmas parade. A new attraction was added in 1999, 'Honey I Shrunk The Audience', making the audience the size of a bug while being invited to Inventor of the Year Award Ceremony. However, the planned Christmas and New Year celebrations were disrupted when a freak storm caused havoc, destroying the Mickey Mouse glass statue that had just been installed for the Lighting Ceremony and many other attractions. Also damaged were trees next to the castle, the top of which developed a pronounced lean, as did many street signs and lamp posts.

Disney's 'Fastpass' system was introduced in 2000, a new service that allowed guests to use their entry passes to obtain a ticket for certain attractions to gain direct entry without queuing. Two new attractions were also opened, 'Indiana Jones et le Temple du péril' and 'Tarzan le Recontre' starring a cast of acrobats along with Tarzan, Jane and all their Jungle friends with music from the movie in different European languages. In 2001 the 'ImagiNations Parade' was replaced by the 'Wonderful World of Disney Parade' which received some criticism for being 'less than spectacular', with only eight parade floats. Also Disney's 'California Adventure' was opened in California. The resort's tenth anniversary saw the opening of the new Walt Disney Studios Park attraction, based on a similar attraction in Florida that had proved to be a success.

André Lacroix from Burger King was appointed as CEO of Disneyland Resort Paris in 2003, to *'take on the challenge of a failing Disney park in Europe and turn it around'*. Increasing investment, he refurbished whole sections of the park and introduced the Jungle Book Carnival in February to increase attendance during the slow months. By 2004 attendance had improved but the company announced that it was still losing money. And even the positive news of 2006, although generally well received, still left questions unanswered. As one commentator put it: *'Would Disney, the stockholders, the banks, or even the French government make the same decision to go ahead if they could wind the clock back to 1987? Is this a story of a fundamentally flawed concept, or was it just mishandled?'*

QUESTIONS

1 What markets are the Disney resorts and parks aiming for?

2 Was Disney's choice of the Paris site a mistake?

3 What aspects of its parks' design did Disney change when it constructed Euro Disney?

4 What did Disney *not* change when it constructed Euro Disney?

5 What were Disney's main mistakes from the conception of the Paris resort through to 2006?

Active case study   Freeman Biotest

ACTIVE CASE

Freeman Biotest, a large company which supplies the food-processing industry, is having problems with one of its process lines, a 'Brayford line'. It is uncertain about whether to replace it with a new 'Brayford line' or to commission a completely new type of process line. Representatives from the marketing, technology, operations and finance teams express their opinions and raise a number of concerns about the implications of each line.

● How would you recommend Freeman Biotest address its need for extra capacity and its problematic process line?

Please refer to the Active case on the CD accompanying this book to listen to the views of those involved.

Applying the principles

HINTS

Some of these exercises can be answered by reading the chapter. Others will require some general knowledge of business activity and some might require an element of investigation. All have hints on how they can be answered on the CD accompanying this book.

1 Visit sites on the Internet that offer (legal) downloadable music using MP3 or other compression formats. Consider the music business supply chain, (a) for the recordings of a well-known popular music artist, and (b) for a less well-known (or even largely unknown) artist struggling to gain recognition.

● How might the transmission of music over the Internet affect each of these artists' sales?

● What implications does electronic music transmission have for record shops?

2 Visit the websites of companies that are in the paper manufacturing/pulp production/packaging industries. Assess the extent to which the companies you have investigated are vertically integrated in the paper supply chain that stretches from foresting through to the production of packaging materials.

3 Many developing nations are challenging the dominance of more traditional Western locations, notably Silicon Valley, for high-tech research and manufacturing. Two examples are Bangalore in India and Shanghai in China. Make a list of all the factors you would recommend a multinational corporation to take into account in assessing the advantages and disadvantages and risks of locating in developing countries. Use this list to compare Bangalore and China for a multinational computer corporation,

(a) siting its research and development facility;

(b) siting a new manufacturing facility.

4 Tesco.com is now the world's largest and by far the most profitable online grocery retailer. In 1996 Tesco.com was alone in developing a 'store-based' supply network strategy. This means that it used its existing stores to assemble customer orders which were placed online. Tesco staff would simply be given printouts of customer orders and then walk round the store picking items off the shelves. The groceries would then be delivered by a local fleet of Tesco vans to customers. By contrast, many new e-grocery entrants and some existing supermarkets pursued a 'warehouse' supply network strategy of building new, large, totally automated and dedicated regional warehouses. Because forecasts for online demand were so high, they believed that the economies of scale of dedicated warehouses would be worth the investment. In the late 1990s Tesco came under criticism for being over-cautious and in 1999 it reviewed its strategy. Tesco concluded that its store-based strategy was correct and persevered. The most famous of the pure e-grocery companies was called WebVan. At the height of the dot-com phenomenon WebVan Group went public with a first-day market capitalization of $7.6 billion. By 2001, having burnt its way through $1.2 billion in capital before filing for bankruptcy, WebVan Group went bust, letting go all of its workers and auctioning off everything from warehouse equipment to software.

- Draw the different supply network strategies for Tesco and companies like WebVan.

- What do you think the economy of scale curves for the Tesco operation and the WebVan operation would look like relative to each other?

- Why do you think WebVan went bust and Tesco was so successful?

Notes on chapter

1 Sources: 'For whom the Dell tolls' (2006), *The Economist,* 13 May; Cellan-Jones, R. (2008) 'Dell aims to reclaim global lead', *BBC Business,* 14 April.

2 Source: BBC news site at www.bbc.co.uk.

3 Source: Zwick, S. (1999) 'World cars', *Time Magazine,* 22 February.

4 Brandenburger, A.M. and Nalebuff, B. (1996) *Coopetition,* Doubleday, New York.

5 Hayes, R.H. and Wheelwright, S.C. (1994) *Restoring our Competitive Edge,* John Wiley.

6 'Thinking outside the box' (2007) *The Economist*, 7 April.

7 Bacon, G., Machan, I. and Dnyse, J. (2008) 'Offshore challenges', *Manufacturing,* The Institute of Electrical Engineers, January.

8 Pil, F.K. and Holweg, M. (2003) 'Exploring scale: the advantages of thinking small', *MIT Sloan Management Review,* wInter.

9 This case was prepared by Nigel Slack of Warwick Business School, Warwick University, United Kingdom, using published sources of information. It does not reflect the views of the Walt Disney Company, which should not be held responsible for the accuracy or interpretation of any of the information or views contained in the case. It is not intended to illustrate either good or bad management practice. Copyright © 2008 Nigel Slack.

Taking it further

Bartlett, C. and Ghoshal, S. (1989) *Managing Across Borders,* Harvard Business School Press. A great introduction to understanding the background to managing international supply networks.

Chopra, S. and Meindl, P. (2000) *Supply Chain Management: Strategy, planning and operations,* Prentice Hall, New Jersey. A good textbook that covers both strategic and operational issues.

Dell, M. (with Catherine Fredman) (1999) *Direct from Dell: Strategies that revolutionized an industry,* Harper Business. Michael Dell explains how his supply network strategy (and other decisions) had such an impact on the industry. Interesting and readable, but not a critical analysis!

Ferdows, K. (1997) 'Making the most of foreign factories', *Harvard Business Review,* March–April. An articulate exposition of why factories that start out as foreign subsidiaries can end up by becoming pivotal to a multinational's success.

Quinn, J.B. (1999) 'Strategic outsourcing: leveraging knowledge capabilities', *Sloan Management Review, Summer*. A bit academic but a good discussion on the importance of 'knowledge' in the outsourcing decision.

Schniederjans, M.J. (1998) *International Facility Location and Acquisition Analysis,* Quorum Books, New York. Very much one for the technically minded.

Useful websites

www.opsman.org Definitions, links and opinion on operations and process management.

www.locationstrategies.com Exactly what the title implies. Good industry discussion.

www.conway.com American location selection site. You can get a flavour of how location decisions are made.

www.transparency.org A leading site for international business (inducing location) that fights corruption.

www.intel.com More details on Intel's 'Copy Exactly' strategy and other capacity strategy issues.

www.outsourcing.com Site of the Institute of Outsourcing. Some good case studies.

www.bath.ac.uk/crisps A centre for research in strategic purchasing and supply. Some interesting papers.

www.outsourcing.co.uk Site of the UK National Outsourcing Association. Some interesting reports, news items, etc.

FURTHER RESOURCES

For further resources including examples, animated diagrams, self-test questions, Excel spreadsheets, active case studies and video materials please explore the CD accompanying this book.

Supplement to Chapter I-3
Forecasting

Introduction

Some forecasts are accurate. We know exactly what time the sun will rise at any given place on earth tomorrow or one day next month or even next year. Forecasting in a business context, however, is much more difficult and therefore prone to error. We do not know precisely how many orders we will receive or how many customers will walk through the door tomorrow, next month or next year. Such forecasts, however, are necessary to help managers make decisions about resourcing the organization for the future.

Forecasting – knowing the options

Simply knowing that demand for your goods or services is rising or falling is not enough in itself. Knowing the rate of change is likely to be vital to business planning. A firm of lawyers may have to decide the point at which, in their growing business, they will have to take on another partner. Hiring a new partner could take months, so they need to be able to forecast when they expect to reach that point and then when they need to start their recruitment drive. The same applies to a plant manager who will need to purchase new plant to deal with rising demand. She may not want to commit to buying an expensive piece of machinery until absolutely necessary but in enough time to order the machine and have it built, delivered, installed and tested. The same is so for governments, whether planning new airports or runway capacity or deciding where and how many primary schools to build.

The first question is to know how far you need to look ahead. This will depend on the options and decisions available to you. Take the example of a local government district where the number of primary-age children (5–11 year olds) is increasing in some areas and declining in other areas within its boundaries. The council is legally obliged to provide school places for all such children. Government officials will have a number of options open to them and they may each have different lead times associated with them. One key step in forecasting is to know the possible options and the lead times required to bring them about (see Table 3.4).

Table 3.4	Options available and lead time required for dealing with changes in numbers of school children
Options available	*Lead time required*
Hire short-term teachers	Hours
Hire staff	
Build temporary classrooms	
Amend school catchment areas	
Build new classrooms	
Build new schools	Years

Individual schools can hire (or lay off) short-term (supply) teachers from a pool, not only to cover for absent teachers but also to provide short-term capacity while more teachers are hired to deal with increases in demand. Acquiring (or dismissing) such temporary cover may require only a few hours' notice. (This is often referred to as short-term capacity management.)

Hiring new (or laying off existing) staff is another option, but both of these may take months to complete (medium-term capacity management).

A shortage of accommodation may be fixed in the short to medium term by hiring or buying temporary classrooms. It may take only a couple of weeks to hire such a building and equip it ready for use.

It may be possible to amend catchment areas between schools to try to balance an increasing population in one area against a declining population in another. Such changes may require lengthy consultation processes.

In the longer term, new classrooms or even new schools may have to be built. The planning, consultation, approval, commissioning, tendering, building and equipping process may take up to five years depending on the scale of the new build.

Knowing the range of options, managers can then decide the time scale for their forecasts; indeed several forecasts might be needed for the short term, medium term and long term.

In essence forecasting is simple

In essence forecasting is easy. To know how many children may turn up at a local school tomorrow, you can use the number that turned up today. In the long term, in order to forecast how many primary-age children will expect to attend a school in five years' time, one need simply look at the birth statistics for the current year for the school's catchment area – see Figure 3.11.

However, such simple extrapolation techniques are prone to error and indeed such approaches have resulted in some local government authorities committing themselves to building schools which five or six years later, when complete, had few children, while other schools were bursting at the seams with temporary classrooms and temporary teachers, often resulting in falling morale and declining educational standards. The reason why such simple approaches are prone to problems is that there are many contextual variables (see Figure 3.12) that will have a potentially significant impact on, for example, the school population five years hence. For example, one minor factor in developed countries, though a major factor in developing countries, might be the death rate in children between birth and five years of age. This may depend upon location, with a slightly higher mortality rate in poorer areas than in more affluent areas. Another more significant factor is immigration and emigration as people move into or out of the local area. This will be affected by housing stock and housing developments, the ebb and flow of jobs and the changing economic prosperity in the area.

One key factor which has an impact on the local birth rate is the amount and type of the housing stock. City centre tenement buildings tend to have a higher proportion of

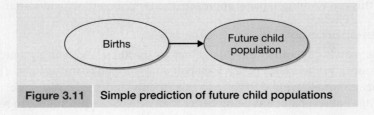

Figure 3.11   Simple prediction of future child populations

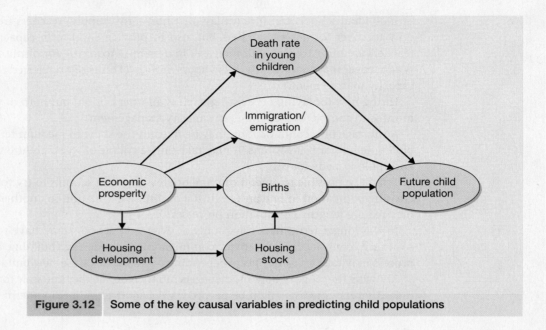

Figure 3.12   Some of the key causal variables in predicting child populations

children per dwelling, for example, than suburban semi-detached houses. So not only will existing housing stock have an impact on the child population but so also will the type of housing developments under construction, planned and proposed.

Approaches to forecasting

There are two main approaches to forecasting. Managers sometimes use qualitative methods based on opinions, past experience and even best guesses. There is also a range of qualitative forecasting techniques available to help managers evaluate trends and causal relationships and make predictions about the future. Also quantitative forecasting techniques can be used to model data. Although no approach or technique will necessarily result in an accurate forecast, a combination of qualitative and quantitative approaches can be used to great effect by bringing together expert judgements and predictive models.

Qualitative methods

Imagine you were asked to forecast the outcome of a forthcoming football match. Simply looking at the teams' performance over the last few weeks and extrapolating it is unlikely to yield the right result. Like many business decisions the outcome will depend on many other factors. In this case the strength of the opposition, their recent form, injuries to players on both sides, the match location and even the weather will influence the outcome. A qualitative approach involves collecting and appraising judgements, options, even best guesses as well as past performance from 'experts' to make a prediction. There are several ways this can be done: a panel approach, the Delphi method, and scenario planning.

Panel approach

Just as panels of football pundits gather to speculate about likely outcomes, so too do politicians, business leaders, stock market analysts, banks and airlines. The panel acts like a focus group allowing everyone to talk openly and freely. Although there is the great advantage of several brains being better than one, it can be difficult to reach a consensus, or sometimes the views of the loudest or highest status may emerge (the bandwagon effect). Although more reliable than one person's views, the panel approach still has the weakness that everybody, even the experts, can get it wrong.

Delphi method

Perhaps the best-known approach to generating forecasts using experts is the Delphi method.[1] This is a more formal method that attempts to reduce the influences from procedures of face-to-face meetings. It employs a questionnaire, emailed or posted to the experts. The replies are analyzed and summarized and returned, anonymously, to all the experts. The experts are then asked to reconsider their original response in the light of the replies and arguments put forward by the other experts. This process is repeated several times to conclude either with a consensus or at least with a narrower range of decisions. One refinement of this approach is to allocate weights to the individuals and their suggestions based on, for example, their experience, their past success in forecasting, or other people's views of their abilities. The obvious problems associated with this method include constructing an appropriate questionnaire, selecting an appropriate panel of experts and trying to deal with their inherent biases.

Scenario planning

One method for dealing with situations of even greater uncertainty is scenario planning. This is usually applied to long-range forecasting, again using a panel. The panel members are usually asked to devise a range of future scenarios. Each scenario can then be discussed and the inherent risks considered. Unlike the Delphi method, scenario planning is not necessarily concerned with arriving at a consensus but with looking at the possible range of options and putting plans in place to try to avoid the ones that are least desired and to take action to follow the most desired.

Quantitative methods

There are two main approaches to quantitative forecasting: time series analysis and causal modelling techniques. Time series analysis examines the pattern of past behaviour of a single phenomenon over time, taking into account reasons for variation in the trend in order to use the analysis to forecast the phenomenon's future behaviour. Causal modelling is an approach that describes and evaluates the complex cause and effect relationships between the key variables (such as in Figure 3.12).

Excel

Time series analysis

Simple time series plot a variable over time, then by removing underlying variations with assignable causes use extrapolation techniques to predict future behaviour. The key weakness with this approach is that it simply looks at past behaviour to predict the future, ignoring causal variables that are taken into account in other methods such as causal modelling or qualitative techniques. For example, suppose a company is attempting to predict the future sales of a product. The past three years' sales, quarter by quarter, are shown in Figure 3.13(a). This series of past sales may be analyzed to indicate future sales. For instance, underlying the series might be a linear upward trend in sales. If this is taken out of the data, as in Figure 3.13(b), we are left with a cyclical seasonal variation. The mean deviation of each quarter from the trend line can now be taken out, to give the average seasonality deviation. What remains is the random variation about the trends and seasonality lines, Figure 3.13(c). Future sales may now be predicted as lying within a band about a projection of the trend, plus the seasonality. The width of the band will be a function of the degree of random variation.

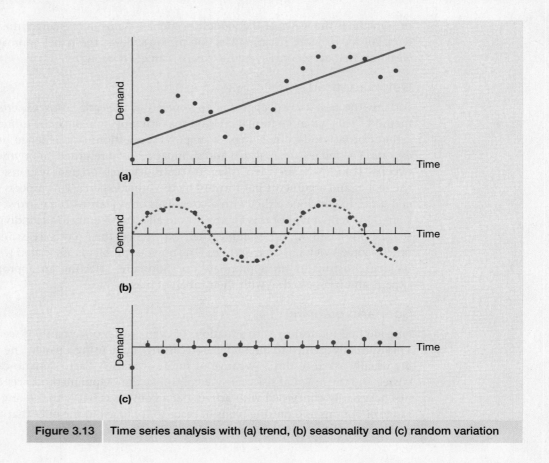

Figure 3.13   Time series analysis with (a) trend, (b) seasonality and (c) random variation

Forecasting unassignable variations The random variations that remain after taking out trend and seasonal effects are without any known or assignable cause. This does not mean that they do not have a cause, but just that we do not know what it is. Nevertheless, some attempt can be made to forecast it, if only on the basis that future events will, in some way, be based on past events. We will examine two of the more common approaches to forecasting that are based on projecting forward from past behaviour. These are:

- moving-average forecasting
- exponentially smoothed forecasting.

The moving-average approach to forecasting takes the previous n periods' actual demand figures, calculates the average demand over the n periods, and uses this average as a forecast for the next period's demand. Any data older than the n periods plays no part in the next period's forecast. The value of n can be set at any level, but is usually in the range 4 to 7.

Example   **Eurospeed parcels using moving-average**

Table 3.5 shows the weekly demand for Eurospeed, a European-wide parcel-delivery company. It measures demand, on a weekly basis, in terms of the number of parcels that it is given to deliver (irrespective of the size of each parcel). Each week, the next week's demand is forecast by taking the moving average of the previous four weeks' actual demand. Thus if the forecast demand for week t is F_t and the actual demand for week t is A_t, then:

$$F_t = \tfrac{1}{4}(A_{t-4} + A_{t-3} + A_{t-2} + A_{t-1})$$

Table 3.5	Actual demand and moving-average forecast (thousands) calculated over a four-week period	
Week (t)	Actual demand (A)	Forecast demand (F)
20	63.3	
21	62.5	
22	67.8	
23	66.0	
24	67.2	64.9
25	69.9	65.9
26	65.6	67.7
27	71.1	66.3
28	68.8	67.3
29	68.4	68.9
30	70.3	68.5
31	72.5	69.7
32	66.7	70.0
33	68.3	69.5
34	67.0	69.5
35		68.6

For example, the forecast for week 35:

$$F_{35} = (72.5 + 66.7 + 68.3 + 67.0)/4$$
$$= 68.8$$

Exponential smoothing There are two significant drawbacks to the moving-average approach to forecasting. First, in its basic form, it gives equal weight to all the previous n periods which are used in the calculations (although this can be overcome by assigning different weights to each of the n periods). Second, and more important, it does not use data from beyond the n periods over which the moving average is calculated. Both these problems are overcome by exponential smoothing, which is also somewhat easier to calculate. The exponential-smoothing approach forecasts demand in the next period by taking into account the actual demand in the current period and the forecast that was previously made for the current period. It does so according to the formula:

$$F_t = \alpha A_{t-1} + (1 - x)F_{t-1}$$

where α = the smoothing constant.

The smoothing constant α is, in effect, the weight that is given to the last (and therefore assumed to be most important) piece of information available to the forecaster. However, the other expression in the formula includes the forecast for the current period which included the previous period's actual demand, and so on. In this way all previous data has a (diminishing) effect on the next forecast.

Example

Eurospeed parcels using exponential smoothing

Table 3.6 shows the data for Eurospeed's parcels forecasts using this exponential-smoothing method, where $\alpha = 0.2$. For example, the forecast for week 35 is:

$$F_{35} = (0.2 \times 67.0) + (0.8 \times 68.3) = 68.04$$

Table 3.6	Actual demand and exponentially smoothed forecast (thousands) calculated with smoothing constant $\alpha = 0.2$	
Week (t)	Actual demand (A)	Forecast demand (F)
20	63.3	60.00
21	62.5	60.66
22	67.8	60.03
23	66.0	61.58
24	67.2	62.83
25	69.9	63.70
26	65.6	64.94
27	71.1	65.07
28	68.8	66.28
29	68.4	66.78
30	70.3	67.12
31	72.5	67.75
32	66.7	68.70
33	68.3	68.30
34	67.0	68.30
35		68.04

The value of α governs the balance between the responsiveness of the forecasts to changes in demand, and the stability of the forecasts. The closer α is to 0 the more forecasts will be dampened by previous forecasts (not very sensitive but stable). Figure 3.14 shows the Eurospeed volume data plotted for a four-week moving average, exponential smoothing with $\alpha = 0.2$ and exponential smoothing with $\alpha = 0.3$.

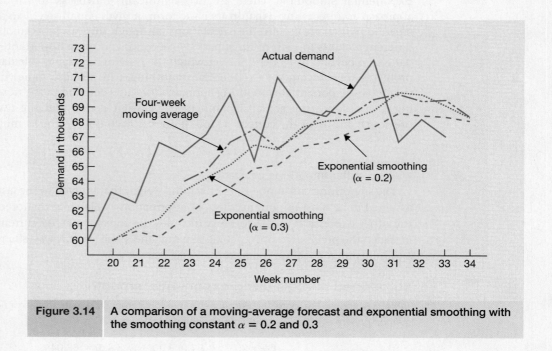

Figure 3.14	A comparison of a moving-average forecast and exponential smoothing with the smoothing constant $\alpha = 0.2$ and 0.3

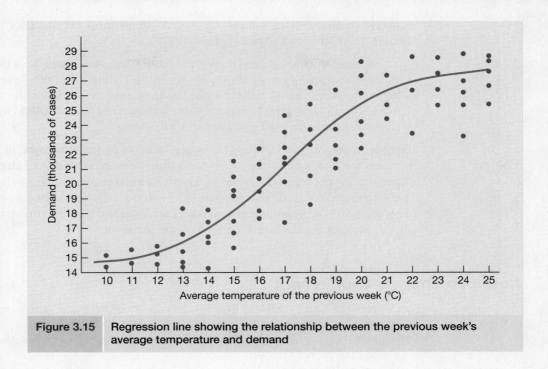

Figure 3.15   Regression line showing the relationship between the previous week's average temperature and demand

Causal models

Causal models often employ complex techniques to understand the strength of relationships between the network of variables and the impact they have on each other. Simple regression models try to determine the 'best fit' expression between two variables. For example, suppose an ice-cream company is trying to forecast its future sales. After examining previous demand, it figures that the main influence on demand at the factory is the average temperature of the previous week. To understand this relationship, the company plots demand against the previous week's temperatures. This is shown in Figure 3.15. Using this graph, the company can make a reasonable prediction of demand, once the average temperature is known, provided that the other conditions prevailing in the market are reasonably stable. If they are not, then these other factors that influence demand will need to be included in the regression model, which becomes increasingly complex.

These more complex networks comprise many variables and relationships, each with its own set of assumptions and limitations. While developing such models and assessing the importance of each of the factors and understanding the network of interrelationships is beyond the scope of this text, many techniques are available to help managers undertake this more complex modelling and also feed data back into the model to further refine and develop it, in particular structural equation modelling.

The performance of forecasting models

Forecasting models are widely used in management decision making, and indeed most decisions require a forecast of some kind, yet the performance of this type of model is far from impressive. Hogarth and Makridakis,[2] in a comprehensive review of the applied management and finance literature, show that the record of forecasters using both judgement and sophisticated mathematical methods is not good. What they do suggest, however, is that certain forecasting techniques perform better under certain circumstances. In short-term forecasting there is:

> . . . considerable inertia in most economic and natural phenomena. Thus the present states of any variables are predictive of the short-term future (i.e., three months or less). Rather simple mechanistic methods, such as those used in time series forecasts, can often make accurate short-term forecasts and even out-perform more theoretically elegant and elaborate approaches used in econometric forecasting.[3]

Long-term forecasting methods, although difficult to judge because of the time lapse between the forecast and the event, do seem to be more amenable to an objective causal approach. In a comparative study of long-term market forecasting methods, Armstrong and Grohman[4] conclude that econometric methods offer more accurate long-range forecasts than do expert opinion or time series analysis, and that the superiority of objective causal methods improves as the time horizon increases.

Notes on chapter supplement

1 Linstone, H.A. and Turoof, M. (1975) *The Delphi Method: Techniques and Applications,* Addison-Wesley.
2 Hogarth, R.M. and Makridakis, S. (1981) 'Forecasting and planning: an evaluation', *Management Science,* Vol. 27, pp. 115–38.
3 Hogarth and Makridakis, *op. cit.*
4 Armstrong, J.S. and Grohman, M.C. (1972) 'A comparative study of methods for long-range market forecasting', *Management Science,* Vol. 19, No. 2, pp. 211–21.

Taking it further

Hoyle, R.H. (ed.) (1995) *Structural Equation Modeling,* Sage, Thousand Oaks, CA. For the specialist.

Maruyama, G.M. (1997) *Basics of Structural Equation Modeling,* Sage, Thousand Oaks, CA. For the specialist.

H4   PROCESS DESIGN 1 – POSITIONING

Introduction

Processes are everywhere. They are the building blocks of all operations, and their design will affect the performance of the whole operation and, eventually, the contribution it makes to its supply network. No one, in any function or part of the business, can fully contribute to its competitiveness if the processes in which they work are poorly designed. It is not surprising then that process design has become such a popular topic in the management press and among consultants. This chapter is the first of two that examine the design of processes. This first one is primarily concerned with how processes and the resources they contain must reflect the volume and variety requirements placed on them (see Figure 4.1). The next chapter examines the more detailed and analytical aspects of process analysis.

Source: Courtesy of Arup

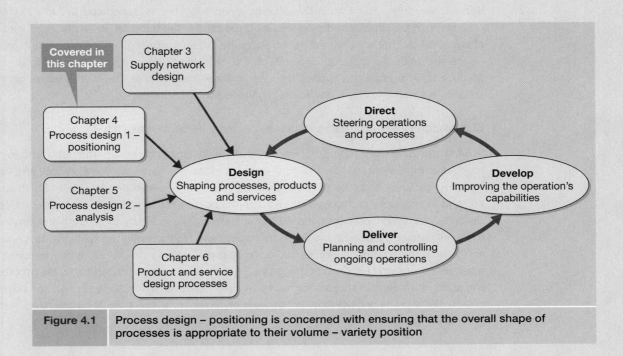

| Figure 4.1 | Process design – positioning is concerned with ensuring that the overall shape of processes is appropriate to their volume – variety position |

Executive summary

VIDEO
further detail

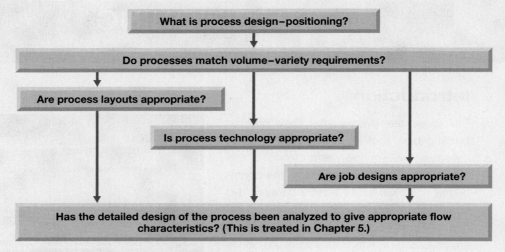

What is process design–positioning?

Do processes match volume–variety requirements?

Are process layouts appropriate?

Is process technology appropriate?

Are job designs appropriate?

Has the detailed design of the process been analyzed to give appropriate flow characteristics? (This is treated in Chapter 5.)

Decision logic chain for process design–positioning

Each chapter is structured around a set of diagnostic questions. These questions suggest what you should ask in order to gain an understanding of the important issues of a topic, and as a result, improve your decision making. An executive summary, addressing these questions, is provided below.

■ What is process design–positioning?

Process design is concerned with conceiving the overall shape of processes and their detailed workings. The first of these tasks (conceiving the overall shape or nature of the process) can be approached by positioning the process in terms of its volume and variety characteristics. The second task (conceiving the detailed workings of the process) is more concerned with the detailed analysis of the objectives, capacity and variability of the process. In this chapter we treat the first of these issues: how the overall nature of the process is determined by its volume–variety position.

■ Do processes match volume–variety requirements?

Volume and variety are particularly influential in the design of processes. They also tend to go together in an inverse relationship. High-variety processes are normally low-volume and vice versa. So processes can be positioned on the spectrum between low volume and high variety, and high volume and low variety. At different points on this spectrum processes can be described as distinct process 'types'. Different terms are used in manufacturing and services to identify these types. Working from low volume and high variety towards high volume and low variety, the process types are project processes, jobbing processes, batch processes, mass processes and continuous processes. The same sequence is characterized as professional services, service shops and mass services. Whatever terminology is used, the overall design of the process must fit its volume–variety position. This is usually summarized in the form of the 'product–process' matrix.

Are process layouts appropriate?

There are different ways in which the different resources within a process (people and technology) can be arranged relative to each other. But however this is done, it should reflect the process's volume–variety position. Again, there are pure 'types' of layout that correspond with the different volume–variety positions. These are fixed position layout, functional layout, cell layout and product layout. Many layouts are hybrids of these pure types, but the type chosen is influenced by the volume and variety characteristics of the process.

Is process technology appropriate?

Process technologies are the machines, equipment and devices that help processes transform materials and information and customers. Process technology is different from the product technology that is embedded with the product or service itself. Again, process technology should reflect volume and variety. In particular, the degree of automation in the technology, the scale and/or scalability of the technology, and the coupling and/or connectivity of the technology, should all be appropriate to volume and variety. Generally, low volume and high variety requires relatively unautomated, general purpose, small-scale and flexible technologies. By contrast, high volume and low variety processes require automated, dedicated, large-scale technologies that are sometimes relatively inflexible.

Are job designs appropriate?

Job design is about how people carry out their tasks within a process. It is particularly important because it governs people's expectations and perceptions of their contribution to the organization as well as being a major factor in shaping the culture of the organization. Some aspects of job design are common to all processes irrespective of their volume and variety position. These are such things as ensuring the safety of everyone affected by the process, ensuring a firm ethical stance, and upholding an appropriate work/life balance. However, other aspects of job design are influenced by volume and variety, in particular the extent of division of labour, the degree to which jobs are defined, and the way in which job commitment is encouraged. Broadly, high variety and low volume processes require broad, relatively undefined jobs with decision-making discretion. Such jobs tend to have intrinsic job commitment. By contrast, high volume and low variety processes tend to require jobs that are relatively narrow in scope and closely defined with relatively little decision-making discretion. This means some deliberative action is needed in the design of the job (such as job enrichment) in order to help maintain commitment to the job.

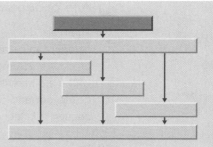

What is process design–positioning?

To 'design' is to conceive the looks, arrangement and workings of something *before it is constructed*. In that sense it is a conceptual exercise. Yet it is one which must deliver a solution that will work in practice. Design is also an activity that can be approached at different levels of detail. One may envisage the general shape and intention of something before getting down to defining its details. However, it is often only through getting to grips with the detail of a design that the feasibility of its overall shape can be assessed. So it is with designing processes. First, one must consider the overall shape and nature of the process. The most common way of doing this is by positioning it according to its volume and variety characteristics. Second, one must analyze the details of the process in order to ensure that it fulfils its objectives effectively. But don't think of this as a simple sequential process. There may be aspects concerned with the broad positioning of the process that will need to be modified following its more detailed analysis.

In this chapter we discuss the more general approach to process design by showing how a process's position on the volume–variety scale will influence its layout and technology, and the design of its jobs. In the next chapter we will discuss the more detailed aspects of process design, in particular its objectives, current configuration, capacity and variability. This is illustrated in Figure 4.2.

Example — **Tesco's store flow processes[1]**

Successful supermarkets, like Tesco, know that the design of their stores has a huge impact on profitability. They must maximize their revenue per square metre and minimize the costs of operating the store, while keeping customers happy. At a basic level, supermarkets have to get the amount of space allocated to the different areas right. Tesco's 'One in front' campaign, for

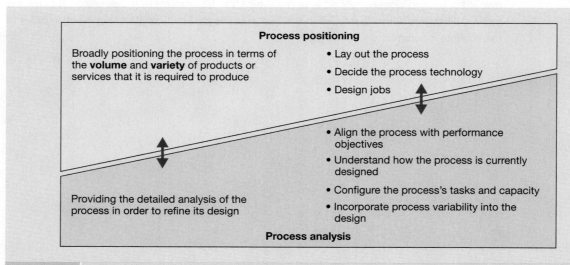

Process positioning

Broadly positioning the process in terms of the **volume** and **variety** of products or services that it is required to produce

- Lay out the process
- Decide the process technology
- Design jobs

- Align the process with performance objectives
- Understand how the process is currently designed
- Configure the process's tasks and capacity
- Incorporate process variability into the design

Providing the detailed analysis of the process in order to refine its design

Process analysis

Figure 4.2 Process design is treated in two parts: Positioning, that sets the broad characteristics of the design; and Analysis, that refines the details of the design

example, tries to avoid long waiting times by opening additional tills if more than one customer is waiting at a checkout. Tesco also uses technology to understand exactly how customers flow through its stores. The 'Smartlane' system from Irisys, a specialist in intelligent infrared technologies, counts the number and type of customers entering the store (in family or other groups known as 'shopping units'), tracks their movement using infrared sensors, and predicts the likely demand at the checkouts up to an hour in advance. The circulation of customers through the store must be correct and the right layout can make customers buy more.

Some supermarkets put their entrance on the left-hand side of a building, with a layout designed to take customers in a clockwise direction around the store. Aisles are made wide to ensure a relatively slow flow of trolleys so that customers pay more attention to the products on display (and buy more). However, wide aisles can come at the expense of reduced shelf space that does not allow a wider range of products to be stocked.

The actual location of all the products is a critical decision, directly affecting the convenience to customers, their level of spontaneous purchase and the cost of filling the shelves. Although the majority of supermarket sales are packaged, tinned or frozen goods, the displays of fruit and vegetables are usually located adjacent to the main entrance, as a signal of freshness and wholesomeness, providing an attractive and welcoming point of entry. Basic products that figure on most people's shopping lists, such as flour, sugar and bread, may be located at the back of the store and apart from each other so that customers have to pass higher-margin items as they search. High-margin items are usually put on shelves at eye level (where they are more likely to be seen) and low-margin products lower down or higher up. Some customers also go a few paces up an aisle before they start looking for what they need. Some supermarkets call the shelves occupying the first metre of an aisle 'dead space', not a place to put impulse-bought goods. But the prime site in a supermarket is the 'gondola-end', the shelves at the end of the aisle. Moving products to this location can increase sales 200 or 300 per cent. Not surprising that suppliers are willing to pay for their products to be located here.

Example Chocolate and visitors are processed by Cadbury's

Flow of chocolate

In the Cadbury's chocolate factory, on the outskirts of Birmingham, UK, chocolate products are manufactured to a high degree of consistency and efficiency. Production processes use specialist technology to meet the technical and capacity requirements of each stage of the process. In the production of Cadbury's Dairy Milk bars, the liquid chocolate is prepared from cocoa beans, fresh milk and sugar using equipment that is connected together with pipes and conveyors. These processes operate continuously, day and night, to ensure consistency of both the chocolate itself and the rate of output. The liquid chocolate is pumped through heated pipework to the moulding

Nuts destined for chocolate products being processed

Customers being processed

section, where it is dispensed into a moving line of precision-made plastic moulds that form the chocolate bars and vibrate them to remove any trapped air bubbles. The moulds are continuously conveyed into a large refrigerator, allowing sufficient time for the chocolate to harden. The next stage inverts the moulds and shakes out the bars. These then pass directly to a set of automated wrapping and packing machines, from where they go to the warehouse.

Flow of customers

Cadbury also have a large visitor centre called 'Cadbury World' alongside the factory (linked to a viewing area which looks onto the packaging area described above). It is a permanent exhibition devoted entirely to chocolate and the part Cadbury has played in its history. The design of the visitor centre uses a single route for all customers. The main exhibition and demonstration areas allow a smooth flow of visitors, avoiding bottlenecks and delays. Entry to the Exhibition Area is by timed ticket, to ensure a constant flow of visitors, who are free to walk around at their preferred speed, but are constrained to keep to the single track through the sequence of displays. On leaving this section, they are directed upstairs to the Chocolate Packaging Plant, where a guide escorts batches of visitors to where they can see the packing processes. The groups are then led down to and around the Demonstration Area, where skilled employees demonstrate small-scale production of handmade chocolates.

What do these two examples have in common?

All operations described in these two examples operate with relatively high volume of demand. The chocolate factory produces identical products flowing using identical processes round the clock. It may make several products but variety is relatively low. The visitor centre, located next door, also has a high volume of visitors, but, unlike chocolate, they have a mind of their own. Yet, the process is designed to constrain the route that visitors take and therefore the variety of their experiences. Even more problematic is the plight of Tesco, again with high volume, but what of its variety? Looked at one way, every customer is different and therefore variety will be extremely high. Yet, because of the way the process is designed, partly to encourage similarity of flow and partly by making customers 'customize' their own service, variety is made to seem very low. For example, checkout processes deal with only two 'products': customers with baskets and customers with trolleys. The important point is that in each case the volume and variety of demand (or how it is interpreted by the operation) has a profound effect on the design of the processes. Just think about the design of a small convenience store, or a small artisan chocolate manufacturer, or even a small visitor experience. Because they have different volume–variety characteristics, they would be designed in very different ways.

Do processes match volume–variety requirements?

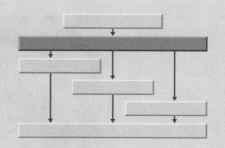

Two factors are particularly important in process design: these are the *volume* and *variety* of the products and services that it processes. Moreover volume and variety are related in so much as low-volume operations processes often have a high variety of products and services, and high-volume operations processes often have a narrow variety of products and services. So, we can *position* processes on a continuum from those that operate under conditions of low volume and high variety, through to those that operate under conditions of high volume and low variety. The volume–variety position of a process influences almost every aspect of its design. Processes with different volume–variety positions will be arranged in different ways, have different flow characteristics, and have different technology and jobs. So, the first steps in process design are to understand how volume and variety shape process characteristics, and to check whether processes have been configured in a manner that is appropriate for their volume–variety position. Think about the volume–variety characteristics of the following examples.

The 'product–process' matrix

The most common method of illustrating the relationship between a process's volume–variety position and its design characteristics is shown in Figure 4.3. Often called the 'product–process' matrix, it can in fact be used for any type of process, whether producing products or services. Its underlying idea of the product–process matrix is that many of the more important elements of process design are strongly related to the volume–variety position of the process. So, for any process, the tasks that it undertakes, the flow of items through the process, the layout of its resources, the technology it uses, and the design of jobs, are all strongly influenced by its volume–variety position. This means that most processes should lie close to the diagonal of the matrix that represents the 'fit' between the process and its volume–variety position. This is called the 'natural' diagonal.[2]

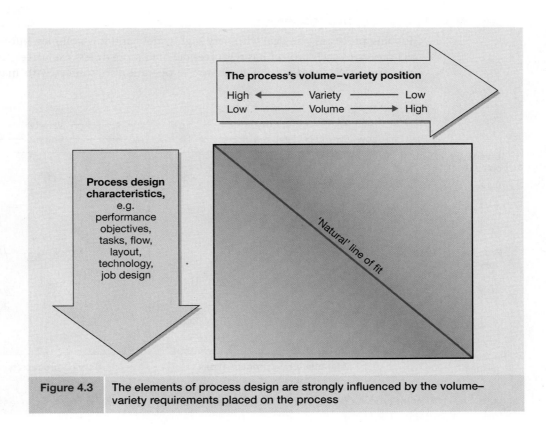

Figure 4.3   The elements of process design are strongly influenced by the volume–variety requirements placed on the process

Process types

Processes that inhabit different points on the diagonal of the product–process matrix are sometimes referred to as 'process types'. Each process type implies differences in the set of tasks performed by the process and in the way materials or information or customers flow through the process. Different terms are sometimes used to identify process types depending on whether they are predominantly manufacturing or service processes and there is some variation in how the names are used. This is especially so in service process types. It is not uncommon to find manufacturing terms used also to describe service processes. Perhaps most importantly, there is some degree of overlap between process types. The different process types are shown in Figure 4.4.

> **Operations principle**
> Process types indicate the position of processes on the volume–variety spectrum.

Project processes

Project processes are those that deal with discrete, usually highly customized products. Often the time scale of making the product is relatively long, as is the interval between the completions of each product. The activities involved in the process may be ill-defined and uncertain, sometimes changing during the process itself. Examples include advertising agencies, shipbuilding, most construction companies and movie production companies, drilling oil wells and installing computer systems. Any process map for project processes will almost certainly be complex, partly because each unit of output is usually large with many activities occurring at the same time and partly because the activities often involve significant discretion to act according to professional judgement. In fact a process map for a whole project would be extremely complex, so rarely would a project be mapped, but small parts may be.

Jobbing processes

Jobbing processes also deal with very high variety and low volumes, but whereas in project processes each project has resources devoted more or less exclusively to it, in jobbing processes each 'product' has to share the operation's resources with many others. The

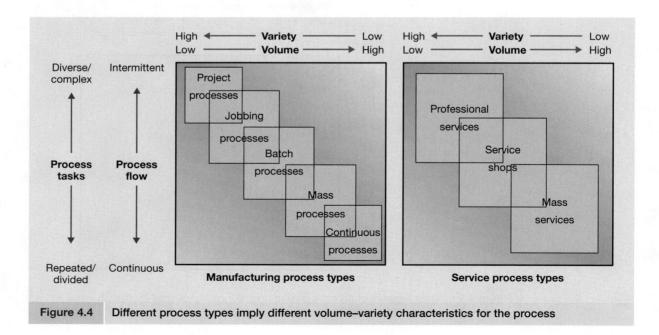

Figure 4.4   Different process types imply different volume–variety characteristics for the process

process will work on a series of products but, although all the products will require the same kind of attention, each will differ in its exact needs. Examples of jobbing processes include many precision engineers such as specialist toolmakers, furniture restorers, 'make-to-measure' tailors, and the printer who produces tickets for the local social event. Jobbing processes produce more and usually smaller items than project processes but, like project processes, the degree of repetition is low. Many jobs could be 'one-offs'. Again, any process map for a jobbing process could be relatively complex for similar reasons to project processes. Although jobbing processes sometimes involve considerable skill, they are usually more predictable than project processes.

Batch processes

Batch processes can look like jobbing processes, but without the degree of variety normally associated with jobbing. As the name implies, batch processes usually produce more than one 'product' at a time. So each part of the operation has periods when it is repeating itself, at least while the 'batch' is being processed. The size of the batch could be just two or three, in which case the batch process would differ little from jobbing, especially if each batch is a totally novel product. Conversely, if the batches are large, and especially if the products are familiar to the operation, batch processes can be fairly repetitive. Because of this, the batch type of process can be found over a wider range of volume and variety levels than other process types. Examples of batch processes include machine tool manufacturing, the production of some special gourmet frozen foods, the manufacture of most of the component parts that go into mass-produced assemblies such as automobiles, and the production of most clothing. Batch process maps may look straightforward, especially if different products take similar routes through the process with relatively standard activities being performed at each stage.

Mass processes

Mass processes produce in high volume, usually with narrow effective variety. An automobile plant, for example, might produce several thousand variants of car if every option of engine size, colour and equipment is taken into account. Yet its effective variety is low because the different variants do not affect the basic process of production. The activities in the automobile plant, like all mass processes, are essentially repetitive and largely predictable. In addition to the automobile plant, examples of mass processes include consumer durable manufacturers, most food processes such as a frozen pizza manufacturer, beer bottling plants and CD production. Process maps for this type of process will be straightforward sequences of activities.

Continuous processes

Continuous processes are one step beyond mass processes in so much as they operate at even higher volume and often have even lower variety. Sometimes they are literally continuous in that their products are inseparable, being produced in an endless flow. Continuous processes are often associated with relatively inflexible, capital-intensive technologies with highly predictable flow. Examples of continuous processes include petrochemical refineries, electricity utilities, steelmaking and Internet server firms. Like mass processes, process maps will show few elements of discretion, and although products may be stored during the process, the predominant characteristic of most continuous processes is of smooth flow from one part of the process to another.

Professional services

Professional services are high-variety, low-volume processes, where customers may spend a considerable time in the service process. Such services usually provide high levels of customization, so contact staff are given considerable discretion. They tend to be people-based rather than equipment-based, with emphasis placed on the process (how the service is delivered) as much as the 'product' (what is delivered). Examples include management consultants, lawyers' practices, architects, doctors' surgeries, auditors, health and safety inspectors and some computer field service operations. Where process maps are used they are likely to be drawn predominantly at a high level. Consultants, for example, frequently use a predetermined set of broad stages, starting with understanding the real nature of the problem through to the implementation of their recommended solutions. This high-level process map guides the nature and sequence of the consultants' activities.

Service shops

Service shops are characterized by levels of customer contact, customization, volume of customers and staff discretion that position them between the extremes of professional and mass services (see next paragraph). Service is provided via a mix of front- and back-office activities. Service shops include banks, high street shops, holiday tour operators, car rental companies, schools, most restaurants, hotels and travel agents. For example, an equipment hire and sales organization may have a range of equipment displayed in front-office outlets, while back-office operations look after purchasing and administration. The front-office staff have some technical training and can advise customers during the process of selling the product. Essentially the customer is buying a fairly standardized 'product' but will be influenced by the process of the sale which is customized to the individual customer's needs.

Mass services

Mass services have many customer transactions and little customization. Such services are often predominantly equipment-based and 'product' oriented, with most value added in the back-office, sometimes with comparatively little judgement needed by front-office staff who may have a closely defined job and follow set procedures. Mass services include supermarkets, a national rail network, airports, and many call centres. For example, airlines move a large number of passengers on their networks. Passengers pick a journey from the range offered. The airline can advise passengers on the quickest or cheapest way to get from A to B, but they cannot 'customize' the service by putting on special flights for them.

Moving off the natural diagonal

A process lying on the natural diagonal of the matrix shown in Figure 4.3 will normally have lower operating costs than one with the same volume–variety position that lies off the diagonal. This is because the diagonal represents the most appropriate process design for any volume–variety position. Processes that are on the right of the 'natural' diagonal would normally be associated with lower volumes and higher variety. This means that they are likely to be more flexible than seems to be warranted by their actual volume–variety position. That is, they are not taking advantage of their ability to standardize their activities. Because of this, their costs are likely to be higher than they would be with a process that was closer to the diagonal. Conversely, processes that are on the left of the diagonal have adopted a position that would normally be used for higher volume and lower variety processes. Processes will therefore be 'over-standardized' and probably too inflexible for their volume–variety position. This lack of flexibility can also lead to high costs because the process will not be able to change from one activity to another as readily as a more flexible process. One note of caution regarding this idea: although logically coherent, it is a conceptual model rather than something that can be 'scaled'. Although it is intuitively

> **Operations principle**
> Moving off the 'natural diagonal' of the product–process matrix will incur excess cost.

obvious that deviating from the diagonal increases costs, the precise amount by which costs will increase is very difficult to determine. Nevertheless, a first step in examining the design of an existing process is to check whether it is on the natural diagonal of the product–process matrix. The volume–variety position of the process may have changed without any corresponding change in its design. Alternatively, design changes may have been introduced without considering their suitability for the process's volume–variety position.

FURTHER EXAMPLE

Example | ### Meter installation[3]

The 'meter installation' unit of a water utility company installed and repaired water meters. The nature of each installation job could vary significantly because the metering requirements of each customer varied and because meters had to be fitted into various different water pipe systems. When a customer requested an installation or repair a supervisor would survey the customer's water system and transfer the results of the survey to the installation team of skilled plumbers. An appointment would then be made for a plumber to visit the customer's location and install or repair the meter on the agreed appointment date. The company decided to install free of charge a new 'standard' remote-reading meter that would replace the wide range of existing meters and could be read automatically using the customer's telephone line. This would save meter reading costs. It also meant a significant increase in work for the unit and more skilled plumbing staff were recruited. The new meter was designed to make installation easier by including universal quick-fit joints that reduced pipe cutting and jointing during installation. As a pilot, it was also decided to prioritize those customers with the oldest meters and conduct trials of how the new meter worked in practice. All other aspects of the installation process were left as they were.

The pilot was not a success. Customers with older meters were distributed throughout the company's area, so staff could not service several customers in one area and had to travel relatively long distances between customers. Also, because customers had not initiated the visit themselves, they were more likely to have forgotten the appointment, in which case plumbers had to return to their base and try to find other work to do. The costs of installation were proving to be far higher than forecast and the plumbers were frustrated at the waste of their time and the now relatively standardized installation job. The company decided to change its process. Rather than replace the oldest meters which were spread around its region, it targeted smaller geographic areas to limit travelling time. It also cut out the survey stage of the process because, using the new meter, 98 per cent of installations could be fitted in one visit, minimizing disruption to the customer and the number of missed appointments. Just as significantly, fully qualified plumbers were often not needed, so installation could be performed by less expensive labour.

This example is illustrated in Figure 4.5. The initial position of the installation process is at point A. The installation unit was required to repair and install a wide variety of meters into a very wide variety of water systems. This needed a survey stage to assess the nature of the job and the use of skilled labour to cope with the complex tasks. The installation of the new type of meter changed the volume–variety position for the process by reducing the variety of jobs tackled by the process and increasing the volume it had to cope with. However, the process was not changed. By choosing a wide geographic area to service, retaining the unnecessary survey stage and hiring over-skilled staff, the company was still defining itself as a high-variety, low-volume 'jobbing' process. The design of the process was appropriate for its old volume–variety position, but not the new one. In effect it had moved to point B in Figure 4.5. It was off the diagonal, with unnecessary flexibility and high operating costs. Redesigning the process to take advantage of the reduced variety and complexity of the job (position C on Figure 4.5) allowed installation to be performed far more efficiently.

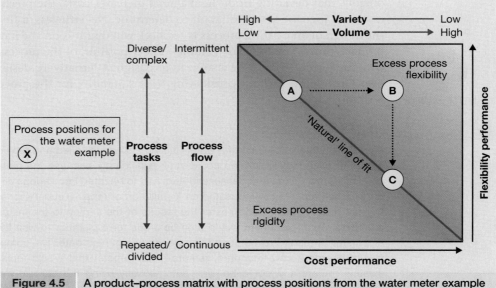

Figure 4.5   A product–process matrix with process positions from the water meter example

Layout, technology and design

If movement down the natural diagonal of the product–process matrix changes the nature of a process, then the key elements of its design will also change. At this broad level, these 'key elements' of the design are the two 'ingredients' that make up processes, technology and people, and the way in which these ingredients are arranged within the process relative to each other. This latter aspect is usually called *layout.* In the remainder of the chapter, we start by discussing layout and then the design decisions that relate to process technology and the jobs that the people within the process undertake.

DIAGNOSTIC QUESTION

Are process layouts appropriate?

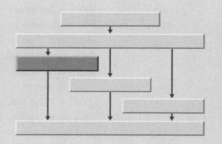

There is little point in having a well-sequenced process if in reality its activities are physically located in a way that involves excessive movement of materials, information or customers. Usually the objective of the layout decision is to minimize movement, but, especially in information transforming process where distance is largely irrelevant, other criteria may dominate. For example, it may be more important to lay out processes such that similar activities or resources are grouped together. So, an international bank may group its foreign exchange dealers together to encourage communication and discussion between them, even though the 'trades' they make are processed in an entirely different location. Some high-visibility processes may fix their layout to emphasize the behaviour of the customers who are being processed.

Layout should reflect volume and variety

Again, the layout of a process is determined partly by its volume and variety characteristics. When volume is very low and variety is relatively high, 'flow' may not be a major issue. For example, in telecommunications satellite manufacture each product is different, and because products 'flow' through the operation very infrequently, it is not worth arranging facilities to minimize the flow of parts through the operation. With higher volume and lower variety, flow becomes a far more important issue. If variety is still high, however, an entirely flow-dominated arrangement is difficult because there will be different flow patterns. For example, a library will arrange its different categories of books and its other services partly to minimize the average distance its customers have to 'flow' through the operation. But, because its customers' needs vary, it will arrange its layout to satisfy the majority of its customers (but perhaps inconvenience a minority). When the variety of products or services reduces to the point where a distinct 'category' with similar requirements becomes evident but variety is still not small, appropriate resources could be grouped into a separate cell. When variety is relatively small and volume is high, flow can become regularized and resources can be positioned to address the (similar) needs of the products or services, as in a classic flow line.

> **Operations principle**
> Resources in low volume-high variety processes should be arranged to cope with irregular flow.

> **Operations principle**
> Resources in high volume-low variety processes should be arranged to cope with smooth, regular flow.

Most practical layouts are derived from only four *basic layout types* that correspond to different positions on the volume–variety spectrum. These are illustrated diagrammatically in Figure 4.6 and are as follows.

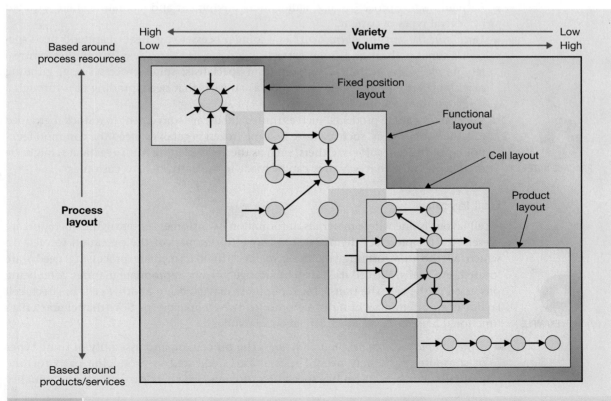

Figure 4.6   Different process layouts are appropriate for different volume–variety combinations

Fixed-position layout

Fixed-position layout is in some ways a contradiction in terms, since the transformed resources do not move between the transforming resources. Instead of materials, information or customers flowing through an operation, the recipient of the processing is stationary and the equipment, machinery, plant and people who do the processing move as necessary. This could be because the product or the recipient of the service is too large to be moved conveniently, or it might be too delicate to move, or perhaps it could object to being moved; for example:

● *Power generator construction* – the product is too large to move.
● *Open-heart surgery* – patients are too delicate to move.
● *High-class restaurant* – customers would object to being moved to where food is prepared.

Functional layout

Functional layout is so called because the functional needs and convenience of the transforming resources that constitute the processes dominate the layout decision. (Confusingly, functional layout can also be called 'process layout'.) In functional layout, similar activities or resources (or those with similar needs) are located together. This may be because it is convenient to group them together, or that their utilization can be improved. It means that when materials, information or customers flow through the operation, they will take a route from activity to activity according to their needs. Usually this makes the flow pattern in the operation complex. Examples of process layouts include:

● *Hospital* – some processes (e.g. radiography equipment and laboratories) are required by several types of patient.
● *Machining the parts for aircraft engines* – some processes (e.g. heat treatment) need specialist support (heat and fume extraction); some processes (e.g. machining centres) require the same technical support from specialists; some processes (e.g. grinding machines) get high machine utilization as all parts that need grinding pass through a single grinding section.

● *Supermarket* – some products, such as tinned goods, are convenient to restock if grouped together. Some areas, such as those holding frozen vegetables, need the common technology of freezer cabinets. Others, such as the areas holding fresh vegetables, might be together because that way they can be made to look attractive to customers.

PRACTICE NOTE

Cell layout

A cell layout is one where materials, information or customers entering the operation are preselected (or preselect themselves) to move to one part of the operation (or cell) in which all the transforming resources, to meet their immediate processing needs, are located. Internally, the cell itself may be arranged in any appropriate manner. After being processed in the cell, the transformed resources may go on to another cell. In effect, cell layout is an attempt to bring some order to the complexity of flow that characterizes functional layout. Examples of cell layouts include:

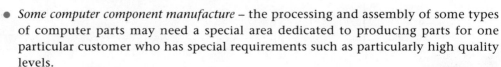

FURTHER EXAMPLE

● *Some computer component manufacture* – the processing and assembly of some types of computer parts may need a special area dedicated to producing parts for one particular customer who has special requirements such as particularly high quality levels.

- *'Lunch' products area in a supermarket* – some customers use the supermarket just to purchase sandwiches, savoury snacks, cool drinks, etc. for their lunch. These products are often located close together in a 'cell' for the convenience of these customers.
- *Maternity unit in a hospital* – customers needing maternity attention are a well-defined group who can be treated together and who are unlikely to need the other facilities of the hospital at the same time that they need the maternity unit.

Product layout

Product layout involves locating people and equipment entirely for the convenience of the transformed resources. Each product, piece of information or customer follows a pre-arranged route in which the sequence of required activities corresponds to the sequence in which the processes have been located. The transformed resources 'flow' along a 'line'. This is why this type of layout is sometimes called flow or line layout. Flow is clear, predictable and therefore relatively easy to control. It is the high volume and standardized requirements of the product or service that allows product layouts. Examples of product layout include:

- *Automobile assembly* – almost all variants of the same model require the same sequence of processes.
- *Self-service cafeteria* – generally the sequence of customer requirements (starter, main course, dessert, drink) is common to all customers, but layout also helps control customer flow.

Layout selection

Getting the process layout right is important, if only because of the cost, difficulty and disruption of making any layout change. It is not an activity many businesses would want to repeat very often. Also, an inappropriate layout could mean that extra cost is incurred *every time* an item is processed. But more than this, an effective layout gives clarity and transparency to the flow of items through a process. There is no better way of emphasizing that everyone's activities are really part of an overall process than by making the flow between activities evident to everyone.

One of the main influences on which type of layout will be appropriate is the nature of the process itself, as summarized in its 'process type'. There is often some confusion between process types and layout types. Layout types are not the same as process types. Process types were described earlier in the chapter and indicate a broad approach to the organization and operation of a process. Layout is a narrower concept but is very clearly linked to process type. Just as process type is governed by volume and variety, so is layout. But for any given process type there are usually at least two alternative layouts. Table 4.1 summarizes the alternative layouts for particular process types. Which of these is selected, or whether some hybrid layout is chosen, depends on the relative importance of the performance objectives of the process, especially cost and flexibility. Table 4.2 summarizes.

Table 4.1   Alternative layout types for each process type

Manufacturing process type	Potential layout types		Service process type
Project	Fixed-position layout Functional layout	Fixed-position layout Functional layout Cell layout	Professional service
Jobbing	Functional layout Cell layout		
Batch	Functional layout Cell layout	Functional layout Cell layout	Service shop
Mass	Cell layout Product layout	Cell layout Product layout	Mass service
Continuous	Product layout		

Table 4.2   The advantages and disadvantages of the basic layout types

	Advantages	Disadvantages
Fixed-position	Very high mix and product flexibility Product or customer not moved or disturbed High variety of tasks for staff	High unit costs Scheduling of space and activities can be difficult Can mean much movement of plant and staff
Functional	High mix and product flexibility Relatively robust if in the case of disruptions Relatively easy supervision of equipment or plant	Low facilities utilization Can have very high work-in-progress or customer queuing Complex flow can be difficult to control
Cell	Can give a good compromise between cost and flexibility for relatively high-variety operations Fast throughput Group work can result in good motivation	Can be costly to rearrange existing layout Can need more plant and equipment Can give lower plant utilization
Product	Low unit costs for high volume Gives opportunities for specialization of equipment Materials or customer movement is convenient	Can have low mix flexibility Not very robust if there is disruption Work can be very repetitive

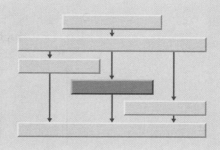

Is process technology appropriate?

Process technologies are the machines, equipment and devices that help processes 'transform' materials and information and customers. This is a particularly important issue because few operations have been unaffected by the advances in process technology over the last two decades. And the pace of technological development is not slowing down. But it is important to distinguish between *process technology* (the machines and devices that help to *create* products and services) and *product technology* (the technology that is embedded within the product or service and creates its specification or functionality). Some process technology, although not used for the actual creation of goods and services, nonetheless plays a key role in *facilitating* their creation. For example, the information technology systems that run planning and control activities can be used to help managers and operators run the processes. Sometimes this type of technology is called *indirect* process technology, and it is becoming increasingly important. Many businesses spend more on the computer systems that run their processes than they do on the direct process technology that creates their products and services.

Process technology should reflect volume and variety

Again, different process technologies will be appropriate for different parts of the volume–variety continuum. High variety–low volume processes generally require process technology that is *general purpose,* because it can perform the wide range of processing activities that high variety demands. High volume–low variety processes can use technology that is more *dedicated* to its narrower range of processing requirements. Within the spectrum from general purpose to dedicated process technologies, three dimensions in particular tend to vary with volume and variety. The first is the extent to which the process technology carries out activities or makes decisions for itself, that is, its degree of 'automation'. The second is the capacity of the technology to process work, that is, its 'scale' or 'scalability'. The third is the extent to which it is integrated with other technologies; that is, its degree of 'coupling' or 'connectivity'. Figure 4.7 illustrates these three dimensions of process technology.[4]

> **Operations principle**
> Process technology in high-volume, low-variety processes is relatively automated, large-scale and closely coupled when compared with that in low-volume, high-variety processes.

The degree of automation of the technology

To some extent, all technology needs human intervention. It may be minimal, for example the interventions for periodic maintenance in a petrochemical refinery. Conversely, the person who operates the technology may be the entire 'brains' of the process, for example the surgeon using keyhole surgery techniques. Generally, processes that have high variety and low volume employ process technology with lower degrees of automation than those with higher volume and lower variety. For example, investment banks trade in highly complex and sophisticated financial 'derivatives', often customized to the needs of individual clients, and each may be worth millions of dollars. The back-office of

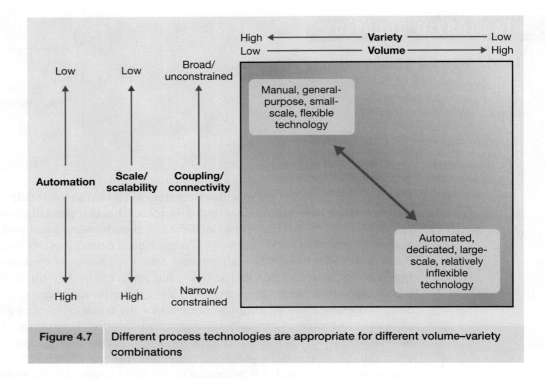

Figure 4.7 Different process technologies are appropriate for different volume–variety combinations

the bank has to process these deals to make sure that payments are made on time, documents are exchanged, and so on. Much of this processing will be done using relatively general-purpose technology such as spreadsheets. Skilled back-office staff are making the decisions rather than the technology. Contrast this with higher-volume, low variety financial products, such as straightforward equity (stock) trades. Most of these products are simple and straightforward and are processed in very high volume of several thousand per day by 'automated' technology.

FURTHER EXAMPLE

The scale/scalability of the technology

There is usually some discretion as to the scale of individual units of technology. For example, the duplicating department of a large office complex may decide to invest in a single, very large, fast copier, or alternatively in several smaller, slower copiers distributed around the operation's various processes. An airline may purchase one or two wide-bodied aircraft or a larger number of smaller aircraft. The advantage of large-scale technologies is that they can usually process items more cheaply than small-scale technologies, but usually need high volume and can cope only with low variety. By contrast, the virtues of smaller-scale technology are often the nimbleness and flexibility that is suited to high-variety, lower-volume processing. For example, four small machines can between them produce four different products simultaneously (albeit slowly), whereas a single large machine with four times the output can produce only one product at a time (albeit faster). Small-scale technologies are also more robust. Suppose the choice is between three small machines and one larger one. In the first case, if one machine breaks down, a third of the capacity is lost, but in the second, capacity is reduced to zero.

The equivalent to scale for some types of information processing technology is *scalability*. By scalability we mean the ability to shift to a different level of useful capacity quickly and cost-effectively. Scalability is similar to absolute scale in so much as it is influenced by the same volume–variety characteristics. IT scalability relies on consistent

IT platform architecture and the high process standardization that is usually associated with high-volume and low-variety operations.

The coupling/connectivity of the technology

Coupling means the linking together of separate activities within a single piece of process technology to form an interconnected processing system. Tight coupling usually gives fast process throughput. For example, in an automated manufacturing system products flow quickly without delays between stages, and inventory will be lower – it can't accumulate when there are no 'gaps' between activities. Tight coupling also means that flow is simple and predictable, making it easier to keep track of parts when they pass through fewer stages, or information when it is automatically distributed to all parts of an information network. However, closely coupled technology can be both expensive (each connection may require capital costs) and vulnerable (a failure in one part of an interconnected system can affect the whole system). The fully integrated manufacturing system constrains parts to flow in a predetermined manner, making it difficult to accommodate products with very different processing requirements. So, coupling is generally more suited to relatively low variety and high volume. Higher-variety processing generally requires a more open and unconstrained level of coupling because different products and services will require a wider range of processing activities.

DIAGNOSTIC QUESTION

Are job designs appropriate?

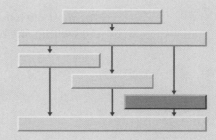

Job design is about how people carry out their tasks within a process. It defines the way they go about their working lives. It positions the expectations of what is required of them, and it influences their perceptions of how they contribute to the organization. It also defines their activities in relation to their work colleagues and it channels the flows of communication between different parts of the operation. But, of most importance, it helps to develop the culture of the organization – its shared values, beliefs and assumptions. Inappropriately designed jobs can destroy the potential of a process to fulfil its objectives, no matter how appropriate its layout or process technology. So jobs must be designed to fit the nature of the process. However, before considering this, it is important to accept that some aspects of job design are common to all processes, irrespective of what they do or how they do it. Consider the following.

- *Safety.* The primary and universal objective of job design is to ensure that all staff performing any task within a process are protected against the possibility of physical or mental harm.
- *Ethical issues.* No individual should be asked to perform any task that either is illegal or (within limits) conflicts with strongly held ethical beliefs.
- *Work/life balance.* All jobs should be structured so as to promote a healthy balance between time spent at work and time away from work.

Note that all these objectives of job design are also likely to improve overall process performance. However, the imperative to follow such objectives for their own sake transcends conventional criteria.

Job design should reflect volume and variety

As with other aspects of process design, the nature and challenges of job design are governed largely by the volume–variety characteristics of a process. An architect designing major construction projects will perform a wide range of very different, often creative and complex tasks, many of which are not defined at the start of the process, and most of which have the potential to give the architect significant job satisfaction. By contrast, someone in the architect's accounts office keying in invoice details has a job that is repetitive, has little variation, is tightly defined and that cannot rely on the intrinsic interest of the task itself to maintain job commitment. These two jobs will have different characteristics because they are part of processes with different volume and variety positions. Three aspects of job design in particular are affected by the volume–variety characteristics of a process: how tasks are to be allocated to each person in the process, the degree of job definition, and the methods used to maintain job commitment. Figure 4.8 illustrates this.

> **Operations principle**
> Job designs in high-volume, low-variety processes are relatively closely defined with little decision-making discretion and needing action to help commitment when compared with those in low-volume, high-variety processes.

How should tasks be allocated? – the division of labour

The most obvious aspect of any individual's job is how big it is, that is how many of the tasks within any process are allocated to an individual. Should a single individual perform

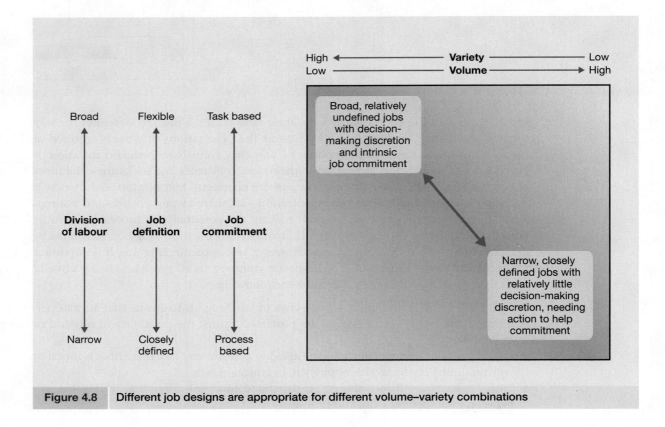

Figure 4.8   Different job designs are appropriate for different volume–variety combinations

the whole of the process? Alternatively, should separate individuals or teams perform each task? Separating tasks into smaller parts between individuals is called the *division of labour*. Perhaps its epitome is the assembly line, where products move along a single path and are built up by operators continually repeating a single task. This is the predominant model of job design in most high volume–low variety processes. For such processes there are some *real advantages* in division-of-labour principles:

- *They promote faster learning*. It is obviously easier to learn how to do a relatively short and simple task than a long and complex one, so new members of staff can be quickly trained and assigned to their tasks.
- *Automation becomes easier*. Substituting technology for labour is considerably easier for short and simple tasks than for long and complex ones.
- *Non-productive work is reduced*. In large, complex tasks the proportion of time between individual value-adding elements can be very high, for example in manufacturing, picking up tools and materials, putting them down again and generally searching and positioning.

There are also *serious drawbacks* to highly divided jobs:

- *The work is monotonous*. Repeating the same task for eight hours a day and five days a week is not fulfilling. This may lead to an increased likelihood of absenteeism, staff turnover and error rates.
- *It can cause physical injury*. The continued repetition of a very narrow range of movements can, in extreme cases, lead to physical injury. The over-use of some parts of the body (especially the arms, hands and wrists) can result in pain and a reduction in physical capability, called repetitive strain injury (RSI).
- *It can mean low flexibility*. Dividing a task into many small parts often gives the job design a rigidity that is difficult to change under changing circumstances. For example, if an assembly line has been designed to make one particular product but then has to change to manufacture a quite different product, the whole line will need redesigning. This will probably involve changing every operator's set of tasks.
- *It can mean poor robustness*. Highly divided jobs imply items passing between several stages. If one of these stages is not working correctly, for example because some equipment is faulty, the whole operation is affected. On the other hand, if each person is performing the whole of the job, any problems will affect only that one person's output.

To what degree should jobs be defined?

Jobs in high-variety processes are difficult to define in anything but the most general terms. Such jobs may require tacit knowledge gained over time and through experience and often require individuals to exercise significant discretion in what they do and how they do it. Some degree of job definition is usually possible and advisable, but it may be stated in terms of the 'outcome' from the task rather than in terms of the activities within the task. For example, the architect's job may be defined in terms of *'achieving overall co-ordination, taking responsibility for articulating the overall vision of the project, ensuring stakeholders are comfortable with the process, etc.'*. By contrast, a process with less variety and higher volume is likely to be defined more closely, with the exact nature of each activity defined and individual staff trained to follow a job step-by-step.

How should job commitment be encouraged?

Many factors may influence job commitment. An individual's job history and expectations, relationships with co-workers and personal circumstances can all be important.

So are the volume and variety characteristics of the process by defining the possible ways in which commitment can be enhanced. In high-variety processes, especially those with a high degree of staff discretion, job commitment is likely to come from the *intrinsic nature of the task* itself. Exercising skill and decision making, for example, can bring their own satisfaction. Of course, commitment can be enhanced through extra responsibility, flexibility in working times and so on, but the main motivator is the job itself. By contrast, low variety–high volume jobs, especially those designed with a high division of labour and little discretion, can be highly alienating. Such jobs have relatively little intrinsic task satisfaction. It has to be *'designed into' the process* by emphasizing the satisfaction to be gained from the performance of the process as a whole. A number of job design approaches have been suggested for achieving this in processes involving relatively repetitive work.

- **Job enlargement** involves allocating a larger number of tasks to individuals, usually by combining tasks that are broadly of the same type as those in the original job. This may not involve more demanding or fulfilling tasks, but it may provide a more complete and therefore slightly more meaningful job. If nothing else, people performing an enlarged job will not repeat themselves as often. For example, suppose that the manufacture of a product has traditionally been split up on an assembly-line basis into 10 equal and sequential jobs. If that job is then redesigned so as to form two parallel assembly lines of five people, each operator would have twice the number of tasks to perform.

- **Job enrichment** like job enlargement, increases the number of tasks in a job, but also implies allocating tasks that involve more decision making, or greater autonomy, and therefore greater control over the job. These could include the maintenance of, and adjustments to, any process technology used, the planning and control of activities within the job, or the monitoring of quality levels. The effect is both to reduce repetition in the job *and* to increase personal development opportunities. So, in the assembly-line example, each operator could also be allocated responsibility for carrying out routine maintenance and such tasks as record-keeping and managing the supply of materials.

- **Job rotation** means moving individuals periodically between different sets of tasks to provide some variety in their activities. When successful, job rotation can increase skill flexibility and make a small contribution to reducing monotony. However, it is not always viewed as beneficial either by management (because it can disrupt the smooth flow of work) or by the people performing the jobs (because it can interfere with their rhythm of work).

- **Empowerment** means enhancing individuals' ability, and sometimes authority, to change how they do their jobs. Some technologically constrained processes, such as those in chemical plants, may limit the extent to which staff can dilute their highly standardized task methods without consultation. Other less defined processes to empowerment may go much further.

- **Team-working** is closely linked to empowerment. Team-based work organization (sometimes called self-managed work teams) is where staff, often with overlapping skills, collectively perform a defined task and have some discretion over how they perform the task. The team may control such things as task allocation between members, scheduling work, quality measurement and improvement, and sometimes even the hiring of staff. Groups are described as 'teams' when the virtues of working together are being emphasized and a shared set of objectives and responsibilities is assumed.

PRACTICE NOTE

Critical commentary

Each chapter contains a short critical commentary on the main ideas covered in the chapter. Its purpose is not to undermine the issues discussed in the chapter, but to emphasize that, although we present a relatively orthodox view of operation, there are other perspectives.

■ Three sets of criticisms could be prompted by the material covered in this chapter. The first relates to the separation of process design into two parts – positioning and analysis. It can reasonably be argued that this separation is artificial in so much as (as is admitted at the beginning of this chapter) the two approaches are very much interrelated. An alternative way of thinking about the topic would be to consider all aspects of the arrangement of resources together. This would include the issues of layout that have been discussed in this chapter together with the more detailed process mapping issues to be described in Chapter 5. The second criticism would challenge the core assumption of the chapter – that many significant process design decisions are influenced primarily by volume and variety. Whereas it is conventional to relate layout and (to a slightly lesser extent) process technology to volume–variety positioning, it is less conventional to do so for issues of job design. Some would argue that the vast majority of job design decisions will not vary significantly with volume and variety. The final criticism is also related to job design. Some academics would argue that our treatment of job design is too influenced by the discredited (in their eyes) principles of the 'scientific' management movement that grew into 'work study' and 'time and motion' management.

Summary checklist

DOWNLOADABLE

This checklist comprises questions that can be usefully applied to any type of operations and reflect the major diagnostic questions used within the chapter.

☐ Do processes match volume–variety requirements?

☐ Are 'process types' understood and do they match volume–variety requirements?

☐ Can processes be positioned on the 'diagonal' of the product–process matrix?

☐ Are the consequences of moving away from the 'diagonal' of the product–process matrix understood?

☐ Are the implications of choosing an appropriate layout, especially the balance between process flexibility and low processing costs, understood?

☐ Are the process layouts appropriate?

☐ Which of the four basic layout types that correspond to different positions on the volume–variety spectrum is appropriate for each process?

☐ Is process technology appropriate?

☐ Is the effect of the three dimensions of process technology (the degree of automation, the scale/scalability and the coupling/connectivity of the technology) understood?

☐ Are job designs appropriate?

☐ Does job design ensure the imperative to design jobs that are safe and ethical, and promote adequate work/life balance?

☐ Is the extent of division of labour in each process appropriate for its volume–variety characteristics?

☐ Is the extent of job definition in each process appropriate for its volume–variety characteristics?

☐ Are job commitment mechanisms in each process appropriate for its volume–variety characteristics?

Case study   North West Constructive Bank – The New Mortgage Centre 1

It had been a long day for Andy Curtis when he emerged from the meeting. In spite of the early May sunshine he looked pale when he gathered his team around him. *'It was terrible in there. The Marketing people gave me a really tough time when I reported our current average turnaround times. They were quite happy to remind me that I had told them our "discount rate" product was killing us operationally and that we had to pull it if we were to survive the reorganization. I've been made to look stupid because now, four weeks after reorganization **and** after the product has been pulled, our turnaround times are even worse. I think they **are** right, we really are a shambles.'* Mary Godfrey, his deputy, was protective of her staff and offended that Marketing was calling her team a shambles. *'It's no use blaming us, the staff are working flat out but we can't seem to make any inroads to the piles of work.'*

Andy Curtis was the Mortgage Operations Manager for North West Constructive Bank (NWCB), a large retail banking group with a mid-sized mortgage business. His main responsibility was running the new applications process in the bank's new mortgage centre. For 12 months Andy had led a project team that had been planning the consolidation of the bank's original three mortgage processing centres into one new site. Prior to the consolidation, the bank's mortgage business had been divided into three regions: 'Northern', 'Southern' and 'Western' applications. *'The driver for the consolidation was to achieve economies of scale. There is no reason why a processing centre need be located close to its market and we could make significant savings by giving up our city centre leases on the three old sites, consolidating all our operations on a single floor of the bank's main headquarters building. We also felt that there would be room to develop more flexibility between the three regions when demand varied.'*

Andy and his team had always known that the merger of the three centres could be difficult; that is why they had planned it for early February, before the spring peak in applications. It was also why they had decided to (at least initially) keep the three regional sets of processing cells located close to each other. Figure 4.9 shows the current layout of the new mortgage floor.

Seven months ago, about halfway through the team's planning process, it became clear that the bank's

Source: Newscast Image Centre

portfolio of mortgage products would be changing. It was accepted that the bank's marketing strategy had been excessively reactive to competitor activity. *'Every time one of our competitors introduced a new mortgage product, we tried to copy them. Sometimes this worked, sometimes it didn't. But we were left with a confusing and incoherent legacy of products that neither our agents nor our branches fully understood. Also, we felt that there was considerable opportunity to develop products that satisfied specific market segments but could fit into a relatively standard back-office process. For example, we will introduce "The Flexible Mortgage", targeted at people with fluctuating incomes, but as far as our back office is concerned, it will require almost the same processing steps as a normal mortgage.'* (Parminder Singh, Mortgage Product Manager) The introduction of the new product portfolio was scheduled to start in June.

Andy's team planning the reorganization of the back office was delighted by the idea of a simplified product portfolio: *'It would make life a lot simpler for us. We can see two operational advantages coming together. First, by consolidating all three centres into one we can get greater economies of scale. Second, the new product portfolio could considerably reduce the variety, and hopefully complexity, of our processing. In hindsight, I am really happy that both the consolidation and the product changes did not happen together. The disruption of the reorganization has been bad enough without having to cope with different products at the same time.'*

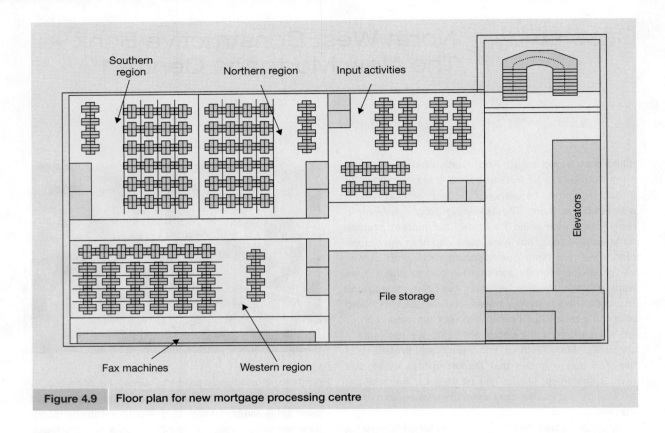

Figure 4.9   Floor plan for new mortgage processing centre

Demand

Applications for new mortgages could arrive through three main channels. Twenty per cent were 'further advances'. These were from existing customers who wanted to extend their borrowing. This type of application came to the new applications process direct from the mortgage businesses sales. The remaining 80 per cent of applications were split evenly between those coming via the branches of the bank and those coming from independent sales agents who usually acted as mortgage brokers for their clients. Demand fluctuated according to the time of year and specific offers. Demand from agents in particular was more volatile as they usually chased the best deals for their clients. The discounted rate product had been seen as very attractive by the market, and the bank's Marketing Department had been delighted at its take-up. Although always intended as a short-term offer, Marketing had wanted the product to continue for another one or two months, but Andy persuaded the board to pull it as originally planned in January. His reasons were largely concerned with reducing the demand on the new applications process during the reorganization. *'The discounted rate product was **too** successful as far as we were concerned. Demand on all three centres had been around 15 per cent higher during the last quarter of the year and I didn't want this to continue into the reorganization*

period. I know it sounds crazy to want less business, but Marketing accepted that it was of marginal profitability and the effect on the processing centres had been disruptive. Our "service level agreement" promise to our agents of achieving an average processing time of 15 days had already slipped to 20 days, and the 17-day promise to our own branches has slipped to 22 days!'

Unfortunately, when the news of the imminent demise of the discounted rate product hit the agents there was a final surge as they persuaded clients to make a fast decision to obtain the discounted rate. To some extent Andy and his team had anticipated some of this surge and had warned of some slippage in turnaround times, but the short-term increase in demand had been larger than expected and now, four weeks later, they certainly hadn't expected things to be getting worse.

The new applications process

The new consolidated site was relatively close to the old southern area centre. Therefore, slightly over 80 per cent of the southern area staff had transferred from the old centres. By contrast, only around 10 per cent in the other teams had worked in the old processing centres. Most of the new staff had experience in financial services operations but were new to mortgage processing.

The processing of a mortgage application involves four sets of activities:

- 'Input' where applications are received and keyed into the computer and initial checks about accompanying evidence are carried out.
- 'Underwriting' where the decision to lend is made.
- 'Offer' where the team liaises with surveyors to obtain surveys.
- 'Completion' where sanction letters are sent to solicitors.

When the processes were moved to the new centre, the only significant change from the old way of working was the grouping together of all the 'keying in' activities associated with the input stage. This was felt to be a fairly risk-free move because all three centres were already using a standardized 'preliminary information screen'. *'Input is a fairly simple activity and there is relatively little difference between different types of product, therefore it makes sense to put them all together. In fact it has worked very well. Bringing the teams together has already allowed us to examine the marginal differences between the ways we used to do it and adopt a method of working that combines different elements of best practice. We have twelve staff in the input section, that is a reduction of seven staff compared to the combined data input staff that were needed in the three separate centres. It has also allowed staff to specialize to some extent, which can be useful at times.'*

The numbers of staff in each team were as follows:

	Northern area	Southern area	Western area
Underwriting	19	22	5
Offer	28	28	12
Completion	14	15	5

All teams had to process a range of products. Every staff member was trained to deal with standard mortgages, but more experienced staff were used for more 'specialist' mortgages such as 'Buy to Let'. There was an ongoing training programme to train all staff to deal with all types of mortgage, but with staff turnover at 11 per cent there would always be some staff who were able to do only the basic work.

Problems with the new process

In spite of his irritation at the recent meeting, Andy Curtis was broadly optimistic about his team's ability to get over their problems. *'Our problem is in fact three sets of problems, all of which have hit us at the same time. First, there is the move itself. That was bound to cause some disruption but I don't think that it has thrown up any particular problems that we were not aware of. It's just that it has created an uncertain and unstable environment in which to cope with our other problems. Second, there is the last-minute rush by agents to take advantage of our discounted rate product before it was withdrawn. This meant an extra load above what we expected and hit us just at the wrong time. I'm not sure who should carry the blame for this. It's probably not useful to even try and allocate blame. I know that Marketing should have forecast the extent of the short-term surge in demand, but there again, there is no reason why we could not have forecast it ourselves. The third problem is probably the most important. Although we have only been operating with the new process and layout for four weeks, it is already clear that it isn't working as well as it should. Or perhaps it would be more accurate to say that we have failed to capitalize on the potential for redesigning the total process that bringing together the three centres has given us.'*

Andy confided his feeling that the underlying process could be improved to his senior team. Together they put together a list of the key problems with the process as they saw them. The main points to emerge from this list were as follows:

- Staff were having to move about more than at the old centres. There, the information was within easy reach of all staff. Now, the files had been consolidated to avoid duplication, so the filing room was further away for most staff.
- This led to another problem. Because of the effort in retrieving a file, staff were developing a habit of keeping it out of the filing system for longer than necessary. They were keeping it on their desk 'in case it was required again'. This made it unavailable to any other member of staff who could need it.
- All the fax machines were located together in one location. This helped to maintain a high utilization of the machines, but again meant that staff had further to walk. Even the Southern Area team, for whom the fax machines are most convenient, resented the other teams constantly walking through their area.
- There was no clarity of flow. The high level of in-process inventory of partially processed applications (both physical files and virtual files on the IT system) resulted in the 'black hole syndrome', with applications disappearing into people's in-trays.
- There was a significant amount of rework required within the system. Putting together the data from the three old centres for the previous year showed that 22.5 per cent of all offers made were either returning to the process for adjustment, or recycled in some way within the process, sometimes more than once. This problem seemed to be continuing at the same rate in the new centre.

'I think our problems come down to two major issues,' Andy told his group. *'First there is the question of getting*

the flow through our process right. One thing that has become clear is that processing a mortgage is a relatively standard task irrespective of whether the customer is from the north or south or west region. The only activity where specialized knowledge matters is at the offer stage where knowledge of the region is required. Nor should the different sales channels matter. We promise a faster turnround time to the agents than to our own branches because, as independents, we need to keep the agents happy. But, if our processing was right, we should be able to offer the same fast throughput time to both the brokers and the branches. We have already put all the input activities together and that has worked well. I don't see why we can't have work flowing from the input section to underwriting, then to offer and then to completion just like a smooth-running assembly line. The existing teams organize themselves so that applications flow from an underwriting stage to an offer stage, then to a completion stage, so why can't we simply do that for the whole operation? At the same time we have to solve the recycling problem. This must be the root cause of a lot of our problems. Ideally, no application should progress beyond the input stage without it being capable of moving smoothly through the rest of the process. One idea may be to put an extra step in the process for agents where we phone the customer to check details at the input stage.'

QUESTIONS

1 Is Andy right that Marketing should have forecast the last-minute surge in demand for the 'discounted rate' product?

2 What appears to be the volume–variety position of the new centre? Is it different from the old centres?

3 How would you recommend that Andy sets about improving the performance of his processes?

This case study is concluded in Chapter 5.

ACTIVE CASE

Active case study   McPherson Charles Solicitors

McPherson Charles, based in Bristol, UK, has rapidly grown to be one of the biggest law firms in the region. The company is embarking upon a 'plans for the future' programme aiming to improve the effectiveness of its operations. Three of the partners, each responsible for a different area (property law, family law, litigation), meet to discuss this but clearly have different ideas about where the priorities of the firm should lie.

● How would you evaluate the existing processes and operations and what would be your recommendation to each partner to ensure future growth for the firm as a whole?

Please refer to the Active case on the CD to listen to the different perspectives and learn more about the operations for which each partner is responsible.

Applying the principles

HINTS

Some of these exercises can be answered by reading the chapter. Others will require some general knowledge of business activity and some might require an element of investigation. All have hints on how they can be answered on the CD accompanying this book.

1 Visit a branch of a retail bank and consider the following questions:

● What categories of service does the bank seem to offer?

● To what extent does the bank design separate processes for each of its types of service?

● What are the different process design objectives for each category of service?

2   Revisit the example at the beginning of this chapter that examines some of the principles behind supermarket lay-out. Then visit a supermarket and observe people's behaviour. You may wish to try to observe which areas they move past slowly and which areas they seem to move past without paying attention to the products. (You may have to exercise some discretion when doing this; people generally don't like to be stalked round the supermarket too obviously.) Try and verify, as far as you can, some of the principles that were outlined in the example.

- If you were to redesign the supermarket, what would you recommend? What do you think, therefore, are the main criteria to be considered in the design of a supermarket layout?
- What competitive or environmental changes may result in the need to change store layouts in the future?
- Will these apply to all supermarkets, or only certain ones, such as town centre stores?

3   Consider a retail bank. It has many services that it could offer through its branch network, using telephone-based call centres, or using an Internet-based service. Choose a service that (like the bank's services) could be delivered in different ways. For example, you could choose education courses (that can be delivered full-time, part-time, by distance learning, by e-learning, etc.), or a library (using a fixed facility, a mobile service, an Internet-based service, etc.), or any other similar service. Evaluate each alternative delivery process in terms of its effect on its customers' experiences.

4   Many universities and colleges around the world are under increasing pressure to reduce the cost per student of their activities. How do you think technology could help operations such as universities to keep their costs down but their quality of education high?

5   Robot-type technology is starting to play a part in some medical surgical procedures. What would it take before you were willing to subject yourself to a robot doctor?

6   Security devices are becoming increasingly high-tech. Most offices and similar buildings have simple security de-vices such as 'swipe cards' that admit only authorized people to the premises. Other technologies are becoming more common (although perhaps more in movies than in reality) such as fingerprint, iris and face scanning. Explore websites that deal with advanced security technology and gain some understanding of their state of development, advantages and disadvantages. Use this understanding to design a security system for an office building with which you are familiar. Remember that any system must allow access to legitimate users of the building (at least to obtain information for which they have clearance) and yet provide maximum security against any unauthorized access to areas and/or information.

Notes on chapter

1   Sources: Paul Walley, our colleague in the Operations Management Group at Warwick Business School; Martin, P. (2000) 'How supermarkets make a meal of you', *Sunday Times,* 4 November.

2   Hayes, R.H. and Wheelwright, S.C. (1984) *Restoring our Competitive Edge,* John Wiley.

3   Example provided by Professor Michael Lewis, Bath University, UK.

4   Typology derived from Slack, N. and Lewis, M.A. (2001) *Operations Strategy,* Financial Times Prentice Hall, Harlow, UK.

Taking it further

Anupindi, R., Chopra, S., Deshmukh, S.D., Van Mieghem, J.A. and Zemel, E. (1999) *Managing Business Process Flows,* Prentice Hall, New Jersey. An excellent, although mathematical, approach to process design in general.

Hammer, M. (1990) 'Reengineering work: don't automate, obliterate', *Harvard Business Review,* July–August. This is the paper that launched the whole idea of business processes and process man-agement in general to a wider managerial audience. Slightly dated but worth reading.

Hopp, W.J. and Spearman, M.L. (2001) *Factory Physics* (2nd edn), McGraw-Hill. Very technical so don't bother with it if you aren't prepared to get into the maths. However, some fascinating analysis, especially concerning Little's Law.

Ramaswamy, R. (1996) *Design and Management of Service Processes,* Addison-Wesley Longman. A relatively technical approach to process design in a service environment.

Shostack, G.L. (1982) 'How to design a service', *European Journal of Marketing,* Vol. 16, No. 1. A far less technical and more experiential approach to design of service processes.

Useful websites

www.opsman.org Definitions, links and opinion on operations and process management.

www.bpmi.org Site of the Business Process Management Initiative. Some good resources including papers and articles.

www.bptrends.com News site for trends in business process management generally. Some interesting articles.

www.bls.gov/oes US Department of Labor employment statistics.

www.fedee.com/hrtrends Federation of European Employers' guide to employment and job trends in Europe.

www.iienet.org The American Institute of Industrial Engineers' site. They are an important professional body for process design and related topics.

www.waria.com A Workflow and Reengineering Association website. Some useful topics.

**FURTHER
RESOURCES**

For further resources including examples, animated diagrams, self-test questions, Excel spreadsheets, active case studies and video materials please explore the CD accompanying this book.

5

PROCESS DESIGN 2 – ANALYSIS

Introduction

The previous chapter set the broad parameters for process design; in particular it showed how volume and variety shape the positioning of the process in terms of layout, process technology and the design of jobs. But this is only the beginning of process design. Within these broad parameters there are many, more detailed decisions to be made that will dictate the way materials, information and customers flow through the process. Do not dismiss these detailed design decisions as merely the 'technicalities' of process design. They are important because they determine the actual performance of the process in practice and eventually its contribution to the performance of the whole business. (See Figure 5.1.)

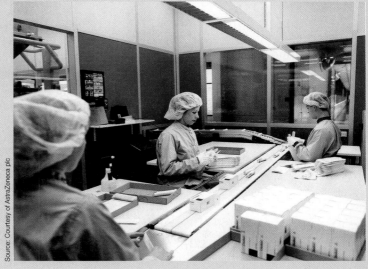

Source: Courtesy of AstraZeneca plc

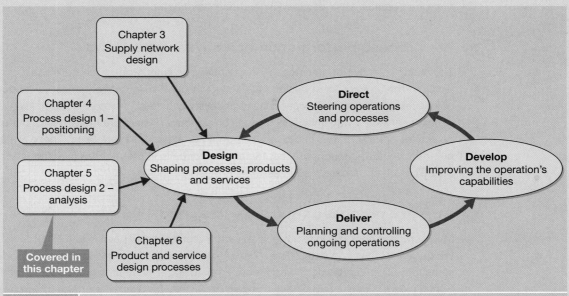

Chapter 3
Supply network design

Chapter 4
Process design 1 – positioning

Chapter 5
Process design 2 – analysis

Covered in this chapter

Chapter 6
Product and service design processes

Design
Shaping processes, products and services

Direct
Steering operations and processes

Develop
Improving the operation's capabilities

Deliver
Planning and controlling ongoing operations

Figure 5.1	Process design–analysis involves calculating the details of the process, in particular its objectives, sequence of activities, allocation of tasks and capacity, and ability to incorporate the effects of variability

Executive summary

VIDEO
further detail

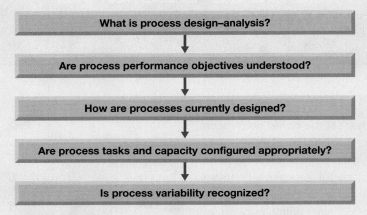

Decision logic chain for process design–analysis

Each chapter is structured around a set of diagnostic questions. These questions suggest what you should ask in order to gain an understanding of the important issues of a topic, and as a result, improve your decision making. An executive summary, addressing these questions, is provided below.

What is process design–analysis?

The analysis stage of process design involves calculating the details of the process, in particular its objectives, sequence of activities, allocation of tasks and capacity, and its ability to incorporate the effects of variability. It is the complementary activity to the broad positioning of processes that was described in the previous chapter.

Are process performance objectives understood?

The major objective of any process in the business is to support the business's overall objectives. Therefore process design must reflect the relative priority of the normal performance objectives: quality, speed, dependability, flexibility and cost. At a more detailed level, process design defines the way units flow through an operation. Therefore more 'micro' performance objectives are also useful in process design. Four in particular are used. These are throughput (or flow) rate, throughput time, the number of units in the process (work in process) and the utilization of process resources.

How are processes currently designed?

Much process design is in fact redesign, and a useful starting point is to fully understand how the current process operates. The most effective way of doing this is to map the process in some way. This can be done at different levels using slightly different mapping techniques. Sometimes it is useful to define the degree of visibility for different parts of the process, indicating how much of the process is transparent to customers.

Are process tasks and capacity configured appropriately?

This is a complex question with several distinct parts. First, it is necessary to understand the task precedence to be incorporated in the process. This defines what activities must occur before others. Second, it is necessary to examine how alternative process design options can incorporate series and parallel configuration. These are sometimes called 'long-thin' and 'short-fat' arrangements. Third, cycle time and process capacity must be calculated. This can help to allocate work evenly between the stages of the process (called balancing). Fourth, the relationship between throughput, cycle time and work in process must be established. This is done using a simple but extremely powerful relationship known as Little's law (throughput time = work in process × cycle time).

Is process variability recognized?

In reality, processes have to cope with variability, in terms of both time and the tasks that are performed within the process. This variability can have very significant effects on process behaviour, usually to reduce process efficiency. Queuing theory can be used to understand this effect. In particular, it is important to understand the relationship between process utilization and the number of units waiting to be processed (or throughput time).

What is process design–analysis?

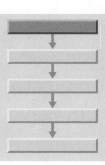

To 'design' is to conceive the looks, arrangement and workings of something *before it is constructed*. Process design should be treated at two levels – the broad, aggregated level and the more detailed level. The previous chapter took a broad approach by relating process design to the volume–variety position of the process. That will have identified the broad process type, and given some guidance as to the layout, process technology and job designs to be used within the process. This chapter takes a more detailed view. However, in working out the details of a process design it is sometimes necessary to revisit the overall broad assumptions under which it is being designed. This is why the detailed analysis of process design covered in the chapter should always be thought through in the context of the broader process positioning issues covered in Chapter 4. The following two examples illustrate processes whose detailed design is important in determining their effectiveness.

Example   ### Processes for even faster food[1]

The quick service restaurant (QSR) industry reckons that the very first drive-through dates back to 1928 when Royce Hailey first promoted the drive-through service at his Pig Stand restaurant in Los Angeles. Customers would simply drive by the back door of the restaurant where the chef would come out and deliver the restaurant's famous 'Barbequed Pig' sandwiches. Today, drive-through processes are slicker and faster. They are also more common: in 1975, McDonald's had no drive-throughs, but now more than 90 per cent of its US restaurants incorporate a drive-through process. In fact 80 per cent of recent fast-food growth has come through the growing number of drive-throughs. Says one industry specialist, *'There are a growing number of customers for whom fast-food is not fast enough. They want to cut waiting time to the very minimum without even getting out of their car. Meeting their needs depends on how smooth we can get the process.'*

The competition to design the fastest and most reliable drive-through process is fierce. Starbucks' drive-throughs have strategically placed cameras at the order boards so that servers can recognize regular customers and start making their order even before it's placed. Burger King has experimented with sophisticated sound systems, simpler menu boards and see-through food bags to ensure greater accuracy (no point in being fast if you don't deliver what the customer ordered). These details matter. McDonald's reckons that its sales increase 1 per cent for every six seconds saved at a drive-through, while a single Burger King restaurant calculated that its takings increased by $15,000 a year each time it reduced queuing time by one second. Menu items must be easy to read and understand. Designing 'combo meals' (burger, fries and a cola), for example, saves time at the ordering stage. But not everyone is thrilled by the boom in drive-throughs. People living in the vicinity may complain of the extra traffic they attract, and the unhealthy image of fast-food combined with a process that does not even make customers get out of their car is, for some, a step too far.

Example   ### 'Factory flow' helps surgery productivity[2]

Even surgery can be seen as a process, and like any process it can be improved. Normally patients remain stationary, with surgeons and other theatre staff performing their tasks around them. But this idea has been challenged by John Petri, an Italian consultant orthopaedic surgeon at a hospital

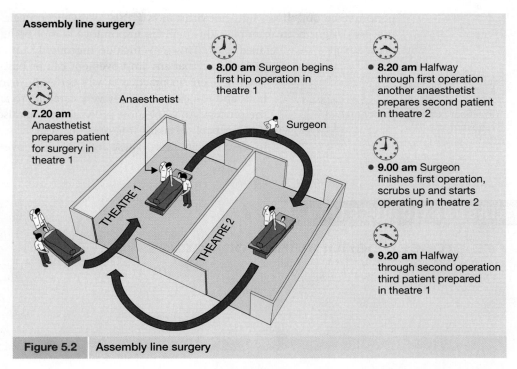

Assembly line surgery

7.20 am Anaesthetist prepares patient for surgery in theatre 1

Anaesthetist

THEATRE 1

THEATRE 2

Surgeon

8.00 am Surgeon begins first hip operation in theatre 1

8.20 am Halfway through first operation another anaesthetist prepares second patient in theatre 2

9.00 am Surgeon finishes first operation, scrubs up and starts operating in theatre 2

9.20 am Halfway through second operation third patient prepared in theatre 1

Figure 5.2	Assembly line surgery

in Norfolk in the UK. Frustrated by spending time drinking tea while patients were prepared for surgery, he redesigned the process so now he moves continually between two theatres. While he is operating on a patient in one theatre, his anaesthetist colleagues are preparing a patient for surgery in another theatre. After finishing with the first patient, the surgeon 'scrubs up', moves to the second operating theatre and begins the surgery on the second patient. While he is doing this the first patient is moved out of the first operating theatre and the third patient is prepared. This method of overlapping operations in different theatres allows him to work for five hours at a time rather than the previous standard three-and-a-half-hour session. '*If you were running a factory,*' says the surgeon, '*you wouldn't allow your most important and most expensive machine to stand idle. The same is true in a hospital.*'

Currently used on hip and knee replacements, this layout would not be suitable for all surgical procedures. But since its introduction the surgeon's waiting list has fallen to zero and his productivity has doubled. '*For a small increase in running costs we are able to treat many more patients,*' said a spokesperson for the hospital management. '*What is important is that clinicians . . . produce innovative ideas and we demonstrate that they are effective.*'

What do these two examples have in common?

Both examples highlight a number of process design issues. The first is that the payback from good process design is clearly significant. Quick-service restaurant operations devote time and effort to the design process, assessing the performance of alternative process designs in terms of efficiency, quality, and above all, throughput time. The return for the hospital is even more dramatic. For a service that offers primarily surgical excellence and quality, being able to achieve the cost benefits of slick process design without compromising quality makes the hospital far better at serving its patients. Also it is difficult to separate the design of the process from the design of the product or service that it produces. The 'combo meal' is designed with the constraints and capabilities of the drive-through process in mind, and even the design of the surgical procedure may need to be adapted marginally to facilitate the new process. An important point here is that, in both cases, processes are designed to be appropriate for the market they are serving. Different market strategies may require different process designs. So a good starting point for any operation is to understand the direct relationship between strategic and process performance objectives. But, notwithstanding this relatively strategic starting point for process design, both examples illustrate the importance of not being afraid to analyze processes at a very detailed level. This may include thoroughly understanding current processes so that any improvement can be based on the reality of what happens in practice. It will certainly involve allocating the tasks and associated capacity very carefully to appropriate parts of the process. And, for most processes, it will also involve a design that is capable of taking into consideration the variability that exists in most human tasks. These are the topics covered in this chapter.

> **Operations principle**
> Processes should always be designed to reflect customer and/or market requirements.

DIAGNOSTIC QUESTION

Are process performance objectives understood?

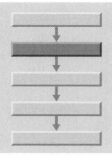

> **Operations principle**
> A process performance can be judged in terms of the levels of quality, speed, dependability, flexibility and cost it achieves.

The whole point of process design is to make sure that the performance of the process is appropriate for whatever it is trying to achieve. For example, if an operation competed primarily on its ability to respond quickly to customer requests, its processes would need to be designed to give fast throughput times. This would minimize the time between customers requesting a product or service and their receiving it. Similarly, if an operation competed on low price, cost-related objectives are likely to dominate its process design. Some kind of logic should link what the operation as a whole is attempting to achieve, and the performance objectives of its individual processes. This is illustrated in Table 5.1.

Process flow objectives

All the strategic performance objectives translate directly to process design as shown in Table 5.1. But, because processes will be managed at a very operational level, process design also needs to consider a more 'micro' and detailed set of objectives. These are largely concerned with flow through the process. When whatever is being 'processed' (we shall refer to these as 'units' irrespective of what they are) enter a process they will progress through a series of activities where they are 'transformed' in some way. Between these activities the units may dwell for some time in inventories, waiting to be transformed by the next activity. This means that the time that a unit spends in the process (its throughput time) will be longer than the sum of all the transforming activities that it passes through. Also the resources that perform the process's activities may not be used all the time because not all units will necessarily require the same activities and the capacity of each resource may not match the demand placed upon it. So neither the units moving through the process nor the resources performing the activities may be fully utilized. Because of this, the way in which units leave the process is unlikely to be exactly the same as the way they arrive at the process. Figure 5.3 illustrates some of the

> **Operations principle**
> Process flow objectives should include throughput rate, throughput time, work-in-process and resource utilization; all of which are interrelated.

Table 5.1	The impact of strategic performance objectives on process design objectives and performance	
Strategic performance objective	*Typical process design objectives*	*Some benefits of good process design*
Quality	• Provide appropriate resources, capable of achieving the specification of product or service • Error-free processing	• Products and service produced 'on-specification' • Less recycling and wasted effort within the process
Speed	• Minimum throughput time • Output rate appropriate for demand	• Short customer waiting time • Low in-process inventory
Dependability	• Provide dependable process resources • Reliable process output timing and volume	• On-time deliveries of products and services • Less disruption, confusion and rescheduling within the process
Flexibility	• Provide resources with an appropriate range of capabilities • Change easily between processing states (what, how or how much is being processed?)	• Ability to process a wide range of products and services • Low cost/fast product and service change • Low cost/fast volume and timing changes • Ability to cope with unexpected events (e.g. supply or a processing failure)
Cost	• Appropriate capacity to meet demand • Eliminate process waste in terms of: – excess capacity – excess process capability – in-process delays – in-process errors – inappropriate process inputs	• Low processing costs • Low resource costs (capital costs) • Low delay/inventory costs (working capital costs)

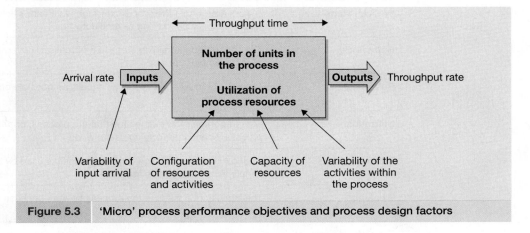

Figure 5.3 'Micro' process performance objectives and process design factors

FURTHER EXAMPLE

'micro' performance flow objectives that describe process flow performance and the process design factors that influence them. The flow objectives are:

● Throughput rate (or flow rate) – the rate at which units emerge from the process, i.e. the number of units passing through the process per unit of time.

- Throughput time – the average elapsed time taken for inputs to move through the process and become outputs.
- The number of units in the process (also called the 'work in process', or in-process inventory), as an average over a period of time.
- The utilization of process resources – the proportion of available time for which the resources within the process are performing useful work.

The design factors that will influence the flow objectives are:

- the variability of input arrival to the process
- the configuration of the resources and activities within the process
- the capacity of the resources at each point in the process
- the variability of the activities within the process.

As we examine each of these design factors, we will be using a number of terms that, although commonly used within process design, need some explanation. These terms will be described in the course of the chapter, but for reference they are summarized in Table 5.2.

Table 5.2	Some common process design terms[3]
Term	**Definition**
Process task	The sum of all the activities that must be performed by the process.
Work content of the process task	The total amount of work within the process task measured in time units.
Activity	A discrete amount of work within the overall process task.
Work content of an activity	The amount of work within an activity measured in time units.
Precedence relationship	The relationship between activities expressed in terms of their dependencies, i.e., whether individual activities must be performed before other activities can be started.
Cycle time	The average time that the process takes between completions of units.
Throughput rate	The number of units completed by the process per unit of time (= 1/cycle time).
Process stage	A work area within the process through which units flow; it may be responsible for performing several activities.
Bottleneck	The capacity-constraining stage in a process; it governs the output from the whole process.
Balancing	The act of allocating activities as equally as possible between stages in the process.
Utilization	The proportion of available time that the process, or part of the process, spends performing useful work.
Starving	Underutilization of a stage within a process caused by inadequate supply from the previous stage.
Blocking	The inability of a stage in the process to work because the inventory prior to the subsequent stage is full.
Throughput time	The elapsed time between a unit entering the process and it leaving the process.
Queue time	The time a unit spends waiting to be processed.

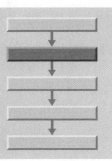

DIAGNOSTIC QUESTION

How are processes currently designed?

> **Operations principle**
> Process mapping is needed to expose the reality of process behaviour.

Existing processes are not always sufficiently well defined or described. Sometimes this is because they have developed over time without ever being formally recorded, or they may have been changed (perhaps improved) informally by the individuals who work in the process. But processes that are not formally defined can be interpreted in different ways, leading to confusion and inhibiting improvement. So, it is important to have some recorded visual descriptor of a process that can be agreed by all those who are involved in it. This is where process mapping comes in.

Process mapping

Process mapping (or process blueprinting as it is sometimes called) at its most basic level involves describing processes in terms of how the activities within the process relate to each other. There are many, broadly similar, techniques that can be used for process mapping. However, all the techniques have two main features:

- They identify the different types of activity that take place during the process.
- They show the flow of materials or people or information through the process (or, put another way, the sequence of activities that materials, people or information are subjected to).

PRACTICE NOTE

Different process mapping symbols are sometimes used to represent different types of activity. They can be arranged in order, and in series or in parallel, to describe any process. And although there is no universal set of symbols used all over the world, some are relatively common. Most derive either from the early days of 'scientific' management around a century ago or, more recently, from information system flowcharting. Figure 5.4 shows some of these symbols.

Example | **Theatre lighting operation**

Figure 5.5 shows one of the processes used in a theatre lighting operation. The company hires out lighting and stage effects equipment to theatrical companies and event organizers. Customers' calls are routed to the store technician. After discussing their requirements, the technician checks the equipment availability file to see whether the equipment can be supplied from the company's own stock on the required dates. If the equipment cannot be supplied in-house, customers may be asked whether they want the company to try and obtain it from other possible suppliers. This offer depends on how busy and how helpful individual technicians are. Sometimes customers decline the offer and a 'Guide to Customers' leaflet is sent to the customer. If the customer does want a search, the technician will call potential suppliers in an attempt to find available equipment. If this is not successful the customer is informed, but if suitable equipment is located it is reserved for delivery to the company's site. If equipment can be supplied from the company's own stores, it is reserved on the equipment availability file and the day before it is required a 'kit wagon' is taken to

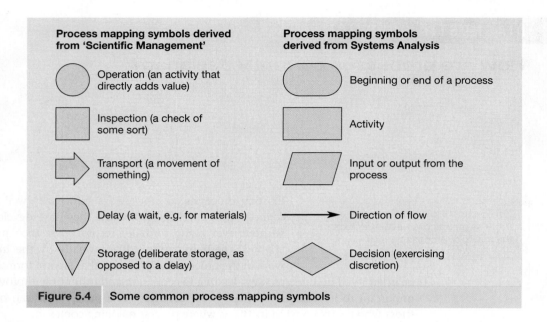

Process mapping symbols derived from 'Scientific Management'

Operation (an activity that directly adds value)

Inspection (a check of some sort)

Transport (a movement of something)

Delay (a wait, e.g. for materials)

Storage (deliberate storage, as opposed to a delay)

Process mapping symbols derived from Systems Analysis

Beginning or end of a process

Activity

Input or output from the process

Direction of flow

Decision (exercising discretion)

Figure 5.4 Some common process mapping symbols

the store where all the required equipment is assembled, taken back to the workshop and checked, and if any equipment is faulty it is repaired at this point. After that it is packed in special cases and delivered to the customer.

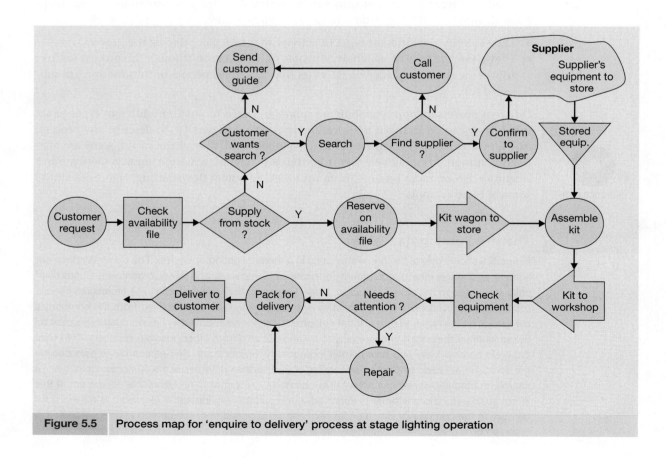

Figure 5.5 Process map for 'enquire to delivery' process at stage lighting operation

Different levels of process mapping

For a large process, drawing process maps at this level of detail can be complex. This is why processes are often mapped at a more aggregated level, called high-level process mapping, before more detailed maps are drawn. Figure 5.6 illustrates this for the total *'supply and install lighting'* process in the stage lighting operation. At the highest level the process can be drawn simply as an input–transformation–output process with materials and customers as its input resources and lighting services as outputs. No details of how inputs are transformed into outputs are included. At a slightly lower or more detailed level, what is sometimes called an outline process map (or chart) identifies the sequence of activities but only in a general way. So the process of *'enquire to delivery'* that is shown in detail in Figure 5.5 is here reduced to a single activity. At the more detailed level, all the activities are shown in a 'detailed process map' (the activities within the process 'install and test' are shown).

Although not shown in Figure 5.6 an even more micro set of process activities could be mapped within each of the detailed process activities. Such a micro detailed process map could specify every single motion involved in each activity. Some quick-service restaurants, for example, do exactly that. In the lighting hire company example most activities would not be mapped in any more detail than that shown in Figure 5.6. Some activities, such as 'return to base', are probably too straightforward to be worth mapping any

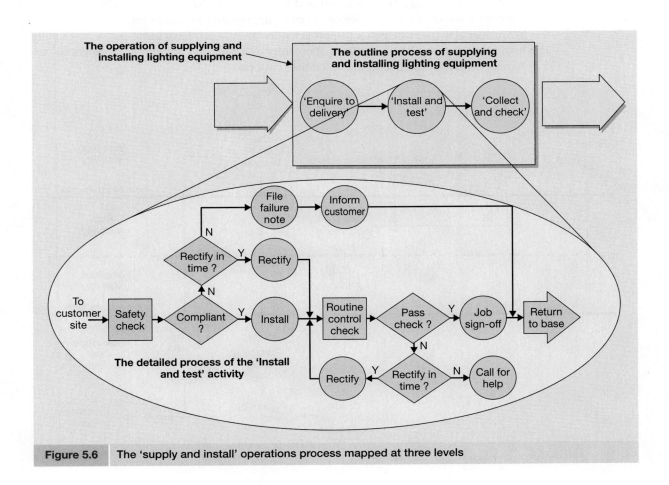

Figure 5.6   The 'supply and install' operations process mapped at three levels

further. Other activities, such as 'rectify faulty equipment', may rely on the technician's skills and discretion to the extent that the activity has too much variation and is too complex to map in detail. Some activities, however, may need mapping in more detail to ensure quality or to protect the company's interests. For example, the activity of safety checking the customer's site to ensure that it is compliant with safety regulations will need specifying in some detail to ensure that the company can prove it exercised its legal responsibilities.

Process visibility

It is sometimes useful to map such processes in a way that makes the degree of visibility of each part of the process obvious.[4] This allows those parts of the process with high visibility to be designed so that they enhance the customer's perception of the process. Figure 5.7 shows yet another part of the lighting equipment company's operation: the 'collect and check' process. The process is mapped to show the visibility of each activity to the customer. Here four levels of visibility are used. There is no hard and fast rule about this; many processes simply distinguish between those activities that the customer *could* see and those that they couldn't. The boundary between these two categories is often called the 'line of visibility'. In Figure 5.7 three categories of visibility are shown. At the very highest level of visibility, above the 'line of interaction', are those activities that involve direct interaction between the lighting company's staff and the customer. Other activities take place at the customer's site or in the presence of the customer but involve less or no direct interaction. Yet further activities (the two transport activities in this case) have some degree of visibility because they take place away from the company's base and are visible to potential customers, but are not visible to the immediate customer.

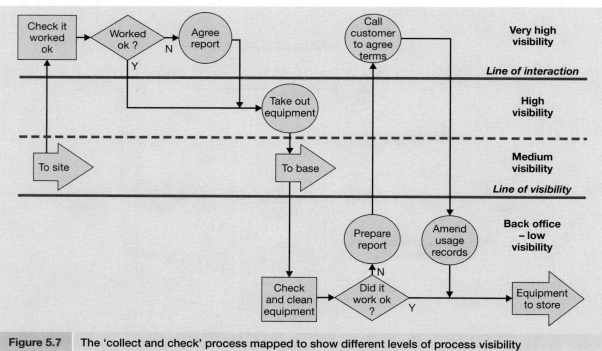

Figure 5.7   The 'collect and check' process mapped to show different levels of process visibility

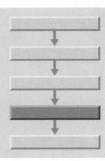

Are process tasks and capacity configured appropriately?

Process maps show how the activities of any particular process are currently arranged and help to suggest how they can be reconfigured. But there are also some general issues that must be understood before processes can be analyzed. These relate to how the total task can be divided up within the process and determine how capacity is allocated. This, in turn, determines the flow through the process.

Getting to grips with process capacity means understanding the following issues:

- task precedence
- series and parallel configurations
- cycle time and process flow
- process balancing
- throughput, cycle time and work in process.

Task precedence

> **Operations principle**
> Process design must respect task precedence.

Any process redesign needs to preserve the inherent precedence of activities within the overall task. Task 'precedence' defines which activities must occur before others, because of the nature of the task itself. At its simplest level task precedence is defined by:

- The individual activities that comprise the total process task
- The relationship between these individual activities.

Task precedence is usually described by using a 'precedence diagram', which, in addition to the above, also includes the following information:

- The time necessary to perform the total task (sometimes known as the 'work content' of the task)
- The time necessary to perform each of the individual activities within the task.

Example Computer repair service centre

A repair service centre receives faulty or damaged computers sent in by customers, repairs them and dispatches them back to the customer. Each computer is subject to the same set of tests and repair activities, and although the time taken to repair each computer will depend on the results of the tests, there is relatively little variation between individual computers.

Table 5.3 defines the process task of testing and repairing the computers in terms of the seven activities that comprise the total task, the relationship between the activities in terms of each activity's 'immediate predecessor', and the time necessary to perform each activity. Figure 5.8 shows the relationship between the activities graphically. This kind of illustration is called the 'precedence diagram' for the process task. It is useful because it indicates how activities *cannot* be sequenced in the eventual process design. For example, the process cannot perform activity 'b' before activity 'a' is completed. However, it does not determine how a process *can* be designed. Yet once the task has been analyzed in this way, activities can be arranged to form the process's general configuration.

Table 5.3   Process task details for the 'computer test and repair' task

Activity code	Activity name	Immediate predecessor	Activity time (minutes)
a	Preliminary test 1	–	5
b	Preliminary test 2	a	6
c	Dismantle	b	4
d	Test and repair 1	c	8
e	Test and repair 2	c	6
f	Test and repair 3	c	4
g	Clean/replace casing elements	d, e, f	10

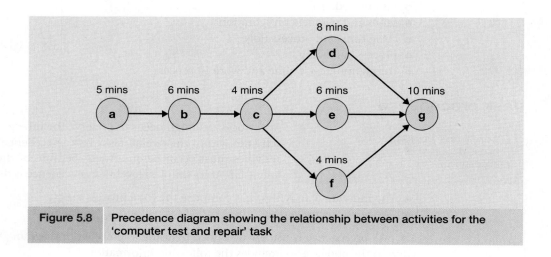

Figure 5.8   Precedence diagram showing the relationship between activities for the 'computer test and repair' task

Series and parallel configurations

FURTHER EXAMPLE

At its simplest level the general configuration of a process involves deciding the extent to which activities are arranged sequentially and the extent to which they are arranged in parallel.

For example, the task illustrated in Figure 5.8 involves seven activities that in total take 43 minutes. Demand is such that the process must be able to complete the test and repair task at the rate of one every 12 minutes in order to meet demand. One possible process design is to arrange the seven activities in a series arrangement of stages. The first question to address is 'How many stages would this type of series arrangement require?' This can be calculated by dividing the total work content of the task by the required cycle time. In this case, number of stages = 43 minutes / 12 minutes = 3.58 stages.

Given the practical difficulties of having a fraction of a stage, this effectively means that the process needs four stages. The next issue is to allocate activities to each stage. Because the output from the whole process will be limited by the stage with most work (the sum of its allocated activities), each stage can have activities allocated to it up to a maximum allocation of 12 minutes. Figure 5.9 illustrates how this could be achieved. The

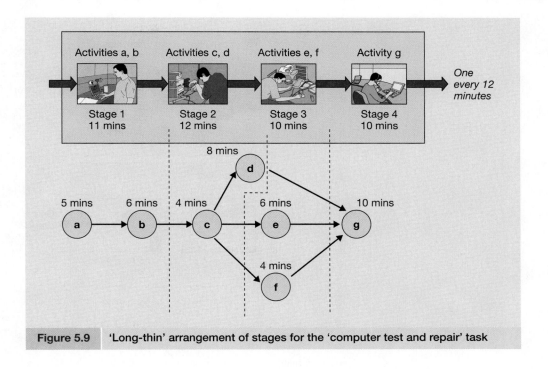

Figure 5.9 'Long-thin' arrangement of stages for the 'computer test and repair' task

longest stage (stage 2 in this case) will limit the output of the total process to one computer every 12 minutes and the other stages will be relatively underloaded.

However, there are other ways of allocating tasks to each stage, and involving the parallel arrangement of activities, that could achieve a similar output rate. For example, the four stages could be arranged as two parallel 'shorter' arrangements with each stage performing approximately half of the activities in the total tasks. This is illustrated in Figure 5.10. It involves two two-stage arrangements, with stage 1 being allocated four activities that amount to 21 minutes of work and the second stage being allocated three activities that amount to 22 minutes of work. So, each arrangement will produce one repaired computer every 22 minutes (governed by the stage with the most work). This means that the two arrangements together will produce two repaired computers every 22 minutes, an average of one repaired computer every 11 minutes.

Loading each stage with more work and arranging the stages in parallel can be taken further. Figure 5.11 illustrates an arrangement where the whole test and repair task is performed at individual stages, all of which are arranged in parallel. Here, each stage will produce one repaired computer every 43 minutes and so together will produce four repaired computers every 43 minutes, an average output rate of one repaired computer every 10.75 minutes.

This simple example represents an important process design issue. Should activities in a process be arranged predominantly in a single-series 'long-thin' configuration, or predominantly in several 'short-fat' parallel configurations, or somewhere in between? (Note that 'long' means the number of stages and 'fat' means the amount of work allocated to each stage.) Most processes will adopt a combination of series and parallel configurations, and in any particular situation there are usually technical constraints that limit either how 'long and thin' or how 'short and fat' the process can be. But there is usually a real choice to be made with a range of possible options. The advantages of each extreme of the long-thin to short-fat spectrum are very different and help to explain why different arrangements are adopted.

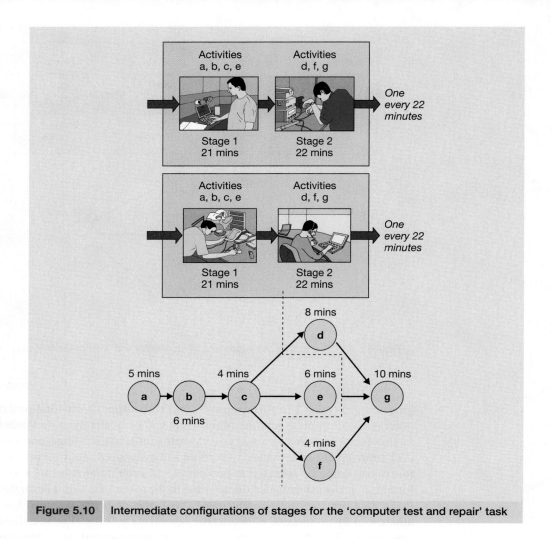

Figure 5.10 Intermediate configurations of stages for the 'computer test and repair' task

The advantages of the series-dominated (long-thin) configuration include:

- *A more controlled flow* through the process that is relatively easy to manage.
- *Simple materials handling* – especially if a product being manufactured is heavy, large or difficult to move.
- *Lower capital requirements*. If a specialist piece of equipment is needed for one element in the job, only one piece of equipment would need to be purchased; on short-fat arrangements every stage would need one.
- *More efficient operation*. If each stage is performing only a small part of the total job, the person at the stage may have a higher proportion of direct productive work as opposed to the non-productive parts of the job, such as picking up tools and materials.

The advantages of the parallel-dominated (short-fat) configuration include:

- *Higher mix flexibility*. If the process needs to produce several types of product or service, each stage could specialize in different types.
- *Higher volume flexibility*. As volume varies, stages can simply be closed down or started up as required.

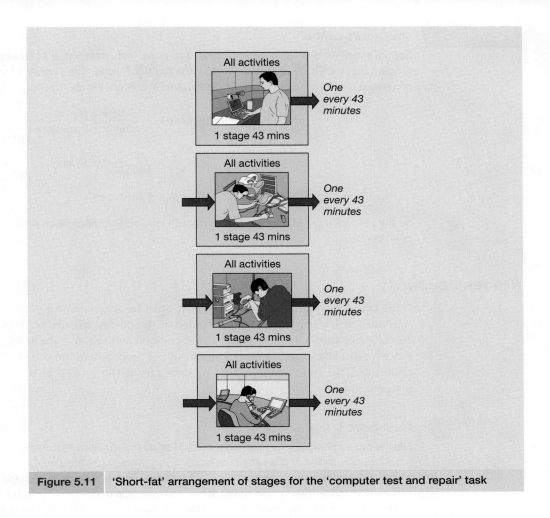

Figure 5.11   'Short-fat' arrangement of stages for the 'computer test and repair' task

- *Higher robustness*. If one stage breaks down or ceases operation in some way, the other parallel stages are unaffected; a long-thin arrangement would cease operating completely.
- *Less monotonous work*. In the computer repair example, the staff in the short-fat arrangement are repeating their tasks only every 43 minutes; in the long-thin arrangement it is every 12 minutes.

Cycle time and process capacity

Operations principle
Process analysis derives from an understanding of the required process cycle time.

The cycle time of a process is the time between completed units emerging from it. Cycle time is a vital factor in process design and has a significant influence on most of the other detailed design decisions. It is usually one of the first things to be calculated because it can be used both to represent the demand placed on a process and the process's capacity. The cycle time also sets the pace or 'drum beat' of the process. However the process is designed it must be able to meet its required cycle time. It is calculated by considering the likely demand for the products or services over a period and the amount of production time available in that period.

Passport office

Suppose the regional government office that deals with passport applications is designing a process that will check applications and issue the documents. The number of applications to be processed is 1600 per week and the time available to process the applications is 40 hours per week.

$$\text{Cycle time for the process} = \frac{\text{time available}}{\text{number to be processed}}$$

$$= \frac{40}{1600} = 0.025 \text{ hours}$$

$$= 1.5 \text{ minutes}$$

So the process must be capable of dealing with a completed application once every 1.5 minutes, or 40 per hour.

Process capacity

If the cycle time indicates the output that must be achieved by a process, the next decision must be how much capacity is needed by the process in order to meet the cycle time. To calculate this, a further piece of information is needed – the work content of the process task. The larger the work content of the process task and the smaller the required cycle time, the more capacity will be necessary if the process is to meet the demand placed upon it.

Example **Passport office**

For the passport office, the total work content of all the activities that make up the total task of checking, processing and issuing a passport is, on average, 30 minutes. So, a process with one person would produce a passport every 30 minutes. That is, one person would achieve a cycle time of 30 minutes. Two people would achieve a cycle time of 30/2 = 15 minutes, and so on.

Therefore the general relationship between the number of people in the process (its capacity in this simple case) and the cycle time of the process is:

$$\frac{\text{Work content}}{N} = \text{cycle time}$$

where N is the number of people in the process. Therefore, in this case,

$$N = \frac{30}{\text{cycle time}} = \frac{30}{1.5} = 20 \text{ people}$$

So, the capacity that this process needs if it is to meet demand is 20 people.

Process balancing

Excel

Balancing a process involves attempting to allocate activities to each stage as equally as possible. Because the cycle time of the whole process is limited by the longest allocation of activity times to an individual stage, the more equally work is allocated, the less time will be 'wasted' at the other stages in the process. In practice it is nearly always impossible to achieve perfect balance, so some degree of imbalance in work allocation between stages will occur. The effectiveness of the balancing activity is measured by balancing loss. This is the time wasted through the unequal allocation of activities as a percentage of the total time invested in processing. This is illustrated in Figure 5.12. Here the computer test and repair task is used to illustrate balancing loss for the 'long-thin' arrangement of four sequential stages and the 'intermediate' arrangement of two parallel two-stage arrangements.

Figure 5.12(a) shows the ideal allocation of activities with each stage perfectly balanced. Here exactly a quarter of the total work content (10.75 minutes) has been allocated to each of the four stages. Every 10.75 minutes each stage performs its activities and passes a computer on to the next stage, or out of the process in the case of stage 4. No stage suffers any idle time and, because the stages are perfectly balanced, balancing loss = 0. In fact, because of the actual times of each activity, it is not possible to equally allocate work to each stage. Figure 5.12(b) shows the best allocation of activities. Most work is allocated to stage 2, so that stage will dictate the cycle time of the whole process. Stage 1 has only 11 minutes of work and so will be idle for $(12 - 11) = 1$ minute every cycle (or alternatively will keep processing one computer every 11 minutes and the build-up of inventory between stage 1 and stage 2 would grow indefinitely). Similarly, stages 3 and 4 have idle time, in both cases $(12 - 10) = 2$ minutes of idle time. They can process one computer only every 12 minutes because stage 2 will pass forward a computer to them only every 12 minutes. So, they are each being starved of work for 2 minutes in every 12 minutes. In practice, stages that are not the bottleneck stage may not actually be idle for a period of time in every cycle. Rather they will slow down the pace of work to match the time of the bottleneck stage. Nevertheless, this is still effective idle time because under conditions of perfect balance they could be performing useful work.

(a) An ideal balance where activities are allocated equally between stages

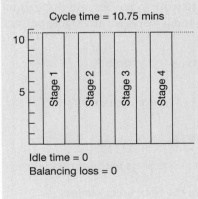

Idle time = 0
Balancing loss = 0

(b) The best achievable balance where activities are allocated between the stages of a four-stage arrangement

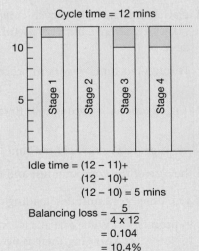

Idle time = $(12 - 11)+$
$(12 - 10)+$
$(12 - 10) = 5$ mins

Balancing loss $= \dfrac{5}{4 \times 12}$
$= 0.104$
$= 10.4\%$

(c) The best achievable balance where activities are allocated between the stages of a two-stage arrangement

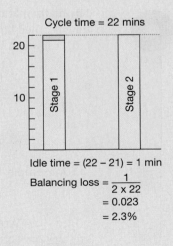

Idle time = $(22 - 21) = 1$ min

Balancing loss $= \dfrac{1}{2 \times 22}$
$= 0.023$
$= 2.3\%$

Figure 5.12 Balancing loss is that proportion of the time invested in processing the product or service that is not used productively. For the 'computer test and repair' process, (a) is the theoretical perfect balance, (b) is the best balance for four stages, and (c) is the best balance for two stages

So, every cycle all four stages are investing an amount of time equivalent to the cycle time to produce one completed computer. The total amount of invested time, therefore, is the number of stages in the process multiplied by the cycle time. In this case, total invested time = 4 × 12 = 48 minutes.

The total idle time for every computer processed is the sum of the idle times at the non-bottleneck stages, in this case 5 minutes.

The balancing loss is the amount of idle time as a percentage of the total invested time. In this case, balancing loss = 5/(4 × 12) = 0.104 = 10.4%.

Figure 5.12(c) makes the same calculation for the intermediate process described earlier. Here too, two-stage arrangements are placed in parallel. Stage 2 has the greatest allocation of work at 22 minutes, and will therefore be the bottleneck of the process. Stage 1 has 21 minutes' worth of work and therefore one minute of idle time every cycle. Because the total invested time in the process in each cycle = 2 × 22 minutes, the balancing loss = 1/(2 × 22) = 0.023 = 2.3%.

PRACTICE NOTE

Throughput, cycle time and work in process

The cycle time of a process is a function of its capacity. For a given amount of work content in the process task, the greater the capacity of the process, the smaller its cycle time. In fact, the capacity of a process is often measured in terms of its cycle time, or more commonly the reciprocal of cycle time that is called 'throughput rate'. So, for example, a theme park ride is described as having a capacity of 1000 customers per hour, or an automated bottling line would be described as having a capacity of 100 bottles a minute, and so on. However, a high level of capacity (short cycle time and fast throughput rate) does not necessarily mean that material, information or customers can move quickly through the process. This will depend on how many other units are contained within the process. If there is a large number of units within the process, they may have to wait in 'work in process' inventories for part of the time they are within the process (throughput time).

Little's law

Excel

The mathematical relationship that relates cycle time to work in process and throughput time is called Little's law.[5] It is simple, but very useful, and it works for any stable process. Little's law can be stated as:

Throughput time = work in process × cycle time

or

Work in process = throughput time × (1/cycle time)

That is,

Work in process = throughput time × throughput rate

For example, in the case of the computer test and repair process with four stages,

Cycle time = 12 minutes (loading on the bottleneck station)

Work in process = 4 units (one at each stage of the process, assuming there is no space for inventory to build up between stages)

Therefore,

Throughput time = work in process × cycle time
= 12 × 4 = 48 minutes

Similarly, for the example of the passport office, suppose the office has a 'clear desk' policy, which means that all desks must be clear of work by the end of the day. How many applications should be loaded onto the process in the morning in order to ensure that every one is completed and desks are clear by the end of the day?

From before,

$$\text{Cycle time} = 1.5 \text{ minutes}$$

From Little's law, assuming a 7.5-hour (450 minute) working day,

$$\text{Throughput time} = \text{work in process} \times \text{cycle time}$$

$$450 \text{ minutes} = \text{work in process} \times 1.5$$

Therefore,

$$\text{Work in process} = 450/1.5 = 300$$

FURTHER EXAMPLE

So, 300 applications can be loaded onto the process in the morning and be cleared by the end of the working day.

Example **Little's law at a seminar**

Mike was totally confident in his judgement: *'You'll never get them back in time,'* he said. *'They aren't just wasting time, the process won't allow them to all have their coffee and get back for 11 o'clock.'* Looking outside the lecture theatre, Mike and his colleague Dick were watching the 20 businessmen who were attending the seminar queuing to be served coffee and biscuits. The time was 10:45 and Dick knew that unless they were all back in the lecture theatre at 11 o'clock there was no hope of finishing his presentation before lunch. *'I'm not sure why you're so pessimistic,'* said Dick. *'They seem to be interested in what I have to say and I think they will want to get back to hear how operations management will change their lives.'* Mike shook his head. *'I'm not questioning their motivation,'* he said, *'I'm questioning the ability of the process out there to get through them all in time. I have been timing how long it takes to serve the coffee and biscuits. Each coffee is being made fresh and the time between the server asking each customer what they want and them walking away with their coffee and biscuits is taking 48 seconds. Remember that, according to Little's Law, throughput equals work in process multiplied by cycle time. If the work in process is the 20 managers in the queue and cycle time is 48 seconds, the total throughput time is going to be 20 multiplied by 0.8 minutes which equals 16 minutes. Add to that sufficient time for the last person to drink their coffee and you must expect a total throughput time of a bit over 20 minutes. You just haven't allowed long enough for the process.'* Dick was impressed. *'Err . . . what did you say that law was called again?'* *'Little's Law,'* said Mike.

Example **Little's law at an IT support unit**

Every year it was the same. All the workstations in the building had to be renovated (tested, new software installed, etc.) and there was only one week in which to do it. The one week fell in the middle of the August vacation period when the renovation process would cause minimum disruption to normal working. Last year the company's 500 workstations had all been renovated within one working week (40 hours). Each renovation last year took on average 2 hours, and 25 technicians had completed the process within the week. This year there would be 530 workstations to renovate but the company's IT support unit had devised a faster testing and renovation routine that would take on average only $1\frac{1}{2}$ hours instead of 2 hours. How many technicians will be needed this year to complete the renovation processes within the week?

Last year:

$$\text{Work in process (WIP)} = 500 \text{ workstations}$$
$$\text{Time available } (T_t) = 40 \text{ hours}$$
$$\text{Average time to renovate} = 2 \text{ hours}$$

Therefore:

$$\text{Throughput rate } (T_r) = 0.5 \text{ hour per technician}$$
$$= 0.5N$$

where N is the number of technicians. Applying Little's law:

$$\text{WIP} = T_t \times T_r$$
$$500 = 40 \times 0.5N$$
$$N = \frac{500}{40 \times 0.5}$$
$$= 25 \text{ technicians}$$

This year:

$$\text{Work in process (WIP)} = 530 \text{ workstations}$$
$$\text{Time available } (T_t) = 40 \text{ hours}$$
$$\text{Average time to renovate} = 1.5 \text{ hours}$$
$$\text{Throughput rate } (T_r) = 1/1.5 \text{ hours per technician}$$
$$= 0.67N$$

where N is the number of technicians. Applying Little's law:

$$\text{WIP} = T_t \times T_r$$
$$530 = 40 \times 0.67N$$
$$N = \frac{530}{40 \times 0.67}$$
$$= 19.88 \text{ technicians}$$

DIAGNOSTIC QUESTION

Is process variability recognized?

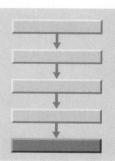

So far in our treatment of process analysis we have assumed that there is no significant variability either in the demand to which the process is expected to respond, or in the time taken for the process to perform its various activities. Clearly, this is not the case in reality. So, it is important to look at the variability that can affect processes and take account of it. However, do not dismiss the deterministic analysis we have been examining up to this point. At worst it provides a good first approximation to analyzing processes, while at best, the relationships that we have discussed do hold for average performance values.

Sources of variability in processes

There are many reasons why variability occurs in processes. A few of these possible sources of variation are listed below.

- The late (or early) arrival of material, information or customers at a stage within the process.
- The temporary malfunction or breakdown of process technology within a stage of the process.
- The necessity for recycling 'misprocessed' materials, information or customers to an earlier stage in the process.
- The misrouting of material, information or customers within the process that then needs to be redirected.
- Each product or service being processed might be different, for example different models of automobile going down the same line.
- Products or services, although essentially the same, might require slightly different treatment. For instance, in the computer test and repair process, the time for some activities will vary depending on the results of the diagnostic checks.
- With any human activity there are slight variations in the physical co-ordination and effort on the part of the person performing the task that result in variation in activity times, even of routine activities.

All these sources of variation within a process will interact with each other, but result in two fundamental types of variability:

- Variability in the demand for processing at an individual stage within the process, usually expressed in terms of variation in the inter-arrival times of units to be processed.
- Variation in the time taken to perform the activities (i.e., process a unit) at each stage.

Activity time variability

> **Operations principle**
> Variability in a process acts to reduce its efficiency.

The effects of variability within a process will depend on whether the movements of units between stages, and hence the inter-arrival times of units at stages, are synchronized or not. For example, consider the computer test and repair process described previously. Figure 5.13 shows the average activity time at each stage of the process, but also the variability around the average time. Suppose that it was decided to

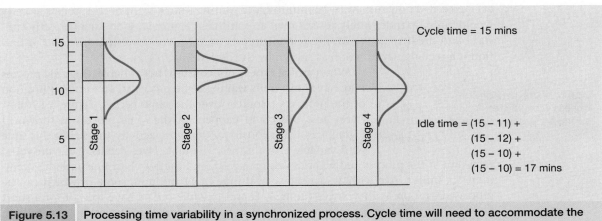

Figure 5.13 Processing time variability in a synchronized process. Cycle time will need to accommodate the longest activity time at any of the stages

synchronize the flow between the four stages by using an indexing conveyor or a simple traffic lights system that ensured all movement between the stages happened simultaneously. The interval between each synchronized movement would have to be set so as to allow all stages to have finished their activities irrespective of whether they had experienced a particularly fast or particularly slow activity time. In this case, from Figure 5.13 that synchronized indexing time would have to be set at 15 minutes. This then becomes the effective cycle time of the process. Note that the effective bottleneck stage is now stage 1 rather than stage 2. Although stage 2 has the longer average activity time (12 minutes), activity 1 with an average activity time of 11 minutes has a degree of variability that results in a maximum activity of 15 minutes. Note also that every stage will experience some degree of idle time, the average idle time at each station being the cycle time minus the average activity time at that station. This reduction in the efficiency of the process is only partly a result of its imbalance. The extra lost time is a result of activity time variability.

This type of effect is not at all uncommon. For example, automobiles are assembled using a moving belt assembly line whose speed is set to achieve a cycle time that can accommodate activity time variability. However, a more common arrangement, especially when processing information or customers, is to move units between stages as soon as the activities performed by each stage are complete. Here, units move through the process in an unsynchronized manner rather than having to wait for an imposed movement time. This means that each stage may spend less time waiting to move their unit forward, but it does introduce more variation in the demand placed on subsequent stations. When movement was synchronized the inter-arrival time of units at each stage was fixed at the cycle time. Without synchronization, the inter-arrival time at each stage will itself be variable.

Arrival time variability

To understand the effect of arrival variability on process performance, it is first useful to examine what happens to process performance in a very simple process as arrival time changes under conditions of no variability. For example, the simple process shown in Figure 5.14 is comprised of one stage that performs exactly 10 minutes of work. Units arrive at the process at a constant and predictable rate. If the arrival rate is one unit every 30 minutes, then the process will be utilized for only 33.33 per cent of the time, and the units will never have to wait to be processed. This is shown as point A on Figure 5.14. If the arrival rate increases to one arrival every 20 minutes, the utilization increases to 50 per cent, and again the units will not have to wait to be processed. This is point B on Figure 5.14. If the arrival rate increases to one arrival every 10 minutes, the process is now fully utilized, but, because a unit arrives just as the previous one has finished being processed, no unit has to wait. This is point C on Figure 5.14. However, if the arrival rate ever exceeded one unit every 10 minutes, the waiting line in front of the process activity would build up indefinitely, as is shown as point D in Figure 5.14. So, in a perfectly constant and predictable world, the relationship between process waiting time and utilization is a rectangular function as shown by the dotted line in Figure 5.14.

Operations principle
Process variability results in simultaneous waiting and resource underutilization.

When arrival time is not constant but variable, then the process may have both units waiting to be processed and underutilization of the process's resources over the same period. Figure 5.15 illustrates how this could happen for the same process as shown in Figure 5.14, with constant 10-minute activity times, but this time with variable arrival times. The table gives details of the arrival of each unit at the process and when it was processed, and the bar chart illustrates it graphically. Six units arrive with an average arrival time of 11 minutes, some of which can be processed as soon as they arrive (units A, D and F) while others have to wait for a short period. Over the same period the process has to wait for work three times.

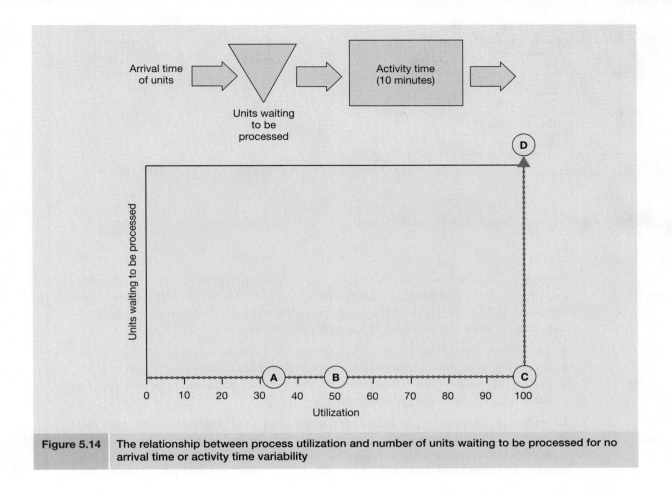

Figure 5.14 The relationship between process utilization and number of units waiting to be processed for no arrival time or activity time variability

During the observed period,

$$\text{Time when a single unit was waiting} = 3 \text{ minutes}$$
$$\text{Elapsed time for processing the six units} = 65 \text{ minutes}$$
$$\text{Average number of units waiting} = 3/65$$
$$= 0.046 \text{ units}$$
$$\text{Process idle time} = 5 \text{ minutes}$$
$$\text{So, process idle percentage} = 5 \times 100/65$$
$$= 7.7\%$$
$$\text{Therefore, process utilization} = 92.3\%$$

This point is shown as point X in Figure 5.16. If the average arrival time were to be changed with the same variability, the dotted line in Figure 5.16 would show the relationship between average waiting time and process utilization. As the process moves closer to 100 per cent utilization the higher the average waiting time will become. To put it another way, the only way to guarantee very low waiting times for the units is to suffer low process utilization.

When both arrival times and activity times are variable, this effect is even more pronounced. And the greater the variability, the more the waiting time utilization deviates from the simple rectangular function of the 'no variability' conditions that was shown in

Unit	Arrival time	Start of activity	End of activity	Wait time
A	0	0	10	0
B	12	12	22	0
C	20	22	32	2
D	34	34	44	0
E	43	44	54	1
F	55	55	65	0

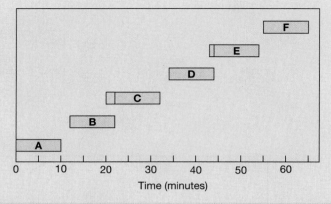

Figure 5.15   Units arriving at a process with variable arrival times and a constant activity time (10 minutes)

Figure 5.14. A set of curves for a typical process is shown in Figure 5.17(a). This phenomenon has important implications for the design of processes. In effect it presents three options to process designers wishing to improve the waiting time or utilization performance of their processes, as shown in Figure 5.17(b). Either:

● Accept long average waiting times and achieve high utilization (point X), or
● Accept low utilization and achieve short average waiting times (point Y), or
● Reduce the variability in arrival times, activity times, or both, and achieve higher utilization and short waiting times (point Z).

To analyze processes with both inter-arrival and activity time variability, queuing or 'waiting line' analysis can be used. This is treated in the supplement to this chapter. But, do not dismiss the relationship shown in Figures 5.16 and 5.17 as some minor technical phenomenon. It is far more than this. It identifies an important choice in process design that

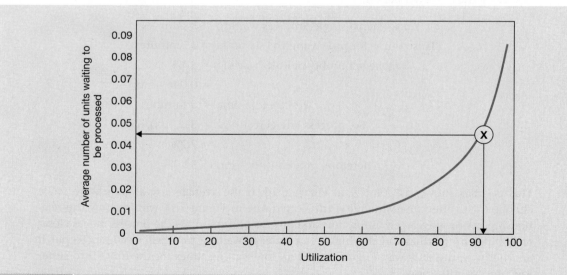

Figure 5.16   The relationship between process utilization and number of units waiting to be processed for the variable arrival times in the example

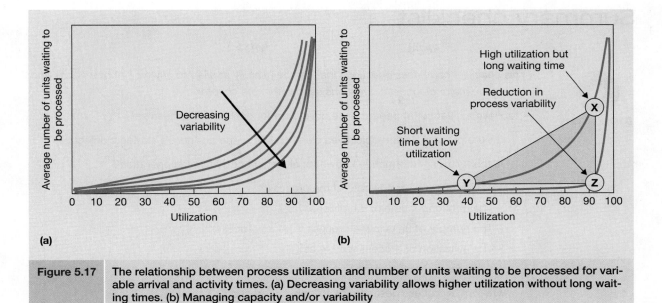

Figure 5.17   The relationship between process utilization and number of units waiting to be processed for variable arrival and activity times. (a) Decreasing variability allows higher utilization without long waiting times. (b) Managing capacity and/or variability

Operations principle
Process design involves some choice between utilization, waiting time and variability reduction.

could have strategic implications. Which is more important to a business – fast throughput time or high utilization of its resources? The only way to have both of these simultaneously is to reduce variability in its processes, which may itself require strategic decisions such as limiting the degree of customization of products or services, or imposing stricter limits on how products or services can be delivered to customers, and so on. It also demonstrates an important point concerned with the day-to-day management of process – the only way to absolutely guarantee 100 per cent utilization of resources is to accept an infinite amount of work in progress and/or waiting time. We will take this point further in Chapter 8 when we deal with capacity management.

Critical commentary

Each chapter contains a short critical commentary on the main ideas covered in the chapter. Its purpose is not to undermine the issues discussed in the chapter, but to emphasize that, although we present a relatively orthodox view of operation, there are other perspectives.

■ There is not too much that would be considered contentious in this chapter. However, some practitioners would reject the idea of mapping processes as they exist currently. Rather, they would advocate a more radical 'clean sheet of paper' approach. Only by doing this, they would say, can one be sufficiently imaginative in the redesign of processes. The other potential point of contention would concern the viability of what we have called 'long-thin' process designs. As was discussed in the previous chapter, this assumes a degree of division of labour and systemization of work that is held by some to be 'dehumanizing'.

Summary checklist

This checklist comprises questions that can be usefully applied to any type of operations and reflect the major diagnostic questions used within the chapter.

☐ Have a clear set of performance objectives for each process been set?

☐ Do the process design objectives clearly relate to the business's strategic objectives?

☐ Is the following information known for all key processes in the operation?

   – The throughput or flow rate of the process?
   – The throughput time of the process?
   – The number of units in the process (work in process)?
   – The utilization of process resources?

☐ Are processes documented using process mapping techniques?

☐ Are formal process descriptions followed in practice?

☐ If not, should the process descriptions be changed or should existing process descriptions be enforced?

☐ Is it necessary for process descriptions to include the degree of visibility at each stage of the process?

☐ Are the details of task precedence known for each process?

☐ Have the advantages and disadvantages of series and parallel configurations been explored?

☐ Is the process balanced? If not, can the bottleneck stages be redesigned to achieve better balance?

☐ Is the relationships between throughput, cycle time and work in process understood (Little's law)?

☐ Are the sources of process variability recognized?

☐ Has the effect of variability been recognized in the design of the process?

Case study   # North West Constructive Bank – The New Mortgage Centre 2

Andy Curtis, the Mortgage Operations Manager for North West Constructive Bank (NWCB), had launched a major investigation into his processes and how they might be redesigned (see Part 1 of this case study in Chapter 4). He had been prompted by the failure of his operation to improve after it had consolidated three separate sites into one location. The staff from the three old centres that covered the northern, southern and western areas of the bank's customer base had been kept largely intact in the new site. Andy and his team suspected that this may have contributed to their failure to improve performance, especially throughput time performance, immediately after the move.

Andy has initiated an investigation that would provide the basic data for a thorough examination of how the mortgage centre's processes could be redesigned. The results of this investigation are shown in Figure 5.18 and Table 5.4. These detail the activities contained within each stage of the overall process together with each activity's immediate predecessor, the type of skills necessary to carry out each activity, the allowed time for each activity (this had varied slightly between the three regional offices, so an average had been taken), and an estimate of the minimum and maximum times necessary to perform each activity.

Also shown for each activity is the percentage of applications that needed to be 'recycled' (applications that contained ambiguities, errors or omissions in the data supplied and therefore had to be returned to a previous activity) or 'rejected' (the mortgage was being refused for some reason). Two of the activities (activity b and activity h) were only necessary for approximately 40 per cent of applications. In addition, Andy had asked each section to make a 'spot check' on how many applications were currently being processed. To his surprise it emerged that around 5000 applications were in-process with most of them in the offer and completion parts of the process. *'I'm not surprised that offers spend a long time in the offer and completion parts of the process,'* explained Andy. *'Those are the sections where we are waiting for the results of surveys or further information from legal representatives to arrive. Nevertheless, it's far too many applications to have just hanging around within the process.'*

Source: Keith Brofsky/PhotoDisc/Getty Images

In addition, 40 minutes is allowed for extra telephone calls, etc., that are not allocated to any specific stage or activity.

Skills required performing the task:

- Credit – Credit assessment skills
- U/R – Underwriting skills
- Local – Knowledge of local property market
- Legal – Knowledge of property law
- Rel. – Relationship skills

All the management team thought that going through the details of each part of the process had been useful. It had produced information that had not been collected before, such as the actual percentage of recycled and rejected applications at each stage. Also it had prompted an interesting debate around the appropriateness of the time allowances for each activity and the sequence of the activities. For example, the underwriting activities had always preceded the offer stage activities in all the centres. Yet there was no technical reason why the underwriting and offer activities could not be performed in parallel. *'When all applications were purely paper-based it would not have been possible to perform activities in parallel unless the documents had been physically copied and even then it would have led to confusion. Now, although there are paper-based files associated with each application, the information system allows real-time*

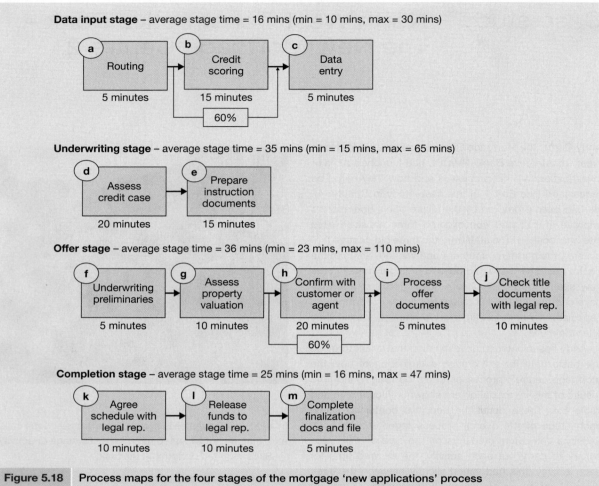

Data input stage – average stage time = 16 mins (min = 10 mins, max = 30 mins)

a. Routing — 5 minutes
b. Credit scoring — 15 minutes (60%)
c. Data entry — 5 minutes

Underwriting stage – average stage time = 35 mins (min = 15 mins, max = 65 mins)

d. Assess credit case — 20 minutes
e. Prepare instruction documents — 15 minutes

Offer stage – average stage time = 36 mins (min = 23 mins, max = 110 mins)

f. Underwriting preliminaries — 5 minutes
g. Assess property valuation — 10 minutes
h. Confirm with customer or agent — 20 minutes (60%)
i. Process offer documents — 5 minutes
j. Check title documents with legal rep. — 10 minutes

Completion stage – average stage time = 25 mins (min = 16 mins, max = 47 mins)

k. Agree schedule with legal rep. — 10 minutes
l. Release funds to legal rep. — 10 minutes
m. Complete finalization docs and file — 5 minutes

Figure 5.18   Process maps for the four stages of the mortgage 'new applications' process

updating of each application file. The only remaining argument in favour of making the underwriting and offer stages sequential is that work carried out on applications that are subsequently rejected or recycled may be wasted. I am also delighted that we have agreed on the time allowances for each activity as well as getting a sense of realistic minimum and maximum times. Even so, I doubt whether it is ever possible in this kind of job to give very precise times. There are just too many different situations that can occur. This is why we have had to incorporate the additional 40 minutes of unallocated time for the whole process. I guess that we could split this between the stages but I'm not sure it would be that helpful. We know that the majority of this extra allowed time is needed in the offer and completion stages rather than the first two stages, but I would rather not fall into the trap of spurious precision.'

Redesigning the process

Three separate options for the design of the process were being actively considered by the management team.

● *Option 1* – Keep the process as it is currently at the new centre, with a common data-input stage serving all regions and with the three regions each having its own underwriting, offer and completion stages working in series. This arrangement had the advantage of not disrupting the existing way of working and of maintaining the organizational coherence of the three teams which were each already developing their own cultures.

● *Option 2* – Reorganize the whole process by abandoning the current regional structure and organizing four sequential teams around each of the four stages of data input, underwriting, offer and completion. This

Table 5.4   **Total activities for all stages of the 'new applications' process**

Stage	Activity code	Activity description	Immediate predecessor	Special skills needed?*	Percentage recycled and rejected	Allowed time	Approx. Min. time	Max. time
Data input	a	Routing	None	None	Recycled 2.2% Rejected 0.5%	5	5	5
	b	Credit scoring (40% of applications only)	a	None	Recycled 0 Rejected 0	15 (6 on average)	10	20
	c	Data entry	b	None	Recycled 0 Rejected 0	5	5	5
Underwriting	d	Assess credit case	c	Credit	Recycled 9.1% Rejected 5%	20	5	45
	e	Prepare instruction docs	d	Credit	Recycled 1.3% Rejected 0	15	10	20
Offer	f	Underwrite prelims	e?	U/R	Recycled 0 Rejected 0	5	5	5
	g	Assess property valuation	f	U/R Local	Recycled 7.7% Rejected 5%	10	8	30
	h	Confirm with customer or agent (40% of applications only)	g	U/R Local Rel.	Recycled 6.4% Rejected 3.2% (of all applications)	20 (8 on average)	10	40
	i	Process offer docs	h	U/R	Recycled 0 Rejected 0	5	5	5
	j	Check title docs with legal rep.	i	U/R Legal Rel.	Recycled 4.5% Rejected 2.8%	8	5	30
Completion	k	Agree schedule with legal rep.	j	Legal Rel.	Recycled 2.8%	10	5	20
	l	Release funds to legal rep.	k	Legal Rel.	Recycled 1.8% Rejected 0	10	8	15
	m	Complete finalization docs and file	l	Legal	Recycled 0.9% Rejected 0	5	3	12
					Total	112		

*See text for abbreviations.

arrangement was seen as being more appropriate for the higher volume that the new combined centre was processing. It would also allow some skills, such as underwriting skills and legal skills, to be developed because of the larger number of staff with these skills working together. However, the team saw two disadvantages of this arrangement. First, it would affect the morale of the existing regionally based teams, especially the southern team who had worked together for many years. Second, for some activities in the offer stage it was still an advantage to have some local

knowledge of the regional property markets. Even if this option were adopted, the offer team would probably still have to retain some local 'cells' within the process.

● *Option 3* – In some ways this was the most radical design option being considered. It involved reorganizing into four teams around the four stages within the process, but operating the underwriting stage and offer stage in parallel. This was seen as risky, especially with such high levels of recycled applications, but offered the advantage of short throughput times.

The recycling problem

Andy had been aware of the problems that existed around the amount of 'rework' even prior to the reorganization. He had already requested an analysis of the reasons behind this recycling. In the previous year a total of 76,250 applications had been received and 60,921 offers were 'issued' (made) by the Mortgage Centre. In the same period a total of 21,735 of these required some recycling at least once during their processing. The majority of these were as a result of documents submitted with the application or information in the application being missing, incomplete, or inaccurate in some way. Some recycles were the result of the customers changing their mind about the details of the mortgage during the processing period; usually this was because they required to borrow a different amount. Some recycling was caused directly by errors made within the Mortgage Centre during earlier stages of the process. The largest single source of errors was those caused by inaccurate or incomplete data capture when initial customer and property information was taken. Agents were far worse at this than the Bank's own branches. Even those errors attributed to customers were often the result of their not being given appropriate guidance by staff at the agents' offices or at branches.

When an application needed recycling within the process, the application and accompanying documents were put in a yellow folder, the customer file on the data base was 'marked' with a yellow tag, and the application was reviewed by the team supervisor, who assessed how it should be treated. Usually this meant sending the application back to an earlier stage in the process. This resulted in a continual 'churn' of some applications being recycled through the process.

'Both rejected and recycled applications cause problems because they represent "wasted" work. Rejections are less serious in the sense that the whole purpose of this process is to "weed out" applications that we don't want to fund. Even so, I wonder whether we could screen these applications out earlier in the process. The recycled applications are more serious. One problem is that, although we know the percentage of applications recycled from each activity, we have no record of where in the process they are recycled to. One option we have is to redefine the very first "routing" activity at the data entry stage and make it an initial screening activity that would try to screen out the applications that were likely to be recycled later in the process. In other words, we should let through only those applications that were unlikely to be recycled. In effect, we would be making the initial routing activity the most important in the whole process. It would mean that we would have to staff the activity with people with a very wide range of skills and allow them sufficient time to do the initial screening, perhaps up to 20 minutes for each application. Whether it is worth doing this depends on the reduction in recycling. Some of the team feel that recycling could be cut down by at least 75 per cent if we did this.'

Staffing levels

The final issue being considered by the team was how many people the process should be employing. By pooling all data entry activity into one stage, the process had already saved 11 staff and there was a general feeling that similar savings could be made throughout the process if it were redesigned according to either Option 2 or Option 3 explained previously. In fact, irrespective of which design option was chosen, the agreed time allowances for the activities seemed to indicate that the process should be able to operate with few people.

Andy realized that his operation was facing a number of decisions. He also realized that none of them was straightforward. 'The real problem we face is that everything is interrelated. The process redesign options we have could affect our ability to reduce the time wasted on recycled applications as well as the number of staff we need. Yet by increasing the investment of staff time and effort in certain parts of the process we may be able to reduce recycling and even achieve an overall reduction in staff. In the long term that is what is important. We need to be able to drive down the cost of processing mortgage applications if we are to survive as an in-house operation. Ours is exactly the sort of process that could be outsourced if we don't provide an effective and efficient service to the business.'

QUESTIONS

1 Does it matter that Andy and his team cannot allocate all the time necessary to process a mortgage application to individual activities?

2 Should the process be redesigned, and if so, which option should be adopted?

3 How could the 'recycling' problem be reduced, and what benefits would this bring?

Active case study   Action Response

ACTIVE CASE

Action Response is a successful charity that provides fast responses to critical situations throughout the world. They are required to process requests for cash quickly and accurately in order to get the money to where it is needed, in time to make a difference. However, complaints about money not getting through quickly enough and rising operational costs are a concern for the charity.

● How would you assess and re-configure the processes employed to improve the responsiveness and efficiency of Action Response?

Please refer to the Active case on the CD accompanying this book to listen to the views of those involved.

Applying the principles

HINTS

Some of these exercises can be answered by reading the chapter. Others will require some general knowledge of business activity and some might require an element of investigation. All have hints on how they can be answered on the CD accompanying this book.

1 Choose a process with which you are familiar. For example, a process at work, registration for a university course, joining a video rental shop service, enrolling at a sports club or gym, registering at a library, obtaining a car parking permit, etc. Map the process that you went through from your perspective, using the process mapping symbols explained in this chapter. Try to map what the 'back-office' process might be (that is the part of the process that is vital to achieving its objective, but that you can't see). You may have to speculate on this but you could talk with someone who knows the process.

● How might the process be improved from your (the customer's) perspective and from the perspective of the operation itself?

2 *'It is a real problem for us,'* said Angnyeta Larson. *'We now have only 10 working days between all the expense claims coming from the departmental co-ordinators and authorizing payments on the next month's payroll. This really is not long enough and we are already having problems during peak times.'* Angnyeta was the department head of the internal financial control department of a metropolitan authority in southern Sweden. Part of her department's responsibilities included checking and processing expense claims from staff throughout the metropolitan authority and authorizing payment to the salaries payroll section. She had 12 staff who were trained to check expense claims and all of them were devoted full-time to processing the claims in the two weeks (10 working days) prior to the deadline for informing the salaries section. The number of claims submitted over the year averaged around 3200, but this could vary between 1000 during the quiet summer months up to 4300 in peak months. Processing claims involved checking receipts, checking that claims met with the strict financial allowances for different types of expenditure, checking all calculations, obtaining more data from the claimant if necessary, and (eventually) sending an approval notification to salaries. The total processing time was on average 20 minutes per claim.

● How many staff does the process need on average, for the lowest demand, and for the highest demand?

● If a more automated process involving electronic submission of claims could reduce the average processing time to 15 minutes, what effect would this have on the required staffing levels?

● If department co-ordinators could be persuaded to submit their batched claims earlier (not always possible for all departments) so that the average time between submission of the claims to the finance department and the deadline for informing salaries section was increased to 15 working days, what effect would this have?

3 The headquarters of a major creative agency offered a service to all its global subsidiaries that included the preparation of a budget estimate that was submitted to potential clients when making a 'pitch' for new work. This service had been offered previously to only a few of the group's subsidiary companies. Now that it was to be offered worldwide, it was deemed appropriate to organize the process of compiling budget estimates on a more systematic basis. It was estimated that the worldwide demand for this service would be around 20 budget estimates per week, and that, on average, the staff who would put together these estimates would be working a 35-hour week. The elements within the total task of compiling a budget estimate are shown in the following table.

Element	Time (mins)	What element(s) must be done prior to this one?
A – obtain time estimate from creatives	20	None
B – obtain account handler's deadlines	15	None
C – obtain production artwork estimate	80	None
D – preliminary budget calculations	65	A, B and C
E – check on client budget	20	D
F – check on resource availability and adjust estimate	80	D
G – complete final budget estimate	80	E and F

● What is the required cycle time for this process?
● How many people will the process require to meet the anticipated demand of 20 estimates per week?
● Assuming that the process is to be designed on a 'long-thin' basis, what elements would each stage be responsible for completing? And what would be the balancing loss for this process?
● Assuming that instead of the long-thin design, two parallel processes are to be designed, each with half the number of stations of the long-thin design, what now would be the balancing loss?

4 A company has decided to manufacture a general-purpose 'smoothing plane', a tool which smoothes and shapes wood. Its engineers estimated the time it would take to perform each element in the assembly process. The marketing department also estimated that the likely demand for the new product would be 98,000 units. The marketing department was not totally confident of its forecast; however, *'a substantial proportion of demand is likely to be export sales, which we find difficult to predict. But whatever demand does turn out to be, we will have to react quickly to meet it. The more we enter these parts of the market, the more we are into impulse buying and the more sales we lose if we don't supply'.*

An idea of the assembly task can be gained from the following table which gives the 'standard time' for each element of the assembly task.

Standard times for each element of assembly task in standard minutes (SM)

Press elements	
Assemble poke	0.12 mins
Fit poke to front	0.10 mins
Rivet adjusting lever to front	0.15 mins
Press adjusting nut screw to front	0.08 mins

Bench elements

Fit adjusting nut to front	0.15 mins
Fit frog screw to front	0.05 mins
Fit knob to base	0.15 mins
Fit handle to base	0.17 mins
Fit front assembly to base	0.15 mins
Assemble blade unit	0.08 mins
Final assembly	0.20 mins

Packing element

Make box, wrap plane, pack	0.20 mins

Total time	**1.60 mins**

All elements must be performed sequentially in the order listed.

The standard costing system at the company involves adding a 150 per cent overhead charge to the direct labour cost of manufacturing the product, and the product would retail for the equivalent of around £35 in Europe where most retailers will sell this type of product for about 70–100 per cent more than they buy it from the manufacturer.

● How many people will be needed to assemble this product?
● Design a process for the assembly operation (to include the fly press work) including the tasks to be performed at each part of the system.
● How might the process design need to be adjusted as demand for this and similar products builds up?

Notes on chapter

1 Source: Horovitz, A. (2002) 'Fast food world ways drive-thru is the way to go', *USA Today*, 3 April.
2 Carr-Brown, J. (2005) 'French factory surgeon cuts NHS queues', *Sunday Times,* 23 October.
3 Not everyone uses exactly the same terminology in this area. For example, some publications use the term 'cycle time' to refer to what we have called 'throughput rate'.
4 The concept of visibility is explained in Shostack, G.L. (1984) 'Designing services that deliver', *Harvard Business Review*, January–February, pp. 133–9.
5 Little's law is best explained in Hopp, W.J. and Spearman, M.L. (2001) *Factory Physics* (2nd edn), McGraw-Hill, New York.

Taking it further

Anupindi, R., Chopra, S., Deshmukh, S.D., Van Mieghem, J.A. and Zemel, E. (1999) *Managing Business Process Flows,* Prentice Hall, New Jersey. An excellent, although mathematical, approach to process design in general.

Hammer, M. (1990) 'Reengineering work: don't automate, obliterate', *Harvard Business Review*, July–August. This is the paper that launched the whole idea of business processes and process management in general to a wider managerial audience. Slightly dated but worth reading.

Ramaswamy, R. (1996) *Design and Management of Service Processes*, Addison-Wesley Longman. A relatively technical approach to process design in a service environment.

Shostack, G.L. (1982) 'How to design a service', *European Journal of Marketing*, Vol. 16, No. 1. A far less technical and more experiential approach to design of service processes.

FURTHER RESOURCES

For further resources including examples, animated diagrams, self-test questions, Excel spreadsheets, active case studies and video materials please explore the CD accompanying this book.

Supplement to Chapter I-5
Queuing analysis

Introduction

Queuing analysis (in many parts of the world it is called 'waiting line'[1] analysis) is often explained purely in terms of customers being processed through service operations. This is misleading. Although queuing analysis can be particularly important in service operations, especially where customers really do 'queue' for service, the approach is useful in any kind of operation. Figure 5.19 shows the general form of queuing analysis.

The general form of queuing analysis

Customers arrive according to some probability distribution and wait to be processed (unless part of the operation is idle); when they have reached the front of the queue, they are processed by one of the m parallel 'servers' (their processing time also being described by a probability distribution), after which they leave the operation. There are many examples of this kind of system. Table 5.5 illustrates some of these. All of these examples can be described by a common set of elements that define their queuing behaviour.

- *The source of customers*, sometimes called the calling population, is the source of supply of customers. In queue management 'customers' are not always human. 'Customers' could for example be trucks arriving at a weighbridge, orders arriving to be processed, machines waiting to be serviced, etc.

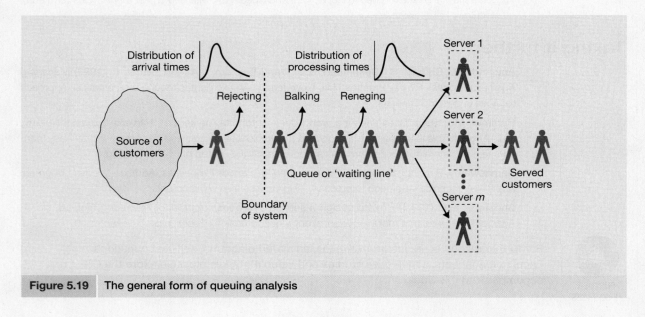

Figure 5.19   The general form of queuing analysis

Table 5.5	Examples of processes that can be analyzed using queuing analysis	
Operation	*Arrivals*	*Processing capacity*
Bank	Customers	Tellers
Supermarket	Shoppers	Checkouts
Hospital clinic	Patients	Doctors
Graphic artist	Commissions	Artists
Custom cake decorators	Orders	Cake decorators
Ambulance service	Emergencies	Ambulances with crews
Telephone switchboard	Calls	Telephonists
Maintenance department	Breakdowns	Maintenance staff

- *The arrival rate* is the rate at which customers needing to be served arrive at the server or servers. Rarely do customers arrive at a steady and predictable rate. Usually there is variability in their arrival rate. Because of this it is necessary to describe arrival rates in terms of probability distributions.
- *The queue.* Customers waiting to be served form the queue or waiting line itself. If there is relatively little limit on how many customers can queue at any time, we can assume that, for all practical purposes, an infinite queue is possible. Sometimes, however, there is a limit to how many customers can be in the queue at any one time.
- *Queue discipline* is the set of rules that determine the order in which customers waiting in the queue are served. Most simple queues, such as those in a shop, use a *first-come-first-served* queue discipline.
- *Servers.* A server is the facility that processes the customers in the queue. In any queuing system there may be any number of servers configured in different ways. In Figure 5.19 servers are configured in parallel, but some systems may have servers in a series arrangement. There is also likely to be variation in how long it takes to process each customer. Therefore processing time, like arrival time, is usually described by a probability distribution.

Calculating queue behaviour

Excel

Management scientists have developed formulae that can predict the steady-state behaviour of different types of queuing system. Unfortunately, many of these formulae are extremely complicated, especially for complex queuing systems, and are beyond the scope of this book. In practice, computer programs are almost always used to predict the behaviour of queuing systems. However, studying queuing formulae can illustrate some useful characteristics of the way queuing systems behave. Moreover, for relatively simple systems, using the formulae (even with some simplifying assumptions) can provide a useful approximation to process performance.

Notation

There are several different conventions for the notation used for different aspects of queuing system behaviour. It is always advisable to check the notation used by different authors before using their formulae. We shall use the following notation:

$$t_a = \text{average time between arrivals}$$
$$r_a = \text{arrival rate (items per unit time)} = 1/t_a$$
$$c_a = \text{coefficient of variation of arrival times}$$
$$m = \text{number of parallel servers at a station}$$

t_e = mean processing time

r_e = processing rate (items per unit time) = m/t_e

c_e = coefficient of variation of process time

u = utilization of station = r_a/r_e = $(r_a t_e)/m$

WIP = average work in process (number of items) in the system

WIP_q = expected work in process (number of items) in the queue

W_q = expected waiting time in the queue

W = expected waiting time in the system (queue time + processing time)

Variability

The concept of variability is central to understanding the behaviour of queues. If there were no variability there would be no need for queues to occur because the capacity of a process could be relatively easily adjusted to match demand. For example, suppose one member of staff (a server) serves customers at a bank counter who always arrive exactly every five minutes (i.e., 12 per hour). Also suppose that every customer takes exactly five minutes to be served, then because

(a) the arrival rate is less than or equal to the processing rate, and
(b) there is no variation,

no customer need ever wait because the next customer will arrive when, or before, the previous customer leaves. That is, WIP_q = 0.

Also, in this case, the server is working all the time, again because exactly as one customer leaves, the next one is arriving. That is, u = 1.

Even with more than one server, the same may apply. For example, if the arrival time at the counter is five minutes (12 per hour) and the processing time for each customer is now always exactly 10 minutes (6 per hour), the counter would need two servers (m = 2), and because

(a) the arrival rate is less than or equal to the processing rate × m, and
(b) there is no variation,

again, WIP_q = 0 and u = 1.

Of course, it is convenient (but unusual) if the arrival rate divided by the processing rate is a whole number. When this is not the case (for this simple example with no variation):

$$\text{Utilization} = \text{processing rate}/(\text{arrival rate} \times m)$$

For example, if arrival rate r_a = 5 minutes, processing rate r_e = 8 minutes, and number of servers m = 2, then:

$$\text{Utilization } u = 8/(5 \times 2) = 0.8 \text{ or } 80\%$$

Incorporating variability

The previous examples were not realistic because they assumed no variation in arrival or processing times. We also need to take into account the variation around these means. To do that, we need to use a probability distribution. Figure 5.20 contrasts two processes with different arrival distributions. The units arriving are shown as people, but they could be jobs arriving at a machine, trucks needing servicing or any other uncertain

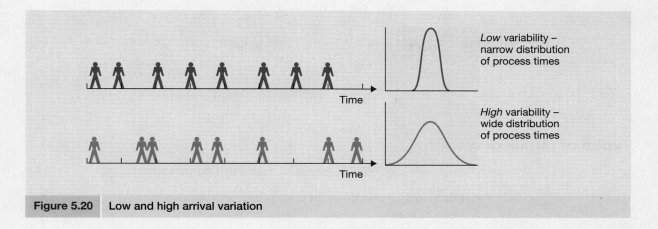

Figure 5.20   Low and high arrival variation

event. The top example shows low variation in arrival time where customers arrive in a relatively predictable manner. The bottom example has the same average number of customers arriving but this time they arrive unpredictably, with sometimes long gaps between arrivals and at other times two or three customers arriving close together. We could do a similar analysis to describe processing times.

In Figure 5.20 high arrival variation has a distribution with a wider spread (called 'dispersion') than the distribution describing lower variability. Statistically the usual measure for indicating the spread of a distribution is its standard deviation, σ. But variation depends not only on standard deviation. For example, a distribution of arrival times may have a standard deviation of 2 minutes. This could indicate very little variation when the average arrival time is 60 minutes. But it would mean a very high degree of variation when the average arrival time is 3 minutes. Therefore to normalize standard deviation, it is divided by the mean of its distribution. This measure is called the coefficient of variation of the distribution. So,

$$c_a = \text{coefficient of variation of arrival times} = \sigma_a/t_a$$

$$c_e = \text{coefficient of variation of processing times} = \sigma_e/t_e$$

Incorporating Little's law

Little's law (described earlier in the chapter) describes the relationship between the cycle time, the work in process and the throughput time of the process. It was denoted by the following simple relationship:

$$\text{Throughput time} = \text{work in process} \times \text{cycle time}$$

or

$$T = \text{WIP} \times C$$

Little's law can help to understand queuing behaviour. Consider the queue in front of the station.

$$\text{Work in process in queue} = \text{arrival rate at queue (equivalent to cycle time)}$$
$$\times \text{waiting time in queue (equivalent to throughput time)}$$

$$\text{WIP}_q = r_a \times W_q$$

and

Waiting time in whole system = waiting time in queue + average process time at station

$$W = W_q + t_e$$

We will use this relationship later to investigate queuing behaviour.

Types of queuing system

Conventionally queuing systems are characterized by four parameters:

A = distribution of arrival times (or more properly interarrival times, the elapsed times between arrivals)
B = distribution of process times
m = number of servers at each station
b = maximum number of items allowed in the system

The most common distributions used to describe A or B are:

- The exponential (or Markovian) distribution, denoted by M
- The general (for example, normal) distribution, denoted by G.

So, for example, an M/G/1/5 queuing system would indicate a system with exponentially distributed arrivals, process times described by a general distribution such as a normal distribution, with one server, and a maximum number of 5 items allowed in the system. This type of notation is called Kendall's Notation.

Queuing theory can help us investigate any type of queuing system, but in order to simplify the mathematics, we shall here deal only with the two most common situations, namely:

- M/M/m – the exponential arrival and processing times with m servers and no maximum limit to the queue
- G/G/m – general arrival and processing distributions with m servers and no limit to the queue.

First we will start by looking at the simple case when $m = 1$.

For M/M/1 queuing systems

The formulae for this type of system are as follows.

$$WIP = \frac{u}{1 - u}$$

Using Little's law,

$$WIP = \text{cycle time/throughput time}$$
$$\text{Throughput time} = WIP \times \text{cycle time}$$

Then

$$\text{Throughput time} = \frac{u}{1 - u} \times \frac{1}{r_a} = \frac{t_e}{1 - u}$$

and since throughput time in the queue = total throughput time – average processing time,

$$W_q = W - t_e$$

$$= \frac{t_e}{1 - u} - t_e$$

$$= \frac{t_e - t_e(1 - u)}{1 - u} = \frac{t_e - t_e - ut_e}{1 - u}$$

$$= \left(\frac{u}{1 - u}\right) t_e$$

Again, using Little's law,

$$\text{WIP}_q = r_a \times W_q = \left(\frac{u}{1 - u}\right) t_e r_a$$

and since

$$u = \frac{r_a}{r_e} = r_a t_e$$

$$r_a = \frac{u}{t_e}$$

then

$$\text{WIP}_q = \frac{u}{1 - u} \times t_e \times \frac{u}{t_e}$$

$$= \frac{u^2}{1 - u}$$

For M/M/m systems

When there are m servers at a station the formula for waiting time in the queue (and therefore all other formulae) needs to be modified. Again, we will not derive these formulae but just state them:

$$W_q = \frac{u^{\sqrt{2(m+1)} - 1}}{m(1 - u)} t_e$$

from which the other formulae can be derived as before.

For G/G/1 systems

The assumption of exponential arrival and processing times is convenient as far as the mathematical derivations of various formulae are concerned. However, in practice, process times in particular are rarely truly exponential. This is why it is important to have some idea of how G/G/1 and G/G/m queues behave. However, exact mathematical relationships are not possible with such distributions. Therefore some kind of approximation is needed. The one here is in common use, and although it is not always accurate, it is so for practical purposes. For G/G/1 systems the formula for waiting time in the queue is as follows:

$$W_q = \left(\frac{c_a^2 + c_e^2}{2}\right)\left(\frac{u}{1 - u}\right) t_e$$

There are two points to make about this equation. The first is that it is exactly the same as the equivalent equation for an M/M/1 system but with a factor to take account of the variability of the arrival and process times. The second is that this formula is sometimes known as the VUT formula because it describes the waiting time in a queue as a function of:

> V (the variability in the queuing system)
> U (the utilization of the queuing system, that is, demand versus capacity), and
> T (the processing times at the station).

In other words, we can reach the intuitive conclusion that queuing time will increase as variability, utilization or processing time increases.

For G/G/m systems

The same modification applies to queuing systems using general equations and m servers. The formula for waiting time in the queue is now as follows:

$$W_q = \left(\frac{c_a^2 + c_e^2}{2} \right) \left(\frac{u^{\sqrt{2(m+1)} - 1}}{m(1 - u)} \right) t_e$$

Example

'I can't understand it. We have worked out our capacity figures and I am sure that one member of staff should be able to cope with the demand. We know that customers arrive at a rate of around six per hour and we also know that any trained member of staff can process them at a rate of eight per hour. So why is the queue so large and the wait so long? Have a look at what is going on there, please.'

Sarah knew that it was probably the variation, both in customers arriving and in how long it took each of them to be processed, that was causing the problem. Over a two-day period when she was told that demand was more or less normal, she timed the exact arrival times and processing times of every customer. Her results were as follows.

> Coefficient of variation of customer arrivals, $c_a = 1$
> Coefficient of variation of processing time, $c_e = 3.5$
> Average arrival rate of customers, $r_a = 6$ per hour
> Therefore, average interarrival time $= 10$ minutes
> Average processing rate, $r_e = 8$ per hour
> Therefore, average processing time $= 7.5$ minutes

> Therefore, utilization of the single server, $u = 6/8 = 0.75$

Using the waiting time formula for a G/G/1 queuing system,

$$W_q = \left(\frac{1 + 12.25}{2} \right) \left(\frac{0.75}{1 - 0.75} \right) \times 7.5$$

$$= 6.625 \times 3 \times 7.5 = 419.06 \text{ mins}$$

$$= 2.48 \text{ hours}$$

Also,

$$\text{WIP}_q = \text{cycle time/throughput time}$$

$$= 6 \times 2.48 = 14.88$$

So, Sarah had found out that the average wait that customers could expect was 2.48 hours and that there would be an average of 14.88 people in the queue.

'Ok, so I see that it's the very high variation in the processing time that is causing the queue to build up. How about investing in a new computer system that would standardize processing time to a greater degree? I have been talking with our technical people and they reckon that, if we invested in a new system, we could cut the coefficient of variation of processing time down to 1.5. What kind of a difference would this make?'

Under these conditions with $c_e = 1.5$

$$W_q = \left(\frac{1 + 2.25}{2}\right)\left(\frac{0.75}{1 - 0.75}\right) \times 7.5$$

$$= 1.625 \times 3 \times 7.5 = 36.56 \text{ mins}$$

$$= 0.61 \text{ hours}$$

Therefore,

$$WIP_q = 6 \times 0.61 = 3.66$$

In other words, reducing the variation of the process time has reduced average queuing time from 2.48 hours to 0.61 hours and has reduced the expected number of people in the queue from 14.88 to 3.66.

Example   A bank wishes to decide how many staff to schedule during its lunch period. During this period customers arrive at a rate of nine per hour and the enquiries that customers have (such as opening new accounts, arranging loans, etc.) take on average 15 minutes to deal with. The bank manager feels that four staff should be on duty during this period but wants to make sure that the customers do not wait more than 3 minutes on average before they are served. The manager has been told by his small daughter that the distributions that describe both arrival and processing times are likely to be exponential. Therefore, $r_a = 9$ per hour, so $t_a = 6.67$ minutes; and $r_e = 4$ per hour, so $t_e = 15$ minutes. The proposed number of servers, $m = 4$, therefore the utilization of the system, $u = 9/(4 \times 4) = 0.5625$.

From the formula for waiting time for an M/M/m system,

$$W_q = \frac{u^{\sqrt{2(m+1)}-1}}{m(1-u)} t_e$$

$$= \frac{0.5625^{\sqrt{10}-1}}{4(1 - 0.5625)} \times 0.25$$

$$= \frac{0.5625^{2.162}}{1.75} \times 0.25$$

$$= 0.042 \text{ hours}$$

$$= 2.52 \text{ minutes}$$

Therefore the average waiting time with four servers would be 2.52 minutes, that is well within the manager's acceptable waiting tolerance.

Notes on chapter supplement

1 Maister, D. (1983) 'The psychology of waiting lines', *Harvard Business Review*, January–February.

Taking it further

Hopp, W.J. and Spearman, M.L. (2001) *Factory Physics* (2nd edn), McGraw-Hill, New York. Very technical so don't bother with it if you aren't prepared to get into the maths. However, some fascinating analysis, especially concerning Little's law.

⊢6 PRODUCT AND SERVICE DESIGN PROCESSES

Introduction

The products and services produced by an operation are its 'public face'. They are how customers judge a business: good products and services equals a good company. Being good at the design of new products and services has always had a strategic impact. What has changed over the last few years is both the speed and scale of *design* changes. And it is now accepted that there is a connection between the design of design processes and the success of those products and services in the marketplace. This is why the processes that design new products and services are so important. (See Figure 6.1.)

Source: Courtesy of BMW Group

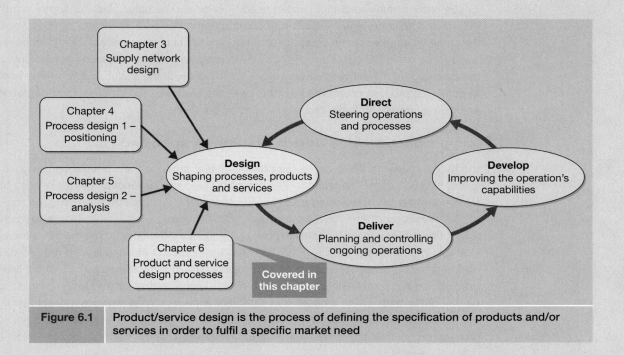

| Figure 6.1 | Product/service design is the process of defining the specification of products and/or services in order to fulfil a specific market need |

Executive summary

VIDEO
further detail

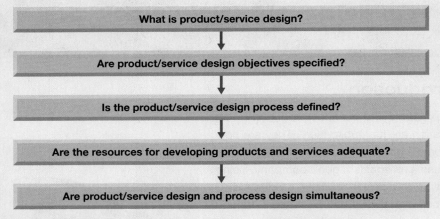

Decision logic chain for product and service design processes

Each chapter is structured around a set of diagnostic questions. These questions suggest what you should ask in order to gain an understanding of the important issues of a topic, and as a result, improve your decision making. An executive summary, addressing these questions, is provided below.

What is product/service design?

Product/service design is the process of defining the specification of products and/or services in order to fulfil a specific market need. It is (or should be) a cross-functional process that must both overcome the traditional communication barriers between functions while at the same time fostering the creativity and innovation that is often necessary in new product and service design. Product and service design is also a process in its own right that must itself be designed. This involves many of the same issues as the design of any other process. In particular, process objectives must be clear, the stages of the process must be defined, and the resources within the process need to be adequate.

Are product/service design objectives specified?

Product and service designs and the processes that produce them should be designed to satisfy market needs. The quality of the design process can be judged in terms of both conformance (no errors in the design) and specification (the effectiveness of the design in achieving its market requirements). Speed in the design process is often called 'time-to-market' (TTM). Short TTM implies that designs can be frequently introduced to the market, achieving strategic impact. Dependability in the design process means meeting launch delivery dates notwithstanding disruptions to the design process. This in turn often requires that the design process is sufficiently flexible to cope with disruptions. The cost of the design process can be thought of both as the amount of budget that is necessary to produce a design, and as the impact of the design on the produced cost of the product or service. As the design process progresses the impact on eventual costs rises faster than the rate at which the design budget is spent.

Is the product/service design process defined?

Although there is no universally agreed set of stages to the design process, almost all stage models start with a general idea or 'concept' and progress through to a fully defined product or service specification. Between these two states the design may pass through stages such as concept generation, concept screening, preliminary design (including consideration of standardization, commonality, modularization and mass customization), design evaluation and improvement, and prototyping and final design.

Are the resources for developing products and services adequate?

All processes, including design processes, need to be designed and resourced adequately. The design principles covered in Chapters 4 and 5 apply equally in product and service design. In particular, resourcing decisions concerning the capacity to devote to the design process, the extent to which the design process is performed in-house and the use of process technologies must be made so as to reflect strategic objectives.

Are product/service design and process design simultaneous?

At the end of the design process, the ongoing operations process that will produce the product or service must itself be designed. Often, it is best to think of designing the ongoing operations process as a continuation of product and service design. Considering all the stages of both product/service and process design together is often called simultaneous design. In recent years simultaneous (or concurrent) design has been used to reduce time-to-market. In particular, four simultaneous design factors can be identified that promote fast time-to-market. These are routinely integrating design process, overlapping design stages, early deployment of strategic decision making to resolve design conflict, and an organizational structure that reflects the nature of the design process.

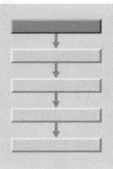

DIAGNOSTIC QUESTION

What is product/service design?

Product/service design is the process of defining the specification of products and/or services in order for them to fulfil a specific market need. The outcome of the product/service design process is a fully detailed product or service that can be produced on an ongoing basis by the operation. This should be a cross-functional process. Contributions are needed from those who understand market requirements, those who understand the technical aspects of the product or service, those with access to cost and investment information, those who can protect the design's intellectual property, and most of all, the operations people who will have to produce the product or service on an ongoing basis. In addition to the usual process design issues that were treated in the previous two chapters, in this type of process there are almost always issues of cross-functional responsibility and communication. Product and service design is also an activity that depends upon imagination, innovation and creativity, attributes that are regarded as almost synonymous with design. And while accepting that design is essentially a creative process, it *is* also a process. And like any process, it must be well designed if it is to contribute to the overall competitiveness of the business.

The following two examples are both design processes. Even though we may not see software as having to be 'designed', the way in which it is specified is essentially a design process. In fact it is probably the most important process for companies like Microsoft. The actual mass production of the software is important, but not at all as important as designing (and redesigning) the software product itself. Similarly, we may not see pharmaceutical products as being 'designed'. Yet, again, they go through a long and rigorous process that leads to their final specification.

| Example | The Daniel Hersheson Blowdry Bar at Top Shop |

Source: Pearson Education Ltd

Even at the chic and stylish end of the hairdressing business, close as it is to the world of changing fashion trends, true innovation and genuinely novel new services are a relative rarity. Yet real service innovation can reap significant rewards, as Daniel and Luke Hersheson, the father and son team behind the Daniel Hersheson salons, fully understand. The Hersheson brand has successfully bridged the gap between salon, photo session and the fashion catwalk. The team first put themselves on the fashion map with a salon in London's Mayfair followed by a salon and spa in Harvey Nichols' flagship London store.

Their latest innovation is the 'Blowdry Bar at Top Shop'. This is a unique concept that is aimed at customers who want fashionable and catwalk-quality styling at an affordable price without the full 'cut and blow dry' treatment. The Hersheson Blowdry Bar was launched in December 2006 in Top Shop's flagship Oxford Circus store to ecstatic press coverage. The four-seater pink pod within the Top Shop store is a scissor-free zone dedicated to styling on the go. Originally seen as a walk-in, no-appointment-necessary format, demand has proved to be so high that an appointment system has been implemented to avoid disappointing customers. Once in the pod, customers can choose from a tailor-made picture menu of nine fashion styles with names like 'The Super Straight', 'The Classic Big and Bouncy' and 'Wavy Gravy'. Typically, the wash and blow-dry takes around 30 minutes. *'It's just perfect for a client who wants to look that bit special for a big night out but who doesn't want a full cut,'* says Ryan Wilkes, one of the stylists at the Blowdry Bar. *'Some clients will "graduate" to become regular customers at the main Daniel Hersheson salons. I have clients who started out using the Blowdry Bar but now also get their hair cut with me in the salon.'*

Partnering with Top Shop is an important element in the design of the service, says Daniel Hersheson. *'We are delighted to be opening the UK's first blow-dry bar at Top Shop. Our philosophy of constantly relating hair back to fashion means we will be perfectly at home in the most creative store on the British High Street.'* Top Shop also recognizes the fit. *'The Daniel Hersheson Blowdry Bar is a really exciting service addition to our Oxford Circus flagship and offers the perfect finishing touch to a great shopping experience at Top Shop,'* says Jane Shepherdson, Brand Director of Top Shop.

But the new service has not just been a success in the market, it also has advantages for the operation itself. *'It's a great opportunity for young stylists not only to develop their styling skills but also to develop the confidence that it takes to interact with clients,'* says George Northwood, Manager of Daniel Hersheson's Mayfair salon. *'You can see a real difference after a trainee stylist has worked in the Blowdry Bar. They learn how to talk to clients, to understand their needs and to advise them. It's the confidence that they gain that is so important in helping them to become fully qualified and successful stylists in their own right.'*

Example

Spangler, Hoover and Dyson[1]

In 1907 a janitor called Murray Spangler put together a pillowcase, a fan, an old biscuit tin and a broom handle. It was the world's first vacuum cleaner. One year later he sold his patented idea to William Hoover whose company went on to dominate the vacuum cleaner market for decades, especially in its United States homeland. Yet between 2002 and 2005 Hoover's market share dropped from 36 per cent to 13.5 per cent. Why? Because a futuristic looking and comparatively expensive rival product, the Dyson vacuum cleaner, had jumped from nothing to over 20 per cent of the market.

Source: Getty News Images/Getty

In fact, the Dyson product dates back to 1978 when James Dyson noticed how the air filter in the spray-finishing room of a company where he had been working was constantly clogging with powder particles (just like a vacuum cleaner bag clogs with dust). So he designed and built an industrial cyclone tower, which removed the powder particles by exerting centrifugal forces. The question intriguing him was, *'Could the same principle work in a domestic vacuum cleaner?'* Five years and five *thousand* prototypes later he had a working design, since praised for its 'uniqueness and functionality'. However, existing vacuum cleaner manufacturers were not as impressed – two rejected the design outright. So Dyson started making his new design himself. Within a few years Dyson cleaners were, in the UK, outselling the rivals which had once rejected them. The aesthetics and functionality of the design help to keep sales growing in spite of a higher retail price. To Dyson, good *'is about looking at everyday things with new eyes and working out how they can be made better. It's about challenging existing technology'*.

Dyson engineers have taken this technology one stage further and developed core separator technology to capture even more microscopic dirt. Dirt now goes through three stages of separation. First, dirt is drawn into a powerful outer cyclone. Centrifugal forces fling larger debris such as pet hair and dust particles into the clear bin at 500Gs (the maximum G-force the human body can take is 8Gs). Second, a further cyclonic stage, the core separator, removes dust particles as small as 0.5 microns from the airflow – particles so small you could fit 200 of them on this full stop. Finally, a cluster of smaller, even faster cyclones generates centrifugal forces of up to 150,000G – extracting particles as small as mould and bacteria.

What do these two examples have in common?

The nature of product and service design, to some extent, will be different in different types of operation; the technical issues will be different, as often will the time scales involved. High fashion products and services may not even exist in three or four years' time. There is also a difference between designing products and designing services, especially high-visibility services where the customer is inside the service, experiencing it. With products, customers judge the attributes of the product itself such as its functionality, its aesthetics, and so on. But with services, customers will judge not only the functionality of what they receive but also the process that they were put through in receiving it. For example, a retail bank may design the products that are available through its branches or its website, and the customer will make a judgement about the usefulness and value of these services. But they will also judge their experience in visiting the branch or using the website. So, whereas for products, the design of the product itself and the design of the process that produces it can be considered as two separate activities (although this may be a mistake, see later), the design of a service cannot be considered independently of the design of the process that creates it.

Yet notwithstanding these differences, the design *process* is essentially very similar irrespective of what is being designed. More importantly, it is a process that is seen as increasingly important. Poor design and development of new services or products in either Daniel Hersheson or Dyson would obviously have serious consequences for the company. Conversely, good design that incorporates innovation and creativity within a well-ordered design process can have a huge strategic impact. But the design activity is still a process that itself must be designed. It has stages that the design must go through. It must be clear about its process objectives and it must be structured and resourced in order to achieve those objectives. Figure 6.2 shows the design activity as a process, with inputs and outputs as in any other process.

> **Operations principle**
> Product and service design is a process and can be managed using the same principles as any other process.

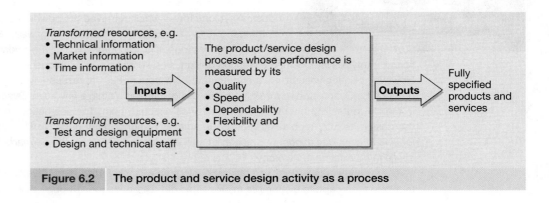

Figure 6.2   The product and service design activity as a process

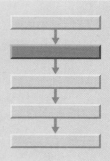

DIAGNOSTIC QUESTION

Are product/service design objectives specified?

> **Operations principle**
> Product/service design processes can be judged in terms of their levels of quality, speed, dependability, flexibility and cost.

Products and services are designed to satisfy market needs, and the process that produces those designs should be assessed in terms of what the market will expect from any process, namely quality, speed, dependability, flexibility and cost. These performance objectives have just as much relevance for the production of new product and service designs as they do for their ongoing production once they are introduced to the market.

What is the quality of product/service design processes?

Design quality is not always easy to define precisely, especially if customers are relatively satisfied with existing products and services. Many software companies talk about the 'I don't know what I want but I'll know when I see it' syndrome, meaning that only when customers use the software are they in a position to articulate what they do or don't require. Nevertheless, it is possible to distinguish high and low quality designs (although this is easier to do in hindsight) by judging them in terms of their ability to meet market requirements. In doing this, the distinction between the specification quality and the conformance quality of designs is important. No business would want a design process that was indifferent to 'errors' in its designs, yet some are more tolerant than others. In the 'design' of pharmaceutical products, for example, the authorities insist on a prolonged and thorough design process. Although withdrawing a drug from the market is unusual, it does occasionally occur. Far more frequent are the 'product recalls' that are relatively common in, say, the automotive industry. Many of these are design related and the result of 'conformance' failures in the design process. The 'specification' quality of design is different. It means the degree of functionality, or experience, or aesthetics, or whatever the product or service is primarily competing on. Some businesses require product or service designs that are relatively basic (although free from errors), while others require designs that are clearly special in terms of the customer response they hope to elicit.

What is the speed of product/service design processes?

Fast product and service design has become the norm in many industries, often because market competition has forced companies to capture the markets' imagination with the frequent introduction of new offerings. Sometimes this is the result of fast-changing consumer fashion. Sometimes it is forced by a rapidly changing technology base. Telecoms products need to be updated frequently because their underlying technology is constantly improving. Sometimes both of these pressures are evident, as in many Internet-based services. But no matter what the motivation, fast design brings a number of advantages.

- *Early market launch.* An ability to design products and services speedily means that they can be introduced to the market earlier and thus earn revenue for longer, and may command price premiums.
- *Starting design late.* Alternatively, starting the design process late rather than introducing a product or service early may have advantages, especially where either the nature of customer demand or the availability of technology is uncertain and dynamic, so fast design allows design decisions to be made closer to the time when they are introduced to the market.
- *Frequent market stimulation.* Fast design allows frequent new or updated product and service introductions.
- *More opportunities for innovation.* Where the underlying technology base is moving fast, short design times allow more windows of opportunity to introduce innovations.

What is the dependability of product/service design processes?

Fast product and service design processes that cannot be relied on to deliver innovations dependably are, in reality, not fast at all. Design schedule slippage can extend design times, but worse, a lack of dependability adds to the uncertainty surrounding the design process. Conversely, processes that are dependable minimize design uncertainty. Unexpected technical difficulties, such as suppliers who themselves do not deliver solutions on time, customers or markets that change during the design process itself, and so on, all contribute to an uncertain and ambiguous design environment. Professional project management (see Chapter 15) of the design process can help to reduce uncertainty and minimize the risk of internal disturbance to the design process and can prevent (or give early warning of) missed deadlines, process bottlenecks and resource shortages. External disturbances to the process will remain, however. These may be minimized through close liaison with suppliers and market or environmental monitoring. Nevertheless, unexpected disruptions will always occur and the more innovative the design, the more likely they are to occur. This is why flexibility within the design process is one of the most important ways in which dependable delivery of new products and services can be ensured.

What is the flexibility of product/service design processes?

Flexibility in product and service design is the ability of the design process to cope with external or internal change. The most common reason for external change is that markets, or specific customers, change their requirements. Although flexibility may not be needed in relatively predictable environments, it is clearly valuable in more fast-moving and volatile environments, where one's own customers and markets change, or where the designs of competitors' products or services dictate a matching or leapfrogging move. Internal changes include the emergence of superior technical solutions. In addition, the increasing complexity and interconnectedness of products and services may require flexibility. A bank, for example, may bundle together a number of separate services for one particular segment of its market. Privileged account holders may obtain special deposit rates, premium credit cards, insurance offers, travel facilities and so on together in the same 'product'. Changing one aspect of this bundle may require changes to be made in other elements. So extending the credit card benefits to include extra travel insurance may also mean the redesign of the separate insurance element of the package. One way of measuring design flexibility is to compare the cost of modifying a product or service design in response to such changes against the consequences to profitability if no changes are made. The higher the cost of modifying a product or service in response to a given change, the lower is the design flexibility.

What is the cost of product/service design processes?

The cost of designing products and services is usually analyzed in a similar way to the on-going cost of producing the goods and services. In other words, cost factors are split up into three categories: the cost of buying the inputs to the process, the cost of providing the labour in the process, and the other general overhead costs of running the process. In most in-house design processes the latter two costs outweigh the former.

One way of thinking about the effect of the other design performance objectives on cost is shown in Figure 6.3. Whether through quality errors, intrinsically slow design processes, a lack of project dependability, or delays caused through inflexible design processes, the end result is that the design is late. Delayed completion of the design results in both more expenditure on the design and delayed (and probably reduced) revenue. The combination of both these effects usually means that the financial breakeven point for a new product or service is delayed by far more than the original delay in the product or service launch.

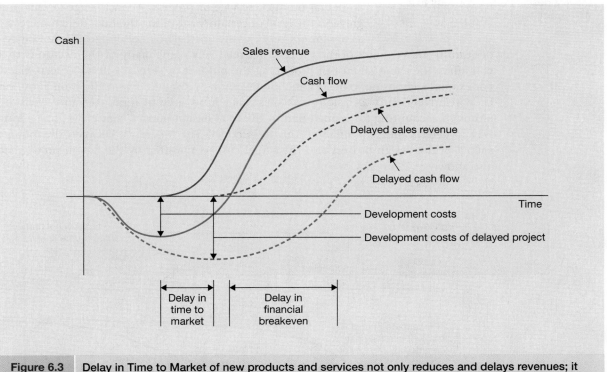

Figure 6.3 Delay in Time to Market of new products and services not only reduces and delays revenues; it also increases the costs of development. The combination of both of these effects usually delays the financial breakeven point far more than the delay in the Time to Market

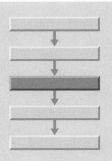

DIAGNOSTIC QUESTION

Is the product/service design process defined?

To produce a fully specified product or service, a potential design must pass through several stages. These form an approximate sequence, although in practice designers will often recycle or backtrack through the stages. The stages in a typical design process are shown in Figure 6.4, although these exact stages are not used by all companies. Different processes are used by different companies. However, there is considerable similarity between the stages used and their sequence. Furthermore, they all have the same underlying principle: that over time an original idea, or 'concept', is refined and made progressively more detailed until it contains sufficient information to be turned into an actual product, service or process. At each stage in this progression the level of certainty regarding the final design increases as design options are discarded. The final design will not be evident until the very end of the process. Yet relatively early, many of the decisions that will affect the eventual cost of producing the product or service will have been made. For example, choosing to make a mobile telephone's case out of a magnesium alloy will be a relatively early decision that may take little investigation. Yet this decision, although accounting for a small part of the total design budget, may have gone a long way to determining the final cost of the product. The difference between the 'budget spend' of the design process and the actual costs committed by the design process are also shown in Figure 6.4.

> **Operations principle**
> Any product/service design process should involve a number of stages that move a design from a 'concept' to a fully specified state.

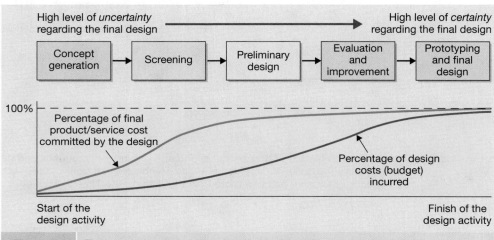

Figure 6.4   The stages in a typical product/service design process. As the process progresses the level of uncertainty regarding the final design is reduced and the percentage of final product or service cost committed by the design increases

Concept generation

Ideas for new products and services can come from anywhere. They are expected to emerge from the parts of the business that have that formal responsibility, such as research and development (R&D) or market research departments, but any business that restricts itself strictly to such internal sources is failing to exploit other, less formal but potentially useful sources. For example, although a business may use formal market research tools such as focus groups, questionnaires, etc., capturing the opinions of the staff who serve customers can often lead to deeper insights into customers' real preferences and opinions than more formal surveys. Similarly, customer complaints may be dealt with at a relatively operational level, whereas in fact they can be a rewarding source of customer opinion that should be making an impact at the more strategic level that sets objectives for product and service design. Closely analyzing competitors' designs (known as reverse engineering) may also help to isolate the key features of the design that are worth emulating. Some (more back-office) aspects of services may be difficult to reverse engineer, but by consumer testing a service it may be possible to make educated guesses about how it has been created. Many service organizations employ 'testers' to check out the services provided by competitors.

Concept screening

Not all concepts will be capable of being developed into products and services. Designers need to be selective. The purpose of concept screening is to take the flow of concepts and evaluate them for their feasibility (can we do it?), acceptability (do we want to do it?) and 'vulnerability' (what are the risks of doing it?). Concepts may have to pass through many different screens, and several functions might be involved (for example marketing, operations and finance). Table 6.1 gives typical feasibility, acceptability and vulnerability questions for each of these three functional filters.

Preliminary design

Having generated one or more appropriate concepts, the next stage is to create preliminary designs. It is at this stage when opportunities arise for reducing the design complexity that can build cost into products and services when they are produced. The most elegant design solutions are often the simplest. However, when an operation produces a variety of products or services (as most do) the range, considered as a whole, can become

Table 6.1	Some typical evaluation questions for marketing, operations and finance		
Evaluation criteria	Marketing	Operations	Finance
Feasibility	Is the market likely to be big enough?	Do we have the capabilities to produce it?	Do we have access to sufficient finance to develop and launch it?
Acceptability	How much market share could it gain?	How much will we have to reorganize our activities to produce it?	How much financial return will there be on our investment?
Vulnerability	What is the risk of it failing in the marketplace?	What is the risk of us being unable to produce it acceptably?	How much money could we lose if things do not go to plan?

complex, again increasing costs. Designers can adopt a number of approaches to reducing inherent design complexity.

Standardization

This is an attempt to overcome the cost of high variety by standardizing products and services, usually by restricting variety to that which has real value for the end customer. Examples include fast-food restaurants, discount supermarkets or telephone-based insurance companies. Similarly, although everybody's body shape is different, garment manufacturers produce clothes in only a limited number of sizes. The range of sizes is chosen to give a reasonable fit for most, but not all, body shapes. Controlling variety is an important issue for most businesses, who can all face the danger of allowing variety to grow excessively. Many organizations have significantly improved their profitability by careful variety reduction, often by assessing the real profit or contribution of each product or service.

Commonality

Common elements are used to simplify design complexity, for example by using the same components across a range of automobiles. Likewise, standardizing the format of information inputs to a process can be achieved by using appropriately designed forms or screen formats. The more that different products and services can be based on common components, the less complex it is to produce them. For example, the European aircraft maker Airbus designed its new generation of civil aircraft with a high degree of commonality with the introduction of fly-by-wire technology. This meant that 10 aircraft models featured virtually identical flight decks, common systems and similar handling characteristics. The advantages of commonality for the airline operators include a much shorter training time for pilots and engineers when they move from one aircraft to another. This offers pilots the possibility of flying a wide range of routes from short-haul to ultra-long-haul and leads to greater efficiencies because common maintenance procedures can be designed with maintenance teams capable of servicing any aircraft in the same family. Also, when up to 90 per cent of all parts are common within a range of aircraft, there is a reduced need to carry a wide range of spare parts.

> **Operations principle**
> A key design process objective should be to reduce the complexity of the design through standardization, commonality and modularization.

Modularization

This involves designing standardized 'subcomponents' of a product or service which can be put together in different ways. It is possible to create wide choice through the fully interchangeable assembly of various combinations of a smaller number of standard sub-assemblies; computers are designed in this way, for example. These standardized modules, or sub-assemblies, can be produced in higher volume, thereby reducing their cost. Similarly, the package holiday industry can assemble holidays to meet a specific customer requirement, from predesigned and purchased air travel, accommodation, insurance, and so on. In education also there is an increasing use of modular courses that allow 'customers' choice but permit each module to have economically viable numbers of students.

Mass customization[2]

Flexibility in design can allow the ability to offer different things to different customers. Normally, high variety means high cost, but some companies have developed their flexibility in such a way that products and services are customized for each individual customer, yet produced in a high-volume, mass production manner that keeps costs down. This approach is called mass customization. Sometimes this is achieved through flexibility in design. For example, Dell is the largest volume producer of personal computers in the world, yet allows each customer to 'design' (albeit in a limited sense) their own configuration. Sometimes flexible technology is used to achieve the same effect. For example Paris Miki, an up-market eyewear retailer that has the largest number of eyewear stores in the world, uses its own 'Mikissimes Design System' to capture a digital image of the customer and analyze facial characteristics. Together with a list of customers' personal preferences, the system then recommends a particular design and displays it on the image of the customer's face. In consultation with the optician the customer can adjust shapes and sizes until the final design is chosen. Within the store the frames are assembled from a range of pre-manufactured components and the lenses ground and fitted to the frames. The whole process takes around an hour.

| Example | ### Customizing for kids[3] |

Reducing design complexity is a principle that applies just as much to services as to products. For example, television programmes are made increasingly with a worldwide market in mind. However, most television audiences around the world have a distinct preference for programmes that respect their regional tastes, culture and of course language. The challenge facing global programme makers therefore is to try and achieve the economies which come as a result of high-volume production while allowing programmes to be customized for different markets. For example, take the programme 'Art Attack!' made for the Disney Channel, a children's TV channel shown around the world. Typically, over 200 episodes of the show are made in six different language versions. About 60 per cent of each show is common across all versions. Shots without speaking or where the presenter's face is not visible are shot separately. For example, if a simple cardboard model is being made, all versions will share the scenes where the presenter's hands only are visible. Commentary in the appropriate language is over-dubbed onto the scenes which are edited seamlessly with other shots of the appropriate presenter. The final product will have the head and shoulders of a Brazilian, French, Italian, German or Spanish presenter flawlessly mixed with the same pair of (British) hands constructing the model. The result is that local viewers in each market see the show as their own. Even though presenters are flown into the UK production studios, the cost of making each episode is only about one third of producing separate programmes for each market.

Design evaluation and improvement

The purpose of this stage in the design activity is to take the preliminary design and see whether it can be improved before the product or service is tested in the market. There are a number of techniques that can be employed at this stage to evaluate and improve the preliminary design. Perhaps the best known is quality function deployment (QFD). The key purpose of QFD is to try to ensure that the eventual design of a product or service actually meets the needs of its customers. Customers may not have been considered explicitly since the concept generation stage, and therefore it is appropriate to check that what is being proposed for the design of the product or service will meet their needs. It is a technique that was developed in Japan at Mitsubishi's Kobe shipyard and used extensively by Toyota, the motor vehicle manufacturer, and its suppliers. It is also known as the 'house of quality' (because of its shape) and the 'voice of the customer' (because of its purpose). The technique tries to capture what the customer needs and how it might be achieved. Figure 6.5 shows a simple QFD matrix used in the design of a promotional USB data storage pen (given away for promotion purposes). It is a formal articulation of how designers see the relationship between the requirements of the customer and the design characteristics of the new product or service.

PRACTICE NOTE

It is at this stage in the process when both creativity and persistence are needed to move from a potentially good idea to a workable design. One product has commemorated the persistence of its design engineers in its company name. Back in 1953 the Rocket Chemical Company set out to create a rust-prevention solvent and degreaser to be used in the aerospace

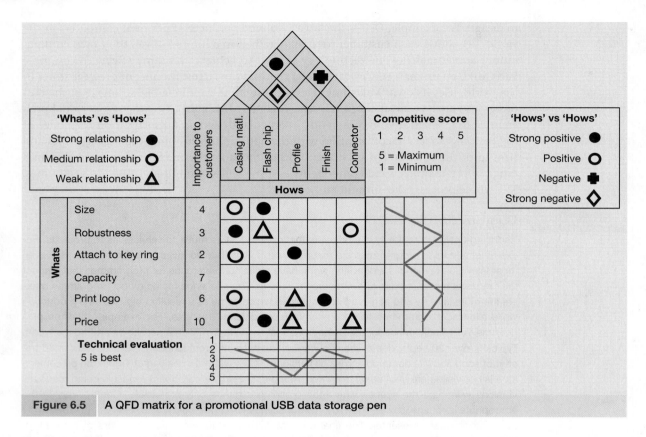

Figure 6.5 A QFD matrix for a promotional USB data storage pen

industry. Working in their lab in San Diego, California, it took them 40 attempts to get the water-displacing formula worked out. So that is what they called the product. WD-40 literally stands for Water Displacement, fortieth attempt. It was the name used in the lab book. Originally used to protect the outer skin of the Atlas Missile from rust and corrosion, the product worked so well that employees kept taking cans home to use for domestic purposes. Soon after, the product was launched with great success into the consumer market.

Prototyping and final design

At around this stage in the design activity it is necessary to turn the improved design into a prototype so that it can be tested. Product prototypes include everything from clay models to computer simulations. Service prototypes may also include computer simulations but also the actual implementation of the service on a pilot basis, for example, retailing organizations piloting new services in a small number of stores in order to test customers' reaction to them. It may also be possible to 'virtually' prototype in much the same way as a physical prototype. This is a familiar idea in some industries such as magazine publishing, where images and text can be rearranged and subjected to scrutiny prior to existing in any physical form, allowing them to be amended right up to the point of production. But, although the means of prototyping may vary, the principle is always the same: do whatever one can to test out the design before any possible errors in the design could damage the business's reputation or finances. This may be as simple as debating the new product or service thoroughly within the business and with customers and/or suppliers. Or, it could involve highly sophisticated mathematical modelling or simulation. The important point is that design should be tested in some way, and the results of those tests fed back into a refined and superior design.

FURTHER EXAMPLE

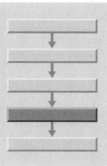

Are the resources for developing products and services adequate?

For any process to operate effectively it must be appropriately designed and resourced. Design processes are no different. The detailed principles of process design that were discussed in Chapters 4 and 5 are as applicable here as they are for any other process in the business. But, in addition, because design processes are often an operation within the business in their own right, there are some more strategic aspects of organizing design processes that need managing. In particular there are the questions of how much capacity to devote to design, how much of the design activity to outsource, and how to organize design-related resources.[4]

> **Operations principle**
> For product/service design processes to be effective they must be adequately resourced.

Is there sufficient product and service design capacity?

As in any other process, the management of capacity involves deciding on the appropriate level of capacity needed by the process, and how capacity can be changed in order to respond to likely changes in demand. Demand in this case is the number of new designs needed by the business. The chief difficulty is that, even in very large companies, the rate of new service or product introduction is not constant. This means that product and service design processes are subjected to uneven internal 'demand' for designs, possibly with several new offerings being introduced to the market close together, while at other times little design is needed. This poses a resourcing problem because the capacity of a design process is often difficult to flex. The expertise necessary for design is embedded within designers, technologists, market analysts, and so on. Some expertise may be able to be hired in as and when it is needed, but much design resource is, in effect, fixed.

Such a combination of varying demand and relatively fixed design capacity leads some organizations to be reluctant to invest in design processes because they see them as an underutilized resource. This may lead to a vicious cycle in which, although there is a short-term need for design resources, companies fail to invest in those resources because many of them (such as skilled design staff) cannot be hired in the short term, which leads to design projects being under-resourced with an increased chance of project overrun or failure to deliver appropriate technical solutions. This in turn may lead to the company losing business or otherwise suffering in the marketplace, which makes the company even less willing to invest in design resources. This issue relates to the relationship between capacity utilization and throughput time that was discussed in Chapter 4. Either the business must accept relatively low utilization of its design resources if it wants to maintain fast time to market, or, if it wants to maintain high levels of design resource utilization, it must accept longer design times, or it must try to reduce the variability in the process in some way. Reducing variability may mean introducing new designs at fixed periods, for example every year. See Figure 6.6.

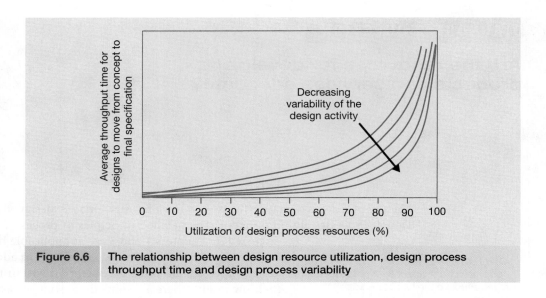

Figure 6.6 The relationship between design resource utilization, design process throughput time and design process variability

Should all design be done in-house?

Just as there are supply networks that produce products and services, there is also a supply network of design knowledge that connects suppliers and customers in the design process. This network of knowledge exchange is sometimes called the 'design (or development) network'. Design processes can adopt any position on a continuum of varying degrees of design engagement with suppliers, from retaining all the design capabilities in-house, to outsourcing all its design work. Between these extremes are varying degrees of internal and external design capability. Figure 6.7 shows some of the more important factors that will vary depending on where a design process is on the continuum. Design resources will be easy to control if they are kept in-house because they are closely aligned with the company's normal organizational structures, but control should be relatively loose because of the extra trust present in working with familiar colleagues. Outsourced design requires greater control and, because it has to be applied at a distance, contracts, often with penalty clauses for delay, may be needed.

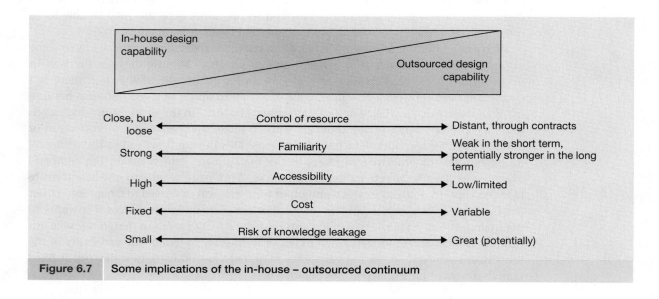

Figure 6.7 Some implications of the in-house – outsourced continuum

The overall cost of in-house versus outsourced design will vary, depending on the firm and the design project. An important difference, however, is that external designs tend to be regarded as a variable cost. The more external resources are used, the more the cost will be. In-house design is more of a fixed cost. Indeed a shift to outsourcing may occur because fixed design costs are viewed as too great. Also, a major driver of this decision can be the risk of knowledge leakage. Firms become concerned that experience gained through collaboration with a supplier of design expertise may be transferred to competitors. There is a paradox here. Businesses usually outsource design primarily because of the supplier's capabilities which are themselves an accumulation of specialist knowledge from working with a variety of customers. Without such knowledge 'leakage' the benefits of the supplier's accumulated design capabilities would not even exist.

Involving customers in design

Few people know the merits and limitations of products and services better than the customers who use them, which makes them an obvious source of feedback. Different types of customer have the potential to provide different types of information. New users can pinpoint more attractive product and service features; those who have switched to a competitor offering can reveal its problems. A particularly interesting group of customers are the so-called 'lead users', who have requirements of a product or service well ahead of the rest of the market, and who will benefit by finding a solution to their requirements. One reported example of lead-user research concerns a new product design manager at Bose, the high quality hi-fi and speaker company. On visiting his local music store he noted the high quality of the background music. He found that the store manager was using Bose speakers designed for home use but had attached metal strips around the speaker boxes so that they could be suspended from the ceiling. Inspired by this, Bose built prototypes of speakers that would satisfy the need for quality in-store speakers. These were taken back to the music store for further testing and eventually led to the company successfully entering the market.

FURTHER EXAMPLE

Is product and service design technology being used?

Process technology has become important in product/service design processes. Simulation software, for example, is now common in the design of everything from transportation services through to chemical factories. These allow developers to make design decisions in advance of the actual product or service being created. They allow designers to work through the experience of using the service or product and learn more about how it might operate in practice. They can explore possibilities, gain insights and, most important, explore the consequences of their decisions.

Computer-aided design (CAD)

The best-known process technology in product design is computer-aided design (CAD). CAD systems store and categorize product and component information and allow designs to be built up on screen, often performing basic engineering calculations to test the appropriateness of proposed design solutions. They provide the computer-aided ability to create a modified product drawing and allow conventionally used shapes to be added swiftly to the computer-based representation of a product. Designs created on screen can be saved and retrieved for later use, enabling a library of standardized part and component designs to be built up. Not only can this dramatically increase the productivity of the design process but it also aids the standardization of parts in the design activity. Often CAD systems come with their own library of standard parts.

Knowledge management technologies

In many professional service firms, such as management consultancies, service design involves the evaluation of concepts and frameworks which can be used in client organizations to diagnose problems, analyze performance, and construct possible solutions. They may include ideas of industry best practice, benchmarks of performance within an industry, and ideas which can be transported across industry boundaries. However, the characteristics of management consulting firms are that they are geographically dispersed and rarely in their offices. The consultants are most of their time in client organizations acquiring knowledge day by day. Yet at the same time it is vital for such companies to avoid 'reinventing the wheel' continually. Any means of collectivizing the cumulative knowledge and experience within the organization must greatly assist the design of new concepts and frameworks. Most consultancy companies attempt to tackle this problem using knowledge management routines based on their intranet capabilities. This allows consultants to put their experience into a common pool, contact other staff within the company who have skills relevant to a current assignment, and identify previous similar assignments. In this way information is integrated into the ongoing knowledge design process within the company and can be tapped by those charged with developing new products.

FURTHER EXAMPLE

Design technologies are particularly useful when the design task is both uncertain and complex. Simulation technologies allow developers to reduce their own uncertainty of how products and services will work in practice. Similarly, knowledge management systems consolidate and juxtapose information on what is happening within the organization, thus presenting a more comprehensive vision and reducing uncertainty. CAD systems also help to deal with complexity by storing data on component details as they develop through various interactions. The absolute size and interrelatedness of some large products require sophisticated CAD systems if they are to be developed effectively. One of the most reported examples was the design of Boeing's 777 aircraft. The powerful CAD system used on this project was credited with Boeing's success in being able to involve its customers in the design process, allow more product configuration flexibility (such as the proportion of seats in each class, etc.), and still bring the huge project successfully to completion.

DIAGNOSTIC QUESTION

Are product/service design and process design simultaneous?

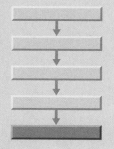

The outputs from the processes that design products and services (finished designs) become important inputs to the processes that produce these products and services on an ongoing basis. This is why it is a mistake to separate the design of products and services from the design of the processes that will produce them. Operations process managers should have some involvement from the initial evaluation of the concept right through

Operations principle
Effective simultaneous design reduces time-to-market.

to the production of the product or service and its introduction to the market. Merging the design of products/services and the processes that create them is sometimes called simultaneous or interactive design. Its benefits come from the elapsed time taken for the whole design activity, from concept through to market introduction – the design's time-to-market (TTM). Reducing time-to-market gives increased competitive advantage. For example, if it takes a business three years to develop a product from concept to market, with a given set of resources, it can introduce a new product only once every three years. If its rival can develop products in two years, it can introduce its (presumably) improved new product once every two years. So the rival does not have to make such radical improvements in performance each time it introduces a new product, because it is introducing its new products more frequently. Shorter TTM means that businesses get more opportunities to improve the performance of their products or services.

The factors that can significantly reduce time-to-market for a product or service include the following:

- bringing 'product/service' and 'process' design together as one integrated process
- overlapping (simultaneous) design of the stages in the combined design process
- early deployment of strategic decision making and resolution of design conflict
- an organizational structure that reflects the nature of the design process.

Bringing product/service and process design together

What looks good as an elegant product or service design may be difficult to produce on an ongoing basis. Conversely, an operations process designed for one set of products and services may be incapable of producing new ones. It clearly makes sense to design products, services and operations processes together. However, the fact that many businesses do not do this is only partly a result of their ignorance or incompetence. There are real barriers to doing it. First, the time scales involved can be very different. Products and services may be modified, or even redesigned, relatively frequently. The processes that will be used to produce those products and services may be far too expensive to modify every time the product or service design changes. Second, the people involved with product or service designs on one hand, and ongoing process design on the other, are likely to be organizationally separate. Finally, it is sometimes not possible to design an ongoing process for the production of products and services until the product or service itself is fully defined.

Yet none of these barriers is insurmountable. Although ongoing processes may not be able to be changed every time there is a product or service design change, they can be designed to cope with a range of potential products and services. The fact that design staff and operations staff are often organizationally separate can also be overcome. Even if it is not sensible to merge the two functions, there are communication and organizational mechanisms to encourage the two functions to work together. Even the claim that ongoing processes cannot be designed until design staff know the nature of products and services they are going to produce is not entirely true. There can be sufficient clues emerging from product and service design for process design staff to be considering how they might modify ongoing processes. This is a fundamental principle of simultaneous design, considered next.

Encouraging simultaneous design

We have described the design process as a set of individual, predetermined stages, with one stage being completed before the next one commences. This step-by-step, or sequential, approach has traditionally been the typical form of product/service design processes.

It has some advantages. It is easy to manage and control design processes organized in this way because each stage is clearly defined. In addition, each stage is completed before the next stage is begun, so each stage can focus its skills and expertise on a limited set of tasks. The main problem of the sequential approach is that it is both time-consuming and costly. When each stage is separate, with a clearly defined set of tasks, any difficulties encountered during the design at one stage might necessitate the design being halted while responsibility moves back to the previous stage. This sequential approach is shown in Figure 6.8(a).

Often there is really little need to wait until the absolute finalization of one stage before starting the next.[5] For example, perhaps while generating the concept, the evaluation activity of screening and selection could be started. It is likely that some concepts could be judged as 'non-starters' relatively early in the process of ideas generation. Similarly, during the screening stage, it is likely that some aspects of the design will become obvious before the phase is finally complete. Therefore, the preliminary work on these parts of the design could be commenced at that point. This principle can be taken right through all the stages, one stage commencing before the previous one has finished, so there is simultaneous or concurrent work on the stages (see Figure 6.8(b)).

We can link this idea with the idea of uncertainty reduction, discussed earlier, when we made the point that uncertainty reduces as the design progresses. This also applies to each stage of the design. If this is so then there must be some degree of certainty which the next stage can take as its starting point prior to the end of the previous stage. In other

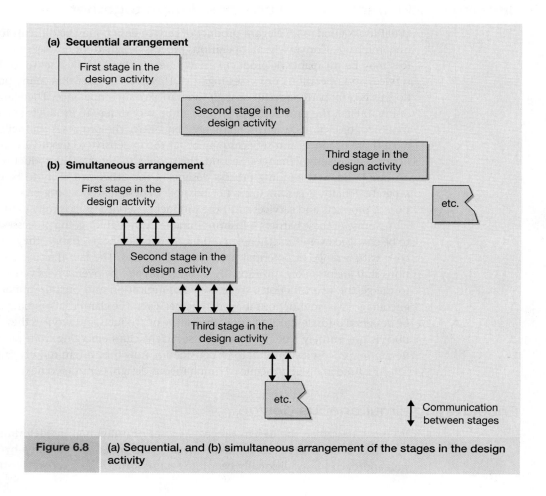

Figure 6.8   (a) Sequential, and (b) simultaneous arrangement of the stages in the design activity

words, designers can be continually reacting to a series of decisions and clues that are given to them by the designers working on the preceding stage. However, this can only work if there is effective communication between each pair of stages.

Deploying strategic intervention and resolving conflicts early

A design decision, once made, need not irrevocably shape the final design. All decisions can be changed, but it becomes increasingly hard to do so as the design process progresses. At the same time, early design decisions are often the most difficult to make because of the high level of uncertainty surrounding what may or may not work as a final design.

This is why the level of debate, and even disagreement, over the characteristics of a design can be at its most heated in the early stages of the process. One approach is to delay decision making in the hope that an obvious 'answer' will emerge. The problem with this is that, if decisions are delayed and this causes changes to be made later in the design process, those changes will be more disruptive later in the process than they would have been earlier. The implications of this are, first, that it is worth trying to reach consensus in the early stages of the design process even if this seems to be delaying the total process in the short term, and second, that strategic intervention into the design process by senior management is particularly needed at these early stages in the process.

> **Operations principle**
> The product/service design process requires strategic attention early, when there is the most potential to affect design decisions.

Unfortunately, there is a tendency for senior managers, after setting the initial objectives of the design process, to 'leave the details' to technical experts. They may only become engaged with the process again in the later stages as problems start to emerge that need reconciliation or extra resources. Figure 6.9 illustrates this in terms of the mismatch between senior management's ability to influence the design process and what, in some organizations, is the actual pattern of intervention.[6]

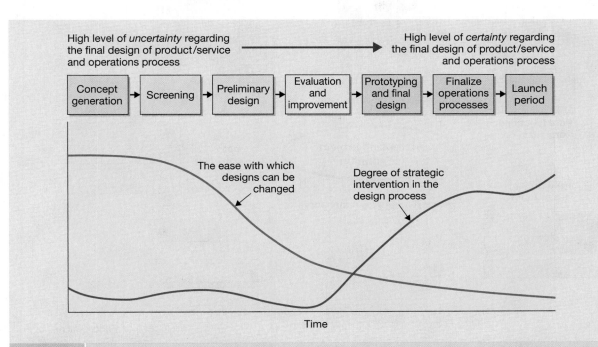

Figure 6.9 The degree of strategic intervention in the design process is often dictated by the need to resolve outstanding conflicts rather than the needs of the design process itself

Organizing design process in a way that reflects the nature of the design

The design process of developing concepts through to market will almost certainly involve people from several different areas of the business who will have some part in making the decisions shaping the final design. Yet any design project will also have an existence of its own. It will have a project name, an individual manager or group of staff who are championing the project, a budget and, hopefully, a clear strategic purpose in the organization. The organizational question is which of these two ideas – the various organizational functions that contribute to the design, or the design project itself – should dominate the way in which the design activity is managed?

There is a range of possible organizational structures – from pure functional to pure project forms. In a pure functional organization, all staff associated with the design project are based unambiguously in their functional groups. There is no project-based group at all. They may be working full-time on the project but all communication and liaison are carried out through their functional manager. The project exists because of agreement between these functional managers. At the other extreme, all the individual members of staff from each function involved in the project could be moved out of their functions and perhaps even co-located (working physically close to each other) in a task force dedicated solely to the project. The task force could be led by a project manager who might hold the entire budget allocated to the design project. Not all members of the task force necessarily have to stay in the team throughout the design period, but a substantial core might see the project through from start to finish. Some members of a design team may even be from other companies. Between these two extremes there are various types of matrix organization with varying emphasis on these two aspects of the organization[7] (see Figure 6.10).

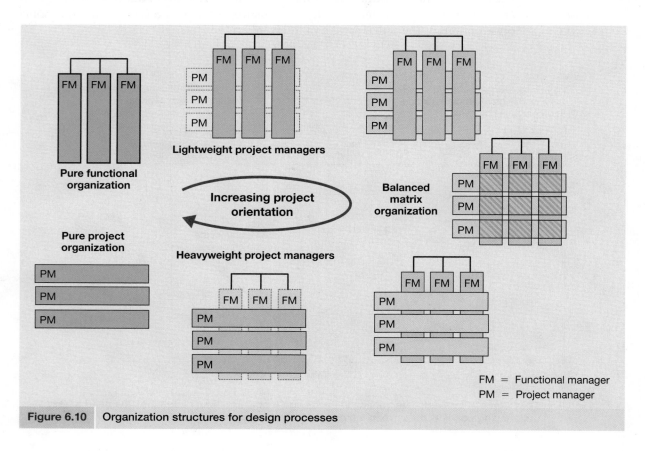

Figure 6.10   Organization structures for design processes

- **Functional organization.** The project is divided into segments and assigned to relevant functional areas and/or groups within functional areas. The project is jointly co-ordinated by functional and senior management.
- **Functional matrix (or lightweight project manager).** A person is formally designated to oversee the project across different functional areas. This person may have limited authority over the functional staff involved and serves primarily to plan and co-ordinate the project. Functional managers retain primary responsibility for their specific segments of the project.
- **Balanced matrix.** A person is assigned to oversee the project and interacts on an equal basis with functional managers. This person and the functional managers jointly direct work flow segments and approve technical and operational decisions.
- **Project matrix (or *heavyweight* project manager).** A manager is assigned to oversee the project and is responsible for the completion of the project. Functional managers' involvement is limited to assigning personnel as needed and providing advisory expertise.
- **Project team (or *tiger* team).** A manager is given responsibility of a project team composed of a core group of personnel from several functional areas and/or groups, assigned on a full-time basis. The functional managers have no formal involvement.

Although there is no clear 'winner' among the alternative organizational structures, there is wide support for structures towards the project end rather than the functional end of the continuum. In one widely respected study, Professors Clark and Fujimoto argued that heavyweight project manager structures and dedicated project teams are the most efficient forms of organization for product competitiveness, shorter lead times and technical efficiency. Other studies, although sometimes more equivocal, have shown that, in terms of the best total outcome from the development process, structures from balanced matrix through to project teams can all give high success rates. Perhaps of more interest is the suitability of the alternative structures for different types of product or service development project. Matrix structures are generally deemed to be appropriate for both simple and highly complex projects. Dedicated project teams, on the other hand, are seen as appropriate for projects with a high degree of uncertainty, where their flexibility becomes valuable.

Functionally based design processes, with resources clustered around a functional specialism, help the development of technical knowledge. Some organizations manage to capture the deep technological and skills development advantages of functional structures, while at the same time co-ordinating between the functions so as to ensure satisfactory delivery of new product and service ideas. Perhaps the best known of these organizations is Toyota. They have a strong, functionally based organization to develop their products. It adopts highly formalized development procedures to communicate between functions and places strict limits on the use of cross-functional teams. But what is really different is their approach to devising an organizational structure for product development that is appropriate for them. The argument that most companies have adopted to justify cross-functional project teams goes something like this: *'Problems with communication between traditional functions have been the main reasons for, in the past, failing to deliver new product and service ideas to specification, on time and to budget. Therefore let us break down the walls between the functions and organize resources around the individual development projects. This will ensure good communication and a market-oriented culture.'* Toyota and similar companies, on the other hand, have taken a different approach. Their argument goes something like this: *'The problem with cross-functional teams is that they can dissipate the carefully nurtured knowledge that exists within specialist functions. The real problem is how to retain this knowledge on which our future product development depends, while overcoming some of the traditional functional barriers which have inhibited communication between the functions. The solution is not to destroy the function but to devise the organizational mechanisms to ensure close control and integrative leadership which will make the functional organization work.'*[8]

Critical commentary

Each chapter contains a short critical commentary on the main ideas covered in the chapter. Its purpose is not to undermine the issues discussed in the chapter, but to emphasize that, although we present a relatively orthodox view of operation, there are other perspectives.

■ The whole process-based approach to product and service design could be interpreted as implying that all new products and services are created in response to a clear and articulated customer need. While this is usually the case, especially for products and services that are similar to (but presumably better than) their predecessors, more radical innovations are often brought about by the innovation itself creating demand. Customers don't usually know that they need something radical. For example, in the late 1970s people were not asking for microprocessors – they did not even know what they were. They were improvised by an engineer in the USA for a Japanese customer who made calculators. Only later did they become the enabling technology for the PC and after that the innumerable devices that now dominate our lives.

■ Nor do all designers agree with the concept of the possible design options being progressively reduced stage by stage. For some it is just too neat and ordered an idea to reflect accurately the creativity, arguments and chaos that sometimes characterize the design activity. First, they argue, managers do not start out with an infinite number of options. No one could process that amount of information – and anyway, designers often have some set solutions in their mind, looking for an opportunity to be used. Second, the number of options being considered often increases as time goes by. This may actually be a good thing, especially if the activity was unimaginatively specified in the first place. Third, the real process of design often involves cycling back, often many times, as potential design solutions raise fresh questions or become dead ends. In summary, the idea of the design funnel does not describe what actually happens in the design activity. Nor does it necessarily even describe what should happen.

Summary checklist

DOWNLOADABLE

This checklist comprises questions that can be usefully applied to any type of operations and reflect the major diagnostic questions used within the chapter.

- [ ] Is the importance of product or service design as a contributor to achieving strategic impact fully understood?
- [ ] Are some functions of the business more committed to product/service design than others?
- [ ] If so, have the barriers to cross-functional commitment been identified and addressed?
- [ ] Is the design process really treated as a process?
- [ ] Is the design process itself designed with the same attention to detail as any other process?
- [ ] Are design objectives specified so as to give a clear priority between quality, speed, dependability, flexibility and cost?
- [ ] Are the stages in the product/service process clearly defined?
- [ ] Are ideas for new products and services captured from all appropriate sources (including employees)?
- [ ] Are potential designs screened in a systematic manner in terms of their feasibility, acceptability and vulnerability?
- [ ] Have all possibilities for design standardization been explored?
- [ ] Have all possibilities for design commonality been explored?
- [ ] Have all possibilities for modularization of design elements been explored?
- [ ] Has the concept of mass customization been linked to the design process?
- [ ] Are potential designs thoroughly evaluated and tested before they could expose the business to financial and/or reputational risk?
- [ ] Is sufficient capacity devoted to the design process?
- [ ] Have all options for outsourcing parts of the design process been explored?
- [ ] Has the possibility of involving customers formally in the design of new products and services been explored?
- [ ] Are design technologies such as CAD and knowledge management used in the design process?
- [ ] Are product/service design and process design considered together as one integrated process?
- [ ] Is overlapping (simultaneous) design of the stages in the process used?
- [ ] Is senior management effort deployed early enough to ensure early resolution of design conflict?
- [ ] Does the organizational structure of the design process reflect its nature?

Case study   Chatsworth – the adventure playground decision

Chatsworth, the home of the 12th Duke and Duchess of Devonshire, is one of the finest and most palatial houses in the UK, set in over 1000 acres of parkland in the Peak District National Park, England. The original house was built over 400 years ago and rebuilt starting in the 17th century. The house is vast, with 175 rooms, lit by over 2000 light bulbs, and with a roof that covers 1.3 acres. Chatsworth's many rooms are full of treasures, including famous works of art by painters including Rembrandt, and tapestries, sculptures, valuable furniture, musical instruments and even 63 antique clocks which need winding every day. The gardens cover over 105 acres, with more than five miles of footpaths that guide visitors past fountains, small and large (the largest is 28 metres high), cascades, streams and ponds, all of which are fed by gravity from four large manmade lakes on the moors above the grounds. The gardens are a mix of formal and informal areas. There are sculptures, statues, rock gardens, a maze and garden views that constantly change with the seasons – all managed and maintained by a small team of 20 gardeners. Both the house and gardens are open from March to December and are just two of the experiences available to visitors. Others include an orangery gift shop, restaurant and farm shop, which are open all year round, and the surrounding park land which is open to visitors for walking, picnics and swimming in the river. The whole estate is owned and managed by an independent charity.

Close to the house and gardens, with a separate admission charge, is the farmyard and adventure playground. The farmyard is a popular attraction for families and provides for close encounters with a variety of livestock, including pigs, sheep, cows, chickens and fish. The staff provide daily milking demonstrations and animal-handling sessions. The woodland adventure playground is accessed through the farmyard and is one of the largest in the country, with a range of frames, bridges, high-level walkways, swings, chutes and slides.

Simon Seligman is the Promotions and Education Manager at Chatsworth. As head of marketing he is closely involved in the design and development of new services and facilities. He explained the way they do this at Chatsworth. *'It is a pretty abstract and organic process. Looking back over the last 25 years we either take occasional great leaps forward or make frequent little shuffles.*

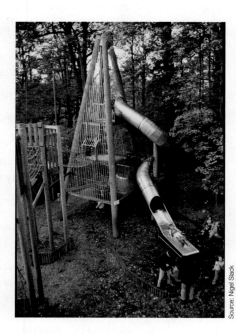

Source: Nigel Slack

The little shuffles tend to be organic changes, usually in response to visitor feedback. The great leaps forward have been the few major changes that we decided we wanted to bring about.'

One of those great leaps forward was the decision to replace the children's adventure playground attached to the farmyard, Simon explained. *'The existing adventure playground was clearly coming to the end of its life and it was time to make a decision about what to do with it. It was costing us about £18,000 each winter to maintain it and these costs were increasing year on year. We believed we could get a better one for around £100,000. The trustees asked me, the deputy estate manager with line responsibility for the farmyard and the farmyard manager to form a group and put forward a report to the trustees setting out all the options. We asked ourselves several detailed questions and some fundamental ones too, such as why are we replacing it, and should we replace it at all? We came up with four options: remove it, do nothing, replace with similar, replace with substantially better.'*

It was felt that removing the playground altogether was a realistic option. The Duke and Duchess had a view that Chatsworth should be true to its roots and traditions.

Whereas one could make an argument for a farmyard being part of a country estate, an adventure playground was considered to fit less well. The down-side would be that the lack of adventure playground, which is a big attraction for families with young children, could have an impact on visitor numbers. However, there would be savings in terms of site maintenance.

The 'do nothing' option would entail patching up the playground each year and absorbing the increasing maintenance costs. This could be a low-impact option, in the short term at least. However, it was felt that this option would simply delay the replace/remove decision by five years at most. The current playground was no longer meeting international safety standards so this could be a good opportunity to replace the playground with something similar. It was estimated that a like-for-like replacement would cost around £100,000. Replacing the playground with a substantially better one would entail a much greater cost but could have an impact on visitor numbers. Simon and his team keep a close eye on their competitors and visit them whenever they can. They reported that several other attractions had first-rate adventure playgrounds. Installing a substantially better playground could provide an opportunity for Chatsworth to leapfrog over them and offer something really special.

'We tried to cost out all four alternatives and estimate what we thought the impact on visitor numbers might be. We presented an interim report to the Duke and the other trustees. We felt that maintaining the status quo was inappropriate and a like-for-like replacement was expensive, especially given that it would attract little publicity and few additional visitors. We strongly recommended two options: either remove the playground or go for a great leap forward. The trustees asked us to bear in mind the "remove" option and take a closer look at the "substantially better" option.'

Three companies were asked to visit the site, propose a new adventure playground and develop a site plan and initial design to a budget of £150,000. All three companies provided some outline proposals for such a figure but they all added that for £200,000 they could provide something really quite special. Furthermore, the team realized that they would have to spend some additional money putting in a new ramp and a lift into the farmyard at an estimated £50,000. It was starting to look like a very expensive project. Simon takes up the story. 'One of the companies came along with a complete idea for the site based on water, which is a recurring theme in the garden at Chatsworth. They had noticed the stream running through the playground and thought it could make a wonderful feature. They told us they were reluctant to put up a single solution but wanted to work with us, really engage with us, to explore what would really work for us and how it could be achieved. They also wanted to take us to visit their German partner who made all the major pieces of equipment. So, over the next few months, together, we worked up a complete proposal for a state-of-the-art adventure playground, including the structural changes in the farmyard. The budget was £250,000. To be honest, it was impossible to know what effect this would have on visitor numbers so in the end we put in a very conservative estimate that suggested that we would make the investment back in seven years. Over the next few years we reckon the playground led to an increase in visitor numbers of 85,000 per year and so we recouped our investment in just three years.'

QUESTIONS

1 What do you think comprised the overall concept for the adventure playground?

2 Describe the four options highlighted in the case study in terms of their feasibility, acceptability and vulnerability.

3 What does the concept of interactive design mean for a service such as the adventure playground described here?

Active case study   Getting Customer #1

ACTIVE CASE

Rellacast AG specializes in the precision die casting of zinc, magnesium and aluminium alloys. It has been asked to develop a component for a large telecoms and internet systems supplier known internally as Customer #1. In fact, Customer #1 is not yet a full customer. However, for some time it has been the most important target customer in the minds of Rellacast's marketing executives.

● How would you advise Rellacast over the development of the component and the dilemmas which emerge to ensure it wins the business of Customer #1?

Please refer to the Active case on the CD accompanying this book to find out more about the company and the decisions they face in the development of the component.

Applying the principles

HINTS

Some study activities can be answered by reading the chapter. Others will require some general knowledge of business activity and some might require an element of investigation. All have hints on how they can be answered on the CD accompanying this book.

1   One product where a very wide range of product types is valued by customers is domestic paint. Most people like to express their creativity in the choice of paints and other decorating products that they use in their homes. Clearly, offering a wide range of paint must have serious cost implications for the companies that manufacture, distribute and sell the product. Visit a store that sells paint and get an idea of the range of products available on the market. How do you think paint manufacturers and retailers manage to design their products and services so as to maintain high variety but keep costs under control?

2   Design becomes particularly important at the interface between products or services and the people that use them. This is especially true for Internet-based services. Consider two types of website:

(a) those that are trying to sell something such as Amazon.com, and
(b) those that are primarily concerned with giving information, for example bbc.co.uk.

For each of these categories, what seems to constitute 'good design'? Find examples of particularly good and particularly poor Web design and explain what makes them good or bad.

3   Visit the website of the UK's Design Council (**www.design-council.org.uk**). There you will find examples of how design has provided innovation in many fields. Look through these examples and find one that you think represents excellence in design and one that you don't like (for example, because it seems trivial, or may not be practical, or for which there is no market, etc.). Prepare a case supporting your view of why one is good and the other bad. In doing this, derive a checklist of questions that could be used to assess the worth of any design idea.

4   How can the design of quick-service restaurant (fast-food) products and services be improved from the point of view of environmental sustainability? Visit two or three fast-food outlets and compare their approach to environmentally sensitive designs.

Notes on chapter

1   Sources include Doran, J. (2006) 'Hoover heading for a sell-off as Dyson sweeps up in America', *The Times*, 4 February.
2   Mass customization was first fully articulated in Pine, B.J. (1993) *Mass Customization: The new frontier in business competition,* Harvard Business School Press, Boston, MA.
3   Source: *The Economist* (2002) 'Think local', 13 April.
4   This section on resourcing is based on material from Slack, N. and Lewis, M.A. (2008) *Operations Strategy,* Second Edition, Financial Times Prentice Hall, Harlow, UK.
5   Wheelwright, S.C. and Clark, K.B. (1995) *Leading Product Development,* Free Press, New York.
6   This idea is based on one presented by Hayes, Wheelwright and Clark, in Hayes, R.H., Wheelwright, S.C. and Clark, K.B. (1988) *Dynamic Manufacturing,* Free Press, New York.
7   From an idea by Hayes, Wheelwright and Clark, *op. cit.*
8   Sobek, D.K. II, Liker, J.K. and Ward, A.K. (1998) 'Another look at how Toyota integrates product development', *Harvard Business Review,* July–August.

Taking it further

Bangle, C. (2001) 'The ultimate creativity machine: How BMW turns art into profit', *Harvard Business Review,* January, pp. 47–55. A good description of how good aesthetic design translates into business success.

Baxter, M. (1995) *Product Design,* Chapman and Hall. Presents a structured framework for product design that will be of interest to practising managers.

Blackburn, J.D. (ed.) (1991) *Time Based Competition: The next battle ground in American manufacturing,* Irwin, Homewood, IL. A good summary of why interactive design gives fast time-to-market and why this is important.

Bruce, M. and Bessant, J. (2002) *Design In Business: Strategic innovation through design,* Financial Times Prentice Hall and The Design Council. Probably one of the best overviews of design in a business context available today.

Bruce, M. and Cooper, R. (2000) *Creative Product Design: A practical guide to requirements capture management,* Wiley, Chichester. Exactly what it says.

Cooper, R. and Chew, W.B. (1996) 'Control tomorrow's costs through today's designs', *Harvard Business Review,* January–February, pp. 88–98. A really good description of why it is important to think about costs at the design stage.

Dyson, J. (1997) *Against the Odds: An autobiography,* Orion Business Books, London. One of Europe's most famous designers gives us his philosophy.

Lowe, A. and Ridgway, K. (2000) 'A user's guide to quality function deployment', *Engineering Management Journal,* June. A good overview of QFD explained in straightforward non-technical language.

Useful websites

www.cfsd.org.uk The Centre for Sustainable Design's site. Some useful resources, but obviously largely confined to sustainability issues.

www.conceptcar.co.uk A site devoted to automotive design. Fun if you like new car designs!

www.betterproductdesign.net A site that acts as a resource for good design practice. Set up by Cambridge University and the Royal College of Art. Some good material that supports all aspects of design.

www.ocw.mit.edu/OcwWeb/Sloan-School-of-Management Good source of open courseware from MIT.

www.design-council.org.uk Site of the UK's Design Council. One of the best sites in the world for design-related issues.

www.nathan.com/ed/glossary/#ED Glossary of design terms.

**FURTHER
RESOURCES**

For further resources including examples, animated diagrams, self-test questions, Excel spreadsheets, active case studies and video materials please explore the CD accompanying this book.

1-7

SUPPLY CHAIN MANAGEMENT

Introduction

An operation's ability to deliver products or services to customers is fundamentally influenced by how its supply chains are managed. Chapter 3 treated the strategic design of supply networks. This chapter considers the planning and control activity for the individual supply chains in the network. Supply chain management is the overarching operations management activity that dictates an operation's *delivery* performance because it controls the flow of products and services from suppliers right through to the end customer. That is why it is the first chapter dealing with the planning and control of delivery. But planning and controlling delivery is a much larger topic and includes capacity management (Chapter 8), inventory management (Chapter 9), resource planning and control (Chapter 10) and lean synchronization (Chapter 11). Figure 7.1 illustrates these 'delivery' topics treated in this chapter.

Source: Courtesy of SAB Miller plc

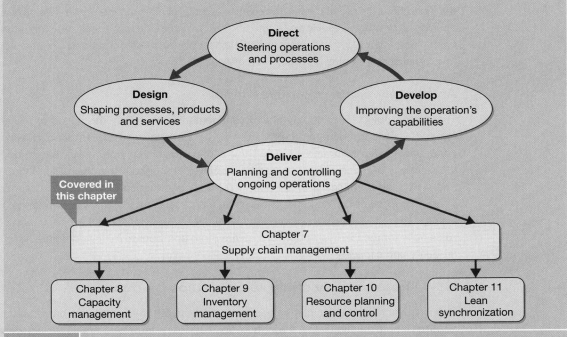

| Figure 7.1 | Supply chain management is the management of the relationships and flows between operations and processes; it is the topic that integrates all the issues concerning the delivery of products and services |

Executive summary

VIDEO
further detail

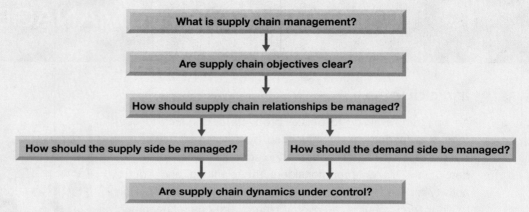

Decision logic chain for supply chain management

Each chapter is structured around a set of diagnostic questions. These questions suggest what you should ask in order to gain an understanding of the important issues of a topic, and as a result, improve your decision making. An executive summary, addressing these questions, is provided below.

What is supply chain management?

Supply chain management is the management of relationships and flows between operations and processes. Technically, it is different from supply network management, which looks at all the operations or processes in a network. Supply chain management refers to a string of operations or processes. However, the two terms are often used interchangeably. Many of the principles of managing external supply chains (flow between operations) are also applicable to internal supply chains (flow between processes).

Are supply chain objectives clear?

The central objective of supply chain management is to satisfy the needs of the end customer. So, each operation in the chain should contribute to whatever mix of quality, speed, dependability, flexibility and cost that the end customer requires. An individual operation's failure in any of these objectives can be multiplied throughout the chain. So, although each operation's performance may be adequate, the performance of the whole chain could be poor. An important distinction is between lean and agile supply chain performance. Broadly, lean (or efficient) supply chains are appropriate for stable 'functional' products and services, while agile (or responsive) supply chains are more appropriate for less predictable innovative products and services.

How should supply chain relationships be managed?

Supply chain relationships can be described on a spectrum from market-based, transactional, 'arms length' relationships, through to close and long-term partnership relationships. Each has its advantages and disadvantages. Developing relationships involves assessing which relationship will provide the best potential for developing overall performance. However, the types of relationships adopted may be dictated by the structure of the market itself. If the number of potential suppliers is small, there are few opportunities to use market mechanisms to gain any kind of advantage.

How should the supply side be managed?

Managing supply side relationships involves three main activities: selecting appropriate suppliers, planning and controlling ongoing supply activity, and supplier development. Supplier selection involves trading off different supplier attributes, often using scoring assessment methods. Managing ongoing supply involves clarifying supply expectations, often using service-level agreements to manage the supply relationships. Supplier development can benefit both suppliers and customers, especially in partnership relationships. Sometimes barriers to this are the mismatches in perception between customers and suppliers.

How should the demand side be managed?

This will depend partly on whether demand is dependent on some known factor and therefore predictable, or independent of any known factor and therefore less predictable. Approaches such as materials requirements planning (MRP) are used in the former case, while approaches such as inventory management are used in the latter case. The increasing outsourcing of physical distribution and the use of new tracking technologies, such as RFID, have brought efficiencies to the movement of physical goods and customer service. But customer service may be improved even more if suppliers take on responsibility for customer development, i.e. helping customers to help themselves.

Are supply chain dynamics under control?

Supply chains have a dynamic of their own that is often called the *bullwhip* effect. It means that relatively small changes at the demand end of the chain increasingly amplify into large disturbances as they move upstream. Three methods can be used to reduce this effect. Information sharing can prevent over-reaction to immediate stimuli and give a better view of the whole chain. Channel alignment through standardized planning and control methods allows for easier co-ordination of the whole chain. Improving the operational efficiency of each part of the chain prevents local errors multiplying to affect the whole chain.

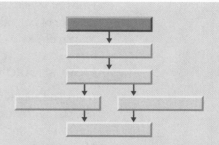

DIAGNOSTIC QUESTION

What is supply chain management?

Supply chain management (SCM) is the management of the relationships and flows between the 'string' of operations and processes that produce value in the form of products and services to the ultimate consumer. It is a holistic approach to managing across the boundaries of companies and of processes. Technically, supply *chains* are different from supply *networks*. A supply network is *all* the operations that are linked together so as to provide goods and services through to end customers. In large supply networks there can be many hundreds of supply chains of linked operations passing through a single operation. The same distinction holds within operations. Internal supply network, and supply chain, management concerns flow between processes or departments. See Figure 7.2. Confusingly, the terms supply network and supply chain management are often used interchangeably.

> **Operations principle**
> The supply chain concept applies to the internal relationships between processes as well as the external relationships between operations.

It is worth emphasizing again that the supply chain concept applies to internal process networks as well as external supply networks. Many of the ideas discussed in the context of the 'operation-to-operation' supply chain also apply to the 'process-to-process' internal supply chain. It is also worth noting that the 'flows' in supply chains are not restricted to

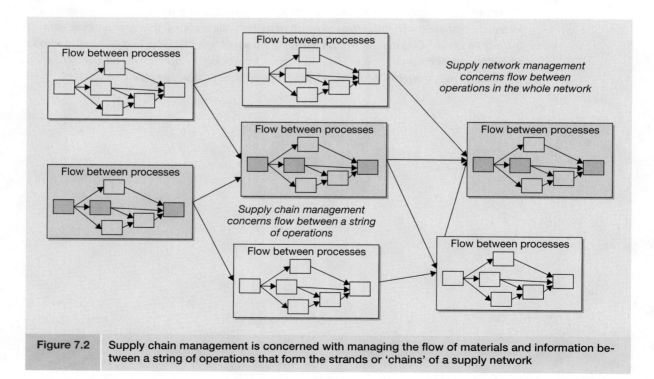

Figure 7.2   Supply chain management is concerned with managing the flow of materials and information between a string of operations that form the strands or 'chains' of a supply network

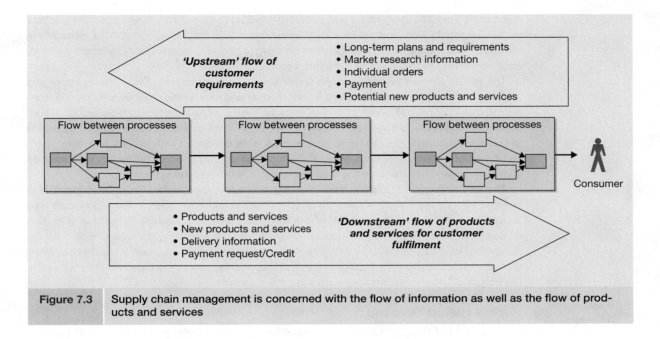

Figure 7.3 Supply chain management is concerned with the flow of information as well as the flow of products and services

the downstream flow of products and services from suppliers through to customers. Although the most obvious failure in supply chain management occurs when downstream flow fails to meet customer requirements, the root cause may be a failure in the upstream flow of information. Modern supply chain management is as much concerned with managing information flows (upstream and downstream) as it is with managing the flow of products and services – see Figure 7.3.

The following two examples of supply chain management illustrate some of the issues that are discussed in this chapter.

Example   Siemens 'SCOR' a success[1]

Siemens AG, with over 450,000 people, sales of around €70 billion and operating in more than 190 countries, is one of the world's top five electrical engineering and electronics companies, pro-

ducing products from mobile phones to power plants. Since the late 1990s Siemens has used the Supply Chain Operations Reference (SCOR) model to improve its supply chain efficiency and process performance. (The SCOR model is explained later in this chapter.) The implementation of the model was initially intended to support the company's move to a considerably stronger focus on e-business. Teams of more than 250 internal change agents were formed, starting to review strategies, opportunities and challenges.

Siemens initially developed what it called its 'Generic Business Process' version of the SCOR model so that it could be applied in all its markets. However, it soon realized that different kinds of business required different supply chain solutions. For example, Siemens used SCOR to streamline the make-to-order processes of its 'Siemens Medical Solutions' business whose Computed Tomography (CT) devices are made in Germany and China. This was a particularly difficult business involving 'make-to-order' functions such as the global management of customer orders, comprehensive and complex material management, customization and production, technical support, worldwide dispatch and logistics, and installation at the customer's site. Yet while Siemens was the clear innovation leader, before the SCOR initiative its inflexible and bureaucratic processes had resulted in long waits for customers, high levels of inventory and high costs. The CT supply chain was not connected, with little common understanding of how processes should work or what its supply objectives should be. Internal operations managers in the supply chain answered to headquarters rather than to end customers and conflicting perform-ance objectives led to fluctuating demands throughout the chain.

The SCOR process helped Siemens tackle these problems directly. Order management and planning and control processes moved from individual and fragmented order handling to the man-agement of all worldwide customer orders, sourcing was simplified and integrated using 22 'A sup-pliers' rather than the 250 used previously, production of small quantities was organized according to customer specifications, strategic partnerships were developed with service providers, quick installation of systems directly delivered to customer sites using qualified CT factory personal was implemented, and 'reverse logistics' was employed to refurbish used systems.

The improvements in supply chain performance were spectacular. Order to delivery time reduced from 22 weeks to 2 weeks, the simplified and transparent order on the factories allowed two production lines to do the work of the four used previously, factory throughput time was reduced from 13 days to 6 days, flexibility was increased tremendously to a level of ±50% orders per month, inventory levels were reduced significantly enabling CT to divest a warehouse, direct shipments non stop from the factory to the customer enabled delivery to customer sites within five working days and also allowed customers to track shipments.

| Example |

Supply risk at Gap Inc.[2]

Gap Inc. is a $15.9 billion leading international retailer selling clothing, accessories and personal care products. Its brands include the Banana Republic, Old Navy and Piperlime names but it is

best known for its chain of Gap stores throughout the United States, United Kingdom, Canada, France, Ireland and Japan as well as Asia and the Middle East. The countries from which it sources its products are similarly international, from Sri Lanka to Lesotho, the United States to El Salvador. But an international supply base carries some significant risks.

In October 2007 evidence appeared in *The Observer*, a British news-paper, that an unauthorized subcontractor had used child workers to make blouses for GapKids at a factory in Delhi. In response Gap immedi-ately issued a statement. *'Earlier this week, the company was informed about an allegation of child labor at a facility in India that was working on one product for GapKids. An investigation was immediately launched. The company noted that a very small portion of a particular order placed with one of its vendors was apparently subcontracted to an unauthorized subcontractor without the company's knowledge or approval. This is in direct violation of the company's agreement with the vendor under its Code of Vendor Conduct. Marka Hansen, president of Gap North America, made the following statement today.*

"We strictly prohibit the use of child labor. This is a non-negotiable for us – and we are deeply concerned and upset by this allegation. As we've demonstrated in the past, Gap has a history of addressing challenges like this head-on, and our approach to this situation will be no exception. In 2006, Gap Inc. ceased business with 23 factories due to code violations. We have 90 people located around the world whose job is to ensure compliance with our Code of Vendor Conduct. As soon as we were alerted to this situation, we stopped the work order and prevented the product from being sold in stores. While violations of our strict prohibition on child labor in factories that produce product for the company are extremely rare, we have called an urgent meeting with our suppliers in the region to reinforce our policies. Gap Inc. has one of the industry's most comprehensive programs in place to fight for workers' rights overseas. We will continue to work with the government, NGOs, trade unions, and other stakeholder organizations in an effort to end the use of child labor."'

Gap's new policy on violations of its child-labour rules may help to limit the damage to its repu-tation as one of the most ethical retailers. Rather than immediately closing supplier factories that employ child workers, it now stops suppliers using children, continues to pay them, but insists suppliers provide them with an education and guarantees them a job once they reach the legal age.

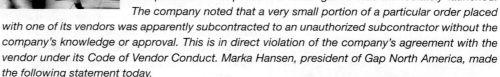

For any company sourcing its products around the world, maintaining a rigorous monitoring regime on faraway subcontractors is never going to be easy. Many of Gap's clothes are made in India, where an estimated 50,000,000 children are employed. Yet the International Labour Organization (ILO) of the United Nations believes all companies could do more. '*If companies are capable of supervising the quality of their products, they should also be able to police their production,*' says Geir Myrstad, head of the ILO's programme to eliminate child labour.

What do these two examples have in common?

The first lesson from these two companies is that they both have good reasons for taking supply chain management seriously. They understand that, no matter how good individual operations or processes are, a business's overall performance is a function of the whole chain of which it is a part. That is why both of these companies put so much effort into managing the whole chain. This does not mean that both companies adopt the same, or even similar, approaches to supply chain management. Each has a slightly different set of priorities. The key issue for Siemens was to improve the performance of one of its supply chains to make it more appropriate for the market that it served. The issue for Gap Inc. in this particular example was to overcome the negative publicity it had received in spite of its very significant efforts to ensure the ethical credentials of its supply network. Between them, these two examples illustrate two of the debates within supply chain management. First, can frameworks such as the SCOR model help to improve supply chain performance? Second, what risks are inherent in the way companies manage their supply chains? The commonality between the two companies is that, although their supply chain issues are different, both have a clear idea of what they are. Similarly, both companies understand the importance of managing relationships. The common theme is the importance of investing in relationships. In addition, both companies have invested in mechanisms for communicating along the supply chain and co-ordinating material and information flows. The rest of this chapter is structured around these three main issues: clarifying supply chain objectives; supply chain relationships, both with suppliers and with customers; and controlling and co-ordinating flow.

DIAGNOSTIC QUESTION

Are supply chain objectives clear?

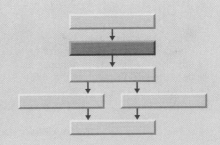

All supply chain management shares one common, and central, objective – to satisfy the end customer. All stages in a chain must eventually include consideration of the final customer, no matter how far an individual operation is from the end customer. When a customer decides to make a purchase, he or she triggers action back along the whole chain. All the businesses in the supply chain pass on portions of that end customer's money to each other, each retaining a margin for the value it has added. Each operation in the chain should be satisfying its own customer, but also making sure that eventually the end customer is also satisfied.

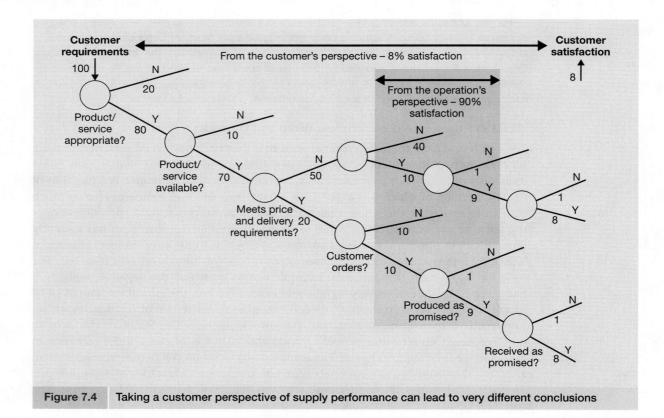

Figure 7.4   Taking a customer perspective of supply performance can lead to very different conclusions

For a demonstration of how end customer perceptions of supply satisfaction can be very different from that of a single operation, examine the customer 'decision tree' in Figure 7.4. It charts the hypothetical progress of 100 customers requiring service (or products) from a business (for example, a printer requiring paper from an industrial paper stockist). Supply performance, as seen by the core operation (the warehouse), is represented by the shaded part of the diagram. It has received 20 orders, 18 of which were 'produced' (shipped to customers) as promised (on time, and in full). However, originally 100 customers may have requested service, 20 of whom found the business did not have appropriate products (did not stock the right paper), 10 of whom could not be served because the products were not available (out of stock), and 50 of whom were not satisfied with the price and/or delivery (of whom 10 placed an order notwithstanding). Of the 20 orders received, 18 were produced as promised (shipped) but two were not received as promised (delayed or damaged in transport). So what seems a 90 per cent supply performance is in fact an 8 per cent performance from the customer's perspective.

> **Operations principle**
> The performance of an operation in a supply chain does not necessarily reflect the performance of the whole supply chain.

This is just one operation in a whole network. Include the cumulative effect of similar reductions in performance for all the operations in a chain, and the probability that the end customer is adequately served could become remote. The point here is not that all supply chains have unsatisfactory supply performances (although most supply chains have considerable potential for improvement). Rather it is that the performance both of the supply chain as a whole, and of its constituent operations, should be judged in terms of how all end customer needs are satisfied.

Supply chain objectives

The objective of supply chain management is to meet the requirements of end customers by supplying appropriate products and services when they are needed, at a competitive cost. Doing this requires the supply chain to achieve appropriate levels of the five operations performance objectives – quality, speed, dependability, flexibility and cost.

Quality

The quality of a product or service when it reaches the customer is a function of the quality performance of every operation in the chain that supplied it. The implication of this is that errors in each stage of the chain can become multiplied in their effect on end customer service. For example, if each of seven stages in a supply chain has a 1 per cent error rate, only 93.2 per cent of products or services will be of good quality on reaching the end customer (i.e. 0.99^7). This is why only by every stage taking some responsibility for its own *and its suppliers'* performance, can a supply chain achieve high end customer quality.

Speed

This has two meanings in a supply chain context. The first is how fast customers can be served (the elapsed time between a customer requesting a product or service and receiving it in full), an important element in any business's ability to compete. However, fast customer response can be achieved simply by over-resourcing or over-stocking within the supply chain. For example, very large stocks in a retail operation can reduce the chances of stock-out to almost zero, so reducing customer waiting time virtually to zero. Similarly, an accounting firm may be able to respond quickly to customer demand by having a very large number of accountants on standby waiting for demand that may (or may not) occur. An alternative perspective on speed is the time taken for goods and services to move through the chain. So, for example, products that move quickly down a supply chain from raw material suppliers through to retailers will spend little time as inventory because, to achieve fast throughput time, material cannot dwell for significant periods as inventory. This in turn reduces the working capital requirements and other inventory costs in the supply chain, so reducing the overall cost of delivering to the end customer. Achieving a balance between speed as responsiveness to customers' demands and speed as fast throughput (although they are not incompatible) will depend on how the supply chain is choosing to compete.

Dependability

Dependability in a supply chain context is similar to speed in so much as one can almost guarantee 'on-time' delivery by keeping excessive resources, such as inventory, within the chain. However, dependability of throughput time is a much more desirable aim because it reduces uncertainty within the chain. If the individual operations in a chain do not deliver as promised on time, there will be a tendency for customers to over-order, or order early, so as to provide some kind of insurance against late delivery. The same argument applies if there is uncertainty regarding the *quantity* of products or services delivered. This is why delivery dependability is often measured as 'on time, in full' in supply chains.

Flexibility

In a supply chain context, this is usually taken to mean the chain's ability to cope with changes and disturbances. Very often this is referred to as supply chain agility. The concept of agility includes previously discussed issues such as focusing on the end customer and ensuring fast throughput and responsiveness to customer needs. But, in addition, agile supply chains are sufficiently flexible to cope with changes, either in the nature of customer demand or in the supply capabilities of operations within the chain.

Cost

FURTHER EXAMPLE

In addition to the costs incurred within each operation to transform its inputs into outputs, the supply chain as a whole incurs additional costs that derive from each operation in a chain doing business with each other. These transaction costs may include such things as the costs of finding appropriate suppliers, setting up contractual agreements, monitoring supply performance, transporting products between operations, holding inventories, and so on. Many of the recent developments in supply chain management, such as partnership agreements or reducing the number of suppliers, are an attempt to minimize transaction costs.

Should supply chains be lean or agile?

A distinction is often drawn between supply chains that are managed to emphasize supply chain efficiency (lean supply chains), and those that emphasize supply chain responsiveness and flexibility (agile supply chains). These two modes of managing supply chains are reflected in an idea proposed by Professor Marshall Fisher of Wharton Business School,[3] that supply chains serving different markets should be managed in different ways. Even companies that have seemingly similar products or services, in fact, may compete in different ways with different products. For example, shoe manufacturers may produce classics that change little over the years, as well as fashion shoes that last only one season. Chocolate manufacturers have stable lines that have been sold for 50 years, but also product 'specials' associated with an event or film release, the latter selling only for a matter of months. Hospitals have routine 'standardized' surgical procedures such as cataract removal, but also have to provide emergency post-trauma surgery. Demand for the former products will be relatively stable and predictable, but demand for the latter will be far more uncertain. Also, the profit margin commanded by the innovative product will probably be higher than that of the more functional product. However, the price (and therefore the margin) of the innovative product may drop rapidly once it has become unfashionable in the market.

The supply chain policies that are seen to be appropriate for functional products and innovative products are termed efficient (or lean), and responsive (or agile) supply chain policies, respectively. Efficient supply chain policies include keeping inventories low, especially in the downstream parts of the network, so as to maintain fast throughput and reduce the amount of working capital tied up in the inventory. What inventory there is in the network is concentrated mainly in the manufacturing operation, where it can keep utilization high and therefore manufacturing costs low. Information must flow quickly up and down the chain from retail outlets back up to the manufacturer so that schedules can be given the maximum amount of time to adjust efficiently. The chain is then managed to make sure that products flow as quickly as possible down the chain to replenish what few stocks are kept downstream.

> **Operations principle**
> Supply chains with different end objectives need managing differently.

> **Operations principle**
> 'Functional' products require lean supply chain management; 'innovative' products require agile supply chain management.

By contrast, responsive supply chain policy stresses high service levels and responsive supply to the end customer. The inventory in the network will be deployed as closely as possible to the customer. In this way, the chain can still supply even when dramatic changes occur in customer demand. Fast throughput from the upstream parts of the chain will still be needed to replenish downstream stocks. But those downstream stocks are needed to ensure high levels of availability to end customers. Figure 7.5 illustrates how the different supply chain policies match the different market requirements implied by functional and innovative products.

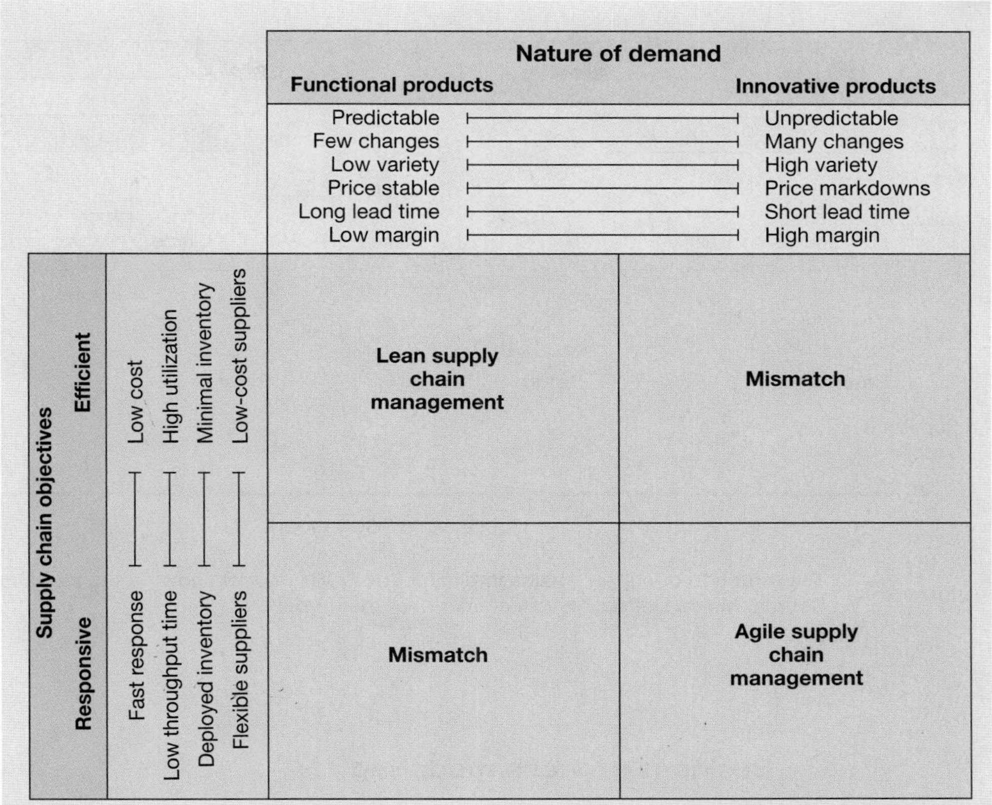

		Nature of demand	
		Functional products	**Innovative products**
		Predictable ⊢————————⊣ Unpredictable Few changes ⊢————————⊣ Many changes Low variety ⊢————————⊣ High variety Price stable ⊢————————⊣ Price markdowns Long lead time ⊢————————⊣ Short lead time Low margin ⊢————————⊣ High margin	

Supply chain objectives

Efficient — Low cost, High utilization, Minimal inventory, Low-cost suppliers

Responsive — Fast response, Low throughput time, Deployed inventory, Flexible suppliers

	Functional products	Innovative products
Efficient	**Lean supply chain management**	**Mismatch**
Responsive	**Mismatch**	**Agile supply chain management**

Figure 7.5   **Matching the operations resources in the supply chain with market requirements**

Source: Adapted from Fisher, M.C. (1997) 'What is the Right Supply Chain for Your Product?' *Harvard Business Review,* March–April, pp. 105–116.

The SCOR model[4]

The Supply Chain Operations Reference (SCOR) model is a broad but highly structured and systematic framework to supply chain improvement that has been developed by the Supply Chain Council (SCC), a global non-profit consortium. The framework uses a methodology, and diagnostic and benchmarking tools that are increasingly widely accepted for evaluating and comparing supply chain activities and their performance. Just as important, the SCOR model allows its users to improve and communicate supply chain management practices within and between all interested parties in the supply chain by using a standard language and a set of structured definitions. The SCC also provides a benchmarking database by which companies can compare their supply chain performance with others in their industries and training classes. Companies that have used the model include BP, AstraZeneca, Shell, SAP AG, Siemens AG and Bayer.

The model uses three well-known individual techniques turned into an integrated approach. These are:

- business process modelling
- benchmarking performance
- best-practice analysis.

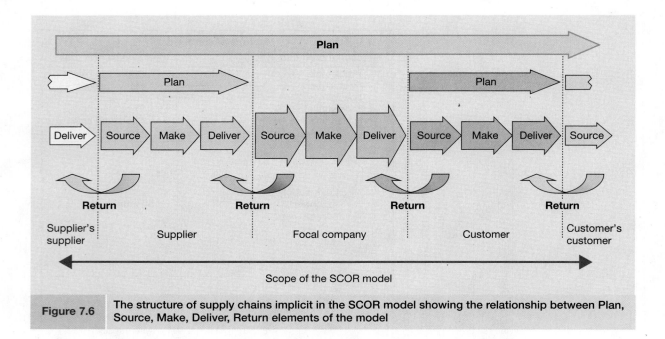

Figure 7.6 The structure of supply chains implicit in the SCOR model showing the relationship between Plan, Source, Make, Deliver, Return elements of the model

Business process modelling

SCOR does not represent organizations or functions but rather a network of processes. Each basic 'link' in the supply chain is made up of five types of process, each being a 'supplier–customer' relationship (see Figure 7.6).

- 'Plan' processes manage each of these customer–supplier links and balance the activity of the supply chain. They are the supply and demand reconciliation process, which includes prioritization when needed.
- 'Source' is the procurement, delivery, receipt and transfer of raw-material items, sub-assemblies, product and/or services.
- 'Make' is the transformation process of adding value to products and services through mixing production operations processes.
- 'Deliver' processes perform all customer-facing order-management and fulfilment activities including outbound logistics.
- 'Return' processes look after the reverse logistics flow of moving material back from end customers up-stream in the supply chain because of product defects or post-delivery customer support.

All these processes are modelled at increasingly detailed levels (see Chapter 4 for a description of the different levels of process analysis). The first level (level 1) identifies the five processes and allows managers to set the scope of the business issues. The SCC advocates the idea that 'if it isn't broken, don't model it'. If no problem has been identified in a particular area, it will be of no significant help to map processes in any further detail. More detailed modelling (level 2) identifies which type of supply chain configuration the company operates, for example make-to-stock, make-to-order or engineer-to-order environment. Yet more detailed process modelling (level 3) is then done in terms of the company's ability to compete successfully in its chosen markets.

Benchmarking performance

Performance metrics in the SCOR model are also structured by level, as is process analysis. Level 1 metrics are the yardsticks by which an organization can measure how successful it is in achieving its desired positioning within the competitive environment, as measured by the performance of a particular supply chain. These level 1 metrics are the key performance indicators of the chain and are created from lower-level diagnostic metrics (called 'diagnostic' or level 2 and level 3 metrics) which are calculated on the performance of lower-level processes. Some metrics do not 'roll up' to level 1 – these are intended to diagnose variations in performance against plan.

Best-practice analysis

Best-practice analysis follows the benchmarking activity that should have measured the performance of the supply chain processes and identified the main performance gaps. Best-practice analysis identifies the activities that need to be performed to close the gaps. SCC members have identified more than 400 'best practices' derived from their experience. The definition of a 'best practice' in the SCOR model is one that:

- is current – neither untested (emerging) nor outdated
- is structured – it has clearly defined goals, scope and processes
- is proven – there has been some clearly demonstrated success
- is repeatable – it has been demonstrated to be effective in various contexts
- has an unambiguous method – the practice can be connected to business processes, operations strategy, technology, supply relationships, and information- or knowledge-management systems
- has a positive impact on results – operations improvement can be linked to KPIs.

The SCOR roadmap

The SCOR model can be implemented by using a five-phase project 'roadmap'. Within this roadmap lies a collection of tools and techniques that both help to implement and support the SCOR framework. In fact, many of these tools are commonly used management-decision tools such as Pareto charts, cause–effect diagrams, maps of material flow, brainstorming, etc.

The roadmap has the five stages as follows.

Phase 1: Discover – involves supply chain definition and prioritization where a 'project charter' sets the scope for the project. This identifies logic groupings of supply chains within the scope of the project. The priorities, based on a weighted rating method, determine which supply chains should be dealt with first. This phase also identifies the resources that are required, identified and secured through business process owners/actors.

Phase 2: Analyze – using data from benchmarking and competitive analysis, the appropriate level of performance metrics is identified, that will define the strategic requirements of each supply chain.

Phase 3: Material flow design – in this phase the project teams have their first go at creating a common understanding of how processes can be developed. The current state of processes is identified and an initial analysis attempts to see where there are opportunities for improvement.

Phase 4: Work and information flow design – the project teams collect and analyze the work involved in all relevant processes (plan, source, make, deliver and return) and map the productivity and yield of all transactions.

Phase 5: Implementation planning – this is the final phase for communicating the findings of the project. Its purpose is to transfer the knowledge of the SCOR team(s) to individual implementation or deployment teams.

Benefits of the SCOR model

Claimed benefits from using the SCOR model include improved process understanding and performance, improved supply chain performance, increased customer satisfaction and retention, a decrease in required capital, better profitability and return on investment, and increased productivity. Although most of these results could arguably be expected when any company starts focusing on business processes improvements, SCOR proponents argue that using the model gives an above-average and supply-focused improvement.

DIAGNOSTIC QUESTION

How should supply chain relationships be managed?

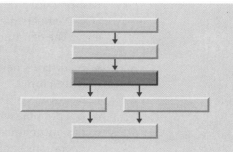

The 'relationship' between operations in a supply chain is the basis on which the exchange of products, services, information and money is conducted. Managing supply chains is about managing relationships, because relationships influence the smooth flow between operations and processes. Different forms of relationship will be appropriate in different circumstances. An obvious but important factor in determining the importance of relationships to any operation is the extent to which they outsource their activities. In Chapter 3 we distinguished between non-vertically integrated operations that outsource almost all activities, and vertically integrated operations that outsource almost nothing. Only extremely vertically integrated businesses are able to ignore the question of how to manage customer–supplier relationships (because they do everything themselves). Initially, we can examine this question by describing two seemingly opposite approaches to managing relationships – arms-length, market-based, *transactional* relationships and close, longer-term, *partnership* relationships.

FURTHER EXAMPLE

Market-based 'transactional' relationships

Transactional relationships involve purchasing goods and services in a 'pure' market fashion, often seeking the 'best' supplier every time it is necessary to make a purchase. Each transaction effectively becomes a separate decision. The relationship may be short term, with no guarantee of further trading between the parties once the goods or services are delivered and payment is made.[5] The *advantages* of traditional market transactional relationships are usually seen as follows:

- They maintain competition between alternative suppliers. This promotes a constant drive between suppliers to provide best value.
- A supplier specializing in a small number of products or services, but supplying them to many customers, can gain natural economies of scale, enabling the supplier to offer

the products and services at a lower price than if customers performed the activities themselves on a smaller scale.

- There is inherent flexibility in outsourced supplies. If demand changes, customers can simply change the number and type of suppliers – a faster and cheaper alternative to redirecting internal activities.
- Innovations can be exploited no matter where they originate. Specialist suppliers are more likely to come up with innovations that can be acquired faster and cheaper than by developing them in-house.

There are, however, *disadvantages* in buying in a totally 'free market' manner:

- Suppliers owe little loyalty to customers. If supply is difficult, there is no guarantee of receiving supply.
- Choosing who to buy from takes time and effort. Gathering sufficient information and making decisions continually are, in themselves, activities that need to be resourced.

Short-term market-based relationships of this type may be appropriate when new companies are being considered as more regular suppliers, or when purchases are one-off or very irregular. For example, the replacement of all the windows in a company's office block would typically involve this type of competitive-tendering market relationship.

Long-term 'partnership' relationships

Partnership relationships in supply chains are sometimes seen as a compromise between vertical integration on the one hand (owning the resources that supply you) and transactional relationships on the other. Partnership relationships are defined as:[6]

> . . . relatively enduring inter-firm cooperative agreements, involving flows and linkages that use resources and/or governance structures from autonomous organizations, for the joint accomplishment of individual goals linked to the corporate mission of each sponsoring firm.

This means that suppliers and customers are expected to co-operate, even to the extent of sharing skills and resources, to achieve joint benefits beyond those they could have achieved by acting alone. At the heart of the concept of partnership lies the issue of the *closeness* of the relationship. Partnerships are close relationships, the degree of which is influenced by a number of factors, as follows:

- *Sharing success* – both partners jointly benefit from the co-operation rather than manoeuvring to maximize their own individual contribution.
- *Long-term expectations* – relatively long-term commitments, but not necessarily permanent ones.
- *Multiple points of contact* – communication not restricted to formal channels, but may take place between many individuals in both organizations.
- *Joint learning* – a relationship commitment to learn from each other's experience.
- *Few relationships* – a commitment on the part of both parties to limit the number of customers or suppliers with whom they do business.

- *Joint co-ordination of activities* – fewer relationships allow joint co-ordination of activities such as the flow of materials or service, payment, and so on.
- *Information transparency* – confidence built through information exchange between the partners.
- *Joint problem solving* – jointly approaching problems can increase closeness over time.
- *Trust* – probably the key element in partnership relationships. In this context, trust means the willingness of one party to relate to the other on the understanding that the relationship will be beneficial to both, even though that cannot be guaranteed. Trust is widely held to be both the key issue in successful partnerships, but also, by far, the most difficult element to develop and maintain.

Which type of relationship?

> **Operations principle**
> All supply chain relationships lie on a spectrum from 'transactional' to 'partnership'.

It is very unlikely that any business will find it sensible to engage exclusively in one type of relationship or another. Most businesses will have a portfolio of, possibly, widely differing relationships. Also, there are degrees to which any particular relationship can be managed on a transactional or partnership basis. The real question is: Where, on the spectrum from transactional to partnership, should each relationship be positioned? And, while there is no simple formula for choosing the 'ideal' form of relationship in each case, there are some important factors that can sway the decision.

The most obvious issue will concern how a business intends to compete in its marketplace. If price is the main competitive factor then the relationship could be determined by which approach offers the highest potential savings. On one hand, market-based transactional relationships could minimize the actual price paid for purchased products and services, while partnerships could minimize the transaction costs of doing business. If a business is competing primarily on product or service innovation, the type of relationship may depend on where innovation is likely to happen. If innovation depends on close collaboration between supplier and customer, partnership relationships are needed. On the other hand, if suppliers are busily competing to out-do each other in terms of their innovations, and especially if the market is turbulent and fast growing (as with many software and Internet-based industries), then it may be preferable to retain the freedom to change suppliers quickly using market mechanisms. However, if markets are very turbulent, partnership relationships may reduce the risks of being unable to secure supply.

The main differences between the two ends of this relationship spectrum concern whether a customer sees advantage in long-term or short-term relationships. Transactional relationships can be either long or short term, but there is no guarantee of anything beyond the immediate transaction. They are appropriate when short-term benefits are important. Many relationships and many businesses are best served by concentrating on the short term (especially if, without short-term success, there is no long term). Partnership relationships are by definition long term. There is a commitment to work together over time to gain mutual advantage. The concept of mutuality is important here. A supplier does not become a 'partner' merely by being called one. True partnership implies mutual benefit, and often mutual sacrifice. Partnership means giving up some freedom of action in order to gain something more beneficial over the long term. If it is not in the culture of a business to give up some freedom of action, it is very unlikely to ever make a success of partnerships.

> **Operations principle**
> True 'partnership' relationships involve mutual sacrifice as well as mutual benefit.

Opportunities to develop relationships can be limited by the structure of the market itself. If the number of potential suppliers is small, there may be few opportunities to use market mechanisms to gain any kind of supply advantage and it would probably be sensible to develop a close relationship with at least one supplier. On the other hand, if there are many potential suppliers, and especially if it is easy to judge the capabilities of the suppliers, transactional relationships are likely to be best.

How should the supply side be managed?

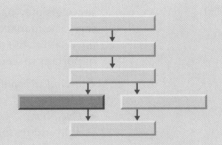

The ability of any process or operation to produce outputs is dependent on the inputs it receives. So good supply management is a necessary (but not sufficient) condition for effective operations management in general. It involves three main activities: selecting appropriate suppliers, planning and controlling the ongoing supply activity, and developing and improving suppliers' capabilities. All three activities are usually the responsibility of the purchasing or procurement function within the business. Purchasing should provide a vital link between the operation itself and its suppliers. They should understand the requirements of all the processes within their own operation and also the capabilities of the suppliers who could potentially provide products and services for the operation.

Supplier selection

Excel

Choosing appropriate suppliers should involve trading off alternative attributes. Rarely are potential suppliers so clearly superior to their competitors that the decision is self-evident. Most businesses find it best to adopt some kind of supplier 'scoring' or assessment procedure. This should be capable of rating alternative suppliers in terms of factors such as the following:

- Range of products or services provided
- Quality of products or services
- Responsiveness
- Dependability of supply
- Delivery and volume flexibility
- Total cost of being supplied
- Ability to supply in the required quantity.

In addition, there are likely to be less quantifiable or longer-term factors that will need taking into consideration. These may include the following:

- Potential for innovation
- Ease of doing business
- Willingness to share risk
- Long-term commitment to supply
- Ability to transfer knowledge as well as products and services.

Choosing suppliers should involve evaluating the relative importance of all these factors. So, for example, a business might choose a supplier who, although more expensive than alternative suppliers, has an excellent reputation for on-time delivery, because that is more appropriate to the way the business competes itself, or because the high level of

> **Operations principle**
> Supplier selection should reflect overall supply chain objectives.

supply dependability allows the business to hold lower stock levels, which may even save costs overall. Other trade-offs may be more difficult to calculate. For example, a potential supplier may have high levels of technical capability, but may be financially weak, with a small but finite risk of going out of business. Other suppliers may have little track record of supplying the products or services required, but show the managerial talent and energy for potential customers to view developing a supply relationship as an investment in future capability. But to make sensible trade-offs it is important to assess four basic capabilities:

- *Technical capability* – the product or service knowledge to supply to high levels of specification.
- *Operations capability* – the process knowledge to ensure consistent, responsive, dependable and reasonable cost supply.
- *Financial capability* – the financial strength to fund the business in both the short term and the long term.
- *Managerial capability* – the management talent and energy to develop supply potential in the future.

Single- or multi-sourcing

A closely linked decision is whether to source each individual product or service from one, or more than one, supplier (single-sourcing or multi-sourcing). Some of the advantages and disadvantages of single- and multi-sourcing are shown in Table 7.1.

Table 7.1	Advantages and disadvantages of single- and multi-sourcing	
	Single-sourcing	**Multi-sourcing**
Advantages	• Potentially better quality because of more supplier quality assurance possibilities • Strong relationships that are more durable • Greater dependency encourages more commitment and effort • Better communication • Easier to co-operate on new product/service development • More economies of scale • Higher confidentiality	• Purchaser can drive price down by competitive tendering • Can switch sources in case of supply failure • Wide sources of knowledge and expertise to tap
Disadvantages	• More vulnerable to disruption if a failure to supply occurs • Individual supplier more affected by volume fluctuations • Supplier might exert upward pressure on prices if no alternative supplier is available	• Difficult to encourage commitment from suppliers • Less easy to develop effective supplier quality assurance • More effort needed to communicate • Suppliers less likely to invest in new processes • More difficult to obtain economies of scale

It may seem as though companies who multi-source do so exclusively for their own short-term benefit. However, this is not always the case: multi-sourcing can have an altruistic motive, or at least one that brings benefits to both supplier and purchaser in the long term. For example, Robert Bosch GmbH, the German automotive components manufacturer and distributor, at one time required that sub-contractors do no more than 20 per cent of their total business with them.[7] This was to prevent suppliers becoming too dependent on them. The purchasing organization could then change volumes up and down without pushing the supplier into bankruptcy. However, despite these perceived advantages, there has been a trend for purchasing functions to reduce their supplier base in terms of numbers of companies supplying any one part or service, mainly because it reduces the costs of transacting business.

Purchasing, the Internet and e-commerce

For some years, electronic means have been used by businesses to confirm purchased orders and ensure payment to suppliers. The rapid development of the Internet, however, opened up the potential for far more fundamental changes in purchasing behaviour. Partly this was as the result of supplier information made available through the Internet. Previously, a purchaser of industrial components may have been predisposed to return to suppliers who had been used before. There was inertia in the purchasing process because of the costs of seeking out new suppliers. By making it easier to search for alternative suppliers, the Internet changes the economics of the search process and offers the potential for wider searches. It also changed the economics of scale in purchasing. Purchasers requiring relatively low volumes find it easier to group together in order to create orders of sufficient size to warrant lower prices. In fact, the influence of the Internet on purchasing behaviour is not confined to *e-commerce*. Usually e-commerce is taken to mean the trade that actually takes place over the Internet. This is usually assumed to be a buyer visiting the seller's website, placing an order for parts and making a payment (also through the site). But the web is also an important source of purchasing information. For every 1 per cent of business transacted directly via the Internet, there may be 5 or 6 per cent of business that, at some point, involved the net, probably with potential buyers using it to compare prices or obtain technical information.

One increasingly common use of Internet technology in purchasing (or *e-procurement* as it is sometimes known) is for large companies, or groups of companies, to link their e-commerce systems into a common 'exchange'. In their more sophisticated form, such an exchange may be linked into the purchasing companies' own information systems (see the explanation of ERP in Chapter 10). Many of the large automotive, engineering and petrochemical companies, for example, have adopted such an approach. Typical of these companies' motives are those put forward by Shell Services International:[8] *'Procurement is an obvious first step in e-commerce. First, buying through the web is so slick and cheap compared to doing it almost any other way. Second, it allows you to aggregate, spend and ask: Why am I spending this money, or shouldn't I be getting a bigger discount? Third, it encourages new services like credit, insurance and accreditation to be built around it.'*

Managing ongoing supply

Managing supply relationships is not just a matter of choosing the right suppliers and then leaving them to get on with day-to-day supply. It is also about ensuring that suppliers are given the right information and encouragement to maintain smooth supply and that internal inconsistency does not negatively affect their ability to supply. A basic requirement is that some mechanism should be set up that ensures the two-way flow of information between customer and supplier. It is easy for both suppliers and customers simply to forget to inform each other of internal developments that could affect supply. Customers may see suppliers as having the responsibility for ensuring appropriate supply 'under any circumstances'. Or, suppliers themselves may be reluctant to inform customers of any potential problems with supply because they see it as risking the relationship. Yet, especially if customer and supplier see themselves as 'partners', the free flow of information, and a mutually supportive tolerance of occasional problems, is the best way to ensure smooth supply. Often day-to-day supplier relationships are damaged because of internal inconsistencies. For example, one part of a business may be asking a supplier for some special service beyond the strict nature of their agreement, whilst another part of the business is not paying suppliers on time.[9]

Service-level agreements

Some organizations bring a degree of formality to supplier relationships by encouraging (or requiring) all suppliers to agree service-level agreements (SLAs). SLAs are formal definitions of the dimensions of service and the relationship between suppliers and the organization. The type of issues covered by such an agreement could include response times, the range of services, dependability of service supply, and so on. Boundaries of responsibility and appropriate performance measures could also be agreed. For example, an SLA between an information systems support unit and a research unit in the laboratories of a large pharmaceutical company could define such performance measures as:

- the types of information network services that may be provided as 'standard'
- the range of special information services that may be available at different periods of the day
- the minimum 'up time', i.e. the proportion of time the system will be available at different periods of the day
- the maximum response time and average response time to get the system fully operational should it fail
- the maximum response time to provide 'special' services, and so on.

Although SLAs are described here as mechanisms for governing the ongoing relationship between suppliers and customers, they often prove inadequate because they are seen as being useful in setting up the terms of the relationship, but then are used only to resolve disputes. For SLAs to work effectively, they must be treated as working documents that establish the details of ongoing relationships *in the light of experience*. Used properly, they are a repository of the knowledge that both sides have gathered through working together. Any SLA that stays unchanged over time is, at the very least, failing to encourage improvement in supply.

How can suppliers be developed?

In any relationship other than pure market-based transactional relationships, it is in a customer's long-term interests to take some responsibility for developing supplier capabilities. Helping a supplier to improve not only enhances the service (and hopefully price) from the supplier; it may also lead to greater supplier loyalty and long-term commitment. This is why some particularly successful businesses (including Japanese automotive manufacturers) invest in supplier development teams whose responsibility is to help suppliers to improve their own operations processes. Of course, committing the resources to help suppliers is worthwhile only if it improves the effectiveness of the supply chain as a whole. Nevertheless, the potential for such enlightened self-interest can be significant.

How customers and suppliers see each other[10]

One of the major barriers to supplier development is the mismatch between how customers and suppliers perceive both what is required and how the relationship is performing. Exploring potential mismatches is often a revealing exercise, for both customers and suppliers. Figure 7.7 illustrates this. It shows that gaps may exist between four sets of ideas. As a customer you (presumably) have an idea about what you really want from a supplier. This may, or may not, be formalized in the form of a service level agreement. But no SLA can capture everything about what is required. There may be a gap between how you as a customer interpret what is required and how the supplier interprets it. This is the *requirements perception gap*. Similarly, as a customer, you (again presumably) have a view on how your supplier is performing in terms of fulfilling your requirements. That may not coincide with how your supplier believes it is performing. This is the *fulfilment perception gap*. Both these gaps are a function of the effectiveness of the communication between supplier and customer. But there are also two other gaps. The gap between what you want from your supplier and how they are performing indicates the type of development that, as a customer, you should be giving to your supplier. Similarly, the gap between your supplier's perceptions of your needs and its performance indicates how they should initially see themselves improving their own performance. Ultimately, of course, their responsibility for improvement should coincide with their customer's views of requirements and performance.

> **Operations principle**
> Unsatisfactory supplier relationships can be caused by requirements and fulfilment perception gaps.

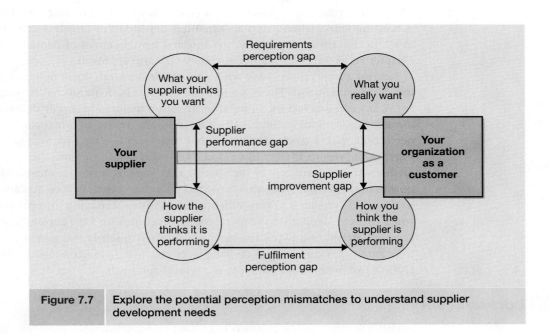

Figure 7.7   Explore the potential perception mismatches to understand supplier development needs

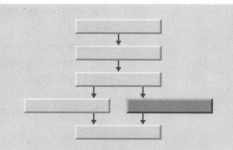

How should the demand side be managed?

The management of demand-side relationships will depend partly on the nature of demand, in particular how uncertain it is. Knowing the exact demands that customers are going to require allows a supplier to plan its own internal processes in a systematic manner. This type of demand is called 'dependent' demand; it is relatively predictable because it is dependent upon some factor which is itself predictable. For example, supplying tyres to an automobile factory involves examining the manufacturing schedules in the car plant and deriving the demand for tyres from these. If 200 cars are to be manufactured on a particular day, then it is simple to calculate that 1000 tyres will be demanded by the car plant (each car has five tyres). Because of this, the tyres can be ordered from the tyre manufacturer to a delivery schedule that is closely in line with the demand for tyres from the plant. In fact, the demand for every part of the car plant will be derived from the assembly schedule for the finished cars. Manufacturing instructions and purchasing requests will all be dependent upon this figure. Managing internal process networks when external demand is dependent is largely a matter of calculating, in as precise a way as possible, the internal consequences of demand. MRP, treated in Chapter 10, is the best-known dependent demand approach.

But not all operations have such predictable demand. Some operations are subject to independent demand. There is a random element in demand that is virtually independent of any obvious factors. Companies are often required to supply demand without having any firm forward visibility of customer orders. A drive-in tyre replacement service will need to manage a stock of tyres. In that sense it is exactly the same task that faced the supplier of tyres to the car plant, but demand is very different. The tyre service cannot predict either the volume or the specific needs of customers. It must make decisions on how many and what type of tyres to stock, based on demand forecasts and in the light of the risks it is prepared to run of being out of stock. Managing internal process networks when external demand is independent involves making 'best guesses' concerning future demand, attempting to put the resources in place to satisfy this demand, and attempting to respond quickly if actual demand does not match the forecast. Inventory planning and control, treated in Chapter 9, is a typical approach.

Logistics services

FURTHER EXAMPLE

Logistics means moving products to customers. Sometimes the term 'physical distribution management' or simply 'distribution' is used as being analogous to logistics. Logistics is now frequently outsourced to 'third party' logistics (or 3PL) providers, which vary in terms of the range and integration of their services. At the simplest level, the 'haulage' and 'storage' businesses either move goods around or store them in warehouses. Clients take responsibility for all planning. Physical distribution companies bring haulage and storage together, collecting clients' products, putting them into storage facilities and delivering them to the end customer as required. 'Contract' logistics service providers tend to have more sophisticated clients with more complex operations. Total 'supply chain management' (or 4PL) providers offer to manage supply chains from end to end, often for several customers simultaneously. Doing this requires a much greater degree of analytical and modelling capability, business process re-engineering and consultancy skills.

Logistics management and the Internet

Internet-based communication has had a significant impact on physical distribution management. Information can be made available more readily along the distribution chain, so that transport companies, warehouses, suppliers and customers can share knowledge of where goods are in the chain (and sometimes where they are going next). This allows the operations within the chain to co-ordinate their activities more readily. It also gives the potential for some significant cost savings. For example, an important issue for transportation companies is back-loading. When the company is contracted to transport goods from A to B, its vehicles may have to return from B to A empty. Back-loading means finding a potential customer who wants their goods transported from B to A in the right time-frame. With the increase in information availability through the Internet, the possibility of finding a back-load increases. Companies that can fill their vehicles on both the outward and return journeys will have significantly lower costs per distance travelled than those whose vehicles are empty for half the total journey. Similarly, Internet-based technology that allows customers visibility of the progress of distribution can be used to enhance the perception of customer service. 'Track-and-trace' technologies, for example, allow package distribution companies to inform and reassure customers that their service is being delivered as promised.

Automatic identification technologies

Tracing the progress of items through a supply chain has involved the use of bar codes to record progress. During manufacture bar codes are used to identify the number of products passing through a particular point in the process. In warehouses, bar codes are used to keep track of how many products are stored at particular locations. But bar codes have disadvantages. It is sometimes difficult to align the item so that the bar code can be read conveniently, items can only be scanned one by one, and the bar code identifies only the *type* of item, not a specific item itself. That is, the code identifies that an item is, say, a can of one type of drink rather than one specific can. These drawbacks can be overcome through the use of 'automated identification' or Auto-ID. Usually this involves Radio Frequency Identification (RFID). Here an Electronic Product Code (ePC) that is a unique number, 96 bits long, is embedded in a memory chip or smart tag. These tags are put on individual items so that each item has its own unique identifying code. At various points during its manufacture, distribution, storage and sale, each smart tag can be scanned by a wireless radio frequency 'reader'. This transmits the item's embedded identity code to a network such as the Internet, describing, for example, when and where it was made, where it has been stored, etc. This information can then be fed into control systems. It is also controversial – see the critical commentary, later.

Customer development

Earlier in the chapter, Figure 7.7 illustrated some of the gaps in perception and performance that can occur between customers and suppliers. The purpose then was to demonstrate the nature of supplier development. The same approach can be used to analyze the nature of requirements and performance with customers. In this case the imperative is to understand customer perceptions, both of their requirements and of their view of your performance, and feed these into your own performance improvement plans. What is less common, but can be equally valuable, is to use these gaps (shown in Figure 7.8) to examine the question of whether customer requirements and perceptions of performance are either accurate or reasonable. For example, customers may be placing demands on suppliers without fully considering their

Operations principle
Unsatisfactory customer relationships can be caused by requirement and fulfilment perception gaps.

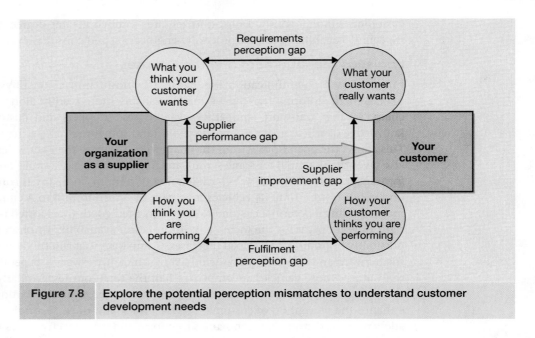

Figure 7.8 **Explore the potential perception mismatches to understand customer development needs**

consequences. It may be that slight modifications in what is demanded would not inconvenience customers and yet would provide significant benefits to suppliers that could then be passed on to customers. Similarly, customers may be incompetent at measuring supplier performance, in which case the benefits of excellent supplier service will not be recognized. So, just as customers have a responsibility to help develop their own supplier's performance, in their own as well as their supplier's interests, suppliers have a responsibility to develop their customer's understanding of how supply should be managed.

DIAGNOSTIC QUESTION

Are supply chain dynamics under control?

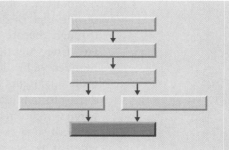

There are dynamics that exist between firms in supply chains that cause errors, inaccuracies and volatility, and these increase for operations further upstream in the supply chain. This effect is known as the Bullwhip Effect,[11] so called because a small disturbance at one end of the chain causes increasingly large disturbances as it works its way towards the end. Its main cause is a perfectly understandable and rational desire by the different links in the supply chain to manage their levels of activity and inventory sensibly. To demonstrate this, examine the production rate and stock levels for the supply chain shown in Table 7.2. This is a four-stage supply chain where an original equipment manufacturer (OEM) is served by three tiers of suppliers. The demand from the OEM's market has been running at a rate of 100 items per period, but in period 2, demand reduces to 95 items per period. All stages in the supply chain work on the principle that they will keep in stock one period's demand. This is a simplification but not a gross one. Many operations gear their inventory levels to their demand rate. The column headed

Table 7.2 Fluctuations of production levels along the supply chain in response to a small change in end-customer demand

Period	Third-tier supplier		Second-tier supplier		First-tier supplier		Original equipment mfr.		Demand
	Prodn.	Stock	Prodn.	Stock	Prodn.	Stock	Prodn.	Stock	
1	100	100	100	100	100	100	100	100	100
		100		100		100		100	
2	20	100	60	100	80[b]	100[a]	90[d]	100	95
		60		80		90[c]		95	
3	180	60	120	80	100	90	95	95	95
		120		100		95		95	
4	60	120	90	100	95	95	95	95	95
		90		95		95		95	
5	100	90	95	95	95	95	95	95	95
		95		95		95		95	
6	95	95	95	95	95	95	95	95	95
		95		95		95		95	

Starting stock (a) + production (b) = finishing stock (c) + demand, that is, production in previous tier down (d): see explanation in text.

All stages in the supply chain keep one period's inventory: c = d.

'stock' for each level of supply shows the starting stock at the beginning of the period and the finishing stock at the end of the period. At the beginning of period 2, the OEM has 100 units in stock (that being the rate of demand up to period 2). Demand in period 2 is 95 and so the OEM knows that it would need to produce sufficient items to finish up at the end of the period with 95 in stock (this being the new demand rate). To do this, it need only manufacture 90 items; these, together with five items taken out of the starting stock, will supply demand and leave a finishing stock of 95 items. The beginning of period 3 finds the OEM with 95 items in stock. Demand is also 95 items and therefore its production rate to maintain a stock level of 95 will be 95 items per period. The original equipment manufacturer now operates at a steady rate of producing 95 items per period. Note, however, that a change in demand of only five items has produced a fluctuation of 10 items in the OEM's production rate.

Carrying this same logic through to the first-tier supplier, at the beginning of period 2, the first-tier supplier has 100 items in stock. The demand that it has to supply in period 2 is derived from the production rate of the OEM. This has dropped down to 90 in period 2. The first-tier supplier therefore has to produce sufficient to supply the demand of 90 items (or the equivalent) and leave one month's demand (now 90 items) as its finishing stock. A production rate of 80 items per month will achieve this. It will therefore start period 3 with an opening stock of 90 items, but the demand from the OEM has now risen to 95 items. It therefore has to produce sufficient to fulfil this demand of 95 items and leave 95 items in stock. To do this, it must produce 100 items in period 3. After period 3 the first-tier supplier then resumes a steady state, producing 95 items per month. Note again, however, that the fluctuation has been even greater than that in the OEM's production rate, decreasing to 80 items a period, increasing to 100 items a period, and then achieving a steady rate of 95 items a period. Extending the logic back to the third-tier supplier, it is clear that the further back up the supply chain an operation is placed, the more drastic are the fluctuations.

This relatively simple demonstration ignores any time lag in material and information flow between stages. In practice there

Operations principle
Demand fluctuations become progressively amplified as their effects work back up the supply chain.

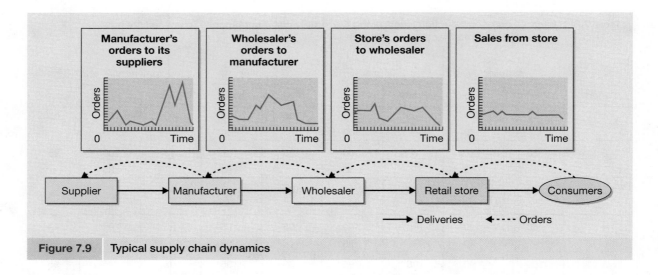

Figure 7.9   Typical supply chain dynamics

will be such a lag, and this will make the fluctuations even more marked. Figure 7.9 shows the net result of all these effects in a typical supply chain. Note the increasing volatility further back in the chain.

Controlling supply chain dynamics

The first step in improving supply chain performance involves attempting to reduce the bullwhip effect. This usually means co-ordinating the activities of the operations in the chain in the following ways.[12]

Share information throughout the supply chain

Operations principle
The bullwhip effect can be reduced by information sharing, aligning planning and control decisions, improving flow efficiency, and better forecasting.

One reason for the bullwhip effect is that each operation in the chain reacts only to the orders placed by its *immediate* customer. They have little overview of what is happening throughout the chain. But if chain-wide information is shared throughout the chain, it is unlikely that such wild fluctuations will occur. With information transmitted throughout the chain, all the operations can monitor true demand, free of distortions. So, for example, information regarding supply problems, or shortages, can be transmitted down the chain so that downstream customers can modify their schedules and sales plans accordingly. For example, the electronic point-of-sale (EPOS) systems, used by many retailers, make information on current demand downstream in the supply chain available to upstream operations. Sales data from checkouts or cash registers is consolidated and transmitted to the warehouses, transportation companies and supplier operations in the supply chain. This means that suppliers can be aware of the 'real' movements in the market.

Align all the channels of information and supply

Channel alignment means the adjustment of scheduling, material movements, stock levels, pricing and other sales strategies so as to bring all the operations in the chain into line with each other. This goes beyond the provision of information. It means that the systems and methods of planning and control decision making are harmonized through the chain. For example, even when using the same information, differences in forecasting methods or purchasing practices can lead to fluctuations in orders between operations in the chain. One way of avoiding this is to allow an upstream supplier to manage the inventories of its downstream customer. This is known as vendor-managed inventory

(VMI). So, for example, a packaging supplier could take responsibility for the stocks of packaging materials held by a food manufacturing customer. In turn, the food manufacturer takes responsibility for the stocks of its products that are held in its customer's (the supermarket's) warehouses.

Increase operational efficiency throughout the chain

'Operational efficiency' in this context means the efforts that each operation in the chain makes to reduce its own complexity, the cost of doing business with other operations in the chain, and its throughput time. The cumulative effect of this is to simplify throughput in the whole chain. For example, imagine a chain of operations whose performance level is relatively poor: quality defects are frequent, the lead time to order products and services is long, delivery is unreliable, and so on. The behaviour of the chain would be a continual sequence of errors and effort wasted in replanning to compensate for the errors. Poor quality would mean extra and unplanned orders being placed, and unreliable delivery and slow delivery lead times would mean high safety stocks. Just as important, most operations managers' time would be spent coping with the inefficiency. By contrast, a chain whose operations had high levels of operations performance would be more predictable and have faster throughput, both of which would help to minimize supply chain fluctuations.

Improve forecasts

Improved forecast accuracy also helps to reduce the bullwhip effect. Bullwhip is caused by the demand pattern, lead times, forecasting mechanisms and the replenishment decisions used to order product from production facilities or suppliers. Improving the accuracy of your forecasts directly reduces the inventory-holding requirements that will achieve customer service-level targets. Reducing lead times means that you need to forecast less far into the future and thus lead times have a large impact on bullwhip and inventory costs. The exact nature of how bullwhip propagates in a supply chain is also dependent on the nature of the demand pattern. Negatively correlated demands require less inventory in the supply chain than do positively correlated demand patterns, for example. But bullwhip is avoidable. By using sophisticated replenishment policies, designed using control engineering principles, many businesses have been able to eliminate bullwhip effects. Sometimes this comes at a cost. Extra inventory may be required in parts of the chain, or customer service levels reduce. But more often bullwhip avoidance creates a 'win–win' situation. It reduces inventory requirements and improves customer service.[13]

Critical commentary

Each chapter contains a short critical commentary on the main ideas covered in the chapter. Its purpose is not to undermine the issues discussed in the chapter, but to emphasize that, although we present a relatively orthodox view of operation, there are other perspectives.

■ This emphasis on understanding the end customer in a supply chain has led some authorities to object to the very term *supply* chain. Rather, they say, they should be referred to as *demand* chains. Their argument is based on the idea that the concept of 'supply' implies a 'push' mentality. Any emphasis on pushing goods through a supply chain should be avoided.

It implies that customers should consume what suppliers see fit to produce. On the other hand, referring to 'demand chains' puts proper emphasis on the importance of seeing customers as pulling demand through the chain. Nevertheless, 'supply chain' is still the most commonly used term.

■ Although the SCOR model is increasingly adopted, it has been criticized for under-emphasizing people issues. The SCOR model assumes, but does not explicitly address, the human resource base skill set, notwithstanding the model's heavy reliance on supply chain knowledge to properly understand the model and methodology. Often external expertise is needed to support the process. This, along with the nature of the SCC membership, implies that the SCOR model may be appropriate only for relatively large companies that are more likely to have the necessary business capabilities to implement the model. Many small to medium-sized companies may find difficulty in handling full-scale model implementation. Some critics would also argue that the model lacks a link to the financial plans of a company, making it very difficult to highlight the benefits obtainable, as well as inhibiting senior management support.

■ The use of technology in supply chain management is not always universally welcomed. Even e-procurement is seen by some as preventing closer partnership-type relationships that, in the long run, may be more beneficial. Similarly, track-and-trace technology is seen by some as a waste of time and money. *'What we need,'* they argue, *'is to know that we can trust the delivery to arrive on time; we do not need the capability to waste our time finding out where the delivery is.'*

■ The idea of Auto-ID also opens up many ethical issues. People see its potential and its dangers in very different ways. Take the following two statements:[14]

'We are on the brink of a revolution of "smart products" that will interconnect everyday objects, consumers and manufacturers in a dynamic cycle of world commerce. . . . The vision of the Auto-ID centre is to create a universal environment in which computers understand the world without help from human beings.'

'Supermarket cards and other retail surveillance devices are merely the opening volley of the marketers' war against consumers. If consumers fail to oppose these practices now our long term prospects may look like something from a dystopian science fiction novel. . . . though many Auto-ID proponents appear focused on inventory and supply chain efficiency, others are developing financial and consumer applications that, if adopted, will have chilling effects on consumers' ability to escape the oppressive surveillance of manufacturers, retailers, and marketers. Of course, government and law enforcement will be quick to use the technology to keep tabs on citizens as well.'

It is this last issue that particularly scares some civil liberties activists. Keeping track of items within a supply chain is a relatively uncontentious issue. Keeping track of items when those items are identified with a particular individual going about their everyday lives is far more problematic. So, beyond the checkout for every arguably beneficial application there is also potential for misuse. For example, smart tags could drastically reduce theft because items could automatically report when they are stolen; their tags serving as a homing device pinpoint their exact location. But, similar technology could be used to trace any citizen, honest or not.

Summary checklist

DOWNLOADABLE

This checklist comprises questions that can be usefully applied to any type of operations and reflect the major diagnostic questions used within the chapter.

- [ ] Is it understood that the performance of any one operation is partly a function of all the other operations in the supply chain?

- [ ] Are supply chain concepts applied internally as well as externally?

- [ ] Are supply chain objectives understood in the context of the whole chain rather than the single operation?

- [ ] Which product or service groups are 'functional' and which are 'innovative'?

- [ ] Therefore, which products or service groups need 'lean' and which need 'agile' supply chain management?

- [ ] Is the position on the 'transactional to partnership' spectrum understood for each customer and supplier relationship?

- [ ] Are customer and supplier relationships at an appropriate point on the 'transactional to partnership' spectrum?

- [ ] Are 'partnership' relationships *really* partnerships or are they just called that?

- [ ] Are suppliers and potential suppliers rigorously assessed using some scoring procedure?

- [ ] Are the trade-offs inherent in supplier selection understood?

- [ ] Is the approach to single- or multi-sourcing appropriate?

- [ ] Is the purchasing activity making full use of Internet-based mechanisms?

- [ ] Are service-level agreements used? And do they develop over time?

- [ ] Is sufficient effort put into supplier development?

- [ ] Are actual and potential mismatches of perception in the supplier relationships explored?

- [ ] Is the difference between dependent and independent demand understood?

- [ ] Is the potential for outsourcing logistics services regularly explored?

- [ ] Could new technologies such as RFID have any benefit?

- [ ] Has the idea of customer development been explored?

- [ ] Have mechanisms for reducing the impact of the bullwhip effect been explored?

- [ ] Has there been a risk assessment to assess supply chain vulnerability?

Case study Supplying fast fashion[15]

Garment retailing has changed. No longer is there a standard look that all retailers adhere to for a whole season. Fashion is fast, complex and furious. Different trends overlap and fashion ideas that are not even on a store's radar screen can become 'must haves' within six months. Many retail businesses with their own brands such as H&M and Zara sell up-to-the-minute fashionability at low prices, in stores that are clearly focused on one particular market. In the world of fast fashion, catwalk designs speed their way into high street stores at prices anyone can afford. The quality of the garment means that it may last only one season, but fast fashion customers don't want yesterday's trends. As *Newsweek* puts it, '. . . *being a "quicker picker-upper" is what made fashion retailers H&M and Zara successful. [They] thrive by practicing the new science of "fast fashion"; compressing product development cycles as much as six times.*' But the retail operations that customers see are only the end part of the supply chain that feeds them. And these have also changed.

At its simplest level, the fast fashion supply chain has four stages. First, the garments are designed, after which they are manufactured and then distributed to the retail outlets where they are displayed and sold in retail operations designed to reflect the businesses' brand values. In this short case we examine two fast fashion operations, Hennes and Mauritz (known as H&M) and Zara, together with United Colors of Benetton (UCB), a similar chain but with a different market positioning.

Benetton

Almost 50 years ago Luciano Benetton took the world of fashion by storm by selling the bright, casual sweaters designed by his sister across Europe (and later the rest of the world), promoted by controversial advertising. By 2005 the Benetton Group was present in 120 countries throughout the world. Selling casual garments, mainly under its United Colors of Benetton (UCB) and its more fashion-oriented Sisley brands, it produces 110 million garments a year, over 90 per cent of them in Europe. Its retail network of over 5000 stores produces revenue of around €2 billion. Benetton products are seen as less 'high fashion' but higher quality and durability, with higher prices, than H&M and Zara.

Source: James Leynse/Corbis

H&M

Established in Sweden in 1947, H&M now sells clothes and cosmetics in over 1000 stores in 21 countries around the world. The business concept is 'fashion and quality at the best price'. With more than 45,000 employees, and revenues of around SEK 60,000 million, its biggest market is Germany, followed by Sweden and the UK. H&M is seen by many as the originator of the fast fashion concept. Certainly it has years of experience at driving down the price of up-to-the-minute fashions. '*We ensure the best price,*' they say, '*by having few middlemen, buying large volumes, having extensive experience of the clothing industry, having a great knowledge of which goods should be bought from which markets, having efficient distribution systems, and being cost-conscious at every stage.*'

Zara

The first store opened almost by accident in 1975 when Amancio Ortega Gaona, a women's pyjama manufacturer, was left with a large cancelled order. The shop he opened was intended only as an outlet for cancelled orders. Now Inditex, the holding group that includes the Zara brand, has over 1300 stores in 39 countries with sales of over €3 billion. The Zara brand accounts for over 75 per cent of the group's total retail sales, and is still based in north-west Spain. By 2003 it had become the world's fastest-growing volume garment retailer. The Inditex group also has several other branded chains, including Pull and Bear, and Massimo Dutti. In total it employs almost 40,000 people in a business that is known for a high degree of vertical integration compared with most fast fashion companies. The company believes that it is its integration along the supply chain that allows it to respond to customer demand quickly and flexibly while keeping stock to a minimum.

Design

All three businesses emphasize the importance of design in this market. Although not *haute couture,* capturing design trends is vital to success. Even the boundary between high and fast fashion is starting to blur. In 2004 H&M recruited high-fashion designer Karl Lagerfeld, previously noted for his work with more exclusive brands. For H&M his designs were priced for value rather than exclusivity: *'Why do I work for H&M? Because I believe in inexpensive clothes, not "cheap" clothes,'* said Lagerfeld. Yet most of H&M's products come from over 100 designers in Stockholm who work with a team of 50 pattern designers, around 100 buyers and a number of budget controllers. The department's task is to find the optimum balance between the three components comprising H&M's business concept – fashion, price and quality. Buying volumes and delivery dates are then decided.

Zara's design functions are organized in a different way from those of most similar companies. Conventionally, the design input comes from three *separate* functions: the designers themselves, market specialists, and buyers who place orders on to suppliers. At Zara the design stage is split into three product areas: women's, men's and children's garments. In each area, designers, market specialists and buyers are co-located in design halls that also contain small workshops for trying out prototype designs. The market specialists in all three design halls are in regular contact with Zara retail stores, discussing customer reaction to new designs. In this way, the retail stores are not the end of the whole supply chain but the beginning of the design stage of the chain. Zara's around 300 designers, whose average age is 26, produce approximately 40,000 items per year of which about 10,000 go into production.

Benetton also has around 300 designers, who not only design for all its brands but also are engaged in researching new materials and clothing concepts. Since 2000 the company has moved to standardize their range globally. At one time more than 20 per cent of its ranges were customized to the specific needs of each country; now only between 5 and 10 per cent of garments are customized. This reduced the number of individual designs offered globally by over 30 per cent, strengthening the global brand image and reducing production costs.

Both H&M and Zara have moved away from the traditional industry practice of offering two 'collections' a year, for Spring/Summer and Autumn/Winter. Their 'seasonless cycle' involves the continual introduction of new products on a rolling basis throughout the year. This allows designers to learn from customers' reactions to their new products and incorporate them quickly into more new products. The most extreme version of this idea is practised by Zara. A garment is designed; a batch is manufactured and 'pulsed' through the supply chain. Often the design is never repeated; it may be modified and another batch produced, but there are no 'continuing' designs as such. Even Benetton has increased the proportion of what it calls 'flash' collections – small collections that are put into its stores during the season.

Manufacturing

At one time Benetton focused its production on its Italian plants. Then it significantly increased its production outside Italy to take advantage of lower labour costs. Non-Italian operations include factories in North Africa, Eastern Europe and Asia. Yet each location operates in a very similar manner. A central, Benetton-owned operation performs some manufacturing operations (especially those requiring expensive technology) and co-ordinates the more labour-intensive production activities that are performed by a network of smaller contractors (often owned and managed by ex-Benetton employees). These contractors may in turn sub-contract some of their activities. The company's central facility in Italy allocates production to each of the non-Italian networks, deciding what and how much each is to produce. There is some specialization, for example jackets are made in Eastern Europe while T-shirts are made in Spain. Benetton also has a controlling share in its main supplier of raw materials, to ensure fast supply to its factories. Benetton is also known for the practice of dyeing garments after assembly rather than using dyed thread or fabric. This postpones decisions about colours until late in the supply process so that there is a greater chance of producing what is needed by the market.

H&M does not have any factories of its own, but instead works with around 750 suppliers. Around half of production takes place in Europe and the rest mainly in Asia. It has 21 production offices around the world that between them are responsible for co-ordinating the suppliers who produce over half a billion items a year for H&M. The relationship between production offices and suppliers is vital, because it allows fabrics to be bought in early. The actual dyeing and cutting of the garments can then be decided at a later stage in the production. The later an order can be placed on suppliers, the less the risk of buying the wrong thing. Average supply lead times vary from three weeks up to six months, depending on the nature of the goods. However, *'The most important thing,'* they say, *'is to find the optimal time to order each item. Short lead times are not always best. For some high-volume fashion basics, it is to our advantage to place orders far in advance. Trendier garments require considerably shorter lead times.'*

Zara's lead times are said to be the fastest in the industry, with a 'catwalk to rack' time as little as 15 days. According to one analyst, this is because they *'own most of the manufacturing capability used to make their products, which they use as a means of exciting and stimulating customer demand'.* About half of Zara's products are produced in its network of 20 Spanish factories, which, as at Benetton, tend to concentrate on the more capital-intensive operations such as cutting and dyeing. Sub-contractors are used for most of the labour-intensive operations such as sewing. Zara buys around 40 per cent of its fabric from its own wholly-owned subsidiary, most of which is in undyed form for dyeing after assembly. Most Zara factories and their sub-contractors work on a single-shift system to retain some volume flexibility.

Distribution

Both Benetton and Zara have invested in highly automated warehouses, close to their main production centres, that store, pack and assemble individual orders for their retail networks. These automated warehouses represent a major investment for both companies. In 2001, Zara caused some press comment by announcing that it would open a second automated warehouse even though, by its own calculations, it was only using about half its existing warehouse capacity.

More recently, Benetton caused some controversy by announcing that it was exploring the use of RFID tags to track its garments.

At H&M, while the stock management is primarily handled internally, physical distribution is sub-contracted. A large part of the flow of goods is routed from the production site to the retail country via H&M's transit terminal in Hamburg. Upon arrival the goods are inspected and allocated to the stores or to the centralized store stock room. The centralized store stock room, within H&M referred to as the 'Call-Off warehouse', replenishes stores on item level according to what is selling.

Retail

All H&M stores (average size, 1300 square metres) are owned and run solely by H&M. The aim is to *'create a comfortable and inspiring atmosphere in the store that makes it simple for customers to find what they want and to feel at home'.* This is similar to Zara stores, although they tend to be smaller (average size, 800 square metres). Perhaps the most remarkable characteristic of Zara stores is that garments rarely stay in the store for longer than two weeks. Because product designs are often not repeated and are produced in relatively small batches, the range of garments displayed in the store can change radically every two or three weeks. This encourages customers both to avoid delaying a purchase and to revisit the store frequently.

Since 2000 Benetton has been reshaping its retail operations. At one time the vast majority of Benetton retail outlets were small shops run by third parties. Now these small stores have been joined by several, Benetton-owned and operated, larger stores (1500 to 3000 square metres). These mega-stores can display the whole range of Benetton products and reinforce the Benetton shopping experience.

QUESTION

1 Compare and contrast the approaches taken by H&M, Benetton and Zara to managing their supply chain.

Active case study   NK Fleet Management

ACTIVE CASE

NK Fleet Management is looking to grow their business. Responsible for managing and servicing car fleets, the company's relationship with its main customer (the vehicle manufacturer) is governed by a set of service level agreements (SLAs). Whilst these agreements are comprehensive, they do not cover all eventualities. In the coming months the company have to respond to various more unusual requests from their customer.

● How would you react to each of the challenges to managing the relationship with their major customer?

Please refer to the Active case on the CD to work through the dilemmas faced by NK Fleet Management.

Applying the principles

Some of these exercises can be answered by reading the chapter. Others will require some general knowledge of business activity and some might require an element of investigation. All have hints on how they can be answered on the CD accompanying this book.

HINTS

1. If you were the owner of a small local retail shop, what criteria would you use to select suppliers for the goods that you wish to stock in your shop? Visit three shops that are local to you and ask the owners how they select their suppliers. In what way were their answers different from what you thought they might be?

2. What is your purchasing strategy? How do you approach buying the products and services that you need (or want)? Classify the types and products and services that you buy and record the criteria you use to purchase each category. Discuss these categories and criteria with others. Why are their views different?

3. Visit a C2C (consumer-to-consumer) auction site (for example eBay) and analyze the function of the site in terms of the way it facilitates transactions. What does such a site have to get right to be successful?

4. The example of the bullwhip effect shown in Table 7.2 shows how a simple 5 per cent reduction in demand at the end of the supply chain causes fluctuations that increase in severity the further back an operation is placed in the chain.

   (a) Using the same logic and the same rules (i.e. all operations keep one period's demand as inventory), what would the effect on the chain be if demand fluctuated period by period between 100 and 95? That is, period 1 has a demand of 100, period 2 has a demand of 95, period 3 of 100, period 4 of 95, and so on.

   (b) What happens if all operations in the supply chain decide to keep only half of each period's demand as inventory?

   (c) Find examples of how supply chains try to reduce this bullwhip effect.

5. Visit the websites of some distribution and logistics companies. For example, you might start with some of the following: **www.eddiestobart.co.uk, www.norbert-dentressangle.com, www.accenture.com** (under 'services' look for supply chain management), **www.logisticsonline.com.**

   - What do you think are the market promises that these companies make to their clients and potential clients?
   - What are the operations capabilities they need in order to fulfil these promises successfully?

Notes on chapter

1. This example was prepared by Carsten Dittrich of the University of Southern Denmark. Siemens case background data: © Siemens Archives 2007. Sources include Siemens homepage web source: http://w1.siemens.com/entry/cc/en/ Special thanks to Dr Christian Frühwald, Partner, Supply Chain Consulting, Siemens Procurement & Logistics Services.
2. Sources: Gap Inc. (2007) 'Gap issues statement on media reports on child labor', corporate website; 'Clean, wholesome and American? A storm over the use of child labour clouds Gap's pristine image', *The Economist,* 1 November 2007.
3. Fisher, M.L. (1997) 'What is the right supply chain for your product', *Harvard Business Review,* March–April.
4. Again, we are grateful to Carsten Dittrich for very significant help with this section.
5. Kapour, V. and Gupta, A. (1997) 'Aggressive sourcing: a free-market approach', *Sloan Management Review,* Fall.

6 Parkhe, A. (1993) 'Strategic alliance structuring', *Academy of Management Journal*, Vol. 36, pp. 794–829.

7 Source: Grad, C. (2000) 'A network of supplies to be woven into the web', *Financial Times*, 9 February.

8 Harney, A. (2000) 'Up close but impersonal', *Financial Times*, 10 March.

9 Lee, L. and Dobler, D.W. (1977) *Purchasing and Materials Management*, McGraw-Hill.

10 Harland, C.M. (1996) 'Supply chain management relationships, chains and networks', *British Journal of Management*, Vol. 1, No. 7.

11 Lee, H.L., Padmanabhan, V. and Whang, S. (1997) 'The bull whip effect in supply chains', *Sloan Management Review*, Spring.

12 Lee *et al., op. cit.*

13 Thanks to Stephen Disney at Cardiff Business School, UK, for help with this section.

14 MIT Auto-ID website, and Albrecht, K. (2002) 'Supermarket cards: tip of the surveillance iceberg', *Denver University Law Review*, June.

15 All data from public sources and reflect period 2004–05.

Taking it further

Bolstorff, P. (2004) 'Supply chain by the numbers', *Logistics Today,* July, pp. 46–50.

Bolstorff, P. and Rosenbaum, R. (2008) *Supply Chain Excellence – a handbook for dramatic improvement using the SCOR model* (2nd edn), American Management Association.

Child, J. and Faulkner, D. (1998) *Strategies of Cooperation: Managing alliances, networks and joint ventures,* Oxford University Press. Very much a strategic view of supply networks, but insightful and readable.

Christopher, M. (1998) *Logistics and Supply Chain Management: Strategies for reducing cost and improving services* (2nd edn), Financial Times Prentice Hall. A comprehensive treatment on supply chain management from a distribution perspective by one of the gurus of supply chain management.

Fisher, M.L. (1997) 'What is the right supply chain for your product?', *Harvard Business Review*, Vol. 75, No. 2. A particularly influential article that explores the issue of how supply chains are not all the same.

Harland, C.M., Lamming, R.C. and Cousins, P. (1999) 'Developing the concept of supply strategy', *International Journal of Operations and Production Management,* Vol. 19, No. 7. An academic paper but one that gives a broad understanding of how supply chain ideas have developed and could develop.

Harrison, A. and van Hoek, R. (2002) *Logistics Management and Strategy,* Financial Times Prentice Hall. A short but readable book that explains many of the modern ideas in supply chain management, including lean supply chains and agile supply chains.

Hines, P. and Rich, N. (1997) 'The seven value stream mapping tools', *International Journal of Operations and Production Management,* Vol. 17, No. 1. Another academic paper, but one that explores some practical techniques that can be used to understand supply chains.

Presutti Jr, W. D. and Mawhinney, J. R. (2007) 'The supply chain finance link', *Supply Chain Management Review,* September, pp. 32–8.

Useful websites

www.cio.com/research/scm/edit/012202_scm Site of CIO's Supply Chain Management Research Center. Topics include procurement and fulfilment, with case studies.

www.stanford.edu/group/scforum/ Stanford University's supply chain forum. Interesting debate.

www.rfidc.com Site of the RFID Centre that contains RFID demonstrations and articles to download.

www.spychips.com Vehemently anti-RFID site. If you want to understand the nature of some activists' concerns over RFID, this site provides the arguments.

www.cips.org The Chartered Institute of Purchasing and Supply (CIPS) is an international organization, serving the purchasing and supply profession and dedicated to promoting best practice. Some good links.

www.supply-chain.org/cs/root/home The Supply Chain Council homepage.

**FURTHER
RESOURCES**

For further resources including examples, animated diagrams, self-test questions, Excel spreadsheets, active case studies and video materials please explore the CD accompanying this book.

8

CAPACITY MANAGEMENT

Introduction

Providing the capability to satisfy current and future demand is a fundamental responsibility of operations management. It is at the heart of trade-offs between customer service and cost. Insufficient capacity leaves customers not served and excess capacity incurs increased costs. In this chapter we deal with *medium-term* capacity management, also sometimes referred to as *aggregate* capacity management. The essence of medium-term capacity management is to reconcile, at a general level, the aggregated supply of capacity with the aggregated level of demand. (See Figure 8.1.)

Source: Catherine Karnow/Corbis

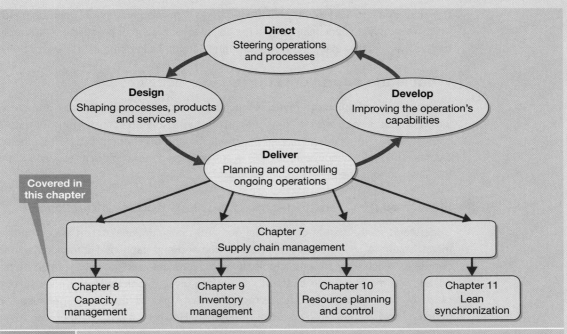

Direct
Steering operations and processes

Design
Shaping processes, products and services

Develop
Improving the operation's capabilities

Deliver
Planning and controlling ongoing operations

Covered in this chapter

Chapter 7
Supply chain management

Chapter 8
Capacity management

Chapter 9
Inventory management

Chapter 10
Resource planning and control

Chapter 11
Lean synchronization

Figure 8.1   Capacity management is the activity of coping with mismatches between demand and the ability to supply demand

Executive summary

VIDEO
further detail

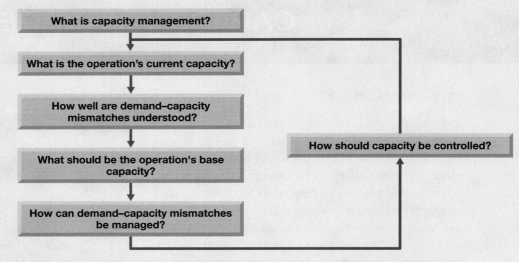

Decision logic chain for capacity management

Each chapter is structured around a set of diagnostic questions. These questions suggest what you should ask in order to gain an understanding of the important issues of a topic, and as a result, improve your decision making. An executive summary, addressing these questions, is provided below.

What is capacity management?

Capacity management is the activity of coping with mismatches between demand and the ability to supply demand. Capacity is the ability an operation or process has to supply its customers. Mismatches can be caused through fluctuations in demand, supply, or both.

What is the operation's current capacity?

Capacity can be difficult to measure because it depends on activity mix, the duration over which output is required and any changes in the actual specification of the output. Often, capacity 'leakage' occurs because of scheduling and other constraints within the operation. Overall equipment effectiveness (OEE) is one method of judging the effectiveness of capacity that incorporates the idea of activity leakage.

How well are demand–capacity mismatches understood?

Understanding the nature of potential demand–capacity mismatches is central to capacity management. A key issue is the nature of demand and capacity fluctuations, especially the degree to which they are predictable. If fluctuations are predictable, they can be planned in advance to minimize their costs. If fluctuations are unpredictable, the main objective is to react to them quickly. Accurate, simple forecasting is an advantage because it converts unpredictable variation into predictable variation. However, a broader approach to enhancing market knowledge generally can reveal more about the options for managing mismatches.

What should be the operation's base capacity?

Capacity planning often involves setting a base level of capacity and then planning capacity fluctuations around it. The level at which base capacity is set depends on three main factors: the relative importance of the operation's performance objectives, the perishability of the operation's outputs, and the degree of variability in demand or supply. High service levels, high perishability of an operation's outputs and a high degree of variability in either demand or supply all indicate a relatively high level of base capacity.

How can demand–capacity mismatches be managed?

Demand–capacity mismatches usually call for some degree of capacity adjustment over time. There are three pure methods of achieving this, although in practice a mixture of all three may be used. A 'level capacity' plan involves no change in capacity and requires that the operation absorb demand–capacity mismatches, usually through under- or over-utilization of its resources, or the use of inventory. The 'chase demand' plan involves the changing of capacity through such methods as overtime, varying the size of the work force, sub-contracting, etc. The 'manage demand' plan involves an attempt to change demand through pricing or promotion methods, or changing product or service mix to reduce fluctuations in activity levels. Yield management is a common method of coping with mismatches when operations have relatively fixed capacities. Cumulative representations are sometimes used to plan capacity.

How should capacity be controlled?

In practice, capacity management is a dynamic process with decisions reviewed period by period. It is essential that capacity decisions made in one period reflect the knowledge accumulated from experiences in previous periods.

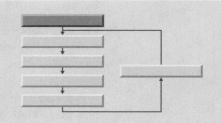

What is capacity management?

Capacity is the output that an operation (or a single process) can deliver in a defined unit of time. It reflects an 'ability to supply', at least in a quantitative sense. Capacity management is the activity of coping with mismatches between the demand on an operation and its ability to supply. Demand is the quantity of products or services that customers request from an operation or process at any point in time. A mismatch between demand and capacity can occur because demand fluctuates over time, or capacity fluctuates over time, or both.

Defining capacity as 'the ability to supply' is taking a broad view of the term. The ability to supply depends not only on the limitations of the previous stage in a supply network, operation or process, but on all the stages up to that point. So, for example, the capacity of an ice cream manufacturer is a function not only of how much ice cream its factories can produce at any point in time, but also of how much packaging material, raw material supplies, and so on, that its suppliers can provide. It may have the capacity to make 10,000 kilograms of ice cream a day, but if its suppliers of dairy produce can supply only 7000 kilos a day, then the effective capacity (in terms of 'ability to supply') is only 7000 kilos per day. Of course, if demand remains steady, any operation will attempt to make sure that its supply capacity does not limit its own ability to supply. But, capacity management is concerned with fluctuations in demand *and* supply. It involves coping with the dynamics of delivering products and services to customers. Balancing the individual capacities of each part of the network is therefore a more difficult, and ever changing, task.

> **Operations principle**
> Any measure of capacity should reflect the ability of an operation or process to supply demand.

It is worth noting that 'coping' with mismatches between demand and capacity may not mean that capacity should match demand. An operation could take the deliberate decision to fail to meet demand, or to fail to fully exploit its ability to supply. For example, a hotel may not make any effort to meet demand in peak periods because doing so would incur unwarranted capital costs. It is therefore content to leave some demand unsatisfied, although it may increase its prices to reflect this. Similarly, a flower grower may not supply the entirety of its potential supply (crop) if doing so would simply depress market prices and reduce its total revenue.

Levels of capacity management

The activity of coping with demand–capacity mismatches needs addressing over various time scales. In the long term, physical capacity needs adjusting to reflect the growth or decline in long-term demand. This task involves 'streaming on' or closing down relatively large units of physical capacity over a time period, possibly stretching into years. This activity was treated when we discussed the design of supply networks in Chapter 3. In addition, and within the physical constraints imposed by long-term capacity, most operations will need to cope with demand–capacity mismatches in the medium term, where 'medium term' may mean anything from one day to one year. It is this level that we discuss in this chapter. In an even shorter term, individual processes may need to cope with demand–capacity mismatches day-by-day or even minute-by-minute. This is an issue for 'resource planning and control', examined in Chapter 10.

The following two examples illustrate the nature of capacity management.

Example   The Penang Mutiara[1]

Source: Courtesy of Mutiara Beach Resort, Penang

One of the vacation regions of the world, South-East Asia has many luxurious hotels. One of the best is the Penang Mutiara, a top-of-the-market hotel which nestles in the lush greenery of Malaysia's Indian Ocean coast. Owned and managed by PERNAS, Malaysia's largest hotel group, the Mutiara has to cope with fluctuating demand, notwithstanding the region's relatively constant benign climate. *'Managing a hotel of this size is an immensely complicated task,'* says the hotel's manager. *'Our customers have every right to be demanding. Quality of service has to be impeccable. Staff must be courteous and yet also friendly towards our guests. And of course they must have the knowledge to be able to answer guests' questions. Most of all, though, great service means anticipating our guests' needs, thinking ahead so that you can identify what, and how much, they are likely to demand.'*

The hotel tries to anticipate guests' needs in a number of ways. If guests have been to the hotel before, their likely preferences will have been noted from their previous visit. *'A guest should not be kept waiting. This is not always easy but we do our best. For example, if every guest in the hotel tonight decided to call room service and request a meal instead of going to the restaurants, our room service department would obviously be grossly overloaded, and customers would have to wait an unacceptably long time before the meals were brought up to their rooms. We can predict this to some extent, but also we keep a close watch on how demand for room service is building up. If we think it's going to get above the level where response time to customers would become unacceptably long, we will call in staff from other restaurants in the hotel. Of course, to do this we have to make sure that our staff are multi-skilled. In fact we have a policy of making sure that restaurant staff can always do more than one job. It's this kind of flexibility which allows us to maintain fast response to the customer.'*

Although the hotel needs to respond to some short-term fluctuations in demand for individual services, it can predict likely demand relatively accurately because, each day, the actual number of guests is known. Most guests book their stay well in advance, so activity levels for the hotel's restaurants and other services can be planned ahead. Demand does vary throughout the year, peaking during holiday periods, and the hotel has to cope with these seasonal fluctuations. They do this partly by using temporary part-time staff. In the back-office parts of the hotel this isn't a major problem. In the laundry, for example, it is relatively easy to put on an extra shift in busy periods by increasing staffing levels. However, this is more of a problem in the parts of the hotel that have direct contact with the customer. New or temporary staff can't be expected to have the same customer contact skills as the regular staff. The solution to this is to keep the temporary staff as far in the background as possible and make sure that only skilled, well-trained staff interact with the customer. So, for example, a waiter who would normally take orders, serve the food and take away the dirty plates would in peak times restrict his or her activities to taking orders and serving the food. The less skilled part of the job, taking away the plates, could be left to temporary staff.

Example   Madame Tussaud's Amsterdam[2]

A short holiday in Amsterdam would not be complete without a visit to Madame Tussaud's located on four upper floors of the city's most prominent department store in Dam Square. With over 600,000 visitors each year, this is the third most popular tourist attraction in Amsterdam, after the flower market and canal trips. On busy days in the summer, the centre can just manage to handle 5000 visitors. On a wet day in January, however, there may only be 300 visitors throughout the whole day. But although *average* demand is predictable, the actual number of customers can fluctuate significantly. For example, unexpectedly poor weather when there are many visitors in Amsterdam can bring tourists flocking to the shelter and entertainment on offer.

Source: Elisabeth Peters/Alamy

In the streets outside, orderly queues of expectant tourists snake along the pavement, looking in at the displays in the store windows. In this public open space, Tussaud's can do little to entertain the visitors, but entrepreneurial buskers and street artists are quick to capitalize on a captive market. On reaching the entrance lobby, individuals, families and groups purchase their admission tickets. The lobby is in the shape of a large horseshoe, with the ticket sales booth in the centre. On winter days or in quiet spells, there will be only one sales assistant, but on busier days, visitors can pay at either side of the ticket booth, to speed up the process. Having paid, the visitors assemble in the lobby outside the two lifts. While waiting in this area, a photographer wanders around offering to take photos of the visitors standing next to life-sized wax figures of famous people. They may also be entertained by living look-alikes of famous personalities who act as guides to groups of visitors in batches of around 25 customers (the capacity of each of the two lifts that take visitors up to the facility). The lifts arrive every four minutes and customers simultaneously disembark, forming one group of about 50 customers who stay together throughout the section.

What do these two examples have in common?

The obvious similarity between both these operations is that they have to cope with fluctuating customer demand. Also both operations have found ways to cope with these fluctuations, at least up to a point. This is good because both operations would suffer in the eyes of their customers and in terms of their own efficiency, if they could not cope. Yet in one important respect the two operations are different. Although both have to cope with variation in demand, and although the demand on both operations is a mixture of the predictable and the unpredictable, the balance between predictable variation in demand and unpredictable variation in demand is different. Demand at the Penang Mutiara is largely predictable. Seasonal fluctuations are related to known holiday periods and most customers book their stays well in advance. Madame Tussaud's, on the other hand, has to cope with demand that is unpredictable to a greater extent. Very short-term changes in the weather can significantly affect its demand.

In both these examples, mismatches between demand and capacity derive from predictable and unpredictable variation in demand. Although the mismatches that occur in most businesses result from demand fluctuations, some operations have to cope with predictable and unpredictable variation in capacity, if it is defined as 'the ability to supply'.

> **Operations principle**
> Capacity management decision should reflect both predictable and unpredictable variations in capacity and demand.

For example, Figure 8.2 shows the demand and capacity variation of two businesses. The first is a domestic appliance repair service. Both demand and capacity vary month by month. Capacity varies because the field service operatives in the business prefer to take their vacations at particular times of the year. Nevertheless, capacity is relatively stable throughout the year. Demand, by contrast, fluctuates more significantly. It would appear that there are two peaks of demand through the year, with peak demand being approximately twice the level of the low point in demand. The second business is a food manufacturer freezing spinach. The demand for this product is relatively constant throughout the year, but the capacity of the business (in terms not of the capacity of its factories, but of its ability to supply) varies significantly. During the growing and harvesting season capacity is high, but it falls off almost to zero for part of the year. Yet, although the mismatch between demand and capacity is driven primarily by fluctuations in demand in the first case, and by capacity in the second case, the essence of the capacity management activity is essentially similar for both.

FURTHER EXAMPLE

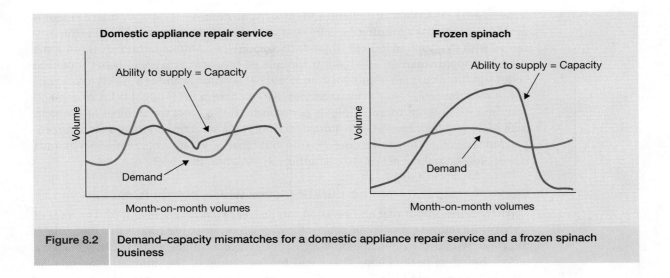

Figure 8.2   Demand–capacity mismatches for a domestic appliance repair service and a frozen spinach business

What is the operation's current capacity?

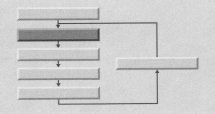

All operations and processes need to know their capacity because if they have too little they cannot meet demand and if they have too much they are paying for more capacity than they need. So a first step in managing capacity is being able to measure current capacity. This sounds simple, but often it is not. In fact, only when the operation is relatively standardized and repetitive is capacity easy to define unambiguously. Any measure of capacity will contain a number of assumptions, each of which may be necessary to give an estimate, but each of which obscures some aspect of reality. Again, taking capacity as 'the ability to supply', these assumptions relate to the mix of products or services supplied, the time over which they are supplied, and the specification of what is supplied.

> **Operations principle**
> Capacity is a function of product/service mix, duration, and product service specification.

Capacity depends on product or service mix

How much an operation can do depends on what it is being required to do. For example, a hospital has a problem in measuring its capacity, partly because there is not a clear relationship between its scale (in terms of the number of beds it has) and the number of patients it treats. If all its patients required relatively minor treatment with only short stays in hospital, it could treat many people per week. Alternatively, if most of its patients required long periods of observation or recuperation, it could treat far fewer. Output depends on the mix of activities in which the hospital is engaged and, because most hospitals perform many different types of activities, output is difficult to predict. Some of the problems caused by variation mix can be partially overcome by using aggregated capacity measures. 'Aggregated' means that different products and services are bundled together in order to get a broad view of demand and capacity. Medium-term capacity management is usually concerned with setting capacity levels in aggregated terms, rather than being concerned with the detail of individual products and services. Although this may mean some degree of approximation, especially if the mix of products or services being produced varies significantly, such approximation is usually acceptable and is a widely used practice in medium-term capacity management. For example, a hotel might think of demand and capacity in terms of 'room nights per month'; this ignores the number of guests in each room and their individual requirements, but it is a good first approximation. A computer manufacturer might measure demand and capacity in terms of the number of units it is capable of making per month, ignoring any variation in models.

Capacity depends on the duration over which output is required

Capacity is the output that an operation can deliver *in a defined unit of time*. The level of activity and output that may be achievable over short periods of time is not the same as the capacity that is sustainable on a regular basis. For example, a tax return processing office, during its peak periods at the end (or beginning) of the financial year, may be capable of processing 120,000 applications a week. It does this by extending the working hours of its staff, discouraging its staff from taking vacations during this period, avoiding any potential disruption to its IT systems (not allowing upgrades during this period, etc.), and maybe just by working hard and intensively. Nevertheless, staff do need vacations, nor can they work long hours continually, and eventually the information system will have to be upgraded. The capacity that is possible to cope with peak times is not sustainable over long periods. Often, capacity is taken to be the level of activity or output that can be sustained over an extended period of time.

Capacity depends on the specification of output

Some operations can increase their output by changing the specification of the product or service (although this is more likely to apply to a service). For example, a postal service may effectively reduce its delivery dependability at peak times. So, during the busy Christmas period, the number of letters delivered the day after being posted may drop from 95 per cent to 85 per cent. This may not always matter to the customer, who understands that the postal service is especially overloaded at this time. Similarly, accounting firms may avoid long 'relationship building' meetings with clients during busy periods. Important though these are, they can usually be deferred to less busy times. The important task is to distinguish between the 'must do' elements of the service that should not be sacrificed and the 'nice to do' parts of the service that can be omitted or delayed in order to increase capacity.

Capacity 'leakage'

Even after allowing for all the difficulties inherent in measuring capacity, the theoretical capacity of a process (the capacity that it was designed to have) is not always achieved in practice. Some reasons for this are, to some extent, predictable. Different products or services may have different requirements, so the process will need to be stopped while it is changed over. Maintenance will need to be performed. Scheduling difficulties could mean further lost time. Not all of these losses are necessarily avoidable; they may occur because of the market and technical demands on the process. However, some of the reduction in capacity can be the result of less predictable events. For example, labour shortages, quality problems, delays in the delivery of bought-in products and services, and machine or system breakdown, can all reduce capacity. This reduction in capacity is sometimes called 'capacity leakage'.

Overall equipment effectiveness[3]

The overall equipment effectiveness (OEE) measure is a popular method of judging the effectiveness of capacity that incorporates the concept of capacity leakage. It is based on three aspects of performance:

- The *time* for which equipment is available to operate
- The *speed*, or throughput rate, of the equipment
- The *quality* of the product or service it produces.

Overall equipment effectiveness is calculated by multiplying an availability rate by a performance (or speed) rate multiplied by a quality rate. Figure 8.3 illustrates this. Some of the reduction in available capacity of a piece of equipment (or any process) is caused by time losses such as setup and changeover losses (when the equipment or process is being prepared for its next activity), and breakdown failures (when the machine is being repaired). Some capacity is lost through speed losses such as when equipment is idling (for example, when it is temporarily waiting for work from another process) and when equipment is being run below its optimum work rate. Finally, not everything processed by a piece of equipment will be error free, so some capacity is lost through quality losses.

Taking the notation in Figure 8.3:

$$OEE = a \times p \times q$$

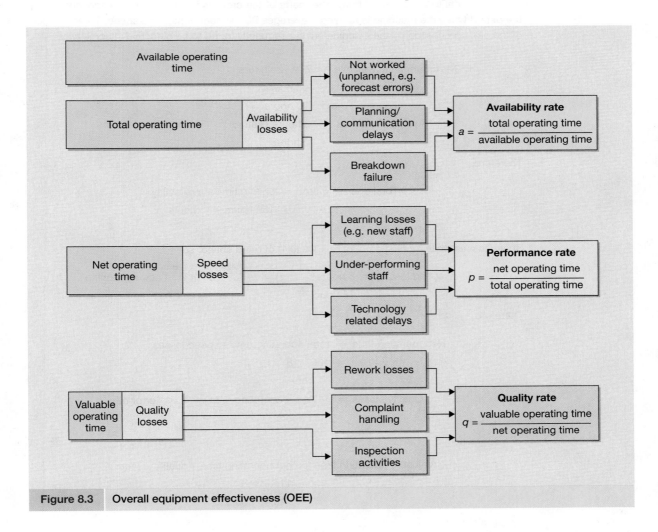

Figure 8.3   Overall equipment effectiveness (OEE)

For equipment to operate effectively, it needs to achieve high levels of performance against all three of these dimensions. Viewed in isolation, these individual metrics are important indicators of plant performance, but they do not give a complete picture of the machine's *overall* effectiveness. This can only be understood by looking at the combined effect of the three measures, calculated by multiplying the three individual metrics together. All these losses to the OEE performance can be expressed in terms of units of time – the design cycle time to produce one good part. So, a reject of one part has an equivalent time loss. In effect, this means that an OEE represents the valuable operating time as a percentage of the capacity something was designed to have.

OEE can be used for service operations and processes, but it is more difficult to do so. Of the three factors (time, speed and quality) only time is straightforward. There is no direct equivalent of speed or throughput rate that is easy to measure objectively. Similarly with quality of output, softer factors such as 'relationship' may be important but, again, difficult to measure. Nevertheless, provided one can accept some degree of approximation, there is no theoretical reason why OEE cannot be used for services.

Worked example

In a typical 7-day period, the planning department programme a particular machine to work for 150 hours, its loading time. Changeovers and setups take an average of 10 hours, and breakdown failures average 5 hours every 7 days. The time when the machine cannot work because it is waiting for material to be delivered from other parts of the process is 5 hours on average, and during the period when the machine is running it averages 90 per cent of its rated speed. Three per cent of the parts processed by the machine are subsequently found to be defective in some way.

$$\text{Maximum time available} = 7 \times 24 \text{ hours}$$
$$= 168 \text{ hours}$$
$$\text{Loading time} = 150 \text{ hours}$$
$$\text{Availability losses} = 10 \text{ hours (setups)} + 5 \text{ hours (breakdowns)}$$
$$= 15 \text{ hours}$$

Therefore,

$$\text{Total operating time} = \text{loading time} - \text{availability}$$
$$= 150 \text{ hours} - 15 \text{ hours}$$
$$= 135 \text{ hours}$$

Speed losses while running amount to 10% (0.1) of rated speed, so

$$\text{Total speed losses} = 5 \text{ hours (idling)} + ((135 - 5) \times 0.1) \text{ hours (running)}$$
$$= 18 \text{ hours}$$

Therefore,

$$\text{Net operating time} = \text{total operating time} - \text{speed losses}$$
$$= 135 - 18$$
$$= 117 \text{ hours}$$
$$\text{Quality losses} = 117 \text{ (net operating time)} \times 0.03 \text{ (error rate)}$$
$$= 3.51 \text{ hours}$$

So,

$$\text{Valuable operating time} = \text{net operating time} - \text{quality losses}$$
$$= 117 - 3.51$$
$$= 113.49 \text{ hours}$$

Therefore,

$$\text{Availability rate} = a = \frac{\text{total operating time}}{\text{available operating time}}$$

$$= \frac{135}{150} = 90\%$$

$$\text{Performance rate} = p = \frac{\text{net operating time}}{\text{total operating time}}$$

$$= \frac{117}{135} = 86.67\%$$

$$\text{Quality rate} = q = \frac{\text{valuable operating time}}{\text{net operating time}}$$

$$= \frac{113.49}{117} = 97\%$$

$$\text{OEE } (a \times p \times q) = 75.6$$

DIAGNOSTIC QUESTION

How well are demand–capacity mismatches understood?

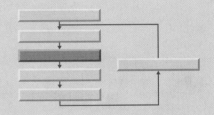

A sound understanding of the nature of potential mismatches between demand and capacity is necessary for effective capacity management. For most businesses, this equates to understanding how demand might vary (although the same logic would apply to variation in capacity). In particular, the balance between predictable and unpredictable variation in demand affects the nature of capacity management. When demand is predictable (usually under conditions of 'dependent demand' – see previous chapter), capacity may need adjusting, but the adjustments can be planned in advance, preferably to minimize the costs of making the change. With unpredictable variation in demand (usually under conditions of 'independent demand'), if an operation is to react to it at all, it must do so quickly; otherwise the change in capacity will have little effect on the operation's ability to cope with the changed demand. Figure 8.4 illustrates how the objective and tasks of capacity management vary depending on the balance between predictable and unpredictable variation.

Enhanced market knowledge makes capacity planning easier

Capacity planning has to cope with mismatches between capacity and demand. Therefore, a deep understanding of the market forces that will generate demand is, if not an absolute prerequisite, nevertheless particularly important. This goes beyond the idea of forecasting as the prediction of uncontrollable events. Enhanced market knowledge is a broader concept and is illustrated in Figure 8.5. When the main characteristic of demand–supply mismatch is unpredictable variation, then forecasting in its conventional sense is important because it converts unpredictable variation into predictable variation. But, when the main

		Unpredictable variation	
		Low	**High**
Predictable variation	**High**	*Objective* – Adjust planned capacity as efficiently as possible *Capacity management tasks* • Evaluate optimum mix of methods for capacity fluctuation • Work on how to reduce cost of putting plan into effect	*Objective* – Adjust planned capacity as efficiently as possible and enhance capability for further fast adjustments *Capacity management tasks* • Combination of those for predictable and unpredictable variation
	Low	*Objective* – Make sure the base capacity is appropriate *Capacity management tasks* • Seek ways of providing steady capacity effectively	*Objective* – Adjust capacity as fast as possible *Capacity management tasks* • Identify sources of extra capacity and/or uses for surplus capacity • Work on how to adjust capacity and/or uses of capacity quickly

Figure 8.4 The nature of capacity management depends on the mixture of predictable and unpredictable demand and capacity variation

Operations principle
The greater an operation's market knowledge, the more capacity management will focus on predictable demand–capacity mismatches.

capacity management is predictable variation, then better forecasting as such is of limited value because demand–supply mismatches are, by definition, already known. What is useful under these circumstances is not so much a knowledge of what demand–supply mismatches will be, but rather how they can be changed.

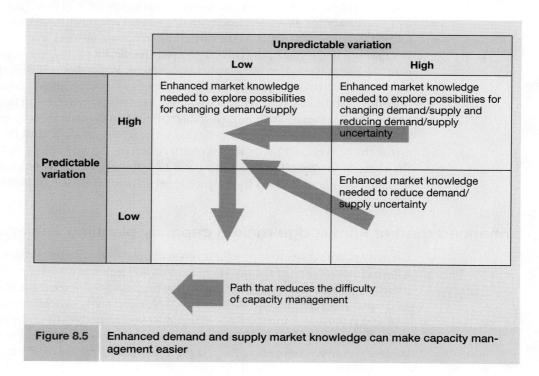

Figure 8.5 Enhanced demand and supply market knowledge can make capacity management easier

So, for example, can a major customer be persuaded to move their demand to a quieter period? Will increasing prices at peak periods shift demand to off-peak periods? Can new storage techniques allow the supply of food ingredients throughout the year?

If capacity management is largely a matter of coping with significant, but predictable, mismatches between demand and supply, then knowledge about how markets can be changed is important. However, when unpredictable variation is high, the first task is to transform variation from unpredictable to predictable through better forecasting. Of course, forecasting cannot eliminate predictable variation, but it is a first step towards minimizing the negative effects of variation on capacity management.

Making forecasts useful for capacity management

Without some understanding of future demand and supply fluctuations, it is not possible to plan effectively for future events, only to react to them. This is why it is important to understand how forecasts are made. Forecasting was discussed in the supplement to Chapter 3, and it clearly helps the capacity management activity to have accurate forecasts. But, in addition to accuracy there are a number of other issues that make forecasts more (or less) useful as an input to capacity planning.

Forecasts can never be perfectly accurate all the time. Yet sometimes forecast errors are more damaging than at other times. For example, if a process is operating at a level close to its maximum capacity, over-optimistic forecasts could lead the process to committing itself to unnecessary capital expenditure to increase its capacity. Inaccurate forecasts for a process operating well below its capacity limit will also result in extra cost, but probably not to the same extent. So the effort put into forecasting should reflect the varying sensitivity to forecast error. Forecasts also need to be expressed in units that are useful for capacity planning. If forecasts are expressed only in money terms and give no indication of the demands that will be placed on an operation's capacity, they will need to be translated into realistic expectations of demand, expressed in the same units as the capacity (for example, machine hours per year, operatives required, space, etc.). Perhaps most importantly, forecasts should give an indication of relative uncertainty. Demand in some periods is more uncertain than others. The importance of this is that the operations managers need an understanding of when increased uncertainty makes it necessary to have reserve capacity. A probabilistic forecast allows this type of judgement between possible plans that would virtually guarantee the operation's ability to meet actual demand, and plans that minimize costs. Ideally, this judgement should be influenced by the nature of the way the business wins orders: price-sensitive markets may require a risk-avoiding cost minimization plan that does not always satisfy peak demand, whereas markets that value responsiveness and service quality may justify a more generous provision of operational capacity. Remember, though, the idea that 'better forecasting' is needed for effective capacity management is only partly true. A better approach would be to say that it is enhanced market knowledge (of both demand and supply) generally that is important.

Better forecasting or better operations responsiveness?

Operations principle
Attempting to increase market knowledge and attempting to increase operations flexibility present alternative approaches to capacity management, but are not mutually exclusive.

The degree of effort (and cost) to devote to forecasting is often a source of heated debate within businesses. This often comes down to two opposing arguments. One goes something like this: *'Of course it is important for forecasts to be as accurate as possible; we cannot plan operations capacity otherwise. This invariably means we finish up with too much capacity (thereby increasing costs), or too little capacity (thereby losing revenue and dissatisfying customers).'* The counter-argument is very different: *'Demand will always be uncertain, that is the nature of demand. Get used to it. The only way to satisfy customers is to make the operation sufficiently responsive to cope with demand, almost irrespective of what it is.'* Both these arguments have some merit, but both are extreme positions. In practice, operations must find some balance between having better forecasts and being able to cope without perfect forecasts.

FURTHER EXAMPLE

Trying to get forecasts right has particular value where the operation finds it difficult or impossible to react to unexpected demand fluctuations in the short term. Internet-based retailers at some holiday times, for example, find it difficult to flex the quantity of goods they have in stock in the short term. Customers may not be willing to wait. On the other hand, other types of operation working in intrinsically uncertain markets may develop fast and flexible processes to compensate for the difficulty in obtaining accurate forecasts. For example, fashion garment manufacturers try to overcome the uncertainty in their market by shortening their response time to new fashion ideas (catwalk to rack time) and the time taken to replenish stocks in the stores (replenishment time). Similarly, when the cost of not meeting demand is very high, processes also have to rely on their responsiveness rather than accurate forecasts. For example, accident and emergency departments in hospitals must be responsive even if it means underutilized resources at times.

DIAGNOSTIC QUESTION

What should be the operation's base capacity?

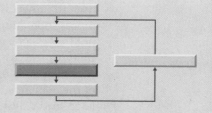

The most common way of planning capacity is to decide on a 'base level' of capacity and then adjust it periodically up or down to reflect fluctuations in demand. In fact, the concept of 'base' capacity is unusual because, although nominally it is the capacity level from which increases and decreases in capacity level are planned, in very unstable markets, where fluctuations are significant, it may never occur. Also, these two decisions of 'what should the base level of capacity be?' and 'how do we adjust capacity around that base to reflect demand?' are interrelated. An operation could set its base level of capacity at such a high level compared to demand that there is no need ever to adjust capacity levels because they will never exceed the base level of capacity. However, this is clearly wasteful, which is why most operations will adjust their capacity level over time. Nevertheless, although the two decisions are interrelated, it is usually worth setting a nominal base level of capacity before going on to consider how it can be adjusted.

> **Operations principle**
> The higher the base level of capacity, the less capacity fluctuation is needed to satisfy demand.

Setting base capacity

The base level of capacity in any operation is influenced by many factors, but should be clearly related to three in particular:

- The relative importance of the operation's performance objectives
- The perishability of the operation's outputs
- The degree of variability in demand or supply.

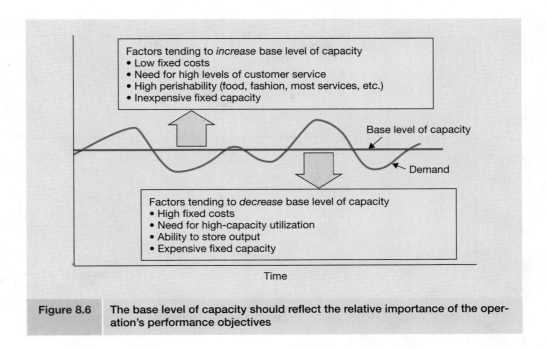

Factors tending to *increase* base level of capacity
- Low fixed costs
- Need for high levels of customer service
- High perishability (food, fashion, most services, etc.)
- Inexpensive fixed capacity

Base level of capacity

Demand

Factors tending to *decrease* base level of capacity
- High fixed costs
- Need for high-capacity utilization
- Ability to store output
- Expensive fixed capacity

Time

Figure 8.6   **The base level of capacity should reflect the relative importance of the operation's performance objectives**

The operation's performance objectives

Base levels of capacity should be set primarily to reflect an operation's performance objectives: see Figure 8.6. For example, setting the base level of capacity high compared to average demand will result in relatively high levels of underutilization of capacity and therefore high costs. This is especially true when an operation's fixed costs are high and therefore the consequences of underutilization are also high. Conversely, high base levels of capacity result in a capacity 'cushion' for much of the time, so the ability to flex output to give responsive customer service will be enhanced. When the output from the operation is capable of being stored, there may also be a trade-off between fixed capital and working capital where base capacity level is set. A high level of base capacity can require considerable investment (unless the cost per unit of capacity is relatively low). Reducing the base level of capacity would reduce the need for capital investment but (where possible) may require inventory to be built up to satisfy future demand and therefore increased levels of working capital. For some operations, building up inventory is either risky because products have a short shelf life (for example perishable food, high performance computers, or fashion items) or impossible because the output cannot be stored at all (most services).

The perishability of the operation's outputs

When either supply or demand is perishable, base capacity will need to be set at a relatively high level because inputs to the operation or outputs from the operation cannot be stored for long periods. For example, a factory that produces frozen fruit will need sufficient freezing, packing and storage capacity to cope with the rate at which the fruit crop is being harvested during its harvesting season. Similarly, a hotel cannot store its accommodation services. If an individual hotel room remains unoccupied, the ability to sell for that night has 'perished'. In fact, unless a hotel is full every single night, its capacity is always going to be higher than the average demand for its services.

The degree of variability in demand or supply

Variability, in either demand or capacity (or processing rate), will reduce the ability of an operation to process its inputs. That is, it will reduce its effective capacity. This effect was

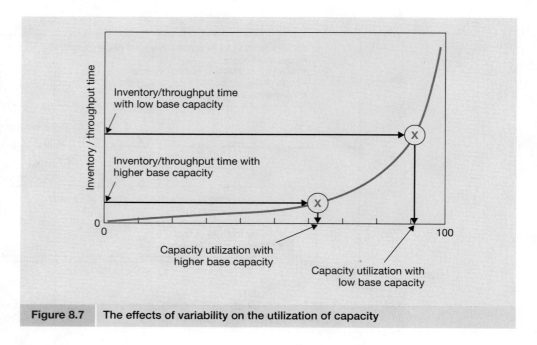

Figure 8.7   The effects of variability on the utilization of capacity

explained in Chapter 5 when the consequences of variability in individual processes were discussed. As a reminder, the greater the variability in arrival time or activity time at a process, the more the process will suffer both high throughput times and reduced utilization. This principle holds true for whole operations, and because long throughput times mean that queues will build up in the operation, high variability also affects inventory levels. This is illustrated in Figure 8.7. The implication of this is that the greater the variability, the more extra capacity will need to be provided to compensate for the reduced utilization of available capacity. Therefore, operations with high levels of variability will tend to set their base level of capacity relatively high in order to provide this extra capacity.

DIAGNOSTIC QUESTION

How can demand–capacity mismatches be managed?

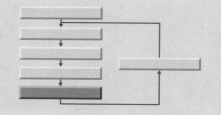

Almost all operations have to cope with varying demand or supply; therefore they will need to consider adjusting capacity around its nominal base level. There are three 'pure' plans available for treating such variation, although in practice most organizations will use a mixture of all of them, even if one plan dominates.

- Ignore demand fluctuations and keep nominal capacity levels constant (level capacity plan).
- Adjust capacity to reflect the fluctuations in demand (chase demand plan).
- Attempt to change demand (demand management).

Level capacity plan

In a level capacity plan, the processing capacity is set at a uniform level throughout the planning period, regardless of the fluctuations in forecast demand. This means that the same number of staff operate the same processes and should therefore be capable of producing the same aggregate output in each period. Where non-perishable materials are processed, but not immediately sold, they can be transferred to finished goods inventory in anticipation of later sales. When inventory is not possible, as in most services, operations demand fluctuations are absorbed through underutilization of the operation's resources and/or and failure to meet demand immediately (see Figure 8.8(a)). The more demand fluctuates, the higher is either inventory or underutilization when using a level capacity plan. Both are expensive, but may be considered if the cost of building inventory is low compared with changing output levels, or in service operations if the opportunity cost of individual lost sales is very high: for example, in the high-margin retailing of jewellery and in (real-) estate agents. Setting capacity below the forecast peak demand level will reduce the degree of underutilization, but, in the periods where demand is expected to exceed capacity, customer service may deteriorate.

Chase demand plan

Chase demand plans attempt to match capacity closely to the varying levels of forecast demand, as in Figure 8.8(b). This is much more difficult to achieve than a level capacity plan, as different numbers of staff, different working hours, and even different amounts of equipment may be necessary in each period. For this reason, pure chase demand plans are unlikely to appeal to operations producing standard, non-perishable products, especially where operations are capital-intensive. The chase demand policy would require a level of physical capacity (as opposed to effective capacity), all of which would be used only occasionally. A pure chase demand plan is more usually adopted by operations that cannot store their output, such as a call centre. It avoids the wasteful provision of excess staff that occurs with a level capacity plan, and yet should satisfy customer demand throughout the planned period. Where inventory is possible, a chase demand policy might be adopted in order to minimize it.

The chase demand approach requires that capacity is adjusted by some means. There are a number of different methods for achieving this, although they may not all be feasible for all types of operation. Some of these methods are shown in Table 8.1.

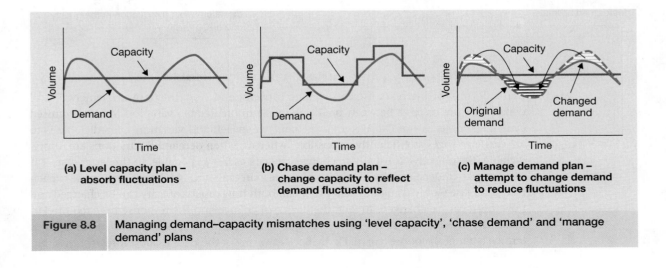

(a) Level capacity plan – absorb fluctuations

(b) Chase demand plan – change capacity to reflect demand fluctuations

(c) Manage demand plan – attempt to change demand to reduce fluctuations

Figure 8.8   Managing demand–capacity mismatches using 'level capacity', 'chase demand' and 'manage demand' plans

Table 8.1 Summary of advantages and disadvantages of some methods of adjusting capacity

Method of adjusting capacity	Advantages	Disadvantages
Overtime – staff working longer than their normal working times	Quickest and most convenient	Extra payment normally necessary, and agreement of staff to work can reduce productivity over long periods
Annualized hours – staff contracting to work a set number of hours per year rather than a set number of hours per week	Without many of the costs associated with overtime, the amount of staff time available to an organization can be varied throughout the year to reflect demand	When very large and unexpected fluctuations in demand are possible, all the negotiated annual working time flexibility can be used before the end of the year
Staff scheduling – arranging working times (start and finish times) to vary the aggregate number of staff available for working at any time	Staffing levels can be adjusted to meet demand without changing job responsibilities or hiring new staff	Providing start and finish (shift) times that both satisfy the need of staff for reasonable working times and shift patterns as well as providing appropriate capacity can be difficult
Varying the size of the workforce – hiring extra staff during periods of high demand and laying them off as demand falls, or 'hire and fire'	Reduces basic labour costs quickly	Hiring costs and possible low productivity while new staff go through the learning curve. Lay-offs may result in severance payments and possible loss of morale in the operation and loss of goodwill in the local labour market
Using part-time staff – recruit staff who work for less than the normal working day (at the busiest periods)	Good method of adjusting capacity to meet predictable short-term demand fluctuations	Expensive if the fixed costs of employment for each employee (irrespective of how long he or she works) are high
Skills flexibility – designing flexibility in job design and job demarcation so that staff can transfer across from less busy parts of the operation	Fast method of reacting to short-term demand fluctuations	Investment in skills training needed and may cause some internal disruption
Sub-contracting/outsourcing – buying, renting or sharing capacity or output from other operations	No disruption to the operation	Can be very expensive because of sub-contractor's margin, and sub-contractor may not be as motivated to give same service or quality. Also a risk of leakage of knowledge
Change output rate – expecting staff (and equipment) to work faster than normal	No need to provide extra resources	Can only be used as a temporary measure, and even then can cause staff dissatisfaction, a reduction in the quality of work, or both

Changing capacity when variation is unpredictable

Both the mix of methods used to change capacity and how they are implemented will depend on the balance between predictable and unpredictable variation. As we discussed earlier, the objective of capacity management when demand variation is predictable is to affect the changes as efficiently as possible, whereas, when demand fluctuations are unpredictable, the objective is usually to change capacity as fast as possible. In the latter case, it is necessary to understand the flexibility of the resources that may be used to increase capacity. In this case we are using flexibility to mean both how much capacity can be changed and how fast it can be changed. In fact, the degree of change and the response time required to make the change are almost always related. The relationship can be shown in what is termed a 'range–response' curve. Figure 8.9 shows one of these for a call centre. It shows that

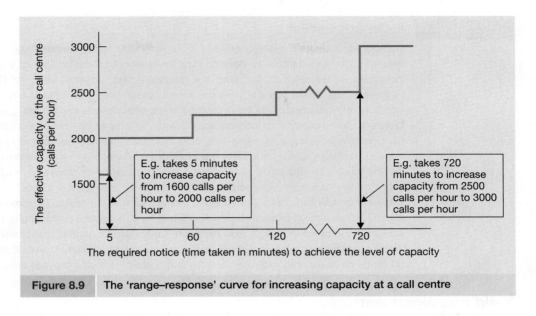

Figure 8.9   The 'range–response' curve for increasing capacity at a call centre

FURTHER EXAMPLE

within a few minutes of demand for the call centre's services increasing, it has the ability to switch a proportion of its calls to the company's other call centres. However, not everyone in these other call centres is trained to take such calls, therefore any further increase in capacity must come from bringing in staff currently not on shift. Eventually, the call centre will hit its limits of physical capacity (computers, telephone lines, etc.). Any further capacity increase will have to wait until more physical capacity is added.

Manage demand plan

The objective of demand management is to change the pattern of demand to bring it closer to available capacity, usually by transferring customer demand from peak periods to quiet periods, as was shown in Figure 8.8(c). There are a number of methods for achieving this.

- *Constraining customer access* – allowing customers access to the operation's products or services only at particular times, for example reservation and appointment systems in hospitals.
- *Price differentials* – adjusting price to reflect demand. That is, increasing prices during periods of high demand and reducing prices during periods of low demand.
- *Scheduling promotion* – varying the degree of market stimulation through promotion and advertising in order to encourage demand during normally low periods.
- *Service differentials* – allowing service levels to reflect demand (implicitly or explicitly), allowing service to deteriorate in periods of high demand and increase in periods of low demand. If this strategy is used explicitly, customers are being educated to expect varying levels of service and hopefully move to periods of lower demand.

A more radical approach attempts to create alternative products or services to fill capacity in quiet periods. It can be an effective demand management method but, ideally, new products or services should meet three criteria: (a) they can be produced on the same processes, (b) they have different demand patterns from existing offerings, and (c) they are sold through similar marketing channels. For example, ski resorts may provide organized mountain activity holidays in the summer, and garden tractor companies may make snow movers in the autumn and winter. However, the apparent benefits of filling capacity in this way must be weighed against the risks of damaging the core product or service, and the operation must be fully capable of serving both markets.

Example	**Hallmark Cards**[4]

Companies that traditionally operate in seasonal markets can demonstrate some considerable ingenuity in their attempts to develop counter-seasonal products. One of the most successful industries in this respect has been the greetings card industry. Mothers' Day, Fathers' Day, Halloween, Valentine's Day and other occasions have all been promoted as times to send (and buy) appropriately designed cards. Now, having run out of occasions to promote, greetings card manufacturers have moved on to 'non-occasion' cards, which can be sent at any time. These have the considerable advantage of being less seasonal, thus making the companies' seasonality less marked. Hallmark Cards has been the pioneer in developing non-occasion cards. Their cards include those intended to be sent from a parent to a child with messages such as 'Would a hug help?', 'Sorry I made you feel bad' and 'You're perfectly wonderful – it's your room that's a mess'. Other cards deal with more serious adult themes such as friendship ('you're more than a friend, you're just like family') or even alcoholism ('this is hard to say, but I think you're a much neater person when you're not drinking'). Now Hallmark Cards have founded a 'loyalty marketing group' that 'helps companies communicate with their customers at an emotional level'. It promotes the use of greetings cards for corporate use, to show that customers and employees are valued.

Yield management

In operations which have relatively fixed capacities, such as airlines and hotels, it is important to use the capacity of the operation for generating revenue to its full potential. One approach used by such operations is called yield management.[5] This is really a collection of methods, some of which we have already discussed, that can be used to ensure that an operation maximizes its potential to generate profit. Yield management is especially useful where:

- capacity is relatively fixed
- the market can be fairly clearly segmented
- the service cannot be stored in any way
- the services are sold in advance
- the marginal cost of making a sale is relatively low.

Airlines, for example, fit all these criteria. They adopt a collection of methods to try to maximize the yield (i.e. profit) from their capacity. Overbooking capacity may be used to compensate for passengers who do not show up for the flight. If the airline does not fill a seat it will lose the revenue from it, so airlines regularly book more passengers onto flights than the aircraft can cope with. However, if more passengers show up than expected, the airline will have a number of upset passengers (although they may be able to offer financial inducements for the passengers to take another flight). By studying past data on flight demand, airlines try to balance the risks of overbooking and underbooking. Operations may also use price discounting at quiet times, when demand is unlikely to fill capacity. Airlines also sell heavily discounted tickets to agents who then themselves take the risk of finding customers for them. This type of service may also be varied. For example, the relative demand for first-class, business-class and economy-class seats varies throughout the year. There is no point discounting tickets in a class for which demand will be high. Yield management tries to adjust the availability of the different classes of seat to reflect their demand. They will also vary the number of seats available in each class by upgrading or even changing the configuration of airline seats.

Using cumulative representations to plan capacity

When an operation's output can be stored, a useful method of assessing the feasibility and consequences of adopting alternative capacity plans is the use of cumulative demand and supply curves. These plot (or calculate) both the cumulative demand on an operation,

Excel

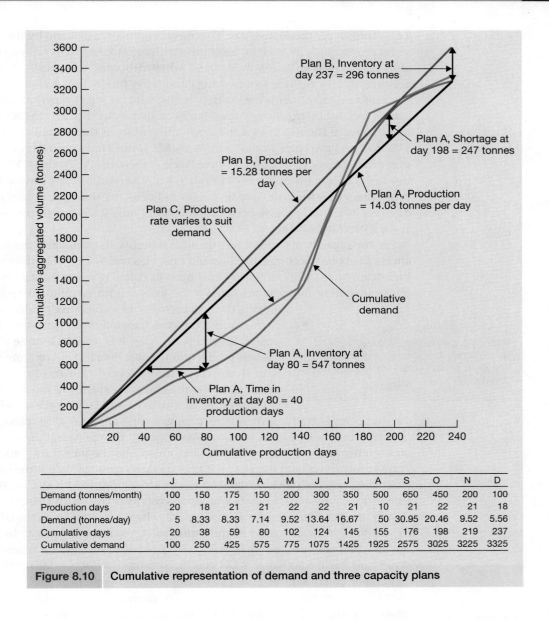

	J	F	M	A	M	J	J	A	S	O	N	D
Demand (tonnes/month)	100	150	175	150	200	300	350	500	650	450	200	100
Production days	20	18	21	21	22	22	21	10	21	22	21	18
Demand (tonnes/day)	5	8.33	8.33	7.14	9.52	13.64	16.67	50	30.95	20.46	9.52	5.56
Cumulative days	20	38	59	80	102	124	145	155	176	198	219	237
Cumulative demand	100	250	425	575	775	1075	1425	1925	2575	3025	3225	3325

Figure 8.10   Cumulative representation of demand and three capacity plans

and its cumulative ability to supply, over time. For example, Figure 8.10 shows the forecast aggregated demand for a chocolate factory that makes confectionery products. Demand for its products in the shops is greatest in December. To meet this demand and allow time for the products to work their way through the supply chain, the factory must supply a demand that peaks in September. But the cumulative representation of demand against available supply time (productive days) shown in Figure 8.10 reveals that, although total demand peaks in September, because of the restricted number of available productive days, the peak demand per productive day occurs a month earlier in August. It also shows that the effective fluctuation in demand over the year is even greater than it seemed. The ratio of monthly peak demand to monthly lowest demand is 6.5:1, but the ratio of peak to lowest demand per productive day is 10:1. Demand per productive day is more relevant to operations managers, because productive days represent the 'ability to supply'.

PRACTICE NOTE

The feasibility and consequences of a capacity plan can be assessed on this basis. Figure 8.10 also shows a level capacity plan (A) that assumes production at a rate of

14.03 tonnes per productive day. This meets cumulative demand by the end of the year, so total over-capacity is equal to or greater than under-capacity. However, if one of the aims of the plan is to supply demand when it occurs, the plan is inadequate. Up to around day 168, the line representing cumulative production is above that representing cumulative demand. This means that at any time during this period, more product has been produced by the factory than has been demanded from it. In fact the vertical distance between the two lines is the level of inventory at that point in time. So by day 80, 1122 tonnes have been produced but only 575 tonnes have been demanded. The surplus of production above demand, or inventory, is therefore 547 tonnes. When the cumulative demand line lies above the cumulative production line, the reverse is true. The vertical distance between the two lines now indicates the shortage, or lack of supply. So by day 198, 3025 tonnes have been demanded but only 2778 tonnes produced. The shortage is therefore 247 tonnes.

For any capacity plan to meet demand as it occurs, its cumulative production line must always lie above the cumulative demand line. This makes it a straightforward task to judge the adequacy of a plan, simply by looking at its cumulative representation. An impression of the inventory implications can also be gained from a cumulative representation by judging the area between the cumulative production and demand curves. This represents the amount of inventory carried over the period. Level capacity plan B is feasible because it always ensures enough production to meet demand at any time throughout the year. However, inventory levels are high using this plan. It may even mean that the chocolate spends so much time in the factory's inventory, that it has insufficient shelf life when it arrives at the company's retail customers. Assuming a 'first-in-first-out' inventory management principle, the time product stays in inventory will be represented by the horizontal line between the demand at the time it is 'demanded' and the time it was produced.

> **Operations principle**
> For any capacity plan to meet demand as it occurs, its cumulative production line must always lie above its cumulative demand line.

Inventory levels (and therefore the time products spend as part of the inventory) can be reduced by adopting a chase demand plan, such as that shown as C in Figure 8.10. This reduces inventory-carrying costs, but incurs costs associated with changing capacity levels. Usually, the marginal cost of making a capacity change increases with the size of the change. For example, if the chocolate manufacturer wishes to increase capacity by 5 per cent, this can be achieved by requesting its staff to work overtime – a simple, fast and relatively inexpensive option. If the change is 15 per cent, overtime cannot provide sufficient extra capacity and temporary staff will need to be employed – a more expensive solution which also would take more time. Increases in capacity of above 15 per cent might only be achieved by sub-contracting some work out. This would be even more expensive.

DIAGNOSTIC QUESTION

How should capacity be controlled?

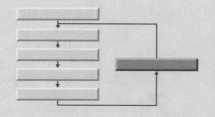

Although planning capacity levels in advance, and even planning how to respond to unexpected changes in demand, is an important part of capacity management, it does not fully reflect the dynamic nature of the activity. Capacity management must react to *actual* demand and *actual* capacity as it occurs. Period by period, operations management considers its forecasts of demand, its understanding of current capacity and, if outputs can be stocked, how much inventory has been carried forward from the previous period. Based on all this information, it makes plans for the following period's capacity. During the next period, demand might or might not be as forecast and the actual capacity of the operation might or might not turn out as planned (because of the capacity leakage discussed earlier). But whatever the actual conditions during that period, at the beginning of the next period the same types of decisions must be made, in the light of the new circumstances. Figure 8.11 shows how this works in practice. It shows the overall performance of an operation's capacity management as a function of the way it manages capacity and the way it manages (or forecasts) demand.

The success of capacity management is generally measured by some combination of costs, revenue, working capital and customer satisfaction (which goes on to influence revenue). This is influenced by the actual capacity available to the operation in any period and the demand for that period. If capacity is in excess of demand, customer demands can be met, but underutilized capacity and possibly inventory will increase costs. If capacity is less than demand, the operation's resources will be fully utilized, but at the expense of being unable to meet all demand. However, some operations are more able to cope than others with any mismatch between actual capacity and actual demand. If the underlying cost structure of the operation is such that fluctuations in output level have relatively little effect on costs, then the operation will be less sensitive to errors in capacity management.

Demand forecasting should always be an ongoing process that incorporates the general market factors which influence demand. In addition, the actual demand that occurs each month should be factored into each period's forecast. In fact, the whole process of capacity control is one of carrying forward, period by period, the decisions and the results of those decisions from one period to the next. In doing so the operation should

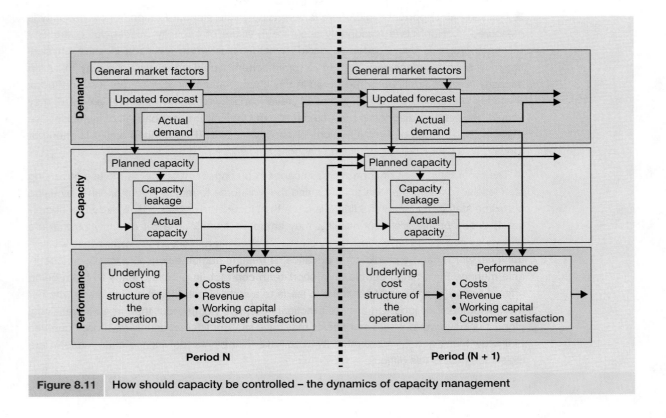

Figure 8.11   How should capacity be controlled – the dynamics of capacity management

be aiming to build up experience of managing demand, managing capacity and adapting the operation to make it less sensitive to mismatches between the two.

Successful capacity control also requires businesses to learn from their handling of previous demand fluctuations. Period by period, operations managers are reacting to a set of stimuli as illustrated in Figure 8.11. Some of these stimuli may be ambiguous, such as the overall objectives of the operation and its approach to risk. Others will be uncertain, such as future demand and (to a lesser extent) future capacity. This is a complex decision-making process that depends on more than the availability and accuracy of information (although this is important). It also depends on the ability to refine decision-making behaviour through learning from past successes and mistakes. For example, some managers may tend to over-react to immediate stimuli by frequently increasing or decreasing capacity as forecasts of future demand are adjusted. If so, some mechanism will need to be put in place that smoothes both forecasts and the response to them.

> **Operations principle**
> The learning from managing capacity in practice should be captured and used to refine both demand forecasting and capacity planning.

Critical commentary

Each chapter contains a short critical commentary on the main ideas covered in the chapter. Its purpose is not to undermine the issues discussed in the chapter, but to emphasize that, although we present a relatively orthodox view of operation, there are other perspectives.

■ For such an important topic, there is surprisingly little standardization in how capacity is measured. Not only is a reasonably accurate measure of capacity needed for operations management, it is also needed to decide whether it is worth investing in extra physical capacity such as machines. Yet not all practitioners would agree with the way in which capacity has been defined or measured in this chapter (although it does represent orthodox practice). One school of thought is that whatever capacity efficiency measures are used, they should be useful as diagnostic measures that can highlight the root causes of inefficient use of capacity. The idea of overall equipment effectiveness (OEE) described earlier is often put forward as a useful way of measuring capacity efficiencies.

■ The other main point of controversy in capacity management concerns the use of varying staff levels. To many, the idea of fluctuating the workforce to match demand, either by using part-time staff or by hiring and firing, is more than just controversial, it is regarded as unethical. It is any business's responsibility, they argue, to engage in a set of activities that are capable of sustaining employment at a steady level. Hiring and firing merely for seasonal fluctuations, which can be predicted in advance, is treating human beings in a totally unacceptable manner. Even hiring people on a short-term contract, in practice, leads to them being offered poorer conditions of service and leads to a state of permanent anxiety as to whether they will keep their jobs. On a more practical note, it is pointed out that, in an increasingly global business world where companies may have sites in different countries, those countries that allow hiring and firing are more likely to have their plants 'downsized' than those where legislation makes this difficult.

Summary checklist

DOWNLOADABLE

This checklist comprises questions that can be usefully applied to any type of operations and reflect the major diagnostic questions used within the chapter.

☐ Is the importance of effective capacity management fully understood?

☐ Is the operation's current capacity measured?

☐ If so, are all the assumptions inherent in the measurement of capacity made fully explicit?

☐ What capacity 'leakage' is normal, and have options for minimizing capacity leakage been explored?

☐ Is there scope for using the overall equipment effectiveness (OEE) measure of capacity?

☐ What is the balance between predictable variation and unpredictable variation in demand and capacity?

☐ Realistically, what potential is there for making unpredictable variability more predictable through better forecasting?

☐ Does an understanding of the market include the extent to which the behaviour of customers and/or suppliers can be influenced to reduce variability?

☐ Does the operations base capacity reflect all the factors that should be influencing its level?

☐ Have alternative methods of adjusting (or not) capacity been fully explored and assessed?

☐ If variation is unpredictable, have methods of speeding up the operation's reaction to demand–capacity mismatches been explored?

☐ Is there scope for using cumulative representations of demand and capacity for planning purposes?

☐ Is the method of deciding period-by-period capacity levels effective?

☐ How does the method of deciding period-by-period capacity levels reflect previous experience?

Case study   Blackberry Hill Farm

'Six years ago I had never heard of agri-tourism. As far as I was concerned, I had inherited the farm and I would be a farmer all my life.' (Jim Walker, Blackberry Hill Farm)

The 'agri-tourism' that Jim was referring to is 'a commercial enterprise at a working farm, or other agricultural centre, conducted for the enjoyment of visitors that generates supplemental income for the owner'. 'Farming has become a tough business,' says Jim. 'Low world prices, a reduction in subsidies, and increasingly uncertain weather patterns have made it a far more risky business than when I first inherited the farm. Yet, because of our move into the tourist trade we are flourishing. Also . . . I've never had so much fun in my life.' But, Jim warns, agri-tourism isn't for everyone. 'You have to think carefully. Do you really want to do it? What kind of life style do you want? How open-minded are you to new ideas? How business-minded are you? Are you willing to put a lot of effort into marketing your business? Above all, do you like working with people? If you would rather be around cows than people, it isn't the business for you.'

History

Blackberry Hill Farm was a 200-hectare mixed farm in the south of England when Jim and Mandy Walker inherited it 15 years ago. It was primarily a cereal-growing operation with a small dairy herd, some fruit and vegetable growing and mixed woodland that was protected by local preservation laws. Six years ago it had become evident to Jim and Mandy that they may have to rethink how the farm was being managed. 'We first started a pick-your-own (PYO) operation because our farm is close to several large

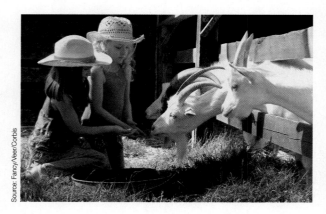

Source: Fancy/Veer/Corbis

centres of population. Also the quantities of fruit and vegetables that we were producing were not large enough to interest the commercial buyers. Entering the PYO market was a reasonable success and in spite of making some early mistakes, it turned our fruit and vegetable growing operation from making a small loss to making a small profit. Most importantly, it gave us some experience of how to deal with customers face-to-face and of how to cope with unpredictable demand. The biggest variable in PYO sales is weather. Most business occurs at the weekends between late spring and early autumn. If rain keeps customers away during part of those weekends, nearly all sales have to occur in just a few days.'

Within a year of opening up the PYO operation Jim and Mandy had decided to reduce the area devoted to cereals and increase their fruit and vegetable growing capability. At the same time they organized a Petting Zoo that allowed children to mix with, feed and touch various animals.

'We already had our own cattle and poultry but we extended the area and brought in pigs and goats. Later we also introduced some rabbits, ponies and donkeys, and even a small bee-keeping operation.' At the same time the farm started building up its collection of 'farm heritage' exhibits. These were static displays of old farm implements and 'recreations' of farming processes together with information displays. This had always been a personal interest of Jim's and it allowed him to convert two existing farm outbuildings to create a 'Museum of Farming Heritage'.

The year after, they introduced tractor rides for visitors around the whole farm and extended the petting zoo and farming tradition exhibits further. But the most significant investment was in the 'Preserving Kitchen'. 'We had been looking for some way of using the surplus fruits and vegetables that we occasionally accumulated and also for some kind of products that we could sell in a farm shop. We started the Preserving Kitchen to make jams and fruit, vegetables and sauces preserved in jars. The venture was an immediate success. We started making just 50 kilograms of preserves a week; within three months that had grown to 300 kilograms a week and we are now producing around 1000 kilograms a week, all under the "Blackberry Hill Farm" label.' The following year the preserving kitchen was extended and a viewing area added. 'It was a great attraction from the beginning,' says Mandy. 'We employed ladies

Table 8.2a   Number of visitors last year

Month	Total visitors	Month	Total visitors
January	1,006	August	15,023
February	971	September	12,938
March	2,874	October	6,687
April	6,622	November	2,505
May	8,905	December	3,777
June	12,304	**Total**	**88,096**
July	14,484	Average	7,341.33

Table 8.2b   Farm opening times*

January to mid-March	Wed – Sun	10.00–16.00
Mid-March to May	Tues – Sun	9.00–18.00
June to September	All week	8.30–19.00
October to November	Tues – Sun	10.00–16.00
December	Tues – Sun	9.00–18.00

*Special evening events at Easter, summer weekends and Christmas.

from the local village to make the preserves. They are all extrovert characters, so when we asked them to dress up in traditional "farmers wives" type clothing they were happy to do it. The visitors love it, especially the good-natured repartee with our ladies. The ladies also enjoy giving informal history lessons when we get school parties visiting us.'

Within the last two years the farm had further extended its preserving kitchen, farm shop, exhibits and petting zoo. It had also introduced a small adventure playground for the children, a café serving drinks and its own produce, a picnic area and a small bakery. The bakery was also open to view by customers and staffed by bakers in traditional dress. *'It's a nice little visitor attraction,'* says Mandy, *'and*

it gives us another opportunity to squeeze more value out of our own products.' Table 8.2a shows last year's visitor numbers, and Table 8.2b lists the farm's opening times.

Demand

The number of visitors to the farm was extremely seasonal. From a low point in January and February, when most people just visited the farm shop, the spring and summer months could be very busy, especially on public holidays. The previous year Mandy had tracked the number of visitors arriving at the farm each day. *'It is easy to record the number of people visiting the farm attractions, because they pay the entrance charge. What we had not done before is include the people who just visited the farm shop and bakery that can be accessed both from within the farm and from the car park. We estimate that the number of people visiting the shop but not the farm ranges from 74 per cent in February down to around 15 per cent in August.'* Figure 8.12 shows the number of visitors in the previous year's August. *'What our figures do not include are those people who visit the shop but don't buy anything. This is unlikely to be a large number.'*

Mandy had also estimated the average stay at the farm and/or farm shop. She reckoned that in winter the average stay was 45 minutes, but in August it climbed to 3.1 hours (see also Figure 8.13).

Current issues

Both Jim and Mandy agreed that their lives had fundamentally changed over the last few years. Income from visitors and from the Blackberry Hill brand of preserves now accounted for 70 per cent of the farm's revenue. More importantly, the whole enterprise was significantly more

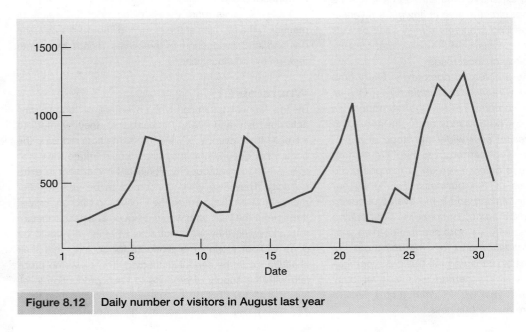

Figure 8.12   Daily number of visitors in August last year

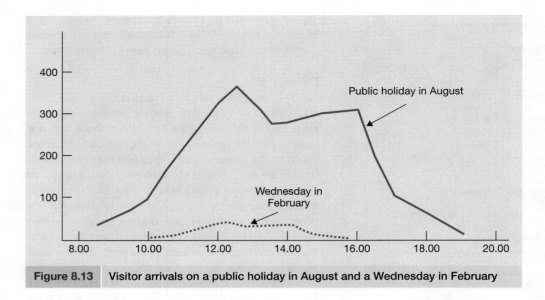

Figure 8.13 Visitor arrivals on a public holiday in August and a Wednesday in February

profitable than it had ever been. Nevertheless, the farm faced a number of issues.

The first was the balance between its different activities. Jim was particularly concerned that the business remained a genuine farm. *'When you look at the revenue per hectare, visitor and production activities bring in far more revenue than conventional agricultural activities. However, if we push the agri-tourism too far we become no better than a theme park. We represent something more than this to our visitors. They come to us partly because of what we represent as well as what we actually do. I am not sure that we would want to grow much more. Anyway, more visitors would mean that we have to extend the car park. That would be expensive, and although it would be necessary, it does not directly bring in any more revenue. There are already parking problems during peak periods and we have had complaints from the police that our visitors park inappropriately on local roads.*

'There is also the problem of complexity. Every time we introduce a new attraction, the whole business gets that little bit more complex to manage. Although we enjoy it tremendously, both Mandy and I are spreading ourselves thinly over an ever widening range of activities.' Mandy was also concerned over this. *'I'm starting to feel that my time is being taken up in managing the day-to-day problems of the business. This does not leave time either for thinking about the overall direction in which we should be going, or spending time talking with the staff. That is why we both see this coming year as a time for consolidation and for smoothing out the day-to-day problems of managing the business, particularly the queuing, which is getting excessive at busy times. That is why this year we are limiting ourselves to just one new venture for the business.'*

Staff management was also a concern for Mandy. The business had grown to over 80 (almost all part-time and seasonal) employees. *'We have become a significant employer in the area. Most of our employees are still local people working part-time for extra income but we are also now employing 20 students during the summer period and, last year, eight agricultural students from Eastern Europe. But now, labour is short in this part of the country and it is becoming more difficult to attract local people, especially to produce Blackberry Hill Farm Preserves. Half of the Preserving Kitchen staff work all year, with the other employed during the summer and autumn periods. But most of them would prefer guaranteed employment throughout the year.'*

Table 8.3 gives more details of some of the issues of managing the facilities at the farm, and Table 8.4 shows the demand and production of preserves month by month through the previous year.

Where next?

By the 'consolidation' and improvement of 'day-to-day' activities Jim and Mandy meant that they wanted to increase their revenue, while at the same time reducing the occasional queues that they knew could irritate their visitors, preferably without any significant investment in extra capacity. They also were concerned to be able to offer more stable employment to the Preserving Kitchen 'ladies' throughout the year, who would produce at a near-constant rate. However, they were not sure whether this could be done without storing the products for so long that their shelf life would be seriously affected. There was no problem with the supply of produce to keep production level: less than 2 per cent of the fruit and vegetables that went into their preserves were actually grown on the farm. The

Table 8.3   The farm's main facilities and some of the issues concerned with managing them

Facility	Issues
Car park	85 car parking spaces, 4 × 40-seater tour bus spaces.
Fixed exhibits, etc. Recreation of old farmhouse kitchen, recreation of barnyard, old-fashioned milking parlour, various small exhibits on farming past and present, adventure playground, ice-cream and snack stands.	• Most exhibits in, or adjacent to, the farm museum. • At peak times helpers are dressed in period costume to entertain visitors. • Feedback indicates customers find exhibits more interesting than they thought they would. • Visitors free to look when they wish absorbs demand from busy facilities.
Tractor rides One tractor towing decorated covered cart with maximum capacity of 30 people, tour takes around 20 minutes on average (including stops). Waits 10 minutes between tours except at peak times when tractor circulates continuously.	• Tractor acts as both transport and entertainment; approximately 60 per cent of visitors stay on for the whole tour, 40 per cent use it as 'hop-on, hop-off' facility. • Overloaded at peak times, long queues building. • Feedback indicates it is popular, except for queuing. • Jim reluctant to invest in further cart and tractor.
Pick-your-own area Largest single facility on the farm. Use local press, dedicated telephone line (answering machine) and website to communicate availability of fruit and vegetables. Checkout and weighing area next to farm shop, also displays picked produce and preserves, etc. for sale.	• Very seasonal and weather dependent, for both supply and demand. • Farm plans for a surplus over visitor demand, uses surplus in preserves. • Six weighing/paying stations at undercover checkout area. Queues develop at peak times. Feedback indicates some dissatisfaction with this. • Can move staff from farm shop to help with checkout in busy periods, but farm shop also tends to be busy at the same time. • Considering using packers at pay stations to speed up the process.
Petting Zoo Accommodation for smaller animals including sheep and pigs. Large animals (cattle, horses) brought to viewing area daily. Visitors can view all animals and handle/stroke most animals under supervision.	• Approximately 50 per cent of visitors view Petting Zoo. • Number of staff in attendance varies between none (off-peak) and five (peak periods). • The area can get congested during peak periods. • Staff need to be skilled at managing children.
Preserving kitchen Boiling vats, mixing vats, jar sterilizing equipment, etc. Visitor viewing area can hold 15 people comfortably. Average length of stay 7 minutes in off-season, 14 minutes in peak season.	• Capacity of kitchen is theoretically 4500 kilograms per month on a 5-day week and 6000 kilograms on a 7-day week. • In practice, capacity varies with season because of interaction with visitors. Can be as low as 5000 kilograms on a 7-day week in summer, or up to 5000 kilograms on a 5-day week in winter. • Shelf-life of products is on average 12 months. • Current storage area can hold 16,000 kilograms.
Bakery Contains mixing and shaping equipment, commercial oven, cooling racks, display stand, etc. Just installed doughnut-making machine. All pastries contain farm's preserved fruit.	• Starting to become a bottleneck since doughnut-making machine installed, visitors like watching it. • Products also on sale at farm shop adjacent to bakery. • Would be difficult to expand this area because of building constraints.
Farm shop and café Started by selling farm's own products exclusively. Now sells a range of products from farms in the region and wider. Started selling frozen menu dishes (lasagne, goulash, etc.) produced off-peak in the preserving kitchen.	• The most profitable part of the whole enterprise, Jim and Mandy would like to extend the retailing and café operation. • Shop includes area for cooking displays, cake decoration, fruit dipping (in chocolate), etc. • Some congestion in shop at peak times but little visitor dissatisfaction. • More significant queuing for café in peak periods. • Considering allowing customers to place orders before they tour the farm's facilities and collect their purchases later. • Retailing more profitable per square metre than café.

Table 8.4	Preserve demand and production (previous year)				
Month	Demand (kg)	Cumulative demand (kg)	Production (kg)	Cumulative product (kg)	Inventory (kg)
January	682	682	4,900	4,900	4,218
February	794	1,476	4,620	9,520	8,044
March	1,106	2,582	4,870	14,390	11,808
April	3,444	6,026	5,590	19,980	13,954
May	4,560	10,586	5,840	25,820	15,234
June	6,014	16,600	5,730	31,550	14,950
July	9,870	26,470	5,710	37,260	10,790
August	13,616	40,086	5,910	43,170	3,084
September	5,040	45,126	5,730	48,900	3,774
October	1,993	47,119	1,570*	50,470	3,351
November	2,652	49,771	2,770*	53,240	3,467
December	6,148	55,919	4,560	57,800	1,881
Average	**4,660**	–	–	–	**7,880**

*Technical problems reduced production level.

remainder were bought at wholesale markets, although this was not generally understood by customers.

Of the many ideas being discussed as candidates for the 'one new venture' for next year, two were emerging as particularly attractive. Jim liked the idea of developing a Maize Maze, a type of attraction that had become increasingly popular in Europe and North America in the last five years. It involved planting a field of maize (corn) and, once grown, cutting through a complex series of paths in the form of a maze. Evidence from other farms indicated that a maze would be extremely attractive to visitors and Jim reckoned that it could account for up to an extra 10,000 visitors during the summer period. Designed as a separate activity with its own admission charge, it would require an investment of around £20,000, but generate more than twice that in admission charges as well as attracting more visitors to the farm itself.

Mandy favoured the alternative idea – that of building up their business in organized school visits. 'Last year we joined the National Association of Farms for Schools. Their advice is that we could easily become one of the top school attractions in this part of England. Educating visitors about farming tradition is already a major part of what we do. And many of our staff have developed the skills to communicate to children exactly what farm life used to be like. We would need to convert and extend one of our existing underused farm outbuildings to make a "school room" and that would cost between £30,000 and £35,000. And although we would need to discount our admission charge substantially, I think we could break even on the investment within around two years.'

QUESTIONS

1 How could the farm's day-to-day operations be improved?

2 What advice would you give Jim and Mandy regarding this year's 'new venture'?

Active case study   Fresh Salads Ltd

ACTIVE CASE

Fresh Salads Ltd is an important division of a privately-owned farming company specializing in vegetable growing and distribution. Its most important customer group is the major UK supermarkets which require fresh produce to be delivered to them 364 days a year.

● Based on the information provided, how would you evaluate the capacity management of the company?

Please refer to the Active case on the CD to find out more about the processes involved in picking and ensuring the delivery of high-quality vegetables to their customers.

Applying the principles

Some of these exercises can be answered by reading the chapter. Others will require some general knowledge of business activity and some might require an element of investigation. All have hints on how they can be answered on the CD accompanying this book.

HINTS

1 A pizza company has a demand forecast for the next 12 months that is shown in the table below. The current work-force of 100 staff can produce 1000 cases of pizzas per month.

(a) Prepare a production plan that keeps the output level. How much warehouse space would the company need for this plan?

(b) Prepare a 'chase demand' plan. What implications would this have for staffing levels, assuming that the maximum amount of overtime would result in production levels only 10 per cent greater than those achieved in normal working hours?

Pizza demand forecast

Month	Demand (cases per month)
January	600
February	800
March	1000
April	1500
May	2000
June	1700
July	1200
August	1100
September	900
October	2500
November	3200
December	900

2 Consider how airlines cope with balancing capacity and demand. In particular, consider the role of yield management. Do this by visiting the website of a low-cost airline, and for a number of flights price the fare that is being charged by the airline from tomorrow onwards. In other words, how much would it cost if you needed to fly tomorrow, how much if you needed to fly next week, how much if you needed to fly in 2 weeks, etc.? Plot the results for different flights and debate the findings.

3 Calculate the overall equipment efficiency (OEE) of the following facilities by investigating their use:

(a) A lecture theatre

(b) A cinema

(c) A coffee machine.

Discuss whether it is worth trying to increase the OEE of these facilities and, if it is, how you would go about it.

4 How should a business work out what it is prepared to pay for increasingly sophisticated weather forecasts?

5 What seem to be the advantages and disadvantages of the strategy adopted by Hallmark Cards described earlier in the chapter? What else could Hallmark do to cope with demand fluctuations?

Notes on chapter

1   Source: Interview with company staff.
2   Source: By kind permission of Dr Willem Bijleveld, Director, Madame Tussaud Scenerama BV, Amsterdam.
3   With special thanks to Philip Godfrey and Cormac Campbell of OEE Consulting Ltd (www.oeeconsulting.com).
4   Sources include Robinette, S. (2001) 'Get emotional', *Harvard Business Review,* May.
5   Kimes, S. (1989) 'Yield management: a tool for capacity-constrained service firms', *Journal of Operations Management,* Vol. 8, No. 4.

Taking it further

Brandimarte, P. and Villa, A. (1999) *Modelling Manufacturing Systems: From aggregate planning to real time control,* Springer, New York. *Very academic, although it does contain some interesting pieces if you need to get 'under the skin' of the subject.*

Buxey, G. (1993) 'Production planning and scheduling for seasonal demand', *International Journal of Operations and Production Management,* Vol. 13, No. 7. *Another academic paper but one that takes an understandable and systematic approach.*

Fisher, M.L., Hammond, J.H. and Obermeyer, W. (1994) 'Making supply meet demand in an uncertain world', *Harvard Business Review,* Vol. 72, No. 3, May–June.

Useful websites

www.dti.gov.uk/er/index Website of the Employment Relations Directorate, which has developed a framework for employers and employees that promotes a skilled and flexible labour market founded on principles of partnership.

www.worksmart.org.uk/index.php This site is from the Trades Union Congress. Its aim is 'to help today's working people get the best out of the world of work'.

www.eoc-law.org.uk This website aims to provide a resource for legal advisors and representatives who are conducting claims on behalf of applicants in sex discrimination and equal pay cases in England and Wales. This site covers employment-related sex discrimination only.

www.dol.gov/index.htm US Department of Labor's site with information regarding using part-time employees.

www.downtimecentral.com Lots of information on overall equipment efficiency (OEE).

FURTHER RESOURCES

> **For further resources including examples, animated diagrams, self-test questions, Excel spreadsheets, active case studies and video materials please explore the CD accompanying this book.**

9

INVENTORY MANAGEMENT

Introduction

Operations managers often have an ambivalent attitude towards inventories. They can be costly, tying up working capital. They are also risky because items held in stock could deteriorate, become obsolete or just get lost. They can also take up valuable space in the operation. On the other hand, they can provide some security in an uncertain environment. Knowing that you have the items in stock is a comforting insurance against unexpected demand. This is the dilemma of inventory management: in spite of the cost and the other disadvantages associated with holding stocks, they do facilitate the smoothing of supply and demand. In fact they exist only because supply and demand are not exactly in harmony with each other. (See Figure 9.1.)

Source: Digital Vision/Getty Images

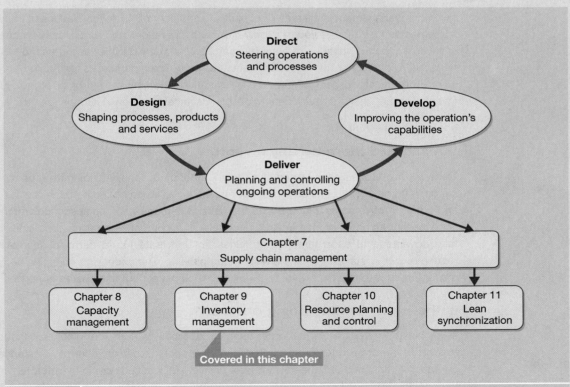

| Figure 9.1 | Inventory management is the activity of planning and controlling accumulations of transformed resources as they move through supply networks, operations and processes |

Executive summary

Decision logic chain for inventory management

Each chapter is structured around a set of diagnostic questions. These questions suggest what you should ask in order to gain an understanding of the important issues of a topic, and as a result, improve your decision making. An executive summary, addressing these questions, is provided below.

What is inventory management?

Inventory management is the activity of planning and controlling accumulations of transformed resources as they move through supply networks, operations and processes. Accumulations of inventory occur because of local mismatches between supplier and demand. All operations have inventories of some kind and inventory management is particularly important where the inventories are central to the operation's objectives and/or of high value. How inventories are managed will determine the balance between customer service and cost objectives.

Why should there be any inventory?

Generally inventory is seen as negative for a number of reasons, including its impact on working capital, the effect it has on throughput times, its ability to obscure problems, the storage and administrative costs it incurs, and the risks of damage and obsolescence. Yet inventory is necessary as an insurance against uncertainty, to compensate for process inflexibility, to take advantage of short-term opportunities, to anticipate future demand, (sometimes) to reduce overall costs, and to fill the distribution pipeline. The underlying objective of inventory management is to minimize inventory while maintaining acceptable customer service.

Is the right quantity being ordered?

A key inventory decision is the 'order quantity' decision. Various formulae exist that attempt to identify the order quantity that minimizes total costs under different circumstances. One approach to this problem, the news vendor problem (discussed later in this chapter), includes the effects of probabilistic demand in determining order quantity.

Are inventory orders being placed at the right time?

Broadly, there are two approaches to this. The reorder point approach is to time reordering at the point in time where stock will fall to zero minus the order lead time. A variation of this is to reorder at the equivalent inventory level (the reorder level approach). Methods of reordering at a fixed point or level are termed continuous review methods because they require continuous monitoring of stock levels. A different approach, called the periodic review approach, places orders at predetermined times, but varies the order depending on the level of inventory at that time. Both continuous and periodic review can be calculated on a probabilistic basis to include safety stocks.

Is inventory being controlled effectively?

The most common inventory control approach is based on the Pareto (at 80:20) curve. It classifies stocked items by their usage value (usage rate multiplied by value). High-usage value items are deemed A class and controlled carefully, whereas low usage value items (B and C class) are controlled less intensely. However, this approach often has to be modified to take account of slow-moving items. Inventory information systems are generally used to keep track of inventory, forecast demand, and place orders automatically.

What is inventory management?

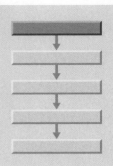

Inventory is the stored accumulation of transformed resources such as materials, information, money, and sometimes customers. Occasionally the term is also used to describe transforming resource, such as rooms in a hotel, or cars in a vehicle-hire firm, but here we use the term exclusively for the accumulation of resources that flow through processes, operations or supply networks. Inventories of customers are normally referred to as 'queues' and were discussed in Chapter 5. Inventory management is the activity of planning and controlling accumulations of the resources that flow through supply networks, operations and processes.

All processes, operations and supply networks have inventories

All processes, operations and supply networks accumulate inventory. Table 9.1 gives some examples, but not all inventories have the same importance. Some in Table 9.1 are relatively trivial. For example, the cleaning materials in the computer assembly operation are of low value and relatively unimportant to the operation. By contrast, inventories of components for assembly are both high value and vital for continued operation. However, cleaning materials would be a far more important item of inventory for an industrial cleaning company, not only because it uses far more of this input, but also because its main operation would stop if it ran out.

Inventory can accumulate between the stages in a process, between the processes in an operation, and between the operations in a supply network. But, wherever inventory

Table 9.1	Examples of inventory held in processes, operations and supply networks
Process, operation or supply network	*Examples of inventory held*
Customer invoicing process	Money, customer and delivery information
Credit card application process	Customer's credit and personal details
Air conditioning systems service process	Spare parts, consumable materials
Hotel	Food items, drinks, toilet items, cleaning materials, customer information
Hospital	Wound dressings, disposable instruments, whole blood, food, drugs, cleaning materials, patient medical records
Computer manufacturer	Components for assembly, peripheral equipment for resale, packaging materials, cleaning materials
Automotive parts distribution network	Automotive parts in main depot, automotive parts at local distribution points
Supermarket supply network	Food and non-food items, packing materials

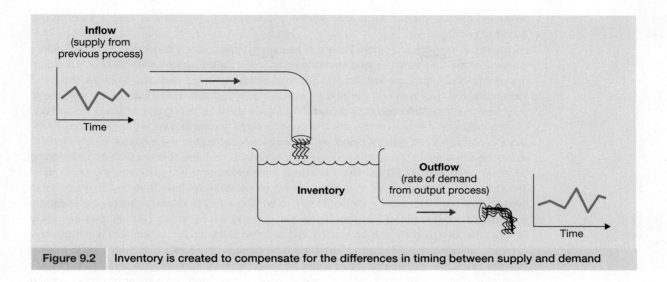

Figure 9.2 Inventory is created to compensate for the differences in timing between supply and demand

accumulates, and whatever is being stored, it will be there because there is a difference in the timing or rate of supply and demand at that point. If the supply of any item occurred exactly when it was demanded, the item would never be stored. A common analogy is the water tank shown in Figure 9.2. If, over time, the rate of supply of water to the tank differs from the rate at which it is demanded, a tank of water (inventory) will be needed to maintain supply. When the rate of supply exceeds the rate of demand, inventory increases; when the rate of demand exceeds the rate of supply, inventory decreases. So if an operation or process can match supply and demand rates, it will also succeed in reducing its inventory levels.

But most organizations must cope with unequal supply and demand, at least at some points in their supply chain. Both organizations in the following examples depend on the ability to manage supply and demand inequality through their inventory management.

| Example | ### The UK's National Blood Service[1] |

No inventory manager likes to run out of stock. But for blood services, such as the UK's National Blood Service (NBS), the consequences of running out of stock can be particularly serious. Many people owe their lives to transfusions that were made possible by the efficient management of blood, stocked in a supply network that stretches from donation centres through to hospital blood banks. The NBS supply chain has three main stages:

- *Collection,* that involves recruiting and retaining blood donors, encouraging them to attend donor sessions (at mobile or fixed locations) and transporting the donated blood to their local blood centre.
- *Processing,* that breaks blood down into its constituent parts (red cells, platelets and plasma) as well over 20 other blood-based 'products'.
- *Distribution,* that transports blood from blood centres to hospitals in response to both routine and emergency requests. Of the Service's 200,000 deliveries a year, about 2500 are emergency deliveries.

Inventory accumulates at all three stages, and in individual hospitals' blood banks. Within the supply chain, around 11.5 per cent of donated red blood cells are lost. Much of this is due to losses in processing, but around 5 per cent is not used because it has 'become unavailable', mainly because it has been stored for too long. Part of the Service's inventory control task is to keep this 'time expired' loss to a minimum. In fact, only small losses occur within the NBS; most blood is lost when it is stored in hospital blood banks that are outside its direct control.

However, it does attempt to provide advice and support to hospitals to enable them to use blood efficiently.

Blood components and products need to be stored under a variety of conditions, but will deteriorate over time. This varies depending on the component; platelets have a shelf life of only five days and demand can fluctuate significantly. This makes stock control particularly difficult. Even red blood cells that have a shelf life of 35 days may not be acceptable to hospitals if they are close to their 'use by date'. Stock accuracy is crucial. Giving a patient the wrong type of blood can be fatal.

At a local level demand can be affected significantly by accidents. One serious accident involving a cyclist used 750 units of blood, which completely exhausted the available supply (miraculously, he survived). Large-scale accidents usually generate a surge of offers from donors wishing to make immediate donations. There is also a more predictable seasonality to the donating of blood, however, with a low period during the summer vacation. Yet there is always an unavoidable tension between maintaining sufficient stocks to provide a very high level of supply dependability to hospitals and minimizing wastage. Unless blood stocks are controlled carefully, they can easily go past the 'use by date' and be wasted. But avoiding outdated blood products is not the only inventory objective at NBS. It also measures the percentage of requests that it was able to meet in full, the percentage of emergency requests delivered within two hours, the percentage of units banked to donors bled, the number of new donors enrolled, and the number of donors waiting longer than 30 minutes before they are able to donate. The traceability of donated blood is also increasingly important. Should any problems with a blood product arise, its source can be traced back to the original donor.

| Example |

Howard Smith Paper Group[2]

The Howard Smith Paper Group operates the most advanced warehousing operation within the European paper merchanting sector, delivering over 120,000 tonnes of paper annually. The function of a paper merchant is to provide the link between the paper producers and the printers or converters who use large quantities of paper. It is a service-driven business, so the role of the operation function is to deliver whatever the salesperson has promised to the customer: the right product, at the right time, at the right place, and in the right quantity. This depends on professional inventory management. The company's operations are divided into two areas: 'logistics', which combines all warehousing and logistics tasks, and 'supply side', which includes inventory planning, and purchasing. Its main stocks are held at the national distribution centre, located in Northampton in central England. This location was chosen because it is at the centre of the company's main customer location and also because it has good access to motorways.

The key to any efficient merchanting operation lies in its ability to do two things well. It must be able to run a set of efficient processes that purchase, store, pick and distribute paper to customers. But also it must make the right decision on how much of each product to stock, how much to order, and when to replenish stocks at the company's 'dark warehouse' which is operational 24 hours per day, 5 days per week. All picking and movement within the dark warehouse is fully automatic and there is no need for any person to enter the high-bay stores and picking area. A warehouse computer system (WCS) controls the whole operation without the need for human input. It manages pallet location and retrieval, robotic crane missions, automatic conveyors, bar code label production and scanning, and all picking routines and priorities. All products are identified by a unique bar code so that accuracy is guaranteed. The unique user log-on ensures that any picking errors can be traced back to the name of the picker, to ensure further errors do not occur. The WCS is linked to the company's Enterprise Resources Planning (ERP) system (we will deal with ERP in Chapter 12), such that once the order has been placed by a customer, the information systems manage the whole process from order placement to order dispatch. These systems also track demand trends and produce regularly updated forecasts, as well as controlling inventory levels and placing orders with paper manufacturers to ensure fast and accurate stock replenishment. This inventory control activity is at the heart of the company's success because it governs the amount of inventory held (a major element in the company's costs) and the service level to customers (which shapes customer satisfaction, and therefore the company's revenue).

What do these two examples have in common?

Both of these organizations depend on their ability to manage inventory. In doing so, both are attempting to manage the trade-off that lies at the heart of all inventory management – balancing the costs of holding stock against the customer service that comes from having appropriate stock levels. Too high stock levels have a cost. This may be simply working capital in the case of the paper merchants, or it could be the cost of blood becoming outdated and being wasted in the blood service. But without an appropriate level of inventory, customers go unserved. This means potentially losing revenue for the paper merchant. A failure to supply for the blood service may have even more drastic consequences. So, for both operations at each point in the inventory system, operations managers need to manage the day-to-day tasks of running the system. Orders will be received from internal or external customers; these will be dispatched and demand will gradually deplete the inventory. Orders will need to be placed for replenishment of the stocks; deliveries will arrive and require storing. In managing the system, three types of decision are needed:

- *How much to order.* Every time a replenishment order is placed, how big should it be? This is sometimes called the volume decision.
- *When to order.* At what point in time, or at what level of stock, should the replenishment order be placed? This is sometimes called the timing decision.
- *How to control the system.* What procedures and routines should be installed to help make these decisions? Should different priorities be allocated to different stock items? How should stock information be stored?

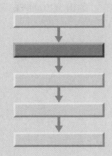

DIAGNOSTIC QUESTION

Why should there be any inventory?

There are plenty of reasons to avoid accumulating inventory where possible.

- Inventory (of products) ties up money, in the form of working capital, which is therefore unavailable for other uses, such as reducing borrowings or making investment in productive fixed assets (we shall expand on the idea of working capital later). In other words, it has an opportunity cost, and at the same time cannot be considered to directly add value.
- Inventory slows throughput in processes, operations and supply networks. While something is stored as inventory it is not progressing, or (usually) having value added to it. Low inventory levels mean that transformed resources move between stages,

processes or operations quickly, while high inventory levels mean that they spend time simply being stored. There is therefore a direct connection between high inventory and long throughput times.

- Inventory hides problems. High levels of inventory 'decouple' the activities of adjacent operations, processes or stages. This prevents problems being evident to anyone other than those immediately affected. This idea is central to the concept of lean synchronization and is treated further in Chapter 13.
- Inventory can become obsolete as alternatives become available.
- Inventory can be damaged, or deteriorate (age, rot, corrode, warp, shop-soil, etc.).
- Inventory can be totally lost, or be very expensive to retrieve, as it gets hidden amongst other inventory.
- Inventory might be hazardous to store (for example flammable solvents, explosives, chemicals and drugs), requiring special facilities and systems.
- Inventory may take up excessive storage space compared to its value (for example packaging and insulation materials).
- Inventory could be duplicated at several different locations, possibly even being reordered at one, whilst excess inventory exists at others. This is not only a common dilemma for chains of retail shops or builders merchants, but also occurs in large hospitals.
- Inventory can involve high administrative and insurance costs.

> **Operations principle**
> Inventory should only accumulate when the advantages of having it outweigh its disadvantages.

FURTHER EXAMPLE

So why have inventory?

All the negative effects of inventory, although very real, are only part of the inventory management activity. An equally powerful case can be based on the reasons why inventory is necessary. When a customer goes elsewhere because just one item is out of stock, or when a major project is waiting for just one small part, the value of inventories seems indisputable. The task of operations management is to allow inventory to accumulate only when its benefits outweigh its disadvantages. The following are some of the benefits of inventory.

Inventory is an insurance against uncertainty

Inventory can act as a buffer against unexpected fluctuations in supply and demand. For example, a retail operation can never forecast demand perfectly over the lead time. It will order goods from its suppliers such that there is always a minimum level of inventory to cover against the possibility that demand will be greater than expected during the time taken to deliver the goods. This is buffer, or safety, inventory. It can also compensate for the uncertainties in the process of the supply of goods into the store. The same applies with the output inventories, which is why hospitals always have a supply of blood, sutures and bandages for immediate response to accident and emergency patients. Similarly, vehicle servicing services, factories and airlines may hold selected critical spare parts inventories so that maintenance staff can repair the most common faults without delay. Again, inventory is being used as an 'insurance' against unpredictable events.

Inventory can counteract a lack of flexibility

Where a wide range of customer options is offered, unless the operation is perfectly flexible, stock will be needed to ensure supply when it is engaged on other activities. This is sometimes called cycle inventory. For example, suppose a baker makes three types of bread. Because of the nature of the mixing and baking process, only one kind of bread can be produced at any time. The baker will have to produce each type of bread in batches large enough to satisfy the demand for each kind of bread between the times when each batch is ready for sale. So, even when demand is steady and predictable, there will always be some inventory to compensate for the intermittent supply of each type of bread.

Inventory allows operations to take advantage of short-term opportunities

Sometimes opportunities arise that necessitate accumulating inventory, even when there is no immediate demand for it. For example, a supplier may be offering a particularly good deal on selected items for a limited time period, perhaps because they want to reduce their own finished goods inventories. Under these circumstances a purchasing department may opportunistically take advantage of the short-term price advantage.

Inventory can be used to anticipate future demands

Medium-term capacity management (covered in Chapter 10) may use inventory to cope with demand–capacity fluctuations. Rather than trying to make a product (such as chocolate) only when it is needed, it is produced throughout the year ahead of demand and put into inventory until it is needed. This type of inventory is called anticipation inventory and is most commonly used when demand fluctuations are large but relatively predictable.

Inventory can reduce overall costs

Holding relatively large inventories may bring savings that are greater than the cost of holding the inventory. This may be when bulk-buying gets the lowest possible cost of inputs, or when large order quantities reduce both the number of orders placed and the associated costs of administration and material handling. This is the basis of the 'economic order quantity' (EOQ) approach that will be treated later in this chapter.

Inventory can increase in value

Sometimes the items held as inventory can increase in value and so become an investment. For example, dealers in fine wines are less reluctant to hold inventory than dealers in wine that does not get better with age. (However, it can be argued that keeping fine wines until they are at their peak is really part of the overall process rather than inventory as such.) A more obvious example is inventories of money. The many financial processes within most organizations will try to maximize the inventory of cash they hold because it is earning them interest.

Inventory fills the processing 'pipeline'

'Pipeline' inventory exists because transformed resources cannot be moved instantaneously between the point of supply and the point of demand. When a retail store places an order, its supplier will 'allocate' the stock to the retail store in its own warehouse, pack it, load it onto its truck, transport it to its destination, and unload it into the retailer's inventory. From the time that stock is allocated (and therefore unavailable to any other customer) to the time it becomes available for the retail store, it is pipeline inventory. Especially in geographically dispersed supply networks, pipeline inventory can be substantial.

Reducing inventory

The objective of most operations managers is to reduce the overall level (and/or cost) of inventory while maintaining an acceptable level of customer service. Table 9.2 identifies some of the ways in which inventory may be reduced.

Table 9.2	Some ways in which inventory may be reduced	
Reason for holding inventory	*Example*	*How inventory could be reduced*
As an insurance against uncertainty	Safety stocks for when demand or supply is not perfectly predictable	• Improve demand forecasting • Tighten supply, e.g. through service-level penalties
To counteract a lack of flexibility	Cycle stock to maintain supply when other products are being made	• Increase flexibility of processes, e.g. by reducing changeover times (see Chapter 11) • Using parallel processes producing output simultaneously (see Chapter 5)
To take advantage of relatively short-term opportunities	Suppliers offer 'time limited' special low-cost offers	• Persuade suppliers to adopt 'everyday low prices' (see Chapter 11)
To anticipate future demands	Build up stocks in low-demand periods for use in high-demand periods	• Increase volume flexibility by moving towards a 'chase demand' plan (see Chapter 8)
To reduce overall costs	Purchasing a batch of products in order to save delivery and administration costs	• Reduce administration costs through purchasing process efficiency gains • Investigate alternative delivery channels that reduce transport costs
To fill the processing 'pipeline'	Items being delivered to customer	• Reduce process time between customer request and dispatch of items • Reduce throughput time in the downstream supply chain (see Chapter 7)

DIAGNOSTIC QUESTION

Is the right quantity being ordered?

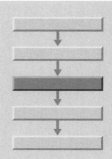

To illustrate this decision, consider how we manage our domestic inventory. We implicitly make decisions on order quantity, that is, how much to purchase at one time, by balancing two sets of costs: the costs associated with going out to purchase the food items and the costs associated with holding the stocks. The option of holding very little or no inventory of food and purchasing each item only when it is needed requires little money because purchases are made only when needed, but involves buying several times a day, which is inconvenient. Conversely, making one journey to the local superstore every few months and purchasing all the provisions we would need until our next visit reduces purchasing time and costs but requires a very large amount of money each time the trip is made – money that could otherwise be in the bank and earning interest. We might also have to invest in extra cupboard units and a very large freezer. Somewhere between these extremes lies an ordering strategy that will minimize the total costs and effort involved in purchasing food.

Inventory costs

A similar range of costs apply in commercial order-quantity decisions as in the domestic situation. These are costs of placing an order, including preparing the documentation, arranging for the delivery to be made, arranging to pay the supplier for the delivery, and the general costs of keeping all the information that allows us to do this. An 'internal order' on processes within an operation has equivalent costs. Price discount costs for large orders or extra costs for small orders may also influence how much to purchase. If inventory cannot supply demand, there will be costs to us incurred by failing to supply customers. External customers may take their business elsewhere. Internal stock-outs could lead to idle time at the next process, inefficiencies and eventually, again, dissatisfied external customers. There are the working capital costs of funding the lag between paying suppliers and receiving payment from customers. Storage costs are the costs associated with physically storing goods, such as renting, heating and lighting a warehouse, as well as insuring the inventory. While stored as inventory there is a risk of obsolescence costs if the inventory is superseded (in the case of a change in fashion) or deteriorates with age (in the case of most foodstuffs).

Some of these costs will decrease as order size is increased; the first three costs (cost of placing an order, price discount costs and stockout costs) are like this. The other costs (working capital, storage and obsolescence costs) generally increase as order size is increased. But it may not be the same organization that incurs each cost. For example, sometimes suppliers agree to hold consignment stock. This means that they deliver large quantities of inventory to their customers to store but will charge for the goods only as and when they are used. In the meantime they remain the supplier's property so do not have to be financed by the customer, who does, however, provide storage facilities.

Inventory profiles

An inventory profile is a visual representation of the inventory level over time. Figure 9.3 shows a simplified inventory profile for one particular stock item in a retail operation. Every time an order is placed, Q items are ordered. The replenishment order arrives in one batch instantaneously. Demand for the item is then steady and perfectly predictable at a

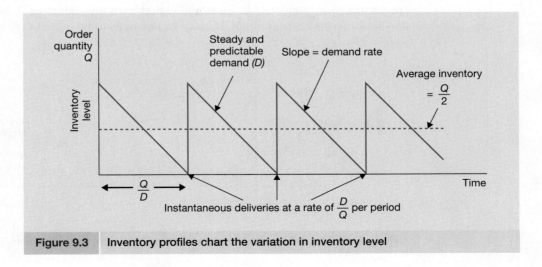

Figure 9.3   Inventory profiles chart the variation in inventory level

rate of D units per month. When demand has depleted the stock of the items entirely, another order of Q items instantaneously arrives, and so on. Under these circumstances:

$$\text{Average inventory} = \frac{Q}{2} \text{ (because the two shaded areas in Figure 9.3 are equal)}$$

$$\text{Time interval between deliveries} = \frac{Q}{D}$$

$$\text{Frequency of deliveries} = \text{reciprocal of the time interval} = \frac{D}{Q}$$

The economic order quantity (EOQ) formula

Excel

The economic order quantity (EOQ) approach attempts to find the best balance between the advantages and disadvantages of holding stock. For example, Figure 9.4 shows two alternative order-quantity policies for an item. Plan A, represented by the blue line, involves ordering in quantities of 400 at a time. Demand in this case is running at 1000 units per year. Plan B, represented by the red line, uses smaller but more frequent replenishment orders. This time only 100 are ordered at a time, with orders being placed four times as often. However, the average inventory for plan B is one-quarter of that for plan A.

To find out whether either of these plans, or some other plan, minimizes the total cost of stocking the item, we need some further information, namely the total cost of holding one unit in stock for a period of time (C_h) and the total costs of placing an order (C_o). In this case the cost of holding stocks is calculated at £1 per item per year and the cost of placing an order is calculated at £20 per order.

We can now calculate total holding costs and ordering costs for any particular ordering plan as follows:

$$\text{Holding costs} = \text{holding cost/unit} \times \text{average inventory}$$

$$= C_h \times \frac{Q}{2}$$

$$\text{Ordering costs} = \text{ordering cost} \times \text{number of orders per period}$$

$$= C_o \times \frac{D}{Q}$$

So,

$$\text{Total cost, } C_t = \frac{C_h Q}{2} + \frac{C_o D}{Q}$$

We can now calculate the costs of adopting plans with different order quantities. These are illustrated in Table 9.3. As we would expect with low values of Q, holding costs are low but ordering costs are high, because orders have to be placed very frequently. As Q

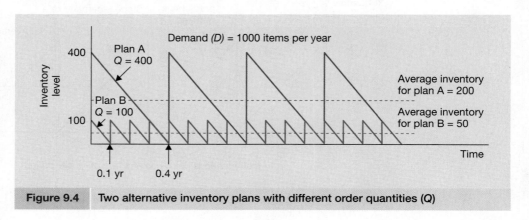

Figure 9.4   Two alternative inventory plans with different order quantities (Q)

Table 9.3 Costs of adoption of plans with different order quantities

Demand (D) = 1000 units per year, holding costs (C_h) = £1 per item per year, order costs (C_o) = £20 per order

Order quantity Q	Holding costs $0.5Q \times C_h$	+	Order costs $(D/Q) \times C_o$	=	Total costs
50	25		$20 \times 20 = 400$		425
100	50		$10 \times 20 = 200$		250
150	75		$6.7 \times 20 = 134$		209
200	100		$5 \times 20 \ \ \ = 100$		200[a]
250	125		$4 \times 20 \ \ \ = \ \ 80$		205
300	150		$3.3 \times 20 = \ \ 66$		216
350	175		$2.9 \times 20 = \ \ 58$		233
400	200		$2.5 \times 20 = \ \ 50$		250

[a] Minimum total cost.

increases, the holding costs increase but the costs of placing orders decrease. In this case the order quantity, Q, which minimizes the sum of holding and order costs, is 200. This 'optimum' order quantity is called the *economic order quantity* (EOQ). This is illustrated graphically in Figure 9.5.

A more elegant method of finding the EOQ is to derive its general expression. This can be done using simple differential calculus as follows. From before:

$$\text{Total cost} = \text{holding cost} + \text{order cost}$$

$$C_t = \frac{C_h Q}{2} + \frac{C_o D}{Q}$$

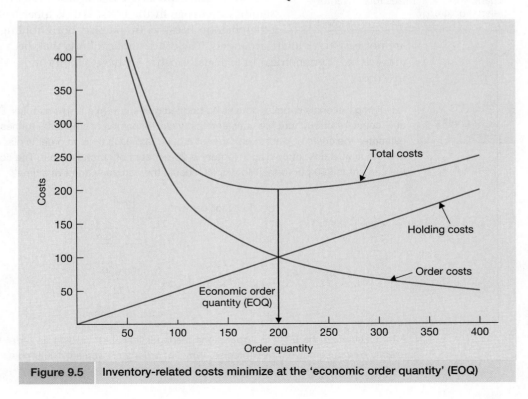

Figure 9.5 Inventory-related costs minimize at the 'economic order quantity' (EOQ)

The rate of change of total cost is given by the first differential of C_t with respect to Q:

$$\frac{dC_t}{dQ} = \frac{C_h}{2} - \frac{C_o D}{Q^2}$$

The lowest cost will occur when $\dfrac{dC_t}{dQ} = 0$, that is:

$$0 = \frac{C_h}{2} - \frac{C_o D}{Q_o^2}$$

where Q_o is the EOQ. Rearranging this expression gives:

$$Q_o = \text{EOQ} = \sqrt{\frac{C_o D}{C_h}}$$

When using the EOQ:

$$\text{Time between orders} = \frac{\text{EOQ}}{D}$$

$$\text{Order frequency} = \frac{D}{\text{EOQ}} \text{ per period}$$

Sensitivity of the EOQ

The graphical representation of the total cost curve in Figure 9.5 shows that, although there is a single value of Q that minimizes total costs, any relatively small deviation from the EOQ will not increase total costs significantly. In other words, costs will be near-optimum provided a value of Q that is reasonably close to the EOQ is chosen. Put another way, small errors in estimating either holding costs or order costs will not result in a significant change in the EOQ. This is a particularly convenient phenomenon because, in practice, both holding and order costs are not easy to estimate accurately. The other implication is that, because the total cost curve is not symmetrical, it is usually better to have slightly more than slightly less inventory.

Operations principle
For any stock replenishment activity there is a theoretical 'optimum' order quantity that minimizes total inventory-related costs.

Worked example

A building materials supplier obtains its bagged cement from a single supplier. Demand is reasonably constant throughout the year, and last year the company sold 2000 tonnes of this product. It estimates the costs of placing an order at around £25 each time an order is placed, and calculates that the annual cost of holding inventory is 20 per cent of purchase cost. The company purchases the cement at £60 per tonne. How much should the company order at a time?

$$\text{EOQ for cement} = \sqrt{\frac{2 C_o D}{C_h}}$$

$$= \sqrt{\frac{2 \times 25 \times 2000}{0.2 \times 60}}$$

$$= \sqrt{\frac{100{,}000}{12}}$$

$$= 91.287 \text{ tonnes}$$

After calculating the EOQ the operations manager feels that placing an order for 91.287 tonnes exactly seems somewhat over-precise. Why not order a convenient 100 tonnes?

Total cost of ordering plan for $Q = 91.287$:

$$= \frac{C_hQ}{2} + \frac{C_oD}{Q}$$

$$= \frac{(0.2 \times 60) \times 91.287}{2} + \frac{25 \times 2000}{91.287}$$

$$= £1095.45$$

Total cost of ordering plan for $Q = 100$:

$$= \frac{(0.2 \times 60) \times 100}{2} + \frac{25 \times 2000}{100}$$

$$= £1100$$

The extra cost of ordering 100 tonnes at a time is £1100 − £1095.45 = £4.55. The operations manager therefore should feel confident in using the more convenient order quantity.

Gradual replacement – the economic batch quantity (EBQ) model

The simple inventory profile shown in Figure 9.3 assumes that each complete replacement order arrives at one point in time. However, replenishment may occur over a time period rather than in one lot, for example where an internal order is placed for a batch of parts to be produced on a machine. The machine will start to produce items and ship them in a more or less continuous stream into inventory, but at the same time demand is removing items from the inventory. Provided the rate at which items are being supplied to the inventory (P) is higher than the demand rate (D), then the inventory will increase. After the batch has been completed the machine will be reset (to produce some other part), and demand will continue to deplete the inventory level until production of the next batch begins. The resulting profile is shown in Figure 9.6. This is typical for inventories supplied by batch processes, and the minimum-cost batch quantity for this profile is called the *economic batch quantity* (EBQ). It is derived as follows:

$$\text{Maximum stock level} = M$$
$$\text{Slope of inventory build-up} = P - D$$

Also, as is clear from Figure 9.6:

$$\text{Slope of inventory build-up} = M \div \frac{Q}{P}$$
$$= \frac{MP}{Q}$$

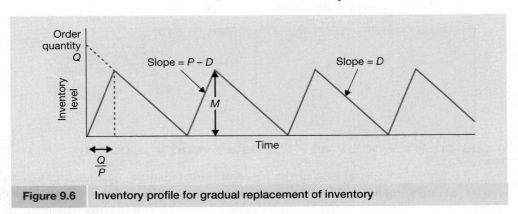

Figure 9.6 Inventory profile for gradual replacement of inventory

So,

$$\frac{MP}{Q} = P - D$$

$$M = \frac{Q(P - D)}{P}$$

$$\text{Average inventory level} = \frac{M}{2}$$

$$= \frac{Q(P - D)}{2P}$$

As before:

$$\text{Total cost} = \text{holding cost} + \text{order cost}$$

$$C_t = \frac{C_h Q(P - D)}{2P} + \frac{C_o D}{Q}$$

$$\frac{dC_t}{dQ} = \frac{C_h(P - D)}{2P} - \frac{C_o D}{Q^2}$$

Again, equating to zero and solving Q gives the minimum-cost order quantity, EBQ:

$$\text{EBQ} = \sqrt{\frac{2C_o D}{C_h(1 - (D/P))}}$$

Worked example

The manager of a bottle-filling plant that bottles soft drinks needs to decide how long a 'run' of each type of drink to process. Demand for each type of drink is reasonably constant at 80,000 per month (a month has 160 production hours). The bottling lines fill at a rate of 3000 bottles per hour, but take an hour to clean and reset between different drinks. The cost (of labour and lost production capacity) of each of these changeovers has been calculated at £100 per hour. Stock-holding costs are counted at £0.1 per bottle per month.

$$D = 80,000 \text{ per month}$$

$$= 500 \text{ per hour}$$

$$\text{EBQ} = \sqrt{\frac{2C_o D}{C_h(1 - (D/P))}}$$

$$= \sqrt{\frac{2 \times 100 \times 80000}{0.1(1 - (500/3000))}}$$

$$= 13,856$$

The staff who operate the lines have devised a method of reducing the changeover time from 1 hour to 30 minutes. How would that change the EBQ?

$$\text{New } C_o = £50$$

$$\text{New EBQ} = \sqrt{\frac{2 \times 50 \times 80000}{0.1(1 - (500/3000))}}$$

$$= 9798$$

If customers won't wait – the news vendor problem

A special case of the inventory order-quantity decision is when an order quantity is purchased for a specific event or time period, after which the items are unlikely to be sold. A simple example of this is the decision taken by a newspaper vendor of how many

Excel

newspapers to stock for the day. If the news vendor should run out of papers, customers will either go elsewhere or decide not to buy a paper that day. Newspapers left over at the end of the day are worthless and demand for the newspapers varies day by day. In deciding how many newspapers to carry, the news vendor is in effect balancing the risk and consequence of running out of newspapers against that of having newspapers left over at the end of the day. Retailers and manufacturers of high-class leisure products, such as some books and popular music CDs, face the same problem. For example, a concert promoter needs to decide how many concert T-shirts to order emblazoned with the logo of the main act. The profit on each T-shirt sold at the concert is £5 and any unsold T-shirts are returned to the company that supplies them, but at a loss to the promoter of £3 per T-shirt. Demand is uncertain but is estimated to be between 200 and 1000. The probabilities of different demand levels are as follows:

Demand level	200	400	600	800
Probability	0.2	0.3	0.4	0.1

How many T-shirts should the promoter order? Table 9.4 shows the profit that the promoter would make for different order quantities and different levels of demand. We can now calculate the *expected* profit that the promoter will make for each order quantity by weighting the outcomes by their probability of occurring.

If the promoter orders 200 T-shirts:

$$\text{Expected profit} = 1000 \times 0.2 + 1000 \times 0.3 + 1000 \times 0.4 + 1000 \times 0.1$$
$$= £1000$$

If the promoter orders 400 T-shirts:

$$\text{Expected profit} = 400 \times 0.2 + 2000 \times 0.3 + 2000 \times 0.4 + 2000 \times 0.1$$
$$= £1680$$

If the promoter orders 600 T-shirts:

$$\text{Expected profit} = -200 \times 0.2 + 1400 \times 0.3 + 3000 \times 0.4 + 3000 \times 0.1$$
$$= £1880$$

If the promoter orders 800 T-shirts:

$$\text{Expected profit} = -800 \times 0.2 + 800 \times 0.3 + 2400 \times 0.4 + 4000 \times 0.1$$
$$= £1440$$

The order quantity that gives the maximum profit is 600 T-shirts, which results in a profit of £1880.

The importance of this approach lies in the way it takes a probabilistic view of part of the inventory calculation (demand), something we shall use again in this chapter.

Table 9.4 Pay-off matrix for T-shirt order quantity (profit or loss in £s)

Demand level	200	400	600	800
Probability	0.2	0.3	0.4	0.1
Promoter orders 200	1000	1000	1000	1000
Promoter orders 400	400	2000	2000	2000
Promoter orders 600	−200	1400	3000	3000
Promoter orders 800	−800	800	2400	4000

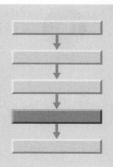

DIAGNOSTIC QUESTION

Are inventory orders being placed at the right time?

When we assumed that orders arrived instantaneously and demand was steady and predictable, the decision on when to place a replenishment order was self-evident. An order would be placed as soon as the stock level reached zero; it would arrive instantaneously and prevent any stock-out occurring. When there is a lag between the order being placed and arriving in the inventory, we can still calculate the timing of a replacement order simply, as shown in Figure 9.7. The lead time for an order to arrive in this case is two weeks, so the reorder point (ROP) is the point at which stock will fall to zero minus the order lead time. Alternatively, we can define the point in terms of the level that the inventory will have reached when a replenishment order needs to be placed. In this case this occurs at a reorder level (ROL) of 200 items.

However, this assumes that both the demand and the order lead time are perfectly predictable. In most cases this is not so. Both demand and the order lead time are likely to vary to produce a profile that looks something like that in Figure 9.8. In these circumstances it is necessary to make the replenishment order somewhat earlier than would be the case in a purely deterministic situation. This will result in, on average, some 'safety' stock (s) still being in the inventory when the replenishment order arrives. The earlier the replenishment order is placed, the higher will be the expected level of safety stock when the replenishment order arrives. But because of the variability of both lead time (t) and demand rate (d), the safety stock at the time of replenishment will vary. The main consideration in setting safety stock is the

> **Operations principle**
> For any stock replenishment activity, the timing of replenishment should reflect the effects of uncertain lead time and uncertain demand during that lead time.

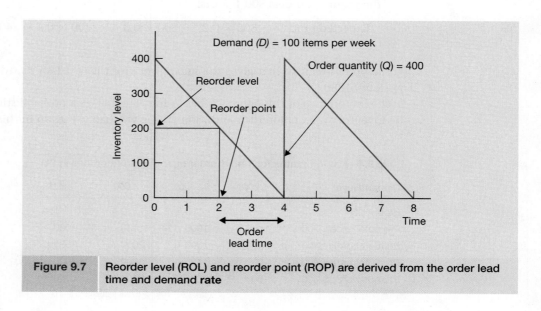

| **Figure 9.7** | Reorder level (ROL) and reorder point (ROP) are derived from the order lead time and demand rate |

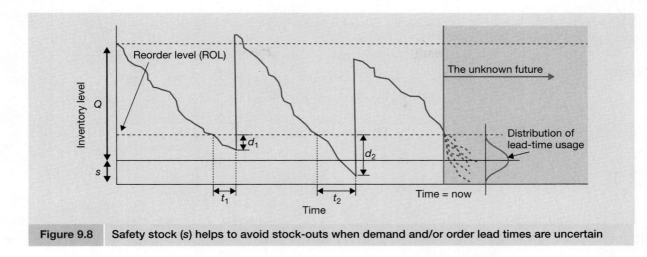

| **Figure 9.8** | **Safety stock (s) helps to avoid stock-outs when demand and/or order lead times are uncertain** |

probability that the stock will not have run out before the replenishment order arrives. This depends on the lead-time usage distribution. This is a combination of the distributions that describe lead-time variation and the demand rate during the lead time. If safety stock is set below the lower limit of this distribution then there will be shortages every single replenishment cycle. If safety stock is set above the upper limit of the distribution, there is no chance of stock-outs occurring. Usually, safety stock is set to give a predetermined likelihood that stock-outs will not occur. Figure 9.8 shows that, in this case, the first replenishment order arrived after t_1, resulting in a lead-time usage of d_1. The second replenishment order took longer, t_2, and demand rate was also higher, resulting in a lead-time usage of d_2. The third order cycle shows several possible inventory profiles for different conditions of lead-time usage and demand rate.

Worked example

An online retailer of running shoes can never be certain of how long, after placing an order, the delivery will take. Examination of previous orders reveals that out of 10 orders, one took one week, two took two weeks, four took three weeks, two took four weeks and one took five weeks. The rate of demand for the shoes also varies between 110 pairs per week and 140 pairs per week. There is a 0.2 probability of the demand rate being either 110 or 140 pairs per week, and a 0.3 chance of demand being either 120 or 130 pairs per week. The company needs to decide when it should place replenishment orders if the probability of a stock-out is to be less than 10 per cent.

Both lead time and the demand rate during the lead time will contribute to the lead-time usage. So the distributions that describe each will need to be combined. Figure 9.9 and Table 9.5 show how this can be done. Taking lead time to be either one, two, three, four or five weeks, and demand rate to be either 110, 120, 130 or 140 pairs per week, and also assuming the two variables to be independent, the distributions can be combined as shown in Table 9.5. Each element in the matrix shows a possible lead-time usage with the probability of its occurrence. So if the lead time is one week and the demand rate is 110 pairs per week, the actual lead-time usage will be $1 \times 110 = 110$ pairs. Since there is a 0.1 chance of the lead time being one week, and a 0.2 chance of demand rate being 110 pairs per week, the probability of both these events occurring is $0.1 \times 0.2 = 0.02$.

We can now classify the possible lead-time usages into histogram form. For example, summing the probabilities of all the lead-time usages that fall within the range 100–199 (all the first column) gives a combined probability of 0.1. Repeating this for subsequent intervals results in Table 9.6.

This shows the probability of each possible range of lead-time usage occurring, but it is the *cumulative* probabilities that are needed to predict the likelihood of stock-out (see Table 9.7).

Setting the reorder level at 600 would mean that there is only a 0.08 (8%) chance of usage being greater than available inventory during the lead time, i.e. there is a less than 10 per cent chance of a stock-out occurring.

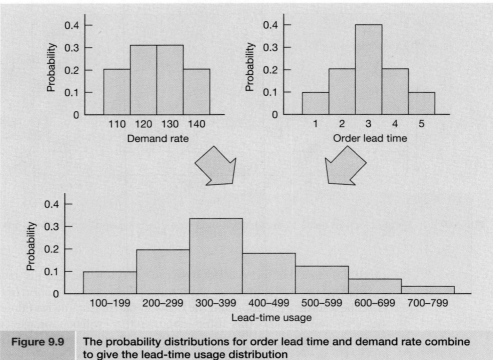

Figure 9.9   The probability distributions for order lead time and demand rate combine to give the lead-time usage distribution

Table 9.5   Matrix of lead-time and demand-rate probabilities

			Lead-time probabilities				
			1	2	3	4	5
			0.1	0.2	0.4	0.2	0.1
Demand-rate probabilities	110	0.2	110 (0.02)	220 (0.04)	330 (0.08)	440 (0.04)	550 (0.02)
	120	0.3	120 (0.03)	240 (0.06)	360 (0.12)	480 (0.06)	600 (0.03)
	130	0.3	130 (0.03)	260 (0.06)	390 (0.12)	520 (0.06)	650 (0.03)
	140	0.2	140 (0.02)	280 (0.04)	420 (0.08)	560 (0.04)	700 (0.02)

Table 9.6   Combined probabilities

Lead-time usage	100–199	200–299	300–399	400–499	500–599	600–699	700–799
Probability	0.1	0.2	0.32	0.18	0.12	0.06	0.02

Table 9.7   Cumulative probabilities

Lead-time usage (x)	100	200	300	400	500	600	700	800
Probability of usage being greater than x	1.0	0.9	0.7	0.38	0.2	0.08	0.02	0

Continuous and periodic review

The approach we have described is often called the continuous review approach. To make the decision in this way the stock level of each item must be reviewed continuously and an order placed when the stock level reaches its reorder level. The virtue of this approach is that, although the timing of orders may be irregular (depending on the variation in demand rate), the order size (Q) is constant and can be set at the optimum economic order quantity. But continually checking inventory levels may be time-consuming. An alternative, and simpler, approach, but one which sacrifices the use of a fixed (and therefore possibly optimum) order quantity, is 'periodic review'. Here, rather than ordering at a predetermined reorder level, the periodic approach orders at a fixed and regular time interval. So the stock level of an item could be found, for example, at the end of every month and a replenishment order placed to bring the stock up to a predetermined level. This level is calculated to cover demand between the replenishment order being placed and the following replenishment order arriving. Safety stocks will also need to be calculated, in a similar manner as before, based on the distribution of usage over this period.

Two-bin and three-bin systems

Keeping track of inventory levels is especially important in continuous review approaches to reordering. A simple and obvious method of indicating when the reorder point has been reached is necessary, especially if there are a large number of items to be monitored. The simple two-bin system involves storing the reorder point quantity plus the safety inventory quantity in the second bin and using parts from the first bin. When the first bin empties, it is the signal to order the next reorder quantity. Different 'bins' are not always necessary to operate this type of system. For example, a common practice in retail operations is to store the second 'bin' quantity upside-down behind or under the first 'bin' quantity. Orders are then placed when the upside-down items are reached.

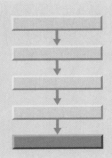

DIAGNOSTIC QUESTION

Is inventory being controlled effectively?

Even probabilistic models are still simplified compared with the complexity of real stock management. Coping with many thousands of stocked items, supplied by many hundreds of different suppliers, with possibly tens of thousands of individual customers, makes for a complex and dynamic operations task. Controlling such complexity requires an approach that discriminates between different items so that each has a degree of control that is appropriate to its importance. It also requires an information system to keep track of inventories.

Inventory priorities – the ABC system

Some stocked items are more important than others. Some might have a high usage rate, so if they ran out many customers would be disappointed. Others might be of particularly high value, so excessively high inventory levels would be particularly expensive. One common way of discriminating between different stock items is to rank them by their usage value (usage rate multiplied by value). Items with a particularly high usage value are deemed to warrant the most careful control, whereas those with low usage values need not be controlled quite so rigorously. Generally, a relatively small proportion of the total range of items contained in an inventory will account for a large proportion of the total usage value. This phenomenon is known as the Pareto, or 80/20 rule. It is called this because, typically, 80 per cent of an operation's sales are accounted for by only 20 per cent of all stocked item types. (This idea is also used elsewhere in operations management, for example as described in Chapter 13.) Here the relationship is used to classify items into A, B or C categories, depending on their usage value.

> **Operations principle**
> Different inventory management decision rules are needed for different classes of inventory.

- Class A items are those 20 per cent or so of high usage value items that account for around 80 per cent of the total usage value.
- Class B items are those of medium usage value, usually the next 30 per cent of items, which often account for around 10 per cent of the total usage value.
- Class C items are those low usage value items which, although comprising around 50 per cent of the total types of items stocked, probably only account for around 10 per cent of the total usage value of the operation.

Although annual usage and value are the two criteria most commonly used to determine a stock classification system, other criteria might also contribute towards the (higher) classification of an item. The consequence of stock-out might give higher priority to some items that would seriously delay or disrupt operations, if they were not in stock. Uncertainty of supply may also give some items priority, as might high obsolescence or deterioration risk.

Worked example

Table 9.8 shows all the parts stored by an electrical wholesaler. The 20 different items stored vary in terms of both their usage per year and their cost per item as shown. However, the wholesaler has ranked the stock items by their usage value per year. The total usage value per year is £5,569,000. From this it is possible to calculate the usage value per year of each item as a percentage of the total usage value, and from that a running cumulative total of the usage value as shown. The wholesaler can then plot the cumulative percentage of all stocked items against the cumulative percentage of their value. So, for example, the part with stock number A/703 is the highest value part and accounts for 25.14 per cent of the total inventory value. As a part, however, it is only one-twentieth or 5 per cent of the total number of items stocked. This item together with the next highest value item (D/012) account for only 10 per cent of the total number of items stocked, yet account for 47.37 per cent of the value of the stock, and so on.

This is shown graphically in Figure 9.10. The first four part numbers (20 per cent of the range) are considered Class A whose usage will be monitored very closely. The next six part numbers (30 per cent of the range) are to be treated as Class B items with slightly less effort devoted to their control. All other items are classed as Class C items whose stocking policy is reviewed only occasionally.

Table 9.8 Warehouse items ranked by usage value

Stock no.	Usage (items/year)	Cost (£/item)	Usage value (£000/year)	% of total value	Cumulative % of total value
A/703	700	2.00	1400	25.14	25.14
D/012	450	2.75	1238	22.23	47.37
A/135	1000	0.90	900	16.16	63.53
C/732	95	8.50	808	14.51	78.04
C/735	520	0.54	281	5.05	83.09
A/500	73	2.30	168	3.02	86.11
D/111	520	0.22	114	2.05	88.16
D/231	170	0.65	111	1.99	90.15
E/781	250	0.34	85	1.53	91.68
A/138	250	0.30	75	1.34	93.02
D/175	400	0.14	56	1.01	94.03
E/001	80	0.63	50	0.89	94.92
C/150	230	0.21	48	0.86	95.78
F/030	400	0.12	48	0.86	96.64
D/703	500	0.09	45	0.81	97.45
D/535	50	0.88	44	0.79	98.24
C/541	70	0.57	40	0.71	98.95
A/260	50	0.64	32	0.57	99.52
B/141	50	0.32	16	0.28	99.80
D/021	20	0.50	10	0.20	100.00
Total			5569	100.00	

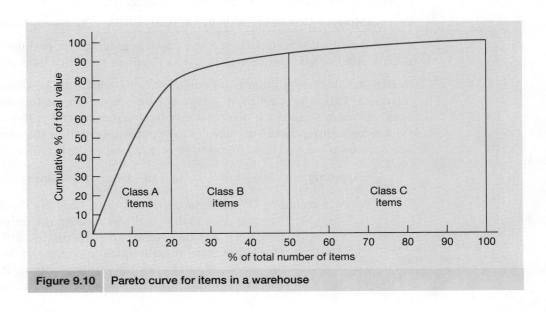

Figure 9.10 Pareto curve for items in a warehouse

Inventory information systems

Most inventories of any significant size are managed by information systems. This is especially so since data capture has been made more convenient through the use of bar code readers, radio frequency identification (RFID) and the point-of-sale recording of sales transactions. Many commercial systems of stock control are available, although they tend to share certain common functions.

- **Updating stock records**. Every time an inventory transaction takes place the position, status and possibly value of the stock will have changed. This information must be recorded so that operations managers can determine their current inventory status at any time.
- **Generating orders**. Both the 'how much' and the 'when to order' decisions can be made by a stock control system. Originally almost all computer systems calculated order quantities by using the EOQ formulae. Now more sophisticated probabilistic algorithms are used, based on examining the marginal return on investing in stock. The system will hold all the information that goes into the ordering algorithm but might periodically check to see whether demand or order lead times, or any of the other parameters, have changed significantly, and recalculate accordingly. The decision on when to order, on the other hand, is a far more routine affair that computer systems make according to whatever decision rules operations managers have chosen to adopt: either continuous review or periodic review.
- **Generating inventory reports**. Inventory control systems can generate regular reports of stock value which can help management monitor its inventory control performance. Similarly, customer service performance, such as the number of stock-outs or the number of incomplete orders, can be regularly monitored. Some reports may be generated on an exception basis. That is, the report is only generated if some performance measure deviates from acceptable limits.
- **Forecasting**. Inventory replenishment decisions should ideally be made with a clear understanding of forecast future demand. Inventory control systems usually compare actual demand against forecast, and adjust forecasts in the light of actual levels of demand.

Common problems with inventory systems

Our description of inventory systems has been based on the assumption that operations

- have a reasonably accurate idea of costs such as holding cost, or order cost, and
- have accurate information that really does indicate the actual level of stock and sales.

In fact data inaccuracy often poses one of the most significant problems for inventory managers. This is because most computer-based inventory management systems are based on what is called the perpetual inventory principle. This is the simple idea that stock records are (or should be) automatically updated every time that items are recorded as having been received into an inventory or taken out of the inventory. So,

Opening stock level + receipts in − dispatches out = new stock level

Any errors in recording these transactions, and/or in handling the physical inventory, can lead to discrepancies between the recorded and actual inventory, and these errors are perpetuated until physical stock checks are made (usually quite infrequently). In practice there are many opportunities for errors to occur, if only because inventory transactions are numerous. This means that it is

Operations principle
The maintenance of data accuracy is vital for the day-to-day effectiveness of inventory management systems.

surprisingly common for the majority of inventory records to be inaccurate. The underlying causes of errors include:

- Keying errors: entering the wrong product code
- Quantity errors: a mis-count of items put into or taken from stock
- Damaged or deteriorated inventory not recorded as such, or not correctly deleted from the records when it is destroyed
- The wrong items being taken out of stock, but the records not being corrected when they are returned to stock
- Delays between the transactions being made and the records being updated
- Items stolen from inventory (common in retail environments, but also not unusual in industrial and commercial inventories).

Critical commentary

Each chapter contains a short critical commentary on the main ideas covered in the chapter. Its purpose is not to undermine the issues discussed in the chapter, but to emphasize that, although we present a relatively orthodox view of operation, there are other perspectives.

■ The approach to determining order quantity that involves optimizing costs of holding stock against costs of ordering stock, typified by the EOQ and EBQ models, has always been subject to criticisms. Originally these concerned the validity of some of the assumptions of the model; more recently they have involved the underlying rationale of the approach itself. Criticisms include that the assumptions included in the EOQ models are simplistic, that the real costs of stock in operations are not as assumed in EOQ models, and that cost minimization is not an appropriate objective for inventory management.

■ The last criticism is particularly significant. Many organizations (such as supermarkets and wholesalers) make most of their revenue and profits simply by holding and supplying inventory. Because their main investment is in the inventory it is critical that they make a good return on this capital, by ensuring that it has the highest possible 'stock turn' and/or gross profit margin. Alternatively, they may also be concerned to maximize the use of space by seeking to maximize the profit earned per square metre. The EOQ model does not address these objectives. Similarly for products that deteriorate or go out of fashion, the EOQ model can result in excess inventory of slower-moving items. In fact the EOQ model is rarely used in such organizations, and there is more likely to be a system of periodic review for regular ordering of replenishment inventory. For example, a typical builders' supply merchant might carry around 50,000 different items of stock (SKUs). However, most of these cluster into larger families of items such as paints, sanitary ware or metal fixings. Single orders are placed at regular intervals for all the required replenishments in the supplier's range, and these are then delivered together at one time. If deliveries are made weekly then, on average, the individual item order quantities will be for only one week's usage. Less popular items, or those with erratic demand patterns, can be individually ordered at the same time, or (when urgent) can be delivered the next day by carrier.

■ The ABC approach to inventory classification is also regarded by some as misleading. Many professional inventory managers point out that it is the slow-moving (C category) items that often pose the greatest challenge in inventory management. Often these slow-moving items, although only accounting for 20 per cent of sales, require a large part (typically between one-half and two-thirds) of the total investment in stock. This is why slow-moving items are a real problem. Moreover, if errors in forecasting or ordering result in excess stock in 'A class' fast-moving items, it is relatively unimportant in the sense that excess stock can be sold quickly. However, excess stock in slow-moving C items will be there a long time. According to some inventory managers, it is the A items that can be left to look after themselves, and the B and even more the C items that need controlling.

Summary checklist

This checklist comprises questions that can be usefully applied to any type of operations and reflect the major diagnostic questions used within the chapter.

☐ Have all inventories been itemized and costed?

☐ Have all the costs and negative effects of inventory been assessed?

☐ What proportion of inventory is there:
　— as an insurance against uncertainty?
　— to counteract a lack of flexibility?
　— to allow operations to take advantage of short-term opportunities?
　— to anticipate future demand?
　— to reduce overall costs?
　— because it can increase in value?
　— because it is in the processing pipeline?

☐ Have methods of reducing inventory in these categories been explored?

☐ Have cost minimization methods been used to determine order quantity?

☐ Do these use a probabilistic estimate of demand?

☐ Have the relative merits of continuous and period inventory review been assessed?

☐ Are probabilistic estimates of demand and lead time used to determine safety stock levels?

☐ Are items controlled by their usage value?

☐ Does the inventory information system integrate all inventory decisions?

Case study   supplies4medics.com

Founded at the height of the 'dotcom bubble' of the late 1990s, **supplies4medics.com** has become one of Europe's most successful direct mail suppliers of medical hardware and consumables to hospitals, doctors' and dentists' surgeries, clinics, nursing homes and other medical-related organizations. Its physical and online catalogues list just over 4000 items, categorized by broad applications such as 'hygiene consumables' and 'surgeons' instruments'. Quoting their website:

'We are the pan-European distributors of wholesale medical and safety supplies . . . We aim to carry everything you might ever need; from nurses' scrubs to medical kits, consumables for operations, first aid kits, safety products, chemicals, fire-fighting equipment, nurse and physicians' supplies, etc. Everything is at affordable prices – and backed by our very superior customer service and support – supplies4medics is your ideal source for all medical supplies. Orders are normally despatched same-day, via our European distribution partner, the Brussels Hub of DHL. You should therefore receive your complete order within one week, but you can request next day delivery if required, for a small extra charge. You can order our printed catalogue on the link at the bottom of this page, or shop on our easy-to-use on-line store.'

Last year turnover grew by over 25 per cent to about €120 million, a cause for considerable satisfaction in the company. However, profit growth was less spectacular; and market research suggested that customer satisfaction, although generally good, was slowly declining. Most worrying, inventory levels had grown faster than sales revenue, in percentage terms. This was putting a strain on cash flow, requiring the company to borrow more cash to fund the rapid growth planned for the next year. Inventory holding is estimated to be costing around 15 per cent per annum, taking account of the cost of borrowing, insurance, and all warehousing overheads.

Pierre Lamouche, the Head of Operations, summarized the situation faced by his department:

'As a matter of urgency, we are reviewing our purchasing and inventory management systems! Most of our existing re-order levels (ROL) and re-order quantities (ROQ) were set several years ago, and have never been recalculated.

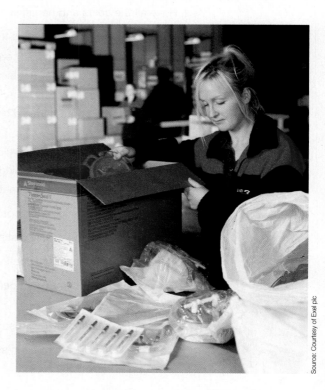

Source: Courtesy of Exel plc

Our focus has been on rapid growth through the introduction of new product lines. For more recently introduced items, the ROQs were based only on forecast sales, which actually can be quite misleading. We estimate that it costs us, on average, €50 to place and administer every purchase order, since most suppliers are still not able to take orders over the Internet or by EDI. In the meantime, sales of some products have grown fast, whilst others have declined. Our average inventory (stock) cover is about 10 weeks, but . . . amazingly . . . we still run out of critical items! In fact, on average, we are currently out of stock of about 500 SKUs (Stock Keeping Units) at any time. As you can imagine, our service level is not always satisfactory with this situation. We really need help to conduct a review of our system, so have employed a mature intern from the local business school to review our system. He has first asked my team to provide information on a random, representative sample of 20 items from the full catalogue range.' (This is reproduced in Table 9.9.)

Table 9.9   Representative sample of 20 catalogue items

Sample number	Catalogue reference number[a]	Sales unit description[b]	Sales unit cost (euro)	Last 12 months' sales (units)	Inventory as at last year end (units)	Reorder quantity (units)
1	11036	Disposable Aprons (10 pk)	2.40	100	0	10
2	11456	Ear-loop Masks (box)	3.60	6000	120	1000
3	11563	Drill Type 164	1.10	220	420	250
4	12054	Incontinence Pads Large	3.50	35400	8500	10000
5	12372	150 ml Syringe	11.30	430	120	100
6	12774	Rectal Speculum 3 Prong	17.40	65	20	20
7	12979	Pocket Organiser Blue	7.00	120	160	500
8	13063	Oxygen Trauma Kit	187.00	40	2	10
9	13236	Zinc Oxide Tape	1.50	1260	0	50
10	13454	Dual Head Stethoscope	6.25	10	16	25
11	13597	Disp. Latex Catheter	0.60	3560	12	20
12	13999	Roll-up Wheelchair Ramp	152.50	12	44	50
13	14068	WashClene Tube	1.40	22500	10500	8000
14	14242	Cervical Collar	12.00	140	24	20
15	14310	Head Wedge	89.00	44	2	10
16	14405	Three-Wheel Scooter	755.00	14	5	5
17	14456	Neonatal Trach. Tube	80.40	268	6	100
18	14675	Mouldable Strip Paste	10.20	1250	172	100
19	14854	Sequential Comp. Pump	430.00	430	40	50
20	24943	Toilet Safety Frame	25.60	560	18	20

[a]Reference numbers are allocated sequentially as new items are added to catalogue.
[b]All quantities are in sales units (e.g. item, box, case, pack).

QUESTIONS

1 Prepare a spreadsheet-based ABC analysis of usage value. Classify as follows:
   A items: top 20% of usage value
   B items: next 30% of usage value
   C items: remaining 50% of usage value.

2 Calculate the inventory weeks for each item, for each classification, and for all the items in total. Does this suggest that the OM's estimate of inventory weeks is correct? If so, what is your estimate of the overall inventory at the end of the base year, and how much might that have increased during the year?

3 Based on the sample, analyze the underlying causes of the availability problem described in the text.

4 Calculate the EOQs for the A items.

5 What recommendations would you give to the company?

Active case study   Rotterdam Serum

ACTIVE CASE

Anders works as a lab technician at Rotterdam Serum, one of the world's primary suppliers of antibody and other sera to the veterinarian and animal care sector. He faces the daunting task of operating the serum inventory. He must ensure that storage conditions are correct, stock is adequately controlled and costs are kept to a minimum.

● As the demand for serum varies, when are you going to place orders to replenish stocks and how much should you be ordering?

Please refer to the Active case on the CD accompanying this book to assess how Anders should manage serum stocks.

Applying the principles

HINTS

Some can be answered by reading the chapter. Others will require some general knowledge of business activity and some might require an element of investigation. All have hints on how they can be answered on the CD accompanying this book.

1 Read the example of the National Blood Service at the beginning of the chapter.

- What are the factors that constitute inventory holding costs, order costs and stock-out costs in a National Blood Service?

- What makes this particular inventory planning and control example so complex?

- How might the National Blood Service inventory management affect its ability to collect blood?

2 Estimate the annual usage value and average inventory level (or value) and space occupied by 20 representative items of food used within your household, or that of your family. Using Pareto analysis, categorize this into usage-value groups (e.g. A, B, C), and calculate the average stock turn for each group.

- Does this analysis indicate a sensible use of capital and space, and if not, what changes might you make to the household's shopping strategy?

3 Obtain the last few years' Annual Report and Accounts (you can usually download these from the company's website) for two materials-processing operations (as opposed to customer or information processing operations) within one industrial sector. Calculate each operation's stock–turnover ratio and the proportion of inventory to current assets over the last few years. Try to explain what you think are the reasons for any differences and trends you can identify, and discuss the likely advantages and disadvantages for the organizations concerned.

4 Visit a large petrol (gas) filling station to meet the manager. Discuss and analyze the inventory planning and control system used for fuel and other items in the shop, such as confectionery and lubricants. You should then obtain data to show how the system is working (for example, reorder points and quantities, use of forecasts to predict patterns of demand) and, if possible, prepare graphs showing fluctuations in inventory levels for the selected products.

5 Using product information obtained from Web searches, compare three inventory management systems (or software packages) that could be purchased by the General Manager of a large state-run hospital who wishes to gain control of inventory throughout the organization.

- What are the claimed benefits of each system, and how do they align to the theories presented in this chapter?

- What disadvantages might be experienced in using these approaches to inventory management, and what resistance might be presented by the hospital's staff, and why?

Notes on chapter

1 Source: NBS website and discussion with association staff.
2 With special thanks to John Mathews, Howard Smith Paper Group.

Taking it further

Flores, B.E. and Whybark, D.C. (1987) 'Implementing multiple criteria ABC analysis', *Journal of Operations Management*, Vol. 7, No. 1. An academic paper but one that gives some useful hints on the practicalities of ABC analysis.

Mather, H. (1984) *How to Really Manage Inventories,* McGraw-Hill. A practical guide by one of the more influential production management authors.

Viale, J.D. (1997) *The Basics of Inventory Management,* Crisp Publications. Very much 'the basics', but that is exactly what most people need.

Wild, T. (2002) *Best Practice in Inventory Management,* Butterworth-Heinemann. A straightforward and readable practice-based approach to the subject.

Useful websites

www.inventoryops.com/dictionary.htm A great source for information on inventory management and warehouse operations.

www.managementhelp.org/ops_mgnt/ops_mgnt.htm General 'private' site on operations management, but with some good content.

www.apics.org Site of APICS: a US 'educational society for resource managers'.

www.inventorymanagement.com Site of the Centre for Inventory Management. Cases and links.

FURTHER RESOURCES

For further resources including examples, animated diagrams, self-test questions, Excel spreadsheets, active case studies and video materials please explore the CD accompanying this book.

|-10

RESOURCE PLANNING AND CONTROL

Introduction

If materials or information or customers are to flow smoothly through processes, operations and supply networks, the value-adding resources at each stage must be managed to avoid unnecessary delay. But also resources must be used efficiently. Attempting to do this is the activity of resource planning and control (see Figure 10.1). It is a subject with many technical issues. We cover the best known of these, Materials Requirements Planning (MRP), in the supplement to this chapter.

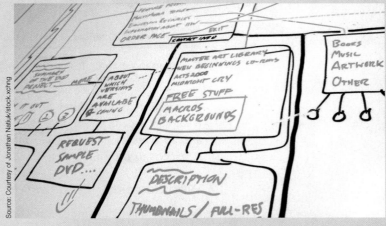

Source: Courtesy of Jonathan Natiuk/stock.xchng

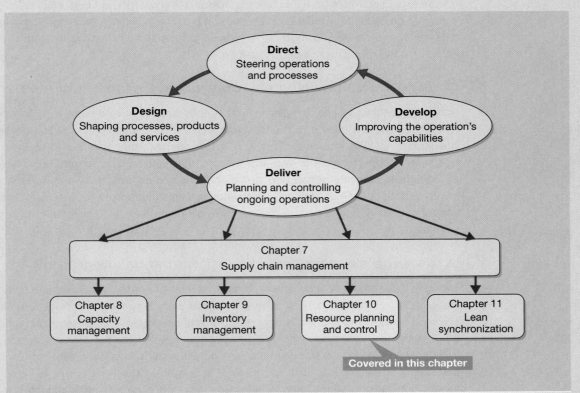

| Figure 10.1 | Resource planning and control is concerned with managing the ongoing allocation of resources and activities to ensure that the operation's processes are efficient and reflect customer demand for products and services |

Executive summary

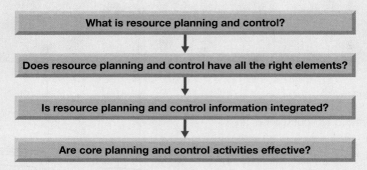

Decision logic chain for resource planning and control

Each chapter is structured around a set of diagnostic questions. These questions suggest what you should ask in order to gain an understanding of the important issues of a topic, and as a result, improve your decision making. An executive summary, addressing these questions, is provided below.

What is resource planning and control?

Resource planning and control is concerned with managing the ongoing allocation of resources and activities to ensure that the operation's processes are both efficient and reflect customer demand for products and services. In practice, planning (deciding what is intended to happen) and control (coping when things do not happen as intended) overlap to such an extent that they are usually treated together.

Does resource planning and control have all the right elements?

Although planning and control systems differ, they tend to have a number of common elements. These are a customer interface that forms a two-way information link between the operation's activities and its customers, a supply interface that does the same thing for the operation's suppliers, a set of overlapping 'core' mechanisms that perform basic tasks such as loading, sequencing, scheduling, and monitoring and control, and a decision mechanism involving both operations staff and information systems that makes or confirms planning and control decisions. It is important that all these elements are effective in their own right and work together.

Is resource planning and control information integrated?

Resource planning and control involves vast amounts of information. Unless all relevant information is integrated, it is difficult to make informed planning and control decisions. The most common method of doing this is through the use of integrated 'enterprise resource planning' (ERP) systems. These are information systems that have grown out of the more specialized and detailed material requirements planning (MRP) systems that have been common in the manufacturing sector for many years. MRP is treated in the supplement to this chapter. Investment in ERP systems often involves large amounts of capital and staff time. It may also mean a significant overhaul of the way the business organizes itself. Not all investments in ERP have proved successful.

Are core planning and control activities effective?

Unless the resource planning and control system makes appropriate decisions at a detailed level, it cannot be effective. These detailed decisions fall into four overlapping categories. Loading is the activity of allocating work to individual processes or stages in the operation. Sequencing is the activity of deciding the order or priority in which a number of jobs will be processed. Scheduling is the activity of producing a detailed timetable showing when activities should start and end. Monitoring and control is the activity of detecting any deviation from what has been planned and acting to cope and re-plan as necessary. The theory of constraints (TOC) is a useful concept in resource planning and control that emphasizes the role of bottleneck stages or processes in planning and control.

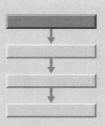

What is resource planning and control?

Resource planning and control is concerned with managing the ongoing allocation of resources and activities to ensure that the operation's processes are both efficient and reflect customer demand for products and services. Planning and control activities are distinct but often overlap. Formally, planning determines what is *intended* to happen at some time in the future, while control is the process of *coping* when things do not happen as intended. Control makes the adjustments that help the operation to achieve the objectives that the plan has set, even when the assumptions on which the plan was based do not hold true.

Look at the resource planning and control activities in the following two organizations. One, Air France, is a very large and very complex network of operations and processes. The other, the service section of a BMW automotive dealership, is far smaller. However, although the challenges are different, the task of planning and controlling each operation's resources is surprisingly similar.

Example   ## Operations control at Air France[1]

'In many ways a major airline can be viewed as one large planning problem which is usually approached as many independent, smaller (but still difficult) planning problems. The list of things

Source: Courtesy of Air France

which need planning seems endless: crews, reservation agents, luggage, flights, through trips, maintenance, gates, inventory, equipment purchases. Each planning problem has its own considerations, its own complexities, its own set of time horizons, its own objectives, but all are interrelated.'

Air France has 80 flight planners covering 24-hour operation in their flight planning office at Roissy, Charles de Gaulle. Their job is to establish the optimum flight routes, anticipate any problems such as weather changes, and minimize fuel consumption. Overall the goals of the flight planning activity are first, and most important, safety, followed by economy and passenger comfort. Increasingly powerful computer programs process the mountain of data necessary to plan the flights, but in the end many decisions still rely on human judgement. Even the most sophisticated expert systems only serve as support for the flight planners. Planning Air France's schedule is a massive job that includes the following.

- *Frequency.* For each airport how many separate services should the airline provide?
- *Fleet assignment.* Which type of plane should be used on each leg of a flight?
- *Banks.* At any airline hub where passengers arrive and may transfer to other flights to continue their journey, airlines like to organize flights into 'banks' of several planes which arrive close together, pause to let passengers change planes, and all depart close together.
- *Block times.* A block time is the elapsed time between a plane leaving the departure gate at an airport and arriving at its gate in the arrival airport. The longer the allowed block time the more likely a plane will keep to schedule even if it suffers minor delays, but the fewer flights can be scheduled.
- *Planned maintenance.* Any schedule must allow time for planes to have time at a maintenance base.

- *Crew planning.* Pilot and cabin crew must be scheduled to allocate pilots to fly planes on which they are licensed and to keep within the maximum 'on duty' allowances.
- *Gate plotting.* If many planes are on the ground at the same time there may be problems in loading and unloading them simultaneously.
- *Recovery.* Many things can cause deviations from any plan in the airline industry. Allowances must be built in that allow for recovery.

For flights within and between Air France's 12 geographic zones, the planners construct a flight plan that will form the basis of the actual flight only a few hours later. All planning documents need to be ready for the flight crew who arrive two hours before the scheduled departure time. Being responsible for passenger safety and comfort, the captain always has the final say and, when satisfied, co-signs the flight plan together with the planning officer.

| Example |

Joanne manages the schedule[2]

Joanne Cheung is the Senior Service Advisor at a premier BMW dealership. She and her team act as the interface between customers who want their cars serviced and repaired, and the 16 techni-

Source: Nigel Slack

cians who carry out the work in their state-of-the-art workshop. *'There are three types of work that we have to organize,'* says Joanne. *'The first is performing repairs on customers' vehicles. They usually want this doing as soon as possible. The second type of job is routine servicing. It is usually not urgent so customers are generally willing to negotiate a time for this. The remainder of our work involves working on the pre-owned cars which our buyer has bought-in to sell on to customers. Before any of these cars can be sold they have to undergo extensive checks. To some extent we treat these categories of work slightly differently. We have to give good service to our internal car buyers, but there is some flexibility in planning these jobs. At the other extreme, emergency repair work for customers has to be fitted into our schedule as quickly as possible. If someone is desperate to have their car repaired at very short notice, we sometimes ask them to drop their car in as early as they can and pick it up as late as possible. This gives us the maximum amount of time to fit it into the schedule.*

'There are a number of service options open to customers. We can book short jobs in for a fixed time and do it while they wait. Most commonly, we ask the customer to leave the car with us and collect it later. To help customers we have ten loan cars which are booked out on a first-come first-served basis. Alternatively, the vehicle can be collected from the customer's home and delivered back there when it is ready. Our four drivers who do this are able to cope with up to twelve jobs a day.

'Most days we deal with 50 to 80 jobs, taking from half-an-hour up to a whole day. To enter a job into our process all Service Advisors have access to the computer-based scheduling system. On-screen it shows the total capacity we have day-by-day, all the jobs that are booked in, the amount of free capacity still available, the number of loan cars available, and so on. We use this to see when we have the capacity to book a customer in, and then enter in all the customer's details. BMW have issued "standard times" for all the major jobs. However, you have to modify these standard times a bit to take account of circumstances. That is where the Service Advisor's experience comes in.

'We keep all the most commonly used parts in stock, but if a repair needs a part which is not in stock, we can usually get it from the BMW parts distributors within a day. Every evening our planning system prints out the jobs to be done the next day and the parts which are likely to be needed for each job. This allows the parts staff to pick out the parts for each job so that the technicians can collect them first thing the next morning without any delay.

'Every day we have to cope with the unexpected. A technician may find that extra work is needed, customers may want extra work doing, and technicians are sometimes ill, which reduces our capacity. Occasionally parts may not be available so we have to arrange with the customer for the vehicle to be rebooked for a later time. Every day up to four or five customers just don't turn up. Usually they have just forgotten to bring their car in so we have to rebook them in at a later time. We can cope with most of these uncertainties because our technicians are flexible in terms of the skills

they have and also are willing to work overtime when needed. Also, it is important to manage customers' expectations. If there is a chance that the vehicle may not be ready for them, it shouldn't come as a surprise when they try and collect it.'

What do these two examples have in common?

The systems set up by Air France and the BMW dealership have a number of common elements. First, there is some kind of acknowledgement that there should be an effective *customer interface* that translates the needs of customers into their implications for the operation. This involved setting the timetable of flights (frequency, timing, etc.) and the interfaces between flights (banks) in Air France. On a more individual scale Joanne needed to judge the degree of urgency of each job and feed back to the customer, managing their expectations where appropriate. Both planning and control systems also have a *supply interface* that translates the operation's plans in terms of the supply of parts, fuel, ground services, crew availability, etc. At the heart of each company's activities is a set of *core mechanics* that load capacity, prioritize, schedule, monitor and control the operation. The aim of this decision making is to reconcile the needs of the customers and the operation's resources in some way. For Joanne this involves attempting to maximize the utilization of her workshop resources while keeping customers satisfied. Air France also has similar objectives with customer comfort and safety being paramount. Also each operation is attempting some *information integration* that involves both computer-assisted information handling and the skills and experience of planning and control staff.

DIAGNOSTIC QUESTION

Does resource planning and control have all the right elements?

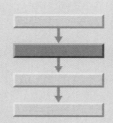

Figure 10.2 illustrates the elements that should be present in all planning and control systems. In more sophisticated systems they may even be extended to include the integration of the core operations resource planning and control task with other functional areas of the firm such as finance, marketing and personnel. We deal with this cross-functional perspective when we discuss Enterprise Resource Planning (ERP) later.

How does the system interface with customers?

The part of the resource planning and control system that manages the way customers interact with the business on a day-to-day basis is called the 'customer interface' or sometimes 'demand management'. This is a set of activities that interface with both individual customers and the market more broadly. Depending on the business, these activities may include customer negotiation, order entry, demand forecasting, order promising, updating customers, keeping customer histories, post-delivery customer service and physical distribution.

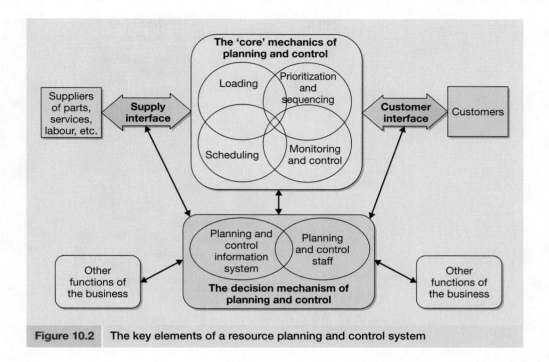

Figure 10.2   The key elements of a resource planning and control system

The customer interface defines the customer experience

The customer interface is important because it defines the nature of the customer experience. It is the public face of the operation (the 'line of visibility' as it was called in Chapter 8). Therefore, it needs to be managed like any other 'customer processing' process, where the quality of the service, as the customer sees it, is defined by the gap between customers' expectations and their perceptions of the service they receive. Figure 10.3 illustrates a typical customer experience of interacting with a planning and control customer interface. The experience itself will start before any customer contact is initiated. Customer expectations will have been influenced by the way the business presents itself through promotional activities, the ease with which channels of communication can be used (for example, design of the website), and so on. The question is: 'Does the communication channel give any indication of the kind of service response (for example, how long will we have to wait?) that the customer can expect?' At the first point of contact when an individual customer requests services or products, their request must be understood, delivery possibly negotiated, and a delivery promise made. Prior to the delivery of the service or product, the customer may or may not change their mind, which in turn may or may not involve renegotiating delivery promises. Similarly, customers may require or value feedback as to the progress of their request. At the point of delivery, not only are the products and services handed over to the customer, but there may also be an opportunity to explain the nature of the delivery and gauge customers' reactions. Following the completion of the delivery there may also be some sort of post-delivery action, such as a phone call to confirm that all is well.

As is usual with such customer experiences, the managing of customer expectations is particularly important in the early stages of the experience. For example, if there is a possibility that a delivery may be late (perhaps because of the nature of the service being requested) then that possibility is established as an element in the customer's

Operations principle
Customers' perceptions of an operation will partially be shaped by the customer interface of its planning and control system.

PRACTICE NOTE

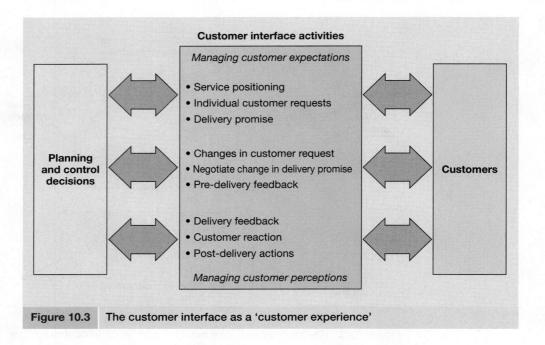

Figure 10.3   The customer interface as a 'customer experience'

expectations. As the experience continues, various interactions with the customer interface serve to build up customer perceptions of the level of support and care exhibited by the operation.

The customer interface should reflect the operation's objectives

In managing a customer's experience, the customer interface element of the planning and control system is, in effect, operationalizing the business's operations objectives. It may have to prioritize one type of customer over another. It may have to encourage some types of customer to transact business more than other (possibly less profitable) types of customer. It will almost certainly have to trade off elements of customer service against the efficiency and utilization of the operations resources. No matter how sophisticated the customer interface technology, or how skilled the customer interface staff, this part of the planning and control system cannot operate effectively without clear priorities derived from the operation's strategic objectives.

The customer interface acts as a trigger function

Acceptance of an order should prompt the customer interface to trigger the operation's processes. Exactly what is triggered will depend on the nature of the business. For example, some building and construction companies, because they are willing to build almost any kind of construction, will keep relatively few of their own resources within the business, but rather hire them in when the nature of the job becomes evident. This is a 'resource-to-order' operation where the customer interface triggers the task of hiring in the relevant equipment (and possibly labour) and purchasing the appropriate materials. If the construction company confined itself to a narrower range of construction tasks, thereby making the nature of demand slightly more predictable, it would be likely to have its own equipment and labour permanently within the operation. Here, accepting a job would only need to trigger the purchase of the materials to be used in the construction, and the business is a 'produce to order' operation. Some construction companies will construct pre-designed standard houses or apartments ahead of any firm demand for them. If demand is high, customers may place requests for houses before they are started or during their construction. In this case, the customer will form a back-log of demand and must wait. However, the company is also taking the risk of holding a stock of unsold houses. Operations of this type are called 'produce-ahead-of-order'.

How does the system interface with suppliers?

The supplier interface provides the link between the activities of the operation itself and those of its suppliers. The timing and level of activities within the operation or process will have implications for the supply of products and services to the operation. Suppliers need to be informed so that they can make products and services available when needed. In effect this is the mirror image of the customer interface. As such, the supplier interface is concerned with managing the supplier experience to ensure appropriate supply. Because the customer is not directly involved in this does not make it any less important. Ultimately, customer satisfaction will be influenced by supply effectiveness because that in turn influences delivery to customers.

Operations principle
An operation's planning and control system can enhance or inhibit the ability of its suppliers to support delivery effectiveness.

Using the expectations–perception gap to judge the quality of the supplier interface function may at first seem strange. After all, suppliers are not customers as such. Yet, it is important to be a 'quality customer' to suppliers because this increases the chances of receiving high-quality service from them. This means that suppliers fully understand one's expectations because they have been made clear and unambiguous.

PRACTICE NOTE

The supplier interface has both a long- and a short-term function. It must be able to cope with different types of long-term supplier relationship, and also handle individual transactions with suppliers. To do the former it must understand the requirements of all the processes within the operation and also the capabilities of the suppliers (in large operations, there could be thousands of suppliers). Figure 10.4 shows a simplified sequence of events in the management of a typical supplier–operation interaction which the supplier interface must facilitate. When the planning and control activity requests supply, the supplier interface must have identified potential suppliers and might also be

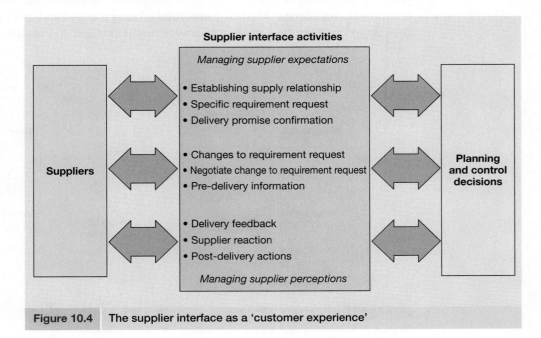

Figure 10.4   The supplier interface as a 'customer experience'

able to suggest alternative materials or services if necessary. Formal request for quotations may be sent to potential suppliers if no supply agreement exists. These requests might be sent to several suppliers or a smaller group, who may be 'preferred' suppliers. Just as it was important to manage customer expectations, it is important to manage supplier expectations, often prior to any formal supply of products or services. This issue was discussed in Chapter 7 as supplier development. To handle individual transactions, the supplier interface will need to issue formal purchase orders. These may be stand-alone documents or, more likely, electronic orders. Whatever the mechanisms, it is an important activity because it often forms the legal basis of the contractual relationship between the operation and its supplier. Delivery promises will need to be formally confirmed. Whilst waiting for delivery, it may be necessary to negotiate changes in supply, or to track progress to get early warning of potential changes to delivery. Also delivery supplier performance needs to be established and communicated, with follow-up as necessary.

How does the system perform basic planning and control calculations?

Resource planning and control requires the reconciliation of supply and demand in terms of the level and timing of activities within an operation or process. To do this, four overlapping activities are performed. These are loading, sequencing, scheduling, and monitoring and control. However, some caution is needed when using these terms. Different organizations may use them in different ways, and even textbooks in the area may adopt different definitions. Although these four activities are very closely interrelated, they do address different aspects of the resource planning and control task. Loading allocates tasks to resources in order to assess *what* level of activity will be expected of each part of the operation. Scheduling is more concerned with *when* the operation or process will do things. Sequencing is a more detailed set of decisions that determines *in what order* jobs pass through processes. Monitoring and control involves checking whether *activities are going to plan* by observing what is actually happening in practice, and making adjustments as necessary. See Figure 10.5. This part of the planning and control system can be regarded as the engine room of the whole system in so much as it calculates the consequences of planning and control decisions. Without understanding how these basic mechanisms work, it is difficult to understand how any operation is being planned and controlled. Because of their importance, we treat the four interrelated activities later in the chapter.

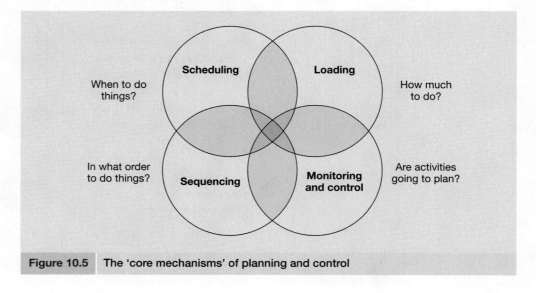

Figure 10.5 The 'core mechanisms' of planning and control

Does the system integrate human with 'automated' decision making?

Although computer-based resource planning and control systems are now widespread in many industries, much of the decision making is still carried out partially by people. This is always likely to be the case because some elements of the task, such as negotiating with customers and suppliers, are difficult to automate. Yet the benefits of computer-aided decision making are difficult to ignore. Unlike humans, computer-based planning and control can cope with immense complexity, both in terms of being able to model the interrelationship between decisions and in terms of being able to store large quantities of information. However, humans are generally better at many of the 'soft' qualitative tasks that can be important in planning and control. In particular, humans are good at the following.

- *Flexibility, adaptability and learning.* Humans can cope with ambiguous, incomplete, inconsistent and redundant goals and constraints. In particular they can deal with the fact that planning and control objectives and constraints may not be stable for longer than a few hours.
- *Communication and negotiation.* Humans are able to understand and sometimes influence the variability inherent in an operation. They can influence job priorities and sometimes processing times. They can negotiate between internal processes and communicate with customers and suppliers in a way that could minimize misunderstanding.
- *Intuition.* Humans can fill in the blanks of missing information that is required to plan and control. They can accumulate the tacit knowledge about what is, and what may be, really happening with the operation's processes.

These strengths of human decision making versus computer decision making provide a clue as to what should be the appropriate degree of automation built into decision making in this area. When planning and controlling stable and relatively straightforward processes that are well understood, decision making can be automated to a greater degree than processes that are complex, unstable and poorly understood.

DIAGNOSTIC QUESTION

Is resource planning and control information integrated?

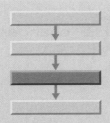

One of the most important issues in resource planning and control is managing the sometimes vast amounts of information generated, not just from the operations function, but from almost every other function of the business. Unless all relevant information is brought together and integrated, it is difficult to make informed planning and control decisions. This is what Enterprise Resource Planning (ERP) is about. It has been defined as *'a complete enterprise wide business solution. The ERP system consists of software support modules such as: marketing and sales, field service, product design and development, production and inventory control, procurement, distribution, industrial facilities management, process design and development, manufacturing,*

> **Operations principle**
> Planning and control systems should integrate information from all relevant organizational functions.

quality, human resources, finance and accounting, and information services. Integration between the modules is stressed without the duplication of information'.[3]

The origins of ERP

Enterprise resource planning has spawned a huge industry devoted to developing the computer systems needed to drive it. The (now) large companies that have grown almost exclusively on the basis of providing ERP systems include SAP, Oracle and Baan. Yet ERP is the one of the latest (and most important) stages in a development that started with Materials Requirements Planning (MRP), an approach that became popular during the 1970s, although the planning and control logic that underlies it had been known for some time. It is a method (simple in principle but complex in execution) of translating a statement of required output into a plan for all the activities that must take place to achieve the required output. What popularized MRP was the availability of computer power to drive the basic planning and control mathematics in a fast, efficient, and most importantly, flexible manner. MRP is treated in the supplement to this chapter. Manufacturing Resource Planning (MRP II) expanded out of MRP during the 1980s. This extended concept has been described as a game plan for planning and monitoring all the resources of a manufacturing company: manufacturing, marketing, finance and engineering. Again, it was a technology innovation that allowed the development. Local Area Networks (LANs) together with increasingly powerful desktop computers allowed a much higher degree of processing power and communication between different parts of a business.

The strength of MRP and MRP II lay always in the fact that it could explore the *consequences* of any changes to what an operation was required to do. So, if demand changed, the MRP system would calculate all the 'knock-on' effects and issue instructions accordingly. The same principle applies to ERP, but on a much wider basis. ERP systems allow decisions and databases from all parts of the organization to be integrated so that the consequences of decisions in one part of the organization are reflected in the planning and control systems of the rest of the organization (see Figure 10.6).

ERP changes the way companies do business

Arguably the most significant issue in the decision by many companies to buy an off-the-shelf ERP system is its compatibility with the company's current business processes and practices. Experience of ERP installation suggests that it is extremely important to make sure that one's current way of doing business will fit (or can be changed to fit) with a standard ERP package. One of the most common reasons for not installing ERP is incompatibility between the assumptions in the software and the operating practice of core business processes. If a business's current processes do not fit, it can either change its processes to fit the ERP package, or modify the software within the ERP package to fit its processes.

> **Operations principle**
> ERP systems are fully effective only if the way a business organizes its processes is aligned with the underlying assumption of its ERP system.

Both of these options involve costs and risks. Changing business practices that are working well will involve reorganization costs as well introducing the potential for errors to creep into the processes. Adapting the software will both slow down the project and introduce potentially dangerous software 'bugs' into the system. It would also make it difficult to upgrade the software later on.

ERP installation can be particularly expensive. Attempting to get new systems and databases to talk to old (sometimes called *legacy*) systems can be very problematic. Not surprisingly, many companies choose to replace most, if not all, their existing systems

PRACTICE NOTE

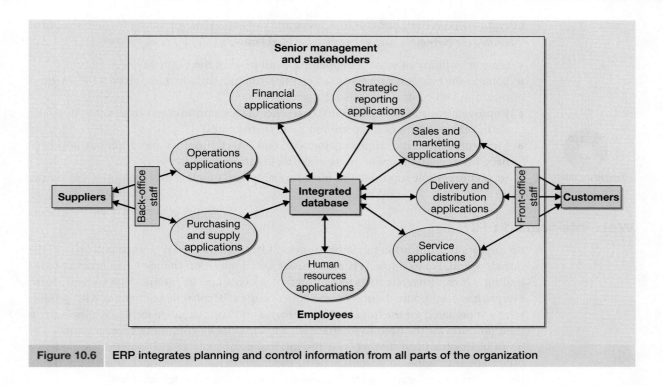

Figure 10.6   ERP integrates planning and control information from all parts of the organization

simultaneously. New common systems and relational databases help to ensure the smooth transfer of data between different parts of the organization. In addition to the integration of systems, ERP usually includes other features which make it a powerful planning and control tool:

● It is based on a client/server architecture; that is, access to the information systems is open to anyone whose computer is linked to central computers.
● It can include decision support facilities that enable operations decision makers to include the latest company information.
● It is often linked to external extranet systems, such as the electronic data interchange (EDI) systems, which are linked to the company's supply chain partners.
● It can be interfaced with standard applications programs which are in common use by most managers, such as spreadsheets, etc.
● Often, ERP systems are able to operate on most common platforms such as Windows NT, UNIX or Linux.

The benefits of ERP

ERP is generally seen as having the potential to significantly improve the performance of many companies in many different sectors. This is partly because of the very much enhanced visibility that information integration gives, but it is also a function of the discipline that ERP demands. Yet this discipline is itself a double-edged sword. On one hand, it 'sharpens up' the management of every process within an organization, allowing best practice (or at least common practice) to be implemented uniformly through the business. No longer will individual idiosyncratic behaviour by one part of a company's operations cause disruption to all other processes. On the other hand, it is the rigidity of this discipline that is both difficult to achieve and (arguably) inappropriate for all parts of the business. Nevertheless, the generally accepted benefits of ERP are as follows.

- Greater visibility of what is happening in all parts of the business.
- Forcing the business process-based changes that potentially make all parts of the business more efficient.
- Improved control of operations that encourages continuous improvement (albeit within the confines of the common process structures).
- More sophisticated communication with customers, suppliers and other business partners, often giving more accurate and timely information.
- Integrating whole supply chains including suppliers' suppliers and customers' customers.

FURTHER EXAMPLE

Web-integrated ERP

An important justification for embarking on ERP is the potential it gives to link up with the outside world. For example, it is much easier for an operation to move into Internet-based trading if it can integrate its external Internet systems into its internal ERP systems. However, as has been pointed out by some critics of the ERP software companies, ERP vendors were not prepared for the impact of e-commerce and had not made sufficient allowance in their products for the need to interface with Internet-based communication channels. The result of this has been that whereas the internal complexity of ERP systems was designed only to be intelligible to systems experts, the Internet has meant that customers and suppliers (who are non-experts) are demanding access to the same information.

One problem is that different types of external company often need different types of information. Customers need to check the progress of their orders and invoicing, whereas suppliers and other partners want access to the details of operations planning and control. Not only that, but they want access all the time. The Internet is always there, but ERP systems are often complex and need periodic maintenance. This can mean that every time the ERP system is taken offline for routine maintenance or other changes, the website also goes offline. To combat this, some companies configure their ERP and e-commerce links in such a way that they can be decoupled so that ERP can be periodically shut down without affecting the company's Web presence.

Supply network ERP

The step beyond integrating internal ERP systems with immediate customers and suppliers is to integrate it with the systems of other businesses throughout the supply network. This is often exceptionally complicated. Not only do different ERP systems have to communicate together, they have to integrate with other types of system. For example, sales and marketing functions often use systems such as Customer Relationship Management (CRM) systems that manage the complexities of customer requirements, promises and transactions. Getting ERP and CRM systems to work together is itself often difficult. Nevertheless, such Web-integrated ERP or 'c-commerce' (Collaborative Commerce) applications are emerging and starting to make an impact on the way companies do business. Although a formidable task, the benefits are potentially great. The costs of communicating between supply network partners could be dramatically reduced and the potential for avoiding errors as information and products move between partners in the supply chain is significant. Yet such transparency also brings risks. If the ERP system of one operation within a supply chain fails for some reason, it may block the effective operation of the whole integrated information system throughout the network.

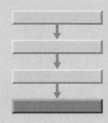

Are core planning and control activities effective?

All resource planning and control activity eventually relies on a set of calculations that guide how much work to load onto different parts of the operation, when different activities should be performed, in what order individual jobs should be done, and how processes can be adjusted if they have deviated from plan. These calculations can be thought of as the 'engine room' of the whole resource planning and control system. Although the algorithms that guide the calculations are often embedded within computer-based systems, it is worth understanding some of the core ideas on which they are based. These fall into four overlapping categories: loading, scheduling, sequencing, and monitoring and control.

Loading

Loading is the amount of work that is allocated to a process stage or the whole process. It is a capacity-related issue that attempts to reconcile how much the operation or the process is expected to do with how much the operation or process can do. Essentially the loading activity calculates the consequences on individual parts of the operation of the operation's overall workload. It may or may not assume realistic capacity limits on what can be loaded. If it does, it is called finite loading; if not, it is called infinite loading. Finite loading is an approach that allocates work to a work centre (a person, a machine or perhaps a group of people or machines) only up to a set limit. This limit is the estimate of capacity for the work centre (based on the times available for loading). Work over and above this capacity is not accepted. Figure 10.7(a) shows that the load on the work centre is not allowed to exceed the capacity limit. Finite loading is particularly relevant for operations where:

> **Operations principle**
> For any given level of demand a planning and control system should be able to indicate the implications for the loading on any part of the operation.

- *it is possible to limit the load* – for example, it is possible to run an appointment system for a general medical practice or a hairdresser;
- *it is necessary to limit the load* – for example, for safety reasons only a finite number of people and weight of luggage are allowed on an aircraft;
- *the cost of limiting the load is not prohibitive* – for example, the cost of maintaining a finite order book at a specialist sports car manufacturer does not adversely affect demand, and may even enhance it.

Infinite loading is an approach to loading work which does not limit accepting work, but instead tries to cope with it. Figure 10.7(b) illustrates a loading pattern where capacity constraints have not been used to limit loading. Infinite loading is relevant for operations where:

- *it is not possible to limit the load* – for example, an accident and emergency department in a hospital should not turn away arrivals needing attention;

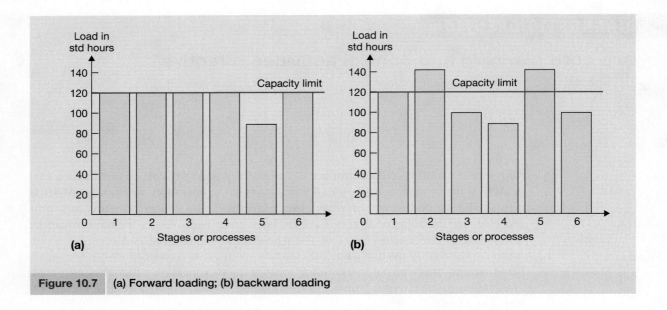

Figure 10.7   (a) Forward loading; (b) backward loading

- *it is not necessary to limit the load* – for example, fast-food outlets are designed to flex capacity up and down to cope with varying arrival rates of customers. During busy periods, customers accept that they must queue for some time before being served. Unless this is extreme, the customers might not go elsewhere;
- *the cost of limiting the load is prohibitive* – for example, if a retail bank turned away customers at the door because a set number were inside, customers would feel less than happy with the service.

In complex planning and control activities where there are multiple stages, each with different capacities and with a varying mix arriving at the facilities, such as a machine shop in an engineering company, the constraints imposed by finite loading make loading calculations complex and not worth the considerable computational power that would be needed.

Sequencing

After the 'loading' of work onto processes, the order or sequence in which it will be worked on needs to be determined. This task is called 'sequencing'. The priorities given to work in an operation are often determined by some predefined set of sequencing rules. Some of these are summarized below.

- **Customer priority.** This allows an important or aggrieved customer, or item, to be prioritized irrespective of their order of arrival. Some banks, for example, give priority to important customers. Accident and Emergency departments in hospitals must rapidly devise a schedule that prioritizes patients presenting symptoms of a serious illness. Hospitals have developed 'triage systems', whereby medical staff hurriedly sort through the patients to determine their relative urgency.
- **Due date (DD).** Work is sequenced according to when it is 'due' for delivery, irrespective of the size of each job or the importance of each customer. For example, a support service in an office block, such as a reprographic unit, may sequence the work according to when the job is needed. Due date sequencing usually improves delivery reliability and average delivery speed, but may not provide optimal productivity.

- **Last in first out (LIFO).** This is usually selected for practical reasons. For example, unloading an elevator is more convenient on a LIFO basis, as there is only one entrance and exit. LIFO has a very adverse effect on delivery speed and reliability.
- **First in first out (FIFO).** Also called 'first come, first served' (FCFS), this is a simple and equitable rule, used especially when queues are evident to customers, as in theme parks.
- **Longest operation time first (LOT).** Executing the longest job first has the advantage of utilizing work centres for long periods, but, although utilization may be high (therefore cost relatively low), this rule does not take into account delivery speed, delivery reliability or flexibility.
- **Shortest operation time first (SOT).** This sends small jobs quickly through the process, so achieving output quickly, and enabling revenue to be generated quickly. Short-term delivery performance may be improved, but productivity and the through-put time of large jobs are likely to be poor.

PRACTICE NOTE

Scheduling

Scheduling is the activity of producing a detailed timetable showing when activities should start and end. Schedules are familiar in many consumer environments, for example a bus schedule that shows the time each bus is due to arrive at each stage of the route. But, although familiar, scheduling is one of the most complex tasks in operations and process management. Schedules may have to deal simultaneously with many activities and several different types of resources, probably with different capabilities and capacities. Also the number of possible schedules increases rapidly as the number of activities and resources increases. If one process has five different jobs to process, any of the five jobs could be processed first and, following that, any one of the remaining four jobs, and so on. This means that there are $5 \times 4 \times 3 \times 2 = 120$ different possible schedules. More generally, for n jobs there are $n!$ (factorial n, or $n \times (n - 1) \times (n - 2) \ldots \times 1$) different ways of scheduling the jobs through a single process or stage. If there is more than one process or stage, there are $(n!)^m$ possible schedules, where n is the number of jobs and m is the number of processes or stages. In practical terms, this means that there are often many millions of feasible schedules, even for relatively small operations. This is why scheduling rarely attempts to provide an 'optimal' solution but rather satisfies itself with an 'acceptable' feasible one.

> **Operations principle**
> An operation's planning and control system should allow for the effects of alternative schedules to be assessed.

Gantt charts

The most common method of scheduling is by use of the Gantt chart. This is a simple device which represents time as a bar, or channel, on a chart. The start and finish times for activities can be indicated on the chart and sometimes the actual progress of the job is also indicated. The advantages of Gantt charts are that they provide a simple visual representation both of what should be happening and of what actually is happening in the operation. Furthermore, they can be used to 'test out' alternative schedules. It is a relatively simple task to represent alternative schedules (even if it is a far from simple task to find a schedule that fits all the resources satisfactorily). Figure 10.8 illustrates a Gantt chart for a specialist software developer. It indicates the progress of several jobs as they are expected to progress through five stages of the process. Gantt charts are not an optimizing tool; they merely facilitate the development of alternative schedules by communicating them effectively.

FURTHER EXAMPLE

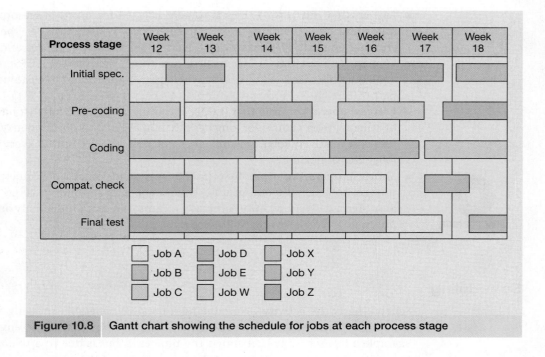

Figure 10.8 Gantt chart showing the schedule for jobs at each process stage

Scheduling work patterns

Where the dominant resource in an operation is its staff, then the schedule of work times effectively determines the capacity of the operation itself. Scheduling needs to make sure enough people are working at any time to provide a capacity appropriate for the level of demand. Operations such as call centres and hospitals, which must respond directly to customer demand, will need to schedule the working hours of their staff with demand in mind. For example, Figure 10.9 shows the scheduling of shifts for a small technical 'hotline' support service for the software company. Its service times are 4.00 hrs to 20.00 hrs on Monday, 4.00 hrs to 22.00 hrs Tuesday to Friday, 6.00 hrs to 22.00 hrs on Saturday, and 10.00 hrs to 20.00 hrs on Sunday. Demand is heaviest Tuesday to Thursday, starts to decrease on Friday, is low over the weekend and starts to increase

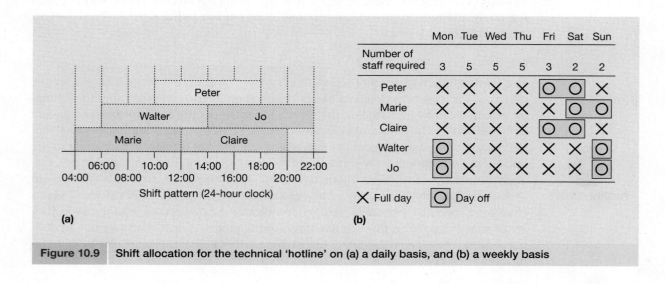

Figure 10.9 Shift allocation for the technical 'hotline' on (a) a daily basis, and (b) a weekly basis

again on Monday. The scheduling task for this kind of problem can be considered over different time scales, two of which are shown in Figure 10.9. During the day, working hours need to be agreed with individual staff members. During the week, days off need to be agreed. During the year, vacations, training periods, and other blocks of time where staff are unavailable need to be agreed. All this has to be scheduled such that:

- capacity matches demand;
- the length of each shift is neither excessively long nor too short to be attractive to staff;
- working at unsocial hours is minimized;
- days off match agreed staff conditions (in this example, staff prefer two consecutive days off every week);
- vacation and other 'time-off' blocks are accommodated;
- sufficient flexibility is built into the schedule to cover for unexpected changes in supply (staff illness) and demand (surge in customer calls).

Scheduling staff times is one of the most complex of scheduling problems. In the relatively simple example shown in Figure 10.9 we have assumed that all staff have the same level and type of skill. In very large operations with many types of skill to schedule and uncertain demand (for example, a large hospital) the scheduling problem becomes extremely complex. Some mathematical techniques are available but most scheduling of this type is, in practice, solved using heuristics (rules of thumb), some of which are incorporated into commercially available software packages.

Theory of constraints (TOC)

An important concept, closely related to scheduling, that recognizes the importance of planning to known capacity constraints, is the theory of constraints (TOC). It focuses scheduling effort on the bottleneck parts of the operation. By identifying the location of constraints, working to remove them, and then looking for the next constraint, an operation is always focusing on the part that critically determines the pace of output. The approach that uses this idea is called optimized production technology (OPT). Its development and its marketing as a proprietary software product were originated by Eliyahu Goldratt.[4] It helps to schedule production systems to the pace dictated by the most heavily loaded resources, that is, bottlenecks. If the rate of activity in any part of the system exceeds that of the bottleneck, then items are being produced that cannot be used. If the rate of working falls below the pace at the bottleneck, then the entire system is underutilized. The 'principles' of underlying OPT demonstrate this focus on bottlenecks.

OPT principles

1 Balance flow, not capacity. It is more important to reduce throughput time rather than achieving a notional capacity balance between stages or processes.
2 The level of utilization of a non-bottleneck is determined by some other constraint in the system, not by its own capacity. This applies to stages in a process, processes in an operation, and operations in a supply network.
3 Utilization and activation of a resource are not the same. According to the TOC a resource is being *utilized* only if it contributes to the entire process or operation creating more output. A process or stage can be *activated* in the sense that it is working, but it may only be creating stock or performing other non-value added activity.
4 An hour lost (not used) at a bottleneck is an hour lost forever out of the entire system. The bottleneck limits the output from the entire process or operation, therefore the underutilization of a bottleneck affects the entire process or operation.

5 An hour saved at a non-bottleneck is a mirage. Non-bottlenecks have spare capacity anyway. Why bother making them even less utilized?

6 Bottlenecks govern both throughput and inventory in the system. If bottlenecks govern flow, then they govern throughput time, which in turn governs inventory.

7 You do not have to transfer batches in the same quantities as you produce them. Flow will probably be improved by dividing large production batches into smaller ones for moving through a process.

8 The size of the process batch should be variable, not fixed. Again, from the EBQ model, the circumstances that control batch size may vary between different products.

9 Fluctuations in connected and sequence-dependent processes add to each other rather than averaging out. So, if two parallel processes or stages are capable of a particular average output rate, in series they will never be able to achieve the same average output rate.

10 Schedules should be established by looking at all constraints simultaneously. Because of bottlenecks and constraints within complex systems, it is difficult to work out schedules according to a simple system of rules. Rather, all constraints need to be considered together.

Monitoring and control

Having created a plan for the operation through loading, sequencing and scheduling, each part of the operation has to be monitored to ensure that activities are happening as planned. Any deviation can be rectified through some kind of intervention in the operation, which itself will probably involve some re-planning. Figure 10.10 illustrates a simple view of control. The output from a work centre is monitored and compared with the plan which indicates what the work centre is supposed to be doing. Deviations from this plan are taken into account through a re-planning activity and the necessary interventions made (on a timely basis) to the work centre which will ensure that the new plan is carried out. Eventually, however, some further deviation from planned activity will be detected and the cycle is repeated.

> **Operations principle**
> A planning and control system should be able to detect deviations from plans within a time scale that allows an appropriate response.

Push and pull control

An element of control is periodic intervention into processes and operations. A key distinction is between intervention signals that push work through processes and operations

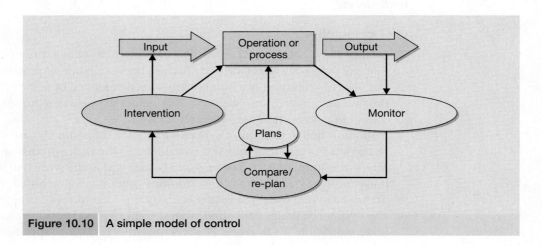

Figure 10.10   A simple model of control

and those that pull work only when it is required. In a *push* system of control, activities are scheduled by means of a central system and completed in line with central instructions, such as an MRP system (see the supplement to this chapter). Each work centre pushes out work without considering whether the succeeding work centre can make use of it. Deviations from plan are noted by the central operations planning and control system, and plans are adjusted as required. In a *pull* system of control, the pace and specification of what is done are set by the succeeding 'customer' workstation, which 'pulls' work from the preceding (supplier) workstation. The customer acts as the only 'trigger' for movement. If a request is not passed back from the customer to the supplier, the supplier cannot produce anything or move any materials. A request from a customer not only triggers production at the supplying stage, but also prompts the supplying stage to request a further delivery from its own suppliers. In this way, demand is transmitted back through the stages from the original point of demand by the original customer.

Push systems of control are more formal and require significant decision making or computing power when it is necessary to re-plan in the light of events. But push control can cope with very significant changes in circumstances such as major shifts in output level or product mix. By contrast, pull control is more self-adjusting in the sense that the

> **Operations principle**
> Pull control reduces the build-up of inventory between processes or stages.

more natural rules that govern the relationships between stages or processes can cope with deviations from plan without reference to any higher decision-making authority. But there are limits to the extent to which this can cope with major fluctuations in demand. Pull control works best when conditions are relatively stable. Understanding the differences between push and pull is also important because they have different effects in terms of their propensities to accumulate inventory. Pull systems are far less likely to result in inventory build-up and therefore have advantages in terms of the lean synchronization of flow (covered in Chapter 13).

Drum, buffer, rope control

The drum, buffer, rope concept comes from the Theory of Constraints (TOC) described earlier. It is an idea that helps to decide exactly *where* control should occur. Again, the TOC emphasizes the role of the bottleneck on work flow. If the bottleneck is the chief constraint, it should be the control point of the whole process. The bottleneck should be the *drum* because it sets the 'beat' for the rest of the process to follow. Because it does not have sufficient capacity, a bottleneck is (or should be) working all the time.

> **Operations principle**
> The constraints of bottleneck processes and activities should be a major input to the planning and control activity.

Therefore, it is sensible to keep a *buffer* of inventory in front of it to make sure that it always has something to work on. Also, because it constrains the output of the whole process, any time lost at the bottleneck will affect the output from the whole process. So it is not worthwhile for the parts of the process before the bottleneck to work to their full capacity. All they would do is produce work that would accumulate further along in the process up to the point where the bottleneck is constraining flow. Therefore, some form of communication between the bottleneck and the input to the process is needed to make sure that activities before the bottleneck do not overproduce. This is called the *rope* (see Figure 10.11).

The degree of difficulty in controlling operations

The simple monitoring control model in Figure 10.10 helps in understanding the basic functions of the monitoring and control activity. But it is a simplification. Some simple technology-dominated processes may approximate to it, but many other operations do not. In fact, the specific criticisms cited in the critical commentary below provide a

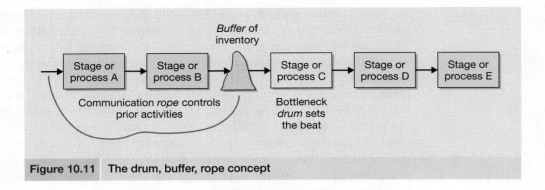

Figure 10.11   The drum, buffer, rope concept

useful set of questions that can be used to assess the degree of difficulty associated with control of any operation:

- Is there consensus over what the operation's objectives should be?
- How well can the output from the operation be measured?
- Are the effects of interventions into the operation predictable?
- Are the operation's activities largely repetitive?

Figure 10.12 illustrates how these four questions can form dimensions of 'controllability'. It shows three different operations. The food processing operation is relatively straightforward to control, while the child care service is particularly difficult. The tax advice service is somewhere in between.

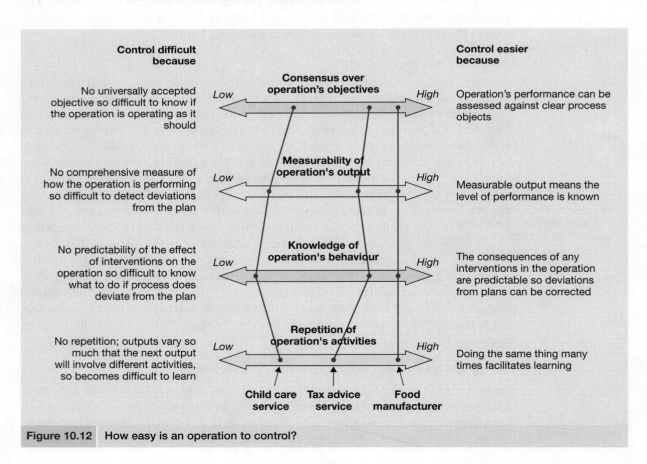

Figure 10.12   How easy is an operation to control?

Critical commentary

Each chapter contains a short critical commentary on the main ideas covered in the chapter. Its purpose is not to undermine the issues discussed in the chapter, but to emphasize that, although we present a relatively orthodox view of operation, there are other perspectives.

■ Far from being the magic ingredient which allows operations to fully integrate all their information, ERP is regarded by some as one of the most expensive ways of getting zero or even negative return on investment. For example, the American chemicals giant, Dow Chemical, spent almost half a billion dollars and seven years implementing an ERP system which became outdated almost as soon as it was implemented. One company, FoxMeyer Drug, claimed that the expense and problems which it encountered in implementing ERP eventually drove it into bankruptcy. One problem is that ERP implementation is expensive. This is partly because of the need to customize the system, understand its implications on the organization, and train staff to use it. Spending on what some call the *ERP ecosystem* (consulting, hardware, networking and complementary applications) has been estimated as being twice the spending on the software itself. But it is not only the expense which has disillusioned many companies, it is also the returns they have had for their investment. Some studies show that the vast majority of companies implementing ERP are disappointed with the effect it has had on their businesses. Certainly many companies find that they have to (sometimes fundamentally) change the way they organize their operations in order to fit in with ERP systems. This organizational impact of ERP (which has been described as the corporate equivalent of root-canal work) can have a significantly disruptive effect on the organization's operations.

■ If one accepts only some of the criticisms of ERP, it does pose the question as to why companies have invested such large amounts of money in it. Partly it was the attraction of turning the company's information systems into a 'smooth running and integrated machine'. The prospect of such organizational efficiency is attractive to most managers, even if it does presuppose a very simplistic model of how organizations work in practice. After a while, although organizations could now see the formidable problems in ERP implementation, the investments were justified on the basis that, 'even if we gain no significant advantage by investing in ERP, we will be placed at a disadvantage by *not* investing in it because all our competitors are doing so'. There is probably some truth in this; sometimes businesses have to invest just to stand still.

■ Most of the perspectives on control taken in this chapter are simplifications of a far more messy reality. They are based on models used to understand mechanical systems such as car engines. But anyone who has worked in real organizations knows that organizations are not machines. They are social systems, full of complex and ambiguous interactions. Simple models such as these assume that operations objectives are always clear and agreed, yet organizations are political entities where different and often conflicting objectives compete. Local government operations, for example, are overtly political. Furthermore, the outputs from operations are not always easily measured. A university may be able to measure the number and qualifications of its students, for example, but it cannot measure the full impact of its education on their future happiness. Also, even if it is possible to work out an appropriate intervention to bring an operation back into 'control', most operations cannot perfectly predict what effect the intervention will have. Even the largest of burger bar chains does not know *exactly* how a new shift allocation system will affect performance. Also, some operations never do the same thing more than once anyway. Most of the work done by construction operations are one-offs. If every output is different, how can 'controllers' ever know what is supposed to happen? Their plans themselves are mere speculation.

Summary checklist

DOWNLOADABLE

This checklist comprises questions that can be usefully applied to any type of operations and reflect the major diagnostic questions used within the chapter.

☐ Is appropriate effort devoted to planning and controlling the operation's resources and activities?

☐ Have any recent failures in planning and control been used to reconsider how the planning and control system operates?

☐ Does the system interface with customers so as to encourage a positive customer experience?

☐ Does the planning and control system interface with suppliers so as to promote a supplier experience that is in the company's long-term interests?

☐ Does the system perform basic planning and control calculations in an appropriate and realistic manner?

☐ Is the balance between human and automated decision making understood and appropriate for the circumstances?

☐ How well is resource planning and control information integrated?

☐ Have the advantages and disadvantages of moving to a sophisticated (but expensive!) ERP system been investigated?

☐ If so, have the possibilities of Web integration and supply chain scope been investigated?

☐ Are bottlenecks accounted for in the way planning and control decisions are made?

☐ If not, have bottlenecks been identified and their effect on the smooth flow of items through the operation been evaluated?

Case study   *subText* Studios, Singapore

'C.K. One' was clearly upset. Since he had founded *sub-Text* in the fast growing South East Asian computer generated imaging (CGI) market, three years ago, this was the first time that he had needed to apologize to his clients. In fact, it had been more than an apology; he had agreed to reduce his fee, though he knew that didn't make up for the delay. He admitted that, up to that point, he hadn't fully realized just how much risk there was, both reputational and financial, in failing to meet schedule dates. It wasn't that either he or his team was unaware of the importance of reliability. On the contrary. 'Imagination', 'expertise' and 'reliability' all figured prominently in their promotional literature, mission statements, and so on. It was just that the 'imagination' and 'expertise' parts had seemed to be the things that had been responsible for their success so far. Of course, it had been bad luck that, after more than a year of perfect reliability (not one late job), the two that had been late in the first quarter of 2004 had been particularly critical. *'They were both for new clients,'* said CK, *'and neither of them indicated just how important the agreed delivery date was to them. We should have known, or found out, I admit. But it's always more difficult with new clients, because without a track record with them, you don't really like even to admit the possibility of being late.'*

Source: Rob Melnychuk/Digital Vision/Getty Images

The company

After studying computer science up to Masters level at the National University of Singapore, C.K. Ong had worked for four years in CGI workshops in and around the Los Angeles area of California and then taken his MBA at Stanford. It was there that his fellow students had named him CK One, partly because of his fondness for the fragrance and partly because his outgoing leadership talents usually left him as the leader of whatever group he was working in. After that, *'the name just kinda stuck'*, even when he returned to Singapore to start *subText* Studios. While in California, CK had observed that a small but growing part of the market for computer-generated imaging services was in the advertising industry. *'Most CGI work is still connected with the movie industry,'* admitted CK. *'However, two important factors have emerged over the last four or five years. First, the Ad agencies have realized that, with one or two notable exceptions, the majority of their output is visually less arresting than most of the* public are used to seeing at the movies. Second, the cost of sophisticated CGI, once something of a barrier to most advertising budgets, is starting to fall rapidly. Partly this is because of cheaper computing power and partly because the scarcity of skilled CGI experts who also have creative talent is starting to rectify itself.' CK had decided to return to Singapore both for family reasons and because the market in the area was growing quickly and, unlike Hong Kong that had a large movie industry with its ancillary service industries, Singapore had few competitors.

The company was set up on a similar but slightly simpler basis to the companies CK had worked for in California. At the heart of the company were the three 'core' departments that dealt sequentially with each job taken on. These three departments were 'Pre-production', 'Production' and 'Post-production'.

- **Pre-production** was concerned with taking and refining the brief as specified by the client, checking with and liaising with the client to iron out any ambiguities in the brief, story-boarding the sequences, and obtaining outline approval of the brief from the client. In addition, pre-production also acted as account liaison with the client and were also responsible for estimating the resources and timing for each job. They also had nominal responsibility for monitoring the job through the remaining two stages, but generally they only did this if the client needed to be consulted during the production and post-production processes. The Supervising Artists in each department were responsible for the control of the jobs in their departments.

- **Production** involved the creation of the imagery itself. This could be a complex and time-consuming process involving the use of state-of-the-art workstations and CGI software. Around 80 per cent of all production work was carried out in-house, but for some jobs other specialist workshops were contracted. This was only done for work that *subText* either could not do, or would find difficult to do. Contracting was hardly ever used simply to increase capacity because the costs of doing so could drastically reduce margins.
- **Post-production** had two functions. The first was to integrate the visual image sequences produced by Production with other effects such as sound effects, music, voice-overs, etc. The second was to cut, edit and generally produce the finished 'product' in the format required by the client.

Each of the three departments employed teams of two people. *'It's a trick I learnt working for a workshop in L.A.,'* said CK. *'Two people working together both enhance the creative process (if you get the right two people!) and provide a discipline for each other. Also, it allows for some flexibility both in the mixing of different talents and in making sure that there is always at least one person from the team present at any time who knows the progress and status of any job.'* Pre-production had two teams, Production three teams, and Post-production two teams. In addition CK himself would sometimes work in the core departments, particularly in Pre-production, when he had the time, although this was becoming less common. His main role was in marketing the company's services and business development generally. *'I am the external face of the company and partly my job is to act as a cut-out, particularly for the Production and Post-production people. The last thing I want is them being disturbed by the clients all the time. I also try and help out around the place when I can, especially with the creative and storyboarding work. The problem with doing this is that, particularly for Pre-production and Post-production, a single extra person assisting does not always help to get the job done faster. In fact, it can sometimes confuse things and slow things down. This is why, for Pre-production and Post-production work, one team is always exclusively devoted to one job. We never allow either one team to be working on two jobs at the same time, or have both teams working on one job. It just doesn't work because of the confusion it creates. That doesn't apply to Production. Usually (but not always) the Production work can be parcelled up so that two or even all three of the teams could be working on different* parts of it at the same time. Provided there is close co-ordination between the teams and provided that they are all committed to pulling it together at the end, there should be a more or less inverse relationship between the number of bodies working on the job and the length of time it takes. In fact, with the infamous "fifty three slash F" job that's exactly what we had to do. However, not withstanding what I just said about shortening the time, we probably did lose some efficiency there by having all three teams working on it.

'We pay our teams in the three core departments a salary based on their experience and a yearly bonus. For that they are expected to, within reason, work until the job is finished. It varies, but most of us work at least ten-hour days relatively frequently. That level of work is factored in to the time estimates we make for each stage of the process. And, although we can be a little inaccurate sometimes, I don't think it's anything to do with a lack of motivation or pace of work. It's just that this type of thing is sometimes difficult to estimate.'

The 'fifty three slash F' job

The 'fifty three slash F' job, recently finished (late) and delivered to the client (dissatisfied), had been the source of much chaos, confusion and recrimination over the last two or three weeks. Although the job was only three days late, it had caused the client (the Singapore office of a US Advertising agency) to postpone a presentation to its own client. Worse, *subText* had given only five days' notice of late delivery, trying until the last to pull back onto schedule.

The full name of the job that had given them so much trouble was 04/53/F. The 04 related to the year in which the job was started, the 53 was the client's reference number and the F the job identifier (at the start of the year the first job would be labelled A, then B, and so forth, with AA, BB, etc., being used subsequently). Table 10.1 shows the data for all the jobs started in 2004 up to the current time (day 58, every working day was numbered throughout the year). Figure 10.13 shows the schedule for this period. The job had been accepted on day 18 and had seemed relatively straightforward, although it was always clear that it would be a long production job. It was also clear that time was always going to be tight. There were 32 days in which to finish a job that was estimated to take 30 days.

'We had been negotiating for this job for two or three weeks and we were delighted to get it. It was important to us because the client, although small in Singapore, had interests all over the world. We saw it as a way into potentially some major business in the future. In hindsight we underestimated how much having three teams working on the production stage of this job at one point or other would increase its complexity. OK, it was not an easy piece of CGI to carry off, but we probably would have been OK if we had organized the CGI stage better. It was

Table 10.1   *subText* Studios Singapore – planning data for day 02 to day 58 2004

Job (04)	Day in	Estimated total time	Actual total time	Due date	Actual delivery	Pre-prod. Est.	Pre-prod. Actual	Prod. Est.	Prod. Actual	Post-prod. Est.	Post-prod. Actual
06/A	–4	29	30	40	34	6	8	11	10	12	12
11/B	–4	22	24	42	31	4	5.5	7	7.5	11	11
04/C	2	31	30.5	43	40	9	9.5	12	13	10	9
54/D	5	28	34	55	58	10	12	12	17	6	5
31/E	15	34	25	68	57	10	11	12	14	12	–
53/F	18	32	49	50	53	6	10	18	28	8	11
24/G	25	26	20	70	–	9	11	9	9	8	–
22/H	29	32	26	70	–	10	12	14	14	8	–
22/I	33	30	11	75	–	10	11	12	–	8	–
09/J	41	36	14	81	–	12	14	14	–	10	–
20/K	49	40	–	89	–	12	–	14	–	14	–

also real bad luck that, in our efforts to deliver the fifty three slash F job on time, we also disrupted the fifty four slash D job that turned out to be the only other new client we have had this year.' (C.K. Ong)

The job had proved difficult from the start. The pre-production stage took longer than estimated, mainly because the client's creative team changed just before the start of *subText* beginning the work. But it was the actual CGI itself that proved to be the major problem. Not only was the task intrinsically difficult, it was difficult to parcel it up into separate packages that could be co-ordinated for working on by the two teams allocated to the job. More

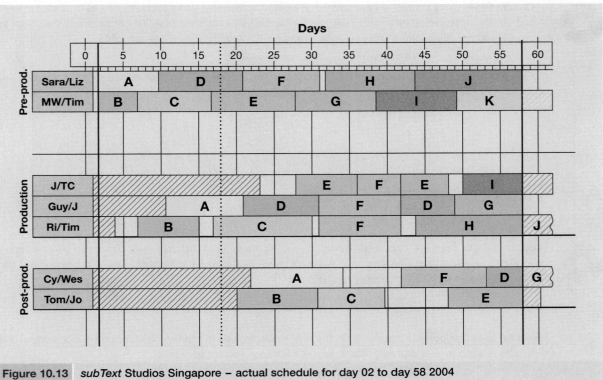

Figure 10.13   *subText* Studios Singapore – actual schedule for day 02 to day 58 2004

seriously, it became apparent, within two or three days of starting the production work, that they would need the help of another studio for some of the effects. Although the other studio was a regular supplier at short notice, this time they were too busy with their own work to help out. Help eventually came from a specialist studio in Hong Kong. *'The subcontracting delay was clearly a problem, but it was only half way through the production phase that we first realized just how much difficulty the fifty three slash F job was in. It was at that stage that we devoted all our production resources to finishing it. Unfortunately, even then, the job was late. The decision eventually to put all three teams on to the fifty three slash F job was not easy because we knew that it would both disrupt other jobs and potentially cause more co-ordination problems. However, when I accept jobs into Production I am accepting that I will try and do whatever it takes to pass it over to Post-production on the date agreed. We did miss out that time, but you can't say we didn't give it everything we've got and technically the job was brilliant, even the client admits that.'* ('TC' Ashwan, Supervising CGI Artist, Production Department)

'No way will we be doing that again'

'No way will we be doing that again,' said CK to the core teams when they met to pick over what had gone wrong. *'We are desperately in need of a more professional approach to keeping track of our activities. There is no point in me telling everyone how good we are if we then let them down. The problem is that I don't want to encourage a "command and control" culture in the studio. We depend on all staff feeling that they have the freedom to explore seemingly crazy options that may just lead to something real special. We aren't a factory. But we do need to get a grip on our estimating so that we have a better idea of how long each job really will take. After that each of the core departments can be responsible for their own planning.'*

QUESTIONS

1 What went wrong with the fifty three slash F job and how could the company avoid making the same mistakes again?

2 What would you suggest that *subText* do to tighten up its planning and control procedures?

Active case study   Coburn Finnegan Accountants

ACTIVE CASE

Coburn Finnegan is a small accountancy practice in the Republic of Ireland with offices in Cork, Limerick and Galway. It is settled on a fairly busy week ahead when, out of the blue, one of its clients calls with an urgent request which forces Mark Williams, the team manager, to re-visit the schedule.

● How would you advise the firm to respond to the request?

Please refer to the Active case on the CD accompanying this book to find out more about the planning and control activities within the firm.

Applying the principles

HINTS

Some of these exercises can be answered by reading the chapter. Others will require some general knowledge of business activity and some might require an element of investigation. All have hints on how they can be answered on the CD accompanying this book.

---

1 (a) Make a list of all the jobs you have to do in the next week. Include in this list jobs relating to your work and/or study, jobs relating to your domestic life, in fact all the things you have to do.

(b) Prioritize all these jobs on a 'most important' to 'least important' basis.

(c) Draw up an outline schedule of exactly when you will do each of these jobs.

(d) At the end of the week compare what your schedule said you *would* do with what you actually *have* done. If there is a discrepancy, why did it occur?

(e) Draw up your own list of planning and control rules from your experience in this exercise in personal planning and control.

2 Revisit the example at the beginning of the chapter which explained how one car dealership planned and controlled its workshop activities. Try to visit a local car servicing operation and talk to them about their approach to planning and control. (Note that it may be less sophisticated than the operation described in the example, or if it is a franchised operation, it may have a different approach from the one described in the example.)

- What do you think the planning and control 'system' (which may or may not be computer-based) has to do well in order to ensure efficient and effective scheduling?

- What do you think are the ideal qualities for people with similar jobs to Joanne Cheung's?

3 From your own experience of making appointments at your General Practitioner's surgery, or by visiting whoever provides you with primary medical care, reflect on how patients are scheduled to see a doctor or nurse.

- What do you think planning and control objectives are for a General Practitioner's surgery?

- How could your own medical practice be improved?

Read the following descriptions of two cinemas, then answer the questions that follow.

Kinepolis in Brussels is one of the largest cinema complexes in the world, with 28 screens, a total of 8000 seats, and four showings of each film every day. It is equipped with the latest projection technology. All the film performances are scheduled to start at the same times every day: 4 pm, 6 pm, 8 pm and 10.30 pm. Most customers arrive in the 30 minutes before the start of the film. Each of the 18 ticket desks has a networked terminal and a ticket printer. For each customer, a screen code is entered to identify and confirm seat availability of the requested film. Then the number of seats required is entered, and the tickets are printed, though these do not allocate specific seat positions. The operator then takes payment by cash or credit card and issues the tickets. This takes an average of 19.5 seconds and a further 5 seconds is needed for the next customer to move forward. An average transaction involves the sale of approximately 1.7 tickets.

4 The UCI cinema in Birmingham has eight screens. The cinema incorporates many 'state-of-the-art' features, including the high-quality THX sound system, fully computerized ticketing and a video games arcade off the main hall. In total the eight screens can seat 1840 people; the capacity (seating) for each screen varies, so the cinema management can allocate the more popular films to the larger screens and use the smaller screens for the less popular films. The starting times of the eight films at UCI are usually staggered by 10 minutes, with the most popular film in each category (children's, drama, comedy, etc.) being scheduled to run first. Because the films are of different durations, and since the manager must try to maximize the utilization of the seating, the scheduling task is complex. Ticket staff are continually aware of the remaining capacity of each 'screen' through their terminals. There are up to four ticket desks open at any one time. The target time per overall transaction is 20 seconds. The average number of ticket sales per transaction is 1.8. All tickets indicate specific seat positions, and these are allocated on a first-come-first-served basis.

(a) Reflect on the main differences between the two cinemas from the perspectives of their operations managers. In other words, what are the advantages and disadvantages of the two different methods of scheduling the films onto the screens?

(b) Find out the running times and classification of eight popular films. Try to schedule these onto the UCI screens, taking account of what popularity you might expect at different times. Allow at least 20 minutes for emptying, cleaning, and admitting the next audience, and 15 minutes for advertising, before the start of the film.

(c) Visit your local cinema (meet the manager if you can). Compare the operations with those at Kinepolis and UCI, particularly in terms of scheduling.

Notes on chapter

1 Sources: Farman, J. (1999) 'Les Coulisses du Vol', Air France. Talk presented by Richard E. Stone, NorthWest Airlines, at the IMA Industrial Problems Seminar, 1998.
2 Source: Interview with Joanne Cheung, Steve Deeley and other staff at Godfrey Hall, BMW Dealership, Coventry.
3 Wallace, T.F. and Kretmar, M.K. (2001) *ERP: Making it happen,* Wiley, New York.
4 Goldratt, E.Y. and Cox, J. (1984) *The Goal,* North River Press.

Taking it further

Goldratt, E.Y. and Cox, J. (1984) *The Goal,* North River Press. Don't read this if you like good novels but do read this if you want an enjoyable way of understanding some of the complexities of scheduling. It particularly applies to the drum, buffer, rope concept described in this chapter and it also sets the scene for the discussion of OPT in Chapter 14.

Pinedo, M. and Chao, X. (1999) *Operations Scheduling with Applications in Manufacturing and Services,* Irwin/McGraw-Hill, New York. Specialist, comprehensive and detailed.

Sule, D.R. (1997) *Industrial Scheduling,* PWSs Publishing Company. Technical and detailed for those who like and/or need technical details.

Vollmann, T.E., Berry, W.L. and Whybark, D.C. (1992) *Manufacturing Planning and Control Systems* (3rd edn), Irwin, Homewood, IL. This is the bible of production planning and control. It deals with all the issues in this part of this textbook.

Useful websites

www.bpic.co.uk Some useful information on general planning and control topics.

www.cio.com/research/erp/edit/erpbasics.html Several descriptions and useful information on ERP-related topics.

www.erpfans.com Yes, even ERP has its own fan club! Debates and links for the enthusiast.

www.sap.com/index.epx *'Helping to build better businesses for more than three decades',* SAP has been the leading worldwide supplier of ERP systems for ages. They should know how to do it by now!

www.sapfans.com Another fan club, this one for SAP enthusiasts.

www.apics.org The American professional and education body that has its roots in planning and control activities.

FURTHER RESOURCES

> **For further resources including examples, animated diagrams, self-test questions, Excel spreadsheets, active case studies and video materials please explore the CD accompanying this book.**

Introduction

Materials Requirements Planning (MRP) is an approach to calculating how many parts or materials of particular types are required and at what times they are required. This requires data files which, when the MRP program is run, can be checked and updated. Figure 10.14 shows how these files relate to each other. The first inputs to MRP are customer orders and forecast demand. MRP performs its calculations based on the combination of these two parts of future demand. All other requirements are derived from, and dependent on, this demand information.

Master production schedule

The master production schedule (MPS) forms the main input to materials requirements planning and contains a statement of the volume and timing of the end products to be made. It drives all the production and supply activities that eventually will come together to form the end products. It is the basis for the planning and utilization of labour and equipment, and it determines the provisioning of materials and cash. The MPS should include all sources of demand, such as spare parts, internal production promises, etc. For example, if a manufacturer of earth excavators plans an exhibition of its products and allows a project team to raid the stores so that it can build two pristine examples to be exhibited, this is likely to leave the factory short of parts. MPS can also be used in service organizations. For example, in a hospital theatre there is a master schedule that contains a statement of which operations are planned and when. This can be used to provision materials for the operations, such as the sterile instruments, blood and dressings. It may also govern the scheduling of staff for operations.

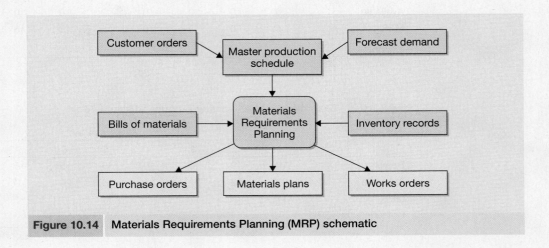

Figure 10.14   Materials Requirements Planning (MRP) schematic

The master production schedule record

Master production schedules are time-phased records of each end product, which contain a statement of demand and currently available stock of each finished item. Using this information, the available inventory is projected ahead in time. When there is insufficient inventory to satisfy forward demand, order quantities are entered on the master schedule line. Table 10.2 is a simplified example of part of a master production schedule for one item. In the first row the known sales orders and any forecast are combined to form 'Demand'. The second row, 'Available', shows how much inventory of this item is expected to be in stock at the end of each weekly period. The opening inventory balance, 'On hand', is shown separately at the bottom of the record. The third row is the master production schedule, or MPS; this shows how many finished items need to be completed and available in each week to satisfy demand.

'Chase demand' or level master production schedules

In the example in Table 10.2, the MPS increases as demand increases and aims to keep available inventory at 0. The master production schedule is 'chasing' demand (see Chapter 8) and so adjusting the provision of resources. An alternative 'levelled' MPS for this situation is shown in Table 10.3. Level scheduling involves averaging the amount required to be completed to smooth out peaks and troughs. It generates more inventory than the previous MPS.

'Available to promise' (ATP)

The master production schedule provides the information to the sales function on what can be promised to customers and when delivery can be promised. The sales function can load known sales orders against the master production schedule and keep track of what is 'available to promise' (ATP) (see Table 10.4). The ATP line in the master production schedule shows the maximum that is still available in any one week, against which sales orders can be loaded.

Table 10.2　Example of a master production schedule

		Week number								
		1	2	3	4	5	6	7	8	9
Demand		10	10	10	10	15	15	15	20	20
Available		20	10	0	0	0	0	0	0	0
MPS		0	0	10	10	15	15	15	20	20
On hand	30									

Table 10.3　Example of a 'level' master production schedule

		Week number								
		1	2	3	4	5	6	7	8	9
Demand		10	10	10	10	15	15	15	20	20
Available		31	32	33	34	30	26	22	13	4
MPS		11	11	11	11	11	11	11	11	11
On hand	30									

Table 10.4   Example of a level master production schedule including 'available to promise'

				Week number					
	1	2	3	4	5	6	7	8	9
Demand	10	10	10	10	15	15	15	20	20
Sales orders	10	10	10	8	4				
Available	31	32	33	34	30	26	22	13	4
ATP	31	1	1	3	7	11	11	11	11
MPS	11	11	11	11	11	11	11	11	11
On hand	30								

The bill of materials (BOM)

From the master schedule, MRP calculates the required volume and timing of assemblies, sub-assemblies and materials. To do this it needs information on what parts are required for each product. This is called the 'bill of materials'. Initially it is simplest to think about these as a product structure. The product structure in Figure 10.15 is a simplified structure showing the parts required to make a simple board game. Different 'levels of assembly' are shown with the finished product (the boxed game) at level 0, the parts and sub-assemblies that go into the boxed game at level 1, the parts that go into the sub-assemblies at level 2, and so on.

A more convenient form of the product structure is the 'indented bill of materials'. Table 10.5 shows the whole indented bill of materials for the board game. The term

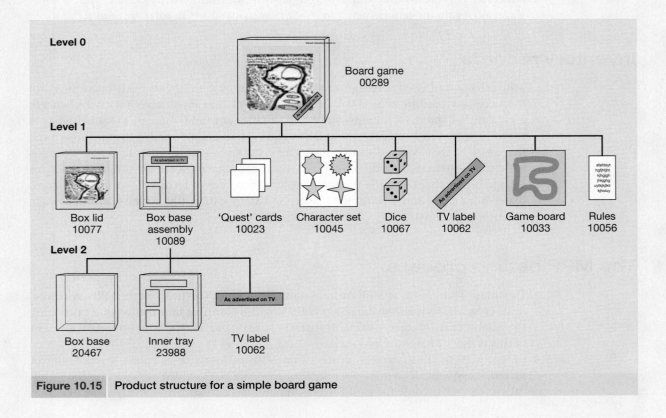

Figure 10.15   Product structure for a simple board game

| Table 10.5 | Indented bill of materials for board game |

Part number: 00289

Description: Board game

Level: 0

Level	Part number	Description	Quantity
0	00289	Board game	1
. 1	10077	Box lid	1
. 1	10089	Box base assembly	1
. . 2	20467	Box base	1
. . 2	10062	TV label	1
. . 2	23988	Inner tray	1
. 1	10023	Quest card set	1
. 1	10045	Character set	1
. 1	10067	Dice	2
. 1	10062	TV label	1
. 1	10033	Game board	1
. 1	10056	Rules booklet	1

'indented' refers to the indentation of the level of assembly, shown in the left-hand column. Multiples of some parts are required; this means that MRP has to know the required number of each part to be able to multiply up the requirements. Also, the same part (for example, the TV label, part number 10062) may be used in different parts of the product structure. This means that MRP has to cope with this commonality of parts and, at some stage, aggregate the requirements to check how many labels in total are required.

Inventory records

MRP calculations need to recognize that some required items may already be in stock. So, it is necessary, starting at level 0 of each bill, to check how much inventory is available of each finished product, sub-assembly and component, and then to calculate what is termed the 'net' requirements, that is the extra requirements needed to supplement the inventory so that demand can be met. This requires that three main inventory records are kept: the item master file, which contains the unique standard identification code for each part or component; the transaction file, which keeps a record of receipts into stock, issues from stock and a running balance; and the location file, which identifies where inventory is located.

The MRP netting process

The information needs of MRP are important, but it is not the 'heart' of the MRP procedure. At its core, MRP is a systematic process of taking this planning information and calculating the volume and timing requirements that will satisfy demand. The most important element of this is the MRP netting process.

Figure 10.16 illustrates the process that MRP performs to calculate the volumes of materials required. The master production schedule is 'exploded', examining the implications of the schedule through the bill of materials, checking how many sub-assemblies

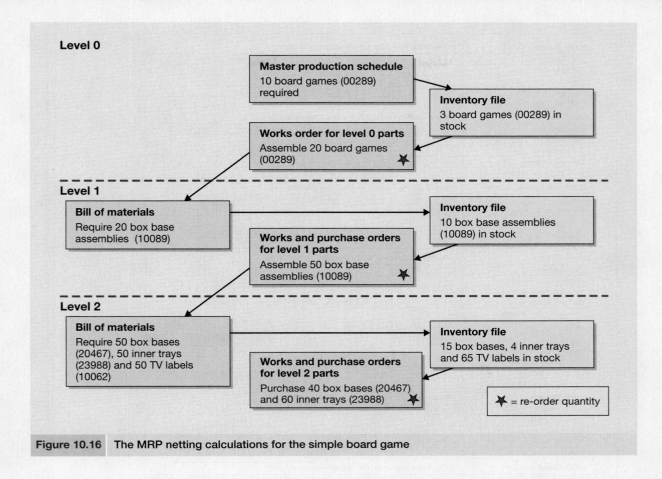

Figure 10.16   The MRP netting calculations for the simple board game

and parts are required. Before moving down the bill of materials to the next level, MRP checks how many of the required parts are already available in stock. It then generates 'works orders', or requests, for the net requirements of items. These form the schedule which is again exploded through the bill of materials at the next level down. This process continues until the bottom level of the bill of materials is reached.

Back-scheduling

In addition to calculating the volume of materials required, MRP also considers when each of these parts is required, that is, the timing and scheduling of materials. It does this by a process called back-scheduling which takes into account the lead time (the time allowed for completion of each stage of the process) at every level of assembly. Again using the example of the board game, assume that 10 board games are required to be finished by a notional planning day which we will term day 20. To determine when we need to start work on all the parts that make up the game, we need to know all the lead times that are stored in MRP files for each part (see Table 10.6).

Using the lead-time information, the programme is worked backwards to determine the tasks that have to be performed and the purchase orders that have to be placed. Given the lead times and inventory levels shown in Table 10.6, the MRP records shown in Figure 10.17 can be derived.

00289: Treasure Hunt game — Assembly lead time = 2 — Re-order quantity = 20

Day Number:	0	1	2	3	4	5	6	7	8	9	10	11	12	13	14	15	16	17	18	19	20
Requirements Gross																					10
Scheduled Receipts																					
On hand Inventory	3	3	3	3	3	3	3	3	3	3	3	3	3	3	3	3	3	3	3	3	13
Planned Order Release																			20		

10077: Box lid — Purchase lead time = 8 — Re-order quantity = 25

Day Number:	0	1	2	3	4	5	6	7	8	9	10	11	12	13	14	15	16	17	18	19	20
Requirements Gross																			20		
Scheduled Receipts																					
On hand Inventory	4	4	4	4	4	4	4	4	4	4	4	4	4	4	4	4	4	4	9	9	9
Planned Order Release											25										

10089: Box base assembly — Assembly lead time = 4 — Re-order quantity = 50

Day Number:	0	1	2	3	4	5	6	7	8	9	10	11	12	13	14	15	16	17	18	19	20
Requirements Gross																			20		
Scheduled Receipts																					
On hand Inventory	10	10	10	10	10	10	10	10	10	10	10	10	10	10	10	10	10	10	40	40	40
Planned Order Release											50										

20467: Box base — Purchase lead time = 12 — Re-order quantity = 40

Day Number:	0	1	2	3	4	5	6	7	8	9	10	11	12	13	14	15	16	17	18	19	20
Requirements Gross															50						
Scheduled Receipts																					
On hand Inventory	15	15	15	15	15	15	15	15	15	15	15	15	15	15	5	5	5	5	5	5	5
Planned Order Release			40																		

23988: Inner tray — Purchase lead time = 14 — Re-order quantity = 60

Day Number:	0	1	2	3	4	5	6	7	8	9	10	11	12	13	14	15	16	17	18	19	20
Requirements Gross															50						
Scheduled Receipts																					
On hand Inventory	4	4	4	4	4	4	4	4	4	4	4	4	4	4	14	14	14	14	14	14	14
Planned Order Release	60																				

10062: TV label — Purchase lead time = 8 — Re-order quantity = 100

Day Number:	0	1	2	3	4	5	6	7	8	9	10	11	12	13	14	15	16	17	18	19	20
Requirements Gross															50				20		
Scheduled Receipts																					
On hand Inventory	65	65	65	65	65	65	65	65	65	65	65	65	65	65	15	15	15	15	95	95	95
Planned Order Release											100										

10023: Quest card set — Purchase lead time = 3 — Re-order quantity = 50

Day Number:	0	1	2	3	4	5	6	7	8	9	10	11	12	13	14	15	16	17	18	19	20
Requirements Gross																			20		
Scheduled Receipts																					
On hand Inventory	4	4	4	4	4	4	4	4	4	4	4	4	4	4	4	4	4	4	34	34	34
Planned Order Release															50						

10045: Character set — Purchase lead time = 3 — Re-order quantity = 50

Day Number:	0	1	2	3	4	5	6	7	8	9	10	11	12	13	14	15	16	17	18	19	20
Requirements Gross																			20		
Scheduled Receipts																					
On hand Inventory	46	46	46	46	46	46	46	46	46	46	46	46	46	46	46	46	46	46	26	26	26
Planned Order Release																					

10067: Dice — Purchase lead time = 5 — Re-order quantity = 80

Day Number:	0	1	2	3	4	5	6	7	8	9	10	11	12	13	14	15	16	17	18	19	20
Requirements Gross																			40		
Scheduled Receipts																					
On hand Inventory	3	3	3	3	3	3	3	3	3	3	3	3	3	3	3	3	3	3	3	3	13
Planned Order Release														80							

10033: Game board — Purchase lead time = 15 — Re-order quantity = 50

Day Number:	0	1	2	3	4	5	6	7	8	9	10	11	12	13	14	15	16	17	18	19	20
Requirements Gross																			20		
Scheduled Receipts																					
On hand Inventory	8	8	8	8	8	8	8	8	8	8	8	8	8	8	8	8	8	8	38	38	38
Planned Order Release			50																		

10056: Rules booklet — Purchase lead time = 3 — Re-order quantity = 80

Day Number:	0	1	2	3	4	5	6	7	8	9	10	11	12	13	14	15	16	17	18	19	20
Requirements Gross																			20		
Scheduled Receipts																					
On hand Inventory	0	0	0	0	0	0	0	0	0	0	0	0	0	0	0	0	0	0	60	60	60
Planned Order Release															80						

Figure 10.17 Extract from the MRP records for the simple board game (lead times indicated by arrows ◄——►)

Table 10.6   Back-scheduling of requirements in MRP

Part no.	Description	Inventory on-hand at day 0	Lead time (days)	Re-order quantity
00289	Board game	3	2	20
10077	Box lid	4	8	25
10089	Box base assembly	10	4	50
20467	Box base	15	12	40
23988	Inner tray	4	14	60
10062	TV label	65	8	100
10023	Quest card set	4	3	50
10045	Character set	46	3	50
10067	Dice	22	5	80
10033	Game board	8	15	50
10056	Rules booklet	0	3	80

MRP capacity checks

The MRP process needs a feedback loop to check whether a plan was achievable and whether it has actually been achieved. Closing this planning loop in MRP systems involves checking production plans against available capacity and, if the proposed plans are not achievable at any level, revising them. All but the simplest MRP systems are now closed-loop systems. They use three planning routines to check production plans against the operation's resources at three levels.

- *Resource requirements plans (RRPs)* involve looking forward in the long term to predict the requirements for large structural parts of the operation, such as the numbers, locations and sizes of new plants.
- *Rough-cut capacity plans (RCCPs)* are used in the medium to short term, to check the master production schedules against known capacity bottlenecks, in case capacity constraints are broken. The feedback loop at this level checks the MPS and key resources only.
- *Capacity requirements plans (CRPs)* are used to look at the day-to-day effects of the works orders issued from the MRP on the loading of individual process stages.

11 LEAN SYNCHRONIZATION

Introduction

Lean synchronization aims to meet demand instantaneously, with perfect quality and no waste. This involves supplying products and services in perfect synchronization with the demand for them, using 'lean' or 'just-in-time' (JIT) principles. These principles were once a radical departure from traditional operations practice, but have now become orthodox in promoting the synchronization of flow through processes, operations and supply networks. (See Figure 11.1.)

Source: Flying Colours Ltd/Digital Vision/Getty Images

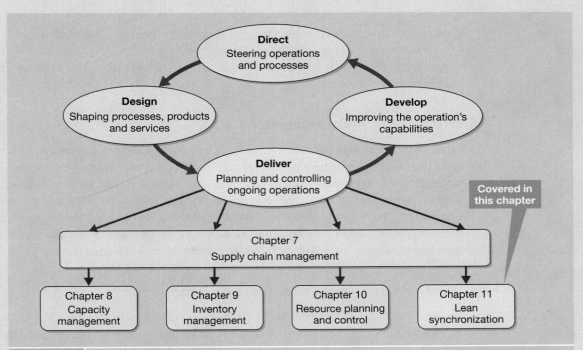

Direct
Steering operations and processes

Design
Shaping processes, products and services

Develop
Improving the operation's capabilities

Deliver
Planning and controlling ongoing operations

Covered in this chapter

Chapter 7
Supply chain management

| Chapter 8 Capacity management | Chapter 9 Inventory management | Chapter 10 Resource planning and control | Chapter 11 Lean synchronization |

Figure 11.1 Lean synchronization is the aim of achieving a flow of products and services that always delivers exactly what customers want, in exact quantities, exactly when needed, exactly where required, and at the lowest possible cost

Executive summary

VIDEO
further detail

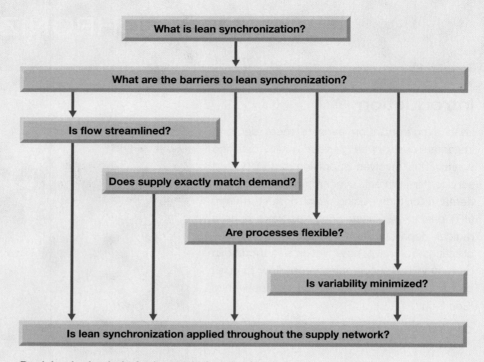

Decision logic chain for lean synchronization

Each chapter is structured around a set of diagnostic questions. These questions suggest what you should ask in order to gain an understanding of the important issues of a topic, and as a result, improve your decision making. An executive summary, addressing these questions, is provided below.

What is lean synchronization?

Lean synchronization is the aim of achieving a flow of products and services that always delivers exactly what customers want, in exact quantities, exactly when needed, exactly where required, and at the lowest possible cost. It is a term that is almost synonymous with terms such as 'just-in-time' (JIT) and 'lean operations principles'. The central idea is that if items flow smoothly, uninterrupted by delays in inventories, not only is throughput time reduced, but the negative effects of in-process inventory are avoided. Inventory is seen as obscuring the problems that exist within processes and therefore inhibiting process improvement.

What are the barriers to lean synchronization?

The aim of lean synchronization can be inhibited in three ways. First is the failure to eliminate waste in all parts of the operation. The causes of waste are more extensive than is generally understood. The second is a failure to involve all the people within the operation in the shared task of smoothing flow and eliminating waste. Japanese proponents of lean synchronization often use a set of 'basic working practices' to ensure involvement. Third is the failure to adopt continuous improvement principles. Because pure lean synchronization is an aim rather than something that can be implemented quickly, it requires the continual application of incremental improvement steps to reach it.

Is flow streamlined?

Long process routes are wasteful and cause delay and inventory build-up. Physically reconfiguring processes to reduce distance travelled and aid co-operation between staff can help to streamline flow. Similarly, ensuring flow visibility helps to make improvement to flow easier. Sometimes this can involve small-scale technologies that can reduce fluctuations in flow volume.

Does supply exactly match demand?

The aim of lean synchronization is to meet demand exactly: neither too much nor too little and only when it is needed. Achieving this often means pull control principles. The most common method of doing this is the use of kanbans, simple signalling devices that prevent the accumulation of excess inventory.

Are processes flexible?

Responding exactly to demand only when it is needed often requires a degree of flexibility in processes, both to cope with unexpected demand and to allow processes to change between different activities without excessive delay. This often means reducing changeover times in technologies.

Is variability minimized?

Variability in processes disrupts flow and prevents lean synchronization. Variability includes quality variability and schedule variability. Statistical process control (SPC) principles are useful in reducing quality variability. Levelled scheduling and mixed modelling can be used to reduce flow variability, and total productive maintenance (TPM) can reduce variability caused by breakdowns.

Is lean synchronization applied throughout the supply network?

The same benefits of lean synchronization that apply within operations can also apply between operations. Furthermore, the same principles that can be used to achieve lean synchronization within operations can be used to achieve it between operations. This is more difficult, partly because of the complexity of flow and partly because supply networks are prone to the type of unexpected fluctuations that are easier to control within operations.

What is lean synchronization?

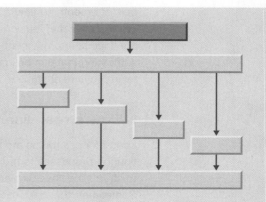

Synchronization means that the flow of products and services always delivers exactly what customers want (perfect quality), in exact quantities (neither too much nor too little), exactly when needed (not too early nor too late), and exactly where required (not to the wrong location). *Lean* synchronization is to do all this at the lowest possible cost. It results in items flowing rapidly and smoothly through processes, operations and supply networks.

The benefits of synchronized flow

The best way to understand how lean synchronization differs from more traditional approaches to managing flow is to contrast the two simple processes in Figure 11.2. The traditional approach assumes that each stage in the process will place its output in an inventory that 'buffers' that stage from the next one downstream in the process. The next stage down will then (eventually) take outputs from the inventory, process them, and pass them through to the next buffer inventory. These buffers are there to 'insulate' each stage from its neighbours, making each stage relatively independent so that if, for example, stage A stops operating for some reason, stage B can continue, at least for a time.

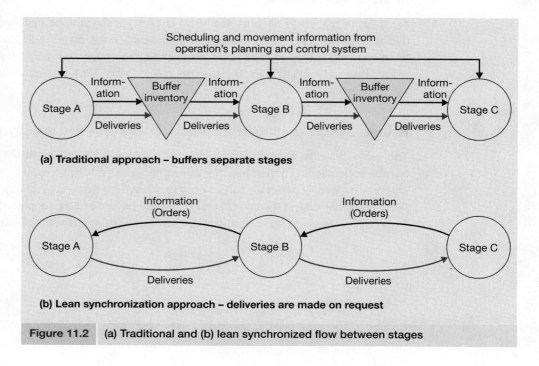

Figure 11.2   (a) Traditional and (b) lean synchronized flow between stages

The larger the buffer inventory, the greater the degree of insulation between the stages. This insulation has to be paid for in terms of inventory and slow throughput times, because items will spend time waiting in the buffer inventories.

The main 'learning' argument against this traditional approach lies in the very conditions it seeks to promote, namely the insulation of the stages from one another. When a problem occurs at one stage, the problem will not immediately be apparent elsewhere in the system. The responsibility for solving the problem will be centred largely on the people within that stage, and the consequences of the problem will be prevented from spreading to the whole system. Contrast this with the pure lean synchronized process illustrated in Figure 11.2. Here items are processed and then passed directly to the next stage 'just-in-time' for them to be processed further. Problems at any stage have a very different effect in such a system. Now if stage A stops processing, stage B will notice immediately and stage C very soon after. Stage A's problem is now quickly exposed to the whole process, which is immediately affected by the problem. This means that the responsibility for solving the problem is no longer confined to the staff at stage A. It is now shared by everyone, considerably improving the chances of the problem being solved, if only because it is now too important to be ignored. In other words, by preventing items accumulating between stages, the operation has increased the chances of the intrinsic efficiency of the plant being improved.

Non-synchronized approaches seek to encourage efficiency by protecting each part of the process from disruption. The lean synchronized approach takes the opposite view. Exposure of the system (although not suddenly, as in our simplified example) to problems can both make them more evident and change the 'motivation structure' of the whole system towards solving the problems. Lean synchronization sees accumulations of inventory as a 'blanket of obscurity' that lies over the production system and prevents problems being noticed. This same argument can be applied when, instead of queues of material, or information (inventory), an operation has to deal with queues of customers. Table 11.1 shows how certain aspects of inventory are analogous to certain aspects of queues.

> **Operations principle**
> When buffer inventory is used to insulate stages or processes it localizes the motivation to improve.

Table 11.1   Inventories of materials. information or customers have similar characteristics

	Inventory		
	Of material (queue of material)	*Of information (queue of information)*	*Of customers (queue of people)*
Cost	Ties up working capital	Less current information and so worth less	Wastes customers' time
Space	Needs storage space	Needs memory capacity	Needs waiting area
Quality	Defects hidden, possible damage	Defects hidden, possible data corruption	Gives negative perception
Decoupling	Makes stages independent	Makes stages independent	Promotes job specialization/ fragmentation
Utilization	Stages kept busy by work in progress	Stages kept busy by work in data queues	Servers kept busy by waiting customers
Co-ordination	Avoids need for synchronization	Avoids need for straight-through processing	Avoids having to match supply and demand

Source: Adapted from Fitzsimmons, J.A. (1990) 'Making continual improvement: a competitive strategy for service firms', *in* Bowen, D.E., Chase, R.B., Cummings, T.G. and Associates (eds), *Service Management Effectiveness*, Jossey-Bass, San Francisco.

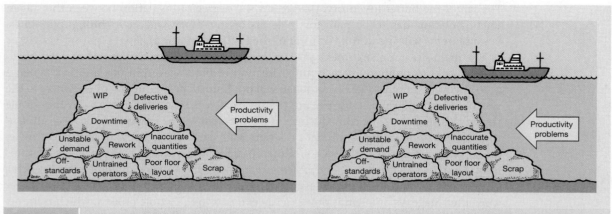

Figure 11.3   Reducing the level of inventory (water) allows operations management (the ship) to see the problems in the operation (the rocks) and work to reduce them

The river and rocks analogy

The idea of obscuring effects of inventory is often illustrated diagrammatically, as in Figure 11.3. The many problems of the operation are shown as rocks in a river bed that cannot be seen because of the depth of the water. The water in this analogy represents the inventory in the operation. Yet, even though the rocks cannot be seen, they slow the progress of the river's flow and cause turbulence. Gradually reducing the depth of the water (inventory) exposes the worst of the problems which can be resolved, after which the water is lowered further, exposing more problems, and so on. The same argument will also apply for the flow between whole processes, or whole operations. For example, stages A, B and C in Figure 11.2 could be a supplier operation, a manufacturer and a customer's operation, respectively.

Synchronization, 'lean' and 'just-in-time'

Different terms are used to describe what here we call lean synchronization. Our shortened definition – *'lean synchronization aims to meet demand instantaneously, with perfect quality and no waste'* – could also be used to describe the general concept of 'lean', or 'just-in-time' (JIT). The concept of 'lean' stresses the elimination of waste, while 'just-in-time' emphasizes the idea of producing items only when they are needed. But all three concepts overlap to a large degree, and no definition fully conveys the full implications for operations practice. Here we use the term lean synchronization because it best describes the impact of these ideas on flow and delivery.

Two companies that have implemented lean synchronization are briefly described below. One is the company that is generally credited with doing most to develop the whole concept; the other is a far smaller craft-based company that nevertheless has derived benefits from adopting some of the principles.

Example   **Toyota**

Seen as the leading practitioner and the main originator of the lean approach, the Toyota Motor Company has progressively synchronized all its processes simultaneously to give high quality, fast throughput and exceptional productivity. It has done this by developing a set of practices that has largely shaped what we now call 'lean' or 'just-in-time' but which Toyota calls the Toyota Production System (TPS). The TPS has two themes, 'just-in-time' and 'jidoka'. Just-in-time is defined as the rapid and co-ordinated movement of parts throughout the production system and supply network

Source: Courtesy of Toyota Motor Manufacturing (UK) Ltd

to meet customer demand. It is operationalized by means of *hei-junka* (levelling and smoothing the flow of items), *kanban* (signalling to the preceding process that more parts are needed) and *nagare* (laying out processes to achieve smoother flow of parts throughout the production process). *Jidoka* is described as 'humanizing the interface between operator and machine'. Toyota's philosophy is that the machine is there to serve the operator's purpose. The operator should be left free to exercise his or her judgement. Jidoka is operationalized by means of fail-safeing (or machine jidoka), line-stop authority (or human jidoka), and visual control (at-a-glance status of production processes and visibility of process standards).

Toyota believes that both just-in-time and jidoka should be applied ruthlessly to the elimination of waste, where waste is defined as 'anything other than the minimum amount of equipment, items, part and workers that are absolutely essential to production'. Fujio Cho of Toyota identified seven types of waste that must be eliminated from all operations processes. They are waste from overproduction, waste from waiting time, transportation waste, inventory waste, processing waste, waste of motion, and waste from product defects. Beyond this, authorities on Toyota claim that its strength lies in understanding the differences between the tools and practices used with Toyota operations and the overall philosophy of their approach to lean synchronization. This is what some have called the apparent paradox of the Toyota production system, 'namely, that activities, connections and production flows in a Toyota factory are rigidly scripted, yet at the same time Toyota's operations are enormously flexible and adaptable. Activities and processes are constantly being challenged and pushed to a higher level of performance, enabling the company to continually innovate and improve'.

One influential study of Toyota identified four rules that guide the design, delivery and development activities within the company.[1]

1 All work shall be highly specified as to content, sequence, timing and outcome.
2 Every customer–supplier connection must be direct and there must be an unambiguous yes or no method of sending requests and receiving responses.
3 The route for every product and service must be simple and direct.
4 Any improvement must be made in accordance with the scientific method, under the guidance of a teacher, and at the lowest possible level in the organization.

Example | ## Lean hospitals[2]

In one of the increasing number of health-care services to adopt lean principles, the Bolton Hospitals National Health Service Trust in the north of the UK has reduced one of its hospital's mortality rate from one injury by more than a third. David Fillingham, Chief Executive of Bolton Hospitals

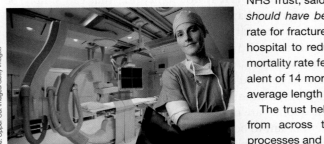

Source: Upper Cut Images/Getty Images

NHS Trust, said, *'We had far more people dying from fractured hips than should have been dying.'* Then the trust greatly reduced its mortality rate for fractured neck of femur by redesigning the patient's stay in the hospital to reduce or remove the waits between 'useful activity'. The mortality rate fell from 22.9 per cent to 14.6 per cent, which is the equivalent of 14 more patients surviving every six months. At the same time, average length of stay fell by a third from 34.6 days to 23.5 days.

The trust held five 'rapid improvement events', involving employees from across the organization who spent several days examining processes and identifying alternative ways to improve them. Some management consultants were also used but strictly in an advisory role. In addition third-party experts were brought in. These included staff from the Royal Air Force, who had been applying lean principles to running aircraft carriers. The value of these outsiders was not only their expertise. *'They asked all sorts of innocent, naïve questions,'* said Mr Fillingham, *'to which, often, no member of staff had an answer.'* Other lean-based improvement initiatives included examining the patient's whole experience from start to finish so that delays (some of which could prove fatal) could be removed on their journey to the operating theatre, radiology processes were speeded up and unnecessary paperwork was eliminated. Cutting the length of stay and reducing process complications should also start to reduce costs, although Mr Fillingham says that it could take several years for the savings to become substantial. Not only that, but staff are also said to benefit from the changes because they can spend more time helping patients rather than doing non-value-added activities.

Meanwhile, at Salisbury District Hospital in the south of the UK, lean principles have reduced delays in waiting for the results of tests from the ultrasound department. Waiting lists have been reduced from 12 weeks to between 2 and zero weeks after an investigation showed that 67 per cent of demand was coming from just 5 per cent of possible ultrasound tests: abdominal, gynaecological and urological. So all work was streamed into routine 'green' streams and complex 'red' ones. This is like having different traffic lanes on a motorway dedicated to different types of traffic, with fast cars in one lane and slow trucks in another. Mixing both types of work is like mixing fast cars and slow-moving trucks in all lanes. The department then concentrated on doing the routine 'green' work more efficiently. For example, the initial date scan used to check the age of a foetus took only two minutes, so a series of five-minute slots was allocated just for these. *'The secret is to get the steady stream of high-volume, low-variety chugging down the ultrasound motorway,'* says Kate Hobson, who runs the department. Streaming routine work in this way has left more time to deal with the more complex jobs, yet staff are not overloaded. They are more likely to leave work on time and also believe that the department is doing a better job, all of which has improved morale, says Kate Hobson. *'I think people feel their day is more structured now. It's not that madness, opening the doors and people coming at you.'*

Nor has this more disciplined approach impaired the department's ability to treat really urgent jobs. In fact, it has stopped leaving space in its schedule for emergencies – the, now standard, short waiting time is usually sufficient for urgent jobs.

What do these two operations have in common?

Here are two types of operation separated by sector, culture, size, location and their route to adopting lean synchronization principles. Toyota took decades to develop a fully integrated and coherent philosophy to managing their operations and have become one of the world's leading and most profitable automotive companies as a result. The two hospitals, on the other hand, adopted and adapted selected ideas from the lean synchronization philosophy and yet still gained benefits. That is because, notwithstanding the differences between the types of operation, the basic principles of lean synchronization remain the same, namely aiming to achieve perfect synchronization through smooth and even flow. But lean synchronization is an *aim*. It is not something that can simply be implemented overnight. These organizations have worked hard at overcoming the barriers to lean synchronization. They can be summarized as the elimination of all waste, the involvement of everyone in the business, and the adoption of a continuous improvement philosophy. The focus on eliminating waste uses four important methods: streamlining flow, making sure that supply matches demand exactly, increasing process flexibility, and reducing the effects of variability. And, although rooted in manufacturing, the techniques of lean or just-in-time philosophies are now being extended to service operations.

Before further discussion it is important to be clear on the distinction between the *aim* (lean synchronization), the *approach to overcoming the barriers* to achieving lean synchronization, the *methods of eliminating waste,* and the various *techniques* that can be used to help eliminate waste. The relationship between these elements is shown in Figure 11.4.

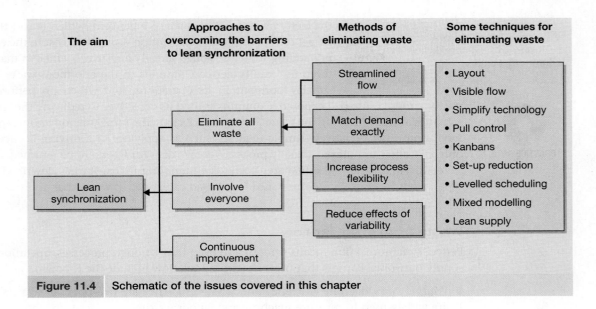

Figure 11.4 Schematic of the issues covered in this chapter

What are the barriers to lean synchronization?

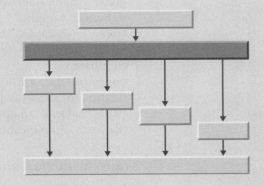

The aim of pure lean synchronization represents an ideal of smooth, uninterrupted flow without delay, waste or imperfection of any kind. The supply and demand between stages in each process, between processes in each operation, and between operations in each supply network are all perfectly synchronized. It represents the ultimate in what customers are looking for from an operation. But first one must identify the barriers to achieving this ideal state. We group these under three headings:

- Failure to eliminate waste in all parts of the operation
- Failure to harness the contribution of all the people within the operation
- Failure to establish improvement as a continuous activity.

The waste elimination barrier

Arguably the most significant part of the lean philosophy is its focus on the elimination of all forms of waste. Waste can be defined as any activity that does not add value. For example, a study by Cummins Worldwide Fortune 500, the engine company, showed that, at best, an engine was being worked on for only 15 per cent of the time it was in

PRACTICE NOTE

the factory.[3] At worst, this fell to 9 per cent, which meant that for 91 per cent of its time, the operation was adding cost to the engine, not adding value. Although already a relatively efficient manufacturer, the results alerted Cummins to the enormous waste which still lay dormant in its operations, and which no performance measure then in use had exposed. Cummins shifted its objectives to reducing the wasteful activities and to enriching the value-added ones. Exactly the same phenomenon applies in service processes. Relatively simple requests, such as applying for a driving licence, may only take a few minutes to actually process, yet take days (or weeks) to be returned.

Identifying waste is the first step towards eliminating it. Toyota has described seven types. Here we consolidate these into four broad categories of waste that apply in many different types of operation.

Waste from irregular flow

Perfect synchronization means smooth and even flow through processes, operations and supply networks. Barriers that prevent streamlined flow include the following.

- *Waiting time.* Machine efficiency and labour efficiency are two popular measures that are widely used to measure machine and labour waiting time, respectively. Less obvious is the time for which items wait as inventory, there simply to keep operators busy.
- *Transport.* Moving items around the plant, together with double and triple handling, does not add value. Layout changes that bring processes closer together, improvements in transport methods and workplace organization can all reduce waste.
- *Process inefficiencies.* The process itself may be a source of waste. Some operations may exist only because of poor component design, or poor maintenance, and so could be eliminated.
- *Inventory.* All inventory should become a target for elimination. However, it is only by tackling the causes of inventory, such as irregular flow, that it can be reduced.
- *Wasted motions.* An operator may look busy but sometimes no value is being added by the work. Simplification of work is a rich source of reduction in the waste of motion.

Waste from inexact supply

Perfect synchronization supplies exactly what is wanted, exactly when it is needed. Any under- or oversupply and any early or late delivery will result in waste. Barriers to achieving an exact match between supply and demand include the following.

- *Overproduction or underproduction.* Supplying more than, or less than, the amount immediately needed by the next stage, process or operation. This is the greatest source of waste according to Toyota.
- *Early or late delivery.* Items should only arrive exactly when they are needed. Early delivery is as wasteful as late delivery.
- *Inventory.* Again, all inventories should become a target for elimination. However, it is only by tackling the causes of inventory, such as inexact supply, that it can be reduced.

Waste from inflexible response

Customer needs can vary, in terms of what they want, how much they want, and when they want it. However, processes usually find it more convenient to change what they do relatively infrequently, because every change implies some kind of cost. That is why hospitals schedule specialist clinics only at particular times, and why machines often make a batch of similar products together. Yet responding to customer demands exactly and instantaneously requires a high degree of process flexibility. Symptoms of inadequate flexibility include the following.

- *Large batches*. Sending a batch of items through a process inevitably increases inventory as the batch moves through the whole process.
- *Delays between activities*. The longer the time (and the cost) of changing over from one activity to another, the more difficult it is to synchronize flow to match customer demand instantaneously.
- *More variation in activity mix than in customer demand*. If the mix of activities in different time periods varies more than customer demand varies, then some 'batching' of activities must be taking place.

Waste from variability

Synchronization implies exact levels of quality. If there is variability in quality levels then customers will not consider themselves as being adequately supplied. Variability, therefore, is an important barrier to achieving synchronized supply. Symptoms of poor variability include the following.

- *Poor reliability of equipment*. Unreliable equipment usually indicates a lack of conformance in quality levels. It also means that there will be irregularity in supplying customers. Either way, it prevents synchronization of supply.
- *Defective products or services*. Waste caused by poor quality is significant in most operations. Service or product errors cause both customers and processes to waste time until they are corrected.

But capacity utilization may be sacrificed in the short term

A paradox in the lean synchronization concept is that adoption may mean some sacrifice of capacity utilization. In organizations that place a high value on the utilization of capacity this can prove particularly difficult to accept. But it is necessary. Return to the process shown in Figure 11.2. When stoppages occur in the traditional system, the buffers allow each stage to continue working and thus achieve high capacity utilization. The high utilization does not necessarily make the system as a whole produce more parts. Often the extra production goes into the large buffer inventories. In a synchronized lean process, any stoppage will affect the rest of the system, causing stoppages throughout the operation. This will necessarily lead to lower capacity utilization, at least in the short term. However, there is no point in producing output just for its own sake. Unless the output is useful and enables the operation as a whole to produce saleable output, there is no point in producing it anyway. In fact, producing just to keep utilization high is not only pointless, it is counter-productive, because the extra inventory produced merely serves to make improvements less likely. Figure 11.5 illustrates the two approaches to capacity utilization.

> **Operations principle**
> Focusing on lean synchronization can initially reduce resource utilization.

The involvement barrier

An organizational culture that supports lean synchronization must place a very significant emphasis on involving everyone in the organization. This approach to people management (sometimes called the 'respect-for-people' system, after a rough translation from the Japanese) is seen by some as the most controversial aspect of the lean philosophy. It encourages (and often requires) team-based problem solving, job enrichment, job rotation and multi-skilling. The intention is to encourage a high degree of personal responsibility, engagement and 'ownership' of the job. Some Japanese companies refer to operationalizing the 'involvement of everyone' principle by adopting 'basic working practices'. They are held to be the basic preparation of the operation and its employees

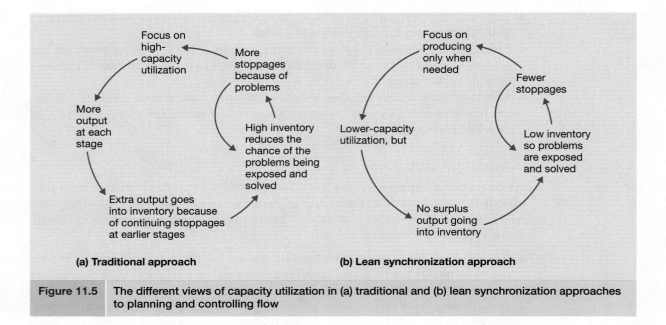

Figure 11.5   The different views of capacity utilization in (a) traditional and (b) lean synchronization approaches to planning and controlling flow

for implementing lean synchronization. They include the following.

- *Discipline.* Work standards that are critical for the safety of staff, the environment and quality, must be followed by everyone all the time.
- *Flexibility.* It should be possible to expand responsibilities to the extent of people's capabilities. This applies as equally to managers as it does to shop-floor personnel. Barriers to flexibility, such as grading structures and restrictive practices, should be removed.
- *Equality.* Unfair and divisive personnel policies should be discarded. Many companies implement the egalitarian message through to company uniforms, consistent pay structures which do not differentiate between full-time staff and hourly-rated staff, and open-plan offices.
- *Autonomy.* Delegate responsibility to people involved in direct activities so that management's task becomes one of supporting processes. Delegation includes giving staff the responsibility for stopping processes in the event of problems, scheduling work, gathering performance monitoring data, and general problem solving.
- *Development of personnel.* Over time, the aim is to create more company members who can support the rigours of being competitive.
- *Quality of working life (QWL).* This may include, for example, involvement in decision making, security of employment, enjoyment and working area facilities.
- *Creativity.* This is one of the indispensable elements of motivation. Creativity in this context means not just doing a job, but also improving how it is done, and building the improvement into the process.
- *Total people involvement.* Staff take on more responsibility to use their abilities to the benefit of the company as a whole. They are expected to participate in activities such as the selection of new recruits, dealing directly with suppliers and customers over schedules, quality issues and delivery information, spending improvement budgets, and planning and reviewing work done each day through communication meetings.

The concept of continuous learning is also central to the 'involvement of everyone' principle. For example, Toyota's approach to involving its employees includes using a learning method that allows employees to discover the Toyota Production System rules through problem solving. So, while the job is being performed, a supervisor/trainer asks a series of questions that gives the employee deeper insights into the work.[4] These questions could be:

- How do you do this work?
- How do you know you are doing this work correctly?
- How do you know that the outcome is free of defects?
- What do you do if you have a problem?

The continuous improvement barrier

Lean synchronization objectives are often expressed as ideals, such as our previous definition: 'to meet demand instantaneously with perfect quality and no waste'. While any operation's current performance may be far removed from such ideals, a fundamental lean belief is that it is possible to get closer to them over time. Without such beliefs to drive progress, lean proponents claim improvement is more likely to be transitory than continuous. This is why the concept of continuous improvement is such an important part of the lean philosophy. If its aims are set in terms of ideals which individual organizations may never fully achieve, then the emphasis must be on the way in which an organization moves closer to the ideal state. The Japanese word that incorporates the idea of continuous improvement is 'kaizen'. It is one of the main pillars of process improvement and is explained fully in Chapter 13.

Techniques to address the four sources of waste

Of the three barriers to achieving lean synchronization (reduce waste, involve everyone, and adopt continuous improvement), the last two are addressed further in Chapter 13. Therefore the rest of this chapter is devoted to what could be called the 'core' of lean synchronization. These are a collection of 'just-in-time' tools and techniques that are the means of cutting out waste. Although many of these techniques are used to reduce waste generally within processes, operations and supply networks, we will group the approaches to reducing waste under four main headings: streamlining flow, matching demand exactly, increasing process flexibility, and reducing the effects of variability.

DIAGNOSTIC QUESTION

Is flow streamlined?

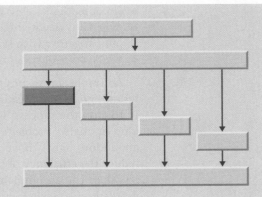

The smooth flow of materials, information and people in the operation is a central idea of lean synchronization. Long process routes provide opportunities for delay and inventory build-up, add no value, and slow down throughput time. So, the first contribution any operation can make to streamlining flow is to reconsider the basic layout of its processes. Primarily, reconfiguring the layout of a process to aid lean synchronization involves moving it down the 'natural diagonal' of process design that was discussed in

Chapter 4. Broadly speaking, this means moving from functional layouts towards cell-based layouts, or from cell-based layouts towards product layouts. Either way, it is necessary to move towards a layout that brings more systematization and control to the process flow. At a more detailed level, typical layout techniques include placing workstations close together so that inventory physically just cannot build up because there is no space for it to do so, and arranging workstations in such a way that all those who contribute to a common activity are in sight of each other and can provide mutual help, for example by facilitating movement between workstations to balance capacity.

> **Operations principle**
> Simple, transparent flow exposes sources of waste.

Examine the shape of process flow

The pattern that flow makes within or between processes is not a trivial issue. Processes that have adopted the practice of curving line arrangements into U-shaped or 'serpentine' arrangements can have a number of advantages (U shapes are usually used for shorter lines and serpentines for longer lines). One authority[5] sees the advantages of this type of flow pattern as *staffing flexibility and balance,* because the U shape enables one person to tend several jobs; *rework,* because it is easy to return faulty work to an earlier station; *free flow,* because long straight lines interfere with cross-travel in the rest of the operation; and *teamwork,* because the shape encourages a team feeling.

Ensure visibility

Appropriate layout also includes the extent to which all movement is transparent to everyone within the process. High visibility of flow makes it easier to recognize potential improvements to flow. It also promotes quality within a process because the more transparent the operation or process, the easier it is for all staff to share in its management and improvement. Problems are more easily detectable and information becomes simple, fast and visual. Visibility measures include the following.

- Clearly indicated process routes using signage
- Performance measures clearly displayed in the workplace
- Coloured lights used to indicate stoppages
- An area is devoted to displaying samples of one's own and competitors' process outputs, together with samples of good and defective output
- Visual control systems (e.g. kanbans, discussed later).

An important technique used to ensure flow visibility is the use of simple, but highly visual signals to indicate that a problem has occurred, together with operational authority to stop the process. For example, on an assembly line, if an employee detects some kind of quality problem, he or she could activate a signal that illuminates a light (called an 'andon' light) above the workstation and stops the line. Although this may seem to reduce the efficiency of the line, the idea is that this loss of efficiency in the short term is less than the accumulated losses of allowing defects to continue in the process. Unless problems are tackled immediately, they may never be corrected.

Use small-scale simple process technology

There may also be possibilities of encouraging smooth streamlined flow through the use of small-scale technologies, that is, using several small units of process technology (for example, machines) rather than one large unit. Small machines have several advantages over large ones. First, they can process different products and services simultaneously. For

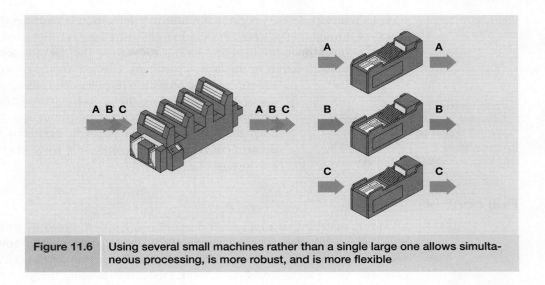

| Figure 11.6 | Using several small machines rather than a single large one allows simultaneous processing, is more robust, and is more flexible |

example, in Figure 11.6 one large machine produces a batch of A, followed by a batch of B, followed by a batch of C. However, if three smaller machines are used they can each produce A, B and/or C simultaneously. The system is also more robust. If one large machine breaks down, the whole system ceases to operate. If one of the three smaller machines breaks down, the system is still operating at two-thirds effectiveness. Small machines are also easily moved, so that layout flexibility is enhanced, and the risks of making errors in investment decisions are reduced. However, investment in capacity may increase in total because parallel facilities are needed, so utilization may be lower (see the earlier arguments).

DIAGNOSTIC QUESTION

Does supply exactly match demand?

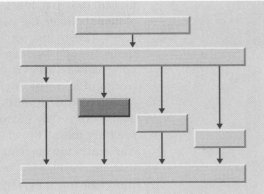

The value of the supply of products or services is always time dependent. Something that is delivered early or late often has less value than something that is delivered exactly when it is needed. We can see many everyday examples of this. For example, parcel delivery companies charge more for guaranteed faster delivery. This is because our real need for the delivery is often for it to be as fast as possible. The closer to instantaneous delivery we can get, the more value the delivery has for us, and the more we are willing to pay for it. In fact delivery of information earlier than it is required can be even more harmful than late delivery because it results in information inventories that serve to confuse flow through the process. For example, an Australian tax office used to receive applications by mail, open the mail and send it through to the relevant department which, after processing it, sent it to the next department. This led to piles of unprocessed applications building up within its processes, causing problems in tracing applications, losing them, sorting through and prioritizing applications, and worst of all, long throughput times. Now they open mail only when the stages in front can process it. Each department requests more work only when they have processed previous work.

> **Operations principle**
> Delivering only and exactly, what is needed and when it is needed, smoothes flow and exposes waste.

Pull control

The exact matching of supply and demand is often best served by using 'pull control' wherever possible (discussed in Chapter 10). At its simplest, consider how some fast-food restaurants cook and assemble food and place it in the warm area only when the customer-facing server has sold an item. Production is being triggered only by real customer demand. Similarly supermarkets usually replenish their shelves only when customers have taken sufficient products off the shelf. The movement of goods from the 'back-office' store to the shelf is triggered only by the 'empty-shelf' demand signal. Some construction companies make it a rule to call for material deliveries to their sites only the day before those items are actually needed. This not only reduces clutter and the chances of theft, it speeds up throughput time and reduces confusion and inventories. The essence of pull control is to let the downstream stage in a process, operation or supply network pull items through the system rather than have them 'pushed' to them by the supplying stage. As Richard Hall, an authority on lean operations put it, *'Don't send nothing nowhere, make 'em come and get it.'*[6]

Kanbans

The use of kanbans is one method of operationalizing pull control. Kanban is the Japanese for card or signal. It is sometimes called the 'invisible conveyor' that controls the transfer of items between the stages of an operation. In its simplest form, it is a card used by a customer stage to instruct its supplier stage to send more items. Kanbans can also take other forms. In some Japanese companies, they are solid plastic markers or even coloured ping-pong balls. Whichever kind of kanban is being used, the principle is always the same: the receipt of a kanban triggers the movement, production or supply of one unit or a standard container of units. If two kanbans are received, this triggers the movement, production or supply of two units or standard containers of units, and so on. Kanbans are the only means by which movement, production or supply can be authorized. Some companies use 'kanban squares'. These are marked spaces on the shop floor or bench that are drawn to fit one or more workpieces or containers. Only the existence of an empty square triggers production at the stage that supplies the square. As one would expect, at Toyota the key control tool is its kanban system. The kanban is seen as serving three purposes:

PRACTICE NOTE

- It is an instruction for the preceding process to send more
- It is a visual control tool to show up areas of overproduction and lack of synchronization
- It is a tool for *kaizen* (continuous improvement). Toyota's rules state that 'the number of kanbans should be reduced over time'.

Are processes flexible?

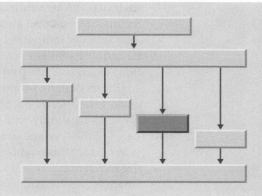

Responding exactly and instantaneously to customer demand implies that operations resources need to be sufficiently flexible to change both what they do and how much they do of it without incurring high cost or long delays. In fact, flexible processes (often with flexible technologies) can significantly enhance smooth and synchronized flow. For example, new publishing technologies allow professors to assemble printed and e-learning course material customized to the needs of individual courses or even individual students. In this case flexibility is allowing customized, small batches to be delivered 'to order'. In another example, a firm of lawyers used to take 10 days to prepare its bills for customers. This meant that customers were not asked to pay until 10 days after the work had been done. Now they use a system that, every day, updates each customer's account. So, when a bill is sent it includes all work up to the day before the billing date. The principle here is that process inflexibility also delays cash flow.

> **Operations principle**
> Change-over flexibility reduces waste and smoothes flow.

Reduce setup times

For many technologies, increasing process flexibility means reducing setup times, defined as the time taken to change the process over from one activity to the next. Compare the time it takes you to change the tyre on your car with the time taken by a Formula 1 team. Setup reduction can be achieved by a variety of methods such as cutting out time taken to search for tools and equipment, the pre-preparation of tasks that delay changeovers, and the constant practice of setup routines. Setup time reduction is also called single minute exchange of dies (SMED), because this was the objective in some manufacturing operations. The other common approach to setup time reduction is to convert work that was previously performed while the machine was stopped (called *internal* work) to work that is performed while the machine is running (called *external* work). There are three major methods of achieving the transfer of internal setup work to external work:[7]

- Pre-prepare equipment instead of having to do it while the process is stopped. Preferably, all adjustment should be carried out externally.
- Make equipment capable of performing all required tasks so that changeovers become a simple adjustment.
- Facilitate the change of equipment, for example by using simple devices such as roller conveyors.

Fast changeovers are particularly important for airlines because they cannot make money from aircraft that are sitting idle on the ground. It is called 'running the aircraft hot' in the industry. For many smaller airlines, the biggest barrier to running hot is that their markets are not large enough to justify passenger flights during the day *and* night. So, in order to avoid aircraft being idle overnight, they must be used in some other way. That was the motive behind Boeing's 737 'Quick Change' (QC) aircraft. With it, airlines have the flexibility to use it for passenger flights during the day and, with less than a one-hour changeover (setup) time, use it as a cargo aeroplane throughout the night. Boeing engineers designed frames that hold entire rows of seats that could smoothly glide on and off the aircraft, allowing 12 seats to be rolled into place at once. When used for cargo, the seats are simply rolled out and replaced by special cargo containers designed to fit the curve of the fuselage and prevent damage to the interior. Before reinstalling the seats the sidewalls are thoroughly cleaned so that, once the seats are in place, passengers cannot tell the difference between a QC aircraft and a normal 737. Airlines such as Aloha Airlines, which serves Hawaii, particularly value the aircraft's flexibility. It allows them to provide frequent reliable services in both passenger and cargo markets. So the aircraft that has been carrying passengers around the islands during the day can be used to ship fresh supplies overnight to the hotels that underpin the tourist industry.

DIAGNOSTIC QUESTION

Is variability minimized?

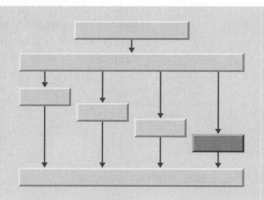

One of the biggest causes of the variability that will disrupt flow and prevent lean synchronization is variation in the quality of items. This is why a discussion of lean synchronization should always include an evaluation of how quality conformance is ensured within processes. In particular, the principles of statistical process control (SPC) can be used to understand quality variability. Chapter 12 and its supplement on SPC examine this subject, so in this section we shall focus on other causes of variability. The first of these is variability in the mix of products and services moving through processes, operations or supply networks.

> **Operations principle**
> Variability in product/service quality, or quantity, or timing, acts against smooth flow and waste elimination.

Level schedules as much as possible

Levelled scheduling (or *heijunka*) means keeping the mix and volume of flow between stages even over time. For example, instead of producing 500 parts in one batch, which would cover the needs for the next three months, levelled scheduling would require the process to make only one piece per hour regularly. Thus, the principle of levelled scheduling is very straightforward; however, the requirements to put it into practice are quite severe, although the benefits resulting from it can be substantial. The move from conventional to levelled scheduling is illustrated in Figure 11.7. Conventionally, if a mix of products were required in a time period (usually a month), a batch size would be calculated for

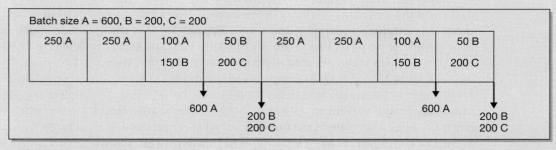

Batch size A = 600, B = 200, C = 200

250 A	250 A	100 A	50 B	250 A	250 A	100 A	50 B
		150 B	200 C			150 B	200 C

600 A   200 B   600 A   200 B
200 C   200 C

(a) Scheduling in large batches

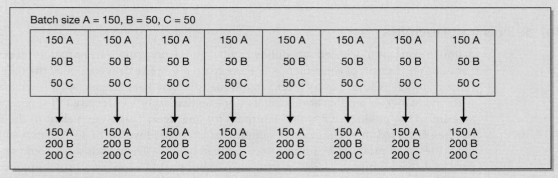

Batch size A = 150, B = 50, C = 50

150 A	150 A	150 A	150 A	150 A	150 A	150 A	150 A
50 B	50 B	50 B	50 B	50 B	50 B	50 B	50 B
50 C	50 C	50 C	50 C	50 C	50 C	50 C	50 C

150 A	150 A	150 A	150 A	150 A	150 A	150 A	150 A
200 B	200 B	200 B	200 B	200 B	200 B	200 B	200 B
200 C	200 C	200 C	200 C	200 C	200 C	200 C	200 C

(b) Levelled scheduling

Figure 11.7   Levelled scheduling equalizes the mix of products made each day

each product and the batches produced in some sequence. Figure 11.7(a) shows three products that are produced in a 20-day time period in a production unit.

> Quantity of product A required = 3000
> Quantity of product B required = 1000
> Quantity of product C required = 1000
> Batch size of product A   =   600
> Batch size of product B   =   200
> Batch size of product C   =   200

Starting at day 1, the unit commences producing product A. During day 3, the batch of 600 of product A is finished and dispatched to the next stage. The batch of Bs is started but is not finished until day 4. The remainder of day 4 is spent making the batch of Cs and both batches are dispatched at the end of that day. The cycle then repeats itself. The consequences of using large batches are first, that relatively large amounts of inventory accumulate within and between the units, and second, that most days are different from one another in terms of what they are expected to produce (in more complex circumstances, no two days would be the same).

Now suppose that the flexibility of the unit could be increased to the point where the batch sizes for the products were reduced to a quarter of their previous levels without loss of capacity (see Figure 11.7(b)):

> Batch size of product A = 150
> Batch size of product B = 50
> Batch size of product C = 50

A batch of each product can now be completed in a single day, at the end of which the three batches are dispatched to their next stage. Smaller batches of inventory are moving between each stage, which will reduce the overall level of work-in-progress in the operation. Just as significant, however, is the effect on the regularity and rhythm of production at the unit. Now every day in the month is the same in terms of what needs to be produced. This makes planning and control of each stage in the operation much easier. For example, if on day 1 of the month the daily batch of As was finished by 11.00 am, and all the batches were successfully completed in the day, then the following day the unit will know that, if it again completes all the As by 11.00 am, it is on schedule. When every day is different, the simple question 'Are we on schedule to complete our production today?' requires some investigation before it can be answered. However, when every day is the same, everyone in the unit can tell whether production is on target by looking at the clock. Control becomes visible and transparent to all, and the advantages of regular, daily schedules can be passed to upstream suppliers.

Level delivery schedules

A similar concept to levelled scheduling can be applied to many transportation processes. For example, a chain of convenience stores may need to make deliveries of all the different types of products it sells every week. Traditionally it may have dispatched a truck loaded with one particular product around all its stores so that each store received the appropriate amount of the product that would last them for one week. This is equivalent to the large batches discussed in the previous example. An alternative would be to dispatch smaller quantities of all products in a single truck more frequently. Then, each store would receive smaller deliveries more frequently, inventory levels would be lower and the system could respond to trends in demand more readily because more deliveries means more opportunity to change the quantity delivered to a store. This is illustrated in Figure 11.8.

Adopt mixed modelling where possible

The principle of levelled scheduling can be taken further to give mixed modelling; that is, a repeated mix of outputs. Suppose that the machines in the production unit can be made so flexible that they achieve the JIT ideal of a batch size of one. The sequence of individual products emerging from the unit could be reduced progressively as illustrated in Figure 11.9. This would produce a steady stream of each product flowing continuously from the unit. However, the sequence of products does not always fall as conveniently as in Figure 11.9. The unit production times for each product are not usually identical and the ratios of required volumes are less convenient. For example, if a process is required to produce products A, B and C in the ratio 8:5:4, it could produce 800 of A, followed by 500 of B, followed by 400 of C, or 80A, 50B and 40C. But ideally, to sequence the products as smoothly as possible, it would produce in the order . . . BACABACABACABACAB . . .

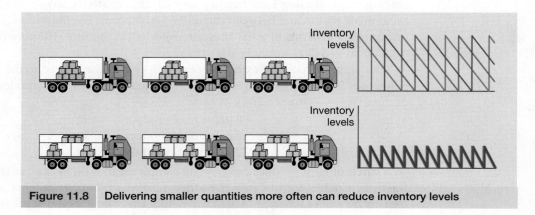

Figure 11.8   Delivering smaller quantities more often can reduce inventory levels

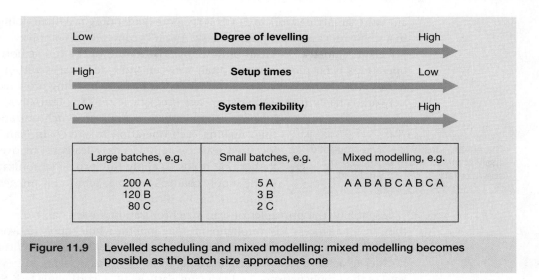

Large batches, e.g.	Small batches, e.g.	Mixed modelling, e.g.
200 A 120 B 80 C	5 A 3 B 2 C	A A B A B C A B C A

Figure 11.9 Levelled scheduling and mixed modelling: mixed modelling becomes possible as the batch size approaches one

repeated . . . repeated . . . etc. Doing this achieves relatively smooth flow (but does rely on significant process flexibility).

Adopt total productive maintenance (TPM)

Total productive maintenance aims to eliminate the variability in operations processes caused by the effect of breakdowns. This is achieved by involving everyone in the search for maintenance improvements. Process owners are encouraged to assume ownership of their machines and to undertake routine maintenance and simple repair tasks. By so doing, maintenance specialists can then be freed to develop higher-order skills for improved maintenance systems. TPM is treated in more detail in Chapter 14.

DIAGNOSTIC QUESTION

Is lean synchronization applied throughout the supply network?

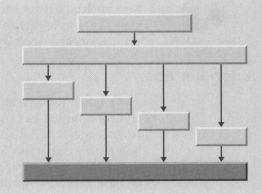

Although most of the concepts and techniques discussed in this chapter are devoted to the management of stages *within* processes and of processes *within* an operation, the same principles can apply to the whole supply chain. In this context, the stages in a process are the whole businesses, operations or processes between which products flow. And as any business starts to approach lean synchronization it will eventually come up against the constraints imposed by the lack of lean synchronization of the other operations in its supply chain. So, achieving further gains must involve trying to spread lean synchronization practice outward to its partners in the chain. Ensuring lean synchronization throughout an entire supply network is clearly a far more demanding task than doing the same within a single process. It is a complex task. And it becomes more complex as more of the supply chain embraces the lean philosophy. The nature of the interaction between whole operations is far more complex than between individual stages within a process. A far more complex mix of products and services is likely to be being provided and the whole network is likely to be subject to a less predictable set of potentially disruptive events.

> **Operations principle**
> The advantages of lean synchronization apply at the level of the process, the operation and the supply network.

Making a supply chain adopt lean synchronization means more than making each operation in the chain lean. A collection of localized lean operations rarely leads to an overall lean chain. Rather one needs to apply the lean synchronization philosophy to the supply chain as a whole. Yet the advantages from truly lean chains can be significant.

Essentially, the principles of lean synchronization are the same for a supply chain as they are for a process. Fast throughput throughout the whole supply network is still valuable and will save cost throughout the supply network. Lower levels of inventory will still make it easier to achieve lean synchronization. Waste is just as evident (and even larger) at the level of the supply network, and reducing waste is still a worthwhile task. Streamlined flow, exact matching of supply and demand, enhanced flexibility and minimal variability are all still tasks that will benefit the whole network. The principles of pull control can work between whole operations in the same way as they can between stages within a single process. In fact, the principles and the techniques of lean synchronization are essentially the same no matter what level of analysis is being used. And because lean synchronization is being implemented on a larger scale, the benefits will also be proportionally greater.

One of the weaknesses of lean synchronization principles is that it is difficult to achieve when conditions are subject to unexpected disturbance (see the critical commentary later). This is especially a problem with applying lean synchronization principles in the context of the whole supply network. Whereas unexpected fluctuations and disturbances do occur within operations, local management has a reasonable degree of control that it can exert in order to reduce them. Outside the operation, within the supply network, fluctuations can also be controlled to some extent (see Chapter 7), but it is far more difficult to do so. Nevertheless, it is generally held that, although the task is more difficult and although it may take longer to achieve, the aim of lean synchronization is just as valuable for the supply network as a whole as it is for an individual operation.

FURTHER EXAMPLE

Lean service

Any attempt to consider how lean ideas apply throughout a whole supply chain must also confront the fact that these chains include service operations, often dealing in intangibles. So how can lean principles be applied in these parts of the chain? The idea of lean factory operations is relatively easy to understand. Waste is evident in over-stocked inventories, excess scrap, badly sited machines, and so on. In services it is less obvious, inefficiencies are more difficult to see. Yet most of the principles and techniques of lean synchronization, although often described in the context of manufacturing operations, are also applicable to service settings. In fact, some of the philosophical underpinning to lean synchronization can also be seen as having its equivalent in the service sector. Take, for example, the role of inventory. The comparison between manufacturing systems that hold large stocks of inventory between stages and those that do not centres on the effect which inventory had on improvement and problem solving. Exactly the same argument can be applied when, instead of queues of material (inventory), an operation has to deal with queues of information, or even customers.

With its customer focus, standardization, continuous quality improvement, smooth flow and efficiency, lean thinking has direct application in all operations, manufacturing or service. Bradley Staats and David Upton of Harvard Business School have studied how lean ideas can be applied in service operations.[8] They make three main points.

- In terms of operations and improvements, the service industries in general are a long way behind manufacturing.
- Not all lean ideas that work in manufacturing can be translated directly into an office context. For example, tools such as empowering manufacturing workers to 'stop the line' when they encounter a problem are not directly replicable when there is no line to stop.
- Adopting lean operations principles alters the way a company learns through changes in problem solving, co-ordination through connections, and pathways and standardization.

Examples of lean service

- Many of the examples of lean philosophy and lean techniques in service industries are directly analogous to those found in manufacturing industries because physical items are being moved or processed in some way. Consider the following examples.
- Supermarkets usually replenish their shelves only when customers have taken sufficient products off the shelf. The movement of goods from the 'back-office' store to the shelf is triggered only by the 'empty-shelf' demand signal. *Principle – pull control.*
- An Australian tax office used to receive applications by mail, open the mail and send it through to the relevant department which, after processing it, sent it to the next department. Now they only open mail when the stages in front can process it. Each department requests more work only when they have processed previous work. *Principle – don't let inventories build up, use pull control.*
- One construction company makes a rule of only calling for material deliveries to its sites the day before materials are needed. This reduces clutter and the chances of theft. *Principle – pull control reduces confusion.*
- Many fast-food restaurants cook and assemble food and place it in the warm area only when the customer-facing server has sold an item. *Principle – pull control reduces throughput time.*

Other examples of lean concepts and methods apply even when most of the service elements are intangible.

- Some websites allow customers to register for a reminder service that automatically e-mails reminders for action to be taken. For example, the day before a partner's birthday, in time to prepare for a meeting, etc. *Principle – the value of delivered information, like delivered items, can be time dependent. Too early and it deteriorates (you forget it), too late and it's useless (because it's too late).*
- A firm of lawyers used to take ten days to prepare its bills for customers. This meant that customers were not asked to pay until ten days after the work had been done. Now the firm uses a system that updates each customer's account every day. So, when a bill is sent it includes all work up to the day before the billing date. *Principle – process delays also delay cash flow, fast throughput improves cash flow.*
- New publishing technologies allow professors to assemble printed and e-learning course material customized to the needs of individual courses or even individual students. *Principle – flexibility allows customization and small batch sizes delivered 'to order'.*

Lean supply chains are like air traffic control systems[9]

The concept of the lean supply chain has been likened to an air traffic control system, in that it attempts to provide continuous, 'real-time visibility and control' to all elements in the chain. This is the secret of how the world's busiest airports handle thousands of departures and arrivals daily. All aircraft are given an identification number that shows up on a radar map. Aircraft approaching an airport are detected by the radar and contacted using radio. The control tower precisely positions the aircraft in an approach pattern which it co-ordinates. The radar detects any small adjustments that are necessary, which are communicated to the aircraft. This real-time visibility and control can optimize airport throughput while maintaining extremely high safety and reliability.

Contrast this to how most supply chains are co-ordinated. Information is captured only periodically, probably once a day, output levels at the various operations in the supply chain are adjusted, and plans are rearranged. But imagine what would happen if this was how the airport operated, with only a 'radar snapshot' once a day. Co-ordinating aircraft with sufficient tolerance to arrange take-offs and landings every two minutes would be out of the question. Aircraft would be jeopardized, or alternatively, if aircraft were spaced further apart to maintain safety, throughput would be drastically reduced. Yet this is how most supply chains have traditionally operated. They use a daily 'snapshot' from their ERP systems (see Chapter 10 for an explanation of ERP). This limited visibility means operations must either space their work out to avoid 'collisions' (i.e. missed customer orders), thereby reducing output, or they must 'fly blind', thereby jeopardizing reliability.

The concept of 'lean supply'

Professor Lamming of Southampton University has proposed a model of customer–supplier relationships that he calls 'lean supply'. Table 11.2 illustrates some of the characteristics of lean supply.

At the time, Lamming saw lean supply as a step beyond the type of partnership relationships that were discussed in Chapter 7. And, although this view is not universally held, the concept of leanness in supply chains remains very influential, along with the concepts of agility and partnership. In particular, it is useful to note Lamming's emphasis on continual improvement in supply chain relationships. This concept of lean supply is not to be thought of as universally benign; in fact, the lean relationships essential for synchronized flow through the chain depend on a significant degree of rigour in relationships between operations. For example, consider how the prices charged by suppliers for products and services are handled over time. Often, in lean supply, price reductions in real terms are planned years in advance (e.g. over the next five years you will achieve a 3 per cent reduction in price, year by year). This then becomes the driver for equivalent reductions in the real cost of supply. The responsibility for reducing cost is shared in so much as customers are expected to co-operate in cost reduction. This may be by co-ordinating purchasing and planning activities so as to reduce the cost of each transaction, or more fundamentally, it may mean customers devoting resources such as 'supplier development engineers' to helping suppliers reduce their costs.

Although not an easy state to achieve, this concept of lean supply can bring advantages to both customers and suppliers. However, the idea of lean supply is often misinterpreted. One particularly common failing is for individual operations in a chain to reduce their inventories, and therefore throughput times, simply by moving stock elsewhere in the chain. Demanding instant delivery from a supplier, 'just-in-time' for when it is needed, could be achieved by a supplier holding excess resources and/or inventory. This may give the appearance of lean supply, but it certainly is not synchronized. The excessive resources and/or inventory in suppliers will add to their costs which will eventually be reflected in the price that is charged to the customer.

Lean and agile

One continuing debate on how lean principles can be applied across the supply chain concerns whether supply networks should be lean or 'agile'. Professor Martin Christopher of Cranfield University defines agility as 'rapid strategic and operational adaptation to large-scale, unpredictable changes in the business environment. Agility implies

Table 11.2   Lamming's lean supply concept

Factor	Lean supply characteristics
Nature of competition	Global operation; local presence
	Dependent upon alliances/collaboration
How suppliers are selected by customers	Early involvement of established supplier
	Joint efforts in target costing/value analysis
	Single *and* dual sourcing
	Supplier provides global benefits
	Re-sourcing as a last resort after attempts to improve
Exchange of information between supplier and customer	True transparency: costs, etc.
	Two-way: discussion of costs and volumes
	Technical and commercial information
	Electronic data interchange
	Kanban system for production deliveries (see earlier in chapter)
Management of capacity	Regionally strategic investments discussed
	Synchronized capacity
	Flexibility to operate with fluctuations
Delivery practice	True just-in-time with kanban triggering deliveries
	Local, long-distance and international JIT
Dealing with price changes	Price reductions based upon cost reductions from the start of the relationship onwards, often pre-planned, and achieved from joint efforts of both supplier and customer
Attitude to quality	Supplier vetting schemes become redundant
	Mutual agreement on quality targets
	Continual interaction and kaizen (see Chapter 13)
	Perfect quality as goal

Source: Adapted from Lamming, R. (1993) *Beyond Partnership: Strategies for innovation and lean supply*, Prentice Hall.

responsiveness from one end of the supply chain to the other. It focuses upon eliminating the barriers to quick response, be they organizational or technical'. Other definitions have agility as meaning the capability to operate profitably in a competitive environment of continually changing customer opportunities.

The clue lies in how the word 'agile' is often defined: it implies being responsive, quick moving, flexible, nimble, active and constantly ready to change. But some proponents of operational agility go further than this. They see agility as also implying a rejection of a planning paradigm that makes any assumption of a predictable future. Like lean, it is more of a philosophy than an approach. Agile encourages a better match to what customers want by placing an emphasis on producing to 'emergent' demand as opposed to rigid plans or schedules. Furthermore, rather than uncertainty and change being seen as things to be 'coped with' or preferably avoided, they should be embraced so that agility becomes changing faster than one's customer. Even the less ambitious approaches to agility see it as more than simply organizational flexibility. It involves an organizational mastery of uncertainty and change, where people within the organization, their capacity to learn from change and their collective knowledge are regarded as the organization's greatest assets because they allow the operation to respond effectively to uncertainty and change. Continually inventing innovative business processes solutions to new market demands becomes a key operations objective.

All this seems very different to the underlying assumptions of the lean philosophy. Again, look at the word: lean means 'thin, having no superfluous fat, skinny, gaunt, undernourished'. Lean attempts to eliminate waste and provide value to the customer throughout the entire supply chain. It thrives on standardization, stability, defined processes and repeatability – not at all the way agility has been described. Lean is also a well-defined (although frequently misunderstood) concept. Agility, on the other hand, is a far newer and less 'operationalized' set of relatively strategic objectives. But some operational-level distinctions can be inferred.

The types of principles needed to support a lean philosophy include such things as simple processes, waste elimination, simple (if any) IT, the use of manual and robust planning and control as well as pull control and kanbans with overall MRP. Agile philosophies, by contrast, require effective demand management to keep close to market needs, a focus on customer relationship management, responsive supply co-ordination, and visibility across the extended supply chain, continuous rescheduling and quick response to changing demand, short planning cycles, integrated knowledge management and fully exploited e-commerce solutions.

So are lean and agile philosophies fundamentally opposed? Well, yes and no. Certainly they have differing emphases. Saying that lean equals synchronized, regular flow and low inventory, and agile equals responsiveness, flexibility and fast delivery, may be something of a simplification, but it more or less captures the distinction between the two. But because they have different objectives and approaches does not mean that they cannot co-exist. Nor does it mean that there is a 'lean versus agile' argument to be resolved. The two approaches may not be complementary, as some consultants claim, but both do belong to the general collection of methodologies available to help companies meet the requirements of their markets. In the same way as it was wrong to think that JIT would replace MRP, so 'agile' is not a substitute for lean.[10]

However, agile and lean are each more appropriate for differing market and product/service conditions. Put simply, if product/service variety or complexity is high and demand predictability low, then you have the conditions in which agile principles keep an operation ready to cope with instability in the business environment. Conversely, if product/service variety is low and demand predictability high, then a lean approach can exploit the stable environment to achieve cost efficiency and dependability. So the two factors of product/service variety or complexity and demand uncertainty influence whether agile or lean principles should dominate. But what of the conditions where complexity and uncertainty are not related in this manner? Figure 11.10 illustrates how complexity and uncertainty affect the adoption of lean, agile and other approaches to organizing the flow in a supply chain.

- When complexity is low and demand uncertainty is also low (operations that produce commodities), lean planning and control is appropriate.
- When complexity is low and demand uncertainty is high (operations that produce fashion-based products/services), agile planning and control is appropriate.
- When complexity is high and demand uncertainty is also high (operations that produce 'super-value' products/services), project or requirements planning and control (for example MRPII, see Chapter 10) is appropriate.
- When product/service complexity is high and demand uncertainty is low (operations that produce consumer durable-type products/services), a combination of agile and lean planning and control is appropriate.

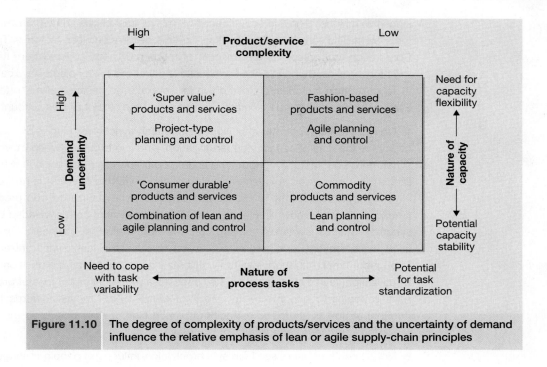

Figure 11.10 The degree of complexity of products/services and the uncertainty of demand influence the relative emphasis of lean or agile supply-chain principles

This last category, shown as the bottom left quadrant in Figure 11.10, has been rather clumsily called 'leagile'. Leagile is based on the idea that both lean and agile practices can be employed within supply chains. It envisages an inventory decoupling point that is the separation between the responsive (and therefore agile) 'front end' of the supply chain that reacts fast and flexibly to customer demand and the efficient (and therefore lean). This is not a new idea and in product-based supply chains involves 'making to *forecast*' before the decoupling point and 'making (or assembling, adapting or finishing) to *order*' after it. The idea has many similarities with the idea of 'mass customization'. However, it is difficult to transpose the idea directly into supply chains that deal exclusively in non-tangible services.

Critical commentary

Each chapter contains a short critical commentary on the main ideas covered in the chapter. Its purpose is not to undermine the issues discussed in the chapter, but to emphasize that, although we present a relatively orthodox view of operation, there are other perspectives.

■ Lean synchronization principles can be taken to an extreme. When just-in-time ideas first started to have an impact on operations practice in the West, some authorities advocated the reduction of between-process inventories to zero. While in the long term this provides the ultimate in motivation for operations managers to ensure the efficiency and reliability of each process stage, it does not admit the possibility of some processes always being intrinsically less than totally reliable. An alternative view is to allow inventories (albeit small ones) around process stages with higher than average uncertainty. This at least allows some protection for the rest of the system. The same ideas apply to just-in-time delivery between factories. The Toyota Motor Corporation, often seen as the epitome of modern JIT, has suffered from its low inter-plant inventory policies. Both the Kobe earthquake and fires in supplier plants have caused production at Toyota's main factories to close down for several days because of a shortage of key parts. Even in the best-regulated manufacturing networks, one cannot always account for such events.

■ One of the most counter-intuitive issues in lean synchronization is the way it appears to downplay the idea of capacity underutilization. And it is true that, when moving towards lean synchronization, fast throughput time and smooth flow *are* more important than the high utilization that can result in inventory build-up. However, this criticism is not really valid in the long term. Remember the relationship between capacity utilization and process throughput time (or inventory), shown in Figure 11.11. The improvement path envisaged by adopting lean synchronization is shown as moving from the state that most businesses find themselves in (high utilization but long throughput times) towards the lean synchronization ideal (short throughput time). Although, inevitably, this means moving towards a position of lower capacity utilization, lean synchronization also stresses a reduction in all types of process variability. As this begins to become reality, the improvement path moves towards the point where throughput time is short and capacity utilization high. It manages to do this because of the reduction in process variability.

■ Not all commentators see lean synchronization-influenced people-management practices as entirely positive. The JIT approach to people management can be viewed as patronizing. It may be, to some extent, less autocratic than some Japanese management practices dating

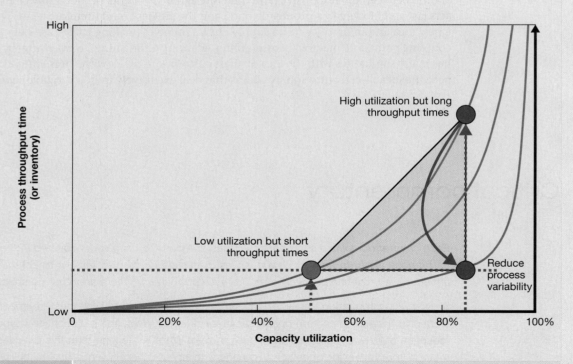

Figure 11.11   Developing lean processes can mean accepting lower utilization in the short to medium term

from earlier times. However, it is certainly not in line with some of the job design philosophies that place a high emphasis on contribution and commitment, described in Chapter 9. Even in Japan the JIT approach is not without its critics. Kamata wrote an autobiographical description of life as an employee at a Toyota plant, called *Japan in the Passing Lane*.[11] His account speaks of 'the inhumanity and the unquestioning adherence' of working under such a system. Similar criticisms have been voiced by some trade union representatives.

■ Any textbook of this type has to segment the ideas and knowledge contained within its subject so as to treat them in such a way as to explain it, to communicate each set of ideas as clearly as possible. Yet doing this inevitably means imposing artificial boundaries between the various topics. No more so than in the case of lean synchronization. There are some particularly evangelical proponents of the lean philosophy who object strongly to separating out the whole concept of lean into a separate chapter. The underlying ideas of lean, they say, have now comprehensively replaced those ideas described as 'traditional' at the beginning of this chapter. Rather, lean principles should be the foundation for the whole of operations and process management. Lean principles have something to tell us about everything in the subject, from quality management to inventory management, from job design to product design. And they are right, of course. Nevertheless, the ideas behind lean synchronization are both counterintuitive enough and important enough to warrant separate treatment. Also lean in its pure form is not necessarily equally applicable to every situation (refer to the discussion about lean and agile), hence the inclusion of this chapter which focuses on this topic. Remember though, lean synchronization is one of those topics (like operations strategy, quality and improvement) that has a particularly strong influence over the whole subject.

Summary checklist

This checklist comprises questions that can be usefully applied to any type of operations and reflect the major diagnostic questions used within the chapter.

- [ ] Are the benefits of attempting to achieve lean synchronization well understood within the business?

- [ ] Notwithstanding that the idea derives from manufacturing operations, have the principles been considered for non-manufacturing processes within the business?

- [ ] Is the extent of waste within operations and processes fully understood?

- [ ] Can flow of items through processes be made more regular?

- [ ] How much inventory of items is building up because of inexact supply?

- [ ] How much waste is caused because of inflexibility in the operation's processes?

- [ ] How much waste is caused because of variability (especially of quality) within the operation's processes?

- [ ] Are capacity utilization performance measures likely to prove a barrier to achieving lean synchronization?

- [ ] Does the culture of the organization encourage the involvement in the improvement process of all people in the organization?

- [ ] Are the ideas of continuous improvement understood?

- [ ] Are the ideas of continuous improvement used in practice?

- [ ] Are the various techniques used to promote lean synchronization understood and practised?

- [ ] Is the concept of lean synchronization applied throughout the supply network?

- [ ] Has the possibility of blending push (such as MRP) and pull (such as lean synchronization) been considered?

Case study   Boys and Boden (B&B)

'There **must** be a better way of running this place!' said Dean Hammond, recently recruited General Manager of B&B, as he finished a somewhat stressful conversation with a complaining customer, a large and loyal local building contractor.

'We had six weeks to make their special staircase, and we are still late. I'll have to persuade one of the joiners to work overtime this weekend to get everything ready for Monday. We never seem to get complaints about quality . . . our men always do an excellent job, but there is usually a big backlog of work, so how can we set priorities? We could do the most profitable work first, or the work for our biggest customers, or the jobs which are most behind. In practice, we try to satisfy everyone as best we can, but inevitably someone's order will be late. On paper, each job should be quite profitable, since we build in a big allowance for waste, and for timber defects. And we know the work content of almost any task we would have to do, and this is the basis of our estimating system. But, overall, the department isn't very profitable in comparison to our other operations, and most problems seem to end up with higher-than-anticipated costs and late deliveries!'

Boys and Boden was a small, successful, privately owned timber and building materials merchant based in a small town. Over the years it had established its large Joinery Department, which made doors, windows, staircases and other timber products, all to the exact special requirements of the customers, comprising numerous local and regional builders. In addition, the joiners would cut and prepare special orders of timber, such as non-standard sections, and special profiles including old designs of skirting board, sometimes at very short notice while the customers waited. Typically, for joinery items, the customer provided simple dimensioned sketches of the required products. These were then passed to the central Estimating/Quotations Department which, in conjunction with the Joinery Manager, calculated costs and prepared a written quotation which was faxed to the customer. This first stage was normally completed within two or three days, but on occasions could take a week or more. On receipt of an order, the original sketches and estimating details were passed back to the Joinery Manager across the yard, who roughly scheduled them into his plan, allocating them to individual craftsmen as they

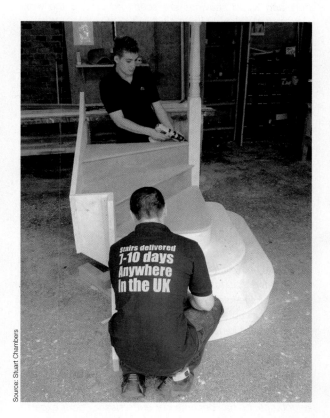

Source: Stuart Chambers

became available. Most of the joiners were capable of making any product, and enjoyed the wide variety of challenging work.

The Joinery Department appeared congested and somewhat untidy, but everyone believed that this was acceptable and normal for job shops, since there was no single flow route for materials. Whatever the design of the item being made, or the quantity, it was normal for the joiner to select the required timber from the storage building across the yard. The timber was then prepared using a planer/thicknesser. After that, the joiner would use a variety of processes, depending on the product. The timber could be machined into different cross-sectional shapes, cut into component lengths using a radial arm saw, have joints formed by hand tools or using a mortise/tenon machine, and so on. Finally the products would be glued and assembled, sanded smooth by hand or machine, and treated with preservatives, stains or varnishes if required. All the large and more expensive machines were grouped together by type (for example, saws) or were single pieces of equipment shared by all 10 or so joiners. Dean described what one might observe on a random visit to the Joinery Department:

'One or two long staircases partly assembled, and crossing several work areas; large door frames on trestles being assembled; stacks of window components for a large contract being prepared and jointed, and so on. Off-cuts and wood shavings are scattered around the work area, but are cleared periodically when they get in the way or form a hazard. The joiners try to fit in with each other over the use of machinery, so are often working on several part-finished items at once. Varnishing or staining has to be done when it's quiet – for example, evenings or weekends – or outside, to avoid dust contamination. Long off-cuts are stacked around the workshop, to be used up on any future occasion when these lengths or sections are required. However, it is often easier to take a new length of timber for each job, so the off-cuts do tend to build up over time. Unfortunately, everything I have described is getting worse as we get busier . . . our sales are increasing so the system is getting more congested. The joiners are almost climbing over each other to do their work. Unfortunately, despite having more orders, the department has remained stubbornly unprofitable.

'Whilst analyzing in detail the lack of profit, we were horrified to find that, for the majority of orders, the actual times booked by the joiners exceeded the estimated times by up to 50 per cent. Sometimes this was attributable to new, inexperienced joiners. Although fully trained and qualified, they might lack the experience needed to complete a complex job in the time an estimator would expect, but there had been no feedback of this to the individual. We put one of these men on doors only; having overcome his initial reluctance, he has become our enthusiastic "door expert", and gets closely involved in quotations too, so he always does his work within the time estimates! However, the main time losses were found to be the result of general delays caused by congestion, interference, double handling and rework to rectify in-process damage. Moreover, we found that a joiner walked an average of nearly 5 km a day, usually carrying around bits of wood.

'When I did my operations management course on my MBA, the professor described the application of cellular manufacturing and JIT. From what I can remember, the idea seemed to be to get better flow, reducing the times and distances in the process, and thus achieving quicker throughput times. That is just what we need, but these concepts were explained in the context of high-volume, repetitive production of bicycles, whereas everything we make is "one-offs". However, although we do make a lot of different staircases, they all use roughly the same process steps:

1 Cutting timber to width and length
2 Sanding
3 Machining
4 Tenoning
5 Manual assembly (glue and wedges).

We have a lot of unused factory floor-space, so it would be relatively easy to set up a self-contained staircase cell. There is huge demand for special stairs in this region, but also a lot of competing small joinery businesses which can beat us on price and lead time. So we go to a lot of trouble quoting for stairs, but only win about 20 per cent of the business. If we got the cell idea to work, we could be more competitive on price and delivery, hence winning more orders. I know we will need a lot more volume to justify establishing the cell, so it's really a case of "chicken and egg!".'

QUESTIONS

1 To what extent could (or should) Dean expect to apply the philosophies and techniques of JIT described in this chapter to the running of a staircase cell?

2 What are likely to be the main categories of costs and benefits in establishing the cell? Are there any non-financial benefits that should be taken into account?

3 At what stage, and how, should Dean sell his idea to the Joinery Manager and the workers?

4 How different would the cell work be to that in the main Joinery Department?

5 Should Dean differentiate the working environment by providing distinctive work-wear, such as T-shirts and distinctively painted machines, in order to reinforce a cultural change?

6 What risks are associated with Dean's proposal?

Active case study   Treating Ann

ACTIVE CASE

Ann is a self-employed designer and decorator. As a result of some sanding work she takes on, she develops a painful lump in her forearm. Little does she realize the processes she will have to go through in order to get the right treatment.

- How would you assess and evaluate the two health systems that she encounters? How close is each to achieving lean synchronization?

Please refer to the Active case on the CD to follow her experience of the health system in the UK and Belgium and her quest to get the right diagnosis and treatment.

Applying the principles

HINTS

Some exercises can be answered by reading the chapter. Others will require some general knowledge of business activity and some might require an element of investigation. All have hints on how they can be answered on the CD accompanying this book.

 1 Re-examine the description of the Toyota production system at the beginning of the chapter.

- (a) List all the different techniques and practices that Toyota adopts. Which of these would you call just-in-time philosophies and which are just-in-time techniques?
- (b) How are operations objectives (quality, speed, dependability, flexibility, cost) influenced by the practices that Toyota adopts?

 2 Consider this record of an ordinary flight.

'Breakfast was a little rushed but left the house at 6.15. Had to return a few minutes later, forgot my passport. Managed to find it and leave (again) by 6.30. Arrived at the airport 7.00, dropped Angela off with bags at terminal and went to the long-term car park. Eventually found a parking space after 10 minutes. Waited 8 minutes for the courtesy bus. Six-minute journey back to the terminal, we start queuing at the check-in counters by 7.24. Twenty-minute wait. Eventually get to check-in and find that we have been allocated seats at different ends of the plane. Staff helpful but takes 8 minutes to sort it out. Wait in queue for security checks for 10 minutes. Security decide I look suspicious and search bags for 3 minutes. Waiting in lounge by 8.05. Spend 1 hour and 5 minutes in lounge reading computer magazine and looking at small plastic souvenirs. Hurrah, flight is called 9.10, takes 2 minutes to rush to the gate and queue for further 5 minutes at gate. Through the gate and on to air bridge that is continuous queue going onto plane, takes 4 minutes but finally in seats by 9.21. Wait for plane to fill up with other passengers for 14 minutes. Plane starts to taxi to runway at 9.35. Plane queues to take-off for 10 minutes. Plane takes off 9.45. Smooth flight to Amsterdam, 55 minutes. Stacked in queue of planes waiting to land for 10 minutes. Touch down at Schiphol Airport 10.50. Taxi to terminal and wait 15 minutes to disembark. Disembark at 11.05 and walk to luggage collection (calling at lavatory on way), arrive luggage collection 11.15. Wait for luggage 8 minutes. Through customs (not searched by Netherlands security who decide I look trustworthy) and to taxi rank by 11.26. Wait for taxi 4 minutes. Into taxi by 11.30, 30 minutes ride into Amsterdam. Arrive at hotel 12.00.'

- (a) Analyze the journey in terms of value-added time (actually going somewhere) and non-value-added time (time spent queuing, etc.).
- (b) Visit the websites of two or three airlines and examine their business-class and first-class services to look for ideas that reduce the non-value-added time for customers who are willing to pay the premium.
- (c) Next time you go on a journey, time each part of the journey and perform a similar analysis.

3 Examine the value-added versus non-value-added times for some other services. For example:

(a) Handing an assignment in for marking if you are currently studying for a qualification (what is the typical elapsed time between handing the assignment in and receiving it back with comments?). How much of this elapsed time do you think is value-added time?

(b) Posting a letter (the elapsed time is between posting the letter in the box and it being delivered to the recipient).

(c) Taking a garment to be professionally dry cleaned.

4 Using an Internet search engine, enter 'kanban', and capture those who use such devices for planning and control. Contrast the ways in which they are used.

5 Consider how setup reduction principles can be used on the following.

(a) Changing a tyre at the side of the road (following a puncture).

(b) Cleaning out an aircraft and preparing it for the next flight between an aircraft on its inbound flight landing and disembarking its passengers, and the same aircraft being ready to take off on its outbound flight.

(c) The time between the finish of one surgical procedure in a hospital's operating theatre, and the start of the next one.

(d) The 'pitstop' activities during a Formula One race (how does this compare to (a) above?).

6 In the chapter the example of Boeing's success in enabling aircraft to convert between passenger and cargo operations was described.

(a) If the changeover between 'passengers' and 'cargo' took 2 hours instead of 1 hour, how much impact do you think it would have on the usefulness of the aircraft?

(b) For an aircraft that carries passengers all the time, what is the equivalent of setup reduction? Why might it be important?

Notes on chapter

1 Spears, S. and Bowen, H.K. (1999) 'Decoding the DNA of the Toyota production system', *Harvard Business Review,* October, pp. 96–106.

2 Source: Mathieson, S.A. (2006) 'NHS should embrace lean times', *The Guardian,* 8 June.

3 Lee, D.C. (1987) 'Set-up time reduction: making JIT work' *in* Voss, C.A. (ed.), *Just-in-Time Manufacture,* IFS/Springer-Verlag.

4 Spears and Bowen, *op. cit.*

5 Harrison, A. (1992) *Just-in-Time Manufacturing in Perspective,* Prentice Hall.

6 Hall, R.W. (1983) *'Zero Inventories',* McGraw-Hill, New York.

7 Yamashina, H. (1992) 'Reducing set-up times makes your company flexible and more competitive', unpublished, quoted in Harrison, *op. cit.*

8 Reported in Hanna, J. (2007) 'Bringing "lean" principles to service industries', *Harvard Business Review,* October.

9 This great metaphor seems to have originated from the consultancy '2think', www.2think.biz/index.htm

10 Kruse, G. (2002) 'IT enabled lean agility', *Control,* November.

11 Kamata, S. (1983) *Japan in the Passing Lane: An insider's account of life in a Japanese auto factory,* Allen & Unwin.

Taking it further

Fiedler, K., Galletly, J.E. and Bicheno, J. (1993) 'Expert advice for JIT implementation', *International Journal of Operations and Production Management,* Vol. 13, No. 6. An academic paper but contains some good advice.

Schonberger, R.J. (1982) *Japanese Manufacturing Techniques: Nine hidden lessons in simplicity,* Free Press, New York. One of the really influential books that established JIT in the West. Now seen as over-simplistic but worth looking at to understand pure JIT.

Schonberger, R.J. (1986) *World Class Manufacturing: The lessons of simplicity applied,* Free Press, New York. As above, but developed further.

Schonberger, R.J. (1996) *World Class Manufacturing: The next decade,* Free Press, New York. As above (and above that) but more speculative.

Spear, S. and Bowen, H.K. (1999) 'Decoding the DNA of the Toyota Production System', *Harvard Business Review,* September–October. Revisits the leading company in terms of JIT practice and re-evaluates the underlying philosophy behind the way it manages its operations. Recommended.

Womack, J.P., Jones, D.T. and Roos, D. (1990) *The Machine that Changed the World,* Rawson Associates. Arguably the most influential book on operations management practice of the last 50 years. Firmly rooted in the automotive sector but did much to establish JIT.

Womack, J.P. and Jones, D.T. (1996) Lean Thinking: Banish waste and create wealth in your corporation, Simon and Schuster. Some of the lessons from 'The Machine that Changed the World' but applied in a broader context.

Useful websites

www.lean.org Site of the Lean Enterprise Unit, set up by one of the founders of the Lean Thinking movement.

www.iee.org/index.cfm The site of the Institution of Electrical Engineers (which includes manufacturing engineers, surprisingly) has material on this and related topics as well as other issues covered in this book.

www.mfgeng.com The manufacturing engineering site.

FURTHER RESOURCES

For further resources including examples, animated diagrams, self-test questions, Excel spreadsheets, active case studies and video materials please explore the CD accompanying this book.

Introduction

All businesses are concerned with quality, usually because they have come to understand that high quality can give a significant competitive advantage. But 'quality management' has come to mean more than avoiding errors. It is also seen as an approach to the way processes should be managed and, more significantly, improved, generally. This is because quality management focuses on the very fundamental of operations and process management – the ability to produce and deliver the products and services that the market requires, in both the short and long term. A grasp of quality-management principles is the foundation of any improvement activity. (See Figure 12.1.)

Source: John A. Rizzo/PhotoDisc/Getty

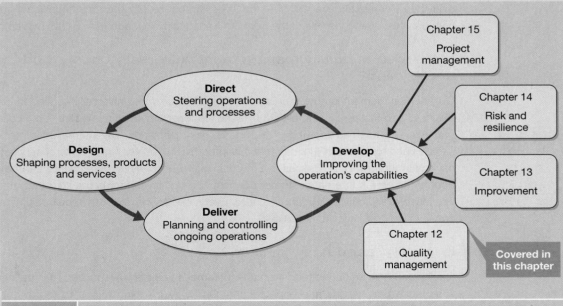

Direct
Steering operations
and processes

Design
Shaping processes, products
and services

Deliver
Planning and controlling
ongoing operations

Develop
Improving the
operation's capabilities

Chapter 15
Project
management

Chapter 14
Risk and
resilience

Chapter 13
Improvement

Chapter 12
Quality
management

Covered in
this chapter

Figure 12.1   **Quality management is the activity of ensuring consistent conformance to customers' expectations**

Executive summary

VIDEO
further detail

Decision logic chain for quality management

Each chapter is structured around a set of diagnostic questions. These questions suggest what you should ask in order to gain an understanding of the important issues of a topic, and as a result, improve your decision making. An executive summary, addressing these questions, is provided below.

What is quality management?

Quality is consistent conformance to customers' expectations. Managing quality means ensuring that an understanding of its importance and the way in which it can be improved is spread throughout the business. It is a subject that has undergone significant development over the last several decades, but arguably the most recent and most significant impact on how quality is managed has come from the total quality management (TQM) movement.

Is the idea of quality management universally understood and applied?

Quality management is now seen as something that can be universally applied throughout a business and that also, by implication, is the responsibility of all managers in the business. In particular, it is seen as applying to all parts of the organization. The internal customer concept can be used to establish the idea that it is important to deliver high quality of service to internal customers (other processes in the business). Service-level agreements can be used to operationalize the internal customer concept. Just as important is the idea that quality also applies to every individual in the business. Everyone has the ability to impair quality, so everyone also has the ability to improve it.

Is 'quality' adequately defined?

Quality needs to be understood from the customer's point of view because it is defined by the customer's perceptions and expectations. One way of doing this is to use a quality gap model. This starts from the fundamental potential gap between customers' expectations and perceptions and deconstructs the various influences on perceptions and expectations. Gaps between these factors can then be used to diagnose possible root causes of quality problems. A further development is to define the quality characteristics of products or services in terms of their functionality, appearance, reliability, durability, recovery and contact.

Is 'quality' adequately measured?

Without measuring quality it is difficult to control it. The various attributes of quality can be measured either as a variable (measured on a continuously variable scale) or as an attribute (a binary, acceptable or not acceptable judgement). One approach to measuring quality is to express all quality-related issues in cost terms. Quality costs are usually categorized as prevention costs (incurred in trying to prevent errors), appraisal costs (associated with checking for errors), internal failure costs (errors that are corrected within the operation), and external failure costs (errors that are experienced by customers). Generally, it is held that increasing expenditure on prevention will bring a more than equivalent reduction in other quality-related costs.

Is 'quality' adequately controlled?

Control means monitoring and responding to any deviations from acceptable levels of quality. One of the most common ways of doing this is through statistical process control (SPC). This technique not only attempts to reduce the variation in quality performance, so as to enhance process knowledge, but also is used to detect deviations outside the 'normal' range of quality variation.

Does quality management always lead to improvement?

Very often quality improvements are not sustained because there is no set of systems and procedures to support and embed them within the operation's day-to-day routines. The best known system for doing this is the ISO 9000 approach adopted now throughout the world. Of the other systems, one of the most widely known is the EFQM excellence model. Once known only as the basis of the European Quality Award, it is now extensively used as a self-assessment tool that allows organizations to assess their own quality systems.

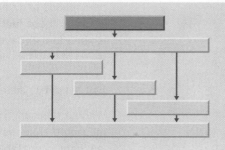

What is quality management?

There are many definitions of 'quality'–'conformance to specification', being 'fit for purpose', 'achieving appropriate specification', and so on. The one we use here is . . . *'quality is consistent conformance to customers' expectations'* because it includes both the idea of quality as *specification* (what the product or service can do) and the idea of quality as *conformance* (there are no errors, so it always does what it is supposed to do). Not surprisingly, for such an important topic, it has a history. Approaches to quality management have always been of interest to any business that aspired to satisfy its customers. Arguably, the most significant of the approaches to quality management was Total Quality Management (TQM) that became popular with all types of business in the late 1970s and 1980s, although it was based on earlier work by several management thinkers. Feigenbaum popularized the term 'total quality management' in 1957. After that it was developed through the work of several 'quality gurus' including Deming, Juran, Ishikawa, Taguchi and Crosby (see *Taking it further* at the end of the main part of the chapter).

TQM can be viewed as a logical extension of the way in which quality-related practice has progressed. Originally quality was achieved by inspection – screening out defects before customers noticed them. Then the 'quality control' (QC) concept developed a more systematic approach to not only detecting but also solving quality problems. 'Quality assurance' (QA) widened the responsibility for quality to include functions other than direct operations, such as Human Resources, Accounting and Marketing. It also made increasing use of more sophisticated statistical quality techniques. TQM included much of what went before but developed its own distinctive themes, especially in its adoption of a more 'all-embracing' approach. Since the fashionable peak of TQM, there has been some decline in its status, yet its ideas, many of which are included in this chapter, have become accepted quality practice. The two businesses described in the following examples both incorporate TQM ideas in their approach to quality, especially their inclusion of every employee.

Example   ## The Four Seasons Hotel, Canary Wharf[1]

Source: Rex Features

The Four Seasons Hotel group has a chain of over 63 properties in 29 countries. Famed for its quality of service, the hotel group has won countless awards, including the prestigious Zagat survey ranking as 'top hotel chain' internationally. From its inception the group has had the same guiding principle, *'to make the quality of our service our competitive advantage'*. Its Golden Rule is 'do to others (guests and staff) as you would wish others to do to you'.

'It may be a simple rule, but it guides the whole organization's approach to quality,' says Karen Earp, General Manager of the Four Seasons in London's Canary Wharf, who was recently voted Hotelier of the Year by one of the most popular trade journals. *'Quality of service is our distinguishing edge. The golden rule means treating your guests with courtesy and intelligence. It also means that treating your employees with humanity and respect encourages them to be equally sensitive to the needs and expectations of guests. When guests come to a Four Seasons Hotel they need to have our assurance that they are going to get exceptional food, great service and a great*

night's sleep. We are not trading in service quality gimmicks. We focus on giving what we call "the exceptional basics". So we listen very carefully to our guests, give a lot of thought to their needs, and provide what they really need. For example, more than anything else, guests value a good night's sleep. We have invested time and research into obtaining the very best beds (they are made especially for us) and we have very strict linen requirements using the very finest cotton sheets. We have even developed a special fold at the end of the bed linen that means very tall people cannot push their feet out of the bottom of the bed. It's this attention to detail that counts in helping a good night's sleep.

'There is no greater contribution than our staff in achieving such high quality of service. They respond to the culture of the organization that encourages three things – creativity, initiative and attitude. The most important of these is attitude. You can teach people the technical skills of the job but it is the attitude of our staff that sets us apart. We try and hire people who take great pride in delivering exceptional service. And attitude leads on to innovation and creativity. For example, we had a well-known person who was staying with us and speaking to a large gathering in the hotel in the evening. He was dressed casually and wearing bright green trainers. One of our staff escorted him to his room and carried his tuxedo for the evening's event. On arriving at the room the guest realized that he had forgotten to bring his formal shoes. Seeing that the guest's feet seemed to be around the same size as his own, our member of staff gave him his own shoes to wear. Not only was that guest delighted, he stood up at the event and told 200 very important people of his delight.'

All Four Seasons hotels use a 'guest history system' to track guests' preferences. If a guest likes particular types of flowers or fruit in their room, or if they like a particular type of wine, it is recorded and these items can be made available on the guest's next visit. Within the limits of privacy, all staff are empowered to make a record on the guest history file of anything that could improve the guest's stay next time.

'Many of our guests are senior managers of high quality businesses themselves, so they know about quality and their standards are very high,' says Karen. 'Our objective is to exceed their expectations. And although **our** *expectation is that we will achieve zero defects, you cannot always do that. Obviously we design our systems to try and prevent errors occurring but it is impossible to prevent all mistakes. We very rarely get formal complaints, but when we do I will always personally see to them myself by talking to the guest or answering any letters. The key is service recovery; this is why empowerment is so important. You have to make sure that all staff know they can turn around any negative experiences into positive ones before the guest leaves. It really is worth the effort. Giving exceptional service pays off in the long run because we get tremendous loyalty from our guests.'*

Example | ## Ryanair[2]

Ryanair was Europe's original, and is still Europe's largest, low-cost airline (LCA). Operating its low-fare, no-frills formula, its team of over 5000 employees and growing fleet of around 170 new Boe-

Source: Peter Titmuss/Alamy

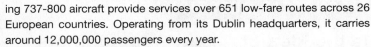

ing 737-800 aircraft provide services over 651 low-fare routes across 26 European countries. Operating from its Dublin headquarters, it carries around 12,000,000 passengers every year.

But Ryanair was not always so successful. Entering the market in early 1985, its early aim was to provide an alternative low-cost service between Ireland and London to the two market leaders, British Airways and Aer Lingus. Ryanair chose this route because it was expanding in both the business and leisure sectors. However, the airline business is marked by economies of scale and Ryanair, then with a small fleet of old-fashioned aircraft, was no match for its larger competitors. The first six years of Ryanair's operation resulted in an IR£20,000,000 loss. In 1991, Ryanair

decided to rework its strategy. *'We patterned Ryanair after Southwest Airlines, the most consistently profitable airline in the US,'* says Michael O'Leary, Ryanair's Chief Executive. *'Southwest founder Herb Kelleher created a formula for success that works by flying only one type of airplane – the 737 – using smaller airports, providing no-frills service on-board, selling tickets directly to customers and offering passengers the lowest fares in the market. We have adapted his model for our marketplace and are now setting the low-fare standard for Europe.'*

Whatever else can be said about Ryanair's strategy, it does not suffer from any lack of clarity. It has grown by offering low-cost basic services and has devised an operations strategy which is in line with its market position. The efficiency of the airline's operations supports its low-cost market position. Turnaround time at airports is kept to a minimum. This is achieved partly because there are no meals to be loaded onto the aircraft and partly through improved employee productivity. All the aircraft in the fleet are identical, giving savings through standardization of parts, maintenance and servicing. It also means large orders to a single aircraft supplier and therefore the opportunity to negotiate prices down. Also, because the company often uses secondary airports, landing and service fees are much lower. Finally, the cost of selling its services is reduced where possible. Ryanair has developed its own low-cost Internet booking service. In addition, the day-to-day experiences of the company's operations managers can modify and refine these strategic decisions. For example, Ryanair changed its baggage-handling contractors at Stansted airport in the UK after problems with misdirecting customers' luggage.

The company's policy on customer service is also clear. *'Our customer service,'* says O'Leary, *'is about the most well defined in the world. We guarantee to give you the lowest air fare. You get a safe flight. You get a normally on-time flight. That's the package. We don't, and won't, give you anything more. Are we going to say sorry for our lack of customer service? Absolutely not. If a plane is cancelled, will we put you up in a hotel overnight? Absolutely not. If a plane is delayed, will we give you a voucher for a restaurant? Absolutely not.'*

What do these two examples have in common?

The guests at the Four Seasons are paying for exceptional service at a top-range hotel and have high expectations. Ryanair, on the other hand, does not aim to offer anything close to a 'luxurious' quality of service. It offers value for money. Quality is 'getting the service you expect, given what you are paying'. Yet both businesses define quality in terms of the expectations and perceptions of customers. This means seeing things *from a customer's point of view.* Customers are seen not as being *external* to the organization but as the most important *part* of it. Both see quality as multifaceted, not a single attribute but a combination of many different things, some of which are difficult to define (for example, a sense that the operation cares for its customers). There is also an emphasis on every part of the business and every individual having responsibility for ensuring quality. The root causes of quality errors may often be people-related but so is excellent quality.

> **Operations principle**
> Quality is multifaceted, its individual elements differ for different operations.

DIAGNOSTIC QUESTION

Is the idea of quality management universally understood and applied?

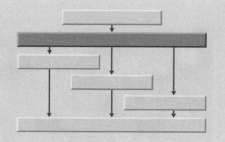

FURTHER EXAMPLE

If an operation is to fully understand customers' expectations and to match or exceed them in a consistent manner, it needs to take a universal or *total* approach to quality. Adopting a universal approach means that an understanding of *why* quality is important and *how* quality can be improved permeates the entire organization. This idea was popularized by proponents of total quality management (TQM), who saw TQM as the ideal unifying philosophy that could unite the whole business behind customer-focused improvement. In particular, two questions are worth asking: first, does quality apply to all parts of the organization? And second, does every person in the organization contribute to quality?

Does quality apply to all parts of the organization?

If quality management is to be effective, every process must work properly together. This is because every process affects and in turn is affected by others. Called the *internal customer concept,* it is recognition that every part of an organization is both an internal customer and, at the same time, an internal supplier for other parts of the organization.

> **Operations principle**
> An appreciation of, involvement in, and commitment to quality should permeate the entire organization.

This means that errors in the service provided within an organization will eventually affect the product or service that reaches the external customer. So, one of the best ways of satisfying external customers is to satisfy internal customers. This means that each process has a responsibility to manage its own internal customer – supplier relationships by clearly defining their own and their customers' exact requirements. In fact the exercise replicates what should be going on for the whole operation and its external customers.

Service-level agreements

Some operations bring a degree of formality to the internal customer concept by requiring processes to agree service-level agreements (SLAs) with each other. SLAs are formal definitions of the service and the relationship between two processes. The type of issues that would be covered by such an agreement could include response times, the range of services, dependability of service supply, and so on. Boundaries of responsibility and appropriate performance measures could also be agreed. For example, an SLA between an information systems help desk and the processes that are its internal customers could define such performance measures as follows:

- The types of information network services that may be provided as 'standard'
- The range of special information services that may be available at different periods of the day
- The minimum 'up time', i.e. the proportion of time the system will be available at different periods of the day
- The maximum response time and average response time to get the system fully operational should it fail
- The maximum response time to provide 'special' services, and so on.

SLAs are best thought of as an approach to deciding service priorities between processes, and as a basis for improving process performance from the internal customers' perspective. At their best they can be the mechanism for clarifying exactly how processes can contribute to the operations as a whole. See the critical commentary at the end of the chapter for a more cynical view.

Does every person in the organization contribute to quality?

A total approach to quality should include every individual in the business. People are the source of both good and bad quality and it is everyone's personal responsibility to get quality right. This applies not only to those people who can affect quality directly and have the capability to make mistakes that are immediately obvious to customers, for example those who serve customers face to face or physically make products. It also applies to those who are less directly involved in producing products and services. The keyboard operator who mis-keys data, or the product designer who fails to investigate thoroughly the conditions under which products will be used in practice, could also set in motion a chain of events that customers eventually see as poor quality.

It follows that, if everyone has the ability to impair quality, they also have the ability to improve it – if only by 'not making mistakes'. But their contribution is expected to go beyond a commitment not to make mistakes; they are expected to bring something positive to the way they perform their jobs. Everyone is capable of improving the way in which they do their own jobs and practically everyone is capable of helping the others in the organization to improve theirs. Neglecting the potential that is inherent in all people is neglecting a powerful source of improvement.

DIAGNOSTIC QUESTION

Is 'quality' adequately defined?

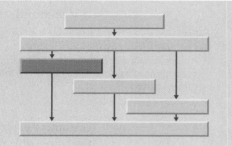

Quality is consistent conformance to customers' expectations. It needs to be understood from a customer's point of view because, to the customer, the quality of a particular product or service is whatever he or she perceives it to be. However, each individual customer's expectations may be different. Past experiences, individual knowledge and history will all shape a customer's individual expectations. Perceptions are not absolute. Exactly the same product or service may be perceived in different ways by different customers. Also, in some situations, customers may be unable to judge the 'technical' specification of the service or product. They may then use surrogate measures as a basis for their perception of quality. For example, after seeking financial advice from an advisor it might be difficult immediately to evaluate the technical quality of the advice, especially if no better solution presents itself. In reality a judgement of the quality of the advice may be based on perceptions of trustworthiness, relationship, the information that was provided, or the way in which it was provided.

Operations principle
Perceived quality is governed by the magnitude and direction of the gap between customers' expectations and their perceptions of a product or service.

Closing the gaps – alignment in quality

If the product or service experience was better than expected then the customer is satisfied and quality is perceived to be high. If the product or service was less than his or her expectations then quality is low and the customer may be dissatisfied. If the product or service matches expectations then the perceived quality of the product or service is seen to be acceptable. These relationships are summarized in Figure 12.2.

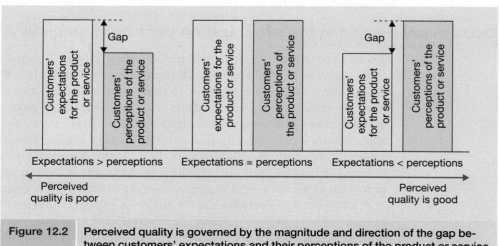

Figure 12.2   Perceived quality is governed by the magnitude and direction of the gap between customers' expectations and their perceptions of the product or service

Both customers' expectations and perceptions are influenced by a number of factors, some of which cannot be controlled by the operation and some of which can, at least to a certain extent. Figure 12.3 shows some of the factors that influence the gap between expectations and perceptions and the potential gaps between some of these factors. This approach to defining quality is called a 'gap model' of quality. The model shown in Figure 12.3 is adapted from one developed by Zeithaml, Berry and Parasuraman,[3] primarily to understand how quality in service operations can be managed and to identify some of the problems in so doing. However, this approach is now also used in all types of operation.

Diagnosing quality problems

Describing perceived quality in this way allows a diagnosis of quality problems. If the perceived quality gap is such that customers' perceptions of the product or service fail to match their expectations of it, then the reason (or reasons) must lie in other gaps elsewhere in the model. Four other gaps could explain a perceived quality gap between customers' perceptions and expectations.

Gap 1: The customer's specification–operation's specification gap

Perceived quality could be poor because there may be a mismatch between the organization's own internal quality specification and the specification which is expected by the customer. For example, a car may be designed to need servicing every 10,000 kilometres but the customer may expect 15,000 kilometre service intervals. An airline may have a policy of charging for drinks during the flight whereas the customer's expectation may be that the drinks would be free.

Gap 2: The concept–specification gap

Perceived quality could be poor because there is a mismatch between the product or service concept and the way the organization has specified the quality of the product or service internally. For example, the concept of a car might have been for an inexpensive, energy-efficient means of transportation, but the inclusion of a catalytic converter may have both added to its cost and made it less energy-efficient.

Gap 3: The quality specification–actual quality gap

Perceived quality could be poor because there is a mismatch between the actual quality of the service or product provided by the operation and its internal quality specification.

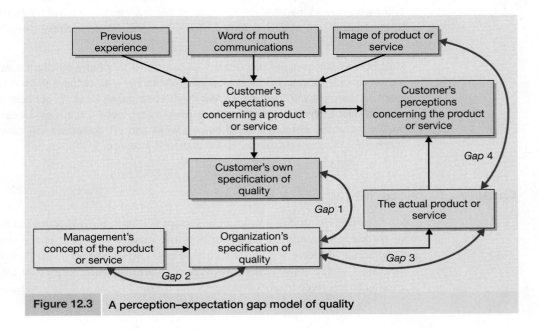

Figure 12.3   A perception–expectation gap model of quality

This may be the result, for example, of an inappropriate or unachievable specification, or of poorly trained or inexperienced personnel, or because effective control systems are not in place to ensure the provision of defined levels of quality. For example if, despite an airline's policy of charging for drinks, some flight crews provide free drinks, they add unexpected costs to the airline and influence customers' expectations for the next flight, when they may be disappointed.

Gap 4: The actual quality–communicated image gap

Perceived quality could also be poor because there is a gap between the organization's external communications or market image and the actual quality of the service or product delivered to the customer. This may be the result of either market positioning setting unachievable expectations in the minds of customers, or operations not providing the level of quality expected by the customer. The advertising campaign for an airline might show a cabin attendant offering to replace a customer's shirt on which food or drink has been spilt, but this service may not always be available.

Example Tea and Sympathy[4]

Defining quality in terms of perception and expectation can sometimes reveal some surprising results. For example, Tea and Sympathy is a British restaurant and café in the heart of New York's West Village. Over the last 10 years it has become a fashionable landmark in a city with one of the broadest ranges of restaurants in the world. Yet it is tiny, around a dozen tables packed into an area little bigger than the average British sitting room. Not only expatriate Brits but also native New Yorkers and celebrities queue to get in. As the only British restaurant in New York, it has a novelty factor,

but also it has become famous for the unusual nature of its service. *'Everyone is treated in the same way,'* says Nicky Perry, one of the two ex-Londoners who run it. *'We have a firm policy that we don't take any shit.'* This robust attitude to the treatment of customers is reinforced by 'Nicky's Rules' that are printed on the menu.

1. Be pleasant to the waitresses – remember Tea and Sympathy girls are always right.
2. You will have to wait outside the restaurant until your entire party is present: no exceptions.
3. Occasionally, you may be asked to change tables so that we can accommodate all of you.
4. If we don't need the table you may stay all day, but if people are waiting it's time to naff off.
5. These rules are strictly enforced. Any argument will incur Nicky's wrath. You have been warned.

Most of the waitresses are also British and enforce Nicky's Rules strictly. If customers object they are thrown out. Nicky says that she has had to train 'her girls' to toughen up. *'I've taught them that when people cross the line they can tear their throats out as far as I'm concerned. What we've discovered over the years is that if you are really sweet, people see it as a weakness.'* People get thrown out of the restaurant about twice a week and yet customers still queue for the genuine shepherd's pie, a real cup of tea, and of course, the service.

Quality characteristics

Much of the 'quality' of a product or service will have been specified in its design. But not all the design details are useful in defining quality. Rather it is the *consequences* of the design that are perceived by customers. These consequences of the design are called *quality characteristics*. Table 12.1 shows a list of quality characteristics that are generally useful applied to a service (flight) and a product (car).

Table 12.1 Quality characteristics for a motor car and an air journey

Quality characteristics	Car	Flight
Functionality – how well the product or service does its job, including its performance and features	Speed, acceleration, fuel consumption, ride quality, road-holding, etc.	Safety and duration of journey, on-board meals and drinks, car and hotel booking services
Appearance – the sensory characteristics of the product or service: its aesthetic appeal, look, feel, sound and smell	Aesthetics, shape, finish, door gaps, etc.	Decor and cleanliness of aircraft, lounges and crew
Reliability – the consistency of the product's or service's performance over time, or the average time for which it performs within its tolerated band of performance	Mean time to failure	Keeping to the published flight times
Durability – the total useful life of the product or service, assuming occasional repair or modification	Useful life (with repair)	Keeping up with trends in the industry
Recovery – the ease with which problems with the product or service can be rectified or resolved	Ease of repair	Resolution of service failures
Contact – the nature of the person-to-person contact which might take place. It could include the courtesy, empathy, sensitivity and knowledge of contact staff	Knowledge and courtesy of sales and service staff	Knowledge, courtesy and sensitivity of airline staff

DIAGNOSTIC QUESTION

Is 'quality' adequately measured?

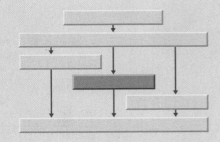

Some quality characteristics are relatively easy to measure. For example, is the gap between a car door and pillar less than 5 mm? Other more difficult-to-measure quality characteristics, such as 'appearance', need to be decomposed into their constituent elements such as 'colour match', 'surface finish' and 'the number of visible scratches', all of which are capable of being measured in a relatively objective manner. They may even be quantifiable. However, decomposing quality characteristics into their measurable sub-components can result in some loss of meaning. A quantified list of 'colour match', the 'smoothness' of the surface finish and the 'number of visible scratches' does not cover factors such as 'aesthetics', a characteristic that is difficult to measure but nonetheless important. Some quality characteristics cannot themselves be measured at all. The 'courtesy' of airline staff, for example, has no objective quantified measure, yet airlines place a great deal of importance on the need to ensure courtesy in their staff. In cases like this, the operation will have to attempt to measure customer *perceptions* of courtesy.

Variables and attributes

The measures used to describe quality characteristics are of two types: variables and attributes. Variable measures are those that can be measured on a continuously variable scale (for example length, diameter, weight or time). Attributes are those that are assessed by judgement and have two states (for example right or wrong, works or does not work, looks OK or not OK). Table 12.2 categorizes some of the measures that might be used for the quality characteristics of the car and the flight.

Measuring the 'costs of quality'

One approach to measuring aggregated quality is to express all quality-related issues in cost terms. This is the 'cost of quality' approach (usually taken to refer to both costs and benefits of quality). These costs of quality are usually categorized as *prevention costs, appraisal costs, internal failure costs* and *external failure costs*. Table 12.3 illustrates the types of factors that are included in these categories.

Table 12.2	Variable and attribute measures for quality characteristics			
Characteristic	*Car*		*Flight*	
	Variable	*Attribute*	*Variable*	*Attribute*
Functionality	Acceleration and braking characteristics from test bed	Is the ride quality satisfactory?	Number of journeys that actually arrived at the destination (i.e. didn't crash!)	Was the food acceptable?
Appearance	Number of blemishes visible on car	Is the colour to specification?	Number of seats not cleaned satisfactorily	Are the crew dressed smartly?
Reliability	Average time between faults	Is the reliability satisfactory?	Proportion of journeys that arrived on time	Were there any complaints?
Durability	Life of the car	Is the useful life as predicted?	Number of times service innovations lagged behind those of competitors	Generally, is the airline updating its services in a satisfactory manner?
Recovery	Time from fault discovered to fault repaired	Is the serviceability of the car acceptable?	Proportion of service failures resolved satisfactorily	Do customers feel that staff deal satisfactorily with complaints?
Contact	Level of help provided by sales staff (1 to 5 scale)	Did customers feel well served (yes or no)?	The extent to which customers feel well treated by staff (1 to 5 scale)	Did customers feel that the staff were helpful (yes or no)?

Table 12.3   Categories of quality-related costs

Category of quality-related cost	Examples in the category
Prevention costs – those costs incurred in trying to prevent problems, failures and errors from occurring in the first place	• Identifying potential problems and putting the process right before poor quality occurs • Designing and improving the design of products and services and processes to reduce quality problems • Training and development of personnel in the best way to perform their jobs • Process control
Appraisal costs – those costs associated with controlling quality to check whether problems or errors have occurred during and after the creation of the product or service	• The setting up of statistical acceptance sampling plans • The time and effort required to inspect inputs, processes and outputs • Obtaining processing inspection and test data • Investigating quality problems and providing quality reports • Conducting customer surveys and quality audits
Internal failure costs – failure costs that are associated with errors dealt with inside the operation	• The cost of scrapped parts and materials • The cost of reworking parts and materials • The lost production time as a result of coping with errors • Lack of concentration due to time spent troubleshooting rather than improvement
External failure costs – failure costs that are associated with errors being experienced by customers	• Loss of customer goodwill affecting future business • Aggrieved customers who may take up time • Litigation (or payments to avoid litigation) • Guarantee and warranty costs • The cost to the company of providing excessive capability (too much coffee in the pack and too much information to a client)

Understand the relationship between quality costs[5]

At one time it was assumed that failure costs were reduced as the money spent on appraisal and prevention was increased. There must be a point beyond which the cost of improving quality exceeds the benefits that it brings. Therefore there must be an optimum amount of quality effort to be applied in any situation that minimizes the total costs of quality. Figure 12.4(a) sums up this idea.

More recently the 'optimum quality effort' approach has been challenged. First, why should any operation accept the *inevitability* of errors? Some occupations seem to be able to accept a zero-defect standard (even if they do not always achieve it). No one accepts the inevitability of pilots crashing a certain proportion of their aircraft, or nurses dropping a certain number of babies. Second, failure costs are generally underestimated. They are usually taken to include the cost of 'reworking' defective products, 're-serving' customers, scrapping parts and materials, the loss of goodwill, warranty costs, etc. These are important, but in practice, the real cost of poor quality should include all the management time wasted in organizing rework and rectification and, more important, the loss of concentration and the erosion of confidence between processes within the operation. Third, it implies that prevention costs are inevitably high. But by stressing the importance of quality to every individual, preventing errors becomes an integral part of everyone's work. More quality is not only achieved by using more inspectors, we all have a

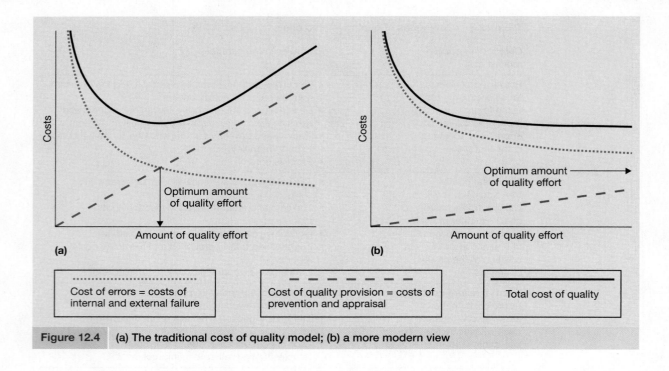

Figure 12.4 (a) The traditional cost of quality model; (b) a more modern view

responsibility for our own quality and all should be capable of 'doing things right first time'. This may incur some costs – training, automatic checks, anything which helps to prevent errors occurring in the first place – but not such a steeply inclined cost curve as in the 'optimum-quality' theory. Finally the 'optimum-quality level' approach, by accepting compromise, does little to challenge operations managers and staff to find ways of improving quality.

Put these corrections into the optimum-quality effort calculation and the picture looks very different (see Figure 12.4(b)). If there is an 'optimum', it is a lot further to the right, in the direction of putting more effort (but not necessarily cost) into quality.

The TQM-influenced quality cost model

TQM rejected the optimum-quality level concept. Rather, it concentrated on how to reduce all known and unknown failure costs. So, rather than placing most emphasis on appraisal (so that 'bad products and service don't get through to the customer'), it emphasized prevention (to stop errors happening in the first place). This has a significant, positive effect on internal failure costs, followed by reductions both in external failure costs and, once confidence has been firmly established, also in appraisal costs. Eventually even prevention costs can be stepped down in absolute terms, though prevention remains a significant cost in relative terms. Figure 12.5 illustrates this idea, showing how initially total quality costs may rise as investment in some aspects of prevention is increased. Once this relationship between categories of quality cost is accepted it shifts the emphasis from a reactive approach to quality (waiting for errors to happen, then screening them out), to a more proactive, 'getting it right first time' approach (doing something before errors happen).

> **Operations principle**
> Effective investment in preventing quality errors can significantly reduce appraisal and failure costs.

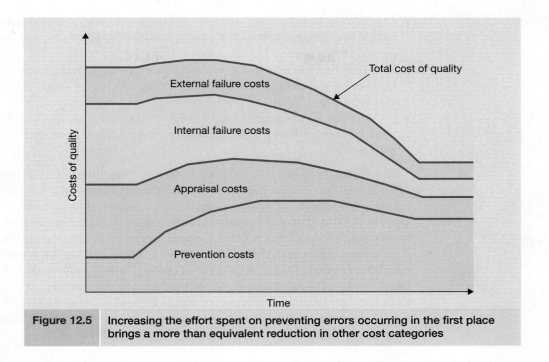

Figure 12.5 Increasing the effort spent on preventing errors occurring in the first place brings a more than equivalent reduction in other cost categories

Is 'quality' adequately controlled?

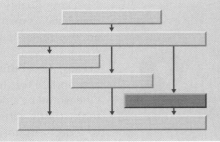

After quality has been defined and measured, processes will need to check that their quality conforms to whatever quality standards are deemed appropriate. This does not necessarily mean checking everything – sampling may be more appropriate.

Check every product and service or take a sample?

There are several reasons why checking everything may not be sensible:

- It could be dangerous to check everything. A doctor, for example, checks just a small sample of blood rather than all of it. The characteristics of this sample are taken to represent those of the rest of the patient's blood.
- Checking of everything might destroy the product or interfere with the service. A lamp manufacturer cannot check the life of every single light bulb leaving the factory; they would all be destroyed. Nor would it be appropriate for a head waiter to check whether customers are enjoying the meal every 30 seconds.
- Checking everything may be too costly. For example, it just might not be feasible to check every single item from a high-volume plastic moulding machine or to check the feelings of every single bus passenger every day.

Even 100 per cent checking will not always guarantee that all defects or problems will be identified.

- Checks may be inherently difficult. Although a doctor may undertake all the correct testing procedures to check for a particular disease, he or she may not necessarily be certain to diagnose it.
- Staff may become fatigued when inspecting repetitive items where it is easy to make mistakes (try counting the number of 'e's on this page. Count them again and see if you get the same score).
- Information may be unreliable. Although all the customers in a restaurant may tell the head waiter that 'everything is fine', they may actually have reservations about their experience.

Sometimes, however, it is necessary to sample everything that is produced by a process or an operation. If a product is so critical that its failure to conform to specification would result in death or injury (for example, some parts that are used in aircraft, or some services within health-care operations) then, although expensive, 100 per cent inspection is necessary. In such cases it is the consequence of non-conformance that is driving the decision to inspect everything. In other cases it may be that the economics of 100 per cent inspection are such that the cost of doing it is relatively small. For example, some labels can be automatically scanned as they are produced at virtually no extra cost. Yet, whenever 100 per cent inspection is adopted, there is another risk – that of classifying something as an error when, in fact, it conforms to specification. This distinction is summarized in what is often referred to as type I and type II errors.

Type I and type II errors

FURTHER EXAMPLE

Checking quality by sampling, although requiring less time than checking everything, does have its own problems. Take the example of someone waiting to cross a street. There are two main options: cross (take some action), or continue waiting (take no action). If there is a break in the traffic and the person crosses, or if that person continues to wait because the traffic is too dense, then a correct decision has been made (the action was appropriate for the circumstances). There are two types of incorrect decisions, or errors. One would be a decision to cross (take some action) when there is not an adequate break in the traffic, resulting in an accident – this is referred to as a type I error. Another would be a decision not to cross even though there was an adequate gap in the traffic – this is called a type II error. Type I errors are those which occur when a decision was made to do something and the situation did not warrant it. Type II errors are those which occur when nothing was done, yet a decision to do something should have been taken as the situation did indeed warrant it. So, there are four outcomes, summarized in Table 12.4.

Statistical process control (SPC)

Excel

The most common method of checking the quality of a sampled product or service so as to make inferences about all the output from a process is called statistical process control (SPC). SPC is concerned with sampling the process during the production of the goods or the delivery of service. Based on this sample, decisions are made as to whether the

Table 12.4	Type I and type II errors for a pedestrian crossing the road	
Decision	**Road conditions**	
	Safe (action was appropriate)	**Unsafe** (action was not appropriate)
Cross (take some action)	Correct decision	**Type I error**
Wait (take no action)	**Type II error**	Correct decision

process is 'in control', that is, operating as it should be. If there seems to be a problem with the process, then it can be stopped (if possible and appropriate) and the problem identified and rectified. For example, an international airport may regularly ask a sample of customers if the cleanliness of its restaurants is satisfactory. If an unacceptable number of customers in one sample are found to be unhappy, airport managers may have to consider improving the procedures that are in place for cleaning tables.

Control charts

The value of SPC is not just to make checks of a single sample but to monitor the results of many samples over a period of time. It does this by using control charts. Control charts record some aspect of quality (or performance generally) over time to see whether the process seems to be performing as it should (called *in control*), or not (called *out of control*). If the process does seem to be going out of control, then steps can be taken *before* there is a problem.

FURTHER EXAMPLE

Figure 12.6 shows typical control charts. Charts that look something like these can be found in almost any operation. They could, for example, represent the percentage of customers in a sample of 1000 who, each week, were dissatisfied with the service they received from two call centres. In chart (a), measured customer dissatisfaction has been steadily increasing over time. There is evidence of a clear (negative) trend that management may wish to investigate. In chart (b), although there is little evidence of any trend in average dissatisfaction, the variability in performance seems to be increasing. Again the operation may want to investigate the causes.

Looking for *trends* is an important use of control charts. If the trend suggests the process is getting steadily worse, then it will be worth investigating the process. If the trend is steadily improving, it may still be worthy of investigation to try to identify what is happening that is making the process better. An even more important use of control charts is to investigate the *variation* in performance.

Why variation is a bad thing

> **Operations principle**
> High levels of variation reduce the ability to detect changes in process performance.

Although a trend such as that shown in Figure 12.6(a) clearly indicates deteriorating performance, the variation shown in Figure 12.6(b) can be just as serious. Variation is a problem because it masks any changes in process behaviour. Figure 12.7 shows the performance of two processes both of which change their behaviour at

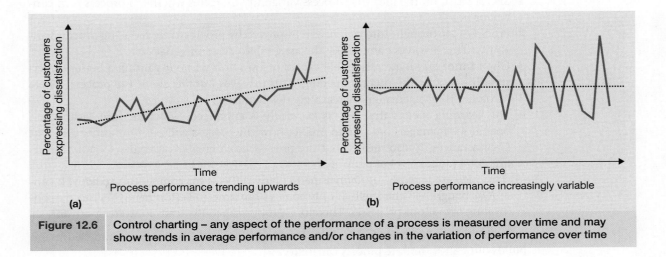

Figure 12.6   Control charting – any aspect of the performance of a process is measured over time and may show trends in average performance and/or changes in the variation of performance over time

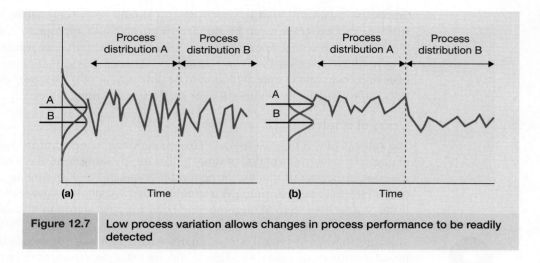

Figure 12.7 Low process variation allows changes in process performance to be readily detected

the same time. The process on the left has such a wide natural variation that it is not immediately apparent that any change has taken place. Eventually it will become apparent, but it may take some time. By contrast, the performance of the process represented by the chart on the right has a far narrower band of variation, so the same change in average performance is more easily noticed. The narrower the variation of a process, the more obvious are any changes that might occur, and the easier it is to make a decision to intervene. SPC is discussed much further in the supplement to this chapter. It is also one of the core ideas in the Six Sigma improvement approach that is discussed in the next chapter.

Process control, learning and knowledge

Operations principle
Statistical-based control gives the potential to enhance process knowledge.

In recent years the role of process control and SPC in particular has changed. Increasingly, it is seen not just as a convenient method of keeping processes in control, but also as an activity that is fundamental to the acquisition of competitive advantage. This is a remarkable shift in the status of SPC. Traditionally it was seen as one of the most *operational,* immediate and 'hands-on' operations management techniques. Yet it is now seen as contributing to an operation's *strategic* capabilities. This is how the logic of the argument goes:

1 SPC is based on the idea that process variability indicates whether a process is in control or not.
2 Processes are brought into *control* and improved by progressively reducing process variability. This involves eliminating the assignable causes of variation.
3 One cannot eliminate assignable causes of variation without gaining a better understanding of how the process operates. This involves *learning* about the process, where its nature is revealed at an increasingly detailed level.
4 This learning means that *process knowledge* is enhanced, which in turn means that operations managers are able to predict how the process will perform under different circumstances. It also means that the process has a greater capability to carry out its tasks at a higher level of performance.
5 This increased *process capability* is particularly difficult for competitors to copy. It cannot be bought 'off-the-shelf'. It only comes from time and effort being invested in controlling operations processes. Therefore, process capability leads to strategic advantage.

In this way, process control leads to learning which enhances process knowledge and builds difficult-to-imitate process capability.

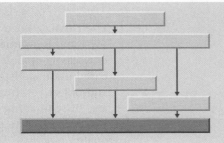

Does quality management always lead to improvement?

No amount of effort put into quality initiatives can guarantee improvement in process performance. In fact some surveys show that up to half of all quality programmes provide only disappointing, if any, permanent improvement. Improving quality is not something that happens simply by getting everyone in an organization to 'think quality'. Very often improvements do not stick because there is no set of systems and procedures to support and embed them into the operation's day-to-day routines. 'Quality systems' are needed.

A quality system is '*the organizational structure, responsibilities, procedures, processes and resources for implementing quality management*'.[6] It should cover all facets of a business's operations and processes, and define the responsibilities, procedures and processes that ensure the implementation of quality improvement. The best-known quality system is ISO 9000.

The ISO 9000 approach

The ISO 9000 series is a set of international standards that establishes requirements for companies' quality management systems. It is being used worldwide to provide a framework for quality assurance. By 2000, ISO 9000 had been adopted by more than a quarter of a million organizations in 143 countries. Originally its purpose was to provide an assurance to the purchasers of products or services by defining the procedures, standards and characteristics of the control system that governed the process that produced them. In 2000, ISO 9000 was substantially revised. Rather than using different standards for different functions within a business, it took a 'process' approach and focused on the outputs from any operation's process, rather than the detailed procedures that had dominated the previous version. This process orientation requires operations to define and record core processes and sub-processes. ISO 9000 (2000) also stresses four other principles.

- Quality management should be customer focused, and customer satisfaction measured using surveys and focus groups. Improvement against customer standards should be documented.
- Quality performance should be measured, and relate to products and services themselves, the processes that created them, and customer satisfaction. Furthermore, measured data should always be analyzed.
- Quality management should be improvement driven. Improvement must be demonstrated in both process performance and customer satisfaction.
- Top management must demonstrate their commitment to maintaining and continually improving management systems. This commitment should include communicating the importance of meeting customer and other requirements, establishing a quality policy and quality objectives, conducting management reviews to ensure the adherence to quality policies, and ensuring the availability of the necessary resources to maintain quality systems.

The Deming Prize

The Deming Prize was instituted by the Union of Japanese Scientists and Engineers in 1951 and is awarded to those companies, initially in Japan, but more recently opened to overseas companies, which have successfully applied 'company-wide quality control' based upon statistical quality control. There are 10 major assessment categories: policy and objectives, organization and its operation, education and its extension, assembling and disseminating of information, analysis, standardization, control, quality assurance, effects and future plans. The applicants are required to submit a detailed description of quality practices. This is a significant activity in itself and some companies claim a great deal of benefit from having done so.

The Malcolm Baldrige National Quality Award

In the early 1980s the American Productivity and Quality Center recommended that an annual prize, similar to the Deming Prize, should be awarded in America. The purpose of the awards was to stimulate American companies to improve quality and productivity, to recognize achievements, to establish criteria for a wider quality effort and to provide guidance on quality improvement. The main examination categories are leadership, information and analysis, strategic quality planning, human resource utilization, quality assurance of products and services, quality results and customer satisfaction. The process, like that of the Deming Prize, includes a detailed application and site visits.

The EFQM Excellence Model[7]

In 1988, 14 leading Western European companies formed the European Foundation for Quality Management (EFQM). An important objective of the EFQM is to recognize quality achievement. Because of this, it launched the European Quality Award (EQA), awarded to the most successful exponent of total quality management in Europe each year. To receive a prize, companies must demonstrate that their approach to total quality management has contributed significantly to satisfying the expectations of customers, employees and others with an interest in the company for the past few years. In 1999, the model on which the European Quality Award was based was modified and renamed

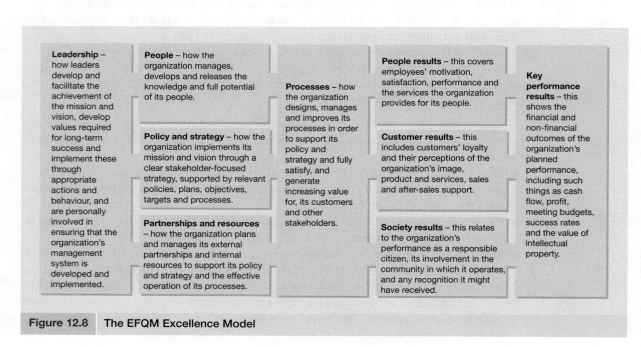

Leadership – how leaders develop and facilitate the achievement of the mission and vision, develop values required for long-term success and implement these through appropriate actions and behaviour, and are personally involved in ensuring that the organization's management system is developed and implemented.

People – how the organization manages, develops and releases the knowledge and full potential of its people.

Policy and strategy – how the organization implements its mission and vision through a clear stakeholder-focused strategy, supported by relevant policies, plans, objectives, targets and processes.

Partnerships and resources – how the organization plans and manages its external partnerships and internal resources to support its policy and strategy and the effective operation of its processes.

Processes – how the organization designs, manages and improves its processes in order to support its policy and strategy and fully satisfy, and generate increasing value for, its customers and other stakeholders.

People results – this covers employees' motivation, satisfaction, performance and the services the organization provides for its people.

Customer results – this includes customers' loyalty and their perceptions of the organization's image, product and services, sales and after-sales support.

Society results – this relates to the organization's performance as a responsible citizen, its involvement in the community in which it operates, and any recognition it might have received.

Key performance results – this shows the financial and non-financial outcomes of the organization's planned performance, including such things as cash flow, profit, meeting budgets, success rates and the value of intellectual property.

Figure 12.8   The EFQM Excellence Model

'The EFQM Excellence Model'. The changes made were not fundamental but did attempt to reflect some new areas of management and quality thinking (for example, partnerships and innovation) and placed more emphasis on customer and market focus. The model is based on the idea that the outcomes of quality management in terms of what it calls 'people results', 'customer results', 'society results' and 'key performance results' are achieved through a number of 'enablers'. These enablers are leadership and constancy of purpose, policy and strategy, how the organization develops its people, partnerships and resources, and the way it organizes its processes. These ideas are incorporated as shown in Figure 12.8. The five 'enablers' are concerned with how results are being achieved, while the four 'results' are concerned with what the company has achieved and is achieving.

Self-assessment

The EFQM defines *self-assessment* as 'a comprehensive, systematic, and regular review of an organization's activities and results referenced against a model of business excellence'. The main advantage of using such models for self-assessment seems to be that companies find it easier to understand some of the more philosophical concepts of quality management when they are translated into specific areas, questions and percentages. Self-assessment also allows organizations to measure their progress in achieving the benefits of quality management.

Critical commentary

Each chapter contains a short critical commentary on the main ideas covered in the chapter. Its purpose is not to undermine the issues discussed in the chapter, but to emphasize that, although we present a relatively orthodox view of operation, there are other perspectives.

■ Quality management has been one of the hottest topics in operations management and one of the most controversial. Much of the debate has centred on the people focus of quality management, especially the rhetoric of employee empowerment central to several modern approaches to quality. In many cases, it can be little more than an increase in employee discretion over minor details of their working practice. Some industrial relations academics argue that TQM rarely affects the fundamental imbalance between managerial control and employees' influence over organizational direction. For example, '. . . there is little evidence that employee influence over corporate decisions which affect them has been, or can ever be, enhanced through contemporary configuration of involvement. In other words, whilst involvement might increase individual task discretion, or open up channels for communication, the involvement programme is not designed to offer opportunities for employees to gain or consolidate control over the broader environment in which their work is located.'[8]

Other criticisms concern the appropriateness of some mechanisms such as service-level agreements (SLAs). Some see the strength of SLAs as the degree of formality they bring to customer–supplier relationships, but there are also drawbacks. The first is that the 'pseudo-contractual' nature of the formal relationship can work against building partnerships. This is especially true if the SLA includes penalties for deviation from service standards. The effect can sometimes be to inhibit rather than encourage joint improvement. The second is that SLAs tend to emphasize the 'hard' and measurable aspects of performance rather than the 'softer' but often more important aspects. So a telephone may be answered within four rings, but how the caller is treated in terms of 'friendliness' may be far more important.

■ Similarly, and notwithstanding its widespread adoption (and its revision to take into account some of its perceived failing), ISO 9000 is not seen as beneficial by all authorities. Criticisms include the following.

● The whole process of documenting processes, writing procedures, training staff and conducting internal audits is expensive and time-consuming.
● Similarly, the time and cost of achieving and maintaining ISO 9000 registration are excessive.
● It is too formulaic. It encourages operations to 'manage by manual', substituting a 'recipe' for a more customized and creative approach to managing operations improvement.

Summary checklist

DOWNLOADABLE

This checklist comprises questions that can be usefully applied to any type of operations and reflect the major diagnostic questions used within the chapter.

☐ Does everyone in the business really believe in the importance of quality, or is it just one of those things that people say without really believing it?

☐ Is there an accepted definition of quality used within the business?

☐ Do people understand that there are many different definitions and approaches to quality, and do they understand why the business has chosen its own particular approach?

☐ Do all parts of the organization understand their contribution to maintaining and improving quality?

☐ Are service-level agreements used to establish concepts of internal customer service?

☐ Is some form of gap model used to diagnose quality problems?

☐ Is quality defined in terms of a series of quality characteristics?

☐ Is quality measured using all relevant quality characteristics?

☐ Is the cost of quality measured?

☐ Are quality costs categorized as prevention, appraisal, internal failure and external failure costs?

☐ Is quality adequately controlled?

☐ Has the idea of statistical process control (SPC) been explored as a mechanism for controlling quality?

☐ Do individual processes have any idea of their own variability of quality performance?

☐ Have quality systems been explored, such as ISO 9000 and the EFQM excellence model?

Case study   Turnround at the Preston plant

'Before the crisis the quality department was just for looks, we certainly weren't used much for problem solving, the most we did was inspection. Data from the quality department was brought to the production meeting and they would all look at it, but no one was looking behind it.' (Quality Manager, Preston Plant)

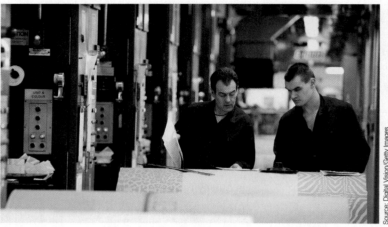

Source: Digital Vision/Getty Images

The Preston plant of Rendall Graphics was located in Preston, Vancouver, across the continent from its headquarters in Massachusetts. The plant had been bought from the Georgetown Corporation by Rendall in March 2000. Precision-coated papers for inkjet printers accounted for the majority of the plant's output, especially paper for specialist uses. The plant used coating machines that allowed precise coatings to be applied. After coating, the conversion department cut the coated rolls to the final size and packed the sheets in small cartons.

The curl problem

In late 1998 Hewlett-Packard (HP), the plant's main customer for inkjet paper, informed the plant of some problems it had encountered with paper curling under conditions of low humidity. There had been no customer complaints to HP, but its own personnel had noticed the problem and wanted it fixed. Over the next seven or eight months a team at the plant tried to solve the problem. Finally, in October 1999 the team made recommendations for a revised and considerably improved coating formulation. By January 2000 the process was producing acceptably. However, 1999 had not been a good year for the plant. Although sales were reasonably buoyant the plant was making a loss of around $2 million for the year. In October 1999, Tom Branton, previously accountant for the business, was appointed as Managing Director.

Slipping out of control

In the spring of 2000, productivity, scrap and rework levels continued to be poor. In response to this the operations management team increased the speed of the line and made a number of changes to operating practice in order to raise productivity.

*'Looking back, changes were made without any proper discipline, and there was no real concept of control. We were always meeting specification, yet we didn't fully understand how close we really were to not being able to make it. The culture here said, "If it's within specification then it's OK" and we were very diligent in making sure that the product which was shipped **was** in specification. However, Hewlett-Packard gets "process charts" that enable them to see more or less exactly what is happening right inside your operation. We were also getting all the reports but none of them were being internalized, we were using them just to satisfy the customer. By contrast, HP have a statistically-based analytical mentality that says to itself, "You might be capable of making this product but we are thinking two or three product generations forward and asking ourselves, will you have the capability then, and do we want to invest in this relationship for the future?"'* (Tom Branton)

The spring of 2000 also saw two significant events. First, Hewlett-Packard asked the plant to bid for the contract to supply a new inkjet platform, known as the Vector project, a contract that would secure healthy orders for several years. The second event was that the plant was acquired by Rendall. *'What did Rendall see when they bought us? They saw a small plant on the Pacific coast losing lots of money.'* (Finance Manager, Preston Plant)

Rendall were not impressed by what it found at the Preston plant. It was making a loss and had only just escaped from incurring a major customer's disapproval over the curl issue. If the plant did not get the Vector contract, its future looked bleak. Meanwhile the chief concern continued to be productivity. But also, once again, there were occasional complaints about quality levels. However, HP's attitude caused some bewilderment to the operations management team. 'When HP asked questions about our process the operations guys would say, "Look, we're making roll after roll of paper, it's within specification. What's the problem?" ' (Quality Manager, Preston Plant).

But it was not until summer that the full extent of HP's disquiet was made. 'I will never forget June of 2000. I was at a meeting with HP in Chicago. It was not even about quality. But during the meeting one of their engineers handed me a control chart, one that we supplied with every batch of product. He said, "Here's your latest control chart. We think you're out of control and you don't know that you're out of control and we think that we are looking at this data more than you are." He was absolutely right, and I fully understood how serious the position was. We had our most important customer telling us we couldn't run our processes just at the time we were trying to persuade them to give us the Vector contract.' (Tom Branton)

The crisis

Tom immediately set about the task of bringing the plant back under control. They first of all decided to go back to the conditions which prevailed in January, when the curl team's recommendations had been implemented. This was the state before productivity pressures had caused the process to be adjusted. At the same time the team worked on ways of implementing unambiguous 'shut-down rules' that would allow operators to decide under what conditions a line should be halted if they were in doubt about the quality of the product they were making.

'At one point in May of 2000 we had to throw away 64 jumbo rolls of out-of-specification product. That's over $100,000 of product scrapped in one run. Basically that was because they had been afraid to shut the line down. Either that or they had tried to tweak the line while it was running to get rid of the defect. The shut-down guidelines in effect say, "We are not going to operate when we are not in a state of control." Until then our operators just couldn't win. If they failed to keep the machines running we would say, "You've got to keep productivity up." If they kept the machines running but had quality problems as a result, we criticized them for making garbage. Now you get into far more trouble for violating process procedures than you do for not meeting productivity targets.' (Engineer, Preston Plant)

This new approach needed to be matched by changes in the way the communications were managed in the plant. 'We did two things that we had never done before. First, each production team started holding daily reviews of control chart data. Second, one day a month we took people away from production and debated the control chart data. Several people got nervous because we were not producing anything. But it was necessary. For the first time you got operators from the three shifts meeting together and talking about the control chart data and other quality issues. Just as significantly, we invited HP up to attend these meetings. Remember these weren't staged meetings, it was the first time these guys had met together and there was plenty of heated discussion, all of which the Hewlett-Packard representatives witnessed.' (Engineer, Preston Plant)

At last something positive was happening in the plant and morale on the shop floor was buoyant. By September 2000 the results of the plant's teams efforts were starting to show results. Process were coming under control, quality levels were improving and, most importantly, personnel both on the shop floor and in the management team were beginning to get into the 'quality mode' of thinking. Paradoxically, in spite of stopping the line periodically, the efficiency of the plant was also improving.

Yet the Preston team did not have time to enjoy their emerging success. In September 2000 the plant learned that it would not get the Vector project because of its recent quality problems. Then Rendall decided to close the plant. 'We were losing millions, we had lost the Vector project, and it was really no surprise. I told the senior management team and said that we would announce it probably in April of 2001. The real irony was that we knew that we had actually already turned the corner.' (Tom Branton)

Notwithstanding the closure decision, the management team in Preston set about the task of convincing Rendall that the plant could be viable. They figured it would take three things. First, it was vital that they continue to improve quality. Progressing with their quality initiative involved establishing full statistical process control (SPC).

Second, costs had to be brought down. Working on cost reduction was inevitably going to be painful. The first task was to get an understanding of what should be an appropriate level of operating costs. 'We went through a zero-based assessment to decide what an ideal plant would look like, and the minimum number of people needed to run it.' (Tom Branton)

By December 2000 there were 40 per cent fewer people in the plant than two months earlier. All departments were affected. The quality department shrank more than most, moving from 22 people down to six. 'When the plant *was considering down-sizing they asked me, "How can we run a lab with six technicians?" I said, "Easy. We just make good paper in the first place, and then we don't have to inspect all the garbage. That alone would save an immense amount of time."'* (Quality Manager, Preston Plant)

Third, the plant had to create a portfolio of new product ideas which could establish a greater confidence in future sales. Several new ideas were under active investigation, the most important of which was 'Protowrap', a wrap for newsprint that could be repulped. It was a product that was technically difficult. However, the plant's newly acquired capabilities allowed the product to be made economically.

Out of the crisis

In spite of their trauma, the plant's management team faced Christmas 2000 with increasing optimism. They had just made a profit for the first time for over two years. By spring 2001 even HP, at a corporate level, was starting to take notice. It was becoming obvious that the Preston plant really had made a major change. More significantly, HP had asked the plant to bid for a new product. April 2001 was a good month for the plant. It had chalked up three months of profitability and HP formally gave the new contract to Preston. Also in April, Rendall reversed their decision to close the plant.

QUESTIONS

1 What are the most significant events in the story of how the plant survived because of its adoption of quality-based principles?

2 The plant's processes eventually were brought under control. What were the main benefits of this?

3 SPC is an operational-level technique of ensuring quality conformance. How many of the benefits of bringing the plant under control would you class as strategic?

Active case study   'You have eight messages'

ACTIVE CASE

The De Noorman hotel prides and distinguishes itself on offering high-quality accommodation and service. After his day off, Andries Claessen, the hotel's General Manager, returns to work to discover a number of phone messages awaiting him. The messages cause him to question how quality is defined and managed in the hotel.

● How would you advise Andries on his questions of quality definition, measurement, control and management and how would you suggest he acts to ensure improvement?

Please refer to the Active case on the CD accompanying this book to listen to the messages and find out more about what Andries decides to do.

Applying the principles

HINTS

Some of these exercises can be answered by reading the chapter. Others will require some general knowledge of business activity and some might require an element of investigation. All have hints on how they can be answered on the CD accompanying this book.

---

1 Using the four categories of quality-related costs, make a list of the costs that fall within each category for the following operations:

(a) A university library

(b) A washing machine manufacturer

(c) A nuclear electricity generating station

(d) A church.

2   Consider how a service-level agreement could be devised for the following:

(a) The service between a library and its general customers

(b) The service given by a motor vehicle rescue service to its customers

(c) The service given by a university audiovisual aids department to both academic staff and students.

3   Using an Internet search engine (such as google.com), look at the consultancy organizations that are selling help and advice on quality management. How do they try to sell quality improvement approaches to prospective customers?

4   Visit the website of the European Foundation for Quality Management (**www.efqm.org**). Look at the companies that have won or been finalists in the European Quality Awards and try to identify the characteristics which make them 'excellent' in the opinion of the EFQM. Investigate how the EFQM promotes its model for self-assessment purposes.

5   Find two products, one a manufactured food item (for example, a pack of breakfast cereals, packet of biscuits, etc.) and the other a domestic electrical item (for example, electric toaster, coffee maker, etc.).

(a) Identify the important quality characteristics for these two products.

(b) How could each of these quality characteristics be specified?

(c) How could each of these quality characteristics be measured?

6   Many organizations check up on their own level of quality by using 'mystery shoppers'. This involves an employee of the company acting the role of a customer and recording how they are treated by the operation. Choose two or three high-visibility operations (for example, a cinema, a department store, the branch of a retail bank, etc.) and discuss how you would put together a mystery shopper approach to testing their quality. This may involve your determining the types of characteristics you would wish to observe, the way in which you would measure these characteristics, an appropriate sampling rate, and so on. Try out your mystery shopper plan by visiting these operations.

Notes on chapter

1   Source: Interview with Karen Earp, General Manager, Four Seasons Canary Wharf Hotel.

2   Sources: Ryanair website; Keenan, S. (2002) "How Ryanair puts passengers in their place,' *The Times,* 19 June.

3   Parasuraman, A. *et al.* (1985) 'A conceptual model of service quality and implications for future research', *Journal of Marketing,* Vol. 49, Fall.

4   Mechling, L. (2002) 'Get ready for a storm in a tea shop', *The Independent,* 8 March, and company website.

5   Source: Plunkett, J.J. and Dale, B.S. (1987) 'A review of the literature in quality-related costs', *International Journal of Quality and Reliability Management,* Vol. 4, No. 1.

6   Dale, B.G. (ed.) (1999) *Managing Quality,* Blackwell, Oxford.

7   Source: the EFQM website (www.efqm.org).

8   Hyman, J. and Mason, B. (1995) *Management Employees Involvement and Participation,* Sage.

Taking it further

Bounds, G., Yorks, L., Adams, M. and Ranney, G. (1994) *Beyond Total Quality Management: Towards the emerging paradigm,* McGraw-Hill. A useful summary of the state of play in total quality management at about the time it was starting to lose its status as the only approach to managing quality.

Crosby, P.B. (1979) *Quality is Free,* McGraw-Hill. One of the gurus. It had a huge impact in its day. Read it if you want to know what all the fuss was about.

Dale, B.G. (ed.) (1999) *Managing Quality,* Blackwell, Oxford. This is the third edition of a book that has long been one of the best respected texts in the area. A comprehensive and balanced guide to the area.

Deming, W.E. (1986) *Out of the Crisis,* MIT Press. Another of the quality gurus, whose work had a similarly huge impact.

Feigenbaum, A.V. (1986) *Total Quality Control,* McGraw-Hill. A more comprehensive book than those by some of the other quality gurus.

Garvin, D.A. (1991) 'How the Baldrige Award really works', *Harvard Business Review,* Vol. 69, No. 6. A look behind the scenes at what counts in getting quality prizes.

Pande, P.S., Neuman, R.P. and Kavanagh, R.R. (2000) *The Six Sigma Way,* McGraw-Hill, New York. There are many books written by consultants for practising managers on the now fashionable Six Sigma Approach (see supplement to chapter). This one is readable and informative.

Useful websites

www.quality-foundation.co.uk The British Quality Foundation is a not-for-profit organization promoting business excellence.

www.juran.com The Juran Institute's mission statement is to provide clients with the concepts, methods and guidance for attaining leadership in quality.

www.asq.org The American Society for Quality site. Good professional insights.

www.quality.nist.gov American Quality Assurance Institute, a well-established institution for all types of business quality assurance.

www.gslis.utexas.edu/~rpollock/tqm.html Non-commercial site on Total Quality Management with some good links.

www.iso.org/iso/en/ISOOnline.frontpage Site of the International Standards Organization that runs the ISO 9000 and ISO 14000 families of standards. ISO 9000 has become an international reference for quality management requirements.

**FURTHER
RESOURCES**

For further resources including examples, animated diagrams, self-test questions, Excel spreadsheets, active case studies and video materials please explore the CD accompanying this book.

Supplement to Chapter I-12
Statistical Process Control (SPC)

Introduction

The purpose of statistical process control (SPC) is both to control process performance, keeping it within acceptable limits, and to improve process performance by reducing the variation in performance from its target level. It does this by applying statistical techniques to understand the nature of performance variation over time. For those who are anxious about the 'statistical' part of SPC, don't be. Essentially SPC is based on principles that are both practical and intuitive. The statistical element is there to help rather than complicate quality decisions.

Variation in process performance

The core instrument in SPC is the control chart. These were explained earlier in the chapter. They are an illustration of the dynamic performance of a process, measuring how some aspect of process performance varies over time. All processes vary to some extent. No machine will give precisely the same result each time it is used. All materials vary a little. People in the process differ marginally in how they do things each time they perform a task. Given this, it is not surprising that any measure of performance quality (whether attribute or variable) will also vary. Variations that derive from these *normal* or *common causes* of variation can never be entirely eliminated (although they can be reduced).

Excel

For example, at a call centre for a utility company, customer care operatives answer queries over accounts, service visits, and so on. The length of time of each call will vary depending on the nature of the enquiry and the customer's needs. There will be some variation around an average call time. When the process of answering and responding to customer enquiries is stable, the computer system that intercepts and allocates calls to customer care operatives could be asked to randomly sample the length of each call. As this data built up, the histogram showing call times could develop as is shown in Figure 12.9. The first calls could lie anywhere within the natural variation of the process but are more likely to be close to the average call length (Figure 12.9(a)). As more calls are measured they would clearly show a tendency to be close to the process average (see Figure 12.9(b) and (c)). Eventually the data will show a smooth histogram that can be drawn into a smoother distribution that will indicate the underlying process variation (the distribution shown in Figure 12.9(f)).

Often this type of variation can be described by a *normal distribution*. (Even if this raw data does not conform to a normal distribution, it can be manipulated to approximate to one by using sampling – see later.) It is a characteristic of normal distributions that 99.7 per cent of the measures will lie within ± 3 standard deviations of the distribution (standard deviation is a measure of how widely the distribution is spread or *dispersed*).

The central limit theorem

Not all processes vary in their performance according to a normal distribution. However, if a sample is taken from any type of distribution, the distribution of the average of the sample (sample mean) *will* approximate to a normal distribution. For example, there is an equal probability of any number between one and six being thrown on a six-sided, unweighted

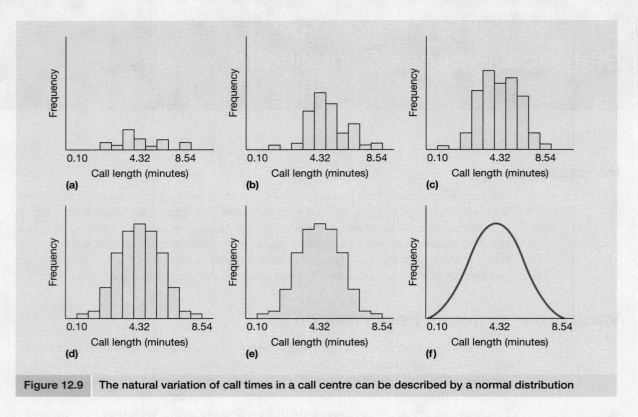

Figure 12.9   The natural variation of call times in a call centre can be described by a normal distribution

die. The distribution is rectangular with an average of 3.5 as shown in Figure 12.10(a). But if a die is thrown (say) six times repeatedly and the average of the six throws calculated, the sample average will also be 3.5, but the standard deviation of the distribution will be the standard deviation of the original rectangular distribution divided by the square of the

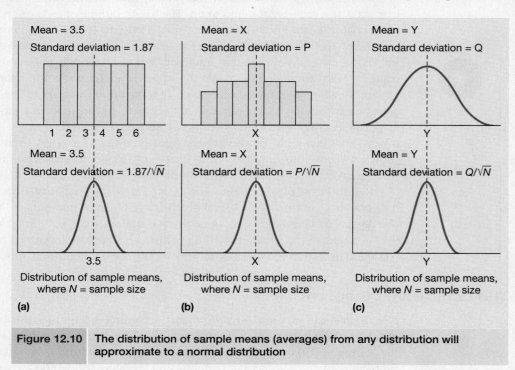

Figure 12.10   The distribution of sample means (averages) from any distribution will approximate to a normal distribution

sample size. More significantly, the shape of the distribution will be close to normal and so can be treated the same way as a normal distribution. This becomes important when control limits are calculated – see later.

Is the process 'in control'?

Not all variation in process performance is the result of common causes. There may be something wrong with the process that is assignable to an abnormal and preventable cause. Machinery may have worn or been set up badly. An untrained person may not be following the prescribed procedure for the process. The causes of such variation are called *assignable* or *abnormal causes*. The question for operations management is whether the results from any particular sample, when plotted on the control chart, simply represent the variation due to *common* causes or due to some specific and correctable *assignable* cause. Figure 12.11(a), for example, shows the control chart for the average call length of samples of customer calls in a utility's call centre. Like any process the results vary, but the last three points seem to be lower than usual. The question is whether this is natural variation or the symptom of some more serious cause. Is the variation the result of common causes, or does it indicate assignable causes (something abnormal) occurring in the process?

To help make this decision, control limits can be added to the control charts that indicate the expected extent of 'common-cause' variation. If any points lie outside these control limits then the process can be deemed *out of control* in the sense that variation is likely to be due to assignable causes. These can be set in a statistically revealing manner based on the probability that the mean of a particular sample will differ by more than a set amount from the mean of the population from which it is taken. Figure 12.11(b) shows the same control chart as Figure 12.11(a) with the addition of control limits put at ±3 standard deviations (of the population of sample means) away from the mean of sample averages. It shows that the probability of the final point on the chart being influenced by an assignable cause is very high indeed. When the process is exhibiting behaviour which is outside its normal 'common-cause' range, it is said to be 'out of control'.

However, we cannot be absolutely certain that the process is out of control. There is a small but finite chance that the point is a rare but natural result at the tail of its distribution. Stopping the process under these circumstances would represent a type I error because the process is actually in control. Alternatively, ignoring a result which in reality is due to an assignable cause is a type II error (see Table 12.5). Control limits that are set at three standard deviations either side of the population mean are called the upper control limit (UCL) and lower control limit (LCL). There is only a 0.3 per cent chance of any sample mean falling outside these limits by chance causes (that is, a chance of a type I error of 0.3 per cent).

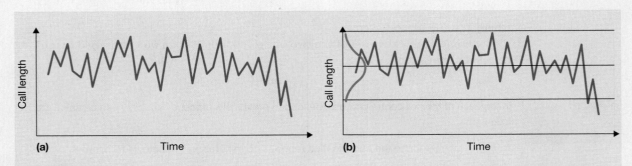

| Figure 12.11 | Control chart for the average call length in a call centre: (a) without control limits; (b) with control limits derived from the natural variation of the process |

Table 12.5 Type I and type II errors in SPC

	Actual process state	
Decision	*In control*	*Out of control*
Stop process	Type I error	Correct decision
Leave alone	Correct decision	Type II error

Process capability

Using control charts to assess whether the process is in control is an important internal benefit of SPC. An equally important question for any operations manager would be: 'Is the variation in the process performance acceptable to external customers?' The answer will depend on the acceptable range of performance that will be tolerated by the customers. This range is called the *specification range*. Returning to the call time example, if the call time is too small then the organization might offend customers. If it is too large, the organization is 'giving away' too much of its time.

Process capability is a measure of the acceptability of the variation of the process. The simplest measure of capability (C_p) is given by the ratio of the specification range to the 'natural' variation of the process (i.e. ±3 standard deviations):

$$C_p = \frac{UTL - LTL}{6s}$$

where   UTL = the upper tolerance limit
LTL = the lower tolerance limit
s = the standard deviation of the process variability.

Generally, if the C_p of a process is greater than 1, it is taken to indicate that the process is 'capable', and a C_p of less than 1 indicates that the process is not 'capable', assuming that the distribution is normal (see Figure 12.12(a), (b) and (c)).

The simple C_p measure assumes that the average of the process variation is at the mid-point of the specification range. Often the process average is offset from the specification range, however (see Figure 12.12(d)). In such cases, *one-sided* capability indices are required to understand the capability of the process:

$$\text{Upper one-sided index } C_{pu} = \frac{UTL - X}{3s}$$

$$\text{Lower one-sided index } C_{pl} = \frac{X - LTL}{3s}$$

where X = the process average.

Sometimes only the lower of the two one-sided indices for a process is used to indicate its capability (C_{pk}):

$$C_{pk} = \min(C_{pu}, C_{pl})$$

Worked example

In the case of the call centre process, described previously, process capability can be calculated as follows:

Suppose the specification range = 16 minutes − 1 minute = 15 minutes

and the natural variation of process = 6 × standard deviation

= 6 × 2 = 12 minutes

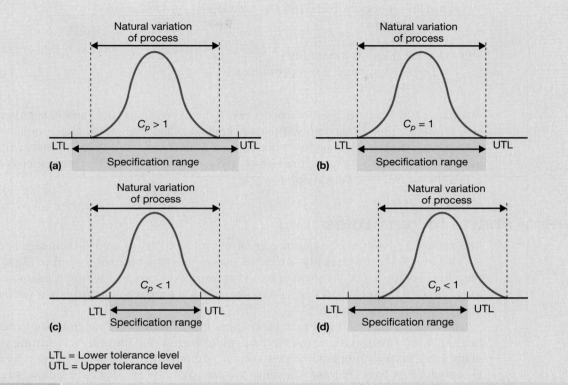

LTL = Lower tolerance level
UTL = Upper tolerance level

Figure 12.12   Process capability compares the natural variation of the process with the specification range that is required

C_p = process capability

$$= \frac{UTL - LTL}{6s}$$

$$= \frac{16 - 1}{6 \times 2} = \frac{15}{12}$$

$$= 1.25$$

If the natural variation of the process changed to have a process average of 7 minutes but the standard deviation of the process remained at 2 minutes:

$$C_{pu} = \frac{16 - 7}{3 \times 2} = \frac{9}{6} = 1.5$$

$$C_{pl} = \frac{7 - 1}{3 \times 2} = \frac{6}{6} = 1.0$$

$$C_{pl} = \min\ (1.5, 1.0)$$

$$= 1.00$$

The Taguchi loss function

Genichi Taguchi has criticized the concept of an acceptable range of variation.[1] He suggested that the consequences of being 'off-target' (that is, deviating from the required process average performance) were inadequately described by simple control limits. Instead, he proposed a quality loss function (QLF) – a mathematical function which includes all the costs of poor quality. These include wastage, repair, inspection, service, warranty and generally what he termed 'loss to society' costs. This loss function is expressed as follows:

$$L = D^2C$$

where L = total loss to society costs
D = deviation from target performance
C = a constant.

Figure 12.13 illustrates the difference between the conventional and Taguchi approaches to interpreting process variability. The more graduated approach of the QLF shows losses increasing quadratically as performance deviates from target. Because of this there will be an appropriate motivation to progressively reduce process variability. This is sometimes called the *target-oriented* quality philosophy.[2]

Control charts for variables

The most commonly used type of control chart employed to control variables is the $\overline{X} - R$ *chart*. In fact this is really two charts in one. One chart is used to control the sample average or mean ($\overline{X}$). The other is used to control the variation within the sample by measuring the range (R). The range is used because it is simpler to calculate than the standard deviation of the sample.

The means ($\overline{X}$) chart can pick up changes in the average output from the process being charted. Changes in the means chart would suggest that the process is drifting generally away from its supposed process average, although the variability inherent in the process may not have changed. The range (R) chart plots the range of each sample, which is the difference between the largest and the smallest measurement in the samples. Monitoring sample range gives an indication of whether the variability of the process is changing, even when the process average remains constant.

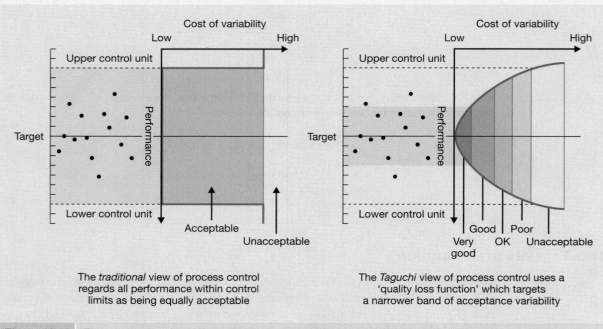

Figure 12.13 The conventional and Taguchi views of the cost of variability

Control limits for variables control chart

As with attributes control charts, a statistical description of how the process operates under normal conditions (when there are no assignable causes) can be used to calculate control limits. The first task in calculating the control limits is to estimate the grand average or population mean $(\overline{\overline{X}})$ and average range $(\overline{R})$ using m samples each of sample size n. The population mean is estimated from the average of a large number (m) of sample means:

$$\overline{\overline{X}} = \frac{\overline{X}_1 + \overline{X}_2 + \cdots \overline{X}_m}{m}$$

The average range is estimated from the ranges of the large number of samples:

$$\overline{R} = \frac{R_1 + R_2 + \cdots R_m}{m}$$

The control limits for the sample means chart are:

$$\text{Upper control limit (LCL)} = \overline{\overline{X}} + A_2\,\overline{R}$$

$$\text{Lower control limit (LCL)} = \overline{\overline{X}} - A_2\,\overline{R}$$

The control limits for the range charts are:

$$\text{Upper control limit (UCL)} = D_4\,\overline{R}$$

$$\text{Lower control limit (LCL)} = D_3\,\overline{R}$$

The factors A_2, D_3 and D_4 vary with sample size and are shown in Table 12.6.

   The LCL for the means chart may be negative (for example, temperature or profit may be less than zero) but it may not be negative for a range chart (or the smallest measurement in the sample would be larger than the largest). If the calculation indicates a negative LCL for a range chart then the LCL should be set to zero.

Worked example

GAM (Groupe À Maquillage) is a contract cosmetics company that manufactures and packs cosmetics and perfumes for other companies. One of its plants operates a filling line that automatically fills plastic bottles with skin cream and seals the bottles with a screw-top cap. The tightness with which the screw-top cap is fixed is an important aspect of quality. If the cap is screwed on too tightly, there is a danger that it will crack; if screwed on too loosely it might come loose. Either

Table 12.6	Factors for the calculation of control limits		
Sample size n	A_2	D_3	D_4
2	1.880	0	3.267
3	1.023	0	2.575
4	0.729	0	2.282
5	0.577	0	2.115
6	0.483	0	2.004
7	0.419	0.076	1.924
8	0.373	0.136	1.864
9	0.337	0.184	1.816
10	0.308	0.223	1.777
12	0.266	0.284	1.716
14	0.235	0.329	1.671
16	0.212	0.364	1.636
18	0.194	0.392	1.608
20	0.180	0.414	1.586
22	0.167	0.434	1.566
24	0.157	0.452	1.548

outcome could cause leakage. The plant had received some complaints of product leakage, possibly caused by inconsistent fixing of the screw-tops. Tightness can be measured by the amount of turning force (torque) that is required to unfasten the tops. The company decided to take samples of the bottles coming out of the filling-line process, test them for their unfastening torque and plot the results on a control chart. Several samples of four bottles are taken during a period when the process is regarded as being in control.

The following data are calculated from this exercise:

$$\text{Grand average of all samples } \overline{\overline{X}} = 812 \text{ g/cm}^3$$

$$\text{Average range of the sample } \overline{R} = 6 \text{ g/cm}^3$$

Control limits for the means $(\overline{X})$ chart were calculated as follows:

$$\text{UCL} = \overline{\overline{X}} + A_2\overline{R}$$

$$= 812 + (A_2 \times 6)$$

From Table 12.6, we know that, for a sample size of four, $A_2 = 0.729$. Thus:

$$\text{UCL} = 812 + (0.729 \times 6)$$

$$= 816.37$$

$$\text{LCL} = \overline{\overline{X}} - (A_2\,\overline{R})$$

$$= 812 - (0.729 \times 6)$$

$$= 807.63$$

Control limits for the range (R) chart were calculated as follows:

$$\text{UCL} = D_4 \times \overline{R}$$

$$= 2.282 \times 6$$

$$= 13.69$$

$$\text{LCL} = D_3 \times \overline{R}$$

$$= 0 \times 6$$

$$= 0$$

After calculating these averages and limits for the control chart, the company regularly took samples of four bottles during production, recorded the measurements and plotted them as shown in Figure 12.14. This control chart reveals that only with difficulty could the process average be kept in control. Occasional operator interventions are required. Also the process range is moving towards (and once exceeds) the upper control limit. The process also seems to be becoming more variable. (After investigation it was discovered that, because of faulty maintenance of the line, skin cream was occasionally contaminating the part of the line that fitted the cap, resulting in erratic tightening of the caps.)

Control charts for attributes

Attributes have only two states – 'right' or 'wrong', for example – so the statistic calculated is the proportion of wrongs (p) in a sample. (This statistic follows a binomial distribution.) Control charts using p are called 'p-charts'. When calculating control limits, the population mean ($\overline{p}$) (the actual, normal or expected proportion of 'defectives') may not be known. Who knows, for example, the actual number of city commuters who are dissatisfied with their journey time? In such cases the population mean can be estimated

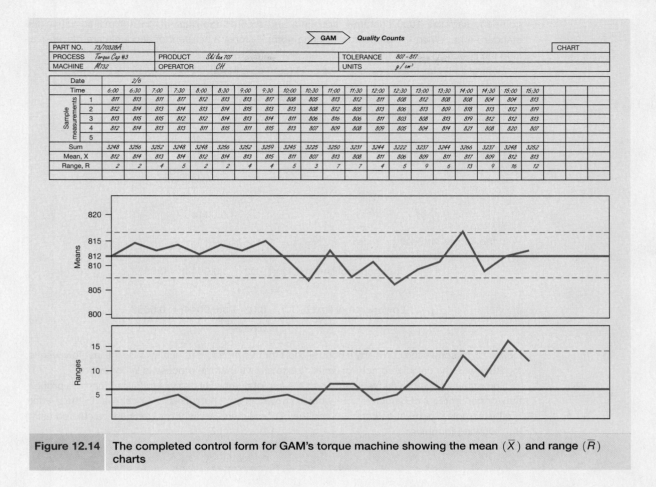

Date		2/6																					
Time		6:00	6:30	7:00	7:30	8:00	8:30	9:00	9:30	10:00	10:30	11:00	11:30	12:00	12:30	13:00	13:30	14:00	14:30	15:00	15:30		
Sample measurements	1	811	813	811	817	812	813	813	817	808	805	813	812	811	808	812	808	808	804	804	813		
	2	812	814	813	814	813	814	815	813	813	808	812	805	813	806	813	809	818	813	812	819		
	3	813	815	815	812	812	814	813	814	811	806	816	806	811	803	808	813	819	812	812	813		
	4	812	814	813	813	811	815	811	815	813	807	809	808	809	805	804	814	821	808	820	807		
	5																						
Sum		3248	3256	3252	3248	3248	3256	3252	3259	3245	3225	3250	3231	3244	3222	3237	3244	3266	3237	3248	3252		
Mean, X		812	814	813	814	812	814	813	815	811	807	813	808	811	806	809	811	817	809	812	813		
Range, R		2	2	4	5	2	2	4	4	5	3	7	7	4	5	9	6	13	9	16	12		

Figure 12.14 The completed control form for GAM's torque machine showing the mean $(\bar{X})$ and range $(\bar{R})$ charts

from the average of the proportion of 'defectives' from m samples each of n items, where m should be at least 30 and n should be at least 100:

$$\bar{p} = \frac{p^1 + p^2 + p^3 \cdots p^n}{m}$$

One standard deviation can then be estimated from:

$$\sqrt{\frac{\bar{p}(1-\bar{p})}{n}}$$

The upper and lower control limits can then be set as:

$$\text{UCL} = \bar{p} + 3 \text{ standard deviations}$$

$$\text{LCL} = \bar{p} - 3 \text{ standard deviations}$$

Of course, the LCL cannot be negative, so when it is calculated to be so it should be rounded up to zero.

Worked example

A credit card company deals with many hundreds of thousands of transactions every week. One of its measures of the quality of service it gives its customers is the dependability with which it mails customers' monthly accounts. The quality standard it sets itself is that accounts should be mailed within two days of the 'nominal post date' which is specified to the customer. Every week the company samples 1000 customer accounts and records the percentage not mailed within the standard time. When the process is working normally, only 2 per cent of accounts are mailed outside the specified period, that is, 2 per cent are 'defective'.

Control limits for the process can be calculated as follows:

$$\text{Mean proportion defective, } \bar{p} = 0.02$$

$$\text{Sample size } n = 1000$$

$$\text{Standard deviation } s = \sqrt{\frac{\bar{p}(1-\bar{p})}{n}}$$

$$= \sqrt{\frac{0.02(0.98)}{1000}}$$

$$= 0.0044$$

With the control limits at $\bar{p} \pm 3s$:

$$\text{Upper control limit (UCL)} = 0.02 + 3(0.0044) = 0.0332$$

$$= 3.32\%$$

$$\text{Lower control limit (LCL)} = 0.02 - 3(0.0044) = 0.0068$$

$$= 0.68\%$$

Figure 12.15 shows the company's control chart for this measure of quality over the last few weeks, together with the calculated control limits. It also shows that the process is in control.

Sometimes it is more convenient to plot the actual number of defects (c) rather than the proportion (or percentage) of defectives, on what is known as a c-chart. This is very similar to the p-chart but the sample size must be constant and the process mean and control limits are calculated using the following formulae:

$$\text{Process mean } \bar{c} = \frac{c_1 + c_2 + c_3 \cdots c_m}{m}$$

$$\text{Control limits} = \bar{c} \pm 3\sqrt{c}$$

where c = number of defects
m = number of samples.

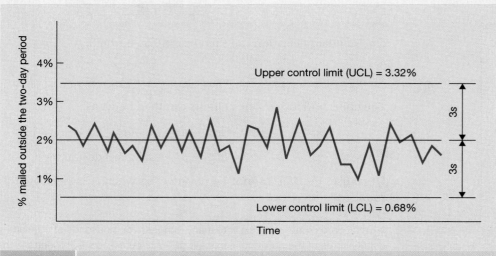

Figure 12.15   Control chart for the percentage of customer accounts which are mailed outside their two-day period

Note on chapter supplement

1. For more details of Taguchi's ideas, see Stuart, G. (1993) *Taguchi Methods: A hands-on approach,* Addison Wesley.

2. Taguchi, G. and Clausing, D. (1990) 'Robust quality', *Harvard Business Review,* Vol. 68, No. 1, pp. 65–75. For more details of the Taguchi approach, see Stuart, *op. cit.*

13

IMPROVEMENT

Introduction

All operations, no matter how well managed, are capable of improvement. In fact in recent years the emphasis has shifted markedly towards making improvement one of the main responsibilities of operations managers. And although the whole of this book is focused on improving the performance of individual processes, operations and whole supply networks, there are some issues that relate to the activity of improvement itself. In any operation, whatever is improved, and however it is done, the overall direction and approach to improvement need to be addressed. (See Figure 13.1.)

Source: Courtesy of LotusHead (www.pixelpusher.co.za)

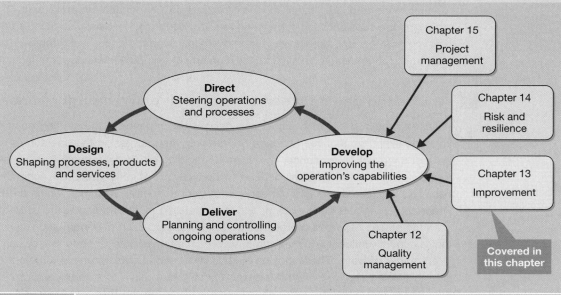

| Figure 13.1 | Improvement is the activity of closing the gap between the current and the desired performance of an operation or process |

Executive summary

VIDEO
further detail

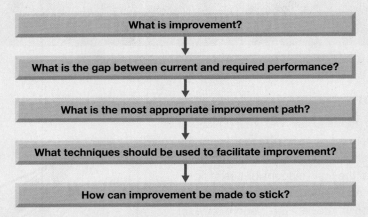

Decision logic chain for improvement

Each chapter is structured around a set of diagnostic questions. These questions suggest what you should ask in order to gain an understanding of the important issues of a topic, and as a result, improve your decision making. An executive summary, addressing these questions, is provided below.

What is improvement?

Improvement is the activity of closing the gap between the current and the desired performance of an operation or process. It is increasingly seen as the ultimate objective for all operations and process management activity. Furthermore, almost all popular operations initiatives in recent years, such as total quality management, lean operations, business process re-engineering and Six Sigma, have all focused on performance improvement. It involves assessing the gaps between current and required performance, balancing the use of continuous improvement and breakthrough improvement, adopting appropriate improvement techniques, and attempting to ensure that the momentum of improvement does not fade over time.

What is the gap between current and required performance?

Assessing the gap between actual and desired performance is the starting point for most improvement. This requires two sets of activities: first, assessing the operation's and each process's current performance; and second, deciding on an appropriate level of target performance. The first activity will depend on how performance is measured within the operation. This involves deciding what aspects of performance to measure, which are the most important aspects of performance, and what detailed measures should be used to assess each factor. The balanced scorecard approach is an approach to performance measurement that is currently influential in many organizations. Setting targets for performance can be done in a number of ways. These include historically based targets, strategic targets that reflect strategic objectives, external performance targets that relate to external and/or competitor operations, and absolute performance targets based on the theoretical upper limit of performance. Benchmarking is an important input to this part of performance improvement.

What is the most appropriate improvement path?

Two improvement paths represent different philosophies of improvement, although both may be appropriate at different times. They are breakthrough improvement and continuous improvement. Breakthrough improvement focused on major and dramatic changes that are intended to result in dramatic increases in performance. The business process re-engineering approach is typical of breakthrough improvement. Continuous improvement focuses on small but never-ending improvements that become part of normal operations life. Its objective is to make improvement part of the culture of the organization. Often continuous improvement involves the use of multi-stage improvement cycles for regular problem solving. The Six Sigma approach to improvement brings many existing ideas together and can be seen as a combination of continuous and breakthrough improvement.

What techniques should be used to facilitate improvement?

Almost all techniques in operations management contribute directly or indirectly to performance improvement. However, some more general techniques have become popularly associated with improvement. These include scatter diagrams (correlation), cause–effect diagrams, Pareto analysis and why–why analysis.

How can improvement be made to stick?

One of the biggest problems in improvement is to preserve improvement momentum over time. One factor that inhibits improvement becoming accepted as a regular part of operations activity is the emphasis on the fashionability of each new improvement approach. Most new improvement ideas contain some worthwhile elements but none will provide the ultimate answer. There must be some overall management of the improvement process that can absorb the best of each new idea. And, although authorities differ to some extent, most emphasize the importance of an improvement strategy, top management support, and training.

What is improvement?

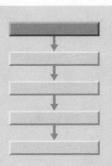

Improvement comes from closing the gap between what you are and what you want to be. In a specifically operations context, it comes from closing the gap between current and desired performance. Performance improvement is the ultimate objective of operations and process management. It has also become the subject of innumerable ideas that have been put forward as particularly effective methods of ensuring improvement. These include many that are described in this book, for example, total quality management (TQM), 'lean' operations, business process re-engineering (BPR), Six Sigma, and so on. All of these, and other, ideas have something to contribute. What is important is that all managers develop an understanding of the underlying elements of improvement. The following two examples illustrate many of these.

> **Operations principle**
> Performance improvement is the ultimate objective of operations and process management.

Example | ### Six Sigma at Xchanging[1]

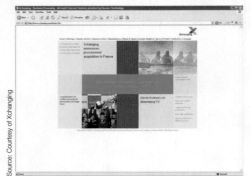

Source: Courtesy of Xchanging

'I think Six Sigma is powerful because of its definition: it is the process of comparing process outputs against customer requirements. Processes operating at less than 3.4 defects per million opportunities means that you must strive to get closer to perfection and it is the customer that defines the goal. Measuring defects per opportunity means that you can actually compare the process of, say, a human resources process with a billing and collection process.' Paul Ruggier, Head of Process at Xchanging, is a powerful advocate of Six Sigma and credits the success of the company, at least partly, to the approach.

Xchanging, created in 1998, is one of a new breed of companies, operating as an outsourcing business for 'back-office' functions for a range of companies, such as Lloyds of London, the insurance centre. Xchanging's business proposition is for the client company to transfer the running of the whole or part of its back office to Xchanging, for either a fixed price or one determined by cost savings achieved. The challenge Xchanging faces is to run that back office in a more effective and efficient manner than the client company had managed in the past. So, the more effective Xchanging is at running the processes, the greater its profit. To achieve these efficiencies Xchanging offers larger scale, a higher level of process expertise, focus and investment in technology. But above all, it offers a Six Sigma approach. *'Everything we do can be broken down into a process,'* says Ruggier, *'It may be more straightforward in a manufacturing business, frankly they've been using a lot of Six Sigma tools and techniques for decades. But the concept of process improvement is relatively new in many service companies. Yet the concept is powerful. Through the implementation of this approach we have achieved 30 per cent productivity improvements in six months.'*

The company also adopts the Six Sigma terminology for its improvement practitioners – Master Black Belts, Black Belts and Green Belts. The status of Black Belt is very much sought after as well as being fulfilling, says, Rebecca Whittaker, who is a Master Black Belt. *'At the end of a project it is about having a process which is redesigned to such an extent, that is simplified and consolidated and people come back and say, "It's so much better than it used to be". It makes their lives better and it makes the business results better and those are the things that make being a Black Belt worthwhile.'*

Rebecca was recruited by Xchanging along with a number of other Master Black Belts as part of a strategic decision to kick-start Six Sigma in the company. It is seen as a particularly responsible position and Master Black Belts are expected to be well versed in the Six Sigma techniques and be able to provide the training and know how to develop other staff within the company. In Rebecca's case she has been working as a Six Sigma facilitator for five years, initially as a Green Belt then as a Black Belt.

Typically a person identified as having the right analytical and interpersonal skills will be taken off their job for at least a year, trained and immersed in the concepts of improvement and then sent to work with line staff as project manager/facilitator. Their role as Black Belt will be to guide the line staff to make improvements in the way they do the job. One of the new Black Belts at Xchanging, Sarah Frost, is keen to stress the responsibility she owes to the people who will have to work in the improvement process. *'Being a Black Belt is about being a project manager. It is about working with the staff and combining our skills in facilitation and our knowledge of the Six Sigma process with their knowledge of the business. You always have to remember that you will go onto another project but they (process staff) will have to live with the new process. It is about building solutions that they can believe in.'*

Example	Taxing quality[2]

Source: Keith Brofsky/PhotoDisc/Getty Images

Operations effectiveness is just as important an issue in public sector operations as it is for commercial companies. People have the right to expect that their taxes are not wasted on inefficient or inappropriate public processes. This is especially true of the tax collecting system, which is never a popular organization in any country, and taxpayers can be especially critical when the tax collection process is not well managed. This was very much on the minds of the Aarhus Region Customs and Tax unit (Aarhus CT) when they developed their improvement initiative. The Aarhus Region is the largest of Denmark's 29 local customs and tax offices. It acts as an agent for central government in collecting taxes while being able to respond to taxpayers' queries. Aarhus CT must *'keep the user (customer) in focus'*, they say. *'Users must pay what is due – no more, no less and on time. But users are entitled to fair control and collection, fast and efficient case work, service and guidance, flexible employees, polite behaviour and a professional telephone service.'* The Aarhus CT approach to managing its performance initiative was built around a number of key points.

- A recognition that poorly designed and managed processes cause waste both internally and externally.
- A determination to adopt a practice of regularly surveying the satisfaction of its users. Employees were also surveyed, both to understand their views on quality and to check that their working environment would help to instil the principles of high performance service.
- Although a not-for-profit organization, performance measures included measuring the organization's adherence to financial targets as well as error reporting.
- Internal processes were redefined and redesigned to emphasize customer needs and internal staff requirements. For example, Aarhus CT was the only tax region in Denmark to develop an independent information process that was used to analyze customers' needs and 'prevent misunderstanding in users' perception of legislation'.
- Internal processes were designed to allow staff the time and opportunity to develop their own skills, exchange ideas with colleagues and take on greater responsibility for management of their own work processes.
- The organization set up what it called its 'Quality Organization' (QO) structure that spanned all divisions and processes. The idea of the QO was to foster staff commitment to continuous improvement and to encourage the development of ideas for improving process performance.

Within the QO was the Quality Group (QG). This consisted of four managers and four process staff, and reported directly to senior management. It also set up a number of improvement groups and suggestion groups consisting of managers as well as process staff. The role of the suggestion groups was to collect and process ideas for improvement which the improvement groups would then analyze and if appropriate implement.

● Aarhus CT were keen to stress that their Quality Groups would eventually become redundant if they were to be successful. In the short term they would maintain a stream of improvement ideas, but in the long term they should have fully integrated the idea of quality improvement into the day-to-day activities of all staff.

What do these two examples have in common?

The improvement initiatives at these two operations, and the way they managed them, is typical of improvement projects. Both measured performance and placed information gathering at the centre of their improvement initiative. Both had a view of improvement targets that related directly to strategic objectives. Both made efforts to collect information that would allow decisions based on evidence rather than opinion. Xchanging adopted a Six Sigma approach, based on hard evidence and analysis. Aarhus CT focused on their customers' perceptions, needs and requirements. This included what customers should not receive as well as what they should receive from the operation. Both companies had to foster an environment that allowed all staff to contribute to improvement, and both came to view improvement not as a 'one-off', but rather as the start of a never-ending cycle of improvement. Most importantly, both had to decide how to organize the whole improvement initiative. Different organizations with different objectives may choose to implement improvement initiatives in a different way. But all will face a similar set of issues to these two operations, even if they choose to make different decisions.

DIAGNOSTIC QUESTION

What is the gap between current and required performance?

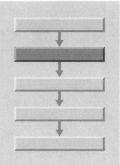

The gap between how an operation or process is currently performing and how it wishes to perform is the key driver of any improvement initiative. The wider the gap, the more importance is likely to be given to improvement. But, in order to harness the gap as a driver of improvement, it must be addressed in some detail, in terms of both exactly what is failing to meet targets, and by how much. Answering these questions depends on the operation's ability to do three things: assess its current performance, derive a set of target levels of performance that the organization can subscribe to, and compare current against target performance in a systematic and graphic manner that demonstrates to everyone the need for improvement.

Assessing current performance – performance measurement

Some kind of *performance measurement* is a prerequisite for judging whether an operation is good, bad or indifferent, although this is not the only reason for investing in effective performance measurement. Without one, it would be impossible to exert any control over an operation on an ongoing basis. However, a performance measurement system that gives no help to ongoing improvement is only partially effective. Performance measurement, as we are treating it here, concerns three generic issues:

Operations principle
Performance measurement is a prerequisite for the assessment of operations performance.

- What factors to include as performance measures?
- Which are the most important performance measures?
- What detailed measures to use?

What factors to include as performance measures?

An obvious starting point for deciding which performance measures to adopt is to use the five generic performance objectives – quality, speed, dependability, flexibility and cost. These can be broken down into more detailed measures, or they can be aggregated into 'composite' measures, such as 'customer satisfaction', 'overall service level' or 'operations agility'. These composite measures may be further aggregated by using measures such as 'achieve market objectives', 'achieve financial objectives', 'achieve operations objectives' or even 'achieve overall strategic objectives'. The more aggregated performance measures have greater strategic relevance in so much as they help to draw a picture of the overall performance of the business, although by doing so they necessarily include many influences outside those that operations performance improvement would normally address. The more detailed performance measures are usually monitored more closely and more often, and although they provide a limited view of an operation's performance, they do provide a more descriptive and complete picture of what should be and what is happening within the operation. In practice, most organizations will choose to use performance targets from throughout the range. This idea is illustrated in Figure 13.2.

Choosing the important performance measures

One of the problems of devising a useful performance measurement system is trying to achieve some balance between having a few key measures on one hand (straightforward and simple, but may not reflect the full range of organizational objectives), or, on the other hand, having many detailed measures (complex and difficult to manage, but capable of conveying many nuances of performance). Broadly, a compromise is reached by making sure that there is a clear link between the operation's overall strategy, the most important (or 'key') performance indicators (KPIs) that reflect strategic objectives, and the bundle of detailed measures that are used to 'flesh out' each key performance indicator. Obviously, unless strategy is well defined then it is difficult to 'target' a narrow range of key performance indicators.

Operations principle
Without strategic clarity, key performance indicators cannot be appropriately targeted.

What detailed measures to use?

The five performance objectives – quality, speed, dependability, flexibility and cost – are really composites of many smaller measures. For example, an operation's cost is derived from many factors which could include the purchasing efficiency of the operation, the efficiency with which it converts materials, the productivity of its staff, the ratio of direct to indirect staff, and so on. All of these measures individually give a partial view of the operation's cost performance, and many of them overlap in terms of the information they include. However, each of them does give a perspective on the cost performance of

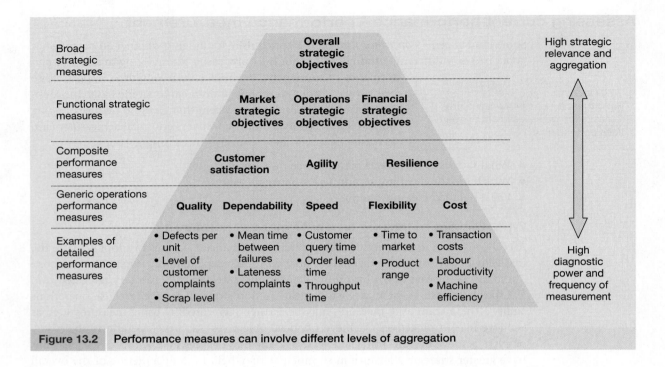

Broad strategic measures		**Overall strategic objectives**			High strategic relevance and aggregation
Functional strategic measures		**Market strategic objectives**	**Operations strategic objectives**	**Financial strategic objectives**	
Composite performance measures		**Customer satisfaction**	**Agility**	**Resilience**	
Generic operations performance measures	**Quality**	**Dependability**	**Speed**	**Flexibility**	**Cost**
Examples of detailed performance measures	• Defects per unit • Level of customer complaints • Scrap level	• Mean time between failures • Lateness complaints	• Customer query time • Order lead time • Throughput time	• Time to market • Product range	• Transaction costs • Labour productivity • Machine efficiency

High diagnostic power and frequency of measurement

Figure 13.2   Performance measures can involve different levels of aggregation

an operation that could be useful either to identify areas for improvement or to monitor the extent of improvement. If an organization regards its 'cost' performance as unsatisfactory, disaggregating it into 'purchasing efficiency', 'operations efficiency', 'staff productivity', etc. might explain the root cause of the poor performance. Table 13.1 shows some of the partial measures which can be used to judge an operation's performance.

The balanced scorecard approach

The balanced scorecard retains traditional financial measures. But financial measures tell the story of past events, an adequate story for industrial age companies for which investments in long-term capabilities [and] customer relationships were not critical for success. These financial measures are inadequate, however, for guiding and evaluating the journey that information age companies must make to create future value through investment in customers, suppliers, employees, processes, technology, and innovation.[3]

Generally operations performance measures have been broadening in their scope. It is now generally accepted that the scope of measurement should, at some level, include external as well as internal, long-term as well as short-term, and 'soft' as well as 'hard' measures. The best-known manifestation of this trend is the 'Balanced Scorecard' approach taken by Kaplan and Norton.[4] As well as including financial measures of performance, in the same way as traditional performance measurement systems, the balanced scorecard approach also attempts to provide the important information that is required to allow the overall strategy of an organization to be reflected adequately in specific performance measures. In addition to financial measures of performance, it also includes more operational measures of customer satisfaction, internal processes, innovation and other improvement activities. In doing so it measures the factors behind financial performance which are seen as the key drivers of future financial success. In

Table 13.1   Some typical partial measures of performance

Performance objective	Some typical measures
Quality	Number of defects per unit Level of customer complaints Scrap level Warranty claims Mean time between failures Customer satisfaction score
Speed	Customer query time Order lead time Frequency of delivery Actual versus theoretical throughput time Cycle time
Dependability	Percentage of orders delivered late Average lateness of orders Proportion of products in stock Mean deviation from promised arrival Schedule adherence
Flexibility	Time needed to develop new products/services Range of products/services Machine changeover time Average batch size Time to increase activity rate Average/maximum capacity Time to change schedules
Cost	Minimum/average delivery time Variance against budget Utilization of resources Labour productivity Added value Efficiency Cost per operation hour

particular, it is argued that a balanced range of measures enables managers to address the following questions (see Figure 13.3):

● How do we look to our shareholders (financial perspective)?
● What must we excel at (internal process perspective)?
● How do our customers see us (the customer perspective)?
● How can we continue to improve and build capabilities (the learning and growth perspective)?

The balanced scorecard attempts to bring together the elements that reflect a business's strategic position, including product or service quality measures, product and service development times, customer complaints, labour productivity, and so on. At the same time it attempts to avoid performance reporting becoming unwieldy by restricting the number of measures and focusing especially on those seen to be essential. The advantages of the approach are that it presents an overall picture of the organization's performance in a single report, and by being comprehensive in the measures of performance it uses, encourages companies to take decisions in the interests of the whole organization rather than sub-optimizing around narrow measures. Developing a balanced scorecard is a complex process and is now the subject of considerable debate. One of the key questions that have to be considered is how specific measures of performance should be designed. Inadequately designed performance measures can result in dysfunctional behaviour, so teams of managers are often used to develop a scorecard which reflects their organization's specific needs.

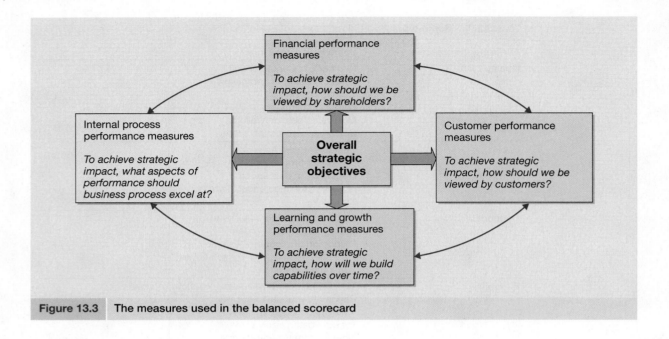

Figure 13.3   The measures used in the balanced scorecard

Setting target performance

A performance measure means relatively little until it is compared against some kind of target. Knowing that only one document in 500 is sent out to customers containing an error tells us relatively little unless we know whether this is better or worse than we were achieving previously, and whether it is better or worse than other similar operations (especially competitors) are achieving. Setting performance targets transforms performance measures into performance 'judgements'. Several approaches to setting targets can be used, including the following.

- *Historically based targets* – targets that compare current against previous performance.
- *Strategic targets* – targets set to reflect the level of performance that is regarded as appropriate to achieve strategic objectives.
- *External performance-based targets* – targets set to reflect the performance that is achieved by similar, or competitor, external operations.
- *Absolute performance targets* – targets based on the theoretical upper limit of performance.

One of the problems in setting targets is that different targets can give very different messages regarding the improvement being achieved. So, for example, in Figure 13.4, one of an operation's performance measures is 'delivery' (in this case defined as the proportion of orders delivered on time). The performance for one month has been measured at 83 per cent, but any judgement regarding performance will be dependent on the performance targets. Using a *historical* target, when compared to last year's performance of 60 per cent, this month's performance of 83 per cent is good. But, if the operation's *strategy* calls for a 95 per cent delivery performance, the actual performance of 83 per cent looks decidedly poor. The company may also be concerned with how they perform against *competitors*' performance. If competitors are currently averaging delivery performances of around 80 per cent the company's performance looks rather good. Finally, the more ambitious managers within the company may wish to at least try and seek perfection. Why not, they argue, use an

> **Operations principle**
> Performance measures only have meaning when compared against targets.

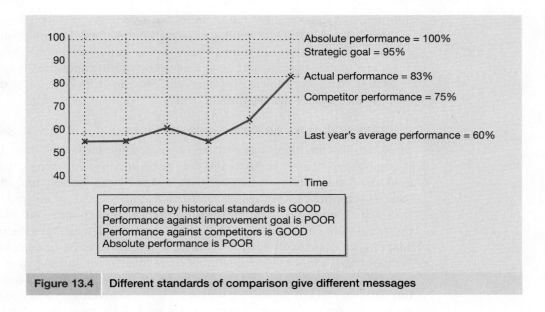

Figure 13.4   Different standards of comparison give different messages

absolute performance standard of 100 per cent delivery on time? Against this standard the company's actual 83 per cent again looks disappointing.

Benchmarking

Benchmarking is 'the process of learning from others' and involves comparing one's own performance or methods against other comparable operations. It is a broader issue than setting performance targets, and includes investigating other organizations' operations practice in order to derive ideas that could contribute to performance improvement. Its rationale is based on the ideas that (a) problems in managing processes are almost certainly shared by processes elsewhere, and (b) there is probably another operation somewhere that has developed a better way of doing things. For example, a bank might learn some things from a supermarket about how it could cope with demand fluctuations during the day. Benchmarking is essentially about stimulating creativity in improvement practice.

Operations principle
Improvement is aided by contextualizing processes and operations.

Types of benchmarking

There are many different types of benchmarking (which are not necessarily mutually exclusive), some of which are listed below:

- *Internal benchmarking* is a comparison between operations or parts of operations which are within the same total organization. For example, a large motor vehicle manufacturer with several factories might choose to benchmark each factory against the others.
- *External benchmarking* is a comparison between an operation and other operations which are part of a different organization.
- *Non-competitive benchmarking* is benchmarking against external organizations which do not compete directly in the same markets.
- *Competitive benchmarking* is a comparison directly between competitors in the same, or similar, markets.
- *Performance benchmarking* is a comparison between the levels of achieved performance in different operations. For example, an operation might compare its own performance

in terms of some or all of our performance objectives – quality, speed, dependability, flexibility and cost – against other organizations' performance in the same dimensions.

● *Practice benchmarking* is a comparison between an organization's operations practices, or ways of doing things, and those adopted by another operation. For example, a large retail store might compare its systems and procedures for controlling stock levels with those used by another department store.

Benchmarking as an improvement tool

Although benchmarking has become popular, some businesses have failed to derive maximum benefit from it. Partly this may be because there are some misunderstandings as to what benchmarking actually entails. First, it is not a 'one-off' project. It is best practised as a continuous process of comparison. Second, it does not provide 'solutions'. Rather, it provides ideas and information that can lead to solutions. Third, it does not involve simply copying or imitating other operations. It is a process of learning and adapting in a pragmatic manner. Fourth, it means devoting resources to the activity. Benchmarking cannot be done without some investment, but this does not necessarily mean allocating exclusive responsibility to a set of highly paid managers. In fact, there can be advantages in organizing staff at all levels to investigate and collate information from benchmarking targets. There are also some basic rules about how benchmarking can be organized.

● A prerequisite for benchmarking success is to understand thoroughly your own processes. Without this it is difficult to compare your processes against those of other companies.

● Look at the information that is available in the public domain. Published accounts, journals, conferences and professional associations can all provide information that is useful for benchmarking purposes.

● Do not discard information because it seems irrelevant. Small pieces of information only make sense in the context of other pieces of information that may emerge subsequently.

● Be sensitive in asking for information from other companies. Don't ask any questions that we would not like to be asked ourselves.

PRACTICE NOTE

Assess the gap between actual and target performance

A comparison of actual and target performance should guide the relative priorities for improvement. A significant aspect of performance is the relative importance of the various performance measures. Because some factor of performance is relatively poor does not mean that it should be improved immediately if current performance as a whole exceeds target performance. In fact, both the relative importance of the various performance measures, and their performance against target, need to be brought together in order to prioritize for improvement. One way of doing this is through the importance–performance matrix.

The importance–performance matrix

As its name implies, the importance–performance matrix positions each aspect of performance on a matrix according to its scores or ratings on how important each aspect of relative performance is, and what performance it is currently achieving. Figure 13.5 shows an importance–performance matrix divided into zones of improvement priority. The first zone boundary is the 'lower bound of acceptability' shown as line AB in Figure 13.5.

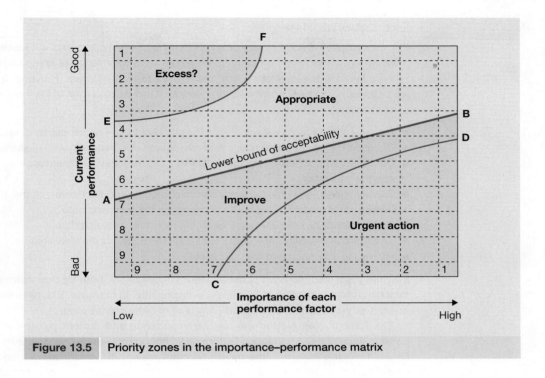

Figure 13.5   Priority zones in the importance–performance matrix

This is the boundary between acceptable and unacceptable current performance. When some aspect of performance is rated as relatively unimportant, this boundary will be low. Most operations are prepared to tolerate lower performance for relatively unimportant performance factors. However, for performance factors that are rated more important, they will be markedly less sanguine at poor or mediocre levels of current performance. Below this minimum bound of acceptability (AB) there is clearly a need for improvement; above this line there is no immediate urgency for any improvement. However, not all factors of performance that fall below the minimum line will be seen as having the same degree of improvement priority. A boundary approximately represented by line CD represents a distinction between an urgent priority zone and a less urgent improvement zone. Similarly, above the line AB, not all competitive factors are regarded as having the same priority. The line EF can be seen as the approximate boundary between performance levels which are regarded as 'good' or 'appropriate' on one hand and those regarded as 'too good' or 'excess' on the other. Segregating the matrix in this way results in four zones which imply very different priorities:

- The 'appropriate' zone. Performance factors in this area lie above the lower bound of acceptability and so should be considered satisfactory.
- The 'improve' zone. Lying below the lower bound of acceptability, any performance factors in this zone must be candidates for improvement.
- The 'urgent-action' zone. These performance factors are important to customers but current performance is unacceptable. They must be considered as candidates for immediate improvement.
- The 'excess?' zone. Performance factors in this area are 'high performing', but are not particularly important. The question must be asked, therefore, whether the resources devoted to achieving such a performance could be used better elsewhere.

PRACTICE NOTE

Example   ## EXL Laboratories

EXL Laboratories is a subsidiary of an electronics company. It carries out research and development as well as technical problem-solving work for a wide range of companies. It is particularly keen to improve the level of service that it gives to its customers. However, it needs to decide which aspect of its performance to improve first. It has devised a list of the most important aspects of its service:

- *The quality of its technical solutions* – the perceived appropriateness by customers.
- *The quality of its communications with customers* – the frequency and usefulness of information.
- *The quality of post-project documentation* – the usefulness of the documentation which goes with the final report.
- *Delivery speed* – the time between customer request and the delivery of the final report.
- *Delivery dependability* – the ability to deliver on the promised date.
- *Delivery flexibility* – the ability to deliver the report on a revised date.
- *Specification flexibility* – the ability to change the nature of the investigation.
- *Price* – the total charge to the customer.

EXL assigns a rating to each of these performance factors, both for their relative importance and for their current performance, as shown in Figure 13.6. In this case, EXL have used a 1 to 9 scale, where 1 is 'very important', or 'good'. Any type of scale can be used.

EXL Laboratories plotted the relative importance and current performance ratings it had given to each of its performance factors on an importance–performance matrix. This is shown in Figure 13.7. It shows that the most important aspect of performance – the ability to deliver sound technical solutions to its customers – falls comfortably within the 'appropriate' zone. Specification flexibility and delivery flexibility are also in the 'appropriate' zone, although only just. Both delivery speed and delivery dependability seem to be in need of improvement as each is below the minimum level of acceptability for their respective importance positions. However, two competitive factors, communications and cost/price, are clearly in need of immediate improvement. These two factors should therefore be assigned the most urgent priority for improvement. The matrix also indicates that the company's documentation could almost be regarded as 'too good'.

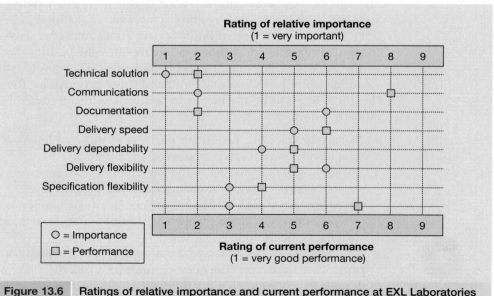

Figure 13.6   Ratings of relative importance and current performance at EXL Laboratories

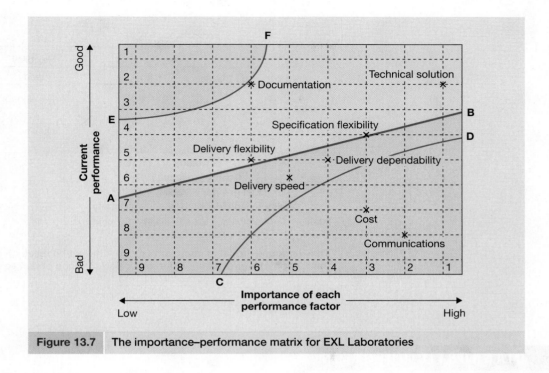

Figure 13.7   The importance–performance matrix for EXL Laboratories

The sandcone theory

As well as approaches that base improvement priority on an operation's specific circumstances, some authorities believe that there is also a generic 'best' sequence of improvement. The best-known theory is called *the sandcone theory*,[5] so called because the sand is analogous to management effort and resources. Building a stable sandcone needs a stable foundation of quality, upon which one can build layers of dependability, speed, flexibility and cost: see Figure 13.8. Building up improvement is thus a cumulative process, not a sequential one. Moving on to the second priority for improvement does not mean dropping the first, and so on. According to the sandcone theory, the first priority should be *quality*, since this is a precondition to all lasting improvement. Only when the operation has reached a minimally acceptable level of quality should it then tackle the next issue, that of internal *dependability*. Importantly, though, moving on to include dependability in the improvement process will actually require further improvement in quality. Once a critical level of dependability is reached, enough to provide some stability to the operation, the next stage is to improve the *speed* of internal throughput, but again only while continuing to improve quality and dependability further. Soon it will become evident that the most effective way to improve speed is through improvements in response *flexibility*, that is, changing things within the operation faster. Again, including flexibility in the improvement process should not divert attention from continuing to work further on quality, dependability and speed. Only now, according to the sandcone theory, should *cost* be tackled head on.

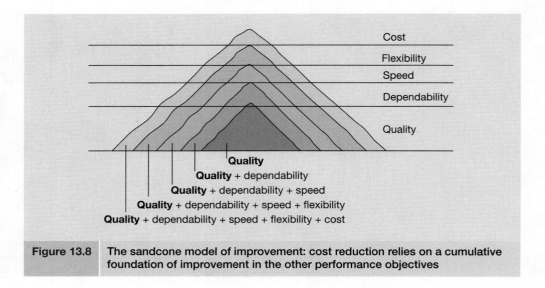

Figure 13.8   The sandcone model of improvement: cost reduction relies on a cumulative foundation of improvement in the other performance objectives

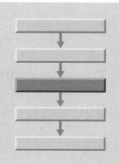

DIAGNOSTIC QUESTION

What is the most appropriate improvement path?

Once the priority of improvement has been determined, an operation must consider the approach or path it wishes to take to reaching its improvement goals. Two paths represent different, and to some extent opposing, philosophies – *breakthrough improvement* and *continuous improvement*. Although they represent different philosophies of improvement, they are not mutually exclusive. Few operations cannot benefit from improving their operations performance on a continuous basis, and few operations would reject investing in a major improvement breakthrough leap in performance if it represented good value. For most operations, both approaches are relevant to some extent, although possibly at different points in time. But to understand how and when each approach is appropriate one must understand their underlying philosophies.

> **Operations principle**
> Breakthrough and continuous improvement are not mutually exclusive.

Breakthrough improvement

Breakthrough (or 'innovation'-based) improvement assumes that the main vehicle of improvement is major and dramatic change in the way the operation works, for example the total reorganization of an operation's process structure, or the introduction of a fully integrated information system. The impact of these improvements represents a step change in practice (and hopefully performance). Such improvements can be expensive,

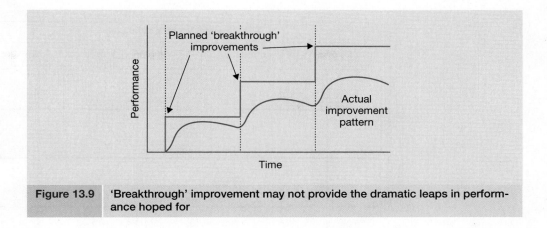

Figure 13.9 'Breakthrough' improvement may not provide the dramatic leaps in performance hoped for

often disrupting the ongoing workings of the operation, and frequently involving changes in the product/service or process technology. The red line in Figure 13.9 illustrates the intended pattern of performance with several breakthrough improvements. The improvement pattern illustrated by the blue line in Figure 13.9 is regarded by some as being more representative of what really occurs when operations rely on pure breakthrough improvement.

The business process re-engineering approach

Typical of the radical breakthrough way of tackling improvement is the business process re-engineering (BPR) approach. It is a blend of a number of ideas such as fast throughput, waste elimination through process flow charting, customer-focused operations, and so on. But it was the potential of information technologies to enable the fundamental redesign of processes that acted as the catalyst in bringing these ideas together. BPR has been defined as *'the fundamental rethinking and radical redesign of business processes to achieve dramatic improvements in critical, contemporary measures of performance, such as cost, quality, service and speed.'*[6]

Underlying the BPR approach is the belief that operations should be organized around the total process that adds value for customers, rather than the functions or activities that perform the various stages of the value-adding activity. (Figure 1.6 in Chapter 1 illustrated this idea.) The core of BPR is a redefinition of the processes within a total operation, to reflect the business processes that satisfy customer needs. Figure 13.10 illustrates this idea. The main principles of BPR have been summarized as follows:[7]

- Rethink business processes in a cross-functional manner that organizes work around the natural flow of information (or materials or customers). This means organizing around outcomes of a process rather than the tasks which go into it.
- Strive for dramatic improvements in the performance by radically rethinking and redesigning the process.
- Have those who use the output from a process perform the process. Check to see whether all internal customers can be their own supplier rather than depending on another function in the business to supply them (which takes longer and separates out the stages in the process).
- Put decision points where the work is performed. Do not separate those who do the work from those who control and manage the work. Control and action are just one more type of supplier–customer relationship that can be merged.

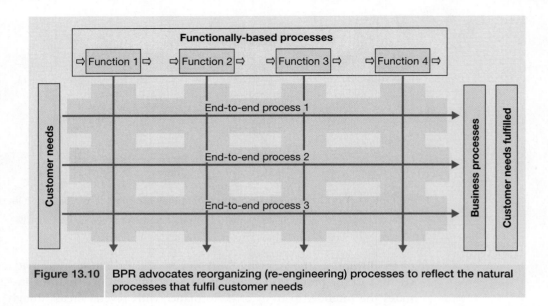

Figure 13.10 BPR advocates reorganizing (re-engineering) processes to reflect the natural processes that fulfil customer needs

Continuous improvement

Continuous improvement, as the name implies, adopts an approach to improving performance that assumes a never-ending series of small incremental improvement steps, for example modifying the way a product is fixed to a machine to reduce changeover time, or simplifying the question sequence when taking a hotel reservation. While there is no guarantee that such small steps towards better performance will be followed by other steps, the whole philosophy of continuous improvement attempts to ensure that they will be. It is also known as *kaizen,* defined by Masaaki Imai (who has been one of the main proponents of continuous improvement) as follows: *'Kaizen means improvement. Moreover, it means improvement in personal life, home life, social life and work life. When applied to the work place, kaizen means continuing improvement involving everyone – managers and workers alike.'*[8]

FURTHER EXAMPLE

Continuous improvement is not concerned with promoting small improvements *per se,* but it does see small improvements as having one significant advantage over large ones – they can be followed relatively painlessly by others. It is not the *rate* of improvement which is important; it is the *momentum* of improvement. It does not matter if successive improvements are small; what does matter is that every month (or week, or quarter, or whatever period is appropriate) some kind of improvement has actually taken place. Continuous improvement does not always come naturally. There are specific abilities, behaviours and actions which need to be consciously developed if continuous improvement is to be sustained over the long term. Bessant and Caffyn[9] distinguish between what they call 'organizational abilities' (the ability to adopt a particular approach to continuous improvement), 'constituent behaviours' (the behaviour that staff adopt) and 'enablers' (the techniques used to progress the continuous improvement effort). They identify six generic organizational abilities, each with its own set of constituent behaviours. These are identified in Table 13.2. Examples of enablers are the improvement techniques described later in this chapter.

Table 13.2 Continuous improvement (CI) abilities and some associated behaviours

Organizational ability	Constituent behaviours
Getting the CI habit Developing the ability to generate sustained involvement in CI	• People use formal problem-finding and solving cycle • People use simple tools and techniques • People use simple measurement to shape the improvement process • Individuals and/or groups initiate and carry through CI activities – they participate in the process • Ideas are responded to in a timely fashion – either implemented or otherwise dealt with • Managers support the CI process through allocation of resources • Managers recognize in formal ways the contribution of employees to CI • Managers lead by example, becoming actively involved in design and implementation of CI • Managers support experiment not by punishing mistakes, but instead by encouraging learning from them
Focusing on CI Generating and sustaining the ability to link CI activities to the strategic goals of the company	• Individuals and groups use the organization's strategic objectives to prioritize improvements • Everyone is able to explain what the operation's strategy and objectives are • Individuals and groups assess their proposed changes against the operation's objectives • Individuals and groups monitor/measure the results of their improvement activity • CI activities are an integral part of the individual's or group's work, not a parallel activity
Spreading the word Generating the ability to move CI activity across organizational boundaries	• People co-operate in cross-functional groups • People understand and share a holistic view (process understanding and ownership) • People are oriented towards internal and external customers in their CI activity • Specific CI projects with outside agencies (customers, suppliers, etc.) take place • Relevant CI activities involve representatives from different organizational levels
CI on the CI system Generating the ability to manage strategically the development of CI	• The CI system is continually monitored and developed • There is a cyclical planning process whereby the CI system is regularly reviewed and amended • There is periodic review of the CI system in relation to the organization as a whole • Senior management make available sufficient resources (time, money, personnel) to support the development of the CI system • The CI system itself is designed to fit within the current structure and infrastructure • When a major organizational change is planned, its potential impact on the CI system is assessed
Walking the talk Generating the ability to articulate and demonstrate CI's values	• The 'management style' reflects commitment to CI values • When something goes wrong, people at all levels look for reasons why, rather than blame individuals • People at all levels demonstrate a shared belief in the value of small steps and that everyone can contribute, by themselves being actively involved in making and recognizing incremental improvements

continued overleaf

444 Chapter I-13 · Improvement

<table>
<tr><td colspan="2">**Table 13.2**   Continuous improvement (CI) abilities and some associated behaviours (*continued*)</td></tr>
</table>

Organizational ability	Constituent behaviours
Building the learning organization Generating the ability to learn through CI activity	• Everyone learns from their experiences, both good and bad • Individuals seek out opportunities for learning/personal development • Individuals and groups at all levels share their learning • The organization captures and shares the learning of individuals and groups • Managers accept and act on all the learning that takes place • Organizational mechanisms are used to deploy what has been learned across the organization

Source: Bessant, J. and Caffyn, S. (1997) 'High involvement innovation', *International Journal of Technology Management*, Vol. 14, No. 1.

Improvement cycle models

An important element of continuous improvement is the idea that improvement can be represented by a never-ending process of repeatedly questioning and re-questioning the detailed working of a process. This is usually summarized by the idea of the *improvement cycle,* of which there are many, including some proprietary models owned by consultancy companies. Two of the more generally used models are the PDCA cycle (sometimes called the Deming Cycle, named after the famous quality 'guru', W.E. Deming), and the DMAIC cycle (made popular by the Six Sigma approach to improvement – see later).

> **Operations principle**
> Continuous improvement necessarily implies a never-ending cycle of analysis and action.

The PDCA cycle

The PDCA cycle model is shown in Figure 13.11(a). It starts with the P (for plan) stage, which involves an examination of the current method or the problem area being studied. This involves collecting and analyzing data so as to formulate a plan of action which is intended to improve performance. (Some of the techniques used to collect and analyze

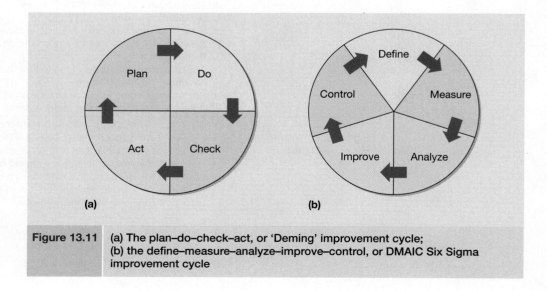

(a)   (b)

Figure 13.11   (a) The plan–do–check–act, or 'Deming' improvement cycle; (b) the define–measure–analyze–improve–control, or DMAIC Six Sigma improvement cycle

data are explained later.) The next step is the D (for do) stage. This is the implementation stage during which the plan is tried out in the operation. This stage may itself involve a mini-PDCA cycle as the problems of implementation are resolved. Next comes the C (for check) stage where the new implemented solution is evaluated to see whether it has resulted in the expected improvement. Finally, at least for this cycle, comes the A (for act) stage. During this stage the change is consolidated or standardized if it has been success-ful. Alternatively, if the change has not been successful, the lessons learned from the 'trial' are formalized before the cycle starts again.

The DMAIC cycle

In some ways this cycle is more intuitively obvious than the PDCA cycle in as much as it fol-lows a more 'experimental' approach. The DMAIC cycle starts with defining the problem or problems, partly to understand the scope of what needs to be done and partly to define exactly the requirements of the process improvement. Often at this stage a formal goal or target for the improvement is set. After definition comes the measurement stage, important because the Six Sigma approach emphasizes the importance of working with hard evidence rather than opinion. It involves validating the problem (to make sure it is really worth solving), using data to refine the problem and measuring exactly what is happening. The analysis stage can be seen as an opportunity to develop hypotheses as to what the root causes of the problem really are. Such hypotheses are validated (or not) by the analysis and the main root causes of the problem identified. Once the causes of the problem are identified, work can begin on improving the process. Ideas are developed to remove the root causes of problems, solutions are tested and those solutions that seem to work are implemented, for-malized and results measured. The improved process needs then to be continually moni-tored and controlled to check that the improved level of performance is sustaining. The then cycle starts again, defining the problems that are preventing further improvement.

The last point in both cycles is the most important – *'the cycle starts again'*. It is only by accepting that in a continuous improvement philosophy these cycles quite literally never stop that improvement becomes part of every person's job.

The differences between breakthrough and continuous improvement

Breakthrough improvement places a high value on creative solutions, and encourages free thinking and individualism. It is a radical philosophy in so much as it fosters an approach to improvement which does not accept many constraints on what is possible. 'Starting with a clean sheet of paper', 'going back to first principles' and 'completely rethinking the system' are all typical breakthrough improvement principles. Continuous improvement, on the other hand, is less ambitious, at least in the short term. It stresses adaptability, teamwork and attention to detail. It is not radical; rather it builds upon the wealth of accumulated experience within the operation itself, often relying primarily on the people who operate the system to improve it. One analogy used to explain this dif-ference is the sprint versus the marathon. Breakthrough improvement is a series of explosive and impressive sprints. Continuous improvement, like marathon running, does not require the expertise and prowess required for sprinting; but it does require that the runner (or operations manager) keeps on going. Yet notwithstanding these differences, it is possible to use both approaches. Large and dramatic improvements can be implemented as and when they seem to promise significant improvement steps, but between such occasions the operation can continue making its quiet and less spectacular 'kaizen' improvements. Table 13.3 lists some of the differences between the two approaches.

> **Operations principle**
> Breakthrough improvement necessarily implies radical and/or extensive change.

Table 13.3	Some features of breakthrough and continuous improvement	
	Breakthrough improvement	**Continuous improvement**
Effect	Short-term but dramatic	Long-term and long-lasting but undramatic
Pace	Big steps	Small steps
Time-frame	Intermittent and non-incremental	Continuous and incremental
Change	Abrupt and volatile	Gradual and constant
Involvement	Select a few 'champions'	Everybody
Approach	Individualism, individual ideas and efforts	Collectivism, group efforts, systems approach
Stimulus	Technological breakthroughs, new inventions, new theories	Conventional know-how and state of the art
Risks	Concentrated – 'all eggs in one basket'	Spread – many projects simultaneously
Practical requirements	Requires large investment but little effort to maintain	Requires little investment but great effort to maintain it
Effort orientations	Technology	People
Evaluation criteria	Results for profit	Process and effects for better results

Source: Based on Imai, M. (1986) *Kaizen – The Key to Japan's Competitive Success*, McGraw-Hill.

The Six Sigma approach to organizing improvement

One approach to improvement that combines breakthrough and continuous philosophies is *Six Sigma*. Although technically the 'Six Sigma' name derives from statistical process control (SPC), and more specifically the concept of process capability, it has now come to mean a much broader approach to improvement. The following definition gives a sense of its modern usage: *'Six Sigma is a comprehensive and flexible system for achieving, sustaining and maximizing business success. Six Sigma is uniquely driven by close understanding of customer needs, disciplined use of facts, data, and statistical analysis, and diligent attention to managing, improving, and reinventing business processes.'* [10]

The Six Sigma concept, therefore, includes many of the issues covered in this and other chapters of this book, for example process design and redesign, balanced scorecard measures, continuous improvement, statistical process control, ongoing process planning and control, and so on. However, at the heart of Six Sigma lies an understanding of the negative effects of variation in all types of business process. This aversion to variation was first popularized by Motorola, the electronics company, which set its objective as 'total customer satisfaction' in the 1980s, then decided that true customer satisfaction would only be achieved when its products were delivered when promised, with no defects, with no early-life failures and no excessive failure in service. To achieve this, they initially focused on removing manufacturing defects, but soon realized that many problems were caused by latent defects, hidden within the design of their products. The only way to eliminate these defects was to make sure that design specifications were tight (i.e. narrow tolerances) and their processes very capable.

FURTHER EXAMPLE

Motorola's Six Sigma quality concept was so named because it required that the natural variation of processes (±3 standard deviations) should be half their specification range. In other words, the specification range of any part of a product or service should be ±6 times the standard deviation of the process. The Greek letter sigma (σ) is often used to indicate the standard deviation of a process, hence the Six Sigma label. The Six Sigma approach also used the measure of 'defects per million *opportunities*' (DPMO). This is the number of defects that the process will produce if there were one million opportunities to do so. So difficult processes with many opportunities for defects can be compared with simple processes with few opportunities for defects.

The Six Sigma approach also holds that improvement initiatives can only be successful if significant resources and training are devoted to their management. It recommends a specially trained cadre of practitioners, many of whom should be dedicated full-time to improving processes as internal consultants. The terms that have become associated with this group of experts (and denote their level of expertise) are Master Black Belt, Black Belt and Green Belt.

- *Master Black Belts* are experts in the use of Six Sigma tools and techniques as well as how such techniques can be used and implemented. They are seen as teachers who can not only guide improvement projects, but also coach and mentor Black Belts and Green Belts. Given their responsibilities, it is expected that Master Black Belts are employed full-time on their improvement activities.
- *Black Belts* take a direct hand in organizing improvement teams, and will usually have undertaken a minimum of 20 to 25 days training and carried out at least one major improvement project. Black Belts are expected to develop their quantitative analytical skills and also act as coaches for Green Belts. Like Master Black Belts, they are dedicated full-time to improvement, and although opinions vary, some organizations recommend one Black Belt for every 100 employees.
- *Green Belts* work within improvement teams, possibly as team leaders. They have less training than Black Belts – typically around 10 to 15 days. Green Belts are not full-time positions. They have normal day-to-day process responsibilities but are expected to spend at least 20 per cent of their time on improvement projects.

Devoting such a large amount of training and time to improvement is a significant investment, especially for small companies. Nevertheless, Six Sigma proponents argue that the improvement activity is generally neglected in most operations and if it is to be taken seriously, it deserves the significant investment implied by the Six Sigma approach. Furthermore, they argue, if operated well, Six Sigma improvement projects run by experienced practitioners can save far more than their cost.

The Work-Out approach[11]

The idea of including all staff in the process of improvement existed before it was recognized as central to high-profile concepts such as total quality management (TQM) or continuous improvement (CI). It has also formed the core of more recent approaches. Perhaps the best known of these is the 'Work-Out' approach that originated (as far as it can be said to be original) in the US conglomerate GE. Jack Welch, the then boss of GE, reputedly developed the approach to recognize that employees were an important source of brainpower for new and creative ideas, and as a mechanism for 'creating an environment that pushes towards a relentless, endless companywide search for a better way to do everything we do'. The Work-Out programme was seen as a way to reduce the bureaucracy often associated with improvement and 'giving every employee, from managers to factory workers, an opportunity to influence and improve GE's day-to-day operations'.

According to Welch, Work-Out was meant to help people stop 'wrestling with the boundaries, the absurdities that grow in large organizations. We're all familiar with those absurdities: too many approvals, duplication, pomposity, waste. Work-Out in essence turned the company upside down, so that the workers told the bosses what to do. That forever changed the way people behaved at the company. Work-Out is also designed to reduce and ultimately eliminate all of the waste hours and energy that organizations like GE typically expend in performing day-to-day operations'. GE also used what it called 'town meetings' of employees (in fact, Work-Out is sometimes also referred to as 'town meetings'). And although Work-Out is as much of a philosophy and approach to improvement as it is a technique, and although its proponents emphasize the need to modify the specifics of the approach to fit the context in which it is applied, there is a broad sequence of activities implied within the approach.

- Staff, other key stakeholders and their manager hold a meeting away from the operation (a so-called 'off-siter').
- At this meeting the manager gives the group the responsibility to solve a problem or set of problems shared by the group but which are ultimately the manager's responsibility.
- The manager then leaves and the group spend time (maybe two or three days) working on developing solutions to the problems, sometimes using outside facilitators.
- At the end of the meeting, the responsible manager (and sometimes the manager's boss) rejoins the group to be presented with its recommendations.
- The manager can respond in three ways to each recommendation; 'yes', 'no', or 'I have to consider it more'. If it is the last response the manager must clarify what further issues must be considered and how and when the decision will be made.

Work-Out programmes are also expensive. Most organizations will need to use outside facilitators. Off-site facilities will also need to be hired and the payroll costs of a sizeable group of people meeting away from work can be substantial, even without considering the potential disruption to everyday activities. But arguably the most important implications of adopting Work-Out are cultural. In its purest form Work-Out as used by General Electric reinforces an underlying culture of fast (and, some would claim, superficial) problem solving. It also relies on full and near universal employee involvement and empowerment together with direct dialogue between managers and their subordinates. What distinguishes the Work-Out approach from the many other group-based problem-solving techniques are some of its underlying cultural values of fast decision making, the idea that managers own the problems and must respond immediately and decisively to team suggestions, and its relative intolerance of staff and managers who are not committed to its values. In fact, it is acknowledged in GE that resistance to the process or outcome is not tolerated and that obstructing the efforts of the Work-Out process is 'a career-limiting move'.

DIAGNOSTIC QUESTION

What techniques should be used to facilitate improvement?

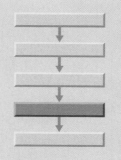

> **Operations principle**
> Improvement is facilitated by relatively simple analytical techniques.

All the techniques described in this book and its supplements can be regarded as 'improvement' techniques. However, some techniques are particularly useful for improving operations and processes generally. Here we select some techniques which either have not been described elsewhere or need to be reintroduced in their role of helping operations improvement particularly.

Scatter diagrams

Scatter diagrams provide a quick and simple method of identifying whether there is evidence of a connection between two sets of data: for example, the time at which you set off for work every morning and how long the journey to work takes. Plotting each journey on a graph with departure time on one axis and journey time on the other could give an indication of whether departure time and journey time are related, and if so, how. Scatter diagrams can be treated in a far more sophisticated manner by quantifying the strength of the relationship between the sets of data. But, however sophisticated the approach, this type of graph only identifies the existence of a relationship, not necessarily the existence of a cause–effect relationship. If the scatter diagram shows a very strong connection between the sets of data, it is important evidence of a cause–effect relationship, but not proof positive. It could be coincidence!

Example   ### Kaston Pyral Services Ltd (1)

Kaston Pyral Services Ltd (KPS) installs and maintains environmental control, heating and air conditioning systems. It has set up an improvement team to suggest ways in which it might improve its levels of customer service. The improvement team had completed its first customer satisfaction survey. The survey asked customers to score the service they received from KPS in several ways. For example, it asked customers to score services on a scale of 1 to 10 on promptness, friendliness, level of advice, etc. Scores were then summed to give a 'total satisfaction score' for each customer – the higher the score, the greater the satisfaction. The spread of satisfaction scores puzzled the team and they considered what factors might be causing such differences in the way their customers viewed them. Two factors were put forward to explain the differences.

1 The number of times in the past year the customer had received a preventive maintenance visit.
2 The number of times the customer had called for emergency service.

All this data was collected and plotted on scatter diagrams as shown in Figure 13.12. Figure 13.12(a) shows that there seems to be a clear relationship between a customer's satisfaction score and the number of times the customer was visited for regular servicing. The scatter diagram in Figure 13.12(b) is less clear. Although all customers who had very high satisfaction scores had made very few emergency calls, so had some customers with low satisfaction scores. As a result of this analysis, the team decided to survey customers' views on its emergency service.

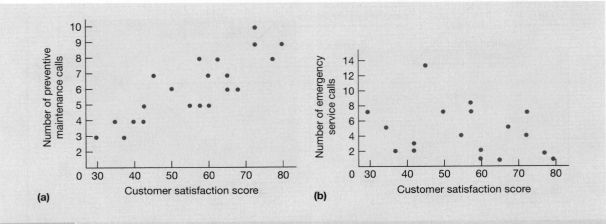

Figure 13.12   Scatter diagrams for customer satisfaction versus (a) number of preventive maintenance calls and (b) number of emergency service calls

Cause–effect diagrams

Cause–effect diagrams are a particularly effective method of helping to search for the root causes of problems. They do this by asking *what, when, where, how* and *why* questions, but also add some possible 'answers' in an explicit way. They can also be used to identify areas where further data is needed. Cause–effect diagrams (which are also known as Ishikawa diagrams) have become extensively used in improvement programmes. This is because they provide a way of structuring group brainstorming sessions. Often the structure involves identifying possible causes under the (rather old-fashioned) headings of machinery, manpower, materials, methods and money. Yet in practice, any categorization that comprehensively covers all relevant possible causes could be used.

FURTHER EXAMPLE

Example   ### Kaston Pyral Services Ltd (2)

The improvement team at KPS was working on a particular area which was proving a problem. Whenever service engineers were called out to perform emergency servicing for a customer, they took with them the spares and equipment which they thought would be necessary to repair the system. Although engineers could never be sure exactly what materials and equipment they would need for a job, they could guess what was likely to be needed and take a range of spares and equipment which would cover most eventualities. Too often, however, the engineers would find that they needed a spare that they had not brought with them. The cause–effect diagram for this particular problem, as drawn by the team, is shown in Figure 13.13.

PRACTICE NOTE

Pareto diagrams

In any improvement process, it is worth distinguishing what is important and what is less so. The purpose of the Pareto diagram (first introduced in Chapter 9) is to distinguish between the 'vital few' issues and the 'trivial many'. It is a relatively straightforward technique which involves arranging items of information on the types of problem or causes of problem into their order of importance (usually measured by 'frequency of occurrence'). This can be used to highlight areas where further decision making will be useful.

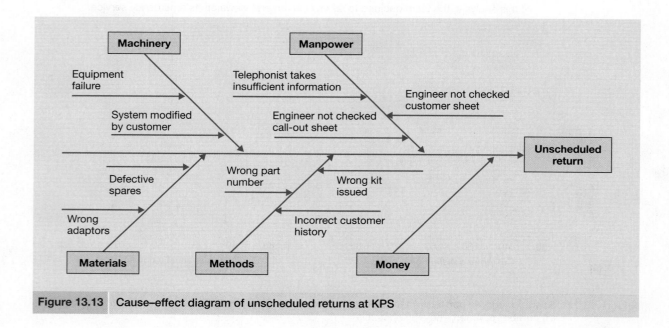

Figure 13.13   Cause–effect diagram of unscheduled returns at KPS

FURTHER EXAMPLE

Pareto analysis is based on the phenomenon of relatively few causes explaining the majority of effects. For example, most revenue for any company is likely to come from relatively few of the company's customers. Similarly, relatively few of a doctor's patients will probably occupy most of his or her time.

Example

Kaston Pyral Services Ltd (3)

The KPS improvement team which was investigating unscheduled returns from emergency servicing (the issue which was described in the cause–effect diagram in Figure 13.13) examined all occasions over the previous 12 months on which an unscheduled return had been made. They categorized the reasons for unscheduled returns as follows:

1 The wrong part had been taken to a job because, although the information which the engineer received was sound, he or she had incorrectly predicted the nature of the fault.
2 The wrong part had been taken to the job because there was insufficient information given when the call was taken.
3 The wrong part had been taken to the job because the system had been modified in some way not recorded on KPS's records.
4 The wrong part had been taken to the job because the part had been incorrectly issued to the engineer by stores.
5 No part had been taken because the relevant part was out of stock.
6 The wrong equipment had been taken for whatever reason.
7 Any other reason.

The relative frequency of occurrence of these causes is shown in Figure 13.14. About a third of all unscheduled returns were due to the first category, and more than half the returns were accounted for by the first and second categories together. It was decided that the problem could best be tackled by concentrating on how to get more information to the engineers which would enable them to predict the causes of failure accurately.

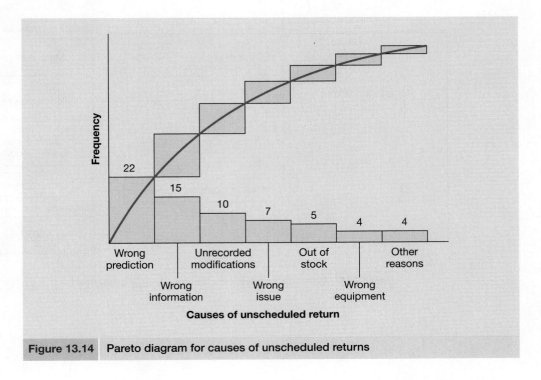

Figure 13.14 Pareto diagram for causes of unscheduled returns

Why–why analysis

Why–why analysis starts by stating the problem and asking *why* that problem has occurred. Once the major reasons for the problem occurring have been identified, each of the major reasons is taken in turn and again the question is asked *why* those reasons have occurred, and so on. This procedure is continued until either a cause seems sufficiently self-contained to be addressed by itself or no more answers to the question 'Why?' can be generated.

Example

Kaston Pyral Services Ltd (4)

The major cause of unscheduled returns at KPS was the incorrect prediction of reasons for the customer's system failure. This is stated as the 'problem' in the why–why analysis in Figure 13.15. The question is then asked, why was the failure wrongly predicted? Three answers are proposed: first, that the engineers were not trained correctly; second, that they had insufficient knowledge of the particular product installed in the customer's location; and third, that they had insufficient knowledge of the customer's particular system with its modifications. Each of these three reasons is taken in turn, and the questions are asked, why is there a lack of training, why is there a lack of product knowledge, why is there a lack of customer knowledge? And so on.

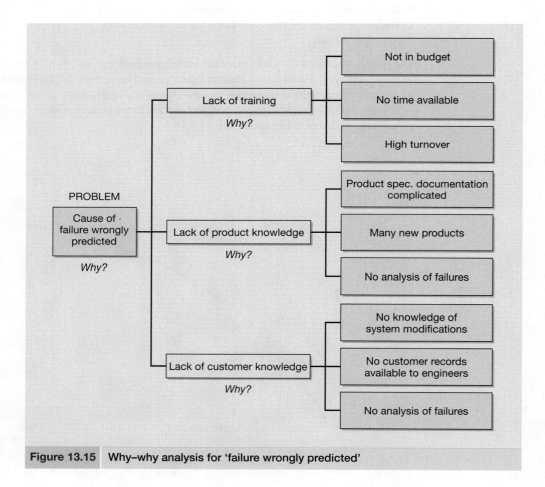

Figure 13.15   Why–why analysis for 'failure wrongly predicted'

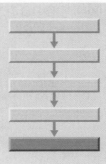

How can improvement be made to stick?

Not all of the improvement initiatives (often launched with high expectations) will go on to fulfil their potential. Even those improvement initiatives that are successfully implemented may lose impetus over time. Sometimes this is because of managers' view of the nature of improvement; at other times it is because managers fail to manage the improvement process adequately.

Avoid becoming a victim of improvement 'fashion'

Improvement has, to some extent, become a fashion industry with new ideas and concepts continually being introduced as offering a novel way to improve business performance. There is nothing intrinsically wrong with this. Fashion stimulates and refreshes through introducing novel ideas. Without it, things would stagnate. The problem lies not with new improvement ideas, but rather with some managers becoming a victim of the process, where some new idea will entirely displace whatever went before. Most new ideas have something to say, but jumping from one fad to another will not only generate a backlash against any new idea, but also destroy the ability to accumulate the experience that comes from experimenting with each one.

> **Operations principle**
> The popularity of an improvement approach is not necessarily an indicator of its effectiveness.

Avoiding becoming an improvement fashion victim is not easy. It requires that those directing the improvement process take responsibility for a number of issues.

- They must take responsibility for improvement as an ongoing activity, rather than becoming champions for only one specific improvement initiative.
- They must take responsibility for understanding the underlying ideas behind each new concept. Improvement is not 'following a recipe' or 'painting by numbers'. Unless one understands *why* improvement ideas are supposed to work, it is difficult to understand *how* they can be made to work properly.
- They must take responsibility for understanding the antecedents to a 'new' improvement idea, because it helps to understand it better and to judge how appropriate it may be for one's own operation.
- They must be prepared to adapt new ideas so that they make sense within the context of their own operation. 'One size' rarely fits all.
- They must take responsibility for the (often significant) education and learning effort that will be needed if new ideas are to be intelligently exploited.
- Above all they must avoid the over-exaggeration and hype that many new ideas attract. Although it is sometimes tempting to exploit the motivational 'pull' of new ideas through slogans, posters and exhortations, carefully thought-out plans will always be superior in the long run, and will help avoid the inevitable backlash that follows 'over-selling' a single approach.

Managing the improvement process

There is no absolute prescription for the way improvement should be managed. Any improvement process should reflect the uniqueness of each operation's characteristics.

> **Operations principle**
> There is no one universal approach to improvement.

What appears to be almost a guarantee of difficulty in managing improvement processes are attempts to squeeze improvement into a standard mould. Nevertheless, there are some aspects of any improvement process that appear to influence its eventual success, and should at least be debated.

Should an improvement *strategy* be defined?

Without thinking through the overall purpose and long-term goals of the improvement process, it is difficult for any operation to know where it is going. Specifically, an improvement strategy should have something to say about the following.

- The competitive priorities of the organization, and how the improvement process is expected to contribute to achieving increased strategic impact
- The roles and responsibilities of the various parts of the organization in the improvement process
- The resources which will be available for the improvement process
- The general approach to, and philosophy of, improvement in the organization.

Yet, too rigid a strategy can become inappropriate if the business's competitive circumstances change, or as the operation learns through experience. But, the careful modification of improvement strategy in the light of experience is not the same as making dramatic changes in improvement strategy as new improvement fashions appear.

What degree of top-management support is required?

For most authorities, the answer is unambiguous – a significant amount. Without top management support, improvement cannot succeed. It is the most crucial factor in almost all the studies of improvement process implementation. It also goes far beyond merely allocating senior resources to the process. Top-management support usually means that senior personnel must:

- understand and believe in the link between improvement and the business's overall strategy
- understand the practicalities of the improvement process and be able to communicate its principles and techniques to the rest of the organization
- be able to participate in the total problem-solving process to improve performance
- formulate and maintain a clear idea of the operation's improvement philosophy.

Should the improvement process be formally supervised?

Some improvement processes fail because they develop an unwieldy 'bureaucracy' to run them. But any process needs to be managed, so all improvement processes will need some kind of group to design, plan and control its efforts. However, a worthwhile goal for many improvement processes is to make themselves 'self-governing' over time. In fact there are significant advantages in terms of people's commitment in giving them responsibility for managing the improvement process. However, even when improvement is driven primarily by self-managing improvement groups, there is a need for some sort of 'repository of knowledge' to ensure that the learning and experience accumulated from the improvement process is not lost.

To what extent should improvement be group-based?

No one can really know a process quite like the people who operate it. They have access to the informal as well as the formal information networks that contain the way processes really work. But, working alone, individuals cannot pool their experience or learn from one another. So improvement processes are almost always based on teams. The issue is how these teams should be formulated, which will depend on the circumstances of the operation, its context and its objectives. For example, *quality circles,* much used in Japan, encountered mixed success in the West. A very different type of team is the '*task force*', or what some US companies call a 'tiger team'. Compared with quality circles, this type of group is far more management directed and focused. Most improvement teams are between these two extremes (see Figure 13.16).

How should success be recognized?

If improvement is so important, it should be recognized, with success, effort and initiative being formally rewarded. The paradox is that, if improvement is to become part of everyday operational life, then why should improvement effort be especially rewarded? One compromise is to devise a recognition and rewards system that responds to improvement initiatives early in the improvement process, but then merges into the operation's normal reward procedures. In this way people are rewarded not just for the efficient and effective running of their processes on an ongoing basis, but also for improving their processes. Then improvement will become an everyday responsibility of all people in the operation.

How much training is required?

Training has two purposes in the development of improvement processes. The first is to provide the necessary skills that will allow staff to solve process problems and implement improvements. The second is to provide an understanding of the appropriate

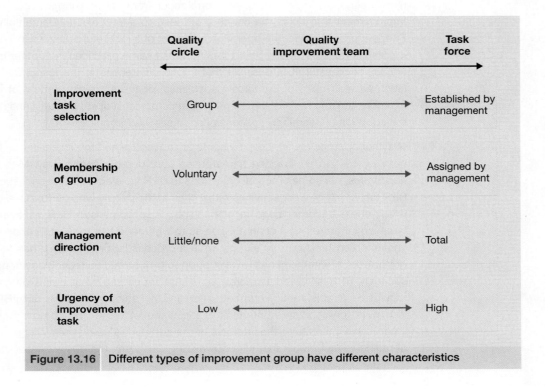

Figure 13.16 Different types of improvement group have different characteristics

interpersonal, group and organizational skills that are needed to 'lubricate' the improvement process. This second objective is more difficult than the first. Training and improvement techniques may take up significant time and effort, but none of this knowledge will be of much use if the organizational context for improvement mitigates against the techniques being used effectively. Although the nature of appropriate organizational development is beyond the scope of this book, it is worth noting that both technique-based skills and organizational skills are enhanced if staff have a basic understanding of the core ideas and principles of operations and process management.

Critical commentary

Each chapter contains a short critical commentary on the main ideas covered in the chapter. Its purpose is not to undermine the issues discussed in the chapter, but to emphasize that, although we present a relatively orthodox view of operation, there are other perspectives.

■ Many of the issues covered in this chapter are controversial, for different reasons. Some criticism concerns the effectiveness of improvement methods. For example, it can be argued that there is a fundamental flaw in the concept of benchmarking. Operations that rely on others to stimulate their creativity, especially those that are in search of 'best practice', are always limiting themselves to currently accepted methods of operating or currently accepted limits to performance. 'Best practice' is not 'best' in the sense that it cannot be bettered; it is only 'best' in the sense that it is the best one can currently find. And accepting what is currently defined as 'best' may prevent operations from ever making the radical breakthrough or improvement that takes the concept of 'best' to a new and fundamentally improved level. Furthermore, because one operation has a set of successful practices in the way it manages it process does not mean that adopting those same practices in another context will prove equally successful. It is possible that subtle differences in the resources within a process (such as staff skills or technical capabilities) or the strategic context of an operation (for example, the relative priorities of performance objectives) will be sufficiently different to make the adoption of seemingly successful practices inappropriate.

■ Other approaches are seen by some as too radical and too insensitive. For example, business process re-engineering has aroused considerable controversy. Most of its critics are academics, but some practical objections to BPR have also been raised, such as the fear that BPR looks only at work activities rather than at the people who perform the work. Because of this, people become 'cogs in a machine'. Also some see BPR as being too imprecise because its proponents cannot agree as to whether it has to be radical or whether it can be implemented gradually, or exactly what a process is, or whether it has to be top-down or bottom-up, or whether it has to be supported by information technology or not. Perhaps most seriously, BPR is viewed as merely an excuse for getting rid of staff. Companies that wish to 'downsize' (that is, reduce numbers of staff within an operation) are using BPR as an excuse. This puts the short-term interests of the shareholders of the company above either their longer-term interests or the interests of the company's employees. Moreover, a combination of radical redesign together with downsizing can mean that the essential core of experience is lost from the operation. This leaves it vulnerable to any marked turbulence since it no longer has the knowledge and experience of how to cope with unexpected changes.

■ Even the more gentle approach of continuous improvement is not universally welcomed. Notwithstanding its implications of empowerment and liberal attitude towards shop-floor staff, it is regarded by some worker representatives as merely a further example of management exploiting workers. Relatively established ideas such as TQM have been defined by its critics as 'management by stress'. Or, even more radically, 'TQM is like putting a vacuum cleaner next to a worker's brain and sucking out ideas. They don't want to rent your knowledge anymore, they want to own it – in the end that makes you totally replaceable.'

Summary checklist

This checklist comprises questions that can be usefully applied to any type of operations and reflect the major diagnostic questions used within the chapter.

☐ Is the importance of performance improvement fully recognized within the operation?

☐ Do all operations and process managers see performance improvement as an integral part of their job?

☐ Is the gap between current and desired performance clearly articulated in all areas?

☐ Is the current performance measurement system seen as forming a basis for improvement?

☐ Does performance measurement focus on factors that reflect the operation's strategic objectives?

☐ Do performance measures allow likely problem areas to be diagnosed?

☐ Is some kind of balanced scorecard approach used that includes financial, internal, customer and learning perspectives?

☐ Is target performance set using an appropriate balance between historical, strategic, external and absolute performance targets?

☐ Are both performance and process methods benchmarked against similar operations and/or processes externally?

☐ Is benchmarking done on a regular basis and seen as an important contribution to improvement?

☐ Is some formal method of comparing actual and desired performance (such as the importance–performance matrix) used?

☐ To what extent does the operation have a predisposition towards breakthrough or continuous improvement?

☐ Have breakthrough improvement approaches such as business process re-engineering been evaluated?

☐ Are continuous improvement methods and problem-solving cycles used within the operation?

☐ If they are, has continuous improvement become a part of everyone's job?

☐ Which 'abilities' and 'associated behaviours' (see Table 13.2) are evident within the operation?

☐ Has the Six Sigma approach to improvement been evaluated?

☐ Are the more common improvement techniques used to facilitate improvement within the operations?

☐ Does the operation show any signs of becoming a fashion victim of the latest improvement approach?

☐ Does the operation have a well thought-through approach to managing improvement?

Case study | Geneva Construction and Risk (GCR)

'This is not going to be like last time. Then, we were adopting an improvement programme because we were told to. This time it's our idea and, if it's successful, it will be us that are telling the rest of the group how to do it.' (Tyko Mattson, Six Sigma Champion, GCR)

Tyko Mattson was speaking as the newly appointed 'Champion' at Geneva Construction and Risk Insurance. He had been charged with 'steering the Six Sigma programme until it is firmly established as part of our ongoing practice'. The previous improvement initiative that he was referring to dated back many years to when GCR's parent company, Wichita Mutual Insurance, had insisted on the adoption of total quality management (TQM) in all its businesses. The TQM initiative had never been pronounced a failure and had managed to make some improvements, especially in customers' perception of the company's levels of service. However, the initiative had 'faded out' during the 1990s and, even though all departments still had to formally report on their improvement projects, their number and impact was now relatively minor.

History

The Geneva Construction Insurance Company was founded in 1922 to provide insurance for building contractors and construction companies, initially in German-speaking Europe and then, because of the emigration of some family members to the USA, in North America. The company had remained relatively small and had specialized in housing construction projects until the early 1950s when it had started to grow, partly because of geographical expansion and partly because it moved into larger (sometimes very large) construction insurance in the industrial, oil, petrochemical and power plant construction areas. In 1983 it had been bought by the Wichita Mutual Group and had absorbed the group's existing construction insurance businesses.

By 2000 it had established itself as one of the leading providers of insurance for construction projects, especially complex, high-risk projects, where contractual and other legal issues, physical exposure and design uncertainty needed 'customized' insurance responses. Providing such insurance needed particular knowledge and skills from specialists including construction underwriters, loss adjusters, engineers, international lawyers and specialist risk consultants. Typically, the company would insure losses resulting

Source: Digital Vision/Getty Images

from contractor failure, related public liability issues, delays in project completion, associated litigation, other litigation (such as ongoing asbestos risks) and negligence issues.

The company's headquarters were in Geneva and housed all major departments including sales and marketing, underwriting, risk analysis, claims and settlement, financial control, general administration, specialist and general legal advice, and business research. There were also 37 local offices around the world, organized into four regional areas: North America, South America, Europe Middle East and Africa, and Asia. These regional offices provided localized help and advice directly to clients and also to the 890 agents that GCR used worldwide.

The previous improvement initiative

When Wichita Mutual had insisted that GCR adopt a TQM initiative, it had gone as far as to specify exactly how it should do it and which consultants should be used to help establish the programme. Tyko Mattson shakes his head as he describes it. *'I was not with the company at that time but, looking back, it's amazing that it ever managed to do any good. You can't impose the structure of an improvement initiative from the top. It has to, at least partially, be shaped by the people who are going to be involved in it. But everything had to be done according to the handbook. The* cost of quality was measured for different departments according to the handbook. Everyone had to learn the improvement techniques that were described in the handbook. Everyone had to be part of a quality circle that was organized according to the handbook. We even had to have annual award ceremonies where we gave out special "certificates of merit" to those quality circles that had achieved the type of improvement that the handbook said they should.' The TQM initiative had been run by the 'Quality Committee', a group of eight people with representatives from all the major departments at head office. Initially, it had spent much of its time setting up the improvement groups and organizing training in quality techniques. However, soon it had become swamped by the work needed to evaluate which improvement suggestions should be implemented. Soon the workload associated with assessing improvement ideas had become so great that the company decided to allocate small improvement budgets to each department on a quarterly basis that they could spend without reference to the quality committee. Projects requiring larger investment or that had a significant impact on other parts of the business still needed to be approved by the committee before they were implemented.

Department improvement budgets were still used within the business and improvement plans were still required from each department on an annual basis. However, the quality committee had stopped meeting by 1994 and the annual award ceremony had become a general communications meeting for all staff at the headquarters. 'Looking back,' said Tyko, 'the TQM initiative faded away for three reasons. First, people just got tired of it. It was always seen as something extra rather than part of normal business life, so it was always seen as taking time away from doing your normal job. Second, many of the supervisory and middle management levels never really bought into it, I guess because they felt threatened. Third, only a very few of the local offices around the world ever adopted the TQM philosophy. Sometimes this was because they did not want the extra effort. Sometimes, however, they would argue that improvement initiatives of this type may be OK for head office processes, but not for the more dynamic world of supporting clients in the field.'

The Six Sigma initiative

Early in 2005 Tyko Mattson, who for the last two years had been overseeing the outsourcing of some of GCR's claims processing to India, had attended a conference on 'Operations Excellence in Financial Services', and had heard several speakers detail the success they had achieved through using a Six Sigma approach to operations improvement. He had persuaded his immediate boss, Marie-Dominique Tomas, the head of claims for the company, to allow him to investigate its applicability to GCR. He had interviewed a number of other financial services that had implemented Six Sigma as well as a number of consultants, and in September 2005 had submitted a report entitled 'What is Six Sigma and how might it be applied in GCR?'. Extracts from this are included in the Appendix. Marie-Dominique Tomas was particularly concerned that they should avoid the mistakes of the TQM initiative. 'Looking back, it is almost embarrassing to see how naive we were. We really did think that it would change the whole way that we did business. And although it did produce some benefits, it absorbed a large amount of time at all levels in the organization. This time we want something that will deliver results without costing too much or distracting us from focusing on business performance. That is why I like Six Sigma. It starts with clarifying business objectives and works from there.'

By late 2005 Tyko's report had been approved both by GCR and by Wichita Mutual's main board. Tyko had been given the challenge of carrying out the recommendations in his report, reporting directly to GCR's executive board. Marie-Dominique Tomas was cautiously optimistic: 'It is quite a challenge for Tyko. Most of us on the executive board remember the TQM initiative and some are still sceptical concerning the value of such initiatives. However, Tyko's gradualist approach and his emphasis on the "three pronged" attack on revenue, costs and risk, impressed the board. We now have to see whether he can make it work.'

Appendix – Extract from *What is Six Sigma and how might it be applied in GCR?'*

Some pitfalls of Six Sigma

Six Sigma is not simple to implement, and is resource hungry. The focus on measurement implies that the process data is available and reasonably robust. If this is not the case it is possible to waste a lot of effort in obtaining process performance data. It may also over-complicate things if advanced techniques are used on simple problems.

It is easier to apply Six Sigma to repetitive processes – characterized by high volume, low variety and low visibility to customers. It is more difficult to apply it to low volume, higher variety and high visibility processes where standardization is harder to achieve and the focus is on managing the variety.

Six Sigma is not a 'quick fix'. Companies that have implemented Six Sigma effectively have not treated it as just another new initiative but as an approach that requires the long-term systematic reduction of waste. Equally, it is not a panacea and should not be implemented as one.

Some benefits of Six Sigma

Companies have achieved significant benefits in reducing cost and improving customer service through implementing Six Sigma.

Six Sigma can reduce process variation, which will have a significant impact on operational risk. It is a tried and tested methodology, which combines the strongest parts of existing improvement methodologies. It lends itself to being customized to fit individual company's circumstances. For example, Mestech Assurance has extended their Six Sigma initiative to examine operational risk processes.

Six Sigma could leverage a number of current initiatives. The risk self-assessment methodology, Sarbanes Oxley, the process library, and our performance metrics work are all laying the foundations for better knowledge and measurement of process data.

Six Sigma – key conclusions for GCR

Six Sigma is a powerful improvement methodology. It is not all new but what it does do successfully is to combine some of the best parts of existing improvement methodologies, tools and techniques. Six Sigma has helped many companies achieve significant benefits. It could help GCR significantly improve risk management because it focuses on driving errors and exceptions out of processes.

Six Sigma has significant advantages over other process improvement methodologies. It engages senior management actively by establishing process ownership and linkage to strategic objectives. This is seen as integral to successful implementation in the literature and by all companies interviewed who had implemented it. It forces a rigorous approach to driving out variance in processes by analyzing the root cause of defects and errors and measuring improvement. It is an 'umbrella' approach, combining all the best parts of other improvement approaches.

Implementing Six Sigma across GCR is not the right approach

Companies that are widely quoted as having achieved the most significant headline benefits from Six Sigma were already relatively mature in terms of process management. Those companies that understood their process capability typically had achieved a degree of process standardization and had an established process improvement culture.

Six Sigma requires significant investment in performance metrics and process knowledge. GCR is probably not yet sufficiently advanced. However, we are working towards a position where key process data are measured and known and this will provide a foundation for Six Sigma.

Why is a targeted implementation recommended?

Full implementation is resource hungry. Dedicated resource and budget for implementation of improvements is required. Even if the approach is modified, resource and budget will still be needed, just to a lesser extent. However, the evidence is that the investment is well worth it and pays back relatively quickly.

There was strong evidence from companies interviewed that the best implementation approach was to pilot Six Sigma, and select failing processes for the pilot. In addition, previous internal piloting of implementations has been successful in GCR – we know this approach works within our culture.

Six Sigma would provide a platform for GCR to build on and evolve over time. It is a way of leveraging the ongoing work on processes, and the risk methodology (being developed by the Operational Risk Group). This diagnostic tool could be blended into Six Sigma, giving GCR a powerful model to drive reduction in process variation and improved operational risk management.

Recommendations

It is recommended that GCR management implement a Six Sigma pilot. The characteristics of the pilot would be as follows:

- A tailored approach to Six Sigma that would fit GCR's objectives and operating environment. Implementing Six Sigma in its entirety would not be appropriate.
- The use of an external partner: GCR does not have sufficient internal Six Sigma expertise, and external experience will be critical to tailoring the approach, and providing training.
- Establishing where GCR's sigma performance is now. Different tools and approaches will be required to advance from 2 to 3 Sigma than those required to move from 3 to 4 Sigma.
- Quantifying the potential benefits. Is the investment worth making? What would a 1 Sigma increase in performance vs. risk be worth to us?
- Keeping the methods simple, if simple will achieve our objectives. As a minimum for us that means Team Based Problem Solving and basic statistical techniques.

Next steps

1 Decide priority and confirm budget and resourcing for initial analysis to develop a Six Sigma risk improvement programme in 2006.

2 Select an external partner experienced in improvement and Six Sigma methodologies.

3 Assess GCR current state to confirm where to start in implementing Six Sigma.

4 Establish how much GCR is prepared to invest in Six Sigma and quantify the potential benefits.

5 Tailor Six Sigma to focus on risk management.

6 Identify potential pilot area(s) and criteria for assessing its suitability.

7 Develop a Six Sigma pilot plan.

8 Conduct and review the pilot programme.

QUESTIONS

1 How does the Six Sigma approach seem to differ from the TQM approach adopted by the company almost 20 years ago?

2 Is Six Sigma a better approach for this type of company?

3 Do you think Tyko can avoid the Six Sigma initiative suffering the same fate as the TQM initiative?

Active case study · Ferndale Sands Conference Centre

ACTIVE CASE

Ferndale Sands Conference Centre is a conference venue of 52 rooms in Victoria State, Australia. They pride themselves on offering supreme quality and service; the *'executive retreat'*. Mario Romano, the owner and General Manager, is furious and alarmed to read a review which threatens their excellent reputation. An urgent meeting is called to address the negative publicity.

● How would you assess the performance of the hotel within different aspects of its business and what path of improvement would you recommend?

Please refer to the Active case on the CD accompanying this book to listen to the views of different staff working for Mario.

Applying the principles

HINTS

Some of these exercises can be answered by reading the chapter. Others will require some general knowledge of business activity and some might require an element of investigation. All have hints on how they can be answered on the CD accompanying this book.

1 Visit a library (for example, a university library) and consider how it could start a performance measurement programme which would enable it to judge the effectiveness with which it organizes its operations. Probably the library lends books on both long-term and short-term loans, keeps an extensive stock of journals, will send off for specialist publications to specialist libraries, and has an extensive online database facility.

● What measures of performance do you think it would be appropriate to use in this kind of operation and what type of performance standards should the library adopt?

2 (a) Devise a benchmarking programme that will benefit the course or programme that you are currently taking (if appropriate). In doing so, decide whether you are going to benchmark against other courses at the same institution, competitor courses at other institutions, or some other point of comparison. Also decide whether you are more interested in the performance of these other courses or the way they organize their processes, or both.

(b) Identify the institutions and courses against which you are going to benchmark your own course.

(c) Collect data on these other courses (visit them, send off for literature, or visit their Internet site).

(d) Compare your own course against these others and draw up a list of implications for the way your course could be improved.

3 Think back to the last product or service failure that caused you some degree of inconvenience. Draw a cause–effect diagram that identifies all the main causes of why the failure could have occurred. Try to identify the frequency with which such causes happen. This could be done by talking with the staff of the operation that provided the service. Draw a Pareto diagram that indicates the relative frequency of each cause of failure. Suggest ways in which the operation could reduce the chances of failure.

4 (a) If you are working in a group, identify a 'high visibility' operation that you all are familiar with. This could be a type of quick-service restaurant, record stores, public transport systems, libraries, etc.

(b) Once you have identified the broad class of operation, visit a number of them and use your experience as customers to identify the main performance factors that are of importance to you as customers, and how each store rates against the others in terms of their performance on these same factors.

(c) Draw an importance–performance diagram for one of the operations that indicates the priority they should be giving to improving their performance.

(d) Discuss the ways in which such an operation might improve its performance and try to discuss your findings with the staff of the operation.

Notes on chapter

1 Source: Discussion with staff at Xchanging, Particular thanks to Clive Buesnel and Paul Ruggier.

2 Source: the EFQM website (www.efqm.org).

3 See Kaplan, R.S. and Norton, D.P. (1996) *The Balanced Scorecard,* Harvard Business School Press, Boston, MA.

4 Kaplan and Norton, *op. cit.*

5 Ferdows, K. and de Meyer, A. (1990) 'Lasting improvement in manufacturing', *Journal of Operations Management,* Vol. 9, No. 2. However, research for this model is mixed. For example, Patricia Nemetz questions the validity of the model, finding more support for the idea that the sequence of improvement is generally dictated by technological (operations resource) or market (requirements) pressures: Nemetz, P. (2002) 'A longitudinal study of strategic choice, multiple advantage, cumulative model and order winner/qualifier view of manufacturing strategy', *Journal of Business and Management,* January.

6 Hammer, M. and Champy, J. (1993) *Re-engineering the Corporation,* Nicholas Brealey Publishing.

7 Hammer, M. (1990) 'Re-engineering work: don't automate, obliterate', *Harvard Business Review,* Vol. 68, No. 4.

8 Imai, M. (1986) *Kaizen – The Key to Japan's Competitive Success,* McGraw-Hill.

9 Bessant, J. and Caffyn, S. (1997) 'High involvement innovation', *International Journal of Technology Management,* Vol. 14, No. 1.

10 Pande, P.S., Neuman, R.P. and Cavanagh, R.R. (2000) *The Six Sigma Way,* McGraw-Hill, New York.

11 For further details of this approach see Schaninger, W.S., Harris, S.G. and Niebuhr, R.L. (2000) 'Adapting General Electric's Workout for use in other organizations: a template', www.isixsigma.com; Quinn, J. (1994) 'What a workout!', *Sales & Marketing Management, Performance Supplement*, November, pp. 58–63; Stewart, T. (1991) 'GE keeps those ideas coming,' *Fortune,* Vol. 124, No. 4, pp. 40–5.

Taking it further

Chang, R.Y. (1995) *Continuous Process Improvement: A practical guide to improving processes for measurable results,* Kogan Page.

Leibfried, K.H.J. and McNair, C.J. (1992) *Benchmarking: A tool for continuous improvement,* HarperCollins. There are many books on benchmarking; this is a comprehensive and practical guide to the subject.

Pande, P.S., Neuman, R.P. and Cavanagh, R. (2002) *Six Sigma Way Team Field Book: An implementation guide for project improvement teams,* McGraw-Hill. Obviously based on the Six Sigma principle and related to the book by the same author team recommended in Chapter 12, this is an unashamedly practical guide to the Six Sigma approach.

Useful websites

www.processimprovement.com Commercial site but some content that could be useful.

www.kaizen-institute.com Professional institute for *kaizen.* Gives some insight into practitioner views.

www.imeche.org.uk/mx/index.asp The Manufacturing Excellence Awards site. Dedicated to rewarding excellence and best practice in UK manufacturing. Obviously manufacturing biased, but some good examples.

www.ebenchmarking.com Benchmarking information.

www.quality.nist.gov American Quality Assurance Institute. Well-established institution for all types of business quality assurance.

www.balancedscorecard.org Site of an American organization with plenty of useful links.

**FURTHER
RESOURCES**

For further resources including examples, animated diagrams, self-test questions, Excel spreadsheets, active case studies and video materials please explore the CD accompanying this book.

Introduction

One obvious way of improving operations performance is by reducing the risk of failure (or of failure causing disruption) within the operation. All operations are subject to the risk of failure of many types, for example technology failure, supplier failure, natural and man-made disasters, and many other causes. A 'resilient' operation or process is one that can prevent failures occurring, minimize their effects, and learn how to recover from them. In an increasingly risky economic, political and social environment, resilience has become an important part of operations and process management, and in some operations – aircraft in flight or electricity supplies to hospitals, or the emergency services where failure can be literally fatal – it is vital. (See Figure 14.1.)

Source: Nigel Slack

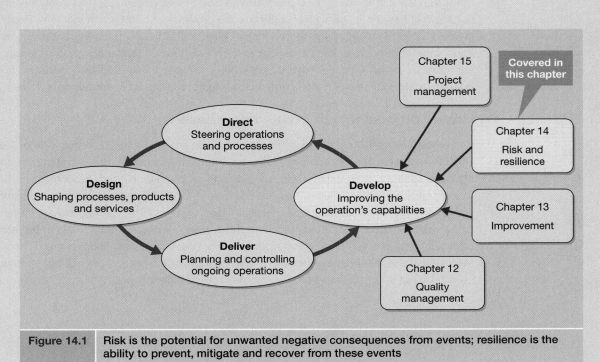

| Figure 14.1 | Risk is the potential for unwanted negative consequences from events; resilience is the ability to prevent, mitigate and recover from these events |

Executive summary

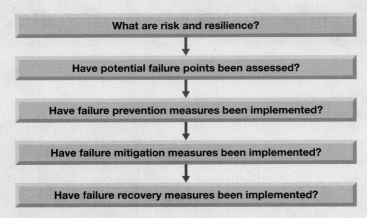

Decision logic chain for risk and resilience

Each chapter is structured around a set of diagnostic questions. These questions suggest what you should ask in order to gain an understanding of the important issues of a topic, and as a result, improve your decision making. An executive summary, addressing these questions, is provided below.

What are risk and resilience?

Risk is the potential for unwanted negative consequences from events. Resilience is the ability to prevent, withstand and recover from those events. Failures can be categorized in terms of the seriousness of their impact and the likelihood of their occurrence. Relatively low impact failures that happen relatively frequently are the province of quality management. Resilience involves attempting to reduce the combined effects of a failure occurring and the negative impact that it may have. It involves four sets of activities: understanding and assessing the seriousness of the potential failures, preventing failures, minimizing their negative consequences (called failure mitigation), and recovering from failure so as to reduce its impact.

Have potential failure points been assessed?

Resilience begins with understanding the possible sources and consequences of failure. Potential sources of failure can be categorized into supply failures, failures that happen inside the operation (further categorized as human, organizational and technology failures), product/service design failures, customer failures and the failures causes by environmental disruption such as weather, crime, terrorism, and so on. Understanding why such failures occur can be aided by post-failure analysis using accident investigation, traceability, complaint analysis, fault tree analysis, and other similar techniques. Judging the likelihood of failure may be relatively straightforward for some well-understood processes, but often has to be carried out on a subjective basis, which is rarely straightforward.

Have failure prevention measures been implemented?

Failure prevention is based on the assumption that it is generally better to avoid failures than suffer their consequences. The main approaches to failure prevention involve designing out the possibility of failure at key points in a process, providing extra but redundant resources that can provide back-up in the case of failure, installing fail-safeing mechanisms that prevent the mistakes which can cause failure, and maintaining processes so as to reduce the likelihood of failure. This last category is particularly important for many operations but can be approached in different ways such as preventive maintenance, condition-based maintenance, and total product maintenance.

Have failure mitigation measures been implemented?

Failure mitigation means isolating a failure from its negative consequences. It can involve a number of 'mitigation actions'. These include ensuring that planning procedures are installed that provide an overarching guide to mitigation as well as demonstrating that failure is taken seriously, economic mitigation using insurance, risk sharing and hedging, spatial or temporal containment that prevents the failure spreading geographically or over time, loss reduction that removes whatever might be harmed by a failure, and substitution that involves providing substitute resources to work on a failure before it becomes serious.

Have failure recovery measures been implemented?

Failure recovery is the set of actions that are taken after the negative effects of failure have occurred and that reduce the impact of the negative effects. Sometimes recovering well from a public failure can even enhance a business's reputation. However, recovery does need to be planned and procedures put in place that can discover when failures have occurred, guide appropriate action to keep everyone informed, capture the lessons learnt from the failure, and plan to absorb the lesson into any future recovery.

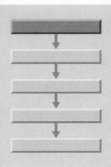

DIAGNOSTIC QUESTION

What are risk and resilience?

Risk is the potential for unwanted negative consequences from some event. Resilience is the ability to prevent, withstand and recover from those events. Things happen in operations, or to operations, that have negative consequences: this is failure. But accepting the fact that failure occurs is not the same thing as accepting failure itself, or ignoring it. Oper-

> **Operations principle**
> Failure will always occur in operations, recognizing this does not imply accepting or ignoring it.

ations do generally attempt to minimize both the likelihood of failure and the effect it will have, although the method of coping with failure will depend on how serious are its negative consequences, and how likely it is to occur. At a minor level, every small error in the delivered product or service from the operation could be considered a failure. The whole area of quality management is con-

cerned with reducing this type of 'failure'. Other failures will have more impact on the operation, even if they do not occur very frequently. A server failure can seriously affect service and therefore customers, which is why system reliability is such an important measure of performance for IT service providers. And, if we class a failure as something that has negative consequences, some are so serious we class them as disasters, such as freak weather conditions, air crashes and acts of terrorism. These 'failures' are treated increasingly seriously by businesses, not necessarily because their likelihood of occurrence is high (although it may be at certain times and in certain places), but because their impact is so negative.

This chapter is concerned with all types of failure other than those with relatively minor consequences. This is illustrated in Figure 14.2. Some of these failures are irritating but relatively unimportant, especially those close to the bottom left-hand corner of the matrix in Figure 14.2. Other failures, especially those close to the top right-hand corner of the matrix, are normally avoided by all businesses because embracing such risks would be clearly foolish. In between these two extremes is where most operations-related risks occur. In this chapter we shall be treating various aspects of these types of failure, and in particular how they can be moved in the direction of the arrows in Figure 14.2. The two examples described next illustrate one organization that paid a high price for not achieving this and another that managed to minimize the effects of one particular failure.

Example

Barings Bank and Nick Leeson[1]

Source: AP/PA Photos

On 3 March 1995 Nick Leeson, the Singapore-based 'rogue trader', was arrested immediately after his flight from the Far East touched down in Frankfurt. Since 27 February, the world's financial community had been in shock after Barings Bank collapsed following the discovery of massive debts. During the nine-month period Leeson spent in a German jail before finally being returned to Singapore to stand trial, auditors, regulators and legislators learnt that although most of the blame for the crash could be placed upon Leeson, whose increasingly risky and fraudulent deals eventually cost Barings $1.3 billion, it was also the bank's inadequate systems for monitoring their trading operations that were equally to blame.

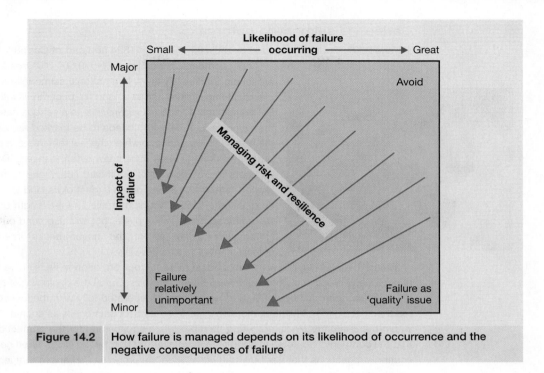

Figure 14.2   How failure is managed depends on its likelihood of occurrence and the negative consequences of failure

In March 1993 Barings Securities and Baring Brothers merged their operations (an action known as solo-consolidation) to form Baring Investment Bank (BIB). Although this had a financial logic, this action effectively created the operations structure that would allow Nick Leeson to get away with illicit dealing until the bank went bust. It enabled Barings to make large loans to its constituent parts without reference to the Bank of England, whose key principle was that no bank should ever risk more money than it can afford to lose. Large exposures (more than 10 per cent of a bank's capital) should be formally reported, yet by the end of 1993 Baring's exposure was nearly 45 per cent of its capital. In July 1992, Leeson opened the trading account 88888 as an 'error account' that is usually used to record sales pending their investigation and clearance. The volume of such trades is normally small and they are quickly cleared from the account. However, Leeson from the outset used account 88888 inappropriately. By the time of the collapse the size of the positions booked in this account was so large that, when market prices moved unfavourably, it caused the collapse of the Baring Group. Funding for positions in the form of cash or securities deposited with an exchange is known as margin. A margin call is a demand from an exchange or broker/dealer for additional cash or collateral to cover that position. In order to finance the SIMEX (Singapore's exchange) margin deposits for account 88888 transactions, Leeson needed funds from other Baring companies. In January 1995, Coopers & Lybrand's annual audit of Barings' Singapore office account picked up a discrepancy in the accounts, so that Barings' management knew that there was a problem, but not exactly where it lay or its size. However, Leeson managed to evade the auditors' questions. Around the same time, SIMEX auditors identified a problem with the 88888 account. By February 1995, Barings Securities was severely worried by events. Up until February 1995, the position might have been recoverable, but thereafter the market fell persistently and losses in account 88888 mounted almost exponentially. Barings' fate was sealed by the absence of either the people or the systems needed to stop the flow of funds to Singapore. By that time the bank was *like a colander, leaking funds to Leeson through a variety of orifices'*. No checks were carried out when money was transferred from one part of Barings to another. Because no apparent risk was involved, the job was allocated to junior clerks. Also because no systems existed for detecting fraudulent activities, it was left up to individuals to pick up and interpret clues.

| Example | Cadbury's salmonella outbreak[2] |

In June 2007, Cadbury, founded by a Quaker family in 1824 and part of Cadbury Schweppes, one of the world's biggest confectionery companies, was fined £1,000,000 plus costs of £152,000 for breaching food safety laws. In a national salmonella outbreak, 42 people, including children aged under 10, became ill with a rare strain of Salmonella montevideo. 'I regard this as a serious case of negligence,' the judge said. 'It therefore needs to be marked as such to emphasize the responsibility and care which the law requires of a company in Cadbury's position.' One prominent lawyer announced: 'Despite Cadbury's attempts to play down this significant fine, make no mistake it was intended to hurt and is one of the largest of its kind to date. This reflects no doubt the company's high profile and the length of time over which the admitted breach took place, but will also send out a blunt warning to smaller businesses of the government's intentions regarding enforcement of food-safety laws.'

Before the hearing, the company had, in fact, apologized, offering its 'sincere regrets' to those affected, and pleaded guilty to nine food-safety offences. But at the beginning of the incident it had not been so open. Although Cadbury said it had co-operated fully with the investigation, it admitted that it failed to notify the authorities of positive tests for salmonella as soon as they were known within the company. While admitting its mistakes, a spokesman for the confectioner emphasized that the company had acted in good faith, a point supported by the judge when he dismissed prosecution suggestions that Cadbury had introduced the procedural changes that led to the outbreak simply as a cost-cutting measure. Cadbury, through its lawyers, said: 'Negligence we admit, but we certainly do not admit that this was done deliberately to save money and nor is there any evidence to support that conclusion.' The judge said Cadbury had accepted that a new testing system, originally introduced to improve safety, was a 'distinct departure from previous practice' and was 'badly flawed and wrong'. In a statement Cadbury said: 'Mistakenly, we did not believe that there was a threat to health and thus any requirement to report the incident to the authorities – we accept that this approach was incorrect. The processes that led to this failure ceased from June last year and will never be reinstated.'

The company was not only hit by the fine and court costs, it had to bear the costs of recalling 1,000,000 bars that may have been contaminated and faced private litigation claims brought by consumers who were affected. Cadbury claimed to have lost around £30,000,000 because of the recall and subsequent safety modifications, not including any private litigation claims. *The Times* reported on the case of Shaun Garratty, one of the people affected. A senior staff nurse, from Rotherham, he spent seven weeks critically ill in the hospital and now fears that his nursing career might be in jeopardy. *The Times* reported him as being 'pleased that Cadbury's had admitted guilt but now wants to know what the firm is going to do for him'. Before the incident, it said, he was a fitness fanatic and went hiking, cycling, mountain biking or swimming twice a week. He always took two bars of chocolate on the trips, usually a Cadbury's Dairy Milk and a Cadbury's Caramel bar. He also ate one as a snack each day at work. 'My gastroenterologist told me if I had not been so fit I would have died,' said Mr. Garratty. 'Six weeks after being in hospital they thought my bowel had perforated and I had to have a laparoscopy. I was told my intestines were inflamed and swollen.' Even after he returned to work he had not fully recovered. According to one medical consultant, the illness had left him with a form of irritable bowel syndrome that he could take 18 months to recover from.

What do these two examples have in common?

Both of these operations suffered failure, in the sense that failure means a disruption to normal operation. In Barings' case it was such a serious failure that the company did not survive. But both companies knew that they risked the type of failure that actually occurred and both companies had procedures in place that attempted to prevent failure occurring. Yet by the time that the extent of the failure at Barings did become evident, its impact had become too great and it could no longer recover. By contrast, Cadbury, although admitting responsibility, did recover.

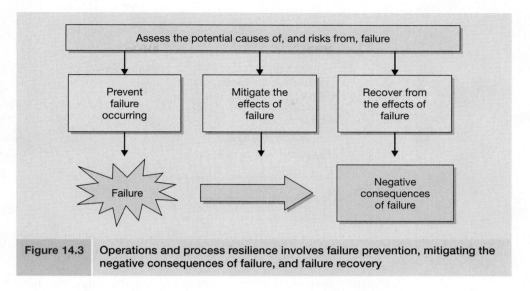

Figure 14.3 Operations and process resilience involves failure prevention, mitigating the negative consequences of failure, and failure recovery

Of course, some operations operate in a more risky environment than others. And, those operations with a high likelihood of failure and/or serious consequences deriving from that failure will need to give it more attention, but operations and process resilience is relevant to all businesses. They must all give attention to the four sets of activities which, in practical terms, resilience includes. The first is concerned with understanding what failures could potentially occur in the operation and assessing their seriousness. The second task is to examine ways of preventing failures occurring. The third is to minimize the negative consequences of failure (called failure or risk 'mitigation'). The final task is to devise plans and procedures that will help the operation to recover from failures when they do occur. The remainder of this chapter deals with these four tasks – see Figure 14.3.

> **Operations principle**
> Resilience is governed by the effectiveness of failure prevention, mitigation and recovery.

DIAGNOSTIC QUESTION

Have potential failure points been assessed?

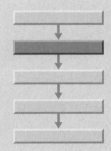

A prerequisite to achieving operations and process resilience is to understand where failure might occur and what the consequences of failure might be, by reviewing all possible causes of failure. Often it is the 'failure to understand failure' that leads to excessive disruption. Each cause of failure also needs to be assessed in terms of the impact it may have. Only then can measures be taken to prevent or minimize the effect of the more important potential failures. The classic approach to assessing potential failures is to inspect and audit operations activities. Unfortunately, inspection and audit cannot, on their own, provide complete assurance that undesirable events will be avoided. The content of the audit has to be appropriate, the checking process has to be

> **Operations principle**
> A 'failure to understand failure' is the root cause of a lack of resilience.

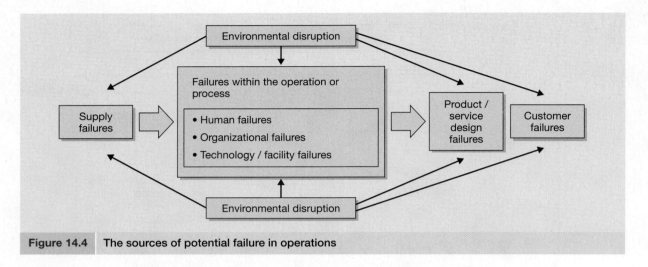

Figure 14.4   The sources of potential failure in operations

sufficiently frequent and comprehensive, and the inspectors have to have sufficient knowledge and experience.

Identify the potential causes of failure

The causes of some failure are purely random, like lightning strikes, and are difficult, if not impossible, to predict. However, the vast majority of failures are not like this. They are caused by something that could have been avoided, which is why, as a minimum starting point, a simple checklist of failure causes is useful. In fact the root cause of most failure is usually human failure of some type; nevertheless, identifying failure sources usually requires a more evident set, such as that illustrated in Figure 14.4. Here, failure sources are classified as failures of supply, internal failures such as those deriving from human organizational and technological sources, failures deriving from the design of products and services, failures deriving from customer failures, and general environmental failures.

Supply failure

Supply failure means any failure in the timing or quality of goods and services delivered into an operation, for example suppliers delivering the wrong or faulty components, outsourced call centres suffering a telecoms failure, disruption to power supplies, and so on. The more an operation relies on suppliers for materials or services, the more it is at risk from failure caused by missing or sub-standard inputs. This is an important source of failure because of increasing dependence on outsourced activities in most industries, and the emphasis on keeping supply chains 'lean' in order to cut costs. For example, in early 2002 Land Rover (a division of the Ford Motor Company) had to cope with a threat to the supply of chassis for its Discovery model when the single company to which it had subcontracted its manufacture became insolvent. The receivers were demanding an upfront payment of around €60,000,000 to continue supply, arguing that they were legally obliged to recover as much money as possible on behalf of creditors. And a single-supplier agreement was a valuable asset.

In this case the outsourcing of a component had made the supply chain more vulnerable. But there are also other factors which have, in recent years, increased the vulnerability of supply. For example, global sourcing usually means that parts are shipped around the world on their journey through the supply chain. Microchips manufactured in Taiwan could be assembled to printed circuit boards in Shanghai which are then finally assembled into a computer in Ireland. At the same time, many industries are suffering increased volatility in demand. Perhaps most significantly there tends to be far less inventory in supply chains that could buffer interruptions to supply. According to one authority on supply chain management, *'Potentially the risk of disruption has increased dramatically as the result of a too-narrow focus on supply chain efficiency at the expense of effectiveness.'*[3]

Human failures

There are two broad types of human failure. The first is where key personnel leave, become ill, die, or in some way cannot fulfil their role. The second is where people are actively doing their job but are making mistakes. Understanding risk in the first type of failure involves identifying the key people without whom operations would struggle to operate effectively. These are not always the most senior individuals, but rather those fulfilling crucial roles that require special skills or tacit knowledge. Human failure through 'mistakes' also comes in two types: errors and violations. 'Errors' are mistakes in judgement; with hindsight, a person should have done something different. For example, if the manager of a sports stadium fails to anticipate dangerous crowding during a championship event, this is an error of judgement. 'Violations' are acts which are clearly contrary to defined operating procedure. For example, if a maintenance engineer fails to clean a filter in the prescribed manner, it is eventually likely to cause failure. Catastrophic failures are often caused by a combination of errors and violations. For example, one kind of accident, where an aircraft appears to be under control and yet still flies into the ground, is very rare (once in two million flights).[4] For this type of failure to occur, first, the pilot has to be flying at the wrong altitude (error); second, the co-pilot would have to fail to cross-check the altitude (violation); third, air traffic controllers would have to miss the fact that the plane was at the wrong altitude (error); and finally, the pilot would have to ignore the ground proximity warning alarm in the aircraft, which can be prone to give false alarms (violation).

Organizational failure

Organizational failure is usually taken to mean failures of procedures and processes and failures that derive from a business's organizational structure and culture. This is a huge potential source of failure and includes almost all operations and process management. In particular, failure in the design of processes (such as bottlenecks causing system overloading) and failures in the resourcing of processes (such as insufficient capacity being provided at peak times) need to be investigated. But there are also many other procedures and processes within an organization that can make failure more likely. For example, remuneration policy may motivate staff to work in a way that, although increasing the financial performance of the organization, also increases its susceptibility to failure. Examples of this can range from salespeople being so incentivized that they make promises to customers that cannot be fulfilled, through to investment bankers being more concerned with profit than the risks of financial overexposure. This type of risk can derive from an organizational culture that minimizes consideration of risk, or it may come from a lack of clarity in reporting relationships; in fact, in the Barings Bank example at the beginning of the chapter, there was some evidence that both these types of failure contributed to its demise.

Technology/facilities failures

By 'technology and facilities' we mean all the IT systems, machines, equipment and buildings of an operation. All are liable to failure, or breakdown. The failure may be only partial, for example a machine that has an intermittent fault. Alternatively, it can be what we normally regard as a breakdown – a total and sudden cessation of operation. Either way, its effects could bring a large part of the operation to a halt. For example, a computer failure in a supermarket chain could paralyze several large stores until it is fixed.

Product/service design failures

In its design stage, a product or service might look fine on paper; only when it has to cope with real circumstances might inadequacies become evident. Of course, during the design process, potential risk of failure should have been identified and 'designed out'. But one only has to look at the number of 'product recalls' or service failures to understand that design failures are far from uncommon. Sometimes this is the result of a trade-off between fast time-to-market performance and the risk of the product or service failing in operation. And, while no reputable business would deliberately market flawed products or services, equally most businesses cannot delay a product or service launch indefinitely to eliminate every single small risk of failure.

Customer failures

Not all failures are (directly) caused by the operation or its suppliers. Customers may 'fail' in that they misuse products and services. For example, an IT system might have been well designed, yet the user could treat it in a way that causes it to fail. Customers are not 'always right'; they can be inattentive and incompetent. However, merely complaining about customers is unlikely to reduce the chances of this type of failure occurring. Most organizations will accept that they have a responsibility to educate and train customers, and to design their products and services so as to minimize the chances of failure.

Environmental disruption

Environmental disruption includes all the causes of failure that lie outside an operation's direct influence. This source of potential failure has risen to near the top of many firms' agenda since 11 September 2001. As operations become increasingly integrated (and increasingly dependent on integrated technologies such as information technologies), businesses are more aware of the critical events and malfunctions that have the potential to interrupt normal business activity and even stop the entire company. Typically, such disasters include the following:

- Hurricanes, floods, lightning, temperature extremes
- Fire
- Corporate crime, theft, fraud, sabotage
- Terrorism, bomb blast, bomb scare or other security attacks
- Contamination of product or processes.

Example   ## Viruses, threats and 30 years of spam[5]

Happy Birthday! 1 May 2008 saw the 30th anniversary of junk electronic mail, or spam as it has become known. It was in 1978 that Gary Thuerk, a Marketing Executive at the Digital Equipment Corporation (DEC), a US mini-computer manufacturer, decided it would be a great sales ploy to let Arpanet (the direct ancestor of the Internet) researchers on the west coast of the USA know that DEC had incorporated the network's protocols directly into one of its operating systems. So Thuerk's secretary typed in all the researchers' addresses and dispatched the message using the e-mail program, which at the time was very primitive. But not all the recipients were happy. Arpanet's rules said that the network could not be used for commercial purposes and not everyone wanted to know about the content of the message; it just seemed intrusive.

Since then unwanted Internet-distributed information has gone on to irritate, infuriate and threaten the whole Internet. For example, on 25 January 2003 the 'SQL Slammer' worm, a rogue program, spread at frightening speed throughout the Internet. It disrupted computers around the world and, at the height of the attack, its effect was such that half the traffic over the Internet was being lost (see Figure 14.5). Thousands of cash dispensers in North America ceased operating and one police force was driven back to using pencils and paper when its dispatching system crashed. Yet security experts believe that the SQL Slammer did more good than harm because it highlighted weaknesses in Internet security processes. Like most rogue software, it exploited a flaw in a

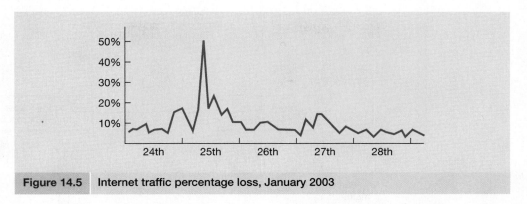

| **Figure 14.5** | Internet traffic percentage loss, January 2003 |

commonly used piece of software. Much commonly used software has security flaws that can be exploited in this way. Software producers issue 'patch' software to fix flaws but this can actually direct Internet terrorists to vulnerable areas in the software, and not all systems managers get around to implementing all patches. Nevertheless, every rogue program that penetrates Internet security systems teaches a valuable lesson to those working to prevent security failures.

Detecting non-evident failure

Not all failures are immediately evident. Small failures may be accumulating for a while before they become evident. Purchasing officers encountering difficulties in using a website may cause them to abandon the purchase. Within an automated materials handling line, debris may periodically accumulate that, in itself, will not cause immediate failure, but could eventually lead to sudden and dramatic failure. Even when such failures are detected, they may not always receive the appropriate attention because there are inadequate failure identification systems, or a lack of managerial support or interest in making improvements. The mechanisms available to seek out failures in a proactive way include machine diagnostic checks, in-process checks, point-of-departure and phone interviews, and customer focus groups.

Post-failure analysis

One of the critical activities of operations and process resilience is to understand why a failure has occurred. This activity is called post-failure analysis. It is used to uncover the root cause of failures. Some techniques for this were described as 'improvement techniques' in Chapter 13. Others include the following.

- **Accident investigation.** Large-scale national disasters like oil tanker spillages and aeroplane accidents are usually investigated using accident investigation, where specifically trained staff analyze the causes of the accident.
- **Failure traceability.** Some businesses (either by choice or because of a legal requirement) adopt traceability procedures to ensure that all their failures (such as contaminated food products) are traceable. Any failures can be traced back to the process which produced them, the components from which they were produced, or the suppliers who provided them.
- **Complaint analysis.** Complaints (and compliments) are a potentially valuable source for detecting the root causes of failures of customer service. Two key advantages of complaints are that they come unsolicited and also they are often very timely pieces of information that can pinpoint problems quickly. Complaint analysis also involves tracking the actual number of complaints over time, which can in itself be indicative of developing problems. The prime function of complaint analysis involves analyzing the 'content' of the complaints to understand better the nature of the failure as it is perceived by the customer.

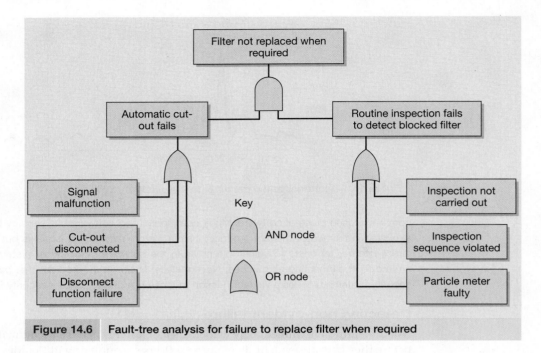

Figure 14.6   Fault-tree analysis for failure to replace filter when required

● **Fault-tree analysis.** This is a logical procedure that starts with a failure or a potential failure and works backwards to identify all the possible causes and therefore the origins of that failure. Fault-tree analysis is made up of branches connected by two types of nodes: AND nodes and OR nodes. The branches below an AND node all need to occur for the event above the node to occur. Only one of the branches below an OR node needs to occur for the event above the node to occur. Figure 14.6 shows a simple tree identifying the possible reasons for a filter in a heating system not being replaced when it should have been.

Likelihood of failure

The difficulty of estimating the chance of a failure occurring varies greatly. Some failures are the result of well-understood phenomena. A combination of rational causal analysis and historical performance data can lead to a relatively accurate estimate of failure occurring. For example, a mechanical component may fail between 10 and 17 months from its installation in 99 per cent of cases. Other types of failure are far more difficult to predict. The chances of a fire in a supplier's plant are (hopefully) low, but how low? There will be some data concerning fire hazards in this type of plant, and one may insist on regular hazard inspection reports from the supplier's insurance providers, but the estimated probability of failure will be both low and subjective.

'Objective' estimates

Estimates of failure based on historical performance can be measured in several ways, including:

● *Failure rates* – how often a failure occurs
● *Reliability* – the chances of a failure occurring
● *Availability* – the amount of available useful operating time.

PRACTICE NOTE

'Failure rate' and 'reliability' are different ways of measuring the same thing – the propensity of an operation, or part of an operation, to fail. Availability is one measure of the consequences of failure in the operation.

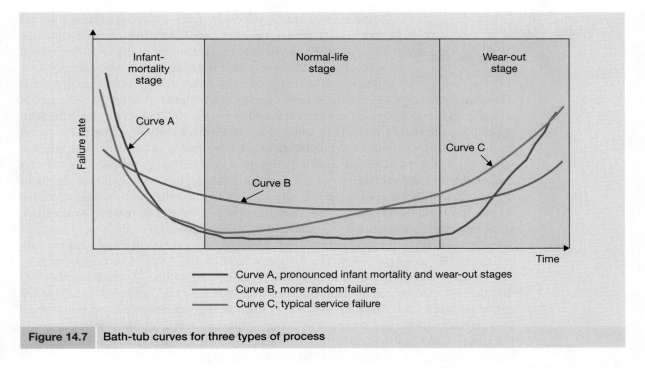

Figure 14.7   Bath-tub curves for three types of process

Sometimes failure is a function of time. For example, the probability of an electric lamp failing is relatively high when it is first used, but if it survives this initial stage, it could still fail at any point, and the longer it survives, the more likely its failure becomes. Most physical parts of an operation behave in a similar manner. The curve which describes failure probability of this type is called the bath-tub curve. It comprises three distinct stages:

● The 'infant-mortality' or 'early-life' stage where early failures occur caused by defective parts or improper use
● The 'normal-life' stage when the failure rate is usually low and reasonably constant, and caused by normal random factors
● The 'wear-out' stage when the failure rate increases as the part approaches the end of its working life and failure is caused by the ageing and deterioration of parts.

Figure 14.7 illustrates three bath-tub curves with slightly different characteristics. Curve A shows a part of the operation which has a high initial infant-mortality failure but then a long, low-failure, normal life followed by the gradually increasing likelihood of failure as it approaches wear-out. Curve B, while having the same stages, is far less predictable. The distinction between the three stages is less clear, with infant-mortality failure subsiding only slowly and a gradually increasing chance of wear-out failure. Failure of the type shown in curve B is far more difficult to manage in a planned manner. The failure of operations which rely more on human resources than on technology, such as some services, can be closer to curve C of Figure 14.7. They may be less susceptible to component wear-out but more so to staff complacency. Without review and regeneration, the service may become tedious and repetitive, and after an initial stage of failure reduction, as problems in the service are ironed out, there can be a long period of increasing failure.

'Subjective' estimates

Failure assessment, even for subjective risks, is increasingly a formal exercise that is carried out using standard frameworks, often prompted by health and safety concerns, environmental regulations, and so on. These frameworks are similar to the formal quality inspection methods associated with quality standards like ISO 9000 (see Chapter 12) that often implicitly assume unbiased objectivity. However, individual attitudes to risk are complex and subject to a wide variety of influences. In fact many studies have demonstrated that people are generally very poor at making risk-related judgements. Consider the success of state and national lotteries. The chances of winning, in nearly every case, are extraordinarily low, and the costs of playing sufficiently significant to make the financial value of the investment entirely negative. If a player has to drive their car in order to purchase a ticket, they may be more likely to be killed or seriously injured than they are to win the top prize. But, although people do not always make rational decisions concerning the chances of failure, this does not mean abandoning the attempt. But it does mean that one must understand the limits to overly rational approaches to failure estimation, for example, how people tend to pay too much attention to dramatic low-probability events, and to overlook routine events.[6]

Even when 'objective' evaluations of risks are used, they may still cause negative consequences. For example, when the oil giant Royal-Dutch Shell took the decision to employ deep-water disposal in the North Sea for their Brent Spar Oil Platform, they felt that they were making a rational operational decision based upon the best available scientific evidence concerning environmental risk. Greenpeace disagreed and put forward an alternative 'objective analysis' showing significant risk from deep-water disposal. Eventually Greenpeace admitted their evidence was flawed but by that time Shell had lost the public relations battle and had altered their plans.

Failure mode and effect analysis

Excel

One of the best-known approaches to assessing the relative significance of failure is failure mode and effect analysis (FMEA). Its objective is to identify the factors that are critical to various types of failure as a means of identifying failures before they happen. It does this by providing a 'checklist' procedure built around three key questions for each possible cause of failure:

- What is the likelihood that failure will occur?
- What would the consequence of the failure be?
- How likely is such a failure to be detected before it affects the customer?

PRACTICE NOTE

Based on a quantitative evaluation of these three questions, a risk priority number (RPN) is calculated for each potential cause of failure. Corrective actions, aimed at preventing failure, are then applied to those causes whose RPN indicates that they warrant priority – see Figure 14.8.

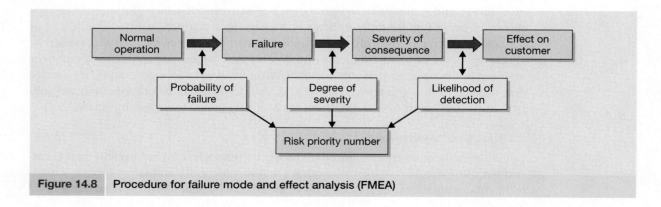

Figure 14.8   Procedure for failure mode and effect analysis (FMEA)

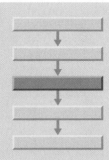

DIAGNOSTIC QUESTION

Have failure prevention measures been implemented?

It is almost always better to avoid failures and negative consequences than have to recover from them, which is why failure prevention is an important part of operations and process resilience. There are a number of approaches to this, including designing out failure points, deploying redundant resources, fail-safeing and maintenance.

Designing out fail points

Process mapping, described in Chapter 5, can be used to 'engineer out' the potential fail points in operations. For example, Figure 14.9 shows a process map for an automobile repair process. The stages in the process that are particularly prone to failure and the stages that are critical to the success of the service have been marked. This will have been done by the staff of this operation metaphorically 'walking themselves through' the process and discussing each stage in turn.

Redundancy

Building in redundancy to an operation means having back-up processes or resources in case of failure. It can be an expensive solution to reduce the likelihood of failure and is generally used when breakdown could have a critical impact. Redundancy means doubling or even tripling some of the elements in a process so that these 'redundant' elements can come into action when one component fails. Nuclear power stations, hospitals and other public buildings have auxiliary or back-up electricity generators ready to operate in case the main electricity supply should fail. Some organizations also have back-up staff held in reserve in case someone does not turn up for work or is held up on one job and is unable to move on to the next. Spacecraft have several back-up computers on board that will not only monitor the main computer but also act as a back-up in case of failure. Human bodies contain two of some organs – kidneys and eyes, for example – both of which are used in 'normal operation' but the body can cope with a failure in one of them. One response to the threat of large failures, such as terrorist activity, has been a rise in the number of companies offering 'replacement office' operations, fully equipped with normal Internet and telephone communications links, and often with access to a company's current management information. Should a customer's main operation be affected by a disaster, business can continue in the replacement facility within days or even hours.

The effect of redundancy can be calculated by the sum of the reliability of the original process component and the likelihood that the back-up component will both be needed and be working.

$$R_{a+b} = R_a + (R_b \times P_{(failure)})$$

where R_{a+b} = reliability of component a with its back-up component b

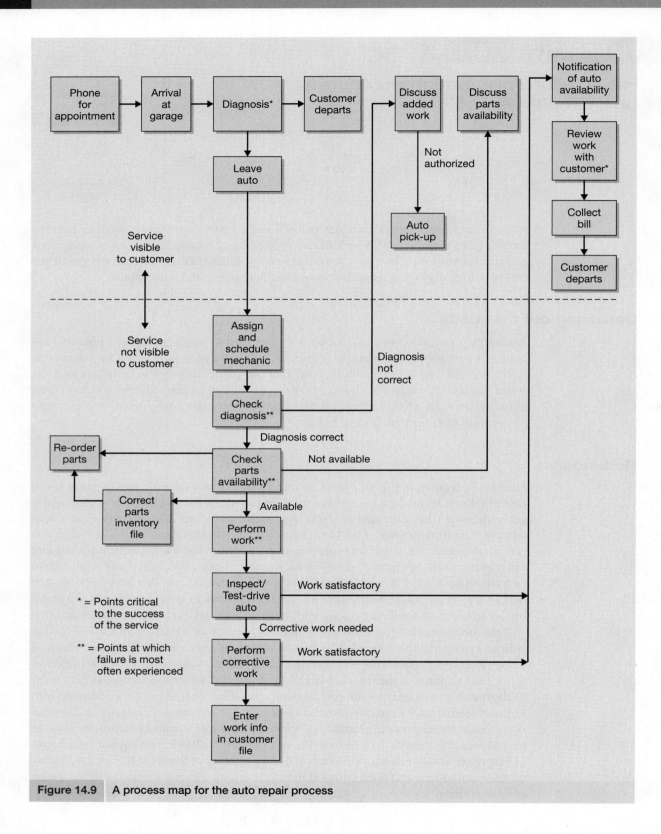

Figure 14.9 A process map for the auto repair process

R_a = reliability of a alone

R_b = reliability of back-up component b

$P_{(failure)}$ = probability that component a will fail and therefore component b will be needed.

So, for example, a food manufacturer has two packing lines, one of which will come into action only if the first line fails. If each line has a reliability of 0.9, the lines working together (each with reliability = 0.9) will have a reliability of $0.9 + [0.9 \times (1 - 0.9)] = 0.99$.

Fail-safeing

The concept of fail-safeing has emerged since the introduction of Japanese methods of operations improvement. Called *poka-yoke* in Japan (from *yokeru* (to prevent) and *poka* (inadvertent errors)), the idea is based on the principle that human mistakes are to some extent inevitable. What is important is to prevent them becoming defects. Poka-yokes are simple (preferably inexpensive) devices or systems which are incorporated into a process to prevent inadvertent operator mistakes resulting in a defect.

> **Operations principle**
> Simple methods of fail-safeing can often be the most cost effective.

FURTHER EXAMPLE

Typical poka-yokes are the following devices:

- Limit switches on machines which allow the machine to operate only if the part is positioned correctly
- Gauges placed on machines through which a part has to pass in order to be loaded onto, or taken off, the machine – an incorrect size or orientation stops the process
- Digital counters on machines to ensure that the correct number of cuts, passes or holes have been machined
- Checklists which have to be filled in, either in preparation for, or on completion of, an activity
- Light beams which activate an alarm if a part is positioned incorrectly.

The same principle can also be applied to service operations, for example:

- Colour-coding cash register keys to prevent incorrect entry in retail operations
- The McDonald's french-fry scoop which picks up the right quantity of fries in the right orientation to be placed in the pack
- Trays used in hospitals with indentations shaped to each item needed for a surgical procedure – any item not back in place at the end of the procedure might have been left in the patient
- The paper strips placed round clean towels in hotels, the removal of which helps housekeepers to tell whether a towel has been used and therefore needs replacing
- The locks on aircraft lavatory doors, which must be turned to switch the light on
- Beepers on ATMs to ensure that customers remove their cards
- Height bars on amusement rides to ensure that customers do not exceed size limitations.

Maintenance

FURTHER EXAMPLE

Maintenance is the term used to cover the way operations and processes try to avoid failure by taking care of their physical facilities. It is particularly important when physical facilities play a central role in the operation, such as at power stations, airlines and petrochemical refineries. There are a number of approaches to maintenance, including the following.

Preventive maintenance (PM)

This attempts to eliminate or reduce the chances of failure by regularly servicing (cleaning, lubricating, replacing and checking) facilities. For example, the engines of passenger aircraft are checked, cleaned and calibrated according to a regular schedule after a set number of flying hours. Taking aircraft away from their regular duties for preventive maintenance is clearly an expensive option for any airline, but the consequences of failure while in service are considerably more serious.

Condition-based maintenance (CBM)

This attempts to perform maintenance only when the facilities require it. For example, continuous process equipment, such as that used in coating photographic paper, is run for long periods in order to achieve the high utilization necessary for cost-effective production. Stopping the machine when it is not strictly necessary to do so would take it out of action for long periods and reduce its utilization. Here condition-based maintenance might involve continuously monitoring the vibrations, or some other characteristic of the line. The results of this monitoring would then be used to decide whether the line should be stopped and the bearings replaced.

Total productive maintenance (TPM)

This is defined as '. . . *the productive maintenance carried out by all employees through small group activities*', where productive maintenance is '. . . *maintenance management which recognizes the importance of reliability, maintenance and economic efficiency in plant design.*'[7] TPM adopts team-working and empowerment principles, as well as a continuous improvement approach to failure prevention. It aims to establish good maintenance practice in operations through the pursuit of 'the five goals of TPM':[7]

1 Examine how the facilities are contributing to the effectiveness of the operation by examining all the losses which occur.
2 Achieve autonomous maintenance by allowing people to take responsibility for at least some of the maintenance tasks.
3 Plan maintenance by having a fully worked out approach to all maintenance activities, including the level of preventive maintenance which is required for each piece of equipment, the standards for condition-based maintenance and the respective responsibilities of operating staff and maintenance staff.
4 Train all staff in relevant maintenance skills so that staff have all the skills to carry out their roles.
5 Avoid maintenance altogether by 'maintenance prevention' (MP), that is, considering failure causes and the maintainability of equipment during its design stage, its manufacture, its installation and its commissioning.

How much maintenance?

Most operations plan their maintenance to include a level of regular preventive maintenance which gives a reasonably low but finite chance of breakdown. Usually the more frequent the preventive maintenance episodes, the less are the chances of a breakdown. Infrequent preventive maintenance will cost little to provide but will result in a high likelihood (and therefore cost) of breakdown. Conversely, very frequent preventive maintenance will be expensive to provide but will reduce the cost of having to provide breakdown maintenance, as shown in Figure 14.10(a). The total cost of maintenance appears to minimize at an 'optimum' level of preventive maintenance. However, this may not reflect reality. The cost of providing preventive maintenance in Figure 14.10(a) assumes that it is carried out by a separate set of people (skilled maintenance staff) whose time is scheduled

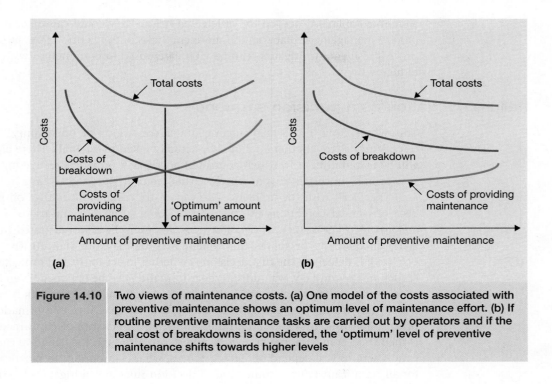

Figure 14.10 Two views of maintenance costs. (a) One model of the costs associated with preventive maintenance shows an optimum level of maintenance effort. (b) If routine preventive maintenance tasks are carried out by operators and if the real cost of breakdowns is considered, the 'optimum' level of preventive maintenance shifts towards higher levels

and accounted for separately from the 'operators' of the facilities. In many operations, however, at least some preventive maintenance can be performed by the operators themselves (which reduces the cost of providing it) and at times that are convenient for the operation (which minimizes the disruption to the operation). Furthermore, the cost of breakdowns could also be higher than is indicated in Figure 14.10(a) because unplanned downtime can take away stability from the operation, preventing it being able to improve itself. Put these two ideas together and the minimizing total curve and maintenance cost curve look more like Figure 14.10(b). The emphasis is shifted towards using more preventive maintenance than is generally thought appropriate.

DIAGNOSTIC QUESTION

Have failure mitigation measures been implemented?

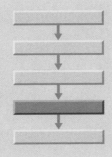

Failure mitigation means isolating a failure from its negative consequences. It is an admission that not all failures can be avoided. However, in some areas of operations management, relying on mitigation, rather than prevention, is unfashionable. For example, 'inspection' practices in quality management were based on the assumption that failures were inevitable and needed to be detected before they could cause harm. Modern total quality management places much more emphasis on prevention. Yet, in operations and process resilience, mitigation can be vital when used in conjunction with prevention in reducing overall risk.

Failure mitigation as a decision sequence

This whole topic involves managing under conditions of uncertainty. There may be uncertainty as to whether a failure has actually taken place at all. There almost certainly will be uncertainty as to which courses of action will provide effective mitigation. There may even be uncertainty as to whether what seems to have worked as a mitigation action really has dealt with the problem. One way of thinking about mitigation is as a series of decisions under conditions of uncertainty. Doing so enables the use of formal decision analysis techniques such as decision trees, for example that illustrated in Figure 14.11. Here, an anomaly of some kind, which may or may not indicate that a failure has occurred, is detected. The first decision is whether to act to try and mitigate the supposed failure or, alternatively, wait until more information can be obtained. Even if mitigation is tried, it may or may not contain the failure. If not, then further action will be needed, which may or may not contain the failure, and so on. If more information is obtained prior to enacting mitigation, then the failure may or may not be confirmed. If mitigation is then tried, it may or may not work, and so on. Although the details of the specific mitigation actions will depend on circumstances, what is important in practical terms is that for all significant failures some kind of decision rules and mitigation planning has been established.

Failure mitigation actions

The nature of the action taken to mitigate failure will obviously depend on the nature of the failure. In most industries technical experts have established a classification of failure mitigation actions that are appropriate for the types of risk likely to be suffered. So, for example, in agriculture, government agencies and industry bodies have published mitigation strategies for such 'failures' as the outbreak of crop disease, contagious animal infections, and so on. Such documents will outline the various mitigation actions that can be taken under different circumstances and detail exactly who are responsible for

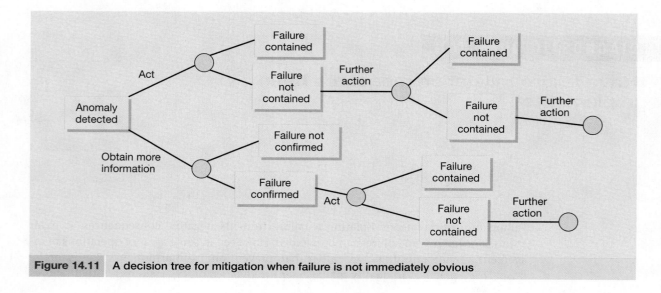

Figure 14.11 A decision tree for mitigation when failure is not immediately obvious

each action. Although these classifications tend to be industry specific, the following generic categorization gives a flavour of the types of mitigation actions that may be generally applicable.

- **Mitigation planning** is the activity of ensuring that all possible failure circumstances have been identified and the appropriate mitigation actions identified. It is the overarching activity that encompasses all subsequent mitigation actions, and may be described in the form of a decision tree or guide rules. Almost certainly there will be some form of escalation that will guide the extra mitigation effort should early actions not prove successful. It is worth noting that mitigation planning, as well an overarching action, also provides mitigation action in its own right. For example, if mitigation planning has identified appropriate training, job design, emergency procedures, and so on, then the financial liability of a business for any losses should a failure occur will be reduced. Certainly businesses that have not planned adequately for failures will be more liable in law for any subsequent losses.

- **Economic mitigation** includes actions such as insurance against losses from failure, spreading the financial consequences of failure, and 'hedging' against failure. Insurance is the best known of these actions and is widely adopted, although ensuring appropriate insurance and effective claims management is a specialized skill in itself. Spreading the financial consequences of failure could involve, for example, spreading the equity holding in supply companies to reduce the financial consequences of such companies failing. Hedging involves creating a portfolio of ventures whose outcomes happen to be correlated so as to reduce total variability. This often takes the form of financial instruments, for example a business may purchase a financial 'hedge' against the price risk of a vital raw material deviating significantly from a set price.

- **Containment (spatial)** means stopping the failure physically spreading to affect other parts of an internal or external supply network. Preventing contaminated food from spreading through the supply chain, for example, will depend on real-time information systems that provide traceability data.

- **Containment (temporal)** means containing the spread of a failure over time. It particularly applies when information about a failure or potential failure needs to be transmitted without undue delay. For example, systems that give advance warning of hazardous weather such as snowstorms must transmit such information to local agencies such as the police and road-clearing organizations in time for them to stop the problem causing excessive disruption.

- **Loss reduction** covers any action that reduces the catastrophic consequences of failure by removing the resources that are likely to suffer those consequences. For example, the road signs that indicate evacuation routes in the event of severe weather, or the fire drills that train employees in how to escape in the event of an emergency, may not reduce the consequences of failure on buildings or physical facilities, but can dramatically help in reducing loss of life or injury.

- **Substitution** means compensating for failure by providing other resources that can substitute for those rendered less effective by the failure. It is a little like the concept of redundancy that was described earlier, but does not always imply excess resources if a failure has not occurred. For example, in a construction project, the risk of encountering unexpected geological problems may be mitigated by the existence of a separate work plan that is invoked only if such problems are found. The resources may come from other parts of the construction project, which will in turn have plans to compensate for their loss.

Table 14.1 gives some examples of each type of failure mitigation action for three failures: the theft of money from one of a company's bank accounts, the failure of a new

Table 14.1   Failure mitigation actions for three failures

Failure mitigation actions	Type of failure		
	Financial failure – theft from company account	Development failure – new technology does not work	Emergency failure – fire at premises
Mitigation planning	Identify different types of theft that have been reported and devise mitigation actions including software to identify anomalous account behaviour	Identify possible types of technology failure and identify contingency technologies together with plans for accessing them	Identify fire hazards and methods of detecting, limiting and extinguishing fires
Economic mitigation	Insure against theft and possibly use several different accounts	Invest in, or form partnership with, supplier of alternative technology	Insure against fire and have more, smaller, premises
Containment (spatial)	'Ring fence' accounts so a deficit in one account cannot be made good from another account	Develop alternative technological solutions for different parts of the development project so that failure in one part does not affect the whole project	Install localized sprinkler systems and fire door barriers
Containment (temporal)	Invest in software that detects signs of possible unusual account behaviour	Build in project milestones that indicate the possibility of eventual development failure	Install alarm systems that indicate the occurrence of fire to everyone who may be affected (including in other premises)
Loss reduction	Build in transfer delays until approval for major withdrawals has been given, also institute plans for recovering stolen money	Ensure the development project can use old technology if new one does not work	Ensure means of egress and employee training are adequate
Substitution	Ensure that reserve funds and staff to manage the transfer can be speedily brought into play	Have fallback work package for devoting extra resources to overcome the new technology failure	Ensure back-up team that can take over from premises rendered inoperative by fire

product technology to work adequately during the new product development process, and the outbreak of fire at a business premises.

Example **Mitigating currency risk[8]**

A multinational consumer goods firm was concerned at the way its operations in certain parts of the world were exposed to currency fluctuations. The company's Russian subsidiary sourced nearly all products from its parent factories in France and Germany, while its main rivals had manufacturing facilities in Russia. Conscious of the potential volatility of the rouble, the firm needed to minimize its operating exposure to a devaluation of the currency that would leave the firm's cost structure at a serious disadvantage compared to its rivals, and without any real option but to increase their prices. In seeking to mitigate against the risk of devaluation, the firm could choose from among various financial and operations-based options. For example, financial tools were available to minimize currency exposure. Most of these allow the operation to reduce the risk of currency fluctuations but involve an 'upfront' cost. Usually, the higher the risk the greater the upfront cost. Alternatively the company may restructure its operations strategy in order to mitigate its currency risk. One option would be to develop its own production facilities within Russia. This may reduce, or even eliminate, the currency risk, although it may introduce other risks. A further option may be to form supply partnerships with other Russian companies. Again, this does not eliminate risks but can shift them to ones which the company feels more able to control. More generally the company may consider creating a portfolio of operations-based strategies, such as developing alternative suppliers in different currency zones, building up excess/flexible capacity in a global production network, and creating more differentiated products that are less price-sensitive.

DIAGNOSTIC QUESTION

Have failure recovery measures been implemented?

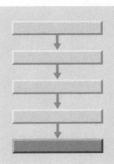

Failure recovery is the set of actions that are taken, after the negative effects of failure have occurred, that reduce the impact of the negative effects. All types of operation can benefit from well-planned recovery. For example, a construction company whose mechanical digger breaks down can have plans in place to arrange a replacement from a hire company. The breakdown might be disruptive, but not as much as it might have been if the operations manager had not worked out what to do. Recovery procedures will also shape customers' perceptions of failure. Even where the customer sees a failure, it may not necessarily lead to dissatisfaction; customers may even accept that things occasionally do go wrong. If there is a metre of snow on the train lines, or if the restaurant is particularly popular, we may accept the fact that something is wrong with the product or service. It is not necessarily the failure itself that leads to dissatisfaction but often the organization's response to the breakdown. Mistakes may be inevitable, but dissatisfied customers are not.

A failure may even be turned into a positive experience. If a flight is delayed by five hours, there is considerable potential for dissatisfaction. But if the airline informs passengers that the aircraft has been delayed by a cyclone at its previous destination, and that arrangements have been made for accommodation at a local hotel with a complimentary meal, passengers might then feel that they have been well treated and even recommend that airline to others. A good recovery can turn angry, frustrated customers into loyal ones. In fact one investigation[9] into customer satisfaction and customer loyalty used four scenarios to test the willingness of customers to use an operation's services again. The four scenarios were:

> **Operations principle**
> Successful failure recovery can yield more benefits than if the failure had not occurred.

1 The service is delivered to meet the customers' expectations and there is full satisfaction.
2 There are faults in the service delivery but the customer does not complain about them.
3 There are faults in the service delivery and the customer complains, but he or she has been fobbed off or mollified. There is no real satisfaction with the service provider.

4 There are faults in the service delivery and the customer complains and feels fully satisfied with the resulting action taken by the service providers.

Customers who are fully satisfied and do not experience any problems (1) are the most loyal, followed by complaining customers whose complaints are resolved successfully (4). Customers who experience problems but don't complain (2) are in third place and last of all come customers who do complain but are left with their problems unresolved and feelings of dissatisfaction (3).

The recovery process

Recovery needs to be a planned process. Organizations therefore need to design appropriate responses to failure, linked to the cost and the inconvenience caused by the failure to their customers. These must first meet the needs and expectations of customers. Such recovery processes need to be carried out either by empowered front-line staff or by trained personnel who are available to deal with recovery in a way which does not interfere with day-to-day service activities. Figure 14.12 illustrates a typical recovery sequence.

Discover

The first thing any manager needs to do when faced with a failure is to discover its exact nature. Three important pieces of information are needed: first of all, what exactly has happened; second, who will be affected by the failure; and third, why did the failure occur? This last point is not intended to be a detailed inquest into the causes of failure (that comes later), but it is often necessary to know something of the causes of failure in case it is necessary to determine what action to take.

Act

The discover stage could take only minutes or even seconds, depending on the severity of the failure. If the failure is a severe one with important consequences, we need to move on to doing something about it quickly. This means carrying out three actions, the first two of which could be carried out in reverse order, depending on the urgency of the situation. First, tell the significant people involved what you are proposing to do about the failure. In service operations this is especially important where the customers need to be kept informed, both for their peace of mind and to demonstrate that something is being done. In all operations, however, it is important to communicate what action is going to

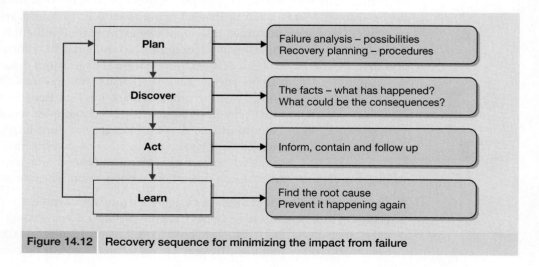

Figure 14.12   Recovery sequence for minimizing the impact from failure

happen so that everyone can set their own recovery plans in motion. Second, the effects of the failure need to be contained in order to stop the consequences spreading and causing further failures. The precise containment actions will depend on the nature of the failure. Third, there needs to be some kind of follow-up to make sure that the containment actions really have contained the failure.

Learn

As discussed earlier in this chapter, the benefits of failure in providing learning opportunities should not be underestimated. In failure planning, learning involves revisiting the failure to find out its root cause and then engineering out the causes of the failure so that it will not happen again.

Plan

Learning the lessons from a failure is not the end of the procedure. Operations managers need formally to incorporate the lessons into their future reactions to failures. This is often done by working through 'in theory' how they would react to failures in the future. Specifically, this involves first identifying all the possible failures which might occur (in a similar way to the FMEA approach). Second, it means formally defining the procedures which the organization should follow in the case of each type of identified failure.

Critical commentary

Each chapter contains a short critical commentary on the main ideas covered in the chapter. Its purpose is not to undermine the issues discussed in the chapter, but to emphasize that, although we present a relatively orthodox view of operation, there are other perspectives.

■ The idea that failure can be detected through in-process inspection is increasingly seen as only partially true. Although inspecting for failures is an obvious first step in detecting them, it is not even close to being 100 per cent reliable. Accumulated evidence from research and practical examples consistently indicates that people, even when assisted by technology, are not good at detecting failure and errors. This applies even when special attention is being given to inspection. For example, airport security was significantly strengthened after 11 September 2001, yet one in ten lethal weapons that were entered into airports' security systems (in order to test them) were not detected. 'There is no such thing as 100 per cent security, we are all human beings,' says Ian Hutcheson, the Director of Security at Airport Operator BAA. No one is advocating abandoning inspection as a failure detection mechanism. Rather it is seen as one of a range of methods of preventing failure.

■ Much of the previous discussion surrounding the prevention of failure has assumed a 'rational' approach. In other words, it is assumed that operations managers and customers alike will put more effort into preventing failures that are either more likely to occur or more serious in their consequences. Yet this assumption is based on a rational response to risk. In fact, being human, managers often respond to the perception of risk rather than its reality. For example, Table 14.2 shows the cost of each life saved by investment in various road and rail transportation safety (in other words, failure prevention) investments. The table shows that investing in improving road safety is very much more effective than investing in rail safety.

Table 14.2 The cost per life saved of various safety (failure prevention) investments

Safety investment	Cost per life (€m)
Advanced train protection system	30
Train protection warning systems	7.5
Implementing recommended guidelines on rail safety	4.7
Implementing recommended guidelines on road safety	1.6
Local authority spending on road safety	0.15

And while no one is arguing for abandoning efforts on rail safety, it is noted by some transportation authorities that actual investment reflects more the public perception of rail deaths (low) compared with road deaths (very high).

Summary checklist

This checklist comprises questions that can be usefully applied to any type of operations and reflect the major diagnostic questions used within the chapter.

- [ ] Does the business have an operations and process resilience policy?
- [ ] Have any possible changes in the business's vulnerability to failure been discussed and accommodated within its failure policy?
- [ ] Have all potential sources of failure been identified?
- [ ] Have any future changes in the sources of failure been identified?
- [ ] Have the impact of all potential sources of failure been assessed?
- [ ] Has the likelihood of each potential failure been assessed?
- [ ] Has the possibility of non-evident failures been addressed?
- [ ] Is post-failure analysis carried out when failure does occur?
- [ ] Are techniques such as failure mode and effect analysis (FMEA) used?
- [ ] Has due attention been paid to the possibility of designing out failure points?
- [ ] Is the concept of redundancy economically viable for any potential failures?
- [ ] Has the idea of fail-safeing (poka-yoke) been considered as a means of reducing the likelihood of failure?
- [ ] Have all approaches to process and technology maintenance been explored?
- [ ] Has the possibility that insufficient maintenance effort is being applied been investigated?
- [ ] Does the operation have a failure mitigation plan?
- [ ] Have the whole range of mitigation actions been thoroughly evaluated?
- [ ] Are specific plans in place for the use of each type of mitigation action?
- [ ] Is a well-planned recovery procedure in place?
- [ ] Does the recovery procedure cover all the steps of discover, act, learn and plan?

Case study

The Chernobyl failure[10]

At 1.24 in the early hours of Saturday morning on 26 April 1986, the worst accident in the history of commercial nuclear power generation occurred. Two explosions in quick succession blew off the 1000-tonne concrete sealing cap of the Chernobyl-4 nuclear reactor. Molten core fragments showered down on the immediate area and fission products were released into the atmosphere. The accident cost probably hundreds of lives and contaminated vast areas of land in the Ukraine.

Many reasons probably contributed to the disaster. Certainly the design of the reactor was not new – around 30 years old at the time of the accident – and had been conceived before the days of sophisticated computer-controlled safety systems. Because of this, the reactor's emergency-handling procedures relied heavily on the skill of the operators. This type of reactor also had a tendency to run 'out of control' when operated at low power. For this reason, the operating procedures for the reactor strictly prohibited it being operated below 20 per cent of its maximum power. It was mainly a combination of circumstance and human error which caused the failure, however. Ironically, the events which led up to the disaster were designed to make the reactor safer. Tests, devised by a specialist team of engineers, were being carried out to evaluate whether the emergency core cooling system (ECCS) could be operated during the 'free-wheeling' run-down of the turbine generator, should an off-site power failure occur. Although this safety device had been tested before, it had not worked satisfactorily and new tests of the modified device were to be carried out with the reactor operating at reduced power throughout the test period. The tests were scheduled for the afternoon of Friday, 25 April 1986 and the plant power reduction began at 1.00 pm. However, just after 2.00 pm, when the reactor was operating at about half its full power, the Kiev controller requested that the reactor should continue supplying the grid with electricity. In fact it was not released from the grid until 11.10 that night. The reactor was due to be shut down for its annual maintenance on the following Tuesday and the Kiev controller's request had in effect shrunk the 'window of opportunity' available for the tests.

The following is a chronological account of the hours up to the disaster, together with an analysis by James Reason, which was published in the Bulletin of the British Psychological Society the following year. Significant

Source: © Vladimir Repik/Reuters/Corbis

operator actions are italicized. These are of two kinds: errors (indicated by an 'E') and procedural violations (marked with a 'V').

25 April 1986

1.00 pm Power reduction started with the intention of achieving 25 per cent power for test conditions.

2.00 pm ECCS disconnected from primary circuit. (This was part of the test plan.)

2.05 pm Kiev controller asked the unit to continue supplying grid. The ECCS was not reconnected (V). (This particular violation is not thought to have contributed materially to the disaster, but it is indicative of a lax attitude on the part of the operators towards the observance of safety procedures.)

11.10 pm The unit was released from the grid and continued power reduction to achieve the 25 per cent power level planned for the test programme.

26 April 1986

12.28 am Operator seriously undershot the intended power setting (E). The power dipped to a dangerous 1 per cent. (The operator had switched off the 'auto-pilot' and had tried to achieve the desired level by manual control.)

1.00 am After a long struggle, the reactor power was finally stabilized at 7 per cent – well below the intended level and well into the low-power danger zone. At this point, the experiment should have been abandoned, but it was not (E). This was the most serious mistake (as opposed to violation): it meant that all subsequent activity would be conducted within the reactor's zone of maximum instability. This was apparently not appreciated by the operators.

1.03 am All eight pumps were started (V). The safety regulations limited the maximum number of pumps in use at any one time to six. This showed a profound misunderstanding of the physics of the reactor. The consequence was that the increased water flow (and reduced steam fraction) absorbed more neutrons, causing more control rods to be withdrawn to sustain even this low level of power.

1.19 am The feedwater flow was increased threefold (V). The operators appear to have been attempting to cope with a falling steam-drum pressure and water level. The result of their actions, however, was to further reduce the amount of steam passing through the core, causing yet more control rods to be withdrawn. They also overrode the steam-drum automatic shut-down (V). The effect of this was to strip the reactor of one of its automatic safety systems.

1.22 am The shift supervisor requested printout to establish how many control rods were actually in the core. The printout indicated only six to eight rods remaining. It was strictly forbidden to operate the reactor with fewer than 12 rods. Yet the shift supervisor decided to continue with the tests (V). This was a fatal decision: the reactor was thereafter without 'brakes'.

1.23 am The steam line valves to No. 8 turbine generator were closed (V). The purpose of this was to establish the conditions necessary for repeated testing, but its consequence was to disconnect the automatic safety trips. This was perhaps the most serious violation of all.

1.24 am An attempt was made to 'scram' the reactor by driving in the emergency shut-off rods, but they jammed within the now warped tubes.

1.24 am Two explosions occurred in quick succession. The reactor roof was blown off and 30 fires started in the vicinity.

1.30 am Duty firemen were called out. Other units were summoned from Pripyat and Chernobyl.

5.00 am Exterior fires had been extinguished, but the graphite fire in the core continued for several days.

The subsequent investigation into the disaster highlighted a number of significant points which contributed to it:

- The test programme was poorly worked out and the section on safety measures was inadequate. Because the ECCS was shut off during the test period, the safety of the reactor was in effect substantially reduced.
- The test plan was put into effect before being approved by the design group who were responsible for the reactor.
- The operators and the technicians who were running the experiment had different and non-overlapping skills.
- The operators, although highly skilled, had probably been told that getting the test completed before the shut-down would enhance their reputation. They were proud of their ability to handle the reactor even in unusual conditions and were aware of the rapidly reducing window of opportunity within which they had to complete the test. They had also probably 'lost any feeling for the hazards involved' in operating the reactor.
- The technicians who had designed the test were electrical engineers from Moscow. Their objective was to solve a complex technical problem. In spite of having designed the test procedures, they probably would not know much about the operation of the nuclear power station itself.

Again, in the words of James Reason: *'Together, they made a dangerous mixture: a group of single-minded but non-nuclear engineers directing a team of dedicated but over-confident operators. Each group probably assumed that the other knew what it was doing. And both parties had little or no understanding of the dangers they were courting, or of the system they were abusing.'*

QUESTIONS

1 What were the root causes which contributed to the ultimate failure?

2 How could failure planning have helped prevent the disaster?

Active case study   Paterford Elevators

ACTIVE CASE

Elevators are one of the many products and services integral to our daily lives and whose smooth performance we take for granted. Yet their efficient operation really does depend on the type of maintenance services offered by companies like Paterford Elevators. Ensuring that elevators run smoothly depends upon an understanding of when they might fail, and for elevators, failure is not just irritating, but is potentially lethal.

- How would you recommend the company improve their maintenance service, whilst ensuring they do not place their customers at risk?

Please refer to the CD to work through the decisions that Paterford Elevators must make to ensure they offer the best service to their customers.

Applying the principles

HINTS

Some of these exercises can be answered by reading the chapter. Others will require some general knowledge of business activity and some might require an element of investigation. All have hints on how they can be answered on the CD accompanying this book.

1　Earlier in this chapter the failure of 'controlled flight into ground' was mentioned. Predominantly, the reason for this is not mechanical failure but human failure such as pilot fatigue. Boeing, which dominates the commercial airline business, has calculated that over 60 per cent of all the accidents which have occurred in the past 10 years had flight crew behaviour as their 'dominant cause'. For this type of failure to occur, a whole chain of minor failures must happen. First, the pilot at the controls has to be flying at the wrong altitude – there is only one chance in a thousand of this. Second, the co-pilot would have to fail to cross-check the altitude – only one chance in a hundred of this. The air traffic controllers would have to miss the fact that the plane was at the wrong altitude (which is not strictly part of their job) – a one-in-ten chance. Finally, the pilot would have to ignore the ground proximity warning alarm in the aircraft (which can be prone to give false alarms) – a one-in-two chance.

- What are your views on the quoted probabilities of each failure described above occurring?
- How would you try to prevent these failures occurring?
- If the probability of each failure occurring could be reduced by a half, what would be the effect on the likelihood of this type of crash occurring?

2　Conduct a survey amongst colleagues, friends and acquaintances of how they cope with the possibility that their computers might 'fail', in terms of either ceasing to operate effectively, or losing data. Discuss how the concept of redundancy applies in such failure.

3　Survey a range of people who own and/or are responsible for the performance of the following pieces of equipment. What is their approach to maintaining them and how is this influenced by the perceived seriousness of any failure?

(a) Motor cars

(b) Central heating systems or air conditioning systems

(c) Domestic appliances such as dishwashers and vacuum cleaners

(d) Furniture

(e) Lighting or lighting systems.

4　Visit the websites of some of the many companies that offer advice and consultancy to companies wishing to review their 'business continuity' plans. Based on your investigation of these sites, identify the key issues in any business continuity plan for the following types of operation:

(a) A university

(b) An airport

(c) A container port

(d) A chemicals manufacturing plant.

In terms of its effectiveness at managing the learning process, how does a university detect failures? What could it do to improve its failure detection processes?

Notes on chapter

1 Drawn primarily from Leeson's own book, *Rogue Trader* (1996), Warner Books, and (the more objective) *The Collapse of Barings: Panic, ignorance and greed* by Stephen Fay (1996), Arrow Books.

2 Sources: Herman, M. and Dearbail, J. (2007) 'Cadbury fined £1 million over salmonella outbreak', *Times Online*, 16 July; Elliott, V. (2007) 'Cadbury admits hygiene failures over salmonella in chocolate bars', *The Times*, 16 June.

3 Christopher, M. (2002) 'Business is failing to manage supply chain vulnerability', *Odessey*, Issue 16, June.

4 Source: 'Air crashes, but surely . . .', *The Economist*, 4 June 1994.

5 Sources: Naughton, J. (2008) 'The typing error that gave us thirty years of spam', *The Observer*, 4 May.

6 Examples taken from Slack, N. and Lewis, M.A. (2002) *Operations Strategy*, Financial Times Prentice Hall, Harlow, UK.

7 Nakajima, S. (1988) *Total Productive Maintenance*, Productivity Press.

8 Example taken from Slack, N. and Lewis, M.A. (2002) *Operations Strategy*, Financial Times Prentice Hall, Harlow, UK.

9 Armistead, C.G. and Clark, G. (1992) *Customer Service and Support*, FT/Pitman Publishing.

10 Based on information from Read, P.P. (1994) *Ablaze: The story of Chernobyl*, Secker and Warburg; and Reason, J. (1987) 'The Chernobyl errors', *Bulletin of the British Psychological Society*, Vol. 4, pp. 201–6.

Taking it further

Dhillon, B.S. (2002) *Engineering Maintenance: A modern approach*, Technomic Publishing Company. A comprehensive book for the enthusiastic that stresses the 'cradle-to-grave' aspects of maintenance.

Heskett, J.L., Sasser, W.E. and Hart, C.W.L. (1990) *Service Breakthroughs: Changing the rules of the game*, Free Press, New York. A general book on managing service operations, but does contain some interesting points on service failure.

HMSO (1995) *An Introduction and a Guide to Business Continuity Management*, HMSO. One of the earliest technical guides to failure and disaster recovery.

Japan Institute (ed.) (1997) *Focused Equipment Improvement to TPM Teams*, Japan Institute of Plant Maintenance. Very much a simple and practical guide to an important element of total productive maintenance.

Löfsten, H. (1999) 'Management of industrial maintenance – Economic evaluation of maintenance policies', *International Journal of Operations and Production Management*, Vol. 19, No. 7. An academic paper, but provides a useful economic rationale for choosing alternative maintenance policies.

Mobley, K. (1999) *Root Cause Failure Analysis*, Butterworth-Heinemann. Root cause failure analysis is one of the more important techniques in reliability and maintenance. This book describes it in detail.

Smith, D.J. (2000) *Reliability, Maintainability and Risk*, Butterworth-Heinemann. A comprehensive and excellent guide to all aspects of maintenance and reliability.

Useful websites

www.smrp.org Site of the Society for Maintenance and Reliability Professionals. Gives an insight into practical issues.

www.sre.org American Society of Reliability Engineers. The newsletters give insights into reliability practice.

www.csob.berry.edu/faculty/jgrout/pokayoke.shtml The poka-yoke page of John Grout. Some great examples, tutorials, etc.

www.rspa.com/spi/SQA.html Lots of resources, involving reliability and poka-yoke.

www.sra.org Site of the Society for Risk Analysis. Very wide scope, but interesting.

FURTHER RESOURCES

For further resources including examples, animated diagrams, self-test questions, Excel spreadsheets, active case studies and video materials please explore the CD accompanying this book.

PROJECT MANAGEMENT

Introduction

This chapter is concerned with managing 'projects'. Some projects are complex and large-scale, have activities involving diverse resources, and last for years. But other 'projects' are far smaller affairs, possibly limited to one part of a business, and may last only a few days. Yet, although the complexity and degree of difficulty involved in managing different types of projects will vary, the essential approach to the task does not. Whether projects are large or small, internal or external, long or short, they all require defining, planning and controlling. (See Figure 15.1.)

Source: Digital Vision/Getty Images

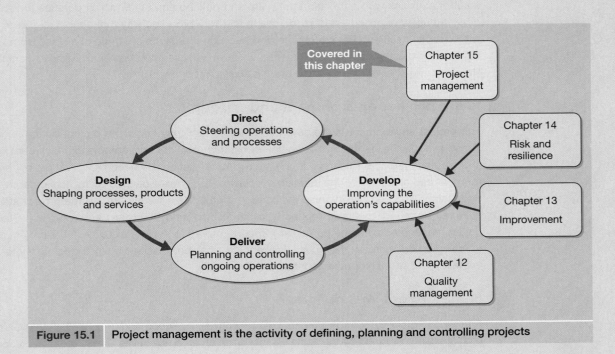

Covered in this chapter

Chapter 15
Project management

Chapter 14
Risk and resilience

Chapter 13
Improvement

Chapter 12
Quality management

Direct
Steering operations and processes

Design
Shaping processes, products and services

Deliver
Planning and controlling ongoing operations

Develop
Improving the operation's capabilities

Figure 15.1   **Project management is the activity of defining, planning and controlling projects**

Executive summary

VIDEO
further detail

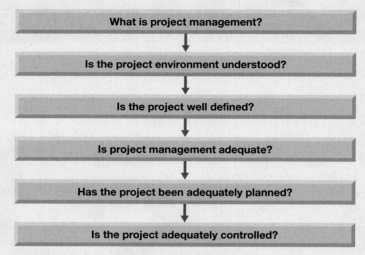

Decision logic chain for project management

Each chapter is structured around a set of diagnostic questions. These questions suggest what you should ask in order to gain an understanding of the important issues of a topic, and as a result, improve your decision making. An executive summary, addressing these questions, is provided below.

What is project management?

Project management is the activity of defining, planning and controlling projects. A project is a set of activities with a defined start point and defined end state, which pursues a defined goal and uses a defined set of resources. It is a very broad activity that almost all managers will become involved in at some time or other. Some projects are large-scale and complex, but most projects, such as implementation of a process improvement, will be far smaller. However, all projects are managed using a similar set of principles.

Is the project environment understood?

The project environment is the sum of all factors that may affect the project during its life. These include the geographical, social, economic, political and commercial environments, and on small projects also include the internal organizational environment. The project environment can also include the intrinsic difficulty of the project defined by its scale, degree of uncertainty, and complexity. Also included in a project's environment are the project stakeholders, those individuals or groups who have some kind of interest in the project. Stakeholder management can be particularly important both to avoid difficulties in the project and to maximize its chances of success. Stakeholders can be classified by their degree of interest in the project and their power to influence it.

Is the project well defined?

A project is defined by three elements: its objectives, its scope and its overall strategy. Most projects can be defined by the relative importance of three objectives. These are cost (keeping the overall project to its original budget), time (finishing the project by the scheduled finish time) and quality (ensuring that the project outcome is as was originally specified). The project scope defines its work content and outcomes. More importantly, it should define what is not included in the project. The project strategy describes the general way in which the project is going to meet its objectives, including significant project milestones and 'stagegates'.

Is project management adequate?

Because of their complexity and the involvement of many different parties, projects need particularly careful managing. In fact, project management is seen as a particularly demanding role with a very diverse set of skills, including technical project management knowledge, interpersonal skills and leadership ability. Very often project managers need the ability to motivate staff who not only report to a manager other than themselves, but also divide their time between several different projects.

Has the project been adequately planned?

Project planning involves determining the cost and duration of the project and the level of resources that it will need. In more detail, it involves identifying the start and finish times of individual activities within the project. Generally, the five stages of project planning include identifying activities, estimating times and resources, identifying relationships and dependencies between activities, identifying time and resource schedule constraints, and fixing the final schedule. However, no amount of planning can prevent the need for replanning as circumstances dictate during the life of the project. Network planning techniques such as critical path analysis (CPA) are often used to aid the project planning process.

Is the project adequately controlled?

Project control involves monitoring the project in order to check its progress, assessing the performance of the project against the project plan, and, if necessary, intervening in order to bring the project back to plan. The process often involves continually assessing the progress of the project in terms of budgeted expenditure and progress towards meeting the project's final goal. It may also involve deciding when to devote extra resources to accelerating (also know as crashing) individual activities within the project. There are a number of proprietary computer-assisted project management packages on the market that range from relatively simple network planning programmes through to complex and integrated 'enterprise project management' (EPRM) systems.

DIAGNOSTIC QUESTION

What is project management?

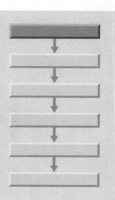

A project is a set of activities with a defined start point and a defined end state, which pursues a defined goal and uses a defined set of resources. What can be defined as a 'project' can vary significantly from relatively small and local activities, through to very large 'put a man on the moon' enterprises. Project management is the activity of defining, planning and controlling projects of any type.

The activity of project management is very broad in so much as it could encompass almost all the operations and process management tasks described in this book. Partly because of this, it could have been treated almost anywhere within the direct, design, delivery, develop, structure of this book. We have chosen to place it in the context of operations and process development because most of the projects that most managers will be involved in are essentially improvement projects. Of course, many projects are vast enterprises with very high levels of resourcing, complexity and uncertainty that will extend over many years. Look around at the civil engineering, social, political and environmental successes (and failures) to see the evidence of major projects. Such projects require professional project management involving high levels of technical expertise and management skills. But so do the smaller, yet important, projects that implement the many and continuous improvements that will determine the strategic impact of operations development. This is why it is equally important to take a rigorous and systematic approach to managing improvement projects as it is to managing major projects.

At this point it is worth pointing out the distinction between 'projects' and 'programmes'. A programme, such as a continuous improvement programme, has no defined end point. Rather it is an ongoing process of change. Individual projects, such as the development of training processes, may be individual sub-sections of an overall programme, such as an integrated skills development programme. Programme management will overlay and integrate the individual projects. Generally, it is a more difficult task in the sense that it requires resource co-ordination, particularly when multiple projects share common resources, as emphasized in the following quotation: *'Managing projects is, it is said, like juggling three balls – cost, quality, and time. Programme management … is like organizing a troupe of jugglers all juggling three balls and swapping balls from time to time.'*[1]

The following two projects illustrate some of the issues in project management.

Example | ### Popping the Millau cork[2]

For decades locals and French motorists had called the little bridge at Millau that was one of the few crossings on the river Tarn 'the Millau cork'. It held up all the traffic on what should have been one of the busiest north–south routes through France. No longer. In place of the little bridge is one of the most impressive and beautiful civil engineering successes of the last century. Lord Foster, the British architect who designed the bridge, described it as an attempt to enhance the natural beauty of the valley through a structure that had the 'delicacy of a butterfly', with the environment dominating the

Source: Jean-Philippe Arles/Reuters/Corbis

scene rather than the bridge. And although the bridge appears to float on the clouds, it has seven pillars and a roadway of $1^1/_2$ miles in length. It is also a remarkable technical achievement. At 300 metres it is the highest road bridge in the world, weighing 36,000 tonnes. The central pillar is higher than the Eiffel Tower, and took only three years to complete, notwithstanding the new engineering techniques that were needed.

Outline plans for the bridge were produced back in 1987. But, because of planning, funding and design considerations, construction did not begin until December 2001. It was completed in December 2004, on time and budget, having proved the effectiveness of its new construction technique. The traditional method of building this type of bridge (called a cable stay bridge) involves building sections of the roadway on the ground and using cranes to put them in position. Because of its height, 300 metres above the valley floor, a new technique had to be developed. First, the towers were built in the usual way, with steel-reinforced concrete. The roadway was built on the high ground at either side of the valley and then pushed forward into space as further sections were added, until it met with precision (to the nearest centimetre) in the centre. This technique had never been tried before and it carried engineering risks, which added to the complexity of the project management task.

It all began with a massive recruitment drive. *'People came from all over France for employment. We knew it would be a long job. We housed them in apartments and houses in and around Millau. Eiffel gave guarantees to all the tenants and a unit was set up to help everyone with the paperwork involved in this. It was not unusual for a worker to be recruited in the morning and have his apartment available the same evening with electricity and a telephone available.'* (Jean-Pierre Martin, Chief Engineer of Groupe Eiffage and director of building) Over 3000 workers – technicians, engineers, crane drivers, carpenters, welders, winchers, metal workers, painters, concrete specialists, and experts in the use of the stays and pylons that would support the bridge – contributed to the project. On the project site, 500 of them, positioned somewhere between the sky and the earth, worked in all weathers to complete the project on time. *'Everyday I would ask myself what was the intense force that united these men,'* said Jean-Pierre Martin. *'They had a very strong sense of pride and they belonged to a community that was to build the most beautiful construction in the world. It was never necessary to shout at them to get them to work. Life on a construction site has many ups and downs. Some days we were frozen. Other days we were subjected to a heatwave. But even on days of bad weather, one had to force them to stay indoors. Yet often they would leave their lodgings to return to work.'*

Many different businesses were involved in building the bridge – Arcelor, Eiffel, Lafarge, Freyssinet, Potain. All of them needed co-ordinating in such a way that they would co-operate towards the common goal, but yet avoid any loss of overall responsibility. Jean-Pierre Martin came up with the idea of nine autonomous work groups. One group was placed at the foot of each of the seven piles that would support the bridge and two others at either end. The motto adopted by the teams was *'rigueur et convivialité'*, rigorous quality and friendly co-operation. *'The difficulty with this type of project is keeping everyone enthusiastic throughout its duration. To make this easier we created these small groups. Each of the nine team's shifts were organized in relays between 7 and 14 hours, and 14 and 21 hours.'* So, to maintain the good atmosphere, no expense was spared to celebrate important events in the construction of the viaduct, for example a pile, or another piece of road completed. Sometimes, to boost the morale of the teams, and to celebrate these important events, Jean-Pierre would organize a *'méchouis'* – a spit roast of lamb, especially popular with the many workers who were of North African origin.

Example   ## Access HK[3]

Access HK is an independent non-profit organization that works to fight inequality and to provide underprivileged children with educational opportunities that are otherwise unaffordable by them. Every summer, Access HK's volunteers, mostly students studying at overseas universities, return to Hong Kong to give a free Summer School to children in need. It was set up in the summer of 2001 by a group of Hong Kong students at leading UK and US universities. Since then it has organized

Source: China Photos/Getty Images

several large-scale events to help underprivileged children, including free four-week Summer Schools during which children are taught in interactive formats on subjects such as the English language, current affairs, speech and drama. Oxford student Ng Kwan-hung, Access HK's external secretary, said: *'We share a common belief that what distinguishes one child from another is not ability but access – access to opportunities, access to education, access to love. All of us realize the importance of a good learning environment for a child's development.'* Chung Tin-Wong, a law student at Oxford and sub-committee member, added: *'We are all dedicated to providing the best education for underprivileged children.'*

Project managing the summer schools is particularly important to Access HK because their opportunities to make a difference to the underprivileged are limited largely to the vacation periods when their student volunteers are available. Project failure would mean waiting until the next year to get another chance. Also, like many charities, the budget is limited with every dollar having to count. Because of this, the student volunteers soon learn some of the arts of the project management, including how to break the project down into four phases for ease of planning and control.

- *Conceptual phase,* during which the Access HK central committee agrees with the Summer School Committee, its direction, aim and goal.
- *Planning phase,* when the Summer School Committee sets the time and cost parameters for the project. The time frame for the Summer School is always tight. Student volunteers become available only after they have completed their summer exams, and the Summer School must be ready to run when the primary school students have their summer break.
- *Definition and design phase,* when the detailed implementation plans for the Summer School are finalized. Communication between the teams of volunteers is particularly important to ensure contributed smooth implementation later. Many of them, although enthusiastic, have little project management experience, and therefore need the support of detailed instructions as to how to carry out their part of the project.
- *Implementation phase.* Again, it is the relative inexperience of the volunteer force that dictates how the Summer School project is implemented. It is important to ensure that control mechanisms are in place that can detect any problems or deviations from the plan quickly, and help to bring it back on target.

'The success of these Summer School projects depends very much on including all our stakeholders in the process,' says one Summer School co-ordinator. *'All our stakeholders are important but they have different interests. The students on the Summer Schools, even if they don't articulate their objectives, need to feel that are benefiting from the experience. Our volunteers are all bright and enthusiastic and are interested in helping to manage the process as well as taking part in it. Access HK wants to be sure that we are doing our best to fulfil their objectives and uphold their reputation. The Hong Kong government have an obvious interest in the success and integrity of the Summer Schools, and the sponsors need to be assured that their donations are being used wisely. In addition the schools who lend us their buildings and many other interested parties all need to be included, in different ways and to different extents, in our project management process.'*

What do these two example have in common?

Not all projects are as large or as complex as the Millau Bridge, but the same issues will occur. Because no single project exists in isolation, the social, political and operational environment must be taken into account. For the Access HK Summer School this means including many different community groups and organizations as well as sponsors. Each project's objectives and scope also need to be clarified with stakeholders. Detailed planning, however, will be the responsibility of those who act as project managers. They are the ones who determine the time and resource commitments that the project will need, as well as identifying the long list of things that could go wrong. Back-up plans will need to be made to minimize the impact of uncertainties. The project management teams for the two examples are very different – professional and experienced in one case, volunteer and inexperienced in the other. But both have elements in common. Both have an objective, a definable end result. Both are temporary in that they have a defined beginning and need a temporary concentration of resources that will be redeployed once their contribution has been completed. Both need to motivate the people involved in the project, both need planning, both need controlling. In other words, both need project managing.

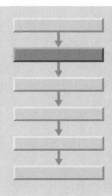

DIAGNOSTIC QUESTION

Is the project environment understood?

The project environment comprises all the factors which may affect the project during its life. It is the context and circumstances in which the project takes place. Understanding the project environment is important because the environment affects the way in which a project will need to be managed and (just as important) the possible dangers that may cause the project to fail. Environmental factors can be considered under the following four headings.

- *Geo-social environment.* Geographical, climatic and cultural factors that may affect the project.
- *Econo-political environment.* The economic, governmental and regulatory factors in which the project takes place.
- *The business environment.* Industrial, competitive, supply network and customer expectation factors that shape the likely objectives of the project.
- *The internal environment.* The individual company's or group's strategy and culture, the resources available, and the interaction with other projects that will influence the project.

FURTHER EXAMPLE

Project difficulty

An important element in the project management environment is the degree of difficulty of the project itself. Three factors have been proposed as determining project difficulty. These are scale, uncertainty and complexity. This is illustrated in Figure 15.2. Large-scale projects involving many different types of resources with durations of many years will be more difficult to manage, both because the resources will need a high level of management effort and because project management objectives must be maintained over a long time period. Uncertainty particularly affects project planning. Ground-breaking projects are likely to be especially uncertain, with ever-changing objectives leading to planning difficulties. When uncertainty is high, the whole project planning process needs to be sufficiently flexible to cope with the consequences of change. Projects with high levels of complexity, such as multi-organizational projects, often require considerable control effort. Their many separate

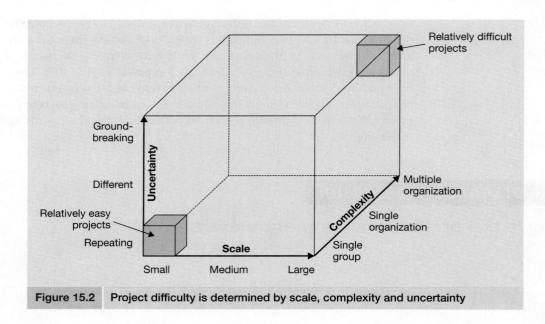

Figure 15.2   Project difficulty is determined by scale, complexity and uncertainty

> **Operations principle**
> The difficulty of managing a project is a function of its scale, complexity and uncertainty.

activities, resources and groups of people involved increase the scope for things to go wrong. Furthermore, as the number of separate activities in a project increases, the ways in which they can impact on each other increase exponentially. This increases the effort involved in monitoring each activity. It also increases the chances of overlooking some part of the project which is deviating from the plan. Most significantly, it increases the 'knock-on' effect of any problem.

Stakeholders

One way of operationalizing the importance of understanding a project's environment is to consider the various 'stakeholders' who have some kind of interest in the project. The stakeholders in any project are the individuals and groups who have an interest in the project process or outcome. All projects will have stakeholders; complex projects will have many. They are likely to have different views on a project's objectives that may conflict with those of other stakeholders. At the very least, different stakeholders are likely to

> **Operations principle**
> All projects have stakeholders with different interests and priorities.

stress different aspects of a project. So, as well as an ethical imperative to include as many people as possible in a project from an early stage, it is often useful in preventing objections and problems later in the project. Moreover, there can be significant direct benefits from using a stakeholder-based approach. Project managers can use the opinions of powerful stakeholders to shape the project at an early stage. This makes it more likely that they will support the project, and also can improve its quality. Communicating with stakeholders early and frequently can ensure that they fully understand the project and understand potential benefits. Stakeholder support may even help to win more resources, making it more likely that projects will be successful. Perhaps most important, one can anticipate stakeholder reaction to various aspects of the project, and plan the actions that could prevent opposition, or build support.

> **Operations principle**
> Project stakeholders have responsibilities as well as rights.

Some (even relatively experienced) project managers are reluctant to include stakeholders in the project management process, preferring to 'manage them at a distance' rather than allowing them to interfere with the project. Others argue that the benefits

Table 15.1 The rights and responsibilities of project stakeholders in one IT company

Rights	Responsibilities
1 To expect developers to learn and speak their language	1 Provide resources (time, money, etc.) to the project team
2 To expect developers to identify and understand their requirements	2 Educate developers about their business
3 To receive explanations of artifacts that developers use as part of working with project stakeholders, such as models they create with them (e.g. user stories or essential prototypes), or artifacts that they present to them (e.g. deployment diagrams)	3 Spend the time to provide and clarify requirements
	4 Be specific and precise about requirements
	5 Make timely decisions
	6 Respect a developer's assessment of cost and feasibility
	7 Set requirement priorities
4 To expect developers to treat them with respect	8 Review and provide timely feedback regarding relevant work artifacts of developers
5 To hear ideas and alternatives for requirements	9 Promptly communicate changes to requirements
6 To describe characteristics that make the product easy to use	10 Own your organization's software processes: to both follow them and actively help to fix them when needed
7 To be presented with opportunities to adjust requirements to permit reuse, reduce development time, or reduce development costs	
8 To be given good-faith estimates	
9 To receive a system that meets their functional and quality needs	

of stakeholder management are too great to ignore and many of the risks can be moderated by emphasizing the responsibilities as well as the rights of project stakeholders. For example, one information technology company formally identifies the rights and responsibilities of project stakeholders as shown in Table 15.1.

Managing stakeholders

PRACTICE NOTE

Managing stakeholders can be a subtle and delicate task, requiring significant social and, sometimes, political skills. But it is based on three basic activities: identifying, prioritizing and understanding the stakeholder group.

- *Identify stakeholders.* Think of all the people who are affected by your work, who have influence or power over it, or have an interest in its successful or unsuccessful conclusion. Although stakeholders may be both organizations and people, ultimately you must communicate with people. Make sure that you identify the correct individual stakeholders within a stakeholder organization.
- *Prioritize stakeholders.* Many people and organizations will be affected by a project. Some of these may have the power either to block or to advance the project. Some may be interested in what you are doing; others may not care. Map out stakeholders using the Power–Interest Grid (see later), and classify them by their power and by their interest in the project.
- *Understand key stakeholders.* It is important to know about key stakeholders. One needs to know how they are likely to feel about and react to the project. One also needs to know how best to engage them in the project and how best to communicate with them.

The power–interest grid

FURTHER EXAMPLE

One approach to discriminating between different stakeholders, and more important, how they should be managed, is to distinguish between their power to influence the project and their interest in doing so. Stakeholders who have the power to exercise a major influence over the project should never be ignored. At the very least, the nature of their interest, and their motivation, should be well understood. But not all stakeholders who have the power to exercise influence over a project will be interested in doing so, and not everyone who is interested in the project has the power to influence it. The power–interest grid, shown in Figure 15.3, classifies stakeholders simply in terms of these two dimensions. Although there will be gradations between them, the two dimensions are useful in providing an indication of how stakeholders can be managed in terms of four categories.

Stakeholders' positions on the grid give an indication of how they might be managed. High-power, interested groups must be fully engaged, with the greatest efforts made to satisfy them. High-power, less interested groups require enough effort to keep them satisfied, but not so much that they become bored or irritated with the message. Low-power, interested groups need to be kept adequately informed, with checks to ensure that no major issues are arising. These groups may be very helpful with the detail of the project. Low-power, less interested groups need monitoring, but without excessive communication. Some key questions that can help in distinguishing high-priority stakeholders include the following.

> **Operations principle**
> Different stakeholder groups will need managing differently.

- What financial or emotional interest do they have in the outcome of the project? Is it positive or negative?
- What motivates them most of all?
- What information do they need?
- What is the best way of communicating with them?
- What is their current opinion of the project?
- Who influences their opinions? Do some of these influencers therefore become important stakeholders in their own right?
- If they are not likely to be positive, what will win them round to support the project?
- If you don't think you will be able to win them round, how will you manage their opposition?

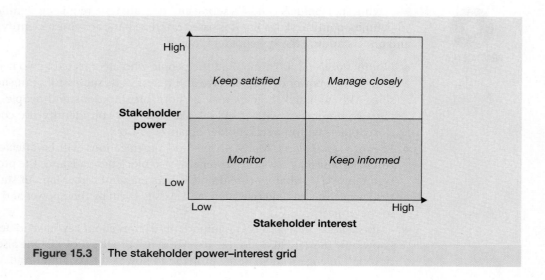

Figure 15.3 The stakeholder power–interest grid

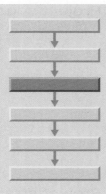

Is the project well defined?

Before starting the complex task of planning and executing a project, it is necessary to be clear about exactly what the project is – its definition. This is not always straightforward, especially in projects with many stakeholders. Three different elements define a project:

- Its *objectives*: the end state that project management is trying to achieve
- Its *scope*: the exact range of the responsibilities taken on by project management
- Its *strategy*: how project management is going to meet its objectives.

Project objectives

PRACTICE NOTE

Objectives help to provide a definition of the end point which can be used to monitor progress and identify when success has been achieved. They can be judged in terms of the five performance objectives – quality, speed, dependability, flexibility and cost. However, flexibility is regarded as a 'given' in most projects which, by definition, are to some extent one-offs, and speed and dependability are compressed to one composite objective – 'time'. This results in what are known as the 'three objectives of project management' – cost, time and quality.

The relative importance of each objective will differ for different projects. Some aerospace projects, such as the development of a new aircraft, which impact on passenger safety, will place a very high emphasis on quality objectives. With other projects, for example a research project that is being funded by a fixed government grant, cost might predominate. Other projects emphasize time: for example, the organization of an open-air music festival has to happen on a particular date if the project is to meet its objectives. In each of these projects, although one objective might be particularly important, the other objectives can never be totally forgotten. Good objectives are those which are clear, measurable and, preferably, quantifiable. Clarifying objectives involves breaking down project objectives into three categories – the purpose, the end results and the success criteria. For example, a project that is expressed in general terms as 'improve the budgeting process' could be broken down into:

> **Operations principle**
> Different projects will place different levels of emphasis on cost, time, and quality objectives.

- *Purpose* – to allow budgets to be agreed and confirmed prior to the annual financial meeting
- *End result* – a report that identifies the causes of budget delay, and which recommends new budgeting processes and systems
- *Success criteria* – the report should be completed by 30 June, meet all departments' needs, and enable integrated and dependable delivery of agreed budget statements. Cost of the recommendations should not exceed $200,000.

Project scope

The scope of a project identifies its work content and its products or outcomes. It is a boundary-setting exercise which attempts to define the dividing line between what each part of the project will do and what it won't do. Defining scope is particularly important when part of a project is being outsourced. A supplier's scope of supply will identify the legal boundaries within which the work must be done. Sometimes the scope of the project is articulated in a formal 'project specification'. This is the written, pictorial and graphical information used to define the output, and the accompanying terms and conditions.

Project strategy

The third part of a project's definition is the project strategy, which defines, in a general rather than a specific way, how the project is going to meet its objectives. It does this in two ways: by defining the phases of the project, and by setting milestones, and/or 'stage-gates'. Milestones are important events during the project's life. Stagegates are the decision points that allow the project to move onto its next phase. A stagegate often launches further activities and therefore commits the project to additional costs, etc. Milestone is a more passive term, which may herald the review of a part-complete project or mark the completion of a stage, but does not necessarily have more significance than a measure of achievement or completeness. At this stage the actual dates for each milestone are not necessarily determined. It is useful, however, to at least identify the significant milestones and stagegates, either to define the boundary between phases or to help in discussions with the project's customer.

DIAGNOSTIC QUESTION

Is project management adequate?

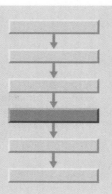

In order to co-ordinate the efforts of many people in different parts of the organization (and often outside it as well), all projects need a project manager. Many of a project manager's activities are concerned with managing human resources. The people working in the project team need a clear understanding of their roles in the (usually temporary) organization. Controlling an uncertain project environment requires the rapid exchange of relevant information with the project stakeholders, both within and outside the organization. People, equipment and other resources must be identified and allocated to the various tasks. Undertaking these tasks successfully makes the management of a project a particularly challenging operations activity.

Project management skills

The project manager is the person responsible for delivering a project. He or she leads and manages the project team, with the responsibility, if not always the authority, to run the project on a day-to-day basis. They are special people. They must possess seemingly opposing skills. They must be able to influence without necessarily having authority, pay attention to details without losing sight of the big picture, establish an open, communicative environment while remaining wedded to project objectives, and be able to hope for the best but plan for the worst.

Operations principle
The activity of project management requires interpersonal as well as technical skills.

PRACTICE NOTE

It is a formidable role. Ideally it involves leading, communicating, organizing, negotiating, managing conflict, motivating, supporting, team building, planning, directing, problem solving, coaching and delegating.

In more formal terms, typical project manager responsibilities include the following.

- Devising and applying an appropriate project management framework for the project
- Managing the production of the required deliverables
- Planning and monitoring the project
- Delegating project roles within agreed reporting structures
- Preparing and maintaining a project plan
- Managing project risks, including the development of contingency plans
- Liaison with programme management (if the project is part of a programme)
- Overall progress and use of resources, initiating corrective action where necessary
- Managing changes to project objectives or details
- Reporting through agreed reporting lines on project progress and stage assessments
- Liaison with senior management to assure the overall direction and integrity of the project
- Adopting technical and quality strategy
- Identifying and obtaining support and advice required for the management of the project
- Managing ongoing project administration
- Conducting post-project evaluation to assess how well the project was executed
- Preparing any follow-on action recommendations as required.

Five characteristics in particular are seen as important in an effective project manager:[4]

- Background and experience which are consistent with the needs of the project
- Leadership and strategic expertise, in order to maintain an understanding of the overall project and its environment, while at the same time working on the details of the project
- Technical expertise in the area of the project in order to make sound technical decisions
- Interpersonal competence and the people skills to take on such roles as project champion, motivator, communicator, facilitator and politician
- Proven managerial ability, in terms of a track record of getting things done.

Managing matrix tensions

In all but the simplest projects, project managers usually need to reconcile the interests of both the project itself and the departments contributing resources to the project. When calling on a variety of resources from various departments, projects are operating in a 'matrix management' environment, where projects cut across organizational boundaries and involve staff who are required to report to their own line manager as well as to the project manager. Figure 15.4 illustrates the type of reporting relationship that usually occurs in matrix management structures running multiple projects. A person in department 1, assigned part-time to projects A and B, will be reporting to three different managers all of whom will have some degree of authority over their activities. This is why

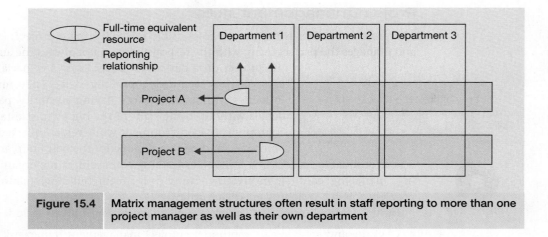

Figure 15.4   Matrix management structures often result in staff reporting to more than one project manager as well as their own department

matrix management requires a high degree of co-operation and communication between all individuals and departments. Although decision-making authority will formally rest with either the project or the departmental manager, most major decisions will need some degree of consensus. Arrangements need to be made that reconcile potential differences between project managers and departmental managers. To function effectively, matrix management structures should have the following characteristics.

- There should be effective channels of communication between all managers involved, with relevant departmental managers contributing to project planning and resourcing decisions.
- There should be formal procedures in place for resolving the management conflicts that do arise.
- Project staff should be encouraged to feel committed to their projects as well as to their own department.
- Project management should be seen as the central co-ordinating role, with sufficient time devoted to planning the project, securing the agreement of the line managers to deliver on time and within budget.

DIAGNOSTIC QUESTION

Has the project been adequately planned?

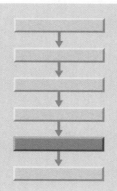

All projects, even the smallest, need some degree of planning. The planning process fulfils four distinct purposes. It determines the cost and duration of the project, it determines the level of resources that will be needed, it helps to allocate work and to monitor progress, and it helps to assess the impact of any changes to the project. It is a vital step

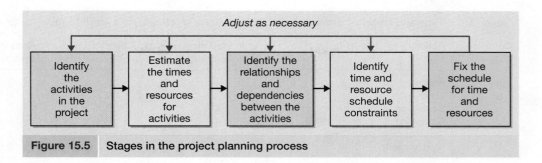

Figure 15.5   Stages in the project planning process

at the start of the project, but it could be repeated several times during the project's life as circumstances change. This is not a sign of project failure or mismanagement. In uncertain projects, in particular, it is a normal occurrence. In fact, later stage plans typically mean that more information is available, and that the project is becoming less uncertain. The process of project planning involves five steps, shown in Figure 15.5.

Identify activities – the work breakdown structure

Some projects are too complex to be planned and controlled effectively unless they are first broken down into manageable portions. This is achieved by structuring the project into a 'family tree' that specifies the major tasks or sub-projects. These in turn are divided up into smaller tasks until a defined, manageable series of tasks, called a work package, is arrived at. Each work package can be allocated its own objectives in terms of time, cost and quality. The output from this is called the work breakdown structure (WBS). The WBS brings clarity and definition to the project planning process. It shows 'how the jigsaw fits together'. It also provides a framework for building up information for reporting purposes.

For example, Figure 15.6 shows the work breakdown structure for a project to design a new information interface (a website screen) for a new sales knowledge management system that is being installed in an insurance company. The project requires co-operation between the company's IT systems department and its sales organization. Three types of activity will be necessary to complete the project: training, installation and testing. Each of these categories is further broken down into specific activities as shown in Figure 15.6.

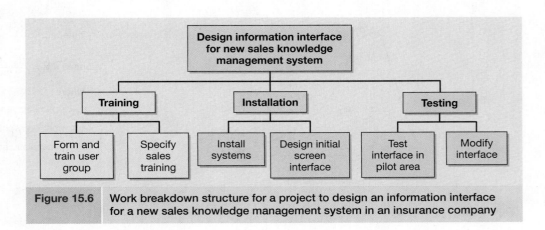

Figure 15.6   Work breakdown structure for a project to design an information interface for a new sales knowledge management system in an insurance company

Table 15.2 Time and resource estimates and relationships for the sales system interface design project

Code	Activity	Immediate predecessor(s)	Duration (days)	Resources (developers)
a	Form and train user group	none	10	3
b	Install systems	none	17	5
c	Specify sales training	a	5	2
d	Design initial screen interface	a	5	3
e	Test interface in pilot area	b, d	25	2
f	Modify interface	c, e	15	3

Estimate times and resources

The next stage in planning is to identify the time and resource requirements of the work packages. Without some idea of how long each part of a project will take and how many resources it will need, it is impossible to define what should be happening at any time during the execution of the project. Estimates are just that, however – a systematic best guess, not a perfect forecast of reality. Estimates may never be perfect but they can be made with some idea of how accurate they might be. Table 15.2 includes time (in days) and resource (in terms of the number of IT developers needed) estimates for the sales system interface design project.

Probabilistic estimates

The amount of uncertainty in a project has a major bearing on the level of confidence which can be placed on an estimate. The impact of uncertainty on estimating times leads some project managers to use a probability curve to describe the estimate. In practice, this is usually a positively skewed distribution, as in Figure 15.7. More uncertainty increases the range of the distribution. The natural tendency of some people is to produce optimistic estimates, but these will have a relatively low probability of being correct because they represent the time which would be taken if everything went well. Most likely estimates have the highest probability of proving correct. Finally, pessimistic estimates assume that almost everything which could go wrong does go wrong. Because of the skewed nature of the distribution, the expected time for the activity will not be the same as the most likely time.

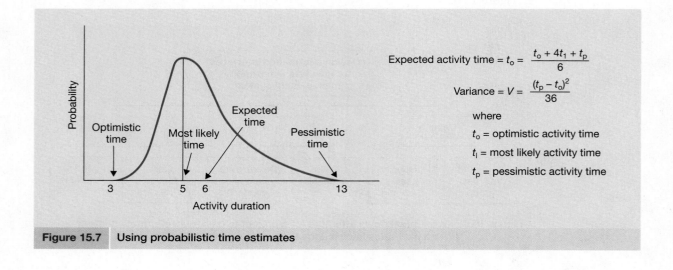

$$\text{Expected activity time} = t_o = \frac{t_o + 4t_1 + t_p}{6}$$

$$\text{Variance} = V = \frac{(t_p - t_o)^2}{36}$$

where

t_o = optimistic activity time

t_l = most likely activity time

t_p = pessimistic activity time

Figure 15.7 Using probabilistic time estimates

Identify the relationships and dependencies between the activities

All the activities which are identified as comprising a project will have some relationship with one another that will depend on the logic of the project. Some activities will, by necessity, need to be executed in a particular order. For example, in the construction of a house, the foundations must be prepared before the walls are built, which in turn must be completed before the roof is put in place. These activities have a dependent or series relationship. Other activities do not have any such dependence on each other. The rear garden of the house could probably be prepared totally independently of the garage being built. These two activities have an independent or parallel relationship.

In the case of the sales system interface design, Table 15.2 provided the basic information that enables the relationships between activities in the project to be established. It did this by identifying the immediate predecessor (or predecessors) for each activity. So, for example, activities **a** and **b** can be started without any of the other activities being completed. Activity **c** cannot begin until activity **a** has been completed, nor can activity **d**. Activity **e** can start only when both activities **b** and **d** have been completed, and activity **f** can start only when activities **c** and **e** have been completed.

Planning tools

Project planning is greatly aided by the use of techniques that help to handle time, resource and relationships complexity. The simplest of these techniques is the *Gantt chart* (or bar chart) which we introduced in Chapter 10. Figure 15.8 shows a Gantt chart for the activities that form the sales system interface project. The bars indicate the start, duration and finish time for each activity. The length of the bar for each activity on a Gantt chart is directly proportional to the calendar time, and so indicates the relative duration of each activity. Gantt charts are the simplest way to exhibit an overall project plan, because they have excellent visual impact and are easy to understand. They are also useful for communicating project plans and status to senior managers as well as for day-to-day project control.

As project complexity increases, it becomes more necessary to identify clearly the relationships between activities, and show the logical sequence in which activities must take place. This is most commonly done by using the *critical path method* (CPM) to clarify the relationships between activities diagrammatically. The first way we can illustrate this is by using arrows to represent each activity in a project. Figure 15.9 shows this for the sales system interface design project. Each activity is represented by an arrow, in this case with the activity code and the duration in days shown next to it. The circles in Figure 15.9 represent

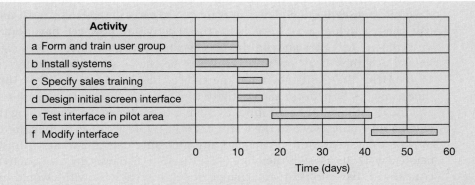

Figure 15.8   Gantt chart for the project to design an information interface for a new sales knowledge management system in an insurance company

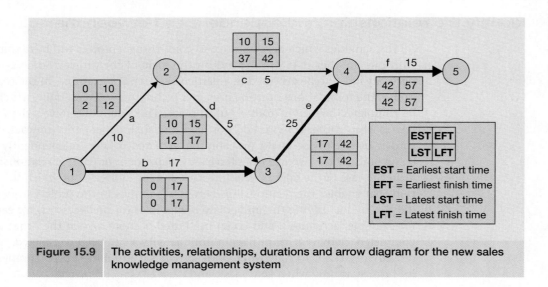

Figure 15.9   The activities, relationships, durations and arrow diagram for the new sales knowledge management system

PRACTICE NOTE

'events'. These are single points in time that have no duration but mark, for example, the start and finish of activities. So, in this case, event 2 represents the event 'activity **a** finishes'. Event 3 represents '*both* activities **b** and **d** finished', and so on.

The diagram shows that there are a number of chains of events that must be completed before the project can be considered as finished (event 5). In this case, activity chains **a–c–f**, **a–d–e–f** and **b–e–f** must all be completed before the project can be considered as finished. The longest of these chains of activities is called the 'critical path' because it represents the shortest time in which the project can be finished, and therefore dictates the project timing. In this case **b–e–f** is the longest path and the earliest the project can finish is after 57 days.

Figure 15.9 also includes information concerning the earliest and latest start and finish times for each activity. This can be derived by following the logic of the arrow diagram forwards by calculating the earliest times an event can take place, and backwards by calculating the latest time an event can take place. So, for example, the earliest the project can finish (event 5) is the sum of all the activities on the critical path, **b–e–f**, 57 days. If we then take 57 days as the latest that we wish the project to finish, the latest activity **f** can start is 57 – 15 = 42, and so on. Activities that lie on the critical path will have the same earliest and latest start times and earliest and latest finish times. That is why these activities are critical. Non-critical activities, however, have some flexibility as to when they start and finish. This flexibility is quantified into a figure that is known as either 'float' or 'slack'. This can be shown diagrammatically, as in Figure 15.10. Here, the Gantt chart for the project has been revisited, but this time the time available to perform each activity (the duration between the earliest start time and the latest finish time for the activity) has been shown. So, combining the network diagram in Figure 15.9 and the Gantt chart in Figure 15.10, activity **c**, for example, is only of 5 days' duration, it can start any time after day 10 and must finish any time before day 42. Its 'float' is therefore (42 – 10) – 5 = 27 days. Obviously, activities on the critical path have no float; any change or delay in these activities would immediately affect the whole project.

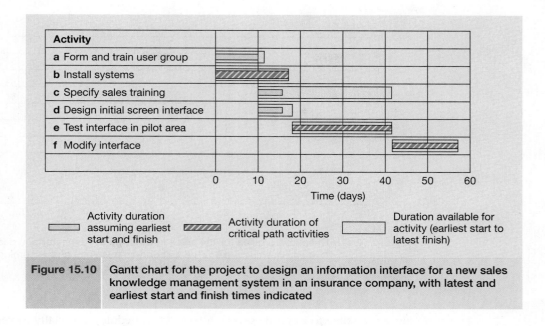

Activity							
a Form and train user group							
b Install systems							
c Specify sales training							
d Design initial screen interface							
e Test interface in pilot area							
f Modify interface							

Time (days)

Activity duration assuming earliest start and finish

Activity duration of critical path activities

Duration available for activity (earliest start to latest finish)

Figure 15.10 Gantt chart for the project to design an information interface for a new sales knowledge management system in an insurance company, with latest and earliest start and finish times indicated

Identify time and resource schedule constraints

Once estimates have been made of the time and effort involved in each activity, and their dependencies identified, it is possible to compare project requirements with the available resources. The finite nature of critical resources – such as staff with special skills – means that they should be taken into account in the planning process. This often has the effect of highlighting the need for more detailed replanning.

The logic that governs project relationships, as shown in the network diagram, is primarily derived from the technical details, but the availability of resources may also impose its own constraints, which can materially affect the relationships between activities. Return to the sales system interface design project. Figure 15.11 shows the resource profile under two different assumptions. The critical path activities (**b–e–f**) form the initial basis of the project's resource profile. These activities have no float and can only take place as shown. However, activities **a**, **c** and **d** are not on the critical path, so project managers have some flexibility as to when these activities occur, and therefore when the resources associated with these activities will be required. From Figure 15.11, if one schedules all activities to start as soon as possible, the resource profile peaks between days 10 and 15 when 10 IT development staff are required. However, if the project manager exploits the float that activity **c** possesses and delays its start until after activity **b** has been completed (day 17), the number of IT developers required by the project does not exceed 8. In this way, float can be used to smooth out resource requirements or make the project fit resource constraints. However, it does impose further resource-constrained logic on the relationship between the activities. So, for example, in this project moving activity **c** as shown in Figure 15.11 results in a further constraint of not starting activity **c** until activity **b** has been completed.

Fix the schedule

Project planners should ideally have a number of alternatives to choose from. The one which best fits project objectives can then be chosen or developed. However, it is not

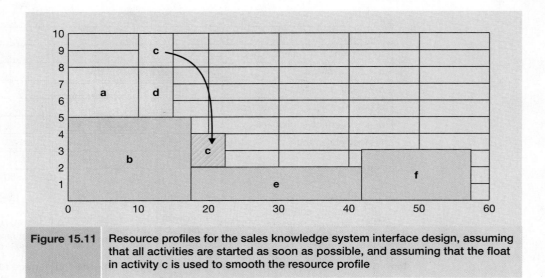

Figure 15.11   Resource profiles for the sales knowledge system interface design, assuming that all activities are started as soon as possible, and assuming that the float in activity c is used to smooth the resource profile

always possible to examine several alternative schedules, especially in very large or very uncertain projects, as the computation could be prohibitive. However, modern computer-based project management software is making the search for the best schedule more feasible.

Variations on simple network planning

There are several variations on the simple critical path method type of network that we have used to illustrate project planning thus far. While it is beyond the scope of this book to enter into much more detail of the various ways that simple network planning can be made more sophisticated, two variants are worth mentioning. The first, activity on node networks, is simply a different approach to drawing the network diagram. The second, programme evaluation and review technique (PERT), does represent an enrichment of the basic network approach.

Activity on node networks

The network we have described so far uses arrows to represent activities and circles at the junctions or nodes of the arrows to represent events. This method is called the activity on arrow (AoA) method. An alternative method of drawing networks is the activity on node (AoN) method. In the AoN representation, activities are drawn as boxes, and arrows are used to define the relationships between them. There are three advantages to the AoN method:

- It is often easier to move from the basic logic of a project's relationships to a network diagram using AoN rather than using the AoA method.
- AoN diagrams do not need dummy activities to maintain the logic of relationships.
- Most of the computer packages which are used in project planning and control use an AoN format.

Figure 15.12 shows the sales system interface design project drawn as an AoN diagram. In this case, we have kept a similar notation to the one used in the original AoA diagram. In addition, each activity box contains information on the description of the activity, its duration and its total float.

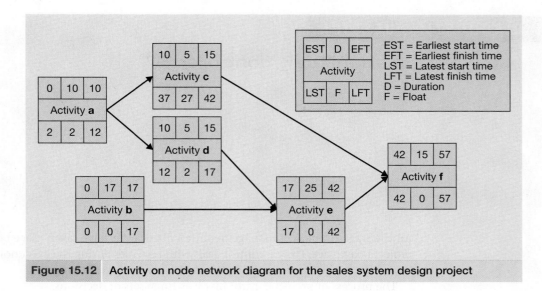

Figure 15.12   Activity on node network diagram for the sales system design project

Programme evaluation and review technique (PERT)

The programme evaluation and review technique, or PERT as it is universally known, had its origins in planning and controlling major defence projects in the US Navy. PERT had its most spectacular gains in the highly uncertain environment of space and defence projects. The technique recognizes that activity durations and costs in project management are not deterministic (fixed), and that probability theory can be applied to estimates, as was shown in Figure 15.7.

Operations principle
Probabilistic activity time estimates facilitate the assessment of a project being completed on time.

In this type of network each activity duration is estimated on an optimistic, a most likely and a pessimistic basis, and the mean and variance of the distribution that describes each activity can be estimated as was shown in Figure 15.7. The results are shown in Table 15.3.

In this case the sum of the expected times for each of the activities on the critical path (b–e–f) is 58.17 days, and the sum of the variances of these three activities is 6.07 days. From this, one could calculate the probability of the project overrunning by different amounts of time.

Table 15.3   PERT parameters for the sales system design project

Code	Activity	Optimistic estimate	Most likely estimate	Pessimistic estimate	Expected time	Variance
a	Form and train user group	8	10	14	10.33	1
b	Install systems	10	17	25	17.17	0.69
c	Specify sales training	4	5	6	5	0.11
d	Design initial screen interface	5	5	5	5	0
e	Test interface in pilot area	22	25	27	24.83	0.69
f	Modify interface	12	15	25	16.17	4.69

DIAGNOSTIC QUESTION

Is the project adequately controlled?

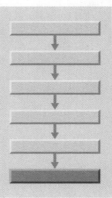

All the stages in project management described so far have taken place before the actual project takes place. Project control deals with activities during the execution of the project. Project control is the essential link between planning and doing.

The process of project control involves three sets of decisions:

- How to monitor the project in order to check on its progress
- How to assess the performance of the project by comparing monitored observations of the project with the project plan
- How to intervene in the project in order to make the changes that will bring it back to plan.

Project monitoring

Project managers have first to decide what they should be looking for as the project progresses. Usually a variety of measures are monitored. To some extent, the measures used will depend on the nature of the project. However, common measures include current expenditure to date, supplier price changes, amount of overtime authorized, technical changes to project, inspection failures, number and length of delays, activities not started on time, missed milestones, etc. Some of these monitored measures affect mainly cost, some mainly time. However, when something affects the quality of the project, there are also time and cost implications. This is because quality problems in project planning and control usually have to be solved in a limited amount of time.

Assessing project performance

A typical planned cost profile of a project through its life is shown in Figure 15.13. At the beginning of a project some activities can be started, but most activities will be dependent on finishing. Eventually, only a few activities will remain to be completed. This pattern of a slow start followed by a faster pace with an eventual tail-off of activity holds true for almost all projects, which is why the rate of total expenditure follows an S-shaped pattern as shown in Figure 15.13, even when the cost curves for the individual activities are linear. It is against this curve that actual costs can be compared in order to check whether the project's costs are being incurred to plan. Figure 15.13 shows the planned and actual cost figures compared in this way. It shows that the project is incurring costs, on a cumulative basis, ahead of what was planned.

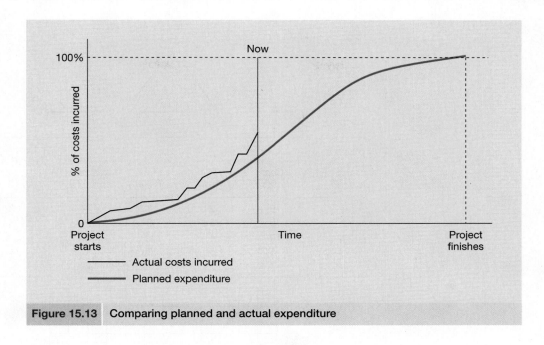

Figure 15.13   Comparing planned and actual expenditure

Intervening to change the project

If the project is obviously out of control in the sense that its costs, quality levels or times are significantly different from those planned, then some kind of intervention is almost certainly likely to be required. The exact nature of the intervention will depend on the technical characteristics of the project, but it is likely to need the advice of all the people who would be affected. Given the interconnected nature of projects – a change to one part of the project will have knock-on effects elsewhere – this means that interventions often require wide consultation. Sometimes intervention is needed even if the project looks to be proceeding according to plan. For example, the schedule and cost for a project may seem to be 'to plan', but when the project managers project activities and cost into the future, they see that problems are very likely to arise. In this case it is the trend of performance which is being used to trigger intervention.

Crashing, or accelerating, activities

Crashing activities is the process of reducing time spans on critical path activities so that the project is completed in less time. Usually, crashing activities incurs extra cost. This can be as a result of the following factors:

● Overtime working
● Additional resources, such as manpower
● Sub-contracting.

Figure 15.14 shows an example of crashing a simple network. For each activity the duration and normal cost are specified, together with the (reduced) duration and (increased)

> **Operations principle**
> Only accelerating activities on the critical path(s) will accelerate the whole project.

cost of crashing them. Not all activities are capable of being crashed; here activity **e** cannot be crashed. The critical path is the sequence of activities **a**, **b**, **c**, **e**. If the total project time is to be reduced, one of the activities on the critical path must be crashed. In order to decide which activity to crash, the 'cost slope' of each

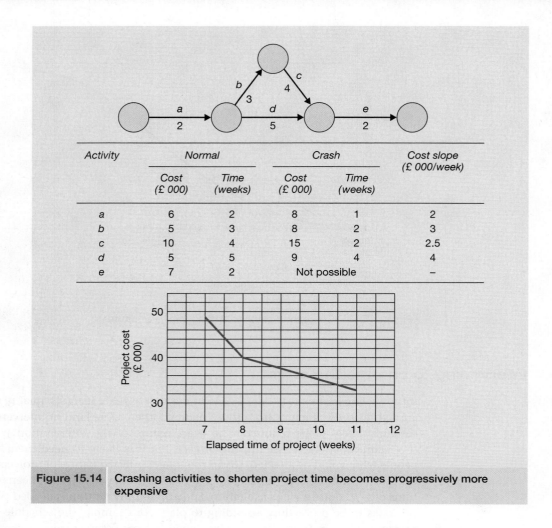

Activity	Normal		Crash		Cost slope (£ 000/week)
	Cost (£ 000)	Time (weeks)	Cost (£ 000)	Time (weeks)	
a	6	2	8	1	2
b	5	3	8	2	3
c	10	4	15	2	2.5
d	5	5	9	4	4
e	7	2	Not possible		–

Figure 15.14 Crashing activities to shorten project time becomes progressively more expensive

is calculated. This is the cost per time period of reducing durations. The most cost-effective way of shortening the whole project then is to crash the activity on the critical path which has the lowest cost slope. This is activity **a**, the crashing of which will cost an extra £2000 and will shorten the project by one week. After this, activity **c** can be crashed, saving a further two weeks and costing an extra £5000. At this point all the activities have become critical and further time savings can only be achieved by crashing two activities in parallel.

The shape of the time–cost curve in Figure 15.14 is entirely typical. Initial savings come relatively inexpensively if the activities with the lowest cost slope are chosen. Later in the crashing sequence the more expensive activities need to be crashed and eventually two or more paths become jointly critical. Inevitably by that point, savings in time can only come from crashing two or more activities on parallel paths.

Computer-assisted project management

For many years, since the emergence of computer-based modelling, increasingly sophisticated software for project planning and control has become available. The rather tedious computation necessary in network planning can be performed relatively easily by project planning models. All they need are the basic relationships between activities together with timing and resource requirements for each activity. Earliest and latest event times, float and other characteristics of a network can be presented, often in the form of a Gantt chart. More significantly, the speed of computation allows for frequent updates to project plans. Similarly, if updated information is both accurate and frequent, such computer-based systems can also provide effective project control data. More recently, the potential for using computer-based project management systems for communication within large and complex projects has been developed in so-called Enterprise Project Management (EPM) systems.

Figure 15.15 illustrates just some of the elements that are integrated within EPM systems. Most of these activities have been treated in this chapter. Project planning involves critical path analysis and scheduling, an understanding of float, and the sending of instructions on when to start activities. Resource scheduling looks at the resource implications of planning decisions and the way projects may have to be changed to accommodate resource constraints. Project control includes simple budgeting and cost management together with more sophisticated earned value control. However, EPM also includes other elements. Project modelling involves the use of project planning methods to explore alternative approaches to a project, identifying where failure might occur and exploring the changes to the project which may have to be made under alternative future scenarios. Project portfolio analysis acknowledges that, for many organizations, several projects have to be managed simultaneously. Usually these share common resources. Therefore, not only delays in one activity within a project affect other activities in that project, they may also have an impact on completely different projects which are relying on the same resource. Finally, integrated EPM systems can help to communicate, both within a project and to outside organizations which may be contributing to the project.

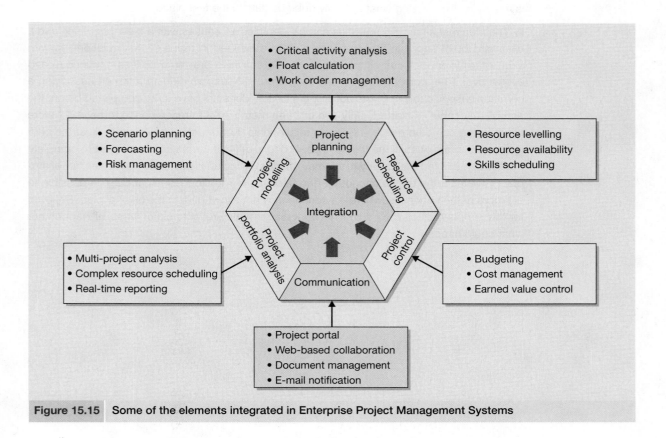

Figure 15.15   Some of the elements integrated in Enterprise Project Management Systems

Much of this communication facility is Web-based. Project portals can allow all stakeholders to transact activities and gain a clear view of the current status of a project. Automatic notification of significant milestones can be made by e-mail. At a very basic level, the various documents that specify parts of the project can be stored in an online library. Some people argue that it is this last element of communication capabilities that is the most useful part of EPM systems.

Critical commentary

Each chapter contains a short critical commentary on the main ideas covered in the chapter. Its purpose is not to undermine the issues discussed in the chapter, but to emphasize that, although we present a relatively orthodox view of operation, there are other perspectives.

■ When project managers talk of 'time estimates', they are really talking about guessing. By definition, planning a project happens in advance of the project itself. Therefore, no one really knows how long each activity will take. Of course, some kind of guess is needed for planning purposes. However, some project managers believe that too much faith is put in time estimates. The really important question, they claim, is not how long will something take, but how long could something take without delaying the whole project. Also, if a single most likely time estimate is difficult to estimate, then using three, as one does for probabilistic estimates, is merely over-analyzing what is highly dubious data in the first place.

■ The idea that all project activities can be identified as entities with a clear beginning and a clear end point and that these entities can be described in terms of their relationship with each other is an obvious simplification. Some activities are more or less continuous and evolve over time. For example, take a simple project such as digging a trench and laying a communications cable in it. The activity 'dig trench' does not have to be completed before the activity 'lay cable' is started. Only two or three metres of the trench needs to be dug before cable laying can commence – a simple relationship, but one that is difficult to illustrate on a network diagram. Also, if the trench is being dug in difficult terrain, the time taken to complete the activity, or even the activity itself, may change, to include rock drilling activities, for example. However, if the trench cannot be dug because of rock formations, it may be possible to dig more of the trench elsewhere – a contingency not allowed for in the original plan. So, even for this simple project, the original network diagram may reflect neither what will happen nor what could happen.

Summary checklist

DOWNLOADABLE

This checklist comprises questions that can be usefully applied to any type of operations and reflect the major diagnostic questions used within the chapter.

- [ ] Have all the factors that could influence the project been identified?
- [ ] Do these factors include both external and internal influences?
- [ ] Has the project been assessed for its intrinsic difficulty by considering its relative scale, uncertainty and complexity, when compared to other projects?
- [ ] Is the importance of stakeholder management fully understood?
- [ ] Have the rights and responsibilities of project stakeholders been defined?
- [ ] Have all stakeholders been identified?
- [ ] Have all stakeholders been prioritized in terms of their relative power and interest?
- [ ] Has sufficient attention been paid to understanding the needs and motivation of key stakeholders?
- [ ] Has the project been well defined?
- [ ] Have the objectives of the project been defined, particularly in terms of the relative importance of cost, time and quality?
- [ ] Has the scope of the project been defined, including the areas that the project will not include?
- [ ] Has the overall strategy of the project been defined in terms of its overall approach, its significant milestones, and any decision gateways that may occur in the project?
- [ ] Have overall project management skills within the business been generally assessed?
- [ ] For this particular project, does the project manager have skills appropriate for the project's intrinsic degree of difficulty?
- [ ] Is sufficient effort being put into the project planning process?
- [ ] Have all activities been identified and expressed in the form of a work breakdown structure?
- [ ] Have all activity times and resources been estimated using the best possible information within the organization?
- [ ] Is there sufficient confidence in the time and resource estimates to make planning meaningful?
- [ ] Have the relationships and dependencies between activities been identified and summarized in the form of a simple network diagram?
- [ ] Have project planning tools, such as critical path analysis, been considered for the project?
- [ ] Have potential resource and time schedule constraints been built into the project plan?
- [ ] Are there mechanisms in place to monitor the progress of the project?
- [ ] Is there a formal mechanism to assess progress against project plans?
- [ ] Have mechanisms for intervening in the project to bring it back to plan been put in place?
- [ ] Is the level of computer-based project management support appropriate for the degree of difficulty of the project?

Case study   United Photonics Malaysia Sdn Bhd

Introduction

Anuar Kamaruddin, COO of United Photonics Malaysia (EPM), was conscious that the project in front of him was one of the most important he had handled for many years. The number and variety of the development projects under way within the company had risen sharply in the last few years, and although they had all seemed important at the time, this one – the 'Laz-skan' project – clearly justified the description given it by the President of United Photonics Corporation, the US parent of UPM: '. . . *the make or break opportunity to ensure the division's long term position in the global instrumentation industry.*'

The United Photonics Group

United Photonics Corporation had been founded in the 1920s (as the Detroit Gauge Company), a general instrument and gauge manufacturer for the engineering industry. By expanding its range into optical instruments in the early 1930s, it eventually moved also into the manufacture of high precision and speciality lenses, mainly for the photographic industry. Its reputation as a specialist lens manufacturer led to such a growth in sales that by 1969 the optical side of the company accounted for about 60 per cent of total business and it ranked as one of the top two or three optics companies of its type in the world. Although its reputation for skilled lens making had not diminished since then, the instrument side of the company had come to dominate sales once again in the 1980s and 1990s.

UPM product range

UPM's product range on the optical side included lenses for inspection systems which were used mainly in the manufacture of microchips. These lenses were sold both to the inspection system manufacturers and to the chip manufacturers themselves. They were very high-precision lenses; however, most of the company's optical products were specialist photographic and cinema lenses. In addition about 15 per cent of the company's optical work was concerned with the development and manufacture of 'one or two off' extremely high-precision lenses for defence contracts, specialist scientific instrumentation, and other optical companies. The group's instrument product range consisted largely of electromechanical assemblies with an increasing emphasis on software-based recording, display

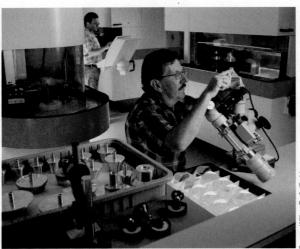

Source: William Taufic/Corbis

and diagnostic abilities. This move towards more software-based products had led the instrument side of the business towards accepting some customized orders. The growth of this part of the instrumentation had resulted in a special development unit being set up – the Customer Services Unit (CSU), which modified, customized or adapted products for those customers who required an unusual product. Often CSU's work involved incorporating the company's products into larger systems for a customer.

In 1995 United Photonics Corporation had set up its first non-North American facility just outside Kuala Lumpur in Malaysia. United Photonics Malaysia Sdn Bhd (UPM) had started by manufacturing sub-assemblies for Photonics instrumentation products, but soon had developed in a laboratory for the modification of United Photonics products for customers throughout the Asian region. This part of the Malaysian business was headed by T.S. Lim, a Malaysian engineer who had taken his postgraduate qualifications at Stanford and three years ago moved back to his native KL to head up the Malaysian outpost of the CSU, reporting directly to Bob Brierly, the Vice-President of Development, who ran the main CSU in Detroit. Over the last three years, T.S. Lim and his small team of engineers had gained quite a reputation for innovative development. Bob Brierly was delighted with their enthusiasm. '*Those guys really do know how to make things happen. They are giving us all a run for our money.*'

The Laz-skan project

The idea for Laz-skan had come out of a project which T.S. Lim's CSU had been involved with in 2004. At that time the CSU had successfully installed a high precision Photonics lens into a character recognition system for a large clearing bank. The enhanced capability which the lens and software modifications had given had enabled the bank to scan documents even when they were not correctly aligned. This had led to CSU proposing the development of a 'vision metrology' device that could optically scan a product at some point in the manufacturing process, and check the accuracy of up to 20 individual dimensions. The geometry of the product to be scanned, the dimensions to be gauged, and the tolerances to be allowed, could all be programmed into the control logic of the device. The T.S. Lim team were convinced that the idea could have considerable potential. The proposal, which the CSU team had called the Laz-skan project, was put to Bob Brierly in August 2004. Brierly both saw the potential value of the idea and was again impressed by the CSU team's enthusiasm. 'To be frank, it was their evident enthusiasm that influenced me as much as anything. Remember that the Malaysian CSU had only been in existence for two years at this time – they were a group of keen but relatively young engineers. Yet their proposal was well thought out and, on reflection, seemed to have considerable potential.'

In November 2004 Lim and his team were allocated funds (outside the normal budget cycle) to investigate the feasibility of the Laz-skan idea. Lim was given one further engineer and a technician, and a three-month deadline to report to the board. In this time he was expected to overcome any fundamental technical problems, assess the feasibility of successfully developing the concept into a working prototype, and plan the development task that would lead to the prototype stage.

The Lim investigation

T.S. Lim, even at the start of his investigation, had some firm views as to the appropriate 'architecture' for the Laz-skan project. By 'architecture' he meant the major elements of the system, their functions, and how they related to each other. The Laz-skan system architecture would consider five major sub-systems: the lens and lens mounting, the vision support system, the display system, the control logic software, and the documentation.

T.S. Lim's first task, once the system's overall architecture was set, was to decide whether the various components in the major sub-systems would be developed in-house, developed by outside specialist companies from UPM's specifications, or bought in as standard units and if necessary modified in-house. Lim and his colleagues made these decisions themselves, while recognizing that a more consultative process might have been preferable. 'I am fully aware that ideally we should have made more use of the expertise within the company to decide how units were to be developed. But within the time available we just did not have the time to explain the product concept, explain the choices, and wait for already busy people to come up with a recommendation. Also there was the security aspect to think of. I'm sure our employees are to be trusted but the more people who know about the project, the more chance there is for leaks. Anyway, we did not see our decisions as final. For example, if we decided that a component was to be bought in and modified for the prototype building stage it does not mean that we can't change our minds and develop a better component in-house at a later stage.' By February 2005, TS's small team had satisfied themselves that the system could be built to achieve their original technical performance targets. Their final task before reporting to Brierly would be to devise a feasible development plan.

Planning the Laz-skan development

As a planning aid the team drew up a network diagram for all the major activities within the project from its start through to completion, when the project would be handed over to Manufacturing Operations. This is shown in Figure 15.16 and the complete list of all events in the diagram is shown in Table 15.4. The durations of all the activities in the project were estimated either by T.S. Lim or (more often) by him consulting a more experienced engineer back in Detroit. While he was reasonably confident in the estimates, he was keen to stress that they were just that – estimates.

Two draughting conventions on these networks need explanation. The three figures in brackets by each activity arrow represent the 'optimistic', 'most likely' and 'pessimistic' times (in weeks) respectively. The figure in the left side of the event circles indicates the earliest time the event could take place, and the figure in the right side of the circles indicates the latest time the event could take place without delaying the whole project. Dotted lines represent 'dummy' activities. These are nominal activities which have no time associated with them and are there either to maintain the logic of the network or for drafting convenience.

(1) The lens (events 5–13–14–15)

The lens was particularly critical since the shape was complex and precision was vital if the system was to perform up to its intended design specification. T.S. Lim was relying heavily upon the skill of the group's expert optics group in Pittsburgh to produce the lens to the required high tolerance. Since what in effect was a trial and error approach was involved in their manufacture, the exact

Table 15.4   Event listing for the Laz-skan project

Event number	Event description
1	Start systems engineering
2	Complete interface transient tests
3	Complete compatibility testing
4	Complete overall architecture block and simulation
5	Complete costing and purchasing tender planning
6	End alignment system design
7	Receive S/T/G, start synch mods
8	Receive Triscan/G, start synch mods
9	Complete B/A mods
10	Complete S/T/G mods
11	Complete Triscan/G mods
12	Start laser subsystem compatibility tests
13	Complete optic design and specification, start lens manufacture
14	Complete lens manufacture, start lens housing S/A
15	Lens S/A complete, start tests
16	Start technical specifications
17	Start help routine design
18	Update engineering mods
19	Complete doc sequence
20	Start vision routines
21	Start interface (tmsic) tests
22	Start system integration compatibility routines
23	Co-ordinate trinsic tests
24	End interface development
25	Complete alignment integration routine
26	Final alignment integration data consolidation
27	Start interface (tmnsic) programming
28	Complete alignment system routines
29	Start tmnsic comparator routines
30	Complete (interface) trinsic coding
31	Begin all logic system tests
32	Start cycle tests
33	Lens S/A complete
34	Start assembly of total system
35	Complete total system assembly
36	Complete final tests and dispatch

time to manufacture would be uncertain. T.S. Lim realized this: '*The lens is going to be a real problem. We just don't know how easy it will be to make the particular geometry and precision we need. The optics people won't commit themselves even though they are regarded as some of the best optics technicians in the world. It is a relief that lens development is not amongst the "critical path" activities.*'

(2) The vision support system (events 6–7–8–12, 9–5, 11)

The vision support system included many components which were commercially available, but considerable engineering effort would be required to modify them. Although the development design and testing of the vision support system was complicated, there was no great uncertainty in the individual activities, or therefore the schedule of completion. If more funds were allocated to their development, some tasks might even be completed ahead of time.

(3) The control software (events 20 to 26, 28)

The control software represented the most complex task, and the most difficult to plan and estimate. In fact, the software development unit had little experience of this type of work but (partly in anticipation of this type of development) had recently recruited a young software engineer with some experience of the type of work which would be needed for Laz-skan. He was confident that any technical problems could be solved even though the system needs were novel, but completion times would be difficult to predict with confidence.

(4) Documentation (events 5–16–17–18–19)

A relatively simple sub-system, 'documentation' included specifying and writing the technical manuals, maintenance routines, online diagnostics, and 'help desk' information. It was a relatively predictable activity, part of which was sub-contracted to technical writers and translation companies in Kuala Lumpur.

(5) The display system (events 29–27–30)

The simplest of the sub-systems to plan, the display system would need to be manufactured entirely outside the company and tested and calibrated on receipt.

Market prospects

In parallel with T.S. Lim's technical investigation, Sales and Marketing had been asked to estimate the market potential of Laz-skan. In a very short time, the Laz-skan

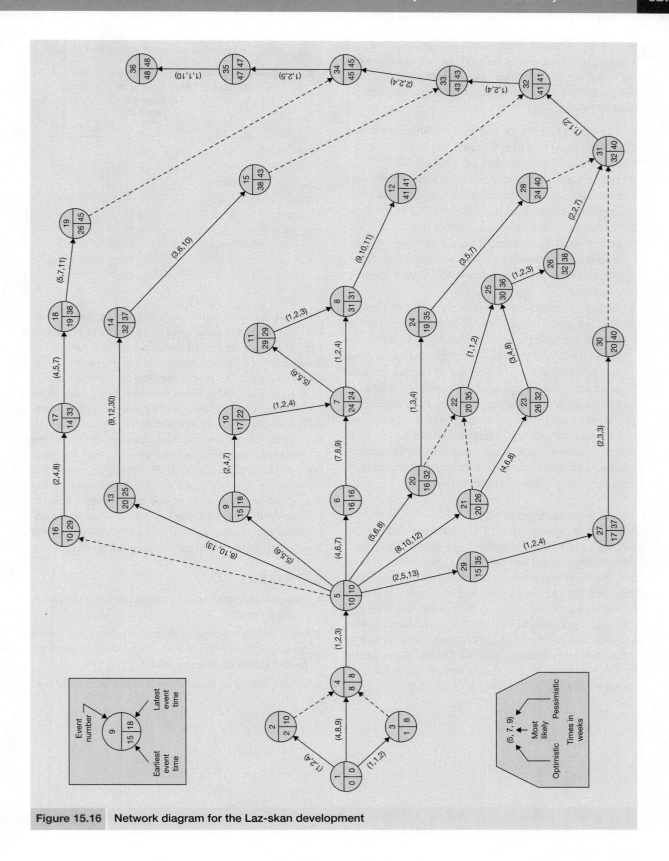

Figure 15.16   Network diagram for the Laz-skan development

project had aroused considerable enthusiasm within the function, to the extent that Halim Ramli, the Asian Marketing Vice President, had taken personal charge of the market study. The major conclusions from this investigation were as follows.

1 The global market for Laz-skan type systems was unlikely to be less than 50 systems per year in 2008, climbing to more than 200 per year by 2012.
2 The volume of the market in financial terms was more difficult to predict, but each system sold was likely to represent around US$300,000 of turnover.
3 Some customization of the system would be needed for most customers. This would mean greater emphasis on commissioning and post-installation service than was necessary for UPM's existing products.
4 Timing the launch of Laz-skan would be important. Two 'windows of opportunity' were critical. The first and most important was the major world trade show in Geneva in April 2006. This show, held every two years, was the most prominent showcase for new products such as Laz-skan. The second related to the development cycles of the original equipment manufacturers who would be the major customers for Laz-skan. Critical decisions would be taken in the autumn of 2006. If Laz-skan was to be incorporated into these companies' products it would have to be available from October 2006.

The Laz-skan go-ahead

At the end of February 2005 UPM considered both the Lim and the Ramli reports. In addition estimates of Laz-skan's manufacturing costs had been sought from George Hudson, the head of Instrument Development. His estimates indicated that Laz-skan's operating contribution would be far higher than those of the company's existing products. The board approved the immediate commencement of the Laz-skan development through to prototype stage, with an initial development budget of US$4,500,000. The objective of the project was to '. . . *build three prototype Laz-skan systems to be "up and running" for April 2006'*.

Table 15.5   Acceleration opportunities for Laz-skan

Activity	Acceleration cost (US$/ week)	Likely maximum activity time, with acceleration (weeks)	Normal most likely time (weeks)
5–6	23,400	3	6
5–9	10,500	2	5
5–13	25,000	8	10
20–24	5,000	2	3
24–28	11,700	3	5
33–34	19,500	1	2

The decision to go ahead was unanimous. Exactly how the project was to be managed provoked far more discussion. The Laz-skan project posed several problems. First, engineers had little experience of working on such a major project. Second, the crucial deadline for the first batch of prototypes meant that some activities might have to be accelerated, an expensive process that would need careful judgement. A very brief investigation into which activities could be accelerated had identified those where acceleration definitely would be possible and the likely cost of acceleration (Table 15.5). Finally, no one could agree either whether there should be a single project leader, which function he or she should come from, or how senior the project leader should be. Anuar Kamaruddin knew that these decisions could affect the success of the project, and possibly the company, for years to come.

QUESTIONS

1 Who do you think should manage the Laz-skan Development Project?
2 What are the major dangers and difficulties that will be faced by the development team as they manage the projects towards its completion?
3 What can they do about these dangers and difficulties?

Active case study   National Trust

ACTIVE CASE

The National Trust of England, Wales and Northern Ireland was formed in 1895 with the objective to preserve places of historic interest or natural beauty for the nation to enjoy. When the local director and his project team take on 'The Workhouse' they know from the outset that it will be one of their more intriguing and challenging projects. Aware of the need for sensitive stakeholder management, the team draws up a list of stakeholders and set out to win them over with their enthusiasm for the project.

● How would you assess their plans for dealing with each one?

Please refer to the Active case on the CD accompanying this book to find out more about the stakeholder groups involved.

Applying the principles

HINTS

Some of these exercises can be answered by reading the chapter. Others will require some general knowledge of business activity and some might require an element of investigation. All have hints on how they can be answered on the CD accompanying this book.

1 The activities, their durations and precedences for designing, writing and installing a bespoke computer database are shown in the table below. Draw a Gantt chart and a network diagram for the project and calculate the fastest time in which the operation might be completed.

Bespoke computer database activities

Activity	Duration (weeks)	Activities that must be completed before it can start
1 Contract negotiation	1	–
2 Discussions with main users	2	1
3 Review of current documentation	5	1
4 Review of current systems	6	2
5 Systems analysis (A)	4	3, 4
6 Systems analysis (B)	7	5
7 Programming	12	5
8 Testing (prelim)	2	7
9 Existing system review report	1	3, 4
10 System proposal report	2	5, 9
11 Documentation preparation	19	5, 8
12 Implementation	7	7, 11
13 System test	3	12
14 Debugging	4	12
15 Manual preparation	5	11

2 Identify a project of which you have been part (for example moving apartments, a holiday, a dramatic production, revision for an examination, etc.).

- Who were the stakeholders in this project?
- What was the overall project objective (especially in terms of the relative importance of cost, quality and time)?
- Were there any resource constraints?
- Looking back, how could you have managed the project better?

3 The Channel Tunnel project was the largest construction project ever undertaken in Europe and the biggest single investment in transport anywhere in the world. The project, which was funded by the private sector, made provision for a 55-year concession for the owners to design, build and run the operation. The Eurotunnel Group awarded the contract to design and build the tunnel to TML (Trans-Manche Link), a consortium of 10 French and British construction companies. For the project managers it was a formidable undertaking. The sheer scale of the project was daunting in itself. The volume of rubble removed from the tunnel increased the size of Britain by the equivalent of 68 football fields. Two main railway tunnels, separated by a service/access tunnel, each 7.6 metres in diameter, run 40 metres below the sea bed. In total there are in excess of 150 kilometres of tunnel. The whole project was never going to be a straightforward management task. During the early negotiations, political uncertainty surrounded the commitment of both governments, and in the planning phase geological issues had to be investigated by a complex series of tests. Even the financing of the project was complex. It required investment by over 200 banks and finance houses, as well as over half a million shareholders. Furthermore, the technical problems posed by the drilling itself and, more importantly, in the commissioning of the tracks and systems within the tunnel needed to be overcome. Yet in spite of some delays and cost overruns, the project ranks as one of the most impressive of the twentieth century.

- What factors made the Channel Tunnel a particularly complex project and how might these have been dealt with?
- What factors contributed to 'uncertainty' in the project and how might these factors have been dealt with?
- Look on the Internet to see what has happened to the Channel Tunnel since it was built. How does this affect your view on the project of building it?

4 Identify your favourite sporting team (Manchester United, the Toulon rugby team, or if you are not a sporting person, choose any team you have heard of).

- What kind of projects do you think they need to manage? For example, merchandising, sponsorship, etc.
- What do you think are the key issues in making a success of managing each of these different types of project?

5 Visit the websites of some companies that have developed computer-based project management software (for example, **primavera.com**, **welcome.com**, **microsoft.com**, or just put 'project management software' in a search engine).

- What appear to be the common elements in the software packages on offer from these companies? Develop a method that could be used by any operation to choose different types of software.

Notes on chapter

1 Reiss, G. (1996) *Programme Management Demystified*, Spon, London.
2 Slack, A. (2005) 'Popping the Millau Cork', translated and adapted from *Le Figaro Entreprises*, 15 December 2004.
3 Source: Organization website.
4 Weiss, J.W. and Wysocki, R.K. (1992) *Five-Phase Project Management: A practical planning and implementation guide*, Addison-Wesley.

Taking it further

There are hundreds of books on project management. They range from the introductory to the very detailed, and from the managerial to the highly mathematical. Here are two general (as opposed to mathematical) books which are worth looking at.

Maylor, H. (2003) *Project Management* (3rd edn), Financial Times Prentice Hall.

Meredith, J.R. and Mantel, S. (1995) *Project Management:* A managerial approach (3rd edn), John Wiley.

Useful websites

www.apm.org.uk The UK Association for Project Management. Contains a description of what professionals consider to be the body of knowledge of project management.

www.pmi.org The Project Management Institute's home page. An American association for professionals. Insights into professional practice.

www.ipma.ch The International Project Management Association, based in Zürich. Some definitions and links.

www.comp.glam.ac.uk/pages/staff/dwfarth/projman.htm#automated A great site with lots of interesting stuff on software, project management and related issues, but also very good for general project management.

**FURTHER
RESOURCES**

For further resources including examples, animated diagrams, self-test questions, Excel spreadsheets, active case studies and video materials please explore the CD accompanying this book.

Part II

Taken from *Financial and Managerial Accounting,* Second Edition by
Charles T. Horngren, Walter T. Harrison, and M. Suzanne Oliver

The Statement of Cash Flows

Learning Objectives/Success Keys

1 Identify the purposes of the Statement of Cash Flows

2 Distinguish among operating, investing, and financing cash flows

3 Prepare the Statement of Cash Flows by the indirect method

4 Prepare the Statement of Cash Flows by the direct method (Appendix 13A)

Why is cash so important? You can probably answer that question from your own experience: It takes cash to pay the bills. You have some income and you have expenses; and these events create cash receipts and payments.

Businesses, including Smart Touch Learning, Inc., and Greg's Groovy Tunes, Inc., work the same way. Net income is a good thing, but Smart Touch and Greg's both need enough cash to pay the bills and run their operations.

This chapter covers cash flows—cash receipts and cash payments. We will see how to prepare the Statement of Cash Flows, starting with the format used by the vast majority of non-public companies; it is called the *indirect method*. Chapter Appendix 13A covers the alternate format of the Statement of Cash Flows, the *direct method*.

The chapter has four distinct sections:

- Introduction: The Statement of Cash Flows
- Preparing the Statement of Cash Flows by the Indirect Method
- Chapter Appendix 13A: Preparing the Statement of Cash Flows by the Direct Method
- Chapter Appendix 13B: Preparing the Statement of Cash Flows Using a Spreadsheet

The focus company throughout the chapter once again is Smart Touch Learning.

Chapter Appendix 13B shows how to use a spreadsheet to prepare the Statement of Cash Flows. This appendix presents the indirect-method spreadsheet first, and the direct-method spreadsheet last—to maintain consistency with the order in which these topics are covered in the chapter.

Introduction: The Statement of Cash Flows

1 Identify the purposes of the Statement of Cash Flows

The Balance Sheet reports financial position. When a comparative Balance Sheet for two periods is presented, it shows whether cash increased or decreased. For example, Smart Touch Learning's comparative Balance Sheet reported the following:

	2011	2010	Increase (Decrease)
Cash..........	$22,000	$42,000	$(20,000)

Smart Touch's cash decreased by $20,000 during 2011. But the Balance Sheet does not show *why* cash decreased. We need the cash-flow statement for that.

The Statement of Cash Flows reports **cash flows**—cash receipts and cash payments. It

- shows where cash came from (receipts) and how cash was spent (payments).
- reports why cash increased or decreased during the period.
- covers a span of time and is dated the same as the Income Statement—"Year Ended December 31, 2011," for example.

The Statement of Cash Flows explains why net income as reported on the Income Statement does not equal the change in the cash balance. In essence the cash flow statement is the communicating link between the accrual based Income Statement and the cash reported on the Balance Sheet.

Exhibit 13-1 illustrates the relationships among the Balance Sheet, the Income Statement, and the Statement of Cash Flows.

How do people use cash-flow information? The Statement of Cash Flows helps

1. **predict future cash flows.** Past cash receipts and payments help predict future cash flows.

2. **evaluate management decisions.** Wise investment decisions help the business prosper, while unwise decisions cause problems. Investors and creditors use cash-flow information to evaluate managers' decisions.

3. **predict ability to pay debts and dividends.** Lenders want to know whether they will collect on their loans. Stockholders want dividends on their investments. The Statement of Cash Flows helps make these predictions.

Cash Equivalents

On a Statement of Cash Flows, *Cash* means more than cash on hand and cash in the bank. *Cash* includes **cash equivalents,** which are highly liquid investments that can be converted into cash quickly. As the name implies, cash equivalents are so close to cash that they are treated as "equals." Examples of cash equivalents are money-market accounts and investments in U.S. government securities. Throughout this chapter, the term *cash* refers to both cash and cash equivalents.

EXHIBIT 13-1 | **Timing of the Financial Statements**

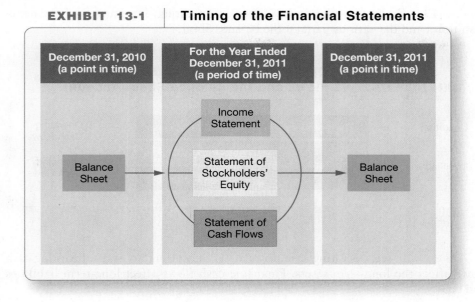

Operating, Investing, and Financing Activities

There are three basic types of cash-flow activities and the Statement of Cash Flows has a section for each:

2 Distinguish among operating, investing, and financing cash flows

- Operating activities
- Investing activities
- Financing activities

   Let us see what each section reports.

Operating Activities

- Is the most important category of cash flows because it reflects the day-to-day operations that determine the future of an organization
- Create revenues, expenses, gains, and losses
- Affect net income on the Income Statement
- Affect current assets and current liabilities on the Balance Sheet

Investing Activities

- Increase and decrease long-term assets, such as computers, software, land, buildings, and equipment
- Include purchases and sales of these assets, plus loans receivable from others and collections of those loans

Financing Activities

- Increase and decrease long-term liabilities and equity
- Include issuing stock, paying dividends, and buying and selling treasury stock
- Include borrowing money and paying off loans

Exhibit 13-2 shows the relationship between operating, investing, and financing cash flows and the various parts of the Balance Sheet.

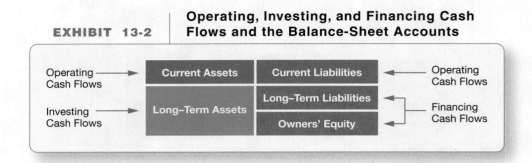

| EXHIBIT 13-2 | Operating, Investing, and Financing Cash Flows and the Balance-Sheet Accounts |

As you can see, operating cash flows affect the current accounts. Investing cash flows affect the long-term assets. Financing cash flows affect long-term liabilities and equity.

Two Formats for Operating Activities

There are two ways to format operating activities on the Statement of Cash Flows:

- The **indirect method** starts with net income and adjusts it to net cash provided by operating activities.
- The **direct method** restates the Income Statement in terms of cash. The direct method shows all the cash receipts and all the cash payments from operating activities.

   The indirect and direct methods:

- use different computations but produce the same amount of cash flow from operations.
- have no effect on investing activities or financing activities.

   Let us begin with the indirect method because most companies use it. To focus on the direct method, go to Appendix 13A.

Preparing the Statement of Cash Flows by the Indirect Method

3 Prepare the Statement of Cash Flows by the indirect method

To prepare the Statement of Cash Flows, you need the Income Statement and both the beginning and the ending Balance Sheets. Consider Smart Touch Learning's financial statements on page 687. To prepare the Statement of Cash Flows by the indirect method follow Steps 1–4:

STEP 1: Lay out the statement format as shown in Exhibit 13-3. Steps 2–4 will complete the Statement of Cash Flows.

EXHIBIT 13-3	**Format of the Statement of Cash Flows:** **Indirect Method**

SMART TOUCH LEARNING, INC.
Statement of Cash Flows
Year Ended December 31, 2011

Cash flows from operating activities:		
Net income		
Adjustments to reconcile net income to net cash provided by		
operating activities:		
+ Depreciation / amortization expense		
+ Loss on sale of long-term assets		
− Gain on sale of long-term assets		
− Increases in current assets other than cash		
+ Decreases in current assets other than cash		
+ Increases in current liabilities		
− Decreases in current liabilities		
Net cash provided by operating activities		
± Cash flows from investing activities:		
+ Cash receipts from sales of long-term assets (investments, land,		
building, equipment, and so on)		
− Purchases of long-term assets		
Net cash provided by (used for) investing activities		
± Cash flows from financing activities:		
+ Cash receipts from issuance of stock		
+ Sale of treasury stock		
− Purchase of treasury stock		
+ Cash receipts from issuance of notes or bonds payable (borrowing)		
− Payment of notes or bonds payable		
− Payment of dividends		
Net cash provided by (used for) financing activities		
= Net increase (decrease) in cash during the year		
+ Cash at December 31, 2010		
= Cash at December 31, 2011		

STEP 2: Compute the change in cash from the comparative Balance Sheet. The change in cash is the "key reconciling figure" for the Statement of Cash Flows. Exhibit 13-8 is the comparative Balance Sheet of Smart Touch Learning, where the top line shows that cash decreased by $20,000 during 2011.

STEP 3: Take net income, depreciation, and any gains or losses from the Income Statement. Exhibit 13-9 gives the 2011 Income Statement of Smart Touch Learning, with the relevant items highlighted.

STEP 4: Complete the Statement of Cash Flows, using data from the Income Statement and the Balance Sheet. The statement is complete only after you have explained all the year-to-year changes in all the accounts on the Balance Sheet.

Let us apply these steps to show the operating activities of Smart Touch Learning. Exhibit 13-4 gives the operating activities section of the Statement of Cash Flows. All items are highlighted for emphasis. That makes it easy to trace the data from one statement to the other.

EXHIBIT 13-4 | **Operating Activities**

	SMART TOUCH LEARNING, INC. Statement of Cash Flows Year Ended December 31, 2011		
	Cash flows from operating activities:		*(Thousands)*
A	Net income		$ 40
	Adjustments to reconcile net income to net cash provided by operating activities:		
B	Depreciation	$ 20	
C	Gain on sale of plant assets	(10)	
D	Increase in accounts receivable	(17)	
	Decrease in inventory	2	
	Increase in accounts payable	40	
	Decrease in accrued liabilities	(5)	30
	Net cash provided by operating activities		70

EXHIBIT 13-5 | **Investing Activities**

	Cash flows from investing activities:		
E	Acquisition of plant assets	$(310)	
F	Cash receipt from sale of plant asset	50	
	Net cash used for investing activities		(260)

EXHIBIT 13-6 | **Financing Activities**

	Cash flows from financing activities:		
I	Cash receipt from issuance of common stock	120	
G	Cash receipt from issuance of notes payable	90	
H	Payment of notes payable	(10)	
J	Purchase of treasury stock	(20)	
K	Payment of dividends	(10)	
	Net cash provided by financing activities		170

EXHIBIT 13-7 | **Net Decrease in Cash and Cash Balance— Completed Statement**

Net decrease in cash		$ (20)
Cash balance, December 31, 2010		42
Cash balance, December 31, 2011		$ 22

Cash Flows from Operating Activities

Operating cash flows begin with net income, taken from the Income Statement.

A Net Income

The Statement of Cash Flows—indirect method—begins with net income because revenues and expenses, which affect net income, produce cash receipts and cash payments. Revenues bring in cash receipts, and expenses must be paid. But net income is accrual based and the cash flows (cash basis net income) do not always equal the accrual basis revenues and expenses. For example, sales *on account* are revenues that increase net income, but the company has not yet collected cash from those sales. Accrued expenses decrease your net income, but you have not paid cash *if the expenses are accrued.*

To go from net income to cash flow from operations, we must make some adjustments to net income on the Statement of Cash Flows. These additions and subtractions follow net income and are labeled *Adjustments to reconcile net income to net cash provided by operating activities.*

EXHIBIT 13-8 | **Comparative Balance Sheet**

SMART TOUCH LEARNING, INC.
Comparative Balance Sheet
December 31, 2011 and 2010

(In thousands)	2011	2010	Increase (Decrease)	
Assets				
Current:				
Cash	$ 22	$ 42	$ (20)	
Accounts receivable	90	73	17	D
Inventory	143	145	(2)	
Plant assets, net	460	210	250	E/F
Total assets	$715	$470	$245	
Liabilities				
Current:			—	
Accounts payable	$ 90	$ 50	$ 40	D
Accrued liabilities	5	10	–5	
Long-term notes payable	160	80	80	G/H
Stockholders' Equity				
Common stock	370	250	120	I
Retained earnings	110	80	30	A/K
Less: Treasury stock	(20)	0	(20)	J
	$715	$470	$245	

EXHIBIT 13-9 | **Income Statement**

SMART TOUCH LEARNING, INC.
Income Statement
Year Ended December 31, 2011

	(In thousands)	
Revenues and gains:		
Sales revenue	$286	
Interest revenue	12	
Dividend revenue	9	
C Gain on sale of plant assets	10	
Total revenues and gains		$317
Expenses:		
Cost of goods sold	$156	
Salary and wage expense	56	
B Depreciation expense	20	
Other operating expense	16	
Interest expense	15	
Income tax expense	14	
Total expenses		277
A Net income		$ 40

B Depreciation, Depletion, and Amortization Expenses

These expenses are added back to net income to reconcile from net income to cash flow from operations. Let us see why this occurs. Depreciation is recorded as follows:

Depreciation expense	(E+)	20,000	
Accumulated depreciation	(CA+)		20,000

You can see that depreciation does not affect cash because there is no Cash account in the journal entry. However, depreciation, like all the other expenses, decreases net income. Therefore, to go from net income to cash flows, we must remove depreciation by adding it back to net income.

Example: Suppose you had only two transactions during the period:

- $40,000 cash sale
- Depreciation expense of $20,000

Accrual basis net income is $20,000 ($40,000 − $20,000). But cash flow from operations is $40,000. To reconcile from net income, $20,000, to cash flow from operations, $40,000, add back depreciation, $20,000. Also add back depletion and amortization expenses because they are similar to depreciation.

C Gains and Losses on the Sale of Assets

Sales of long-term assets such as land and buildings are investing activities, and these sales usually create a gain or a loss. The gain or loss is included in net income, which is already in the operating section of the cash flow statement. Gains and losses require an adjustment to cash flow from operating activities: The gain or loss must be removed from net income on the Statement of Cash Flows so the total cash from the transaction can be shown in the investing section.

Exhibit 13-4 includes an adjustment for a gain. During 2011 Smart Touch sold equipment and there was a gain of $10,000 on the sale. The gain was included in the calculation of net income on the Income Statement, so the gain must be removed from operating cash flows. The gain made net income bigger, so it is deducted from the operating section. On the other hand, a loss on the sale of plant assets would make net income smaller, so it would be added back to net income.

D Changes in the Current Assets and the Current Liabilities

Most current assets and current liabilities result from operating activities. For example,

- accounts receivable result from sales,
- inventory relates to cost of goods sold, and so on.

Changes in the current accounts create adjustments to net income on the cash-flow statement, as follows:

↑ Current assets   ↓ Cash

1. **An increase in a current asset other than cash causes a decrease in cash.** It takes cash to acquire assets. If Accounts receivable, Inventory, or Prepaid expenses increased, then cash decreased. Therefore, subtract the increase in the current asset from net income to get cash flow from operations. For example, Smart Touch's Accounts Receivable went up by $17,000. That increase in the current asset shows as a decrease in cash on the cash flow statement (Exhibit 13-4).

2. **A decrease in a current asset other than cash causes an increase in cash.** Smart Touch's Inventory decreased by $2,000. What caused the decrease? Smart Touch must have sold some inventory, and collected cash. Therefore, we add the decrease in Inventory of $2,000 in the cash flow statement (Exhibit 13-4).

↓ **Current assets** ↑ **Cash**

3. **A decrease in a current liability causes a decrease in cash.** The payment of a current liability decreases cash. Therefore, we subtract decreases in current liabilities from net income to get cash flow from operations. Smart Touch's Accrued liabilities went down $5,000. That change shows up as a $5,000 decrease in cash flows in Exhibit 13-4.

↓ **Current liabilities** ↓ **Cash**

4. **An increase in a current liability causes an increase in cash.** Smart Touch's Accounts payable increased by $40,000. This means that cash was not spent at the time the expense was incurred, but rather it will be paid at a later time—resulting in a liability. Accordingly, even though net income was reduced by the expense, cash was not reduced. However, cash will be reduced later when Smart Touch pays off its liability. Therefore, an increase in a current liability is *added* to net income in the Statement of Cash Flows (Exhibit 13-4).

↑ **Current liabilities** ↑ **Cash**

Evaluating Cash Flows from Operating Activities

During 2011, Smart Touch Learning's operations provided net cash flow of $70,000. This amount exceeds net income (due to the various adjustments discussed in sections B, C, and D). However, to fully evaluate a company's cash flows, we must also examine its investing and financing activities. Exhibit 13-4 shows the completed operating activities section.

Stop & Think...

The operating activities represent the core of the day to day results of any business. Remember when we learned the difference between accrual and cash basis accounting? All the operating activities section represents is a cash basis income statement. With the indirect method, we indirectly back into cash basis—that is, we start with accrual basis net income and adjust it back to cash basis "operating" cash flows (cash basis net income).

Cash Flows from Investing Activities

Investing activities affect long-term assets, such as Plant assets and Investments. These are shown for Smart Touch in Exhibit 13-5. Let us see how to compute the investing cash flows.

Computing Acquisitions and Sales of Plant Assets

Companies keep a separate account for each asset. But for computing investing cash flows, it is helpful to combine all the plant assets into a single Plant assets account. We subtract Accumulated depreciation from the assets' cost in order to work with a single net figure for plant assets, such as Plant assets, net—$460,000. This simplifies the computations.

To illustrate, observe that Smart Touch Learning's

- Balance Sheet reports plant assets, net of depreciation, of $460,000 at the end of 2011 and $210,000 at the end of 2010 (Exhibit 13-8).
- Income Statement shows depreciation expense of $20,000 and a $10,000 gain on sale of plant assets (Exhibit 13-9).

Also, assume that Smart Touch's acquisitions of plant assets during 2011 totaled $310,000. **E**

This gives us an incomplete T-account as follows:

Plant assets, net

12/31/10 Bal	210,000		
		Depreciation (from Inc Stmt)	20,000
Acquisitions	310,000	Sales	?
12/31/11 Bal	460,000		

We also know that Smart Touch sold some older plant assets because there was a gain on sale of assets reported on the Income Statement. We don't care about the gain itself, we need to know the cash amount of the sale. Remember, we are looking for cash movement. How much cash did the business receive from the sale of plant assets? First, let us look at the cost of the sold assets. This will be the missing value in our Plant assets, net T-account.

12/31/10 Bal + Acquisitions − Depreciation − Sales? = 12/31/11 Bal
210,000   +   310,000   −   20,000   − Sales? = 460,000
500,000   − Sales? = 460,000
Sales   = 40,000

So our completed T-account is as follows:

Plant assets, net

12/31/10 Bal	210,000		
		Depreciation (from Inc Stmt)	20,000
Acquisitions	310,000	Sales	40,000
12/31/11 Bal	460,000		

Cash received from selling plant assets can be computed by using the journal entry approach:

Cash	?????	
Gain on sale of plant assets (from the Income Statement)		10,000
Plant assets (from the T-account)		40,000

The book-value information comes from the Plant assets (Net) account on the Balance Sheet. The gain or loss comes from the Income Statement. The missing amount must be the cash received from the sale.

So, we compute the cash receipt from the sale as follows:

Cash = $10,000 Gain + $40,000 Plant assets, net
Cash = $50,000

The cash receipt from the sale of plant assets of $50,000 is shown as item **F** in the investing activities section of the Statement of Cash Flows (see Exhibit 13-7).

Exhibit 13-10 summarizes the computation of the investing cash flows. Items to be computed are shown in color.

EXHIBIT 13-10 | Computing Cash Flows from Investing Activities

Cash Receipts

From sale of plant assets	Beginning plant assets (net)	+ Acquisition	− Depreciation Expense	− Book value of assets sold	= Ending plant assets (net)	

$$\text{Cash receipt} = \text{Book value of assets sold} \begin{cases} + & \text{Gain on sale} \\ \text{or} \\ - & \text{Loss on sale} \end{cases}$$

Cash Payments

For acquisition of plant assets	Beginning plant assets (net)	+ Acquisition	− Depreciation Expense	− Book value of assets sold	= Ending plant assets (net)

Cash Flows from Financing Activities

Financing activities affect the liability and owners' equity accounts, such as Long-Term notes payable, Bonds payable, Common stock, and Retained earnings. These are shown for Smart Touch in Exhibit 13-8.

Computing Issuances and Payments of Long-Term Notes Payable

The beginning and ending balances of Notes payable or Bonds payable are taken from the Balance Sheet. If either the amount of new issuances or payments is known, the other amount can be computed. For Smart Touch Learning, new issuances of notes payable total $90,000 (Shown as item **G** in Exhibit 13-6). The computation of note payments uses the Long-Term notes payable account, with amounts from Smart Touch Learning's Balance Sheet in Exhibit 13-8 to create the following incomplete T-account:

Long-Term notes payable

Notes payments	?	12/31/10 Bal	80,000
		New notes issued	90,000
		12/31/11 Bal	160,000

Then, solve for the missing payments value:

12/31/10 Bal + New Notes Issued − Payments? = 12/31/11 Bal
80,000 + 90,000 − Payments? = 160,000
170,000 − Payments? = 160,000
Payments = 10,000

Complete the T-Account:

Long-Term notes payable

Notes payments	10,000	12/31/10 Bal	80,000
		New notes issued	90,000
		12/31/11 Bal	160,000

The payment of $10,000 as an outflow of cash is shown on the Statement of Cash Flows. (See item **H** in Exhibit 13-6).

Computing Issuances of Stock and Purchases of Treasury Stock

Cash flows for these financing activities can be determined by analyzing the stock accounts. For example, the amount of a new issuance of common stock is determined from Common stock. Using data from Exhibit 13-8, the incomplete Common stock T-account is as follows:

Common stock			
		12/31/10 Bal	250,000
Retirements	?	Issuance	?
		12/31/11 Bal	370,000

We would have to be told if there were any stock retirements. Since there were not, we know the balance change must be represented by new stock issuances.
Solving for the missing value is completed as follows:

12/31/10 Bal + Issuance of Stock? – Retirements? = 12/31/11 Bal

250,000   + Issuance of Stock? –   0   = 370,000

Issuance of Stock = 120,000

The completed T-Account for Common stock is as follows:

Common stock			
		12/31/10 Bal	250,000
Retirements	0	Issuance	120,000
		12/31/11 Bal	370,000

Therefore, the new stock issuance shows as $120,000 positive cash flows in the financing section of the statement (item **I** in Exhibit 13-6).

The last item that changed on Smart Touch Learning's Balance Sheet was Treasury stock. The T-account balances from the Treasury stock account on the Balance sheet show the following:

Treasury stock			
12/31/10 Bal	0		
Purchases	?	Sales	?
12/31/11 Bal	20,000		

Since we were not told that any Treasury stock was sold, we must assume that 100% of the account change represents new acquisitions of Treasury stock. Solving for the amount, the equation follows:

12/31/10 Bal + Purchases? – Sales? = 12/31/11 Bal

0   + Purchases? – 0   = 20,000

Purchases = 20,000

Completing the T-account, we have the following:

Treasury stock			
12/31/10 Bal	0		
Purchases	20,000	Sales	0
12/31/11 Bal	20,000		

So, $20,000 is shown as a cash outflow in the financing section of the cash flow statement for purchase of treasury stock (item **J** in Exhibit 13-6).

Computing Dividend Payments

The amount of dividend payments can be computed by analyzing the Retained earnings account. First we input the balances from the Balance Sheet:

Retained earnings

		12/31/10 Bal	80,000
Net loss	?	Net income	?
Dividend declarations	?		
		12/31/11 Bal	110,000

Retained earnings increases when companies earn net income. Retained earnings decreases when companies have a net loss and when they declare dividends. We know that Smart Touch earned net income of $40,000 from the Income Statement in Exhibit 13-9.

Retained earnings

		12/31/10 Bal	80,000
Net loss	?	Net income	40,000
Dividend declarations	?		
		12/31/11 Bal	110,000

Therefore, the missing value must be the amount of dividends Smart Touch declared. Solving for the value is as follows:

12/31/10 Bal + Net Income – Dividends Declared = 12/31/11 Bal
80,000 + 40,000 – Dividends Declared = 110,000
120,000 – Dividends Declared = 110,000
Dividends Declared = 10,000

So our final Retained earnings T-account shows the following:

Retained earnings

		12/31/10 Bal	80,000
		Net income	40,000
Dividend declarations	10,000		
		12/31/11 Bal	110,000

A stock dividend has *no* effect on Cash and is *not* reported on the cash-flow statement. Smart Touch had no stock dividends—only cash dividends. Exhibit 13-11 on page 16 summarizes the computation of cash flows from financing activities, highlighted in color.

Net Change in Cash and Cash Balances

The next line of the cash flow statement (underneath Net cash provided by financing activities in Exhibit 13-7) represents the total change in cash for the period. In the case of Smart Touch Learning, it is the net decrease in cash balances of $20,000 for the year. The decrease in cash of $20,000 is also represented by the following:

(amounts in thousands)

Net cash provided by Operating activities	–	Net cash used by Investing activities	+	Net cash provided by Financing activities		Net decrease in Cash
70	–	260	+	170	=	–20

EXHIBIT 13-11 | **Computing Cash Flows from Financing Activities**

Cash Receipts

From issuance of notes payable	Beginning notes payable	+	Cash receipt from issuance of notes payable	−	Payment of notes payable	=	Ending notes payable
From issuance of stock	Beginning stock	+	Cash receipt from issuance of new stock			=	Ending stock

Cash Payments

Of notes payable	Beginning notes payable	+	Cash receipt from issuance of notes payable	−	Payment of notes payable	=	Ending notes payable
To purchase treasury stock	Beginning treasury stock	+	Cost of treasury stock purchased			=	Ending treasury stock
Of dividends	Beginning retained earnings	+	Net income	−	Dividends Declared	=	Ending retained earnings

Next, the beginning cash from December 31, 2010, is listed at $42,000. The net decrease of $20,000 from beginning cash of $42,000 equals the ending cash balance on December 31, 2011, of $22,000. This is the key to the Statement of Cash Flows—it explains why the cash balance for Smart Touch decreased by $20,000, even though the company reported net income for the year.

Stop & Think...

Most of you probably have a checking or savings account. Think about how the balance changes from month to month. It does not always change because you have earned revenues or incurred expenses (operating). Sometimes it changes because you buy a long-lasting asset, such as a TV (investing). Sometimes it changes because you make a payment on your car note (financing). It is the same with business; business bank accounts do not change only because they earn revenue or incur expenses (operating). The cash flow statement explains all the reasons that cash changed (operating, investing, and financing).

Noncash Investing and Financing Activities

Companies make investments that do not require cash. They also obtain financing other than cash. Such transactions are called noncash investing and financing activities, and appear in a separate part of the cash flow statement. Our Smart Touch example did not include transactions of this type because the company did not have any noncash transactions during the year. So, to illustrate them, let us consider the three noncash transactions for Greg's Groovy Tunes. How would they be reported? First, we gather the noncash activity for the company:

1 Acquired $300,000 building by issuing stock
2 Acquired $70,000 land by issuing notes payable
3 Paid $100,000 note payable by issuing common stock

Now, we consider each transaction individually.

1. Greg's Groovy Tunes issued common stock of $300,000 to acquire a building. The journal entry to record the purchase would be as follows:

Building (A+)	300,000	
Common stock (Q+)		300,000

This transaction would not be reported on the cash-flow statement because no cash was paid. But the building and the common stock are important.

The purchase of the building is an investing activity. The issuance of common stock is a financing activity. Taken together, this transaction is a *noncash investing and financing activity*.

2. The second transaction listed indicates that Greg's Groovy Tunes acquired $70,000 of land by issuing a note. The journal entry to record the purchase would be as follows:

Land (A+)	70,000	
Notes payable (L+)		70,000

This transaction would not be reported on the cash-flow statement because no cash was paid. But the land and the notes payable are important.

The purchase of the land is an investing activity. The issuance of the note is a financing activity. Taken together, this transaction is a *noncash investing and financing activity*.

3. The third transaction listed indicates that Greg's Groovy Tunes exchanged $100,000 of debt by issuing common stock. The journal entry to record the purchase would be as follows:

Notes payable (L–)	100,000	
Common stock (Q+)		100,000

This transaction would not be reported on the cash-flow statement because no cash was paid. But the notes payable and the stock issuance are important.

The payment on the note and the issuance of the common stock are both financing activities. Taken together, this transaction, even though it is two financing transactions, is reported in the *noncash investing and financing activities*.

Noncash investing and financing activities can be reported in a separate schedule that accompanies the Statement of Cash Flows. Exhibit 13-12 on page 18 illustrates noncash investing and financing activities for Greg's Groovy Tunes (all amounts are assumed). This information either follows the cash-flow statement or can be disclosed in a note.

EXHIBIT 13-12 | **Noncash Investing & Financing Activities**

GREG'S GROOVY TUNES
Statement of Cash Flows—partial
Year Ended December 31, 2011

	(In thousands)
Noncash investing and financing activities:	
Acquisition of building by issuing common stock	$300
Acquisition of land by issuing note payable	70
Payment of note payable by issuing common stock	100
Total noncash investing and financing activities	$470

Measuring Cash Adequacy: Free Cash Flow

Throughout this chapter we have focused on cash flows from operating, investing, and financing activities. Some investors want to know how much cash a company can "free up" for new opportunities. **Free cash flow** is the amount of cash available from operations after paying for planned investments in long-term assets. Free cash flow can be computed as follows:

Free cash flow =	Net cash provided by operating activities	–	Cash payments planned for investments in plant, equipment, and other long-term assets

Many companies use free cash flow to manage their operations. Suppose Greg's Groovy Tunes expects net cash provided by operations of $200,000. Assume Greg's Groovy Tunes plans to spend $160,000 to modernize its production facilities. In this case, Greg's Groovy Tunes' free cash flow would be $40,000 ($200,000 – $160,000). If a good investment opportunity comes along, Greg's Groovy Tunes should have $40,000 to invest.

Now let us put into practice what you have learned about the Statement of Cash Flows prepared by the indirect method.

II-14 Financial Statement Analysis

Learning Objectives/Success Keys

1 Perform a horizontal analysis of financial statements

2 Perform a vertical analysis of financial statements

3 Prepare and use common-size financial statements

4 Compute the standard financial ratios

Now that you have learned some of the "how-to's" of financial statement preparation, we are going to show you how to analyze financial statements. We will be using our Smart Touch Learning, Inc., company for the first half of this chapter. Then in the second part of the chapter we will shift over to Greg's Groovy Tunes, Inc., to round out your introduction to financial statement analysis.

To get started, take a look at Smart Touch Learning's comparative income statement, as shown in Exhibit 14-1 on the following page.

You can see that 2014 was an incredible year for the company. Net income was over three times the net income of 2013, and investors were very happy.

Investors and creditors cannot evaluate a company by examining only one year's data. This is why most financial statements cover at least two periods, like the Smart Touch Learning income statement. In fact, most financial analysis covers trends of three to five years. This chapter shows you how to use some of the analytical tools for charting a company's progress through time.

To do that, we need some way to compare a company's performance

a. from year to year.

b. with a competing company, like **Learning Tree**.

c. with the education and training industry.

EXHIBIT 14-1 | **Comparative Income Statement, Smart Touch Learning, Inc.**

		(In millions)	2014	2013
		Revenues (same as Net sales)	$3,189	$1,466
		Expenses:		
		Cost of revenues (same as Cost of goods sold)	1,458	626
		Sales and marketing expense	246	120
		General and administrative expense	140	57
		Research and development expense	225	91
		Other expense	470	225
		Income before income tax	650	347
		Income tax expense	251	241
		Net income	$ 399	$ 106

SMART TOUCH LEARNING, INC.*
Income Statement (Adapted)
Year Ended December 31, 2014 and 2013

*All values are assumed.

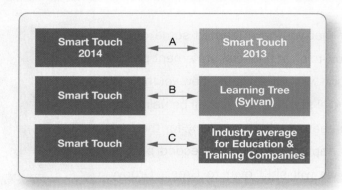

Then we will have a better idea of how to judge Smart Touch Learning's present situation and predict what might happen in the near future.

There are two main ways to analyze financial statements:

- Horizontal analysis provides a year-to-year comparison of a company's performance in different periods.
- Another technique, vertical analysis, is the standard way to compare different companies. Let us begin with horizontal analysis.

Horizontal Analysis

1 Perform a horizontal analysis of financial statements

Many decisions hinge on whether the numbers—in sales, expenses, and net income—are increasing or decreasing. Have sales and other revenues risen from last year? By how much? Sales may have increased by $20,000, but considered alone, this fact is not very helpful. The *percentage change* in sales over time is more relative and, therefore, more helpful. It is better to know that sales increased by 20% than to know that sales increased by $20,000.

The study of percentage changes in comparative statements is called **horizontal analysis**. Computing a percentage change in comparative statements requires two steps:

1. Compute the dollar amount of the change from the earlier period to the later period.

2. Divide the dollar amount of change by the earlier period amount. We call the earlier period the base period.

Illustration: Smart Touch Learning, Inc.

Horizontal analysis is illustrated for Smart Touch Learning as follows (dollar amounts in millions):

	2014	2013	Increase (Decrease) Amount	Percentage
Revenues (same as net sales).........	$3,189	$1,466	$1,723	117.5%

Sales increased by an incredible 117.5% during 2014, computed as follows:

STEP 1: Compute the dollar amount of change in sales from 2014 to 2013:

2014   2013   Increase
$3,189 – $1,466 = $1,723

STEP 2: Divide the dollar amount of change by the base-period amount. This computes the percentage change for the period:

$$\text{Percentage change} = \frac{\text{Dollar amount of change}}{\text{Base-year amount}}$$

$$= \frac{\$1,723}{\$1,466} = 1.175 = 117.5\%$$

Completed horizontal analyses for Smart Touch's financial statements are shown in the following exhibits:

- Exhibit 14-2 Income Statement
- Exhibit 14-3 Balance Sheet

EXHIBIT 14-2 | **Comparative Income Statement—Horizontal Analysis**

SMART TOUCH LEARNING, INC.*
Income Statement (Adapted)
Year Ended December 31, 2014 and 2013

(Dollar amounts in millions)	2014	2013	Increase (Decrease) Amount	Percentage
Revenues	$3,189	$1,466	$1,723	117.5%
Cost of revenues	1,458	626	832	132.9
Gross profit	1,731	840	891	106.1
Operating expenses:				
Sales and marketing expense	246	120	126	105.0
General and administrative expense	140	57	83	145.6
Research and development expense	225	91	134	147.3
Other expense	470	225	245	108.9
Income before income tax	650	347	303	87.3
Income tax expense	251	241	10	4.1
Net income	$ 399	$ 106	$ 293	276.4

*All values are assumed.

EXHIBIT 14-3 | **Comparative Balance Sheet—Horizontal Analysis**

SMART TOUCH LEARNING, INC.*
Balance Sheet (Adapted)
December 31, 2014 and 2013

(Dollar amounts in millions)	2014	2013	Increase (Decrease) Amount	Increase (Decrease) Percentage
Assets				
Current Assets:				
Cash and cash equivalents	$ 427	$149	$ 278	186.6%
Other current assets	2,266	411	1,855	451.3
Total current assets	2,693	560	2,133	380.9
Property, plant, and equipment, net	379	188	191	101.6
Intangible assets, net	194	106	88	83.0
Other assets	47	17	30	176.5
Total assets	$3,313	$871	$2,442	280.4
Liabilities				
Current Liabilities:				
Accounts payable	$ 33	$ 46	$ (13)	(28.3)%
Other current liabilities	307	189	118	62.4
Total current liabilities	340	235	105	44.7
Long-term liabilities	44	47	(3)	(6.4)
Total liabilities	384	282	102	36.2
Stockholders' Equity				
Capital stock	1	45	(44)	(97.8)
Retained earnings and other equity	2,928	544	2,384	438.2
Total stockholders' equity	2,929	589	2,340	397.3
Total liabilities and equity	$3,313	$871	$2,442	280.4

*All values are assumed.

Horizontal Analysis of the Income Statement

Smart Touch's comparative income statement reveals exceptional growth during 2014. An increase of 100% occurs when an item doubles, so Smart Touch's 117.5% increase in revenues means that revenues more than doubled.

The item on Smart Touch's income statement with the slowest growth rate is income tax expense. Income taxes increased by only 4.1%. On the bottom line, net income grew by an incredible 276.4%. That is real progress!

Horizontal Analysis of the Balance Sheet

Smart Touch's comparative balance sheet also shows rapid growth in assets, with total assets increasing by 280.4%. That means total assets almost tripled in one year. Very few companies grow that fast.

Smart Touch's liabilities grew more slowly. Total liabilities increased by 36.2%, and Accounts payable actually decreased, as indicated by the liability figures in parentheses. This is another indicator of positive growth for Smart Touch.

Trend Percentages

Trend percentages are a form of horizontal analysis. Trends indicate the direction a business is taking. How have sales changed over a five-year period? What trend does net income show? These questions can be answered by trend percentages over a period, such as three to five years.

Trend percentages are computed by selecting a base year. The base-year amounts are set equal to 100%. The amounts for each subsequent year are expressed as a percentage of the base amount. To compute trend percentages, divide each item for the following years by the base-year amount.

$$\text{Trend \%} = \frac{\text{Any year \$}}{\text{Base year \$}} \times 100$$

Let us assume Smart Touch's total revenues were $1,000 million in 2010 and rose to $3,189 million in 2014. To illustrate trend analysis, let us review the trend of net sales during 2010–2014, with dollars in millions. The base year is 2010, so that year's percentage is set equal to 100.

(In millions)	2014	2013	2012	2011	2010
Net sales..................	$3,189	1,466	1,280	976	1,000
Trend percentages	318.9%	146.6%	128%	97.6%	100%

We want trend percentages for the five-year period 2010–2014. We compute these by dividing each year's amount by the 2010 net sales amount.

Net sales decreased a little in 2011 and then the rate of growth increased from 2012–2014.

You can perform a trend analysis on any one or multiple item(s) you consider important. Trend analysis is widely used to predict the future.

Vertical Analysis

As we have seen, horizontal analysis and trend percentages highlight changes in an item from year to year, or over *time*. But no single technique gives a complete picture of a business, so we also need vertical analysis.

2 Perform a vertical analysis of financial statements

Vertical analysis of a financial statement shows the relationship of each item to its base amount, which is the 100% figure. Every other item on the statement is then reported as a percentage of that base. For the income statement, net sales is the base.

$$\text{Vertical analysis \%} = \frac{\text{Each income-statement item}}{\text{Revenues (net sales)}} \times 100$$

Exhibit 14-4 on the following page shows the completed vertical analysis of Smart Touch Learning's 2014 income statement.

In this case, the vertical-analysis percentage for Smart Touch's cost of revenues is 45.7% of net sales ($1,458/$3,189 = 0.457). This means that for every $1 in net sales, almost 46 cents is spent on cost of revenue.

On the bottom line, Smart Touch's net income is 12.5% of revenues. That is extremely good. Suppose under normal conditions a company's net income is 10% of revenues. A drop to 4% may cause the investors to be alarmed and sell their stock.

Exhibit 14-5 on the following page the vertical analysis of Smart Touch's balance sheet.

The base amount (100%) is total assets. The base amount is also total liabilities and equity, because they are exactly the same number, $3,313. (Recall that they should always be the same number because of the accounting equation.)

EXHIBIT 14-4 | **Comparative Income Statement—Vertical Analysis**

SMART TOUCH LEARNING, INC.*
Income Statement (Adapted)
Year Ended December 31, 2014

(Dollar amounts in millions)	Amount	Percent of Total
Revenues	$3,189	100.0%
Cost of revenues	1,458	45.7
Gross profit	1,731	54.3
Operating expenses:		
Sales and marketing expense	246	7.7
General and administrative expense	140	4.4
Research and development expense	225	7.1
Other expense	470	14.7
Income before income tax	650	20.4
Income tax expense	251	7.9
Net income	$ 399	12.5%

*All values are assumed.

EXHIBIT 14-5 | **Comparative Balance Sheet—Vertical Analysis**

SMART TOUCH LEARNING, INC.*
Balance Sheet (Adapted)
December 31, 2014

(Dollar amount in millions)	Amount	Percent of Total
Assets		
Current Assets:		
Cash and cash equivalents	$ 427	12.9%
Other current assets	2,266	68.4
Total current assets	2,693	81.3
Property, plant, and equipment, net	379	11.4
Intangible assets, net	194	5.9
Other assets	47	1.4
Total assets	$3,313	100.0%
Liabilities		
Current Liabilities:		
Accounts payable	$ 33	1.0%
Other current liabilities	307	9.3
Total current liabilities	340	10.3
Long-term liabilities	44	1.3
Total liabilities	384	11.6
Stockholders' Equity		
Common stock	1	0.0
Retained earnings and other equity	2,928	88.4
Total stockholders' equity	2,929	88.4
Total liabilities and equity	$3,313	100.0%

*All values are assumed.

The vertical analysis of Smart Touch's balance sheet reveals several interesting things:

- Current assets make up 81.3% of total assets. For most companies this percentage is closer to 30%. The 81.3% of current assets represent a great deal of liquidity.

- Property, plant, and equipment make up only 11.4% of total assets. This percentage is low because of the nature of Smart Touch's business. Smart Touch's Web-based operations do not require lots of buildings and equipment.

- Total liabilities are only 11.6% of total assets, and stockholders' equity makes up 88.4% of total assets. Most of Smart Touch's equity is retained earnings and other equity—signs of a strong company because most of the equity is internally generated rather than externally generated (through stock share sales).

How Do We Compare One Company with Another?

Horizontal analysis and vertical analysis provide lots of useful data about a company. As we have seen, Smart Touch's percentages depict a very successful company. But the data apply only to one business.

3 Prepare and use common-size financial statements

To compare Smart Touch Learning to another company we can use a common-size statement. A **common-size statement** reports only percentages—the same percentages that appear in a vertical analysis. By only reporting percentages, it removes dollar value bias when comparing the companies. **Dollar value bias** is the bias one sees from comparing numbers in absolute (dollars) rather than relative (percentage) terms. For us, $1 million seems like a lot. For some large companies, it is immaterial. For example, Smart Touch's common-size income statement comes directly from the percentages in Exhibit 14-4.

We can use a common-size income statement to compare Smart Touch Learning and Learning Tree on profitability. The companies compete in the service-learning industry. Which company earns a higher percentage of revenues as profits for its shareholders? Exhibit 14-6 gives both companies' common-size income statements for 2014 so that we may compare them on a relative, not absolute basis.

EXHIBIT 14-6 | **Common-Size Income Statement**
Smart Touch vs. Learning Tree

SMART TOUCH vs. LEARNING TREE* Common-Size Income Statement Year ended Dec. 31, 2014	Smart Touch	Learning Tree
Revenues	100.0%	100.0%
Cost of revenues	45.7	36.3
Gross profit	54.3	63.7
Sales and marketing expense	7.7	21.8
General and administrative expense	4.4	7.3
Research and development expense	7.1	10.3
Other expense (income)	14.7	(11.5)
Income before income tax	20.4	35.8
Income tax expense	7.9	12.3
Net income	12.5%	23.5%

*All values are assumed.

Exhibit 14-6 shows that Learning Tree was more profitable than Smart Touch in 2014. Learning Tree's gross profit percentage is 63.7%, compared to Smart Touch's 54.3%. This means that Learning Tree is getting more profit from every dollar than Smart Touch. And, most importantly, Learning Tree's percentage of net income to revenues is 23.5%. That means almost one-fourth of Learning Tree's revenues end up as profits for the company's stockholders. Smart Touch's percentage of net income to revenues, on the other hand, is 12.5%. Both are excellent percentages; however, the common-size statement highlights Learning Tree's advantages over Smart Touch.

Benchmarking

Benchmarking is the practice of comparing a company with other leading companies. There are two main types of benchmarks in financial statement analysis.

Benchmarking Against a Key Competitor

Exhibit 14-6 uses a key competitor, Learning Tree, to compare Smart Touch's profitability. The two companies compete in the same industry, so Learning Tree serves as an ideal benchmark for Smart Touch. The graphs in Exhibit 14-7 highlight the profitability difference between the companies. Focus on the segment of the graphs showing net income. Learning Tree is clearly more profitable than Smart Touch.

EXHIBIT 14-7 | **Graphical Analysis of Common-Size Income Statement Smart Touch Learning vs. Learning Tree**

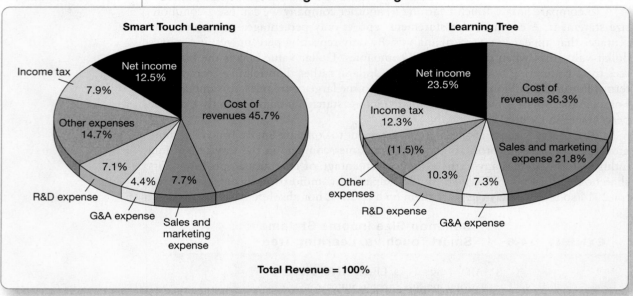

Benchmarking Against the Industry Average

The industry average can also serve as a very useful benchmark for evaluating a company. An industry comparison would show how Smart Touch is performing alongside the average for the e-learning industry. *Annual Statement Studies*, published by The Risk Management Association, provides common-size statements for most industries. To compare Smart Touch to the industry average, simply insert the industry-average common-size income statement in place of Learning Tree in Exhibit 14-6.

Stop & Think...

When you are driving down any road, how do you know how fast you can travel? The speed limit sign. You compare the speed at which you are traveling in your car to that speed limit sign. That is the same concept as benchmarking. The industry averages, for example, are the "sign" and your company results are the "speed at which you are traveling." Sometimes your company is going faster than other companies. Sometimes it is going slower.

Now let us put your learning to practice. Work the summary problem, which reviews the concepts from the first half of this chapter.

Summary Problem 1

Requirements

Perform a horizontal analysis and a vertical analysis of the comparative income statement of Kimball Corporation, which makes iPod labels. State whether 2011 was a good year or a bad year, and give your reasons.

KIMBALL CORPORATION Comparative Income Statement Years Ended December 31, 2011 and 2010		
	2011	**2010**
Net sales	$275,000	$225,000
Expenses:		
Cost of goods sold	$194,000	$165,000
Engineering, selling, and administrative expenses	54,000	48,000
Interest expense	5,000	5,000
Income tax expense	9,000	3,000
Other expense (income)	1,000	(1,000)
Total expenses	263,000	220,000
Net income	$ 12,000	$ 5,000

Solution

KIMBALL CORPORATION Horizontal Analysis of Comparative Income Statement Years Ended December 31, 2011 and 2010				
			Increase (Decrease)	
	2011	**2010**	**Amount**	**Percent**
Net sales	$275,000	$225,000	$50,000	22.2%
Expenses:				
Cost of goods sold	$194,000	$165,000	$29,000	17.6
Engineering, selling, and administrative expenses	54,000	48,000	6,000	12.5
Interest expense	5,000	5,000	—	—
Income tax expense	9,000	3,000	6,000	200.0
Other expense (income)	1,000	(1,000)	2,000	—*
Total expenses	263,000	220,000	43,000	19.5
Net income	$ 12,000	$ 5,000	$ 7,000	140.0%

*Percentage changes are typically not computed for shifts from a negative to a positive amount, and vice versa.

The horizontal analysis shows that total revenues increased 22.2%. Total expenses increased by 19.5%, and net income rose by 140%.

KIMBALL CORPORATION
Vertical Analysis of Comparative Income Statement
Years Ended December 31, 2011 and 2010

	2011		2010	
	Amount	Percent	Amount	Percent
Net sales	$275,000	100.0%	$225,000	100.0%
Expenses:				
Cost of goods sold	$194,000	70.5	$165,000	73.3
Engineering, selling, and administrative expenses	54,000	19.6	48,000	21.3
Interest expense	5,000	1.8	5,000	2.2
Income tax expense	9,000	3.3	3,000	1.4**
Other expense (income)	1,000	0.4	(1,000)	(0.4)
Total expenses	263,000	95.6	220,000	97.8
Net income	$ 12,000	4.4%	$ 5,000	2.2%

**Number is rounded up.

The vertical analysis shows decreases in the percentages of net sales consumed by
- cost of goods sold (from 73.3% to 70.5%);
- engineering, selling, and administrative expenses (from 21.3% to 19.6%).

These two items are Kimball's largest dollar expenses, so their percentage decreases are important.

The 2011 net income rose to 4.4% of sales, compared with 2.2% the preceding year. The analysis shows that 2011 was significantly better than 2010.

Using Ratios to Make Decisions

Online financial databases, such as **Lexis/Nexis** and the **Dow Jones News Retrieval Service**, provide data on thousands of companies. Suppose you want to compare some companies' recent earnings histories. You might want to compare companies' returns on stockholders' equity. The computer could then search the databases and give you the names of the 20 companies with the highest return on equity. You can use any ratio for searching that is relevant to a particular decision.

4   Compute the standard financial ratios

Remember, however, that no single ratio tells the whole picture of any company's performance. Different ratios explain different aspects of a company. The ratios we discuss in this chapter may be classified as follows:

1. Measuring ability to pay current liabilities

2. Measuring ability to sell inventory and collect receivables

3. Measuring ability to pay long-term debt

4. Measuring profitability

5. Analyzing stock as an investment

Measuring Ability to Pay Current Liabilities

Working capital is defined as follows:

> **Working capital = Current assets − Current liabilities**

Working capital measures the ability to meet short-term obligations with current assets. Two decision tools based on working-capital data are the *current ratio* and the *acid-test ratio*.

Current Ratio

The most widely used ratio is the *current ratio*, which is current assets divided by current liabilities. The current ratio measures ability to pay current liabilities with current assets.

Exhibit 14-8 on the following page gives the comparative income statement and balance sheet of Greg's Groovy Tunes, which we will be using in the remainder of this chapter.

The current ratios of Greg's Groovy Tunes, at December 31, 2012 and 2011, follow, along with the average for the entertainment industry:

Formula	Greg's Groovy Tunes' Current Ratio 2012	Greg's Groovy Tunes' Current Ratio 2011	Industry Average
Current ratio = $\dfrac{\text{Current assets}}{\text{Current liabilities}}$	$\dfrac{\$262,000}{\$142,000} = 1.85$	$\dfrac{\$236,000}{\$126,000} = 1.87$	.60

A high current ratio indicates that the business has sufficient current assets to maintain normal business operations. Compare Greg's Groovy Tunes' current ratio of 1.85 for 2012 with the industry average of .60.

What is an acceptable current ratio? The answer depends on the industry. The norm for companies in most industries is around 1.50, as reported by The Risk Management Association. Greg's Groovy Tunes' current ratio of 1.85 is strong. Keep in mind that we would not want to see a current ratio that is too high, say 25.0. This would indicate that the company is too liquid and, therefore, is not using its assets effectively.

EXHIBIT 14-8 | **Comparative Financial Statements**

GREG'S GROOVY TUNES, INC.
Comparative Income Statement
Years Ended December 31, 2012 and 2011

		2012	2011
	Net sales	$858,000	$803,000
	Cost of goods sold	513,000	509,000
	Gross profit	345,000	294,000
	Operating expenses:		
	Selling expenses	126,000	114,000
	General expenses	118,000	123,000
	Total operating expenses	244,000	237,000
	Income from operations	101,000	57,000
	Interest revenue	4,000	—
	Interest (expense)	(24,000)	(14,000)
	Income before income taxes	81,000	43,000
	Income tax expense	33,000	17,000
	Net income	**$ 48,000**	**$ 26,000**

GREG'S GROOVY TUNES, INC.
Comparative Balance Sheet
December 31, 2012 and 2011

	2012	2011
Assets		
Current Assets:		
Cash	$ 29,000	$ 32,000
Accounts receivable, net	114,000	85,000
Inventories	113,000	111,000
Prepaid expenses	6,000	8,000
Total current assets	262,000	236,000
Long-term investments	18,000	9,000
Property, plant, and equipment, net	507,000	399,000
Total assets	$787,000	$644,000
Liabilities		
Current Liabilities:		
Notes payable	$ 42,000	$ 27,000
Accounts payable	73,000	68,000
Accrued liabilities	27,000	31,000
Total current liabilities	142,000	126,000
Long-term notes payable	289,000	198,000
Total liabilities	431,000	324,000
Stockholders' Equity		
Common stock, no par	186,000	186,000
Retained earnings	170,000	134,000
Total stockholders' equity	356,000	320,000
Total liabilities and equity	$787,000	$644,000

Acid-Test Ratio

The *acid-test* (or *quick*) *ratio* tells us whether the entity could pay all its current liabilities if they came due immediately. That is, could the company pass this *acid test*?

To compute the acid-test ratio, we add cash, short-term investments, and net current receivables (accounts and notes receivable, net of allowances) and divide this sum by current liabilities. Inventory and prepaid expenses are *not* included in the acid test because they are the least-liquid current assets. Greg's Groovy Tunes' acid-test ratios for 2012 and 2011 follow:

Formula	Greg's Groovy Tunes' Acid-Test Ratio		Industry Average
	2012	2011	
Acid-test ratio $=$ $\dfrac{\text{Cash + Short-term investments + Net current receivables}}{\text{Current liabilities}}$	$\dfrac{\$29,000 + \$0 + \$114,000}{\$142,000} = 1.01$	$\dfrac{\$32,000 + \$0 + \$85,000}{\$126,000} = 0.93$	.46

The company's acid-test ratio improved during 2012 and is significantly better than the industry average. The norm for the acid-test ratio ranges from 0.20 for shoe retailers to 1.00 for manufacturers of equipment, as reported by The Risk Management Association. An acid-test ratio of 0.90 to 1.00 is acceptable in most industries.

Measuring Ability to Sell Inventory and Collect Receivables

The ability to sell inventory and collect receivables is fundamental to business. In this section, we discuss three ratios that measure the company's ability to sell inventory and collect receivables.

Inventory Turnover

The inventory turnover ratio measures the number of times a company sells its average level of inventory during a year. A high rate of turnover indicates ease in selling inventory; a low rate indicates difficulty. A value of 4 means that the company sold its average level of inventory four times—once every three months—during the year. If the company were a seasonal company, this would be a good ratio because it would mean it turned its inventory over each season, on average.

To compute inventory turnover, we divide cost of goods sold by the average inventory for the period. We use the cost of goods sold—not sales—because both cost of goods sold and inventory are stated *at cost*. Sales at *retail* are not comparable with inventory at *cost*.

Greg's Groovy Tunes' inventory turnover for 2012 is as follows:

Formula	Greg's Groovy Tunes' Inventory Turnover	Industry Average
Inventory turnover $=$ $\dfrac{\text{Cost of goods sold}}{\text{Average inventory}}$	$\dfrac{\$513,000}{\$112,000} = 4.6$	27.65

Cost of goods sold comes from the income statement (Exhibit 14-8). Average inventory is figured by adding the beginning inventory ($111,000) to the ending inventory ($113,000) and dividing by two. (See the balance sheet, Exhibit 14-8.)

Inventory turnover varies widely with the nature of the business. For example, most manufacturers of farm machinery have an inventory turnover close to three times a year. In contrast, companies that remove natural gas from the ground hold their inventory for a very short period of time and have an average turnover of 30.

Greg's Groovy Tunes' turnover of 4.6 times a year is very low for its industry, which has an average turnover of 27.65 times per year. This ratio has identified an area that Greg's Groovy Tunes needs to improve.

Accounts Receivable Turnover

The **accounts receivable turnover ratio** measures the ability to collect cash from credit customers. The higher the ratio, the faster the cash collections. But a receivable turnover that is too high may indicate that credit is too tight, causing the loss of sales to good customers.

To compute accounts receivable turnover, divide net credit sales by average net accounts receivable. Average net accounts receivable is figured by adding the beginning accounts receivable balance ($85,000) and the ending balance ($114,000), then dividing by 2:

$$(\$85,000 + \$114,000)/2 = \$99,500$$

Greg's Groovy Tunes' accounts receivable turnover ratio for 2012 is computed as follows:

Formula	Greg's Groovy Tunes' Accounts Receivable Turnover	Industry Average
Accounts receivable turnover $= \dfrac{\text{Net credit sales}}{\text{Average net accounts receivable}}$	$\dfrac{\$858,000}{\$99,500} = 8.6$	29.10

Greg's receivable turnover of 8.6 times per year is much slower than the industry average of 29.1. Why the difference? Greg's is a fairly new business that sells to established people who pay their accounts over time. Further, this turnover coincides with the lower than average inventory turnover. So, Greg's may achieve a higher receivable turnover by increasing its inventory turnover ratio.

Days' Sales in Receivables

The *days'-sales-in-receivables* ratio also measures the ability to collect receivables. Days' sales in receivables tell us how many days' sales remain in Accounts receivable. To compute the ratio, we can follow a logical two-step process:

1. Divide net sales by 365 days to figure average sales for one day.

2. Divide this average day's sales amount into average net accounts receivable.

The data to compute this ratio for Greg's Groovy Tunes for 2012 are taken from the income statement and the balance sheet (Exhibit 14-8):

Formula	Greg's Groovy Tunes' Days' Sales in Accounts Receivable	Industry Average
Days' sales in *average* Accounts receivable:		
1. One day's sales $= \dfrac{\text{Net sales}}{365 \text{ days}}$	$\dfrac{\$858,000}{365 \text{ days}} = \$2,351$	
2. Days' sales in average accounts receivable $= \dfrac{\text{Average net accounts receivable}}{\text{One day's sales}}$	$\dfrac{\$99,500}{\$2,351} = 42 \text{ days}$	25

Average accounts receivable was calculated in the previous ratio example at $99,500.

Greg's Groovy Tunes' ratio tells us that 42 average days' sales remain in Accounts receivable and need to be collected. The company's days'-sales-in-receivables ratio is much higher (worse) than the industry average of 25 days. This is probably because Greg's collects its own receivables rather than paying a collection agency to collect for the company. Without the customers' good paying habits, the company's cash flow would suffer.

Measuring Ability to Pay Long-Term Debt

The ratios discussed so far yield insight into current assets and current liabilities. They help us measure ability to sell inventory, collect receivables, and pay current liabilities. Most businesses also have long-term debt. Two key indicators of a business's ability to pay long-term liabilities are the *debt ratio* and the *times-interest-earned ratio*.

Debt Ratio

A loan officer at Metro Bank is evaluating loan applications from two companies. Both companies have asked to borrow $500,000 and have agreed to repay the loan over a five-year period. The first firm already owes $600,000 to another bank. The second owes only $100,000. If all else is equal, the bank is more likely to lend money to Company 2 because that company owes less than Company 1.

This relationship between total liabilities and total assets—called the *debt ratio*—shows the proportion of assets financed with debt. If the debt ratio is 1, then all the assets are financed with debt. A debt ratio of 0.50 means that half the assets are financed with debt and the other half is financed by the owners of the business. The higher the debt ratio, the higher the company's financial risk.

The debt ratios for Greg's Groovy Tunes at the ends of 2012 and 2011 follow:

| Formula | Greg's Groovy Tunes' Debt Ratio | | Industry Average |
	2012	2011	
Debt ratio = $\dfrac{\text{Total liabilities}}{\text{Total assets}}$	$\dfrac{\$431,000}{\$787,000} = 0.55$	$\dfrac{\$324,000}{\$644,000} = 0.50$	0.69

Greg's debt ratio in 2012 of 0.55 is not very high. The Risk Management Association reports that the average debt ratio for most companies ranges from 0.57 to 0.67, with relatively little variation from company to company. Greg's debt ratio indicates a fairly low-risk position compared with the industry average debt ratio of 0.69.

Times-Interest-Earned Ratio

The debt ratio says nothing about the ability to pay interest expense. Analysts use the **times-interest-earned ratio** to relate income to interest expense. This ratio is also called the **interest-coverage ratio**. It measures the number of times operating income can cover (pay) interest expense. A high interest-coverage ratio indicates ease in paying interest expense; a low ratio suggests difficulty.

To compute this ratio, we divide income from operations (operating income) by interest expense. Calculation of Greg's times-interest-earned ratio follows:

| Formula | Greg's Groovy Tunes' Times-Interest-Earned Ratio | | Industry Average |
	2012	2011	
Times-interest-earned ratio = $\dfrac{\text{Income from operations}}{\text{Interest expense}}$	$\dfrac{\$101,000}{\$24,000} = 4.21$	$\dfrac{\$57,000}{\$14,000} = 4.07$	7.80

The company's times-interest-earned ratio of around 4.00 is significantly lower than the average for the industry of 7.80 times but is slightly better than the average U.S. business. The norm for U.S. business, as reported by The Risk Management Association, falls in the range of 2.0 to 3.0. When you consider Greg's debt ratio and its times-interest-earned ratio, Greg's Groovy Tunes appears to have little difficulty *servicing its debt*, that is, paying liabilities.

Measuring Profitability

The fundamental goal of business is to earn a profit. Ratios that measure profitability are reported in the business press. We will examine four profitability measures.

Rate of Return on Net Sales

In business, the term *return* is used broadly as a measure of profitability. Consider a ratio called the **rate of return on net sales,** or simply **return on sales.** (The word *net* is usually omitted for convenience, even though net sales is used to compute the ratio.) This ratio shows the percentage of each sales dollar earned as net income. Greg's Groovy Tunes' rate of return on sales follows:

Formula	Greg's Groovy Tunes' Rate of Return on Sales		Industry Average
	2012	2011	
$\dfrac{\text{Rate of return}}{\text{on sales}} = \dfrac{\text{Net income}}{\text{Net sales}}$	$\dfrac{\$48,000}{\$858,000} = 0.056$	$\dfrac{\$26,000}{\$803,000} = 0.032$	.017

Companies strive for a high rate of return on sales. The higher the rate of return, the more sales dollars end up as profit. The increase in Greg's return on sales from 2011 to 2012 is significant and identifies the company as more successful than the average education service provider whose rate of return is .017.

Rate of Return on Total Assets

The *rate of return on total assets*, or simply *return on assets*, measures a company's success in using assets to earn a profit. Two groups finance a company's assets.

- Creditors have loaned money to the company, and they earn interest.
- Shareholders have invested in stock, and their return is net income.

The sum of interest expense and net income divided by total assets is the return to the two groups that have financed the company's assets. Average total assets is the average of beginning and ending total assets from the comparative balance sheet:

$$(\$644,000 + \$787,000)/2 = \$715,500$$

Computation of the return-on-assets ratio for Greg's Groovy Tunes follows:

Formula	Greg's Groovy Tunes' 2012 Rate of Return on Total Assets	Industry Average
$\dfrac{\text{Rate of return}}{\text{on assets}} = \dfrac{\begin{array}{c}\text{Net} \\ \text{income}\end{array} + \begin{array}{c}\text{Interest} \\ \text{expense}\end{array}}{\text{Average total assets}}$	$\dfrac{\$48,000 + \$24,000}{\$715,500} = 0.101$	.0599

Greg's Groovy Tunes' return-on-assets ratio of .101 is much better than the industry average of .0599.

Rate of Return on Common Stockholders' Equity

A popular measure of profitability is *rate of return on common stockholders' equity*, often shortened to *return on equity*. This ratio shows the relationship between net income and common stockholders' equity—how much income is earned for each $1 invested by the common shareholders.

To compute this ratio, we first subtract preferred dividends from net income to get net income available to the common stockholders. (Greg's does not have any preferred stocks issued, so preferred dividends are zero.) Then divide net income available to common stockholders by average common equity during the year. Common equity is total stockholders' equity minus preferred equity. Average equity is the average of the beginning and ending balances.

$$($356,000 + $320,000)/2 = $338,000$$

The 2012 rate of return on common stockholders' equity for Greg's Groovy Tunes follows:

	Formula	Greg's Groovy Tunes' 2012 Rate of Return on Common Stockholders' Equity	Industry Average
Rate of return on common stockholders' equity	$= \dfrac{\text{Net income} - \text{Preferred dividends}}{\text{Average common stockholders' equity}}$	$\dfrac{\$48,000 - \$0}{\$338,000} = 0.142$	.105

Greg's return on equity of 0.142 is higher than its return on assets of 0.101. This difference results from borrowing at one rate—say, 8%—and investing the money to earn a higher rate, such as the firm's 14.2% return on equity. This practice is called **trading on the equity**, or using *leverage*. It is directly related to the debt ratio. The higher the debt ratio, the higher the leverage. Companies that finance operations with debt are said to *leverage* their positions.

During good times, leverage increases profitability. But leverage can have a negative impact on profitability as well. Therefore, leverage is a double-edged sword, increasing profits during good times but compounding losses during bad times. Compare Greg's Groovy Tunes' return on equity with the industry average of 0.105. Once again, Greg's Groovy Tunes is performing much better than the average company in its industry. A return on equity of 15% to 20% year after year is considered good in most industries. At 14.2%, Greg's is doing well.

Earnings per Share of Common Stock

Earnings per share of common stock, or simply *earnings per share (EPS)*, is perhaps the most widely quoted of all financial statistics. EPS is the only ratio that must appear on the face of the income statement. EPS is the amount of net income earned for each share of the company's outstanding *common* stock. Recall that

Outstanding stock = Issued stock − Treasury stock

Earnings per share is computed by dividing net income available to common stockholders by the number of common shares outstanding during the year. Preferred dividends are subtracted from net income because the preferred stockholders have the first claim to dividends. Greg's Groovy Tunes has no preferred stock outstanding and, therefore, paid no preferred dividends.

The firm's EPS for 2012 and 2011 follow. (Note that Greg's had 10,000 shares of common stock outstanding throughout both years.)

| | | Earnings per Share | | Industry |
	Formula	2012	2011	Average
Earnings per share of common stock	$= \dfrac{\text{Net income} - \text{Preferred dividends}}{\text{Number of shares of common stock outstanding}}$	$\dfrac{\$48{,}000 - \$0}{10{,}000} = \$4.80$	$\dfrac{\$26{,}000 - \$0}{10{,}000} = \$2.60$	$9.76

Greg's Groovy Tunes' EPS increased significantly in 2012 (by almost 85%). Its stockholders should not expect this big a boost in EPS every year. Most companies strive to increase EPS by 10%–15% annually, and leading companies do so. But even the most successful companies have an occasional bad year. EPS for the industry at $9.76 is a little over twice Greg's Groovy Tunes' 2012 EPS. Therefore, Greg's Groovy Tunes needs to work on continuing to increase EPS so that it is more competitive with other companies in its industry.

Analyzing Stock Investments

Investors purchase stock to earn a return on their investment. This return consists of two parts: (1) gains (or losses) from selling the stock at a price above or below purchase price and (2) dividends. The ratios we examine in this section help analysts evaluate stock investments.

Price/Earnings Ratio

The **price/earnings ratio** is the ratio of the market price of a share of common stock to the company's earnings per share. It shows the market price of $1 of earnings. This ratio, abbreviated P/E, appears in *The Wall Street Journal* stock listings.

Calculations for the P/E ratios of Greg's Groovy Tunes follow. The market price of its common stock was $60 at the end of 2012 and $35 at the end of 2011. These prices for real companies can be obtained from a financial publication, a stockbroker, or the company's Web site.

| | | Greg's Groovy Tunes' Price/Earnings Ratio | | Industry |
	Formula	2012	2011	Average
P/E ratio	$= \dfrac{\text{Market price per share of common stock}}{\text{Earnings per share}}$	$\dfrac{\$60.00}{\$4.80} = 12.5$	$\dfrac{\$35.00}{\$2.60} = 13.5$	17.79

Greg's P/E ratio of 12.5 means that the company's stock is selling at 12.5 times one year's earnings. The decline from the 2011 P/E ratio of 13.5 is no cause for alarm because the market price of the stock is not under Greg's Groovy Tunes' control. Net income is more controllable, and net income increased during 2012.

II-20 Capital Investment Decisions and the Time Value of Money

Learning Objectives/ Success Keys

1 Describe the importance of capital investments and the capital budgeting process

2 Use the payback and accounting rate of return methods to make capital investment decisions

3 Use the time value of money to compute the present and future values of single lump sums and annuities

4 Use discounted cash flow models to make capital investment decisions

Music DVDs and learning DVDs seem to have little or nothing to do with accounting. But every part of the growth and expansion of Smart Touch Learning and Greg's Groovy Tunes began first with the decision—do we spend the money to expand the business?

In this chapter, we will see how companies like Smart Touch and Greg's Groovy Tunes use capital investment analysis techniques to decide which long-term capital investments to make.

Capital Budgeting

The process of making capital investment decisions is often referred to as **capital budgeting**. Companies make capital investments when they acquire *capital assets*—assets used for a long period of time. Capital investments include buying new equipment, building new plants, automating production, and developing major commercial Web sites. In addition to affecting operations for many years, capital investments usually require large sums of money.

Capital investment decisions affect all businesses as they try to become more efficient by automating production and implementing new technologies. Grocers and retailers, such as **Wal-Mart**, have invested in expensive self-scan check-out machines, while airlines, such as **Delta** and **Continental**, have invested in self check-in kiosks. These new technologies cost money. How do managers decide whether these expansions in plant and equipment will be good investments? They use capital budgeting analysis. Some companies, such as **Georgia Pacific**, employ staff solely dedicated to capital budgeting analysis. They spend thousands of hours a year determining which capital investments to pursue.

1 Describe the importance of capital investments and the capital budgeting process

Four Popular Methods of Capital Budgeting Analysis

In this chapter, we discuss four popular methods of analyzing potential capital investments:

1. Payback period
2. Accounting rate of return (ARR)
3. Net present value (NPV)
4. Internal rate of return (IRR)

The first two methods, payback period and accounting rate of return, are fairly quick and easy and work well for capital investments that have a relatively short life span, such as computer equipment and software that may have a useful life of only three to five years. Payback period and accounting rate of return are also used to screen potential investments from those that are less desirable. The payback period provides management with valuable information on how fast the cash invested will be recouped. The accounting rate of return shows the effect of the investment on the company's accrual-based income. However, these two methods are inadequate if the capital investments have a longer life span. Why? Because these methods do not consider the time value of money. The last two methods, net present value and internal rate of return, factor in the time value of money so they are more appropriate for longer-term capital investments, such as Smart Touch's expansion to manufacturing DVDs. Management often uses a combination of methods to make final capital investment decisions.

Capital budgeting is not an exact science. Although the calculations these methods require may appear precise, remember that they are based on predictions about an uncertain future—estimates. These estimates must consider many unknown factors, such as changing consumer preferences, competition, the state of the economy, and government regulations. The further into the future the decision extends, the more likely that actual results will differ from predictions. Long-term decisions are riskier than short-term decisions.

Focus on Cash Flows

Generally accepted accounting principles (GAAP) are based on accrual accounting, but capital budgeting focuses on cash flows. The desirability of a capital asset depends on its ability to generate net cash inflows—that is, inflows in excess of outflows—over the asset's useful life. Recall that operating income based on accrual accounting contains noncash expenses, such as depreciation expense and bad-debt expense. The capital investment's *net cash inflows,* therefore, will differ from its operating income. Of the four capital budgeting methods covered in this chapter, only the accounting rate of return method uses accrual-based accounting income. The other three methods use the investment's projected *net cash inflows.*

What do the projected *net cash inflows* include? Cash *inflows* include future cash revenue generated from the investment, any future savings in ongoing cash operating costs resulting from the investment, and any future residual value of the asset. To determine the investment's *net* cash inflows, the inflows are *netted* against the investment's *future cash outflows,* such as the investment's ongoing cash operating costs and refurbishment, repairs, and maintenance costs. The initial investment itself is also a significant cash outflow. However, in our calculations, *we will always consider the amount of the investment separately from all other cash flows related to the investment.* The projected net cash inflows are "given" in our examples and in the assignment material. In reality, much of capital investment analysis revolves around projecting these figures as accurately as possible using input from employees throughout the organization (production, marketing, and so forth, depending on the type of capital investment).

Capital Budgeting Process

The first step in the capital budgeting process is to identify potential investments—for example, new technology and equipment that may make the company more efficient, competitive, and/or profitable. Employees, consultants, and outside sales vendors often offer capital investment proposals to management. After identifying potential capital investments, managers project the investments' net cash inflows and then analyze the investments using one or more of the four capital budgeting methods previously described. Sometimes the analysis involves a two-stage process. In the first stage, managers screen the investments using one or both of the methods that do *not* incorporate the time value of money: payback period or accounting rate of return. These simple methods quickly weed out undesirable investments. Potential investments that "pass stage one" go on to a second stage of analysis. In the second stage, managers further analyze the potential investments using the net present value and/or internal rate of return methods. Because these methods consider the time value of money, they provide more accurate information about the potential investment's profitability.

Some companies can pursue all of the potential investments that meet or exceed their decision criteria. However, because of limited resources, other companies must engage in **capital rationing,** and choose among alternative capital investments. Based on the availability of funds, managers determine if and when to make specific capital investments. For example, management may decide to wait three years to buy a certain piece of equipment because it considers other investments more important. In the intervening three years, the company will reassess whether it should still invest in the equipment. Perhaps technology has changed, and even better equipment is available. Perhaps consumer tastes have changed so the company no longer needs the equipment. Because of changing factors, long-term capital budgets are rarely set in stone.

Most companies perform **post-audits** of their capital investments. After investing in the assets, they compare the actual net cash inflows generated from the investment to the projected net cash inflows. Post-audits help companies determine whether the investments are going as planned and deserve continued support, or whether they should abandon the project and sell the assets. Managers also use feedback from post-audits to better estimate net cash flow projections for future projects. If managers expect routine post-audits, they will more likely submit realistic net cash flow estimates with their capital investment proposals.

Using Payback and Accounting Rate of Return to Make Capital Investment Decisions

Payback Period

Payback is the length of time it takes to recover, in net cash inflows, the cost of the capital outlay. The payback model measures how quickly managers expect to recover their investment dollars. All else being equal, the shorter the payback period the more attractive the asset. Computing the payback period depends on whether net cash inflows are equal each year, or whether they differ over time. We consider each in turn.

2 Use the payback and accounting rate of return methods to make capital investment decisions

Payback with Equal Annual Net Cash Inflows

Smart Touch Learning is considering investing $240,000 in hardware and software to upgrade its website to provide a business-to-business (B2B) portal. Employees throughout the company will use the B2B portal to access company-approved suppliers. Smart Touch expects the portal to save $60,000 a year for each of the six years of its useful life. The savings will arise from reducing the number of purchasing personnel the company employs and from lower prices on the goods and services purchased. Net cash inflows arise from an increase in revenues, a decrease in expenses, or both. In Smart Touch's case, the net cash inflows result from lower expenses.

When net cash inflows are equal each year, managers compute the payback period as shown in Exhibit 20-1.

EXHIBIT 20-1	Calculating Payback Period— Equal Cash Flows

$$\text{Payback period} = \frac{\text{Amount invested}}{\text{Expected annual net cash inflow}}$$

Smart Touch computes the investment's payback as follows:

$$\text{Payback period for B2B portal} = \frac{\$240,000}{\$60,000} = 4 \text{ years}$$

Exhibit 20-2 verifies that Smart Touch expects to recoup the $240,000 investment in the B2B portal by the end of year 4, when the accumulated net cash inflows total $240,000.

Smart Touch is also considering investing $240,000 to upgrade its Web site. The company expects the upgraded Web site to generate $80,000 in net cash inflows each year of its three-year life. The payback period is computed as follows:

$$\text{Payback period for Web site development} = \frac{\$240,000}{\$80,000} = 3 \text{ years}$$

Exhibit 20-2 verifies that Smart Touch will recoup the $240,000 investment for the Web site upgrade by the end of year 3, when the accumulated net cash inflows total $240,000.

EXHIBIT 20-2 | **Payback—Equal Annual Net Cash Inflows**

		Net Cash Inflows			
		B2B Portal		Web Site Upgrade	
Year	Amount Invested	Annual	Accumulated	Annual	Accumulated
0	240,000	—	—	—	—
1	—	$60,000	$ 60,000	$80,000	$ 80,000
2	—	60,000	120,000	80,000	160,000
3	—	60,000	180,000	80,000	240,000
4	—	60,000	240,000		
5	—	60,000	300,000		
6	—	60,000	360,000		

Payback with Unequal Net Cash Inflows

The payback equation in Exhibit 20-1 only works when net cash inflows are the same each period. When periodic cash flows are unequal, you must total net cash inflows until the amount invested is recovered. Assume that Smart Touch is considering an alternate investment, the Z80 portal. The Z80 portal differs from the B2B portal and the Web site in two respects: (1) It has *unequal* net cash inflows during its life and (2) it has a $30,000 residual value at the end of its life. The Z80 portal will generate net cash inflows of $100,000 in year 1, $80,000 in year 2, $50,000 each year in years 3 through 5, $30,000 in year 6, and $30,000 when it is sold at the end of its life. Exhibit 20-3 shows the payback schedule for these unequal annual net cash inflows.

EXHIBIT 20-3 | **Payback: Unequal Annual Net Cash Inflows**

		Net Cash Inflows Z80 Portal	
Year	Amount Invested	Annual	Accumulated
0	$240,000	—	—
1	—	100,000	$100,000
2	—	80,000	180,000
3	—	50,000	230,000
4	—	50,000	280,000
5	—	50,000	330,000
6	—	30,000	360,000
6–Residual Value		30,000	390,000

By the end of year 3, the company has recovered $230,000 of the $240,000 initially invested, so it is only $10,000 short of payback. Because the expected net cash inflow in year 4 is $50,000, by the end of year 4 the company will have recovered *more* than the initial investment. Therefore, the payback period is somewhere between three and four years. Assuming that the cash flow occurs evenly throughout the fourth year, the payback period is calculated as follows:

$$\text{Payback} = 3 \text{ years} + \frac{\$10,000 \text{ (amount needed to complete recovery in year 4)}}{\$50,000 \text{ (net cash inflow in year 4)}}$$

$$= 3.2 \text{ years}$$

Criticism of the Payback Period Method

A major criticism of the payback method is that it focuses only on time, not on profitability. The payback period considers only those cash flows that occur *during* the payback period. This method ignores any cash flows that occur *after* that period. For example, Exhibit 20-2 shows that the B2B portal will continue to generate net cash inflows for two years after its payback period. These additional net cash inflows amount to $120,000 ($60,000 × 2 years), yet the payback method ignores this extra cash. A similar situation occurs with the Z80 portal. As shown in Exhibit 20-3, the Z80 portal will provide an additional $150,000 of net cash inflows, including residual value, after its payback period of 3.2 years ($390,000 total accumulated cash inflows – $240,000 amount invested). However, the Web site's useful life, as shown in Exhibit 20-2, is the *same* as its payback period (three years). No cash flows are ignored, yet the Web site will merely cover its cost and provide no profit. Because this is the case, the company has no financial reason to invest in the Web site.

Exhibit 20-4 compares the payback period of the three investments. As the exhibit illustrates, the payback method does not consider the asset's profitability. The method only tells management how quickly it will recover the cash. Even though the Web site has the shortest payback period, both the B2B portal and the Z80 portal are better investments because they provide profit. The key point is that the investment with the shortest payback period is best *only if all other factors are the same*. Therefore, managers usually use the payback method as a screening device to "weed out" investments that will take too long to recoup. They rarely use payback period as the sole method for deciding whether to invest in the asset. When using the payback period method, managers are guided by following decision rule:

DECISION RULE: Payback Period

Investments with shorter payback periods are more desirable, *all else being equal*.

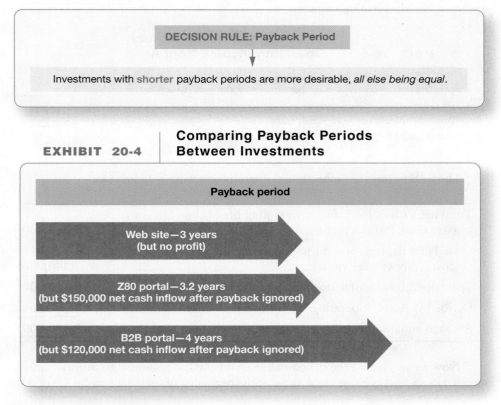

EXHIBIT 20-4 | **Comparing Payback Periods Between Investments**

Payback period

Web site—3 years (but no profit)

Z80 portal—3.2 years (but $150,000 net cash inflow after payback ignored)

B2B portal—4 years (but $120,000 net cash inflow after payback ignored)

Stop & Think...

Let us say you loan $50 to a friend today (a Friday). The friend says he will pay you $25 next Friday when he gets paid and another $25 the following Friday. What is your payback period? The friend will pay you back in 2 weeks.

Accounting Rate of Return (ARR)

Companies are in business to earn profits. One measure of profitability is the **accounting rate of return (ARR)** on an asset. The formula for calculating ARR is shown in Exhibit 20-5.

EXHIBIT 20-5	Calculating Accounting Rate of Return

$$\text{Accounting rate of return} = \frac{\text{Average annual operating income from an asset}}{\text{Average amount invested in an asset}}$$

The ARR focuses on the *operating income, not the net cash inflow,* an asset generates. The ARR measures the *average* rate of return over the asset's entire life. Let us first consider investments with no residual value.

Recall the B2B portal, which costs $240,000, has equal annual net cash inflows of $60,000, a six-year useful life, and no (zero) residual value.

Let us look at the average annual operating income in the numerator first. The average annual operating income of an asset is simply the asset's total operating income over the course of its operating life divided by its lifespan (number of years). Operating income is based on *accrual accounting.* Therefore, any noncash expenses, such as depreciation expense, must be subtracted from the asset's net cash inflows to arrive at its operating income. Exhibit 20-6 displays the formula for calculating average annual operating income.

EXHIBIT 20-6	Calculating Average Annual Operating Income from Asset

Total net cash inflows during operating life of the asset	A
Less: Total depreciation during operating life of the asset (Cost − Residual Value)	B
Total operating income during operating life	(A − B)
Divide by: Asset's operating life in years	C
Average annual operating income from asset	[(A − B)/C]

The B2B portal's average annual operating income is as follows:

Total net cash inflows during operating life of the asset ($60,000 × 6 years)	$ 360,000
Less: Total depreciation during operating life of asset (cost − any salvage value)	(240,000)
Total operating income during operating life	$ 120,000
Divide by: Asset's operating life (in years)	÷ 6 years
Average annual operating income from asset	$ 20,000

Now let us look at the denominator of the ARR equation. The *average* amount invested in an asset is its *net book value* at the beginning of the asset's useful life plus the net book value at the end of the asset's useful life divided by two. Another way to say that is the asset's cost plus the asset's residual value divided by two. The net book value of the asset decreases each year because of depreciation, as shown in Exhibit 20-6.

Because the B2B portal does not have a residual value, the *average* amount invested is $120,000 [($240,000 cost + 0 residual value) ÷ 2].

We calculate the B2B's ARR as:

$$\text{Accounting rate of return} = \frac{\$20,000}{(\$240,000 + \$0)/2} = \frac{\$20,000}{\$120,000} = 0.167 = 16.70\%$$

Now consider the Z80 portal (data from Exhibit 20-3). Recall that the Z80 portal differed from the B2B portal only in that it had unequal net cash inflows during its life and a $30,000 residual value at the end of its life. Its average annual operating income is calculated as follows:

Total net cash inflows *during* operating life of asset (does not include the residual value at end of life) (Year 1 + Year 2, etc.)	$ 360,000
Less: Total depreciation during operating life of asset (cost – any salvage value) ($240,000 cost – $30,000 residual value)	(210,000)
Total operating income during operating life of asset................	$ 150,000
Divide by: Asset's operating life (in years)	÷ 6 years
Average annual operating income from asset	$ 25,000

Notice that the Z80 portal's average annual operating income of $25,000 is higher than the B2B portal's operating income of $20,000. Since the Z80 asset has a residual value at the end of its life, less depreciation is expensed each year, leading to a higher average annual operating income.

Now let us calculate the denominator of the ARR equation, the average amount invested in the asset. For the Z80, the average asset investment is as follows:

Average amount invested	=	(Amount invested in asset	+	Residual value)/2		
$135,000	=	($240,000	+	$30,000)	/2	

We calculate the Z80's ARR as follows:

$$\text{Accounting rate of return} = \frac{\$25,000}{(\$240,000 + \$30,000)/2} = \frac{\$25,000}{\$135,000} = 0.185 = 18.5\%$$

Companies that use the ARR model set a minimum required accounting rate of return. If Smart Touch requires an ARR of at least 20%, then its managers would not approve an investment in the B2B portal or the Z80 portal because the ARR for both investments is less than 20%.

The decision rule is as follows:

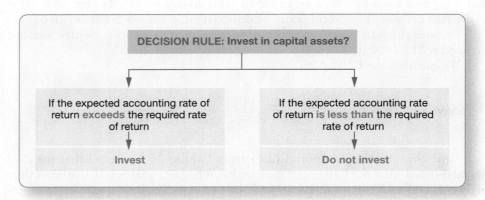

In summary, the payback period focuses on the time it takes for the company to recoup its cash investment but ignores all cash flows occurring after the payback period. Because it ignores any additional cash flows (including any residual value), the method does not consider the profitability of the project.

The ARR, however, measures the profitability of the asset over its entire life using accrual accounting figures. It is the only method that uses accrual accounting rather than net cash inflows in its computations. The payback period and ARR methods are simple and quick to compute so managers often use them to screen out undesirable investments. However, both methods ignore the time value of money.

Decision Guidelines

CAPITAL BUDGETING

Amazon.com started as a virtual retailer. It held no inventory. Instead, it bought books and CDs only as needed to fill customer orders. As the company grew, its managers decided to invest in their own warehouse facilities. Why? Owning warehouse facilities allows **Amazon.com** to save money by buying in bulk. Also, shipping all items in the customer's order in one package, from one location, saves shipping costs. Here are some of the guidelines **Amazon.com's** managers used as they made the major capital budgeting decision to invest in building warehouses.

Decision	Guidelines
• Why is this decision important?	Capital budgeting decisions typically require large investments and affect operations for years to come.
• What method shows us how soon we will recoup our cash investment?	The payback method shows managers how quickly they will recoup their investment. This method highlights investments that are too risky due to long payback periods. However, it does not reveal any information about the investment's profitability.
• Does any method consider the impact of the investment on accrual accounting income?	The accounting rate of return is the only capital budgeting method that shows how the investment will affect accrual accounting income, which is important to financial statement users. All other methods of capital investment analysis focus on the investment's net cash inflows.
• How do we compute the payback period if cash flows are *equal*?	$$\text{Payback period} = \frac{\text{Amount invested}}{\text{Expected annual net cash inflow}}$$
• How do we compute the payback period if cash flows are *unequal*?	Accumulate net cash inflows until the amount invested is recovered.
• How do we compute the ARR?	$$\text{Accounting rate of return} = \frac{\text{Average annual operating income from asset}}{\text{Average amount invested in asset}}$$

Summary Problem 1

Reality-max is considering buying a new bar-coding machine for its Austin, Texas, plant. The company screens its potential capital investments using the payback period and accounting rate of return methods. If a potential investment has a payback period of less than four years and a minimum 12% accounting rate of return, it will be considered further. The data for the machine follow:

Cost of machine	$48,000
Estimated residual value...	$ 0
Estimated annual net cash inflow (each year for 5 years)	$13,000
Estimated useful life	5 years

Requirements

1. Compute the bar-coding machine's payback period.
2. Compute the bar-coding machine's ARR.
3. Should Reality-max turn down this investment proposal or consider it further?

Solution

Requirement 1

$$\text{Payback period} = \frac{\text{Amount invested}}{\text{Expected annual net cash inflow}} = \frac{\$48,000}{\$13,000} = 3.7 \text{ years (rounded)}$$

Requirement 2

$$\text{Accounting rate of return} = \frac{\text{Average annual operating income from asset}}{\text{Average amount invested in asset}}$$

$$= \frac{\$3,400^*}{(\$48,000 + \$0)/2}$$

$$= \frac{\$3,400}{\$24,000}$$

$$= 0.142 \text{ (rounded)}$$

$$= 14.2\%$$

*Total net cash inflows during life ($13,000 × 5 years)	$ 65,000
Less: total depreciation during life	(48,000)
Total operating income during life	$ 17,000
Divided by: life of the asset	÷ 5 years
Average annual operating income	$ 3,400

Requirement 3

The bar-coding machine proposal passes both initial screening tests. The payback period is slightly less than four years, and the accounting rate of return is higher than 12%. Reality-max should further analyze the proposal using a method that incorporates the time value of money.

A Review of the Time Value of Money

A dollar received today is worth more than a dollar to be received in the future. Why? Because you can invest today's dollar and earn extra income. The fact that invested money earns income over time is called the *time value of money*, and this explains why we would prefer to receive cash sooner rather than later. The time value of money means that the timing of capital investments' net cash inflows is important. Two methods of capital investment analysis incorporate the time value of money: the NPV and IRR. This section reviews time value of money to make sure you have a firm foundation for discussing these two methods.

3 | Use the time value of money to compute the present and future values of single lump sums and annuities

Factors Affecting the Time Value of Money

The time value of money depends on several key factors:

1. the principal amount (p)
2. the number of periods (n)
3. the interest rate (i)

The principal (p) refers to the amount of the investment or borrowing. Because this chapter deals with capital investments, we will primarily discuss the principal in terms of investments. However, the same concepts apply to borrowings (which we covered in Chapter 7). We state the principal as either a single lump sum or an annuity. For example, if you win the lottery, you have the choice of receiving all the winnings now (a single lump sum) or receiving a series of equal payments for a period of time in the future (an annuity). An **annuity** is a stream of *equal installments* made at *equal time intervals under the same interest rate*.[1]

The number of periods (n) is the length of time from the beginning of the investment until termination. All else being equal the shorter the investment period the lower the total amount of interest earned. If you withdraw your savings after four years, rather than five years, you will earn less interest. In this chapter, the number of periods is stated in years.[2]

The interest rate (i) is the annual percentage earned on the investment. **Simple interest** means that interest is calculated *only* on the principal amount. **Compound interest** means that interest is calculated on the principal *and* on all interest earned to date. *Compound interest assumes that all interest earned will remain invested and earn additional interest at the same interest rate.* Exhibit 20-7 compares simple interest

EXHIBIT 20-7	Simple Versus Compound Interest for a Principal Amount of $10,000, at 6%, over 5 Years

Year	Simple Interest Calculation	Simple Interest	Compound Interest Calculation	Compound Interest
1	$10,000 × 6% =	$ 600	$10,000 × 6% =	$ 600
2	$10,000 × 6% =	600	($10,000 + 600) × 6% =	636
3	$10,000 × 6% =	600	($10,000 + 600 + 636) × 6% =	674
4	$10,000 × 6% =	600	($10,000 + 600 + 636 + 674) × 6% =	715
5	$10,000 × 6% =	600	($10,000 + 600 + 636 + 674 + 715) × 6% =	758
	Total interest	$3,000	Total interest	$3,383

---

[1] An *ordinary annuity* is an annuity in which the installments occur at the *end* of each period. An *annuity due* is an annuity in which the installments occur at the beginning of each period. Throughout this chapter we use ordinary annuities since they are better suited to capital budgeting cash flow assumptions.
[2] The number of periods can also be stated in days, months, or quarters. If so, the interest rate needs to be adjusted to reflect the number of time periods in the year.

(6%) on a five-year, $10,000 CD with interest compounded yearly (rounded to the near-est dollar). As you can see, the amount of compound interest earned yearly grows as the base on which it is calculated (principal plus cumulative interest to date) grows. Over the life of this investment, the total amount of compound interest is about 10% more than the total amount of simple interest. Most investments yield compound interest so we assume compound interest, rather than simple interest, for the rest of this chapter.

Fortunately, time value calculations involving compound interest do not have to be as tedious as those shown in Exhibit 20-7. Formulas and tables (or proper use of business calculators programmed with these formulas, or spreadsheet software such as Microsoft Excel) simplify the calculations. In the next sections, we will dis-cuss how to use these tools to perform time value calculations.

Future Values and Present Values: Points Along the Time Line

Consider the time line in Exhibit 20-8. The future value or present value of an investment simply refers to the value of an investment at different points in time.

| **EXHIBIT 20-8** | **Present Value and Future Value Along the Time Continuum** |

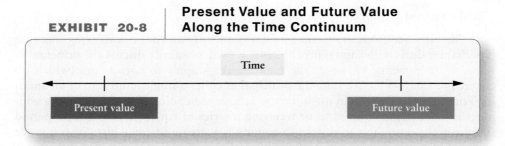

We can calculate the future value or the present value of any investment by knowing (or assuming) information about the three factors we listed earlier: (1) the principal amount, (2) the period of time, and (3) the interest rate. For example, in Exhibit 20-7, we calculated the interest that would be earned on (1) a $10,000 principal, (2) invested for five years, (3) at 6% interest. The future value of the investment is sim-ply its worth at the end of the five-year time frame—the original principal *plus* the interest earned. In our example, the future value of the investment is as follows:

$$\text{Future value} = \text{Principal} + \text{Interest earned}$$
$$= \$10{,}000 + \$3{,}383$$
$$= \$13{,}383$$

If we invest $10,000 *today*, its *present value* is simply $10,000. So another way of stating the future value is as follows:

$$\text{Future value} = \text{Present value} + \text{Interest earned}$$

We can rearrange the equation as follows:

$$\text{Present value} = \text{Future value} - \text{Interest earned}$$
$$\$10{,}000 = \$13{,}383 - \$3{,}383$$

The only difference between present value and future value is the amount of interest that is earned in the intervening time span.

Future Value and Present Value Factors

Calculating each period's compound interest, as we did in Exhibit 20-7, and then adding it to the present value to figure the future value (or subtracting it from the future value to figure the present value) is tedious. Fortunately, mathematical formulas have been developed that specify future values and present values for unlimited combinations of interest rates (i) and time periods (n). Separate formulas exist for single lump-sum investments and annuities.

These formulas are programmed into most business calculators so that the user only needs to correctly enter the principal amount, interest rate, and number of time periods to find present or future values. These formulas are also programmed into spreadsheets functions in Microsoft Excel. Because the specific steps to operate business calculators differ between brands, we will use tables instead. These tables contain the results of the formulas for various interest rate and time period combinations.

The formulas and resulting tables are shown in Appendix B at the end of this book:

1. Present Value of $1 (Appendix B, Table A, p. B-1)—*used for lump-sum amounts*

2. Present Value of Annuity of $1 (Appendix B, Table B, p. B-3)—*used for annuities*

3. Future Value of $1 (Appendix B, Table C, p. B-5)—*used for lump-sum amounts*

4. Future Value of Annuity of $1 (Appendix B, Table D, p. B-6)—*used for annuities*

Take a moment to look at these tables because we are going to use them throughout the rest of the chapter. Note that the columns are interest rates (i) and the rows are periods (n).

The data in each table, known as future value factors (FV factors) and present value factors (PV factors), are for an investment (or loan) of $1. To find the future value of an amount other than $1, you simply multiply the FV factor by the present amount. To find the present value of an amount other than $1, you multiply the PV factor by the future amount.

The annuity tables are derived from the lump-sum tables. For example, the Annuity PV factors (in the Present Value of Annuity of $1 table) are the *sums* of the PV factors found in the Present Value of $1 tables for a given number of time periods. The annuity tables allow us to perform "one-step" calculations rather than separately computing the present value of each annual cash installment and then summing the individual present values.

Calculating Future Values of Single Sums and Annuities Using FV Factors

Let us go back to our $10,000 lump-sum investment. If we want to know the future value of the investment five years from now at an interest rate of 6%, we determine the FV factor from the table labeled Future Value of $1 (Appendix B, Table C). We use this table for lump-sum amounts. We look down the 6% column, and across the 5 periods row, and find the future value factor is 1.338. We finish our calculations as follows:

Future value = Principal amount × (FV factor for $i = 6\%$, $n = 5$)
= $10,000 × (1.338)
= $13,380

This figure materially agrees with our earlier calculation of the investment's future value of $13,383 in Exhibit 20-7. (The difference of $3 is due to two facts:

(1) The tables round the FV and PV factors to three decimal places and (2) we rounded our earlier yearly interest calculations in Exhibit 20-7 to the nearest dollar.)

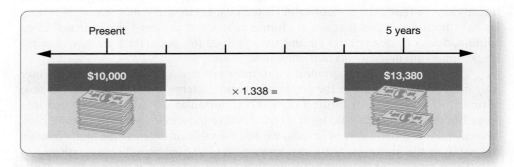

Let us also consider our alternative investment strategy, investing $2,000 at the end of each year for five years. The procedure for calculating the future value of an *annuity* is quite similar to calculating the future value of a lump-sum amount. This time, we use the Future Value of Annuity of $1 table (Appendix B, Table D). Assuming 6% interest, we once again look down the 6% column. Because we will be making five annual installments, we look across the row marked 5 periods. The Annuity FV factor is 5.637. We finish the calculation as follows:

Future value = Amount of each cash installment × (Annuity FV factor for i = 6%, n = 5)

= $2,000 × (5.637)

= $11,274

This is considerably less than the future value of $13,380 of the lump sum of $10,000, even though we have invested $10,000 out-of-pocket either way.

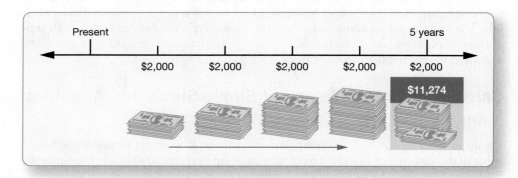

Calculating Present Values of Single Sums and Annuities Using PV Factors

The process for calculating present values—often called discounting cash flows—is similar to the process for calculating future values. The difference is the point in time at which you are assessing the investment's worth. Rather than determining its value at a future date, you are determining its value at an earlier point in time (today). For our example, let us assume you have just won the lottery after purchasing one $5 lottery ticket. The state offers you the following three payout options for your after-tax prize money:

Option #1: $1,000,000 now

Option #2: $150,000 at the end of each year for the next 10 years

Option #3: $2,000,000 10 years from now

Which alternative should you take? You might be tempted to wait 10 years to "double" your winnings. You may be tempted to take the money now and spend it. However, let us assume you plan to prudently invest all money received—no matter when you receive it—so that you have financial flexibility in the future (for example, for buying a house, retiring early, or taking exotic vacations). How can you choose among the three payment alternatives, when the total amount of each option varies ($1,000,000 versus $1,500,000 versus $2,000,000) and the timing of the cash flows varies (now versus some each year versus later)? Comparing these three options is like comparing apples to oranges—we just cannot do it—unless we find some common basis for comparison. Our common basis for comparison will be the prize-money's worth at a certain point in time—namely, today. In other words, if we convert each payment option to its *present value*, we can compare apples to apples.

We already know the principal amount and timing of each payment option, so the only assumption we will have to make is the interest rate. The interest rate will vary, depending on the amount of risk you are willing to take with your investment. Riskier investments (such as stock investments) command higher interest rates; safer investments (such as FDIC-insured bank deposits) yield lower interest rates. Let us say that after investigating possible investment alternatives, you choose an investment contract with an 8% annual return. We already know that the present value of Option #1 is $1,000,000. Let us convert the other two payment options to their present values so that we can compare them. We will need to use the Present Value of Annuity of $1 table (Appendix B, Table B) to convert payment Option #2 (since it is an annuity) and the Present Value of $1 table (Appendix B, Table A) to convert payment Option #3 (since it is a single-lump-sum). To obtain the PV factors, we will look down the 8% column and across the 10 period row. Then, we finish the calculations as follows:

Option #2

Present value = Amount of each cash installment × (Annuity PV factor for $i = 8\%$, $n = 10$)

Present value = $150,000 × (6.710)

Present value = $1,006,500

Option #3

Present value = Principal amount × (PV factor for $i = 8\%$, $n = 10$)

Present value = $2,000,000 × (0.463)

Present value = $926,000

Exhibit 20-9 shows that we have converted each payout option to a common basis—its worth *today*—so we can make a valid comparison among the options. Based on this comparison, we should choose Option #2 because its worth, in today's dollars, is the highest of the three options.

Now that you have reviewed time value of money concepts, we will discuss the two capital budgeting methods that incorporate the time value of money: net present value (NPV) and internal rate of return (IRR).

EXHIBIT 20-9	Present Value of Lottery Payout Options

Payment Options	Present Value of Lottery Payout ($i = 8\%$, $n = 10$)
Option #1	$1,000,000
Option #2	$1,006,500
Option #3	$ 926,000

Using Discounted Cash Flow Models to Make Capital Budgeting Decisions

4 Use discounted cash flow models to make capital investment decisions

Neither the payback period nor the ARR recognizes the time value of money. That is, these models fail to consider the *timing* of the net cash inflows an asset generates. *Discounted cash flow models*—the NPV and the IRR—overcome this weakness. These models incorporate compound interest by assuming that companies will reinvest future cash flows when they are received. Over 85% of large industrial firms in the United States use discounted cash-flow methods to make capital investment decisions. Companies that provide services also use these models.

The NPV and IRR methods rely on present value calculations to *compare* the amount of the investment (the investment's initial cost) with its expected net cash inflows. Recall that an investment's *net cash inflows* includes all *future* cash flows related to the investment, such as future increased sales or cost savings netted against the investment's cash operating costs. Because the cash outflow for the investment occurs *now*, but the net cash inflows from the investment occur in the *future*, companies can only make valid "apple-to-apple" comparisons if they convert the cash flows to the *same point in time*—namely the present value. Companies use the present value to make the comparison (rather than the future value) because the investment's initial cost is already stated at its present value.[3]

As shown in Exhibit 20-10, in a favorable investment, the present value of the investment's net cash inflows exceeds the initial cost of the investment. In terms of our earlier lottery example, the lottery ticket turned out to be a "good investment" because the present value of its net cash inflows (the present value of the lottery payout under *any* of the three payout options) exceeded the cost of the investment (the lottery ticket cost $5 to purchase). Let us begin our discussion by taking a closer look at the NPV method.

Net Present Value (NPV)

Greg's Groovy Tunes is considering producing CD players and digital video recorders (DVRs). The products require different specialized machines that each cost $1 million. Each machine has a five-year life and zero residual value. The two products have different patterns of predicted net cash inflows, as shown in Exhibit 20-11.

The CD-player project generates more net cash inflows, but the DVR project brings in cash sooner. To decide how attractive each investment is, we find its **net present value (NPV)**. The NPV is the *net difference* between the present value of the

---

[3] If the investment is to be purchased through lease payments, rather than a current cash outlay, we would still use the current cash price of the investment as its initial cost. If no current cash price is available, we would discount the future lease payments back to their present value to estimate the investment's current cash price.

| EXHIBIT 20-10 | Comparing the Present Value of an Investment's Net Cash Inflows Against the Investment's Initial Cost |

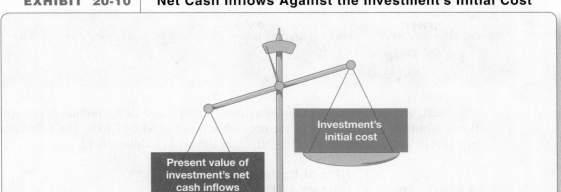

| EXHIBIT 20-11 | Expected Cash Flows for Two Projects |

	Annual Net Cash Inflows	
Year	CD Players	DVRs
1	$ 305,450	$ 500,000
2	$ 305,450	350,000
3	$ 305,450	300,000
4	$ 305,450	250,000
5	$ 305,450	40,000
Total	$1,527,250	$1,440,000

investment's net cash inflows and the investment's cost (cash outflows). We *discount* the net cash inflows—just as we did in the lottery example—using Greg's minimum desired rate of return. This rate is called the **discount rate** because it is the interest rate used for the present value calculations. It is also called the **required rate of return** because the investment must meet or exceed this rate to be acceptable. The discount rate depends on the riskiness of investments. The higher the risk, the higher the discount (interest) rate. Greg's discount rate for these investments is 14%.

We then compare the present value of the net cash inflows to the investment's initial cost to decide which projects meet or exceed management's minimum desired rate of return. In other words, management is deciding whether the $1 million option is worth more (because the company would give it up now to invest in the project) or whether the project's future net cash inflows are worth more. Management can only make a valid comparison between the two sums of money by comparing them at the *same* point in time—namely, at their present value.

NPV with Equal Periodic Net Cash Inflows (Annuity)

Greg's expects the CD-player project to generate $305,450 of net cash inflows each year for five years. Because these cash flows are equal in amount, and occur every year, they are an annuity. Therefore, we use the Present Value of Annuity of $1 table (Appendix B, Table B) to find the appropriate Annuity PV factor for $i = 14\%$, $n = 5$.

The present value of the net cash inflows from Greg's CD-player project is as follows:

Present value = Amount of each cash net cash inflow × (Annuity PV factor for *i* = 14%, *n* = 5)

   = $305,450 × (3.433)

   = $1,048,610

Next, we simply subtract the investment's initial cost of $1 million (cash outflows) from the present value of the net cash inflows of $1,048,610. The difference of $48,610 is the *net* present value (NPV), as shown in Exhibit 20-12.

EXHIBIT 20-12 | **NPV of Equal Net Cash Inflows—CD-Player Project**

Time		Annuity PV Factor (*i* = 14%, *n* = 5)	Net Cash Inflow	Present Value
1–5 yrs	Present value of annuity of equal annual net cash inflows for 5 years at 14%	3.433* ×	$305,450 =	$ 1,048,610
0	Investment			(1,000,000)
	Net present value of the CD-player project			$ 48,610

*Annuity PV Factor is found in Appendix B, Table B.

A *positive* NPV means that the project earns *more* than the required rate of return. A negative NPV means that the project earns less than the required rate of return. This leads to the following decision rule:

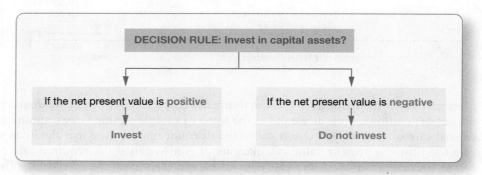

In Greg's Groovy Tunes' case, the CD-player project is an attractive investment. The $48,610 positive NPV means that the CD-player project earns *more than* Greg's Groovy Tunes' 14% target rate of return.

Another way managers can use present value analysis is to start the capital budgeting process by computing the total present value of the net cash inflows from the project to determine the *maximum* the company can invest in the project and still earn the target rate of return. For Greg's, the present value of the net cash inflows is $1,048,610. This means that Greg's Groovy Tunes can invest a maximum of $1,048,610 and still earn the 14% target rate of return (i.e., if Greg's invests $1,048,610, NPV will be 0 and return will be exactly 14%). Because Greg's Groovy Tunes' managers believe they can undertake the project for $1 million, the project is an attractive investment.

NPV with Unequal Periodic Net Cash Inflows

In contrast to the CD-player project, the net cash inflows of the DVR project are unequal—$500,000 in year 1, $350,000 in year 2, and so on. Because these amounts vary by year, Greg's Groovy Tunes' managers *cannot* use the annuity table to compute the present value of the DVR project. They must compute the present value of each individual year's net cash inflows *separately (as separate lump sums received in different years)*, using the Present Value of $1 table (Appendix B, Table A). Exhibit 20-13 shows that the $500,000 net cash inflow received in year 1 is discounted using a PV factor of $i = 14\%$, $n = 1$, while the $350,000 net cash inflow received in year 2 is discounted using a PV factor of $i = 14\%$, $n = 2$, and so forth. After separately discounting each of the five year's net cash inflows, we add each result to find that the *total* present value of the DVR project's net cash inflows is $1,078,910. Finally, we subtract the investment's cost of $1 million (cash outflows) to arrive at the DVR project's NPV: $78,910.

EXHIBIT 20-13 | **NPV with Unequal Net Cash Inflows—DVR Project**

Year		PV Factor ($i = 14\%$)		Net Cash Inflow		Present Value
	Present value of each year's net cash inflows discounted at 14%					
1	Year 1 ($n = 1$)	0.877†	×	$500,000	=	$ 438,500
2	Year 2 ($n = 2$)	0.769	×	350,000	=	269,150
3	Year 3 ($n = 3$)	0.675	×	300,000	=	202,500
4	Year 4 ($n = 4$)	0.592	×	250,000	=	148,000
5	Year 5 ($n = 5$)	0.519	×	40,000	=	20,760
	Total present value of net cash inflows					1,078,910
0	Investment					(1,000,000)
	Net present value of the DVR project					$ 78,910

†PV Factors are found in Appendix B, Table A.

Because the NPV is positive, Greg's Groovy Tunes expects the DVR project to earn more than the 14% target rate of return, making this an attractive investment.

Stop & Think...

Assume you win the lottery today and you have the choice of taking $1,000,000 today or $120,000 a year for the next 10 years. If you think that you can earn 6%, which option should you take? That is the key to NPV. We must find the NPV of the $120,000 annuity at 6% (PV factor is 7.360) to compare. The value of the $120,000 annuity today is $883,200, which is less than the $1,000,000. So, you should take the $1,000,000 payout today rather than the $120,000 annuity.

Capital Rationing and the Profitability Index

Exhibits 20-12 and 20-13 show that both the CD player and DVR projects have positive NPVs. Therefore, both are attractive investments. Because resources are limited, companies are not always able to invest in all capital assets that meet their investment criteria. This is called *capital rationing*. For example, Greg's may not have the funds to invest in both the DVR and CD-player projects at this time. In this case, Greg's should choose the DVR project because it yields a higher NPV. The DVR project should earn an additional $78,910 beyond the 14% required rate of return, while the CD-player project returns an additional $48,610.

This example illustrates an important point. The CD-player project promises more *total* net cash inflows. But the *timing* of the DVR cash flows—loaded near the beginning of the project—gives the DVR investment a higher NPV. The DVR project is more attractive because of the time value of money. Its dollars, which are received sooner, are worth more now than the more-distant dollars of the CD-player project.

If Greg's had to choose between the CD and DVR project, the company would choose the DVR project because it yields a higher NPV ($78,910). However, comparing the NPV of the two projects is *only* valid because both projects require the same initial cost—$1 million. In contrast, Exhibit 20-14 summarizes three capital investment options faced by Smart Touch. Each capital project requires a different initial investment. All three projects are attractive because each yields a positive NPV. Assuming Smart Touch can only invest in one project at this time, which one should it choose? Project B yields the highest NPV, but it also requires a larger initial investment than the alternatives.

EXHIBIT 20-14 | **Smart Touch Capital Investment Options**

Year	Project A	Project B	Project C
Present value of net cash inflows	$ 150,000	$ 238,000	$ 182,000
Investment	(125,000)	(200,000)	(150,000)
Net present value (NPV)	$ 25,000	$ 38,000	$ 32,000

To choose among the projects, Smart Touch computes the **profitability index** (also known as the **present value index**). The profitability index is computed as follows:

Profitability index = Present value of net cash inflows ÷ Investment

The profitability index computes the number of dollars returned for every dollar invested, *with all calculations performed in present value dollars*. It allows us to compare alternative investments in present value terms (like the NPV method), but it also considers differences in the investments' initial cost. Let us compute the profitability index for all three alternatives.

Present value of net cash inflows	÷ Investment	= Profitability index
Project A: $150,000	÷ $125,000 =	1.20
Project B: $238,000	÷ $200,000 =	1.19
Project C: $182,000	÷ $150,000 =	1.21

The profitability index shows that Project C is the best of the three alternatives because it returns $1.21 (in present value dollars) for every $1.00 invested. Projects A and B return slightly less.

Let us also compute the profitability index for Greg's Groovy Tunes' CD-player and DVR projects:

CD-player: $1,048,610 ÷ $1,000,000 = 1.048
DVR: $1,078,910 ÷ $1,000,000 = 1.078

The profitability index confirms our prior conclusion that the DVR project is more profitable than the CD-player project. The DVR project returns $1.078 (in present value dollars) for every $1.00 invested (beyond the 14% return already used to discount the cash flows). We did not need the profitability index to determine that the DVR project was preferable because both projects required the same investment ($1 million).

NPV of a Project with Residual Value

Many assets yield cash inflows at the end of their useful lives because they have residual value. Companies discount an investment's residual value to its present value when determining the *total* present value of the project's net cash inflows. The residual value is discounted as a single lump sum—not an annuity—because it will be received only once, when the asset is sold. In short, it is just another type of cash inflow of the project.

Suppose Greg's expects that the CD project equipment will be worth $100,000 at the end of its five-year life. To determine the CD-player project's NPV, we discount the residual value of $100,000 using the Present Value of $1 table ($i = 14\%$, $n = 5$). (See Appendix B, Table A, page B-1.) We then *add* its present value of $51,900 to the present value of the CD project's other net cash inflows we calculated in Exhibit 20-13 ($1,048,610). This gives the new net present value calculation as shown in Exhibit 20-15 below:

EXHIBIT 20-15 | **NPV of a Project with Residual Value**

Year		PV Factor ($i = 14\%$, $n = 5$)		Net Cash Inflow		Present Value
1–5	Present value of annuity	3.433	×	$305,450	=	$ 1,048,610
5	Present value of residual value (single lump sum)	0.519	×	$100,000	=	51,900
	Total present value of net cash inflows					$ 1,100,510
0	Investment					$(1,000,000)
	Net present value (NPV)					$ 100,510

Because of the expected residual value, the CD-player project is now more attractive than the DVR project. If Greg's could pursue only the CD or DVR project, it would now choose the CD project, because its NPV of $100,510 is higher than the DVR project's NPV of $78,910, and both projects require the same investment of $1 million.

Sensitivity Analysis

Capital budgeting decisions affect cash flows far into the future. Greg's managers might want to know whether their decision would be affected by any of their major assumptions, for example,

- changing the discount rate from 14% to 12% or to 16%.
- changing the net cash flows by 10%.

After reviewing the basic information for NPV analysis, managers perform sensitivity analyses to recalculate and review the results.

Internal Rate of Return (IRR)

Another discounted cash flow model for capital budgeting is the internal rate of return. The **internal rate of return (IRR)** is the rate of return (based on discounted cash flows) a company can expect to earn by investing in the project. *It is the interest rate that makes the NPV of the investment equal to zero.*

Let us look at this concept in another light by substituting in the definition of NPV:

Present value of the investment's net cash inflows – Investment's cost (Present value of cash outflows) = 0

In other words, the IRR is the *interest rate* that makes the cost of the investment equal to the present value of the investment's net cash inflows. The higher the IRR, the more desirable the project.

IRR with Equal Periodic Net Cash Inflows (Annuity)

Let us first consider Greg's CD-player project, which would cost $1 million and result in five equal yearly cash inflows of $305,450. We compute the IRR of an investment with equal periodic cash flows (annuity) by taking the following steps:

1. The IRR is the interest rate that makes the cost of the investment *equal to* the present value of the investment's net cash inflows, so we set up the following equation:

Investment's cost = Present value of investment's net cash inflows
Investment's cost = Amount of each equal net cash inflow × Annuity PV factor (*i* = ?, *n* = given)

2. Next, we plug in the information we do know—the investment cost, $1,000,000, the equal annual net cash inflows, $305,450, no residual value, and the number of periods (five years):

$1,000,000 = $305,450 × Annuity PV factor (*i* = ?, *n* = 5)

3. We then rearrange the equation and solve for the Annuity PV factor (*i* = ?, *n* = 5):

$1,000,000 ÷ $305,450 = Annuity PV factor (*i* = ?, *n* = 5)
3.274 = Annuity PV factor (*i* = ?, *n* = 5)

4. Finally, we find the interest rate that corresponds to this Annuity PV factor. Turn to the Present Value of Annuity of $1 table (Appendix B, Table B). Scan the row corresponding to the project's expected life—five years, in our example. Choose the column(s) with the number closest to the Annuity PV factor you calculated in step 3. The 3.274 annuity factor is in the 16% column. Therefore, the IRR of the CD-player project is 16%. Greg's expects the project to earn an internal rate of return of 16% over its life. Exhibit 20-16 confirms this result: Using a 16% discount rate, the project's NPV is zero. In other words, 16% is the discount rate that makes the investment cost equal to the present value of the investment's net cash inflows.

EXHIBIT 20-16 | **IRR—CD-Player Project**

Years		Annuity PV Factor (*i* = 16%, *n* = 5)	Net Cash Inflow	Total Present Value
1–5	Present value of annuity of equal annual net cash inflows for 5 years at 16%	3.274 ×	$305,450 =	$1,000,000[†]
0	Investment			(1,000,000)
	Net present value of the CD-player project			$ 0[‡]

†Slight rounding error.
‡The zero difference proves that the IRR is 16%.

To decide whether the project is acceptable, compare the IRR with the minimum desired rate of return. The decision rule is as follows:

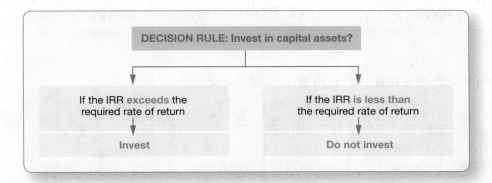

Recall that Greg's Groovy Tunes' required rate of return is 14%. Because the CD project's IRR (16%) is higher than the hurdle rate (14%), Greg's would invest in the project.

In the CD-player project, the exact Annuity PV factor (3.274) appears in the Present Value of an Annuity of $1 table (Appendix B, Table B). Many times, the exact factor will not appear in the table. For example, let us find the IRR of Smart Touch's B2B Web portal. Recall the B2B portal had a six-year life with annual net cash inflows of $60,000. The investment costs $240,000. We find its Annuity PV factor using the same steps:

Investment's cost	= Present value of investment's net cash inflows
Investment's cost	= Amount of each equal net cash inflow × Annuity PV factor (i = ?, n = given)
$240,000	= $60,000 × Annuity PV factor (i = ?, n = 6)
$240,000 ÷ $60,000	= Annuity PV factor (i = ?, n = 6)
4.00	= Annuity PV factor (i = ?, n = 6)

Now look in the Present Value of Annuity of $1 table in the row marked 6 periods (Appendix B, Table B). You will not see 4.00 under any column. The closest two factors are 3.889 (at 14%) and 4.111 (at 12%). Thus, the B2B portal's IRR must be somewhere between 12% and 14%. If we need a more precise figure, we could interpolate, or use a business calculator or Microsoft Excel to find the portal's exact IRR of 12.978%. If Smart Touch had a 14% required rate of return, it would *not* invest in the B2B portal because the portal's IRR is less than 14%.

IRR with Unequal Periodic Cash Flows

Because the DVR project has unequal cash inflows, Greg's cannot use the Present Value of Annuity of $1 table to find the asset's IRR. Rather, Greg's must use a trial-and-error procedure to determine the discount rate making the project's NPV equal to zero. For example, because the company's minimum required rate of return is 14%, Greg's might start by calculating whether the DVR project earns at least 14%. Recall from Exhibit 20-13 that the DVR's NPV using a 14% discount rate is $78,910. Since the NPV is *positive*, the IRR must be *higher* than 14%. Greg's continues the trial-and-error process using *higher* discount rates until the company finds the rate that brings the net present value of the DVR project to *zero*. Exhibit 20-17 shows that at 16%, the DVR has an NPV of $40,390. Therefore, the IRR must be higher than 16%. At 18%, the NPV is $3,980, which is very close to zero. Thus, the IRR must be slightly higher than 18%. If we use a business calculator, rather than the trial-and-error procedure, we would find the IRR is 18.23%.

EXHIBIT 20-17 | **Finding the DVR's IRR Through Trial-and-Error**

Years		Net Cash Inflow		PV Factor (for $i = 16\%$)		Present Value at 16%	Net Cash Inflow		PV Factor (for $i = 18\%$)		Present Value at 18%
1	Inflows	$500,000	×	0.862*	=	$ 431,000	$500,000	×	0.847*	=	$ 423,500
2	Inflows	350,000	×	0.743	=	260,050	350,000	×	0.718	=	251,300
3	Inflows	300,000	×	0.641	=	192,300	300,000	×	0.609	=	182,700
4	Inflows	250,000	×	0.552	=	138,000	250,000	×	0.516	=	129,000
5	Inflows	40,000	×	0.476	=	19,040	40,000	×	0.437	=	17,480
	Total present value of net cash inflows					$ 1,040,390					$ 1,003,980
0	Investment					(1,000,000)					(1,000,000)
	Net present value (NPV)					$ 40,390					$ 3,980

*PV Factors are found in Appendix B, Table A.

The DVR's internal rate of return is higher than Greg's 14% required rate of return so the DVR project is attractive.

Comparing Capital Budgeting Methods

We have discussed four capital budgeting methods commonly used by companies to make capital investment decisions. Two of these methods do not incorporate the time value of money: payback period and ARR. Exhibit 20-18 summarizes the similarities and differences between these two methods.

EXHIBIT 20-18 | **Capital Budgeting Methods That *Ignore* the Time Value of Money**

Payback period	Accounting rate of return
• Simple to compute	• The only method that uses accrual accounting figures
• Focuses on the time it takes to recover the company's cash investment	• Shows how the investment will affect operating income, which is important to financial statement users
• Ignores any cash flows occurring after the payback period, including any residual value	• Measures the profitability of the asset over its entire life
• Highlights risks of investments with longer cash recovery periods	• Ignores the time value of money
• Ignores the time value of money	

The discounted cash-flow methods are superior because they consider both the time value of money and profitability. These methods compare an investment's initial cost (cash outflow) with its future net cash inflows—all converted to the *same point in time*—the present value. Profitability is built into the discounted cash-flow methods because they consider *all* cash inflows and outflows over the project's life. Exhibit 20-19 considers the similarities and differences between the two discounted cash-flow methods.

EXHIBIT 20-19 | **Capital Budgeting Methods That *Incorporate* the Time Value of Money**

Net present value	Internal rate of return
• Incorporates the time value of money and the asset's net cash flows over its entire life	• Incorporates the time value of money and the asset's net cash flows over its entire life
• Indicates whether or not the asset will earn the company's minimum required rate of return	• Computes the project's unique rate of return
• Shows the excess or deficiency of the asset's present value of net cash inflows over its initial investment cost	• No additional steps needed for capital rationing decisions
• The profitability index should be computed for capital rationing decisions when the assets require different initial investments	

Managers often use more than one method to gain different perspectives on risks and returns. For example, Smart Touch Learning could decide to pursue capital projects with positive NPVs, provided that those projects have a payback of four years or fewer.

Decision Guidelines

CAPITAL BUDGETING

Here are more of the guidelines **Amazon.com's** managers used as they made the major capital budgeting decision to invest in building warehouses.

Decision	Guideline
• Which capital budgeting methods are best?	Discounted cash-flow methods (NPV and IRR) are best because they incorporate both profitability and the time value of money.
• Why do the NPV and IRR models use the present value?	Because an investment's cash inflows and cash outflows occur at different points in time, they must be converted to a common point in time to make a valid comparison (that is, to determine whether inflows exceed cash outflows). These methods use the *present* value as the common point in time.
• How do we know if investing in warehouse facilities will be worthwhile?	An investment in warehouse facilities may be worthwhile if the NPV is positive or the IRR exceeds the required rate of return.
• How do we compute the net present value with	
• equal annual cash flows?	Compute the present value of the investment's net cash inflows using the Present Value of an Annuity of $1 table and then subtract the investment's cost.
• unequal annual cash flows?	Compute the present value of each year's net cash inflows using the Present Value of $1 (lump sum) table, sum the present values of the inflows, and then subtract the investment's cost.
• How do we compute the internal rate of return with	
• equal annual cash flows?	Find the interest rate that yields the following PV factor:

$$\text{Annuity PV factor} = \frac{\text{Investment cost}}{\text{Expected annual net cash inflow}}$$

• unequal annual cash flows?	Trial and error, spreadsheet software, or business calculator

II-23 Performance Evaluation and the Balanced Scorecard

Learning Objectives/ Success Keys

1 Explain why and how companies decentralize

2 Explain why companies use performance evaluation systems

3 Describe the balanced scorecard and identify key performance indicators for each perspective

4 Use performance reports to evaluate cost, revenue, and profit centers

5 Use ROI, RI, and EVA to evaluate investment centers

To deliver over 3.6 billion packages a year in over 200 countries, **United Parcel Service (UPS)** employs over 370,000 people. But how does management successfully guide the actions of all of these employees? First, it divides—or decentralizes—the company into three segments: domestic packaging, international packaging, and non-packaging services (such as supply chain and logistics). It further breaks each packaging segment into geographic regions and each region into districts. Management gives each district manager authority to make decisions for his or her own district. Because top management wants *every* employee to know how his or her day-to-day job contributes to the company's goals, it implemented a system, called the balanced scorecard, for communicating strategy to all district managers and employees. Management can also use the balanced scorecard to measure whether each district is meeting its goals and to assess where it should make changes. According to one **UPS** executive, "The balanced scorecard provided a road map—the shared vision of our future goals—with action elements that let *everyone* contribute to our success." After reading this article, Smart Touch's CEO, Sheena Bright, wants to learn more about this managerial tool.

In 2000, *Forbes* named **UPS** the "Company of the Year" and in 2004, *Fortune* rated **UPS** as the "World's Most Admired Company in its Industry" for the sixth consecutive year.[1]

Many companies, like **UPS**, decentralize their operations into subunits. Decentralization provides large companies with many advantages. Because top management is not directly involved in running the day-to-day operations of each subunit, it needs a system—such as the balanced scorecard—for communicating the company's strategy to subunit managers and for measuring how well the subunits are achieving their goals. Let us first take a look at the advantages and disadvantages of decentralization.

Decentralized Operations

In a small company, the owner or top manager often makes all planning and operating decisions. Small companies are most often considered to be **Centralized companies** because centralizing decision making is easier due to the smaller scope of their operations. However, when a company grows, it is impossible for a single person to manage the entire organization's daily operations. Therefore, most companies decentralize as they grow. These are called **decentralized companies.**

Companies decentralize by splitting their operations into different divisions or operating units. Top management delegates decision-making responsibility to the unit managers. Top management determines the type of decentralization that best suits the company's strategy. For example, decentralization may be based on geographic area, product line, customer base, business function, or some other business characteristic. **Citizen's Bank** segments its operations by state (different geographic areas). **Sherwin-Williams** segments by customer base (commercial and consumer paint divisions). **PepsiCo** segments by brands (**Pepsi, Frito-Lay, Quaker, Gatorade, and Tropicana**). And UPS segmented first by function (domestic packaging, international packaging, and nonpackaging services), then by geographic area. Smart Touch Learning thinks it will segment by product line (DVDs and Web-based learning).

1 Explain why and how companies decentralize

---

[1]*Sources*: Robert Kaplan and David Norton, *The Strategy-Focused Organization: How Balanced Scorecard Companies Thrive in the New Business Environment*, Harvard Business School Press, Boston, 2001, pp. 21–22, 239–241; UPS Web site.

Advantages of Decentralization

What advantages does decentralization offer large companies? Let us take a look.

Frees Top Management Time

By delegating responsibility for daily operations to unit managers, top management can concentrate on long-term strategic planning and higher-level decisions that affect the entire company. It also naturally places the decision makers (top management) closer to the source of the decisions.

Supports Use of Expert Knowledge

Decentralization allows top management to hire the expertise each business unit needs to excel in its own specific operations. For example, decentralizing by state allows **Citizens Bank** to hire managers with specialized knowledge of the banking laws in each state. Such specialized knowledge can help unit managers make better decisions, than could the company's top managers, about product and business improvements within the business unit (state).

Improves Customer Relations

Unit managers focus on just one segment of the company. Therefore, they can maintain closer contact with important customers than can upper management. Thus, decentralization often leads to improved customer relations and quicker customer response time.

Provides Training

Decentralization also provides unit managers with training and experience necessary to become effective top managers. For example, in politics, presidential candidates often have experience as senators or state governors. Likewise, companies often choose CEOs based on their past performance as division managers.

Improves Motivation and Retention

Empowering unit managers to make decisions increases managers' motivation and retention. This improves job performance and satisfaction.

Disadvantages of Decentralization

Despite its advantages, decentralization can also cause potential problems, including those outlined in this section.

Duplication of Costs

Decentralization may cause the company to duplicate certain costs or assets. For example, each business unit may hire its own payroll department and purchase its own payroll software. Companies can often avoid such duplications by providing centralized services. For example, **Doubletree Hotels** segments its business by property, yet each property shares one centralized reservations office and one centralized Web site.

Problems Achieving Goal Congruence

Goal congruence occurs when unit managers' goals align with top management's goals. Decentralized companies often struggle to achieve goal congruence. Unit managers may not fully understand the "big picture" of the company. They may make decisions that are good for their division but could harm another division or the rest of the company. For example, the purchasing department may buy cheaper components to decrease product cost. However, cheaper components may hurt the product line's quality, and the company's brand, *as a whole*, may suffer. Later in this chapter, we will see how managerial accountants can design performance evaluation systems that encourage goal congruence.

As Exhibit 23-1 illustrates, the many advantages of decentralization usually outweigh the disadvantages.

| EXHIBIT 23-1 | **Advantages Outweigh Disadvantages** |

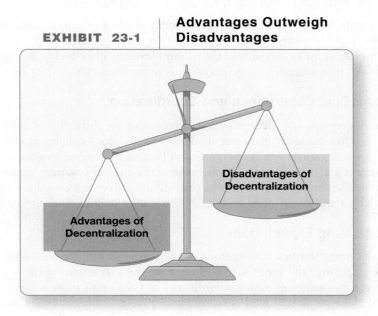

Responsibility Centers

Decentralized companies delegate responsibility for specific decisions to each subunit, creating responsibility centers. Recall that a *responsibility center* is a part or subunit of an organization whose manager is accountable for specific activities. Exhibit 23-2 reviews the four most common types of responsibility centers.

| EXHIBIT 23-2 | **The Four Most Common Types of Responsibility Centers** |

Responsibility Center	Manager is responsible for...	Examples
Cost center	Controlling costs	Production line at Dell Computer; legal department and accounting departments at Nike
Revenue center	Generating sales revenue	Midwest sales region at Pace Foods; central reservation office at Delta
Profit center	Producing profit through generating sales and controlling costs	Product line at Anheuser-Busch; individual Home Depot stores
Investment center	Producing profit and managing the division's invested capital	Company divisions, such as Walt Disney World Resorts and Toon Disney

Performance Measurement

 2   Explain why companies use performance evaluation systems

Once a company decentralizes operations, top management is no longer involved in running the subunits' day-to-day operations. Performance evaluation systems provide top management with a framework for maintaining control over the entire organization.

Goals of Performance Evaluation Systems

When companies decentralize, top management needs a system to communicate its goals to subunit managers. Additionally, top management needs to determine whether the decisions being made at the subunit level are effectively meeting company goals. We will now consider the primary goals of performance evaluation systems.

Promoting Goal Congruence and Coordination

As previously mentioned, decentralization increases the difficulty of achieving goal congruence. Unit managers may not always make decisions consistent with the overall goals of the organization. A company will be able to achieve its goals only if each unit moves, in a synchronized fashion, toward the overall company goals. The performance measurement system should provide incentives for coordinating the subunits' activities and direct them toward achieving the overall company goals.

Communicating Expectations

To make decisions that are consistent with the company's goals, unit managers must know the goals and the specific part their unit plays in attaining those goals. The performance measurement system should spell out the unit's most critical objectives. Without a clear picture of what management expects, unit managers have little to guide their daily operating decisions.

Motivating Unit Managers

Unit managers are usually motivated to make decisions that will help to achieve top management's expectations. For additional motivation, upper management may offer bonuses to unit managers who meet or exceed performance targets. Top management must exercise extreme care in setting performance targets. For example, a manager measured solely by his ability to control costs may take whatever actions are necessary to achieve that goal, including sacrificing quality or customer service. But such actions would *not* be in the best interests of the firm as a whole. Therefore, upper management must consider the ramifications of the performance targets it sets for unit managers.

Providing Feedback

In decentralized companies, top management is no longer involved in the day-to-day operations of each subunit. Performance evaluation systems provide upper management with the feedback it needs to maintain control over the entire organization, even though it has delegated responsibility and decision-making authority to unit managers. If targets are not met at the unit level, upper management will take corrective actions, ranging from modifying unit goals (if the targets were unrealistic) to replacing the unit manager (if the targets were achievable, but the manager failed to reach them).

Benchmarking

Performance evaluation results are often used for benchmarking, which is the practice of comparing the company's achievements against the best practices in the industry. Comparing results against industry benchmarks is often more revealing than comparing results against budgets. To survive, a company must keep up with its competitors. Benchmarking helps the company determine whether or not it is performing at least as well as its competitors.

Stop & Think...

Do companies, such as **UPS**, only benchmark subunit performance against competitors and industry standards?

Answer: No. Companies also benchmark performance against the subunit's past performance. Historical trend data (measuring performance over time) helps managers assess whether their decisions are improving, having no effect, or adversely affecting subunit performance. Some companies also benchmark performance against other subunits with similar characteristics.

Limitations of Financial Performance Measurement

In the past, performance measurement revolved almost entirely around *financial* performance. Until 1995, 95% of **UPS's** performance measures were financial. On the one hand, this focus makes sense because the ultimate goal of a company is to generate profit. On the other hand, *current* financial performance tends to reveal the results of *past* actions rather than indicate *future* performance. For this reason, financial measures tend to be **lag indicators** (after the fact), rather than **lead indicators** (future predictors). Management needs to know the results of past decisions, but it also needs to know how current decisions may affect the future. To adequately assess the company, managers need both lead indicators and lag indicators.

Another limitation of financial performance measures is that they tend to focus on the company's short-term achievements, rather than on long-term performance. Why is this the case? Because financial statements are prepared on a monthly, quarterly, or annual basis. To remain competitive, top management needs clear signals that assess and predict the company's performance over longer periods of time.

The Balanced Scorecard

In the early 1990s, Robert Kaplan and David Norton introduced the **balanced scorecard**.[2] The balanced scorecard recognizes that management must consider *both* financial performance measures (which tend to measure the results of actions already taken—lag indicators) and operational performance measures (which tend to drive future performance—lead indicators) when judging the performance of a company and its subunits. These measures should be linked with the company's goals and its strategy for achieving those goals. The balanced scorecard represents a major shift in corporate performance measurement. Rather than treating financial indicators as the sole measure of performance, companies recognize that they are only one measure among a broader set. Keeping score of operating measures *and* traditional financial measures gives management a "balanced" view of the organization.

3 Describe the balanced scorecard and identify key performance indicators for each perspective

---

[2]Robert Kaplan and David Norton, "The Balanced Scorecard—Measures That Drive Performance," *Harvard Business Review on Measuring Corporate Performance*, Boston, 1991, pp. 123–145; Robert Kaplan and David Norton, *Translating Strategy into Action: The Balanced Scorecard*, Boston, Harvard Business School Press, 1996.

Kaplan and Norton use the analogy of an airplane pilot to illustrate the necessity for a balanced scorecard approach to performance evaluation. The pilot of an airplane cannot rely on only one factor, such as wind speed, to fly a plane. Rather, the pilot must consider other critical factors, such as altitude, direction, and fuel level. Likewise, management cannot rely on only financial measures to guide the company. Management needs to consider other critical factors, such as customer satisfaction, operational efficiency, and employee excellence. Similar to the way a pilot uses cockpit instruments to measure critical factors, management uses *key performance indicators*—such as customer satisfaction ratings and revenue growth—to measure critical factors that affect the success of the company. As shown in Exhibit 23-3, **key performance indicators (KPIs)** are summary performance measures that help managers assess whether the company is achieving its goals.

EXHIBIT 23-3 | **Linking Company Goals to Key Performance Indicators**

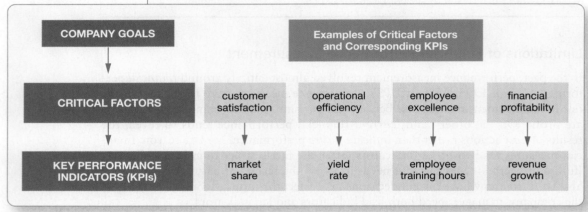

The Four Perspectives of the Balanced Scorecard

The balanced scorecard views the company from four different perspectives, each of which evaluates a specific aspect of organizational performance:

1. Financial perspective
2. Customer perspective
3. Internal business perspective
4. Learning and growth perspective

Exhibit 23-4 on the following page illustrates how the company's strategy affects, and, in turn, is affected by all four perspectives. Additionally, it shows the cause-and-effect relationship linking the four perspectives.

Companies that adopt the balanced scorecard usually have specific objectives they wish to achieve within each of the four perspectives. Once management clearly identifies the objectives, it develops KPIs that will assess how well the objectives are being achieved. To focus attention on the most critical elements and prevent information overload, management should use only a few KPIs for each perspective. Let us now look at each of the perspectives and discuss the links between them.

Financial Perspective

This perspective helps managers answer the question, "How do we look to shareholders?" The ultimate goal of companies is to generate income for their owners. Therefore, company strategy revolves around increasing the company's profits through increasing revenue growth and increasing productivity. Companies grow revenue through introducing new products, gaining new customers, and increasing

EXHIBIT 23-4 | **The Four Perspectives of the Balanced Scorecard**

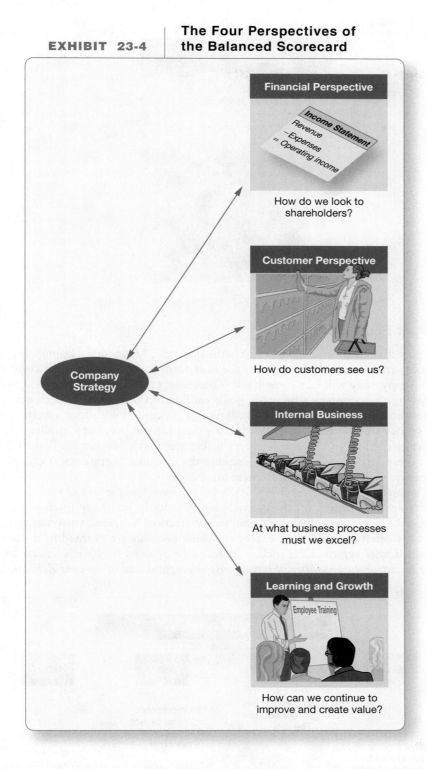

sales to existing customers. Companies increase productivity through reducing costs and using the company's assets more efficiently. Managers may implement seemingly sensible strategies and initiatives, but the test of their judgment is whether these decisions increase company profits. The financial perspective focuses management's attention on KPIs that assess financial objectives, such as revenue growth and cost cutting. Some commonly used KPIs include: *sales revenue growth, gross margin growth,* and *return on investment.* The latter portion of this chapter discusses in detail the most commonly used financial perspective KPIs.

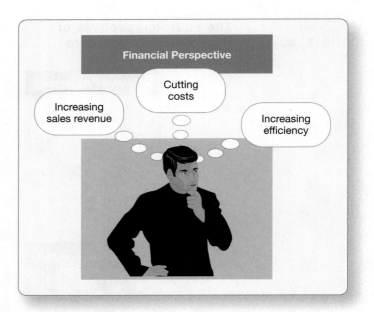

Customer Perspective

This perspective helps managers evaluate the question, "How do customers see us?" Customer satisfaction is a top priority for long-term company success. If customers are not happy, they will not come back. Therefore, customer satisfaction is critical to achieving the company's financial goals outlined in the financial perspective of the balanced scorecard. Customers are typically concerned with four specific product or service attributes: (1) the product's price, (2) the product's quality, (3) the sales service quality, and (4) the product's delivery time (the shorter the better). Since each of these attributes is critical to making the customer happy, most companies have specific objectives for each of these attributes.

Businesses commonly use KPIs, such as *customer satisfaction ratings*, to assess how they are performing on these attributes. No doubt you have filled out a customer satisfaction survey. Because customer satisfaction is crucial, customer satisfaction ratings often determine the extent to which bonuses are granted to restaurant managers. Other typical KPIs include *percentage of market share, increase in the number of customers, number of repeat customers*, and *rate of on-time deliveries*.

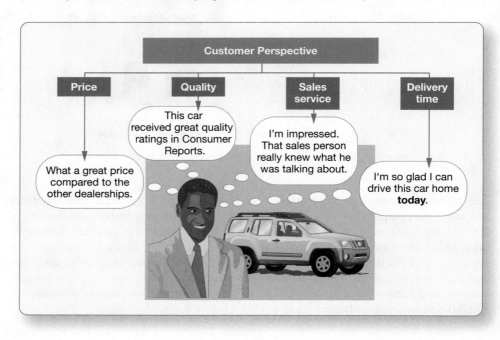

Internal Business Perspective

This perspective helps managers address the question, "At what business processes must we excel to satisfy customer and financial objectives?" The answer to this question incorporates three factors: innovation, operations, and post-sales service. All three factors critically affect customer satisfaction, which will affect the company's financial success.

Satisfying customers once does not guarantee future success, which is why the first important factor of the internal business perspective is innovation. Customers' needs and wants change as the world around them changes. Just a couple of years ago, digital cameras, flat-panel computer monitors, plasma screen televisions, and digital video recorders (DVRs) did not exist. Companies must continually improve existing products (such as adding cameras to cell phones) and develop new products (such as iPods and portable DVD players) to succeed in the future. Companies commonly assess innovation using KPIs, such as the *number of new products developed* or *new-product development time*.

The second important factor of the internal business perspective is operations. Efficient and effective internal operations allow the company to meet customers' needs and expectations. For example, the time it takes to manufacture a product (*manufacturing cycle time*) affects the company's ability to deliver quickly to meet a customer's demand. Production efficiency (*number of units produced per hour*) and product quality (*defect rate*) also affect the price charged to the customer. To remain competitive, companies must be at least as good as the industry leader at those internal operations that are essential to their business.

The third factor of the internal business perspective is post-sales service. How well does the company service customers after the sale? Claims of excellent post-sales service help to generate more sales. Management assesses post-sales service through the following typical KPIs: *number of warranty claims received, average repair time*, and *average wait time on the phone for a customer service representative*.

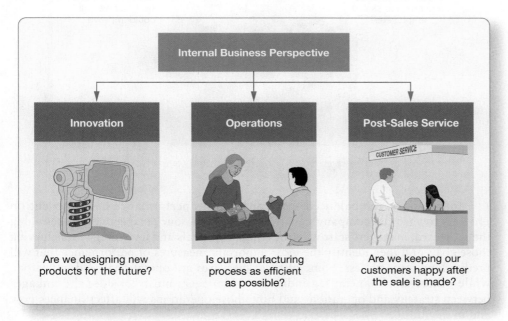

Innovation	Operations	Post-Sales Service
Are we designing new products for the future?	Is our manufacturing process as efficient as possible?	Are we keeping our customers happy after the sale is made?

Learning and Growth Perspective

This perspective helps managers assess the question, "How can we continue to improve and create value?" The learning and growth perspective focuses on three factors: (1) employee capabilities, (2) information system capabilities, and (3) the company's "climate for action." The learning and growth perspective lays the foundation needed to improve internal business operations, sustain customer satisfaction, and generate financial success. Without skilled employees, updated technology, and a positive corporate culture, the company will not be able to meet the objectives of the other perspectives.

Let us consider each of these factors. First, because most routine work is automated, employees are freed up to be critical and creative thinkers who, therefore, can help achieve the company's goals. The learning and growth perspective measures employees' skills, knowledge, motivation, and empowerment. KPIs typically include *hours of employee training*, *employee satisfaction*, *employee turnover*, and *number of employee suggestions implemented*. Second, employees need timely and accurate information on customers, internal processes, and finances; therefore, other KPIs measure the maintenance and improvement of the company's information system. For example, KPIs might include the *percentage of employees having online access to information about customers*, and the *percentage of processes with real-time feedback on quality, cycle time, and cost*. Finally, management must create a corporate culture that supports communication, change, and growth. For example, **UPS** used the balanced scorecard to communicate strategy to every employee and to show each employee how his or her daily work contributed to company success.

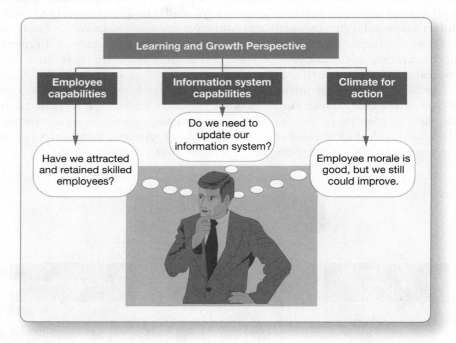

In summary, the balanced scorecard focuses performance measurement on progress toward the company's goals in each of the four perspectives. In designing the scorecard, managers start with the company's goals and its strategy for achieving those goals and then identify the *most* important measures of performance that will predict long-term success. Some of these measures are operational lead indicators, while others are financial lag indicators. Managers must consider the linkages between strategy and operations and how those operations will affect finances now and in the future.

So far, we have looked at why companies decentralize, why they need to measure subunit performance, and how the balanced scorecard can help. In the second half of the chapter, we will focus on how companies measure the financial perspective of the balanced scorecard.

Decision Guidelines

UPS had to make the following types of decisions when it decentralized and developed its balanced scorecard for performance evaluation.

Decision	Guidelines
• On what basis should the company be decentralized?	The manner of decentralization should fit the company's strategy. Many companies decentralize based on geographic region, product line, business function, or customer type.
• Will decentralization have any negative impact on the company?	Decentralization usually provides many benefits; however, decentralization also has potential drawbacks: • Subunits may duplicate costs or assets. • Subunit managers may not make decisions that are favorable to the entire company.
• How can responsibility accounting be incorporated at decentralized companies?	Subunit managers are given responsibility for specific activities and are only held accountable for the results of those activities. Subunits generally fall into one of the following four categories according to their responsibilities: 1. Cost centers—responsible for controlling costs 2. Revenue centers—responsible for generating revenue 3. Profit centers—responsible for controlling costs and generating revenue 4. Investment centers—responsible for controlling costs, generating revenue, and efficiently managing the division's invested capital (assets)
• Is a performance evaluation system necessary?	While not mandatory, most companies will reap many benefits from implementing a well-designed performance evaluation system. Such systems will promote goal congruence, communicate expectations, motivate managers, provide feedback, and enable benchmarking.
• Should the performance evaluation system include lag or lead measures?	Better performance evaluation systems include *both* lag and lead measures. Lag measures indicate the results of past actions, while lead measures a project's future performance.
• What are the four balanced scorecard perspectives?	1. Financial perspective 2. Customer perspective 3. Internal Business perspective 4. Learning and Growth perspective
• Must all four perspectives be included in the company's balanced scorecard?	Every company's balanced scorecard will be unique to its business and strategy. Because each of the four perspectives is causally linked, most companies will benefit from developing performance measures for each of the four perspectives.

Summary Problem 1

The balanced scorecard gives performance perspective from 4 different viewpoints.

Requirements

1. Each of the following describes a key performance indicator. Determine which of the following balanced scorecard perspectives is being addressed (financial, customer, internal business, or learning and growth):
   a. Employee turnover
   b. Earnings per share
   c. Percentage of on-time deliveries
   d. Revenue growth rate
   e. Percentage of defects discovered during manufacturing
   f. Number of warranties claimed
   g. New product development time
   h. Number of repeat customers
   i. Number of employee suggestions implemented

2. Read the following company initiatives and determine which of the balanced scorecard perspectives is being addressed (financial, customer, internal business, learning and growth):
   a. Purchasing efficient production equipment
   b. Providing employee training
   c. Updating retail store lighting
   d. Paying quarterly dividends
   e. Updating the company's information system

Solution

Requirement 1
   a. Learning and growth
   b. Financial
   c. Customer
   d. Financial
   e. Internal business
   f. Internal business
   g. Internal business
   h. Customer
   i. Learning and growth

Requirement 2
   a. Internal business
   b. Learning and growth
   c. Customer
   d. Financial
   e. Learning and growth

Measuring the Financial Performance of Cost, Revenue, and Profit Centers

In this half of the chapter we will take a more detailed look at how companies measure the financial perspective of the balanced scorecard for different subunits of the company. We will focus now on the financial performance measurement of each type of responsibility center.

Responsibility accounting performance reports capture the financial performance of cost, revenue, and profit centers. Recall from Chapter 21 that responsibility accounting performance reports compare *actual* results with *budgeted* amounts and display a variance, or difference, between the two amounts. Because *cost centers* are only responsible for controlling costs, their performance reports only include information on actual versus budgeted *costs*. Likewise, performance reports for *revenue centers* only contain actual versus budgeted *revenue*. However, *profit centers* are responsible for both controlling costs and generating revenue. Therefore, their performance reports contain actual and budgeted information on both their *revenues and costs*.

Cost center performance reports typically focus on the *flexible budget variance*—the difference between actual results and the flexible budget (as described in Chapter 22). Exhibit 23-5 shows an example of a cost center performance report for a regional payroll processing department of Smart Touch Learning. Because the payroll processing department only incurs expenses and does not generate revenue, it is classified as a cost center.

4 Use performance reports to evaluate cost, revenue, and profit centers

EXHIBIT 23-5	Example of Cost Center Performance Report

SMART TOUCH LEARNING, INC. Payroll Processing Department Performance Report July 2011				
	Actual	Flexible Budget	Flexible Budget Variance (U or F)	% Variance* (U of F)
Salary and wages	$18,500	$18,000	$ 500 U	2.8% U
Payroll benefits	6,100	5,000	1,100 U	22.0% U
Equipment depreciation	3,000	3,000	0	0%
Supplies	1,850	2,000	150 F	7.5% F
Other expenses	1,900	2,000	100 F	5.0% F
Total expenses	$31,350	$30,000	$1,350 U	4.5% U

*Flexible budget variance/flexible budget

Managers use management by exception to determine which variances in the performance report are worth investigating. For example, management may only investigate variances that exceed a certain dollar amount (for example, over $1,000) or a certain percentage of the budgeted figure (for example, over 10%). Smaller variances signal that operations are close to target and do not require management's immediate attention. For example, in the cost center performance report illustrated in Exhibit 23-5, management might only investigate "payroll benefits" because the variance exceeds both $1,000 and 10%. Companies that use standard costs can compute price and efficiency variances, as described in Chapter 22, to better understand why significant flexible budget variances occurred.

Revenue center performance reports often highlight both the flexible budget variance and the sales volume variance. The performance report for the specialty DVD department of Smart Touch Learning might look similar to Exhibit 23-6, with detailed sales volume and revenue shown for each brand and type of DVD sold. (For simplicity, the exhibit shows volume and revenue for only one item.) The cash register barcoding system provides management with the sales volume and sales revenue generated by individual products.

EXHIBIT 23-6	Example of a Revenue Center Performance Report

SMART TOUCH LEARNING, INC.
Specialty DVD Department Performance Report
July 2011

Sales revenue	Actual Sales	Flexible Budget Variance	Flexible Budget	Sales Volume Variance	Static (Master) Budget
Number of DVDs	2,480	–0–	2,480	155 (F)	2,325
Specialty DVDs	$40,920	$3,720 (U)	$44,640	$2,790 (F)	$41,850

Recall from Chapter 22 that the sales volume variance is due strictly to volume differences—selling more or fewer units (DVDs) than originally planned. The flexible budget variance, however, is due strictly to differences in the sales price—selling units for a higher or lower price than originally planned. Both the sales volume variance and the flexible budget variance help revenue center managers understand why they have exceeded or fallen short of budgeted revenue.

Managers of profit centers are responsible for both generating revenue and controlling costs so their performance reports include both revenues and expenses. Exhibit 23-7 shows an example of a profit center performance report for the DVD department.

EXHIBIT 23-7	Example of a Profit Center Performance Report

SMART TOUCH LEARNING, INC.
DVD—Performance Report
July 2011

	Actual	Flexible Budget	Flexible Budget Variance	% Variance
Sales revenue	$5,243,600	$5,000,000	$243,600 F	4.9% F
Operating expenses	4,183,500	4,000,000	183,500 U	4.6% U
Income from operations before service department charges	1,060,100	1,000,000	60,100 F	6.0% F
Service department charges (allocated)	84,300	75,000	9,300 U	12.4% U
Income from operations	$ 975,800	$ 925,000	$ 50,800 F	5.5% F

Notice how this profit center performance report contains a line called "Service department charges." Recall that one drawback of decentralization is that subunits may duplicate costs or assets. Many companies avoid this problem by providing centralized service departments where several subunits, such as profit centers, share assets or costs. For example, the payroll processing cost center shown in Exhibit 23-5 serves all of Smart Touch Learning. In addition to centralized payroll departments, companies often provide centralized human resource departments, legal departments, and information systems.

When subunits share centralized services, should those services be "free" to the subunits? If they are free, the subunit's performance report will *not* include any charge for using those services. However, if they are not free, the performance report will show a charge, as you see in Exhibit 23-7. Most companies charge subunits for their use of centralized services because the subunit would incur a cost to buy those services on its own. For example, if Smart Touch Learning did not operate a centralized payroll department, the DVD Department would have to hire its own payroll department personnel and purchase computers, payroll software, and supplies necessary to process the department's payroll. As an alternative, it could outsource payroll to a company, such as **Paychex** or **ADP**. In either event, the department would incur a cost for processing payroll. It only seems fair that the department is charged for using the centralized payroll processing department. Appendix 23A at the end of this chapter describes how companies allocate service department costs between subunits. Because the charges are the result of allocation, rather than a direct cost of the profit center, they are usually shown on a separate line rather than "buried" in the subunit's other operating expenses.

Regardless of the type of responsibility center, performance reports should focus on information, not blame. Analyzing budget variances helps managers understand the underlying *reasons* for the unit's performance. Once management understands these reasons, it may be able to take corrective actions. But some variances are uncontrollable. For example, the 2005 hurricanes in the Gulf Coast increased prices of gasoline (due to damaged oil refineries) and building materials (as people repaired hurricane-damaged homes). These price increases resulted in unfavorable cost variances for many companies. Managers should not be held accountable for conditions they cannot control. Responsibility accounting can help management identify the causes of variances, thereby allowing them to determine what was controllable, and what was not.

We have just looked at the detailed financial information presented in responsibility accounting performance reports. In addition to these *detailed* reports, upper management often uses *summary* measures—financial KPIs—to assess the financial performance of cost, revenue, and profit centers. Examples include the *cost per unit of output* (for cost centers), *revenue growth* (for revenue centers), and *gross margin growth* (for profit centers). KPIs, such as these, are used to address the financial perspective of the balanced scorecard for cost, revenue, and profit centers. In the next section we will look at the most commonly used KPIs for investment centers.

Stop & Think...

We have just seen that companies like Smart Touch Learning use responsibility accounting performance reports to evaluate the financial performance of cost, revenue, and profit centers. Are these types of responsibility reports sufficient for evaluating the financial performance of investment centers? Why or why not?

Answer: Investment centers are responsible not only for generating revenue and controlling costs, but also for efficiently managing the subunit's invested capital. The performance reports we have just seen address how well the subunits control costs and generate revenue, but they do not address how well the subunits manage their assets. Therefore, these performance reports will be helpful but not sufficient for evaluating investment center performance.

Measuring the Financial Performance of Investment Centers

Investment centers are typically large divisions of a company, such as the media division of **Amazon.com** or of Smart Touch Learning. The duties of an investment center manager are similar to those of a CEO. The CEO is responsible for maximizing income, in relation to the company's invested capital, by using company assets

5   Use ROI, RI, and EVA to evaluate investment centers

efficiently. Likewise, investment center managers are responsible not only for generating profit but also for making the best use of the investment center's assets.

How does an investment center manager influence the use of the division's assets? An investment center manager has the authority to open new stores or close old stores. The manager may also decide how much inventory to hold, what types of investments to make, how aggressively to collect accounts receivable, and whether to invest in new equipment. In other words, the manager has decision-making responsibility over all of the division's assets.

Companies cannot evaluate investment centers the way they evaluate profit centers, based only on operating income. Why? Because income does not indicate how *efficiently* the division is using its assets. The financial evaluation of investment centers must measure two factors: (1) how much income the division is generating and (2) how efficiently the division is using its assets.

Consider Smart Touch Learning. In addition to its DVD Division, it also has an online e-learning Division. Operating income, total assets, and sales for the two divisions follow (in thousands of dollars):

Smart Touch Learning	e-learning	DVD
Operating income	$ 450,000	$ 975,800
Total assets	2,500,000	6,500,000
Sales	7,500,000	5,243,600

Based on operating income alone, the DVD Division (with operating income of $975,800) appears to be more profitable than the e-learning Division (with operating income of $450,000). However, this comparison is misleading because it does not consider the assets invested in each division. The DVD Division has more assets to use for generating income than does the e-learning Division.

To adequately evaluate an investment center's financial performance, companies need summary performance measures—or KPIs—that include *both* the division's operating income *and* its assets. (See Exhibit 23-8.) In the next sections, we discuss three commonly used performance measures: return on investment (ROI), residual income (RI), and economic value added (EVA). All three measures incorporate both the division's assets and its operating income. For simplicity, we will leave the word *divisional* out of the equations. However, keep in mind that all of the equations use divisional data when evaluating a division's performance.

EXHIBIT 23-8 | **Summary Performance Measures (KPIs) for Investment Centers**

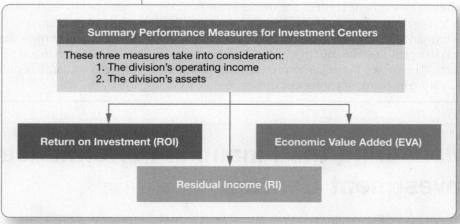

Return on Investment (ROI)

Return on Investment (ROI) is one of the most commonly used KPIs for evaluating an investment center's financial performance. Companies typically define ROI as follows:

$$\text{ROI} = \frac{\text{Operating income}}{\text{Total assets}}$$

ROI measures the amount of income an investment center earns relative to the amount of its assets. Let us calculate each division's ROI:

$$\text{e-learning Division ROI} = \frac{\$450,000}{\$2,500,000} = 18\%$$

$$\text{DVD Division ROI} = \frac{975,800}{\$6,500,000} = 15\%$$

Although the DVD Division has a higher operating income than the e-learning Division, the DVD Division is actually *less* profitable than the e-learning Division when we consider that the DVD Division has more assets from which to generate its profit.

If you had $1,000 to invest, would you rather invest it in the DVD Division or the e-learning Division? The DVD Division earns a profit of $0.15 on every $1.00 of assets, but the e-learning Division earns $0.18 on every $1.00 of assets. When top management decides how to invest excess funds, it often considers each division's ROI. A division with a higher ROI is more likely to receive extra funds because it has a history of providing a higher return.

In addition to comparing ROI across divisions, management also compares a division's ROI across time to determine whether the division is becoming more or less profitable in relation to its assets. Additionally, management often benchmarks divisional ROI with other companies in the same industry to determine how each division is performing compared to its competitors.

To determine what is driving a division's ROI, management often restates the ROI equation in its expanded form. Notice that Sales is incorporated in the denominator of the first term, and in the numerator of the second term. When the two terms are multiplied together, Sales cancels out, leaving the original ROI formula.

$$\text{ROI} = \frac{\text{Operating income}}{\text{Sales}} \times \frac{\text{Sales}}{\text{Total assets}} = \frac{\text{Operating income}}{\text{Total assets}}$$

Why do managers rewrite the ROI formula this way? Because it helps them better understand how they can improve their ROI. The first term in the expanded equation is called the **profit margin**:

$$\text{Profit margin} = \frac{\text{Operating income}}{\text{Sales}}$$

The profit margin shows how much operating income the division earns on every $1.00 of sales, so this term focuses on profitability. Let us calculate each division's sales margin:

$$\text{e-learning Division's profit margin} = \frac{\$450,000}{\$7,500,000} = 6\%$$

$$\text{DVD Division's profit margin} = \frac{\$975,800}{\$5,243,600} = 19\%$$

The e-learning Division has a profit margin of 6%, meaning that it earns a profit of $0.06 on every $1.00 of sales. The DVD Division, however, is much more profitable with a profit margin of 19%, earning $0.19 on every $1.00 of sales.

Capital turnover is the second term of the expanded ROI equation:

$$\text{Capital turnover} = \frac{\text{Sales}}{\text{Total assets}}$$

Capital turnover shows how efficiently a division uses its assets to generate sales. Rather than focusing on profitability, capital turnover focuses on efficiency. Let us calculate each division's capital turnover:

$$\text{e-learning Division's capital turnover} = \frac{\$7,500,000}{\$2,500,000} = 3$$

$$\text{DVD Division's capital turnover} = \frac{\$5,243,600}{\$6,500,000} = 0.80$$

The e-learning Division has a capital turnover of 3. This means that the e-learning Division generates $3.00 of sales with every $1.00 of assets. The DVD Division's capital turnover is only 0.80. The DVD Division generates only $0.80 of sales with every $1.00 of assets. The e-learning Division uses its assets much more efficiently in generating sales than the DVD Division.

Let us put the two terms back together in the expanded ROI equation:

	Profit margin	×	Capital turnover	= ROI
e-learning Division:	6%	×	3	= 18%
DVD Division:	19%	×	0.80	= 15%

As you can see, the expanded ROI equation gives management more insight into the division's ROI. Management can now see that the DVD is more profitable on its sales (19%) than the e-learning Division, but the e-learning Division is doing a better job of generating sales with its assets (capital turnover of 3) than the DVD Division (capital turnover of 0.80). Consequently, the e-learning Division has a higher ROI of 18%.

If a manager is not satisfied with his division's capital turnover rate, how can he improve it? He might try to eliminate nonproductive assets, for example, by being more aggressive in collecting accounts receivables or decreasing inventory levels. He might decide to change retail-store layout to generate sales.

What if management is not satisfied with the current profit margin? To increase the profit margin, management must increase the operating income earned on every dollar of sales. Management may cut product costs or selling and administrative costs, but it needs to be careful when trimming costs. Cutting costs in the short term can hurt long-term ROI. For example, sacrificing quality or cutting back on research and development could decrease costs in the short run, but may hurt long-term sales. The balanced scorecard helps management carefully consider the consequences of cost-cutting measures before acting on them.

ROI has one major drawback. Evaluating division managers based solely on ROI gives them an incentive to adopt *only* projects that will maintain or increase their current ROI. Let us say that top management has set a company-wide target ROI of 16%. Both divisions are considering investing in in-store video display equipment that shows customers how to use featured products. This equipment will increase sales because customers are more likely to buy the products when they see these infomercials. The equipment would cost each division $100,000 and is expected to provide each division with $17,000 of annual income. The *equipment's* ROI is as follows:

$$\text{Equipment ROI} = \frac{\$17,000}{\$100,000} = 17\%$$

Upper management would want the divisions to invest in this equipment since the equipment will provide a 17% ROI, which is higher than the 16% target rate. But what will the managers of the divisions do? Because the DVD Division currently has an ROI of 15%, the new equipment (with its 17% ROI) will *increase* the division's *overall* ROI. Therefore, the DVD Division manager will buy the equipment. However, the e-learning Division currently has an ROI of 18%. If the e-learning Division invests in the equipment, its *overall* ROI will *decrease*. Therefore, the manager of the e-learning Division will probably turn down the investment. In this case, goal congruence is *not* achieved— only one division will invest in equipment. Yet top management wants both divisions to invest in the equipment because the equipment return exceeds the 16% target ROI. Next, we discuss a performance measure that overcomes this problem with ROI.

Residual Income (RI)

Residual income (RI) is another commonly used KPI for evaluating an investment center's financial performance. Similar to ROI, RI considers both the division's operating income and its total assets. RI measures the division's profitability and the efficiency with which the division uses its assets. RI also incorporates another piece of information: top management's target rate of return (such as the 16% target return in the previous example). The target rate of return is the minimum acceptable rate of return that top management expects a division to earn with its assets.

RI compares the division's operating income with the minimum operating income expected by top management *given the size of the division's assets*. A positive RI means that the division's operating income exceeds top management's target rate of return. A negative RI means the division is not meeting the target rate of return. Let us look at the RI equation and then calculate the RI for both divisions using the 16% target rate of return from the previous example.

RI = Operating income – Minimum acceptable income

In this equation, the minimum acceptable income is defined as top management's target rate of return multiplied by the division's total assets. Therefore,

RI = Operating income − (Target rate of return × Total assets)

e-learning Division RI = $450,000 − (16% × $2,500,000)
= $450,000 − $400,000
= $50,000

The positive RI indicates that the e-learning Division exceeded top management's 16% target return expectations. The RI calculation also confirms what we learned about the e-learning Division's ROI. Recall that the e-learning Division's ROI was 18%, which is higher than the targeted 16%.

Let us also calculate the RI for the DVD Division:

DVD Division RI = $975,800 − (16% × $6,500,000)
= $975,800 − $1,040,000
= $(64,200)

The DVD Division's RI is negative. This means that the DVD Division did not use its assets as effectively as top management expected. Recall that the DVD Division's ROI of 15% fell short of the target rate of 16%.

Why would a company prefer to use RI over ROI for performance evaluation? The answer is that RI is more likely to lead to goal congruence than ROI. Let us once again consider the video display equipment that both divisions could buy. In both divisions, the equipment is expected to generate a 17% return. If the divisions are evaluated based on ROI, we learned that the DVD Division will buy the equipment because it will increase the division's ROI. The e-learning Division, on the other hand, will probably not buy the equipment because it will lower the division's ROI.

However, if management evaluates divisions based on RI rather than ROI, what will the divisions do? The answer depends on whether the project yields a positive or negative RI. Recall that the equipment would cost each division $100,000, but will provide $17,000 of operating income each year. The RI provided by *just* the equipment would be as follows:

Equipment RI = $17,000 − ($100,000 × 16%)
= $17,000 − $16,000
= $1,000

If purchased, this equipment will *improve* each division's current RI by $1,000. As a result, both divisions will be motivated to invest in the equipment. Goal congruence is achieved because both divisions will take the action that top management desires. That is, both divisions will invest in the equipment.

Another benefit of RI is that management may set different target returns for different divisions. For example, management might require a higher target rate of return from a division operating in a riskier business environment. If the DVD industry were riskier than the e-learning industry, top management might decide to set a higher target return—perhaps 17%—for the DVD Division.

Economic Value Added (EVA)

Economic Value Added (EVA) is a special type of RI calculation. Unlike the RI calculation we have just discussed, EVA looks at a division's RI through the eyes of the company's primary stakeholders: its investors and long-term creditors (such as bondholders). Since these stakeholders provide the company's capital, management often wishes to evaluate how efficiently a division is using its assets from these two stakeholders' viewpoints. EVA calculates RI for these stakeholders by specifically considering the following:

1. The income available to these stakeholders

2. The assets used to generate income for these stakeholders

3. The minimum rate of return required by these stakeholders (referred to as the **weighted average cost of capital**, or WACC)

Let us compare the EVA equation with the RI equation and then explain the differences in more detail:

RI = Operating income   – (Total assets   × Target rate of return)
EVA = After-tax operating income – [(Total assets – Current liabilities) × WACC%]

Both equations calculate whether any income was created by the division above and beyond expectations. They do this by comparing actual income with the minimum acceptable income. But note the differences in the EVA calculation:

1. The EVA calculation uses *after-tax operating income*, which is the income left over after subtracting income taxes. Why? Because the portion of income paid to the government is not available to investors and long-term creditors.

2. *Total assets is reduced by current liabilities*. Why? Because funds owed to short-term creditors, such as suppliers (accounts payable) and employees (wages payable), will be paid in the immediate future and will not be available for generating income in the long run. The division is not expected to earn a return for investors and long-term creditors on those funds that will soon be paid out to short-term creditors.

3. The *WACC* replaces management's target rate of return. Since EVA focuses on investors and creditors, it is *their* expected rate of return that should be used, not management's expected rate of return. The WACC, which represents the minimum rate of return expected by *investors and long-term creditors*, is based on the company's cost of raising capital from both groups of stakeholders. The riskier the business, the higher the expected return. Detailed WACC computations are discussed in advanced accounting and finance courses.

In summary, EVA incorporates all the elements of RI from the perspective of investors and long-term creditors. Now that we have walked through the equation's components, let us calculate EVA for the e-learning and DVD Divisions discussed earlier. We will need the following additional information:

Effective income tax rate	30%
WACC	13%
e-learning Division's current liabilities	$150,000
DVD Division's current liabilities	$250,000

The 30% effective income tax rate means that the government takes 30% of the company's income, leaving only 70% to the company's stakeholders. Therefore, we calculate *after-tax operating income* by multiplying the division's operating income by 70% (100% – effective tax rate of 30%).

$$EVA = \text{After-tax operating income} - [(\text{Total assets} - \text{Current liabilities}) \times \text{WACC\%}]$$

$$
\begin{aligned}
\text{e-learning Division EVA} &= (\$450{,}000 \times 70\%) - [(\$2{,}500{,}000 - \$150{,}000) \times 13\%] \\
&= \$315{,}000 - (\$2{,}350{,}000 \times 13\%) \\
&= \$315{,}000 - \$305{,}500 \\
&= \$9{,}500
\end{aligned}
$$

$$
\begin{aligned}
\text{DVD Division EVA} &= (\$975{,}800 \times 70\%) - [(\$6{,}500{,}000 - 250{,}000) \times 13\%] \\
&= \$683{,}060 - (\$6{,}250{,}000 \times 13\%) \\
&= \$683{,}060 - \$812{,}500 \\
&= \$(129{,}440)
\end{aligned}
$$

These EVA calculations show that the e-learning Division has generated income in excess of expectations for its investors and long-term debt-holders, whereas the DVD Division has not.

Many firms, such as **Coca-Cola, Amazon.com,** and **J.C. Penney,** measure the financial performance of their investment centers using EVA. EVA promotes goal congruence, just as RI does. Additionally, EVA looks at the income generated by the division in excess of expectations, solely from the perspective of investors and long-term creditors. Therefore, EVA specifically addresses the financial perspective of the balanced scorecard that asks, "How do we look to shareholders?"

Exhibit 23-9 summarizes the three performance measures and some of their advantages.

EXHIBIT 23-9 | **Three Investment Center Performance Measures: A Summary**

ROI:

Equation	$\text{ROI} = \dfrac{\text{Operating income}}{\text{Sales}} \times \dfrac{\text{Sales}}{\text{Total assets}} = \dfrac{\text{Operating income}}{\text{Total assets}}$
Advantages	• The expanded equation provides management with additional information on profitability and efficiency • Management can compare ROI across divisions and with other companies • ROI is useful for resource allocation

RI:

Equation	RI = Operating income − (Total assets × Target rate of return)
Advantages	• Promotes goal congruence better than ROI • Incorporates management's minimum required rate of return • Management can use different target rates of return for divisions with different levels of risk

EVA:

Equation	EVA = (After-tax operating income) − [(Total assets − Current liabilities) × WACC%]
Advantages	• Considers income generated for investors and long-term creditors in excess of their expectations • Promotes goal congruence

Limitations of Financial Performance Measures

We have just finished looking at three KPIs (ROI, RI, and EVA) commonly used to evaluate the financial performance of investment centers. As discussed in the following sections, all of these measures have drawbacks that management should keep in mind when evaluating the financial performance of investment centers.

Measurement Issues

The ROI, RI, and EVA calculations appear to be very straightforward; however, management must make some decisions before these calculations can be made. For example, all three equations use the term *total assets*. Recall that total assets is a balance sheet figure, which means that it is a snapshot at any given point in time. Because the total assets figure will be *different* at the beginning of the period and at the end of the period, most companies choose to use a simple average of the two figures in their ROI, RI, and EVA calculations.

Management must also decide if it really wants to include *all* assets in the total asset figure. Many firms, such as **Wal-mart,** are continually buying land on which to build future retail outlets. Until those stores are built and opened, the land (including any construction in progress) is a nonproductive asset, which is not adding to the company's operating income. Including nonproductive assets in the total asset figure will naturally drive down the ROI, RI, and EVA figures. Therefore, some firms will not include nonproductive assets in these calculations.

Another asset measurement issue is whether to use the gross book value of assets (the historical cost of the assets), or the net book value of assets (historical cost less accumulated depreciation). Many firms will use the net book value of assets because the figure is consistent with and easily pulled from the balance sheet. Because depreciation expense factors into the firm's operating income, the net book value concept is also consistent with the measurement of operating income. However, using the net book value of assets has a definite drawback. Over time, the net book value of assets decreases because accumulated depreciation continues to grow until the assets are fully depreciated. Therefore, ROI, RI, and EVA get *larger* over time *simply because of depreciation* rather than from actual improvements in operations. In addition, the rate of this depreciation effect will depend on the depreciation method used.

In general, calculating ROI based on the net book value of assets gives managers incentive to continue using old, outdated equipment because its low net book value results in a higher ROI. However, top management may want the division to invest in new technology to create operational efficiency (internal business perspective of the balanced scorecard) or to enhance its information systems (learning and growth perspective). The long-term effects of using outdated equipment may be devastating, as competitors use new technology to produce and sell at lower cost. Therefore, to create *goal congruence*, some firms prefer calculating ROI based on the gross book value of assets. The same general rule holds true for RI and EVA calculations: All else being equal, using net book value will increase RI and EVA over time.

Short-Term Focus

One serious drawback of financial performance measures is their short-term focus. Companies usually prepare performance reports and calculate ROI, RI, and EVA figures over a one-year time frame or less. If upper management uses a short time frame, division managers have an incentive to take actions that will lead to an immediate increase in these measures, even if such actions may not be in the company's long-term interest (such as cutting back on R&D or advertising). On the other hand, some potentially positive actions considered by subunit managers may take longer than one year to generate income at the targeted level. Many product life cycles start slow, even incurring losses in the early stages, before generating profit. If managers are measured on short-term financial performance only, they may not introduce new products because they are not willing to wait several years for the positive effect to show up in their financial performance measures.

As a potential remedy, management can measure financial performance using a longer time horizon, such as three to five years. Extending the time frame gives subunit managers the incentive to think long term rather than short term and make decisions that will positively impact the company over the next several years.

The limitations of financial performance measures confirm the importance of the balanced scorecard. The deficiencies of financial measures can be overcome by taking a broader view of performance—including KPIs from all four balanced scorecard perspectives rather than concentrating on only the financial measures.

Decision Guidelines

When managers at **UPS** developed the financial perspective of their balanced scorecard, they had to make decisions such as the examples that follow.

Decision	Guidelines
• How should the financial section of the balanced scorecard be measured for cost, revenue, and profit centers?	Responsibility accounting performance reports measure the financial performance of cost, revenue, and profit centers. These reports typically highlight the variances between budgeted and actual performance.
• How should the financial section of the balanced scorecard be measured for investment centers?	Investment centers require measures that take into account the division's operating income *and* the division's assets. Typical measures include the following: • Return on investment (ROI) • Residual income (RI) • Economic value added (EVA)
• How is ROI computed and interpreted?	$$\text{ROI} = \text{Operating income} \div \text{Total assets}$$ ROI measures the amount of income earned by a division relative to the size of its assets—the higher, the better.
• Can managers learn more by writing the ROI formula in its expanded form?	In its expanded form, ROI is written as follows: $$\text{ROI} = \text{Profit margin} \times \text{Capital turnover}$$ where, $$\text{Profit margin} = \text{Operating income} \div \text{Sales}$$ $$\text{Capital turnover} = \text{Sales} \div \text{Total assets}$$ Profit margin focuses on profitability (the amount of income earned on every dollar of sales), while capital turnover focuses on efficiency (the amount of sales generated with every dollar of assets).
• How is RI computed and interpreted?	$$\text{RI} = \text{Operating income} - \left(\text{Target rate of return} \times \text{Total assets} \right)$$ If RI is positive, the division is earning income at a rate that exceeds management's minimum expectations.
• How does EVA differ from RI?	EVA is a special type of RI calculation that focuses on the income (in excess of expectations) created by the division for two specific stakeholders: investors and long-term creditors.
• When calculating ROI, RI, or VA, are there any measurement issues of concern?	If the net book value of assets is used to measure total assets, ROI, RI, and EVA will "artificially" rise over time due to the depreciation of the assets. Using gross book value to measure total assets eliminates this measurement issue. Many firms use the average balance of total assets, rather than the beginning or ending balance of assets, when they calculate ROI, RI, and EVA.

Appendix 18A

Variable Costing and Absorption Costing

Up to this point, we have focused on the income statements that companies report to the public under the generally accepted accounting principles (GAAP). GAAP requires that we assign both variable and fixed manufacturing costs to products. This approach is called **absorption costing** because products absorb both fixed and variable manufacturing costs. Supporters of absorption costing argue that companies cannot produce products without incurring fixed costs, so these costs are an important part of product costs. Financial accountants usually prefer absorption costing.

The alternate method is called variable costing. **Variable costing** assigns only variable manufacturing costs to products. Fixed costs are considered *period costs* and are *expensed immediately* because the company incurs these fixed costs whether or not it produces any products or services. In variable costing, fixed costs are not product costs. Management accountants often prefer variable costing for their planning and control decisions.

The key difference between absorption costing and variable costing is that:

- Absorption costing considers fixed manufacturing costs as inventoriable product costs.
- Variable costing considers fixed manufacturing costs as period costs (expenses).

All other costs are treated the same way under both absorption and variable costing:

- Variable manufacturing costs are inventoriable products costs.
- All nonmanufacturing costs—both fixed and variable—are period costs and are expensed immediately when incurred.

Exhibit 18A-1 summarizes the difference between variable and absorption costing, with the differences shown in color.

EXHIBIT 18A-1 | Differences Between Absorption Costing and Variable Costing

Type of Cost	Absorption Costing	Variable Costing
Product Costs (Capitalized as Inventory until expensed as Cost of Goods Sold)	Direct materials Direct labor Variable manufacturing overhead Fixed manufacturing overhead	Direct materials Direct labor Variable manufacturing overhead
Period Costs (Expensed in period incurred)	Variable nonmanufacturing costs Fixed nonmanufacturing costs	Fixed manufacturing overhead Variable nonmanufacturing costs Fixed nonmanufacturing costs
Income Statement Format	Conventional income statement, as in Chapters 1–16	Contribution margin income statement

Applying Variable Costing Versus Absorption Costing: Limonade

To see how absorption costing and variable costing differ, let us consider the following example. Limonade incurs the following costs for its powdered sports beverage mix in March 2010:

Direct materials cost per case	$ 8.00
Direct labor cost per case	$ 3.00
Variable manufacturing overhead cost per case	$ 2.00
Total fixed manufacturing overhead costs	$50,000
Total fixed selling and administrative costs	$25,000
Cases of powdered mix produced	10,000
Cases of powdered mix sold	8,000
Sale price per case of powdered mix	$ 25

There were no beginning inventories, so Limonade has 2,000 cases of powdered mix in ending inventory (10,000 cases produced − 8,000 cases sold).

What is Limonade's inventoriable product cost per case under absorption costing and variable costing?

	Absorption Costing	Variable Costing
Direct materials	$ 8.00	$ 8.00
Direct labor	3.00	3.00
Variable manufacturing overhead	2.00	2.00
Fixed manufacturing overhead ($50,000/10,000 cases)	5.00	
Total cost per case	**$18.00**	**$13.00**

The only difference between absorption and variable costing is that fixed manufacturing overhead is a product cost under absorption costing, but a period cost under variable costing. This is why the cost per case is $5 higher under absorption (total cost of $18) than under variable costing ($13).

Exhibit 18A-2 on the following page shows the income statements using absorption costing and variable costing. The exhibit also shows the calculation for ending inventory at March 31, 2010.

Absorption costing income is higher because of the differing treatments of fixed manufacturing cost. Look at the two ending inventory amounts:

- $36,000 under absorption costing
- $26,000 under variable costing

This $10,000 difference results because ending inventory under absorption costing holds $10,000 of fixed manufacturing cost that got expensed under variable costing, as follows:

Units of ending finished goods inventory		Fixed manufacturing cost per unit		Difference in ending inventory
2,000	×	$5	=	$10,000

EXHIBIT 18A-2 — Absorption Costing and Variable Costing Income Statements and Ending Inventory Amount

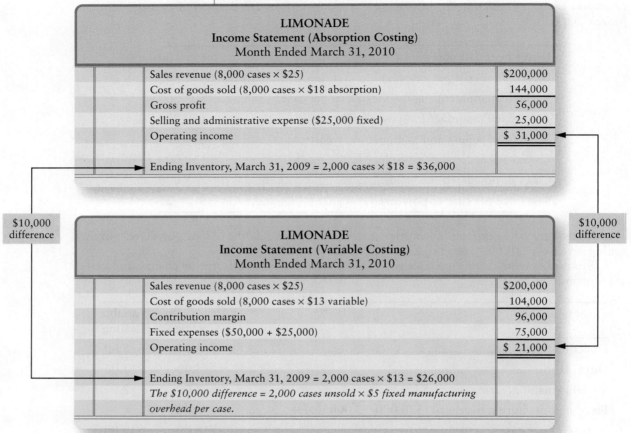

LIMONADE
Income Statement (Absorption Costing)
Month Ended March 31, 2010

Sales revenue (8,000 cases × $25)	$200,000
Cost of goods sold (8,000 cases × $18 absorption)	144,000
Gross profit	56,000
Selling and administrative expense ($25,000 fixed)	25,000
Operating income	$ 31,000

Ending Inventory, March 31, 2009 = 2,000 cases × $18 = $36,000

$10,000 difference

LIMONADE
Income Statement (Variable Costing)
Month Ended March 31, 2010

Sales revenue (8,000 cases × $25)	$200,000
Cost of goods sold (8,000 cases × $13 variable)	104,000
Contribution margin	96,000
Fixed expenses ($50,000 + $25,000)	75,000
Operating income	$ 21,000

Ending Inventory, March 31, 2009 = 2,000 cases × $13 = $26,000
The $10,000 difference = 2,000 cases unsold × $5 fixed manufacturing overhead per case.

Production Exceeds Sales Limonade produced 10,000 units and sold only 8,000 units, leaving 2,000 units in ending inventory. Whenever production exceeds sales, as for Limonade, absorption costing will produce more reported income.

Sales Exceed Production Companies sometimes sell more units of inventory than they produced that period. How can they do that? By drawing down inventories built up in prior periods. In these situations, inventory quantities decrease, and fixed costs in the earlier inventory get expensed under variable costing. That leads to the opposite result: Variable costing will produce more reported income whenever sales exceed production.

Absorption Costing and Manager Incentives

Suppose the Limonade manager receives a bonus based on absorption costing income. Will the manager increase or decrease production? The manager knows that absorption costing assigns each case of Limonade $5 of fixed manufacturing overhead.

- For every case that is produced but not sold, absorption costing "hides" $5 of fixed overhead in ending inventory (an asset).

- The more cases added to inventory, the more fixed overhead is "hidden" in ending inventory at the end of the month.

- The more fixed overhead in ending inventory, the smaller the cost of goods sold and the higher the operating income.

To maximize the bonus under absorption costing, the manager may increase production to build up inventory.

This incentive directly conflicts with the just-in-time philosophy, which emphasizes minimal inventory levels. Companies that have adopted just-in-time should either: (1) evaluate their managers based on variable costing income, or (2) use strict controls to prevent inventory buildup.

Part III

Taken from *Crafting and Executing Strategy: The Quest for Competitive Advantage: Concepts and Cases,* Sixteenth Edition, by Arthur Thompson, A.J. Strickland III, and John Gamble (2007), The McGraw-Hill Companies.

Evaluating a Company's External Environment

Analysis is the critical starting point of strategic thinking.

—Kenichi Ohmae
Consultant and Author

Things are always different—the art is figuring out which differences matter.

—Laszlo Birinyi
Investments Manager

Competitive battles should be seen not as one-shot skirmishes but as a dynamic multiround game of moves and countermoves.

—Anil K. Gupta
Professor

anagers are not prepared to act wisely in steering a company in a different direction or altering its strategy until they have a deep understanding of the pertinent factors surrounding the company's situation. As indicated in the opening paragraph of Chapter 1, one of the three central questions that managers must address in evaluating their company's business prospects is "What's the company's present situation?" Two facets of a company's situation are especially pertinent: (1) the industry and competitive environment in which the company operates and the forces acting to reshape this environment, and (2) the company's own market position and competitiveness—its resources and capabilities, its strengths and weaknesses vis-à-vis rivals, and its windows of opportunity.

Insightful diagnosis of a company's external and internal environment is a prerequisite for managers to succeed in crafting a strategy that is an excellent fit with the company's situation, is capable of building competitive advantage, and holds good prospect for boosting company performance—the three criteria of a winning strategy. As depicted in Figure 3.1, the task of crafting a strategy thus should always begin with an appraisal of the company's external and internal situation (as a basis for developing strategic vision of where the company needs to head), then move toward an evaluation of the most promising alternative strategies and business models, and culminate in choosing a specific strategy.

This chapter presents the concepts and analytical tools for zeroing in on those aspects of a single-business company's external environment that should be considered in making strategic choices. Attention centers on the competitive arena in which a company operates, the drivers of market change, and what rival companies are doing. In Chapter 4 we explore the methods of evaluating a company's internal circumstances and competitiveness.

THE STRATEGICALLY RELEVANT COMPONENTS OF A COMPANY'S EXTERNAL ENVIRONMENT

All companies operate in a "macroenvironment" shaped by influences emanating from the economy at large; population demographics; societal values and lifestyles; governmental legislation and regulation; technological factors; and, closer to home, the

Figure 3.1 **From Thinking Strategically about the Company's Situation to Choosing a Strategy**

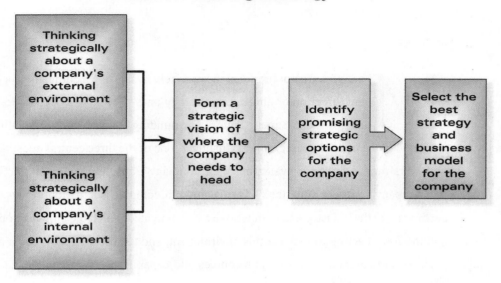

industry and competitive arena in which the company operates (see Figure 3.2). Strictly speaking, a company's macroenvironment includes *all relevant factors and influences* outside the company's boundaries; by relevant, we mean important enough to have a bearing on the decisions the company ultimately makes about its direction, objectives, strategy, and business model. Strategically relevant influences coming from the outer ring of the macroenvironment can sometimes have a high impact on a company's business situation and have a very significant impact on the company's direction and strategy. The strategic opportunities of cigarette producers to grow their business are greatly reduced by antismoking ordinances and the growing cultural stigma attached to smoking. Motor vehicle companies must adapt their strategies (especially as concerns the fuel mileage of their vehicles) to customer concerns about gasoline prices. The demographics of an aging population and longer life expectancies are having a dramatic impact on the business prospects and strategies of health care and prescription drug companies. Companies in most all industries have to craft strategies that are responsive to environmental regulations, growing use of the Internet and broadband technology, and energy prices. Companies in the food-processing, restaurant, sports, and fitness industries have to pay special attention to changes in lifestyles, eating habits, leisure-time preferences, and attitudes toward nutrition and exercise in fashioning their strategies.

Happenings in the outer ring of the macroenvironment may occur rapidly or slowly, with or without advance warning. The impact of outer-ring factors on a company's choice of strategy can range from big to small. But even if the factors in the outer ring of the macroenvironment change slowly or have such a comparatively low impact on a company's situation that only the edges of a company's direction and strategy are affected, there are enough strategically relevant outer-ring trends and events to justify a watchful eye. As company managers scan the external environment, they must be alert for potentially important outer-ring developments, assess their impact and influence, and adapt the company's direction and strategy as needed.

Figure 3.2   **The Components of a Company's Macroenvironment**

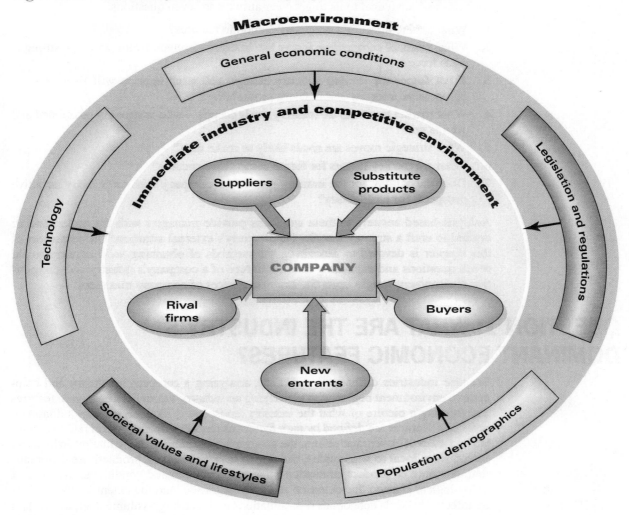

However, the factors and forces in a company's macroenvironment having the *biggest* strategy-shaping impact typically pertain to the company's immediate industry and competitive environment—competitive pressures, the actions of rival firms, buyer behavior, supplier-related considerations, and so on. Consequently, it is on a company's industry and competitive environment that we concentrate our attention in this chapter.

THINKING STRATEGICALLY ABOUT A COMPANY'S INDUSTRY AND COMPETITIVE ENVIRONMENT

To gain a deep understanding of a company's industry and competitive environment, managers do not need to gather all the information they can find and spend lots of time digesting it. Rather, the task is much more focused. Thinking strategically about a company's industry and competitive environment entails using some well-defined concepts and analytical tools to get clear answers to seven questions:

1. What are the industry's dominant economic features?
2. What kinds of competitive forces are industry members facing and how strong is each force?
3. What forces are driving industry change and what impacts will they have on competitive intensity and industry profitability?
4. What market positions do industry rivals occupy—who is strongly positioned and who is not?
5. What strategic moves are rivals likely to make next?
6. What are the key factors for future competitive success?
7. Does the outlook for the industry present the company with sufficiently attractive prospects for profitability?

Analysis-based answers to these questions provide managers with the understanding needed to craft a strategy that fits the company's external situation. The remainder of this chapter is devoted to describing the methods of obtaining solid answers to the seven questions and explaining how the nature of a company's industry and competitive environment weighs upon the strategic choices of company managers.

QUESTION 1: WHAT ARE THE INDUSTRY'S DOMINANT ECONOMIC FEATURES?

Because industries differ so significantly, analyzing a company's industry and competitive environment begins with identifying an industry's dominant economic features and forming a picture of what the industry landscape is like. An industry's dominant economic features are defined by such factors as market size and growth rate, the number and sizes of buyers and sellers, the geographic boundaries of the market (which can extend from local to worldwide), the degree to which sellers' products are differentiated, the pace of product innovation, market supply/demand conditions, the pace of technological change, the extent of vertical integration, and the extent to which costs are affected by scale economies (i.e., situations in which large-volume operations result in lower unit costs) and learning/experience curve effects (i.e., situations in which costs decline as a company gains knowledge and experience). Table 3.1 provides a convenient summary of what economic features to look at and the corresponding questions to consider in profiling an industry's landscape.

Getting a handle on an industry's distinguishing economic features not only sets the stage for the analysis to come but also promotes understanding of the kinds of strategic moves that industry members are likely to employ. For example, in industries characterized by one product advance after another, companies must invest in research and development (R&D) and develop strong product innovation capabilities—a strategy of continuous product innovation becomes a condition of survival in such industries as video games, mobile phones, and pharmaceuticals. An industry that has recently passed through the rapid-growth stage and is looking at single-digit percentage increases in buyer demand is likely to be experiencing a competitive shake-out and much stronger strategic emphasis on cost reduction and improved customer service.

In industries like semiconductors, strong *learning/experience curve effects* in manufacturing cause unit costs to decline about 20 percent each time *cumulative* production

Table 3.1 **What to Consider in Identifying an Industry's Dominant Economic Features**

Economic Feature	Questions to Answer
Market size and growth rate	• How big is the industry and how fast is it growing? • What does the industry's position in the life cycle (early development, rapid growth and takeoff, early maturity and slowing growth, saturation and stagnation, decline) reveal about the industry's growth prospects?
Number of rivals	• Is the industry fragmented into many small companies or concentrated and dominated by a few large companies? • Is the industry going through a period of consolidation to a smaller number of competitors?
Scope of competitive rivalry	• Is the geographic area over which most companies compete local, regional, national, multinational, or global? • Is having a presence in the foreign country markets becoming more important to a company's long-term competitive success?
Number of buyers	• Is market demand fragmented among many buyers? • Do some buyers have bargaining power because they purchase in large volume?
Degree of product differentiation	• Are the products of rivals becoming more differentiated or less differentiated? • Are increasingly look-alike products of rivals causing heightened price competition?
Product innovation	• Is the industry characterized by rapid product innovation and short product life cycles? • How important is R&D and product innovation? • Are there opportunities to overtake key rivals by being first-to-market with next-generation products?
Supply/demand conditions	• Is a surplus of capacity pushing prices and profit margins down? • Is the industry overcrowded with too many competitors? • Are short supplies creating a sellers' market?
Pace of technological change	• What role does advancing technology play in this industry? • Are ongoing upgrades of facilities/equipment essential because of rapidly advancing production process technologies? • Do most industry members have or need strong technological capabilities?
Vertical integration	• Do most competitors operate in only one stage of the industry (parts and components production, manufacturing and assembly, distribution, retailing) or do some competitors operate in multiple stages? • Is there any cost or competitive advantage or disadvantage associated with being fully or partially integrated?
Economies of scale	• Is the industry characterized by economies of scale in purchasing, manufacturing, advertising, shipping, or other activities? • Do companies with large-scale operations have an important cost advantage over small-scale firms?
Learning/experience curve effects	• Are certain industry activities characterized by strong learning/experience curve effects ("learning by doing") such that unit costs decline as a company's experience in performing the activity builds? • Do any companies have significant cost advantages because of their learning/experience in performing particular activities?

volume doubles. With a 20 percent experience curve effect, if the first 1 million chips cost $100 each, the unit cost would be $80 (80 percent of $100) by a production volume of 2 million, the unit cost would be $64 (80 percent of $80) by a production volume of 4 million, and so on.[1] The bigger the learning/experience curve effect, the bigger the cost advantage of the company with the largest *cumulative* production volume.

Thus, when an industry is characterized by important learning/experience curve effects (or by economies of scale), industry members are strongly motivated to adopt volume-increasing strategies to capture the resulting cost-saving economies and maintain their competitiveness. Unless small-scale firms succeed in pursuing strategic options that allow them to grow sales sufficiently to remain cost-competitive with larger-volume rivals, they are unlikely to survive. The bigger the learning/experience curve effects and/or scale economies in an industry, the more imperative it becomes for competing sellers to pursue strategies to win additional sales and market share—the company with the biggest sales volume gains sustainable competitive advantage as the low-cost producer.

QUESTION 2: WHAT KINDS OF COMPETITIVE FORCES ARE INDUSTRY MEMBERS FACING?

The character, mix, and subtleties of the competitive forces operating in a company's industry are never the same from one industry to another. Far and away the most powerful and widely used tool for systematically diagnosing the principal competitive pressures in a market and assessing the strength and importance of each is the *five-forces model of competition.*[2] This model, depicted in Figure 3.3, holds that the state of competition in an industry is a composite of competitive pressures operating in five areas of the overall market:

1. Competitive pressures associated with the market maneuvering and jockeying for buyer patronage that goes on among *rival sellers* in the industry.
2. Competitive pressures associated with the threat of *new entrants* into the market.
3. Competitive pressures coming from the attempts of companies in other industries to win buyers over to their own *substitute products.*
4. Competitive pressures stemming from *supplier* bargaining power and supplier–seller collaboration.
5. Competitive pressures stemming from *buyer* bargaining power and seller–buyer collaboration.

The way one uses the five-forces model to determine the nature and strength of competitive pressures in a given industry is to build the picture of competition in three steps:

- *Step 1:* Identify the specific competitive pressures associated with each of the five forces.
- *Step 2:* Evaluate how strong the pressures comprising each of the five forces are (fierce, strong, moderate to normal, or weak).
- *Step 3:* Determine whether the collective strength of the five competitive forces is conducive to earning attractive profits.

Figure 3.3 **The Five-Forces Model of Competition: A Key Analytical Tool**

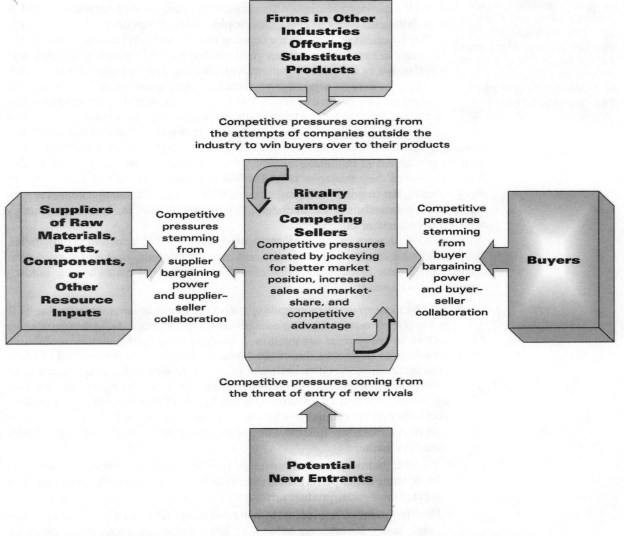

Source: Adapted from Michael E. Porter, "How Competitive Forces Shape Strategy," *Harvard Business Review* 57, no. 2 (March–April 1979), pp. 137–45.

Competitive Pressures Associated with the Jockeying among Rival Sellers

The strongest of the five competitive forces is nearly always the market maneuvering and jockeying for buyer patronage that goes on among rival sellers of a product or service. In effect, *a market is a competitive battlefield* where there's no end to the jockeying for buyer patronage. Rival sellers are prone to employ whatever weapons they

Core Concept
Competitive jockeying among industry rivals is ever changing, as rivals initiate fresh offensive and defensive moves and emphasize first one mix of competitive weapons and then another in efforts to improve their market positions.

have in their business arsenal to improve their market positions, strengthen their market position with buyers, and earn good profits. The challenge is to craft a competitive strategy that, at the very least, allows a company to hold its own against rivals and that, ideally, *produces a competitive edge over rivals.* But competitive contests are ongoing and dynamic. When one firm makes a strategic move that produces good results, its rivals typically respond with offensive or defensive countermoves, shifting their strategic emphasis from one combination of product attributes, marketing tactics, and capabilities to another. This pattern of action and reaction, move and countermove, adjust and readjust produces a continually evolving competitive landscape in which the market battle ebbs and flows, sometimes takes unpredictable twists and turns, and produces winners and losers. But the winners—the current market leaders—have no guarantees of continued leadership; their market success is no more durable than the power of their strategies to fend off the strategies of ambitious challengers. In every industry, the ongoing jockeying of rivals leads to one or another companies gaining or losing momentum in the marketplace according to whether their latest strategic maneuvers succeed or fail.

Figure 3.4 shows a sampling of competitive weapons that firms can deploy in battling rivals and indicates the factors that influence the intensity of their rivalry. A brief discussion of some of the factors that influence the tempo of rivalry among industry competitors is in order:[3]

- *Rivalry intensifies when competing sellers are active in launching fresh actions to boost their market standing and business performance.* One indicator of active rivalry is lively price competition, a condition that puts pressure on industry members to drive costs out of the business and threatens the survival of high-cost companies. Another indicator of active rivalry is rapid introduction of next-generation products—when one or more rivals frequently introduce new or improved products, competitors that lack good product innovation capabilities feel considerable competitive heat to get their own new and improved products into the marketplace quickly. Other indicators of active rivalry among industry members include:
  - Whether industry members are racing to differentiate their products from rivals by offering better performance features or higher quality or improved customer service or a wider product selection.
  - How frequently rivals resort to such marketing tactics as special sales promotions, heavy advertising, rebates, or low-interest-rate financing to drum up additional sales.
  - How actively industry members are pursuing efforts to build stronger dealer networks or establish positions in foreign markets or otherwise expand their distribution capabilities and market presence.
  - How hard companies are striving to gain a market edge over rivals by developing valuable expertise and capabilities that rivals are hard pressed to match.

  Normally, competitive jockeying among rival sellers is active and fairly intense because competing companies are highly motivated to launch whatever fresh actions and creative market maneuvers they can think of to try to strengthen their market positions and business performance.

- *Rivalry intensifies as the number of competitors increases and as competitors become more equal in size and capability.* Rivalry is not as vigorous in microprocessors for PCs, where Advanced Micro Devices (AMD) is one of the few

Figure 3.4 **Weapons for Competing and Factors Affecting the Strength of Rivalry**

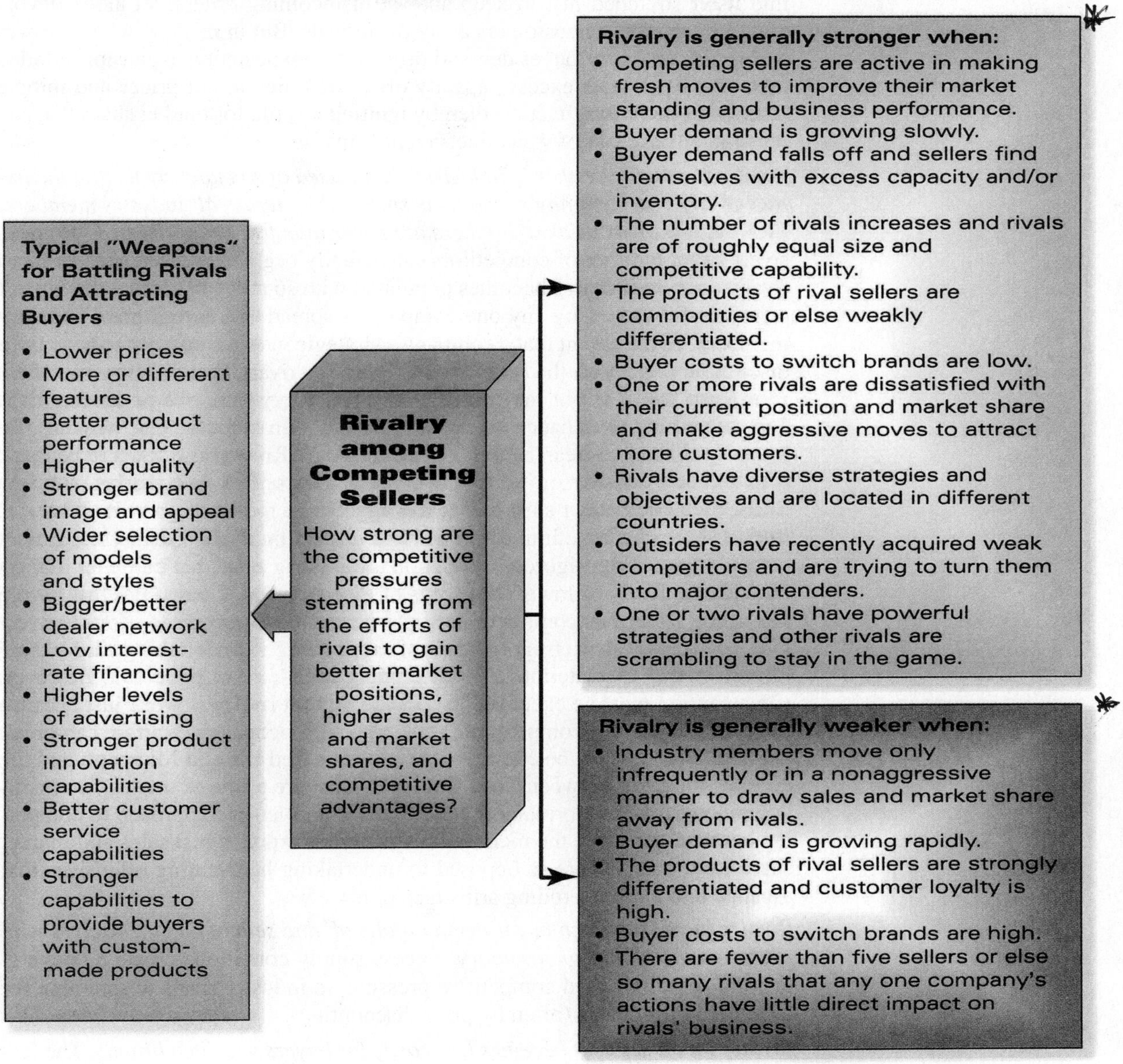

Typical "Weapons" for Battling Rivals and Attracting Buyers

- Lower prices
- More or different features
- Better product performance
- Higher quality
- Stronger brand image and appeal
- Wider selection of models and styles
- Bigger/better dealer network
- Low interest-rate financing
- Higher levels of advertising
- Stronger product innovation capabilities
- Better customer service capabilities
- Stronger capabilities to provide buyers with custom-made products

Rivalry among Competing Sellers

How strong are the competitive pressures stemming from the efforts of rivals to gain better market positions, higher sales and market shares, and competitive advantages?

Rivalry is generally stronger when:
- Competing sellers are active in making fresh moves to improve their market standing and business performance.
- Buyer demand is growing slowly.
- Buyer demand falls off and sellers find themselves with excess capacity and/or inventory.
- The number of rivals increases and rivals are of roughly equal size and competitive capability.
- The products of rival sellers are commodities or else weakly differentiated.
- Buyer costs to switch brands are low.
- One or more rivals are dissatisfied with their current position and market share and make aggressive moves to attract more customers.
- Rivals have diverse strategies and objectives and are located in different countries.
- Outsiders have recently acquired weak competitors and are trying to turn them into major contenders.
- One or two rivals have powerful strategies and other rivals are scrambling to stay in the game.

Rivalry is generally weaker when:
- Industry members move only infrequently or in a nonaggressive manner to draw sales and market share away from rivals.
- Buyer demand is growing rapidly.
- The products of rival sellers are strongly differentiated and customer loyalty is high.
- Buyer costs to switch brands are high.
- There are fewer than five sellers or else so many rivals that any one company's actions have little direct impact on rivals' business.

challengers to Intel, as it is in fast-food restaurants, where numerous sellers are actively jockeying for buyer patronage. Up to a point, the greater the number of competitors, the greater the probability of fresh, creative strategic initiatives. In addition, when rivals are nearly equal in size and capability, they can usually compete on a fairly even footing, making it harder for one or two firms to win commanding market shares and confront weaker market challenges from rivals.

- *Rivalry is usually stronger in slow-growing markets and weaker in fast-growing markets.* Rapidly expanding buyer demand produces enough new business for all industry members to grow. Indeed, in a fast-growing market, a company may find itself stretched just to keep abreast of incoming orders, let alone devote resources to stealing customers away from rivals. But in markets where growth is sluggish or where buyer demand drops off unexpectedly, expansion-minded firms and firms with excess capacity often are quick to cut prices and initiate other sales-increasing tactics, thereby igniting a battle for market share that can result in a shake-out of weak, inefficient firms.

- *Rivalry is usually weaker in industries comprised of so many rivals that the impact of any one company's actions is spread thin across all industry members; likewise, it is often weak when there are fewer than five competitors.* A progressively larger number of competitors can actually begin to weaken head-to-head rivalry once an industry becomes populated with so many rivals that the impact of successful moves by any one company is spread thin across many industry members. To the extent that a company's strategic moves ripple out to have little discernible impact on the businesses of its many rivals, then industry members soon learn that it is not imperative to respond every time one or another rival does something to enhance its market position—an outcome that weakens the intensity of head-to-head battles for market share. Rivalry also *tends* to be weak if an industry consists of just two or three or four sellers. In a market with few rivals, each competitor soon learns that aggressive moves to grow its sales and market share can have immediate adverse impact on rivals' businesses, almost certainly provoking vigorous retaliation and risking an all-out battle for market share that is likely to lower the profits of all concerned. Companies that have a few strong rivals thus come to understand the merits of *restrained* efforts to wrest sales and market share from competitors as opposed to undertaking hard-hitting offensives that escalate into a profit-eroding arms-race or price war. However, some caution must be exercised in concluding that rivalry is weak just because there are only a few competitors. Thus, although occasional warfare can break out (the fierceness of the current battle between Red Hat and Microsoft and the decades-long war between Coca-Cola and Pepsi are prime examples), competition among the few normally produces a live-and-let-live approach to competing because rivals see the merits of restrained efforts to wrest sales and market share from competitors as opposed to undertaking hard-hitting offensives that escalate into a profit-eroding arms race or price war.

- *Rivalry increases when buyer demand falls off and sellers find themselves with excess capacity and/or inventory.* Excess supply conditions create a "buyers' market," putting added competitive pressure on industry rivals to scramble for profitable sales levels (often by price discounting).

- *Rivalry increases as it becomes less costly for buyers to switch brands.* The less expensive it is for buyers to switch their purchases from the seller of one brand to the seller of another brand, the easier it is for sellers to steal customers away from rivals. But the higher the costs buyers incur to switch brands, the less prone they are to brand switching. Even if consumers view one or more rival brands as more attractive, they may not be inclined to switch because of the added time and inconvenience or the psychological costs of abandoning a familiar brand. Distributors and retailers may not switch to the brands of rival manufacturers because they are hesitant to sever long-standing supplier relationships, incur any technical support costs or retraining expenses in making the switchover, go to the trouble of testing the quality and reliability of the rival brand, or devote resources to marketing the new brand (especially if the brand is lesser known).

Apple Computer, for example, has been unable to convince PC users to switch from Windows-based PCs because of the time burdens and inconvenience associated with learning Apple's operating system and because so many Windows-based applications will not run on a MacIntosh due to operating system incompatibility. Consequently, unless buyers are dissatisfied with the brand they are presently purchasing, high switching costs can significantly weaken the rivalry among competing sellers.

- *Rivalry increases as the products of rival sellers become more standardized and diminishes as the products of industry rivals become more strongly differentiated.* When the offerings of rivals are identical or weakly differentiated, buyers have less reason to be brand-loyal—a condition that makes it easier for rivals to convince buyers to switch to their offering. And since the brands of different sellers have comparable attributes, buyers can shop the market for the best deal and switch brands at will. In contrast, strongly differentiated product offerings among rivals breed high brand loyalty on the part of buyers—because many buyers view the attributes of certain brands as better suited to their needs. Strong brand attachments make it tougher for sellers to draw customers away from rivals. Unless meaningful numbers of buyers are open to considering new or different product attributes being offered by rivals, the high degrees of brand loyalty that accompany strong product differentiation work against fierce rivalry among competing sellers. *The degree of product differentiation also affects switching costs.* When the offerings of rivals are identical or weakly differentiated, it is usually easy and inexpensive for buyers to switch their purchases from one seller to another. Strongly differentiated products raise the probability that buyers will find it costly to switch brands.

- *Rivalry is more intense when industry conditions tempt competitors to use price cuts or other competitive weapons to boost unit volume.* When a product is perishable, seasonal, or costly to hold in inventory, competitive pressures build quickly any time one or more firms decide to cut prices and dump supplies on the market. Likewise, whenever fixed costs account for a large fraction of total cost, such that unit costs tend to be lowest at or near full capacity, then firms come under significant pressure to cut prices or otherwise try to boost sales whenever they are operating below full capacity. Unused capacity imposes a significant cost-increasing penalty because there are fewer units over which to spread fixed costs. The pressure of high fixed costs can push rival firms into price concessions, special discounts, rebates, low-interest-rate financing, and other volume-boosting tactics.

- *Rivalry increases when one or more competitors become dissatisfied with their market position and launch moves to bolster their standing at the expense of rivals.* Firms that are losing ground or in financial trouble often pursue aggressive (or perhaps desperate) turnaround strategies that can involve price discounts, more advertising, acquisition of or merger with other rivals, or new product introductions—such strategies can turn competitive pressures up a notch.

- *Rivalry becomes more volatile and unpredictable as the diversity of competitors increases in terms of visions, strategic intents, objectives, strategies, resources, and countries of origin.* A diverse group of sellers often contains one or more mavericks willing to try novel or high-risk or rule-breaking market approaches, thus generating a livelier and less predictable competitive environment. Globally competitive markets often contain rivals with different views about where the industry is headed and a willingness to employ perhaps radically different competitive approaches. Attempts by cross-border rivals to gain stronger footholds in each other's domestic markets usually boost the intensity of rivalry, especially when the aggressors have lower costs or products with more attractive features.

- *Rivalry increases when strong companies outside the industry acquire weak firms in the industry and launch aggressive, well-funded moves to transform their newly acquired competitors into major market contenders.* A concerted effort to turn a weak rival into a market leader nearly always entails launching well-financed strategic initiatives to dramatically improve the competitor's product offering, excite buyer interest, and win a much bigger market share—actions that, if successful, put added pressure on rivals to counter with fresh strategic moves of their own.

- *A powerful, successful competitive strategy employed by one company greatly intensifies the competitive pressures on its rivals to develop effective strategic responses or be relegated to also-ran status.*

Rivalry can be characterized as *cutthroat* or *brutal* when competitors engage in protracted price wars or habitually employ other aggressive tactics that are mutually destructive to profitability. Rivalry can be considered *fierce* to *strong* when the battle for market share is so vigorous that the profit margins of most industry members are squeezed to bare-bones levels. Rivalry can be characterized as *moderate* or *normal* when the maneuvering among industry members, while lively and healthy, still allows most industry members to earn acceptable profits. Rivalry is *weak* when most companies in the industry are relatively well satisfied with their sales growth and market shares, rarely undertake offensives to steal customers away from one another, and have comparatively attractive earnings and returns on investment.

Competitive Pressures Associated with the Threat of New Entrants

Several factors determine whether the threat of new companies entering the marketplace poses significant competitive pressure (see Figure 3.5). One factor relates to the size of the pool of likely entry candidates and the resources at their command. As a rule, the bigger the pool of entry candidates, the stronger the threat of potential entry. This is especially true when some of the likely entry candidates have ample resources and the potential to become formidable contenders for market leadership. Frequently, the strongest competitive pressures associated with potential entry come not from outsiders, but from current industry participants looking for growth opportunities. *Existing industry members are often strong candidates for entering market segments or geographic areas where they currently do not have a market presence.* Companies already well established in certain product categories or geographic areas often possess the resources, competencies, and competitive capabilities to hurdle the barriers of entering a different market segment or new geographic area.

A second factor concerns whether the likely entry candidates face high or low entry barriers. High barriers reduce the competitive threat of potential entry, while low barriers make entry more likely, especially if the industry is growing and offers attractive profit opportunities. The most widely encountered barriers that entry candidates must hurdle include:[4]

- *The presence of sizable economies of scale in production or other areas of operation*—When incumbent companies enjoy cost advantages associated with

Figure 3.5 **Factors Affecting the Threat of Entry**

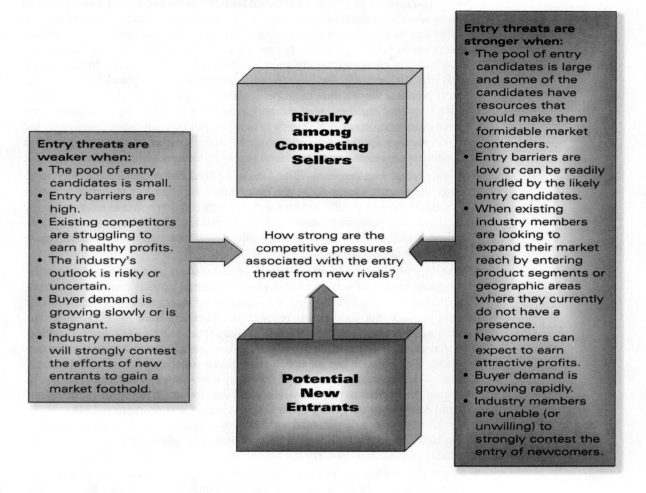

Entry threats are weaker when:
- The pool of entry candidates is small.
- Entry barriers are high.
- Existing competitors are struggling to earn healthy profits.
- The industry's outlook is risky or uncertain.
- Buyer demand is growing slowly or is stagnant.
- Industry members will strongly contest the efforts of new entrants to gain a market foothold.

Rivalry among Competing Sellers

How strong are the competitive pressures associated with the entry threat from new rivals?

Potential New Entrants

Entry threats are stronger when:
- The pool of entry candidates is large and some of the candidates have resources that would make them formidable market contenders.
- Entry barriers are low or can be readily hurdled by the likely entry candidates.
- When existing industry members are looking to expand their market reach by entering product segments or geographic areas where they currently do not have a presence.
- Newcomers can expect to earn attractive profits.
- Buyer demand is growing rapidly.
- Industry members are unable (or unwilling) to strongly contest the entry of newcomers.

large-scale operation, outsiders must either enter on a large scale (a costly and perhaps risky move) or accept a cost disadvantage and consequently lower profitability. Trying to overcome the disadvantages of small size by entering on a large scale at the outset can result in long-term overcapacity problems for the new entrant (until sales volume builds up), and it can so threaten the market shares of existing firms that they launch strong defensive maneuvers (price cuts, increased advertising and sales promotion, and similar blocking actions) to maintain their positions and make things hard on a newcomer.

- *Cost and resource disadvantages not related to scale of operation*—Aside from enjoying economies of scale, there are other reasons why existing firms may have low unit costs that are hard to replicate by newcomers. Industry incumbents can have cost advantages that stem from learning/experience curve effects, the possession of key patents or proprietary technology, partnerships with the best and cheapest suppliers of raw materials and components, favorable locations, and low fixed costs (because they have older facilities that have been mostly depreciated).

- *Strong brand preferences and high degrees of customer loyalty*—The stronger the attachment of buyers to established brands, the harder it is for a newcomer to break into the marketplace. In such cases, a new entrant must have the financial resources to spend enough on advertising and sales promotion to overcome customer loyalties and build its own clientele. Establishing brand recognition and building customer loyalty can be a slow and costly process. In addition, if it is difficult or costly for a customer to switch to a new brand, a new entrant must persuade buyers that its brand is worth the switching costs. To overcome switching-cost barriers, new entrants may have to offer buyers a discounted price or an extra margin of quality or service. All this can mean lower expected profit margins for new entrants, which increases the risk to start-up companies dependent on sizable early profits to support their new investments.

- *High capital requirements*—The larger the total dollar investment needed to enter the market successfully, the more limited the pool of potential entrants. The most obvious capital requirements for new entrants relate to manufacturing facilities and equipment, introductory advertising and sales promotion campaigns, working capital to finance inventories and customer credit, and sufficient cash to cover start-up costs.

- *The difficulties of building a network of distributors or retailers and securing adequate space on retailers' shelves*—A potential entrant can face numerous distribution channel challenges. Wholesale distributors may be reluctant to take on a product that lacks buyer recognition. Retailers have to be recruited and convinced to give a new brand ample display space and an adequate trial period. When existing sellers have strong, well-functioning distributor or retailer networks, a newcomer has an uphill struggle in squeezing its way in. Potential entrants sometimes have to "buy" their way into wholesale or retail channels by cutting their prices to provide dealers and distributors with higher markups and profit margins or by giving them big advertising and promotional allowances. As a consequence, a potential entrant's own profits may be squeezed unless and until its product gains enough consumer acceptance that distributors and retailers are anxious to carry it.

- *Restrictive regulatory policies*—Government agencies can limit or even bar entry by requiring licenses and permits. Regulated industries like cable TV, telecommunications, electric and gas utilities, radio and television broadcasting, liquor retailing, and railroads entail government-controlled entry. In international markets, host governments commonly limit foreign entry and must approve all foreign investment applications. Stringent government-mandated safety regulations and environmental pollution standards are entry barriers because they raise entry costs.

- *Tariffs and international trade restrictions*—National governments commonly use tariffs and trade restrictions (antidumping rules, local content requirements, quotas, etc.) to raise entry barriers for foreign firms and protect domestic producers from outside competition.

- *The ability and inclination of industry incumbents to launch vigorous initiatives to block a newcomer's successful entry*—Even if a potential entrant has or can acquire the needed competencies and resources to attempt entry, it must still worry about the reaction of existing firms.[5] Sometimes, there's little that incumbents can do to throw obstacles in an entrant's path—for instance, existing restaurants have little in their arsenal to discourage a new restaurant from opening or to dissuade people from trying the new restaurant. But there are times when incumbents do all they can to make it difficult for a new entrant, using price cuts, increased advertising, product improvements, and whatever else they can think of to prevent the entrant from building a clientele. Cable TV companies vigorously fight the entry of satellite TV companies; Sony and Nintendo have mounted strong defenses to thwart Microsoft's entry in video games with its Xbox; existing hotels try to combat the opening of new hotels with loyalty programs, renovations of their own, the addition of new services, and so on. A potential entrant can have second thoughts when financially strong incumbent firms send clear signals that they will give newcomers a hard time.

Whether an industry's entry barriers ought to be considered high or low depends on the resources and competencies possessed by the pool of potential entrants. Companies with sizable financial resources, proven competitive capabilities, and a respected brand name may be able to hurdle an industry's entry barriers rather easily. Small start-up enterprises may find the same entry barriers insurmountable. Thus, how hard it will be for potential entrants to compete on a level playing field is always relative to the financial resources and competitive capabilities of likely entrants. For example, when Honda opted to enter the U.S. lawn-mower market in competition against Toro, Snapper, Craftsman, John Deere, and others, it was easily able to hurdle entry barriers that would have been formidable to other newcomers because it had long-standing expertise in gasoline engines and because its well-known reputation for quality and durability gave it instant credibility with shoppers looking to buy a new lawn mower. Honda had to spend relatively little on advertising to attract buyers and gain a market foothold, distributors and dealers were quite willing to handle the Honda lawn-mower line, and Honda had ample capital to build a U.S. assembly plant.

In evaluating whether the threat of additional entry is strong or weak, company managers must look at (1) how formidable the entry barriers are for each type of potential entrant—start-up enterprises, specific candidate companies in other industries, and current industry participants looking to expand their market reach—and (2) how attractive the growth and profit prospects are for new entrants. Rapidly growing market demand and high potential profits act as magnets, motivating potential entrants to commit the resources needed to hurdle entry barriers.[6] When profits are sufficiently attractive, entry barriers are unlikely to be an effective entry deterrent. At most, they limit the pool of candidate entrants to enterprises with the requisite competencies and resources and with the creativity to fashion a strategy for competing with incumbent firms.

Hence, *the best test of whether potential entry is a strong or weak competitive force in the marketplace is to ask if the industry's growth and profit prospects are strongly attractive to potential entry candidates.* When the answer is no, potential entry is a weak competitive force. When the answer is yes and there are entry candidates with sufficient expertise and resources, then potential entry adds significantly to competitive pressures in the marketplace. The stronger the threat of entry, the more that incumbent firms are driven to seek ways to fortify their positions against newcomers, pursuing strategic moves not only to protect their market shares but also to make entry more costly or difficult.

One additional point: *The threat of entry changes as the industry's prospects grow brighter or dimmer and as entry barriers rise or fall.* For example, in the pharmaceutical industry the expiration of a key patent on a widely prescribed drug virtually guarantees that one or more drug makers will enter with generic offerings of their own. Growing use of the Internet for shopping is making it much easier for Web-based retailers to enter into competition

High entry barriers and weak entry threats today do not always translate into high entry barriers and weak entry threats tomorrow.

against such well-known retail chains as Sears, Circuit City, and Barnes and Noble. In international markets, entry barriers for foreign-based firms fall as tariffs are lowered, as host governments open up their domestic markets to outsiders, as domestic wholesalers and dealers seek out lower-cost foreign-made goods, and as domestic buyers become more willing to purchase foreign brands.

Competitive Pressures from the Sellers of Substitute Products

Companies in one industry come under competitive pressure from the actions of companies in a closely adjoining industry whenever buyers view the products of the two industries as good substitutes. For instance, the producers of sugar experience competitive pressures from the sales and marketing efforts of the makers of artificial sweeteners. Similarly, the producers of eyeglasses and contact lenses are currently facing mounting competitive pressures from growing consumer interest in corrective laser surgery. Newspapers are feeling the competitive force of the general public turning to cable news channels for late-breaking news and using Internet sources to get information about sports results, stock quotes, and job opportunities. The makers of videotapes and VCRs have watched demand evaporate as more and more consumers have been attracted to substitute use of DVDs and DVD recorders/players. Traditional providers of telephone service like BellSouth, AT&T, Verizon, and Qwest are feeling enormous competitive pressure from cell phone providers, as more and more consumers find cell phones preferable to landline phones.

Just how strong the competitive pressures are from the sellers of substitute products depends on three factors:

1. *Whether substitutes are readily available and attractively priced.* The presence of readily available and attractively priced substitutes creates competitive pressure by placing a ceiling on the prices industry members can charge without giving customers an incentive to switch to substitutes and risking sales erosion.[7] This price ceiling, at the same time, puts a lid on the profits that industry members can earn unless they find ways to cut costs. When substitutes are cheaper than an industry's product, industry members come under heavy competitive pressure to reduce their prices and find ways to absorb the price cuts with cost reductions.

2. *Whether buyers view the substitutes as being comparable or better in terms of quality, performance, and other relevant attributes.* The availability of substitutes inevitably invites customers to compare performance, features, ease of use, and other attributes as well as price. For example, ski boat manufacturers are experiencing strong competition from personal water-ski craft because water sports enthusiasts see personal water skis as fun to ride and less expensive. The users of paper cartons constantly weigh the performance trade-offs with plastic containers and metal cans. Camera users consider the convenience and performance trade-offs when deciding whether to substitute a digital camera for a film-based camera. Competition from good-performing substitutes unleashes competitive pressures on industry participants to incorporate new performance features and attributes that makes their product offerings more competitive.

3. *Whether the costs that buyers incur in switching to the substitutes are high or low.* High switching costs deter switching to substitutes, while low switching costs make it easier for the sellers of attractive substitutes to lure buyers to their offering.[8] Typical switching costs include the time and inconvenience that may be involved, the costs of additional equipment, the time and cost in testing the quality

Figure 3.6 **Factors Affecting Competition from Substitute Products**

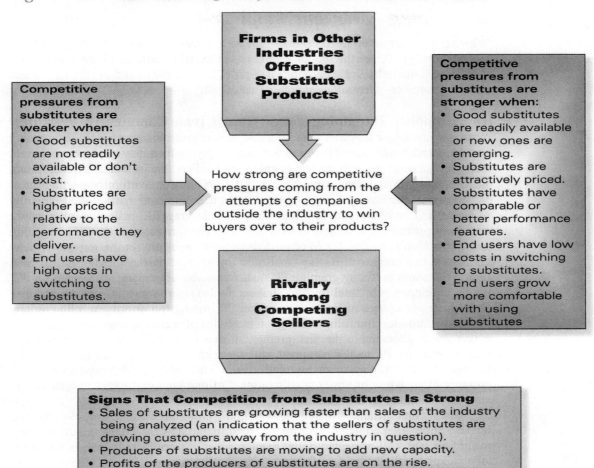

and reliability of the substitute, the psychological costs of severing old supplier relationships and establishing new ones, payments for technical help in making the changeover, and employee retraining costs. High switching costs can materially weaken the competitive pressures that industry members experience from substitutes unless the sellers of substitutes are successful in offsetting the high switching costs with enticing price discounts or additional performance enhancements.

Figure 3.6 summarizes the conditions that determine whether the competitive pressures from substitute products are strong, moderate, or weak.

As a rule, the lower the price of substitutes, the higher their quality and performance, and the lower the user's switching costs, the more intense the competitive pressures posed by substitute products. Other market indicators of the competitive strength of substitute products include (1) whether the sales of substitutes are growing faster than the sales of the industry being analyzed (a sign that the sellers of substitutes may be drawing customers away from the industry in question), (2) whether the producers of substitutes are moving to add new capacity, and (3) whether the profits of the producers of substitutes are on the rise.

Competitive Pressures Stemming from Supplier Bargaining Power and Supplier–Seller Collaboration

Whether supplier–seller relationships represent a weak or strong competitive force depends on (1) whether the major suppliers can exercise sufficient bargaining power to influence the terms and conditions of supply in their favor, and (2) the nature and extent of supplier–seller collaboration in the industry.

How Supplier Bargaining Power Can Create Competitive Pressures

Whenever the major suppliers to an industry have considerable leverage in determining the terms and conditions of the item they are supplying, then they are in a position to exert competitive pressure on one or more rival sellers. For instance, Microsoft and Intel, both of which supply personal computer (PC) makers with products that most PC users consider essential, are known for using their dominant market status not only to charge PC makers premium prices but also to leverage PC makers in other ways. Microsoft pressures PC makers to load only Microsoft products on the PCs they ship and to position the icons for Microsoft software prominently on the screens of new computers that come with factory-loaded software. Intel pushes greater use of Intel microprocessors in PCs by granting PC makers sizable advertising allowances on PC models equipped with "Intel Inside" stickers; it also tends to give PC makers that use the biggest percentages of Intel chips in their PC models top priority in filling orders for newly introduced Intel chips. Being on Intel's list of preferred customers helps a PC maker get an allocation of the first production runs of Intel's latest and greatest chips and thus get new PC models equipped with these chips to market ahead of rivals who are heavier users of chips made by Intel's rivals. The ability of Microsoft and Intel to pressure PC makers for preferential treatment of one kind or another in turn affects competition among rival PC makers.

Several other instances of supplier bargaining power are worth citing. Small-scale retailers must often contend with the power of manufacturers whose products enjoy prestigious and well-respected brand names; when a manufacturer knows that a retailer needs to stock the manufacturer's product because consumers expect to find the product on the shelves of retail stores where they shop, the manufacturer usually has some degree of pricing power and can also push hard for favorable shelf displays. Motor vehicle manufacturers typically exert considerable power over the terms and conditions with which they supply new vehicles to their independent automobile dealerships. The operators of franchised units of such chains as McDonald's, Dunkin' Donuts, Pizza Hut, Sylvan Learning Centers, and Hampton Inns must frequently agree not only to source some of their supplies from the franchisor at prices and terms favorable to that franchisor but also to operate their facilities in a manner largely dictated by the franchisor.

Strong supplier bargaining power is a competitive factor in industries where unions have been able to organize the workforces of some industry members but not others; those industry members that must negotiate wages, fringe benefits, and working conditions with powerful unions (which control the supply of labor) often find themselves with higher labor costs than their competitors with nonunion labor forces. The bigger the gap between union and nonunion labor costs in an industry, the more that unionized industry members must scramble to find ways to relieve the competitive pressure associated with their disadvantage on labor costs. High labor costs are proving a huge competitive liability to unionized supermarket chains like Kroger and Safeway in trying to combat the market share gains being made by Wal-Mart in supermarket retailing—Wal-Mart has a nonunion workforce, and the prices for supermarket items at its Supercenters tend to run 5 to 20 percent lower than those at unionized supermarket chains.

The factors that determine whether any of the suppliers to an industry are in a position to exert substantial bargaining power or leverage are fairly clear-cut:[9]

- *Whether the item being supplied is a commodity that is readily available from many suppliers at the going market price.* Suppliers have little or no bargaining power or leverage whenever industry members have the ability to source their requirements at competitive prices from any of several alternative and eager suppliers, perhaps dividing their purchases among two or more suppliers to promote lively competition for orders. The suppliers of commodity items have market power only when supplies become quite tight and industry members are so eager to secure what they need that they agree to terms more favorable to suppliers.

- *Whether a few large suppliers are the primary sources of a particular item.* The leading suppliers may well have pricing leverage unless they are plagued with excess capacity and are scrambling to secure additional orders for their products. Major suppliers with good reputations and strong demand for the items they supply are harder to wring concessions from than struggling suppliers striving to broaden their customer base or more fully utilize their production capacity.

- *Whether it is difficult or costly for industry members to switch their purchases from one supplier to another or to switch to attractive substitute inputs.* High switching costs signal strong bargaining power on the part of suppliers, whereas low switching costs and ready availability of good substitute inputs signal weak bargaining power. Soft-drink bottlers, for example, can counter the bargaining power of aluminum can suppliers by shifting or threatening to shift to greater use of plastic containers and introducing more attractive plastic container designs.

- *Whether certain needed inputs are in short supply.* Suppliers of items in short supply have some degree of pricing power, whereas a surge in the availability of particular items greatly weakens supplier pricing power and bargaining leverage.

- *Whether certain suppliers provide a differentiated input that enhances the performance or quality of the industry's product.* The more valuable that a particular input is in terms of enhancing the performance or quality of the products of industry members or of improving the efficiency of their production processes, the more bargaining leverage its suppliers are likely to possess.

- *Whether certain suppliers provide equipment or services that deliver valuable cost-saving efficiencies to industry members in operating their production processes.* Suppliers who provide cost-saving equipment or other valuable or necessary production-related services are likely to possess bargaining leverage. Industry members that do not source from such suppliers may find themselves at a cost disadvantage and thus under competitive pressure to do so (on terms that are favorable to the suppliers).

- *Whether suppliers provide an item that accounts for a sizable fraction of the costs of the industry's product.* The bigger the cost of a particular part or component, the more opportunity for the pattern of competition in the marketplace to be affected by the actions of suppliers to raise or lower their prices.

- *Whether industry members are major customers of suppliers.* As a rule, suppliers have less bargaining leverage when their sales to members of this one industry constitute a big percentage of their total sales. In such cases, the well-being of suppliers is closely tied to the well-being of their major customers.

Suppliers then have a big incentive to protect and enhance their customers' competitiveness via reasonable prices, exceptional quality, and ongoing advances in the technology of the items supplied.

- *Whether it makes good economic sense for industry members to integrate backward and self-manufacture items they have been buying from suppliers.* The make-or-buy issue generally boils down to whether suppliers who specialize in the production of a particular part or component and make them in volume for many different customers have the expertise and scale economies to supply as good or better component at a lower cost than industry members could achieve via self-manufacture. Frequently, it is difficult for industry members to self-manufacture parts and components more economically than they can obtain them from suppliers who specialize in making such items. For instance, most producers of outdoor power equipment (lawn mowers, rotary tillers, leaf blowers, etc.) find it cheaper to source the small engines they need from outside manufacturers who specialize in small-engine manufacture rather than make their own engines because the quantity of engines they need is too small to justify the investment in manufacturing facilities, master the production process, and capture scale economies. Specialists in small-engine manufacture, by supplying many kinds of engines to the whole power equipment industry, can obtain a big enough sales volume to fully realize scale economies, become proficient in all the manufacturing techniques, and keep costs low. As a rule, suppliers are safe from the threat of self-manufacture by their customers *until* the volume of parts a customer needs becomes large enough for the customer to justify backward integration into self-manufacture of the component. Suppliers also gain bargaining power when they have the resources and profit incentive to integrate forward into the business of the customers they are supplying and thus become a strong rival.

Figure 3.7 summarizes the conditions that tend to make supplier bargaining power strong or weak.

How Seller–Supplier Partnerships Can Create Competitive Pressures

In more and more industries, sellers are forging strategic partnerships with select suppliers in efforts to (1) reduce inventory and logistics costs (e.g., through just-in-time deliveries), (2) speed the availability of next-generation components, (3) enhance the quality of the parts and components being supplied and reduce defect rates, and (4) squeeze out important cost savings for both themselves and their suppliers. Numerous Internet technology applications are now available that permit real-time data sharing, eliminate paperwork, and produce cost savings all along the supply chain. The many benefits of effective seller–supplier collaboration can translate into competitive advantage for industry members that do the best job of managing supply chain relationships.

Dell Computer has used strategic partnering with key suppliers as a major element in its strategy to be the world's lowest-cost supplier of branded PCs, servers, and workstations. Because Dell has managed its supply chain relationships in ways that contribute to a low-cost, high-quality competitive edge in components supply, it has put enormous pressure on its PC rivals to try to imitate its supply chain management practices. Effective partnerships with suppliers on the part of one or more industry members can thus become a major source of competitive pressure for rival firms.

The more opportunities that exist for win–win efforts between a company and its suppliers, the less their relationship is characterized by who has the upper hand in

Figure 3.7 **Factors Affecting the Bargaining Power of Suppliers**

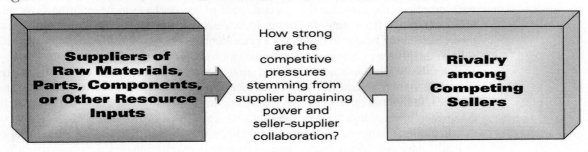

Supplier bargaining power is stronger when:
- Industry members incurs high costs in switching their purchases to alternative suppliers.
- Needed inputs are in short supply (which gives suppliers more leverage in setting prices).
- A supplier has a differentiated input that enhances the quality or performance of sellers' products or is a valuable or critical part of sellers' production process.
- There are only a few suppliers of a particular input.
- Some suppliers threaten to integrate forward into the business of industry members and perhaps become a powerful rival.

Supplier bargaining power is weaker when:
- The item being supplied is a commodity that is readily available from many suppliers at the going market price.
- Seller switching costs to alternative suppliers are low.
- Good substitute inputs exist or new ones emerge.
- There is a surge in the availability of supplies (thus greatly weakening supplier pricing power).
- Industry members account for a big fraction of suppliers' total sales and continued high volume purchases are important to the well-being of suppliers.
- Industry members are a threat to integrate backward into the business of suppliers and to self-manufacture their own requirements.
- Seller collaboration or partnering with selected suppliers provides attractive win–win opportunities.

bargaining with the other. Collaborative partnerships between a company and a supplier tend to last so long as the relationship is producing valuable benefits for both parties. Only if a supply partner is falling behind alternative suppliers is a company likely to switch suppliers and incur the costs and trouble of building close working ties with a different supplier.

Competitive Pressures Stemming from Buyer Bargaining Power and Seller–Buyer Collaboration

Whether seller–buyer relationships represent a weak or strong competitive force depends on (1) whether some or many buyers have sufficient bargaining leverage to obtain price concessions and other favorable terms and conditions of sale, and (2) the extent and competitive importance of seller–buyer strategic partnerships in the industry.

How Buyer Bargaining Power Can Create Competitive Pressures   As with suppliers, the leverage that certain types of buyers have in negotiating favorable terms can range from weak to strong. Individual consumers, for example, rarely have much bargaining power in negotiating price concessions or other favorable terms with sellers; the primary exceptions involve situations in which price haggling is customary, such as the purchase of new and used motor vehicles, homes, and certain big-ticket items like luxury watches, jewelry, and pleasure boats. For most consumer goods and services, individual buyers have no bargaining leverage—their option is to pay the seller's posted price or take their business elsewhere.

In contrast, large retail chains like Wal-Mart, Best Buy, Staples, and Home Depot typically have considerable negotiating leverage in purchasing products from manufacturers because of manufacturers' need for broad retail exposure and the most appealing shelf locations. Retailers may stock two or three competing brands of a product but rarely all competing brands, so competition among rival manufacturers for visibility on the shelves of popular multistore retailers gives such retailers significant bargaining strength. Major supermarket chains like Kroger, Safeway, and Royal Ahold, which provide access to millions of grocery shoppers, have sufficient bargaining power to demand promotional allowances and lump-sum payments (called slotting fees) from food products manufacturers in return for stocking certain brands or putting them in the best shelf locations. Motor vehicle manufacturers have strong bargaining power in negotiating to buy original equipment tires from Goodyear, Michelin, Bridgestone/Firestone, Continental, and Pirelli not only because they buy in large quantities but also because tire makers believe they gain an advantage in supplying replacement tires to vehicle owners if their tire brand is original equipment on the vehicle. "Prestige" buyers have a degree of clout in negotiating with sellers because a seller's reputation is enhanced by having prestige buyers on its customer list.

Even if buyers do not purchase in large quantities or offer a seller important market exposure or prestige, they gain a degree of bargaining leverage in the following circumstances:[10]

- *If buyers' costs of switching to competing brands or substitutes are relatively low*—Buyers who can readily switch brands or source from several sellers have more negotiating leverage than buyers who have high switching costs. When the products of rival sellers are virtually identical, it is relatively easy for buyers to switch from seller to seller at little or no cost and anxious sellers may be willing to make concessions to win or retain a buyer's business.

- *If the number of buyers is small or if a customer is particularly important to a seller*—The smaller the number of buyers, the less easy it is for sellers to find alternative buyers when a customer is lost to a competitor. The prospect of losing a customer not easily replaced often makes a seller more willing to grant concessions of one kind or another.

- *If buyer demand is weak and sellers are scrambling to secure additional sales of their products*—Weak or declining demand creates a "buyers' market"; conversely, strong or rapidly growing demand creates a "sellers' market" and shifts bargaining power to sellers.

- *If buyers are well informed about sellers' products, prices, and costs*—The more information buyers have, the better bargaining position they are in. The mushrooming availability of product information on the Internet is giving added bargaining power to individuals. Buyers can easily use the Internet to compare prices and features of vacation packages, shop for the best interest rates on mortgages and loans, and find the best prices on big-ticket items such as digital cameras. Bargain-hunting individuals can shop around for the best deal on the Internet and use that information to negotiate a better deal from local retailers; this method is becoming commonplace in buying new and used motor vehicles. Further, the Internet has created opportunities for manufacturers, wholesalers, retailers, and sometimes individuals to join online buying groups to pool their purchasing power and approach vendors for better terms than could be gotten individually. A multinational manufacturer's geographically scattered purchasing groups can use Internet technology to pool their orders with parts and components suppliers and bargain for volume discounts. Purchasing agents at some companies are banding together at third-party Web sites to pool corporate purchases to get better deals or special treatment.

- *If buyers pose a credible threat of integrating backward into the business of sellers*—Companies like Anheuser-Busch, Coors, and Heinz have integrated backward into metal can manufacturing to gain bargaining power in obtaining the balance of their can requirements from otherwise powerful metal can manufacturers. Retailers gain bargaining power by stocking and promoting their own private-label brands alongside manufacturers' name brands. Wal-Mart, for example, has elected to compete against Procter & Gamble (P&G), its biggest supplier, with its own brand of laundry detergent, called Sam's American Choice, which is priced 25 to 30 percent lower than P&G's Tide.

- *If buyers have discretion in whether and when they purchase the product*—Many consumers, if they are unhappy with the present deals offered on major appliances or hot tubs or home entertainment centers, may be in a position to delay purchase until prices and financing terms improve. If business customers are not happy with the prices or security features of bill-payment software systems, they can either delay purchase until next-generation products become available or attempt to develop their own software in-house. If college students believe that the prices of new textbooks are too high, they can purchase used copies.

Figure 3.8 highlights the factors causing buyer bargaining power to be strong or weak.

A final point to keep in mind is that *not all buyers of an industry's product have equal degrees of bargaining power with sellers*, and some may be less sensitive than others to price, quality, or service differences. For example, independent tire retailers have less bargaining power in purchasing tires than do Honda, Ford, and DaimlerChrysler (which buy in much larger quantities), and they are also less sensitive to quality. Motor vehicle manufacturers are very particular about tire quality and tire performance because of the effects on vehicle performance, and they drive a hard bargain with tire manufacturers on both price and quality. Apparel manufacturers confront significant bargaining power when selling to big retailers like JCPenney, Macy's, or L. L. Bean but they can command much better prices selling to small owner-managed apparel boutiques.

How Seller–Buyer Partnerships Can Create Competitive Pressures   Partnerships between sellers and buyers are an increasingly important element of the competitive picture in *business-to-business relationships* (as opposed to business-to-consumer relationships). Many sellers that provide items to business customers have found it in their mutual interest to collaborate closely on such matters as just-in-time deliveries, order processing, electronic invoice payments, and data sharing. Wal-Mart, for example, provides the manufacturers with which it does business (like Procter & Gamble) with daily sales at each of its stores so that the manufacturers can maintain sufficient inventories at Wal-Mart's distribution centers to keep the shelves at each Wal-Mart store amply stocked. Dell has partnered with its largest PC customers to create

Figure 3.8 **Factors Affecting the Bargaining Power of Buyers**

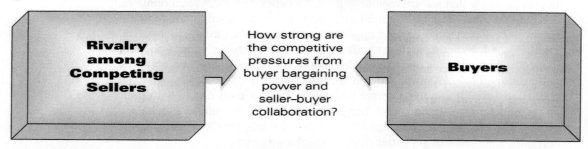

Buyer bargaining power is stronger when:
• Buyer switching costs to competing brands or substitute products are low.
• Buyers are large and can demand concessions when purchasing large quantities.
• Large-volume purchases by buyers are important to sellers.
• Buyer demand is weak or declining.
• There are only a few buyers—so that each one's business is important to sellers.
• Identity of buyer adds prestige to the seller's list of customers.
• Quantity and quality of information available to buyers improves.
• Buyers have the ability to postpone purchases until later if they do not like the present deals being offered by sellers.
• Some buyers are a threat to integrate backward into the business of sellers and become an important competitor.

Buyer bargaining power is weaker when:
• Buyers purchase the item infrequently or in small quantities.
• Buyer switching costs to competing brands are high.
• There is a surge in buyer demand that creates a "sellers' market."
• A seller's brand reputation is important to a buyer.
• A particular seller's product delivers quality or performance that is very important to buyer and that is not matched in other brands.
• Buyer collaboration or partnering with selected sellers provides attractive win–win opportunities.

online systems for over 50,000 corporate customers, providing their employees with information on approved product configurations, global pricing, paperless purchase orders, real-time order tracking, invoicing, purchasing history, and other efficiency tools. Dell loads a customer's software at the factory and installs asset tags so that customer setup time is minimal; it also helps customers upgrade their PC systems to next-generation hardware and software. Dell's partnerships with its corporate customers have put significant competitive pressure on other PC makers.

Is the Collective Strength of the Five Competitive Forces Conducive to Good Profitability?

Scrutinizing each of the five competitive forces one by one provides a powerful diagnosis of what competition is like in a given market. Once the strategist has gained an understanding of the specific competitive pressures comprising each force and determined whether these pressures constitute a strong, moderate, or weak competitive force, the next step is to evaluate the collective strength of the five forces and determine whether the state of competition is conducive to good profitability. Is the collective impact of the five competitive forces stronger than "normal"? Are some of the competitive forces sufficiently strong to undermine industry profitability? Can companies in this industry reasonably expect to earn decent profits in light of the prevailing competitive forces?

Is the Industry Competitively Attractive or Unattractive?   *As a rule, the stronger the collective impact of the five competitive forces, the lower the combined profitability of industry participants.* The most extreme case of a competitively unattractive industry is when all five forces are producing strong competitive pressures: Rivalry among sellers is vigorous, low entry barriers allow new rivals to gain a market foothold, competition from substitutes is intense, and both suppliers and customers are able to exercise considerable bargaining leverage. Fierce to strong competitive pressures coming from all five directions nearly always drive industry profitability to unacceptably low levels, frequently producing losses for many industry members and forcing some out of business. But an industry can be competitively unattractive even when not all five competitive forces are strong. Intense competitive pressures from just two or three of the five forces may suffice to destroy the conditions for good profitability and prompt some companies to exit the business. The manufacture of disk drives, for example, is brutally competitive; IBM recently announced the sale of its disk drive business to Hitachi, taking a loss of over $2 billion on its exit from the business. Especially intense competitive conditions seem to be the norm in tire manufacturing and apparel, two industries where profit margins have historically been thin.

> The stronger the forces of competition, the harder it becomes for industry members to earn attractive profits.

In contrast, when the collective impact of the five competitive forces is moderate to weak, an industry is competitively attractive in the sense that industry members can reasonably expect to earn good profits and a nice return on investment. The ideal competitive environment for earning superior profits is one in which both suppliers and customers are in weak bargaining positions, there are no good substitutes, high barriers block further entry, and rivalry among present sellers generates only moderate competitive pressures. Weak competition is the best of all possible worlds for also-ran companies because even they can usually eke out a decent profit—if a company can't make a decent profit when competition is weak, then its business outlook is indeed grim.

In most industries, the collective strength of the five competitive forces is somewhere near the middle of the two extremes of very intense and very weak, typically ranging from slightly stronger than normal to slightly weaker than normal and typically allowing well-managed companies with sound strategies to earn attractive profits.

Matching Company Strategy to Competitive Conditions   Working through the five-forces model step by step not only aids strategy makers in assessing whether the intensity of competition allows good profitability but also promotes sound strategic thinking about how to better match company strategy to the specific competitive character of the marketplace. Effectively matching a company's strategy to prevailing competitive conditions has two aspects:

> A company's strategy is increasingly effective the more it provides some insulation from competitive pressures and shifts the competitive battle in the company's favor.

1. Pursuing avenues that shield the firm from as many of the different competitive pressures as possible.
2. Initiating actions calculated to produce sustainable competitive advantage, thereby shifting competition in the company's favor, putting added competitive pressure on rivals, and perhaps even defining the business model for the industry.

But making headway on these two fronts first requires identifying competitive pressures, gauging the relative strength of each of the five competitive forces, and gaining a deep enough understanding of the state of competition in the industry to know which strategy buttons to push.

QUESTION 3: WHAT FACTORS ARE DRIVING INDUSTRY CHANGE AND WHAT IMPACTS WILL THEY HAVE?

An industry's present conditions don't necessarily reveal much about the strategically relevant ways in which the industry environment is changing. All industries are characterized by trends and new developments that gradually or speedily produce changes important enough to require a strategic response from participating firms. A popular hypothesis states that industries go through a life cycle of takeoff, rapid growth, early maturity and slowing growth, market saturation, and stagnation or decline. This hypothesis helps explain industry change—but it is far from complete.[11] There are more causes of industry change than an industry's normal progression through the life cycle—these need to be identified and their impacts understood.

The Concept of Driving Forces

Core Concept
Industry conditions change because important forces are *driving* industry participants (competitors, customers, or suppliers) to alter their actions; the ***driving forces*** in an industry are the *major underlying causes* of changing industry and competitive conditions—they have the biggest influence on how the industry landscape will be altered. Some driving forces originate in the outer ring of macroenvironment and some originate from the inner ring.

While it is important to track where an industry is in the life cycle, there's more analytical value in identifying the other factors that may be even stronger drivers of industry and competitive change. The point to be made here is that industry and competitive conditions change because forces are enticing or pressuring certain industry participants (competitors, customers, suppliers) to alter their actions in important ways.[12] The most powerful of the change agents are called **driving forces** because they have the biggest influences in reshaping the industry landscape and altering competitive conditions. Some driving forces originate in the outer ring of the company's macroenvironment (see Figure 3.2), but most originate in the company's more immediate industry and competitive environment.

Driving-forces analysis has three steps: (1) identifying what the driving forces are; (2) assessing whether the drivers of change are, on the whole, acting to make the industry more or less attractive; and (3) determining what strategy changes are needed to prepare for the impacts of the driving forces. All three steps merit further discussion.

Identifying an Industry's Driving Forces

Many developments can affect an industry powerfully enough to qualify as driving forces. Some drivers of change are unique and specific to a particular industry situation, but most drivers of industry and competitive change fall into one of the following categories:[13]

- *Emerging new Internet capabilities and applications*—Since the late 1990s, the Internet has woven its way into everyday business operations and the social fabric of life all across the world. Mushrooming Internet use, growing acceptance of Internet shopping, the emergence of high-speed Internet service and Voice over Internet Protocol (VoIP) technology, and an ever-growing series of Internet applications and capabilities have been major drivers of change in industry after industry. Companies are increasingly using online technology (1) to collaborate closely with suppliers and streamline their supply chains and (2) to revamp internal operations and squeeze out cost savings. Manufacturers can use their Web sites to access customers directly rather than distribute exclusively through traditional wholesale and retail channels. Businesses of all types can use Web stores to extend their geographic reach and vie for sales in areas where they formerly did not have a presence. The ability of companies to reach consumers via the Internet increases the number of rivals a company faces and often escalates rivalry by pitting pure online sellers against combination brick-and-click sellers against pure brick-and-mortar sellers. The Internet gives buyers unprecedented ability to research the product offerings of competitors and shop the market for the best value. Mounting ability of consumers to download music from the Internet via either file sharing or online music retailers has profoundly and re-shaped the music industry and the business of traditional brick-and-mortar music retailers. Widespread use of e-mail has forever eroded the business of providing fax services and the first-class mail delivery revenues of government postal services worldwide. Videoconferencing via the Internet can erode the demand for business travel. Online course offerings at universities have the potential to revolutionize higher education. The Internet of the future will feature faster speeds, dazzling applications, and over a billion connected gadgets performing an array of functions, thus driving further industry and competitive changes. But Internet-related impacts vary from industry to industry. The challenges here are to assess precisely how emerging Internet developments are altering a particular industry's landscape and to factor these impacts into the strategy-making equation.

- *Increasing globalization*—Competition begins to shift from primarily a regional or national focus to an international or global focus when industry members begin seeking out customers in foreign markets or when production activities begin to migrate to countries where costs are lowest. Globalization of competition really starts to take hold when one or more ambitious companies precipitate a race for worldwide market leadership by launching initiatives to expand into more and more country markets. Globalization can also be precipitated by the blossoming of consumer demand in more and more countries and by the actions of government officials in many countries to reduce trade barriers or open up once-closed markets to foreign competitors, as is occurring in many parts of Europe, Latin America, and Asia. Significant differences in labor costs among countries give manufacturers a strong incentive to locate plants for labor-intensive products in low-wage countries and use these plants to supply market demand across the world. Wages in China, India, Singapore, Mexico, and Brazil, for example, are about one-fourth those in the United States, Germany, and Japan. The forces of globalization are sometimes such a strong driver that companies find it highly advantageous, if not necessary, to spread their operating reach into more and more country markets. Globalization is very much a driver of industry change in such industries as credit cards, cell phones, digital cameras, golf and ski equipment, motor vehicles, steel, petroleum, personal computers, video games, public accounting, and textbook publishing.

- *Changes in an industry's long-term growth rate*—Shifts in industry growth up or down are a driving force for industry change, affecting the balance between industry supply and buyer demand, entry and exit, and the character and strength of competition. An upsurge in buyer demand triggers a race among established firms and newcomers to capture the new sales opportunities; ambitious companies with trailing market shares may see the upturn in demand as a golden opportunity to launch offensive strategies to broaden their customer base and move up several notches in the industry standings. A slowdown in the rate at which demand is growing nearly always portends mounting rivalry and increased efforts by some firms to maintain their high rates of growth by taking sales and market share away from rivals. If industry sales suddenly turn flat or begin to shrink after years of rising at double-digit levels, competition is certain to intensify as industry members scramble for the available business and as mergers and acquisitions result in industry consolidation to a smaller number of competitively stronger participants. Stagnating sales usually prompt both competitively weak and growth-oriented companies to sell their business operations to those industry members who elect to stick it out; as demand for the industry's product continues to shrink, the remaining industry members may be forced to close inefficient plants and retrench to a smaller production base—all of which results in a much-changed competitive landscape.

- *Changes in who buys the product and how they use it*—Shifts in buyer demographics and new ways of using the product can alter the state of competition by opening the way to market an industry's product through a different mix of dealers and retail outlets; prompting producers to broaden or narrow their product lines; bringing different sales and promotion approaches into play; and forcing adjustments in customer service offerings (credit, technical assistance, maintenance, and repair). The mushrooming popularity of downloading music from the Internet, storing music files on PC hard drives, and burning custom discs has forced recording companies to reexamine their distribution strategies and raised questions about the future of traditional retail music stores; at the same time, it has stimulated sales of disc burners and blank discs. Longer life expectancies and growing percentages of relatively well-to-do retirees are driving changes in such industries as health care, prescription drugs, recreational living, and vacation travel. The growing percentage of households with PCs and Internet access is opening opportunities for banks to expand their electronic bill-payment services and for retailers to move more of their customer services online.

- *Product innovation*—Competition in an industry is always affected by rivals racing to be first to introduce one new product or product enhancement after another. An ongoing stream of product innovations tends to alter the pattern of competition in an industry by attracting more first-time buyers, rejuvenating industry growth, and/or creating wider or narrower product differentiation among rival sellers. Successful new product introductions strengthen the market positions of the innovating companies, usually at the expense of companies that stick with their old products or are slow to follow with their own versions of the new product. Product innovation has been a key driving force in such industries as digital cameras, golf clubs, video games, toys, and prescription drugs.

- *Technological change and manufacturing process innovation*—Advances in technology can dramatically alter an industry's landscape, making it possible to produce new and better products at lower cost and opening up whole new industry frontiers. For instance, Voice over Internet Protocol (VoIP) technology has spawned low-cost, Internet-based phone networks that are stealing large numbers of customers away from traditional telephone companies worldwide (whose higher cost technology depends on hardwired connections via overhead and underground telephone lines). Flat-screen technology for PC monitors is killing the demand for conventional cathode ray tube (CRT) monitors. Liquid crystal display (LCD), plasma screen technology, and high-definition technology are precipitating a revolution in the television industry and driving use of cathode ray technology (CRT) into the background. MP3 technology is transforming how people listen to music. Digital technology is driving huge changes in the camera and film industries. Satellite radio technology is allowing satellite radio companies with their largely commercial-free programming to draw millions of listeners away from traditional radio stations whose revenue streams from commercials are dependent on audience size. Technological developments can also produce competitively significant changes in capital requirements, minimum efficient plant sizes, distribution channels and logistics, and learning/experience curve effects. In the steel industry, ongoing advances in electric arc minimill technology (which involve recycling scrap steel to make new products) have allowed steelmakers with state-of-the-art minimills to gradually expand into the production of more and more steel products, steadily taking sales and market share from higher-cost integrated producers (which make steel from scratch using iron ore, coke, and traditional blast furnace technology). Nucor Corporation, the leader of the minimill technology revolution in the United States, began operations in 1970 and has ridden the wave of technological advances in minimill technology to become the biggest U.S. steel producer (as of 2004) and ranks among the lowest-cost producers in the world. In a space of 30 years, advances in minimill technology have changed the face of the steel industry worldwide.

- *Marketing innovation*—When firms are successful in introducing new ways to *market* their products, they can spark a burst of buyer interest, widen industry demand, increase product differentiation, and lower unit costs—any or all of which can alter the competitive positions of rival firms and force strategy revisions. Online marketing is shaking up competition in electronics (where there are dozens of online electronics retailers, often with deep-discount prices) and office supplies (where Office Depot, Staples, and Office Max are using their Web sites to market office supplies to corporations, small businesses, schools and universities, and government agencies). Increasing numbers of music artists are marketing their recordings at their own Web sites rather than entering into contracts with recording studios that distribute through online and brick-and-mortar music retailers.

- *Entry or exit of major firms*—The entry of one or more foreign companies into a geographic market once dominated by domestic firms nearly always shakes up competitive conditions. Likewise, when an established domestic firm from another industry attempts entry either by acquisition or by launching its own start-up venture, it usually applies its skills and resources in some innovative fashion that pushes competition in new directions. Entry by a major firm thus often produces a new ball game, not only with new key players but also with new rules for competing. Similarly, exit of a major firm changes the competitive structure by reducing the number of market leaders (perhaps increasing the dominance of the leaders who remain) and causing a rush to capture the exiting firm's customers.

- *Diffusion of technical know-how across more companies and more countries—* As knowledge about how to perform a particular activity or execute a particular manufacturing technology spreads, the competitive advantage held by firms originally possessing this know-how erodes. Knowledge diffusion can occur through scientific journals, trade publications, on-site plant tours, word of mouth among suppliers and customers, employee migration, and Internet sources. It can also occur when those possessing technological knowledge license others to use that knowledge for a royalty fee or team up with a company interested in turning the technology into a new business venture. Quite often, technological know-how can be acquired by simply buying a company that has the wanted skills, patents, or manufacturing capabilities. In recent years, *rapid technology transfer across national boundaries has been a prime factor in causing industries to become more globally competitive.* As companies worldwide gain access to valuable technical know-how, they upgrade their manufacturing capabilities in a long-term effort to compete head-on with established companies. Cross-border technology transfer has made the once domestic industries of automobiles, tires, consumer electronics, telecommunications, computers, and others increasingly global.

- *Changes in cost and efficiency—*Widening or shrinking differences in the costs among key competitors tend to dramatically alter the state of competition. The low cost of fax and e-mail transmission has put mounting competitive pressure on the relatively inefficient and high-cost operations of the U.S. Postal Service—sending a one-page fax is cheaper and far quicker than sending a first-class letter; sending e-mail is faster and cheaper still. In the steel industry, the lower costs of companies using electric-arc furnaces to recycle scrap steel into new steel products has forced traditional manufacturers that produce steel from iron ore using blast furnace technology to overhaul their plants and to withdraw totally from making those steel products where they could no longer be cost competitive. Shrinking cost differences in producing multifeatured mobile phones is turning the mobile phone market into a commodity business and causing more buyers to base their purchase decisions on price.

- *Growing buyer preferences for differentiated products instead of a commodity product (or for a more standardized product instead of strongly differentiated products)—*When buyer tastes and preferences start to diverge, sellers can win a loyal following with product offerings that stand apart from those of rival sellers. In recent years, beer drinkers have grown less loyal to a single brand and have begun to drink a variety of domestic and foreign beers; as a consequence, beer manufacturers have introduced a host of new brands and malt beverages with different tastes and flavors. Buyer preferences for motor vehicles are becoming increasingly diverse, with few models generating sales of more than 250,000 units annually. When a shift from standardized to differentiated products occurs, the driver of change is the contest among rivals to cleverly outdifferentiate one another.

  However, buyers sometimes decide that a standardized, budget-priced product suits their requirements as well as or better than a premium-priced product with lots of snappy features and personalized services. Online brokers, for example, have used the lure of cheap commissions to attract many investors willing to place their own buy–sell orders via the Internet; growing acceptance of online trading has put significant competitive pressures on full-service brokers whose business model has always revolved around convincing clients of the value of asking for personalized advice from professional brokers and paying their high commission fees to make trades. Pronounced shifts toward greater product standardization usually spawn lively price competition and force rival sellers to drive down their costs to maintain profitability. The lesson here is that competition is driven partly by whether the market forces in motion are acting to increase or decrease product differentiation.

- *Reductions in uncertainty and business risk*—An emerging industry is typically characterized by much uncertainty over potential market size, how much time and money will be needed to surmount technological problems, and what distribution channels and buyer segments to emphasize. Emerging industries tend to attract only risk-taking entrepreneurial companies. Over time, however, if the business model of industry pioneers proves profitable and market demand for the product appears durable, more conservative firms are usually enticed to enter the market. Often, these later entrants are large, financially strong firms looking to invest in attractive growth industries.

  Lower business risks and less industry uncertainty also affect competition in international markets. In the early stages of a company's entry into foreign markets, conservatism prevails and firms limit their downside exposure by using less risky strategies like exporting, licensing, joint marketing agreements, or joint ventures with local companies to accomplish entry. Then, as experience accumulates and perceived risk levels decline, companies move more boldly and more independently, making acquisitions, constructing their own plants, putting in their own sales and marketing capabilities to build strong competitive positions in each country market, and beginning to link the strategies in each country to create a more globalized strategy.

- *Regulatory influences and government policy changes*—Government regulatory actions can often force significant changes in industry practices and strategic approaches. Deregulation has proved to be a potent pro-competitive force in the airline, banking, natural gas, telecommunications, and electric utility industries. Government efforts to reform Medicare and health insurance have become potent driving forces in the health care industry. In international markets, host governments can drive competitive changes by opening their domestic markets to foreign participation or closing them to protect domestic companies. Note that this driving force is spawned by forces in a company's macroenvironment.

- *Changing societal concerns, attitudes, and lifestyles*—Emerging social issues and changing attitudes and lifestyles can be powerful instigators of industry change. Growing antismoking sentiment has emerged as a major driver of change in the tobacco industry; concerns about terrorism are having a big impact on the travel industry. Consumer concerns about salt, sugar, chemical additives, saturated fat, cholesterol, carbohydrates, and nutritional value have forced food producers to revamp food-processing techniques, redirect R&D efforts into the use of healthier ingredients, and compete in developing nutritious, good-tasting products. Safety concerns have driven product design changes in the automobile, toy, and outdoor power equipment industries, to mention a few. Increased interest in physical fitness has spawned new industries in exercise equipment, biking, outdoor apparel, sports gyms and recreation centers, vitamin and nutrition supplements, and medically supervised diet programs. Social concerns about air and water pollution have forced industries to incorporate expenditures for controlling pollution into their cost structures. Shifting societal concerns, attitudes, and lifestyles alter the pattern of competition, usually favoring those

Table 3.2 **The Most Common Driving Forces**

1. Emerging new Internet capabilities and applications
2. Increasing globalization
3. Changes in an industry's long-term growth rate
4. Changes in who buys the product and how they use it
5. Product innovation
6. Technological change and manufacturing process innovation
7. Marketing innovation
8. Entry or exit of major firms
9. Diffusion of technical know-how across more companies and more countries
10. Changes in cost and efficiency
11. Growing buyer preferences for differentiated products instead of a commodity product (or for a more standardized product instead of strongly differentiated products)
12. Reductions in uncertainty and business risk
13. Regulatory influences and government policy changes
14. Changing societal concerns, attitudes, and lifestyles

players that respond quickly and creatively with products targeted to the new trends and conditions. As with the preceding driving force, this driving force springs from factors at work in a company's macroenvironment.

Table 3.2 lists these 14 most common driving forces.

That there are so many different potential driving forces explains why it is too simplistic to view industry change only in terms of moving through the different stages in an industry's life cycle and why a full understanding of all types of change drivers is a fundamental part of industry analysis. However, while many forces of change may be at work in a given industry, no more than three or four are likely to be true driving forces powerful enough to qualify as the *major determinants* of why and how the industry is changing. Thus company strategists must resist the temptation to label every change they see as a driving force; the analytical task is to evaluate the forces of industry and competitive change carefully enough to separate major factors from minor ones.

Assessing the Impact of the Driving Forces

An important part of driving-forces analysis is to determine whether the collective impact of the driving forces will be to increase or decrease market demand, make competition more or less intense, and lead to higher or lower industry profitability.

Just identifying the driving forces is not sufficient, however. The second, and more important, step in driving-forces analysis is to determine whether the prevailing driving forces are, on the whole, acting to make the industry environment more or less attractive. Answers to three questions are needed here:

1. Are the driving forces collectively acting to cause demand for the industry's product to increase or decrease?
2. Are the driving forces acting to make competition more or less intense?
3. Will the combined impacts of the driving forces lead to higher or lower industry profitability?

Getting a handle on the collective impact of the driving forces usually requires looking at the likely effects of each force separately, since the driving forces may not all be pushing change in the same direction. For example, two driving forces may be acting to spur demand for the industry's product while one driving force may be working to curtail demand. Whether the net effect on industry demand is up or down hinges on which driving forces are the more powerful. The analyst's objective here is to get a good grip on what external factors are shaping industry change and what difference these factors will make.

Developing a Strategy That Takes the Impacts of the Driving Forces into Account

The third step of driving-forces analysis—where the real payoff for strategy making comes—is for managers to draw some conclusions about what strategy adjustments will be needed to deal with the impacts of the driving forces. The real value of doing driving-forces analysis is to gain better understanding of what strategy adjustments will be needed to cope with the drivers of industry change and the impacts they are likely to have on market demand, competitive intensity, and industry profitability. In short, the strategy-making challenge that flows from driving-forces analysis is what to do to prepare for the industry and competitive changes being wrought by the driving forces. Indeed, without understanding the forces driving industry change and the impacts these forces will have on the character of the industry environment and on the company's business over the next one to three years, managers are ill-prepared to craft a strategy tightly matched to emerging conditions. Similarly, if managers are uncertain about the implications of one or more driving forces, or if their views are incomplete or off base, it's difficult for them to craft a strategy that is responsive to the driving forces and their consequences for the industry. So driving-forces analysis is not something to take lightly; it has practical value and is basic to the task of thinking strategically about where the industry is headed and how to prepare for the changes ahead.

> Driving-forces analysis, when done properly, pushes company managers to think about what's around the corner and what the company needs to be doing to get ready for it.

> The real payoff of driving-forces analysis is to help managers understand what strategy changes are needed to prepare for the impacts of the driving forces.

QUESTION 4: WHAT MARKET POSITIONS DO RIVALS OCCUPY—WHO IS STRONGLY POSITIONED AND WHO IS NOT?

Since competing companies commonly sell in different price/quality ranges, emphasize different distribution channels, incorporate product features that appeal to different types of buyers, have different geographic coverage, and so on, it stands to reason that some companies enjoy stronger or more attractive market positions than other companies. Understanding which companies are strongly positioned and which are weakly positioned is an integral part of analyzing an industry's competitive structure. The best technique for revealing the market positions of industry competitors is **strategic group mapping.**[14] This analytical tool is useful for comparing the market positions of each firm separately or for grouping them into like positions when an industry has so many competitors that it is not practical to examine each one in depth.

> **Core Concept**
> **Strategic group mapping** is a technique for displaying the different market or competitive positions that rival firms occupy in the industry.

Using Strategic Group Maps to Assess the Market Positions of Key Competitors

A **strategic group** consists of those industry members with similar competitive approaches and positions in the market.[15] Companies in the same strategic group can resemble one another in any of several ways: They may have comparable product-line breadth, sell in the same price/quality range, emphasize the same distribution channels, use essentially the same product attributes to appeal to similar types of buyers, depend on identical technological approaches, or offer buyers similar services and technical assistance.[16] An industry contains only one strategic group when all sellers pursue essentially identical strategies and have comparable market positions. At the other extreme, an industry may contain as many strategic groups as there are competitors when each rival pursues a distinctively different competitive approach and occupies a substantially different market position.

> **Core Concept**
> A **strategic group** is a cluster of industry rivals that have similar competitive approaches and market positions.

The procedure for constructing a *strategic group map* is straightforward:

- Identify the competitive characteristics that differentiate firms in the industry. Typical variables are price/quality range (high, medium, low); geographic coverage (local, regional, national, global); degree of vertical integration (none, partial, full); product-line breadth (wide, narrow); use of distribution channels (one, some, all); and degree of service offered (no-frills, limited, full).
- Plot the firms on a two-variable map using pairs of these differentiating characteristics.
- Assign firms that fall in about the same strategy space to the same strategic group.
- Draw circles around each strategic group, making the circles proportional to the size of the group's share of total industry sales revenues.

This produces a two-dimensional diagram like the one for the retailing industry in Illustration Capsule 3.1.

Several guidelines need to be observed in mapping the positions of strategic groups in the industry's overall strategy space.[17] First, the two variables selected as axes for the map should *not* be highly correlated; if they are, the circles on the map will fall along a diagonal and strategy makers will learn nothing more about the relative positions of competitors than they would by considering just one of the variables. For instance, if companies with broad product lines use multiple distribution channels while companies with narrow lines use a single distribution channel, then looking at broad versus narrow product lines reveals just as much about who is positioned where as looking at single versus multiple distribution channels; that is, one of the variables is redundant. Second, the variables chosen as axes for the map should expose big differences in how rivals position themselves to compete in the marketplace. This, of course, means analysts must identify the characteristics that differentiate rival firms and use these differences as variables for the axes and as the basis for deciding which firm belongs in which strategic group. Third, the variables used as axes don't have to be either quantitative or continuous; rather, they can be discrete variables or defined in terms of distinct classes and combinations. Fourth, drawing the sizes of the circles on the map proportional to the combined sales of the firms in each strategic group allows the map to reflect the relative sizes of each strategic group. Fifth, if more than two good competitive variables can be used as axes for the map, several maps can be drawn to give different exposures to the competitive positioning relationships present

Illustration Capsule 3.1

Comparative Market Positions of Selected Retail Chains: A Strategic Group Map Application

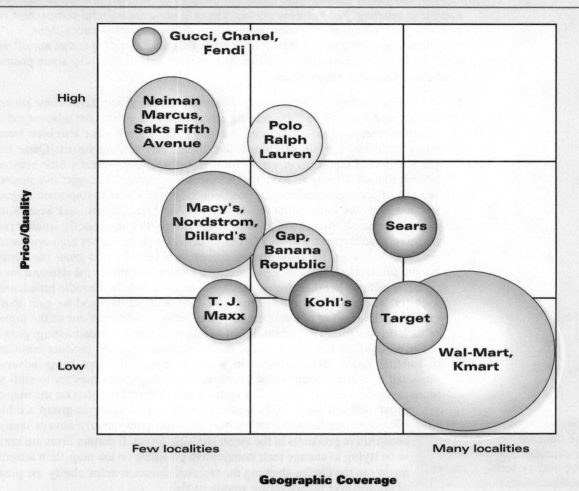

Note: Circles are drawn roughly proportional to the sizes of the chains, based on revenues.

in the industry's structure. Because there is not necessarily one best map for portraying how competing firms are positioned in the market, it is advisable to experiment with different pairs of competitive variables.

What Can Be Learned from Strategic Group Maps?

Strategic group maps are revealing in several respects. The most important has to do with which rivals are similarly positioned and are thus close rivals and which are distant rivals. Generally speaking, *the closer strategic groups are to each other on the*

Strategic group maps reveal which companies are close competitors and which are distant competitors.

map, the stronger the cross-group competitive rivalry tends to be. Although firms in the same strategic group are the closest rivals, the next closest rivals are in the immediately adjacent groups.[18] Often, firms in strategic groups that are far apart on the map hardly compete at all. For instance, Wal-Mart's clientele, merchandise selection, and pricing points are much too different to justify calling them close competitors of Neiman Marcus or Saks Fifth Avenue in retailing. For the same reason, Timex is not a meaningful competitive rival of Rolex, and Subaru is not a close competitor of Lincoln or Mercedes-Benz.

The second thing to be gleaned from strategic group mapping is that *not all positions on the map are equally attractive.* Two reasons account for why some positions can be more attractive than others:

1. *Prevailing competitive pressures and industry driving forces favor some strategic groups and hurt others.*[19] Discerning which strategic groups are advantaged and disadvantaged requires scrutinizing the map in light of what has also been learned from the prior analysis of competitive forces and driving forces. Quite often the strength of competition varies from group to group—there's little reason to believe that all firms in an industry feel the same degrees of competitive pressure, since their strategies and market positions may well differ in important respects. For instance, the competitive battle among Wal-Mart, Target, and Sears/Kmart (Kmart acquired Sears in 2005) is more intense (with consequently smaller profit margins) than the rivalry among Gucci, Chanel, Fendi, and other high-end fashion retailers. Likewise, industry driving forces may be acting to grow the demand for the products of firms in some strategic groups and shrink the demand for the products of firms in other strategic groups—as is the case in the radio broadcasting industry where satellite radio firms like XM and Sirius stand to gain market ground at the expense of commercial-based radio broadcasters due to the impacts of such driving forces as technological advances in satellite broadcasting, growing buyer preferences for more diverse radio programming, and product innovation in satellite radio devices. Firms in strategic groups that are being adversely impacted by intense competitive pressures or driving forces may try to shift to a more favorably situated group. But shifting to a different position on the map can prove difficult when entry barriers for the target strategic group are high. Moreover, attempts to enter a new strategic group nearly always increase competitive pressures in the target strategic group. If certain firms are known to be trying to change their competitive positions on the map, then attaching arrows to the circles showing the targeted direction helps clarify the picture of competitive maneuvering among rivals.

Core Concept
Not all positions on a strategic group map are equally attractive.

2. *The profit potential of different strategic groups varies due to the strengths and weaknesses in each group's market position.* The profit prospects of firms in different strategic groups can vary from good to ho-hum to poor because of differing growth rates for the principal buyer segments served by each group, differing degrees of competitive rivalry within strategic groups, differing degrees of exposure to competition from substitute products outside the industry, and differing degrees of supplier or customer bargaining power from group to group.

Thus, part of strategic group map analysis always entails drawing conclusions about where on the map is the "best" place to be and why. Which companies/strategic groups are destined to prosper because of their positions? Which companies/strategic groups seem destined to struggle because of their positions? What accounts for why some parts of the map are better than others?

QUESTION 5: WHAT STRATEGIC MOVES ARE RIVALS LIKELY TO MAKE NEXT?

Unless a company pays attention to what competitors are doing and knows their strengths and weaknesses, it ends up flying blind into competitive battle. As in sports, scouting the opposition is essential. *Competitive intelligence* about rivals' strategies, their latest actions and announcements, their resource strengths and weaknesses, the efforts being made to improve their situation, and the thinking and leadership styles of their executives is valuable for predicting or anticipating the strategic moves competitors are likely to make next in the marketplace. Having good information to predict the strategic direction and likely moves of key competitors allows a company to prepare defensive countermoves, to craft its own strategic moves with some confidence about what market maneuvers to expect from rivals, and to exploit any openings that arise from competitors' missteps or strategy flaws.

> Good scouting reports on rivals provide a valuable assist in anticipating what moves rivals are likely to make next and outmaneuvering them in the marketplace.

Identifying Competitors' Strategies and Resource Strengths and Weaknesses

Keeping close tabs on a competitor's strategy entails monitoring what the rival is doing in the marketplace, what its management is saying in company press releases, information posted on the company's Web site (especially press releases and the presentations management has recently made to securities analysts), and such public documents as annual reports and 10-K filings, articles in the business media, and the reports of securities analysts. (Figure 1.1 in Chapter 1 indicates what to look for in identifying a company's strategy.) Company personnel may be able to pick up useful information from a rival's exhibits at trade shows and from conversations with a rival's customers, suppliers, and former employees.[20] Many companies have a competitive intelligence unit that sifts through the available information to construct up-to-date strategic profiles of rivals—their current strategies, resource strengths and competitive capabilities, competitive shortcomings, press releases, and recent executive pronouncements. Such profiles are typically updated regularly and made available to managers and other key personnel.

Those who gather competitive intelligence on rivals, however, can sometimes cross the fine line between honest inquiry and unethical or even illegal behavior. For example, calling rivals to get information about prices, the dates of new product introductions, or wage and salary levels is legal, but misrepresenting one's company affiliation during such calls is unethical. Pumping rivals' representatives at trade shows is ethical only if one wears a name tag with accurate company affiliation indicated. Avon Products at one point secured information about its biggest rival, Mary Kay Cosmetics (MKC), by having its personnel search through the garbage bins outside MKC's headquarters.[21] When MKC officials learned of the action and sued, Avon claimed it did nothing illegal, since a 1988 Supreme Court case had ruled that trash left on public property (in this case, a sidewalk) was anyone's for the taking. Avon even produced a videotape of its removal of the trash at the MKC site. Avon won the lawsuit—but Avon's action, while legal, scarcely qualifies as ethical.

In sizing up competitors, it makes sense for company strategists to make three assessments:

1. Which competitor has the best strategy? Which competitors appear to have flawed or weak strategies?

2. Which competitors are poised to gain market share, and which ones seem destined to lose ground?

3. Which competitors are likely to rank among the industry leaders five years from now? Do one or more up-and-coming competitors have powerful strategies and sufficient resource capabilities to overtake the current industry leader?

The industry's *current* major players are generally easy to identify, but some of the leaders may be plagued with weaknesses that are causing them to lose ground; other notable rivals may lack the resources and capabilities to remain strong contenders given the superior strategies and capabilities of up-and-coming companies. In evaluating which competitors are favorably or unfavorably positioned to gain market ground, company strategists need to focus on why there is potential for some rivals to do better or worse than other rivals. Usually, a competitor's prospects are a function of

> Today's market leaders don't automatically become tomorrow's.

whether it is in a strategic group that is being favored or hurt by competitive pressures and driving forces, whether its strategy has resulted in competitive advantage or disadvantage, and whether its resources and capabilities are well suited for competing on the road ahead.

Predicting Competitors' Next Moves

Predicting the next strategic moves of competitors is the hardest yet most useful part of competitor analysis. Good clues about what actions a specific company is likely to undertake can often be gleaned from how well it is faring in the marketplace, the problems or weaknesses it needs to address, and how much pressure it is under to improve its financial performance. Content rivals are likely to continue their present strategy with only minor fine-tuning. Ailing rivals can be performing so poorly that fresh strategic moves are virtually certain. Ambitious rivals looking to move up in the industry ranks are strong candidates for launching new strategic offensives to pursue emerging market opportunities and exploit the vulnerabilities of weaker rivals.

Since the moves a competitor is likely to make are generally predicated on the views their executives have about the industry's future and their beliefs about their firm's situation, it makes sense to closely scrutinize the public pronouncements of rival company executives about where the industry is headed and what it will take to be successful, what they are saying about their firm's situation, information from the grapevine about what they are doing, and their past actions and leadership styles. Other considerations in trying to predict what strategic moves rivals are likely to make next include the following:

- Which rivals badly need to increase their unit sales and market share? What strategic options are they most likely to pursue: lowering prices, adding new models and styles, expanding their dealer networks, entering additional geographic markets, boosting advertising to build better brand-name awareness, acquiring a weaker competitor, or placing more emphasis on direct sales via their Web site?

- Which rivals have a strong incentive, along with the resources, to make major strategic changes, perhaps moving to a different position on the strategic group map? Which rivals are probably locked in to pursuing the same basic strategy with only minor adjustments?

- Which rivals are good candidates to be acquired? Which rivals may be looking to make an acquisition and are financially able to do so?

- Which rivals are likely to enter new geographic markets?
- Which rivals are strong candidates to expand their product offerings and enter new product segments where they do not currently have a presence?

To succeed in predicting a competitor's next moves, company strategists need to have a good feel for each rival's situation, how its managers think, and what the rival's best strategic options are. Doing the necessary detective work can be tedious and time-consuming, but scouting competitors well enough to anticipate their next moves allows managers to prepare effective countermoves (perhaps even beat a rival to the punch) and to take rivals' probable actions into account in crafting their own best course of action.

> Managers who fail to study competitors closely risk being caught napping when rivals make fresh and perhaps bold strategic moves.

QUESTION 6: WHAT ARE THE KEY FACTORS FOR FUTURE COMPETITIVE SUCCESS?

An industry's **key success factors (KSFs)** are those competitive factors that most affect industry members' ability to prosper in the marketplace—the particular strategy elements, product attributes, resources, competencies, competitive capabilities, and market achievements that spell the difference between being a strong competitor and a weak competitor—and sometimes between profit and loss. KSFs by their very nature are so important to future competitive success that *all firms* in the industry must pay close attention to them or risk becoming an industry also-ran. To indicate the significance of KSFs another way, how well a company's product offering, resources, and capabilities measure up against an industry's KSFs determines just how financially and competitively successful that company will be. Identifying KSFs, in light of the prevailing and anticipated industry and competitive conditions, is therefore always a top-priority analytical and strategy-making consideration. Company strategists need to understand the industry landscape well enough to separate the factors most important to competitive success from those that are less important.

> **Core Concept**
> **Key success factors** are the product attributes, competencies, competitive capabilities, and market achievements with the greatest impact on future competitive success in the marketplace.

In the beer industry, the KSFs are full utilization of brewing capacity (to keep manufacturing costs low), a strong network of wholesale distributors (to get the company's brand stocked and favorably displayed in retail outlets where beer is sold), and clever advertising (to induce beer drinkers to buy the company's brand and thereby pull beer sales through the established wholesale/retail channels). In apparel manufacturing, the KSFs are appealing designs and color combinations (to create buyer interest) and low-cost manufacturing efficiency (to permit attractive retail pricing and ample profit margins). In tin and aluminum cans, because the cost of shipping empty cans is substantial, one of the keys is having can-manufacturing facilities located close to end-use customers. Key success factors thus vary from industry to industry, and even from time to time within the same industry, as driving forces and competitive conditions change. Table 3.3 lists the most common types of industry key success factors.

An industry's key success factors can usually be deduced from what was learned from the previously described analysis of the industry and competitive environment. Which factors are most important to future competitive success flow directly from the industry's dominant characteristics, what competition is like, the impacts of the driving forces, the comparative market positions of industry members, and the likely

Table 3.3 **Common Types of Industry Key Success Factors**

Technology-related KSFs	• Expertise in a particular technology or in scientific research (important in pharmaceuticals, Internet applications, mobile communications, and most high-tech industries) • Proven ability to improve production processes (important in industries where advancing technology opens the way for higher manufacturing efficiency and lower production costs)
Manufacturing-related KSFs	• Ability to achieve scale economies and/or capture learning/experience curve effects (important to achieving low production costs) • Quality control know-how (important in industries where customers insist on product reliability) • High utilization of fixed assets (important in capital-intensive, high-fixed-cost industries) • Access to attractive supplies of skilled labor • High labor productivity (important for items with high labor content) • Low-cost product design and engineering (reduces manufacturing costs) • Ability to manufacture or assemble products that are customized to buyer specifications
Distribution-related KSFs	• A strong network of wholesale distributors/dealers • Strong direct sales capabilities via the Internet and/or having company-owned retail outlets • Ability to secure favorable display space on retailer shelves
Marketing-related KSFs	• Breadth of product line and product selection • A well-known and well-respected brand name • Fast, accurate technical assistance • Courteous, personalized customer service • Accurate filling of buyer orders (few back orders or mistakes) • Customer guarantees and warranties (important in mail-order and online retailing, big-ticket purchases, new product introductions) • Clever advertising
Skills and capability-related KSFs	• A talented workforce (important in professional services like accounting and investment banking) • National or global distribution capabilities • Product innovation capabilities (important in industries where rivals are racing to be first-to-market with new product attributes or performance features) • Design expertise (important in fashion and apparel industries) • Short delivery time capability • Supply chain management capabilities • Strong e-commerce capabilities—a user-friendly Web site and/or skills in using Internet technology applications to streamline internal operations
Other types of KSFs	• Overall low costs (not just in manufacturing) so as to be able to meet customer expectations of low price • Convenient locations (important in many retailing businesses) • Ability to provide fast, convenient after-the-sale repairs and service • A strong balance sheet and access to financial capital (important in newly emerging industries with high degrees of business risk and in capital-intensive industries) • Patent protection

next moves of key rivals. In addition, the answers to three questions help identify an industry's key success factors:

1. On what basis do buyers of the industry's product choose between the competing brands of sellers? That is, what product attributes are crucial?
2. Given the nature of competitive rivalry and the competitive forces prevailing in the marketplace, what resources and competitive capabilities does a company need to have to be competitively successful?
3. What shortcomings are almost certain to put a company at a significant competitive disadvantage?

Only rarely are there more than five or six key factors for future competitive success. And even among these, two or three usually outrank the others in importance. Managers should therefore bear in mind the purpose of identifying key success factors—to determine which factors are most important to future competitive success—and resist the temptation to label a factor that has only minor importance a KSF. To compile a list of every factor that matters even a little bit defeats the purpose of concentrating management attention on the factors truly critical to long-term competitive success.

Correctly diagnosing an industry's KSFs raises a company's chances of crafting a sound strategy. The goal of company strategists should be to design a strategy aimed at stacking up well on all of the industry's future KSFs and trying to be *distinctively better* than rivals on one (or possibly two) of the KSFs. Indeed, companies that stand out or excel on a particular KSF are likely to enjoy a stronger market position—*being distinctively better than rivals on one or two key success factors tends to translate into competitive advantage.* Hence, using the industry's KSFs as *cornerstones* for the company's strategy and trying to gain sustainable competitive advantage by excelling at one particular KSF is a fruitful competitive strategy approach.[22]

> **Core Concept**
> A sound strategy incorporates the intent to stack up well on all of the industry's key success factors and to excel on one or two KSFs.

QUESTION 7: DOES THE OUTLOOK FOR THE INDUSTRY PRESENT THE COMPANY WITH AN ATTRACTIVE OPPORTUNITY?

The final step in evaluating the industry and competitive environment is to use the preceding analysis to decide whether the outlook for the industry presents the company with a sufficiently attractive business opportunity. The important factors on which to base such a conclusion include:

*   The industry's growth potential.
*   Whether powerful competitive forces are squeezing industry profitability to subpar levels and whether competition appears destined to grow stronger or weaker.
*   Whether industry profitability will be favorably or unfavorably affected by the prevailing driving forces.
*   The degrees of risk and uncertainty in the industry's future.
*   Whether the industry as a whole confronts severe problems—regulatory or environmental issues, stagnating buyer demand, industry overcapacity, mounting competition, and so on.

- The company's competitive position in the industry vis-à-vis rivals. (Being a well-entrenched leader or strongly positioned contender in a lackluster industry may present adequate opportunity for good profitability; however, having to fight a steep uphill battle against much stronger rivals may hold little promise of eventual market success or good return on shareholder investment, even though the industry environment is attractive.)

- The company's potential to capitalize on the vulnerabilities of weaker rivals, perhaps converting a relatively unattractive *industry* situation into a potentially rewarding *company* opportunity.

- Whether the company has sufficient competitive strength to defend against or counteract the factors that make the industry unattractive.

- Whether continued participation in this industry adds importantly to the firm's ability to be successful in other industries in which it may have business interests.

> **Core Concept**
> The degree to which an industry is attractive or unattractive is not the same for all industry participants and all potential entrants; the attractiveness of the opportunities an industry presents depends heavily on whether a company has the resource strengths and competitive capabilities to capture them.

As a general proposition, *if an industry's overall profit prospects are above average, the industry environment is basically attractive; if industry profit prospects are below average, conditions are unattractive.* However, it is a mistake to think of a particular industry as being equally attractive or unattractive to all industry participants and all potential entrants. Attractiveness is relative, not absolute, and conclusions one way or the other have to be drawn from the perspective of a particular company. Industries attractive to insiders may be unattractive to outsiders. Companies on the outside may look at an industry's environment and conclude that it is an unattractive business for them to get into, given the prevailing entry barriers, the difficulty of challenging current market leaders with their particular resources and competencies, and the opportunities they have elsewhere. Industry environments unattractive to weak competitors may be attractive to strong competitors. A favorably positioned company may survey a business environment and see a host of opportunities that weak competitors cannot capture.

When a company decides an industry is fundamentally attractive and presents good opportunities, a strong case can be made that it should invest aggressively to capture the opportunities it sees and to improve its long-term competitive position in the business. When a strong competitor concludes an industry is relatively unattractive and lacking in opportunity, it may elect to simply protect its present position, investing cautiously if at all and looking for opportunities in other industries. A competitively weak company in an unattractive industry may see its best option as finding a buyer, perhaps a rival, to acquire its business.

Key Points

Thinking strategically about a company's external situation involves probing for answers to the following seven questions:

1. *What are the industry's dominant economic features?* Industries differ significantly on such factors as market size and growth rate, the number and relative sizes of both buyers and sellers, the geographic scope of competitive rivalry, the degree of product differentiation, the speed of product innovation, demand–supply conditions, the extent of vertical integration, and the extent of scale economies and learning-curve effects. In addition to setting the stage for the analysis to come,

identifying an industry's economic features also promotes understanding of the kinds of strategic moves that industry members are likely to employ.

2. *What kinds of competitive forces are industry members facing, and how strong is each force?* The strength of competition is a composite of five forces: (1) competitive pressures stemming from the competitive jockeying and market maneuvering among industry rivals, (2) competitive pressures associated with the market inroads being made by the sellers of substitutes, (3) competitive pressures associated with the threat of new entrants into the market, (4) competitive pressures stemming from supplier bargaining power and supplier–seller collaboration, and (5) competitive pressures stemming from buyer bargaining power and seller–buyer collaboration. The nature and strength of the competitive pressures associated with these five forces have to be examined force by force to identify the specific competitive pressures they each comprise and to decide whether these pressures constitute a strong or weak competitive force. The next step in competition analysis is to evaluate the collective strength of the five forces and determine whether the state of competition is conducive to good profitability. Working through the five-forces model step by step not only aids strategy makers in assessing whether the intensity of competition allows good profitability but also promotes sound strategic thinking about how to better match company strategy to the specific competitive character of the marketplace. Effectively matching a company's strategy to the particular competitive pressures and competitive conditions that exist has two aspects: (1) pursuing avenues that shield the firm from as many of the prevailing competitive pressures as possible, and (2) initiating actions calculated to produce sustainable competitive advantage, thereby shifting competition in the company's favor, putting added competitive pressure on rivals, and perhaps even defining the business model for the industry.

3. *What factors are driving industry change and what impact will they have on competitive intensity and industry profitability?* Industry and competitive conditions change because forces are in motion that create incentives or pressures for change. The first phase is to identify the forces that are driving change in the industry; the most common driving forces include the Internet and Internet technology applications, globalization of competition in the industry, changes in the long-term industry growth rate, changes in buyer composition, product innovation, entry or exit of major firms, changes in cost and efficiency, changing buyer preferences for standardized versus differentiated products or services, regulatory influences and government policy changes, changing societal and lifestyle factors, and reductions in uncertainty and business risk. The second phase of driving-forces analysis is to determine whether the driving forces, taken together, are acting to make the industry environment more or less attractive. Are the driving forces causing demand for the industry's product to increase or decrease? Are the driving forces acting to make competition more or less intense? Will the driving forces lead to higher or lower industry profitability?

4. *What market positions do industry rivals occupy—who is strongly positioned and who is not?* Strategic group mapping is a valuable tool for understanding the similarities, differences, strengths, and weaknesses inherent in the market positions of rival companies. Rivals in the same or nearby strategic groups are close competitors, whereas companies in distant strategic groups usually pose little or no immediate threat. The lesson of strategic group mapping is that some positions on the map are more favorable than others. The profit potential of different strategic groups varies due to strengths and weaknesses in each group's market

position. Often, industry driving forces and competitive pressures favor some strategic groups and hurt others.

5. *What strategic moves are rivals likely to make next?* This analytical step involves identifying competitors' strategies, deciding which rivals are likely to be strong contenders and which are likely to be weak, evaluating rivals' competitive options, and predicting their next moves. Scouting competitors well enough to anticipate their actions can help a company prepare effective countermoves (perhaps even beating a rival to the punch) and allows managers to take rivals' probable actions into account in designing their own company's best course of action. Managers who fail to study competitors risk being caught unprepared by the strategic moves of rivals.

6. *What are the key factors for future competitive success?* An industry's key success factors (KSFs) are the particular strategy elements, product attributes, competitive capabilities, and business outcomes that spell the difference between being a strong competitor and a weak competitor—and sometimes between profit and loss. KSFs by their very nature are so important to competitive success that *all firms* in the industry must pay close attention to them or risk becoming an industry also-ran. Correctly diagnosing an industry's KSFs raises a company's chances of crafting a sound strategy. The goal of company strategists should be to design a strategy aimed at stacking up well on all of the industry KSFs and trying to be *distinctively better* than rivals on one (or possibly two) of the KSFs. Indeed, using the industry's KSFs as *cornerstones* for the company's strategy and trying to gain sustainable competitive advantage by excelling at one particular KSF is a fruitful competitive strategy approach.

7. *Does the outlook for the industry present the company with sufficiently attractive prospects for profitability?* If an industry's overall profit prospects are above average, the industry environment is basically attractive; if industry profit prospects are below average, conditions are unattractive. Conclusions regarding industry attractive are a major driver of company strategy. When a company decides an industry is fundamentally attractive and presents good opportunities, a strong case can be made that it should invest aggressively to capture the opportunities it sees and to improve its long-term competitive position in the business. When a strong competitor concludes an industry is relatively unattractive and lacking in opportunity, it may elect to simply protect its present position, investing cautiously if at all and looking for opportunities in other industries. A competitively weak company in an unattractive industry may see its best option as finding a buyer, perhaps a rival, to acquire its business. On occasion, an industry that is unattractive overall is still very attractive to a favorably situated company with the skills and resources to take business away from weaker rivals.

A competently conducted industry and competitive analysis generally tells a clear, easily understood story about the company's external environment. Different analysts can have varying judgments about competitive intensity, the impacts of driving forces, how industry conditions will evolve, how good the outlook is for industry profitability, and the degree to which the industry environment offers the company an attractive business opportunity. However, while no method can guarantee that all analysts will come to identical conclusions about the state of industry and competitive conditions and an industry's future outlook, this doesn't justify shortcutting hardnosed strategic analysis and relying instead on opinion and casual observation. Managers become better strategists when they know what questions to pose and what tools to use. This is why this chapter has concentrated on suggesting the right questions to ask, explaining concepts and analytical approaches, and indicating the kinds of things to look for. There's no substitute for doing cutting edge strategic thinking about a company's external situation—anything less weakens managers' ability to craft strategies that are well matched to industry and competitive conditions.

Exercises

1. As the owner of a fast-food enterprise seeking a loan from a bank to finance the construction and operation of three new store locations, you have been asked to provide the loan officer with a brief analysis of the competitive environment in fast food. Draw a five-forces diagram for the fast-food industry, and briefly discuss the nature and strength of each of the five competitive forces in fast food. Do whatever Internet research is required to expand your understanding of competition in the fast-food industry and do a competent five-forces analysis.

2. Based on the strategic group map in Illustration Capsule 3.1: Who are Polo Ralph Lauren's closest competitors? Between which two strategic groups is competition the strongest? Why do you think no retailers are positioned in the upper right-hand corner of the map? Which company/strategic group faces the weakest competition from the members of other strategic groups?

3. With regard to the ice cream industry, which of the following factors might qualify as possible driving forces capable of causing fundamental change in the industry's structure and competitive environment?

    a. Increasing sales of frozen yogurt and frozen sorbets.

    b. The potential for additional makers of ice cream to enter the market.

    c. Growing consumer interest in low-calorie/low-fat/low-carb/sugar-free dessert alternatives.

    d. A slowdown in consumer purchases of ice cream products.

    e. Rising prices for milk, sugar, and other ice cream ingredients.

    f. A decision by Häagen-Dazs to increase its prices by 10 percent.

    g. A decision by Ben & Jerry's to add five new flavors to its product line.

Evaluating a Company's Resources and Competitive Position

Before executives can chart a new strategy, they must reach common understanding of the company's current position.

—W. Chan Kim and Rene Mauborgne

The real question isn't how well you're doing today against your own history, but how you're doing against your competitors.

—Donald Kress

Organizations succeed in a competitive marketplace over the long run because they can do certain things their customers value better than can their competitors.

—Robert Hayes, Gary Pisano, and David Upton

Only firms who are able to continually build new strategic assets faster and cheaper than their competitors will earn superior returns over the long term.

—C. C. Markides and P. J. Williamson

I n Chapter 3 we described how to use the tools of industry and competitive analysis to assess a company's external environment and lay the groundwork for matching a company's strategy to its external situation. In this chapter we discuss the techniques of evaluating a company's resource capabilities, relative cost position, and competitive strength vis-á-vis its rivals. The analytical spotlight will be trained on five questions:

1. How well is the company's present strategy working?

2. What are the company's resource strengths and weaknesses, and its external opportunities and threats?

3. Are the company's prices and costs competitive?

4. Is the company competitively stronger or weaker than key rivals?

5. What strategic issues and problems merit front-burner managerial attention?

We will describe four analytical tools that should be used to probe for answers to these questions—SWOT analysis, value chain analysis, benchmarking, and competitive strength assessment. All four are valuable techniques for revealing a company's competitiveness and for helping company managers match their strategy to the company's own particular circumstances.

QUESTION 1: HOW WELL IS THE COMPANY'S PRESENT STRATEGY WORKING?

In evaluating how well a company's present strategy is working, a manager has to start with what the strategy is. Figure 4.1 shows the key components of a single-business company's strategy. The first thing to pin down is the company's competitive approach. Is the company striving to be a low-cost leader *or* stressing ways to differentiate its product offering from rivals? Is it concentrating its efforts on serving a broad spectrum of customers *or* a narrow market niche? Another strategy-defining consideration is the firm's competitive scope within the industry—what its geographic market coverage is and whether it operates in just a single stage of the industry's production/distribution chain or is vertically integrated across several stages. Another good indication of the company's strategy is whether the company has made moves recently to improve its competitive position and performance—for instance, by cutting prices, improving design, stepping up advertising, entering a new geographic market (domestic or foreign),

Figure 4.1 **Identifying the Components of a Single-Business Company's Strategy**

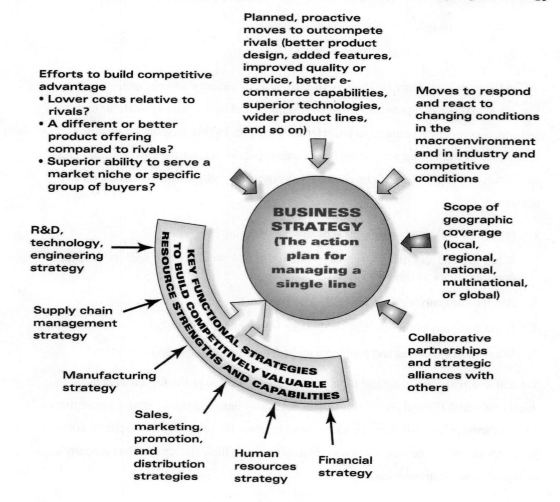

or merging with a competitor. The company's functional strategies in R&D, production, marketing, finance, human resources, information technology, and so on further characterize company strategy.

While there's merit in evaluating the strategy from a *qualitative* standpoint (its completeness, internal consistency, rationale, and relevance), the best *quantitative* evidence of how well a company's strategy is working comes from its results. The two best empirical indicators are (1) whether the company is achieving its stated financial and strategic objectives, and (2) whether the company is an above-average industry performer. Persistent shortfalls in meeting company performance targets and weak performance relative to rivals are reliable warning signs that the company suffers from poor strategy making, less-than-competent strategy execution, or both. Other indicators of how well a company's strategy is working include:

- Whether the firm's sales are growing faster, slower, or about the same pace as the market as a whole, thus resulting in a rising, eroding, or stable market share.

- Whether the company is acquiring new customers at an attractive rate as well as retaining existing customers.
- Whether the firm's profit margins are increasing or decreasing and how well its margins compare to rival firms' margins.
- Trends in the firm's net profits and return on investment and how these compare to the same trends for other companies in the industry.
- Whether the company's overall financial strength and credit rating are improving or on the decline.
- Whether the company can demonstrate continuous improvement in such internal performance measures as days of inventory, employee productivity, unit cost, defect rate, scrap rate, misfilled orders, delivery times, warranty costs, and so on.
- How shareholders view the company based on trends in the company's stock price and shareholder value (relative to the stock price trends at other companies in the industry).
- The firm's image and reputation with its customers.
- How well the company stacks up against rivals on technology, product innovation, customer service, product quality, delivery time, price, getting newly developed products to market quickly, and other relevant factors on which buyers base their choice of brands.

The stronger a company's current overall performance, the less likely the need for radical changes in strategy. The weaker a company's financial performance and market standing, the more its current strategy must be questioned. Weak performance is almost always a sign of weak strategy, weak execution, or both.

> The stronger a company's financial performance and market position, the more likely it has a well-conceived, well-executed strategy.

Table 4.1 provides a compilation of the financial ratios most commonly used to evaluate a company's financial performance and balance sheet strength.

QUESTION 2: WHAT ARE THE COMPANY'S RESOURCE STRENGTHS AND WEAKNESSES AND ITS EXTERNAL OPPORTUNITIES AND THREATS?

Appraising a company's resource strengths and weaknesses and its external opportunities and threats, commonly known as **SWOT analysis,** provides a good overview of whether the company's overall situation is fundamentally healthy or unhealthy. Just as important, a first-rate SWOT analysis provides the basis for crafting a strategy that capitalizes on the company's resources, aims squarely at capturing the company's best opportunities, and defends against the threats to its well-being.

> **Core Concept**
> **SWOT analysis** is a simple but powerful tool for sizing up a company's resource capabilities and deficiencies, its market opportunities, and the external threats to its future well-being.

Identifying Company Resource Strengths and Competitive Capabilities

A *resource strength* is something a company is good at doing or an attribute that enhances its competitiveness in the marketplace. Resource strengths can take any of several forms:

Table 4.1 **Key Financial Ratios: How to Calculate Them and What They Mean**

Ratio	How Calculated	What It Shows
Profitability ratios		
1. Gross profit margin	$$\frac{\text{Sales} - \text{Cost of goods sold}}{\text{Sales}}$$	Shows the percentage of revenues available to cover operating expenses and yield a profit. Higher is better, and the trend should be upward.
2. Operating profit margin (or return on sales)	$$\frac{\text{Sales} - \text{Operating expenses}}{\text{Sales}}$$ or $$\frac{\text{Operating income}}{\text{Sales}}$$	Shows the profitability of current operations without regard to interest charges and income taxes. Higher is better, and the trend should be upward.
3. Net profit margin (or net return on sales)	$$\frac{\text{Profits after taxes}}{\text{Sales}}$$	Shows after-tax profits per dollar of sales. Higher is better, and the trend should be upward.
4. Return on total assets	$$\frac{\text{Profits after taxes} + \text{Interest}}{\text{Total assets}}$$	A measure of the return on total investment in the enterprise. Interest is added to after-tax profits to form the numerator since total assets are financed by creditors as well as by stockholders. Higher is better, and the trend should be upward.
5. Return on stockholders' equity	$$\frac{\text{Profits after taxes}}{\text{Total stockholders' equity}}$$	Shows the return stockholders are earning on their investment in the enterprise. A return in the 12–15 percent range is "average," and the trend should be upward.
6. Earnings per share	$$\frac{\text{Profits after taxes}}{\text{Number of shares of common stock outstanding}}$$	Shows the earnings for each share of common stock outstanding. The trend should be upward, and the bigger the annual percentage gains, the better.
Liquidity ratios		
1. Current ratio	$$\frac{\text{Current assets}}{\text{Current liabilities}}$$	Shows a firm's ability to pay current liabilities using assets that can be converted to cash in the near term. Ratio should definitely be higher than 1.0; ratios of 2 or higher are better still.
2. Quick ratio (or acid-test ratio)	$$\frac{\text{Current assets} - \text{Inventory}}{\text{Current liabilities}}$$	Shows a firm's ability to pay current liabilities without relying on the sale of its inventories.
3. Working capital	Current assets – Current liabilities	Bigger amounts are better because the company has more internal funds available to (1) pay its current liabilities on a timely basis and (2) finance inventory expansion, additional accounts receivable, and a larger base of operations without resorting to borrowing or raising more equity capital.
Leverage ratios		
1. Debt-to-assets ratio	$$\frac{\text{Total debt}}{\text{Total assets}}$$	Measures the extent to which borrowed funds have been used to finance the firm's operations. Low fractions or ratios are better—high fractions indicate overuse of debt and greater risk of bankruptcy.

(*Continued*)

Table 4.1 **Continued**

Ratio	How Calculated	What It Shows
2. Debt-to-equity ratio	$\dfrac{\text{Total debt}}{\text{Total stockholders' equity}}$	Should usually be less than 1.0. High ratios (especially above 1.0) signal excessive debt, lower creditworthiness, and weaker balance sheet strength.
3. Long-term debt-to-equity ratio	$\dfrac{\text{Long-term debt}}{\text{Total stockholders' equity}}$	Shows the balance between debt and equity in the firm's *long-term* capital structure. Low ratios indicate greater capacity to borrow additional funds if needed.
4. Times-interest-earned (or coverage) ratio	$\dfrac{\text{Operating income}}{\text{Interest expenses}}$	Measures the ability to pay annual interest charges. Lenders usually insist on a minimum ratio of 2.0, but ratios above 3.0 signal better creditworthiness.
Activity ratios		
1. Days of inventory	$\dfrac{\text{Inventory}}{\text{Cost of goods sold} \div 365}$	Measures inventory management efficiency. Fewer days of inventory are usually better.
2. Inventory turnover	$\dfrac{\text{Cost of goods sold}}{\text{Inventory}}$	Measures the number of inventory turns per year. Higher is better.
3. Average collection period	$\dfrac{\text{Accounts receivable}}{\text{Total sales} \div 365}$ or $\dfrac{\text{Accounts receivable}}{\text{Average daily sales}}$	Indicates the average length of time the firm must wait after making a sale to receive cash payment. A shorter collection time is better.
Other important measures of financial performance		
1. Dividend yield on common stock	$\dfrac{\text{Annual dividends per share}}{\text{Current market price per share}}$	A measure of the return that shareholders receive in the form of dividends. A "typical" dividend yield is 2–3%. The dividend yield for fast-growth companies is often below 1% (may be even 0); the dividend yield for slow-growth companies can run 4–5%.
2. Price/earnings ratio	$\dfrac{\text{Current market price per share}}{\text{Earnings per share}}$	P/E ratios above 20 indicate strong investor confidence in a firm's outlook and earnings growth; firms whose future earnings are at risk or likely to grow slowly typically have ratios below 12.
3. Dividend payout ratio	$\dfrac{\text{Annual dividends per share}}{\text{Earnings per share}}$	Indicates the percentage of after-tax profits paid out as dividends.
4. Internal cash flow	After tax profits + Depreciation	A quick and rough estimate of the cash a company's business is generating after payment of operating expenses, interest, and taxes. Such amounts can be used for dividend payments or funding capital expenditures.

- *A skill, specialized expertise, or competitively important capability*—skills in low-cost operations, technological expertise, expertise in defect-free manufacture, proven capabilities in developing and introducing innovative products, cutting-edge supply chain management capabilities, expertise in getting new products to market quickly, strong e-commerce expertise, expertise in providing consistently good customer service, excellent mass merchandising skills, or unique advertising and promotional talents.

- *Valuable physical assets*—state-of-the-art plants and equipment, attractive real estate locations, worldwide distribution facilities, or ownership of valuable natural resource deposits.

- *Valuable human assets and intellectual capital*—an experienced and capable workforce, talented employees in key areas, cutting-edge knowledge in technology or other important areas of the business, collective learning embedded in the organization and built up over time, or proven managerial know-how.[1]

- *Valuable organizational assets*—proven quality control systems, proprietary technology, key patents, state-of-the-art systems for doing business via the Internet, ownership of important natural resources, a cadre of highly trained customer service representatives, a strong network of distributors or retail dealers, sizable amounts of cash and marketable securities, a strong balance sheet and credit rating (thus giving the company access to additional financial capital), or a comprehensive list of customers' e-mail addresses.

- *Valuable intangible assets*—a powerful or well-known brand name, a reputation for technological leadership, or strong buyer loyalty and goodwill.

- *An achievement or attribute that puts the company in a position of market advantage*—low overall costs relative to competitors, market share leadership, a superior product, a wider product line than rivals, wide geographic coverage, or award-winning customer service.

- *Competitively valuable alliances or cooperative ventures*—fruitful partnerships with suppliers that reduce costs and/or enhance product quality and performance; alliances or joint ventures that provide access to valuable technologies, specialized know-how, or geographic markets.

> **Core Concept**
> A company's resource strengths represent *competitive assets* and are big determinants of its competitiveness and ability to succeed in the marketplace.

A company's resource strengths represent its endowment of *competitive assets*. The caliber of a firm's resource strengths is a big determinant of its competitiveness—whether it has the wherewithal to be a strong competitor in the marketplace or whether its capabilities and competitive strengths are modest, thus relegating it to a trailing position in the industry.[2] Plainly, a company's resource strengths may or may not enable it to improve its competitive position and financial performance.

Assessing a Company's Competencies and Capabilities—What Activities Does It Perform Well?

One of the most important aspects of appraising a company's resource strengths has to do with its competence level in performing key pieces of its business—such as supply chain management, research and development (R&D), production, distribution, sales and marketing, and customer service. Which activities does it perform especially well? And are there any activities it performs better than rivals? A company's proficiency in conducting different facets of its operations can range from merely a competence in performing an activity to a core competence to a distinctive competence:

1. A **competence** is something an organization is good at doing. It is nearly always the product of experience, representing an accumulation of learning and the buildup

of proficiency in performing an internal activity. Usually a company competence originates with deliberate efforts to develop the organizational ability to do something, however imperfectly or inefficiently. Such efforts involve selecting people with the requisite knowledge and skills, upgrading or expanding individual abilities as needed, and then molding the efforts and work products of individuals into a cooperative group effort to create organizational ability. Then, as experience builds, such that the company gains proficiency in performing the activity consistently well and at an acceptable cost, the ability evolves into a true competence and company capability. Some competencies relate to fairly specific skills and expertise (like just-in-time inventory control or low-cost manufacturing efficiency or picking locations for new stores or designing an unusually appealing and user-friendly Web site); they spring from proficiency in a single discipline or function and may be performed in a single department or organizational unit. Other competencies, however, are inherently multidisciplinary and cross-functional—they are the result of effective collaboration among people with different expertise working in different organizational units. A competence in continuous product innovation, for example, comes from teaming the efforts of people and groups with expertise in market research, new product R&D, design and engineering, cost-effective manufacturing, and market testing.

> **Core Concept**
> A *competence* is an activity that a company has learned to perform well.

2. A **core competence** is a proficiently performed internal activity that is *central* to a company's strategy and competitiveness. A core competence is a more valuable resource strength than a competence because of the well-performed activity's core role in the company's strategy and the contribution it makes to the company's success in the marketplace. A core competence can relate to any of several aspects of a company's business: expertise in integrating multiple technologies to create families of new products, know-how in creating and operating systems for cost-efficient supply chain management, the capability to speed new or next-generation products to market, good after-sale service capabilities, skills in manufacturing a high-quality product at a low cost, or the capability to fill customer orders accurately and swiftly. A company may have more than one core competence in its resource portfolio, but rare is the company that can legitimately claim more than two or three core competencies. Most often, *a core competence is knowledge-based, residing in people and in a company's intellectual capital and not in its assets on the balance sheet.* Moreover, a core competence is more likely to be grounded in cross-department combinations of knowledge and expertise rather than being the product of a single department or work group. 3M Corporation has a core competence in product innovation—its record of introducing new products goes back several decades and new product introduction is central to 3M's strategy of growing its business. Ben & Jerry's Homemade, a subsidiary of Unilever, has a core competence in creating unusual flavors of ice cream and marketing them with catchy names like Chunky Monkey, Wavy Gravy, Chubby Hubby, The Gobfather, Dublin Mudslide, and Marsha Marsha Marshmallow.

> **Core Concept**
> A *core competence* is a *competitively important* activity that a company performs better than other internal activities.

3. A **distinctive competence** is a competitively valuable activity that a company *performs better than its rivals.* A distinctive competence thus signifies even greater proficiency than a core competence. But what is especially important about a distinctive competence is that the company enjoys *competitive superiority*

> **Core Concept**
> A *distinctive competence* is a competitively important activity that a company performs better than its rivals—it thus represents *a competitively superior resource strength.*

in performing that activity—a distinctive competence represents a level of proficiency that rivals do not have. Because a distinctive competence represents uniquely strong capability relative to rival companies, it qualifies as a *competitively superior resource strength* with competitive advantage potential. This is particularly true when the distinctive competence enables a company to deliver standout value to customers (in the form of lower costs and prices or better product performance or superior service). Toyota has worked diligently over several decades to establish a distinctive competence in low-cost, high-quality manufacturing of motor vehicles; its "lean production" system is far superior to that of any other automaker's, and the company is pushing the boundaries of its production advantage with a new type of assembly line—called the Global Body line—that costs 50 percent less to install and can be changed to accommodate a new model for 70 percent less than its previous production system.[3] Starbucks' distinctive competence in innovative coffee drinks and store ambience has propelled it to the forefront among coffee retailers.

The conceptual differences between a competence, a core competence, and a distinctive competence draw attention to the fact that a company's resource strengths and competitive capabilities are not all equal.[4] Some competencies and competitive capabilities merely enable market survival because most rivals have them—indeed, not having a competence or capability that rivals have can result in competitive disadvantage. If an apparel company does not have the competence to produce its apparel items cost-efficiently, it is unlikely to survive given the intensely price-competitive nature of the apparel industry. Every Web retailer requires a basic competence in designing an appealing and user-friendly Web site.

Core competencies are *competitively* more important resource strengths than competencies because they add power to the company's strategy and have a bigger positive impact on its market position and profitability. Distinctive competencies are even more competitively important. A distinctive competence is a competitively potent resource strength for three reasons: (1) it gives a company competitively valuable capability that is unmatched by rivals, (2) it has potential for being the cornerstone of the company's strategy, and (3) it can produce a competitive edge in the marketplace since it represents a level of proficiency that is superior to rivals. It is always easier for a company to build competitive advantage when it has a distinctive competence in performing an activity important to market success, when rival companies do not have offsetting competencies, and when it is costly and time-consuming for rivals to imitate the competence. A distinctive competence is thus potentially the mainspring of a company's success—unless it is trumped by more powerful resources possessed by rivals.

> **Core Concept**
> A distinctive competence is a competitively potent resource strength for three reasons: (1) it gives a company competitively valuable capability that is unmatched by rivals, (2) it can underpin and add real punch to a company's strategy, and (3) it is a basis for sustainable competitive advantage.

What Is the Competitive Power of a Resource Strength?

It is not enough to simply compile a list of a company's resource strengths and competitive capabilities. What is most telling about a company's resource strengths, individually and collectively, is how powerful they are in the marketplace. The competitive power of a resource strength is measured by how many of the following four tests it can pass:[5]

1. *Is the resource strength hard to copy?* The more difficult and more expensive it is to imitate a company's resource strength, the greater its potential competitive

value. Resources tend to be difficult to copy when they are unique (a fantastic real estate location, patent protection), when they must be built over time in ways that are difficult to imitate (a brand name, mastery of a technology), and when they carry big capital requirements (a cost-effective plant to manufacture cutting-edge microprocessors). Wal-Mart's competitors have failed miserably in their attempts over the past two decades to match Wal-Mart's super-efficient state-of-the-art distribution capabilities. Hard-to-copy strengths and capabilities are valuable competitive assets, adding to a company's market strength and contributing to sustained profitability.

2. *Is the resource strength durable—does it have staying power?* The longer the competitive value of a resource lasts, the greater its value. Some resources lose their clout in the marketplace quickly because of the rapid speeds at which technologies or industry conditions are moving. The value of Eastman Kodak's resources in film and film processing is rapidly being undercut by the growing popularity of digital cameras. The investments that commercial banks have made in branch offices is a rapidly depreciating asset because of growing use of direct deposits, debit cards, automated teller machines, and telephone and Internet banking options.

3. *Is the resource really competitively superior?* Companies have to guard against pridefully believing that their core competencies are distinctive competencies or that their brand name is more powerful than the brand names of rivals. Who can really say whether Coca-Cola's consumer marketing prowess is better than Pepsi-Cola's or whether the Mercedes-Benz brand name is more powerful than that of BMW or Lexus? Although many retailers claim to be quite proficient in product selection and in-store merchandising, a number run into trouble in the marketplace because they encounter rivals whose competencies in product selection and in-store merchandising are better than theirs. Apple's operating system for its MacIntosh PCs is by most accounts a world beater (compared to Windows XP), but Apple has failed miserably in converting its resource strength in operating system design into competitive success in the global PC market—it is an also-ran with a paltry 2–3 percent market share worldwide.

4. *Can the resource strength be trumped by the different resource strengths and competitive capabilities of rivals?* Many commercial airlines have invested heavily in developing the resources and capabilities to offer passengers safe, reliable flights at convenient times, along with an array of in-flight amenities. However, Southwest Airlines and JetBlue in the United States and Ryanair and easyJet in Europe have been quite successful deploying their resources in ways that enable them to provide commercial air services at radically lower fares. Amazon.com's strengths in online retailing of books have put a big dent in the business prospects of brick-and-mortar bookstores. Whole Foods Market has a resource lineup that enables it to merchandise a dazzling array of natural and organic food products in a supermarket setting, thus putting strong competitive pressure on Kroger, Safeway, Albertson's, and other prominent supermarket chains. The prestigious brand names of Cadillac and Lincoln have faded because Mercedes, BMW, Audi, and Lexus have used their resources to design, produce, and market more appealing luxury vehicles.

The vast majority of companies are not well endowed with standout resource strengths, much less with one or more competitively superior resources (or distinctive competencies) capable of passing all four tests with high marks. Most firms have a mixed bag of resources—one or two quite valuable, some good, many satisfactory to mediocre.

Companies in the top tier of their industry may have as many as two core competencies in their resource strength lineup. But only a few companies, usually the strongest industry leaders or up-and-coming challengers, have a resource strength that truly qualifies as a distinctive competence. Even so, a company can still marshal the resource strengths to be competitively successful without having a competitively superior resource or distinctive competence. A company can achieve considerable competitive vitality, maybe even competitive advantage, from a collection of good-to-adequate resource strengths that collectively give it competitive power in the marketplace. A number of fast-food chains—for example, Wendy's, Taco Bell, and Subway—have achieved a respectable market position competing against McDonald's with satisfactory sets of resource strengths and no apparent distinctive competence. The same can be said for Lowe's, which competes against industry leader Home Depot, and such regional banks as Compass, State Street, Keybank, PNC, BB&T, and AmSouth, which increasingly find themselves in competition with the top five U.S. banks—JPMorgan Chase, Bank of America, Citibank, Wachovia, and Wells Fargo.

> **Core Concept**
> A company's ability to succeed in the marketplace hinges to a considerable extent on the competitive power of its resources—the set of competencies, capabilities, and competitive assets at its command.

Identifying Company Resource Weaknesses and Competitive Deficiencies

A *resource weakness*, or *competitive deficiency*, is something a company lacks or does poorly (in comparison to others) or a condition that puts it at a disadvantage in the marketplace. A company's resource weaknesses can relate to (1) inferior or unproven skills, expertise, or intellectual capital in competitively important areas of the business; (2) deficiencies in competitively important physical, organizational, or intangible assets; or (3) missing or competitively inferior capabilities in key areas. *Internal weaknesses are thus shortcomings in a company's complement of resources and represent competitive liabilities.* Nearly all companies have competitive liabilities of one kind or another. Whether a company's resource weaknesses make it competitively vulnerable depends on how much they matter in the marketplace and whether they are offset by the company's resource strengths.

> **Core Concept**
> A company's resource strengths represent competitive assets; its resource weaknesses represent competitive liabilities.

Table 4.2 lists the kinds of factors to consider in compiling a company's resource strengths and weaknesses. Sizing up a company's complement of resource capabilities and deficiencies is akin to constructing a *strategic balance sheet,* where resource strengths represent *competitive assets* and resource weaknesses represent *competitive liabilities.* Obviously, the ideal condition is for the company's competitive assets to outweigh its competitive liabilities by an ample margin—a 50–50 balance is definitely not the desired condition!

Identifying a Company's Market Opportunities

Market opportunity is a big factor in shaping a company's strategy. Indeed, managers can't properly tailor strategy to the company's situation without first identifying its market opportunities and appraising the growth and profit potential each one holds. Depending on the prevailing circumstances, a company's opportunities can be plentiful or scarce, fleeting or lasting, and can range from wildly attractive (an absolute "must" to pursue) to marginally interesting (because the growth and profit potential are questionable) to unsuitable (because there's not a good match with the company's

Table 4.2 **What to Look for in Identifying a Company's Strengths, Weaknesses, Opportunities, and Threats**

Potential Resource Strengths and Competitive Capabilities	Potential Resource Weaknesses and Competitive Deficiencies
• A powerful strategy	• No clear strategic direction
• Core competencies in _____	• Resources that are not well matched to industry key success factors
• A distinctive competence in _____	• No well-developed or proven core competencies
• A product that is strongly differentiated from those of rivals	• A weak balance sheet; burdened with too much debt
• Competencies and capabilities that are well matched to industry key success factors	• Higher overall unit costs relative to key competitors
• A strong financial condition; ample financial resources to grow the business	• Weak or unproven product innovation capabilities
• Strong brand-name image/company reputation	• A product/service with ho-hum attributes or features inferior to those of rivals
• An attractive customer base	• Too narrow a product line relative to rivals
• Economy of scale and/or learning/experience curve advantages over rivals	• Weak brand image or reputation
• Proprietary technology/superior technological skills/important patents	• Weaker dealer network than key rivals and/or lack of adequate global distribution capability
• Superior intellectual capital relative to key rivals	• Behind on product quality, R&D, and/or technological know-how
• Cost advantages over rivals	• In the wrong strategic group
• Strong advertising and promotion	• Losing market share because . . .
• Product innovation capabilities	• Lack of management depth
• Proven capabilities in improving production processes	• Inferior intellectual capital relative to leading rivals
• Good supply chain management capabilities	• Subpar profitability because . . .
• Good customer service capabilities	• Plagued with internal operating problems or obsolete facilities
• Better product quality relative to rivals	• Behind rivals in e-commerce capabilities
• Wide geographic coverage and/or strong global distribution capability	• Short on financial resources to grow the business and pursue promising initiatives
• Alliances/joint ventures with other firms that provide access to valuable technology, competencies, and/or attractive geographic markets	• Too much underutilized plant capacity

Potential Market Opportunities	Potential External Threats to a Company's Future Prospects
• Openings to win market share from rivals	• Increasing intensity of competition among industry rivals—may squeeze profit margins
• Sharply rising buyer demand for the industry's product	• Slowdowns in market growth
• Serving additional customer groups or market segments	• Likely entry of potent new competitors
• Expanding into new geographic markets	• Loss of sales to substitute products
• Expanding the company's product line to meet a broader range of customer needs	• Growing bargaining power of customers or suppliers
• Using existing company skills or technological know-how to enter new product lines or new businesses	• A shift in buyer needs and tastes away from the industry's product
• Online sales	• Adverse demographic changes that threaten to curtail demand for the industry's product
• Integrating forward or backward	• Vulnerability to unfavorable industry driving forces
• Falling trade barriers in attractive foreign markets	• Restrictive trade policies on the part of foreign governments
• Acquiring rival firms or companies with attractive technological expertise or capabilities	• Costly new regulatory requirements
• Entering into alliances or joint ventures to expand the firm's market coverage or boost its competitive capability	
• Openings to exploit emerging new technologies	

resource strengths and capabilities). A checklist of potential market opportunities is included in Table 4.2.

While stunningly big or "golden" opportunities appear fairly frequently in volatile, fast-changing markets (typically due to important technological developments or rapidly shifting consumer preferences), they are nonetheless hard to see before most all companies in the industry identify them. The more volatile and thus unpredictable market conditions are, the more limited a company's ability to do market reconnaissance and spot important opportunities much ahead of rivals—there are simply too many variables in play for managers to peer into the fog of the future, identify one or more upcoming opportunities, and get a jump on rivals in pursuing it.[6] In mature markets, unusually attractive market opportunities emerge sporadically, often after long periods of relative calm—but future market conditions may be less foggy, thus facilitating good market reconnaissance and making emerging opportunities easier for industry members to detect. But in both volatile and stable markets, the rise of a golden opportunity is almost never under the control of a single company or manufactured by company executives—rather, it springs from the simultaneous alignment of several external factors. For instance, in China the recent upsurge in demand for motor vehicles was spawned by a convergence of many factors—increased disposable income, rising middle-class aspirations, a major road-building program by the government, the demise of employer-provided housing, and easy credit.[7] But golden opportunities are nearly always seized rapidly—and the companies that seize them are usually those that have been actively waiting, staying alert with diligent market reconnaissance, and preparing themselves to capitalize on shifting market conditions by patiently assembling an arsenal of competitively valuable resources—talented personnel, technical know-how, strategic partnerships, and a war chest of cash to finance aggressive action when the time comes.[8]

> A company is well advised to pass on a particular market opportunity unless it has or can acquire the resources to capture it.

In evaluating a company's market opportunities and ranking their attractiveness, managers have to guard against viewing every *industry* opportunity as a *company* opportunity. Not every company is equipped with the resources to successfully pursue each opportunity that exists in its industry. Some companies are more capable of going after particular opportunities than others, and a few companies may be hopelessly outclassed. *The market opportunities most relevant to a company are those that match up well with the company's financial and organizational resource capabilities, offer the best growth and profitability, and present the most potential for competitive advantage.*

Identifying the External Threats to a Company's Future Profitability

Often, certain factors in a company's external environment pose *threats* to its profitability and competitive well-being. Threats can stem from the emergence of cheaper or better technologies, rivals' introduction of new or improved products, the entry of lower-cost foreign competitors into a company's market stronghold, new regulations that are more burdensome to a company than to its competitors, vulnerability to a rise in interest rates, the potential of a hostile takeover, unfavorable demographic shifts, adverse changes in foreign exchange rates, political upheaval in a foreign country where the company has facilities, and the like. A list of potential threats to a company's future profitability and market position is shown in Table 4.2.

External threats may pose no more than a moderate degree of adversity (all companies confront some threatening elements in the course of doing business), or they may be so imposing as to make a company's situation and outlook quite tenuous. On rare occasions, market shocks can give birth to a *sudden-death* threat that throws a company into an immediate crisis and battle to survive. Many of the world's major airlines have been plunged into unprecedented financial crisis by the perfect storm of the September 11, 2001, terrorist attacks, rising prices for jet fuel, mounting competition from low-fare carriers, shifting traveler preferences for low fares as opposed to lots of in-flight amenities, and out-of-control labor costs. It is management's job to identify the threats to the company's future prospects and to evaluate what strategic actions can be taken to neutralize or lessen their impact.

What Do the SWOT Listings Reveal?

SWOT analysis involves more than making four lists. The two most important parts of SWOT analysis are *drawing conclusions* from the SWOT listings about the company's overall situation, and *translating these conclusions into strategic actions* to better match the company's strategy to its resource strengths and market opportunities, to correct the important weaknesses, and to defend against external threats. Figure 4.2 shows the three steps of SWOT analysis.

Just what story the SWOT listings tell about the company's overall situation is often revealed in the answers to the following sets of questions:

> Simply making lists of a company's strengths, weaknesses, opportunities, and threats is not enough; the payoff from SWOT analysis comes from the conclusions about a company's situation and the implications for strategy improvement that flow from the four lists.

- Does the company have an attractive set of resource strengths? Does it have any strong core competencies or a distinctive competence? Are the company's strengths and capabilities well matched to the industry key success factors? Do they add adequate power to the company's strategy, or are more or different strengths needed? Will the company's current strengths and capabilities matter in the future?

- How serious are the company's weaknesses and competitive deficiencies? Are they mostly inconsequential and readily correctable, or could one or more prove fatal if not remedied soon? Are some of the company's weaknesses in areas that relate to the industry's key success factors? Are there any weaknesses that if uncorrected, would keep the company from pursuing an otherwise attractive opportunity? Does the company have important resource gaps that need to be filled for it to move up in the industry rankings and/or boost its profitability?

- Do the company's resource strengths and competitive capabilities (its competitive assets) outweigh its resource weaknesses and competitive deficiencies (its competitive liabilities) by an attractive margin?

- Does the company have attractive market opportunities that are well suited to its resource strengths and competitive capabilities? Does the company lack the resources and capabilities to pursue any of the most attractive opportunities?

- Are the threats alarming, or are they something the company appears able to deal with and defend against?

Figure 4.2 **The Three Steps of SWOT Analysis: Identify, Draw Conclusions, Translate into Strategic Action**

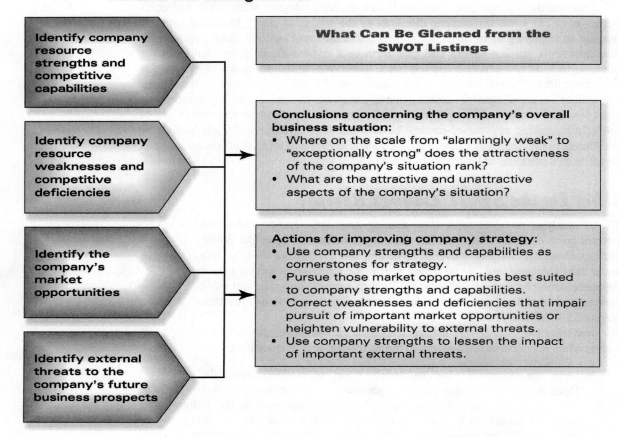

- All things considered, how strong is the company's overall situation? Where on a scale of 1 to 10 (1 being alarmingly weak and 10 exceptionally strong) should the firm's position and overall situation be ranked? What aspects of the company's situation are particularly attractive? What aspects are of the most concern?

The final piece of SWOT analysis is to translate the diagnosis of the company's situation into actions for improving the company's strategy and business prospects. The following questions point to implications the SWOT listings have for strategic action:

- Which competitive capabilities need to be strengthened immediately, so as to add greater power to the company's strategy and boost sales and profitability? Do new types of competitive capabilities need to be put in place to help the company better respond to emerging industry and competitive conditions? Which resources and capabilities need to be given greater emphasis, and which merit less emphasis? Should the company emphasize leveraging its existing resource strengths and capabilities, or does it need to create new resource strengths and capabilities?

- What actions should be taken to reduce the company's competitive liabilities? Which weaknesses or competitive deficiencies are in urgent need of correction?

- Which market opportunities should be top priority in future strategic initiatives (because they are good fits with the company's resource strengths and competitive capabilities, present attractive growth and profit prospects, and/or offer the best potential for securing competitive advantage)? Which opportunities should be ignored, at least for the time being (because they offer less growth potential or are not suited to the company's resources and capabilities)?
- What should the company be doing to guard against the threats to its well-being?

A company's resource strengths should generally form the cornerstones of strategy because they represent the company's best chance for market success.[9] As a rule, strategies that place heavy demands on areas where the company is weakest or has unproven ability are suspect and should be avoided. If a company doesn't have the resources and competitive capabilities around which to craft an attractive strategy, managers need to take decisive remedial action either to upgrade existing organizational resources and capabilities and add others as needed or to acquire them through partnerships or strategic alliances with firms possessing the needed expertise. Plainly, managers have to look toward correcting competitive weaknesses that make the company vulnerable, hold down profitability, or disqualify it from pursuing an attractive opportunity.

At the same time, sound strategy making requires sifting through the available market opportunities and aiming strategy at capturing those that are most attractive and suited to the company's circumstances. Rarely does a company have the resource depth to pursue all available market opportunities simultaneously without spreading itself too thin. How much attention to devote to defending against external threats to the company's market position and future performance hinges on how vulnerable the company is, whether there are attractive defensive moves that can be taken to lessen their impact, and whether the costs of undertaking such moves represent the best use of company resources.

QUESTION 3: ARE THE COMPANY'S PRICES AND COSTS COMPETITIVE?

Company managers are often stunned when a competitor cuts its price to "unbelievably low" levels or when a new market entrant comes on strong with a very low price. The competitor may not, however, be "dumping" (an economic term for selling at prices that are below cost), buying its way into the market with a super-low price, or waging a desperate move to gain sales—it may simply have substantially lower costs. One of the most telling signs of whether a company's business position is strong or precarious is whether its prices and costs are competitive with industry rivals. For a company to compete successfully, its costs must be *in line* with those of close rivals.

> The higher a company's costs are above those of close rivals, the more competitively vulnerable it becomes.

Price–cost comparisons are especially critical in a commodity-product industry where the value provided to buyers is the same from seller to seller, price competition is typically the ruling market force, and low-cost companies have the upper hand. But even in industries where products are differentiated and competition centers on the different attributes of competing brands as much as on price, rival companies have to keep their costs in line and make sure that any added costs they incur, and any price premiums they charge, create ample value that buyers are willing to pay extra for.

While some cost disparity is justified so long as the products or services of closely competing companies are sufficiently differentiated, a high-cost firm's market position becomes increasingly vulnerable the more its costs exceed those of close rivals.

Two analytical tools are particularly useful in determining whether a company's prices and costs are competitive: value chain analysis and benchmarking.

The Concept of a Company Value Chain

> **Core Concept**
> A company's *value chain* identifies the primary activities that create customer value and the related support activities.

Every company's business consists of a collection of activities undertaken in the course of designing, producing, marketing, delivering, and supporting its product or service. All of the various activities that a company performs internally combine to form a **value chain**—so called because the underlying intent of a company's activities is to do things that ultimately *create value for buyers*. A company's value chain also includes an allowance for profit because a markup over the cost of performing the firm's value-creating activities is customarily part of the price (or total cost) borne by buyers—unless an enterprise succeeds in creating and delivering sufficient value to buyers to produce an attractive profit, it can't survive for long.

As shown in Figure 4.3, a company's value chain consists of two broad categories of activities: the *primary activities* that are foremost in creating value for customers and the requisite *support activities* that facilitate and enhance the performance of the primary activities.[10] For example, the primary value-creating activities for a maker of bakery goods include supply chain management, recipe development and testing, mixing and baking, packaging, sales and marketing, and distribution; related support activities include quality control, human resource management, and administration. A wholesaler's primary activities and costs deal with merchandise selection and purchasing, inbound shipping and warehousing from suppliers, and outbound distribution to retail customers. The primary activities for a department store retailer include merchandise selection and buying, store layout and product display, advertising, and customer service; its support activities include site selection, hiring and training, and store maintenance, plus the usual assortment of administrative activities. A hotel chain's primary activities and costs are in site selection and construction, reservations, operation of its hotel properties (check-in and check-out, maintenance and housekeeping, dining and room service, and conventions and meetings), and managing its lineup of hotel locations; principal support activities include accounting, hiring and training hotel staff, advertising, building a brand and reputation, and general administration. Supply chain management is a crucial activity for Nissan and Amazon.com but is not a value chain component at Google or a TV and radio broadcasting company. Sales and marketing are dominant activities at Procter & Gamble and Sony but have minor roles at oil drilling companies and natural gas pipeline companies. Delivery to buyers is a crucial activity at Domino's Pizza but comparatively insignificant at Starbucks. Thus, what constitutes a primary or secondary activity varies according to the specific nature of a company's business, meaning that you should view the listing of the primary and support activities in Figure 4.3 as illustrative rather than definitive.

A Company's Primary and Support Activities Identify the Major Components of Its Cost Structure   Segregating a company's operations into different types of primary and support activities is the first step in understanding its cost structure. Each activity in the value chain gives rise to costs and ties up assets.

Figure 4.3 **A Representative Company Value Chain**

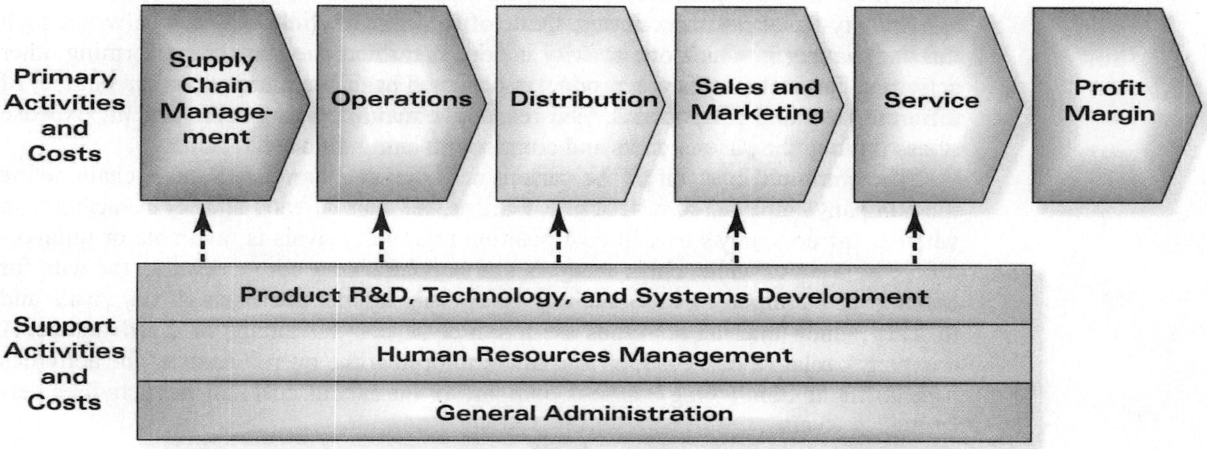

PRIMARY ACTIVITIES

- **Supply chain management**—activities, costs, and assets associated with purchasing fuel, energy, raw materials, parts and components, merchandise, and consumable items from vendors; receiving, storing, and disseminating inputs from suppliers; inspection; and inventory management.

- **Operations**—activities, costs, and assets associated with converting inputs into final product from (production, assembly, packaging, equipment maintenance, facilities, operations, quality assurance, environmental protection).

- **Distribution**—activities, costs, and assets dealing with physically distributing the product to buyers (finished goods warehousing, order processing, order picking and packing, shipping, delivery vehicle operations, establishing and maintaining a network of dealers and distributors).

- **Sales and marketing**—activities, costs, and assets related to sales force efforts, advertising and promotion, market research and planning, and dealer/distributor support.

- **Service**—activities, costs, and assets associated with providing assistance to buyers, such as installation, spare parts delivery, maintenance and repair, technical assistance, buyer inquiries, and complaints.

SUPPORT ACTIVITIES

- **Product R&D, technology, and systems development**—activities, costs, and assets relating to product R&D, process R&D, process design improvement, equipment design, computer software development, telecommunications systems, computer-assisted design and engineering, database capabilities, and development of computerized support systems.

- **Human resources management**—activities, costs, and assets associated with the recruitment, hiring, training, development, and compensation of all types of personnel; labor relations activities; and development of knowledge-based skills and core competencies.

- **General administration**—activities, costs, and assets relating to general management, accounting and finance, legal and regulatory affairs, safety and security, management information systems, forming strategic alliances and collaborating with strategic partners, and other overhead functions.

Source: Based on the discussion in Michael E. Porter, *Competitive Advantage* (New York: Free Press, 1985), pp. 37–43.

Assigning the company's operating costs and assets to each individual activity in the chain provides cost estimates and capital requirements—a process that accountants call activity-based cost accounting. Quite often, there are links between activities such that the manner in which one activity is done can affect the costs of performing other activities. For instance, how a product is designed has a huge impact on the number of different parts and components, their respective manufacturing costs, and the expense of assembling the various parts and components into a finished product.

The combined costs of all the various activities in a company's value chain define the company's internal cost structure. Further, the cost of each activity contributes to whether the company's overall cost position relative to rivals is favorable or unfavorable. The tasks of value chain analysis and benchmarking are to develop the data for comparing a company's costs activity-by-activity against the costs of key rivals and to learn which internal activities are a source of cost advantage or disadvantage. A company's relative cost position is a function of how the overall costs of the activities it performs in conducting business compare to the overall costs of the activities performed by rivals.

Why the Value Chains of Rival Companies Often Differ

A company's value chain and the manner in which it performs each activity reflect the evolution of its own particular business and internal operations, its strategy, the approaches it is using to execute its strategy, and the underlying economics of the activities themselves.[11] Because these factors differ from company to company, the value chains of rival companies sometimes differ substantially—a condition that complicates the task of assessing rivals' relative cost positions. For instance, music retailers like Blockbuster and Musicland, which purchase CDs from recording studios and wholesale distributors and sell them in their own retail store locations, have value chains and cost structures different from those of rival online music stores like Apple's iTunes and Musicmatch, which sell downloadable music files directly to music shoppers. Competing companies may differ in their degrees of vertical integration. The operations component of the value chain for a manufacturer that *makes* all of its own parts and assembles them into a finished product differs from the operations component of a rival producer that *buys* the needed parts from outside suppliers and performs assembly operations only. Likewise, there is legitimate reason to expect value chain and cost differences between a company that is pursuing a low-cost/low-price strategy and a rival that is positioned on the high end of the market. The costs of certain activities along the low-cost company's value chain should indeed be relatively low, whereas the high-end firm may understandably be spending relatively more to perform those activities that create the added quality and extra features of its products.

Moreover, cost and price differences among rival companies can have their origins in activities performed by suppliers or by distribution channel allies involved in getting the product to end users. Suppliers or wholesale/retail dealers may have excessively high cost structures or profit margins that jeopardize a company's cost-competitiveness even though its costs for internally performed activities are competitive. For example, when determining Michelin's cost-competitiveness vis-à-vis Goodyear and Bridgestone in supplying replacement tires to vehicle owners, we have to look at more than whether Michelin's tire manufacturing costs are above or below Goodyear's and Bridgestone's. Let's say that a motor vehicle owner looking for a new set of tires has to pay $400 for a set of Michelin tires and only $350 for a set of Goodyear or Bridgestone tires. Michelin's $50 price disadvantage can stem not only from higher manufacturing costs (reflecting, perhaps, the added costs of Michelin's strategic efforts to build a better-quality tire with more performance features) but also from (1) differences in what the three tire makers pay their suppliers for materials and tire-making components, and (2) differences in the operating efficiencies, costs, and markups of Michelin's wholesale–retail dealer outlets versus those of Goodyear and Bridgestone.

The Value Chain System for an Entire Industry

As the tire industry example makes clear, a company's value chain is embedded in a larger system of activities that includes the value chains of its suppliers and the value chains of whatever distribution channel allies it uses in getting its product or service to end users.[12] Suppliers' value chains are relevant because suppliers perform activities and incur costs in creating and delivering the purchased inputs used in a company's own value-creating activities. The costs, performance features, and quality of these inputs influence a company's own costs and product differentiation capabilities. Anything a company can do to help its suppliers' drive down the costs of their value chain activities or improve the quality and performance of the items being supplied can enhance its own competitiveness—a powerful reason for working collaboratively with suppliers in managing supply chain activities.[13]

The value chains of forward channel partners and/or the customers to whom a company sells are relevant because (1) the costs and margins of a company's distributors and retail dealers are part of the price the ultimate consumer pays, and (2) the activities that distribution allies perform affect customer satisfaction. For these reasons, companies normally work closely with their forward channel allies (who are their direct customers) to perform value chain activities in mutually beneficial ways. For instance, motor vehicle manufacturers work closely with their local automobile dealers to keep the retail prices of their vehicles competitive with rivals' models and to ensure that owners are satisfied with dealers' repair and maintenance services. Some aluminum can producers have constructed plants next to beer breweries and deliver cans on overhead conveyors directly to the breweries' can-filling lines; this has resulted in significant savings in production scheduling, shipping, and inventory costs for both container producers and breweries.[14] Many automotive parts suppliers have built plants near the auto assembly plants they supply to facilitate just-in-time deliveries, reduce warehousing and shipping costs, and promote close collaboration on parts design and production scheduling. Irrigation equipment companies, suppliers of grape-harvesting and winemaking equipment, and firms making barrels, wine bottles, caps, corks, and labels all have facilities in the California wine country to be close to the nearly 700 winemakers they supply.[15] The lesson here is that a company's value chain activities are often closely linked to the value chains of their suppliers and the forward allies or customers to whom they sell.

As a consequence, *accurately assessing a company's competitiveness from the perspective of the consumers who ultimately use its products or services thus requires that company managers understand an industry's entire value chain system for delivering a product or service to customers, not just the company's own value chain.* A typical industry value chain that incorporates the value chains of suppliers and forward channel allies (if any) is shown in Figure 4.4. However, industry value chains

> A company's cost-competitiveness depends not only on the costs of internally performed activities (its own value chain) but also on costs in the value chains of its suppliers and forward channel allies.

Figure 4.4   **Representative Value Chain for an Entire Industry**

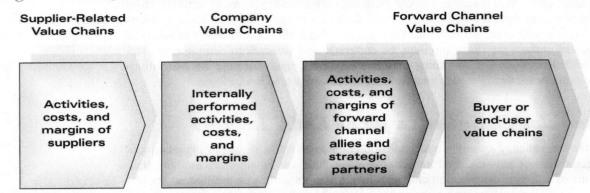

Source: Based in part on the single-industry value chain displayed in Michael E. Porter, *Competitive Advantage* (New York: Free Press, 1985), p. 35.

vary significantly by industry. The primary value chain activities in the pulp and paper industry (timber farming, logging, pulp mills, and papermaking) differ from the primary value chain activities in the home appliance industry (parts and components manufacture, assembly, wholesale distribution, retail sales). The value chain for the soft-drink industry (processing of basic ingredients and syrup manufacture, bottling and can filling, wholesale distribution, advertising, and retail merchandising) differs from that for the computer software industry (programming, disk loading, marketing, distribution). Producers of bathroom and kitchen faucets depend heavily on the activities of wholesale distributors and building supply retailers in winning sales to homebuilders and do-it-yourselfers, but producers of papermaking machines internalize their distribution activities by selling directly to the operators of paper plants. Illustration Capsule 4.1 shows representative costs for various activities performed by the producers and marketers of music CDs.

Activity-Based Costing: A Tool for Assessing a Company's Cost Competitiveness

Once the company has identified its major value chain activities, the next step in evaluating its cost competitiveness involves determining the costs of performing specific value chain activities, using what accountants call activity-based costing.[16] Traditional accounting identifies costs according to broad categories of expenses—wages and salaries, employee benefits, supplies, maintenance, utilities, travel, depreciation, R&D, interest, general administration, and so on. But activity-based cost accounting involves establishing expense categories for specific value chain activities and assigning costs to the activity responsible for creating the cost. An illustrative example is shown in Table 4.3 on page 116. Perhaps 25 percent of the companies that have explored the feasibility of activity-based costing have adopted this accounting approach.

Illustration Capsule 4.1

Estimated Value Chain Costs for Recording and Distributing Music CDs through Traditional Music Retailers

The following table presents the representative costs and markups associated with producing and distributing a music CD retailing for $15 in music stores (as opposed to Internet sources).

Value Chain Activities and Costs in Producing and Distributing a CD		
1. Record company direct production costs:		$2.40
Artists and repertoire	$0.75	
Pressing of CD and packaging	1.65	
2. Royalties		0.99
3. Record company marketing expenses		1.50
4. Record company overhead		1.50
5. Total record company costs		6.39
6. Record company's operating profit		1.86
7. Record company's selling price to distributor/wholesaler		8.25
8. Average wholesale distributor markup to cover distribution activities and profit margins		1.50
9. Average wholesale price charged to retailer		9.75
10. Average retail markup over wholesale cost		5.25
11. Average price to consumer at retail		$15.00

Source: Developed from information in "Fight the Power," a case study prepared by Adrian Aleyne, Babson College, 1999.

The degree to which a company's costs should be disaggregated into specific activities depends on how valuable it is to develop cross-company cost comparisons for narrowly defined activities as opposed to broadly defined activities. Generally speaking, cost estimates are needed at least for each broad category of primary and secondary activities, but finer classifications may be needed if a company discovers that it has a cost disadvantage vis-à-vis rivals and wants to pin down the exact source or activity causing the cost disadvantage. It can also be necessary to develop cost estimates for activities performed in the competitively relevant portions of suppliers' and customers' value chains—which requires going to outside sources for reliable cost information.

Once a company has developed good cost estimates for each of the major activities in its value chain, and perhaps has cost estimates for subactivities within each primary/secondary value chain activity, then it is ready to see how its costs for these activities compare with the costs of rival firms. This is where benchmarking comes in.

Table 4.3 **The Difference between Traditional Cost Accounting and Activity-Based Cost Accounting: A Supply Chain Activity Example**

Traditional Cost Accounting Categories for Supply Chain Activities		Cost of Performing Specific Supply Chain Activities Using Activity-Based Cost Accounting	
Wages and salaries	$450,000	Evaluate supplier capabilities	$150,000
Employee benefits	95,000	Process purchase orders	92,000
Supplies	21,500	Collaborate with suppliers on just-in-time deliveries	180,000
Travel	12,250		
Depreciation	19,000	Share data with suppliers	69,000
Other fixed charges (office space, utilities)	112,000	Check quality of items purchased	94,000
Miscellaneous operating expenses	40,250	Check incoming deliveries against purchase orders	50,000
	$750,000	Resolve disputes	15,000
		Conduct internal administration	100,000
			$750,000

Source: Developed from information in Terence P. Par, "A New Tool for Managing Costs," *Fortune,* June 14, 1993, pp. 124–29.

Benchmarking: A Tool for Assessing Whether a Company's Value Chain Costs Are in Line

Core Concept
Benchmarking is a potent tool for learning which companies are best at performing particular activities and then using their techniques (or "best practices") to improve the cost and effectiveness of a company's own internal activities.

Many companies today are **benchmarking** their costs of performing a given activity against competitors' costs (and/or against the costs of a noncompetitor that efficiently and effectively performs much the same activity in another industry). *Benchmarking is a tool that allows a company to determine whether its performance of a particular function or activity represents the "best practice" when both cost and effectiveness are taken into account.*

Benchmarking entails comparing how different companies perform various value chain activities—how materials are purchased, how suppliers are paid, how inventories are managed, how products are assembled, how fast the company can get new products to market, how the quality control function is performed, how customer orders are filled and shipped, how employees are trained, how payrolls are processed, and how maintenance is performed—and then making cross-company comparisons of the costs of these activities.[17] The objectives of benchmarking are to identify the best practices in performing an activity, to learn how other companies have actually achieved lower costs or better results in performing benchmarked activities, and to take action to improve a company's competitiveness whenever benchmarking reveals that its costs and results of performing an activity are not on a par with what other companies (either competitors or noncompetitors) have achieved.

Xerox became one of the first companies to use benchmarking when, in 1979, Japanese manufacturers began selling midsize copiers in the United States for $9,600 each—less than Xerox's production costs.[18] Xerox management suspected its Japanese competitors were dumping, but it sent a team of line managers to Japan, including the head of manufacturing, to study competitors' business processes and costs. With the aid of Xerox's joint venture partner in Japan, Fuji-Xerox, which knew the competitors well, the team found that Xerox's costs were excessive due to gross inefficiencies in the company's manufacturing processes and business practices. The findings triggered a major internal effort at Xerox to become cost-competitive and prompted Xerox to begin benchmarking 67 of its key work processes against companies identified as employing the best practices. Xerox quickly decided not to restrict its benchmarking efforts to its office equipment rivals but to extend them to any company regarded as world class in performing *any activity* relevant to Xerox's business. Other companies quickly picked up on Xerox's approach. Toyota managers got their idea for just-in-time inventory deliveries by studying how U.S. supermarkets replenished their shelves. Southwest Airlines reduced the turnaround time of its aircraft at each scheduled stop by studying pit crews on the auto racing circuit. Over 80 percent of Fortune 500 companies reportedly use benchmarking for comparing themselves against rivals on cost and other competitively important measures.

The tough part of benchmarking is not whether to do it, but rather how to gain access to information about other companies' practices and costs. Sometimes benchmarking can be accomplished by collecting information from published reports, trade groups, and industry research firms and by talking to knowledgeable industry analysts, customers, and suppliers. Sometimes field trips to the facilities of competing or noncompeting companies can be arranged to observe how things are done, ask questions, compare practices and processes, and perhaps exchange data on productivity, staffing levels, time requirements, and other cost components—but the problem here is that such companies, even if they agree to host facilities tours and answer questions, are unlikely to share competitively sensitive cost information. Furthermore, comparing one company's costs to another's costs may not involve comparing apples to apples if the two companies employ different cost accounting principles to calculate the costs of particular activities.

> Benchmarking the costs of company activities against rivals provides hard evidence of whether a company is cost-competitive.

However, a third and fairly reliable source of benchmarking information has emerged. The explosive interest of companies in benchmarking costs and identifying best practices has prompted consulting organizations (e.g., Accenture, A. T. Kearney, Benchnet—The Benchmarking Exchange, Towers Perrin, and Best Practices) and several councils and associations (e.g., the American Productivity and Quality Center, the Qualserve Benchmarking Clearinghouse, and the Strategic Planning Institute's Council on Benchmarking) to gather benchmarking data, distribute information about best practices, and provide comparative cost data without identifying the names of particular companies. Having an independent group gather the information and report it in a manner that disguises the names of individual companies avoid having the disclosure of competitively sensitive data and lessens the potential for unethical behavior on the part of company personnel in gathering their own data about competitors. Illustration Capsule 4.2 presents a widely recommended code of conduct for engaging in benchmarking that is intended to help companies avoid any improprieties in gathering and using benchmarking data.

Strategic Options for Remedying a Cost Disadvantage

Value chain analysis and benchmarking can reveal a great deal about a firm's cost competitiveness. Examining the costs of a company's own value chain activities and comparing them to rivals' indicates who has how much of a cost advantage or

Illustration Capsule 4.2
Benchmarking and Ethical Conduct

Because discussions between benchmarking partners can involve competitively sensitive data, conceivably raising questions about possible restraint of trade or improper business conduct, many benchmarking organizations urge all individuals and organizations involved in benchmarking to abide by a code of conduct grounded in ethical business behavior. Among the most widely used codes of conduct is the one developed by the American Productivity and Quality Center and advocated by the Qualserve Benchmarking Clearinghouse; it is based on the following principles and guidelines:

- Avoid discussions or actions that could lead to or imply an interest in restraint of trade, market and/or customer allocation schemes, price fixing, dealing arrangements, bid rigging, or bribery. Don't discuss costs with competitors if costs are an element of pricing.

- Refrain from the acquisition of trade secrets from another by any means that could be interpreted as improper including the breach or inducement of a breach of any duty to maintain secrecy. Do not disclose or use any trade secret that may have been obtained through improper means or that was disclosed by another in violation of duty to maintain its secrecy or limit its use.

- Be willing to provide the same type and level of information that you request from your benchmarking partner to your benchmarking partner.

- Communicate fully and early in the relationship to clarify expectations, avoid misunderstanding, and establish mutual interest in the benchmarking exchange.

- Be honest and complete.

- Treat benchmarking interchange as confidential to the individuals and companies involved. Information must not be communicated outside the partnering organizations without the prior consent of the benchmarking partner who shared the information.

- Use information obtained through benchmarking only for purposes stated to the benchmarking partner.

- The use or communication of a benchmarking partner's name with the data obtained or practices observed requires the prior permission of that partner.

- Respect the corporate culture of partner companies and work within mutually agreed-on procedures.

- Use benchmarking contacts designated by the partner company, if that is the company's preferred procedure.

- Obtain mutual agreement with the designated benchmarking contact on any hand-off of communication or responsibility to other parties.

- Make the most of your benchmarking partner's time by being fully prepared for each exchange.

- Help your benchmarking partners prepare by providing them with a questionnaire and agenda prior to benchmarking visits.

- Follow through with each commitment made to your benchmarking partner in a timely manner.

- Understand how your benchmarking partner would like to have the information he or she provides handled and used, and handle and use it in that manner.

Note: Identification of firms, organizations, and contacts visited is prohibited without advance approval from the organization.

Sources: The American Productivity and Quality Center, www.apqc.org, and the Qualserve Benchmarking Clearinghouse, www.awwa.org (accessed September 14, 2005).

disadvantage and which cost components are responsible. Such information is vital in strategic actions to eliminate a cost disadvantage or create a cost advantage. One of the fundamental insights of value chain analysis and benchmarking is that *a company's competitiveness on cost depends on how efficiently it manages its value chain activities relative to how well competitors manage theirs.*[19] There are three main areas in a company's overall value chain where important differences in the costs of competing firms can occur: a company's own activity segments, suppliers' part of the industry value chain, and the forward channel portion of the industry chain.

Remedying an Internal Cost Disadvantage   When a company's cost disadvantage stems from performing internal value chain activities at a higher cost than key rivals, then managers can pursue any of several strategic approaches to restore cost parity:[20]

1. Implement the use of best practices throughout the company, particularly for high-cost activities.

2. Try to eliminate some cost-producing activities altogether by revamping the value chain. Examples include cutting out low-value-added activities or bypassing the value chains and associated costs of distribution allies and marketing directly to end users. Dell has used this approach in PCs, and airlines have begun bypassing travel agents by getting passengers to purchase their tickets directly at airline Web sites.

3. Relocate high-cost activities (such as manufacturing) to geographic areas—such as China, Latin America, or Eastern Europe—where they can be performed more cheaply.

4. See if certain internally performed activities can be outsourced from vendors or performed by contractors more cheaply than they can be done in-house.

5. Invest in productivity-enhancing, cost-saving technological improvements (robotics, flexible manufacturing techniques, state-of-the-art electronic networking).

6. Find ways to detour around the activities or items where costs are high—computer chip makers regularly design around the patents held by others to avoid paying royalties; automakers have substituted lower-cost plastic and rubber for metal at many exterior body locations.

7. Redesign the product and/or some of its components to facilitate speedier and more economical manufacture or assembly.

8. Try to make up the internal cost disadvantage by reducing costs in the supplier or forward channel portions of the industry value chain—usually a last resort.

Remedying a Supplier-Related Cost Disadvantage   Supplier-related cost disadvantages can be attacked by pressuring suppliers for lower prices, switching to lower-priced substitute inputs, and collaborating closely with suppliers to identify mutual cost-saving opportunities.[21] For example, just-in-time deliveries from suppliers can lower a company's inventory and internal logistics costs and may also allow its suppliers to economize on their warehousing, shipping, and production scheduling costs—a win–win outcome for both. In a few instances, companies may find that it is cheaper to integrate backward into the business of high-cost suppliers and make the item in-house instead of buying it from outsiders. If a company strikes out in wringing savings out of its high-cost supply chain activities, then it must resort to finding cost savings either in-house or in the forward channel portion of the industry value chain to offset its supplier-related cost disadvantage.

Remedying a Cost Disadvantage Associated with Activities Performed by Forward Channel Allies   There are three main ways to combat a cost disadvantage in the forward portion of the industry value chain:

1. Pressure dealer-distributors and other forward channel allies to reduce their costs and markups so as to make the final price to buyers more competitive with the prices of rivals.

2. Work closely with forward channel allies to identify win–win opportunities to reduce costs. For example, a chocolate manufacturer learned that by shipping its bulk chocolate in liquid form in tank cars instead of 10-pound molded bars, it could not only save its candy bar manufacturing customers the costs associated with unpacking and melting but also eliminate its own costs of molding bars and packing them.

3. Change to a more economical distribution strategy, including switching to cheaper distribution channels (perhaps direct sales via the Internet) or perhaps integrating forward into company-owned retail outlets.

If these efforts fail, the company can either try to live with the cost disadvantage or pursue cost-cutting earlier in the value chain system.

Translating Proficient Performance of Value Chain Activities into Competitive Advantage

Performing value chain activities in ways that give a company the capabilities to either outmatch the competencies and capabilities of rivals or else beat them on costs are two good ways to secure competitive advantage.

A company that does a *first-rate job* of managing its value chain activities *relative to competitors* stands a good chance of achieving sustainable competitive advantage. As shown in Figure 4.5, outmanaging rivals in performing value chain activities can be accomplished in either or both of two ways: (1) by astutely developing core competencies and maybe a distinctive competence that rivals don't have or can't quite match and that are instrumental in helping it deliver attractive value to customers, and/or (2) by simply doing an overall better job than rivals of lowering its combined costs of performing all the various value chain activities, such that it ends up with a low-cost advantage over rivals.

The first of these two approaches begins with management efforts to build more organizational expertise in performing certain competitively important value chain activities, deliberately striving to develop competencies and capabilities that add power to its strategy and competitiveness. If management begins to make selected competencies and capabilities cornerstones of its strategy and continues to invest resources in building greater and greater proficiency in performing them, then over time one (or maybe several) of the targeted competencies/capabilities may rise to the level of a core competence. Later, following additional organizational learning and investments in gaining still greater proficiency, a core competence could evolve into a distinctive competence, giving the company superiority over rivals in performing an important value chain activity. Such superiority, if it gives the company significant competitive clout in the marketplace, can produce an attractive competitive edge over rivals and, more important, prove difficult for rivals to match or offset with competencies and capabilities of their own making. As a general rule, it is substantially harder for rivals to achieve best-in-industry proficiency in performing a key value chain activity than it is for them to clone the features and attributes of a hot-selling product or service.[22] This is especially true when a company with a distinctive competence avoids becoming complacent and works diligently to maintain its industry-leading expertise and capability. GlaxoSmithKline, one of the world's most competitively capable pharmaceutical companies, has built its business position around expert performance of a few competitively crucial activities: extensive R&D to achieve first discovery of new drugs, a carefully constructed approach to patenting, skill in gaining rapid and thorough clinical clearance through regulatory bodies, and unusually strong distribution and sales-force

Figure 4.5 **Translating Company Performance of Value Chain Activities into Competitive Advantage**

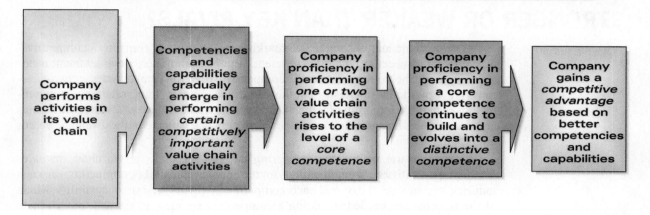

Option 1: Beat rivals in performing value chain activities more proficiently

Company performs activities in its value chain → Competencies and capabilities gradually emerge in performing *certain competitively important* value chain activities → Company proficiency in performing *one or two* value chain activities rises to the level of a *core competence* → Company proficiency in performing a core competence continues to build and evolves into a *distinctive competence* → Company gains a *competitive advantage* based on better competencies and capabilities

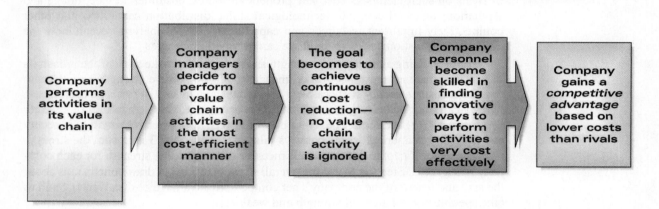

Option 2: Beat rivals in performing value chain activities more cheaply

Company performs activities in its value chain → Company managers decide to perform value chain activities in the most cost-efficient manner → The goal becomes to achieve continuous cost reduction—no value chain activity is ignored → Company personnel become skilled in finding innovative ways to perform activities very cost effectively → Company gains a *competitive advantage* based on lower costs than rivals

capabilities.[23] FedEx's astute management of its value chain has produced unmatched competencies and capabilities in overnight package delivery.

The second approach to building competitive advantage entails determined management efforts to be cost-efficient in performing value chain activities. Such efforts have to be ongoing and persistent, and they have to involve each and every value chain activity. The goal must be continuous cost reduction, not a one-time or on-again/off-again effort. Companies whose managers are truly committed to low-cost performance of value chain activities and succeed in engaging company personnel to discover innovative ways to drive costs out of the business have a real chance of gaining a durable low-cost edge over rivals. It is not as easy as it seems to imitate a company's low-cost practices. Companies like Wal-Mart, Dell, Nucor Steel, Southwest Airlines,

Toyota, and French discount retailer Carrefour have been highly successful in managing their value chains in a low-cost manner.

QUESTION 4: IS THE COMPANY COMPETITIVELY STRONGER OR WEAKER THAN KEY RIVALS?

Using value chain analysis and benchmarking to determine a company's competitiveness on price is necessary but not sufficient. A more comprehensive assessment needs to be made of the company's overall competitive strength. The answers to two questions are of particular interest: First, how does the company rank relative to competitors on each of the important factors that determine market success? Second, all things considered, does the company have a net competitive advantage or disadvantage versus major competitors?

An easy-to-use method for answering the two questions posed above involves developing quantitative strength ratings for the company and its key competitors on each industry key success factor and each competitively pivotal resource capability. Much of the information needed for doing a competitive strength assessment comes from previous analyses. Industry and competitive analysis reveals the key success factors and competitive capabilities that separate industry winners from losers. Benchmarking data and scouting key competitors provide a basis for judging the competitive strength of rivals on such factors as cost, key product attributes, customer service, image and reputation, financial strength, technological skills, distribution capability, and other competitively important resources and capabilities. SWOT analysis reveals how the company in question stacks up on these same strength measures.

Step 1 in doing a competitive strength assessment is to make a list of the industry's key success factors and most telling measures of competitive strength or weakness (6 to 10 measures usually suffice). Step 2 is to rate the firm and its rivals on each factor. Numerical rating scales (e.g., from 1 to 10) are best to use, although ratings of stronger (+), weaker (−), and about equal (=) may be appropriate when information is scanty and assigning numerical scores conveys false precision. Step 3 is to sum the strength ratings on each factor to get an overall measure of competitive strength for each company being rated. Step 4 is to use the overall strength ratings to draw conclusions about the size and extent of the company's net competitive advantage or disadvantage and to take specific note of areas of strength and weakness.

Table 4.5 provides two examples of competitive strength assessment, using the hypothetical ABC Company against four rivals. The first example employs an *unweighted rating system*. With unweighted ratings, each key success factor/competitive strength measure is assumed to be equally important (a rather dubious assumption). Whichever company has the highest strength rating on a given measure has an implied competitive edge on that factor; the size of its edge is mirrored in the margin of difference between its rating and the ratings assigned to rivals—a rating of 9 for one company versus ratings of 5, 4, and 3, respectively, for three other companies indicates a bigger advantage than a rating of 9 versus ratings of 8, 7, and 6. Summing a company's ratings on all the measures produces an overall strength rating. The higher a company's overall strength rating, the stronger its overall competitiveness versus rivals. The bigger the difference between a company's overall rating and the scores of *lower-rated* rivals, the greater its implied *net competitive advantage.* Conversely, the bigger the difference between a company's overall rating and the scores of *higher-rated* rivals, the greater its implied

Table 4.5 **Illustrations of Unweighted and Weighted Competitive Strength Assessments**

A. An Unweighted Competitive Strength Assessment

Key Success Factor/Strength Measure	Strength Rating (Scale: 1 = Very weak; 10 = Very strong)				
	ABC Co.	Rival 1	Rival 2	Rival 3	Rival 4
Quality/product performance	8	5	10	1	6
Reputation/image	8	7	10	1	6
Manufacturing capability	2	10	4	5	1
Technological skills	10	1	7	3	8
Dealer network/distribution capability	9	4	10	5	1
New product innovation capability	9	4	10	5	1
Financial resources	5	10	7	3	1
Relative cost position	5	10	3	1	4
Customer service capabilities	5	7	10	1	4
Unweighted overall strength rating	**61**	**58**	**71**	**25**	**32**

B. A Weighted Competitive Strength Assessment
(Rating Scale: 1 = Very weak; 10 = Very strong)

Key Success Factor/Strength Measure	Importance Weight	ABC Co.		Rival 1		Rival 2		Rival 3		Rival 4	
		Strength Rating	Score	Strength Rating	Score	Strength Rating	Score	Strength Rating	Score	Strength Rating	Score
Quality/product performance	0.10	8	0.80	5	0.50	10	1.00	1	0.10	6	0.60
Reputation/image	0.10	8	0.80	7	0.70	10	1.00	1	0.10	6	0.60
Manufacturing capability	0.10	2	0.20	10	1.00	4	0.40	5	0.50	1	0.10
Technological skills	0.05	10	0.50	1	0.05	7	0.35	3	0.15	8	0.40
Dealer network/distribution capability	0.05	9	0.45	4	0.20	10	0.50	5	0.25	1	0.05
New product innovation capability	0.05	9	0.45	4	0.20	10	0.50	5	0.25	1	0.05
Financial resources	0.10	5	0.50	10	1.00	7	0.70	3	0.30	1	0.10
Relative cost position	0.30	5	1.50	10	3.00	3	0.95	1	0.30	4	1.20
Customer service capabilities	0.15	5	0.75	7	1.05	10	1.50	1	0.15	4	0.60
Sum of importance weights	1.00										
Weighted overall strength rating		61	**5.95**	58	**7.70**	71	**6.85**	25	**2.10**	32	**3.70**

net competitive disadvantage. Thus, ABC's total score of 61 (see the top half of Table 4.5) signals a much greater net competitive advantage over Rival 4 (with a score of 32) than over Rival 1 (with a score of 58) but indicates a moderate net competitive disadvantage against Rival 2 (with an overall score of 71).

However, a better method is a *weighted rating system* (shown in the bottom half of Table 4.5) because the different measures of competitive strength are unlikely to be equally important. In an industry where the products/services of rivals are virtually identical, for instance, having low unit costs relative to rivals is nearly always the most important determinant of competitive strength. In an industry with strong product differentiation, the most significant measures of competitive strength may be brand awareness, amount of advertising, product attractiveness, and distribution capability. In a weighted rating system each measure of competitive strength is assigned a weight based on its perceived importance in shaping competitive success. A weight could be as high as 0.75 (maybe even higher) in situations where one particular competitive variable is overwhelmingly decisive, or a weight could be as low as 0.20 when two or three strength measures are more important than the rest. Lesser competitive strength indicators can carry weights of 0.05 or 0.10. No matter whether the differences between the importance weights are big or little, *the sum of the weights must equal 1.0.*

> A weighted competitive strength analysis is conceptually stronger than an unweighted analysis because of the inherent weakness in assuming that all the strength measures are equally important.

Weighted strength ratings are calculated by rating each competitor on each strength measure (using the 1 to 10 rating scale) and multiplying the assigned rating by the assigned weight (a rating of 4 times a weight of 0.20 gives a weighted rating, or score, of 0.80). Again, the company with the highest rating on a given measure has an implied competitive edge on that measure, with the size of its edge reflected in the difference between its rating and rivals' ratings. The weight attached to the measure indicates how important the edge is. Summing a company's weighted strength ratings for all the measures yields an overall strength rating. Comparisons of the weighted overall strength scores indicate which competitors are in the strongest and weakest competitive positions and who has how big a net competitive advantage over whom.

Note in Table 4.5 that the unweighted and weighted rating schemes produce different orderings of the companies. In the weighted system, ABC Company drops from second to third in strength, and Rival 1 jumps from third to first because of its high strength ratings on the two most important factors. Weighting the importance of the strength measures can thus make a significant difference in the outcome of the assessment.

Interpreting the Competitive Strength Assessments

Competitive strength assessments provide useful conclusions about a company's competitive situation. The ratings show how a company compares against rivals, factor by factor or capability by capability, thus revealing where it is strongest and weakest, and against whom. Moreover, the overall competitive strength scores indicate how all the different factors add up—whether the company is at a net competitive advantage or disadvantage against each rival. The firm with the largest overall competitive strength rating enjoys the strongest competitive position, with the size of its net competitive advantage reflected by how much its score exceeds the scores of rivals.

> High competitive strength ratings signal a strong competitive position and possession of competitive advantage; low ratings signal a weak position and competitive disadvantage.

In addition, the strength ratings provide guidelines for designing wise offensive and defensive strategies. For example, consider the ratings and weighted scores in the bottom half of Table 4.5. If ABC Company wants to go on the offensive to win additional sales and market share, such an offensive probably needs to be aimed directly at winning customers away from Rivals 3 and 4 (which have lower overall strength scores) rather than Rivals 1 and 2 (which have higher overall strength scores). Moreover, while ABC has high ratings for quality/product performance (an 8 rating), reputation/image (an 8 rating), technological skills (a 10 rating), dealer network/distribution capability (a 9 rating), and new product innovation capability (a 9 rating), these strength measures have low importance weights—meaning that ABC has strengths in areas that don't translate into much competitive clout in the marketplace. Even so, it outclasses Rival 3 in all five areas, plus it enjoys lower costs than Rival 3: On relative cost position ABC has a 5 rating versus a 1 rating for Rival 3—and relative cost position carries the highest importance weight of all the strength measures. ABC also has greater competitive strength than Rival 3 as concerns customer service capabilities (which carries the second-highest importance weight). Hence, because ABC's strengths are in the very areas where Rival 3 is weak, ABC is in good position to attack Rival 3—it may well be able to persuade a number of Rival 3's customers to switch their purchases over to ABC's product.

But in mounting an offensive to win customers away from Rival 3, ABC should note that Rival 1 has an excellent relative cost position—its rating of 10, combined with the importance weight of 0.30 for relative cost, means that Rival 1 has meaningfully lower costs in an industry where low costs are competitively important. Rival 1 is thus strongly positioned to retaliate against ABC with lower prices if ABC's strategy offensive ends up drawing customers away from Rival 1. Moreover, Rival 1's very strong relative cost position vis-à-vis all the other companies arms it with the ability to use its lower-cost advantage to underprice all of its rivals and gain sales and market share at their expense. If ABC wants to defend against its vulnerability to potential price cutting by Rival 1, then it needs to aim a portion of its strategy at lowering its costs.

> A company's competitive strength scores pinpoint its strengths and weaknesses against rivals and point directly to the kinds of offensive/defensive actions it can use to exploit its competitive strengths and reduce its competitive vulnerabilities.

The point here is that a competitively astute company should use the strength assessment in deciding what strategic moves to make—which strengths to exploit in winning business away from rivals and which competitive weaknesses to try to correct. When a company has important competitive strengths in areas where one or more rivals are weak, it makes sense to consider offensive moves to exploit rivals' competitive weaknesses. When a company has important competitive weaknesses in areas where one or more rivals are strong, it makes sense to consider defensive moves to curtail its vulnerability.

QUESTION 5: WHAT STRATEGIC ISSUES AND PROBLEMS MERIT FRONT-BURNER MANAGERIAL ATTENTION?

The final and most important analytical step is to zero in on exactly what strategic issues that company managers need to address—and resolve—for the company to be more financially and competitively successful in the years ahead. This step involves drawing on the results of both industry and competitive analysis and the evaluations of the company's own competitiveness. The task here is to get a clear fix on exactly what strategic and competitive challenges confront the company, which of the company's competitive shortcomings need fixing, what obstacles stand in the way of improving the company's competitive position in the marketplace, and what specific problems

Zeroing in on the strategic issues a company faces and compiling a "worry list" of problems and roadblocks creates a strategic agenda of problems that merit prompt managerial attention.

Actually deciding upon a strategy and what specific actions to take is what comes *after* developing the list of strategic issues and problems that merit front-burner management attention.

A good strategy must contain ways to deal with all the strategic issues and obstacles that stand in the way of the company's financial and competitive success in the years ahead.

merit front-burner attention by company managers. *Pinpointing the precise things that management needs to worry about sets the agenda for deciding what actions to take next to improve the company's performance and business outlook.*

The "worry list" of issues and problems that have to be wrestled with can include such things as *how* to stave off market challenges from new foreign competitors, *how* to combat the price discounting of rivals, *how* to reduce the company's high costs and pave the way for price reductions, *how* to sustain the company's present rate of growth in light of slowing buyer demand, *whether* to expand the company's product line, *whether* to correct the company's competitive deficiencies by acquiring a rival company with the missing strengths, *whether* to expand into foreign markets rapidly or cautiously, *whether* to reposition the company and move to a different strategic group, *what to do* about growing buyer interest in substitute products, and *what to do* to combat the aging demographics of the company's customer base. The worry list thus always centers on such concerns as "how to . . .," "what to do about . . .," and "whether to . . ."—the purpose of the worry list is to identify the specific issues/problems that management needs to address, not to figure out what specific actions to take. Deciding what to do—which strategic actions to take and which strategic moves to make—comes later (when it is time to craft the strategy and choose from among the various strategic alternatives).

If the items on the worry list are relatively minor—which suggests the company's strategy is mostly on track and reasonably well matched to the company's overall situation—then company managers seldom need to go much beyond fine-tuning of the present strategy. If, however, the issues and problems confronting the company are serious and indicate the present strategy is not well suited for the road ahead, the task of crafting a better strategy has got to go to the top of management's action agenda.

Key Points

There are five key questions to consider in analyzing a company's own particular competitive circumstances and its competitive position vis-à-vis key rivals:

1. *How well is the present strategy working?* This involves evaluating the strategy from a qualitative standpoint (completeness, internal consistency, rationale, and suitability to the situation) and also from a quantitative standpoint (the strategic and financial results the strategy is producing). The stronger a company's current overall performance, the less likely the need for radical strategy changes. The weaker a company's performance and/or the faster the changes in its external situation (which can be gleaned from industry and competitive analysis), the more its current strategy must be questioned.

2. *What are the company's resource strengths and weaknesses, and its external opportunities and threats?* A SWOT analysis provides an overview of a firm's situation and is an essential component of crafting a strategy tightly matched to the company's situation. The two most important parts of SWOT analysis are (*a*) drawing conclusions about what story the compilation of strengths, weaknesses, opportunities, and threats tells about the company's overall situation, and

(b) acting on those conclusions to better match the company's strategy, to its resource strengths and market opportunities, to correct the important weaknesses, and to defend against external threats. A company's resource strengths, competencies, and competitive capabilities are strategically relevant because they are the most logical and appealing building blocks for strategy; resource weaknesses are important because they may represent vulnerabilities that need correction. External opportunities and threats come into play because a good strategy necessarily aims at capturing a company's most attractive opportunities and at defending against threats to its well-being.

3. *Are the company's prices and costs competitive?* One telling sign of whether a company's situation is strong or precarious is whether its prices and costs are competitive with those of industry rivals. Value chain analysis and benchmarking are essential tools in determining whether the company is performing particular functions and activities cost-effectively, learning whether its costs are in line with competitors, and deciding which internal activities and business processes need to be scrutinized for improvement. Value chain analysis teaches that how competently a company manages its value chain activities relative to rivals is a key to building a competitive advantage based on either better competencies and competitive capabilities or lower costs than rivals.

4. *Is the company competitively stronger or weaker than key rivals?* The key appraisals here involve how the company matches up against key rivals on industry key success factors and other chief determinants of competitive success and whether and why the company has a competitive advantage or disadvantage. Quantitative competitive strength assessments, using the method presented in Table 4.5, indicate where a company is competitively strong and weak, and provide insight into the company's ability to defend or enhance its market position. As a rule a company's competitive strategy should be built around its competitive strengths and should aim at shoring up areas where it is competitively vulnerable. When a company has important competitive strengths in areas where one or more rivals are weak, it makes sense to consider offensive moves to exploit rivals' competitive weaknesses. When a company has important competitive weaknesses in areas where one or more rivals are strong, it makes sense to consider defensive moves to curtail its vulnerability.

5. *What strategic issues and problems merit front-burner managerial attention?* This analytical step zeros in on the strategic issues and problems that stand in the way of the company's success. It involves using the results of both industry and competitive analysis and company situation analysis to identify a "worry list" of issues to be resolved for the company to be financially and competitively successful in the years ahead. The worry list always centers on such concerns as "how to . . .," "what to do about . . .," and "whether to . . ."—the purpose of the worry list is to identify the specific issues/problems that management needs to address. Actually deciding upon a strategy and what specific actions to take is what comes after the list of strategic issues and problems that merit front-burner management attention is developed.

Good company situation analysis, like good industry and competitive analysis, is a valuable precondition for good strategy making. A competently done evaluation of a company's resource capabilities and competitive strengths exposes strong and weak points in the present strategy and how attractive or unattractive the company's competitive position is and why. Managers need such understanding to craft a strategy that is well suited to the company's competitive circumstances.

Exercises

1. Review the information in Illustration Capsule 4.1 concerning the costs of the different value chain activities associated with recording and distributing music CDs through traditional brick-and-mortar retail outlets. Then answer the following questions:

   a. Does the growing popularity of downloading music from the Internet give rise to a new music industry value chain that differs considerably from the traditional value chain? Explain why or why not.

   b. What costs are cut out of the traditional value chain or bypassed when *online music retailers* (Apple, Sony, Microsoft, Musicmatch, Napster, Cdigix, and others) sell songs directly to online buyers? (Note: In 2005, online music stores were selling download-only titles for $0.79 to $0.99 per song and $9.99 for most albums.)

   c. What costs would be cut out of the traditional value chain or bypassed in the event that *recording studios* sell downloadable files of artists' recordings directly to online buyers?

   d. What happens to the traditional value chain if more and more music lovers use peer-to-peer file-sharing software to download music from the Internet to play music on their PCs or MP3 players or make their own CDs? (Note: It was estimated that, in 2004, about 1 billion songs were available for online trading and file sharing via such programs as Kazaa, Grokster, Shareaza, BitTorrent, and eDonkey, despite the fact that some 4,000 people had been sued by the Recording Industry Association of America for pirating copyrighted music via peer-to-peer file sharing.)

2. Using the information in Table 4.1 and the following financial statement information for Avon Products, calculate the following ratios for Avon for both 2003 and 2004:

   a. Gross profit margin.

   b. Operating profit margin.

   c. Net profit margin.

   d. Return on total assets.

   e. Return on stockholders' equity.

   f. Debt-to-equity ratio.

   g. Times-interest-earned.

   h. Days of inventory.

   i. Inventory turnover ratio.

   j. Average collection period.

   Based on these ratios, did Avon's financial performance improve, weaken, or remain about the same from 2003 to 2004?

Avon Products Inc., Consolidated Statements of Income
(in millions, except per share data)

	Years Ended December 31	
	2004	2003
Net sales	$7,656.2	$6,773.7
Other revenue	91.6	71.4
Total revenue	7,747.8	6,845.1
Costs, expenses and other:		
Cost of sales	2,911.7	2,611.8
Marketing, distribution and administrative expenses	3,610.3	3,194.4
Special charges, net	(3.2)	(3.9)
Operating profit	1,229.0	1,042.8
Interest expense	33.8	33.3
Interest income	(20.6)	(12.6)
Other expense (income), net	28.3	28.6
Total other expenses	41.5	49.3
Income before taxes and minority interest	1,187.5	993.5
Income taxes	330.6	318.9
Income before minority interest	856.9	674.6
Minority interest	(10.8)	(9.8)
Net income	$ 846.1	$ 664.8
Earnings per share:		
Basic	$ 1.79	$ 1.41
Diluted	$ 1.77	$ 1.39
Weighted-average shares outstanding (in millions):		
Basic	472.35	471.08
Diluted	477.96	483.13

Avon Products Inc. Consolidated Balance Sheets (in millions)

	December 31	
	2004	2003
Current assets		
Cash, including cash equivalents of $401.2 and $373.8	$ 769.6	$ 694.0
Accounts receivable (less allowances of $101.0 and $81.1)	599.1	553.2
Inventories	740.5	653.4
Prepaid expenses and other	397.2	325.5
Total current assets	$2,506.4	$2,226.1
Property, plant and equipment, at cost:		
Land	$ 61.7	$ 58.6
Buildings and improvements	886.8	765.9
Equipment	1,006.7	904.4
	1,955.2	1,728.9
Less accumulated depreciation	(940.4)	(873.3)
	1,014.8	855.6
Other assets	626.9	499.9
Total assets	$4,148.1	$3,581.6
Liabilities and shareholders' equity		
Current liabilities		
Debt maturing within one year	$ 51.7	$ 244.1
Accounts payable	490.1	400.1
Accrued compensation	164.5	149.5
Other accrued liabilities	360.1	332.6
Sales and taxes other than income	154.4	139.5
Income taxes	304.7	341.2
Total current liabilities	$1,525.5	$1,607.0
Long-term debt	$ 866.3	$ 877.7
Employee benefit plans	620.6	502.1
Deferred income taxes	12.1	50.6
Other liabilities (including minority interest of $42.5 and $46.0)	173.4	172.9
Total liabilities	$3,197.9	$3,210.3

(*Continued*)

	December 31	
	2004	2003
Shareholders' equity		
Common stock, par value $.25—authorized 1,500 shares; issued 728.61 and 722.25 shares	182.2	90.3
Additional paid-in capital	1,356.8	1,188.4
Retained earnings	2,693.5	2,202.4
Accumulated other comprehensive loss	(679.5)	(729.4)
Treasury stock, at cost—257.08 and 251.66 shares	(2,602.8)	(2,380.4)
Total shareholders' equity	950.2	371.3
Total liabilities and shareholders' equity	$4,148.1	$3,581.6

Source: Avon Products Inc., 2004 10-K

chapter five

The Five Generic Competitive Strategies

Which One to Employ?

Competitive strategy is about being different. It means deliberately choosing to perform activities differently or to perform different activities than rivals to deliver a unique mix of value.

—Michael E. Porter

Strategy . . . is about first analyzing and then experimenting, trying, learning, and experimenting some more.

**—Ian C. McMillan and
Rita Gunther McGrath**

Winners in business play rough and don't apologize for it. The nicest part of playing hardball is watching your competitors squirm.

**—George Stalk Jr. and
Rob Lachenauer**

The essence of strategy lies in creating tomorrow's competitive advantages faster than competitors mimic the ones you possess today.

—Gary Hamel and C. K. Prahalad

This chapter describes the *five basic competitive strategy options*—which of the five to employ is a company's first and foremost choice in crafting an overall strategy and beginning its quest for competitive advantage. A company's **competitive strategy** deals exclusively with the specifics of management's game plan for competing successfully—its specific efforts to please customers, its offensive and defensive moves to counter the maneuvers of rivals, its responses to whatever market conditions prevail at the moment, its initiatives to strengthen its market position, and its approach to securing a competitive advantage vis-à-vis rivals. Companies the world over are imaginative in conceiving competitive strategies to win customer favor. At most companies the aim, quite simply, is to do a significantly better job than rivals of providing what buyers are looking for and thereby secure an upper hand in the marketplace.

A company achieves competitive advantage whenever it has some type of edge over rivals in attracting buyers and coping with competitive forces. There are many routes to competitive advantage, but they all involve giving buyers what they perceive as superior value compared to the offerings of rival sellers. Superior value can mean a good product at a lower price; a superior product that is worth paying more for; or a best-value offering that represents an attractive combination of price, features, quality, service, and other appealing attributes. Delivering superior value—whatever form it takes—nearly always requires performing value chain activities differently than rivals and building competencies and resource capabilities that are not readily matched.

THE FIVE GENERIC COMPETITIVE STRATEGIES

There are countless variations in the competitive strategies that companies employ, mainly because each company's strategic approach entails custom-designed actions to fit its own circumstances and industry environment. The custom-tailored nature of each company's strategy makes the chances remote that any two companies—even companies in the same industry—will employ strategies that are exactly alike in every detail. Managers at different companies always have a slightly different spin on future market conditions and how to best align their company's strategy with these conditions; moreover, they have different notions of how they intend to outmaneuver rivals and what strategic options make the most sense for their particular company. However, when one strips away the details to get at the real substance, the biggest and most important differences among competitive strategies boil down to (1) whether a company's market target is broad or narrow, and (2) whether the company is pursuing a competitive advantage linked to low costs or product differentiation. Five distinct competitive strategy approaches stand out:[1]

1. *A low-cost provider strategy*—striving to achieve lower overall costs than rivals and appealing to a broad spectrum of customers, usually by underpricing rivals.

2. *A broad differentiation strategy*—seeking to differentiate the company's product offering from rivals' in ways that will appeal to a broad spectrum of buyers.

3. *A best-cost provider strategy*—giving customers more value for their money by incorporating good-to-excellent product attributes at a lower cost than rivals; the target is to have the lowest (best) costs and prices compared to rivals offering products with comparable attributes.

Figure 5.1   **The Five Generic Competitive Strategies: Each Stakes Out a Different Market Position**

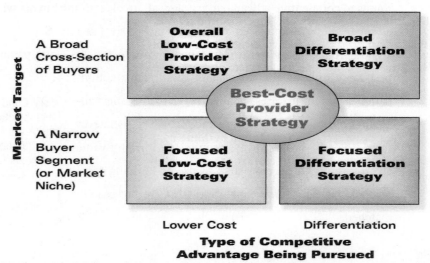

Source: This is an author-expanded version of a three-strategy classification discussed in Michael E. Porter, *Competitive Strategy: Techniques for Analyzing Industries and Competitors* (New York: Free Press, 1980), pp. 35–40.

4. *A focused (or market niche) strategy based on low costs*—concentrating on a narrow buyer segment and outcompeting rivals by having lower costs than rivals and thus being able to serve niche members at a lower price.

5. *A focused (or market niche) strategy based on differentiation*—concentrating on a narrow buyer segment and outcompeting rivals by offering niche members customized attributes that meet their tastes and requirements better than rivals' products.

Each of these five generic competitive approaches stakes out a different market position, as shown in Figure 5.1. Each involves distinctively different approaches to competing and operating the business. The remainder of this chapter explores the ins and outs of the five generic competitive strategies and how they differ.

LOW-COST PROVIDER STRATEGIES

Striving to be the industry's overall low-cost provider is a powerful competitive approach in markets with many price-sensitive buyers. A company achieves low-cost leadership when it becomes the industry's lowest-cost provider rather than just being one of perhaps several competitors with comparatively low costs. A low-cost provider's strategic target is meaningfully lower costs than rivals—but not necessarily the absolutely lowest possible cost. In striving for a cost advantage over rivals, managers must take care to include features and services that buyers consider essential—*a product offering that is too frills-free sabotages the attractiveness of the company's product and can turn buyers off even if it is priced lower than competing products.* For maximum effectiveness, companies employing a low-cost provider strategy need to achieve their cost advantage in ways difficult for rivals to copy or match. If rivals find it relatively easy or inexpensive to imitate the leader's low-cost methods, then the leader's advantage will be too short-lived to yield a valuable edge in the marketplace.

> **Core Concept**
> A low-cost leader's basis for competitive advantage is lower overall costs than competitors. Successful low-cost leaders are exceptionally good at finding ways to drive costs out of their businesses.

A company has two options for translating a low-cost advantage over rivals into attractive profit performance. Option 1 is to use the lower-cost edge to underprice competitors and attract price-sensitive buyers in great enough numbers to increase total profits. The trick to profitably underpricing rivals is either to keep the size of the price cut smaller than the size of the firm's cost advantage (thus reaping the benefits of both a bigger profit margin per unit sold and the added profits on incremental sales) or to generate enough added volume to increase total profits despite thinner profit margins (larger volume can make up for smaller margins provided the underpricing of rivals brings in enough extra sales). Option 2 is to maintain the present price, be content with the present market share, and use the lower-cost edge to earn a higher profit margin on each unit sold, thereby raising the firm's total profits and overall return on investment.

Illustration Capsule 5.1 describes Nucor Corporation's strategy for gaining low-cost leadership in manufacturing a variety of steel products.

The Two Major Avenues for Achieving a Cost Advantage

To achieve a low-cost edge over rivals, a firm's cumulative costs across its overall value chain must be lower than competitors' cumulative costs—and the means of achieving

Illustration Capsule 5.1

Nucor Corporation's Low-Cost Provider Strategy

Nucor Corporation is the world's leading minimill producer of such steel products as carbon and alloy steel bars, beams, sheet, and plate; steel joists and joist girders; steel deck; cold finished steel; steel fasteners; metal building systems; and light gauge steel framing. In 2004, it had close to $10 billion in sales, 9,000 employees, and annual production capacity of nearly 22 million tons, making it the largest steel producer in the United States and one of the 10 largest in the world. The company has pursued a strategy that has made it among the world's lowest-cost producers of steel and has allowed the company to consistently outperform its rivals in terms of financial and market performance.

Nucor's low-cost strategy aims to give it a cost and pricing advantage in the commodity-like steel industry and leaves no part of the company's value chain neglected. The key elements of the strategy include the following:

- Using electric arc furnaces where scrap steel and directly reduced iron ore are melted and then sent to a continuous caster and rolling mill to be shaped into steel products, thereby eliminating an assortment of production processes from the value chain used by traditional integrated steel mills. Nucor's minimill value chain makes the use of coal, coke, and iron ore unnecessary; cuts investment in facilities and equipment (eliminating coke ovens, blast furnaces, basic oxygen furnaces, and ingot casters); and requires fewer employees than integrated mills.

- Striving hard for continuous improvement in the efficiency of its plants and frequently investing in state-of-the-art equipment to reduce unit costs. Nucor is known for its technological leadership and its aggressive pursuit of production process innovation.

- Carefully selecting plant sites to minimize inbound and outbound shipping costs and to take advantage of low rates for electricity (electric arc furnaces are heavy users of electricity). Nucor tends to avoid locating new plants in geographic areas where labor unions are a strong influence.

- Hiring a nonunion workforce that uses team-based incentive compensation systems (often opposed by unions). Operating and maintenance employees and supervisors are paid weekly bonuses based on the productivity of their work group. The size of the bonus is based on the capabilities of the equipment employed and ranges from 80 percent to 150 percent of an employee's base pay; no bonus is paid if the equipment is not operating. Nucor's compensation program has boosted the company's labor productivity to levels nearly double the industry average while rewarding productive employees with annual compensation packages that exceed what their union counterparts earn by as much as 20 percent. Nucor has been able to attract and retain highly talented, productive, and dedicated employees. In addition, the company's healthy culture and results-oriented self-managed work teams allow the company to employ fewer supervisors than what would be needed with an hourly union workforce.

- Heavily emphasizing consistent product quality and has rigorous quality systems.

- Minimizing general and administrative expenses by maintaining a lean staff at corporate headquarters (fewer than 125 employees) and allowing only four levels of management between the CEO and production workers. Headquarters offices are modestly furnished and located in an inexpensive building. The company minimizes reports, paperwork, and meetings to keep managers focused on value-adding activities. Nucor is noted not only for its streamlined organizational structure but also for its frugality in travel and entertainment expenses—the company's top managers set the example by flying coach class, avoiding pricey hotels, and refraining from taking customers out for expensive dinners.

In 2001–2003, when many U.S. producers of steel products were in dire economic straits because of weak demand for steel and deep price discounting by foreign rivals, Nucor began acquiring state-of-the-art steelmaking facilities from bankrupt or nearly bankrupt rivals at bargain-basement prices, often at 20 to 25 percent of what it cost to construct the facilities. This has given Nucor much lower depreciation costs than rivals having comparable plants.

Nucor management's outstanding execution of its low-cost strategy and its commitment to drive down costs throughout its value chain has allowed it to compete aggressively on price, earn higher profit margins than rivals, and grow its business at a considerably faster rate than its integrated steel mill rivals.

Source: Company annual reports, news releases, and Web site.

the cost advantage must be durable. There are two ways to accomplish this:[2]

1. Do a better job than rivals of performing value chain activities more cost-effectively.
2. Revamp the firm's overall value chain to eliminate or bypass some cost-producing activities.

Let's look at each of the two approaches to securing a cost advantage.

Cost-Efficient Management of Value Chain Activities For a company to do a more cost-efficient job of managing its value chain than rivals, managers must launch a concerted, ongoing effort to ferret out cost-saving opportunities in every part of the value chain. No activity can escape cost-saving scrutiny, and all company personnel must be expected to use their talents and ingenuity to come up with innovative and effective ways to keep costs down. All avenues for performing value chain activities at a lower cost than rivals have to be explored. Attempts to outmanage rivals on cost commonly involve such actions as:

1. *Striving to capture all available economies of scale.* Economies of scale stem from an ability to lower unit costs by increasing the scale of operation—there are many occasions when a large plant is more economical to operate than a small or medium-size plant or when a large distribution warehouse is more cost efficient than a small warehouse. Often, manufacturing economies can be achieved by using common parts and components in different models and/or by cutting back on the number of models offered (especially slow-selling ones) and then scheduling longer production runs for fewer models. In global industries, making separate products for each country market instead of selling a mostly standard product worldwide tends to boost unit costs because of lost time in model changeover, shorter production runs, and inability to reach the most economic scale of production for each country model.
2. *Taking full advantage of learning/experience curve effects.* The cost of performing an activity can decline over time as the learning and experience of company personnel builds. Learning/experience curve economies can stem from debugging and mastering newly introduced technologies, using the experiences and suggestions of workers to install more efficient plant layouts and assembly procedures, and the added speed and effectiveness that accrues from repeatedly picking sites for and building new plants, retail outlets, or distribution centers. Aggressively managed low-cost providers pay diligent attention to capturing the benefits of learning and experience and to keeping these benefits proprietary to whatever extent possible.
3. *Trying to operate facilities at full capacity.* Whether a company is able to operate at or near full capacity has a big impact on units costs when its value chain contains activities associated with substantial fixed costs. Higher rates of capacity utilization allow depreciation and other fixed costs to be spread over a larger unit volume, thereby lowering fixed costs per unit. The more capital-intensive the business, or the higher the percentage of fixed costs as a percentage of total costs, the more important that full-capacity operation becomes because there's such a stiff unit-cost penalty for underutilizing existing capacity. In such cases, finding ways to operate close to full capacity year-round can be an important source of cost advantage.
4. *Pursuing efforts to boost sales volumes and thus spread such costs as R&D, advertising, and selling and administrative costs out over more units.* The more units

a company sells, the more it lowers its unit costs for R&D, sales and marketing, and administrative overhead.

5. *Improving supply chain efficiency.* Many companies pursue cost reduction by partnering with suppliers to streamline the ordering and purchasing process via online systems, reduce inventory carrying costs via just-in-time inventory practices, economize on shipping and materials handling, and ferret out other cost-saving opportunities. A company with a core competence (or better still a distinctive competence) in cost-efficient supply chain management can sometimes achieve a sizable cost advantage over less adept rivals.

6. *Substituting the use of low-cost for high-cost raw materials or component parts.* If the costs of raw materials and parts are too high, a company can either substitute the use of lower-cost items or maybe even design the high-cost components out of the product altogether.

7. *Using online systems and sophisticated software to achieve operating efficiencies.* Data sharing, starting with customer orders and going all the way back to components production, coupled with the use of enterprise resource planning (ERP) and manufacturing execution system (MES) software, can make custom manufacturing just as cheap as mass production—and sometimes cheaper. Online systems and software can also greatly reduce production times and labor costs. Lexmark used ERP and MES software to cut its production time for inkjet printers from four hours to 24 minutes. Southwest Airlines uses proprietary software to schedule flights and assign flight crews cost-effectively.

8. *Adopting labor-saving operating methods.* Examples of ways for a company to economize on labor costs include the following: installing labor-saving technology, shifting production from geographic areas where labor costs are high to geographic areas where labor costs are low, avoiding the use of union labor where possible (because of work rules that can stifle productivity and because of union demands for above-market pay scales and costly fringe benefits), and using incentive compensation systems that promote high labor productivity.

9. *Using the company's bargaining power vis-à-vis suppliers to gain concessions.* Many large enterprises (e.g., Wal-Mart, Home Depot, the world's major motor vehicle producers) have used their bargaining clout in purchasing large volumes to wrangle good prices on their purchases from suppliers. Having greater buying power than rivals can be an important source of cost advantage.

10. *Being alert to the cost advantages of outsourcing and vertical integration.* Outsourcing the performance of certain value chain activities can be more economical than performing them in-house if outside specialists, by virtue of their expertise and volume, can perform the activities at lower cost. Indeed, outsourcing has in recent years become a widely used cost-reduction approach. However, there can be times when integrating the activities of either suppliers or distribution channel allies can allow an enterprise to detour suppliers or buyers who have an adverse impact on costs because of their considerable bargaining power.

In addition to the above means of achieving lower costs than rivals, managers can also achieve important cost savings by deliberately opting for an inherently economical strategy keyed to a frills-free product offering. For instance, a company can bolster its attempts to open up a durable cost advantage over rivals by:

- Having lower specifications for purchased materials, parts, and components than rivals do. Thus, a maker of personal computers (PCs) can use the cheapest hard drives, microprocessors, monitors, DVD drives, and other components it can find so as to end up with lower production costs than rival PC makers.

- Distributing the company's product only through low-cost distribution channels and avoiding high-cost distribution channels.
- Choosing to use the most economical method for delivering customer orders (even if it results in longer delivery times).

These strategy-related means of keeping costs low don't really involve "outmanaging" rivals, but they can nonetheless contribute materially to becoming the industry's low-cost leader.

Revamping the Value Chain to Curb or Eliminate Unnecessary Activities

Dramatic cost advantages can emerge from finding innovative ways to cut back on or entirely bypass certain cost-producing value chain activities. There are six primary ways companies can achieve a cost advantage by reconfiguring their value chains:

1. *Cutting out distributors and dealers by selling directly to customers.* Selling directly and bypassing the activities and costs of distributors or dealers can involve (1) having the company's own direct sales force (which adds the costs of maintaining and supporting a sales force but may well be cheaper than accessing customers through distributors or dealers) and/or (2) conducting sales operations at the company's Web site (Web site operations may be substantially cheaper than distributor or dealer channels). Costs in the wholesale/retail portions of the value chain frequently represent 35–50 percent of the price final consumers pay. There are several prominent examples in which companies have instituted a sell-direct approach to cutting costs out of the value chain. Software developers allow customers to download new programs directly from the Internet, eliminating the costs of producing and packaging CDs and cutting out the host of activities, costs, and markups associated with shipping and distributing software through wholesale and retail channels. By cutting all these costs and activities out of the value chain, software developers have the pricing room to boost their profit margins and still sell their products below levels that retailers would have to charge. The major airlines now sell most of their tickets directly to passengers via their Web sites, ticket counter agents, and telephone reservation systems, allowing them to save hundreds of millions of dollars in commissions once paid to travel agents.

2. *Replacing certain value chain activities with faster and cheaper online technology.* In recent years the Internet and Internet technology applications have become powerful and pervasive tools for conducting business and reengineering company and industry value chains. For instance, Internet technology has revolutionized supply chain management, turning many time-consuming and labor-intensive activities into paperless transactions performed instantaneously. Company procurement personnel can—with only a few mouse clicks—check materials inventories against incoming customer orders, check suppliers' stocks, check the latest prices for parts and components at auction and e-sourcing Web sites, and check FedEx delivery schedules. Various e-procurement software packages streamline the purchasing process by eliminating paper documents such as requests for quotations, purchase orders, order acceptances, and shipping notices. There's software that permits the relevant details of incoming customer orders to be instantly shared with the suppliers of needed parts and components. All this facilitates

just-in-time deliveries of parts and components and matching the production of parts and components to assembly plant requirements and production schedules, cutting out unnecessary activities and producing savings for both suppliers and manufacturers. Retailers can install online systems that relay data from cash register sales at the check-out counter back to manufacturers and their suppliers. Manufacturers can use online systems to collaborate closely with parts and components suppliers in designing new products and shortening the time it takes to get them into production. Online systems allow warranty claims and product performance problems involving supplier components to be instantly relayed to the relevant suppliers so that corrections can be expedited. Online systems have the further effect of breaking down corporate bureaucracies and reducing over-head costs. The whole back-office data management process (order processing, invoicing, customer accounting, and other kinds of transaction costs) can be handled fast, accurately, and with less paperwork and fewer personnel.

3. *Streamlining operations by eliminating low-value-added or unnecessary work steps and activities.* Examples include using computer-assisted design techniques, standardizing parts and components across models and styles, having suppliers collaborate to combine parts and components into modules so that products can be assembled in fewer steps, and shifting to an easy-to-manufacture product design. At Wal-Mart, some items supplied by manufacturers are delivered directly to retail stores rather than being routed through Wal-Mart's distribution centers and delivered by Wal-Mart trucks; in other instances, Wal-Mart unloads incoming shipments from manufacturers' trucks arriving at its distribution centers directly onto outgoing Wal-Mart trucks headed to particular stores without ever moving the goods into the distribution center. Many supermarket chains have greatly reduced in-store meat butchering and cutting activities by shifting to meats that are cut and packaged at the meat-packing plant and then delivered to their stores in ready-to-sell form.

4. *Relocating facilities so as to curb the need for shipping and handling activities.* Having suppliers locate facilities adjacent to the company's plant or locating the company's plants or warehouses near customers can help curb or eliminate shipping and handling costs.

5. *Offering a frills-free product.* Deliberately restricting a company's product offering to the essentials can help the company cut costs associated with snazzy attributes and a full lineup of options and extras. Activities and costs can also be eliminated by incorporating fewer performance and quality features into the product and by offering buyers fewer services. Stripping extras like first-class sections, meals, and reserved seating is a favorite technique of budget airlines like Southwest, Ryanair (Europe), easyJet (Europe), and Gol (Brazil).

6. *Offering a limited product line as opposed to a full product line.* Pruning slow-selling items from the product lineup and being content to meet the needs of most buyers rather than all buyers can eliminate activities and costs associated with numerous product versions and wide selection.

Illustration Capsule 5.2 describes how Wal-Mart has managed its value chain in the retail grocery portion of its business to achieve a dramatic cost advantage over rival supermarket chains and become the world's biggest grocery retailer.

Examples of Companies That Revamped Their Value Chains to Reduce Costs Iowa Beef Packers (IBP), now a subsidiary of Tyson Foods, pioneered the

Illustration Capsule 5.2

How Wal-Mart Managed Its Value Chain to Achieve a Huge Low-Cost Advantage over Rival Supermarket Chains

Wal-Mart has achieved a very substantial cost and pricing advantage over rival supermarket chains both by revamping portions of the grocery retailing value chain and by out-managing its rivals in efficiently performing various value chain activities. Its cost advantage stems from a series of initiatives and practices:

- Instituting extensive information sharing with vendors via online systems that relay sales at its checkout counters directly to suppliers of the items, thereby providing suppliers with real-time information on customer demand and preferences (creating an estimated 6 percent cost advantage). It is standard practice at Wal-Mart to collaborate extensively with vendors on all aspects of the purchasing and store delivery process to squeeze out mutually beneficial cost savings. Procter & Gamble, Wal-Mart's biggest supplier, went so far as to integrate its enterprise resource planning (ERP) system with Wal-Mart's.

- Pursuing global procurement of some items and centralizing most purchasing activities so as to leverage the company's buying power (creating an estimated 2.5 percent cost advantage).

- Investing in state-of-the-art automation at its distribution centers, efficiently operating a truck fleet that makes daily deliveries to Wal-Mart's stores, and putting assorted other cost-saving practices into place at its headquarters, distribution centers, and stores (resulting in an estimated 4 percent cost advantage).

- Striving to optimize the product mix and achieve greater sales turnover (resulting in about a 2 percent cost advantage).

- Installing security systems and store operating procedures that lower shrinkage rates (producing a cost advantage of about 0.5 percent).

- Negotiating preferred real estate rental and leasing rates with real estate developers and owners of its store sites (yielding a cost advantage of 2 percent).

- Managing and compensating its workforce in a manner that produces lower labor costs (yielding an estimated 5 percent cost advantage)

Altogether, these value chain initiatives give Wal-Mart an approximately 22 percent cost advantage over Kroger, Safeway, and other leading supermarket chains. With such a sizable cost advantage, Wal-Mart has been able to underprice its rivals and become the world's leading supermarket retailer in little more than a decade.

Source: Developed by the authors from information at www.wal-mart.com (accessed September 15, 2004) and in Marco Iansiti and Roy Levien, "Strategy as Ecology," *Harvard Business Review* 82, no. 3 (March 2004), p. 70.

development of a cheaper value chain system in the beef-packing industry.[3] The traditional cost chain involved raising cattle on scattered farms and ranches; shipping them live to labor-intensive, unionized slaughtering plants; and then transporting whole sides of beef to grocery retailers whose butcher departments cut them into smaller pieces and packaged them for sale to grocery shoppers. IBP revamped the traditional chain with a radically different strategy: It built large automated plants employing nonunion workers near cattle supplies. Near the plants it arranged to set up large feed lots (or holding pens) where cattle were fed grain for a short time to fatten them up prior to slaughter. The meat was butchered at the processing plant into small, high-yield cuts. Some of the trimmed and boned cuts were vacuum-sealed in plastic casings for further butchering in supermarket meat departments, but others were trimmed and/or boned, put in plastic-sealed ready-to-sell trays, boxed, and shipped to retailers. IBP's strategy was to increase the volume of prepackaged, "case-ready" cuts that retail grocers could unpack from boxes and place directly into the meat case. In addition, IBP provided meat retailers with individually wrapped quick-frozen steaks, as well as precooked roasts, beef tip, and meatloaf selections that could be prepared in a matter of minutes. Iowa Beef's inbound cattle transportation expenses, traditionally a major cost item, were cut significantly by avoiding the weight losses that occurred when live animals were shipped long distances just prior to slaughter. Sizable major outbound shipping cost savings were achieved by not having to ship whole sides of beef, which had a high waste factor. Meat retailers had to do far less butchering to stock their meat cases. IBP value chain revamping was so successful that the company became the largest U.S. meatpacker.

Southwest Airlines has reconfigured the traditional value chain of commercial airlines to lower costs and thereby offer dramatically lower fares to passengers. Its mastery of fast turnarounds at the gates (about 25 minutes versus 45 minutes for rivals) allows its planes to fly more hours per day. This translates into being able to schedule more flights per day with fewer aircraft, allowing Southwest to generate more revenue per plane on average than rivals. Southwest does not offer in-flight meals, assigned seating, baggage transfer to connecting airlines, or first-class seating and service, thereby eliminating all the cost-producing activities associated with these features. The company's fast, user-friendly online reservation system facilitates e-ticketing and reduces staffing requirements at telephone reservation centers and airport counters. Its use of automated check-in equipment reduces staffing requirements for terminal check-in.

Dell has created the best, most cost-efficient value chain in the global personal computer industry. Whereas Dell's major rivals (Hewlett-Packard, Lenovo, Sony, and Toshiba) produce their models in volume and sell them through independent resellers and retailers, Dell has elected to market directly to PC users, building its PCs to customer specifications as orders come in and shipping them to customers within a few days of receiving the order. Dell's value chain approach has proved cost-effective in coping with the PC industry's blink-of-an-eye product life cycle. The build-to-order strategy enables the company to avoid misjudging buyer demand for its various models and being saddled with quickly obsolete excess components and finished-goods inventories—all parts and components are obtained on a just-in-time basis from vendors, many of which deliver their items to Dell assembly plants several times a day in volumes matched to the Dell's daily assembly schedule. Also, Dell's sell-direct strategy slices reseller/retailer costs and margins out of the value chain (although some of these savings are offset by the cost of Dell's direct marketing and customer support activities—functions that would otherwise be performed by resellers and retailers). Partnerships with suppliers that facilitate just-in-time deliveries of components and minimize Dell's inventory costs, coupled with Dell's extensive use of e-commerce technologies further reduce Dell's costs. Dell's value chain approach is widely considered to have made it the global low-cost leader in the PC industry.

The Keys to Success in Achieving Low-Cost Leadership

To succeed with a low-cost-provider strategy, company managers have to scrutinize each cost-creating activity and determine what factors cause costs to be high or low. Then they have to use this knowledge to keep the unit costs of each activity low, exhaustively pursuing cost efficiencies throughout the value chain. They have to be proactive in restructuring the value chain to eliminate nonessential work steps and low-value activities. Normally, low-cost producers work diligently to create cost-conscious corporate cultures that feature broad employee participation in continuous cost improvement efforts and limited perks and frills for executives. They strive to operate with exceptionally small corporate staffs to keep administrative costs to a minimum.

Many successful low-cost leaders also use benchmarking to keep close tabs on how their costs compare with rivals and firms performing comparable activities in other industries.

But while low-cost providers are champions of frugality, they are usually aggressive in investing in resources and capabilities that promise to drive costs out of the business. Wal-Mart, one of the foremost practitioners of low-cost leadership, employs state-of-the-art technology throughout its operations—its distribution facilities are an automated showcase, it uses online systems to order goods from suppliers and manage inventories, it equips its stores with cutting-edge sales-tracking and check-out systems, and it sends daily point-of-sale data to 4,000 vendors. Wal-Mart's information and communications systems and capabilities are more sophisticated than those of virtually any other retail chain in the world.

> Success in achieving a low-cost edge over rivals comes from outmanaging rivals in figuring out how to perform value chain activities most cost effectively and eliminating or curbing non essential value chain activities

Other companies noted for their successful use of low-cost provider strategies include Lincoln Electric in arc welding equipment, Briggs & Stratton in small gasoline engines, Bic in ballpoint pens, Black & Decker in power tools, Stride Rite in footwear, Beaird-Poulan in chain saws, and General Electric and Whirlpool in major home appliances.

When a Low-Cost Provider Strategy Works Best

A competitive strategy predicated on low-cost leadership is particularly powerful when:

1. *Price competition among rival sellers is especially vigorous*—Low-cost providers are in the best position to compete offensively on the basis of price, to use the appeal of lower price to grab sales (and market share) from rivals, to win the business of price-sensitive buyers, to remain profitable in the face of strong price competition, and to survive price wars.

2. *The products of rival sellers are essentially identical and supplies are readily available from any of several eager sellers*—Commodity-like products and/or ample supplies set the stage for lively price competition; in such markets, it is less efficient, higher-cost companies whose profits get squeezed the most.

3. *There are few ways to achieve product differentiation that have value to buyers*—When the differences between brands do not matter much to buyers, buyers are nearly always very sensitive to price differences and shop the market for the best price.

4. *Most buyers use the product in the same ways*—With common user requirements, a standardized product can satisfy the needs of buyers, in which case low selling price, not features or quality, becomes the dominant factor in causing buyers to choose one seller's product over another's.

5. *Buyers incur low costs in switching their purchases from one seller to another*—Low switching costs give buyers the flexibility to shift purchases to lower-priced sellers having equally good products or to attractively priced substitute products. A low-cost leader is well positioned to use low price to induce its customers not to switch to rival brands or substitutes.

6. *Buyers are large and have significant power to bargain down prices*—Low-cost providers have partial profit-margin protection in bargaining with high-volume buyers, since powerful buyers are rarely able to bargain price down past the survival level of the next most cost-efficient seller.

7. *Industry newcomers use introductory low prices to attract buyers and build a customer base*—The low-cost leader can use price cuts of its own to make it harder

A low-cost provider is in the best position to win the business of price-sensitive buyers, set the floor on market price, and still earn a profit.

for a new rival to win customers; the pricing power of the low-cost provider acts as a barrier for new entrants.

As a rule, the more price-sensitive buyers are, the more appealing a low-cost strategy becomes. A low-cost company's ability to set the industry's price floor and still earn a profit erects protective barriers around its market position.

The Pitfalls of a Low-Cost Provider Strategy

Perhaps the biggest pitfall of a low-cost provider strategy is getting carried away with overly aggressive price cutting and ending up with lower, rather than higher, profitability. A low-cost/low-price advantage results in superior profitability only if (1) prices are cut by less than the size of the cost advantage or (2) the added gains in unit sales are large enough to bring in a bigger total profit despite lower margins per unit sold. A company with a 5 percent cost advantage cannot cut prices 20 percent, end up with a volume gain of only 10 percent, and still expect to earn higher profits!

A second big pitfall is not emphasizing avenues of cost advantage that can be kept proprietary or that relegate rivals to playing catch-up. The value of a cost advantage depends on its sustainability. Sustainability, in turn, hinges on whether the company achieves its cost advantage in ways difficult for rivals to copy or match.

A low-cost provider's product offering must always contain enough attributes to be attractive to prospective buyers—low price, by itself, is not always appealing to buyers.

A third pitfall is becoming too fixated on cost reduction. Low cost cannot be pursued so zealously that a firm's offering ends up being too features-poor to generate buyer appeal. Furthermore, a company driving hard to push its costs down has to guard against misreading or ignoring increased buyer interest in added features or service, declining buyer sensitivity to price, or new developments that start to alter how buyers use the product. A low-cost zealot risks losing market ground if buyers start opting for more upscale or features-rich products.

Even if these mistakes are avoided, a low-cost competitive approach still carries risk. Cost-saving technological breakthroughs or the emergence of still-lower-cost value chain models can nullify a low-cost leader's hard-won position. The current leader may have difficulty in shifting quickly to the new technologies or value chain approaches because heavy investments lock it in (at least temporarily) to its present value chain approach.

BROAD DIFFERENTIATION STRATEGIES

Core Concept
The essence of a broad differentiation strategy is to be unique in ways that are valuable to a wide range of customers.

Differentiation strategies are attractive whenever buyers' needs and preferences are too diverse to be fully satisfied by a standardized product or by sellers with identical capabilities. A company attempting to succeed through differentiation must study buyers' needs and behavior carefully to learn what buyers consider important, what they think has value, and what they are willing to pay for. Then the company has to incorporate buyer-desired attributes into its product or service offering that will clearly set it apart from rivals. Competitive advantage results once a sufficient number of buyers become strongly attached to the differentiated attributes.

Successful differentiation allows a firm to:

- Command a premium price for its product, and/or
- Increase unit sales (because additional buyers are won over by the differentiating features), and/or

- Gain buyer loyalty to its brand (because some buyers are strongly attracted to the differentiating features and bond with the company and its products).

Differentiation enhances profitability whenever the extra price the product commands outweighs the added costs of achieving the differentiation. Company differentiation strategies fail when buyers don't value the brand's uniqueness and when a company's approach to differentiation is easily copied or matched by its rivals.

Types of Differentiation Themes

Companies can pursue differentiation from many angles: a unique taste (Dr Pepper, Listerine); multiple features (Microsoft Windows, Microsoft Office); wide selection and one-stop shopping (Home Depot, Amazon.com); superior service (FedEx); spare parts availability (Caterpillar); engineering design and performance (Mercedes, BMW); prestige and distinctiveness (Rolex); product reliability (Johnson & Johnson in baby products); quality manufacture (Karastan in carpets, Michelin in tires, Toyota and Honda in automobiles); technological leadership (3M Corporation in bonding and coating products); a full range of services (Charles Schwab in stock brokerage); a complete line of products (Campbell's soups); and top-of-the-line image and reputation (Ralph Lauren and Starbucks).

The most appealing approaches to differentiation are those that are hard or expensive for rivals to duplicate. Indeed, resourceful competitors can, in time, clone almost any product or feature or attribute. If Coca-Cola introduces a vanilla-flavored soft drink, so can Pepsi; if Ford offers a 50,000-mile bumper-to-bumper warranty on its new vehicles, so can Volkswagen and Nissan. If Nokia introduces cell phones with cameras and Internet capability, so can Motorola and Samsung. As a rule, differentiation yields a longer-lasting and more profitable competitive edge when it is based on product innovation, technical superiority, product quality and reliability, comprehensive customer service, and unique competitive capabilities. Such differentiating attributes tend to be tough for rivals to copy or offset profitably, and buyers widely perceive them as having value.

> Easy-to-copy differentiating features cannot produce sustainable competitive advantage; differentiation based on competencies and capabilities tend to be more sustainable.

Where along the Value Chain to Create the Differentiating Attributes

Differentiation is not something hatched in marketing and advertising departments, nor is it limited to the catchalls of quality and service. Differentiation opportunities can exist in activities all along an industry's value chain; possibilities include the following:

- *Supply chain activities* that ultimately spill over to affect the performance or quality of the company's end product. Starbucks gets high ratings on its coffees partly because it has very strict specifications on the coffee beans purchased from suppliers.

- *Product R&D activities* that aim at improved product designs and performance features, expanded end uses and applications, more frequent first-on-the-market victories, wider product variety and selection, added user safety, greater recycling capability, or enhanced environmental protection.

- *Production R&D and technology-related activities* that permit custom-order manufacture at an efficient cost; make production methods safer for the environment; or improve product quality, reliability, and appearance. Many manufacturers have developed flexible manufacturing systems that allow different models and product versions to be made on the same assembly line. Being able to provide buyers with made-to-order products can be a potent differentiating capability.

- *Manufacturing activities* that reduce product defects, prevent premature product failure, extend product life, allow better warranty coverages, improve economy of use, result in more end-user convenience, or enhance product appearance. The quality edge enjoyed by Japanese automakers stems partly from their distinctive competence in performing assembly-line activities.

- *Distribution and shipping activities* that allow for fewer warehouse and on-the-shelf stockouts, quicker delivery to customers, more accurate order filling, and/or lower shipping costs.

- *Marketing, sales, and customer service activities* that result in superior technical assistance to buyers, faster maintenance and repair services, more and better product information provided to customers, more and better training materials for end users, better credit terms, quicker order processing, or greater customer convenience.

Managers need keen understanding of the sources of differentiation and the activities that drive uniqueness to evaluate various differentiation approaches and design durable ways to set their product offering apart from those of rival brands.

The Four Best Routes to Competitive Advantage via a Broad Differentiation Strategy

While it is easy enough to grasp that a successful differentiation strategy must entail creating buyer value in ways unmatched by rivals, the big issue in crafting a differentiation strategy is which of four basic routes to take in delivering unique buyer value via a broad differentiation strategy. Usually, building a sustainable competitive advantage via differentiation involves pursuing one of four basic routes to delivering superior value to buyers.

One route is to *incorporate product attributes and user features that lower the buyer's overall costs of using the company's product.* Making a company's product more economical for a buyer to use can be done by reducing the buyer's raw materials waste (providing cut-to-size components), reducing a buyer's inventory requirements (providing just-in-time deliveries), increasing maintenance intervals and product reliability so as to lower a buyer's repair and maintenance costs, using online systems to reduce a buyer's procurement and order processing costs, and providing free technical support. Rising costs for gasoline have dramatically spurred the efforts of motor vehicle manufacturers worldwide to introduce models with better fuel economy and reduce operating costs for motor vehicle owners.

A second route is to *incorporate features that raise product performance.*[4] This can be accomplished with attributes that provide buyers greater reliability, ease of use, convenience, or durability. Other performance-enhancing options include making the company's product or service cleaner, safer, quieter, or more maintenance-free than rival brands. Cell phone manufacturrs are in a race to introduce next-generation phones with trendsetting features and options.

A third route to a differentiation-based competitive advantage is to *incorporate features that enhance buyer satisfaction in noneconomic or intangible ways.* Goodyear's Aquatread tire design appeals to safety-conscious motorists wary of slick roads. Rolls Royce, Ralph Lauren, Gucci, Tiffany, Cartier, and Rolex have differentiation-based competitive advantages linked to buyer desires for status, image, prestige, upscale fashion, superior craftsmanship, and the finer things in life. L. L. Bean makes its mail-order customers feel secure in their purchases by providing an unconditional guarantee with no time limit: "All of our products are guaranteed to give 100 percent satisfaction in every way. Return anything purchased from us at any time if it proves otherwise. We will replace it, refund your purchase price, or credit your credit card, as you wish."

The fourth route is to *deliver value to customers by differentiating on the basis of competencies and competitive capabilities that rivals don't have or can't afford to match.*[5] The importance of cultivating competencies and capabilities that add power to a company's resource strengths and competitiveness comes into play here. Core and/or distinctive competencies not only enhance a company's ability to compete successfully in the marketplace but can also be unique in delivering value to buyers. There are numerous examples of companies that have differentiated themselves on the basis of capabilities. Because Fox News and CNN have the capability to devote more air time to breaking news stories and get reporters on the scene very quickly compared to the major networks, many viewers turn to the cable networks when a major news event occurs. Microsoft has stronger capabilities to design, create, distribute, and advertise an array of software products for PC applications than any of its rivals. Avon and Mary Kay Cosmetics have differentiated themselves from other cosmetics and personal care companies by assembling a sales force numbering in the hundreds of thousands that gives them direct sales capability—their sales associates can demonstrate products to interested buyers, take their orders on the spot, and deliver the items to buyers' homes. Japanese automakers have the capability to satisfy changing consumer preferences for one vehicle style versus another because they can bring new models to market faster than American and European automakers.

> **Core Concept**
> A differentiator's basis for competitive advantage is either a product/service offering whose attributes differ significantly from the offerings of rivals or a set of capabilities for delivering customer value that rivals don't have.

The Importance of Perceived Value and Signaling Value

Buyers seldom pay for value they don't perceive, no matter how real the unique extras may be.[6] Thus, the price premium commanded by a differentiation strategy reflects *the value actually delivered* to the buyer and *the value perceived* by the buyer (even if not actually delivered). Actual and perceived value can differ whenever buyers have trouble assessing what their experience with the product will be. Incomplete knowledge on the part of buyers often causes them to judge value based on such signals as price (where price connotes quality), attractive packaging, extensive ad campaigns (i.e., how well-known the product is), ad content and image, the quality of brochures and sales presentations, the seller's facilities, the seller's list of customers, the firm's market share, the length of time the firm has been in business, and the professionalism, appearance, and personality of the seller's employees. Such signals of value may be as important as actual value (1) when the nature of differentiation is subjective or hard to quantify, (2) when buyers are making a first-time purchase, (3) when repurchase is infrequent, and (4) when buyers are unsophisticated.

When a Differentiation Strategy Works Best

Differentiation strategies tend to work best in market circumstances where:

- *Buyer needs and uses of the product are diverse*—Diverse buyer preferences present competitors with a bigger window of opportunity to do things differently and set themselves apart with product attributes that appeal to particular buyers. For instance, the diversity of consumer preferences for menu selection, ambience, pricing, and customer service gives restaurants exceptionally wide latitude in creating a differentiated product offering. Other companies having many ways to strongly differentiate themselves from rivals include the publishers of magazines, the makers of motor vehicles, and the manufacturers of cabinetry and countertops.

- *There are many ways to differentiate the product or service and many buyers perceive these differences as having value*—There is plenty of room for retail apparel competitors to stock different styles and quality of apparel merchandise but very little room for the makers of paper clips, copier paper, or sugar to set their products apart. Likewise, the sellers of different brands of gasoline or orange juice have little differentiation opportunity compared to the sellers of high-definition TVs, patio furniture, or breakfast cereal. Unless different buyers have distinguishably different preferences for certain features and product attributes, profitable differentiation opportunities are very restricted.

- *Few rival firms are following a similar differentiation approach*—The best differentiation approaches involve trying to appeal to buyers on the basis of attributes that rivals are not emphasizing. A differentiator encounters less head-to-head rivalry when it goes its own separate way in creating uniqueness and does not try to outdifferentiate rivals on the very same attributes—when many rivals are all claiming "Ours tastes better than theirs" or "Ours gets your clothes cleaner than theirs," the most likely result is weak brand differentiation and "strategy overcrowding"—a situation in which competitors end up chasing the same buyers with very similar product offerings.

- *Technological change is fast-paced and competition revolves around rapidly evolving product features*—Rapid product innovation and frequent introductions of next-version products not only provide space for companies to pursue separate differentiating paths but also heighten buyer interest. In video game hardware and video games, golf equipment, PCs, cell phones, and MP3 players, competitors are locked into an ongoing battle to set themselves apart by introducing the best next-generation products—companies that fail to come up with new and improved products and distinctive performance features quickly lose out in the marketplace. In network TV broadcasting in the United States, NBC, ABC, CBS, Fox, and several others are always scrambling to develop a lineup of TV shows that will win higher audience ratings and pave the way for charging higher advertising rates and boosting ad revenues.

The Pitfalls of a Differentiation Strategy

Differentiation strategies can fail for any of several reasons. *A differentiation strategy is always doomed when competitors are able to quickly copy most or all of the appealing product attributes a company comes up with.* Rapid imitation means that no rival achieves differentiation, since whenever one firm introduces some aspect of uniqueness that strikes the fancy of buyers, fast-following copycats quickly reestablish similarity. This is why a firm must search out sources of uniqueness that are time-consuming or burdensome for rivals to match if it hopes to use differentiation to win a competitive edge over rivals.

A second pitfall is that the company's differentiation strategy produces a ho-hum market reception because buyers see little value in the unique attributes of a company's product. Thus, even if a company sets the attributes of its brand apart from the brands of rivals, its strategy can fail because of trying to differentiate on the basis of something that does not deliver adequate value to buyers (such as lowering a buyer's cost to use the product or enhancing a buyer's well-being). Anytime many potential buyers look at a company's differentiated product offering and conclude "So what?" the company's differentiation strategy is in deep trouble—buyers will likely decide the product is not worth the extra price, and sales will be disappointingly low.

The third big pitfall of a differentiation strategy is overspending on efforts to differentiate the company's product offering, thus eroding profitability. Company efforts to achieve differentiation nearly always raise costs. The trick to profitable differentiation is either to keep the costs of achieving differentiation below the price premium the differentiating attributes can command in the marketplace (thus increasing the profit margin per unit sold) or to offset thinner profit margins per unit by selling enough additional units to increase total profits. If a company goes overboard in pursuing costly differentiation efforts and then unexpectedly discovers that buyers are unwilling to pay a sufficient price premium to cover the added costs of differentiation, it ends up saddled with unacceptably thin profit margins or even losses. The need to contain differentiation costs is why many companies add little touches of differentiation that add to buyer satisfaction but are inexpensive to institute. Upscale restaurants often provide valet parking. Ski resorts provide skiers with complimentary coffee or hot apple cider at the base of the lifts in the morning and late afternoon. FedEx, UPS, and many catalog and online retailers have installed software capabilities that allow customers to track packages in transit. Some hotels and motels provide free continental breakfasts, exercise facilities, and in-room coffeemaking amenities. Publishers are using their Web sites to deliver supplementary educational materials to the buyers of their textbooks. Laundry detergent and soap manufacturers add pleasing scents to their products.

Other common pitfalls and mistakes in crafting a differentiation strategy include:[7]

- *Overdifferentiating so that product quality or service levels exceed buyers' needs.* Even if buyers like the differentiating extras, they may not find them sufficiently valuable for their purposes to pay extra to get them. Many shoppers shy away from buying top-of-the-line items because they have no particular interest in all the bells and whistles; for them, a less deluxe model or style makes better economic sense.

- *Trying to charge too high a price premium.* Even if buyers view certain extras or deluxe features as nice to have, they may still conclude that the added cost is excessive relative to the value they deliver. A differentiator must guard against turning off would-be buyers with what is perceived as price gouging. Normally, the bigger the price premium for the differentiating extras, the harder it is to keep buyers from switching to the lower-priced offerings of competitors.

- *Being timid and not striving to open up meaningful gaps in quality or service or performance features vis-à-vis the products of rivals.* Tiny differences between rivals' product offerings may not be visible or important to buyers. If a company wants to generate the fiercely loyal customer following needed to earn superior profits and open up a differentiation-based competitive advantage over rivals, then its strategy must result in strong rather than weak product differentiation. In markets where differentiators do no better than achieve weak product differentiation (because the attributes of rival brands are fairly similar in the minds of many buyers), customer loyalty to any one brand is weak, the costs of buyers to switch to rival brands are fairly low, and no one company has enough of a market edge that it can get by with charging a price premium over rival brands.

A low-cost provider strategy can defeat a differentiation strategy when buyers are satisfied with a basic product and don't think extra attributes are worth a higher price.

BEST-COST PROVIDER STRATEGIES

Core Concept
The competitive advantage of a best-cost provider is lower costs than rivals in incorporating upscale attributes, putting the company in a position to underprice rivals whose products have similar upscale attributes.

Best-cost provider strategies aim at giving customers *more value for the money*. The objective is to deliver superior value to buyers by satisfying their expectations on key quality/features/performance/service attributes and beating their expectations on price (given what rivals are charging for much the same attributes). *A company achieves best-cost status from an ability to incorporate attractive or upscale attributes at a lower cost than rivals.* The attractive attributes can take the form of appealing features, good-to-excellent product performance or quality, or attractive customer service. When a company has the resource strengths and competitive capabilities to incorporate these upscale attributes into its product offering *at a lower cost than rivals,* it enjoys best-cost status—it is the low-cost provider *of an upscale product.*

Being a best-cost provider is different from being a low-cost provider because the additional upscale features entail additional costs (that a low-cost provider can avoid by offering buyers a basic product with few frills). As Figure 5.1 indicates, best-cost provider strategies stake out a middle ground between pursuing a low-cost advantage and a differentiation advantage and between appealing to the broad market as a whole and a narrow market niche. From a competitive positioning standpoint, best-cost strategies are thus a *hybrid,* balancing a strategic emphasis on low cost against a strategic emphasis on differentiation (upscale features delivered at a price that constitutes superior value).

The competitive advantage of a best-cost provider is its capability to include upscale attributes at a lower cost than rivals whose products have comparable attributes. A best-cost provider can use its low-cost advantage to underprice rivals whose products have similar upscale attributes—it is usually not difficult to entice customers away from rivals charging a higher price for an item with highly comparable features, quality, performance, and/or customer service attributes. To achieve competitive advantage with a best-cost provider strategy, it is critical that a company have the resources and capabilities to incorporate upscale attributes at a lower cost than rivals. In other words, it must be able to (1) incorporate attractive features at a lower cost than rivals whose products have similar features, (2) manufacture a good-to-excellent quality product at a lower cost than rivals with good-to-excellent product quality, (3) develop a product that delivers good-to-excellent performance at a lower cost than rivals whose products also entail good-to-excellent performance, or (4) provide attractive customer service at a lower cost than rivals who provide comparably attractive customer service.

What makes a best-cost provider strategy so appealing is being able to incorporate upscale attributes at a lower cost than rivals and then using the company's low-cost advantage to underprice rivals whose products have similar upscale attributes.

The target market for a best-cost provider is value-conscious buyers—buyers that are looking for appealing extras at an appealingly low price. Value-hunting buyers (as distinct from buyers looking only for bargain-basement prices) often constitute a very sizable part of the overall market. Normally, value-conscious buyers are willing to pay a fair price for extra features, but they shy away from paying top dollar for items having all the bells and whistles. It is the desire to cater to *value-conscious buyers* as opposed to *budget-conscious buyers* that sets a best-cost provider apart from a low-cost provider—the two strategies aim at distinguishably different market targets.

When a Best-Cost Provider Strategy Works Best

A best-cost provider strategy works best in markets where buyer diversity makes product differentiation the norm and where many buyers are also sensitive to price and value. This is because a best-cost provider can position itself near the middle of the market with either a medium-quality product at a below-average price or a high-quality product at an average or slightly higher price. Often, substantial numbers of buyers prefer midrange products rather than the cheap, basic products of low-cost producers or the expensive products of top-of-the-line differentiators. But unless a company has the resources, know-how, and capabilities to incorporate upscale product or service attributes at a lower cost than rivals, adopting a best-cost strategy is ill advised—a winning strategy must always be matched to a company's resource strengths and capabilities.

Illustration Capsule 5.3 describes how Toyota has applied the principles of a best-cost provider strategy in producing and marketing its Lexus brand.

The Big Risk of a Best-Cost Provider Strategy

A company's biggest vulnerability in employing a best-cost provider strategy is getting squeezed between the strategies of firms using low-cost and high-end differentiation strategies. Low-cost providers may be able to siphon customers away with the appeal of a lower price (despite their less appealing product attributes). High-end differentiators may be able to steal customers away with the appeal of better product attributes (even though their products carry a higher price tag). Thus, to be successful, a best-cost provider must offer buyers *significantly* better product attributes in order to justify a price above what low-cost leaders are charging. Likewise, it has to achieve *significantly* lower costs in providing upscale features so that it can outcompete high-end differentiators on the basis of a *significantly* lower price.

FOCUSED (OR MARKET NICHE) STRATEGIES

What sets focused strategies apart from low-cost leadership or broad differentiation strategies is concentrated attention on a narrow piece of the total market. The target segment, or niche, can be defined by geographic uniqueness, by specialized requirements in using the product, or by special product attributes that appeal only to niche members. Community Coffee, the largest family-owned specialty coffee retailer in the United States, is a company that focused on a geographic market niche; despite having a national market share of only 1.1 percent, Community has won a 50 percent share of the coffee business in supermarkets in southern Louisiana in competition

Illustration Capsule 5.3

Toyota's Best-Cost Producer Strategy for Its Lexus Line

Toyota Motor Company is widely regarded as a low-cost producer among the world's motor vehicle manufacturers. Despite its emphasis on product quality, Toyota has achieved low-cost leadership because it has developed considerable skills in efficient supply chain management and low-cost assembly capabilities, and because its models are positioned in the low-to-medium end of the price spectrum, where high production volumes are conducive to low unit costs. But when Toyota decided to introduce its new Lexus models to compete in the luxury-car market, it employed a classic best-cost provider strategy. Toyota took the following four steps in crafting and implementing its Lexus strategy:

- Designing an array of high-performance characteristics and upscale features into the Lexus models so as to make them comparable in performance and luxury to other high-end models and attractive to Mercedes, BMW, Audi, Jaguar, Cadillac, and Lincoln buyers.

- Transferring its capabilities in making high-quality Toyota models at low cost to making premium-quality Lexus models at costs below other luxury-car makers. Toyota's supply chain capabilities and low-cost assembly know-how allowed it to incorporate high-tech performance features and upscale quality into Lexus models at substantially less cost than comparable Mercedes and BMW models.

- Using its relatively lower manufacturing costs to underprice comparable Mercedes and BMW models. Toyota believed that with its cost advantage it could price attractively equipped Lexus cars low enough to draw price-conscious buyers away from Mercedes and BMW and perhaps induce dissatisfied Lincoln and Cadillac owners to switch to a Lexus. Lexus's pricing advantage over Mercedes and BMW was sometimes quite significant. For example, in 2006 the Lexus RX 330, a midsized SUV, carried a sticker price in the $36,000–$45,000 range (depending on how it was equipped), whereas variously equipped Mercedes M-class SUVs had price tags in the $50,000–$65,000 range and a BMW X5 SUV could range anywhere from $42,000 to $70,000, depending on the optional equipment chosen.

- Establishing a new network of Lexus dealers, separate from Toyota dealers, dedicated to providing a level of personalized, attentive customer service unmatched in the industry.

Lexus models have consistently ranked first in the widely watched J. D. Power & Associates quality survey, and the prices of Lexus models are typically several thousand dollars below those of comparable Mercedes and BMW models—clear signals that Toyota has succeeded in becoming a best-cost producer with its Lexus brand.

against Starbucks, Folger's, Maxwell House, and asserted specialty coffee retailers. Community Coffee's geographic version of a focus strategy has allowed it to capture sales in excess of $100 million annually by catering to the tastes of coffee drinkers across an 11-state region. Examples of firms that concentrate on a well-defined market niche keyed to a particular product or buyer segment include Animal Planet and the History Channel (in cable TV); Google (in Internet search engines); Porsche (in sports cars); Cannondale (in top-of-the-line mountain bikes); Domino's Pizza (in pizza delivery); Enterprise Rent-a-Car (a specialist in providing rental cars to repair garage customers); Bandag (a specialist in truck tire recapping that promotes its recaps aggressively at over 1,000 truck stops), CGA Inc. (a specialist in providing insurance to cover the cost of lucrative hole-in-one prizes at golf tournaments); Match.com (the world's largest online dating service); and Avid Technology (the world leader in digital technology products to create 3D animation and to edit films, videos, TV broadcasts, video games, and audio recordings). Microbreweries, local bakeries, bed-and-breakfast inns, and local owner-managed retail boutiques are all good examples of enterprises that have scaled their operations to serve narrow or local customer segments.

A Focused Low-Cost Strategy

A focused strategy based on low cost aims at securing a competitive advantage by serving buyers in the target market niche at a lower cost and lower price than rival competitors. This strategy has considerable attraction when a firm can lower costs significantly by limiting its customer base to a well-defined buyer segment. The avenues to achieving a cost advantage over rivals also serving the target market niche are the same as for low-cost leadership—outmanage rivals in keeping the costs of value chain activities contained to a bare minimum and search for innovative ways to reconfigure the firm's value chain and bypass or reduce certain value chain activities. The only real difference between a low-cost provider strategy and a focused low-cost strategy is the size of the buyer group that a company is trying to appeal to—the former involves a product offering that appeals broadly to most all buyer groups and market segments whereas the latter at just meeting the needs of buyers in a narrow market segment.

Focused low-cost strategies are fairly common. Producers of private-label goods are able to achieve low costs in product development, marketing, distribution, and advertising by concentrating on making generic items imitative of name-brand merchandise and selling directly to retail chains wanting a basic house brand to sell to price-sensitive shoppers. Several small printer-supply manufacturers have begun making low-cost clones of the premium-priced replacement ink and toner cartridges sold by Hewlett-Packard, Lexmark, Canon, and Epson; the clone manufacturers dissect the cartridges of the name-brand companies and then reengineer a similar version that won't violate patents. The components for remanufactured replacement cartridges are aquired from various outside sources, and the clones are then marketed at prices as much as 50 percent below the name-brand cartridges. Cartridge remanufacturers have been lured to focus on this market because replacement cartridges constitute a multibillion-dollar business with considerable profit potential given their low costs and the premium pricing of the name-brand companies. Illustration Capsule 5.4 describes how Motel 6 has kept its costs low in catering to budget-conscious travelers.

A Focused Differentiation Strategy

A focused strategy keyed to differentiation aims at securing a competitive advantage with a product offering carefully designed to appeal to the unique preferences and needs of a narrow, well-defined group of buyers (as opposed to a broad differentiation strategy aimed at many buyer groups and market segments). Successful use of a focused differentiation strategy depends on the existence of a buyer segment that is looking for special product attributes or seller capabilities and on a firm's ability to stand apart from rivals competing in the same target market niche.

Companies like Godiva Chocolates, Chanel, Gucci, Rolls-Royce, Häagen-Dazs, and W. L. Gore (the maker of Gore-Tex) employ successful differentiation-based focused strategies targeted at upscale buyers wanting products and services with world-class attributes. Indeed, most markets contain a buyer segment willing to pay a big price premium for the very finest items available, thus opening the strategic window for some competitors to pursue differentiation-based focused strategies aimed at the very top of the market pyramid. Another successful focused differentiator is Trader Joe's, a 150-store East and West Coast "fashion food retailer" that is a combination gourmet deli and grocery warehouse.[8] Customers shop Trader Joe's as much for entertainment as for conventional grocery items—the store stocks out-of-the-ordinary culinary treats like raspberry salsa, salmon burgers, and jasmine fried rice,

Illustration Capsule 5.4
Motel 6's Focused Low-Cost Strategy

Motel 6 caters to price-conscious travelers who want a clean, no-frills place to spend the night. To be a low-cost provider of overnight lodging, Motel 6 (1) selects relatively inexpensive sites on which to construct its units (usually near interstate exits and high-traffic locations but far enough away to avoid paying prime site prices); (2) builds only basic facilities (no restaurant or bar and only rarely a swimming pool); (3) relies on standard architectural designs that incorporate inexpensive materials and low-cost construction techniques; and (4) provides simple room furnishings and decorations. These approaches lower both investment costs and operating costs. Without restaurants,

bars, and all kinds of guest services, a Motel 6 unit can be operated with just front-desk personnel, room cleanup crews, and skeleton building-and-grounds maintenance.

To promote the Motel 6 concept with travelers who have simple overnight requirements, the chain uses unique, recognizable radio ads done by nationally syndicated radio personality Tom Bodett; the ads describe Motel 6's clean rooms, no-frills facilities, friendly atmosphere, and dependably low rates (usually under $40 a night).

Motel 6's basis for competitive advantage is lower costs than competitors in providing basic, economical overnight accommodations to price-constrained travelers.

as well as the standard goods normally found in supermarkets. What sets Trader Joe's apart is not just its unique combination of food novelties and competitively priced grocery items but also its capability to turn an otherwise mundane grocery excursion into a whimsical treasure hunt that is just plain fun.

Illustration Capsule 5.5 describes Progressive Insurance's focused differentiation strategy.

When a Focused Low-Cost or Focused Differentiation Strategy Is Attractive

A focused strategy aimed at securing a competitive edge based on either low cost or differentiation becomes increasingly attractive as more of the following conditions are met:

- The target market niche is big enough to be profitable and offers good growth potential.

- Industry leaders do not see that having a presence in the niche is crucial to their own success—in which case focusers can often escape battling head-to-head against some of the industry's biggest and strongest competitors.

- It is costly or difficult for multisegment competitors to put capabilities in place to meet the specialized needs of buyers comprising the target market niche and at the same time satisfy the expectations of their mainstream customers.

- The industry has many different niches and segments, thereby allowing a focuser to pick a competitively attractive niche suited to its resource strengths and capabilities. Also, with more niches, there is more room for focusers to avoid each other in competing for the same customers.

Progressive Insurance's Focused Differentiation Strategy in Auto Insurance

Progressive Insurance has fashioned a strategy in auto insurance focused on people with a record of traffic violations who drive high-performance cars, drivers with accident histories, motorcyclists, teenagers, and other so-called high-risk categories of drivers that most auto insurance companies steer away from. Progressive discovered that some of these high-risk drivers are affluent and pressed for time, making them less sensitive to paying premium rates for their car insurance. Management learned that it could charge such drivers high enough premiums to cover the added risks, plus it differentiated Progressive from other insurers by expediting the process of obtaining insurance and decreasing the annoyance that such drivers faced in obtaining insurance coverage. Progressive pioneered the low-cost direct sales model of allowing customers to purchase insurance online and over the phone.

Progressive also studied the market segments for insurance carefully enough to discover that some motorcycle owners were not especially risky (middle-aged suburbanites who sometimes commuted to work or used their motorcycles mainly for recreational trips with their friends). Progressive's strategy allowed it to become a leader in the market for luxury-car insurance for customers who appreciated Progressive's streamlined approach to doing business.

In further differentiating and promoting Progressive policies, management created teams of roving claims adjusters who would arrive at accident scenes to assess claims and issue checks for repairs on the spot. Progressive introduced 24-hour claims reporting, now an industry standard. In addition, it developed a sophisticated pricing system so that it could quickly and accurately assess each customer's risk and weed out unprofitable customers.

By being creative and excelling at the nuts and bolts of its business, Progressive has won a 7 percent share of the $150 billion market for auto insurance and has the highest underwriting margins in the auto-insurance industry.

Sources: www.progressiveinsurance.com; Ian C. McMillan, Alexander van Putten, and Rita Gunther McGrath, "Global Gamesmanship," *Harvard Business Review* 81, no. 5 (May 2003), p. 68; and *Fortune*, May 16, 2005, p. 34.

- Few, if any, other rivals are attempting to specialize in the same target segment—a condition that reduces the risk of segment overcrowding.
- The focuser has a reservoir of customer goodwill and loyalty (accumulated from having catered to the specialized needs and preferences of niche members over many years) that it can draw on to help stave off ambitious challengers looking to horn in on its business.

The advantages of focusing a company's entire competitive effort on a single market niche are considerable, especially for smaller and medium-sized companies that may lack the breadth and depth of resources to tackle going after a broad customer base with a "something for everyone" lineup of models, styles, and product selection. eBay has made a huge name for itself and very attractive profits for shareholders by focusing its attention on online auctions—at one time a very small niche in the overall auction business that eBay's focus strategy turned into the dominant piece of the global auction industry. Google has capitalized on its specialized expertise in Internet search engines to become one of the most spectacular growth companies of the past 10 years. Two hippie entrepreneurs, Ben Cohen and Jerry Greenfield, built Ben & Jerry's Homemade into an impressive business by focusing their energies and resources solely on the superpremium segment of the ice cream market.

The Risks of a Focused Low-Cost or Focused Differentiation Strategy

Focusing carries several risks. One is the chance that competitors will find effective ways to match the focused firm's capabilities in serving the target niche—perhaps by coming up with products or brands specifically designed to appeal to buyers in the target niche or by developing expertise and capabilities that offset the focuser's strengths. In the lodging business, large chains like Marriott and Hilton have launched multibrand strategies that allow them to compete effectively in several lodging segments simultaneously. Marriott has flagship hotels with a full complement of services and amenities that allow it to attract travelers and vacationers going to major resorts, it has J. W. Marriot hotels usually located in downtown metropolitan areas that cater to business travelers; the Courtyard by Marriott brand is for business travelers looking for moderately priced lodging; Marriott Residence Inns are designed as a home away from home for travelers staying five or more nights; and the 530 Fairfield Inn locations cater to travelers looking for quality lodging at an affordable price. Similarly, Hilton has a lineup of brands (Conrad Hotels, Doubletree Hotels, Embassy Suite Hotels, Hampton Inns, Hilton Hotels, Hilton Garden Inns, and Homewood Suites) that enable it to operate in multiple segments and compete head-to-head against lodging chains that operate only in a single segment. Multibrand strategies are attractive to large companies like Marriott and Hilton precisely because they enable a company to enter a market niche and siphon business away from companies that employ a focus strategy.

A second risk of employing a focus strategy is the potential for the preferences and needs of niche members to shift over time toward the product attributes desired by the majority of buyers. An erosion of the differences across buyer segments lowers entry barriers into a focuser's market niche and provides an open invitation for rivals in adjacent segments to begin competing for the focuser's customers. A third risk is that the segment may become so attractive it is soon inundated with competitors, intensifying rivalry and splintering segment profits.

THE CONTRASTING FEATURES OF THE FIVE GENERIC COMPETITIVE STRATEGIES: A SUMMARY

Deciding which generic competitive strategy should serve as the framework for hanging the rest of the company's strategy is not a trivial matter. Each of the five generic competitive strategies positions the company differently in its market and competitive environment. Each establishes a central theme for how the company will endeavor to outcompete rivals. Each creates some boundaries or guidelines for maneuvering as market circumstances unfold and as ideas for improving the strategy are debated. Each points to different ways of experimenting and tinkering with the basic strategy—for example, employing a low-cost leadership strategy means experimenting with ways that costs can be cut and value chain activities can be streamlined, whereas a broad differentiation strategy means exploring ways to add new differentiating features or to perform value chain activities differently if the result is to add value for customers in ways they are willing to pay for. Each entails differences in terms of product line, production emphasis, marketing emphasis, and means of sustaining the strategy—as shown in Table 5.1.

Table 5.1 **Distinguishing Features of the Five Generic Competitive Strategies**

	Low-Cost Provider	Broad Differentiation	Best-Cost Provider	Focused Low-Cost Provider	Focused Differentiation
Strategic target	• A broad cross-section of the market	• A broad cross-section of the market	• Value-conscious buyers	• A narrow market niche where buyer needs and preferences are distinctively different	• A narrow market niche where buyer needs and preferences are distinctively different
Basis of competitive advantage	• Lower overall costs than competitors	• Ability to offer buyers something attractively different from competitors	• Ability to give customers more value for the money	• Lower overall cost than rivals in serving niche members	• Attributes that appeal specifically to niche members
Product line	• A good basic product with few frills (acceptable quality and limited selection)	• Many product variations, wide selection; emphasis on differentiating features	• Items with appealing attributes; assorted upscale features	• Features and attributes tailored to the tastes and requirements of niche members	• Features and attributes tailored to the tastes and requirements of niche members
Production emphasis	• A continuous search for cost reduction without sacrificing acceptable quality and essential features	• Build in whatever differentiating features buyers are willing to pay for; strive for product superiority	• Build in upscale features and appealing attributes at lower cost than rivals	• A continuous search for cost reduction while incorporating features and attributes matched to niche member preferences	• Custom-made products that match the tastes and requirements of niche members
Marketing emphasis	• Try to make a virtue out of product features that lead to low cost	• Tout differentiating features • Charge a premium price to cover the extra costs of differentiating features	• Tout delivery of best value • Either deliver comparable features at a lower price than rivals or else match rivals on prices and provide better features	• Communicate attractive features of a budget-priced product offering that fits niche buyers' expectations	• Communicate how product offering does the best job of meeting niche buyers' expectations
Keys to sustaining the strategy	• Economical prices/good value • Strive to manage costs down, year after year, in every area of the business	• Stress constant innovation to stay ahead of imitative competitors • Concentrate on a few key differentiating features	• Unique expertise in simultaneously managing costs down while incorporating upscale features and attributes	• Stay committed to serving the niche at lowest overall cost; don't blur the firm's image by entering other market segments or adding other products to widen market appeal	• Stay committed to serving the niche better than rivals; don't blur the firm's image by entering other market segments or adding other products to widen market appeal

Thus, a choice of which generic strategy to employ spills over to affect several aspects of how the business will be operated and the manner in which value chain activities must be managed. Deciding which generic strategy to employ is perhaps the most important strategic commitment a company makes—it tends to drive the rest of the strategic actions a company decides to undertake.

One of the big dangers in crafting a competitive strategy is that managers, torn between the pros and cons of the various generic strategies, will opt for *stuck-in-the-middle strategies* that represent compromises between lower costs and greater differentiation and between broad and narrow market appeal. Compromise or middle-ground strategies rarely produce sustainable competitive advantage or a distinctive competitive position—a well-executed, best-cost producer strategy is the only compromise between low cost and differentiation that succeeds. Usually, companies with compromise strategies end up with a middle-of-the-pack industry ranking—they have average costs, some but not a lot of product differentiation relative to rivals, an average image and reputation, and little prospect of industry leadership. Having a competitive edge over rivals is the single most dependable contributor to above-average company profitability. Hence, only if a company makes a strong and unwavering commitment to one of the five generic competitive strategies does it stand much chance of achieving sustainable competitive advantage that such strategies can deliver if properly executed.

Key Points

Early in the process of crafting a strategy company managers have to decide which of the five basic competitive strategies to employ—overall low-cost, broad differentiation, best-cost, focused low-cost, or focused differentiation.

In employing a low-cost provider strategy and trying to achieve a low-cost advantage over rivals, a company must do a better job than rivals of cost-effectively managing value chain activities and/or find innovative ways to eliminate or bypass cost-producing activities. Low-cost provider strategies work particularly well when the products of rival sellers are virtually identical or very weakly differentiated and supplies are readily available from eager sellers, when there are not many ways to differentiate that have value to buyers, when many buyers are price sensitive and shop the market for the lowest price, and when buyer switching costs are low.

Broad differentiation strategies seek to produce a competitive edge by incorporating attributes and features that set a company's product/service offering apart from rivals in ways that buyers consider valuable and worth paying for. Successful differentiation allows a firm to (1) command a premium price for its product, (2) increase unit sales (because additional buyers are won over by the differentiating features), and/or (3) gain buyer loyalty to its brand (because some buyers are strongly attracted to the differentiating features and bond with the company and its products). Differentiation strategies work best in markets with diverse buyer preferences where there are big windows of opportunity to strongly differentiate a company's product offering from those of rival brands, in situations where few other rivals are pursuing a similar differentiation approach, and in circumstances where companies are racing to bring out the most appealing next-generation product. A differentiation strategy is doomed when competitors are able to quickly copy most or all of the appealing product attributes a company comes up with, when a company's differentiation efforts meet with a ho-hum or "so what" market reception, or when a company erodes profitability by overspending on efforts to differentiate its product offering.

Best-cost provider strategies combine a strategic emphasis on low cost with a strategic emphasis on more than minimal quality, service, features, or performance. The aim is to create competitive advantage by giving buyers more value for the money—an approach that entails matching close rivals on key quality/service/features/performance attributes and beating them on the costs of incorporating such attributes into the product or service. A best-cost provider strategy works best in markets where buyer diversity makes product differentiation the norm and where many buyers are also sensitive to price and value.

A focus strategy delivers competitive advantage either by achieving lower costs than rivals in serving buyers comprising the target market niche or by developing specialized ability to offer niche buyers an appealingly differentiated offering than meets their needs better than rival brands. A focused strategy based on either low cost or differentiation becomes increasingly attractive when the target market niche is big enough to be profitable and offers good growth potential, when it is costly or difficult for multi-segment competitors to put capabilities in place to meet the specialized needs of the target market niche and at the same time satisfy the expectations of their mainstream customers, when there are one or more niches that present a good match with a focuser's resource strengths and capabilities, and when few other rivals are attempting to specialize in the same target segment.

Deciding which generic strategy to employ is perhaps the most important strategic commitment a company makes—it tends to drive the rest of the strategic actions a company decides to undertake and it sets the whole tone for the pursuit of a competitive advantage over rivals.

Exercises

1. Go to www.google.com and do a search for "low-cost producer." See if you can identify five companies that are pursuing a low-cost strategy in their respective industries.

2. Using the advanced search function at www.google.com, enter "best-cost producer" in the exact-phrase box and see if you can locate three companies that indicate they are employing a best-cost producer strategy.

3. Go to BMW's Web site (www.bmw.com) click on the link for BMW Group. The site you find provides an overview of the company's key functional areas, including R&D and production activities. Explore each of the links on the Research & Development page—People & Networks, Innovation & Technology, and Mobility & Traffic—to better understand the company's approach. Also review the statements under Production focusing on vehicle production and sustainable production. How do these activities contribute to BMW's differentiation strategy and the unique position in the auto industry that BMW has achieved?

4. Which of the five generic competitive strategies do you think the following companies are employing (do whatever research at the various company Web sites might be needed to arrive at and support your answer):
   a. The Saturn division of General Motors
   b. Abercrombie & Fitch
   c. Amazon.com
   d. Home Depot
   e. Mary Kay Cosmetics
   f. *USA Today*

chapter seven

Competing in Foreign Markets

You have no choice but to operate in a world shaped by globalization and the information revolution. There are two options: Adapt or die.

—Andrew S. Grove
Former Chairman, Intel Corporation

You do not choose to become global. The market chooses for you; it forces your hand.

—Alain Gomez
CEO, Thomson SA

[I]ndustries actually vary a great deal in the pressures they put on a company to sell internationally.

—Niraj Dawar and Tony Frost
Professors, Richard Ivey School of Business

A ny company that aspires to industry leadership in the 21st century must think in terms of global, not domestic, market leadership. The world economy is globalizing at an accelerating pace as countries previously closed to foreign companies open up their markets, as the Internet shrinks the importance of geographic distance, and as ambitious, growth-minded companies race to build stronger competitive positions in the markets of more and more countries. Companies in industries that are already globally competitive or in the process of becoming so are under the gun to come up with a strategy for competing successfully in foreign markets.

This chapter focuses on strategy options for expanding beyond domestic boundaries and competing in the markets of either a few or a great many countries. The spotlight will be on four strategic issues unique to competing multinationally:

1. Whether to customize the company's offerings in each different country market to match the tastes and preferences of local buyers or to offer a mostly standardized product worldwide.

2. Whether to employ essentially the same basic competitive strategy in all countries or modify the strategy country by country.

3. Where to locate the company's production facilities, distribution centers, and customer service operations so as to realize the greatest location advantages.

4. How to efficiently transfer the company's resource strengths and capabilities from one country to another in an effort to secure competitive advantage.

In the process of exploring these issues, we will introduce a number of core concepts—multicountry competition, global competition, profit sanctuaries, and cross-market subsidization. The chapter includes sections on cross-country differences in cultural, demographic, and market conditions; strategy options for entering and competing in foreign markets; the growing role of alliances with foreign partners; the importance of locating operations in the most advantageous countries; and the special circumstances of competing in such emerging markets as China, India, Brazil, Russia, and Eastern Europe.

WHY COMPANIES EXPAND INTO FOREIGN MARKETS

A company may opt to expand outside its domestic market for any of four major reasons:

1. *To gain access to new customers*—Expanding into foreign markets offers potential for increased revenues, profits, and long-term growth and becomes an especially attractive option when a company's home markets are mature. Firms like Cisco Systems, Dell, Sony, Nokia, Avon, and Toyota, which are racing for global leadership in their respective industries, are moving rapidly and aggressively to extend their market reach into all corners of the world.

2. *To achieve lower costs and enhance the firm's competitiveness*—Many companies are driven to sell in more than one country because domestic sales volume is not large enough to fully capture manufacturing economies of scale or learning/experience curve effects and thereby substantially improve the firm's cost-competitiveness. The relatively small size of country markets in Europe explains why companies like Michelin, BMW, and Nestlé long ago began selling their products all across Europe and then moved into markets in North America and Latin America.

3. *To capitalize on its core competencies*—A company may be able to leverage its competencies and capabilities into a position of competitive advantage in foreign markets as well as just domestic markets. Nokia's competencies and capabilities in mobile phones have propelled it to global market leadership in the wireless telecommunications business. Wal-Mart is capitalizing on its considerable expertise in discount retailing to expand into China, Latin America, and parts of Europe—Wal-Mart executives believe the company has tremendous growth opportunities in China.

4. *To spread its business risk across a wider market base*—A company spreads business risk by operating in a number of different foreign countries rather than depending entirely on operations in its domestic market. Thus, if the economies of certain Asian countries turn down for a period of time, a company with operations across much of the world may be sustained by buoyant sales in Latin America or Europe.

In a few cases, companies in industries based on natural resources (e.g., oil and gas, minerals, rubber, and lumber) often find it necessary to operate in the international arena because attractive raw material supplies are located in foreign countries.

The Difference Between Competing Internationally and Competing Globally

Typically, a company will start to compete internationally by entering just one or maybe a select few foreign markets. Competing on a truly global scale comes later, after the company has established operations on several continents and is racing against rivals for global market leadership. Thus, there is a meaningful distinction between the competitive scope of a company that operates in a few foreign countries (with perhaps modest ambitions to enter several more country markets) and a company that markets its products in 50 to 100 countries and is expanding its operations into additional country markets annually. The former is most accurately termed an *international competitor*, whereas the latter qualifies as a *global competitor*. In the discussion that follows, we'll continue to make a distinction between strategies for competing internationally and strategies for competing globally.

CROSS-COUNTRY DIFFERENCES IN CULTURAL, DEMOGRAPHIC, AND MARKET CONDITIONS

Regardless of a company's motivation for expanding outside its domestic markets, the strategies it uses to compete in foreign markets must be situation-driven. Cultural, demographic, and market conditions vary significantly among the countries of the world.[1] Cultures and lifestyles are the most obvious areas in which countries differ; market demographics and income levels are close behind. Consumers in Spain do not have the same tastes, preferences, and buying habits as consumers in Norway; buyers differ yet again in Greece, Chile, New Zealand, and Taiwan. Less than 20 percent of the populations of Brazil, India, and China have annual purchasing power equivalent to $25,000. Middle-class consumers represent a much smaller portion of the population in these and other emerging countries than in North America, Japan, and much of Western Europe—China's middle class numbers about 125 million out of a population of 1.3 billion.[2]

Sometimes product designs suitable in one country are inappropriate in another—for example, in the United States electrical devices run on 110-volt systems, but in some European countries the standard is a 240-volt system, necessitating the use of different electrical designs and components. In France consumers prefer top-loading washing machines, while in most other European countries consumers prefer front-loading machines. Northern Europeans want large refrigerators because they tend to shop once a week in supermarkets; southern Europeans can get by on small refrigerators because they shop daily. In parts of Asia refrigerators are a status symbol and may be placed in the living room, leading to preferences for stylish designs and colors—in India bright blue and red are popular colors. In other Asian countries household space is constrained and many refrigerators are only four feet high so that the top can be used for storage. In Hong Kong the preference is for compact European-style appliances, but in Taiwan large American-style appliances are more popular. In Italy, most people use automatic washing machines but prefer to hang the clothes out to dry on a clothesline—there is a strongly entrenched tradition and cultural belief that sun-dried clothes are fresher, which virtually shuts down any opportunities for appliance makers to market clothes dryers in Italy. In China, many parents are reluctant to purchase personal computers (PCs) even when they can afford them because of concerns that their children will be distracted from their schoolwork by surfing the Web, playing PC-based video games, and downloading and listening to pop music.

Similarly, market growth varies from country to country. In emerging markets like India, China, Brazil, and Malaysia, market growth potential is far higher than in the more mature economies of Britain, Denmark, Canada, and Japan. In automobiles, for example, the potential for market growth is explosive in China, where 2005 sales of new vehicles amounted to less than 5 million in a country with 1.3 billion people. In India there are efficient, well-developed national channels for distributing trucks, scooters, farm equipment, groceries, personal care items, and other packaged products to the country's 3 million retailers, whereas in China distribution is primarily local and there is no national network for distributing most products. The marketplace is intensely competitive in some countries and only moderately contested in others. Industry driving forces may be one thing in Spain, quite another in Canada, and different yet again in Turkey or Argentina or South Korea.

One of the biggest concerns of companies competing in foreign markets is whether to customize their offerings in each different country market to match the tastes and preferences of local buyers or whether to offer a mostly standardized product worldwide. While making products that are closely matched to local tastes makes them more appealing to local buyers, customizing a company's products country by country may have the effect of raising production and distribution costs due to the greater variety of designs and components, shorter production runs, and the complications of added inventory handling and distribution logistics. Greater standardization of a global company's product offering, however, can lead to scale economies and experience/learning curve effects, thus contributing to the achievement of a low-cost advantage. *The tension between the market pressures to localize a company's product offerings country by country and the competitive pressures to lower costs is one of the big strategic issues that participants in foreign markets have to resolve.*

Aside from the basic cultural and market differences among countries, a company also has to pay special attention to location advantages that stem from country-to-country variations in manufacturing and distribution costs, the risks of adverse shifts in exchange rates, and the economic and political demands of host governments.

Gaining Competitive Advantage Based on Where Activities Are Located

Differences in wage rates, worker productivity, inflation rates, energy costs, tax rates, government regulations, and the like create sizable variations in manufacturing costs from country to country. Plants in some countries have major manufacturing cost advantages because of lower input costs (especially labor), relaxed government regulations, the proximity of suppliers, or unique natural resources. In such cases, the low-cost countries become principal production sites, with most of the output being exported to markets in other parts of the world. Companies that build production facilities in low-cost countries (or that source their products from contract manufacturers in these countries) have a competitive advantage over rivals with plants in countries where costs are higher. The competitive role of low manufacturing costs is most evident in low-wage countries like China, India, Pakistan, Cambodia, Vietnam, Mexico, Brazil, Guatemala, the Philippines, and several countries in Africa that have become production havens for manufactured goods with high labor content (especially textiles and apparel). Labor costs in China averaged about $0.70 an hour in 2004–2005 versus about $1.50 in Russia, $4.60 in Hungary, $4.90 in Portugal, $16.50 in Canada, $21.00 in the United States, $23.00 in Norway, and $25.00 in Germany.[3] China is fast becoming the manufacturing capital of the world—virtually all of the world's major manufacturing companies now have facilities in China, and China attracted more foreign direct investment in 2002 and 2003 than any other country in the world. Likewise, concerns about short delivery times and low shipping costs make some countries better locations than others for establishing distribution centers.

The quality of a country's business environment also offers locational advantages—the governments of some countries are anxious to attract foreign investments and go all out to create a business climate that outsiders will view as favorable. A good example is Ireland, which has one of the world's most pro-business environments. Ireland offers companies very low corporate tax rates, has a government that is responsive to the needs of industry, and aggressively recruits high-tech manufacturing facilities and multinational companies. Such policies were a significant force in making Ireland the most dynamic, fastest-growing nation in Europe during the 1990s. Ireland's policies were a major factor in Intel's decision to choose Leixlip, County Kildare, as the site for a $2.5 billion chip manufacturing plant that employs over 4,000 people. Another locational advantage is the clustering of suppliers of components and capital equipment; infrastructure suppliers (universities, vocational training providers, research enterprises); trade associations; and makers of complementary products in a geographic area—such clustering can be an important source of cost savings in addition to facilitating close collaboration with key suppliers.

The Risks of Adverse Exchange Rate Shifts

The volatility of exchange rates greatly complicates the issue of geographic cost advantages. Currency exchange rates often move up or down 20 to 40 percent annually. Changes of this magnitude can either totally wipe out a country's low-cost advantage or transform a former high-cost location into a competitive-cost location. For instance, in the mid-1980s, when the dollar was strong relative to the Japanese yen (meaning that $1 would purchase, say, 125 yen as opposed to only 100 yen), Japanese heavy-equipment maker Komatsu was able to undercut U.S.-based Caterpillar's prices by as much as 25 percent, causing Caterpillar to lose sales and market share. But starting in 1985, when exchange rates began to shift and the dollar grew steadily weaker against the yen (meaning that $1 was worth fewer and fewer yen, and that a Komatsu product made in Japan at a cost of 20 million yen translated into costs of many more dollars than before), Komatsu had to raise its prices to U.S. buyers six times over two years. With its competitiveness against Komatsu restored because of the weaker dollar and Komatsu's higher prices, Caterpillar regained sales and market share. *The lesson of fluctuating exchange rates is that companies that export goods to foreign countries always gain in competitiveness when the currency of the country in which the goods are manufactured is weak. Exporters are disadvantaged when the currency of the country where goods are being manufactured grows stronger.* Sizable long-term shifts in exchange rates thus shuffle the global cards of which rivals have the upper hand in the marketplace and which countries represent the low-cost manufacturing location.

> **Core Concept**
> Companies with manufacturing facilities in a particular country are more cost-competitive in exporting goods to world markets when the local currency is weak (or declines in value relative to other currencies); their competitiveness erodes when the local currency grows stronger relative to the currencies of the countries to which the locally made goods are being exported.

As a further illustration of the risks associated with fluctuating exchange rates, consider the case of a U.S. company that has located manufacturing facilities in Brazil (where the currency is reals—pronounced *ray-alls*) and that exports most of the Brazilian-made goods to markets in the European Union (where the currency is euros). To keep the numbers simple, assume that the exchange rate is 4 Brazilian reals for 1 euro and that the product being made in Brazil has a manufacturing cost of 4 Brazilian reals (or 1 euro). Now suppose that for some reason the exchange rate shifts from 4 reals per euro to 5 reals per euro (meaning that the real has declined in value and that the euro is stronger). Making the product in Brazil is now more cost-competitive because a Brazilian good costing 4 reals to produce has fallen to only 0.8 euros at the new exchange rate. If, in contrast, the value of the Brazilian real grows stronger in relation to the euro—resulting in an exchange rate of 3 reals to 1 euro—the same good costing 4 reals to produce now has a cost of 1.33 euros. Clearly, the attraction of manufacturing a good in Brazil and selling it in Europe is far greater when the euro is strong (an exchange rate of 1 euro for 5 Brazilian reals) than when the euro is weak and exchanges for only 3 Brazilian reals.

Insofar as U.S.-based manufacturers are concerned, declines in the value of the U.S. dollar against foreign currencies act to reduce or eliminate whatever cost advantage foreign manufacturers might have over U.S. manufacturers and can even prompt foreign companies to establish production plants in the United States. Likewise, a weak euro enhances the cost competitiveness of companies manufacturing goods in Europe for export to foreign markets; a strong euro versus other currencies weakens the cost competitiveness of European plants that manufacture goods for export.

In 2002, when the Brazilian real declined in value by about 25 percent against the dollar, the euro, and several other currencies, the ability of companies with manufacturing plants in Brazil to compete in world markets was greatly enhanced—of course, in the future years this windfall gain in cost advantage might well be eroded by sustained rises in the value of the Brazilian real against these same currencies. Herein lies the risk: *Currency exchange rates are rather unpredictable, swinging first one way and then another way, so the competitiveness of any company's facilities in any country is partly dependent on whether exchange rate changes over time have a favorable or unfavorable cost impact.* Companies producing goods in one country for export abroad always improve their cost competitiveness when the country's currency grows weaker relative to currencies of the countries where the goods are being exported to, and they find their cost competitiveness eroded when the local currency grows stronger. In contrast, domestic companies that are under pressure from lower-cost imported goods become more cost competitive when their currency grows weaker in relation to the currencies of the countries where the imported goods are made—in other words, a U.S. manufacturer views a weaker U.S. dollar as a *favorable exchange rate shift* because such shifts help make its costs more competitive versus those of foreign rivals.

> **Core Concept**
> Fluctuating exchange rates pose significant risks to a company's competitiveness in foreign markets. Exporters win when the currency of the country where goods are being manufactured grows weaker, and they lose when the currency grows stronger. Domestic companies under pressure from lower-cost imports are benefited when their government's currency grows weaker in relation to the countries where the imported goods are being made.

Host Governments' Policies

National governments enact all kinds of measures affecting business conditions and the operation of foreign companies in their markets. Host governments may set local content requirements on goods made inside their borders by foreign-based companies, have rules and policies that protect local companies from foreign competition, put restrictions on exports to ensure adequate local supplies, regulate the prices of imported and locally produced goods, enact deliberately burdensome procedures and requirements for imported goods to pass customs inspection, and impose tariffs or quotas on the imports of certain goods—until 2002, when it joined the World Trade Organization, China imposed a 100 percent tariff on motor vehicle imports. The European Union imposes quotas on textile and apparel imports from China, as a measure to protect European producers in southern Europe. India imposed excise taxes on newly purchased motor vehicles in 2005 ranging from 24 to 40 percent—a policy that has significantly dampened the demand for new vehicles in India (though down from as much as 50 percent in prior years). Governments may or may not have burdensome tax structures, stringent environmental regulations, or strictly enforced worker safety standards. Sometimes outsiders face a web of regulations regarding technical standards, product certification, prior approval of capital spending projects, withdrawal of funds from the country, and required minority (sometimes majority) ownership of foreign company operations by local companies or investors. A few governments may be hostile to or suspicious of foreign companies operating within their borders. Some governments provide subsidies and low-interest loans to domestic companies to help them compete against foreign-based companies. Other governments, anxious to obtain new plants and jobs, offer foreign companies a helping hand in the form of subsidies, privileged market access, and technical assistance. All of these possibilities explain why the managers of companies opting to compete in foreign markets have to take a close look at a country's politics and policies toward business in general, and foreign companies in particular, in deciding which country markets to participate in and which ones to avoid.

THE CONCEPTS OF MULTICOUNTRY COMPETITION AND GLOBAL COMPETITION

There are important differences in the patterns of international competition from industry to industry.[4] At one extreme is **multicountry competition,** in which there's so much cross-country variation in market conditions and in the companies contending for leadership that the market contest among rivals in one country is not closely connected to the market contests in other countries. The standout features of multicountry competition are that (1) buyers in different countries are attracted to different product attributes, (2) sellers vary from country to country, and (3) industry conditions and competitive forces in each national market differ in important respects. Take the banking industry in Italy, Brazil, and Japan as an example—the requirements and expectations of banking customers vary among the three countries, the lead banking competitors in Italy differ from those in Brazil or in Japan, and the competitive battle going on among the leading banks in Italy is unrelated to the rivalry taking place in Brazil or Japan. Thus, with multicountry competition, rival firms battle for national championships, and winning in one country does not necessarily signal the ability to fare well in other countries. In multicountry competition, the power of a company's strategy and resource capabilities in one country may not enhance its competitiveness to the same degree in other countries where it operates. Moreover, any competitive advantage a company secures in one country is largely confined to that country; the spillover effects to other countries are minimal to nonexistent. Industries characterized by multicountry competition include radio and TV broadcasting, consumer banking, life insurance, apparel, metals fabrication, many types of food products (coffee, cereals, breads, canned goods, frozen foods), and retailing.

> **Core Concept**
> *Multicountry competition*
> exists when competition in one national market is not closely connected to competition in another national market—there is no global or world market, just a collection of self-contained country markets.

At the other extreme is **global competition,** in which prices and competitive conditions across country markets are strongly linked and the term *global market* has true meaning. In a globally competitive industry, much the same group of rival companies competes in many different countries, but especially so in countries where sales volumes are large and where having a competitive presence is strategically important to building a strong global position in the industry. Thus, a company's competitive position in one country both affects and is affected by its position in other countries. In global competition, a firm's overall competitive advantage grows out of its entire worldwide operations; the competitive advantage it creates at its home base is supplemented by advantages growing out of its operations in other countries (having plants in low-wage countries, being able to transfer expertise from country to country, having the capability to serve customers who also have multinational operations, and brand-name recognition in many parts of the world). Rival firms in globally competitive industries vie for worldwide leadership. Global competition exists in motor vehicles, television sets, tires, mobile phones, personal computers, copiers, watches, digital cameras, bicycles, and commercial aircraft.

> **Core Concept**
> *Global competition* exists when competitive conditions across national markets are linked strongly enough to form a true international market and when leading competitors compete head to head in many different countries.

An industry can have segments that are globally competitive and segments in which competition is country by country.[5] In the hotel/motel industry, for example, the low- and medium-priced segments are characterized by multicountry competition—competitors serve travelers mainly within the same country. In the business and luxury segments, however, competition is more globalized. Companies like Nikki, Marriott, Sheraton, and Hilton have hotels at many international locations, use worldwide reservation systems, and establish common quality and service standards to gain marketing advantages in serving businesspeople and other travelers who make frequent international trips. In lubricants, the marine engine segment is globally competitive—ships move from port to port and require the same oil everywhere they stop. Brand reputations in marine lubricants have a global scope, and successful marine engine lubricant producers (ExxonMobil, BP Amoco, and Shell) operate globally. In automotive motor oil, however, multicountry competition dominates—countries have different weather conditions and driving patterns, production of motor oil is subject to limited scale economies, shipping costs are high, and retail distribution channels differ markedly from country to country. Thus, domestic firms—like Quaker State and Pennzoil in the United States and Castrol in Great Britain—can be leaders in their home markets without competing globally.

It is also important to recognize that an industry can be in transition from multicountry competition to global competition. In a number of today's industries—beer and major home appliances are prime examples—leading domestic competitors have begun expanding into more and more foreign markets, often acquiring local companies or brands and integrating them into their operations. As some industry members start to build global brands and a global presence, other industry members find themselves pressured to follow the same strategic path—especially if establishing multinational operations results in important scale economies and a powerhouse brand name. As the industry consolidates to fewer players, such that many of the same companies find themselves in head-to-head competition in more and more country markets, global competition begins to replace multicountry competition.

At the same time, consumer tastes in a number of important product categories are converging across the world. Less diversity of tastes and preferences opens the way for companies to create global brands and sell essentially the same products in most all countries of the world. Even in industries where consumer tastes remain fairly diverse, companies are learning to use "custom mass production" to economically create different versions of a product and thereby satisfy the tastes of people in different countries.

In addition to taking the obvious cultural and political differences between countries into account, a company has to shape its strategic approach to competing in foreign markets according to whether its industry is characterized by multicountry competition, global competition, or a transition from one to the other.

STRATEGY OPTIONS FOR ENTERING AND COMPETING IN FOREIGN MARKETS

There are a host of generic strategic options for a company that decides to expand outside its domestic market and compete internationally or globally:

1. *Maintain a national (one-country) production base and export goods to foreign markets*, using either company-owned or foreign-controlled forward distribution channels.

2. *License foreign firms to use the company's technology or to produce and distribute the company's products.*

3. *Employ a franchising strategy.*

4. *Follow a multicountry strategy,* varying the company's strategic approach (perhaps a little, perhaps a lot) from country to country in accordance with local conditions and differing buyer tastes and preferences.

5. *Follow a global strategy,* using essentially the same competitive strategy approach in all country markets where the company has a presence.

6. *Use strategic alliances or joint ventures with foreign companies as the primary vehicle for entering foreign markets* and perhaps also using them as an ongoing strategic arrangement aimed at maintaining or strengthening its competitiveness.

The following sections discuss the first five options in more detail; the sixth option is discussed in a separate section later in the chapter.

Export Strategies

Using domestic plants as a production base for exporting goods to foreign markets is an excellent initial strategy for pursuing international sales. It is a conservative way to test the international waters. The amount of capital needed to begin exporting is often quite minimal; existing production capacity may well be sufficient to make goods for export. With an export strategy, a manufacturer can limit its involvement in foreign markets by contracting with foreign wholesalers experienced in importing to handle the entire distribution and marketing function in their countries or regions of the world. If it is more advantageous to maintain control over these functions, however, a manufacturer can establish its own distribution and sales organizations in some or all of the target foreign markets. Either way, a home-based production and export strategy helps the firm minimize its direct investments in foreign countries. Such strategies are commonly favored by Chinese, Korean, and Italian companies—products are designed and manufactured at home and then distributed through local channels in the importing countries; the primary functions performed abroad relate chiefly to establishing a network of distributors and perhaps conducting sales promotion and brand awareness activities.

Whether an export strategy can be pursued successfully over the long run hinges on the relative cost competitiveness of the home-country production base. In some industries, firms gain additional scale economies and experience/learning curve benefits from centralizing production in one or several giant plants whose output capability exceeds demand in any one country market; obviously, a company must export to capture such economies. However, an export strategy is vulnerable when (1) manufacturing costs in the home country are substantially higher than in foreign countries where rivals have plants, (2) the costs of shipping the product to distant foreign markets are relatively high, or (3) adverse shifts occur in currency exchange rates. Unless an exporter can both keep its production and shipping costs competitive with rivals and successfully hedge against unfavorable changes in currency exchange rates, its success will be limited.

Licensing Strategies

Licensing makes sense when a firm with valuable technical know-how or a unique patented product has neither the internal organizational capability nor the resources to enter foreign markets. Licensing also has the advantage of avoiding the risks of committing resources to country markets that are unfamiliar, politically volatile, economically unstable, or otherwise risky. By licensing the technology or the production rights to foreign-based firms, the firm does not have to bear the costs and risks of entering foreign markets on its own, yet it is able to generate income from royalties. The big disadvantage of licensing is the risk of providing valuable technological know-how to foreign companies and thereby losing some degree of control over its use; monitoring licensees and safeguarding the company's proprietary know-how can prove quite difficult in some circumstances. But if the royalty potential is considerable and the companies to whom the licenses are being granted are both trustworthy and reputable, then licensing can be a very attractive option. Many software and pharmaceutical companies use licensing strategies.

Franchising Strategies

While licensing works well for manufacturers and owners of proprietary technology, franchising is often better suited to the global expansion efforts of service and retailing enterprises. McDonald's, Yum! Brands (the parent of Pizza Hut, KFC, and Taco Bell), The UPS Store, Jani-King International (the world's largest commercial cleaning franchisor), Roto-Rooter, 7-Eleven, and Hilton Hotels have all used franchising to build a presence in foreign markets. Franchising has much the same advantages as licensing. The franchisee bears most of the costs and risks of establishing foreign locations; a franchisor has to expend only the resources to recruit, train, support, and monitor franchisees. The big problem a franchisor faces is maintaining quality control; foreign franchisees do not always exhibit strong commitment to consistency and standardization, especially when the local culture does not stress the same kinds of quality concerns. Another problem that can arise is whether to allow foreign franchisees to make modifications in the franchisor's product offering so as to better satisfy the tastes and expectations of local buyers. Should McDonald's allow its franchised units in Japan to modify Big Macs slightly to suit Japanese tastes? Should the franchised KFC units in China be permitted to substitute spices that appeal to Chinese consumers? Or should the same menu offerings be rigorously and unvaryingly required of all franchisees worldwide?

Localized Multicountry Strategies or a Global Strategy?

The issue of whether to vary the company's competitive approach to fit specific market conditions and buyer preferences in each host country or whether to employ essentially the same strategy in all countries is perhaps the foremost strategic issue that companies must address when they operate in two or more foreign markets. Figure 7.1 shows a company's options for resolving this issue.

Core Concept
A *localized* or *multicountry* strategy is one where a company varies its product offering and competitive approach from country to country in an effort to be responsive to differing buyer preferences and market conditions.

Think-Local, Act-Local Approaches to Strategy Making The bigger the differences in buyer tastes, cultural traditions, and market conditions in different countries, the stronger the case for a think-local, act-local approach to strategy making, in which a company tailors its product offerings and perhaps its basic competitive strategy to fit buyer tastes and market conditions in each country where it opts to compete. The strength of employing a set of *localized* or *multicountry strategies* is that the company's actions and business approaches are deliberately crafted to accommodate the

Figure 7.1 **A Company's Strategic Options for Dealing with Cross-Country Variations in Buyer Preferences and Market Conditions**

Strategic Posturing Options	Ways to Deal with Cross-Country Variations in Buyer Preferences and Market Conditions
Think Local, Act Local	**Employ localized strategies—one for each country market:** ■ Tailor the company's competitive approach and product offering to fit specific market conditions and buyer preferences in each host country. ■ Delegate strategy making to local managers with firsthand knowledge of local conditions.
Think Global, Act Global	**Employ same strategy worldwide:** ■ Pursue *the same basic competitive strategy theme* (low-cost, differentiation, best-cost, or focused) *in all country markets*—a global strategy. ■ Offer the same products worldwide, with only very minor deviations from one country to another when local market conditions so dictate. ■ Utilize the same capabilities, distribution channels, and marketing approaches worldwide. ■ Coordinate strategic actions from central headquarters
Think Global, Act Local	**Employ a combination global-local strategy:** ■ Employ essentially *the same basic competitive strategy theme* (low-cost, differentiation, best-cost, or focused) in *all country markets*. ■ Develop the capability to customize product offerings and sell different product versions in different countries (perhaps even under different brand names). ■ Give local managers the latitude to adapt the global approach as needed to accommodate local buyer preferences and be responsive to local market and competitive conditions.

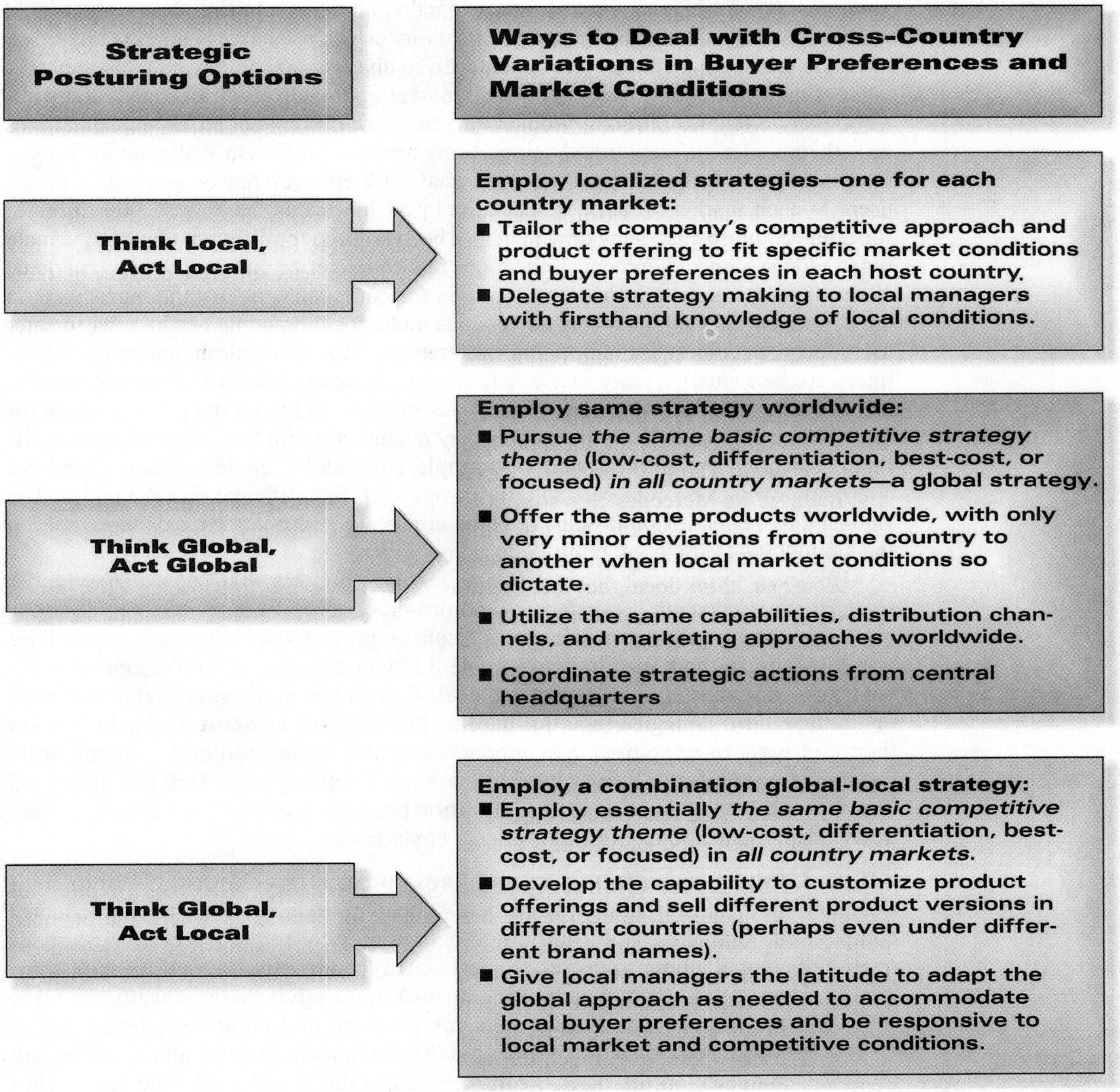

differing tastes and expectations of buyers in each country and to stake out the most attractive market positions vis-à-vis local competitors. A think-local, act-local approach means giving local managers considerable strategy-making latitude. It means having plants produce different product versions for different local markets, and adapting marketing and distribution to fit local customs and cultures. The bigger the country-to-country variations, the more that a company's overall strategy is a collection of its localized country strategies rather than a common or global strategy.

A think-local, act-local approach to strategy making is essential when there are significant country-to-country differences in customer preferences and buying habits, when there are significant cross-country differences in distribution channels and marketing methods, when host governments enact regulations requiring that products sold locally meet strict manufacturing specifications or performance standards, and when the trade restrictions of host governments are so diverse and complicated that they preclude a uniform, coordinated worldwide market approach. With localized strategies, a company often has different product versions for different countries and sometimes sells them under different brand names. Sony markets a different Walkman in Norway than in Sweden to better meet the somewhat different preferences and habits of the users in each market. Castrol, a specialist in oil lubricants, has over 3,000 different formulas of lubricants, many of which have been tailored for different climates, vehicle types and uses, and equipment applications that characterize different country markets. In the food products industry, it is common for companies to vary the ingredients in their products and sell the localized versions under local brand names in order to cater to country-specific tastes and eating preferences. Motor vehicle manufacturers routinely produce smaller, more fuel-efficient vehicles for markets in Europe where roads are often narrower and gasoline prices two or three times higher than they produce for the North American market; the models they manufacture for the Asian market are different yet again. DaimlerChrysler, for example, equips all of the Jeep Grand Cherokees and many of its Mercedes cars sold in Europe with fuel-efficient diesel engines. The Buicks that General Motors sells in China are small compacts, whereas those sold in the United States are large family sedans and SUVs.

However, think-local, act-local strategies have two big drawbacks: They hinder transfer of a company's competencies and resources across country boundaries (since the strategies in different host countries can be grounded in varying competencies and capabilities), and they do not promote building a single, unified competitive advantage—especially one based on low cost. Companies employing highly localized or multicountry strategies face big hurdles in achieving low-cost leadership *unless* they find ways to customize their products and *still* be in position to capture scale economies and experience/learning curve effects. Companies like Dell Computer and Toyota, because they have mass customization production capabilities, can cost effectively adapt their product offerings to local buyer tastes.

Think-Global, Act-Global Approaches to Strategy Making While multicountry or localized strategies are best suited for industries where multicountry competition dominates and a fairly high degree of local responsiveness is competitively imperative, global strategies are best suited for globally competitive industries. A *global strategy* is one in which the company's approach is predominantly the same in all countries—it sells the same products under the same brand names everywhere, uses much the same distribution channels in all countries, and competes on the basis of the same capabilities and marketing approaches worldwide. Although the company's strategy or product offering may be adapted in very minor ways to accommodate specific situations in a few host countries, the company's fundamental competitive approach (low-cost, differentiation, best-cost, or focused) remains very much intact worldwide, and local managers stick close to the global strategy. A think-global, act-global strategic theme prompts company managers to integrate and coordinate the company's strategic moves worldwide and to expand into most if not all nations where there is significant buyer demand. It puts considerable strategic

> **Core Concept**
> A *global strategy* is one where a company employs the same basic competitive approach in all countries where it operates, sells much the same products everywhere, strives to build global brands, and coordinates its actions worldwide.

emphasis on building a *global* brand name and aggressively pursuing opportunities to transfer ideas, new products, and capabilities from one country to another.[6] Indeed, with a think global, act global approach to strategy making, a company's operations in each country can be viewed as experiments that result in learning and in capabilities that may merit transfer to other country markets.

Whenever country-to-country differences are small enough to be accommodated within the framework of a global strategy, a global strategy is preferable to localized strategies because a company can more readily unify its operations and focus on establishing a brand image and reputation that is uniform from country to country. Moreover, with a global strategy a company is better able to focus its full resources on building the resource strengths and capabilities to secure a sustainable low-cost or differentiation-based competitive advantage over both domestic rivals and global rivals racing for world market leadership. Figure 7.2 summarizes the basic differences between a localized or multicountry strategy and a global strategy.

Think-Global, Act-Local Approaches to Strategy Making Often, a company can accommodate cross-country variations in buyer tastes, local customs, and market conditions with a think-global, act-local approach to developing strategy. This middle-ground approach entails using the same basic competitive theme (low-cost, differentiation, best-cost, or focused) in each country but allowing local managers the latitude to (1) incorporate whatever country-specific variations in product attributes are needed to best satisfy local buyers and (2) make whatever adjustments in production, distribution, and marketing are needed to be responsive to local market conditions and compete successfully against local rivals. Slightly different product versions sold under the same brand name may suffice to satisfy local tastes, and it may be feasible to accommodate these versions rather economically in the course of designing and manufacturing the company's product offerings. The build-to-order component of Dell's strategy in PCs for example, makes it simple for Dell to be responsive to how buyers in different parts of the world want their PCs equipped. However, Dell has not wavered in its strategy to sell directly to customers rather than through local retailers, even though the majority of buyers in countries such as China are concerned about ordering online and prefer to personally inspect PCs at stores before making a purchase.

As a rule, most companies that operate multinationally endeavor to employ as global a strategy as customer needs and market conditions permit. Philips Electronics, the Netherlands-based electronics and consumer products company, operated successfully with localized strategies for many years but has recently begun moving more toward a unified strategy within the European Union and within North America.[7] Whirlpool has been globalizing its low-cost leadership strategy in home appliances for over 15 years, striving to standardize parts and components and move toward worldwide designs for as many of its appliance products as possible. But it has found it necessary to continue producing significantly different versions of refrigerators, washing machines, and cooking appliances for consumers in different regions of the world because the needs and tastes of local buyers for appliances of different sizes and designs have not converged sufficiently to permit standardization of Whirlpool's product offerings worldwide. General Motors began an initiative in 2004 to insist that its worldwide units share basic parts and work together to design vehicles that can be sold, with modest variations, anywhere around the world; by reducing the types of radios used in its cars and trucks from 270 to 50, it expected to save 40 percent in radio costs.

Illustration Capsule 7.1 on page 209 describes how two companies localize their strategies for competing in country markets across the world.

Figure 7.2   **How a Localized or Multicountry Strategy Differs from a Global Strategy**

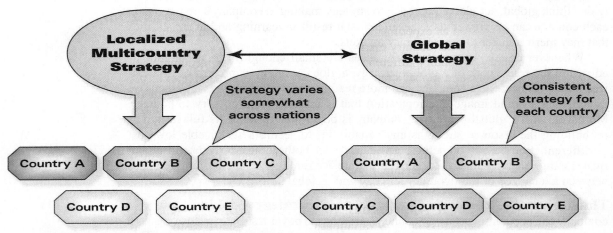

- ■ Customize the company's competitive approach as needed to fit market and business circumstances in each host country—strong responsiveness to local conditions.
- ■ Sell different product versions in different countries under different brand names—adapt product attributes to fit buyer tastes and preferences country by country.
- ■ Scatter plants across many host countries, each producing product versions for local markets.
- ■ Preferably use local suppliers (some local sources may be required by host government).
- ■ Adapt marketing and distribution to local customs and culture of each country.
- ■ Transfer competencies and capabilities from country to country where feasible.
- ■ Give country managers fairly wide strategy-making latitude and autonomy over local operations.

- ■ Pursue same basic competitive strategy worldwide (low-cost, differentiation, best-cost, focused low-cost, focused differentiation), with minimal responsiveness to local conditions.
- ■ Sell same products under same brand name worldwide; focus efforts on building global brands as opposed to strengthening local/regional brands sold in local/regional markets.
- ■ Locate plants on basis of maximum locational advantage, usually in countries where production costs are lowest but plants may be scattered if shipping costs are high or other locational advantages dominate.
- ■ Use best suppliers from anywhere in world.
- ■ Coordinate marketing and distribution worldwide; make minor adaptation to local countries where needed.
- ■ Compete on basis of same technologies, competencies, and capabilities worldwide; stress rapid transfer of new ideas, products, and capabilities to other countries.
- ■ Coordinate major strategic decisions worldwide; expect local managers to stick close to global strategy.

Illustration Capsule 7.1

Multicountry Strategies at Electronic Arts and Coca-Cola

ELECTRONIC ARTS' MULTICOUNTRY STRATEGY IN VIDEO GAMES

Electronic Arts (EA), the world's largest independent developer and marketer of video games, designs games that are suited to the differing tastes of game players in different countries and also designs games in multiple languages. EA has two major design studios—one in Vancouver, British Columbia, and one in Los Angeles—and smaller design studios in San Francisco, Orlando, London, and Tokyo. This dispersion of design studios helps EA to design games that are specific to different cultures—for example, the London studio took the lead in designing the popular FIFA Soccer game to suit European tastes and to replicate the stadiums, signage, and team rosters; the U.S. studio took the lead in designing games involving NFL football, NBA basketball, and NASCAR racing. No other game software company had EA's ability to localize games or to launch games on multiple platforms in multiple countries in multiple languages. EA's game Harry Potter and the Chamber of Secrets was released simultaneously in 75 countries, in 31 languages, and on seven platforms.

COCA-COLA'S MULTICOUNTRY STRATEGY IN BEVERAGES

Coca-Cola strives to meet the demands of local tastes and cultures, offering 300 brands in some 200 countries. Its network of bottlers and distributors is distinctly local, and the company's products and brands are formulated to cater to local tastes. The ways in which Coca-Cola's local operating units bring products to market, the packaging that is used, and the company's advertising messages are all intended to match the local culture and fit in with local business practices. Many of the ingredients and supplies for Coca-Cola's products are sourced locally.

Sources: Information posted at www.ea.com and www.cocacola.com (accessed September 2004).

THE QUEST FOR COMPETITIVE ADVANTAGE IN FOREIGN MARKETS

There are three important ways in which a firm can gain competitive advantage (or offset domestic disadvantages) by expanding outside its domestic market:[8] One, it can use location to lower costs or achieve greater product differentiation. Two, it can transfer competitively valuable competencies and capabilities from its domestic markets to foreign markets. And three, it can use cross-border coordination in ways that a domestic-only competitor cannot.

Using Location to Build Competitive Advantage

To use location to build competitive advantage, a company must consider two issues: (1) whether to concentrate each activity it performs in a few select countries or to disperse performance of the activity to many nations, and (2) in which countries to locate particular activities.[9]

When to Concentrate Activities in a Few Locations   Companies tend to concentrate their activities in a limited number of locations in the following circumstances:

> Companies that compete multinationally can pursue competitive advantage in world markets by locating their value chain activities in whatever nations prove most advantageous.

- *When the costs of manufacturing or other activities are significantly lower in some geographic locations than in others*—For example, much of the world's athletic footwear is manufactured in Asia (China and Korea) because of low labor costs; much of the production of motherboards for PCs is located in Taiwan because of both low costs and the high-caliber technical skills of the Taiwanese labor force.

- *When there are significant scale economies*—The presence of significant economies of scale in components production or final assembly means that a company can gain major cost savings from operating a few superefficient plants as opposed to a host of small plants scattered across the world. Important marketing and distribution economies associated with multinational operations can also yield low-cost leadership. In situations where some competitors are intent on global dominance, being the worldwide low-cost provider is a powerful competitive advantage. Achieving low-cost provider status often requires a company to have the largest worldwide manufacturing share, with production centralized in one or a few world-scale plants in low-cost locations. Some companies even use such plants to manufacture units sold under the brand names of rivals. Manufacturing share (as distinct from brand share or market share) is significant because it provides more certain access to production-related scale economies. Japanese makers of VCRs, microwave ovens, TVs, and DVD players have used their large manufacturing share to establish a low-cost advantage.[10]

- *When there is a steep learning curve associated with performing an activity in a single location*—In some industries experience/learning curve effects in parts manufacture or assembly are so great that a company establishes one or two large plants from which it serves the world market. The key to riding down the learning curve is to concentrate production in a few locations to increase the accumulated volume at a plant (and thus the experience of the plant's workforce) as rapidly as possible.

- *When certain locations have superior resources, allow better coordination of related activities, or offer other valuable advantages*—A research unit or a sophisticated production facility may be situated in a particular nation because of its pool of technically trained personnel. Samsung became a leader in memory chip technology by establishing a major R&D facility in Silicon Valley and transferring the know-how it gained back to headquarters and its plants in South Korea. Where just-in-time inventory practices yield big cost savings and/or where an assembly firm has long-term partnering arrangements with its key suppliers, parts manufacturing plants may be clustered around final assembly plants. An assembly plant may be located in a country in return for the host government's allowing freer import of components from large-scale, centralized parts plants located elsewhere. A customer service center or sales office may be opened in a particular country to help cultivate strong relationships with pivotal customers located nearby.

When to Disperse Activities Across Many Locations   There are several instances when dispersing activities is more advantageous than concentrating them. Buyer-related activities—such as distribution to dealers, sales and advertising, and after-sale service—usually must take place close to buyers. This means physically locating the capability to perform such activities in every country market where a global firm has major customers (unless buyers in several adjoining countries can be served quickly from a nearby central location). For example, firms that make mining and oil-drilling equipment maintain operations in many international locations to support customers' needs for speedy equipment repair and technical assistance. The four biggest public accounting firms have numerous international offices to service the foreign operations of their multinational corporate clients. A global competitor that effectively disperses its buyer-related activities can gain a service-based competitive edge in world markets over rivals whose buyer-related activities are more concentrated—this is one reason the Big Four public accounting firms (PricewaterhouseCoopers, KPMG, Deloitte & Touche, and Ernst & Young) have been so successful relative to regional and national firms. Dispersing activities to many locations is also competitively advantageous when high transportation costs, diseconomies of large size, and trade barriers make it too expensive to operate from a central location. Many companies distribute their products from multiple locations to shorten delivery times to customers. In addition, it is strategically advantageous to disperse activities to hedge against the risks of fluctuating exchange rates; supply interruptions (due to strikes, mechanical failures, and transportation delays); and adverse political developments. Such risks are greater when activities are concentrated in a single location.

The classic reason for locating an activity in a particular country is low cost.[11] Even though multinational and global firms have strong reason to disperse buyer-related activities to many international locations, such activities as materials procurement, parts manufacture, finished goods assembly, technology research, and new product development can frequently be decoupled from buyer locations and performed wherever advantage lies. Components can be made in Mexico; technology research done in Frankfurt; new products developed and tested in Phoenix; and assembly plants located in Spain, Brazil, Taiwan, or South Carolina. Capital can be raised in whatever country it is available on the best terms.

Using Cross-Border Transfers of Competencies and Capabilities to Build Competitive Advantage

One of the best ways for a company with valuable competencies and resource strengths to secure competitive advantage is to use its considerable resource strengths to enter additional country markets. A company whose resource strengths prove particularly potent in competing successfully in newly entered country markets not only grows sales and profits but also may find that its competitiveness is sufficiently enhanced to produce competitive advantage over one or more rivals and contend for global market leadership. Transferring competencies, capabilities, and resource strengths from country to country contributes to the development of broader or deeper competencies and capabilities—ideally helping a company achieve dominating depth in some competitively valuable area. Dominating depth in a competitively valuable capability, resource, or value chain activity is a strong basis for sustainable competitive advantage over other multinational or global competitors, and especially so over domestic-only competitors. A one-country customer base is often too small to support the resource buildup needed to achieve such depth; this is particularly true when the market is just emerging and sophisticated resources have not been required.

Whirlpool, the leading global manufacturer of home appliances, with plants in 14 countries and sales in 170 countries, has used the Internet to create a global information technology platform that allows the company to transfer key product innovations and production processes across regions and brands quickly and effectively. Wal-Mart is slowly but forcefully expanding its operations with a strategy that involves transferring its considerable domestic expertise in distribution and discount retailing to store operations recently established in China, Japan, Latin America, and Europe. Its status as the largest, most resource-deep, and most sophisticated user of distribution/ retailing know-how has served it well in building its foreign sales and profitability. But Wal-Mart is not racing madly to position itself in many foreign markets; rather, it is establishing a strong presence in select country markets and learning how to be successful in these before tackling entry into other countries well-suited to its business model.

However, cross-border resource transfers are not a guaranteed recipe for success. Philips Electronics sells more color TVs and DVD recorders in Europe than any other company does; its biggest technological breakthrough was the compact disc, which it invented in 1982. Philips has worldwide sales of about 38 billion euros, but as of 2005 Philips had lost money for 17 consecutive years in its U.S. consumer electronics business. In the United States, the company's color TVs and DVD recorders (sold under the Magnavox and Philips brands) are slow sellers. Philips notoriously lags in introducing new products into the U.S. market and has been struggling to develop an able sales force that can make inroads with U.S. electronics retailers and change its image as a low-end brand.

Using Cross-Border Coordination to Build Competitive Advantage

Coordinating company activities across different countries contributes to sustainable competitive advantage in several different ways.[12] Multinational and global competitors can choose where and how to challenge rivals. They may decide to retaliate against an aggressive rival in the country market where the rival has its biggest sales volume or its best profit margins in order to reduce the rival's financial resources for competing in other country markets. They may also decide to wage a price-cutting offensive against weak rivals in their home markets, capturing greater market share and subsidizing any short-term losses with profits earned in other country markets.

If a firm learns how to assemble its product more efficiently at, say, its Brazilian plant, the accumulated expertise can be quickly communicated via the Internet to assembly plants in other world locations. Knowledge gained in marketing a company's product in Great Britain can readily be exchanged with company personnel in New Zealand or Australia. A global or multinational manufacturer can shift production from a plant in one country to a plant in another to take advantage of exchange rate fluctuations, to enhance its leverage with host-country governments, and to respond to changing wage rates, components shortages, energy costs, or changes in tariffs and quotas. Production schedules can be coordinated worldwide; shipments can be diverted from one distribution center to another if sales rise unexpectedly in one place and fall in another.

Using online systems, companies can readily gather ideas for new and improved products from customers and company personnel all over the world, permitting informed decisions about what can be standardized and what should be customized. Likewise, online systems enable multinational companies to involve their best design and engineering personnel (wherever they are located) in collectively coming up with next-generation products—it is easy for company personnel in one location to use the Internet to collaborate closely with personnel in other locations in performing all sorts of strategically relevant activities. Efficiencies can also be achieved by shifting workloads from where they are unusually heavy to locations where personnel are underutilized. Whirlpool's efforts to link its product R&D and manufacturing operations in North America, Latin America, Europe, and Asia allowed it to accelerate the discovery of innovative appliance features, coordinate the introduction of these features in the appliance products marketed in different countries, and create a cost-efficient worldwide supply chain. Whirlpool's conscious efforts to integrate and coordinate its various operations around the world have helped it become a low-cost producer and also speed product innovations to market, thereby giving Whirlpool an edge over rivals in designing and rapidly introducing innovative and attractively priced appliances worldwide.

Furthermore, a multinational company that consistently incorporates the same differentiating attributes in its products worldwide has enhanced potential to build a global brand name with significant power in the marketplace. The reputation for quality that Honda established worldwide first in motorcycles and then in automobiles gave it competitive advantage in positioning Honda lawn mowers at the upper end of the U.S. outdoor power equipment market—the Honda name gave the company immediate credibility with U.S. buyers of power equipment and enabled it to become an instant market contender without all the fanfare and cost of a multimillion-dollar ad campaign to build brand awareness.

PROFIT SANCTUARIES, CROSS-MARKET SUBSIDIZATION, AND GLOBAL STRATEGIC OFFENSIVES

Profit sanctuaries are country markets (or geographic regions) in which a company derives substantial profits because of its strong or protected market position. McDonald's serves about 50 million customers daily at nearly 32,000 locations in 119 countries on five continents; not surprisingly, its biggest profit sanctuary is the United States, which generated 61.2 percent of 2004 profits, despite accounting for just 34.2 percent of 2004 revenues. Nike, which markets its products in 160 countries, has two big profit sanctuaries: the United States (where it earned 41.5 percent of its operating profits in 2005) and Europe, the Middle East, and Africa (where it earned 34.8 percent of 2005 operating profits). Discount retailer Carrefour, which has stores across much of Europe plus stores in Asia and the Americas, also has two principal profit sanctuaries; its biggest is in France (which in 2004 accounted for 49.2 percent of revenues and 60.8 percent of earnings before interest and taxes), and its second biggest is Europe outside of France (which in 2004 accounted for 37.3 percent of revenues and 33.1 percent of earnings before interest and taxes). Japan is the chief profit sanctuary for most Japanese companies because trade barriers erected by the Japanese government effectively block foreign companies from competing for a large share of Japanese sales. Protected from the threat of foreign competition in their home market, Japanese companies can safely charge somewhat higher prices to their Japanese customers and thus earn attractively large profits on sales made in Japan. In most cases, a company's biggest and most strategically crucial profit sanctuary is its home market, but international and global companies may also enjoy profit sanctuary status in other nations where they have a strong competitive position, big sales volume, and attractive profit margins. Companies that compete globally are likely to have more profit sanctuaries than companies that compete in just a few country markets; a domestic-only competitor, of course, can have only one profit sanctuary (see Figure 7.3).

Core Concept
Companies with large, protected *profit sanctuaries* have competitive advantage over companies that don't have a protected sanctuary. Companies with multiple profit sanctuaries have a competitive advantage over companies with a single sanctuary.

Figure 7.3 **Profit Sanctuary Potential of Domestic-Only, International, and Global Competitors**

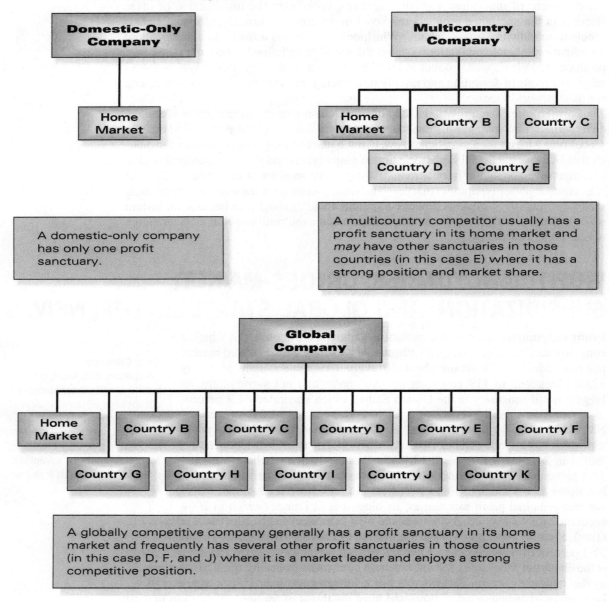

A domestic-only company has only one profit sanctuary.

A multicountry competitor usually has a profit sanctuary in its home market and *may* have other sanctuaries in those countries (in this case E) where it has a strong position and market share.

A globally competitive company generally has a profit sanctuary in its home market and frequently has several other profit sanctuaries in those countries (in this case D, F, and J) where it is a market leader and enjoys a strong competitive position.

Using Cross-Market Subsidization to Wage a Strategic Offensive

Profit sanctuaries are valuable competitive assets, providing the financial strength to support strategic offensives in selected country markets and fuel a company's race for global market leadership. The added financial capability afforded by multiple profit sanctuaries gives a global or multicountry competitor the financial strength to wage a market offensive against a domestic competitor whose only profit sanctuary is its home market. Consider the case of a purely domestic company in competition with a company that has multiple profit sanctuaries and that is racing for global market leadership. The global company has the flexibility of lowballing its prices in the domestic company's home market and grabbing market share at the domestic company's expense, subsidizing razor-thin margins or even losses with the healthy profits earned in its profit sanctuaries—a practice called **cross-market subsidization.** The global company can adjust the depth of its price cutting to move in and capture market share quickly, or it can shave prices slightly to make gradual market inroads (perhaps over a decade or more) so as not to threaten domestic firms precipitously or trigger protectionist government actions. If the domestic company retaliates with matching price cuts, it exposes its entire revenue and profit base to erosion; its profits can be squeezed substantially and its competitive strength sapped, even if it is the domestic market leader.

> **Core Concept**
> ***Cross-market subsidization—*** supporting competitive offensives in one market with resources and profits diverted from operations in other markets—is a powerful competitive weapon.

Offensive Strategies Suitable for Competing in Foreign Markets

Companies that compete in multiple foreign markets can, of course, fashion an offensive strategy based on any of the approaches discussed in Chapter 6 (pages 160–193)—these types of offensive strategies are universally applicable and are just as suitable for competing in foreign markets as for domestic markets. But there are three additional types of offensive strategies that are suited to companies competing in foreign markets:[13]

- *Attack a foreign rival's profit sanctuaries.* Launching an offensive in a country market where a rival earns its biggest profits can put the rival on the defensive, forcing it to perhaps spend more on marketing/advertising, trim its prices, boost product innovation efforts, or otherwise undertake actions that raise its costs and erode its profits. If a company's offensive succeeds in eroding a rival's profits in its chief profit sanctuary, the rival's financial resources may be sufficiently weakened to enable the attacker to gain the upper hand and build market momentum. While attacking a rival's profit sanctuary violates the principle of attacking competitor weaknesses instead of competitor strengths, it can nonetheless prove valuable when there is special merit in pursuing actions that cut into a foreign rival's profit margins and force it to defend a market that is important to its competitive well-being. This is especially true when the attacker has important resource strengths and profit sanctuaries of its own that it can draw on to support its offensive.

- *Employ cross-market subsidization to win customers and sales away from select rivals in select country markets.* This can be a particularly attractive offensive strategy for companies that compete in multiple country markets with multiple products (several brands of cigarettes or different brands of food products). Competing in multiple country markets gives a company the luxury of drawing upon the resources, profits, and cash flows derived from particular country markets (especially its profit sanctuaries) to support offensives aimed at winning customers away from select rivals in those country markets that it wants either to enter or to boost its sales and market share. Alternatively, a company whose product lineup consists of different items can shift resources from a product category where it is competitively strong and resource deep (say soft drinks) to add firepower to an offensive in those countries with bright growth prospects in another product category (say bottled water or fruit juices).

- *Dump goods at cut-rate prices in the markets of foreign rivals.* A company is said to be dumping when it sells its goods in foreign markets at prices that are (1) well below the prices at which it normally sells in its home market or (2) well below its full costs per unit. Companies that engage in dumping usually keep their selling prices high enough to cover variable costs per unit, thereby limiting their losses on each unit to some percentage of fixed costs per unit. Dumping can be an appealing offensive strategy in either of two instances. One is when dumping drives down the price so far in the targeted country that domestic firms are quickly put in dire financial straits and end up declaring bankruptcy or being driven out of business—for dumping to pay off in this instance, however, the dumping company needs to have deep enough financial pockets to cover any losses from selling at below-market prices, and the targeted domestic companies need to be financially weak. The second instance in which dumping becomes an attractive strategy is when a company with unused production capacity discovers that it is cheaper to keep producing (as long as the selling prices cover average variable costs per unit) than it is to incur the costs associated with idle plant capacity. By keeping its plants operating at or near capacity, a dumping company not only may be able to cover variable costs and earn a contribution to fixed costs but also may be able to use its below-market prices to draw price-sensitive customers away from foreign rivals, then attentively court these new customers and retain their business when prices later begin a gradual rise back to normal market levels. Thus, dumping may prove useful as a way of entering the market of a particular foreign country and establishing a customer base.

> **Core Concept**
> Three strategy offensives that are particularly suitable for competing in foreign markets involve (1) attacking a foreign rival's profit sanctuaries, (2) employing cross-market subsidization, and (3) dumping.

However, dumping strategies run a high risk of host government retaliation on behalf of the adversely affected domestic companies. Indeed, as the trade among nations has mushroomed over the past 10 years, most governments have joined the World Trade Organization (WTO), which promotes fair trade practices among nations and actively polices dumping. The WTO allows member governments to take actions against dumping wherever there is material injury to domestic competitors. In 2002, for example, the U.S. government imposed tariffs of up to 30 percent on selected steel products that Asian and European steel manufacturers were said to be selling at ultra-low prices in the U.S. market. Canada recently investigated charges that companies in Austria, Belgium, France, Germany, Poland and China were dumping supplies of laminate flooring in Canada to the detriment of Canadian producers and concluded that companies in France and China were indeed selling such flooring in Canada at unreasonably low prices.[14] Most all governments can be expected to retaliate against dumping by imposing special tariffs on goods being imported from the countries of the guilty companies. Companies deemed guilty of dumping frequently come under pressure from their government to cease and desist, especially if the tariffs adversely affect innocent companies based in the same country or if the advent of special tariffs raises the specter of a trade war.

A company desirous of employing some type of offensive strategy in foreign markets is well advised to observe the principles for employing offensive strategies in general. For instance, it usually wise to attack foreign rivals on grounds that pit the challenger's competitive strengths against the defender's weaknesses and vulnerabilities. As a rule, trying to steal customers away from foreign rivals with strategies aimed at besting rivals where they are strongest stand a lower chance of succeeding than strategies that attack their competitive weaknesses, especially when the challenger has resource strengths that enable it to exploit rivals' weaknesses and when its attack involves an element of surprise.[15] It nearly always makes good strategic sense to use the challenger's core competencies and best competitive capabilities to spearhead the offensive. Furthermore, strategic offensives in foreign markets should, as a general rule, be predicated on exploiting the challenger's core competencies and best competitive capabilities. The ideal condition for a strategic offensive is when the attacker's resource strengths give it a competitive advantage over the targeted foreign rivals. The only two exceptions to these offensive strategy principles come when a competitively strong company with deep financial pockets sees considerable benefit in attacking a foreign rival's profit sanctuary and/or has the ability to employ cross-market subsidization— both of these offensive strategies can involve attacking a foreign rival's strengths (but they also are grounded in important strengths of the challenger and don't fall into the trap of challenging a competitively strong rival with a strategic offensive based on unproven expertise or inferior technology or a relatively unknown brand name or other resource weaknesses).

STRATEGIC ALLIANCES AND JOINT VENTURES WITH FOREIGN PARTNERS

Strategic alliances, joint ventures, and other cooperative agreements with foreign companies are a favorite and potentially fruitful means for entering a foreign market or strengthening a firm's competitiveness in world markets.[16] Historically, export-minded firms in industrialized nations sought alliances with firms in less-developed countries to import and market their products locally—such arrangements were often necessary to win approval for entry from the host country's government. Both Japanese and American companies are actively forming alliances with European companies to strengthen their ability to compete in the 25-nation European Union (and the five countries that are seeking to become EU members) and to capitalize on the opening up of Eastern European markets. Many U.S. and European companies are allying with Asian companies in their efforts to enter markets in China, India, Malaysia, Thailand, and other Asian countries. Companies in Europe, Latin America, and Asia are using alliances and joint ventures as a means of strengthening their mutual ability to compete across a wider geographical area—for instance, all the countries in the European Union or whole continents or most all country markets where there is sizable demand for the industry's product. Many foreign companies, of course, are particularly interested in strategic partnerships that will strengthen their ability to gain a foothold in the U.S. market.

Cross-border alliances have proved to be popular and viable vehicles for companies to edge their way into the markets of foreign countries.

However, cooperative arrangements between domestic and foreign companies have strategic appeal for reasons besides gaining better access to attractive country markets.[17] A second big appeal of cross-border alliances is to capture economies of scale in production and/or marketing—cost reduction can be the difference that allows a company to be cost-competitive. By joining forces in producing components, assembling models, and marketing their products, companies can realize cost savings not achievable with their own small volumes. A third motivation for entering into a cross-border alliance is to fill gaps in technical expertise and/or knowledge of local markets (buying habits and product preferences of consumers, local customs, and so on). Allies learn much from one another in performing joint research, sharing technological know-how, studying one another's manufacturing methods, and understanding how to tailor sales and marketing approaches to fit local cultures and traditions. Indeed, one of the win–win benefits of an alliance is to learn from the skills, technological know-how, and capabilities of alliance partners and implant the knowledge and know-how of these partners in personnel throughout the company.

A fourth motivation for cross-border alliances is to share distribution facilities and dealer networks, thus mutually strengthening their access to buyers. A fifth benefit is that cross-border allies can direct their competitive energies more toward mutual rivals and less toward one another; teaming up may help them close the gap on leading companies. A sixth driver of cross-border alliances comes into play when companies desirous of entering a new foreign market conclude that alliances with local companies are an effective way to tap into a partner's local market knowledge and help it establish working relationships with key officials in the host-country government.[18] And, finally, alliances can be a particularly useful way for companies across the world to gain agreement on important technical standards—they have been used to arrive at standards for DVD players, assorted PC devices, Internet-related technologies, high-definition televisions, and mobile phones.

> Cross-border alliances enable a growth-minded company to widen its geographic coverage and strengthen its competitiveness in foreign markets while, at the same time, offering flexibility and allowing a company to retain some degree of autonomy and operating control.

What makes cross-border alliances an attractive strategic means of gaining the above types of benefits (as compared to acquiring or merging with foreign-based companies to gain much the same benefits) is that entering into alliances and strategic partnerships to gain market access and/or expertise of one kind or another allows a company to preserve its independence (which is not the case with a merger), retain veto power over how the alliance operates, and avoid using perhaps scarce financial resources to fund acquisitions. Furthermore, an alliance offers the flexibility to readily disengage once its purpose has been served or if the benefits prove elusive, whereas an acquisition is more permanent sort of arrangement (although the acquired company can, of course, be divested).[19]

Illustration Capsule 7.2 provides six examples of cross-border strategic alliances.

The Risks of Strategic Alliances with Foreign Partners

Alliances and joint ventures with foreign partners have their pitfalls, however. Cross-border allies typically have to overcome language and cultural barriers and figure out how to deal with diverse (or perhaps conflicting) operating practices. The communication, trust-building, and coordination costs are high in terms of management time.[20] It is not unusual for there to be little personal chemistry among some of the key people on whom success or failure of the alliance depends—the rapport such personnel need to work well together may never emerge. And even if allies are able to develop productive personal relationships, they can still have trouble reaching mutually agreeable ways to deal with key issues or resolve differences. There is a natural tendency for allies to struggle to collaborate effectively in competitively sensitive areas, thus spawning suspicions on both sides about forthright exchanges of information and expertise. Occasionally, the egos of corporate executives can clash—an alliance between Northwest Airlines and KLM Royal Dutch Airlines resulted in a bitter feud among both companies' top officials (who, according to some reports, refused to speak to each other).[21] In addition, there is the thorny problem of getting alliance partners to sort through issues and reach decisions fast enough to stay abreast of rapid advances in technology or fast-changing market conditions.

Illustration Capsule 7.2
Six Examples of Cross-Border Strategic Alliances

1. Two auto firms, Renault of France and Nissan of Japan, formed a broad-ranging global partnership in 1999 and then strengthened and expanded the alliance in 2002. The initial objective was to gain sales for new Nissan vehicles introduced in the European market, but the alliance now extends to full cooperation in all major areas, including the use of common platforms, joint development and use of engines and transmissions, fuel cell research, purchasing and use of common suppliers, and exchange of best practices. When the alliance was formed in 1999, Renault acquired a 36.8 percent ownership stake in Nissan; this was extended to 44.4 percent in 2002 when the alliance was expanded. Also, in 2002, the partners formed a jointly and equally owned strategic management company, named Renault-Nissan, to coordinate cooperative efforts.

2. Intel, the world's largest chip maker, has formed strategic alliances with leading software application providers and computer hardware providers to bring more innovativeness and expertise to the architecture underlying Intel's family of microprocessors and semiconductors. Intel's partners in the effort to enhance Intel's next-generation products include SAP, Oracle, SAS, BEA, IBM, Hewlett-Packard, Dell, Microsoft, Cisco Systems, and Alcatel. One of the alliances between Intel and Cisco involves a collaborative effort in Hong Kong to build next-generation infrastructure for Electronic Product Code/Radio Frequency Identification (EPC/RFID) solutions used to link manufacturers and logistics companies in the Hong Kong region with retailers worldwide. Intel and France-based Alcatel (a leading provider of fixed and mobile broadband access products, marketed in 130 countries) formed an alliance in 2004 to advance the definition, standardization, development, integration, and marketing of WiMAX broadband services solutions. WiMAX was seen as a cost-effective wireless or mobile broadband solution for deployment in both emerging markets and developed countries when, for either economic or technical reasons, it was not feasible to provide urban or rural customers with hardwired DSL broadband access.

3. Verio, a subsidiary of Japan-based NTT Communications and one of the leading global providers of Web hosting services and IP data transport, operates with the philosophy that in today's highly competitive and challenging technology market, companies must gain and share skills, information, and technology with technology leaders across the world. Believing that no company can be all things to all customers in the Web hosting industry, Verio executives have developed an alliance-oriented business model that combines the company's core competencies with the skills and products of best-of-breed technology partners. Verio's strategic partners include Accenture, Cisco Systems, Microsoft, Sun Microsystems,

Oracle, Arsenal Digital Solutions (a provider of worry-free tape backup, data restore, and data storage services), Internet Security Systems (a provider of firewall and intrusion detection systems), and Mercantec (a developer of storefront and shopping cart software). Verio management believes that its portfolio of strategic alliances allows it to use innovative, best-of-class technologies in providing its customers with fast, efficient, accurate data transport and a complete set of Web hosting services. An independent panel of 12 judges recently selected Verio as the winner of the Best Technology Foresight Award for its efforts in pioneering new technologies.

4. Toyota and First Automotive Works, China's biggest automaker, entered into an alliance in 2002 to make luxury sedans, sport-utility vehicles (SUVs), and minivehicles for the Chinese market. The intent was to make as many as 400,000 vehicles annually by 2010, an amount equal to the number that Volkswagen, the company with the largest share of the Chinese market, was making as of 2002. The alliance envisioned a joint investment of about $1.2 billion. At the time of the announced alliance, Toyota was lagging behind Honda, General Motors, and Volkswagen in setting up production facilities in China. Capturing a bigger share of the Chinese market was seen as crucial to Toyota's success in achieving its strategic objective of having a 15 percent share of the world's automotive market by 2010.

5. Airbus Industrie was formed by an alliance of aerospace companies from Britain, Spain, Germany, and France that included British Aerospace, Daimler-Benz Aerospace, and Aerospatiale. The objective of the alliance was to create a European aircraft company capable of competing with U.S.-based Boeing Corporation. The alliance has proved highly successful, infusing Airbus with the know-how and resources to compete head-to-head with Boeing for world leadership in large commercial aircraft (over 100 passengers).

6. General Motors, DaimlerChrysler, and BMW have entered into an alliance to develop a hybrid gasoline-electric engine that is simpler and less expensive to produce than the hybrid engine technology being pioneered by Toyota. Toyota, the acknowledged world leader in hybrid engines, is endeavoring to establish its design as the industry standard by signing up other automakers to use it. But the technology favored by the General Motors/DaimlerChrysler/BMW alliance is said to be less costly to produce and easier to configure for large trucks and SUVs than Toyota's (although it is also less fuel efficient). Europe's largest automaker, Volkswagen, has allied with Porsche to pursue the development of hybrid engines. Ford Motor and Honda, so far, have elected to go it alone in developing hybrid engine technology.

Sources: Company Web sites and press releases; Yves L. Doz and Gary Hamel, *Alliance Advantage: The Art of Creating Value through Partnering* (Boston, MA: Harvard Business School Press, 1998); and Norihiko Shirouzu and Jathon Sapsford, "As Hybrid Cars Gain Traction, Industry Battles over Designs," *The Wall Street Journal,* October 19, 2005, pp. A1, A9B.

It requires many meetings of many people working in good faith over time to iron out what is to be shared, what is to remain proprietary, and how the cooperative arrangements will work. Often, once the bloom is off the rose, partners discover they have conflicting objectives and strategies, deep differences of opinion about how to proceed, or important differences in corporate values and ethical standards. Tensions build up, working relationships cool, and the hoped-for benefits never materialize.[22]

Even if the alliance becomes a win–win proposition for both parties, there is the danger of becoming overly dependent on foreign partners for essential expertise and competitive capabilities. If a company is aiming for global market leadership and needs to develop capabilities of its own, then at some juncture cross-border merger or acquisition may have to be substituted for cross-border alliances and joint ventures.

> Strategic alliances are more effective in helping establish a beachhead of new opportunity in world markets than in achieving and sustaining global leadership.

One of the lessons about cross-border alliances is that they are more effective in helping a company establish a beachhead of new opportunity in world markets than they are in enabling a company to achieve and sustain global market leadership. Global market leaders, while benefiting from alliances, usually must guard against becoming overly dependent on the assistance they get from alliance partners—otherwise, they are not masters of their own destiny.

When a Cross-Border Alliance May Be Unnecessary

Experienced multinational companies that market in 50 to 100 or more countries across the world find less need for entering into cross-border alliances than do companies in the early stages of globalizing their operations.[23] Multinational companies make it a point to develop senior managers who understand how "the system" works in different countries; these companies can also avail themselves of local managerial talent and know-how by simply hiring experienced local managers and thereby detouring the hazards of collaborative alliances with local companies. If a multinational enterprise with considerable experience in entering the markets of different countries wants to detour the hazards and hassles of allying with local businesses, it can simply assemble a capable management team consisting of both senior managers with considerable international experience and local managers. The responsibilities of its own in-house managers with international business savvy are (1) to transfer technology, business practices, and the corporate culture into the company's operations in the new country market, and (2) to serve as conduits for the flow of information between the corporate office and local operations. The responsibilities of local managers are (1) to contribute needed understanding of the local market conditions, local buying habits, and local ways of doing business, and (2) in many cases, to head up local operations.

Hence, one cannot automatically presume that a company needs the wisdom and resources of a local partner to guide it through the process of successfully entering the markets of foreign countries. Indeed, experienced multinationals often discover that local partners do not always have adequate local market knowledge—much of the so-called experience of local partners can predate the emergence of current market trends and conditions, and sometimes their operating practices can be archaic.[24]

Tailoring Strategy to Fit Specific Industry and Company Situations

Strategy is all about combining choices of what to do and what not to do into a system that creates the requisite fit between what the environment needs and what the company does.

—**Costas Markides**

Competing in the marketplace is like war. You have injuries and casualties, and the best strategy wins.

—**John Collins**

It is much better to make your own products obsolete than allow a competitor to do it.

—**Michael A. Cusamano and Richard W. Selby**

In a turbulent age, the only dependable advantage is reinventing your business model before circumstances force you to.

—**Gary Hamel and Liisa Välikangas**

P rior chapters have emphasized the analysis and options that go into matching a company's choice of strategy to (1) industry and competitive conditions and (2) its own resource strengths and weaknesses, competitive capabilities, opportunities and threats, and market position. But there's more to be revealed about the hows of matching the choices of strategy to a company's circumstances. This chapter looks at the strategy-making task in 10 commonly encountered situations:

1. Companies competing in emerging industries.

2. Companies competing in rapidly growing markets.

3. Companies competing in maturing industries.

4. Companies competing in stagnant or declining industries.

5. Companies competing in turbulent, high-velocity markets.

6. Companies competing in fragmented industries.

7. Companies striving to sustain rapid growth.

8. Companies in industry leadership positions.

9. Companies in runner-up positions.

10. Companies in competitively weak positions or plagued by crisis conditions.

We selected these situations to shed still more light on the factors that managers need to consider in tailoring a company's strategy. When you finish this chapter, you will have a stronger grasp of the factors that managers have to weigh in choosing a strategy and what the pros and cons are for some of the heretofore unexplored strategic options that are open to a company.

STRATEGIES FOR COMPETING IN EMERGING INDUSTRIES

An emerging industry is one in the formative stage. Examples include Voice over Internet Protocol (VoIP) telephone communications, high-definition TV, assisted living for the elderly, online education, organic food products, e-book publishing, and electronic banking. Many companies striving to establish a strong foothold in an emerging industry are start-up enterprises busily engaged in perfecting technology, gearing up operations, and trying to broaden distribution and gain buyer acceptance. Important product design issues or technological problems may still have to be worked out. The business models and strategies of companies in an emerging industry are unproved—they may look promising but may or may not ever result in attractive profitability.

The Unique Characteristics of an Emerging Industry

Competing in emerging industries presents managers with some unique strategy-making challenges:[1]

- Because the market is in its infancy, there's usually much speculation about how it will function, how fast it will grow, and how big it will get. The little historical information available is virtually useless in making sales and profit projections. There's lots of guesswork about how rapidly buyers will be attracted and how much they will be willing to pay. For example, there is much uncertainty about how many users of traditional telephone service will be inclined to switch over to VoIP telephone technology and how rapidly any such switchovers will occur.

- In many cases, much of the technological know-how underlying the products of emerging industries is proprietary and closely guarded, having been developed in-house by pioneering firms. In such cases, patents and unique technical expertise are key factors in securing competitive advantage. In other cases, numerous companies have access to the requisite technology and may be racing to perfect it, often in collaboration with others. In still other instances, there can be competing technological approaches, with much uncertainty over whether multiple technologies will end up competing alongside one another or whether one approach will ultimately win out because of lower costs or better performance—such a battle is currently under way in the emerging market for gasoline-electric hybrid engines (where demand is mushrooming because of greater fuel efficiency without a loss of power and acceleration). Toyota has pioneered one design; an alliance among General Motors, DaimlerChrysler, and BMW is pursuing another design; a Volkswagen-Porsche alliance is looking at a third technological approach; and Ford and Honda have their own slightly different hybrid engine designs.

- Just as there may be uncertainties surrounding an emerging industry's technology, there may also be no consensus regarding which product attributes will prove decisive in winning buyer favor. Rivalry therefore centers on each firm's efforts to get the market to ratify its own strategic approach to technology, product design, marketing, and distribution. Such rivalry can result in wide differences in product quality and performance from brand to brand.

- Since in an emerging industry all buyers are first-time users, the marketing task is to induce initial purchase and to overcome customer concerns about product features, performance reliability, and conflicting claims of rival firms.

- Many potential buyers expect first-generation products to be rapidly improved, so they delay purchase until technology and product design mature and second- or third-generation products appear on the market.

- Entry barriers tend to be relatively low, even for entrepreneurial start-up companies. Large, well-known, opportunity-seeking companies with ample resources and competitive capabilities are likely to enter if the industry has promise for explosive growth or if its emergence threatens their present business. For instance, many traditional local telephone companies, seeing the potent threat of wireless communications technology and VoIP, have opted to enter the mobile communications business and begin offering landline customers a VoIP option.

- Strong experience/learning curve effects may be present, allowing significant price reductions as volume builds and costs fall.
- Sometimes firms have trouble securing ample supplies of raw materials and components (until suppliers gear up to meet the industry's needs).
- Undercapitalized companies, finding themselves short of funds to support needed R&D and get through several lean years until the product catches on, end up merging with competitors or being acquired by financially strong outsiders looking to invest in a growth market.

Strategy Options for Emerging Industries

The lack of established rules of the game in an emerging industry gives industry participants considerable freedom to experiment with a variety of different strategic approaches. Competitive strategies keyed either to low cost or differentiation are usually viable. Focusing makes good sense when resources and capabilities are limited and the industry has too many technological frontiers or too many buyer segments to pursue at once. Broad or focused differentiation strategies keyed to technological or product superiority typically offer the best chance for early competitive advantage.

> **Core Concept**
> Companies in an emerging industry have wide latitude in experimenting with different strategic approaches.

In addition to choosing a competitive strategy, companies in an emerging industry usually have to fashion a strategy containing one or more of the following actions:[2]

1. Push to perfect the technology, improve product quality, and develop additional attractive performance features. Out-innovating the competition is often one of the best avenues to industry leadership.

2. Consider merging with or acquiring another firm to gain added expertise and pool resource strengths.

3. As technological uncertainty clears and a dominant technology emerges, try to capture any first-mover advantages by adopting it quickly. However, while there's merit in trying to be the industry standard-bearer on technology and to pioneer the dominant product design, firms have to beware of betting too heavily on their own preferred technological approach or product design—especially when there are many competing technologies, R&D is costly, and technological developments can quickly move in surprising new directions.

4. Acquire or form alliances with companies that have related or complementary technological expertise as a means of helping outcompete rivals on the basis of technological superiority.

5. Pursue new customer groups, new user applications, and entry into new geographical areas (perhaps using strategic partnerships or joint ventures if financial resources are constrained).

6. Make it easy and cheap for first-time buyers to try the industry's first-generation product.

7. As the product becomes familiar to a wide portion of the market, shift the advertising emphasis from creating product awareness to increasing frequency of use and building brand loyalty.

8. Use price cuts to attract the next layer of price-sensitive buyers into the market.

9. Form strategic alliances with key suppliers whenever effective supply chain management provides important access to specialized skills, technological capabilities, and critical materials or components.

Young companies in emerging industries face four strategic hurdles: (1) raising the capital to finance initial operations until sales and revenues take off, profits appear, and cash flows turn positive; (2) developing a strategy to ride the wave of industry growth (what market segments and competitive advantages to go after?); (3) managing the rapid expansion of facilities and sales in a manner that positions them to contend for industry leadership; and (4) defending against competitors trying to horn in on their success.[3] Up-and-coming companies can help their cause by selecting knowledgeable members for their boards of directors and by hiring entrepreneurial managers with experience in guiding young businesses through the start-up and takeoff stages. *A firm that develops solid resource capabilities, an appealing business model, and a good strategy has a golden opportunity to shape the rules and establish itself as the recognized industry front-runner.*

But strategic efforts to win the early race for growth and market share leadership in an emerging industry have to be balanced against the longer-range need to build a durable competitive edge and a defendable market position.[4] The initial front-runners in a fast-growing emerging industry that shows signs of good profitability will almost certainly have to defend their positions against ambitious challengers striving to overtake the current market leaders. Well-financed outsiders can be counted on to enter with aggressive offensive strategies once industry sales take off, the perceived risk of investing in the industry lessens, and the success of current industry members becomes apparent. Sometimes a rush of new entrants, attracted by the growth and profit potential, overcrowds the market and forces industry consolidation to a smaller number of players. Resource-rich latecomers, aspiring to industry leadership, may become major players by acquiring and merging the operations of weaker competitors and then using their own perhaps considerable brand name recognition to draw customers and build market share. Hence, the strategies of the early leaders must be aimed at competing for the long haul and making a point of developing the resources, capabilities, and market recognition needed to sustain early successes and stave off competition from capable, ambitious newcomers.

STRATEGIES FOR COMPETING IN RAPIDLY GROWING MARKETS

Companies that have the good fortune to be in an industry growing at double-digit rates have a golden opportunity to achieve double-digit revenues and profit growth. If market demand is expanding 20 percent annually, a company can grow 20 percent annually simply by doing little more than contentedly riding the tide of market growth—it has to simply be aggressive enough to secure enough new customers to realize a 20 percent gain in sales, not a particularly impressive strategic feat. What is more interesting, however, is to craft a strategy that enables sales to grow at 25 or 30 percent when the overall market is growing by 20 percent, such that the company's market share and competitive position improve relative to rivals, on average. Should a company's strategy only deliver sales growth of 12 percent in a market growing at

> In a fast-growing market, a company needs a strategy predicated on growing faster than the market average, so that it can boost its market share and improve its competitive standing vis-à-vis rivals.

20 percent, then it is actually losing ground in the marketplace—a condition that signals a weak strategy and an unappealing product offering. The point here is that, in a rapidly growing market, a company must aim its strategy at producing gains in revenue that exceed the market average; otherwise, the best it can hope for is to maintain its market standing (if it is able to boost sales at a rate equal to the market average) and its market standing may indeed erode if its sales rise by less than the market average.

To be able to grow at a pace exceeding the market average, a company generally must have a strategy that incorporates one or more of the following elements:

- *Driving down costs per unit so as to enable price reductions that attract droves of new customers.* Charging a lower price always has strong appeal in markets where customers are price-sensitive, and lower prices can help push up buyers demand by drawing new customers into the marketplace. But since rivals can lower their prices also, a company must really be able to drive its unit costs down *faster than rivals*, such that it can use its low-cost advantage to underprice rivals. The makers of liquid crystal display (LCD) and high-definition TVs are aggressively pursuing cost reduction to bring the prices of their TV sets down under $1,000 and thus make their products more affordable to more consumers.

- *Pursuing rapid product innovation, both to set a company's product offering apart from rivals and to incorporate attributes that appeal to growing numbers of customers.* Differentiation strategies, when keyed to product attributes that draw in large numbers of new customers, help bolster a company's reputation for product superiority and lay the foundation for sales gains in excess of the overall rate of market growth. If the market is one where technology is advancing rapidly and product life cycles are short, then it becomes especially important to be first-to-market with next-generation products. But product innovation strategies require competencies in R&D and new product development and design, plus organizational agility in getting new and improved products to market quickly. At the same time they are pursuing cost reductions, the makers of LCD and high-definition TVs are pursuing all sorts of product improvements to enhance product quality and performance and boost screen sizes, so as to match or beat the picture quality and reliability of conventional TVs (with old-fashioned cathode-ray tubes) and drive up sales at an even faster clip.

- *Gaining access to additional distribution channels and sales outlets.* Pursuing wider distribution access so as to reach more potential buyers is a particularly good strategic approach for realizing above-average sales gains. But usually this requires a company to be a first-mover in positioning itself in new distribution channels and forcing rivals into playing catch-up.

- *Expanding the company's geographic coverage.* Expanding into areas, either domestic or foreign, where the company does not have a market presence can also be an effective way to reach more potential buyers and pave the way for gains in sales that outpace the overall market average.

- *Expanding the product line to add models/styles that appeal to a wider range of buyers.* Offering buyers a wider selection can be an effective way to draw new customers in numbers sufficient to realize above-average sales gains. Makers of MP3 players and cell phones are adding new models to stimulate buyer demand; Starbucks is adding new drinks and other menu selections to build store traffic; and marketers of VoIP technology are rapidly introducing a wider variety of plans to broaden their appeal to customers with different calling habits and needs.

STRATEGIES FOR COMPETING IN MATURING INDUSTRIES

A *maturing industry* is one that is moving from rapid growth to significantly slower growth. An industry is said to be *mature* when nearly all potential buyers are already users of the industry's products and growth in market demand closely parallels that of the population and the economy as a whole. In a mature market, demand consists mainly of replacement sales to existing users, with growth hinging on the industry's abilities to attract the few remaining new buyers and to convince existing buyers to up their usage. Consumer goods industries that are mature typically have a growth rate under 5 percent—roughly equal to the growth of the customer base or economy as a whole.

How Slowing Growth Alters Market Conditions

An industry's transition to maturity does not begin on an easily predicted schedule. Industry maturity can be forestalled by the emergence of new technological advances, product innovations, or other driving forces that keep rejuvenating market demand. Nonetheless, when growth rates do slacken, the onset of market maturity usually produces fundamental changes in the industry's competitive environment:[5]

1. *Slowing growth in buyer demand generates more head-to-head competition for market share.* Firms that want to continue on a rapid-growth track start looking for ways to take customers away from competitors. Outbreaks of price cutting, increased advertising, and other aggressive tactics to gain market share are common.

2. *Buyers become more sophisticated, often driving a harder bargain on repeat purchases.* Since buyers have experience with the product and are familiar with competing brands, they are better able to evaluate different brands and can use their knowledge to negotiate a better deal with sellers.

3. *Competition often produces a greater emphasis on cost and service.* As sellers all begin to offer the product attributes buyers prefer, buyer choices increasingly depend on which seller offers the best combination of price and service.

4. *Firms have a "topping-out" problem in adding new facilities.* Reduced rates of industry growth mean slowdowns in capacity expansion for manufacturers— adding too much plant capacity at a time when growth is slowing can create oversupply conditions that adversely affect manufacturers' profits well into the future. Likewise, retail chains that specialize in the industry's product have to cut back on the number of new stores being opened to keep from saturating localities with too many stores.

5. *Product innovation and new end-use applications are harder to come by.* Producers find it increasingly difficult to create new product features, find further uses for the product, and sustain buyer excitement.

6. *International competition increases.* Growth-minded domestic firms start to seek out sales opportunities in foreign markets. Some companies, looking for ways to cut costs, relocate plants to countries with lower wage rates. Greater product standardization and diffusion of technological know-how reduce entry barriers and make it possible for enterprising foreign companies to become serious market contenders in more countries. Industry leadership passes to companies that succeed in building strong competitive positions in most of the world's major geographic markets and in winning the biggest global market shares.

7. *Industry profitability falls temporarily or permanently.* Slower growth, increased competition, more sophisticated buyers, and occasional periods of overcapacity put pressure on industry profit margins. Weaker, less-efficient firms are usually the hardest hit.

8. *Stiffening competition induces a number of mergers and acquisitions among former competitors, driving industry consolidation to a smaller number of larger players.* Inefficient firms and firms with weak competitive strategies can achieve respectable results in a fast-growing industry with booming sales. But the intensifying competition that accompanies industry maturity exposes competitive weakness and throws second- and third-tier competitors into a survival-of-the-fittest contest.

Strategies that Fit Conditions in Maturing Industries

As the new competitive character of industry maturity begins to hit full force, any of several strategic moves can strengthen a firm's competitive position: pruning the product line, improving value chain efficiency, trimming costs, increasing sales to present customers, acquiring rival firms, expanding internationally, and strengthening capabilities.[6]

Pruning Marginal Products and Models   A wide selection of models, features, and product options sometimes has competitive value during the growth stage, when buyers' needs are still evolving. But such variety can become too costly as price competition stiffens and profit margins are squeezed. Maintaining many product versions works against achieving design, parts inventory, and production economies at the manufacturing levels and can increase inventory stocking costs for distributors and retailers. In addition, the prices of slow-selling versions may not cover their true costs. Pruning marginal products from the line opens the door for cost savings and permits more concentration on items whose margins are highest and/or where a firm has a competitive advantage. General Motors has been cutting slow-selling models and brands from its lineup of offerings—it has eliminated the entire Oldsmobile division and is said to be looking at whether it can eliminate its Saab lineup. Textbook publishers are discontinuing publication of those books that sell only a few thousand copies annually (where profits are marginal at best) and instead focusing their resources on texts that generate sales of at least 5,000 copies per edition.

Improving Value Chain Efficiency   Efforts to reinvent the industry value chain can have a fourfold payoff: lower costs, better product or service quality, greater capability to turn out multiple or customized product versions, and shorter design-to-market cycles. Manufacturers can mechanize high-cost activities, redesign production lines to improve labor efficiency, build flexibility into the assembly process so that customized product versions can be easily produced, and increase use of advanced technology (robotics, computerized controls, and automated assembly). Suppliers of parts and components, manufacturers, and distributors can collaboratively deploy online systems and product coding techniques to streamline activities and achieve cost savings all along the value chain—from supplier-related activities all the way through distribution, retailing, and customer service.

Trimming Costs   Stiffening price competition gives firms extra incentive to drive down unit costs. Company cost-reduction initiatives can cover a broad front. Some of the most frequently pursued options are pushing suppliers for better prices, implementing tighter supply chain management practices, cutting low-value activities out of the value chain, developing more economical product designs, reengineering internal processes using e-commerce technology, and shifting to more economical distribution arrangements.

Increasing Sales to Present Customers   In a mature market, growing by taking customers away from rivals may not be as appealing as expanding sales to existing customers. Strategies to increase purchases by existing customers can involve adding more sales promotions, providing complementary items and ancillary services, and finding more ways for customers to use the product. Convenience stores, for example, have boosted average sales per customer by adding video rentals, automated teller machines, gasoline pumps, and deli counters.

Acquiring Rival Firms at Bargain Prices   Sometimes a firm can acquire the facilities and assets of struggling rivals quite cheaply. Bargain-priced acquisitions can help create a low-cost position if they also present opportunities for greater operating efficiency. In addition, an acquired firm's customer base can provide expanded market coverage and opportunities for greater scale economies. The most desirable acquisitions are those that will significantly enhance the acquiring firm's competitive strength.

Expanding Internationally   As its domestic market matures, a firm may seek to enter foreign markets where attractive growth potential still exists and competitive pressures are not so strong. Many multinational companies are expanding into such emerging markets as China, India, Brazil, Argentina, and the Philippines, where the long-term growth prospects are quite attractive. Strategies to expand internationally also make sense when a domestic firm's skills, reputation, and product are readily transferable to foreign markets. For example, even though the U.S. market for soft drinks is mature, Coca-Cola has remained a growth company by upping its efforts to penetrate emerging markets where soft-drink sales are expanding rapidly.

Building New or More Flexible Capabilities   The stiffening pressures of competition in a maturing or already mature market can often be combated by strengthening the company's resource base and competitive capabilities. This can mean adding new competencies or capabilities, deepening existing competencies to make them harder to imitate, or striving to make core competencies more adaptable to changing customer requirements and expectations. Microsoft has responded to challenges by such competitors as Google and Linux by expanding its competencies in search engine software and revamping its entire approach to programming next-generation operating systems. Chevron has developed a best-practices discovery team and a best-practices resource map to enhance the speed and effectiveness with which it is able to transfer efficiency improvements from one oil refinery to another.

Strategic Pitfalls in Maturing Industries

Perhaps the biggest strategic mistake a company can make as an industry matures is steering a middle course between low cost, differentiation, and focusing—blending efforts to achieve low cost with efforts to incorporate differentiating features and efforts to focus on a limited target market. Such strategic compromises typically leave the firm *stuck in the middle* with a fuzzy strategy, too little commitment to winning a competitive advantage, an average image with buyers, and little chance of springing into the ranks of the industry leaders.

Other strategic pitfalls include being slow to mount a defense against stiffening competitive pressures, concentrating more on protecting short-term profitability than on building or maintaining long-term competitive position, waiting too long to respond to price cutting by rivals, overexpanding in the face of slowing growth, overspending on advertising and sales promotion efforts in a losing effort to combat the growth slowdown, and failing to pursue cost reduction soon enough or aggressively enough.

STRATEGIES FOR COMPETING IN STAGNANT OR DECLINING INDUSTRIES

Many firms operate in industries where demand is growing more slowly than the economy-wide average or is even declining. The demand for an industry's product can decline for any of several reasons: (1) advancing technology gives rise to better-performing substitute products (slim LCD monitors displace bulky CRT monitors; DVD players replace VCRs; wrinkle-free fabrics replace the need for laundry/dry-cleaning services) or lower costs (cheaper synthetics replace expensive leather); (2) the customer group shrinks (baby foods are in less demand when birthrates fall); (3) changing lifestyles and buyer tastes (cigarette smoking and wearing dress hats go out of vogue); (4) the rising costs of complementary products (higher gasoline prices drive down purchases of gas-guzzling vehicles).[7] The most attractive declining industries are those in which sales are eroding only slowly, there are pockets of stable or even growing demand, and some market niches present good profit opportunities. But in some stagnant or declining industries, decaying buyer demand precipitates a desperate competitive battle among industry members for the available business, replete with price discounting, costly sales promotions, growing amounts of idle plant capacity, and fast-eroding profit margins. It matters greatly whether buyer demand falls gradually or sharply and whether competition proves to be fierce or moderate.

Businesses competing in stagnant or declining industries have to make a fundamental strategic choice—whether to remain committed to the industry for the long term despite the industry's dim prospects or whether to pursue an end-game strategy to withdraw gradually or quickly from the market. Deciding to stick with the industry despite eroding market demand can have considerable merit. Stagnant demand by itself is not enough to make an industry unattractive. Market demand may be decaying slowly. Some segments of the market may still present good profit opportunities. Cash flows from operations may still remain strongly positive. Strong competitors may well be able to grow and boost profits by taking market share from weaker competitors.[8] Furthermore, the acquisition or exit of weaker firms creates opportunities for the remaining companies to capture greater market share. On the one hand, striving to become the market leader and be one of the few remaining companies in a declining industry can lead to above-average profitability even though overall market demand is stagnant or eroding. On the other hand, if the market environment of a declining industry is characterized by bitter warfare for customers and lots of overcapacity, such that companies are plagued with heavy operating losses, then an early exit makes much more strategic sense.

If a company decides to stick with a declining industry—because top management is encouraged by the remaining opportunities or sees merit in striving for market share

It is erroneous to assume that companies in a declining industry are doomed to having declining revenues and profits.

leadership (or even just being one of the few remaining companies in the industry), then its three best strategic alternatives are usually the following:[9]

1. *Pursue a focused strategy aimed at the fastest-growing or slowest-decaying market segments within the industry.* Stagnant or declining markets, like other markets, are composed of numerous segments or niches. Frequently, one or more of these segments is growing rapidly (or at least decaying much more slowly), despite stagnation in the industry as a whole. An astute competitor who zeros in on fast-growing segments and does a first-rate job of meeting the needs of buyers comprising these segments can often escape stagnating sales and profits and even gain decided competitive advantage. For instance, both Ben & Jerry's and Häagen-Dazs have achieved success by focusing on the growing luxury or superpremium segment of the otherwise stagnant market for ice cream; revenue growth and profit margins are substantially higher for high-end ice creams sold in supermarkets and in scoop shops than is the case in other segments of the ice cream market. Companies that focus on the one or two most attractive market segments in a declining business may well decide to ignore the other segments altogether—withdrawing from them entirely or at least gradually or rapidly disinvesting in them. But the key is to *move aggressively* to establish a strong position in the most attractive parts of the stagnant or declining industry.

2. *Stress differentiation based on quality improvement and product innovation.* Either enhanced quality or innovation can rejuvenate demand by creating important new growth segments or inducing buyers to trade up. Successful product innovation opens up an avenue for competing that bypasses meeting or beating rivals' prices. Differentiation based on successful innovation has the additional advantage of being difficult and expensive for rival firms to imitate. New Covent Garden Soup has met with success by introducing packaged fresh soups for sale in major supermarkets, where the typical soup offerings are canned or dry mixes. Procter & Gamble has rejuvenated sales of its toothbrushes with its new line of Crest battery-powered spin toothbrushes, and it has revitalized interest in tooth care products with a series of product innovations related to teeth whitening. Bread makers are fighting declining sales of white breads that use bleached flour by introducing all kinds of whole-grain breads (which have far more nutritional value).

3. *Strive to drive costs down and become the industry's low-cost leader.* Companies in stagnant industries can improve profit margins and return on investment by pursuing innovative cost reduction year after year. Potential cost-saving actions include (*a*) cutting marginally beneficial activities out of the value chain; (*b*) outsourcing functions and activities that can be performed more cheaply by outsiders; (*c*) redesigning internal business processes to exploit cost-reducing e-commerce technologies; (*d*) consolidating underutilized production facilities; (*e*) adding more distribution channels to ensure the unit volume needed for low-cost production; (*f*) closing low-volume, high-cost retail outlets; and (*g*) pruning marginal products from the firm's offerings. Japan-based Asahi Glass (a low-cost producer of flat glass), PotashCorp and IMC Global (two low-cost leaders in potash production), Alcan Aluminum, Nucor Steel, and Safety Components International (a low-cost producer of air bags for motor vehicles) have all been successful in driving costs down in competitively tough and largely stagnant industry environments.

These three strategic themes are not mutually exclusive.[10] Introducing innovative versions of a product can create a fast-growing market segment. Similarly, relentless pursuit of greater operating efficiencies permits price reductions that create price-conscious growth segments. Note that all three themes are spinoffs of the five generic competitive strategies, adjusted to fit the circumstances of a tough industry environment.

End-Game Strategies for Declining Industries

An *end-game strategy* can take either of two paths: (1) a *slow-exit strategy* that involves a gradual phasing down of operations coupled with an objective of getting the most cash flow from the business even if it means sacrificing market position or profitability and (2) a *fast-exit* or *sell-out-quickly strategy* to disengage from the industry during the early stages of the decline and recover as much of the company's investment as possible for deployment elsewhere.[11]

A Slow-Exit Strategy   With a slow-exit strategy, *the key objective is to generate the greatest possible harvest of cash from the business for as long as possible.* Management either eliminates or severely curtails new investment in the business. Capital expenditures for new equipment are put on hold or given low financial priority (unless replacement needs are unusually urgent); instead, efforts are made to stretch the life of existing equipment and make do with present facilities as long as possible. Old plants with high costs may be retired from service. The operating budget is chopped to a rock-bottom level. Promotional expenses may be cut gradually, quality reduced in not-so-visible ways, nonessential customer services curtailed, and maintenance of facilities held to a bare minimum. The resulting increases in cash flow (and perhaps even bottom-line profitability and return on investment) compensate for whatever declines in sales might be experienced. Withering buyer demand is tolerable if sizable amounts of cash can be reaped in the interim. If and when cash flows dwindle to meager levels as sales volumes decay, the business can be sold or, if no buyer can be found, closed down.

A Fast-Exit Strategy   The challenge of a sell-out-quickly strategy is to find a buyer willing to pay an agreeable price for the company's business assets. Buyers may be scarce since there's a tendency for investors to shy away from purchasing a stagnant or dying business. And even if willing buyers appear, they will be in a strong bargaining position once it's clear that the industry's prospects are permanently waning. How much prospective buyers will pay is usually a function of how rapidly they expect the industry to decline, whether they see opportunities to rejuvenate demand (at least temporarily), whether they believe that costs can be cut enough to still produce attractive profit margins or cash flows, whether there are pockets of stable demand where buyers are not especially price sensitive, and whether they believe that fading market demand will weaken competition (which could enhance profitability) or trigger strong competition for the remaining business (which could put pressure on profit margins). Thus, the expectations of prospective buyers will tend to drive the price they are willing to pay for the business assets of a company wanting to sell out quickly.

STRATEGIES FOR COMPETING IN TURBULENT, HIGH-VELOCITY MARKETS

Many companies operate in industries characterized by rapid technological change, short product life cycles, the entry of important new rivals, lots of competitive maneuvering by rivals, and fast-evolving customer requirements and expectations—all occurring in a manner that creates swirling market conditions. Since news of this or that important competitive development arrives daily, it is an imposing task just to monitor and assess developing events. High-velocity change is plainly the prevailing condition in computer/server hardware and software, video games, networking, wireless tele-communications, medical equipment, biotechnology, prescription drugs, and online retailing.

Ways to Cope with Rapid Change

The central strategy-making challenge in a turbulent market environment is managing change.[12] As illustrated in Figure 8.1, a company can assume any of three strategic postures in dealing with high-velocity change:[13]

- *It can react to change.* The company can respond to a rival's new product with a better product. It can counter an unexpected shift in buyer tastes and buyer demand by redesigning or repackaging its product, or shifting its advertising emphasis to different product attributes. Reacting is a defensive strategy and is therefore unlikely to create fresh opportunity, but it is nonetheless a necessary component in a company's arsenal of options.

- *It can anticipate change.* The company can make plans for dealing with the expected changes and follow its plans as changes occur (fine-tuning them as may be needed). Anticipation entails looking ahead to analyze what is likely to occur and then preparing and positioning for that future. It entails studying buyer behavior, buyer needs, and buyer expectations to get insight into how the market will evolve, then lining up the necessary production and distribution capabilities ahead of time. Like reacting to change, anticipating change is still fundamentally defensive in that forces outside the enterprise are in the driver's seat. Anticipation, however, can open up new opportunities and thus is a better way to manage change than just pure reaction.

- *It can lead change.* Leading change entails initiating the market and competitive forces that others must respond to—it is an offensive strategy aimed at putting a company in the driver's seat. Leading change means being first to market with an important new product or service. It means being the technological leader, rushing next-generation products to market ahead of rivals, and having products whose features and attributes shape customer preferences and expectations. It means proactively seeking to shape the rules of the game.

A sound way to deal with turbulent market conditions is to try to lead change with proactive strategic moves while at the same time trying to anticipate and prepare for upcoming changes and being quick to react to unexpected developments.

As a practical matter, a company's approach to managing change should, ideally, incorporate all three postures (though not in the same proportion). The best-performing companies in high-velocity markets consistently seek to lead change with proactive strategies that often entail the flexibility to pursue any of several strategic options, depending on how the market actually evolves. Even so, an environment of relentless change makes it incumbent on any company to anticipate and prepare for the future and to react quickly to unpredictable or uncontrollable new developments.

Strategy Options for Fast-Changing Markets

Competitive success in fast-changing markets tends to hinge on a company's ability to improvise, experiment, adapt, reinvent, and regenerate as market and competitive conditions shift rapidly and sometimes unpredictably.[14] It has to constantly reshape its

Figure 8.1 **Meeting the Challenge of High-Velocity Change**

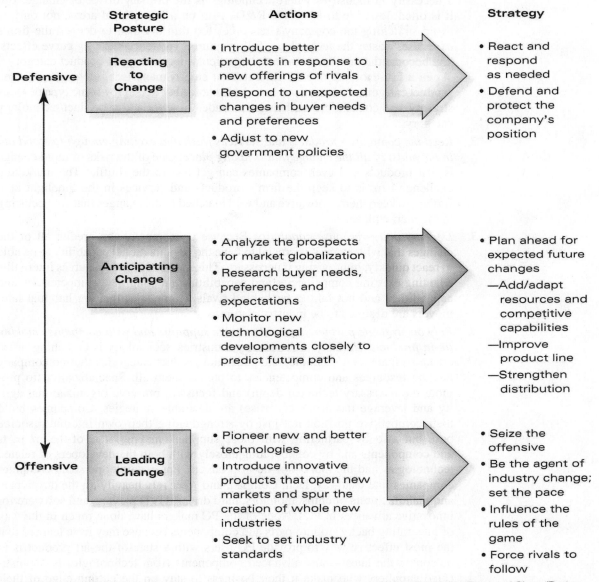

Source: Adapted from Shona L. Brown and Kathleen M. Eisenhardt, *Competing on the Edge: Strategy as Structured Chaos* (Boston, MA: Harvard Business School Press, 1998) p. 5.

strategy and its basis for competitive advantage. While the process of altering offensive and defensive moves every few months or weeks to keep the overall strategy closely matched to changing conditions is inefficient, the alternative—a fast-obsolescing strategy—is worse. The following five strategic moves seem to offer the best payoffs:

1. *Invest aggressively in R&D to stay on the leading edge of technological know-how.* Translating technological advances into innovative new products (and remaining

close on the heels of whatever advances and features are pioneered by rivals) is a necessity in industries where technology is the primary driver of change. But it is often desirable to focus the R&D effort on a few critical areas, not only to avoid stretching the company's resources too thin but also to deepen the firm's expertise, master the technology, fully capture experience/learning curve effects, and become the dominant leader in a particular technology or product category.[15] When a fast-evolving market environment entails many technological areas and product categories, competitors have little choice but to employ some type of focus strategy and concentrate on being the leader in a particular product/technology category.

2. *Keep the company's products and services fresh and exciting enough to stand out in the midst of all the change that is taking place.* One of the risks of rapid change is that products and even companies can get lost in the shuffle. The marketing challenge here is to keep the firm's products and services in the limelight and, further, to keep them innovative and well matched to the changes that are occurring in the marketplace.

3. *Develop quick-response capability.* Because no company can predict all of the changes that will occur, it is crucial to have the organizational capability to be able to react quickly, improvising if necessary. This means shifting resources internally, adapting existing competencies and capabilities, creating new competencies and capabilities, and not falling far behind rivals. Companies that are habitual late-movers are destined to be industry also-rans.

4. *Rely on strategic partnerships with outside suppliers and with companies making tie-in products.* In many high-velocity industries, technology is branching off to create so many new technological paths and product categories that no company has the resources and competencies to pursue them all. Specialization (to promote the necessary technical depth) and focus (to preserve organizational agility and leverage the firm's expertise) are desirable strategies. Companies build their competitive position not just by strengthening their own internal resource base but also by partnering with those suppliers making state-of-the-art parts and components and by collaborating closely with both the developers of related technologies and the makers of tie-in products. For example, personal computer companies like Gateway, Dell, Compaq, and Acer rely heavily on the developers and manufacturers of chips, monitors, hard drives, DVD players, and software for innovative advances in PCs. None of the PC makers have done much in the way of integrating backward into parts and components because they have learned that the most effective way to provide PC users with a state-of-the-art product is to outsource the latest, most advanced components from technologically sophisticated suppliers who make it their business to stay on the cutting edge of their specialization and who can achieve economies of scale by mass-producing components for many PC assemblers. An outsourcing strategy also allows a company the flexibility to replace suppliers that fall behind on technology or product features or that cease to be competitive on price. The managerial challenge here is to strike a good balance between building a rich internal resource base that, on the one hand, keeps the firm from being at the mercy of its suppliers and allies and, on the other hand, maintains organizational agility by relying on the resources and expertise of capable (and perhaps best-in-world) outsiders.

5. *Initiate fresh actions every few months, not just when a competitive response is needed.* In some sense, change is partly triggered by the passage of time rather

than solely by the occurrence of events. A company can be proactive by making time-paced moves—introducing a new or improved product every four months, rather than when the market tapers off or a rival introduces a next-generation model.[16] Similarly, a company can expand into a new geographic market every six months rather than waiting for a new market opportunity to present itself; it can also refresh existing brands every two years rather than waiting until their popularity wanes. The keys to successfully using time pacing as a strategic weapon are choosing intervals that make sense internally and externally, establishing an internal organizational rhythm for change, and choreographing the transitions. 3M Corporation has long pursued an objective of having 25 percent of its revenues come from products less than four years old, a force that established the rhythm of change and created a relentless push for new products. Recently, the firm's CEO upped the tempo of change at 3M by increasing the goal from 25 to 30 percent.

Cutting-edge know-how and first-to-market capabilities are very valuable competitive assets in fast-evolving markets. Moreover, action-packed competition demands that a company have quick reaction times and flexible, adaptable resources—organizational agility is a huge competitive asset. Even so, companies will make mistakes and take some actions that do not work out well. When a company's strategy doesn't seem to be working well, it has to quickly regroup—probing, experimenting, improvising, and trying again and again until it finds something that strikes the right chord with buyers and that puts it in sync with market and competitive realities.

STRATEGIES FOR COMPETING IN FRAGMENTED INDUSTRIES

A number of industries are populated by hundreds, even thousands, of small and medium-sized companies, many privately held and none with a substantial share of total industry sales.[17] The standout competitive feature of a fragmented industry is the absence of market leaders with king-sized market shares or widespread buyer recognition. Examples of fragmented industries include book publishing, landscaping and plant nurseries, real estate development, convenience stores, banking, health and medical care, mail order catalog sales, computer software development, custom printing, kitchen cabinets, trucking, auto repair, restaurants and fast food, public accounting, apparel manufacture and apparel retailing, paperboard boxes, hotels and motels, and furniture.

Reasons for Supply-Side Fragmentation

Any of several reasons can account for why the supply side of an industry comprises hundreds or even thousands of companies:

- *The product or service is delivered at neighborhood locations so as to be conveniently accessible to local residents.* Retail and service businesses, for example, are inherently local—gas stations and car washes, pharmacies, dry-cleaning services, nursing homes, auto repair firms, furniture stores, flower shops, and lawn care enterprises. Whenever it takes thousands of locations to adequately serve the market, the way is opened for many enterprises to be engaged in providing products/services to local residents and businesses (and such enterprises can operate at just one location or at multiple locations).

- *Buyer preferences and requirements are so diverse that very large numbers of firms can easily coexist trying to accommodate differing buyer tastes, expectations, and pocketbooks.* This is true in the market for apparel, where there are thousands of apparel manufacturers making garments of various styles and price ranges. There's a host of different hotels and restaurants in places like New York City, London, Buenos Aires, Mexico City, and Tokyo. The software development industry is highly fragmented because there are so many types of software applications and because the needs and expectations of software users are so highly diverse—hence, there's ample market space for a software company to concentrate its attention on serving a particular market niche.

- *Low entry barriers allow small firms to enter quickly and cheaply.* Such tends to be the case in many areas of retailing, residential real estate, insurance sales, beauty shops, and the restaurant business.

- *An absence of scale economies permits small companies to compete on an equal cost footing with larger firms.* The markets for business forms, interior design, kitchen cabinets, and picture framing are fragmented because buyers require relatively small quantities of customized products; since demand for any particular product version is small, sales volumes are not adequate to support producing, distributing, or marketing on a scale that yields cost advantages to a large-scale firm. A locally owned pharmacy can be cost competitive with the pharmacy operations of large drugstore chains like Walgreen's or Rite Aid or CVS. Small trucking companies can be cost-competitive with companies that have huge truck fleets. A local pizzeria is not cost-disadvantaged in competing against such chains as Pizza Hut, Domino's, and Papa John's.

- *The scope of the geographic market for the industry's product or service is transitioning from national to global.* A broadening of geographic scope puts companies in more and more countries in the same competitive market arena (as in the apparel industry, where increasing numbers of garment makers across the world are shifting their production operations to low-wage countries and then shipping their goods to retailers in several countries).

- *The technologies embodied in the industry's value chain are exploding into so many new areas and along so many different paths that specialization is essential just to keep abreast in any one area of expertise.* Technology branching accounts for why the manufacture of electronic parts and components is fragmented and why there's fragmentation in prescription drug research.

- *The industry is young and crowded with aspiring contenders.* In most young industries, no firm has yet developed the resource base, competitive capabilities, and market recognition to command a significant market share (as in online e-tailing).

Competitive Conditions in a Fragmented Industry

Competitive rivalry in fragmented industries can vary from moderately strong to fierce. Low barriers tend to make entry of new competitors an ongoing threat. Competition from substitutes may or may not be a major factor. The relatively small size of companies in fragmented industries puts them in a relatively weak position to bargain with powerful suppliers and buyers, although sometimes they can become members of a cooperative formed for the purpose of using their combined leverage to negotiate better sales and purchase terms. In such an environment, the best a firm can expect is to cultivate a loyal customer base and grow a bit faster than the industry average.

Some fragmented industries consolidate over time as growth slows and the market matures. The stiffer competition that accompanies slower growth produces a shake-out of weak, inefficient firms and a greater concentration of larger, more visible sellers. Others remain atomistic because it is inherent in their businesses. And still others remain stuck in a fragmented state because existing firms lack the resources or ingenuity to employ a strategy powerful enough to drive industry consolidation.

Strategy Options for Competing in a Fragmented Industry

In fragmented industries, firms generally have the strategic freedom to pursue broad or narrow market targets and low-cost or differentiation-based competitive advantages. Many different strategic approaches can exist side by side (unless the industry's product is highly standardized or a commodity—like concrete blocks, sand and gravel, or paperboard boxes). Fragmented industry environments are usually ideal for focusing on a well-defined market niche—a particular geographic area or buyer group or product type. In an industry that is fragmented due to highly diverse buyer tastes or requirements, focusing usually offers more competitive advantage potential than trying to come up with a product offering that has broad market appeal.

Some of the most suitable strategy options for competing in a fragmented industry include:

- *Constructing and operating "formula" facilities*—This strategic approach is frequently employed in restaurant and retailing businesses operating at multiple locations. It involves constructing standardized outlets in favorable locations at minimum cost and then operating them cost-effectively. This is a favorite approach for locally owned fast-food enterprises and convenience stores that have multiple locations serving a geographically limited market area. Major fast-food chains like Yum! Brands—the parent of Pizza Hut, Taco Bell, KFC, Long John Silver's, and A&W restaurants—and big convenience store retailers like 7-Eleven have, of course, perfected the formula facilities strategy.

- *Becoming a low-cost operator*—When price competition is intense and profit margins are under constant pressure, companies can stress no-frills operations featuring low overhead, high-productivity/low-cost labor, lean capital budgets, and dedicated pursuit of total operating efficiency. Successful low-cost producers in a fragmented industry can play the price-discounting game and still earn profits above the industry average. Many e-tailers compete on the basis of bargain prices; so do budget motel chains like Econo Lodge, Super 8, and Days Inn.

- *Specializing by product type*—When a fragmented industry's products include a range of styles or services, a strategy to focus on one product or service category can be effective. Some firms in the furniture industry specialize in only one furniture type such as brass beds, rattan and wicker, lawn and garden, or Early American. In auto repair, companies specialize in transmission repair, body work, or speedy oil changes.

- *Specializing by customer type*—A firm can stake out a market niche in a fragmented industry by catering to those customers who are interested in low prices,

Illustration Capsule 8.1
Exertris's Focus Strategy in the Fragmented Exercise Equipment Industry

The exercise equipment industry is largely fragmented from a global perspective—there are hundreds of companies across the world making exercise and fitness products of one kind or another. The window of opportunity for employing a focus strategy is big. In 2001, three fitness enthusiasts in Great Britain came up with a novel way to make exercise more interesting. Their idea was to create an exercise bike equipped with a video game console, a flat-screen display, and an on-board PC that allowed users to play a video game while doing their workout.

After creating a prototype and forming a company called Exertris, the three fitness entrepreneurs approached a product design company for help in turning the prototype into a marketable product. The design company quickly determined that the task was not trivial and required significant additional product development. But the company was enthusiastic about the product and put up the capital to fund the venture as a minority partner. The partners set a goal of having six prototypes ready in time for a major leisure products trade show scheduled to be held in the United Kingdom in several months. The design company assumed responsibility for engineering the product, finding a contract manufacturer, and managing the supply chain; certain other specialty tasks were outsourced. The three cofounders concentrated on developing gaming software where the exerciser's pedaling performance had direct consequences for particular elements of the game; for example, the exerciser had to pedal harder to power a spaceship's weapon systems or move cards around in a game of Solitaire.

The Exertris bike won the "best new product" award at the trade show. It featured four games (Gems, Orbit, Solitaire, and Space Tripper), and new games and features could be added as they were released. Exercisers could play solo or competitively against other people, with the option of handicapping for multiplayer games. The recommended workout included an automatic warm-up and cool-down period. The bike had an armrest, a monitor, and a seat that optimized posture. The LCD display used the latest 3D graphics, and the on-board PC (positioned under the mounting step) used Microsoft Windows XP Embedded and was compatible with Polar heart rate monitors. Earphones were optional, and the game pad and menu control were sweat-proof and easy to clean.

Production by contract manufacturers started soon after the show. In the ensuing months, the Exertris bike was well received by gyms and fitness enthusiasts (for whom the addictive nature of video games broke the monotony and made exercise time fly by). The first interactive fitness arcade featuring 25 linked Exertris Interactive Bikes opened in Great Britain in April 2003. In 2005, the Exertris exercise bike was being marketed online in Great Britain at Amazon's Web site (www.amazon-leisure.co.uk) at a price of £675 (or about $1,150); it could also be purchased at Broadcast Vision Entertainment's online store. Exertris's strategy of focusing on this one niche product in exercise equipment was, however, producing unexpectedly weak results—sales were much slower than initially expected.

Sources: Information posted at www.betterproductdesign.com (accessed October 14, 2005), www.embedded-resources.com (accessed October 14, 2005), and www.broadcastvision.com (accessed December 31, 2005).

unique product attributes, customized features, carefree service, or other extras. A number of restaurants cater to take-out customers; others specialize in fine dining, and still others cater to the sports bar crowd. Bed-and-breakfast inns cater to a particular type of traveler/vacationer (and also focus on a very limited geographic area).

- *Focusing on a limited geographic area*—Even though a firm in a fragmented industry can't win a big share of total industrywide sales, it can still try to dominate a local or regional geographic area. Concentrating company efforts on a limited territory can produce greater operating efficiency, speed delivery and customer services, promote strong brand awareness, and permit saturation advertising, while avoiding the diseconomies of stretching operations out over a much wider area. Several locally owned banks, drugstores, and sporting goods retailers successfully operate multiple locations within a limited geographic area. Numerous local restaurant operators have pursued operating economies by opening anywhere from 4 to 10 restaurants (each with each its own distinctive theme and menu) scattered across a single metropolitan area like Atlanta or Denver or Houston.

Illustration Capsule 8.1 describes how a new start-up company in Great Britain has employed a product niche type of focus strategy in the fragmented exercise equipment industry.

STRATEGIES FOR SUSTAINING RAPID COMPANY GROWTH

Companies that strive to grow their revenues and earnings at double-digit rates year after year (or at rates exceeding the overall market average so that they are growing faster than rivals and gaining market share) generally have to craft *a portfolio of strategic initiatives* covering three horizons:[18]

- *Horizon 1: "Short-jump" strategic initiatives to fortify and extend the company's position in existing businesses*—Short-jump initiatives typically include adding new items to the company's present product line, expanding into new geographic areas where the company does not yet have a market presence, and launching offensives to take market share away from rivals. The objective is to capitalize fully on whatever growth potential exists in the company's present business arenas.

- *Horizon 2: "Medium-jump" strategic initiatives to leverage existing resources and capabilities by entering new businesses with promising growth potential*—Growth companies have to be alert for opportunities to jump into new businesses where there is promise of rapid growth and where their experience, intellectual capital, and technological know-how will prove valuable in gaining rapid market penetration. While Horizon 2 initiatives may take a back seat to Horizon 1 initiatives as long as there is plenty of untapped growth in the company's present businesses, they move to the front as the onset of market maturity dims the company's growth prospects in its present business(es).

- *Horizon 3: "Long-jump" strategic initiatives to plant the seeds for ventures in businesses that do not yet exist*—Long-jump initiatives can entail pumping funds into long-range R&D projects, setting up an internal venture capital fund to invest in promising start-up companies attempting to create the industries of the future, or acquiring a number of small start-up companies experimenting with technologies and product ideas that complement the company's present businesses. Intel, for example, set up a multibillion-dollar venture fund to invest in over 100 different projects and start-up companies, the intent being to plant seeds for Intel's future, broadening its base as a global leader in supplying building blocks for PCs and the worldwide Internet economy. Royal Dutch/Shell, with over $140 billion in revenues and over 100,000 employees, spent over $20 million on rule-breaking, game-changing ideas put forth by free-thinking employees; the objective was to inject a new spirit of entrepreneurship into the company and sow the seeds of faster growth.[19]

Figure 8.2   **The Three Strategy Horizons for Sustaining Rapid Growth**

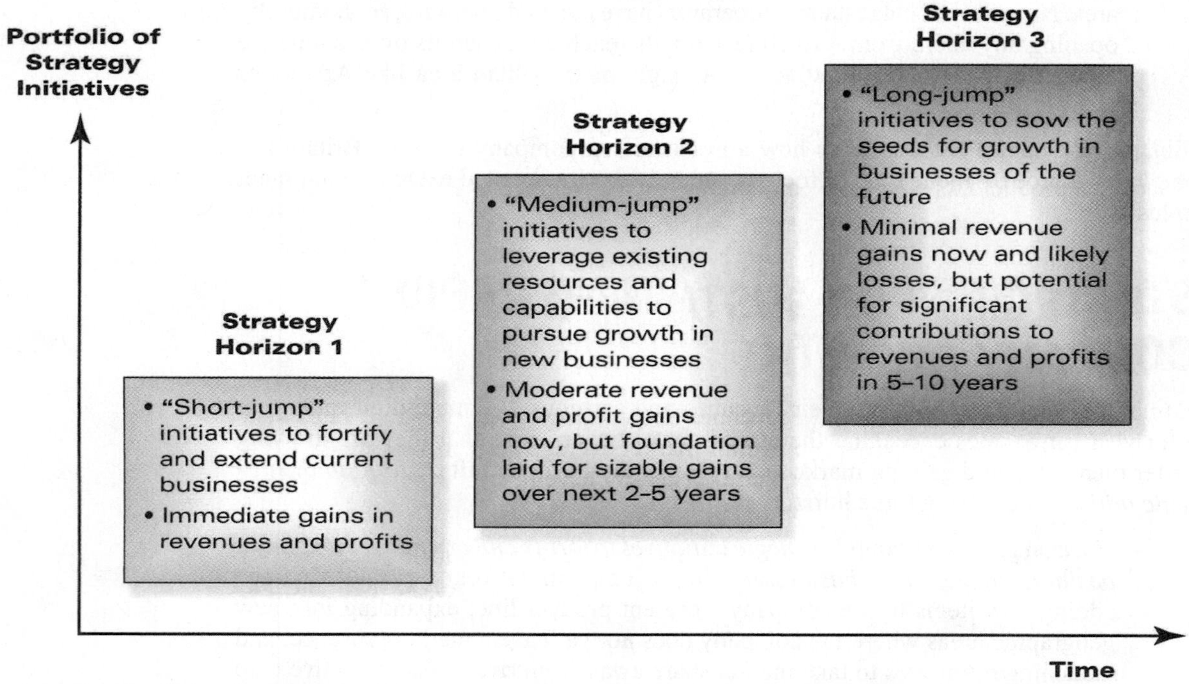

Portfolio of Strategy Initiatives

Strategy Horizon 1
- "Short-jump" initiatives to fortify and extend current businesses
- Immediate gains in revenues and profits

Strategy Horizon 2
- "Medium-jump" initiatives to leverage existing resources and capabilities to pursue growth in new businesses
- Moderate revenue and profit gains now, but foundation laid for sizable gains over next 2–5 years

Strategy Horizon 3
- "Long-jump" initiatives to sow the seeds for growth in businesses of the future
- Minimal revenue gains now and likely losses, but potential for significant contributions to revenues and profits in 5–10 years

Time

Source: Adapted from Eric D. Beinhocker, "Robust Adaptive Strategies," *Sloan Management Review* 40. No. 3 (Spring 1999), p. 101.

The three strategy horizons are illustrated in Figure 8.2. Managing such a portfolio of strategic initiatives to sustain rapid growth is not easy, however. The tendency of most companies is to focus on Horizon 1 strategies and devote only sporadic and uneven attention to Horizon 2 and 3 strategies. But a recent McKinsey & Company study of 30 of the world's leading growth companies revealed a relatively balanced portfolio of strategic initiatives covering all three horizons. The lesson of successful growth companies is that keeping a company's record of rapid growth intact over the long term entails crafting a diverse population of strategies, ranging from short-jump incremental strategies to grow present businesses to long-jump initiatives with a 5- to 10-year growth payoff horizon.[20] Having a mixture of short-jump, medium-jump, and long-jump initiatives not only increases the odds of hitting a few home runs but also provides some protection against unexpected adversity in present or newly entered businesses.

The Risks of Pursuing Multiple Strategy Horizons

There are, of course, risks to pursuing a diverse strategy portfolio aimed at sustained growth. A company cannot, of course, place bets on every opportunity that appears on its radar screen, lest it stretch its resources too thin. And medium-jump and long-jump initiatives can cause a company to stray far from its core competencies and end up trying to compete in businesses for which it is ill-suited. Moreover, it can be difficult to achieve competitive advantage in medium- and long-jump product families and businesses that prove not to mesh well with a company's present businesses and resource strengths. The payoffs of long-jump initiatives often prove elusive; not all of the seeds a company sows will bear fruit, and only a few may evolve into truly significant contributors to the company's revenue and profit growth. The losses from those long-jump ventures that do not take root may significantly erode the gains from those that do, resulting in disappointingly modest gains in overall profits.

STRATEGIES FOR INDUSTRY LEADERS

The competitive positions of industry leaders normally range from "stronger than average" to "powerful." Leaders typically are well known, and strongly entrenched leaders have proven strategies (keyed either to low-cost leadership or to differentiation). Some of the best-known industry leaders are Anheuser-Busch (beer), Starbucks (coffee drinks), Microsoft (computer software), Callaway (golf clubs), McDonald's (fast food), Procter & Gamble (laundry detergents and soaps), Campbell's (canned soups), Gerber (baby food), Hewlett-Packard (printers), Sony (video game consoles), Black & Decker (power tools), Intel (semiconductors and chip sets), Wal-Mart and Carrefour (discount retailing), Amazon.com (online shopping), eBay (online auctions), Apple (MP3 players), and Ocean Spray (cranberries).

The main strategic concern for a leader revolves around how to defend and strengthen its leadership position, perhaps becoming the dominant leader as opposed to just a leader. However, the pursuit of industry leadership and large market share is primarily important because of the competitive advantage and profitability that accrue to being the industry's biggest company. Three contrasting strategic postures are open to industry leaders:[21]

1. *Stay-on-the-offensive strategy*—The central goal of a stay-on-the-offensive strategy is to be a first-mover and a proactive market leader.[22] It rests on the principle that playing hardball, moving early and frequently, and forcing rivals into a catch-up mode is the surest path to industry prominence and potential market dominance—as the saying goes, the best defense is a good offense. Furthermore, *an offensive-minded industry leader relentlessly concentrates on achieving a competitive advantage over rivals and then widening this advantage over time to achieve extreme competitive advantage.*[23] Being the industry standard setter thus requires being impatient with the status quo, seizing the initiative, and pioneering continuous improvement and innovation—this can mean being first-to-market with technological improvements, new or better products, more attractive performance features, quality enhancements, or customer service improvements. It can mean aggressively seeking out ways to cut operating costs, ways to establish competitive capabilities that rivals cannot match, or ways to make it easier and less costly for potential customers to switch their purchases from runner-up firms to the leader's own products. It can mean aggressively attacking the profit sanctuaries of important rivals, perhaps with bursts of advertising or price-cutting or approaching its customers with special deals.[24]

> The governing principle underlying an industry leader's use of a stay-on-the-offensive strategy is to be an action-oriented first-mover, impatient with the status quo.

A low-cost leader must set the pace for cost reduction, and a differentiator must constantly initiate new ways to keep its product set apart from the brands of imitative rivals in order to be the standard against which rivals' products are judged. The array of options for a potent stay-on-the-offensive strategy can also include initiatives to expand overall industry demand—spurring the creation of new families of products, making the product more suitable for consumers in emerging-country markets, discovering new uses for the product, attracting new users of the product, and promoting more frequent use.

Illustration Capsule 8.2
ESPN's Strategy to Dominate Sports Entertainment

Via a series of offensive initiatives over the past 10 years, ESPN has parlayed its cable TV sports programming franchise into a dominating and pervasive general store of sports entertainment. The thrust of ESPN's strategy has been to stay on the offensive by (1) continually enhancing its program offerings and (2) extending the ESPN brand into a host of cutting-edge sports businesses. Examples of ESPN's enhanced product offering include the ESPY Awards for top achievements in sports, the X Games (an annual extreme sports competition for both winter and summer sports), the addition of *Monday Night Football* (starting in 2006), making new movies to show on ESPN, and producing its own shows (such as *ESPN Hollywood, Cold Pizza,* and *Bound for Glory*). The appeal of ESPN's programming was so powerful that ESPN was able to charge cable operators an estimated $2.80 per subscriber per month—nearly twice as much as the next most popular cable channel (CNN, for instance, was only able to command a monthly fee of roughly $0.40 per subscriber).

But the most important element of ESPN's strategic offensive had been to start up a series of new ESPN-branded businesses—all of which were brainstormed by ESPN's entrepreneurially talented management team. The company's brand extension offensive has produced nine TV channels (the most prominent of which are ESPN, ESPN2, ESPN Classic, ESPNews, and ESPN Desportes); the ESPN radio network, with 700 affiliate stations; ESPN. com (which in 2005 attracted some 16 million unique visitors monthly to view its bazaar of wide-ranging sports stories and information); *ESPN: The Magazine* (with a fast-growing base of 1.8 million subscribers that could in time overtake the barely growing 3.3 million subscriber base of longtime leader *Sports Illustrated*); ESPN Motion (an online video service); ESPN360 (which offers sports information and video-clip programming tailored for broadband providers—it had 5 million subscribers in 2005 and was available from 14 broadband providers); Mobile ESPN (an ESPN-branded cell phone service provided in partnership with Sprint Nextel); ESPN Zones (nine sports-themed restaurants in various cities); ESPN branded video games (video game developer Electronic Arts has 15-year licensing rights to use the ESPN name for a series of sports-related games), and a business unit that distributes ESPN sports programming in 11 languages in over 180 countries.

In 2005, the empire of ESPN consisted of some 50 different businesses that generated annual revenues in excess of $5 billion and hefty annual operating profits of about $2 billion—about 40 percent of its revenues came from advertising and 60 percent from subscriptions and distribution fees. ESPN, a division of Disney, was one of Disney's most profitable and fastest-growing operations (Disney was also the parent of ABC Broadcasting).

So far, ESPN's stay-a-step-ahead strategy had left lesser rivals in the dust. But Comcast, the largest U.S. cable operator, with 22 million subscribers, was maneuvering to create its own cable TV sports channel; Comcast already owned the Philadelphia 76ers, the Philadelphia Flyers, and a collection of regional sports networks in cities from Philadelphia to Chicago to Los Angeles. And Rupert Murdoch's expansion-minded News Corporation, a worldwide media conglomerate whose many businesses included Fox Broadcasting and DIRECTV, was said to be looking at melding its 15 regional U.S. sports channels into a national sports channel.

Source: Developed from information in Tom Lowry, "ESPN the Zone," *BusinessWeek,* October 17, 2005, pp. 66–78.

A stay-on-the-offensive strategy cannot be considered successful unless it results in growing sales and revenues faster than the industry as a whole and wresting market share from rivals—a leader whose sales growth is only 5 percent in a market growing at 8 percent is losing ground to some of its competitors. Only if an industry's leader's market share is already so dominant that it presents a threat of antitrust action (a market share under 60 percent is usually safe) should an industry leader deliberately back away from aggressively pursuing market share gains.

Illustration Capsule 8.2 describes ESPN's stay-on-the-offensive strategy to dominate the sports entertainment business.

2. *Fortify-and-defend strategy*—The essence of "fortify and defend" is to make it harder for challengers to gain ground and for new firms to enter. The goals of a strong defense are to hold on to the present market share, strengthen current market position, and protect whatever competitive advantage the firm has. Specific defensive actions can include:

- Attempting to raise the competitive ante for challengers and new entrants via increased spending for advertising, higher levels of customer service, and bigger R&D outlays.
- Introducing more product versions or brands to match the product attributes that challenger brands have or to fill vacant niches that competitors could slip into.
- Adding personalized services and other extras that boost customer loyalty and make it harder or more costly for customers to switch to rival products.
- Keeping prices reasonable and quality attractive.
- Building new capacity ahead of market demand to discourage smaller competitors from adding capacity of their own.
- Investing enough to remain cost-competitive and technologically progressive.
- Patenting the feasible alternative technologies.
- Signing exclusive contracts with the best suppliers and dealer/distributors.

A fortify-and-defend strategy best suits firms that have already achieved industry dominance and don't wish to risk antitrust action. It is also well suited to situations where a firm wishes to milk its present position for profits and cash flow because the industry's prospects for growth are low or because further gains in market share do not appear profitable enough to go after. But a fortify-and-defend strategy always entails trying to grow as fast as the market as a whole (to stave off market-share slippage) and requires reinvesting enough capital in the business to protect the leader's ability to compete.

    3. *Muscle-flexing strategy*—Here a dominant leader plays competitive hardball (presumably in an ethical and competitively legal manner) when smaller rivals rock the boat with price cuts or mount new market offensives that directly threaten its position. Specific responses can include quickly matching and perhaps exceeding challengers' price cuts, using large promotional campaigns to counter challengers' moves to gain market share, and offering better deals to their major customers. Dominant leaders may also court distributors assiduously to dissuade them from carrying rivals' products, provide salespersons with documented information about the weaknesses of competing products, or try to fill any vacant positions in their own firms by making attractive offers to the better executives of rivals that get out of line.

    The leader may also use various arm-twisting tactics to pressure present customers not to use the products of rivals. This can range from simply forcefully communicating its displeasure should customers opt to use the products of rivals to pushing them to agree to exclusive arrangements in return for better prices to charging them a higher price if they use any competitors' products. As a final resort, a leader may grant certain customers special discounts or preferred treatment if they do not use any products of rivals.

    The obvious risks of a muscle-flexing strategy are running afoul of laws prohibiting monopoly practices and unfair competition and using bullying tactics that arouse adverse public opinion. Microsoft paid Real Networks $460 million in 2005 to resolve all of Real Network's antitrust complaints and settle a long-standing feud over Microsoft's repeated bullying of PC makers to include Windows Media Player instead of Real's media player as standard installed software on their PCs. In 2005 AMD filed an antitrust suit against Intel, claiming that Intel unfairly and monopolistically coerced 38 named companies on three continents in efforts to get them to use Intel chips instead of AMD chips in the computer products they manufactured or marketed. Consequently, a company that throws its weight around to protect and enhance its market dominance has got to be judicious, lest it cross the line from allowable muscle-flexing to unethical or illegal competitive bullying.

STRATEGIES FOR RUNNER-UP FIRMS

Runner-up, or second-tier, firms have smaller market shares than first-tier industry leaders. Some runner-up firms are often advancing market challengers, employing offensive strategies to gain market share and build a stronger market position. Other runner-up competitors are focusers, seeking to improve their lot by concentrating their attention on serving a limited portion of the market. There are, of course, always a number of firms in any industry that are destined to be perennial runners-up, either because they are content to follow the trendsetting moves of the market leaders or because they lack the resources and competitive strengths to do much better in the marketplace than they are already doing. But it is erroneous to view runner-up firms as inherently less profitable or unable to hold their own against the biggest firms. Many small and medium-sized firms earn healthy profits and enjoy good reputations with customers.

Obstacles for Firms with Small Market Shares

There are times when runner-up companies face significant hurdles in contending for market leadership. In industries where big size is definitely a key success factor, firms with small market shares have four obstacles to overcome: (1) less access to economies of scale in manufacturing, distribution, or marketing and sales promotion; (2) difficulty in gaining customer recognition (since the products and brands of the market leaders are much better known); (3) less money to spend on mass-media advertising; and (4) limited funds for capital expansion or making acquisitions.[25] Some runner-up companies may be able to surmount these obstacles. Others may not. When significant scale economies give large-volume competitors a dominating cost advantage, small-share firms have only two viable strategic options: initiate offensive moves aimed at building sufficient sales volume to approach the scale economies and lower unit costs enjoyed by larger rivals or withdraw from the business (gradually or quickly) because of the inability to achieve low enough costs to compete effectively against the market leaders.

Offensive Strategies to Build Market Share

A runner-up company desirous of closing in on the market leaders has to make some waves in the marketplace if it wants to make big market share gains—this means coming up with distinctive strategy elements that set it apart from rivals and draw buyer attention. If a challenger has a 5 percent market share and needs a 15 to 20 percent share to contend for leadership and earn attractive profits, it requires a more creative approach to competing than just "Try harder" or "Follow in the footsteps of current industry leaders." Rarely can a runner-up significantly improve its competitive position by imitating the strategies of leading firms. A cardinal rule in offensive strategy is to avoid attacking a leader head-on with an imitative strategy, regardless of the resources and staying power an underdog may have.[26] What an aspiring challenger really needs is a strategy aimed at building a competitive advantage of its own (and certainly a strategy capable of quickly eliminating any important competitive disadvantages).

The best "mover-and-shaker" offensives for a second-tier challenger aiming to join the first-tier ranks usually involve one of the following five approaches:

1. Making a series of acquisitions of smaller rivals to greatly expand the company's market reach and market presence. *Growth via acquisition* is perhaps the most frequently used strategy employed by ambitious runner-up companies to form an enterprise that has greater competitive strength and a larger share of the overall market. For an enterprise to succeed with this strategic approach, senior management must be skilled in quickly assimilating the operations of the acquired companies, eliminating duplication and overlap, generating efficiencies and cost savings, and structuring the combined resources in ways that create substantially stronger competitive capabilities. Many banks and public accounting firms owe their growth during the past decade to acquisition of smaller regional and local banks. Likewise, a number of book publishers have grown by acquiring small publishers, and public accounting firms have grown by acquiring lesser-sized accounting firms with attractive client lists.

2. Finding innovative ways to dramatically drive down costs and then using the attraction of lower prices to win customers from higher-cost, higher-priced rivals. This is a necessary offensive move when a runner-up company has higher costs than larger-scale enterprises (either because the latter possess scale economies or have benefited from experience/learning curve effects). A challenger firm can pursue aggressive cost reduction by eliminating marginal activities from its value chain, streamlining supply chain relationships, improving internal operating efficiency, using various e-commerce techniques, and merging with or acquiring rival firms to achieve the size needed to capture greater scale economies.

3. Crafting an attractive differentiation strategy based on premium quality, technological superiority, outstanding customer service, rapid product innovation, or convenient online shopping options.

4. Pioneering a leapfrog technological breakthrough—an attractive option if an important technological breakthrough is within a challenger's reach and rivals are not close behind.

5. Being first-to-market with new or better products and building a reputation for product leadership. A strategy of product innovation has appeal if the runner-up company possesses the necessary resources—cutting-edge R&D capability and organizational agility in speeding new products to market.

Other possible, but likely less effective, offensive strategy options include (1) outmaneuvering slow-to-change market leaders in adapting to evolving market conditions and customer expectations and (2) forging productive strategic alliances with key distributors, dealers, or marketers of complementary products.

Without a potent offensive strategy to capture added market share, runner-up companies have to patiently nibble away at the lead of market leaders and build sales at a moderate pace over time.

Other Strategic Approaches for Runner-Up Companies

There are five other strategies that runner-up companies can employ.[27] While none of the five is likely to move a company from second-tier to first-tier status, all are capable of producing attractive profits and returns for shareholders.

Vacant-Niche Strategy   A version of a focused strategy, the vacant-niche strategy involves concentrating on specific customer groups or end-use applications that market leaders have bypassed or neglected. An ideal vacant niche is of sufficient size and scope to be profitable, has some growth potential, is well suited to a firm's own capabilities, and for one reason or another is hard for leading firms to serve. Two examples where vacant-niche strategies have worked successfully are (1) regional commuter airlines serving cities with too few passengers to fill the large jets flown by major airlines and (2) health-food producers (like Health Valley, Hain, and Tree of Life) that cater to local health-food stores—a market segment that until recently has been given little attention by such leading companies as Kraft, Nestlé, and Unilever.

Specialist Strategy   A specialist firm trains its competitive effort on one technology, product or product family, end use, or market segment (often one in which buyers have special needs). The aim is to train the company's resource strengths and capabilities on building competitive advantage through leadership in a specific area. Smaller companies that successfully use this focused strategy include Formby's (a specialist in stains and finishes for wood furniture, especially refinishing); Blue Diamond (a California-based grower and marketer of almonds); Cuddledown (a specialty producer and retailer of down and synthetic comforters, featherbeds, and other bedding products); and American Tobacco (a leader in chewing tobacco and snuff). Many companies in high-tech industries concentrate their energies on being the clear leader in a particular technological niche; their competitive advantage is superior technological depth, technical expertise that is highly valued by customers, and the capability to consistently beat out rivals in pioneering technological advances.

Superior Product Strategy   The approach here is to use a differentiation-based focused strategy keyed to superior product quality or unique attributes. Sales and marketing efforts are aimed directly at quality-conscious and performance-oriented buyers. Fine craftsmanship, prestige quality, frequent product innovations, and/or close contact with customers to solicit their input in developing a better product usually undergird the superior product approach. Some examples include Samuel Adams in beer, Tiffany in diamonds and jewelry, Chicago Cutlery in premium-quality kitchen knives, Baccarat in fine crystal, Cannondale in mountain bikes, Bally in shoes, and Patagonia in apparel for outdoor recreation enthusiasts.

Distinctive-Image Strategy   Some runner-up companies build their strategies around ways to make themselves stand out from competitors. A variety of distinctive-image strategies can be used: building a reputation for charging the lowest prices (Dollar General), providing high-end quality at a good price (Orvis, Lands' End, and L. L. Bean), going all out to give superior customer service (Four Seasons hotels), incorporating unique product attributes (Omega-3 enriched eggs), making a product with disctinctive styling (General Motors' Hummer), or devising unusually creative advertising (AFLAC's duck ads on TV). Other examples include Dr Pepper's strategy in calling attention to its distinctive taste, Apple Computer's making it easier and more interesting for people to use its Macintosh PCs, and Mary Kay Cosmetics' distinctive use of the color pink.

Content Follower Strategy   Content followers deliberately refrain from initiating trendsetting strategic moves and from aggressive attempts to steal customers away from the leaders. Followers prefer approaches that will not provoke competitive retaliation, often opting for focus and differentiation strategies that keep them out of the leaders' paths. They react and respond rather than initiate and challenge. They prefer defense to offense. And they rarely get out of line with the leaders on price. They are content to simply maintain their market position, albeit sometimes struggling to do so. Followers have no urgent strategic questions to confront beyond "What strategic changes are the leaders initiating and what do we need to do to follow along and maintain our present position?" The marketers of private-label products tend to be followers, imitating many of the newly introduced features of name brand products and content to sell to price-conscious buyers at prices modestly below those of well-known brands.

STRATEGIES FOR WEAK AND CRISIS-RIDDEN BUSINESSES

A firm in an also-ran or declining competitive position has four basic strategic options. If it can come up with the financial resources, it can launch a turnaround strategy keyed either to "low-cost" or "new" differentiation themes, pouring enough money and talent into the effort to move up a notch or two in the industry rankings and become a respectable market contender within five years or so. It can employ a fortify-and-defend strategy, using variations of its present strategy and fighting hard to keep sales, market share, profitability, and competitive position at current levels. It can opt for a fast-exit strategy and get out of the business, either by selling out to another firm or by closing down operations if a buyer cannot be found. Or it can employ an end-game or slow-exit strategy, keeping reinvestment to a bare-bones minimum and taking actions to maximize short-term cash flows in preparation for orderly market withdrawal.

Turnaround Strategies for Businesses in Crisis

Turnaround strategies are needed when a business worth rescuing goes into crisis. The objective is to arrest and reverse the sources of competitive and financial weakness as quickly as possible. Management's first task in formulating a suitable turnaround strategy is to diagnose what lies at the root of poor performance. Is it an unexpected downturn in sales brought on by a weak economy? An ill-chosen competitive strategy? Poor execution of an otherwise viable strategy? High operating costs? Important resource deficiencies? An overload of debt? The next task is to decide whether the business can be saved or whether the situation is hopeless. Understanding what is wrong with the business and how serious its strategic problems are is essential because different diagnoses lead to different turnaround strategies.

Some of the most common causes of business trouble are taking on too much debt, overestimating the potential for sales growth, ignoring the profit-depressing effects of an overly aggressive effort to "buy" market share with deep price cuts, being burdened with heavy fixed costs because weak sales don't permit near-full capacity utilization, betting on R&D efforts but failing to come up with effective innovations, betting on technological long shots, being too optimistic about the ability to penetrate new markets, making frequent changes in strategy (because the previous strategy didn't work out), and being overpowered by more successful rivals. Curing these kinds of problems and achieving a successful business turnaround can involve any of the following actions:

- Selling off assets to raise cash to save the remaining part of the business.
- Revising the existing strategy.
- Launching efforts to boost revenues.

- Pursuing cost reduction.
- Using a combination of these efforts.

Selling Off Assets   Asset-reduction strategies are essential when cash flow is a critical consideration and when the most practical ways to generate cash are (1) through sale of some of the firm's assets (plant and equipment, land, patents, inventories, or profitable subsidiaries) and (2) through retrenchment (pruning of marginal products from the product line, closing or selling older plants, reducing the workforce, withdrawing from outlying markets, cutting back customer service). Sometimes crisis-ridden companies sell off assets not so much to unload losing operations as to raise funds to save and strengthen the remaining business activities. In such cases, the choice is usually to dispose of noncore business assets to support strategy renewal in the firm's core businesses.

Strategy Revision   When weak performance is caused by bad strategy, the task of strategy overhaul can proceed along any of several paths: (1) shifting to a new competitive approach to rebuild the firm's market position; (2) overhauling internal operations and functional-area strategies to better support the same overall business strategy; (3) merging with another firm in the industry and forging a new strategy keyed to the newly merged firm's strengths; and (4) retrenching into a reduced core of products and customers more closely matched to the firm's strengths. The most appealing path depends on prevailing industry conditions, the firm's particular strengths and weaknesses, its competitive capabilities vis-à-vis rival firms, and the severity of the crisis. A situation analysis of the industry, the major competitors, and the firm's own competitive position is a prerequisite for action. As a rule, successful strategy revision must be tied to the ailing firm's strengths and near-term competitive capabilities and directed at its best market opportunities.

Boosting Revenues   Revenue-increasing turnaround efforts aim at generating increased sales volume. The chief revenue-building options include price cuts, increased advertising, a bigger sales force, added customer services, and quickly achieved product improvements. Attempts to increase revenues and sales volumes are necessary (1) when there is little or no room in the operating budget to cut expenses and still break even, and (2) when the key to restoring profitability is increased use of existing capacity. If buyers are not especially price-sensitive (because many are strongly attached to various differentiating features in the company's product offering), the quickest way to boost short-term revenues may be to raise prices rather than opt for volume-building price cuts. A price increase in the 2–4 percent range may well be feasible if the company's prices are already below those of key rivals.

Cutting Costs   Cost-reducing turnaround strategies work best when an ailing firm's value chain and cost structure are flexible enough to permit radical surgery, when operating inefficiencies are identifiable and readily correctable, when the firm's costs are obviously bloated, and when the firm is relatively close to its break-even point. Accompanying a general belt-tightening can be an increased emphasis on paring administrative overheads, elimination of nonessential and low-value-added activities in the firm's value chain, modernization of existing plant and equipment to gain greater productivity, delay of nonessential capital expenditures, and debt restructuring to reduce interest costs and stretch out repayments.

Illustration Capsule 8.3
Sony's Turnaround Strategy—Will It Work?

Electronics was once Sony's star business, but Sony's electronics business was a huge money-loser in 2003–2004, pushing the company's stock price down about 65 percent. Once the clear leader in top-quality TVs, in 2005 Sony lagged miserably behind Samsung, Panasonic, and Sharp in popular flat-panel LCD and plasma TVs, where sales were growing fastest. Apple Computer's iPod players had stolen the limelight in the handheld music market, where Sony's Walkman had long ruled.

In the fall of 2005, Sony management announced a turnaround strategy. Howard Stringer, a dual American and British citizen who was named Sony's CEO in early 2005 and was the first foreigner ever to head Sony, unveiled a plan centered on cutting 10,000 jobs (about 6 percent of Sony's workforce), closing 11 of Sony's 65 manufacturing plants, and shrinking or eliminating 15 unprofitable

electronics operations by March 2008 (the unprofitable operations were not identified). These initiatives were projected to reduce costs by $1.8 billion. In addition to the cost cuts, Sony said it would focus on growing its sales of "champion products" like the next-generation Sony PlayStation 3 video game console, a newly introduced line of Bravia LCD TVs, and Walkman MP3 music players.

Analysts were not impressed by the turnaround plan. Standard & Poor's cut its credit rating for Sony, citing doubts about the company's turnaround strategy and forecasting "substantially" lower profitability and cash flow in fiscal 2005. Moody's put Sony on its watch list for a credit rating downgrade. Other analysts said Stringer's strategy lacked vision and creativity because it was in the same mold as most corporate streamlining efforts.

Sources: Company press releases; Yuri Kageyama, "Sony Announcing Turnaround Strategy," www.yahoo.com (accessed October 20, 2005); *Mainichi Daily News,* October 14, 2005 (accessed on Google News, October 20, 2005); and "Sony to Cut 10,000 Jobs," www.cnn.com (accessed October 20, 2005).

Combination Efforts   Combination turnaround strategies are usually essential in grim situations that require fast action on a broad front. Likewise, combination actions frequently come into play when new managers are brought in and given a free hand to make whatever changes they see fit. The tougher the problems, the more likely it is that the solutions will involve multiple strategic initiatives—see the story of turnaround efforts at Sony in Illustration Capsule 8.3.

The Chances of a Successful Turnaround Are Not High   Turnaround efforts tend to be high-risk undertakings; some return a company to good profitability, but most don't. A landmark study of 64 companies found no successful turnarounds among the most troubled companies in eight basic industries.[28] Many of the troubled businesses waited too long to begin a turnaround. Others found themselves short of both the cash and entrepreneurial talent needed to compete in a slow-growth industry characterized by a fierce battle for market share. Better-positioned rivals simply proved too strong to defeat in a long, head-to-head contest. Even when successful, turnaround may involve numerous attempts and management changes before long-term competitive viability and profitability are finally restored. A recent study found that troubled companies that did nothing and elected to wait out hard times had only a 10 percent chance of recovery.[29] This same study also found that, of the companies studied, the chances of recovery were boosted 190 percent if the turnaround strategy involved buying assets that strengthened the company's business in its core markets; companies that both bought assets or companies in their core markets while selling off noncore assets increased their chances of recovery by 250 percent.

Harvest Strategies for Weak Businesses

When a struggling company's chances of pulling off a successful turnaround are poor, the wisest option may be to forget about trying to restore the company's competitiveness and profitability and, instead employ a *harvesting strategy* that aims at generating the largest possible cash flows from the company's operations for as long as possible. A losing effort to transform a competitively weak company into a viable market contender has little appeal when there are opportunities to generate potentially sizable amounts of cash by running the business in a manner calculated to either maintain the status quo or even let the business slowly deteriorate over a long period.

As is the case with a slow-exit strategy, a harvesting strategy entails trimming operating expenses to the bone and spending the minimum amount on capital projects to keep the business going. Internal cash flow becomes the key measure of how well the company is performing, and top priority is given to cash-generating actions. Thus,

> The overriding objective of a harvesting strategy is to maximize short-term cash flows from operations.

advertising and promotional costs are kept at minimal levels; personnel who leave for jobs elsewhere or retire may not be replaced; and maintenance is performed with an eye toward stretching the life of existing facilities and equipment. Even though a harvesting strategy is likely to lead to a gradual decline in the company's business over time, the ability to harvest sizable amounts of cash in the interim makes such an outcome tolerable.

The Conditions That Make a Harvesting Strategy Attractive   A strategy of harvesting the cash flows from a weak business is a reasonable option in the following circumstances:[30]

1. *When industry demand is stagnant or declining and there's little hope that either market conditions will improve*—The growing popularity of digital cameras has forever doomed market demand for camera film.

2. *When rejuvenating the business would be too costly or at best marginally profitable*—A struggling provider of dial-up Internet access is likely to realize more benefit from harvesting than from a losing effort to grow its business in the face of the unstoppable shift to high-speed broadband service.

3. *When trying to maintain or grow the company's present sales is becoming increasingly costly*—A money-losing producer of pipe tobacco and cigars is unlikely to make market headway in gaining sales and market share against the top-tier producers (which have more resources to compete for the business that is still available).

4. *When reduced levels of competitive effort will not trigger an immediate or rapid falloff in sales*—the makers of corded telephones will not likely experience much of a decline in sales if they spend all of their R&D and marketing budgets on wireless phone systems.

5. *When the enterprise can redeploy the freed resources in higher-opportunity areas*—The makers of food products with "bad-for-you" ingredients (saturated fats, high transfats, and sugar) are better off devoting their resources to the development, production, and sale of "good-for-you" products (those with no transfats, more fiber, and good types of carbohydrates).

6. *When the business is not a crucial or core component of a diversified company's overall lineup of businesses*—Harvesting a sideline business and perhaps

hastening its decay is strategically preferable to harvesting a mainline or core business (where even a gradual decline may not be a very attractive outcome).

The more of these six conditions that are present, the more ideal the business is for harvesting.

Liquidation: The Strategy of Last Resort

Sometimes a business in crisis is too far gone to be salvaged and presents insufficient harvesting potential to be interesting. Closing down a crisis-ridden business and liquidating its assets is sometimes the best and wisest strategy. But it is also the most unpleasant and painful strategic alternative due to the hardships of job eliminations and the economic effects of business closings on local communities. Nonetheless, in hopeless situations, an early liquidation effort usually serves owner-stockholder interests better than an inevitable bankruptcy. Prolonging the pursuit of a lost cause further erodes an organization's resources and leaves less to salvage, not to mention the added stress and potential career impairment for all the people involved. The problem, of course, is differentiating between when a turnaround is achievable and when it isn't. It is easy for owners or managers to let their emotions and pride overcome sound judgment when a business gets in such deep trouble that a successful turnaround is remote.

10 COMMANDMENTS FOR CRAFTING SUCCESSFUL BUSINESS STRATEGIES

Company experiences over the years prove again and again that disastrous strategies can be avoided by adhering to good strategy-making principles. We've distilled the lessons learned from the strategic mistakes companies most often make into 10 commandments that serve as useful guides for developing sound strategies:

1. *Place top priority on crafting and executing strategic moves that enhance the company's competitive position for the long term.* The glory of meeting one quarter's or one year's financial performance targets quickly fades, but an ever-stronger competitive position pays off year after year. Shareholders are never well served by managers who let short-term financial performance considerations rule out strategic initiatives that will meaningfully bolster the company's longer-term competitive position and competitive strength. The best way to ensure a company's long-term profitability is with a strategy that strengthens the company's long-term competitiveness and market position.

2. *Be prompt in adapting to changing market conditions, unmet customer needs, buyer wishes for something better, emerging technological alternatives, and new initiatives of competitors.* Responding late or with too little often puts a company in the precarious position of having to play catch-up. While pursuit of a consistent strategy has its virtues, adapting strategy to changing circumstances is normal and necessary. Moreover, long-term strategic commitments to achieve top quality or lowest cost should be interpreted relative to competitors' products as well as customers' needs and expectations; the company should avoid singlemindedly striving to make the absolute highest-quality or lowest-cost product no matter what.

3. *Invest in creating a sustainable competitive advantage.* Having a competitive edge over rivals is the single most dependable contributor to above-average profitability.

As a general rule, a company must play aggressive offense to build competitive advantage and aggressive defense to protect it.

4. *Avoid strategies capable of succeeding only in the most optimistic circumstances.* Expect competitors to employ countermeasures and expect times of unfavorable market conditions. A good strategy works reasonably well and produces tolerable results even in the worst of times.

5. *Consider that attacking competitive weakness is usually more profitable and less risky than attacking competitive strength.* Attacking capable, resourceful rivals is likely to fail unless the attacker has deep financial pockets and a solid basis for competitive advantage despite the strengths of the competitor being attacked.

6. *Strive to open up very meaningful gaps in quality or service or performance features when pursuing a differentiation strategy.* Tiny differences between rivals' product offerings may not be visible or important to buyers.

7. *Be wary of cutting prices without an established cost advantage.* Price cuts run the risk that rivals will retaliate with matching or deeper price cuts of their own. The best chance for remaining profitable if the price-cutting contest turns into a price war is to have lower costs than rivals.

8. *Don't underestimate the reactions and the commitment of rival firms.* Rivals are most dangerous when they are pushed into a corner and their well-being is threatened.

9. *Avoid stuck-in-the-middle strategies that represent compromises between lower costs and greater differentiation and between broad and narrow market appeal.* Compromise strategies rarely produce sustainable competitive advantage or a distinctive competitive position—a well-executed best-cost producer strategy is the only exception in which a compromise between low cost and differentiation succeeds. Companies with compromise strategies most usually end up with average costs, an average product, an average reputation, and *no distinctive image in the marketplace.* Lacking any strategy element that causes them to stand out in the minds of buyers, companies with compromise strategies are destined for a middle-of-the-pack industry ranking, with little prospect of ever becoming an industry leader.

10. *Be judicious in employing aggressive moves to wrest market share away from rivals that often provoke retaliation in the form of escalating marketing and sales promotion, a furious race to be first-to-market with next-version products or a price war—to the detriment of everyone's profits.* Aggressive moves to capture a bigger market share invite cutthroat competition, especially when many industry members, plagued with high inventories and excess production capacity, are also scrambling for additional sales.

Key Points

The lessons of this chapter are that (1) some strategic options are better suited to certain specific industry and competitive environments than others and (2) some strategic options are better suited to certain specific company situations than others. Crafting a strategy tightly matched to a company's situation thus involves being alert to which strategy alternatives are likely to work well and which alternatives are unlikely to work well. Specifically:

1. What basic type of industry environment (emerging, rapid-growth, mature/slow-growth, stagnant/declining, high-velocity/turbulent, fragmented) does the company operate in? What strategic options and strategic postures are usually best suited to this generic type of environment?

2. What position does the firm have in the industry (leader, runner-up, or weak/distressed)? Given this position, which strategic options merit strong consideration and which options should definitely be ruled out?

In addition, creating a tight strategy-situation fit entails considering all the external and internal situational factors discussed in Chapters 3 and 4 and then revising the list of strategy options accordingly to take account of competitive conditions, industry driving forces, the expected moves of rivals, and the company's own competitive strengths and weaknesses. Listing the pros and cons of the candidate strategies is nearly always a helpful step. In weeding out the least attractive strategic alternatives and weighing the pros and cons of the most attractive ones, the answers to four questions often help point to the best course of action:

1. What kind of competitive edge can the company realistically achieve, given its resource strengths, competencies, and competitive capabilities? Is the company in a position to lead industry change and set the rules by which rivals must compete?

2. Which strategy alternative best addresses all the issues and problems the firm confronts.

3. Are any rivals particularly vulnerable and, if so, what sort of an offensive will it take to capitalize on these vulnerabilities? Will rivals counterattack? What can be done to blunt their efforts?

4. Are any defensive actions needed to protect against rivals' likely moves or other external threats to the company's future profitability?

In picking and choosing among the menu of strategic options, there are four pitfalls to avoid:

1. Designing an overly ambitious strategic plan—one that overtaxes the company's resources and capabilities.

2. Selecting a strategy that represents a radical departure from or abandonment of the cornerstones of the company's prior success—a radical strategy change need not be rejected automatically, but it should be pursued only after careful risk assessment.

3. Choosing a strategy that goes against the grain of the organization's culture.

4. Being unwilling to commit wholeheartedly to one of the five competitive strategies—picking and choosing features of the different strategies usually produces so many compromises between low cost, best cost, differentiation, and focusing that the company fails to achieve any kind of advantage and ends up stuck in the middle.

Table 8.1 provides a generic format for outlining a strategic action plan for a single-business enterprise. It contains all of the pieces of a comprehensive strategic action plan that we discussed at various places in these first eight chapters.

Table 8.1 **Sample Format for a Strategic Action Plan**

1. Strategic Vision and Mission	5. Supporting Functional Strategies • Production
2. Strategic Objectives • Short-term	• Marketing/sales
• Long-term	• Finance
3. Financial Objectives • Short-term	• Personnel/human resources
	• Other

• Long-term	6. Recommended Actions to Improve
	   Company Performance
	   • Immediate

4. Overall Business Strategy	• Longer-range

Exercises

1. Listed below are 10 industries. Classify each one as (*a*) emerging, (*b*) rapid-growth, (*c*) mature/slow-growth, (*d*) stagnant/declining, (*e*) high-velocity/turbulent, and (*f*) fragmented. Do research on the Internet, if needed, to locate information on industry conditions and reach a conclusion on what classification to assign each of the following:

    a. Exercise and fitness industry.

    b. Dry-cleaning industry.

    c. Poultry industry.

    d. Camera film and film-developing industry.

    e. Wine, beer, and liquor retailing.

    f. Watch industry.

    g. Cell-phone industry.

    h. Recorded music industry (DVDs, CDs, tapes).

    i. Computer software industry.

    j. Newspaper industry.

2. Toyota overtook Ford Motor Company in 2003 to become the world's second-largest maker of motor vehicles, behind General Motors. Toyota is widely regarded as having aspirations to overtake General Motors as the global leader in motor vehicles within the next 10 years. Do research on the Internet or in the library to determine what strategy General Motors is pursuing to maintain its status as the industry leader. Then research Toyota's strategy to overtake General Motors.

3. Review the discussion in Illustration Capsule 8.1 concerning the focused differentiation strategy that Exertris has employed in the exercise equipment industry. Then answer the following:

   a. What reasons can you give for why sales of the Exertris exercise bike have not taken off?

   b. What strategic actions would you recommend to the cofounders of Exertris to spark substantially greater sales of its innovative exercise bike and overcome the apparent market apathy for its video-game-equipped exercise bike? Should the company consider making any changes in its product offering? What distribution channels should it emphasize? What advertising and promotional approaches should be considered? How can it get gym owners to purchase or at least try its bikes?

   c. Should the company just give up on its product innovation (because the bike is not ever likely to get good reception in the marketplace)? Or should the cofounders try to sell their fledgling business to another exercise equipment company with a more extensive product line and wider geographic coverage?

4. Review the information in Illustration Capsule 8.3 concerning the turnaround strategy Sony launched in the fall of 2005. Go to the company's Web site and check out other Internet sources to see how Sony's strategy to revitalize its electronics business is coming along. Does your research indicate that Sony's turnaround strategy is a success or a failure, or is it still too early to tell? Explain.

5. Yahoo competes in an industry characterized by high-velocity change. Read the company's press releases at http://yhoo.client.shareholder.com/releases.cfm and answer the following questions:

   a. Does it appear that the company has dealt with change in the industry by reacting to change, anticipating change, or leading change? Explain.

   b. What are its key strategies for competing in fast-changing markets? Describe them.

Part IV

Taken from *Operations & Supply Management,* Twelfth Edition, by F. Robert Jacobs, Richard B. Chase, and Nicholas J. Aquilano (2008). The McGraw-Hill Companies.

chapter

SERVICE PROCESSES

MY WEEK AS A ROOM-SERVICE WAITER AT THE RITZ

This was to be my first real test. After completing a two-day orientation program and spending the same number of days shadowing Stephen Posner, a veteran Ritz-Carlton room-service waiter, I was going to take the lead on delivering a dinner order. As we headed up the service elevator with a light meal for two—a cheeseburger, a salad, a beer, and a bottle of mineral water—I again went over in my head Steve's instruction on what to say and do. He noticed my furrowed brow. "Don't be so serious," he said, as I awkwardly maneuvered the room-service cart down the hall. "Feel out the guests and try to match their mood."

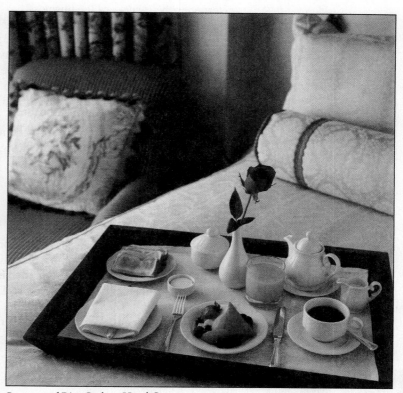

Courtesy of Ritz-Carlton Hotel Company.

I knocked on the door of Room 1036 and swallowed: "Good evening. In-room dining." A cheerful woman opened the door and I pushed, rather than pulled, the jiggling and tinkling cart over the threshold—nearly tipping over the bottle of San Pellegrino in the process. When the woman, who was watching a game show on television with her husband, learned from Steve that I was in training, she tried to put me at ease with some conversation about the program. But I didn't have the excess mental capacity required for casual banter. I was focused on my task.

"Would you like me to open the water for you?" I asked.

"Oh, sure, if you'd like to," said the woman.

Then I stood there, slightly slack jawed, hands behind my back, surveying the cart and trying to recall what my checklist said to do next. The woman stood there looking at me expectantly. Steve stood there looking at me quizzically. Ah, I know! Explain what I've brought for them. "You have a Caesar salad and a grilled beef burger with cheese, medium rare," I said, lifting up the warming cover. "And I brought some extra mustard and ketchup, in case you need it." Steve, having finally despaired of my ever opening the San Pellegrino, deftly stepped forward and did it himself. "Please don't hesitate to call us if you need anything else," I said, as we prepared to leave. The woman smiled. I forgot to offer to open the Heineken. As Steve and I stepped into the hallway, he closed the door behind us and said: "We have a few things to talk about on the way downstairs." →

The delivery of food at the Ritz-Carlton is just the visible portion of a series of service design decisions that emanate from their service strategy. The best service companies, like the Ritz-Carlton, understand that how well they manage the details of every stage of their operations determines the success of the business.

In this chapter, after some preliminary comments about services, we address the issue of service delivery system design, starting with the notion of customer contact as a way of classifying service operations. Next we discuss service organization design, service strategy, and service focus and describe how marketing and operations interrelate to achieve (or fail to achieve) competitive advantage. We also look at a service-system design matrix that can define the broad features of a service process, and at service blueprints as a way of designing the precise steps of a process. In the latter part of the chapter, we present three service designs used in service industries and discuss how service guarantees can be used as "design drivers." The chapter ends with two service organization case studies.

Service

THE NATURE OF SERVICES

A glance at the management book section in your local bookstore gives ample evidence of the concern for service among practitioners. The way we now view service parallels the way we view quality: The *customer* is (or should be) the focal point of all decisions and actions of the service organization. This philosophy is captured nicely in the service triangle in Exhibit 8.1. Here the customer is the center of things—the service strategy, the systems, and the employees who serve him or her. From this view, the organization exists

The Service Triangle

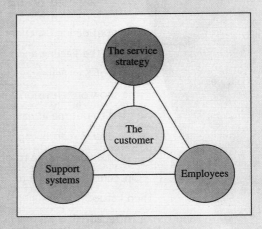

to serve the customer, and the systems and the employees exist to facilitate the process of service. Some suggest that the service organization also exists to serve the workforce because they generally determine how the service is perceived by the customers. Relative to the latter point, the customer gets the kind of service that management deserves; in other words, how management treats the worker is how the worker will treat the public. If the workforce is well trained and well motivated by management, they will do good jobs for their customers.

The role of operations in the triangle is a major one. Operations is responsible for service systems (procedures, equipment, and facilities) and is responsible for managing the work of the service workforce, who typically make up the majority of employees in large service organizations. But before we discuss this role in depth, it is useful to classify services to show how the customer affects the operations function.

AN OPERATIONAL CLASSIFICATION OF SERVICES

Service organizations are generally classified according to who the customer is, for example, individuals or other businesses, and to the service they provide (financial services, health services, transportation services, and so on). These groupings, though useful in presenting aggregate economic data, are not particularly appropriate for OSM purposes because they tell us little about the process. Manufacturing, by contrast, has fairly evocative terms to classify production activities (such as intermittent and continuous production); when applied to a manufacturing setting, they readily convey the essence of the process. Although it is possible to describe services in these same terms, we need one additional item of information to reflect the fact that the customer is involved in the production system. That item, which we believe operationally distinguishes one service system from another in its production function, is the extent of customer contact in the creation of the service.

Customer contact refers to the physical presence of the customer in the system, and *creation of the service* refers to the work process involved in providing the service itself. *Extent of contact* here may be roughly defined as the percentage of time the customer must be in the system relative to the total time it takes to perform the customer service. Generally speaking, the greater the percentage of contact time between the service system and the customer, the greater the degree of interaction between the two during the production process.

From this conceptualization, it follows that service systems with a high degree of customer contact are more difficult to control and more difficult to rationalize than those with a low degree of customer contact. In high-contact systems, the customer can affect the time of demand, the exact nature of the service, and the quality, or perceived quality, of service because the customer is involved in the process.

High and low degree of customer contact

Exhibit 8.2 describes the implications of this distinction. Here we see that each design decision is impacted by whether the customer is present during service delivery. We also see that when work is done behind the scenes (in this case, in a bank's processing center), it is performed on customer surrogates—reports, databases, and invoices. We can thus design it according to the same principles we would use in designing a factory—to maximize the amount of items processed during the production day.

There can be tremendous diversity of customer influence and, hence, system variability within high-contact service systems. For example, a bank branch offers both simple services such as cash withdrawals that take just a minute or so and complicated services such as loan application preparation that can take in excess of an hour. Moreover, these activities may range from being self-service through an ATM, to coproduction where bank personnel and the customer work as a team to develop the loan application.

Courtesy of Ryan McVay/Getty Images USA, Inc.

exhibit 8.2 Major Differences between High- and Low-Contact Systems in a Bank

DESIGN DECISION	HIGH-CONTACT SYSTEM (A BRANCH OFFICE)	LOW-CONTACT SYSTEM (A CHECK PROCESSING CENTER)
Facility location	Operations must be near the customer.	Operations may be placed near supply, transport, or labor.
Facility layout	The facility should accommodate the customer's physical and psychological needs and expectations.	The facility should focus on production efficiency.
Product design	Environment as well as the physical product define the nature of the service.	The customer is not in the service environment, so the product can be defined by fewer attributes.
Process design	Stages of production process have a direct, immediate effect on the customer.	The customer is not involved in the majority of processing steps.
Scheduling	The customer is in the production schedule and must be accommodated.	The customer is concerned mainly with completion dates.
Production planning	Orders cannot be stored, so smoothing production flow will result in loss of business.	Both backlogging and production smoothing are possible.
Worker skills	The direct workforce constitutes a major part of the service product and so must be able to interact well with the public.	The direct workforce need only have technical skills.
Quality control	Quality standards are often in the eye of the beholder and, thus, are variable.	Quality standards are generally measurable and, thus, fixed.
Time standards	Service time depends on customer needs, so time standards are inherently loose.	Work is performed on customer surrogates (such as forms), so time standards can be tight.
Wage payment	Variable output requires time-based wage systems.	"Fixable" output permits output-based wage systems.
Capacity planning	To avoid lost sales, capacity must be set to match peak demand.	Storable output permits capacity at some average demand level.

DESIGNING SERVICE ORGANIZATIONS

Cross Functional

In designing service organizations we must remember one distinctive characteristic of services: We cannot inventory services. Unlike manufacturing, where we can build up inventory during slack periods for peak demand and thus maintain a relatively stable level of employment and production planning, in services we must (with a few exceptions) meet demand as it arises. Consequently, in services capacity becomes a dominant issue. Think about the many service situations you find yourself in—for example, eating in a restaurant or going to a Saturday night movie. Generally speaking, if the restaurant or the theater is full, you will decide to go someplace else. So, an important design parameter in services is "What capacity should we aim for?" Too much capacity generates excessive costs. Insufficient capacity leads to lost customers. In these situations, of course, we seek the assistance of marketing. This is one reason we have discount airfares, hotel specials on weekends, and so on. This is also a good illustration of why it is difficult to separate the operations management functions from marketing in services.

Waiting line models, which are discussed in Chapter 8A, provide a powerful mathematical tool for analyzing many common service situations. Questions such as how many tellers we should have in a bank or how many telephone lines we need in an Internet service operation can be analyzed with these models. These models can be easily implemented using spreadsheets.

Several major factors distinguish service design and development from typical manufactured product development. First, the process and the product must be developed simultaneously; indeed, in services, the process is the product. (We say this with the general recognition that many manufacturers are using such concepts as concurrent engineering and DFM [design for manufacture] as approaches to more closely link product design and process design.)

Second, although equipment and software that support a service can be protected by patents and copyrights, a service operation itself lacks the legal protection commonly available to goods production. Third, the service package, rather than a definable good, constitutes the major output of the development process. Fourth, many parts of the service package are often defined by the training individuals receive before they become part of the service organization. In particular, in professional service organizations (PSOs) such as law firms and hospitals, prior certification is necessary for hiring. Fifth, many service organizations can change their service offerings virtually overnight. Routine service organizations (RSOs) such as barbershops, retail stores, and restaurants have this flexibility.

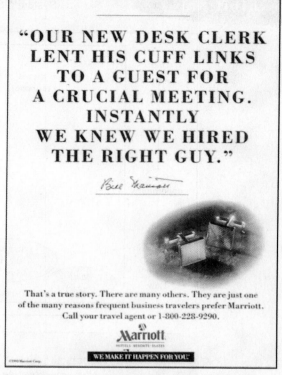

MARRIOTT REWARDS EMPLOYEES WHO PROVIDE SUPERIOR CUSTOMER SERVICE AND GIVES EMPLOYEES DECISION-MAKING AUTHORITY. THE COMPANY MAILS OUT ONE MILLION QUESTIONNAIRES A YEAR TO KEEP INFORMED ABOUT CUSTOMER SATISFACTION AND SERVICE GAPS.

STRUCTURING THE SERVICE ENCOUNTER: SERVICE-SYSTEM DESIGN MATRIX

Service encounters can be configured in a number of different ways. The service-system design matrix in Exhibit 8.3 identifies six common alternatives.

The top of the matrix shows the degree of customer/server contact: the *buffered core*, which is physically separated from the customer; the *permeable system*, which is penetrable by the customer via phone or face-to-face contact; and the *reactive system*, which is both penetrable and reactive to the customer's requirements. The left side of the matrix shows what we believe to be a logical marketing proposition, namely, that the greater the amount of contact, the greater the sales opportunity; the right side shows the impact on production efficiency as the customer exerts more influence on the operation.

The entries within the matrix list the ways in which service can be delivered. At one extreme, service contact is by mail; customers have little interaction with the system. At the other extreme, customers "have it their way" through face-to-face contact. The remaining four entries in the matrix contain varying degrees of interaction.

As one would guess, production efficiency decreases as the customer has more contact (and therefore more influence) on the system. To offset this, the face-to-face contact provides high sales opportunity to sell additional products. Conversely, low contact, such as mail, allows the system to work more efficiently because the customer is unable to significantly affect (or disrupt) the system. However, there is relatively little opportunity for additional product sales.

There can be some shifting in the positioning of each entry. For our first example, consider the "Internet and on-site technology" entry in the matrix. The Internet clearly buffers

exhibit 8.3   Service-System Design Matrix

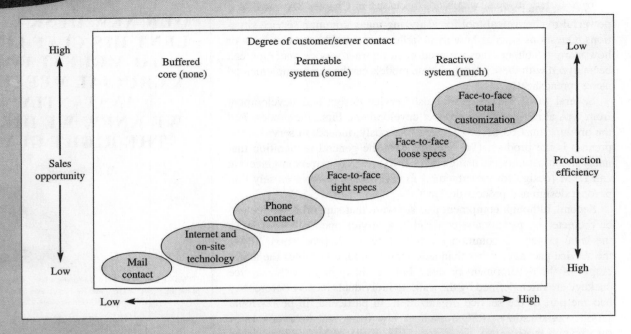

Characteristics of Workers, Operations, and Innovations Relative to the Degree of Customer/Service Contact

Degree of customer/server contact

Low ← ———————————————————————— → High

Worker requirements	Clerical skills	Helping skills	Verbal skills	Procedural skills	Trade skills	Diagnostic skills
Focus of operations	Paper handling	Demand management	Scripting calls	Flow control	Capacity management	Client mix
Technological innovations	Office automation	Routing methods	Computer databases	Electronic aids	Self-serve	Client/worker teams

the company from the customer, but interesting opportunities are available to provide relevant information and services to the customer. Because the website can be programmed to intelligently react to the inputs of the customer, significant opportunities for new sales may be possible. In addition, the system can be made to interface with real employees when the customer needs assistance that goes beyond the programming of the website. The Internet is truly a revolutionary technology when applied to the services that need to be provided by a company.

Another example of shifting in the positioning of an entry can be shown with the "face-to-face tight specs" entry in the matrix. This entry refers to those situations where there is little variation in the service process—neither customer nor server has much discretion in creating the service. Fast-food restaurants and Disneyland come to mind. Face-to-face loose specs refers to situations where the service process is generally understood but there are options in how it will be performed or in the physical goods that are part of it. A full-service restaurant and a car sales agency are examples. Face-to-face total customization refers to service encounters whose specifications must be developed through some interaction between the customer and server. Legal and medical services are of this type, and the degree to which the resources of the system are mustered for the service determines whether the system is reactive, possibly to the point of even being proactive, or merely permeable. Examples would be the mobilization of an advertising firm's resources in preparation for an office visit by a major client or an operating team scrambling to prepare for emergency surgery.

The changes in workers, operations, and types of technical innovations as the degree of customer/service system contact changes are described in the bottom of Exhibit 8.3. For worker requirements, the relationships between mail contact and clerical skills, Internet technology and helping skills, and phone contact and verbal skills are self-evident. Face-to-face tight specs require procedural skills in particular, because the worker must follow the routine in conducting a generally standardized, high-volume process. Face-to-face loose specs frequently call for trade skills (bank teller, draftsperson, maitre d', dental hygienist) to finalize the design for the service. Face-to-face total customization tends to call for diagnostic skills of the professional to ascertain the needs or desires of the client.

STRATEGIC USES OF THE MATRIX

The matrix in Exhibit 8.3 has both operational and strategic uses. The operational uses are reflected in their identification of worker requirements, focus of operations, and innovations previously discussed. The strategic uses include

1. Enabling systematic integration of operations and marketing strategy. Trade-offs become more clear-cut, and, more important, at least some of the major design variables are crystallized for analysis purposes. For example, the matrix indicates that it would make little sense relative to sales for a service firm to invest in high-skilled workers if it plans to operate using tight specs.
2. Clarifying exactly which combination of service delivery the firm is in fact providing. As the company incorporates the delivery options listed on the diagonal, it is becoming diversified in its production process.
3. Permitting comparison with how other firms deliver specific services. This helps to pinpoint a firm's competitive advantage.
4. Indicating evolutionary or life cycle changes that might be in order as the firm grows. Unlike the product–process matrix for manufacturing, however, where natural growth moves in one direction (from workcenter to assembly line as volume increases), evolution of service delivery can move in either direction along the diagonal as a function of a sales–efficiency trade-off.

Cross Functional

SERVICE BLUEPRINTING AND FAIL-SAFING

Just as is the case with manufacturing process design, the standard tool for service process design is the flowchart. Recently, the service gurus have begun calling the flowchart a service blueprint to emphasize the importance of process design. A unique feature of the service blueprint is the distinction made between the high customer contact aspects of the service (the parts of the process that the customer sees) and those activities that the customer does not see. This distinction is made with a "line of visibility" on the flowchart.

Service blueprint

Exhibit 8.4 is a blueprint of a typical automobile service operation. Each activity that makes up a typical service encounter is mapped into the flowchart. To better show the entity that controls the activities, levels are shown in the flowchart. The top level consists of activities that are under the control of the customer. Next are those activities performed by the service manager in handling the customer. The third level is the repair activities performed in the garage; the lowest level is the internal accounting activity.

Service

Basic blueprinting describes the features of the service design but does not provide any direct guidance for how to make the process conform to that design. An approach to this problem is the application of poka-yokes—procedures that block the inevitable mistake from becoming a service defect.[1] Poka-yokes (roughly translated from

Poka-yokes

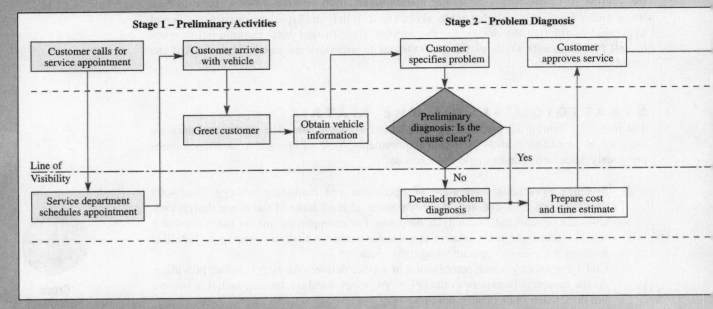

exhibit 8.4   Fail-Safing an Automotive Service Operation

FAILURE: CUSTOMER FORGETS THE NEED FOR SERVICE. POKA-YOKE: SEND AUTOMATIC REMINDERS WITH A 5 PERCENT DISCOUNT.

FAILURE: CUSTOMER CANNOT FIND SERVICE AREA, OR DOES NOT FOLLOW PROPER FLOW. POKA-YOKE: CLEAR AND INFORMATIVE SIGNAGE DIRECTING CUSTOMERS.

FAILURE: CUSTOMER HAS DIFFICULTY COMMUNICATING PROBLEM. POKA-YOKE: JOINT INSPECTION—SERVICE ADVISER REPEATS HIS/HER UNDERSTANDING OF THE PROBLEM FOR CONFIRMATION OR ELABORATION BY THE CUSTOMER.

FAILURE: CUSTOMER DOES NOT UNDERSTAND THE NECESSARY SERVICE. POKA-YOKE: PREPRINTED MATERIAL FOR MOST SERVICES, DETAILING WORK, REASONS, AND POSSIBLY A GRAPHIC REPRESENTATION.

FAILURE: CUSTOMER ARRIVAL UNNOTICED. POKA-YOKE: USE A BELL CHAIN TO SIGNAL ARRIVALS.

FAILURE: CUSTOMERS NOT SERVED IN ORDER OF ARRIVAL. POKA-YOKE: PLACE NUMBERED MARKERS ON CARS AS THEY ARRIVE. FAILURE: VEHICLE INFORMATION INCORRECT AND PROCESS IS TIME-CONSUMING. POKA-YOKE: MAINTAIN CUSTOMER DATABASE AND PRINT FORMS WITH HISTORICAL INFORMATION.

FAILURE: INCORRECT DIAGNOSIS OF THE PROBLEM. POKA-YOKE: HIGH-TECH CHECKLISTS, SUCH AS EXPERT SYSTEMS AND DIAGNOSTIC EQUIPMENT.

FAILURE: INCORRECT ESTIMATE. POKA-YOKE: CHECKLISTS ITEMIZING COSTS BY COMMON REPAIR TYPES.

the Japanese as "avoid mistakes") are common in factories (see Chapter 9, "Quality Management," for examples) and consist of such things as fixtures to ensure that parts can be attached only in the right way, electronic switches that automatically shut off equipment if a mistake is made, kitting of parts prior to assembly to make sure the right quantities are used, and checklists to ensure that the right sequence of steps is followed.

There are many applications of poka-yokes to services as well. These can be classified into warning methods, physical or visual contact methods, and by what we call the *Three T's*—the Task to be done (Was the car fixed right?), the Treatment accorded to the customer (Was the service manager courteous?), and the Tangible or environmental features of the service facility (Was the waiting area clean and comfortable?). Finally (unlike in manufacturing), service poka-yokes often must be applied to fail-safing the actions of the customer as well as the service worker.

Poka-yoke examples include height bars at amusement parks; indented trays used by surgeons to ensure that no instruments are left in the patient; chains to configure waiting lines; take-a-number systems; turnstiles; beepers on ATMs to warn people to take their cards out of the machine; beepers at restaurants to make sure customers do not miss their table calls;

FAILURE: CUSTOMER NOT LOCATED.
POKA-YOKE: ISSUE BEEPERS TO
CUSTOMERS WHO WISH TO LEAVE
FACILITY.

FAILURE: BILL IS ILLEGIBLE.
POKA-YOKE: TOP COPY TO
CUSTOMER, OR PLAIN PAPER BILL.

FAILURE: FEEDBACK NOT OBTAINED.
POKA-YOKE: CUSTOMER SATISFACTION
POSTCARD GIVEN TO CUSTOMER WITH KEYS
TO VEHICLE.

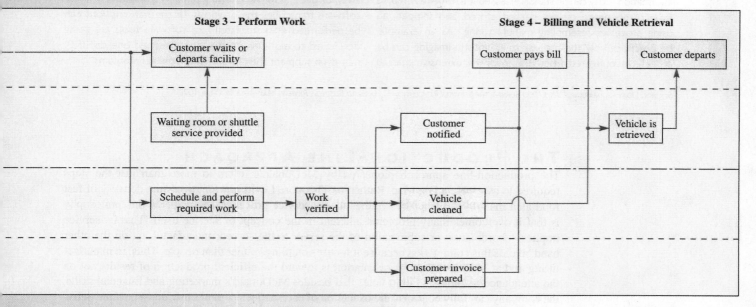

FAILURE: SERVICE SHUTTLE IS INCONVENIENT.
POKA-YOKE: SEATING IN AVAILABLE SHUTTLES IS ALLOCATED
WHEN SCHEDULING APPOINTMENTS. LACK OF FREE SPACE
INDICATES THAT CUSTOMERS NEEDING SHUTTLE SERVICE SHOULD
BE SCHEDULED FOR ANOTHER TIME.
FAILURE: PARTS ARE NOT IN STOCK.
POKA-YOKE: LIMIT SWITCHES ACTIVATE SIGNAL LAMPS WHEN
PART LEVEL FALLS BELOW ORDER POINT.

FAILURE: VEHICLE NOT CLEANED CORRECTLY.
POKA-YOKE: PERSON RETRIEVING VEHICLE INSPECTS,
ORDERS A TOUCH-UP IF NECESSARY, AND REMOVES
FLOOR MAT IN PRESENCE OF CUSTOMER.

FAILURE: VEHICLE TAKES TOO LONG TO ARRIVE.
POKA-YOKE: WHEN CASHIER ENTERS CUSTOMER'S
NAME TO PRINT THE BILL, INFORMATION IS
ELECTRONICALLY SENT TO RUNNERS WHO RETRIEVE
VEHICLE WHILE THE CUSTOMER IS PAYING.

mirrors on telephones to ensure a "smiling voice"; reminder calls for appointments; locks on airline lavatory doors that activate lights inside; small gifts in comment card envelopes to encourage customers to provide feedback about a service; and pictures of what "a clean room" looks like for kindergarten children.

Exhibit 8.4 illustrates how a typical automobile service operation might be fail-safed using poka-yokes. As a final comment, although these procedures cannot guarantee the level of error protection found in the factory, they still can reduce such errors in many service situations.

THREE CONTRASTING SERVICE DESIGNS

Three contrasting approaches to delivering on-site service are the production-line approach, made famous by McDonald's Corporation; the self-service approach, made famous by ATMs and gas stations; and the personal-attention approach, made famous by Nordstrom Department Stores and the Ritz-Carlton Hotel Company.

INFORMATION PRODUCTION LINE

In a recent *Harvard Business Review* article, Uday Karmarkar discusses a different kind of production line made possible by technology. "Forget about the information highway, Moore's Law, and the wonders of wirelessness. Rather think of technology as creating an information assembly line—information today can be standardized, built to order, assembled from components, picked, packed, stored, and shipped, all using processes resembling manufacturing." As an example, he describes how the process of diagnostic imaging can be entirely reconfigured from one involving extensive manual activities with a patient being moved through a hospital to one where "a patient can be scanned at a convenient location by a technologist operating a machine out of a storefront or even a mobile trailer. The images can be sent electronically to the diagnosing radiologist, who may be in a clinic many miles away, or directly to the referring physician. Voice recognition software transcribes the diagnosis, or the transcriptions can be performed offshore. Intelligent software tools are being developed to aid in the actual diagnosis, and one day they may even supplant the radiologist for certain problems."

SOURCE: UDAY KARMARKAR, "WILL YOU SURVIVE THE SERVICES REVOLUTION?" *HARVARD BUSINESS REVIEW*, MAY–JUNE 2004, P. 102.

THE PRODUCTION-LINE APPROACH

The production-line approach pioneered by McDonald's refers to more than just the steps required to assemble a Big Mac. Rather, as Theodore Levitt notes, it treats the delivery of fast food as a manufacturing process rather than a service process.[2] The value of this philosophy is that it overcomes many problems inherent in the concept of service itself. That is, service implies subordination or subjugation of the server to the served; manufacturing, on the other hand, avoids this connotation because it focuses on things rather than people. Thus, in manufacturing and at McDonald's, "the orientation is toward the efficient production of results not on the attendance on others." Levitt notes that besides McDonald's marketing and financial skills, the company carefully controls "the execution of each outlet's central function—the rapid delivery of a uniform, high-quality mix of prepared foods in an environment of obvious cleanliness, order, and cheerful courtesy. The systematic substitution of equipment for people, combined with the carefully planned use and positioning of technology, enables McDonald's to attract and hold patronage in proportions no predecessor or imitator has managed to duplicate."

Levitt cites several aspects of McDonald's operations to illustrate the concepts. Note the extensive use of what we term poka-yokes.

Service

- The McDonald's french fryer allows cooking of the optimum number of french fries at one time.
- A wide-mouthed scoop is used to pick up the precise amount of french fries for each order size. (The employee never touches the product.)
- Storage space is expressly designed for a predetermined mix of prepackaged and premeasured products.
- Cleanliness is pursued by providing ample trash cans in and outside each facility. (Larger outlets have motorized sweepers for the parking area.)
- Hamburgers are wrapped in color-coded paper.
- Through painstaking attention to total design and facilities planning, everything is built integrally into the (McDonald's) machine itself—into the technology of the system. The only choice available to the attendant is to operate it exactly as the designers intended. Using our service-system design matrix (Exhibit 8.3), we would categorize this as a face-to-face tight spec service.

THE SELF-SERVICE APPROACH

In contrast to the production-line approach, C. H. Lovelock and R. F. Young propose that the service process can be enhanced by having the customer take a greater role in the production of the service.[3] Company websites, automatic teller machines, self-service gas stations, salad bars, and e-tickets are approaches that shift the service burden to the consumer. Based on our service-system design matrix, these are great examples of the use of Internet and on-site technology. Many customers like self-service because it puts them in control. For others, this philosophy requires some selling on the part of the service organization to convince customers that it helps them. To this end, Lovelock and Young propose a number of steps, including developing customer trust; promoting the benefits of cost, speed, and convenience; and following up to make sure that the procedures are being effectively used. In essence, this turns customers into "partial employees" who must be trained in what to do and, as noted earlier, must be "fail-safed" in case of mistake.

THE PERSONAL-ATTENTION APPROACH

An interesting contrast in the way personal attention is provided can be seen in Nordstrom Department Stores and the Ritz-Carlton Hotel Company.

At Nordstrom, a rather loose, unstructured process relies on developing a relationship between the individual salesperson and the customer (this is a face-to-face with total customization service). At the Ritz-Carlton, the process is virtually scripted, and the information system rather than the employee keeps track of the guest's (customer's) personal preferences (this is a face-to-face loose spec example). Tom Peters describes Nordstrom's approach here:

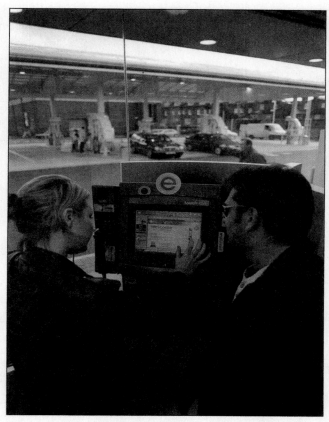

BP AMOCO PROVIDES PAY-AT-THE-PUMP SERVICES AS WELL AS THE NEW "BP ATTENDANT." CUSTOMERS CAN USE TOUCH SCREENS TO LOG ON TO THE INTERNET TO VIEW LOCAL WEATHER REPORTS AND TRAFFIC INFORMATION WHILE FILLING UP.
Courtesy of BP P.L.C.

> After several visits to a store's men's clothing department, a customer's suit still did not fit. He wrote the company president, who sent a tailor to the customer's office with a new suit for fitting. When the alterations were completed, the suit was delivered to the customer—free of charge.
>
> This incident involved the $1.3 billion, Seattle-based Nordstrom, a specialty clothing retailer. Its sales per square foot are about five times that of a typical department store. Who received the customer's letter and urged the extreme (by others' standards) response? Co-chairman John Nordstrom.
>
> The frontline providers of this good service are well paid. Nordstrom's salespersons earn a couple of bucks an hour more than competitors, plus a 6.75 percent commission. Its top salesperson moves over $1 million a year in merchandise. Nordstrom lives for its customers and salespeople. Its only official organization chart puts the customer at the top, followed by sales and sales support people. Next come department managers, then store managers, and the board of directors at the very bottom.
>
> Salespersons religiously carry a "personal book," where they record voluminous information about each of their customers; senior, successful salespeople often have three or four bulging books, which they carry everywhere, according to Betsy Sanders, the vice president who orchestrated the firm's wildly successful penetration of the tough southern California market. "My objective is to get one new personal customer a day," says a budding Nordstrom star. The system helps him do just that. He has a virtually unlimited budget to send cards, flowers, and thank-you notes to customers. He also is encouraged to shepherd his customer to any department in the store to assist in a successful shopping trip.
>
> He also is abetted by what may be the most liberal returns policy in this or any other business: Return *anything,* no questions asked. Sanders says that "trusting customers," or "our bosses" as she repeatedly calls them, is

exhibit 8.5   The Ritz-Carlton Hotel Company (Three Steps of Service)

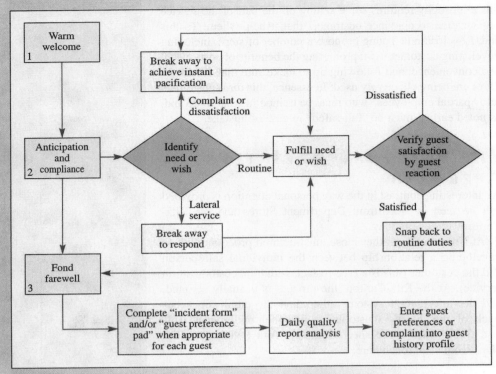

SOURCE: RITZ-CARLTON MALCOLM BALDRIGE NATIONAL QUALITY AWARD APPLICATION SUMMARY, 1993, P. 11.

vital to the Nordstrom philosophy. President Jim Nordstrom told the *Los Angeles Times,* "I don't care if they roll a Goodyear tire into the store. If they say they paid $200, give them $200 (in cash) for it." Sanders acknowledges that a few customers rip the store off—"rent hose from us," to use a common insider's line. But this is more than offset by goodwill from the 99 percent-plus who benefit from the "No Problem at Nordstrom" logo that the company lives up to with unmatched zeal.

No bureaucracy gets in the way of serving the customer. Policy? Sanders explains to a dumbfounded group of Silicon Valley executives, "I know this drives the lawyers nuts, but our whole 'policy manual' is just one sentence, 'Use your own best judgment at all times.'" One store manager offers a translation: "Don't chew gum. Don't steal from us."[4]

The Ritz-Carlton approach is described in the following excerpts from the company's Baldrige Award Application Summary and discussions with Scott Long of Ritz-Carlton's Huntington Hotel in Pasadena, California. Exhibit 8.5 shows the formalized service procedure (the Three Steps of Service). Exhibit 8.6 displays the information system used to capture data about guests ("The Ritz-Carlton Repeat Guest History Program"). Note that the three steps of service are integrated into the guest history information system.

Systems for the collection and utilization of customer reaction and satisfaction are widely deployed and extensively used throughout the organization. Our efforts are centered on various customer segments and product lines.

Our approach is the use of systems which allow every employee to collect and utilize quality-related data on a daily basis. These systems provide critical, responsive data which include:

(1) On-line guest preference information;

The Ritz-Carlton Repeat Guest History Program (An Aid to Highly Personalized Service Delivery)

exhibit 8.6

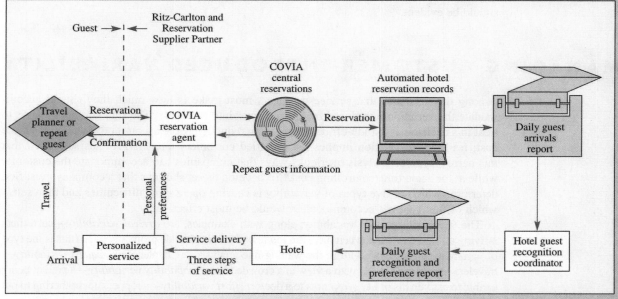

SOURCE: *RITZ-CARLTON MALCOLM BALDRIGE NATIONAL QUALITY AWARD APPLICATION SUMMARY,* 1993, P. 6.

(2) Quantity of error free products and services;

(3) Opportunities for quality improvement.

Our automated property management systems enable the on-line access and utilization of guest preference information at the individual customer level. All employees collect and input this data, and use the data as part of their service delivery with individual guests.

Our quality production reporting system is a method of aggregating hotel level data from nearly two dozen sources into a summary format. It serves as an early warning system and facilitates analysis. The processes

SEVEN CHARACTERISTICS OF A WELL-DESIGNED SERVICE SYSTEM

1 **Each element of the service system is consistent with the operating focus of the firm.** For example, when the focus is on speed of delivery, each step in the process should help foster speed.

2 **It is user-friendly.** This means that the customer can interact with it easily—that is, it has good signage, understandable forms, logical steps in the process, and service workers available to answer questions.

3 **It is robust.** That is, it can cope effectively with variations in demand and resource availability. For example, if the computer goes down, effective backup systems are in place to permit service to continue.

4 **It is structured so that consistent performance by its people and systems is easily maintained.** This means the tasks required of the workers are doable, and the supporting technologies are truly supportive and reliable.

5 **It provides effective links between the back office and the front office so that nothing falls between the cracks.** In football parlance, there should be "no fumbled handoffs."

6 **It manages the evidence of service quality in such a way that customers see the value of the service provided.** Many services do a great job behind the scenes but fail to make this visible to the customer. This is particularly true where a service improvement is made. Unless customers are made aware of the improvement through explicit communication about it, the improved performance is unlikely to gain maximum impact.

7 **It is cost-effective.** There is minimum waste of time and resources in delivering the service. Even if the service outcome is satisfactory, customers are often put off by a service company that appears inefficient.

employees use to identify quality opportunities for improvement are standardized in a textbook, and available throughout our organization.[5]

No matter what approach is taken to design a service, the need for the service characteristics shown in the box titled "Seven Characteristics of a Well-Designed Service System" should be evident.

MANAGING CUSTOMER-INTRODUCED VARIABILITY

Among the decisions that service managers must make is how much they should accommodate the variation introduced by the customer into a process. The standard approach is to treat this decision as a trade-off between cost and quality. More accommodation implies more cost; less accommodation implies less-satisfied customers. Francis Frei has suggested that this narrow type of analysis overlooks ways that companies can accommodate the customer while at the same time controlling cost.[6] To develop these, she says that a company must first determine which of five types of variability is causing operational difficulties and then select which of four types of accommodation would be most effective.

The five basic types of variability, along with examples, are *arrival variability*—customers arriving at a store at times when there are too few clerks to provide prompt service (this is the type of variability that is dealt with in the waiting-line analysis in Chapter 8A); *request variability*—travelers requesting a room with a view at a crowded hotel; *capability variability*—a patient being unable to explain his or her symptoms to a doctor; *effort variability*—shoppers not bothering to put

exhibit 8.7   Strategies for Managing Customer-Introduced Variability

	Classic Accommodation	Low-Cost Accommodation	Classic Reduction	Uncompromised Reduction
Arrival	• Make sure plenty of employees are on hand	• Hire lower-cost labor • Automate tasks • Outsource customer contact • Create self-service options	• Require reservations • Provide off-peak pricing • Limit service availability	• Create complementary demand to smooth arrivals without requiring customers to change their behavior
Request	• Make sure many employees with specialized skills are on hand • Train employees to handle many kinds of requests	• Hire lower-cost specialized labor • Automate tasks • Create self-service options	• Require customers to make reservations for specific types of service • Persuade customers to compromise their requests • Limit service breadth	• Limit service breadth • Target customers on the basis of their requests
Capability	• Make sure employees are on hand who can adapt to customers' varied skill levels • Do work for customers	• Hire lower-cost labor • Create self-service options that require no special skills	• Require customers to increase their level of capability before they use the service	• Target customers on the basis of their capability
Effort	• Make sure employees are on hand who can compensate for customers' lack of effort • Do work for customers	• Hire lower-cost labor • Create self-service options with extensive automation	• Use rewards and penalties to get customers to increase their effort	• Target customers on the basis of motivation • Use a normative approach to get customers to increase their effort
Subjective Preference	• Make sure employees are on hand who can diagnose differences in expectations and adapt accordingly	• Create self-service options that permit customization	• Persuade customers to adjust their expectations to match the value proposition	• Target customers on the basis of their subjective preferences

SOURCE: FRANCIS X. FREI, "BREAKING THE TRADE-OFF BETWEEN EFFICIENCY AND SERVICE," *HARDVARD BUSINESS REVIEW* 84, NO. 11 (NOVEMBER 2006), P. 97.

their shopping carts in a designated area in a supermarket parking lot; and *subjective preference variability*—one bank customer interpreting a teller addressing him by his first name as a sign of warmth, while another customer feels that such informality is unbusinesslike.

The four basic accommodation strategies are *classic accommodation*, which entails, for example, extra employees or additional employee skills to compensate for variations among customers; *low-cost accommodation*, which uses low-cost labor, outsourcing, and self-service to cut the cost of accommodation; *classic reduction*, which requires, for example, customers to engage in more self-service, use reservation systems, or adjust their expectations; and *uncompromised reduction*, which uses knowledge of the customer to develop procedures that enable good service, while minimizing the variation impact on the service delivery system. Exhibit 8.7 illustrates the tactics that are useful in each of the four accommodation categories.

As we can see from Exhibit 8.7, effective management of variability generally requires a company to influence customer behavior. Netflix provides an example of how this was done to deal with the variation in rental times for DVDs. While competitor Blockbuster uses a classic reduction approach of late fees for late returns (which generates tension with the customer), the Netflix subscription model allows customers to keep the DVD for as long as they want. A customer's incentive to return them is being able to get the next movie on his or her request list. This approach thereby accommodates the customer's behavior and at the same time assures revenues.

APPLYING BEHAVIORAL SCIENCE TO SERVICE ENCOUNTERS

Effective management of service encounters requires that managers understand customer perceptions as well as the technical features of service processes. Chase and Dasu[7] suggest applying behavioral concepts to enhance customer perceptions of three aspects of the encounter: *the flow of the service experience* (what's happening), *the flow of time* (how long it seems to take), and *judging encounter performance* (what you thought about it later). Looking at the service encounter from this perspective has led to the following six behaviorally based principles for service encounter design and management.

1. **The front end and the back end of the encounter are not created equal.** It is widely believed that the start and finish of a service or the so-called service bookends are equally weighted in the eyes of the customer. A good deal of research indicates that this is not the case. While it is essential to achieve a base level of satisfactory performance at the beginning so that the customer remains throughout the service, a company is likely to be better off with a relatively weak start and a modest upswing on the end than having a great start and a so-so ending. This ties in with two important findings from behavioral decision theory: the preference for improvement and the dominant effect of the ending in our recollections. The disproportionate influence of the ending gives rise to a corollary principle—that is, end on an up note. Examples of companies that "finish strong": Malaysian Airlines, which lavishes attention on baggage collection and ground transportation, in order to leave the customer with a good feeling; a kitchen cabinet company that ties bright bows on all the installed work, and leaves behind a vase of flowers; cruise lines that end each day with raffles, contests, and shows, end the cruise with the captain's dinner, and pass out keepsakes or bottles of wine upon reaching the home port. All of these strategies are designed to make the final interaction a good one. In a similar vein, relative to unpleasant experiences, researchers have found that prolonging of a colonoscopy by painlessly leaving the colon scope for about a minute after the procedure was completed produced significant improvements in how patients perceived the procedure. (Note here that we are actually extending the duration of discomfort, yet the overall perception is superior to immediate cessation of the procedure!)

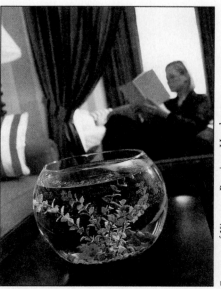

THE HOTEL MONACO IN CHICAGO AIMS TO IMPRESS ITS GUESTS THROUGHOUT THEIR STAY. GUESTS ARE GIVEN THEIR OWN PET GOLDFISH TO MAKE THEM FEEL AT HOME.

2. **Segment the pleasure; combine the pain.** Breaking up may be hard to do, but depending upon the type of encounter, it might be the best thing to do. Events seem longer when they are segmented. This suggests that we want to break pleasant experiences into multiple stages and combine unpleasant ones into a single stage. Thus, it makes sense to, say, reduce the number of stages in a visit to a clinic, even if it extends the time of the visit somewhat, and to provide two 90-second rides at Disneyland rather than one three-minute ride.

3. **Let the customer control the process.** Giving people control over how a process is to be conducted enhances their satisfaction with it. In the medical area, allowing people to choose which arm a blood sample is drawn from reduces the perceived pain of the procedure. For certain repair jobs, allowing people to select a future date they want it to be scheduled may be preferred to doing it right away.

4. **Pay attention to norms and rituals.** Deviations from norms are likely to be overly blamed for failures. This is particularly true for professional services whose processes and outcomes are not clearly ascertainable by the client, and hence adherence to norms is the central basis for evaluation. Consulting firms are expected to make presentations to the boss, even if he or she has little or nothing to do with the problem being studied. At such presentations, all members of the client team are to be lauded for their assistance even if they were less than helpful in accomplishing the work.

5. **People are easier to blame than systems.** When things go wrong, people's gut reaction is to blame the server rather than the system. We want to put a human face on the problem. This is seen especially in complex services where what goes on behind the scenes or in the system is difficult for the customer to untangle. The gate agent is frequently blamed for not allowing a late arrival to get on the plane, even though it is a rule of the airline association that no one can board 15 minutes before departure. (A corollary to this principle is that "a miss is worse than a mile." That is, if someone arrives late for a service, it's better not to say, "too bad, you just missed it.")

6. **Let the punishment fit the crime in service recovery.** How do you make up for an encounter error? Research suggests that the most appropriate recovery action depends upon whether it is a task (outcome) error or a treatment (interpersonal process) error. A botched task calls for material compensation, while poor treatment from a server calls for an apology. Reversing these recovery actions is unlikely to be effective. For example, having a copying job done poorly at a copy store, of course, calls for a quick apology, but more important for quick rework and perhaps some compensation for the customer's inconvenience. On the other hand, if the copying job is done correctly, but the clerk is rude, a sincere apology from the store manager and the clerk is far more likely to result in a satisfied customer than a free coupon or other minor tangible form of compensation.

SERVICE GUARANTEES AS DESIGN DRIVERS

The phrase "Positively, absolutely, overnight" is an example of a service guarantee most of us know by heart. Hiding behind such marketing promises of service satisfaction is a set of actions that must be taken by the operations organization to fulfill these promises.

Service guarantees

Thousands of companies have launched service guarantees as a marketing tool designed to provide peace of mind for customers unsure about trying their service. From an operations perspective, a service guarantee can be used not only as an improvement tool but also at the design stage to focus the firm's delivery system squarely on the things it must do well to satisfy the customer.

Even professional service firms such as Rath and Strong Consulting have service guarantees. (Theirs allows the client to choose from a menu of payouts if they do not—for example—cut lead time by x percent. Menu options include refunds and no charge for overtime work to get the job done.)

The elements of a good service guarantee are that it is unconditional (no small print); meaningful to the customer (the payoff fully covers the customer's dissatisfaction); easy to understand and communicate (for employees as well as customers); and painless to invoke (given proactively).[8]

Recent research on service guarantees has provided the following conclusions about them:[9]

1. Any guarantee is better than no guarantee. The most effective guarantees are big deals. They put the company at risk in the eyes of the customer.
2. Involve the customer as well as employees in the design.
3. Avoid complexity or legalistic language. Use big print, not small print.
4. Do not quibble or wriggle when a customer invokes the guarantee.
5. Make it clear that you are happy for customers to invoke the guarantee.

An issue of growing importance in service relates to the ethical and possibly legal responsibility of a company to actually provide the service that is promised. For example, is an airline responsible for transporting a passenger with a guaranteed reservation, even though the flight has been overbooked? Or consider the Internet service provider's responsibility to provide enough telephone lines so that customers do not receive busy signals when they try to connect to the service. These are difficult issues because having excess capacity is expensive. Demand can be nearly impossible to predict with great accuracy, thus making the estimates of needed capacity difficult.

A very powerful tool—waiting line analysis—is available to help better understand the relationships between the factors that drive a service system. These factors include the average number of customers that arrive over a period of time, the average time that it takes to serve each customer, the number of servers, and information about the size of the customer population. Waiting line models have been developed that allow the estimation of expected waiting time and expected resource utilization. This is the topic of Chapter 8A.

CONCLUSION

In this chapter, we have shown how service businesses are in many ways very similar to manufacturing businesses. Likewise is the need for trade-offs in developing a focus. Focus, for example, is important to success, just as it was with the design of manufacturing systems.

The service-system design matrix is in many ways similar to the product–process matrix we used to categorize manufacturing operations. Further, the tools of flow diagrams and capacity analysis are similar as well.

Services are, however, very different compared to manufacturing when we consider the high degree of personalization often required, the speed of delivery needed, the direct customer contact, and the inherent variability of the service encounter. The buffering and scheduling mechanisms that we have available to smooth the demand placed on a manufacturing operation are often not available to the service operation. Services generally require much higher levels of capacity relative to demand. In addition, they place a greater need for flexibility on the part of the workers involved in providing the services.

KEY TERMS

High and low degree of customer contact The physical presence of the customer in the system and the percentage of time the customer must be in the system relative to the total time it takes to perform the service.

Service blueprint The flowchart of a service process, emphasizing what is visible and what is not visible to the customer.

Poka-yokes Procedures that prevent mistakes from becoming defects. They are commonly found in manufacturing but also can be used in service processes.

Service guarantee A promise of service satisfaction backed up by a set of actions that must be taken to fulfill the promise.

REVIEW AND DISCUSSION QUESTIONS

1   Who is the "customer" in a jail? A cemetery? A summer camp for children?

2   How have price and variety competition changed McDonald's basic formula for success?

3   Could a service firm use a production-line approach or self-serve design and still keep a high customer focus (personal attention)? Explain and support your answer with examples.

4   Why should a manager of a bank home office be evaluated differently than a manager of a bank branch?

5   Identify the high-contact and low-contact operations of the following services:
    a. A dental office.
    b. An airline.
    c. An accounting office.
    d. An automobile agency.
    e. Amazon.com

6   Are there any service businesses that won't be affected by knowledge outsourcing?

7   Relative to the behavioral science discussion, what practical advice do you have for a hotel manager to enhance the ending of a guest's stay in the hotel?

8   List some occupations or sporting events where the ending is a dominant element in evaluating success.

9   Behavioral scientists suggest that we remember events as snapshots, not movies. How would you apply this to designing a service?

10 Some suggest that customer expectation is the key to service success. Give an example from your own experience to support or refute this assertion.

11 Where would you place a drive-in church, a campus food vending machine, and a bar's automatic mixed drink machine on the service-system design matrix?

12 Can a manufacturer have a service guarantee in addition to a product guarantee?

13 Suppose you were the manager of a restaurant and you were told honestly that a couple eating dinner had just seen a mouse. What would you say to them? How would you recover from this service crisis?

14 What strategy do the following organizations seem to use to manage customer-introduced variability?
    a. eBay
    b. Ritz-Carlton Hotels
    c. New airline check-in procedures

PROBLEMS

1   Place the following functions of a department store on the service-system design matrix: mail order (that is, catalog), phone order, hardware, stationery, apparel, cosmetics, customer service (such as taking complaints).

2   Do the same as in the previous problem for a hospital with the following activities and relationships: physician/patient, nurse/patient, billing, medical records, lab tests, admissions, diagnostic tests (such as X-rays).

3   Perform a quick service audit the next time you go shopping at a department store. Evaluate the three T's of service: the Task, the Treatment, and the Tangible features of the service on a scale of 1 (poor), 3 (average), and 5 (excellent). Remember that the tangible features include the environment, layout, and appearance of the store, not the goods you purchased.

4   SYSTEM DESCRIPTION EXERCISE
    The beginning step in studying a productive system is to develop a description of that system. Once a system is described, we can better determine why the system works well or poorly and recommend production-related improvements. Because most of us are familiar with fast-food restaurants, try your hand at describing the production system employed at, say, a McDonald's. In doing so, answer the following questions:

    a. What are the important aspects of the service package?
    b. Which skills and attitudes are needed by the service personnel?
    c. How can customer demand be altered?
    d. Provide a rough-cut blueprint of the delivery system. (It is not necessary to provide execution times. Just diagram the basic flow through the system.) Critique the blueprint. Are there any unnecessary steps or can failure points be eliminated?
    e. Can the customer/provider interface be changed to include more technology? More self-serve?
    f. Which measures are being used to evaluate the service? Which could be used?

5 What are the differences between high and low customer contact service (CCS) businesses, in general, for the dimensions listed below? (Example—Facility Layout: in a high CCS, the facility would be designed to enhance the feelings and comfort of the customer while in a low CCS, the facility would be designed for efficient processing.)

	Low CCS Businesses	High CCS Businesses
Worker skill		
Capacity utilization		
Level of automation		

CASE: PIZZA USA: AN EXERCISE IN TRANSLATING CUSTOMER REQUIREMENTS INTO PROCESS DESIGN REQUIREMENTS

A central theme of contemporary operations management is *focus on the customer*. This is commonly understood to mean that if a company does focus on its customers and if it is able to consistently deliver what the customer wants in a cost-effective manner, then the company should be successful. The hard part is to be able to truly understand what the customer wants. Translating what the customer wants into a deliverable product (meaning some combination of goods and services) and designing a set of processes that will consistently deliver the product in a cost-effective manner are every bit as difficult. Finally, connecting the management of these products and processes to obtain desired business outcomes of the organization is a further challenge.

The following exercise will try to illustrate how difficult all of this can be.

THE SETTING

Pizza USA is a chain of pizza restaurants that currently offers sit-down and take-out service. Many customers have said that they would buy more pizzas from Pizza USA if it offered a delivery service. This exercise is in two parts. In Part I, you play the customer. In Part II, you play the manager at Pizza USA who is responsible for developing the pizza delivery process design requirements.

PART I

To start with, you have to think *like* a customer. This should be easy since you probably have experience with *ordering pizza to be delivered*. Put that experience to work! Make a list of the attributes of *pizza delivery* that are important to you AS A CUSTOMER!

As we said, this should be easy. Right? Or is it? In devising your list, consider the following:

What must a pizza delivery service accomplish so that you are reasonably satisfied? Beyond your being reasonably satisfied, what could a pizza delivery service do that would make it really unique and create a differential advantage? In other words, what could a pizza delivery service do that might cause you to ALWAYS order from one particular service (and, perhaps, to pay more for the privilege)?

As you develop your list, remember that you are considering *only the delivery service* and NOT the pizza itself. Assume that this pizza restaurant can make whatever kind of pizza (and side items) that you want.

PART II

Now, put on your *"Pizza USA manager's hat."* For this part of the exercise, you will be teamed with some other students. First, using the lists of all of your team members, create a master list. Next, try to group the items on your list under a series of major headings; for example, "condition of the delivered pizza" or "quick, on-time delivery" or "order accuracy," and so on. Finally, make a list of the "pizza delivery process design requirements" that your pizza delivery process will have to meet. As you do this, think about measurable standards; in other words, what would you measure in order to ensure that your process is operating effectively and efficiently? Why do you think that these measures will be useful?

Here's an example of how a part of this analysis could go. One customer requirement may be that *the pizza should be hot when it is delivered*. The fact is that as soon as the pizza comes out of the oven, it starts to cool. So, how could you keep the pizza from dropping below some minimum temperature before you hand it to your customer?

ASSIGNMENT

1 Make a list of pizza delivery attributes that are important to you as a customer.
2 Combine your list with the lists of a few other class members and categorize the items under a series of major headings.
3 Make a list of pizza delivery process design requirements. Associate with each requirement a measure that would ensure that the process meets the requirement.
4 Design a process that meets your requirements. Describe it by using a flowchart similar to those shown in Exhibits 8.4, 8.5, and 8.6.

SOURCE: SPECIAL THANKS TO MARK IPPOLITO OF INDIANA UNIVERSITY–PURDUE UNIVERSITY INDIANAPOLIS FOR CONTRIBUTING THIS EXERCISE.

CASE: CONTACT CENTERS SHOULD TAKE A LESSON FROM LOCAL BUSINESSES

There are now three bagel shops in my hometown, two of which are fairly rudimentary in nature: They sell bagels, cream cheese, and coffee. Good bagels, but nothing fancy.

The third store is part of a large, Boston-area chain, and the bagels there are also good. The store often has children's entertainment and has a large seating area with games, free newspapers, and room to spread out and relax. Last, and most important, it has a system that consists of a conveyor belt running across the length of the counter—between the register and the "schmearing" operation—with a huge circular saw in the center. As bagels are ordered, they are tossed onto the conveyor, sliced in half by the saw, and travel at high speed to the end of the conveyor. In other words, store number three isn't just a bagel store; it's entertainment as well.

But that store has lost my business . . . At least 30 percent of the time we order from this store, the order is wrong. And the schmearers at store number three are probably the most stressed cream cheese–appliers ever. The look of terror on their faces from the constant pressure of the sliced bagels whizzing down the conveyor toward them is similar to the look I've seen on the faces of customer service reps in oh-so-many call centers.

Does this happen in your call center? Think about it. The system that makes store number three so very profitable just cost it what I'd argue is a pretty profitable customer.

There's also a hardware store in my hometown (actually, two). In the next town, there is a Home Depot, which I've frequented many a weekend, but not anymore. Our kitchen sink had been leaking on and off for six months, though the leak had been patched. The prospect of standing in line at Home Depot yet again, waiting for service and searching through what seemed like thousands of O-rings to find the right one, was not what I had planned for the weekend.

So I changed my plan and went to my local hardware store. As expected, the prices were at least two times what Home Depot charges, but the service was fabulous, particularly the part when the plumbing department manager suggested a little trick that would prevent the O-ring from failing. I took my expensive O-ring, went home, tried his suggestion, and five minutes later was finished. Not a drop since.

QUESTIONS

1   What lessons are there from these two examples for contact (call) center managers?
2   What are the dilemmas posed in solving these problems in the context of a call center?

SOURCE: MODIFIED FROM CHRIS SELLAND, *CUSTOMER RELATIONSHIP MANAGEMENT* 8, NO. 4 (APRIL 2004), P. 22.

SELECTED BIBLIOGRAPHY

Baker, S., and M. Kripalani. "Software: Will Outsourcing Hurt America's Supremacy?" *BusinessWeek*, March 1, 2004, pp. 85–94.

Bitran, G. R., and J. Hoech. "The Humanization of Service: Respect at the Moment of Truth." *Sloan Management Review*, Winter 1990, pp. 89–96.

Chase, R. B. "The Customer Contact Approach to Services: Theoretical Bases and Practical Extensions." *Operations Research* 21, no. 4 (1981), pp. 698–705.

———. "The Mall Is My Factory: Reflections of a Service Junkie." *Production and Operations Management* 5, no. 4 (Winter 1996), pp. 298–308.

Chase, R. B., and U. Apte. "A History of Research in Service Operations: What's the Big Idea?" *Journal of Operations Management*, March 2007, pp. 375–86.

Chase, R. B., and S. Dasu. "Want to Perfect Your Company's Service? Use Behavioral Science." *Harvard Business Review* 72, no. 6 (May–June 2001), pp. 78–84.

Chase, R. B., and D. M. Stewart. "Make Your Service Fail-Safe." *Sloan Management Review*, Spring 1994, pp. 35–44.

Finsthal, T. W. "My Employees Are My Service Guarantee." *Harvard Business Review*, July–August 1989, pp. 28–33.

Fitzsimmons, J. A., and M. J. Fitzsimmons. *Service Management: Operations, Strategy, and Information Technology*. 5th ed. New York: Irwin/McGraw-Hill, 2006.

Goldhar, J.; Y. Braunstein; and D. Berg. "Services Innovation in the 21st Century: It All Begins with Defining Services vs. Products and Factory vs. Service Operations." University of California–Berkeley, Service Innovation Conference, April 26–28, 2007.

Heskett, J. L.; W. E. Sasser; and L. A. Schlesinger. *The Service Profit Chain: How Leading Companies Link Profit and Growth to Loyalty, Satisfaction, and Value*. New York: Free Press, 1997.

Karmarkar, U. "Will You Survive the Services Revolution?" *Harvard Business Review*, May–June 2004, pp. 99–107.

Metters, R.; K. King-Metters; and M. Pullman. *Successful Service Operations Management*. 2nd ed. Mason OH: Thomson South-Western Publishing, 2005.

Poisant, J. *Creating and Sustaining a Superior Customer Service Organization: A Book about Taking Care of the People Who Take Care of the Customers*. Westport, CT: Quorum Books, 2002.

Sampson, S. E., and C. M. Froehle. "Foundations and Implications of a Proposed Unified Services Theory." *Production and Operations Management*, Summer 2006, pp. 329–42.

Sawhney, M.; S. Balasubramanian; and V. V. Krishnan. "Creating Growth with Services." *MIT Sloan Management Review*, Winter 2004, pp. 34–43.

Schmenner, R. W. *Service Operations Management*. Englewood Cliffs, NJ: Prentice Hall, 1995.

Zemke, R., and C. Bell. *Service Magic: The Art of Amazing Your Customers*. Chicago: Dearborn, 2003.

FOOTNOTES

1 R. B. Chase and D. M. Stewart, "Make Your Service Fail-Safe," *Sloan Management Review*, Spring 1994, pp. 35–44.

2 T. Levitt, "Production-Line Approach to Service," *Harvard Business Review* 50, no. 5 (September–October 1972), pp. 41–52.

3 C. H. Lovelock and R. F. Young, "Look to Customers to Increase Productivity," *Harvard Business Review* 57, no. 2 (March–April 1979), pp. 168–78.

4 T. Peters, *Quality!* (Palo Alto, CA: TPC Communications, 1986), pp. 10–12.

5 *Ritz-Carlton Malcolm Baldrige National Quality Award Application Summary*, 1993, p. 6.

6 Francis X. Frei, "Breaking the Trade-Off between Efficiency and Service," *Harvard Business Review* 84, no. 11 (November 2006), pp. 93–101.

7 Richard B. Chase and Sriram Dasu, "Want to Perfect Your Company's Service? Use Behavioral Science," *Harvard Business Review* 72, no. 6 (May–June 2001), pp. 78–84.

8 C. W. L. Hart, "The Power of Unconditional Service Guarantees," *Harvard Business Review* 56, no. 4 (July–August 1988), p. 55.

9 Gordon H. G. McDougall, T. Levesque, and P. VanderPlaat, "Designing the Service Guarantee: Unconditional or Specific?" *The Journal of Service Marketing* 12, no. 4 (1998), pp. 278–93.

chapter 8A

WAITING LINE ANALYSIS

chapter 8A

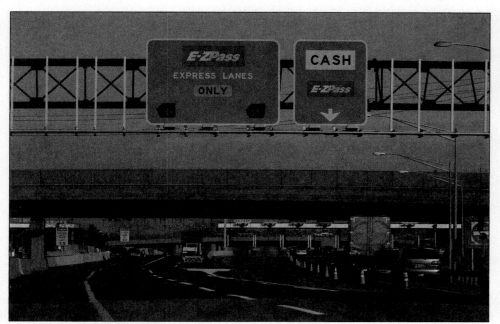

THE E-Z PASS TOLL COLLECTION SYSTEM IN NEW JERSEY USES AN "E-TAG" INSTALLED IN CARS. A RECEIVING ANTENNA AT THE TOLL PLAZA READS THE E-TAG, WHICH CAN BE PREPAID OR LINKED TO A CREDIT CARD. E-Z PASS INCREASES THE TOLL COLLECTION CAPACITY BY 250–300 PERCENT PER LANE.

Courtesy of Affiliated Computer Services.

Understanding waiting lines or queues and learning how to manage them is one of the most important areas in operations management. It is basic to creating schedules, job design, inventory levels, and so on. In our service economy, we wait in line every day, from driving to work to checking out at the supermarket. We also encounter waiting lines at factories—jobs wait in lines to be worked on at different machines, and machines themselves wait their turn to be overhauled. In short, waiting lines are pervasive.

Queues

We will discuss the basic elements of waiting line problems and provide standard steady-state formulas for solving them. These formulas, arrived at through queuing theory, enable planners to analyze service requirements and establish service facilities appropriate to stated conditions. Queuing theory is broad enough to cover such dissimilar delays as those encountered by customers in a shopping mall or aircraft in a holding pattern awaiting landing slots.

ECONOMICS OF THE WAITING LINE PROBLEM

A central problem in many service settings is the management of waiting time. The manager must weigh the added cost of providing more rapid service (more traffic lanes, additional landing strips, more checkout stands) against the inherent cost of waiting.

Frequently, the cost trade-off decision is straightforward. For example, if we find that the total time our employees spend in the line waiting to use a copying machine would otherwise be spent in productive activities, we could compare the cost of installing one additional machine to the value of employee time saved. The decision could then be reduced to dollar terms, and the choice easily made.

Service

On the other hand, suppose that our waiting line problem centers on demand for beds in a hospital. We can compute the cost of additional beds by summing the costs for building construction, additional equipment required, and increased maintenance. But what is on the other side of the scale? Here we are confronted with the problem of trying to place a dollar figure on a patient's need for a hospital bed that is unavailable. While we can estimate lost hospital income, what about the human cost arising from this lack of adequate hospital care?

THE PRACTICAL VIEW OF WAITING LINES

Before we proceed with a technical presentation of waiting line theory, it is useful to look at the intuitive side of the issue to see what it means. Exhibit 8A.1 shows arrivals at a service facility (such as a bank) and service requirements at that facility (such as tellers and loan

exhibit 8A.1   Arrival and Service Profiles

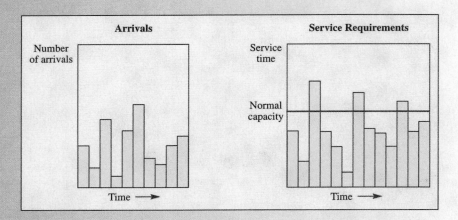

Service

officers). One important variable is the number of arrivals over the hours that the service system is open. From the service delivery viewpoint, customers demand varying amounts of service, often exceeding normal capacity. We can control arrivals in a variety of ways. For example, we can have a short line (such as a drive-in at a fast-food restaurant with only several spaces), we can establish specific hours for specific customers, or we can run specials. For the server, we can affect service time by using faster or slower servers, faster or slower machines, different tooling, different material, different layout, faster setup time, and so on.

The essential point is waiting lines are *not* a fixed condition of a productive system but are to a very large extent within the control of the system management and design. Useful suggestions for managing queues based on research in the banking industry are the following:

- **Segment the customers.**   If a group of customers need something that can be done very quickly, give them a special line so that they do not have to wait for the slower customers.
- **Train your servers to be friendly.**   Greeting the customer by name or providing another form of special attention can go a long way toward overcoming the negative feeling of a long wait. Psychologists suggest that servers be told when to invoke specific friendly actions such as smiling when greeting customers, taking orders, and giving change (for example, in a convenience store). Tests using such specific behavioral actions have shown significant increases in the perceived friendliness of the servers in the eyes of the customer.
- **Inform your customers of what to expect.**   This is especially important when the waiting time will be longer than normal. Tell them why the waiting time is longer than usual and what you are doing to alleviate the wait.
- **Try to divert the customer's attention when waiting.**   Providing music, a video, or some other form of entertainment may help distract the customers from the fact that they are waiting.
- **Encourage customers to come during slack periods.**   Inform customers of times when they usually would not have to wait; also tell them when the peak periods are—this may help smooth the load.

THE QUEUING SYSTEM

Service

Queuing system

The queuing system consists essentially of three major components: (1) the source population and the way customers arrive at the system, (2) the servicing system, and (3) the condition of the customers exiting the system (back to source population or not?), as seen in Exhibit 8A.2. The following sections discuss each of these areas.

Components of a Queuing System

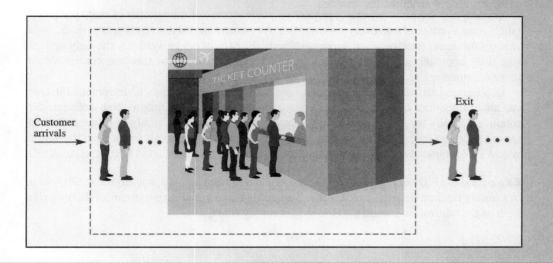

Customer arrivals · · · Exit · · ·

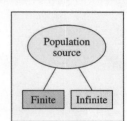

Interactive Operations Management

CUSTOMER ARRIVALS

Arrivals at a service system may be drawn from a *finite* or an *infinite* population. The distinction is important because the analyses are based on different premises and require different equations for their solution.

Population source

Finite Infinite

Finite Population A *finite population* refers to the limited-size customer pool that will use the service and, at times, form a line. The reason this finite classification is important is that when a customer leaves its position as a member for the population (a machine breaking down and requiring service, for example), the size of the user group is reduced by one, which reduces the probability of the next occurrence. Conversely, when a customer is serviced and returns to the user group, the population increases and the probability of a user requiring service also increases. This finite class of problems requires a separate set of formulas from that of the infinite population case.

As an example, consider a group of six machines maintained by one repairperson. When one machine breaks down, the source population is reduced to five, and the chance of one of the remaining five breaking down and needing repair is certainly less than when six machines were operating. If two machines are down with only four operating, the probability of another breakdown is again changed. Conversely, when a machine is repaired and returned to service, the machine population increases, thus raising the probability of the next breakdown.

Infinite Population An *infinite population* is large enough in relation to the service system so that the population size caused by subtractions or additions to the population (a customer needing service or a serviced customer returning to the population) does not significantly affect the system probabilities. If, in the preceding finite explanation, there were 100 machines instead of 6, then if one or two machines broke down, the probabilities for the next breakdowns would not be very different and the assumption could be made without a great deal of error that the population (for all practical purposes) was infinite. Nor would the formulas for "infinite" queuing problems cause much error if applied to a physician with 1,000 patients or a department store with 10,000 customers.

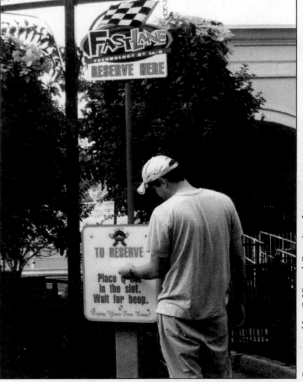

SIX FLAGS' FAST LANE USERS PURCHASE LOW-TECH, GO-TO-THE-HEAD-OF-THE-LINE PAPER TICKETS OR A HIGH-TECH, ELECTRONIC "Q-BOT" DEVICE. Q-BOTS ARE BEEPERS THAT SERVE AS VIRTUAL PLACEHOLDERS. THEY VIBRATE AND FLASH A TEXT MESSAGE WHEN IT'S TIME TO REPORT TO THE RIDE.

Courtesy of Lo-Q Virtual Queuing, Inc.

DISTRIBUTION OF ARRIVALS

When describing a waiting system, we need to define the manner in which customers or the waiting units are arranged for service.

Arrival rate

Waiting line formulas generally require an *arrival rate*, or the number of units per period (such as an average of one every six minutes). A *constant* arrival distribution is periodic, with exactly the same time between successive arrivals. In productive systems, the only arrivals that truly approach a constant interval period are those subject to machine control. Much more common are *variable* (random) arrival distributions.

In observing arrivals at a service facility, we can look at them from two viewpoints: First, we can analyze the time between successive arrivals to see if the times follow some statistical distribution. Usually we assume that the time between arrivals is exponentially distributed. Second, we can set some time length (T) and try to determine how many arrivals might enter the system within T. We typically assume that the number of arrivals per time unit is Poisson distributed.

Exponential distribution

Exponential Distribution   In the first case, when arrivals at a service facility occur in a purely random fashion, a plot of the interarrival times yields an *exponential distribution* such as that shown in Exhibit 8A.3. The probability function is

[8A.1] $$f(t) = \lambda e^{-\lambda t}$$

where λ is the mean number of arrivals per time period.

The cumulative area beneath the curve in Exhibit 8A.3 is the summation of equation (8A.1) over its positive range, which is $e^{-\lambda t}$. This integral allows us to compute the probabilities of arrivals within a specified time. For example, for the case of single arrivals to a waiting line ($\lambda = 1$), the following table can be derived either by solving $e^{-\lambda t}$ or by using Appendix D. Column 2 shows the probability that it will be more than t minutes until the next arrival. Column 3 shows the probability of the next arrival within t minutes (computed as 1 minus column 2)

(1)	(2)	(3)
	PROBABILITY THAT THE NEXT ARRIVAL WILL OCCUR IN	PROBABILITY THAT THE NEXT ARRIVAL WILL OCCUR IN
t (MINUTES)	t MINUTES OR MORE (FROM APPENDIX D OR SOLVING e^{-t})	t MINUTES OR LESS [1− COLUMN (2)]
0	1.00	0
0.5	0.61	0.39
1.0	0.37	0.63
1.5	0.22	0.78
2.0	0.14	0.86

exhibit 8A.3   Exponential Distribution

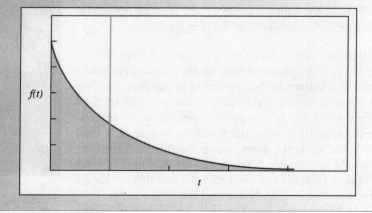

Poisson Distribution for $\lambda T = 3$

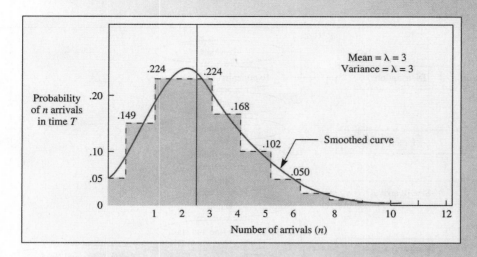

Poisson Distribution In the second case, where one is interested in the number of arrivals during some time period T, the distribution appears as in Exhibit 8A.4 and is obtained by finding the probability of exactly n arrivals during T. If the arrival process is random, the distribution is the Poisson, and the formula is

Poisson distribution

[8A.2]
$$P_T(n) = \frac{(\lambda T)^n e^{-\lambda T}}{n!}$$

Equation (8A.2) shows the probability of exactly n arrivals in time T.[1] For example, if the mean arrival rate of units into a system is three per minute ($\lambda = 3$) and we want to find the probability that exactly five units will arrive within a one-minute period ($n = 5$, $T = 1$), we have

$$P_1(5) = \frac{(3 \times 1)^5 e^{-3 \times 1}}{5!} = \frac{3^5 e^{-3}}{120} = 2.025 e^{-3} = 0.101$$

That is, there is a 10.1 percent chance that there will be five arrivals in any one-minute interval.

Although often shown as a smoothed curve, as in Exhibit 8A.4, the Poisson is a discrete distribution. (The curve becomes smoother as n becomes large.) The distribution is discrete because n refers, in our example, to the number of arrivals in a system, and this must be an integer. (For example, there cannot be 1.5 arrivals.)

Also note that the exponential and Poisson distributions can be derived from one another. The mean and variance of the Poisson are equal and denoted by λ. The mean of the exponential is $1/\lambda$, and its variance is $1/\lambda^2$. (Remember that the time between arrivals is exponentially distributed and the number of arrivals per unit of time is Poisson distributed.)

Other arrival characteristics include arrival patterns, size of arrival units, and degree of patience. (See Exhibit 8A.5.)

Arrival patterns. The arrivals at a system are far more controllable than is generally recognized. Barbers may decrease their Saturday arrival rate (and supposedly shift it to other days of the week) by charging an extra $1 for adult haircuts or charging adult prices for children's haircuts. Department stores run sales during the off-season or hold one-day-only sales in part for purposes of control. Airlines offer excursion and off-season rates for similar reasons. The simplest of all arrival-control devices is the posting of business hours.

Customer Arrivals in Queues

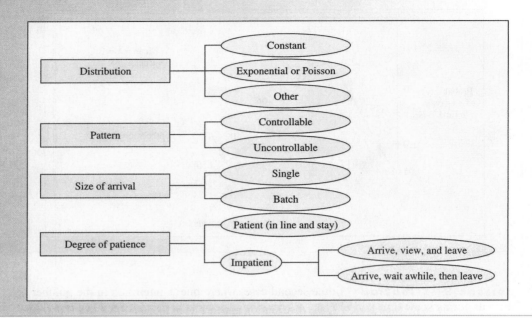

Some service demands are clearly uncontrollable, such as emergency medical demands on a city's hospital facilities. But even in these situations, arrivals at emergency rooms in specific hospitals are controllable to some extent by, say, keeping ambulance drivers in the service region informed of the status of their respective host hospitals.

Size of arrival units.   A *single arrival* may be thought of as one unit. (A unit is the smallest number handled.) A single arrival on the floor of the New York Stock Exchange (NYSE) is 100 shares of stock; a single arrival at an egg-processing plant might be a dozen eggs or a flat of 2½ dozen; a single arrival at a restaurant is a single person.

A *batch arrival* is some multiple of the unit, such as a block of 1,000 shares on the NYSE, a case of eggs at the processing plant, or a party of five at a restaurant.

Degree of patience.   A *patient* arrival is one who waits as long as necessary until the service facility is ready to serve him or her. (Even if arrivals grumble and behave impatiently, the fact that they wait is sufficient to label them as patient arrivals for purposes of waiting line theory.)

There are two classes of *impatient* arrivals. Members of the first class arrive, survey both the service facility and the length of the line, and then decide to leave. Those in the second class arrive, view the situation, join the waiting line, and then, after some period of time, depart. The behavior of the first type is termed *balking,* while the second is termed *reneging.*

THE QUEUING SYSTEM: FACTORS

The queuing system consists primarily of the waiting line(s) and the available number of servers. Here we discuss issues pertaining to waiting line characteristics and management, line structure, and service rate. Factors to consider with waiting lines include the line length, number of lines, and queue discipline.

Length.   In a practical sense, an infinite line is simply one that is very long in terms of the capacity of the service system. Examples of *infinite potential length* are a line of vehicles backed up for miles at a bridge crossing and customers who must form a line around the block as they wait to purchase tickets at a theater.

Gas stations, loading docks, and parking lots have *limited line capacity* caused by legal restrictions or physical space characteristics. This complicates the waiting line problem not only in service system utilization and waiting line computations but also in the shape of the actual arrival distribution. The arrival denied entry into the line because of lack of space may rejoin the population for a later try or may seek service elsewhere. Either action makes an obvious difference in the finite population case.

Number of lines.   A single line or single file is, of course, one line only. The term *multiple lines* refers to the single lines that form in front of two or more servers or to single lines that converge at some central redistribution point. The disadvantage of multiple lines in a busy facility is that arrivals often shift lines if several previous services have been of short duration or if those customers currently in other lines appear to require a short service time.

Queue discipline.   A queue discipline is a priority rule or set of rules for determining the order of service to customers in a waiting line. The rules selected can have a dramatic effect on the system's overall performance. The number of customers in line, the average waiting time, the range of variability in waiting time, and the efficiency of the service facility are just a few of the factors affected by the choice of priority rules.

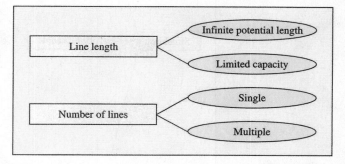

Probably the most common priority rule is first come, first served (FCFS). This rule states that customers in line are served on the basis of their chronological arrival; no other characteristics have any bearing on the selection process. This is popularly accepted as the fairest rule, although in practice it discriminates against the arrival requiring a short service time.

Reservations first, emergencies first, highest-profit customer first, largest orders first, best customers first, longest waiting time in line, and soonest promised date are other examples of priority rules. There are two major practical problems in using any rule: One is ensuring that customers know and follow the rule. The other is ensuring that a system exists to enable employees to manage the line (such as take-a-number systems).

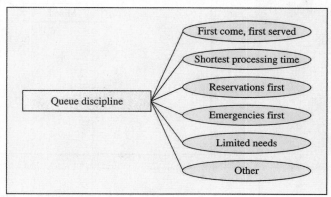

Service Time Distribution   Another important feature of the waiting structure is the time the customer or unit spends with the server once the service has started. Waiting line formulas generally specify service rate as the capacity of the server in number of units per time period (such as 12 completions per hour) and *not* as service time, which might average five minutes each. A constant service time rule states that each service takes exactly the same time. As in constant arrivals, this characteristic is generally limited to machine-controlled operations.

Service rate

When service times are random, they can be approximated by the exponential distribution. When using the exponential distribution as an approximation of the service times, we will refer to μ as the average number of units or customers that can be served per time period.

Line Structures   As Exhibit 8A.6 shows, the flow of items to be serviced may go through a single line, multiple lines, or some mixture of the two. The choice of format depends partly on the volume of customers served and partly on the restrictions imposed by sequential requirements governing the order in which service must be performed.

1. **Single channel, single phase.**   This is the simplest type of waiting line structure, and straightforward formulas are available to solve the problem for standard distribution patterns of arrival and service. When the distributions are nonstandard, the problem is easily solved by computer simulation. A typical example of a single-channel, single-phase situation is the one-person barbershop.

Line Structures

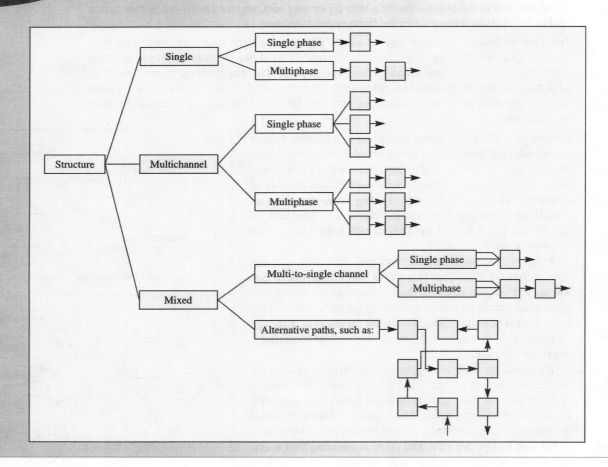

2. **Single channel, multiphase.** A car wash is an illustration because a series of services (vacuuming, wetting, washing, rinsing, drying, window cleaning, and parking) is performed in a fairly uniform sequence. A critical factor in the single-channel case with service in series is the amount of buildup of items allowed in front of each service, which in turn constitutes separate waiting lines.

3. **Multichannel, single phase.** Tellers' windows in a bank and checkout counters in high-volume department stores exemplify this type of structure. The difficulty with this format is that the uneven service time given each customer results in unequal speed or flow among the lines. This results in some customers being served before others who arrived earlier, as well as in some degree of line shifting. Varying this structure to ensure the servicing of arrivals in chronological order would require forming a single line, from which, as a server becomes available, the next customer in the queue is assigned.

 The major problem of this structure is that it requires rigid control of the line to maintain order and to direct customers to available servers. In some instances, assigning numbers to customers in order of their arrival helps alleviate this problem.

4. **Multichannel, multiphase.** This case is similar to the preceding one except that two or more services are performed in sequence. The admission of patients in a hospital follows this pattern because a specific sequence of steps is usually followed: initial contact at the admissions desk, filling out forms, making identification tags, obtaining a room assignment, escorting the patient to the room, and so forth. Because several servers are usually available for this procedure, more than one patient at a time may be processed.

5. **Mixed.** Under this general heading we consider two subcategories: (1) multiple-to-single channel structures and (2) alternative path structures. Under (1), we find either lines

that merge into one for single-phase service, as at a bridge crossing where two lanes merge into one, or lines that merge into one for multiphase service, such as subassembly lines feeding into a main line. Under (2), we encounter two structures that differ in directional flow requirements. The first is similar to the multichannel–multiphase case, except that (a) there may be switching from one channel to the next after the first service has been rendered and (b) the number of channels and phases may vary—again—after performance of the first service.

EXITING THE QUEUING SYSTEM

Once a customer is served, two exit fates are possible: (1) The customer may return to the source population and immediately become a competing candidate for service again or (2) there may be a low probability of reservice. The first case can be illustrated by a machine that has been routinely repaired and returned to duty but may break down again; the second can be illustrated by a machine that has been overhauled or modified and has a low probability of reservice over the near future. In a lighter vein, we might refer to the first as the "recurring-common-cold case" and to the second as the "appendectomy-only-once case."

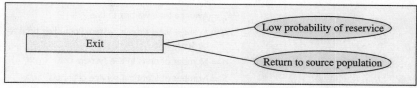

It should be apparent that when the population source is finite, any change in the service performed on customers who return to the population modifies the arrival rate at the service facility. This, of course, alters the characteristics of the waiting line under study and necessitates reanalysis of the problem.

WAITING LINE MODELS

In this section we present four sample waiting line problems followed by their solutions. Each has a slightly different structure (see Exhibit 8A.7) and solution equation (see Exhibit 8A.8). There are more types of models than these four, but the formulas and solutions become quite complicated, and those problems are generally solved using computer simulation. Also, in using these formulas, keep in mind that they are steady-state formulas derived on the assumption that the process under study is ongoing. Thus, they may provide inaccurate results when applied to processes where the arrival rates and/or service rates change over time. The Excel Spreadsheet QueueModel.xls, developed by John McClain of Cornell University and included on the DVD-ROM, can be used to solve these problems.

Excel: Queue

Here is a quick preview of our four problems to illustrate each of the four waiting line models in Exhibits 8A.7 and 8A.8.

Properties of Some Specific Waiting Line Models

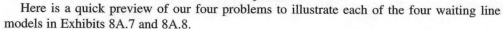

MODEL	LAYOUT	SERVICE PHASE	SOURCE POPULATION	ARRIVAL PATTERN	QUEUE DISCIPLINE	SERVICE PATTERN	PERMISSIBLE QUEUE LENGTH	TYPICAL EXAMPLE
1	Single channel	Single	Infinite	Poisson	FCFS	Exponential	Unlimited	Drive-in teller at bank; one-lane toll bridge
2	Single channel	Single	Infinite	Poisson	FCFS	Constant	Unlimited	Roller coaster rides in amusement park
3	Multichannel	Single	Infinite	Poisson	FCFS	Exponential	Unlimited	Parts counter in auto agency
4	Single channel	Single	Finite	Poisson	FCFS	Exponential	Unlimited	Machine breakdown and repair in a factory

exhibit 8A.8

Notations for Equations

INFINITE QUEUING NOTATION: MODELS 1–3	FINITE QUEUING NOTATION: MODEL 4
λ = Arrival rate	D = Probability that an arrival must wait in line
μ = Service rate	F = Efficiency factor, a measure of the effect of having to wait in line
$\frac{1}{\mu}$ = Average service time	H = Average number of units being serviced
$\frac{1}{\lambda}$ = Average time between arrivals	J = Population source less those in queuing system $(N - n)$
ρ = Ratio of total arrival rate to service rate for a single server $\left(\frac{\lambda}{\mu}\right)^*$	L = Average number of units in line
L_q = Average number waiting in line	S = Number of service channels
L_s = Average number in system (including any being served)	n = Average number of units in queuing system (including the one being served)
W_q = Average time waiting in line	N = Number of units in population source
W_s = Average total time in system (including time to be served)	P_n = Probability of exactly n units in queuing system
	T = Average time to perform the service
n = Number of units in the system	U = Average time between customer service requirements
S = Number of identical service channels	
P_n = Probability of exactly n units in system	W = Average waiting time in line
P_w = Probability of waiting in line	X = Service factor, or proportion of service time required

*For single-server queues, this is equivalent to utilization.

Equations for Solving Four Model Problems

Model 1
$$L_q = \frac{\lambda^2}{\mu(\mu - \lambda)} \qquad W_q = \frac{L_q}{\lambda} \qquad P_n = \left(1 - \frac{\lambda}{\mu}\right)\left(\frac{\lambda}{\mu}\right)^n \qquad P_o = \left(1 - \frac{\lambda}{\mu}\right)$$
$$L_s = \frac{\lambda}{\mu - \lambda} \qquad W_s = \frac{L_s}{\lambda} \qquad \rho = \frac{\lambda}{\mu}$$
[8A.3]

Model 2
$$L_q = \frac{\lambda^2}{2\mu(\mu - \lambda)} \qquad W_q = \frac{L_q}{\lambda}$$
$$L_s = L_q + \frac{\lambda}{\mu} \qquad W_s = \frac{L_s}{\lambda}$$
[8A.4]

(Exhibit 8A.9 provides the value of L_q given λ/μ and the number of servers S.)

Model 3
$$L_s = L_q + \lambda/\mu \qquad W_s = L_s/\lambda$$
$$W_q = L_q/\lambda \qquad P_w = L_q\left(\frac{S\mu}{\lambda} - 1\right)$$
[8A.5]

Model 4 is a finite queuing situation that is most easily solved by using finite tables. These tables, in turn, require the manipulation of specific terms.

Model 4
$$X = \frac{T}{T + U} \qquad H = FNX \qquad L = N(1 - F) \qquad n = L + H$$
$$P_n = \frac{N!}{(N - n)!} X^n P_o \qquad\qquad J = NF(1 - X)$$
$$W = \frac{L(T + U)}{N - L} = \frac{LT}{H} \qquad F = \frac{T + U}{T + U + W}$$
[8A.6]

Problem 1: Customers in line. A bank wants to know how many customers are waiting for a drive-in teller, how long they have to wait, the utilization of the teller, and what the service rate would have to be so that 95 percent of the time there will not be more than three cars in the system at any time.

Problem 2: Equipment selection.   A franchise for Robot Car Wash must decide which equipment to purchase out of a choice of three. Larger units cost more but wash cars faster. To make the decision, costs are related to revenue.

Problem 3: Determining the number of servers.   An auto agency parts department must decide how many clerks to employ at the counter. More clerks cost more money, but there is a savings because mechanics wait less time.

Problem 4: Finite population source.   Whereas the previous models assume a large population, finite queuing employs a separate set of equations for those cases where the calling customer population is small. In this last problem, mechanics must service four weaving machines to keep them operating. Based on the costs associated with machines being idle and the costs of mechanics to service them, the problem is to decide how many mechanics to use.

EXAMPLE 8A.1: Customers in Line

Western National Bank is considering opening a drive-through window for customer service. Management estimates that customers will arrive at the rate of 15 per hour. The teller who will staff the window can service customers at the rate of one every three minutes.

Part 1   Assuming Poisson arrivals and exponential service, find

1. Utilization of the teller.
2. Average number in the waiting line.
3. Average number in the system.
4. Average waiting time in line.
5. Average waiting time in the system, including service.

Service

SOLUTION—Part 1

1. The average utilization of the teller is (using Model 1)

$$\rho = \frac{\lambda}{\mu} = \frac{15}{20} = 75 \text{ percent}$$

2. The average number in the waiting line is

$$L_q = \frac{\lambda^2}{\mu(\mu - \lambda)} = \frac{(15)^2}{20(20 - 15)} = 2.25 \text{ customers}$$

3. The average number in the system is

$$L_s = \frac{\lambda}{\mu - \lambda} = \frac{15}{20 - 15} = 3 \text{ customers}$$

4. Average waiting time in line is

$$W_q = \frac{L_q}{\lambda} = \frac{2.25}{15} = 0.15 \text{ hour, or 9 minutes}$$

5. Average waiting time in the system is

$$W_s = \frac{L_s}{\lambda} = \frac{3}{15} = 0.2 \text{ hour, or 12 minutes}$$

Excel:
Queue.xls

EXAMPLE 8A.1: (Continued)

Part 2   Because of limited space availability and a desire to provide an acceptable level of service, the bank manager would like to ensure, with 95 percent confidence, that no more than three cars will be in the system at any time. What is the present level of service for the three-car limit? What level of teller use must be attained and what must be the service rate of the teller to ensure the 95 percent level of service?

SOLUTION—Part 2

The present level of service for three or fewer cars is the probability that there are 0, 1, 2, or 3 cars in the system. From Model 1, Exhibit 8A.8,

$$P_n = \left(1 - \frac{\lambda}{\mu}\right)\left(\frac{\lambda}{\mu}\right)^n$$

at $n = 0$, $P_0 = (1 - 15/20)$ $(15/20)^0 = 0.250$

at $n = 1$, $P_1 = (1/4)$ $(15/20)^1 = 0.188$

at $n = 2$, $P_2 = (1/4)$ $(15/20)^2 = 0.141$

at $n = 3$, $P_3 = (1/4)$ $(15/20)^3 = \underline{0.105}$

0.684   or   68.5 percent

The probability of having more than three cars in the system is 1.0 minus the probability of three or fewer cars $(1.0 - 0.685 = 31.5$ percent).

For a 95 percent service level of three or fewer cars, this states that $P_0 + P_1 + P_2 + P_3 = 95$ percent.

$$0.95 = \left(1 - \frac{\lambda}{\mu}\right)\left(\frac{\lambda}{\mu}\right)^0 + \left(1 - \frac{\lambda}{\mu}\right)\left(\frac{\lambda}{\mu}\right)^1 + \left(1 - \frac{\lambda}{\mu}\right)\left(\frac{\lambda}{\mu}\right)^2 + \left(1 - \frac{\lambda}{\mu}\right)\left(\frac{\lambda}{\mu}\right)^3$$

$$0.95 = \left(1 - \frac{\lambda}{\mu}\right)\left[1 + \frac{\lambda}{\mu} + \left(\frac{\lambda}{\mu}\right)^2 + \left(\frac{\lambda}{\mu}\right)^3\right]$$

We can solve this by trial and error for values of λ/μ. If $\lambda/\mu = 0.50$,

$$0.95 \overset{?}{=} 0.5(1 + 0.5 + 0.25 + 0.125)$$

$$0.95 \neq 0.9375$$

With $\lambda/\mu = 0.45$,

$$0.95 \overset{?}{=} (1 - 0.45)(1 + 0.45 + 0.203 + 0.091)$$

$$0.95 \neq 0.96$$

With $\lambda/\mu = 0.47$,

$$0.95 \overset{?}{=} (1 - 0.47)(1 + 0.47 + 0.221 + 0.104) = 0.95135$$

$$0.95 \approx 0.95135$$

Therefore, with the utilization $\rho = \lambda/\mu$ of 47 percent, the probability of three or fewer cars in the system is 95 percent.

To find the rate of service required to attain this 95 percent service level, we simply solve the equation $\lambda/\mu = 0.47$, where $\lambda =$ number of arrivals per hour. This gives $\mu = 32$ per hour. That is, the teller must serve approximately 32 people per hour (a 60 percent increase over the original 20-per-hour capability) for 95 percent confidence that not more than three cars will be in the system. Perhaps service may be speeded up by modifying the method of service, adding another teller, or limiting the types of transactions available at the drive-through window. Note that with the condition of 95 percent confidence that three or fewer cars will be in the system, the teller will be idle 53 percent of the time. ●

EXAMPLE 8A.2: Equipment Selection

The Robot Company franchises combination gas and car wash stations throughout the United States. Robot gives a free car wash for a gasoline fill-up or, for a wash alone, charges $0.50. Past experience shows that the number of customers that have car washes following fill-ups is about the same as for a wash alone. The average profit on a gasoline fill-up is about $0.70, and the cost of the car wash to Robot is $0.10. Robot stays open 14 hours per day.

Robot has three power units and drive assemblies, and a franchisee must select the unit preferred. Unit I can wash cars at the rate of one every five minutes and is leased for $12 per day. Unit II, a larger unit, can wash cars at the rate of one every four minutes but costs $16 per day. Unit III, the largest, costs $22 per day and can wash a car in three minutes.

The franchisee estimates that customers will not wait in line more than five minutes for a car wash. A longer time will cause Robot to lose the gasoline sales as well as the car wash sale.

If the estimate of customer arrivals resulting in washes is 10 per hour, which wash unit should be selected?

Service

**Excel:
Queue.xls**

SOLUTION

Using unit I, calculate the average waiting time of customers in the wash line (μ for unit I $= 12$ per hour). From the Model 2 equations (Exhibit 8A.8),

$$L_q = \frac{\lambda^2}{2\mu(\mu - \lambda)} = \frac{10^2}{2(12)(12 - 10)} = 2.08333$$

$$W_q = \frac{L_q}{\lambda} = \frac{2.08333}{10} = 0.208 \text{ hour, or } 12\tfrac{1}{2} \text{ minutes}$$

For unit II at 15 per hour,

$$L_q = \frac{10^2}{2(15)(15 - 10)} = 0.667$$

$$W_q = \frac{0.667}{10} = 0.0667 \text{ hour, or 4 minutes}$$

If waiting time is the only criterion, unit II should be purchased. But before we make the final decision, we must look at the profit differential between both units.

With unit I, some customers would balk and renege because of the $12\tfrac{1}{2}$-minute wait. And, although this greatly complicates the mathematical analysis, we can gain some estimate of lost sales with unit I by increasing $W_q = 5$ minutes or $\frac{1}{12}$ hour (the average length of time customers will wait) and solving for λ. This would be the effective arrival rate of customers:

$$W_q = \frac{L_q}{\lambda} = \left(\frac{\lambda^2/2\mu(\mu - \lambda)}{\lambda} \right)$$

$$W_q = \frac{\lambda}{2\mu(\mu - \lambda)}$$

$$\lambda = \frac{2W_q\mu^2}{1 + 2W_q\mu} = \frac{2\left(\frac{1}{12}\right)(12)^2}{1 + 2\left(\frac{1}{12}\right)(12)} = 8 \text{ per hour}$$

Therefore, because the original estimate of λ was 10 per hour, an estimated 2 customers per hour will be lost. Lost profit of 2 customers per hour $\times$ 14 hours $\times \frac{1}{2}$($0.70 fill-up profit $+$ $0.40 wash profit) $=$ $15.40 per day.

Because the additional cost of unit II over unit I is only $4 per day, the loss of $15.40 profit obviously warrants installing unit II.

The original five-minute maximum wait constraint is satisfied by unit II. Therefore, unit III is not considered unless the arrival rate is expected to increase. ●

Service

**Excel:
Queue.xls**

EXAMPLE 8A.3: Determining the Number of Servers

In the service department of the Glenn-Mark Auto Agency, mechanics requiring parts for auto repair or service present their request forms at the parts department counter. The parts clerk fills a request while the mechanic waits. Mechanics arrive in a random (Poisson) fashion at the rate of 40 per hour, and a clerk can fill requests at the rate of 20 per hour (exponential). If the cost for a parts clerk is $6 per hour and the cost for a mechanic is $12 per hour, determine the optimum number of clerks to staff the counter. (Because of the high arrival rate, an infinite source may be assumed.)

SOLUTION

First, assume that three clerks will be used because having only one or two clerks would create infinitely long lines (since $\lambda = 40$ and $\mu = 20$). The equations for Model 3 from Exhibit 8A.8 will be used here. But first we need to obtain the average number in line using the table of Exhibit 8A.9. Using the table and values $\lambda/\mu = 2$ and $S = 3$, we obtain $L_q = 0.8888$ mechanic.

At this point, we see that we have an average of 0.8888 mechanic waiting all day. For an eight-hour day at $12 per hour, there is a loss of mechanic's time worth 0.8888 mechanic × $12 per hour × 8 hours = $85.32.

Our next step is to reobtain the waiting time if we add another parts clerk. We then compare the added cost of the additional employee with the time saved by the mechanics. Again, using the table of Exhibit 8A.9 but with $S = 4$, we obtain

$L_q = 0.1730$ mechanic in line

$0.1730 \times \$12 \times 8$ hours $= \$16.61$ cost of a mechanic waiting in line

Value of mechanics' time saved is $85.32 - $16.61 $= \$68.71$

Cost of an additional parts clerk is 8 hours × $6/hour $=$ 48.00

Cost of reduction by adding fourth clerk $= \$20.71$

This problem could be expanded to consider the addition of runners to deliver parts to mechanics; the problem then would be to determine the optimal number of runners. This, however, would have to include the added cost of lost time caused by errors in parts receipts. For example, a mechanic would recognize a wrong part at the counter and obtain immediate correction, whereas the parts runner might not. ●

Service

**Excel:
Queue.xls**

EXAMPLE 8A.4: Finite Population Source

Studies of a bank of four weaving machines at the Loose Knit textile mill have shown that, on average, each machine needs adjusting every hour and that the current servicer averages $7\frac{1}{2}$ minutes per adjustment. Assuming Poisson arrivals, exponential service, and a machine idle time cost of $40 per hour, determine if a second servicer (who also averages $7\frac{1}{2}$ minutes per adjustment) should be hired at a rate of $7 per hour.

SOLUTION

This is a finite queuing problem that can be solved by using finite queuing tables. (See Exhibit 8A.10.) The approach in this problem is to compare the cost of machine downtime (either waiting in line or being serviced) and of one repairer to the cost of machine downtime and two repairers. We do this by finding the average number of machines that are in the service system and multiplying this number by the downtime cost per hour. To this we add the repairers' cost.

Before we proceed, we first define some terms:

$N =$ Number of machines in the population

$S =$ Number of repairers

$T =$ Time required to service a machine

$U =$ Average time a machine runs before requiring service

$X =$ Service factor, or proportion of service time required for each machine ($X = T/(T + U)$)

Expected Number of People Waiting in Line (L_q) for Various Values of S and λ/μ

	NUMBER OF SERVICE CHANNELS, S														
λ/μ	1	2	3	4	5	6	7	8	9	10	11	12	13	14	15
0.10	0.0111														
0.15	0.0264	0.0006													
0.20	0.0500	0.0020													
0.25	0.0833	0.0039													
0.30	0.1285	0.0069													
0.35	0.1884	0.0110													
0.40	0.2666	0.0166													
0.45	0.3681	0.0239	0.0019												
0.50	0.5000	0.0333	0.0030												
0.55	0.6722	0.045	0.0043												
0.60	0.9090	0.0593	0.0061												
0.65	1.2071	0.0767	0.0084												
0.70	1.6333	0.0976	0.0112												
0.75	2.2500	0.1227	0.0147												
0.80	3.2000	0.1523	0.0189												
0.85	4.8165	0.1873	0.0239	0.0031											
0.90	8.1000	0.2285	0.0300	0.0041											
0.95	18.0500	0.2767	0.0371	0.0053											
1.0		0.3333	0.0454	0.0067											
1.2		0.6748	0.0940	0.0158											
1.4		1.3449	0.1778	0.0324	0.0059										
1.6		2.8441	0.3128	0.0604	0.0121										
1.8		7.6731	0.5320	0.1051	0.0227	0.0047									
2.0			0.8888	0.1730	0.0390	0.0090									
2.2			1.4907	0.2770	0.066	0.0158									
2.4			2.1261	0.4205	0.1047	0.0266	0.0065								
2.6			4.9322	0.6581	0.1609	0.0425	0.0110								
2.8			12.2724	1.0000	0.2411	0.0659	0.0180								
3.0				1.5282	0.3541	0.0991	0.0282	0.0077							
3.2				2.3855	0.5128	0.1452	0.0427	0.0122							
3.4				3.9060	0.7365	0.2085	0.0631	0.0189							
3.6				7.0893	1.0550	0.2947	0.0912	0.0283	0.0084						
3.8				16.9366	1.5181	0.4114	0.1292	0.0412	0.0127						
4.0					2.2164	0.5694	0.1801	0.0590	0.0189						
4.2					3.3269	0.7837	0.2475	0.0827	0.0273	0.0087					
4.4					5.2675	1.0777	0.3364	0.1142	0.0389	0.0128					
4.6					9.2885	1.4857	0.4532	0.1555	0.0541	0.0184					
4.8					21.6384	2.0708	0.6071	0.2092	0.0742	0.0260					
5.0						2.9375	0.8102	0.2785	0.1006	0.0361	0.0125				
5.2						4.3004	1.0804	0.3680	0.1345	0.0492	0.0175				
5.4						6.6609	1.4441	0.5871	0.1779	0.0663	0.0243	0.0085			
5.6						11.5178	1.9436	0.6313	0.2330	0.0683	0.0330	0.0119			
5.8						26.3726	2.6481	0.8225	0.3032	0.1164	0.0443	0.0164			
6.0							3.6878	1.0707	0.3918	0.1518	0.0590	0.0224			
6.2							5.2979	1.3967	0.5037	0.1964	0.0775	0.0300	0.0113		
6.4							8.0768	1.8040	0.6454	0.2524	0.1008	0.0398	0.0153		
6.6							13.7992	2.4198	0.8247	0.3222	0.1302	0.0523	0.0205		
6.8							31.1270	3.2441	1.0533	0.4090	0.1666	0.0679	0.0271	0.0105	
7.0								4.4471	1.3471	0.5172	0.2119	0.0876	0.0357	0.0141	
7.2								6.3133	1.7288	0.6521	0.2677	0.1119	0.0463	0.0187	
7.4								9.5102	2.2324	0.8202	0.3364	0.1420	0.0595	0.0245	0.0097
7.6								16.0379	2.9113	1.0310	0.4211	0.1789	0.0761	0.0318	0.0129
7.8								35.8956	3.8558	1.2972	0.5250	0.2243	0.0966	0.0410	0.0168
8.0									5.2264	1.6364	0.6530	0.2796	0.1214	0.0522	0.0220
8.2									7.3441	2.0736	0.8109	0.3469	0.1520	0.0663	0.0283
8.4									10.9592	2.6470	1.0060	0.4288	0.1891	0.0834	0.0361
8.6									18.3223	3.4160	1.2484	0.5236	0.2341	0.1043	0.0459
8.8									40.6824	4.4805	1.5524	0.6501	0.2885	0.1208	0.0577
9.0										6.0183	1.9366	0.7980	0.3543	0.1603	0.0723
9.2										8.3869	2.4293	0.9788	0.4333	0.1974	0.0899
9.4										12.4183	3.0732	1.2010	0.5267	0.2419	0.1111
9.6										20.6160	3.9318	1.4752	0.5437	0.2952	0.1367
9.8										45.4769	5.1156	1.8165	0.7827	0.3699	0.16731
10											6.8210	2.2465	0.9506	0.4352	0.2040

exhibit 8A.10   Finite Queuing Tables

POPULATION 4

X	S	D	F	X	S	D	F	X	S	D	F
.015	1	.045	.999		1	.479	.899	.400	3	.064	.992
.022	1	.066	.998	.180	2	.088	.991		2	.372	.915
.030	1	.090	.997		1	.503	.887		1	.866	.595
.034	1	.102	.996	.190	2	.098	.990	.420	3	.074	.990
.038	1	.114	.995		1	.526	.874		2	.403	.903
.042	1	.126	.994	.200	3	.008	.999		1	.884	.572
.046	1	.137	.993		2	.108	.988	.440	3	.085	.986
.048	1	.143	.992	.200	1	.549	.862		2	.435	.891
.052	1	.155	.991	.210	3	.009	.999		1	.900	.551
.054	1	.161	.990		2	.118	.986	.460	3	.097	.985
.058	1	.173	.989		1	.572	.849		2	.466	.878
.060	1	.179	.988	.220	3	.011	.999		1	.914	.530
.062	1	.184	.987		2	.129	.984	.480	3	.111	.983
.064	1	.190	.986		1	.593	.835		2	.498	.864
.066	1	.196	.985	.230	3	.012	.999	.480	1	.926	.511
.070	2	.014	.999		2	.140	.982	.500	3	.125	.980
	1	.208	.984		1	.614	.822		2	.529	.850
.075	2	.016	.999	.240	3	.014	.999		1	.937	.492
	1	.222	.981		2	.151	.980	.520	3	.141	.976
.080	2	.018	.999		1	.634	.808		2	.561	.835
	1	.237	.978	.250	3	.016	.999		1	.947	.475
.085	2	.021	.999		2	.163	.977	.540	3	.157	.972
	1	.251	.975		1	.654	.794		2	.592	.820
.090	2	.023	.999	.260	3	.018	.998		1	.956	.459
	1	.265	.972		2	.175	.975	.560	3	.176	.968
.095	2	.026	.999		1	.673	.780		2	.623	.805
	1	.280	.969	.270	3	.020	.998		1	.963	.443
.100	2	.028	.999		2	.187	.972	.580	3	.195	.964
	1	.294	.965		1	.691	.766		2	.653	.789
.105	2	.031	.998	.280	3	.022	.99s8		1	.969	.429
	1	.308	.962		2	.200	.968	.600	3	.216	.959
.110	2	.034	.998		1	.708	.752		2	.682	.774
	1	.321	.958	.290	3	.024	.998		1	.975	.415
.115	2	.037	.998		2	.213	.965	.650	3	.275	.944
	1	.335	.954		1	.725	.738		2	.752	.734
.120	2	.041	.997	.300	3	.027	.997		1	.985	.384
	1	.349	.950		2	.226	.962	.700	3	.343	.926
.125	2	.044	.997		1	.741	.724		2	.816	.695
	1	.362	.945	.310	3	.030	.997		1	.991	.357
.130	2	.047	.997		2	.240	.958	.750	3	.422	.905
	1	.376	.941		1	.756	.710		2	.871	.657
.135	2	.051	.996	.320	3	.033	.997		1	.996	.333
	1	.389	.936		2	.254	.954	.800	3	.512	.880
.140	2	.055	.996		1	.771	.696		2	.917	.621
	1	.402	.931	.330	3	.036	.996		1	.998	.312
.145	2	.058	.995		2	.268	.950	.850	3	.614	.852
	1	.415	.926		1	.785	.683		2	.954	.587
.150	2	.062	.995	.340	3	.039	.996		1	.999	.294
	1	.428	.921		2	.282	.945	.900	3	.729	.821
.155	2	.066	.994		1	.798	.670		2	.979	.555
	1	.441	.916	.360	3	.047	.994	.950	3	.857	.786
.160	2	.071	.994		2	.312	.936		2	.995	.526
	1	.454	.910		1	.823	.644				
.165	2	.075	.993	.380	3	.055	.993				
	1	.466	.904		2	.342	.926				
.170	2	.079	.993		1	.846	.619				

L = Average number of machines waiting in line to be serviced

H = Average number of machines being serviced

The values to be determined from the finite tables are

D = Probability that a machine needing service will have to wait

F = Efficiency factor, which measures the effect of having to wait in line to be serviced

The tables are arranged according to three variables: N, population size; X, service factor; and S, the number of service channels (repairers in this problem). To look up a value, first find the table for the correct N size, then search the first column for the appropriate X, and finally find the line for S. Then read off D and F. (In addition to these values, other characteristics about a finite queuing system can be found by using the finite formulas.)

To solve the problem, consider Case I with one repairer and Case II with two repairers.

Case I: One repairer. From problem statement,

$N = 4$

$S = 1$

$T = 7\frac{1}{2}$ minutes

$U = 60$ minutes

$$X = \frac{T}{T+U} = \frac{7.5}{7.5+60} = 0.111$$

From Exhibit 8A.10, which displays the table for $N = 4$, F is interpolated as being approximately 0.957 at $X = 0.111$ and $S = 1$.

The number of machines waiting in line to be serviced is L, where

$$L = N(1 - F) = 4(1 - 0.957) = 0.172 \text{ machine}$$

The number of machines being serviced is H, where

$$H = FNX = 0.957(4)(0.111) = 0.425 \text{ machine}$$

Exhibit 8A.11 shows the cost resulting from unproductive machine time and the cost of the repairer.

Case II: Two repairers. From Exhibit 8A.10, at $X = 0.111$ and $S = 2$, $F = 0.998$.

The number of machines waiting in line, L, is

$$L = N(1 - F) = 4(1 - 0.998) = 0.008 \text{ machine}$$

The number of machines being serviced, H, is

$$H = FNX = 0.998(4)(0.111) = 0.443 \text{ machine}$$

The costs for the machines being idle and for the two repairers are shown in Exhibit 8A.11. The final column of that exhibit shows that retaining just one repairer is the better choice. ●

A Comparison of Downtime Costs for Service and Repair of Four Machines

NUMBER OF REPAIRERS	NUMBER OF MACHINES DOWN $(H + L)$	COST PER HOUR FOR MACHINES DOWN $[(H + L) \times \$40/\text{HOUR}]$	COST OF REPAIRERS ($\$7/\text{HOUR}$ EACH)	TOTAL COST PER HOUR
1	0.597	$23.88	$ 7.00	$30.88
2	0.451	18.04	14.00	32.04

APPROXIMATING CUSTOMER WAITING TIME[2]

Good news for managers. All you need is the mean and standard deviation to compute average waiting time! Some good research has led to a "quick and dirty" mathematical approximation to the queuing models illustrated earlier in the chapter. What's nice about the approximation is that it does not assume a particular arrival rate or service distribution. All that is needed is the mean and standard deviation of the interarrival time and the service time. We will not burden you with all the details of how the approximations were derived, just how to use the formulas.

First, you will need to collect some data on your service time. The service time is the amount of time that it takes to serve each customer. Keep in mind that you want to collect your data during a period of time that fairly represents what you expect to happen during the period that you are concerned about. For example, if you want to know how many bank tellers you should have to service customers on Friday around the lunch period, collect your data during that period. This will ensure that the transactions being performed are similar to those that you expect in the future. You can use a stop watch to time how long it takes to serve each customer. Using these data, calculate the mean and standard deviation of the service time.

Recall from your statistics that the mean is

[8A.7]
$$\overline{X} = \sum_{i=1}^{N} x_i / N$$

where x_i = observed value and N = total number of observed values.

The standard deviation is

$$s = \sqrt{\frac{\sum_{i=1}^{N} (x_i - \overline{X})^2}{N - 1}}$$

Next, capture data on the amount of time between the arrivals of each new customer during the period of time you are studying. This is called the interarrival time. From the data, calculate the mean and standard deviation of the interarrival time. From these calculations, we have

$\overline{X}_s$ = Mean service time

$\overline{X}_a$ = Mean interarrival time

S_s = Standard deviation of the service time sample

S_a = Standard deviation of the interarrival time sample

Next, define the following:

C_s = Coefficient of variation of service time = $\dfrac{S_S}{\overline{X}_S}$

C_a = Coefficient of variation of interarrival time = $\dfrac{S_a}{\overline{X}_a}$

λ = Customer arrival rate = $\dfrac{1}{\overline{X}_a}$

μ = Customer service rate = $\dfrac{1}{\overline{X}_s}$

Now, we can calculate some statistics about our system. First, define S as the number of servers that we intend to use. Then,

ρ = Utilization of the servers = $\dfrac{\lambda}{S\mu}$

L_q = Expected length of the waiting line = $\dfrac{\rho^{\sqrt{2(S+1)}}}{1-\rho} \times \dfrac{C_a^2 + C_s^2}{2}$

$$L_s = \text{Expected number of people in the system} = L_q + S\rho$$

$$W_q = \text{Expected time waiting in line} = \frac{L_q}{\lambda}$$

$$W_s = \text{Expected time in the system} = \frac{L_s}{\lambda}$$

The utilization (ρ) is the percentage of time that the servers are expected to be busy. Often companies that provide high service target this number at between 70 and 80 percent depending on the amount of variance there is in the customer arrival and service rates. L_q is how long the queue is expected to be, and W_q is how long a customer is expected to have to wait in the queue. L_s and W_s are the expected number of customers in the system and the expected time that a customer is in the system. These statistics consider that the total number of customers and the total waiting time must include those that are actually being served.

EXAMPLE 8A.5: Waiting Line Approximation

Let's consider an example of a call center that takes orders for a mail order business. During the peak period, the average time between call arrivals ($\overline{X}_a$) is 0.5 minute with a standard deviation (S_a) of 0.203 minute. The average time to service a call ($\overline{X}_s$) is 4 minutes and the standard deviation of the service time (S_s) is 2.5 minutes. If the call center is using 9 operators to service calls, how long would you expect customers to wait before being serviced? What would be the impact of adding an additional operator?

SOLUTION

W_q is the time that we expect a customer to wait before being served. The best way to do these calculations is with a spreadsheet. The spreadsheet "Queue_Models.xls" on the DVD-ROM can be easily used. The following steps are needed for the calculation of the customer wait time.

Excel: Queue.xls

Step 1. Calculate expected customer arrival rate (λ), service rate per server (μ), and coefficient of variation for the interarrival time (C_a) and service time (C_s).

$$\lambda = \frac{1}{\overline{X}_a} = \frac{1}{0.5} = 2 \text{ customers per minute}$$

$$\mu = \frac{1}{\overline{X}_s} = \frac{1}{4} = 0.25 \text{ customer per minute}$$

$$C_a = \frac{S_a}{\overline{X}_a} = \frac{0.203}{0.5} = 0.406$$

$$C_s = \frac{S_s}{\overline{X}_s} = \frac{2.5}{4} = 0.625$$

Step 2. Calculate the expected server utilization (σ).

$$\rho = \frac{\lambda}{S\mu} = \frac{2}{9 \times 0.25} = 0.888889 \qquad \text{(Operators are expected to be busy 89 percent of the time.)}$$

Step 3. Calculate the expected number of people waiting (L_q) and the length of the wait (W_q).

$$L_q = \frac{\rho^{\sqrt{2(S+1)}}}{1-\rho} \times \frac{C_a^2 + C_s^2}{2} = \frac{0.888889^{\sqrt{2(9+1)}}}{1 - 0.888889} \times \frac{0.406^2 + 0.625^2}{2} = 1.476064 \text{ customers}$$

(This is the number of customers that we expect to be waiting on hold.)

$$W_q = \frac{L_q}{\lambda} = \frac{1.476064}{2} = 0.738032 \text{ minute}$$

On average, we expect customers to wait 44 seconds (0.738032×60) before talking to an operator.

For 10 operators, the calculations are as follows:

$$\rho = \frac{\lambda}{S\mu} = \frac{2}{10 \times 0.25} = 0.8 \qquad \text{(Operators are expected to be busy 80 percent of the time.)}$$

$$L_q = \frac{\rho^{\sqrt{2(S+1)}}}{1 - \rho} \times \frac{C_a^2 + C_s^2}{2} = \frac{0.8^{\sqrt{2(10+1)}}}{1 - 0.8} \times \frac{0.406^2 + 0.625^2}{2} = 0.487579 \text{ customer}$$

$$W_q = \frac{L_q}{\lambda} = \frac{0.487579}{2} = 0.24379 \text{ minute}$$

With 10 operators, the waiting time is cut one-third to 14.6 seconds. If you add two operators (bringing the total to 11), the waiting time in queue is 6.4 seconds. Adding the first additional operator has a significant impact on customer wait time. ●

This approximation is useful for many typical queuing situations. It is easy to implement using a spreadsheet such as the "Queue_Models.xls" spreadsheet on the DVD-ROM included with the book. Keep in mind that the approximation assumes that the population to be served is large and customers arrive one at a time. The approximation can be useful for a quick analysis of a queuing situation.

COMPUTER SIMULATION OF WAITING LINES

Some waiting line problems that seem simple on first impression turn out to be extremely difficult or impossible to solve. Throughout this chapter, we have been treating waiting line situations that are independent; that is, either the entire system consists of a single phase or else each service that is performed in a series is independent. (This could happen if the output of one service location is allowed to build up in front of the next one so that this, in essence, becomes a calling population for the next service.) When a series of services is performed in sequence where the output rate of one becomes the input rate of the next, we can no longer use the simple formulas. This is also true for any problem where conditions do not meet the requirements of the equations, as specified in Exhibit 8A.8. The technique best suited to solving this type of problem is computer simulation. We treat the topic of modeling and simulation in Chapter 17A.

CONCLUSION

Waiting line problems both challenge and frustrate those who try to solve them. The basic objective is to balance the cost of waiting with the cost of adding more resources. For a service system, this means that the utilization of a server may be quite low to provide a short waiting time to the customer. One main concern in dealing with waiting line problems is which procedure or priority rule to use in selecting the next product or customer to be served.

Many queuing problems appear simple until an attempt is made to solve them. This chapter has dealt with the simpler problems. When the situation becomes more complex, when there are multiple phases, or where services are performed only in a particular sequence, computer simulation is necessary to obtain the optimal solution.

KEY TERMS

Queue A line of waiting persons, jobs, things, or the like.

Queuing system Consists of three major components: (1) the source population and the way customers arrive at the system, (2) the serving systems, and (3) how customers exit the system.

Arrival rate The expected number of customers that arrive each period.

Exponential distribution A probability distribution often associated with interarrival times.

Poisson distribution Probability distribution often used to describe the number of arrivals during a given time period.

Service rate The capacity of a server measured in number of units that can be processed over a given time period.

FORMULA REVIEW

Exponential distribution

[8A.1]
$$f(t) = \lambda e^{-\lambda t}$$

Poisson distribution

[8A.2]
$$P_T(n) = \frac{(\lambda T)^n e^{-\lambda T}}{n!}$$

Model 1 (See Exhibit 8A.8.)

$$L_q = \frac{\lambda^2}{\mu(\mu - \lambda)} \qquad W_q = \frac{L_q}{\lambda} \qquad P_n = \left(1 - \frac{\lambda}{\mu}\right)\left(\frac{\lambda}{\mu}\right)^n \qquad P_o = \left(1 - \frac{\lambda}{\mu}\right)$$

[8A.3]

$$L_s = \frac{\lambda}{\mu - \lambda} \qquad W_s = \frac{L_s}{\lambda} \qquad \rho = \frac{\lambda}{\mu}$$

Model 2

$$L_q = \frac{\lambda^2}{2\mu(\mu - \lambda)} \qquad W_q = \frac{L_q}{\lambda}$$

[8A.4]

$$L_s = L_q + \frac{\lambda}{\mu} \qquad W_s = \frac{L_s}{\lambda}$$

Model 3

$$L_s = L_q + \lambda/\mu \qquad W_s = L_s/\lambda$$

[8A.5]

$$W_q = L_q/\lambda \qquad P_w = L_q\left(\frac{S\mu}{\lambda} - 1\right)$$

Model 4

$$X = \frac{T}{T + U} \qquad H = FNX \qquad L = N(1 - F) \qquad n = L + H$$

[8A.6]

$$P_n = \frac{N!}{(N - n)!}X^n P_0 \qquad J = NF(1 - X)$$

$$W = \frac{L(T + U)}{N - L} = \frac{LT}{H} \qquad F = \frac{T + U}{T + U + W}$$

Waiting time approximation

$$\bar{X} = \sum_{i=1}^{N} x_i \Big/ N \qquad s = \sqrt{\frac{\sum_{i=1}^{N}(x_i - \bar{X})^2}{N - 1}}$$

$$C_s = \frac{S_s}{\bar{X}_s} \qquad C_a = \frac{S_a}{\bar{X}_a} \qquad \lambda = \frac{1}{\bar{X}_a} \qquad \mu = \frac{1}{\bar{X}_s}$$

[8A.7]

$$\rho = \frac{\lambda}{S\mu}$$

$$L_q = \frac{\rho^{\sqrt{2(S+1)}}}{1 - \rho} \times \frac{C_a^2 + C_s^2}{2}$$

$$L_s = L_q + S\rho$$

$$W_q = \frac{L_q}{\lambda}$$

$$W_s = \frac{L_s}{\lambda}$$

SOLVED PROBLEMS

SOLVED PROBLEM 1

**Excel:
Queue.xls**

Quick Lube Inc. operates a fast lube and oil change garage. On a typical day, customers arrive at the rate of three per hour and lube jobs are performed at an average rate of one every 15 minutes. The mechanics operate as a team on one car at a time.

Assuming Poisson arrivals and exponential service, find

a. Utilization of the lube team.
b. The average number of cars in line.
c. The average time a car waits before it is lubed.
d. The total time it takes to go through the system (that is, waiting in line plus lube time).

Solution

$\lambda = 3, \mu = 4$

a. Utilization $\rho = \frac{\lambda}{\mu} = \frac{3}{4} = 75\%$.

b. $L_q = \frac{\lambda^2}{\mu(\mu - \lambda)} = \frac{3^2}{4(4 - 3)} = \frac{9}{4} = 2.25$ cars in line.

c. $W_q = \frac{L_q}{\lambda} = \frac{2.25}{3} = 0.75$ hour, or 45 minutes.

d. $W_s = \frac{L_s}{\lambda} = \frac{\lambda}{\mu - \lambda} \Big/ \lambda = \frac{3}{4 - 3} \Big/ 3 = 1$ hour (waiting + lube).

SOLVED PROBLEM 2

**Excel:
Queue.xls**

American Vending Inc. (AVI) supplies vended food to a large university. Because students often kick the machines out of anger and frustration, management has a constant repair problem. The machines break down on an average of three per hour, and the breakdowns are distributed in a Poisson manner. Downtime costs the company $25 per hour per machine, and each maintenance worker gets $4 per hour. One worker can service machines at an average rate of five per hour, distributed exponentially; two workers working together can service seven per hour, distributed exponentially; and a team of three workers can do eight per hour, distributed exponentially.

What is the optimal maintenance crew size for servicing the machines?

Solution

Case I—One worker:

$\lambda = 3$/hour Poisson, $\mu = 5$/hour exponential
There is an average number of machines in the system of

$$L_s = \frac{\lambda}{\mu - \lambda} = \frac{3}{5 - 3} = \frac{3}{2} = 1\frac{1}{2} \text{ machines}$$

Downtime cost is $25 × 1.5 = $37.50 per hour; repair cost is $4.00 per hour; and total cost per hour for 1 worker is $37.50 + $4.00 = $41.50.

$$\text{Downtime } (1.5 \times \$25) = \$37.50$$
$$\text{Labor } (1 \text{ worker} \times \$4) = \underline{\quad 4.00}$$
$$\underline{\$41.50}$$

Case II—Two workers:

$\lambda = 3, \mu = 7$

$$L_s = \frac{\lambda}{\mu - \lambda} = \frac{3}{7 - 3} = 0.75 \text{ machine}$$

$$\text{Downtime } (0.75 \times \$25) \quad = \$18.75$$
$$\text{Labor } (2 \text{ workers} \times \$4.00) = \underline{\quad 8.00}$$
$$\underline{\$26.75}$$

Case III—Three workers:

$\lambda = 3, \mu = 8$

$$L_s = \frac{\lambda}{\mu - \lambda} = \frac{3}{8 - 3} = \frac{3}{5} = 0.60 \text{ machine}$$

$$\text{Downtime } (0.60 \times \$25) = \$15.00$$
$$\text{Labor } (3 \text{ workers} \times \$4) = \underline{\quad 12.00}$$
$$\underline{\$27.00}$$

Comparing the costs for one, two, or three workers, we see that Case II with two workers is the optimal decision.

SOLVED PROBLEM 3

American Bank has a single automated teller machine (ATM) located in a shopping center. Data were collected during a period of peak usage on Saturday afternoon, and it was found that the average time between customer arrivals is 2.1 minutes with a standard deviation of 0.8 minute. It also was found it takes an average of 1.9 minutes for a customer to complete a transaction with a standard deviation of 2 minutes. Approximately how long will customers need to wait in line during the peak usage period?

**Excel:
Queue.xls**

Solution

Step 1. Calculate expected customer arrival rate (λ), service rate per server (μ), and coefficient of variation for the arrival distribution (C_a) and service distribution (C_s).

$$\lambda = \frac{1}{\bar{X}_a} = \frac{1}{2.1} = 0.47619 \text{ customer per minute}$$

$$\mu = \frac{1}{\bar{X}_s} = \frac{1}{1.9} = 0.526316 \text{ customer per minute}$$

$$C_a = \frac{S_a}{\bar{X}_a} = \frac{0.8}{2.1} = 0.380952$$

$$C_s = \frac{S_s}{\bar{X}_s} = \frac{2}{1.9} = 1.052632$$

Step 2. Calculate the expected server utilization (ρ)

$$\rho = \frac{\lambda}{S\mu} = \frac{0.47619}{1 \times 0.526316} = 0.904762 \qquad \text{(Operators are expected to be busy 90.5 percent of the time.)}$$

Step 3. Calculate the expected number of people waiting (L_q) and the length of the wait (W_q).

$$L_q = \frac{\rho^{\sqrt{2(S+1)}}}{1-\rho} \times \frac{C_a^2 + C_s^2}{2} = \frac{0.904762^{\sqrt{2(1+1)}}}{1 - 0.904762} \times \frac{0.380952^2 + 1.052632^2}{2}$$

$= 5.385596$ customer   (This is the number of customers that we expect to be waiting on hold.)

$$W_q = \frac{L_q}{\lambda} = \frac{5.385596}{0.47619} = 11.30975 \text{ minutes}$$

On average we expect customers to wait 11 minutes and 19 seconds (0.30975×60) before having access to the ATM.

REVIEW AND DISCUSSION QUESTIONS

1. Cultural factors affect waiting lines. For example, fast checkout lines (e.g., 10 items or less) are uncommon in Japan. Why do you think this is so?
2. How many waiting lines did you encounter during your last airline flight?
3. Distinguish between a *channel* and a *phase*.
4. What is the major cost trade-off that must be made in managing waiting line situations?
5. Which assumptions are necessary to employ the formulas given for Model 1?
6. In what way might the first-come, first-served rule be unfair to the customer waiting for service in a bank or hospital?
7. Define, in a practical sense, what is meant by an *exponential service time*.
8. Would you expect the exponential distribution to be a good approximation of service times for
   a. Buying an airline ticket at the airport?
   b. Riding a merry-go-round at a carnival?
   c. Checking out of a hotel?
   d. Completing a midterm exam in your OSM class?
9. Would you expect the Poisson distribution to be a good approximation of
   a. Runners crossing the finish line in the Boston Marathon?
   b. Arrival times of the students in your OSM class?
   c. Arrival times of the bus to your stop at school?

PROBLEMS

1. Students arrive at the Administrative Services Office at an average of one every 15 minutes, and their requests take on average 10 minutes to be processed. The service counter is staffed by only one clerk, Judy Gumshoes, who works eight hours per day. Assume Poisson arrivals and exponential service times.
   a. What percentage of time is Judy idle?
   b. How much time, on average, does a student spend waiting in line?
   c. How long is the (waiting) line on average?
   d. What is the probability that an arriving student (just before entering the Administrative Services Office) will find at least one other student waiting in line?
2. The managers of the Administrative Services Office estimate that the time a student spends waiting in line costs them (due to goodwill loss and so on) $10 per hour. To reduce the time a student spends waiting, they know that they need to improve Judy's processing time (see Problem 1). They are currently considering the following two options:
   a. Install a computer system, with which Judy expects to be able to complete a student request 40 percent faster (from 2 minutes per request to 1 minute and 12 seconds, for example).
   b. Hire another temporary clerk, who will work at the same rate as Judy.
   If the computer costs $99.50 to operate per day, while the temporary clerk gets paid $75 per day, is Judy right to prefer the hired help? Assume Poisson arrivals and exponential service times.
3. Sharp Discounts Wholesale Club has two service desks, one at each entrance of the store. Customers arrive at each service desk at an average of one every six minutes. The service rate at each service desk is four minutes per customer.
   a. How often (what percentage of time) is each service desk idle?
   b. What is the probability that both service clerks are busy?
   c. What is the probability that both service clerks are idle?
   d. How many customers, on average, are waiting in line in front of each service desk?
   e. How much time does a customer spend at the service desk (waiting plus service time)?

4 Sharp Discounts Wholesale Club is considering consolidating its two service desks (see Problem 3) into one location, staffed by two clerks. The clerks will continue to work at the same individual speed of four minutes per customer.

   a. What is the probability of waiting in line?

   b. How many customers, on average, are waiting in line?

   c. How much time does a customer spend at the service desk (waiting plus service time)?

   d. Do you think the Sharp Discounts Wholesale Club should consolidate the service desks?

5 Burrito King (a new fast-food franchise opening up nationwide) has successfully automated burrito production for its drive-up fast-food establishments. The Burro-Master 9000 requires a constant 45 seconds to produce a batch of burritos. It has been estimated that customers will arrive at the drive-up window according to a Poisson distribution at an average of one every 50 seconds. To help determine the amount of space needed for the line at the drive-up window, Burrito King would like to know the expected average time in the system, the average line length (in cars), and the average number of cars in the system (both in line and at the window).

6 The Bijou Theater in Hermosa Beach, California, shows vintage movies. Customers arrive at the theater line at the rate of 100 per hour. The ticket seller averages 30 seconds per customer, which includes placing validation stamps on customers' parking lot receipts and punching their frequent watcher cards. (Because of these added services, many customers don't get in until after the feature has started.)

   a. What is the average customer time in the system?

   b. What would be the effect on customer time in the system of having a second ticket taker doing nothing but validations and card punching, thereby cutting the average service time to 20 seconds?

   c. Would system waiting time be less than you found in *b* if a second window was opened with each server doing all three tasks?

7 To support National Heart Week, the Heart Association plans to install a free blood pressure testing booth in El Con Mall for the week. Previous experience indicates that, on the average, 10 persons per hour request a test. Assume arrivals are Poisson from an infinite population. Blood pressure measurements can be made at a constant time of five minutes each. Assume the queue length can be infinite with FCFS discipline.

   a. What average number in line can be expected?

   b. What average number of persons can be expected to be in the system?

   c. What is the average amount of time that a person can expect to spend in line?

   d. On the average, how much time will it take to measure a person's blood pressure, including waiting time?

   e. On weekends, the arrival rate can be expected to increase to over 12 per hour. What effect will this have on the number in the waiting line?

8 A cafeteria serving line has a coffee urn from which customers serve themselves. Arrivals at the urn follow a Poisson distribution at the rate of three per minute. In serving themselves, customers take about 15 seconds, exponentially distributed.

   a. How many customers would you expect to see on the average at the coffee urn?

   b. How long would you expect it to take to get a cup of coffee?

   c. What percentage of time is the urn being used?

   d. What is the probability that three or more people are in the cafeteria?

   e. If the cafeteria installs an automatic vendor that dispenses a cup of coffee at a constant time of 15 seconds, how does this change your answers to *a* and *b*?

9 An engineering firm retains a technical specialist to assist four design engineers working on a project. The help that the specialist gives engineers ranges widely in time consumption. The specialist has some answers available in memory; others require computation, and still others require significant search time. On the average, each request for assistance takes the specialist one hour.

   The engineers require help from the specialist on the average of once each day. Because each assistance takes about an hour, each engineer can work for seven hours, on the average, without assistance. One further point: Engineers needing help do not interrupt if the specialist is already involved with another problem.

   Treat this as a finite queuing problem and answer the following questions:

   a. How many engineers, on average, are waiting for the technical specialist for help?

   b. What is the average time that an engineer has to wait for the specialist?

   c. What is the probability that an engineer will have to wait in line for the specialist?

10 L. Winston Martin (an allergist in Tucson) has an excellent system for handling his regular patients who come in just for allergy injections. Patients arrive for an injection and fill out a

name slip, which is then placed in an open slot that passes into another room staffed by one or two nurses. The specific injections for a patient are prepared, and the patient is called through a speaker system into the room to receive the injection. At certain times during the day, patient load drops and only one nurse is needed to administer the injections.

Let's focus on the simpler case of the two—namely, when there is one nurse. Also, assume that patients arrive in a Poisson fashion and the service rate of the nurse is exponentially distributed. During this slower period, patients arrive with an interarrival time of approximately three minutes. It takes the nurse an average of two minutes to prepare the patients' serum and administer the injection.

a. What is the average number you would expect to see in Dr. Martin's facilities?

b. How long would it take for a patient to arrive, get an injection, and leave?

c. What is the probability that there will be three or more patients on the premises?

d. What is the utilization of the nurse?

e. Assume three nurses are available. Each takes an average of two minutes to prepare the patients' serum and administer the injection. What is the average total time of a patient in the system?

11 The Judy Gray Income Tax Service is analyzing its customer service operations during the month prior to the April filing deadline. On the basis of past data, it has been estimated that customers arrive according to a Poisson process with an average interarrival time of 12 minutes. The time to complete a return for a customer is exponentially distributed with a mean of 10 minutes. Based on this information, answer the following questions:

a. If you went to Judy, how much time would you allow for getting your return done?

b. On average, how much room should be allowed for the waiting area?

c. If Judy stayed in the office 12 hours per day, how many hours on average, per day, would she be busy?

d. What is the probability that the system is idle?

e. If the arrival rate remained unchanged, but the average time in system must be 45 minutes or less, what would need to be changed?

12 A graphics reproduction firm has four units of equipment that are automatic but occasionally become inoperative because of the need for supplies, maintenance, or repair. Each unit requires service roughly twice each hour, or, more precisely, each unit of equipment runs an average of 30 minutes before needing service. Service times vary widely, ranging from a simple service (such as pressing a restart switch or repositioning paper) to more involved equipment disassembly. The average service time, however, is five minutes.

Equipment downtime results in a loss of $20 per hour. The one equipment attendant is paid $6 per hour.

Using finite queuing analysis, answer the following questions:

a. What is the average number of units in line?

b. What is the average number of units still in operation?

c. What is the average number of units being serviced?

d. The firm is considering adding another attendant at the same $6 rate. Should the firm do it?

13 Benny the Barber owns a one-chair shop. At barber college, they told Benny that his customers would exhibit a Poisson arrival distribution and that he would provide an exponential service distribution. His market survey data indicate that customers arrive at a rate of two per hour. It will take Benny an average of 20 minutes to give a haircut. Based on these figures, find the following:

a. The average number of customers waiting.

b. The average time a customer waits.

c. The average time a customer is in the shop.

d. The average utilization of Benny's time.

14 Bobby the Barber is thinking about advertising in the local newspaper since he is idle 45% of the time. Currently, customers arrive on average every 40 minutes. What does the arrival rate need to be for Bobby to be busy 85% of the time?

15 Benny the Barber (see Problem 13) is considering the addition of a second chair. Customers would be selected for a haircut on a FCFS basis from those waiting. Benny has assumed that both barbers would take an average of 20 minutes to give a haircut and that business would remain unchanged with customers arriving at a rate of two per hour. Find the following information to help Benny decide if a second chair should be added:

a. The average number of customers waiting.

b. The average time a customer waits.

c. The average time a customer is in the shop.

16 Customers enter the camera department of a store at the average rate of six per hour. The department is staffed by one employee, who takes an average of six minutes to serve each arrival. Assume this is a simple Poisson arrival, exponentially distributed service time situation.

    a. As a casual observer, how many people would you expect to see in the camera department (excluding the clerk)? How long would a customer expect to spend in the camera department (total time)?

    b. What is the utilization of the clerk?

    c. What is the probability that there are more than two people in the camera department (excluding the clerk)?

    d. Another clerk has been hired for the camera department who also takes an average of six minutes to serve each arrival. How long would a customer expect to spend in the department now?

17 Cathy Livingston, bartender at the Tucson Racquet Club, can serve drinks at the rate of one every 50 seconds. During a hot evening recently, the bar was particularly busy and every 55 seconds someone was at the bar asking for a drink.

    a. Assuming that everyone in the bar drank at the same rate and that Cathy served people on a first-come, first-served basis, how long would you expect to have to wait for a drink?

    b. How many people would you expect to be waiting for drinks?

    c. What is the probability that three or more people are waiting for drinks?

    d. What is the utilization of the bartender (how busy is she)?

    e. If the bartender is replaced with an automatic drink dispensing machine, how would this change your answer in part *a*?

18 An office employs several clerks who originate documents and one operator who enters the document information in a word processor. The group originates documents at a rate of 25 per hour. The operator can enter the information with average exponentially distributed time of two minutes. Assume the population is infinite, arrivals are Poisson, and queue length is infinite with FCFS discipline.

    a. Calculate the percentage utilization of the operator.

    b. Calculate the average number of documents in the system.

    c. Calculate the average time in the system.

    d. Calculate the probability of four or more documents being in the system.

    e. If another clerk were added, the document origination rate would increase to 30 per hour. What would this do to the word processor workload? Show why.

19 A study-aid desk staffed by a graduate student has been established to answer students' questions and help in working problems in your OSM course. The desk is staffed eight hours per day. The dean wants to know how the facility is working. Statistics show that students arrive at a rate of four per hour and the distribution is approximately Poisson. Assistance time averages 10 minutes, distributed exponentially. Assume population and line length can be infinite and queue discipline is FCFS.

    a. Calculate the percentage utilization of the graduate student.

    b. Calculate the average number of students in the system.

    c. Calculate the average time in the system.

    d. Calculate the probability of four or more students being in line or being served.

    e. Before a test, the arrival of students increases to six per hour on the average. What does this do to the average length of the line?

20 At the California border inspection station, vehicles arrive at the rate of 10 per minute in a Poisson distribution. For simplicity in this problem, assume that there is only one lane and one inspector, who can inspect vehicles at the rate of 12 per minute in an exponentially distributed fashion.

    a. What is the average length of the waiting line?

    b. What is the average time that a vehicle must wait to get through the system?

    c. What is the utilization of the inspector?

    d. What is the probability that when you arrive there will be three or more vehicles ahead of you?

21 The California border inspection station (see Problem 20) is considering the addition of a second inspector. The vehicles would wait in one lane and then be directed to the first available inspector. Arrival rates would remain the same (10 per minute) and the new inspector would process vehicles at the same rate as the first inspector (12 per minute).

    a. What would be the average length of the waiting line?

    b. What would be the average time that a vehicle must wait to get through the system?

If a second lane was added (one lane for each inspector):

    c. What would be the average length of the waiting line?

    d. What would be the average time that a vehicle must wait to get through the system?

22 During the campus Spring Fling, the bumper car amusement attraction has a problem of cars becoming disabled and in need of repair. Repair personnel can be hired at the rate of $20 per hour, but they only work as one team. Thus, if one person is hired, he or she works alone; two or three people work together on the same repair.

One repairer can fix cars in an average time of 30 minutes. Two repairers take 20 minutes, and three take 15 minutes. While these cars are down, lost income is $40 per hour. Cars tend to break down at the rate of two per hour.

How many repairers should be hired?

23 A toll tunnel has decided to experiment with the use of a debit card for the collection of tolls. Initially, only one lane will be used. Cars are estimated to arrive at this experimental lane at the rate of 750 per hour. It will take exactly four seconds to verify the debit card.

a. In how much time would you expect the customer to wait in line, pay with the debit card, and leave?

b. How many cars would you expect to see in the system?

24 You are planning a bank. You plan for six tellers. Tellers take 15 minutes per customer with a standard deviation of 7 minutes. Customers arrive one every three minutes according to an exponential distribution (recall that the standard deviation is equal to the mean). Every customer that arrives eventually gets serviced.

a. On average, how many customers would be waiting in line?

b. On average, how long would a customer spend in the bank?

c. If a customer arrived, saw the line, and decided not to get in line, that customer has _____.

d. A customer who enters the line but decides to leave the line before getting service is said to have _____.

25 You are planning the new layout for the local branch of the Sixth Ninth Bank. You are considering separate cashier windows for the three different classes of service. Each class of service would be separate with its own cashiers and customers. Oddly enough, each class of service, while different, has exactly the same demand and service times. People for one class of service arrive every four minutes and arrival times are exponentially distributed (the standard deviation is equal to the mean). It takes seven minutes to service each customer, and the standard deviation of the service times is three minutes. You assign two cashiers to each type of service.

a. On average, how long will each line be at each of the cashier windows?

b. On average how long will a customer spend in the bank (assume they enter, go directly to one line, and leave as soon as service is complete).

You decide to consolidate all the cashiers so they can handle all types of customers without increasing the service times.

c. What will happen to the amount of time each cashier spends idle? (increase, decrease, stay the same, depends on _____)

d. What will happen to the average amount of time a customer spends in the bank? (increase, decrease, stay the same, depends on _____)

26 A local fast-food restaurant wants to analyze its drive-through window. At this time, the only information known is the average number of customers in the system (4.00) and the average time a customer spends at the restaurant (1.176 minutes). What are the arrival rate and the service rate?

CASE: COMMUNITY HOSPITAL EVENING OPERATING ROOM

The American College of Surgeons has developed criteria for determining operating room standards in the United States. Level I and II trauma centers are required to have in-house operating room (OR) staff 24 hours per day. So a base level of a single OR team available 24 hours a day is mandatory. During normal business hours, a hospital will typically have additional OR teams available since surgery is scheduled during these times and these additional teams can be used in an emergency. An important decision, though, must be made concerning the availability of a backup team during the evening hours.

A backup team is needed during the evening hours if the probability of having two or more cases simultaneously is significant. "Significant" is difficult to judge, but for the purposes of this case assume that a backup OR team should be employed if the expected probability of two or more cases occurring simultaneously is greater than 1 percent.

A real application was recently studied by doctors at the Columbia University College of Physicians and Surgeons in Stamford, CT.[3] The doctors studied emergency OR patients that arrived after 11 P.M. and before 7 A.M. during a one-year period. During this time period, there were 62 patients that required OR treatment. The average service time was 80.79 minutes.

In analyzing the problem, think about this as a single-channel, single-phase system with Poisson arrivals and exponential service times.

QUESTIONS

1 Calculate the average customer arrival rate and service rate per hour.
2 Calculate the probability of zero patients in the system (P0), probability of one patient (P1), and the probability

of two or more patients simultaneously arriving during the night shift.
3 Using a criterion that if the probability is greater than 1 percent, a backup OR team should be employed, make a recommendation to hospital administration.

SELECTED BIBLIOGRAPHY

Gross, D., and C. M. Harris. *Fundamentals of Queuing Theory*. New York: Wiley, 1997.

Hillier, F. S., et al. *Queuing Tables and Graphs*. New York: Elsevier–North Holland, 1981.

Kleinrock, L., and R. Gail. *Queuing Systems: Problems and Solutions*. New York: Wiley, 1996.

Winston, W. L., and S. C. Albright. *Practical Management Science: Spreadsheet Modeling and Application*. New York: Duxbury, 2000.

FOOTNOTES

1 $n!$ is defined as $n(n-1)(n-2)\cdots(2)(1)$.
2 We are indebted to Gilvan Souza of the Robert H. Smith School of Business, University of Maryland, for his help with this section.
3 J. B. Tucker, J. E. Barone, J. Cecere, R. G. Blabey, and C. K. Rha, "Using Queuing Theory to Determine Operating Room Staffing Needs," *Journal of Trauma*, 46, no. 1 (1999), pp. 71–79.

chapter

LOGISTICS AND FACILITY LOCATION

FedEx: A LEADING GLOBAL LOGISTICS COMPANY

Service

Supply Chain

FedEx provides a host of logistics solutions to its customers. Those services are segmented on the basis of types of customer needs, ranging from turnkey distribution centers to full-scale logistics services that incorporate expedited delivery. Following are some of the major services provided to the business customer:

- **FedEx Distribution Centers:** These centers provide turnkey warehousing services to businesses, using a network of warehouses in the United States and abroad. This service is targeted particularly at time-critical businesses. Goods stored in these centers are continuously available for 24-hour deliveries.

Courtesy of FedEx.

- **FedEx Returns Management:** FedEx Return solutions are designed to streamline the return area of a company's supply chain. These process-intelligent tools give customers services that offer pickup, delivery, and online status tracking for items that need to be returned.

- **Other Value-Added Services:** FedEx offers many other value-added services to its customers. One example is a merge-in-transit service offered to many customers that require rapid delivery. For example, under the merge-in-transit program, for a shipper of computers, FedEx could store peripheral products such as monitors and printers in its Memphis air hub and match those products up with the computer en route to a customer.

LOGISTICS

Supply Chain

A major issue in designing a great supply chain for manufactured goods is determining the way those items are moved from the manufacturing plant to the customer. For consumer products, this often involves moving product from the manufacturing plant to a warehouse and then to a retail store. You probably do not think about this often, but consider all those items with "Made in China" on the label. That sweatshirt probably has made a trip longer than you may ever make. If you live in Chicago in the United States and the sweatshirt is made in the Fujian region of China, that sweatshirt traveled over 6,600 miles, or 10,600 kilometers, nearly halfway around the world, to get to the retail store where you bought it. To keep the price of the sweatshirt down, that trip must be made as efficiently as possible. There is no telling how that sweatshirt made the trip. It might have been flown in an airplane or might have traveled in a combination of vehicles, possibly going by truck part of the way and by boat or plane the rest. Logistics is about this movement of goods through the supply chain.

Logistics

The Association for Operations Management defines logistics as "the art and science of obtaining, producing, and distributing material and product in the proper place and in proper quantities." This is a fairly broad definition, and this chapter will focus on how to analyze where we locate warehouses and plants and how to evaluate the movement of materials to and from those locations. The term international logistics

International logistics

refers to managing these functions when the movement is on a global scale. Clearly, if the China-made sweatshirt is sold in the United States or Europe, this involves international logistics.

There are companies that specialize in logistics, such as United Parcel Service (UPS), Federal Express (FedEx), and DHL. These global companies are in the business of moving everything from flowers to industrial equipment. Today a manufacturing company most often will contract with one of those companies to handle many of its logistics functions. In this case, those transportation companies often are called a third-party logistics company. The

Third-party logistics company

most basic function would be simply moving the goods from one place to another. The logistics company also may provide additional services such as warehouse management, inventory control, and other customer service functions.

Logistics is big business, accounting for 8 to 9 percent of the U.S. gross domestic product, and growing. Today's modern, efficient warehouse and distribution centers are the heart of logistics. These centers are carefully managed and efficiently operated to ensure the secure storage and quick flow of goods, services, and related information from the point of origin to the point of consumption.

DECISIONS RELATED TO LOGISTICS

The problem of deciding how best to transport goods from plants to customers is a complex one that affects the cost of a product. Major trade-offs related to the cost of transporting the product, speed of delivery, and flexibility to react to changes are involved. Information systems play a major role in coordinating activities and include activities such as allocating resources, managing inventory levels, scheduling, and order tracking. A full discussion of these systems is beyond the scope of this book, but we cover basic inventory control and scheduling in later chapters.

Logistics-System Design Matrix: Framework Describing Logistics Processes   exhibit 11.1

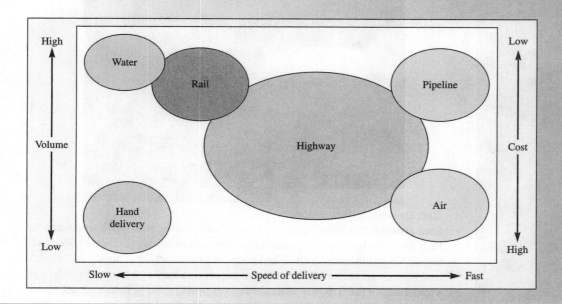

A key decision area is deciding how material will be transported. The Logistics-System Design Matrix shown in Exhibit 11.1 depicts the basic alternatives. There are six widely recognized modes of transportation: highway (trucks), water (ships), air (aircraft), rail (trains), pipelines, and hand delivery. Each mode is uniquely suited to handle certain types of products, as described next:

- **Highway (truck).**   Actually, few products are moved without some highway transportation. The highway offers great flexibility for moving goods to virtually any location not separated by water. Size of the product, weight, and liquid or bulk can all be accommodated with this mode.
- **Water (ship).**   Very high capacity and very low cost, but transit times are slow, and large areas of the world are not directly accessible to water carriers. This mode is especially useful for bulk items such as oil, coal, and chemical products.
- **Air.**   Fast but expensive. Small, light, expensive items are most appropriate for this mode of transportation.

Courtesy of Corbis Images.

Courtesy of F. Schussler/Photolink/Getty Images.

Courtesy of Ryan McVay/Getty Images.

Courtesy of F. Schussler/Photolink/Getty Images.

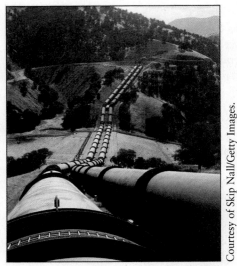

Courtesy of Skip Nall/Getty Images.

Cross-docking

Hub-and-spoke systems

- **Rail (trains).** This is a fairly low-cost alternative, but transit times can be long and may be subject to variability. The suitability of rail can vary depending on the rail infrastructure. The European infrastructure is highly developed, making this an attractive alternative compared to trucks, while in the U.S., the infrastructure has declined over the last 50 years, making it less attractive.
- **Pipelines.** This is highly specialized and limited to liquids, gases, and solids in slurry forms. No packaging is needed and the costs per mile are low. The initial cost to build a pipeline is very high.
- **Hand Delivery.** This is the last step in many supply chains. Getting the product in the customer's hand is a relatively slow and costly activity due to the high labor content.

Few companies use a single mode of transportation. Multimodal solutions are the norm, and finding the correct multimode strategies can be a significant problem. The problem of coordination and scheduling the carriers requires comprehensive information systems capable of tracking goods through the system. Standardized containers often are used so that a product can be transferred efficiently from a truck to an airplane or ship.

Cross-Docking Special consolidation warehouses are used when shipments from various sources are pulled together and combined into larger shipments with a common destination. This improves the efficiency of the entire system. Cross-docking is an approach used in these consolidation warehouses, where rather than making larger shipments, large shipments are broken down into small shipments for local delivery in an area. This often can be done in a coordinated manner so that the goods never are stored in inventory.

Retailers receive shipments from many suppliers in their regional warehouses and immediately sort those shipments for delivery to individual stores by using cross-docking systems coordinated by computerized control systems. This results in a minimal amount of inventory being carried in the warehouses.

Hub-and-spoke systems combine the idea of consolidation and that of cross-docking. Here the warehouse is referred to as a "hub" and its sole purpose is sorting goods. Incoming goods are sorted immediately to consolidation areas, where each area is designated for shipment to a specific location. Hubs are located in strategic locations near the geographic center of the region they are to serve to minimize the distance a good must travel.

Designing these system is an interesting and complex task. The following section focuses on the plant and warehouse location problem as representative of the types of logistics decisions that need to be made. Logistics is a broad topic, and its elements evolve as the value-added services provided by major logistics vendors expand. Having the proper network design is fundamental to efficiency in the industry.

ISSUES IN FACILITY LOCATION

The problem of facility location is faced by both new and existing businesses, and its solution is critical to a company's eventual success. An important element in designing a company's supply chain is the location of its facilities. For instance, 3M has moved a significant part of its corporate activity, including R&D, to the more temperate climate of Austin, Texas. Toys "Я" Us has opened a location in Japan as a part of its global strategy. Disney chose Paris, France, for its European theme park, and BMW assembles the Z3 sports car in South Carolina. Manufacturing and service companies' location decisions are guided by a variety of criteria defined by competitive imperatives. Criteria that influence manufacturing plant and warehouse location planning are discussed next.

Global

Proximity to customers.   For example, Japan's NTN Drive Shafts built a major plant in Columbus, Indiana, to be closer to major automobile manufacturing plants in the United States—whose buyers want their goods delivered yesterday. Such proximity also helps ensure that customer needs are incorporated into products being developed and built.

Business climate.   A favorable business climate can include the presence of similar-sized businesses, the presence of companies in the same industry, and, in the case of international locations, the presence of other foreign companies. Probusiness government legislation and local government intervention to facilitate businesses locating in an area via subsidies, tax abatements, and other support are also factors.

Total costs.   The objective is to select a site with the lowest total cost. This includes regional costs, inbound distribution costs, and outbound distribution costs. Land, construction, labor, taxes, and energy costs make up the regional costs. In addition, there are hidden costs that are difficult to measure. These involve (1) excessive moving of preproduction material between locations before final delivery to the customers and (2) loss of customer responsiveness arising from locating away from the main customer base.

Courtesy of Alcoa, Inc.

ALCOA'S PORTLAND, VICTORIA, AUSTRALIA, PLANT IS ONE OF OVER TWO DOZEN SMELTERS PRODUCING PRIMARY ALUMINUM FOR ALCOA. THE CREATION OF PARKLANDS AROUND THE PLANT SITE HAS EARNED THE TITLE "SMELTER IN THE PARK," AND THE ONLY CERTIFICATION AS A VIABLE HABITAT GRANTED OUTSIDE THE U.S. BY THE WILDLIFE HABITAT ENHANCEMENT COUNCIL.

CONVENIENCE DRIVES HONDA DECISION

Honda announced that it will build its sixth assembly plant in Greensburg, Indiana. As the *Chicago Tribune* put it, the decision was based on "Location, location, location. Indiana had it. Illinois and Ohio didn't." Honda will invest $550 million to build the operation, which will employ 2,000 workers when it starts producing 200,000 vehicles annually in 2008. What specific vehicles or models will be built in Greensburg was not announced, but it will be a "flex plant" capable of producing multiple models.

Courtesy of the *Chicago Tribune*.

While Indiana officials confirmed promising Honda $141.5 million in incentives, Larry Jutte, a company executive, rejected the idea that handouts were a factor. "It wasn't a matter of incentives offered; that was never a consideration. It was a matter of logistics, the human factor, the infrastructure, and the location." He said the decision was based on being in close proximity to suppliers of parts, particularly the source of four-cyclinder engines from Honda's operation in Anna, Ohio. The 1,700-acre Greensburg site is near I-74 and about 50 miles southwest of Indianapolis and will be built with expansion as a possibility. Altogether, so far, Honda has invested $9 billion locating facilities in North America.

An interesting sidelight is that this plant will now be close to the Indy 500. "For more than 50 years, racing has been a key part of the Honda culture, and we use racing to help train our engineers," said Koichi Kondo, president and CEO of American Honda. "Last month the winning car at the Indy 500 was powered by a Honda engine. In fact all 33 cars in the race were powered by Honda engines." Amazingly, in the 2006 race, for the first time ever, there were no engine failures during the Indy 500. Kondo said Honda and Indiana are beginning a long race together.

SOURCES: "CONVENIENCE DRIVES INDIANA TO VICTORY," *CHICAGO TRIBUNE*—BUSINESS, JUNE 29, 2006; http://blogs.edmunds.com/; http://corporate.honda.com/press.

Infrastructure. Adequate road, rail, air, and sea transportation is vital. Energy and telecommunications requirements also must be met. In addition, the local government's willingness to invest in upgrading infrastructure to the levels required may be an incentive to select a specific location.

Quality of labor. The educational and skill levels of the labor pool must match the company's needs. Even more important are the willingness and ability to learn.

Suppliers. A high-quality and competitive supplier base makes a given location suitable. The proximity of important suppliers' plants also supports lean manufacturing methods.

Other facilities. The location of other plants or distribution centers of the same company may influence a new facility's location in the network. Issues of product mix and capacity are strongly interconnected to the location decision in this context.

Free trade zone

Global

Free trade zones. A foreign trade zone or a free trade zone is typically a closed facility (under the supervision of the customs department) into which foreign goods can be brought without being subject to the normal customs requirements. There are about 260 such free trade zones in the United States today. Such specialized locations also exist in other countries. Manufacturers in free trade zones can use imported components in the final product and delay payment of customs duties until the product is shipped into the host country.

Political risk. The fast-changing geopolitical scenes in numerous nations present exciting, challenging opportunities. But the extended phase of transformation that many countries are undergoing makes the decision to locate in those areas extremely difficult. Political risks in both the country of location and the host country influence location decisions.

Government barriers. Barriers to enter and locate in many countries are being removed today through legislation. Yet many nonlegislative and cultural barriers should be considered in location planning.

Trading blocs. The Central America Free Trade Agreement (CAFTA) is one of the new trading blocs in our hemisphere. Such agreements influence location decisions, both within and outside trading bloc countries. Firms typically locate, or relocate, within a bloc to take advantage of new market opportunities or lower total costs afforded by the trading agreement. Other companies (those outside the trading bloc countries) decide on locations within the bloc so as not to be disqualified from competing in the new market. Examples include the location of various Japanese auto manufacturing plants in Europe before 1992 as well as recent moves by many communications and financial services companies into Mexico in a post-NAFTA environment.

Trading blocs

Environmental regulation. The environmental regulations that impact a certain industry in a given location should be included in the location decision. Besides measurable cost implications, these regulations influence the relationship with the local community.

Host community. The host community's interest in having the plant in its midst is a necessary part of the evaluation process. Local educational facilities and the broader issue of quality of life are also important.

Competitive advantage. An important decision for multinational companies is the nation in which to locate the home base for each distinct business. Porter suggests that a company can have different home bases for distinct businesses or segments. Competitive advantage is created at a home base where strategy is set, the core product and process technology are created, and a critical mass of production takes place. So a company should move its home base to a country that stimulates innovation and provides the best environment for global competitiveness.[1] This concept also can be applied to domestic companies seeking to gain sustainable competitive advantage. It partly explains the southeastern states' recent emergence as the preferred corporate destination within the United States (that is, their business climate fosters innovation and low-cost production).

Global

PLANT LOCATION METHODS

As we will see, there are many techniques available for identifying potential sites for plants or other types of facilities. The process required to narrow the decision down to a particular area can vary significantly depending on the type of business we are in and the competitive pressures that must be considered. As we have discussed, there are often many different criteria that need to be considered when selecting from the set of feasible sites.

In this section, we sample three different types of techniques that have proved to be very useful to many companies. The first is the *factor-rating system* that allows us to consider many different types of criteria using simple point-rating scales. Next, we consider the *transportation method* of linear programming, a powerful technique for estimating the cost of using a network of plants and warehouses. Following this, we consider the *centroid method,* a technique often used by communications companies (cell phone providers) to locate their transmission towers. Finally, later in the chapter we consider how service firms such as McDonald's and State Farm Insurance use statistical techniques to find desirable locations for their facilities.

FACTOR-RATING SYSTEMS

Factor-rating systems are perhaps the most widely used of the general location techniques because they provide a mechanism to combine diverse factors in an easy-to-understand format.

Factor-rating systems

By way of example, a refinery assigned the following range of point values to major factors affecting a set of possible sites:

	RANGE
Fuels in region	0 to 330
Power availability and reliability	0 to 200
Labor climate	0 to 100
Living conditions	0 to 100
Transportation	0 to 50
Water supply	0 to 10
Climate	0 to 50
Supplies	0 to 60
Tax policies and laws	0 to 20

Each site was then rated against each factor and a point value was selected from its assigned range. The sums of assigned points for each site were then compared. The site with the most points was selected.

A major problem with simple point-rating schemes is that they do not account for the wide range of costs that may occur within each factor. For example, there may be only a few hundred dollars' difference between the best and worst locations on one factor and several thousands of dollars' difference between the best and the worst on another. The first factor may have the most points available to it but provide little help in making the location decision; the second may have few points available but potentially show a real difference in the value of locations. To deal with this problem, it has been suggested that points possible for each factor be derived using a weighting scale based on standard deviations of costs rather than simply total cost amounts. In this way, relative costs can be considered.

TRANSPORTATION METHOD OF LINEAR PROGRAMMING

Transportation method

The transportation method is a special linear programming method. (Note that linear programming is developed in detail in Chapter 2A.) It gets its name from its application to problems involving transporting products from several sources to several destinations. The two common objectives of such problems are either (1) minimize the cost of shipping n units to m destinations or (2) maximize the profit of shipping n units to m destinations.

Interactive Operations Management

EXAMPLE 11.1: U.S. Pharmaceutical Company

Suppose the U.S. Pharmaceutical Company has four factories supplying the warehouses of four major customers and its management wants to determine the minimum-cost shipping schedule for its monthly output to these customers. Factory supply, warehouse demands, and shipping costs per case for these drugs are shown in Exhibit 11.2.

exhibit 11.2   Data for U.S. Pharmaceutical Transportation Problem

FACTORY	SUPPLY	WAREHOUSE	DEMAND	FROM	SHIPPING COSTS PER CASE (IN DOLLARS) To COLUMBUS	To ST. LOUIS	To DENVER	To LOS ANGELES
Indianapolis	15	Columbus	10	Indianapolis	$25	$35	$36	$60
Phoenix	6	St. Louis	12	Phoenix	55	30	25	25
New York	14	Denver	15	New York	40	50	80	90
Atlanta	11	Los Angeles	9	Atlanta	30	40	66	75

Transportation Matrix for U.S. Pharmaceutical Problem

exhibit 11.3

From \ To	Columbus	St. Louis	Denver	Los Angeles	Factory supply
Indianapolis	25	35	36	60	15
Phoenix	55	30	25	25	6
New York	40	50	80	90	14
Atlanta	30	40	66	75	11
Destination requirements	10	12	15	9	46 46

Excel® Screen Showing the U.S. Pharmaceutical Problem

exhibit 11.4

Microsoft Excel - US Pharmaceutical.xls

File Edit View Insert Format Tools Data Window Help

F20   = =SUM(B16:E19)

	A	B	C	D	E	F
1	From/To	Columbus	St. Louis	Denver	Los Angeles	Factory Supply
2	Indianapolis	25	35	36	60	15
3	Phoenix	55	30	25	25	6
4	New York	40	50	80	90	14
5	Atlanta	30	40	66	75	11
6	Requirements	10	12	15	9	
7						
8	Candidate Solution					Total Shipped
9	Indianapolis	0	0	15	0	15
10	Phoenix	0	0	0	6	6
11	New York	10	4	0	0	14
12	Atlanta	0	8	0	3	11
13	Total Supplied	10	12	15	9	
14						
15	Cost Calculations					
16	Indianapolis	0	0	540	0	
17	Phoenix	0	0	0	150	
18	New York	400	200	0	0	
19	Atlanta	0	320	0	225	
20					Total Cost	$1,835
21						
22						

US Pharmaceutical

Ready   NUM

Excel: US Pharmaceutical.xls

The transportation matrix for this example appears in Exhibit 11.3, where supply availability at each factory is shown in the far right column and the warehouse demands are shown in the bottom row. The shipping costs are shown in the small boxes within the cells. For example, the cost to ship one unit from the Indianapolis factory to the customer warehouse in Columbus is $25.

Tutorial: Transportation Method Solver

SOLUTION

This problem can be solved by using Microsoft® Excel's® Solver function. Exhibit 11.4 shows how the problem can be set up in the spreadsheet. Cells B6 through E6 contain the requirement for each customer warehouse. Cells F2 through F5 contain the amount that can be supplied from each plant. Cells B2 through E5 are the cost of shipping one unit for each potential plant and warehouse combination.

Cells for the solution of the problem are B9 through E12. These cells can initially be left blank when setting up the spreadsheet. Column cells F9 through F12 are the sum of each row, indicating how much is actually being shipped from each factory in the candidate solution. Similarly, row cells B13 through E13 are sums of the amount being shipped to each customer in the candidate solution. The Excel® Sum function can be used to calculate these values.

The cost of the candidate solution is calculated in cells B16 through E19. Multiplying the amount shipped in the candidate solution by the cost per unit of shipping over that particular route makes this calculation. For example, multiplying B2 by B9 in cell B16 gives the cost of shipping between Indianapolis and Columbus for the candidate solution. The total cost shown in cell F20 is the sum of all these individual costs.

To solve the problem, the Excel® Solver application needs to be accessed. The Solver is found by selecting Tools and then Solver from the Excel® menu (in Excel 2007, Solver is accessed through the Data tab). A screen similar to what is shown below should appear. If you cannot find Solver at that location, the required add-in might not have been added when Excel® was initially installed on your computer. Solver can easily be added if you have your original Excel® installation disk.

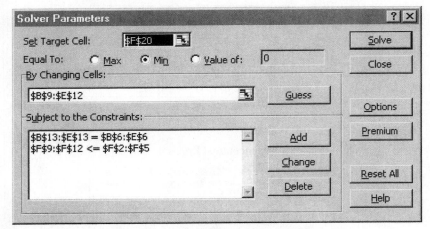

EXCEL® SCREEN SHOTS FROM MICROSOFT® EXCEL © 2003 MICROSOFT CORPORATION.

Solver parameters now need to be set. First, set the target cell. This is the cell where the total cost associated with the solution is calculated. In our sample problem, this is cell F20. Next we need to indicate that we are minimizing this cell. Selecting the "Min" button does this. The location of our solution is indicated in the "By Changing Cells" Text box. These cells are B9 through E12 in our example.

Next, we need to indicate the constraints for our problem. For our transportation problem, we need to be sure that customer demand is met and that we do not exceed the capacity of our manufacturing plants. To ensure that demand is met, click on "Add" and highlight the range of cells where we have calculated the total amount being shipped to each customer. This range is B13 to E13 in our example. Next, select "=" indicating that we want the amount shipped to equal demand. Finally, on the right side, enter the range of cells where the actual customer demand is stated in our spreadsheet. This range is B6 to E6 in our example.

The second set of constraints that ensures that the capacity of our manufacturing plants is not exceeded is entered similarly. The range of cells that indicated how much is being shipped from each factory is F9 to F12. These values need to be less than or equal to (<=) the capacity of each factory, which is in cells F2 to F5. To set up the Solver, a few options need to be set as well. Click on the "Options" button and the following screen should appear:

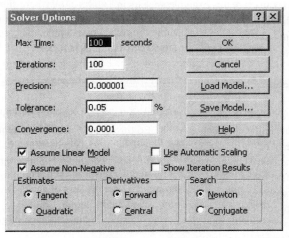

Two options need to be set for solving transportation problems. First, we need "Assume Linear Model." This tells the Solver that there are no nonlinear calculations in our spreadsheet. This is important because the

Solver can use a very efficient algorithm to calculate the optimal solution to this problem if this condition exists. Next, the "Assume Non-Negative" box needs to be checked. This tells Solver that the values in our solution need to be greater than or equal to zero. In transportation problems, shipping negative quantities does not make any sense. Click "OK" to return to the main Solver box, and then click "Solve" to actually solve the problem. Solver will notify you that it found a solution. Indicate that you want that solution saved. Finally, click OK to go back to the main spreadsheet. The solution should be in cells B9 to E12.

The transportation method can be used to solve many different types of problems if it is applied innovatively. For example, it can be used to test the cost impact of different candidate locations on the entire production–distribution network. To do this, we might add a new row that contains the unit shipping cost from a factory in a new location, say, Dallas, to the existing set of customer warehouses, along with the total amount it could supply. We could then solve this particular matrix for minimum total cost. Next, we would replace the factory located in Dallas in the same row of the matrix with a factory at a different location, Houston, and again solve for minimum total cost. Assuming the factories in Dallas and Houston would be identical in other important respects, the location resulting in the lowest total cost for the network would be selected.

For additional information about using the Solver, see Chapter 2A, "Linear Programming Using the Excel Solver." ●

CENTROID METHOD

The centroid method is a technique for locating single facilities that considers the existing facilities, the distances between them, and the volumes of goods to be shipped. The technique is often used to locate intermediate or distribution warehouses. In its simplest form, this method assumes that inbound and outbound transportation costs are equal and it does not include special shipping costs for less than full loads.

Another major application of the centroid method today is the location of communication towers in urban areas. Examples include radio, TV, and cell phone towers. In this application, the goal is to find sites that are near clusters of customers, thus ensuring clear radio signals.

The centroid method begins by placing the existing locations on a coordinate grid system. Coordinates are usually based on longitude and latitude measures due to the rapid adoption of GPS systems for mapping locations. To keep it simple for our examples, we use arbitrary X, Y coordinates. Exhibit 11.5 shows an example of a grid layout.

Centroid method

Grid Map for Centroid Example

exhibit 11.5

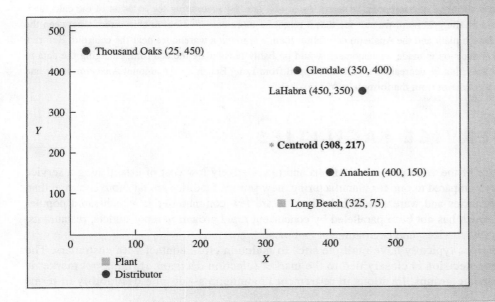

SHIPPING VOLUMES	
LOCATIONS	GALLONS OF GASOLINE PER MONTH (000,000)
Long Beach	1,500
Anaheim	250
LaHabra	450
Glendale	350
Thousand Oaks	45

Excel:
Centroid_method.xls

The centroid is found by calculating the X and Y coordinates that result in the minimal transportation cost. We use the formulas

$$C_x = \frac{\sum d_{ix} V_i}{\sum V_i} \qquad C_y = \frac{\sum d_{iy} V_i}{\sum V_i}$$

where

$C_x = X$ coordinate of the centroid

$C_y = Y$ coordinate of the centroid

$d_{ix} = X$ coordinate of the ith location

$d_{iy} = Y$ coordinate of the ith location

$V_i =$ Volume of goods moved to or from the ith location

EXAMPLE 11.2: HiOctane Refining Company

The HiOctane Refining Company needs to locate an intermediate holding facility between its refining plant in Long Beach and its major distributors. Exhibit 11.5 shows the coordinate map and the amount of gasoline shipped to or from the plant and distributors.

In this example, for the Long Beach location (the first location), $d_{1x} = 325$, $d_{1y} = 75$, and $V_1 = 1,500$.

SOLUTION

Using the information in Exhibit 11.5, we can calculate the coordinates of the centroid:

$$C_x = \frac{(325 \times 1,500) + (400 \times 250) + (450 \times 450) + (350 \times 350) + (25 \times 450)}{1,500 + 250 + 450 + 350 + 450}$$

$$= \frac{923,750}{3,000} = 307.9$$

$$C_y = \frac{(75 \times 1,500) + (150 \times 250) + (350 \times 450) + (400 \times 350) + (450 \times 450)}{1,500 + 250 + 450 + 350 + 450}$$

$$= \frac{650,000}{3,000} = 216.7$$

This gives management the X and Y coordinates of approximately 308 and 217, respectively, and provides an initial starting point to search for a new site. By examining the location of the calculated centroid on the grid map, we can see that it might be more cost-efficient to ship directly between the Long Beach plant and the Anaheim distributor than to ship via a warehouse near the centroid. Before a location decision is made, management would probably recalculate the centroid, changing the data to reflect this (that is, decrease the gallons shipped from Long Beach by the amount Anaheim needs and remove Anaheim from the formula). ●

LOCATING SERVICE FACILITIES

Because of the variety of service firms and the relatively low cost of establishing a service facility compared to one for manufacturing, new service facilities are far more common than new factories and warehouses. Indeed, there are few communities in which rapid population growth has not been paralleled by concurrent rapid growth in retail outlets, restaurants, municipal services, and entertainment facilities.

Services typically have multiple sites to maintain close contact with customers. The location decision is closely tied to the market selection decision. If the target market is college-age groups, locations in retirement communities—despite desirability in terms

LESS THAN TWO MILES FROM TWIN CITIES INTERNATIONAL AIRPORT, WITH FOUR MAJOR HIGHWAYS INTERSECTING THE 78-ACRE PROPERTY, BLOOMINGTON'S MALL OF AMERICA HAS BECOME GLOBALLY RECOGNIZED AS THE LARGEST ENTERTAINMENT AND RETAIL COMPLEX IN THE UNITED STATES. SERVING OVER 28 MILLION PEOPLE WITHIN A ONE-DAY DRIVE AS WELL AS MANY MORE AS A DESTINATION, THE MALL EMPLOYS MORE THAN 12,000 PEOPLE AND TOTAL TRAFFIC IS BETWEEN 35 AND 42 MILLION VISITS YEARLY. VISITORS SPEND AN AVERAGE OF THREE HOURS IN THE MALL, WHICH IS THREE TIMES THE NATIONAL AVERAGE FOR SHOPPING MALLS.

Courtesy of the Mall of America.

of cost, resource availability, and so forth—are not viable alternatives. Market needs also affect the number of sites to be built and the size and characteristics of the sites. Whereas manufacturing location decisions are often made by minimizing costs, many service location decision techniques maximize the profit potential of various sites. Next, we present a multiple regression model that can be used to help select good sites.

EXAMPLE 11.3: Screening Hotel Location Sites

Selecting good sites is crucial to a hotel chain's success. Of the four major marketing considerations (price, product, promotion, and location), location and product have been shown to be most important for multisite firms. As a result, hotel chain owners who can pick good sites quickly have a distinct competitive advantage.

Exhibit 11.6 shows the initial list of variables included in a study to help a hotel chain screen potential locations for its new hotels. Data were collected on 57 existing sites. Analysis of the data identified the variables that correlated with operating profit in two years. (See Exhibit 11.7.)

SOLUTION

A *regression model* (see Chapter 13) was constructed. Its final form was

$$\text{Profitability} = 39.05 - 5.41 \times \text{State population per inn (1,000)}$$

$$+ 5.86 \times \text{Price of the inn}$$

$$- 3.91 \times \text{Square root of the median income of the area (1,000)}$$

$$+ 1.75 \times \text{College students within four miles}$$

The model shows that profitability is affected by market penetration, positively affected by price, negatively affected by higher incomes (the inns do better in lower-median-income areas), and positively affected by colleges nearby.

The hotel chain implemented the model on a spreadsheet and routinely uses the spreadsheet to screen potential real estate acquisitions. The founder and president of the hotel chain has accepted the model's validity and no longer feels obligated to personally select the sites.

This example shows that a specific model can be obtained from the requirements of service organizations and used to identify the most important features in site selection. ●

exhibit 11.6   Independent Variables Collected for the Initial Model-Building Stage

CATEGORY	NAME	DESCRIPTION
Competitive	INNRATE	Inn price
	PRICE	Room rate for the inn
	RATE	Average competitive room rate
	RMS 1	Hotel rooms within 1 mile
	RMSTOTAL	Hotel rooms within 3 miles
	ROOMSINN	Inn rooms
Demand generators	CIVILIAN	Civilian personnel on base
	COLLEGE	College enrollment
	HOSP 1	Hospital beds within 1 mile
	HOSPTOTL	Hospital beds within 4 miles
	HVYIND	Heavy industrial employment
	LGTIND	Light industrial acreage
	MALLS	Shopping mall square footage
	MILBLKD	Military base blocked
	MILITARY	Military personnel
	MILTOT	MILITARY + CIVILIAN
	OFC 1	Office space within 1 mile
	OFCTOTAL	Office space within 4 miles
	OFCCBD	Office space in Central Business District
	PASSENGR	Airport passengers enplaned
	RETAIL	Scale ranking of retail activity
	TOURISTS	Annual tourists
	TRAFFIC	Traffic count
	VAN	Airport van
Demographic	EMPLYPCT	Unemployment percentage
	INCOME	Average family income
	POPULACE	Residential population
Market awareness	AGE	Years inn has been open
	NEAREST	Distance to nearest inn
	STATE	State population per inn
	URBAN	Urban population per inn
Physical	ACCESS	Accessibility
	ARTERY	Major traffic artery
	DISTCBD	Distance to downtown
	SIGNVIS	Sign visibility

exhibit 11.7   A Summary of the Variables That Correlated with Operating Margin

VARIABLE	YEAR 1	YEAR 2
ACCESS	.20	
AGE	.29	.49
COLLEGE		.25
DISTCBD		−.22
EMPLYPCT	−.22	−.22
INCOME		−.23
MILTOT		.22
NEAREST	−.51	
OFCCBD	.30	
POPULACE	.30	.35
PRICE	.38	.58
RATE		.27
STATE	−.32	−.33
SIGNVIS	.25	
TRAFFIC	.32	
URBAN	−.22	−.26

CONCLUSION

In this chapter, the focus was on locating the manufacturing and distribution sites in the supply chain. Certainly, the term *logistics* is more comprehensive in scope and includes not only the design issues addressed in this chapter, but also the more comprehensive problem involved with moving goods through the supply chain.

In the chapter, we covered common techniques for designing the supply chain. Linear programming, in particular the transportation method, is a useful way to structure these logistics design problems. The problems can be easily solved using the Excel Solver; how to do this is covered in the chapter. Dramatic changes in the global business environment have placed a premium on making decisions relating to how products will be sourced and delivered. These decisions need to be made quickly and must be based on the actual costs involved. Cost modeling using spreadsheets when combined with optimization is a powerful tool for analysis of these problems.

The chapter also briefly looked at locating service facilities such as restaurants and retail stores by using regression analysis. These problems are challenging, and spreadsheet modeling is again an important analysis tool.

KEY TERMS

Logistics (1) In an industrial context, the art and science of obtaining, producing, and distributing material and product in the proper place and in the proper quantities. (2) In a military sense (where it has greater usage), its meaning also can include the movement of personnel.

International logistics All functions concerned with the movement of materials and finished goods on a global scale.

Third-party logistics company A company that manages all or part of another company's product delivery operations.

Cross-docking An approach used in consolidation warehouses where rather than making larger shipments, large shipments are broken down into small shipments for local delivery in an area.

Hub-and-spoke systems Systems that combine the idea of consolidation and that of cross-docking.

Free trade zone A closed facility (under the supervision of government customs officials) into which foreign goods can be brought without being subject to the payment of normal import duties.

Trading bloc A group of countries that agree on a set of special arrangements governing the trading of goods between member countries. Companies may locate in places affected by the agreement to take advantage of new market opportunities.

Factor-rating system An approach for selecting a facility location by combining a diverse set of factors. Point scales are developed for each criterion. Each potential site is then evaluated on each criterion, and the points are combined to calculate a rating for the site.

Transportation method A special linear programming method that is useful for solving problems involving transporting products from several sources to several destinations.

Centroid method A technique for locating single facilities that considers the existing facilities, the distances between them, and the volumes of goods to be shipped.

FORMULA REVIEW

Centroid

$$C_x = \frac{\sum d_{ix} V_i}{\sum V_i} \qquad C_y = \frac{\sum d_{iy} V_i}{\sum V_i}$$

SOLVED PROBLEM

Cool Air, a manufacturer of automotive air conditioners, currently produces its XB-300 line at three different locations: Plant A, Plant B, and Plant C. Recently, management decided to build all compressors, a major product component, in a separate dedicated facility, Plant D.

exhibit 11.8

Plant Location Matrix

**Excel:
Centroid_method**

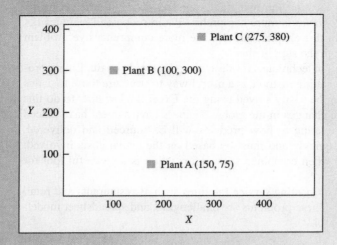

PLANT	QUANTITY OF COMPRESSORS REQUIRED BY EACH PLANT
	COMPRESSORS REQUIRED PER YEAR
A	6,000
B	8,200
C	7,000

Using the centroid method and the information displayed in Exhibit 11.8, determine the best location for Plant D. Assume a linear relationship between volumes shipped and shipping costs (no premium charges).

Solution

$$d_{1x} = 150 \qquad d_{1y} = 75 \qquad V_1 = 6,000$$

$$d_{2x} = 100 \qquad d_{2y} = 300 \qquad V_2 = 8,200$$

$$d_{3x} = 275 \qquad d_{3y} = 380 \qquad V_3 = 7,000$$

$$C_x = \frac{\sum d_{ix} V_i}{\sum V_i} = \frac{(150 \times 6,000) + (100 \times 8,200) + (275 \times 7,000)}{6,000 + 8,200 + 7,000} = 172$$

$$C_y = \frac{\sum d_{iy} V_i}{\sum V_i} = \frac{(75 \times 6,000) + (300 \times 8,200) + (380 \times 7,000)}{21,200} = 262.7$$

Plant D[C_x, C_y] = D[172, 263]

REVIEW AND DISCUSSION QUESTIONS

1 What motivations typically cause firms to initiate a facilities location or relocation project?
2 List five major reasons why a new electronic components manufacturing firm should move into your city or town.
3 How do facility location decisions differ for service facilities and manufacturing plants?
4 What are the pros and cons of relocating a small or midsized manufacturing firm (that makes mature products) from the United States to Mexico in the post-NAFTA environment?
5 If you could locate your new software development company anywhere in the world, which place would you choose, and why?

PROBLEMS

1 Refer to the information given in the solved problem. Suppose management decides to shift 2,000 units of production from Plant B to Plant A. Does this change the proposed location of Plant D, the compressor production facility? If so, where should Plant D be located?
2 A small manufacturing facility is being planned that will feed parts to three heavy manufacturing facilities. The locations of the current plants with their coordinates and volume requirements are given in the following table:

PLANT LOCATION	COORDINATES (x, y)	VOLUME (PARTS PER YEAR)
Peoria	300, 320	4,000
Decatur	375, 470	6,000
Joliet	470, 180	3,000

Use the centroid method to determine the best location for this new facility.

3   Bindley Corporation has a one-year contract to supply motors for all washing machines produced by Rinso Ltd. Rinso manufactures the washers at four locations around the country: New York, Fort Worth, San Diego, and Minneapolis. Plans call for the following numbers of washing machines to be produced at each location:

New York	50,000
Fort Worth	70,000
San Diego	60,000
Minneapolis	80,000

Bindley has three plants that can produce the motors. The plants and production capacities are

Boulder	100,000
Macon	100,000
Gary	150,000

Due to varying production and transportation costs, the profit Bindley earns on each 1,000 units depends on where they were produced and where they were shipped. The following table gives the accounting department estimates of the dollar profit per unit. (Shipment will be made in lots of 1,000.)

	SHIPPED TO			
PRODUCED AT	NEW YORK	FORT WORTH	SAN DIEGO	MINNEAPOLIS
Boulder	7	11	8	13
Macon	20	17	12	10
Gary	8	18	13	16

Given profit maximization as a criterion, Bindley would like to determine how many motors should be produced at each plant and how many motors should be shipped from each plant to each destination.

a. Develop a transportation grid for this problem.

b. Find the optimal solution using Microsoft® Excel.

4   Rent'R Cars is a multisite car rental company in the city. It is trying out a new "return the car to the location most convenient for you" policy to improve customer service. But this means that the company has to constantly move cars around the city to maintain required levels of vehicle availability. The supply and demand for economy cars, and the total cost of moving these vehicles between sites, are shown below.

From \ To	D	E	F	G	Supply
A	$9	$8	$6	$5	50
B	9	8	8	0	40
C	5	3	3	10	75
Demand	50	60	25	30	165 / 165

a. Find the solution that minimizes moving costs using Microsoft® Excel.

b. What would you have to do to the costs to assure that A always sends a car to D as part of the optimal solution?

5   A local manufacturer of wire harnesses is considering merging its three production facilities located in the same county into one new facility. Using the centroid method, determine the best location for the new facility. It is fair to assume a linear relationship between amount shipped and shipping costs.

The plan matrix is shown below with coordinates:

LOCATION	COORDINATES	UNITS PER YEAR
Jasper	150, 100	6500
Huntingburg	100, 400	7500
Celestine	300, 350	8000

6   Whirlpool Appliances produces refrigerators in Los Angeles and Detroit and supplies refrigerators to customers in Houston and Tampa. The costs of shipping a refrigerator between various points are listed below. Los Angeles can produce up to 2,900 units and Detroit up to 2,000. Determine how to best use your Los Angeles and Detroit capacity to minimize shipping costs.

UNIT SHIPPING COSTS

FROM/TO	LA	DETROIT	ATLANTA	HOUSTON	TAMPA
LA		$140	$100	$90	$225
Detroit	$145		$111	$110	$119
Atlanta	$105	$115		$113	$78
Houston	$89	$109	$121		
Tampa	$210	$117	$82		

7   The Peoples Credit Union has two check processing sites. Site 1 can process 10,000 checks per day, and site 2 can process 6000 checks per day. The credit union processes three types of checks: business, salary and personal. The processing cost per check depends on the site, as listed below. Each day 5000 checks of each type must be processed. Determine how to minimize the daily cost of processing checks using Excel.

	BUSINESS	SALARY	PERSONAL
Site 1	$0.05	$0.04	$0.02
Site 2	$0.03	$0.04	$0.05

CASE: APPLICHEM—THE TRANSPORTATION PROBLEM

Applichem management is faced with the difficult problem of allocating to its customers the capacity of manufacturing plants that are located around the world. Management has long recognized that the manufacturing plants differ greatly in efficiency but has had little success in improving the operations of the inefficient plants. At this time, management has decided to focus on how best to use the capacity of its plants given the differences in manufacturing costs that currently exist. They recognize that this study may result in the significant reduction of output or possibly the shutting down of one or more of the existing plants.

Applichem makes a product called Release-ease. Plastics molding manufacturers use this chemical product. Plastic parts are made by injecting hot plastic into a mold made in the shape of the part. After the plastic has sufficiently cooled, the fresh part is removed from the mold and the mold is then reused to make subsequent parts. Release-ease is a dry powder, applied as part of

the manufacturing process, that makes it easy to remove the part from the mold.

Applichem has made the product since the early 1950s, and demand has been consistent over time. A recent study by Applichem's market research team has indicated that demand for Release-ease should be fairly steady for the next five years. Although Applichem does have some competition, particularly in the European markets, management feels that as long as they can provide a quality product at a competitive cost, customers should stick with Applichem. Release-ease sells at an average price of $1.00 per pound.

The company owns plants capable of making Release-ease in the following cities: Gary, Indiana; Windsor, Ontario, Canada; Frankfurt, Germany; Mexico City, Mexico; Caracas, Venezuela; and Osaka, Japan. Although the plants are focused on meeting demand for the immediate surrounding regions, there is considerable exporting and importing of product for various reasons. The following table contains data on how demand has been met during the past year:

PRODUCT MADE AND SHIPPED DURING PAST YEAR (×100,000 POUNDS)

FROM/TO	MEXICO	CANADA	VENEZUELA	EUROPE	UNITED STATES	JAPAN
Mexico City	3.0		6.3			7.9
Windsor, Ontario		2.6				
Caracas			4.1			
Frankfurt			5.6	20.0	12.4	
Gary					14.0	
Osaka						4.0

Differences in the technologies used in the plants and in local raw material and labor costs created significant differences in the cost to produce Release-ease in the various locations. These costs may change dramatically due to currency valuation and labor law changes in some of the countries. This is especially true in Mexico and Venezuela. The capacity of each plant also differs at each location, and management has no interest in increasing capacity anywhere at this time. The following table gives details on the costs to produce and capacity of each plant:

PLANT PRODUCTION COSTS AND CAPACITY

PLANT	PRODUCTION COST (PER 1,000 LBS)	PLANT CAPACITY (×100,000 LBS)
Mexico City	95.01	22.0
Windsor, Ontario	97.35	3.7
Caracas	116.34	4.5
Frankfurt	76.69	47.0
Gary	102.93	18.5
Osaka	153.80	5.0

In considering how best to use the capacity of its plants, Applichem management needs to consider the cost of shipping product from one customer region to another. Applichem now commonly ships product in bulk around the world, but it is expensive.

The costs involved are not only the transportation costs but also import duties that are assessed by customs in some countries. Applichem is committed to meeting demand, though, and sometimes this is done even though profit might not be made on all orders.

The following table details the demand in each country, the cost to transport product from each plant to each country, and the current import duty rate levied by each country. (These percentages do not reflect current duties.) Import duty is calculated on the approximate production plus transportation cost of product brought into the country. (For example, if the production and shipping cost for 1,000 pounds of Release-ease shipped into Venezuela were $100, the import duty would be $100 × 0.5 = $50.)

TRANSPORTATION COST (PER 1,000 LBS), IMPORT DUTIES, AND DEMANDS FOR RELEASE-EASE

PLANT/COUNTRY	MEXICO	CANADA	VENEZUELA	EUROPE	UNITED STATES	JAPAN
Mexico City	0	11.40	7.00	11.00	11.00	14.00
Windsor, Ontario	11.00	0	9.00	11.50	6.00	13.00
Caracas	7.00	10.00	0	13.00	10.40	14.30
Frankfurt	10.00	11.50	12.50	0	11.20	13.30
Gary	10.00	6.00	11.00	10.00	0	12.50
Osaka	14.00	13.00	12.50	14.20	13.00	0
Total demand (×100,000 lbs)	3.0	2.6	16.0	20.0	26.4	11.9
Import duty	0.0%	0.0%	50.0%	9.5%	4.5%	6.0%

QUESTIONS

Given all these data, set up a spreadsheet (Applichem.xls is a start) and answer the following questions for management:

1 Evaluate the cost associated with the way Applichem's plant capacity is currently being used.
2 Determine the optimal use of Applichem's plant capacity using the Solver in Excel.
3 What would you recommend that Applichem management do? Why?

Excel: Applichem

SOURCE: THIS CASE IS ROUGHLY BASED ON DATA CONTAINED IN "APPLICHEM (A)," HARVARD BUSINESS SCHOOL, 9-685-051.

SELECTED BIBLIOGRAPHY

Drezner, Z., and H. Hamacher. *Facility Location: Applications and Theory*. Berlin: Springer Verlag, 2004.

Goldsby, T. J., and R. Martichenko. *Lean Six Sigma Logistics: Strategic Development to Operational Success*. Fort Landerdale, FL: J. Ross Publishing, 2005.

Murphy, P. R., and D. Wood. *Contemporary Logistics*. 9th ed. Upper Saddle River, NJ: Prentice Hall, 2007.

FOOTNOTE

1 M. E. Porter, "The Competitive Advantage of Nation," *Harvard Business Review*, March–April 1990.

Part V

Taken from The *Harvard Business Review*

Strategy and Society
The Link Between Competitive Advantage and Corporate Social Responsibility

by Michael E. Porter and Mark R. Kramer

Governments, activists, and the media have become adept at holding companies to account for the social consequences of their activities. Myriad organizations rank companies on the performance of their corporate social responsibility (CSR), and, despite sometimes questionable methodologies, these rankings attract considerable publicity. As a result, CSR has emerged as an inescapable priority for business leaders in every country.

Many companies have already done much to improve the social and environmental consequences of their activities, yet these efforts have not been nearly as productive as they could be—for two reasons. First, they pit business against society, when clearly the two are interdependent. Second, they pressure companies to think of corporate social responsibility in generic ways instead of in the way most appropriate to each firm's strategy.

The fact is, the prevailing approaches to CSR are so fragmented and so disconnected from business and strategy as to obscure many of the greatest opportunities for companies to benefit society. If, instead, corporations were to analyze their prospects for social responsibility using the same frameworks that guide their core business choices, they would discover that CSR can be much more than a cost, a constraint, or a charitable deed—it can be a source of opportunity, innovation, and competitive advantage.

In this article, we propose a new way to look at the relationship between business and society that does not treat corporate success and social welfare as a zero-sum game. We introduce a framework companies can use to identify all of the effects, both positive and negative, they have on society; determine which ones to address; and suggest effective ways to do so. When looked at strategically, corporate social responsibility can become a source of tremendous social progress, as the business applies its considerable resources, expertise, and insights to activities that benefit society.

The Emergence of Corporate Social Responsibility

Heightened corporate attention to CSR has not been entirely voluntary. Many companies

Michael E. Porter is the Bishop William Lawrence University Professor at Harvard University; he is based at Harvard Business School in Boston. He is a frequent contributor to HBR, and his most recent article is "Seven Surprises for New CEOs" (October 2004). **Mark R. Kramer** (mark.kramer@fsg-impact.org) is the managing director of FSG Social Impact Advisors, an international non profit consulting firm, and a senior fellow in the CSR Initiative at Harvard's John F. Kennedy School of Government in Cambridge, Massachusetts. Porter and Kramer are the cofounders of both FSG Social Impact Advisors and the Center for Effective Philanthropy, a nonprofit research organization.

awoke to it only after being surprised by public responses to issues they had not previously thought were part of their business responsibilities. Nike, for example, faced an extensive consumer boycott after the *New York Times* and other media outlets reported abusive labor practices at some of its Indonesian suppliers in the early 1990s. Shell Oil's decision to sink the *Brent Spar,* an obsolete oil rig, in the North Sea led to Greenpeace protests in 1995 and to international headlines. Pharmaceutical companies discovered that they were expected to respond to the AIDS pandemic in Africa even though it was far removed from their primary product lines and markets. Fast-food and packaged food companies are now being held responsible for obesity and poor nutrition.

Activist organizations of all kinds, both on the right and the left, have grown much more aggressive and effective in bringing public pressure to bear on corporations. Activists may target the most visible or successful companies merely to draw attention to an issue, even if those corporations actually have had little impact on the problem at hand. Nestlé, for example, the world's largest purveyor of bottled water, has become a major target in the global debate about access to fresh water, despite the fact that Nestlé's bottled water sales consume just 0.0008% of the world's fresh water supply. The inefficiency of agricultural irrigation, which uses 70% of the world's supply annually, is a far more pressing issue, but it offers no equally convenient multinational corporation to target.

Debates about CSR have moved all the way into corporate boardrooms. In 2005, 360 different CSR-related shareholder resolutions were filed on issues ranging from labor conditions to global warming. Government regulation increasingly mandates social responsibility reporting. Pending legislation in the UK, for example, would require every publicly listed company to disclose ethical, social, and environmental risks in its annual report. These pressures clearly demonstrate the extent to which external stakeholders are seeking to hold companies accountable for social issues and highlight the potentially large financial risks for any firm whose conduct is deemed unacceptable.

While businesses have awakened to these risks, they are much less clear on what to do

about them. In fact, the most common corporate response has been neither strategic nor operational but cosmetic: public relations and media campaigns, the centerpieces of which are often glossy CSR reports that showcase companies' social and environmental good deeds. Of the 250 largest multinational corporations, 64% published CSR reports in 2005, either within their annual report or, for most, in separate sustainability reports—supporting a new cottage industry of report writers.

Such publications rarely offer a coherent framework for CSR activities, let alone a strategic one. Instead, they aggregate anecdotes about uncoordinated initiatives to demonstrate a company's social sensitivity. What these reports leave out is often as telling as what they include. Reductions in pollution, waste, carbon emissions, or energy use, for example, may be documented for specific divisions or regions but not for the company as a whole. Philanthropic initiatives are typically described in terms of dollars or volunteer hours spent but almost never in terms of impact. Forward-looking commitments to reach explicit performance targets are even rarer.

This proliferation of CSR reports has been paralleled by growth in CSR ratings and rankings. While rigorous and reliable ratings might constructively influence corporate behavior, the existing cacophony of self-appointed scorekeepers does little more than add to the confusion. (See the sidebar "The Ratings Game.")

In an effort to move beyond this confusion, corporate leaders have turned for advice to a growing collection of increasingly sophisticated nonprofit organizations, consulting firms, and academic experts. A rich literature on CSR has emerged, though what practical guidance it offers corporate leaders is often unclear. Examining the primary schools of thought about CSR is an essential starting point in understanding why a new approach is needed to integrating social considerations more effectively into core business operations and strategy.

Four Prevailing Justifications for CSR

Broadly speaking, proponents of CSR have used four arguments to make their case: moral obligation, sustainability, license to operate, and reputation. The moral appeal—arguing that companies have a duty to be good citizens and to "do the right thing"—is prominent in the goal of Business for Social Responsibility, the leading nonprofit CSR business association in the United States. It asks that its members "achieve commercial success in ways that honor ethical values and respect people, communities, and the natural environment." Sustainability emphasizes environmental and community stewardship. An excellent definition was developed in the 1980s by Norwegian Prime Minister Gro Harlem Brundtland and used by the World Business Council for Sustainable Development: "Meeting the needs of the present without compromising the ability of future generations to meet their own needs." The notion of license to operate derives from the fact that every company needs tacit or explicit permission from governments, communities, and numerous other stakeholders to do business. Finally, reputation is used by many companies to justify CSR initiatives on the grounds that they will improve a company's image, strengthen its brand, enliven morale, and even raise the value of its stock. These justifications have advanced thinking in the field, but none offers sufficient guidance for the difficult choices corporate leaders must make. Consider the practical limitations of each approach.

The CSR field remains strongly imbued with a moral imperative. In some areas, such as honesty in filing financial statements and operating within the law, moral considerations are easy to understand and apply. It is the nature of moral obligations to be absolute mandates, however, while most corporate social choices involve balancing competing values, interests, and costs. Google's recent entry into China, for example, has created an irreconcilable conflict between its U.S. customers' abhorrence of censorship and the legal constraints imposed by the Chinese government. The moral calculus needed to weigh one social benefit against another, or against its financial costs, has yet to be developed. Moral principles do not tell a pharmaceutical company how to allocate its revenues among subsidizing care for the indigent today, developing cures for the future, and providing dividends to its investors.

The principle of sustainability appeals to enlightened self-interest, often invoking the so-called triple bottom line of economic, social, and environmental performance. In other words, companies should operate in ways that secure long-term economic performance by avoiding short-term behavior that is socially detrimental or environmentally wasteful. The principle works best for issues that coincide with a company's economic or regulatory interests. DuPont, for example, has saved over $2 billion from reductions in energy use since 1990. Changes to the materials McDonald's uses to wrap its food have reduced its solid waste by 30%. These were smart business decisions entirely apart from their environmental benefits. In other areas,

The Ratings Game

Measuring and publicizing social performance is a potentially powerful way to influence corporate behavior—assuming that the ratings are consistently measured and accurately reflect corporate social impact. Unfortunately, neither condition holds true in the current profusion of CSR checklists.

The criteria used in the rankings vary widely. The Dow Jones Sustainability Index, for example, includes aspects of economic performance in its evaluation. It weights customer service almost 50% more heavily than corporate citizenship. The equally prominent FTSE4Good Index, by contrast, contains no measures of economic performance or customer service at all. Even when criteria happen to be the same, they are invariably weighted differently in the final scoring.

Beyond the choice of criteria and their weightings lies the even more perplexing question of how to judge whether the criteria have been met. Most media, nonprofits, and investment advisory organizations have too few resources to audit a universe of complicated global corporate activities. As a result, they tend to use measures for which data are readily and inexpensively available, even though they may not be good proxies for the social or environmental effects they are intended to reflect. The Dow Jones Sustainability Index, for example, uses the size of a company's board as a measure of community involvement, even though size and involvement may be entirely unrelated.[1]

Finally, even if the measures chosen accurately reflect social impact, the data are frequently unreliable. Most ratings rely on surveys whose response rates are statistically insignificant, as well as on self-reported company data that have not been verified externally. Companies with the most to hide are the least likely to respond. The result is a jumble of largely meaningless rankings, allowing almost any company to boast that it meets some measure of social responsibility—and most do.

1. For a fuller discussion of the problem of CSR ratings, see Aaron Chatterji and David Levine, "Breaking Down the Wall of Codes: Evaluating Non-Financial Performance Measurement," *California Management Review,* Winter 2006.

however, the notion of sustainability can become so vague as to be meaningless. Transparency may be said to be more "sustainable" than corruption. Good employment practices are more "sustainable" than sweatshops. Philanthropy may contribute to the "sustainability" of a society. However true these assertions are, they offer little basis for balancing long-term objectives against the short-term costs they incur. The sustainability school raises questions about these trade-offs without offering a framework to answer them. Managers without a strategic understanding of CSR are prone to postpone these costs, which can lead to far greater costs when the company is later judged to have violated its social obligation.

The license-to-operate approach, by contrast, is far more pragmatic. It offers a concrete way for a business to identify social issues that matter to its stakeholders and make decisions about them. This approach also fosters constructive dialogue with regulators, the local citizenry, and activists—one reason, perhaps, that it is especially prevalent among companies that depend on government consent, such as those in mining and other highly regulated and extractive industries. That is also why the approach is common at companies that rely on the forbearance of their neighbors, such as those, like chemical manufacturing, whose operations are noxious or environmentally hazardous. By seeking to satisfy stakeholders, however, companies cede primary control of their CSR agendas to outsiders. Stakeholders' views are obviously important, but these groups can never fully understand a corporation's capabilities, competitive positioning, or the trade-offs it must make. Nor does the vehemence of a stakeholder group necessarily signify the importance of an issue—either to the company or to the world. A firm that views CSR as a way to placate pressure groups often finds that its approach devolves into a series of short-term defensive reactions—a never-ending public relations palliative with minimal value to society and no strategic benefit for the business.

Finally, the reputation argument seeks that strategic benefit but rarely finds it. Concerns about reputation, like license to operate, focus on satisfying external audiences. In consumer-oriented companies, it often leads to high-profile cause-related marketing campaigns. In stigmatized industries, such as chemicals and energy, a company may instead pursue social responsibility initiatives as a form of insurance, in the hope that its reputation for social consciousness will temper public criticism in the event of a crisis. This rationale once again risks confusing public relations with social and business results.

A few corporations, such as Ben & Jerry's, Newman's Own, Patagonia, and the Body Shop, have distinguished themselves through an extraordinary long-term commitment to social responsibility. But even for these companies, the social impact achieved, much less the business benefit, is hard to determine. Studies of the effect of a company's social reputation on consumer purchasing preferences or on stock market performance have been inconclusive at best. As for the concept of CSR as insurance, the connection between the good deeds and consumer attitudes is so indirect as to be impossible to measure. Having no way to quantify the benefits of these investments puts such CSR programs on shaky ground, liable to be dislodged by a change of management or a swing in the business cycle.

All four schools of thought share the same weakness: They focus on the tension between business and society rather than on their interdependence. Each creates a generic rationale that is not tied to the strategy and operations of any specific company or the places in which it operates. Consequently, none of them is sufficient to help a company identify, prioritize, and address the social issues that matter most or the ones on which it can make the biggest impact. The result is oftentimes a hodgepodge of uncoordinated CSR and philanthropic activities disconnected from the company's strategy that neither make any meaningful social impact nor strengthen the firm's long-term competitiveness. Internally, CSR practices and initiatives are often isolated from operating units—and even separated from corporate philanthropy. Externally, the company's social impact becomes diffused among numerous unrelated efforts, each responding to a different stakeholder group or corporate pressure point.

The consequence of this fragmentation is a tremendous lost opportunity. The power of corporations to create social benefit is dissipated, and so is the potential of companies to take actions that would support both their communities and their business goals.

The prevailing approaches to CSR are so disconnected from business as to obscure many of the greatest opportunities for companies to benefit society.

Mapping Social Opportunities

The interdependence of a company and society can be analyzed with the same tools used to analyze competitive position and develop strategy. In this way, the firm can focus its particular CSR activities to best effect. Rather than merely acting on well-intentioned impulses or reacting to outside pressure, the organization can set an affirmative CSR agenda that produces maximum social benefit as well as gains for the business.

   These two tools should be used in different ways. When a company uses the value chain to chart all the social consequences of its activities, it has, in effect, created an inventory of problems and opportunities—mostly operational issues—that need to be investigated, prioritized, and addressed. In general, companies should attempt to clear away as many negative value-chain social impacts as possible. Some company activities will prove to offer opportunities for social and strategic distinction.

   In addressing competitive context, companies cannot take on every area in the diamond. Therefore, the task is to identify those areas of social context with the greatest strategic value. A company should carefully choose from this menu one or a few social initiatives that will have the greatest shared value: benefit for both society and its own competitiveness.

Looking Inside Out: Mapping the Social Impact of the Value Chain

The *value chain* depicts all the activities a company engages in while doing business. It can be used as a framework to identify the positive and negative social impact of those activities. These "inside-out" linkages may range from hiring and layoff policies to greenhouse gas emissions, as the partial list of examples illustrated here demonstrates.

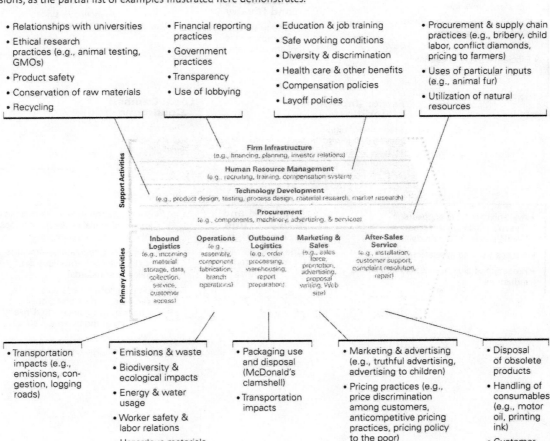

Source: Michael E. Porter, *Competitive Advantage: Creating and Sustaining Superior Performance*, 1985

Looking Outside In: Social Influences on Competitiveness

In addition to understanding the social ramifications of the value chain, effective CSR requires an understanding of the social dimensions of the company's competitive context—the "outside-in" linkages that affect its ability to improve productivity and execute strategy. These can be understood using the *diamond framework,* which shows how the conditions at a company's locations (such as transportation infrastructure and honestly enforced regulatory policy) affect its ability to compete.

- Availability of human resources (Marriott's job training)
- Access to research institutions and universities (Microsoft's Working Connections)
- Efficient physical infrastructure
- Efficient administrative infrastructure
- Availability of scientific and technological infrastructure (Nestlé's knowledge transfer to milk farmers)
- Sustainable natural resources (GrupoNueva's water conservation)
- Efficient access to capital

- Fair and open local competition (e.g., the absence of trade barriers, fair regulations)
- Intellectual property protection
- Transparency (e.g., financial reporting, corruption: Extractive Industries Transparency Initiative)
- Rule of law (e.g., security, protection of property, legal system)
- Meritocratic incentive systems (e.g., antidiscrimination)

Context for Firm Strategy and Rivalry

The rules and incentives that govern competition

Factor (Input) Conditions

Presence of high-quality, specialized inputs available to firms

Local Demand Conditions

The nature and sophistication of local customer needs

- Availability of local suppliers (Sysco's locally grown produce; Nestlé's milk collection dairies)
- Access to firms in related fields
- Presence of clusters instead of isolated industries

Related and Supporting Industries

The local availability of supporting industries

- Sophistication of local demand (e.g. appeal of social value propositions: Whole Foods' customers)
- Demanding regulatory standards (California auto emissions & mileage standards)
- Unusual local needs that can be served nationally and globally (Urbi's housing financing, Unilever's "bottom of the pyramid" strategy)

Source: Michael E. Porter, *The Competitive Advantage of Nations,* 1990

Integrating Business and Society

To advance CSR, we must root it in a broad understanding of the interrelationship between a corporation and society while at the same time anchoring it in the strategies and activities of specific companies. To say broadly that business and society need each other might seem like a cliché, but it is also the basic truth that will pull companies out of the muddle that their current corporate-responsibility thinking has created.

Successful corporations need a healthy society. Education, health care, and equal opportunity are essential to a productive workforce. Safe products and working conditions not only attract customers but lower the internal costs of accidents. Efficient utilization of land, water, energy, and other natural resources makes business more productive. Good government, the rule of law, and property rights are essential for efficiency and innovation. Strong regulatory standards protect both consumers and competitive companies from exploitation. Ultimately, a healthy society creates expanding demand for business, as more human needs are met and aspirations grow. Any business that pursues its ends at the expense of the society in which it operates will find its success to be illusory and ultimately temporary.

At the same time, a healthy society needs successful companies. No social program can rival the business sector when it comes to creating the jobs, wealth, and innovation that improve standards of living and social conditions over time. If governments, NGOs, and other participants in civil society weaken the ability of business to operate productively, they may win battles but will lose the war, as corporate and regional competitiveness fade, wages stagnate, jobs disappear, and the wealth that pays taxes and supports nonprofit contributions evaporates.

Leaders in both business and civil society have focused too much on the friction between them and not enough on the points of intersection. The mutual dependence of corporations and society implies that both business decisions and social policies must follow the principle of *shared value*. That is, choices must benefit both sides. If either a business or a society pursues policies that benefit its interests at the expense of the other, it will find itself on a dangerous path. A temporary gain to one will undermine the long-term prosperity of both.[1]

To put these broad principles into practice, a company must integrate a social perspective into the core frameworks it already uses to understand competition and guide its business strategy.

Identifying the points of intersection. The interdependence between a company and society takes two forms. First, a company impinges upon society through its operations in the normal course of business: These are *inside-out linkages*.

Virtually every activity in a company's value chain touches on the communities in which the firm operates, creating either positive or negative social consequences. (For an example of this process, see the exhibit "Looking Inside Out: Mapping the Social Impact of the Value Chain.") While companies are increasingly aware of the social impact of their activities (such as hiring practices, emissions, and waste disposal), these impacts can be more subtle and variable than many managers realize. For one thing, they depend on location. The same manufacturing operation will have very different social consequences in China than in the United States.

A company's impact on society also changes over time, as social standards evolve and science progresses. Asbestos, now understood as a serious health risk, was thought to be safe in the early 1900s, given the scientific knowledge then available. Evidence of its risks gradually mounted for more than 50 years before any company was held liable for the harms it can cause. Many firms that failed to anticipate the consequences of this evolving body of research have been bankrupted by the results. No longer can companies be content to monitor only the obvious social impacts of today. Without a careful process for identifying evolving social effects of tomorrow, firms may risk their very survival.

Not only does corporate activity affect society, but external social conditions also influence corporations, for better and for worse. These are *outside-in linkages*.

Every company operates within a competitive context, which significantly affects its ability to carry out its strategy, especially in the long run. Social conditions form a key part of this context. Competitive context garners far less attention than value chain impacts but can have far greater strategic importance for both companies and societies. Ensuring the health

An affirmative corporate social agenda moves from mitigating harm to reinforcing corporate strategy through social progress.

of the competitive context benefits both the company and the community.

Competitive context can be divided into four broad areas: first, the quantity and quality of available business inputs—human resources, for example, or transportation infrastructure; second, the rules and incentives that govern competition—such as policies that protect intellectual property, ensure transparency, safeguard against corruption, and encourage investment; third, the size and sophistication of local demand, influenced by such things as standards for product quality and safety, consumer rights, and fairness in government purchasing; fourth, the local availability of supporting industries, such as service providers and machinery producers. Any and all of these aspects of context can be opportunities for CSR initiatives. (See the exhibit "Looking Outside In: Social Influences on Competitiveness.") The ability to recruit appropriate human resources, for example, may depend on a number of social factors that companies can influence, such as the local educational system, the availability of housing, the existence of discrimination (which limits the pool of workers), and the adequacy of the public health infrastructure.[2]

Choosing which social issues to address. No business can solve all of society's problems or bear the cost of doing so. Instead, each company must select issues that intersect with its particular business. Other social agendas are best left to those companies in other industries, NGOs, or government institutions that are better positioned to address them. The essential test that should guide CSR is not whether a cause is worthy but whether it presents an opportunity to create shared value— that is, a meaningful benefit for society that is also valuable to the business.

Our framework suggests that the social issues affecting a company fall into three categories, which distinguish between the many worthy causes and the narrower set of social issues that are both important and strategic for the business.

Generic social issues may be important to society but are neither significantly affected by the company's operations nor influence the company's long-term competitiveness. *Value chain social impacts* are those that are significantly affected by the company's activities in the ordinary course of business. *Social dimensions of competitive context* are factors in the external environment that significantly affect the underlying drivers of competitiveness in those places where the company operates. (See the exhibit "Prioritizing Social Issues.")

Every company will need to sort social issues into these three categories for each of its business units and primary locations, then rank them in terms of potential impact. Into which category a given social issue falls will vary from business unit to business unit, industry to industry, and place to place.

Supporting a dance company may be a generic social issue for a utility like Southern California Edison but an important part of the competitive context for a corporation like American Express, which depends on the high-end entertainment, hospitality, and tourism cluster. Carbon emissions may be a generic social issue for a financial services firm like Bank of America, a negative value chain impact for a transportation-based company like UPS, or both a value chain impact and a competitive context issue for a car manufacturer like Toyota. The AIDS pandemic in Africa may be a generic social issue for a U.S. retailer like Home Depot, a value chain impact for a pharmaceutical company like GlaxoSmithKline, and a competitive context issue for a mining company like Anglo American that depends on local labor in Africa for its operations.

Even issues that apply widely in the economy, such as diversity in hiring or conservation of energy, can have greater significance for some industries than for others. Health care benefits, for example, will present fewer challenges for software development or biotech-

Prioritizing Social Issues

Generic Social Issues	Value Chain Social Impacts	Social Dimensions of Competitive Context
Social issues that are not significantly affected by a company's operations nor materially affect its long-term competitiveness.	Social issues that are significantly affected by a company's activities in the ordinary course of business.	Social issues in the external environment that significantly affect the underlying drivers of a company's competitiveness in the locations where it operates.

nology firms, where workforces tend to be small and well compensated, than for companies in a field like retailing, which is heavily dependent on large numbers of lower-wage workers.

Within an industry, a given social issue may cut differently for different companies, owing to differences in competitive positioning. In the auto industry, for example, Volvo has chosen to make safety a central element of its competitive positioning, while Toyota has built a competitive advantage from the environmental benefits of its hybrid technology. For an individual company, some issues will prove to be important for many of its business units and locations, offering opportunities for strategic corporatewide CSR initiatives.

Where a social issue is salient for many companies across multiple industries, it can often be addressed most effectively through cooperative models. The Extractive Industries Transparency Initiative, for example, includes 19 major oil, gas, and mining companies that have agreed to discourage corruption through full public disclosure and verification of all corporate payments to governments in the countries in which they operate. Collective action by all major corporations in these industries prevents corrupt governments from undermining social benefit by simply choosing not to deal with the firms that disclose their payments.

Creating a corporate social agenda. Categorizing and ranking social issues is just the means to an end, which is to create an explicit and affirmative corporate social agenda. A corporate social agenda looks beyond community expectations to opportunities to achieve social and economic benefits simultaneously. It moves from mitigating harm to finding ways to reinforce corporate strategy by advancing social conditions.

Such a social agenda must be responsive to stakeholders, but it cannot stop there. A substantial portion of corporate resources and attention must migrate to truly strategic CSR. (See the exhibit "Corporate Involvement in Society: A Strategic Approach.") It is through strategic CSR that the company will make the most significant social impact and reap the greatest business benefits.

Responsive CSR. Responsive CSR comprises two elements: acting as a good corporate citizen, attuned to the evolving social concerns of stakeholders, and mitigating existing or anticipated adverse effects from business activities.

Good citizenship is a sine qua non of CSR, and companies need to do it well. Many worthy local organizations rely on corporate contributions, while employees derive justifiable pride from their company's positive involvement in the community.

The best corporate citizenship initiatives involve far more than writing a check: They specify clear, measurable goals and track results over time. A good example is GE's program to adopt underperforming public high schools near several of its major U.S. facilities. The company contributes between $250,000 and $1 million over a five-year period to each school and makes in-kind donations as well. GE managers and employees take an active role by working with school administrators to assess needs and mentor or tutor students. In an independent study of ten schools in the program between 1989 and 1999, nearly all showed significant improvement, while the graduation rate in four of the five worst-performing schools doubled from an average of 30% to 60%.

Effective corporate citizenship initiatives such as this one create goodwill and improve relations with local governments and other important constituencies. What's more, GE's employees feel great pride in their participation. Their effect is inherently limited, however. No matter how beneficial the program is, it remains incidental to the company's business, and the direct effect on GE's recruiting and re-

Corporate Involvement in Society: A Strategic Approach

Generic Social Impacts	Value Chain Social Impacts	Social Dimensions of Competitive Context
Good citizenship	Mitigate harm from value chain activities	Strategic philanthropy that leverages capabilities to improve salient areas of competitive context
Responsive CSR	Transform value-chain activities to benefit society while reinforcing strategy	**Strategic CSR**

tention is modest.

The second part of responsive CSR—mitigating the harm arising from a firm's value chain activities—is essentially an operational challenge. Because there are a myriad of possible value chain impacts for each business unit, many companies have adopted a checklist approach to CSR, using standardized sets of social and environmental risks. The Global Reporting Initiative, which is rapidly becoming a standard for CSR reporting, has enumerated a list of 141 CSR issues, supplemented by auxiliary lists for different industries.

These lists make for an excellent starting point, but companies need a more proactive and tailored internal process. Managers at each business unit can use the value chain as a tool to identify systematically the social impacts of the unit's activities in each location. Here operating management, which is closest to the work actually being done, is particularly helpful. Most challenging is to anticipate impacts that are not yet well recognized. Consider B&Q, an international chain of home supply centers based in England. The company has begun to analyze systematically tens of thousands of products in its hundreds of stores against a list of a dozen social issues—from climate change to working conditions at its suppliers' factories—to determine which products pose potential social responsibility risks and how the company might take action before any external pressure is brought to bear.

For most value chain impacts, there is no need to reinvent the wheel. The company should identify best practices for dealing with each one, with an eye toward how those practices are changing. Some companies will be more proactive and effective in mitigating the wide array of social problems that the value chain can create. These companies will gain an edge, but—just as for procurement and other operational improvements—any advantage is likely to be temporary.

Strategic CSR. For any company, strategy must go beyond best practices. It is about choosing a unique position—doing things differently from competitors in a way that lowers costs or better serves a particular set of customer needs. These principles apply to a company's relationship to society as readily as to its relationship to its customers and rivals.

Strategic CSR moves beyond good corporate citizenship and mitigating harmful value chain impacts to mount a small number of initiatives whose social and business benefits are large and distinctive. Strategic CSR involves both inside-out and outside-in dimensions working in tandem. It is here that the opportunities for shared value truly lie.

Many opportunities to pioneer innovations to benefit both society and a company's own competitiveness can arise in the product offering and the value chain. Toyota's response to concerns over automobile emissions is an example. Toyota's Prius, the hybrid electric/gasoline vehicle, is the first in a series of innovative car models that have produced competitive advantage and environmental benefits. Hybrid engines emit as little as 10% of the harmful pollutants conventional vehicles produce while consuming only half as much gas. Voted 2004 Car of the Year by *Motor Trend* magazine, Prius has given Toyota a lead so substantial that Ford and other car companies are licensing the technology. Toyota has created a unique position with customers and is well on its way to establishing its technology as the world standard.

Urbi, a Mexican construction company, has prospered by building housing for disadvantaged buyers using novel financing vehicles such as flexible mortgage payments made through payroll deductions. Crédit Agricole, France's largest bank, has differentiated itself by offering specialized financial products related to the environment, such as financing packages for energy-saving home improvements and for audits to certify farms as organic.

Strategic CSR also unlocks shared value by investing in social aspects of context that strengthen company competitiveness. A symbiotic relationship develops: The success of the company and the success of the community become mutually reinforcing. Typically, the more closely tied a social issue is to the company's business, the greater the opportunity to leverage the firm's resources and capabilities, and benefit society.

Microsoft's Working Connections partnership with the American Association of Community Colleges (AACC) is a good example of a shared-value opportunity arising from investments in context. The shortage of information technology workers is a significant constraint on Microsoft's growth; currently, there are more than 450,000 unfilled IT positions in the United States alone. Community colleges, with

An affirmative corporate social agenda moves from mitigating harm to reinforcing corporate strategy through social progress.

an enrollment of 11.6 million students, representing 45% of all U.S. undergraduates, could be a major solution. Microsoft recognizes, however, that community colleges face special challenges: IT curricula are not standardized, technology used in classrooms is often outdated, and there are no systematic professional development programs to keep faculty up to date.

Microsoft's $50 million five-year initiative was aimed at all three problems. In addition to contributing money and products, Microsoft sent employee volunteers to colleges to assess needs, contribute to curriculum development, and create faculty development institutes. Note that in this case, volunteers and assigned staff were able to use their core professional skills to address a social need, a far cry from typical volunteer programs. Microsoft has achieved results that have benefited many communities while having a direct—and potentially significant—impact on the company.

Integrating inside-out and outside-in practices. Pioneering value chain innovations and addressing social constraints to competitiveness are each powerful tools for creating economic and social value. However, as our examples illustrate, the impact is even greater if they work together. Activities in the value chain can be performed in ways that reinforce improvements in the social dimensions of context. At the same time, investments in competitive context have the potential to reduce constraints on a company's value chain activities. Marriott, for example, provides 180 hours of paid classroom and on-the-job training to chronically unemployed job candidates. The company has combined this with support for local community service organizations, which identify, screen, and refer the candidates to

Integrating Company Practice and Context: Nestlé's Milk District

Nestlé's approach to working with small farmers exemplifies the symbiotic relationship between social progress and competitive advantage. Ironically, while the company's reputation remains marred by a 30-year-old controversy surrounding sales of infant formula in Africa, the corporation's impact in developing countries has often been profoundly positive.

Consider the history of Nestlé's milk business in India. In 1962, the company wanted to enter the Indian market, and it received government permission to build a dairy in the northern district of Moga. Poverty in the region was severe; people were without electricity, transportation, telephones, or medical care. A farmer typically owned less than five acres of poorly irrigated and infertile soil. Many kept a single buffalo cow that produced just enough milk for their own consumption. Sixty percent of calves died newborn. Because farmers lacked refrigeration, transportation, or any way to test for quality, milk could not travel far and was frequently contaminated or diluted.

Nestlé came to Moga to build a business, not to engage in CSR. But Nestlé's value chain, derived from the company's origins in Switzerland, depended on establishing local sources of milk from a large, diversified base of small farmers. Establishing that value chain in Moga required Nestlé to transform the competitive context in ways that created tremendous shared value for both the company and the region.

Nestlé built refrigerated dairies as collection points for milk in each town and sent its trucks out to the dairies to collect the milk. With the trucks went veterinarians, nutritionists, agronomists, and quality assurance experts. Medicines and nutritional supplements were provided for sick animals, and monthly training sessions were held for local farmers. Farmers learned that the milk quality depended on the cows' diet, which in turn depended on adequate feed crop irrigation. With financing and technical assistance from Nestlé, farmers began to dig previously unaffordable deep-bore wells. Improved irrigation not only fed cows but increased crop yields, producing surplus wheat and rice and raising the standard of living.

When Nestlé's milk factory first opened, only 180 local farmers supplied milk. Today, Nestlé buys milk from more than 75,000 farmers in the region, collecting it twice daily from more than 650 village dairies. The death rate of calves has dropped by 75%. Milk production has increased 50-fold. As the quality has improved, Nestlé has been able to pay higher prices to farmers than those set by the government, and its steady biweekly payments have enabled farmers to obtain credit. Competing dairies and milk factories have opened, and an industry cluster is beginning to develop.

Today, Moga has a significantly higher standard of living than other regions in the vicinity. Ninety percent of the homes have electricity, and most have telephones; all villages have primary schools, and many have secondary schools. Moga has five times the number of doctors as neighboring regions. The increased purchasing power of local farmers has also greatly expanded the market for Nestlé's products, further supporting the firm's economic success.

Nestlé's commitment to working with small farmers is central to its strategy. It enables the company to obtain a stable supply of high-quality commodities without paying middlemen. The corporation's other core products—coffee and cocoa—are often grown by small farmers in developing countries under similar conditions. Nestlé's experience in setting up collection points, training farmers, and introducing better technology in Moga has been repeated in Brazil, Thailand, and a dozen other countries, including, most recently, China. In each case, as Nestlé has prospered, so has the community.

Marriott. The net result is both a major benefit to communities and a reduction in Marriott's cost of recruiting entry-level employees. Ninety percent of those in the training program take jobs with Marriott. One year later, more than 65% are still in their jobs, a substantially higher retention rate than the norm.

When value chain practices and investments in competitive context are fully integrated, CSR becomes hard to distinguish from the day-to-day business of the company. Nestlé, for example, works directly with small farmers in developing countries to source the basic commodities, such as milk, coffee, and cocoa, on which much of its global business depends. (See the sidebar "Integrating Company Practice and Context: Nestlé's Milk District.") The company's investment in local infrastructure and its transfer of world-class knowledge and technology over decades has produced enormous social benefits through improved health care, better education, and economic development, while giving Nestlé direct and reliable access to the commodities it needs to maintain a profitable global business. Nestlé's distinctive strategy is inseparable from its social impact.

Creating a social dimension to the value proposition. At the heart of any strategy is a unique value proposition: a set of needs a company can meet for its chosen customers that others cannot. The most strategic CSR occurs when a company adds a social dimension to its value proposition, making social impact integral to the overall strategy.

Consider Whole Foods Market, whose value proposition is to sell organic, natural, and healthy food products to customers who are passionate about food and the environment. Social issues are fundamental to what makes Whole Foods unique in food retailing and to its ability to command premium prices. The company's sourcing emphasizes purchases from local farmers through each store's procurement process. Buyers screen out foods containing any of nearly 100 common ingredients that the company considers unhealthy or environmentally damaging. The same standards apply to products made internally. Whole Foods' baked goods, for example, use only unbleached and unbromated flour.

Whole Foods' commitment to natural and environmentally friendly operating practices extends well beyond sourcing. Stores are constructed using a minimum of virgin raw materi-

als. Recently, the company purchased renewable wind energy credits equal to 100% of its electricity use in all of its stores and facilities, the only *Fortune* 500 company to offset its electricity consumption entirely. Spoiled produce and biodegradable waste are trucked to regional centers for composting. Whole Foods' vehicles are being converted to run on biofuels. Even the cleaning products used in its stores are environmentally friendly. And through its philanthropy, the company has created the Animal Compassion Foundation to develop more natural and humane ways of raising farm animals. In short, nearly every aspect of the company's value chain reinforces the social dimensions of its value proposition, distinguishing Whole Foods from its competitors.

Not every company can build its entire value proposition around social issues as Whole Foods does, but adding a social dimension to the value proposition offers a new frontier in competitive positioning. Government regulation, exposure to criticism and liability, and consumers' attention to social issues are all persistently increasing. As a result, the number of industries and companies whose competitive advantage can involve social value propositions is constantly growing. Sysco, for example, the largest distributor of food products to restaurants and institutions in North America, has begun an initiative to preserve small, family-owned farms and offer locally grown produce to its customers as a source of competitive differentiation. Even large global multinationals—such as General Electric, with its "ecomagination" initiative that focuses on developing water purification technology and other "green" businesses, and Unilever, through its efforts to pioneer new products, packaging, and distribution systems to meet the needs of the poorest populations—have decided that major business opportunities lie in integrating business and society.

Organizing for CSR

Integrating business and social needs takes more than good intentions and strong leadership. It requires adjustments in organization, reporting relationships, and incentives. Few companies have engaged operating management in processes that identify and prioritize social issues based on their salience to business operations and their importance to the

Typically the more closely tied a social issue is to a company's business, the greater the opportunity to leverage the firm's resources—and benefit society.

company's competitive context. Even fewer have unified their philanthropy with the management of their CSR efforts, much less sought to embed a social dimension into their core value proposition. Doing these things requires a far different approach to both CSR and philanthropy than the one prevalent today. Companies must shift from a fragmented, defensive posture to an integrated, affirmative approach. The focus must move away from an emphasis on image to an emphasis on substance.

The current preoccupation with measuring stakeholder satisfaction has it backwards. What needs to be measured is social impact. Operating managers must understand the importance of the outside-in influence of competitive context, while people with responsibility for CSR initiatives must have a granular understanding of every activity in the value chain. Value chain and competitive-context investments in CSR need to be incorporated into the performance measures of managers with P&L responsibility. These transformations require more than a broadening of job definition; they require overcoming a number of long-standing prejudices. Many operating managers have developed an ingrained us-versus-them mind-set that responds defensively to the discussion of any social issue, just as many NGOs view askance the pursuit of social value for profit. These attitudes must change if companies want to leverage the social dimension of corporate strategy.

Strategy is always about making choices, and success in corporate social responsibility is no different. It is about choosing which social issues to focus on. The short-term performance pressures companies face rule out indiscriminate investments in social value creation. They suggest, instead, that creating shared value should be viewed like research and development, as a long-term investment in a company's future competitiveness. The billions of dollars already being spent on CSR and corporate philanthropy would generate far more benefit to both business and society if consistently invested using the principles we have outlined.

While responsive CSR depends on being a good corporate citizen and addressing every social harm the business creates, strategic CSR is far more selective. Companies are called on to address hundreds of social issues, but only a few represent opportunities to make a real difference to society or to confer a competitive advantage. Organizations that make the right choices and build focused, proactive, and integrated social initiatives in concert with their core strategies will increasingly distance themselves from the pack.

The Moral Purpose of Business

By providing jobs, investing capital, purchasing goods, and doing business every day, corporations have a profound and positive influence on society. The most important thing a corporation can do for society, and for any community, is contribute to a prosperous economy. Governments and NGOs often forget this basic truth. When developing countries distort rules and incentives for business, for example, they penalize productive companies. Such countries are doomed to poverty, low wages, and selling off their natural resources. Corporations have the know-how and resources to change this state of affairs, not only in the developing world but also in economically disadvantaged communities in advanced economies.

This cannot excuse businesses that seek short-term profits deceptively or shirk the social and environmental consequences of their actions. But CSR should not be only about what businesses have done that is wrong—important as that is. Nor should it be only about making philanthropic contributions to local charities, lending a hand in time of disaster, or providing relief to society's needy—worthy though these contributions may be. Efforts to find shared value in operating practices and in the social dimensions of competitive context have the potential not only to foster economic and social development but to change the way companies and society think about each other. NGOs, governments, and companies must stop thinking in terms of "corporate social responsibility" and start thinking in terms of "corporate social integration."

Perceiving social responsibility as building shared value rather than as damage control or as a PR campaign will require dramatically different thinking in business. We are convinced, however, that CSR will become increasingly important to competitive success.

Corporations are not responsible for all the world's problems, nor do they have the resources to solve them all. Each company can identify the particular set of societal problems that it is best equipped to help resolve and from which it can gain the greatest competitive benefit. Addressing social issues by creating shared value will lead to self-sustaining solutions that do not depend on private or government subsidies. When a well-run business applies its vast resources, expertise, and management talent to problems that it understands and in which it has a stake, it can have a greater impact on social good than any other institution or philanthropic organization.

1. An early discussion of the idea of CSR as an opportunity rather than a cost can be found in David Grayson and Adrian Hodges, *Corporate Social Opportunity* (Greenleaf, 2004).

2. For a more complete discussion of the importance of competitive context and the diamond model, see Michael E. Porter and Mark R. Kramer, "The Competitive Advantage of Corporate Philanthropy," HBR December 2002. See also Michael Porter's book *The Competitive Advantage of Nations* (The Free Press, 1990) and his article "Locations, Clusters, and Company Strategy," in *The Oxford Handbook of Economic Geography,* edited by Gordon L. Clark, Maryann P. Feldman, and Meric S. Gertler (Oxford University Press, 2000).

Reprint R0612D
To order, see the next page
or call 800-988-0886 or 617-783-7500
or go to www.hbr.org

Further Reading

The *Harvard Business Review*
Paperback Series

Here are the landmark ideas—both
contemporary and classic—that have
established *Harvard Business Review* as required
reading for businesspeople around the globe.
Each paperback includes eight of the leading
articles on a particular business topic. The
series includes over thirty titles, including the
following best-sellers:

**Harvard Business Review on Brand
Management**
Product no. 1445

Harvard Business Review on Change
Product no. 8842

Harvard Business Review on Leadership
Product no. 8834

**Harvard Business Review on Managing
People**
Product no. 9075

**Harvard Business Review on Measuring
Corporate Performance**
Product no. 8826

For a complete list of the *Harvard Business
Review* paperback series, go to www.hbr.org.

Harvard Business Review

Stable and paranoid, systematic and experimental, formal and frank: The success of Toyota, a pathbreaking six-year study reveals, is due as much to its ability to embrace contradictions like these as to its manufacturing prowess.

The Contradictions That Drive Toyota's Success

by Hirotaka Takeuchi, Emi Osono, and Norihiko Shimizu

Stable and paranoid, systematic and experimental, formal and frank: The success of Toyota, a pathbreaking six-year study reveals, is due as much to its ability to embrace contradictions like these as to its manufacturing prowess.

The Contradictions That Drive Toyota's Success

by Hirotaka Takeuchi, Emi Osono, and Norihiko Shimizu

No executive needs convincing that Toyota Motor Corporation has become one of the world's greatest companies because of the Toyota Production System (TPS). The unorthodox manufacturing system enables the Japanese giant to make the planet's best automobiles at the lowest cost and to develop new products quickly. Not only have Toyota's rivals such as Chrysler, Daimler, Ford, Honda, and General Motors developed TPS-like systems, organizations such as hospitals and postal services also have adopted its underlying rules, tools, and conventions to become more efficient. An industry of lean-manufacturing experts have extolled the virtues of TPS so often and with so much conviction that managers believe its role in Toyota's success to be one of the few enduring truths in an otherwise murky world.

Like many beliefs about Toyota, however, this doesn't serve executives well. It's a half-truth, and half-truths are dangerous. We studied Toyota for six years, during which time we visited facilities in 11 countries, attended nu-

merous company meetings and events, and analyzed internal documents. We also conducted 220 interviews with former and existing Toyota employees, ranging from shop-floor workers to Toyota's president, Katsuaki Watanabe. Our research shows that TPS is necessary but is by no means sufficient to account for Toyota's success.

Quite simply, TPS is a "hard" innovation that allows the company to keep improving the way it manufactures vehicles; in addition, Toyota has mastered a "soft" innovation that relates to corporate culture. The company succeeds, we believe, because it creates contradictions and paradoxes in many aspects of organizational life. Employees have to operate in a culture where they constantly grapple with challenges and problems and must come up with fresh ideas. That's why Toyota constantly gets better. The hard and the soft innovations work in tandem. Like two wheels on a shaft that bear equal weight, together they move the company forward. Toyota's culture of contradictions plays as important a role in its success as TPS does, but rivals and experts have so far overlooked it.

Toyota believes that efficiency alone cannot guarantee success. Make no mistake: No company practices Taylorism better than Toyota does. What's different is that the company views employees not just as pairs of hands but as knowledge workers who accumulate *chie*—the wisdom of experience—on the company's front lines. Toyota therefore invests heavily in people and organizational capabilities, and it garners ideas from everyone and everywhere: the shop floor, the office, the field.

At the same time, studies of human cognition show that when people grapple with opposing insights, they understand the different aspects of an issue and come up with effective solutions. So Toyota deliberately fosters contradictory viewpoints within the organization and challenges employees to find solutions by transcending differences rather than resorting to compromises. This culture of tensions generates innovative ideas that Toyota implements to pull ahead of competitors, both incrementally and radically.

In the following pages, we will describe some key contradictions that Toyota fosters. We will also show how the company unleashes six forces, three of which drive it to experiment and expand while three help it to preserve its values and identity. Finally, we will briefly describe how other companies can learn to thrive on contradictions.

A Culture of Contradictions

Most outsiders find Toyota unfathomable because it doesn't bear any of the telltale signs of a successful enterprise. In fact, it resembles a failing or stagnant giant in several ways. Toyota pays relatively low dividends and hoards cash, which smacks of inefficiency. From 1995 to 2006, Toyota's dividends averaged only 20% of earnings. For instance, its 2006 payout of 21.3% was on par with that of smaller rivals, such as Nissan's 22.9% and Hyundai-Kia's 17.4%, but far behind (the then) Daimler-Chrysler's 47.5%. At the same time, it had accumulated $20 billion of cash, leading some analysts to call it Toyota Bank.

Most of Toyota's senior executives are Japanese men, whereas top management in successful Western corporations is more diverse. The company's roots are in a rural suburb of Nagoya called Mikawa, and they run deep, ac-

counting for its managers' humility and strong work ethic. Toyota doesn't plan to relocate its headquarters to Tokyo as rivals like Honda have done. By any standard, the company pays executives very little. In 2005, Toyota's top executives earned only one-tenth as much as Ford's. Their compensation was lower than that of their counterparts at the 10 largest automobile companies, save Honda. Toyota managers also rise through the hierarchy slowly: In 2006, the company's executive vice presidents were on average 61 years old—close to the retirement age at many non-Japanese companies.

Another oddity at Toyota is the influence the founding Toyoda family wields even though it controls just 2% of the company's stock. The Toyodas appear to have a say in most key decisions, but it isn't clear why they exert power. The company's presidents came mostly from the family's ranks for decades, and although three nonfamily executives have been president over the past 13 years, there's speculation that the next president will once again be a Toyoda.

Toyota doesn't merely have some odd characteristics—it is steeped in contradictions and paradoxes. During the first phase of our research, we uncovered six major contradictory tendencies, one of which influences company strategy and the others Toyota's organizational culture.

Toyota moves slowly, yet it takes big leaps. For example, the company started production in the United States gradually. It began in 1984 by forming a joint venture with GM called New United Motor Manufacturing, in Fremont, California, and opened its first plant in Kentucky four years later. However, the launch of the Prius in Japan in 1997 was a huge leap. Toyota came up with a hybrid engine that combined the power of an internal combustion engine with the environmental friendliness of an electric motor much earlier than rivals.

Toyota grows steadily, yet it is a paranoid company. In the early 1950s, the company faced near bankruptcy, but over the past 40 years, the company has recorded steady sales and market-share growth. Despite this enviable stability, senior executives constantly hammer home messages such as "Never be satisfied" and "There's got to be a better way." A favorite saying of former chairperson

Hirotaka Takeuchi (htakeuchi@ics.hit-u.ac.jp) is a professor; **Emi Osono** (osono@ics.hit-u.ac.jp) is an associate professor; and **Norihiko Shimizu** (nshimizu@ics.hit-u.ac.jp) is a visiting professor at Hitotsubashi University's Graduate School of International Corporate Strategy in Tokyo. This article is adapted from their book *Extreme Toyota: Radical Contradictions That Drive Success at the World's Best Manufacturer*, forthcoming from John Wiley & Sons.

Hiroshi Okuda is "Reform business when business is good," and Watanabe is fond of pointing out that "No change is bad."

Toyota's operations are efficient, but it uses employees' time in seemingly wasteful ways. You would be amazed to see how many people attend a meeting at Toyota even though most of them don't participate in the discussions. The company assigns many more employees to offices in the field than rivals do, and its senior executives spend an inordinate amount of time visiting dealers. Toyota also uses a large number of multilingual coordinators—a post that Carlos Ghosn abolished at Nissan soon after he became CEO in 2001—to help break down barriers between its headquarters and international operations.

Toyota is frugal, but it splurges on key areas. Only Wal-Mart can match Toyota's reputation for penny pinching. In Japan, the company turns off the lights in its offices at lunchtime. Staff members often work together in one large room, with no partitions between desks, due to the high cost of office space in Japan. At the same time, Toyota spends huge sums of money on manufacturing facilities, dealer networks, and human resource development. For instance, since 1990, it has invested $22 billion in production centers and support facilities in the United States and Europe, and for the past six years, it has spent $170 million annually competing in the Formula One circuit.

Toyota insists internal communications be simple, yet it builds complex social networks. It's an unwritten Toyota rule that employees must keep language simple when communicating with each other. When making presentations, they summarize background information, objectives, analysis, action plans, and expected results on a single sheet of paper. At the same time, Toyota fosters a complex web of social networks because it wants "everybody to know everything." The company develops horizontal links between employees across functional and geographic boundaries, grouping them by specializations and year of entry; creates vertical relationships across hierarchies through teaching relationships and mentoring; and fosters informal ties by inviting employees to join clubs based on birthplaces, sports interests, hobbies, and so on.

Toyota has a strict hierarchy, but it gives employees freedom to push back. Voicing contrarian opinions, exposing problems, not blindly following bosses' orders—these are all permissible employee behaviors. Watanabe, who recounts how he fought with his bosses as he rose through the ranks, often says, "Pick a friendly fight." We were surprised to hear criticism about the company and senior management in our interviews, but employees didn't seem worried. They felt they were doing the right thing by offering executives constructive criticism.

Once we realized that contradictions are central to Toyota's success, we tried to identify the underlying forces that cause them. However, digging into Toyota is like peeling an onion: You uncover layer after layer, but you never seem to reach the center. After we had written a half-dozen case studies, a pattern finally emerged. We identified six forces that cause contradictions inside the company. Three forces of expansion lead Toyota to instigate change and improvement. Not surprisingly, they make the organization more diverse, complicate decision making, and threaten its control and communications systems. To prevent the winds of change from blowing down the organization, Toyota also harnesses three forces of integration. They stabilize the company, help employees make sense of the environment in which they operate, and perpetuate Toyota's values and culture.

Forces of Expansion

"This is how we do things here" is a common refrain in every organization. Established practices become standardized and create efficiencies. Over time, however, those methods can prevent the adoption of new ideas. Toyota prevents rigidity from creeping in by forcing employees to think about how to reach new customers, new segments, and new geographic areas and how to tackle the challenges of competitors, new ideas, and new practices.

Impossible goals. By setting near-unattainable goals, Toyota's senior executives push the company to break free from established routines. This practice goes back to Toyota's genesis. In 1937, the founder, Kiichiro Toyoda, wanted to produce automobiles in Japan without using foreign technology. It seemed like an impossible goal; even mighty *zaibatsu* such as Mitsubishi and Mitsui had decided against entering the automobile industry at that stage because of the investments they

Three Forces of Expansion

Three forces of expansion lead the company to instigate change and improvement

- Impossible goals
- Local customization
- Experimentation

would have to make. Toyoda dared to—and the rest is history.

Toyota often sets tough goals to raise employees' consciousness and self-worth. Consider the company's global strategy: Meet every customer need and provide a full line in every market. It's impossible for any company to do that. Besides, the strategy runs contrary to management thinking, which espouses the merits of making trade-offs. Strategy guru Michael E. Porter, for instance, says that the essence of strategy is choosing what not to do. However, Toyota tries to cater to every segment because of its belief that a car contributes to making people happy. It's reminiscent of Henry Ford's desire to make automobiles affordable to American families of moderate means so that they might enjoy "the blessings of happy hours spent in God's great open spaces." Toyota has set itself the goal of delivering "a full line in every market" to make employees feel they serve a useful purpose. *Toyota Value*, the document that outlines the company's beliefs, says it best: "We are always optimizing to enhance the happiness of every customer as well as to build a better future for people, society, and the planet we share. This is our duty. This is Toyota."

Many of Toyota's goals are purposely vague, allowing employees to channel their energies in different directions and forcing specialists from different functions to collaborate across the rigid silos in which they usually work. For example, Watanabe has said that his goal is to build a car that makes the air cleaner, prevents accidents, makes people healthier and happier when they drive it, and gets you from coast to coast on one tank of gas (see "Lessons from Toyota's Long Drive," HBR July–August 2007). Zenji Yasuda, a former Toyota senior managing director, points out the wisdom of painting with broad strokes. "If he makes [the goal] more concrete, employees won't be able to exercise their full potential. The vague nature of this goal confers freedom to researchers to open new avenues of exploration; procurement to look for new and unknown suppliers who possess needed technology; and sales to consider the next steps needed to sell such products."

Local customization. Toyota doesn't modify its automobiles to local needs; it customizes both products and operations to the level of consumer sophistication in each country. This strategy pushes Toyota out of Japan, where it is dominant, and into overseas markets, where it has often been the underdog. Following the strategy increases operational complexity, but it maximizes employees' creativity since they have to develop new technologies, new ways of marketing, and new supply chains. Nissan and Honda follow the same strategy, but less rigorously: In 2006, Toyota offered 94 models in Japan—almost three times as many as Nissan's 35 and Honda's 30 models. Pursuing local customization also exposes Toyota to the sophistication of local tastes. For instance, when it introduced the subcompact Yaris in 1999, Toyota had to offer advanced technology, greater safety, roomier interiors, and better fuel efficiency to live up to European customers' expectations.

Local customization forces Toyota to push the envelope in numerous ways. For instance, the company faced complex challenges in 1998 when it developed the Innovative International Multipurpose Vehicle (IMV) platform. Toyota engineers had to design the platform to meet the needs of consumers in more than 140 countries in Asia, Europe, Africa, Oceania, Central and South America, and the Middle East. The IMV platform is used for three vehicle types—trucks, minivans, and sport utility vehicles—so Toyota can minimize design and production costs. Notably, the IMV-based vehicles were the first that Toyota produced overseas without first making them in Japan, which led to the decentralized development of production know-how, manufacturing technology, and production planning technologies. Since 2004, Toyota has produced IMV-based models in Thailand, Indonesia, Argentina, and South Africa while India, the Philippines, and Malaysia manufacture them for their own markets.

The IMV also rendered the Made-in-Japan concept irrelevant to the Toyota brand. Many executives thought it was risky to relinquish the label since it had become synonymous with quality. However, executive vice president Akio Toyoda, then in charge of sales and production in Asia, launched a personal crusade to persuade employees that the company should replace Made in Japan with Made by Toyota.

Experimentation. Toyota's eagerness to experiment helps it clear the hurdles that stand in the way of achieving near-impossible goals.

People test hypotheses and learn from the consequent successes and failures. By encouraging employees to experiment, Toyota moves out of its comfort zone and into uncharted territory.

Toyota has found that a practical way to achieve the impossible is to think deeply but take small steps—and never give up. It first breaks down a big goal into manageable challenges. Then it experiments to come up with new initiatives and processes for handling the more difficult components of each challenge. This pragmatic approach to innovation yields numerous learning opportunities. Consider, for instance, Toyota's path for developing the Prius. In 1993, the company decided to develop a car that would be environmentally friendly and easy to use. The development team, called G21, first came up with a car that delivered a 50% improvement in fuel efficiency. Toyota's senior executives rejected the prototype and demanded a 100% improvement. That was unachievable using even the most advanced gasoline and diesel engines or even fuel cell technology–based engines. The G21 team had no choice but to tap a hybrid technology that one of the company's laboratories was developing. Sure enough, the first engine wouldn't start. When a subsequent model did, the prototype moved only a few hundred yards down the test track before coming to a dead halt. In later models, the battery pack shut down whenever it became too hot or cold. Despite these setbacks, Toyota didn't stop working on the project and unveiled a hybrid concept car at the 1995 Tokyo Motor Show. Its executives knew that alternative power train technologies were emerging, but the fact that the Prius would be an interim solution didn't deter them. They believed the project was worth the investment because Toyota would learn a lot in the process.

Toyota organizes experiments using strict routines, as is widely known. It has refined Plan-Do-Check-Act (PDCA), the continuous-improvement process used throughout the business world, into the Toyota Business Practices (TBP) process. The eight-step TBP lays out a path for employees to challenge the status quo: clarify the problem; break down the problem; set a target; analyze the root cause; develop countermeasures; see countermeasures through; monitor both results and processes; and standardize successful processes. Similarly, the A3 report, named for a sheet of paper 11 inches by 17 inches, is a succinct communication tool. As we mentioned earlier, it forces employees to capture the most essential information needed to solve a problem on a single sheet that they can disseminate widely.

What sets Toyota's culture apart is the way it encourages employees to be forthcoming about the mistakes they make or the problems they face. By encouraging open communication as a core value for decades, Toyota has made its culture remarkably tolerant of failure.

Forces of Integration

As Toyota expands, it has to deal with a greater variety of perspectives from the growing number of employees and customers in many markets. In addition, the quality of internal communications deteriorates, and it becomes difficult to coordinate operations across markets and product groups. How does the company cope with the hazards of constant change and growth? We found three forces of integration that allow Toyota to stick to its mission. They perpetuate its culture and stabilize the company's expansion and transformation.

Values from the founders. Over the decades, several people have developed Toyota's values: Sakichi Toyoda, who created the parent Toyoda Automatic Loom Works; Kiichiro Toyoda, Sakichi's son and founder of the Toyota Motor Corporation; Taiichi Ohno, the TPS's creator; Eiji Toyoda, Kiichiro's first cousin and a former Toyota president; Shotaro Kamiya, who developed the company's sales network; and Shoichiro Toyoda, Kiichiro's son and another former president. The values include the mind-set of continuous improvement (*kaizen*); respect for people and their capabilities; teamwork; humility; putting the customer first; and the importance of seeing things firsthand (*genchi genbutsu*).

Toyota inculcates these values in employees by demonstrating their everyday relevance through on-the-job training and through stories that managers tell succeeding generations of employees. Although it is a complex organization, we believe four simple beliefs have kept the company from losing its way.

Tomorrow will be better than today. Toyota has succeeded in the long term because of its naive optimism. Its employees see obstacles as challenges that energize them to do better. They really believe that Toyota will make tomorrow a better day than today was. An attitude

Three Forces of Integration

Three forces of integration stabilize the company's expansion and transformation
- Values from the founders
- Up-and-in people management
- Open communication

of never being satisfied with the status quo explains why employees conduct experiments all the time.

Everybody should win. The company has stressed teamwork as a guiding principle since its early days. When a problem arises, each member of the team is accountable and has the authority and responsibility to find a solution. The practice started on the factory floor and has spread throughout the corporation.

Genchi genbutsu. At a recent conference, Toyota's chairperson Fujio Cho translated *genchi genbutsu* as "Have you seen it yourself?" The implication is that if you have not seen something firsthand, your knowledge about it is suspect. Toyota's senior executives hold themselves to the same standard, emphasizing the importance of the tacit knowledge rooted in each employee's actions and experiences. By visiting a factory and a dealership when he was in St. Petersburg, Cho commanded respect not just by talking about *genchi genbutsu* but by practicing it.

Customers first, dealers second—and manufacturer last. Toyota believes its success depends on maintaining the trust of dealers and customers, and it goes to extraordinary lengths to forge lasting relationships with them. Even on the factory floor, supervisors drive home to workers that it isn't the company but customers that pay their salaries.

Up-and-in people management. Many companies either promote employees or ask them to leave—up-or-out, as the practice is called. Toyota rarely weeds out underperformers, focusing instead on upgrading their capabilities. In fact, Toyota is still committed to long-term employment—as all Japanese companies once were. During the 1997 Asian financial crisis, for instance, Toyota's Thailand operation weathered four straight years of losses with no job cuts. The order had come down from then president Hiroshi Okuda: "Cut all costs, but don't touch any people." In August 1998, Moody's lowered Toyota's credit rating from AAA to AA1, citing the guarantee of lifetime employment. Even though the downgrade increased Toyota's interest payments by $220 million a year, company executives told the rating agency that it would not abandon its commitment.

Toyota prefers on-the-job training to off-the-job programs. During their initial training, employees are given the freedom to make judgment calls. They have to adhere to a broad set of guidelines rather than follow a strict set of rules. The company adds more context to employees' perspectives by asking them to think as if they were two levels higher in the organization. Toyota trains employees in problem-solving methods during their first 10 years with the company. Another feature of its people management policies is the role exemplary employees play as mentors. They shoulder the responsibility of developing a cadre of managers who learn through experimentation, and pass on Toyota's values by sharing personal experiences—a modern-day apprenticeship system.

When Toyota evaluates managers, it usually emphasizes process performance and learning over results. The company looks at how managers achieved their goals; how they handled issues; how they fostered organizational skills; and how they developed, motivated, and empowered people. The company uses five kinds of criteria, all of which are fuzzy and subjective. For instance, one category it employs is personal magnetism (*jinbo*), which captures how much trust and respect the manager has earned from others. *Jinbo* is a vague criterion that is open to interpretation and impossible to quantify; you can evaluate people on it only if you have worked closely with them. Another quintessentially Toyota measure of manager performance is persistence or resilience. The company sees this as part of its DNA, describing it as *nebari tsuyosa*, which translates, literally, as adhesive strength.

Toyota's evaluation criteria are particularly relevant in automobile manufacturing, where various types of expertise are essential to success. It's not the kind of company where a few shine. Watanabe says that "every single person is the main actor on the stage." When Toyota promotes employees, it doesn't praise them. Instead, senior executives deliver a message along these lines: "Congratulations on your promotion. Many others were within a hair's breadth of being selected. Keep that in mind as you do your job." This is to instill humility in employees by reminding them that their success is due in part to the efforts of equally accomplished colleagues.

Open communication. Toyota operates 50 manufacturing facilities outside Japan, sells vehicles in more than 170 countries, and employs close to 300,000 people. Despite its size

Characteristics of Toyota Executives

- Willingness to listen and learn from others
- Enthusiasm for constantly making improvements
- Comfort with working in teams
- Ability to take action quickly to solve a problem
- Interest in coaching other employees
- Modesty

and reach, Toyota still functions like a small-town company. Its top executives operate on the assumption that "everybody knows everybody else's business."

Information flows freely up and down the hierarchy and across functional and seniority levels, extending outside the organization to suppliers, customers, and dealers. Typical of traditional Eastern business practice, personal relationships are of primary importance, and Toyota's networks are human rather than virtual. Employees must cultivate the skill of listening intently to opinions in an open environment. The result is a web of relationships that former executive vice president Yoshimi Inaba calls the "nerve system." Like the human body's central nervous system, Toyota transmits information swiftly across the entire organization.

Even in a Toyota plant, executives deliver and receive information by going to the front lines in person. For instance, the head of the Takaoka and Tsutsumi plants, Takahiro Fujioka, is on the factory floor every day and joins workers for drinks in the evening (*nomikai*) sometimes as often as four times a week. Similarly, senior sales people share information with dealers and learn about customer tastes by visiting them. Toyota uses this system to avoid the pitfalls of poor communication typical of big organizations. We identified five elements that underpin Toyota's unique communications system.

Disseminate know-how laterally. The slogan "Let's *yokoten*" is often heard in the corridors of Toyota. *Yokoten*, which is short for *yokoni tenkaisuru*, literally means unfold or open out sideways. At Toyota, communication is viral and knowledge is diffused in all directions. The company has found that one of the best ways to ensure good communications is to have everyone work together in a large room with no partitions (*obeya*). The concept originated in Japan because of the perennial shortage of office space, which we mentioned earlier, but the company now uses it all over the world. Project teams also post information on the walls of a dedicated situation room for everyone to see—a practice known as *mieruka* (visualization).

Give people the freedom to voice contrary opinions. Toyota's communication system works because the organization is open to criticism. Employees feel safe, even empowered, to voice contrary opinions and contradict superiors. Each individual in Toyota is expected to act according to what he or she thinks is right. Every employee enjoys the prerogative to ignore the boss's orders or not take them too seriously. Confronting your boss is acceptable; bringing bad news to the boss is encouraged; and ignoring the boss is often excused. In many of our interviews, employees told us how local operations had succeeded by refusing to obey orders or ignoring what headquarters had advised. For instance, the head of Toyota Motor Sales, U.S.A., Yukitoshi Funo, told us candidly: "Before I was sent to the U.S. in 1997 [as senior vice president], I made the rounds of several top executives in Japan. They told me to increase the number of sales outlets. These were executive vice presidents and managing directors. I went to the market to see the situation. Increasing the number of dealerships would have caused more intense competition and threatened proper management of dealerships. I decided to ignore everything those top executives told me."

Have frequent face-to-face interactions. Although there are no reprisals if local operations don't act on headquarters' advice or if subordinates disobey orders from supervisors, refusing to listen to others is a serious offense. Toyota's system functions only when information from the source is available to everybody in the organization. The emphasis is therefore on interactions at the scene (*genba*). For instance, Tony Fujita, former vice president of Toyota Motor Sales, U.S.A., believes that Toyota distinguishes itself from American carmakers by listening to dealers. "Other carmakers have meetings with dealers, but I think Toyota is unique in the frequency and the seriousness of what we discuss [with them]."

Make tacit knowledge explicit. Another element in Toyota's nerve system is the practice of converting experiential or tacit knowledge into an explicit form to be shared throughout the organization. When Fujio Cho was president, Toyota put into writing the founders' wisdom that had until then been passed down orally. Senior executives evaluated sayings and anecdotes and identified two core values as the pillars of *The Toyota Way 2001:* continuous improvement (*kaizen*) and respect for people.

Create support mechanisms. In 2002, the company set up the Toyota Institute and the

Confronting your boss is acceptable; bringing bad news to the boss is encouraged; and ignoring the boss is often excused.

Global Knowledge Center at Toyota City in Japan and Torrance, California, respectively. Together with the University of Toyota, established four years earlier at Torrance by Toyota Motor Sales, U.S.A., these formal mechanisms support Toyota's communication networks by disseminating best practices and company values. In addition, employees are encouraged to join a wide variety of informal groups, as we mentioned earlier. Every employee belongs to several committees (*iinkai*), self-organizing study groups (*jishuken*), and other social groups, of which there are close to 20 in the company. This helps create a multilayered communication network at Toyota.

Emulating Toyota

People often ask us, "Tell me one thing I should learn from Toyota." That misses the point. Emulating Toyota isn't about copying any one practice; it's about creating a culture. That takes time. It requires resources. And it isn't easy. First, companies have no choice but to embrace contradictions as a way of life. Most enterprises stop growing because they stick to processes and practices their past successes have generated. However, old methods also lead to institutional rigidities. Companies can overcome them by trying to reach new markets or by tackling fresh challenges. Second, companies must develop routines to resolve contradictions. Toyota uses numerous tools such as the Plan-Do-Check-Act model, the eight-step Toyota Business Practices process, the A3 reporting system, and the widely known ask-why-five-times routine. Unless companies teach employees how to deal with problems rigorously and systematically, they won't be able to harness the power of contradictions. Third, companies must encourage employees to voice contrary opinions. Top managements must be open to criticism and hearing opposing viewpoints if they want new ideas.

• • •

Should companies try to do as Toyota does? We believe they should. Toyota's culture of contradictions places humans, not machines, at the center of the company. As such, the company will be imperfect, and there will always be room for improvement. In that sense, Toyota's model mirrors human creativity. Can you say the same about your company?

Reprint R0806F
To order, see the next page
or call 800-988-0886 or 617-783-7500
or go to www.hbr.org

Further Reading

The *Harvard Business Review*
Paperback Series

Here are the landmark ideas—both
contemporary and classic—that have
established *Harvard Business Review* as required
reading for businesspeople around the globe.
Each paperback includes eight of the leading
articles on a particular business topic. The
series includes over thirty titles, including the
following best-sellers:

**Harvard Business Review on Brand
Management**
Product no. 1445

Harvard Business Review on Change
Product no. 8842

Harvard Business Review on Leadership
Product no. 8834

**Harvard Business Review on Managing
People**
Product no. 9075

**Harvard Business Review on Measuring
Corporate Performance**
Product no. 8826

For a complete list of the *Harvard Business
Review* paperback series, go to www.hbr.org.

Harvard Business Review

www.hbr.org

Research shows that enterprises fail at execution because they go straight to structural reorganization and neglect the most powerful drivers of effectiveness— decision rights and information flow.

The Secrets to Successful Strategy Execution

by Gary L. Neilson, Karla L. Martin, and Elizabeth Powers

Included with this full-text *Harvard Business Review* article:

The Secrets to Successful Strategy Execution

The Idea in Brief

A brilliant strategy may put you on the competitive map. But only solid execution keeps you there. Unfortunately, most companies struggle with implementation. That's because they overrely on structural changes, such as reorganization, to execute their strategy.

Though structural change has its place in execution, it produces only short-term gains. For example, one company reduced its management layers as part of a strategy to address disappointing performance. Costs plummeted initially, but the layers soon crept back in.

Research by Neilson, Martin, and Powers shows that execution exemplars focus their efforts on two levers far more powerful than structural change:

- **Clarifying decision rights**—for instance, specifying who "owns" each decision and who must provide input

- **Ensuring information flows where it's needed**—such as promoting managers laterally so they build networks needed for the cross-unit collaboration critical to a new strategy

Tackle decision rights and information flows first, and only then **alter organizational structures** and **realign incentives** to *support* those moves.

The Idea in Practice

The following levers matter *most* for successful strategy execution:

DECISION RIGHTS

- Ensure that everyone in your company knows which decisions and actions they're responsible for.

▶ Example:
In one global consumer-goods company, decisions made by divisional and geographic leaders were overridden by corporate functional leaders who controlled resource allocations. Decisions stalled. Overhead costs mounted as divisions added staff to create bulletproof cases for challenging corporate decisions. To support a new strategy hinging on sharper customer focus, the CEO designated accountability for profits unambiguously to the divisions.

- Encourage higher-level managers to delegate operational decisions.

▶ Example:
At one global charitable organization, country-level managers' inability to delegate led to decision paralysis. So the leadership team encouraged country managers to delegate standard operational tasks. This freed these managers to focus on developing the strategies needed to fulfill the organization's mission.

INFORMATION FLOW

- Make sure important information about the competitive environment flows quickly to corporate headquarters. That way, the top team can identify patterns and promulgate best practices throughout the company.

▶ Example:
At one insurance company, accurate information about projects' viability was censored as it moved up the hierarchy. To improve information flow to senior levels of management, the company took steps to create a more open, informal culture.

Top executives began mingling with unit leaders during management meetings and held regular brown-bag lunches where people discussed the company's most pressing issues.

- Facilitate information flow across organizational boundaries.

▶ Example:
To better manage relationships with large, cross-product customers, a B2B company needed its units to talk with one another. It charged its newly created customer-focused marketing group with encouraging cross-company communication. The group issued regular reports showing performance against targets (by product and geography) and supplied root-cause analyses of performance gaps. Quarterly performance-management meetings further fostered the trust required for collaboration.

- Help field and line employees understand how their day-to-day choices affect your company's bottom line.

▶ Example:
At a financial services firm, salespeople routinely crafted customized one-off deals with clients that cost the company more than it made in revenues. Sales didn't understand the cost and complexity implications of these transactions. Management addressed the information misalignment by adopting a "smart customization" approach to sales. For customized deals, it established standardized back-office processes (such as risk assessment). It also developed analytical support tools to arm salespeople with accurate information on the cost implications of their proposed transactions. Profitability improved.

Research shows that enterprises fail at execution because they go straight to structural reorganization and neglect the most powerful drivers of effectiveness—decision rights and information flow.

The Secrets to Successful Strategy Execution

by Gary L. Neilson, Karla L. Martin, and Elizabeth Powers

A brilliant strategy, blockbuster product, or breakthrough technology can put you on the competitive map, but only solid execution can keep you there. You have to be able to deliver on your intent. Unfortunately, the majority of companies aren't very good at it, by their own admission. Over the past five years, we have invited many thousands of employees (about 25% of whom came from executive ranks) to complete an online assessment of their organizations' capabilities, a process that's generated a database of 125,000 profiles representing more than 1,000 companies, government agencies, and not-for-profits in over 50 countries. Employees at three out of every five companies rated their organization weak at execution—that is, when asked if they agreed with the statement "Important strategic and operational decisions are quickly translated into action," the majority answered no.

Execution is the result of thousands of decisions made every day by employees acting according to the information they have and their own self-interest. In our work helping more than 250 companies learn to execute more effectively, we've identified four fundamental building blocks executives can use to influence those actions—clarifying decision rights, designing information flows, aligning motivators, and making changes to structure. (For simplicity's sake we refer to them as decision rights, information, motivators, and structure.)

In efforts to improve performance, most organizations go right to structural measures because moving lines around the org chart seems the most obvious solution and the changes are visible and concrete. Such steps generally reap some short-term efficiencies quickly, but in so doing address only the symptoms of dysfunction, not its root causes. Several years later, companies usually end up in the same place they started. Structural change can and should be part of the path to improved execution, but it's best to think of it as the capstone, not the cornerstone, of any organizational transformation. In fact, our research shows that actions having to do with decision rights and information are far more important—about twice as effective—as improvements made to the other two building blocks. (See the exhibit "What Matters Most to Strategy Execution.")

Take, for example, the case of a global consumer packaged-goods company that lurched down the reorganization path in the early 1990s. (We have altered identifying details in this and other cases that follow.) Disappointed with company performance, senior management did what most companies were doing at that time: They restructured. They eliminated some layers of management and broadened spans of control. Management-staffing costs quickly fell by 18%. Eight years later, however, it was déjà vu. The layers had crept back in, and spans of control had once again narrowed. In addressing only structure, management had attacked the visible symptoms of poor performance but not the underlying cause—how people made decisions and how they were held accountable.

This time, management looked beyond lines and boxes to the mechanics of how work got done. Instead of searching for ways to strip out costs, they focused on improving execution—and in the process discovered the true reasons for the performance shortfall. Managers didn't have a clear sense of their respective roles and responsibilities. They did not intuitively understand which decisions were theirs to make. Moreover, the link between performance and rewards was weak. This was a company long on micromanaging and second-guessing, and short on accountability. Middle managers spent 40% of their time justifying and reporting upward or questioning the tactical decisions of their direct reports.

Armed with this understanding, the company designed a new management model that established who was accountable for what and made the connection between performance and reward. For instance, the norm at this company, not unusual in the industry, had been to promote people quickly, within 18 months to two years, before they had a chance to see their initiatives through. As a result, managers at every level kept doing their old jobs even after they had been promoted, peering over the shoulders of the direct reports who were now in charge of their projects and, all too frequently, taking over. Today, people stay in their positions longer so they can follow

through on their own initiatives, and they're still around when the fruits of their labors start to kick in. What's more, results from those initiatives continue to count in their performance reviews for some time after they've been promoted, forcing managers to live with the expectations they'd set in their previous jobs. As a consequence, forecasting has become more accurate and reliable. These actions did yield a structure with fewer layers and greater spans of control, but that was a side effect, not the primary focus, of the changes.

The Elements of Strong Execution

Our conclusions arise out of decades of practical application and intensive research. Nearly five years ago, we and our colleagues set out to gather empirical data to identify the actions that were most effective in enabling an organization to implement strategy. What particular ways of restructuring, motivating, improving information flows, and clarifying decision rights mattered the most? We started by drawing up a list of 17 traits, each corresponding to one or more of the four building blocks we knew could enable effective execution—traits like the free flow of information across organizational boundaries or the degree to which senior leaders refrain from getting involved in operating decisions. With these factors in mind, we developed an online profiler that allows individuals to assess the execution capabilities of their organizations. Over the next four years or so, we collected data from many thousands of profiles, which in turn allowed us to more precisely calibrate the impact of each trait on an organization's ability to execute. That allowed us to rank all 17 traits in order of their relative influence. (See the exhibit "The 17 Fundamental Traits of Organizational Effectiveness.)

Ranking the traits makes clear how important decision rights and information are to effective strategy execution. The first eight traits map directly to decision rights and information. Only three of the 17 traits relate to structure, and none of those ranks higher than 13th. We'll walk through the top five traits here.

1. Everyone has a good idea of the decisions and actions for which he or she is responsible. In companies strong on execution, 71% of individuals agree with this statement; that figure drops to 32% in organizations weak on execution.

Gary L. Neilson (gary.neilson@booz.com) is a senior vice president in the Chicago office of Booz & Company, a management-consulting firm. He is a coauthor of "The Passive-Aggressive Organization" (HBR, October 2005). Karla L. Martin (karla.martin@booz.com) is a principal in the firm's San Francisco office. Elizabeth Powers (elizabeth.powers@booz.com) is a principal in the New York office.

Blurring of decision rights tends to occur as a company matures. Young organizations are generally too busy getting things done to define roles and responsibilities clearly at the outset. And why should they? In a small company, it's not so difficult to know what other people are up to. So for a time, things work out well enough. As the company grows, however, executives come and go, bringing in with them and taking away different expectations, and over time the approval process gets ever more convoluted and murky. It becomes increasingly unclear where one person's accountability begins and another's ends.

One global consumer-durables company found this out the hard way. It was so rife with people making competing and conflicting decisions that it was hard to find anyone below the CEO who felt truly accountable for profitability. The company was organized into 16 product divisions aggregated into three geographic groups—North America, Europe, and International. Each of the divisions was charged with reaching explicit performance targets, but functional staff at corporate headquarters controlled spending targets—how R&D dollars were allocated, for instance. Decisions made by divisional and geographic leaders were routinely overridden by functional leaders. Overhead costs began to mount as the divisions added staff to help them create bulletproof cases to challenge corporate decisions.

Decisions stalled while divisions negotiated with functions, each layer weighing in with questions. Functional staffers in the divisions (financial analysts, for example) often deferred to their higher-ups in corporate rather than their division vice president, since functional leaders were responsible for rewards and promotions. Only the CEO and his executive team had the discretion to resolve disputes. All of these symptoms fed on one another and collectively hampered execution—until a new CEO came in.

The new chief executive chose to focus less on cost control and more on profitable growth by redefining the divisions to focus on consumers. As part of the new organizational model, the CEO designated accountability for profits unambiguously to the divisions and also gave them the authority to draw on functional activities to support their goals (as well as more control of the budget). Corporate

functional roles and decision rights were recast to better support the divisions' needs and also to build the cross-divisional links necessary for developing the global capabilities of the business as a whole. For the most part, the functional leaders understood the market realities—and that change entailed some adjustments to the operating model of the business. It helped that the CEO brought them into the organizational redesign process, so that the new model wasn't something imposed on them as much as it was something they engaged in and built together.

2. Important information about the competitive environment gets to headquarters quickly. On average, 77% of individuals in strong-execution organizations agree with this statement, whereas only 45% of those in weak-execution organizations do.

Headquarters can serve a powerful function in identifying patterns and promulgating best practices throughout business segments and geographic regions. But it can play this coordinating role only if it has accurate and up-to-date market intelligence. Otherwise, it will tend to impose its own agenda and policies rather than defer to operations that are much closer to the customer.

Consider the case of heavy-equipment manufacturer Caterpillar.[1] Today it is a highly successful $45 billion global company, but a generation ago, Caterpillar's organization was so badly misaligned that its very existence was threatened. Decision rights were hoarded at the top by functional general offices located at headquarters in Peoria, Illinois, while

What Matters Most to Strategy Execution

When a company fails to execute its strategy, the first thing managers often think to do is restructure. But our research shows that the fundamentals of good execution start with clarifying decision rights and making sure information flows where it needs to go. If you get those right, the correct structure and motivators often become obvious.

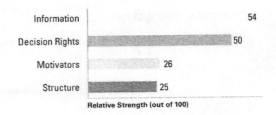

	Relative Strength (out of 100)
Information	54
Decision Rights	50
Motivators	26
Structure	25

The 17 Fundamental Traits of Organizational Effectiveness

From our survey research drawn from more than 26,000 people in 31 companies, we have distilled the traits that make organizations effective at implementing strategy. Here they are, in order of importance.

RANK	ORGANIZATION TRAIT	STRENGTH INDEX (OUT OF 100)
1	Everyone has a good idea of the decisions and actions for which he or she is responsible.	81
2	Important information about the competitive environment gets to headquarters quickly.	68
3	Once made, decisions are rarely second-guessed.	58
4	Information flows freely across organizational boundaries.	58
5	Field and line employees usually have the information they need to understand the bottom-line impact of their day-to-day choices.	55
6	Line managers have access to the metrics they need to measure the key drivers of their business.	48
7	Managers up the line get involved in operating decisions.	32
8	Conflicting messages are rarely sent to the market.	32
9	The individual performance-appraisal process differentiates among high, adequate, and low performers.	32
10	The ability to deliver on performance commitments strongly influences career advancement and compensation.	32
11	It is more accurate to describe the culture of this organization as "persuade and cajole" than "command and control."	29
12	The primary role of corporate staff here is to support the business units rather than to audit them.	29
13	Promotions can be lateral moves (from one position to another on the same level in the hierarchy).	29
14	Fast-track employees here can expect promotions more frequently than every three years.	23
15	On average, middle managers here have five or more direct reports.	19
16	If the firm has a bad year, but a particular division has a good year, the division head would still get a bonus.	13
17	Besides pay, many other things motivate individuals to do a good job.	10

BUILDING BLOCKS ▨ Decision Rights ☐ Information ▨ Motivators ▨ Structure

much of the information needed to make those decisions resided in the field with sales managers. "It just took a long time to get decisions going up and down the functional silos, and they really weren't good business decisions; they were more functional decisions," noted one field executive. Current CEO Jim Owens, then a managing director in Indonesia, told us that such information that did make it to the top had been "whitewashed and varnished several times over along the way." Cut off from information about the external market, senior executives focused on the organization's internal workings, overanalyzing issues and second-guessing decisions made at lower levels, costing the company opportunities in fast-moving markets.

Pricing, for example, was based on cost and determined not by market realities but by the pricing general office in Peoria. Sales representatives across the world lost sale after sale to Komatsu, whose competitive pricing consistently beat Caterpillar's. In 1982, the company posted the first annual loss in its almost-60-year history. In 1983 and 1984, it lost $1 million a day, seven days a week. By the end of 1984, Caterpillar had lost a billion dollars. By 1988, then-CEO George Schaefer stood atop an entrenched bureaucracy that was, in his words, "telling me what I wanted to hear, not what I needed to know." So, he convened a task force of "renegade" middle managers and tasked them with charting Caterpillar's future.

Ironically, the way to ensure that the right information flowed to headquarters was to make sure the right decisions were made much further down the organization. By delegating operational responsibility to the people closer to the action, top executives were free to focus on more global strategic issues. Accordingly, the company reorganized into business units, making each accountable for its own P&L statement. The functional general offices that had been all-powerful ceased to exist, literally overnight. Their talent and expertise, including engineering, pricing, and manufacturing, were parceled out to the new business units, which could now design their own products, develop their own manufacturing processes and schedules, and set their own prices. The move dramatically decentralized decision rights, giving the units control over market decisions. The business unit P&Ls were now measured consistently across the enter-

prise, as return on assets became the universal measure of success. With this accurate, up-to-date, and directly comparable information, senior decision makers at headquarters could make smart strategic choices and trade-offs rather than use outdated sales data to make ineffective, tactical marketing decisions.

Within 18 months, the company was working in the new model. "This was a revolution that became a renaissance," Owens recalls, "a spectacular transformation of a kind of sluggish company into one that actually has entrepreneurial zeal. And that transition was very quick because it was decisive and it was complete; it was thorough; it was universal, worldwide, all at one time."

3. Once made, decisions are rarely second-guessed. Whether someone is second-guessing depends on your vantage point. A more senior and broader enterprise perspective can add value to a decision, but managers up the line may not be adding incremental value; instead, they may be stalling progress by redoing their subordinates' jobs while, in effect, shirking their own. In our research, 71% of respondents in weak-execution companies thought that decisions were being second-guessed, whereas only 45% of those from strong-execution organizations felt that way.

Recently, we worked with a global charitable organization dedicated to alleviating poverty. It had a problem others might envy: It was suffering from the strain brought on by a rapid growth in donations and a corresponding increase in the depth and breadth of its program offerings. As you might expect, this nonprofit was populated with people on a mission who took intense personal ownership of projects. It did not reward the delegation of even the most mundane administrative tasks. Country-level managers, for example, would personally oversee copier repairs. Managers' inability to delegate led to decision paralysis and a lack of accountability as the organization grew. Second-guessing was an art form. When there was doubt over who was empowered to make a decision, the default was often to have a series of meetings in which no decision was reached. When decisions were finally made, they had generally been vetted by so many parties that no one person could be held accountable. An effort to expedite decision-making through restructuring—by collocating key leaders with subject-matter

About the Data

We tested organizational effectiveness by having people fill out an online diagnostic, a tool comprising 19 questions (17 that describe organizational traits and two that describe outcomes).

To determine which of the 17 traits in our profiler are most strongly associated with excellence in execution, we looked at 31 companies in our database for which we had responses from at least 150 individual (anonymously completed) profiles, for a total of 26,743 responses. Applying regression analysis to each of the 31 data sets, we correlated the 17 traits with our measure of organizational effectiveness, which we defined as an affirmative response to the outcome statement, "Important strategic and operational decisions are quickly translated into action." Then we ranked the traits in order, according to the number of data sets in which the trait exhibited a significant correlation with our measure of success within a 90% confidence interval. Finally, we indexed the result to a 100-point scale. The top trait— "Everyone has a good idea of the decisions and actions for which he or she is responsible"—exhibited a significant positive correlation with our success indicator in 25 of the 31 data sets, for an index score of 81.

experts in newly established central and regional centers of excellence—became instead another logjam. Key managers still weren't sure of their right to take advantage of these centers, so they didn't.

The nonprofit's management and directors went back to the drawing board. We worked with them to design a decision-making map, a tool to help identify where different types of decisions should be taken, and with it they clarified and enhanced decision rights at all levels of management. All managers were then actively encouraged to delegate standard operational tasks. Once people had a clear idea of what decisions they should and should not be making, holding them accountable for decisions felt fair. What's more, now they could focus their energies on the organization's mission. Clarifying decision rights and responsibilities also improved the organization's ability to track individual achievement, which helped it chart new and appealing career-advancement paths.

4. Information flows freely across organizational boundaries. When information does not flow horizontally across different parts of the company, units behave like silos, forfeiting economies of scale and the transfer of best practices. Moreover, the organization as a whole loses the opportunity to develop a cadre of up-and-coming managers well versed in all aspects of the company's operations. Our research indicates that only 21% of respondents from weak-execution companies thought information flowed freely across organizational boundaries whereas 55% of those from strong-execution firms did. Since scores for even the strong companies are pretty low, though, this is an issue that most companies can work on.

A cautionary tale comes from a business-to-business company whose customer and product teams failed to collaborate in serving a key segment: large, cross-product customers. To manage relationships with important clients, the company had established a customer-focused marketing group, which developed customer outreach programs, innovative pricing models, and tailored promotions and discounts. But this group issued no clear and consistent reports of its initiatives and progress to the product units and had difficulty securing time with the regular cross-unit management to discuss key performance issues. Each product unit communicated and

planned in its own way, and it took tremendous energy for the customer group to understand the units' various priorities and tailor communications to each one. So the units were not aware, and had little faith, that this new division was making constructive inroads into a key customer segment. Conversely (and predictably), the customer team felt the units paid only perfunctory attention to its plans and couldn't get their cooperation on issues critical to multiproduct customers, such as potential trade-offs and volume discounts.

Historically, this lack of collaboration hadn't been a problem because the company had been the dominant player in a high-margin market. But as the market became more competitive, customers began to view the firm as unreliable and, generally, as a difficult supplier, and they became increasingly reluctant to enter into favorable relationships.

Once the issues became clear, though, the solution wasn't terribly complicated, involving little more than getting the groups to talk to one another. The customer division became responsible for issuing regular reports to the product units showing performance against targets, by product and geographic region, and for supplying a supporting root-cause analysis. A standing performance-management meeting was placed on the schedule every quarter, creating a forum for exchanging information face-to-face and discussing outstanding issues. These moves bred the broader organizational trust required for collaboration.

5. Field and line employees usually have the information they need to understand the bottom-line impact of their day-to-day choices. Rational decisions are necessarily bounded by the information available to employees. If managers don't understand what it will cost to capture an incremental dollar in revenue, they will always pursue the incremental revenue. They can hardly be faulted, even if their decision is—in the light of full information—wrong. Our research shows that 61% of individuals in strong-execution organizations agree that field and line employees have the information they need to understand the bottom-line impact of their decisions. This figure plummets to 28% in weak-execution organizations.

We saw this unhealthy dynamic play out at a large, diversified financial-services client,

Second-guessing was an art form: When decisions were finally made, they had generally been vetted by so many parties that no one person could be held accountable.

which had been built through a series of successful mergers of small regional banks. In combining operations, managers had chosen to separate front-office bankers who sold loans from back-office support groups who did risk assessments, placing each in a different reporting relationship and, in many cases, in different locations. Unfortunately, they failed to institute the necessary information and motivation links to ensure smooth operations. As a result, each pursued different, and often competing, goals.

For example, salespeople would routinely enter into highly customized one-off deals with clients that cost the company more than they made in revenues. Sales did not have a clear understanding of the cost and complexity implications of these transactions. Without sufficient information, sales staff believed that the back-end people were sabotaging their deals, while the support groups considered the front-end people to be cowboys. At year's end, when the data were finally reconciled, management would bemoan the sharp increase in operational costs, which often erased the profit from these transactions.

Executives addressed this information misalignment by adopting a "smart customization" approach to sales. They standardized the end-to-end processes used in the majority of deals and allowed for customization only in select circumstances. For these customized deals, they established clear back-office processes and analytical support tools to arm salespeople with accurate information on the cost implications of the proposed transactions. At the same time, they rolled out common reporting standards and tools for both the front- and back-office operations to ensure that each group had access to the same data and metrics when making decisions. Once each side understood the business realities confronted by the other, they cooperated more effectively, acting in the whole company's best interests—and there were no more year-end surprises.

Creating a Transformation Program

The four building blocks that managers can use to improve strategy execution—decision rights, information, structure, and motivators—are inextricably linked. Unclear decision rights not only paralyze decision making but also impede information flow, divorce perfor-

mance from rewards, and prompt workarounds that subvert formal reporting lines. Blocking information results in poor decisions, limited career development, and a reinforcement of structural silos. So what to do about it?

Since each organization is different and faces a unique set of internal and external variables, there is no universal answer to that question. The first step is to identify the sources of the problem. In our work, we often begin by having a company's employees take our profiling survey and consolidating the results. The more people in the organization who take the survey, the better.

Once executives understand their company's areas of weakness, they can take any number of actions. The exhibit, "Mapping Improvements to the Building Blocks: Some Sample Tactics" shows 15 possible steps that can have an impact on performance. (The options listed represent only a sampling of the dozens of choices managers might make.) All of these actions are geared toward strengthening one or more of the 17 traits. For example, if you were to take steps to "clarify and streamline decision making" you could potentially strengthen two traits: "Everyone has a good idea of the decisions and actions for which he or she is responsible," and "Once made, decisions are rarely second-guessed."

You certainly wouldn't want to put 15 initiatives in a single transformation program. Most organizations don't have the managerial capacity or organizational appetite to take on more than five or six at a time. And as we've stressed, you should first take steps to address decision rights and information, and then design the necessary changes to motivators and structure to support the new design.

To help companies understand their shortcomings and construct the improvement program that will have the greatest impact, we have developed an organizational-change simulator. This interactive tool accompanies the profiler, allowing you to try out different elements of a change program virtually, to see which ones will best target your company's particular area of weakness. (For an overview of the simulation process, see the sidebar "Test Drive Your Organization's Transformation.")

To get a sense of the process from beginning to end—from taking the diagnostic profiler, to

To help companies construct an improvement program with the greatest impact, we've developed an organizational-change simulator.

formulating your strategy, to launching your organizational transformation—consider the experience of a leading insurance company we'll call Goodward Insurance. Goodward was a successful company with strong capital reserves and steady revenue and customer growth. Still, its leadership wanted to further enhance execution to deliver on an ambitious five-year strategic agenda that included aggressive targets in customer growth, revenue increases, and cost reduction, which would require a new level of teamwork. While there were pockets of cross-unit collaboration within the company, it was far more common for each unit to focus on its own goals, making it diffi-

cult to spare resources to support another unit's goals. In many cases there was little incentive to do so anyway: Unit A's goals might require the involvement of Unit B to succeed, but Unit B's goals might not include supporting Unit A's effort.

The company had initiated a number of enterprisewide projects over the years, which had been completed on time and on budget, but these often had to be reworked because stakeholder needs hadn't been sufficiently taken into account. After launching a shared-services center, for example, the company had to revisit its operating model and processes when units began hiring shadow staff to focus on priority work that the center wouldn't expedite. The center might decide what technology applications, for instance, to develop on its own rather than set priorities according to what was most important to the organization.

In a similar way, major product launches were hindered by insufficient coordination among departments. The marketing department would develop new coverage options without asking the claims-processing group whether it had the ability to process the claims. Since it didn't, processors had to create expensive manual work-arounds when the new kinds of claims started pouring in. Nor did marketing ask the actuarial department how these products would affect the risk profile and reimbursement expenses of the company, and for some of the new products, costs did indeed increase.

To identify the greatest barriers to building a stronger execution culture, Goodward Insurance gave the diagnostic survey to all of its 7,000-plus employees and compared the organization's scores on the 17 traits with those from strong-execution companies. Numerous previous surveys (employee-satisfaction, among others) had elicited qualitative comments identifying the barriers to execution excellence. But the diagnostic survey gave the company quantifiable data that it could analyze by group and by management level to determine which barriers were most hindering the people actually charged with execution. As it turned out, middle management was far more pessimistic than the top executives in their assessment of the organization's execution ability. Their input became especially critical to the change agenda ultimately adopted.

Mapping Improvements to the Building Blocks: Some Sample Tactics

Companies can take a host of steps to improve their ability to execute strategy. The 15 here are only some of the possible examples. Every one strengthens one or more of the building blocks executives can use to improve their strategy-execution capability: clarifying decision rights, improving information, establishing the right motivators, and restructuring the organization.

- Focus corporate staff on supporting business-unit decision making.
- Clarify and streamline decision making at each operating level.
- Focus headquarters on important strategic questions.
- Create centers of excellence by consolidating similar functions into a single organizational unit.
- Assign process owners to coordinate activities that span organizational functions.
- Establish individual performance measures.
- Improve field-to-headquarters information flow.
- Define and distribute daily operating metrics to the field or line.
- Create cross-functional teams.
- Introduce differentiating performance awards.
- Expand nonmonetary rewards to recognize exceptional performers.
- Increase position tenure.
- Institute lateral moves and rotations.
- Broaden spans of control.

BUILDING BLOCKS ■ Decision Rights ☐ Information ▨ Motivators ▪ Structure

Through the survey, Goodward Insurance uncovered impediments to execution in three of the most influential organizational traits:

• **Information did not flow freely across organizational boundaries.** Sharing information was never one of Goodward's hallmarks, but managers had always dismissed the mounting anecdotal evidence of poor cross-divisional information flow as "some other group's problem." The organizational diagnostic data, however, exposed such plausible deniability as an inadequate excuse. In fact, when the CEO reviewed the profiler results with his direct reports, he held up the chart on cross-group information flows and declared, "We've been discussing this problem for several years, and yet you always say that it's so-and-so's problem, not mine. Sixty-seven percent of [our] respondents said that they do not think information flows freely across divisions. This is not so-and-so's problem—it's our problem. You just don't get results that low [unless it comes] from everywhere. We are all on the hook for fixing this."

Contributing to this lack of horizontal information flow was a dearth of lateral promotions. Because Goodward had always promoted up rather than over and up, most middle and senior managers remained within a single group. They were not adequately apprised of the activities of the other groups, nor did they have a network of contacts across the organization.

• **Important information about the competitive environment did not get to headquarters quickly.** The diagnostic data and

Test-Drive Your Organization's Transformation

You know your organization could perform better. You are faced with dozens of levers you could conceivably pull if you had unlimited time and resources. But you don't. You operate in the real world.

How, then, do you make the most-educated and cost-efficient decisions about which change initiatives to implement? We've developed a way to test the efficacy of specific actions (such as clarifying decision rights, forming cross-functional teams, or expanding nonmonetary rewards) without risking significant amounts of time and money. You can go to www.simulator-orgeffectiveness.com to assemble and try out various five-step organizational-change programs and assess which would be the most effective and efficient in improving execution at your company.

You begin the simulation by selecting one of seven organizational profiles that most resembles the current state of your organization. If you're not sure, you can take a five-minute diagnostic survey. This online survey automatically generates an organizational profile and baseline execution-effectiveness score. (Although 100 is a perfect score, nobody is perfect; even the most effective companies often score in the 60s and 70s.)

Having established your baseline, you use the simulator to chart a possible course you'd like to take to improve your execution capabilities by selecting five out of a possible 28 actions. Ideally, these moves should directly address the weakest links in your organizational profile. To help you make the right choices, the simulator offers insights that shed further light on how a proposed action influences particular organizational elements.

Once you have made your selections, the simulator executes the steps you've elected and processes them through a web-based engine that evaluates them using empirical relationships identified from 31 companies representing more than 26,000 data observations. It then generates a bar chart indicating how much your organization's execution score has improved and where it now stands in relation to the highest-performing companies from our research and the scores of other people like you who have used the simulator starting from the same original profile you did. If you wish, you may then advance to the next round and pick another five actions. What you will see is illustrated below.

The beauty of the simulator is its ability to consider—consequence-free—the impact on execution of endless combinations of possible actions. Each simulation includes only two rounds, but you can run the simulation as many times as you like. The simulator has also been used for team competition within organizations, and we've found that it engenders very engaging and productive dialogue among senior executives.

While the simulator cannot capture all of the unique situations an organization might face, it is a useful tool for assessing and building a targeted and effective organization-transformation program. It serves as a vehicle to stimulate thinking about the impact of various changes, saving untold amounts of time and resources in the process.

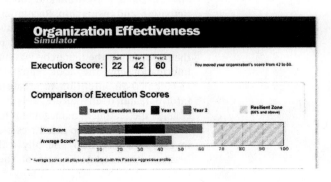

subsequent surveys and interviews with middle management revealed that the wrong information was moving up the org chart. Mundane day-to-day decisions were escalated to the executive level—the top team had to approve midlevel hiring decisions, for instance, and bonuses of $1,000—limiting Goodward's agility in responding to competitors' moves, customers' needs, and changes in the broader marketplace. Meanwhile, more important information was so heavily filtered as it moved up the hierarchy that it was all but worthless for rendering key verdicts. Even if lower-level managers knew that a certain project could never work for highly valid reasons, they would not communicate that dim view to the top team. Nonstarters not only started, they kept going. For instance, the company had a project under way to create new incentives for its brokers. Even though this approach had been previously tried without success, no one spoke up in meetings or stopped the project because it was a priority for one of the top-team members.

• **No one had a good idea of the decisions and actions for which he or she was responsible.** The general lack of information flow extended to decision rights, as few managers understood where their authority ended and another's began. Accountability even for day-to-day decisions was unclear, and managers did not know whom to ask for clarification. Naturally, confusion over decision rights led to second-guessing. Fifty-five percent of respondents felt that decisions were regularly second-guessed at Goodward.

To Goodward's credit, its top executives immediately responded to the results of the diagnostic by launching a change program targeted at all three problem areas. The program integrated early, often symbolic, changes with longer-term initiatives, in an effort to build momentum and galvanize participation and ownership. Recognizing that a passive-aggressive attitude toward people perceived to be in power solely as a result of their position in the hierarchy was hindering information flow, they took immediate steps to signal their intention to create a more informal and open culture. One symbolic change: the seating at management meetings was rearranged. The top executives used to sit in a separate section, the physical space between them and the rest of the room

fraught with symbolism. Now they intermingled, making themselves more accessible and encouraging people to share information informally. Regular brown-bag lunches were established with members of the C-suite, where people had a chance to discuss the overall culture-change initiative, decision rights, new mechanisms for communicating across the units, and so forth. Seating at these events was highly choreographed to ensure that a mix of units was represented at each table. Icebreaker activities were designed to encourage individuals to learn about other units' work.

Meanwhile, senior managers commenced the real work of remedying issues relating to information flows and decision rights. They assessed their own informal networks to understand how people making key decisions got their information, and they identified critical gaps. The outcome was a new framework for making important decisions that clearly specifies who owns each decision, who must provide input, who is ultimately accountable for the results, and how results are defined. Other longer-term initiatives include:

• Pushing certain decisions down into the organization to better align decision rights with the best available information. Most hiring and bonus decisions, for instance, have been delegated to immediate managers, so long as they are within preestablished boundaries relating to numbers hired and salary levels. Being clear about who needs what information is encouraging cross-group dialogue.

• Identifying and eliminating duplicative committees.

• Pushing metrics and scorecards down to the group level, so that rather than focus on solving the mystery of *who* caused a problem, management can get right to the root cause of *why* the problem occurred. A well-designed scorecard captures not only outcomes (like sales volume or revenue) but also leading indicators of those outcomes (such as the number of customer calls or completed customer plans). As a result, the focus of management conversations has shifted from trying to explain the past to charting the future—anticipating and preventing problems.

• Making the planning process more inclusive. Groups are explicitly mapping out the ways their initiatives depend on and affect one another; shared group goals are assigned accordingly.

• Enhancing the middle management career path to emphasize the importance of lateral moves to career advancement.

Goodward Insurance has just embarked on this journey. The insurer has distributed ownership of these initiatives among various groups and management levels so that these efforts don't become silos in themselves. Already, solid improvement in the company's execution is beginning to emerge. The early evidence of success has come from employee-satisfaction surveys: Middle management responses to the questions about levels of cross-unit collaboration and clarity of decision making have improved as much as 20 to 25 percentage points. And high performers are already reaching across boundaries to gain a broader understanding of the full business, even if it doesn't mean a better title right away.

• • •

Execution is a notorious and perennial challenge. Even at the companies that are best at it—what we call "resilient organizations"—

just two-thirds of employees agree that important strategic and operational decisions are quickly translated into action. As long as companies continue to attack their execution problems primarily or solely with structural or motivational initiatives, they will continue to fail. As we've seen, they may enjoy short-term results, but they will inevitably slip back into old habits because they won't have addressed the root causes of failure. Such failures can almost always be fixed by ensuring that people truly understand what they are responsible for and who makes which decisions—and then giving them the information they need to fulfill their responsibilities. With these two building blocks in place, structural and motivational elements will follow.

---

1. The details for this example have been taken from Gary L. Neilson and Bruce A. Pasternack, *Results: Keep What's Good, Fix What's Wrong, and Unlock Great Performance* (Random House, 2005).

Reprint R0806C
To order, see the next page
or call 800-988-0886 or 617-783-7500
or go to www.hbr.org

The Secrets to Successful Strategy Execution

Further Reading

ARTICLE
Mastering the Management System
by Robert S. Kaplan and David P. Norton
Harvard Business Review
January 2008
Product no. R0801D

It's hard to balance pressing operational concerns with long-term strategic priorities. But balance is critical: World-class processes won't produce success without the right strategic direction, and the best strategy won't get anywhere without strong operations to execute it. To manage both strategy and operations, companies must take five steps: 1) Develop strategy, based on the company's mission and values and its strengths, weaknesses, and competitive environment. 2) Translate the strategy into objectives and initiatives linked to performance metrics. 3) Create an operational plan to accomplish the objectives and initiatives. 4) Put the plan into action, monitoring its effectiveness. 5) Test the strategy by analyzing cost, profitability, and correlations between strategy and performance. Update as necessary.

BOOK CHAPTER
Build Execution into Strategy
by W. Chan Kim and Renée Mauborgne
Harvard Business School Press
October 2006
Product no. 1635BC

The authors identify an additional lever essential for strategy execution: the alignment of people behind a strategy. Incentives don't in themselves create alignment. You also need a culture of trust and commitment. This chapter, from *Blue Ocean Strategy: How to Create Uncontested Market Space and Make the Competition Irrelevant*, shows how to build such a culture, particularly by establishing fair strategy-formulation processes. When people perceive a process as fair, they go beyond the call of duty and take initiative in executing the strategy. To create a fair strategy-formulation process: 1) Involve people in the strategic decisions that affect them, by asking for their input. 2) Explain why final strategic decisions were made. 3) Clearly state the new behaviors you expect from people and what will happen if they fail to fulfill them.

Harvard Business Review

www.hbr.org

Leaders who successfully transform businesses do eight things right (and they do them in the right order).

Leading Change
Why Transformation Efforts Fail

by John P. Kotter

Leaders who successfully transform businesses do eight things right (and they do them in the right order).

BEST OF HBR

Leading Change
Why Transformation Efforts Fail

by John P. Kotter

Editor's Note: Guiding change may be the ultimate test of a leader—no business survives over the long term if it can't reinvent itself. But, human nature being what it is, fundamental change is often resisted mightily by the people it most affects: those in the trenches of the business. Thus, leading change is both absolutely essential and incredibly difficult.

Perhaps nobody understands the anatomy of organizational change better than retired Harvard Business School professor John P. Kotter. This article, originally published in the spring of 1995, previewed Kotter's 1996 book *Leading Change*. It outlines eight critical success factors—from establishing a sense of extraordinary urgency, to creating short-term wins, to changing the culture ("the way we do things around here"). It will feel familiar when you read it, in part because Kotter's vocabulary has entered the lexicon and in part because it contains the kind of home truths that we recognize, immediately, as if we'd always known them. A decade later, his work on leading change remains definitive.

Over the past decade, I have watched more than 100 companies try to remake themselves into significantly better competitors. They have included large organizations (Ford) and small ones (Landmark Communications), companies based in the United States (General Motors) and elsewhere (British Airways), corporations that were on their knees (Eastern Airlines), and companies that were earning good money (Bristol-Myers Squibb). These efforts have gone under many banners: total quality management, reengineering, rightsizing, restructuring, cultural change, and turnaround. But, in almost every case, the basic goal has been the same: to make fundamental changes in how business is conducted in order to help cope with a new, more challenging market environment.

A few of these corporate change efforts have been very successful. A few have been utter failures. Most fall somewhere in between, with a distinct tilt toward the lower end of the scale. The lessons that can be drawn are interesting and will probably be relevant to even more organizations in the increasingly competitive business environment of the coming decade.

The most general lesson to be learned from the more successful cases is that the change process goes through a series of phases that, in total, usually require a considerable length of time. Skipping steps creates only the illusion of speed and never produces a satisfying result. A second very general lesson is that critical mistakes in any of the phases can have a devastating impact, slowing momentum and negating hard-won gains. Perhaps because we have relatively little experience in renewing organizations, even very capable people often make at least one big error.

Error 1: Not Establishing a Great Enough Sense of Urgency

Most successful change efforts begin when some individuals or some groups start to look hard at a company's competitive situation, market position, technological trends, and financial performance. They focus on the potential revenue drop when an important patent expires, the five-year trend in declining margins in a core business, or an emerging market that everyone seems to be ignoring. They then find ways to communicate this information broadly and dramatically, especially with respect to crises, potential crises, or great opportunities that are very timely. This first step is essential because just getting a transformation program started requires the aggressive cooperation of many individuals. Without motivation, people won't help, and the effort goes nowhere.

Compared with other steps in the change process, phase one can sound easy. It is not. Well over 50% of the companies I have watched fail in this first phase. What are the reasons for that failure? Sometimes executives underestimate how hard it can be to drive people out of their comfort zones. Sometimes they grossly overestimate how successful they have already been in increasing urgency. Sometimes they lack patience: "Enough with the preliminaries; let's get on with it." In many cases, executives become paralyzed by the downside possibilities. They worry that employees with seniority will become defensive, that morale will drop, that events will spin out of control, that short-term business results will be jeopardized, that the stock will sink, and that they will be blamed for creating a crisis.

A paralyzed senior management often comes from having too many managers and not enough leaders. Management's mandate is to minimize risk and to keep the current system operating. Change, by definition, requires creating a new system, which in turn always demands leadership. Phase one in a renewal process typically goes nowhere until enough real leaders are promoted or hired into senior-level jobs.

Transformations often begin, and begin well, when an organization has a new head who is a good leader and who sees the need for a major change. If the renewal target is the entire company, the CEO is key. If change is needed in a division, the division general manager is key. When these individuals are not new leaders, great leaders, or change champions, phase one can be a huge challenge.

Bad business results are both a blessing and a curse in the first phase. On the positive side, losing money does catch people's attention. But it also gives less maneuvering room. With good business results, the opposite is true: Convincing people of the need for change is much harder, but you have more resources to help make changes.

But whether the starting point is good performance or bad, in the more successful cases I have witnessed, an individual or a group always facilitates a frank discussion of potentially unpleasant facts about new competition, shrinking margins, decreasing market share, flat earnings, a lack of revenue growth, or other relevant indices of a declining competitive position. Because there seems to be an almost universal human tendency to shoot the bearer of bad news, especially if the head of the organization is not a change champion, executives in these companies often rely on outsiders to bring unwanted information. Wall Street analysts, customers, and consultants can all be helpful in this regard. The purpose of all this activity, in the words of one former CEO of a large European company, is "to make the status quo seem more dangerous than launching into the unknown."

In a few of the most successful cases, a group has manufactured a crisis. One CEO deliberately engineered the largest accounting loss in the company's history, creating huge pressures from Wall Street in the process. One division president commissioned first-ever customer satisfaction surveys, knowing full well that the

Now retired, **John P. Kotter** was the Konosuke Matsushita Professor of Leadership at Harvard Business School in Boston.

results would be terrible. He then made these findings public. On the surface, such moves can look unduly risky. But there is also risk in playing it too safe: When the urgency rate is not pumped up enough, the transformation process cannot succeed, and the long-term future of the organization is put in jeopardy.

When is the urgency rate high enough? From what I have seen, the answer is when about 75% of a company's management is honestly convinced that business as usual is totally unacceptable. Anything less can produce very serious problems later on in the process.

Error 2: Not Creating a Powerful Enough Guiding Coalition

Major renewal programs often start with just one or two people. In cases of successful trans-

formation efforts, the leadership coalition grows and grows over time. But whenever some minimum mass is not achieved early in the effort, nothing much worthwhile happens.

It is often said that major change is impossible unless the head of the organization is an active supporter. What I am talking about goes far beyond that. In successful transformations, the chairman or president or division general manager, plus another five or 15 or 50 people, come together and develop a shared commitment to excellent performance through renewal. In my experience, this group never includes all of the company's most senior executives because some people just won't buy in, at least not at first. But in the most successful cases, the coalition is always pretty powerful—in terms of titles,

EIGHT STEPS TO TRANSFORMING YOUR ORGANIZATION

1 Establishing a Sense of Urgency
 • Examining market and competitive realities
 • Identifying and discussing crises, potential crises, or major opportunities

2 Forming a Powerful Guiding Coalition
 • Assembling a group with enough power to lead the change effort
 • Encouraging the group to work together as a team

3 Creating a Vision
 • Creating a vision to help direct the change effort
 • Developing strategies for achieving that vision

4 Communicating the Vision
 • Using every vehicle possible to communicate the new vision and strategies
 • Teaching new behaviors by the example of the guiding coalition

5 Empowering Others to Act on the Vision
 • Getting rid of obstacles to change
 • Changing systems or structures that seriously undermine the vision
 • Encouraging risk taking and nontraditional ideas, activities, and actions

6 Planning for and Creating Short-Term Wins
 • Planning for visible performance improvements
 • Creating those improvements
 • Recognizing and rewarding employees involved in the improvements

7 Consolidating Improvements and Producing Still More Change
 • Using increased credibility to change systems, structures, and policies that don't fit the vision
 • Hiring, promoting, and developing employees who can implement the vision
 • Reinvigorating the process with new projects, themes, and change agents

8 Institutionalizing New Approaches
 • Articulating the connections between the new behaviors and corporate success
 • Developing the means to ensure leadership development and succession

information and expertise, reputations, and relationships.

In both small and large organizations, a successful guiding team may consist of only three to five people during the first year of a renewal effort. But in big companies, the coalition needs to grow to the 20 to 50 range before much progress can be made in phase three and beyond. Senior managers always form the core of the group. But sometimes you find board members, a representative from a key customer, or even a powerful union leader.

Because the guiding coalition includes members who are not part of senior management, it tends to operate outside of the normal hierarchy by definition. This can be awkward, but it is clearly necessary. If the existing hierarchy were working well, there would be no need for a major transformation. But since the current system is not working, reform generally demands activity outside of formal boundaries, expectations, and protocol.

A high sense of urgency within the managerial ranks helps enormously in putting a guiding coalition together. But more is usually required. Someone needs to get these people together, help them develop a shared assessment of their company's problems and opportunities, and create a minimum level of trust and communication. Off-site retreats, for two or three days, are one popular vehicle for accomplishing this task. I have seen many groups of five to 35 executives attend a series of these retreats over a period of months.

Companies that fail in phase two usually underestimate the difficulties of producing change and thus the importance of a powerful guiding coalition. Sometimes they have no history of teamwork at the top and therefore undervalue the importance of this type of coalition. Sometimes they expect the team to be led by a staff executive from human resources, quality, or strategic planning instead of a key line manager. No matter how capable or dedicated the staff head, groups without strong line leadership never achieve the power that is required.

Efforts that don't have a powerful enough guiding coalition can make apparent progress for a while. But, sooner or later, the opposition gathers itself together and stops the change.

Error 3: Lacking a Vision

In every successful transformation effort that I have seen, the guiding coalition develops a picture of the future that is relatively easy to communicate and appeals to customers, stockholders, and employees. A vision always goes beyond the numbers that are typically found in five-year plans. A vision says something that helps clarify the direction in which an organization needs to move. Sometimes the first draft comes mostly from a single individual. It is usually a bit blurry, at least initially. But after the coalition works at it for three or five or even 12 months, something much better emerges through their tough analytical thinking and a little dreaming. Eventually, a strategy for achieving that vision is also developed.

In one midsize European company, the first pass at a vision contained two-thirds of the basic ideas that were in the final product. The concept of global reach was in the initial version from the beginning. So was the idea of becoming preeminent in certain businesses. But one central idea in the final version—getting out of low value-added activities—came only after a series of discussions over a period of several months.

Without a sensible vision, a transformation effort can easily dissolve into a list of confusing and incompatible projects that can take the organization in the wrong direction or nowhere at all. Without a sound vision, the reengineering project in the accounting department, the new 360-degree performance appraisal from the human resources department, the plant's quality program, the cultural change project in the sales force will not add up in a meaningful way.

In failed transformations, you often find plenty of plans, directives, and programs but no vision. In one case, a company gave out four-inch-thick notebooks describing its change effort. In mind-numbing detail, the books spelled out procedures, goals, methods, and deadlines. But nowhere was there a clear and compelling statement of where all this was leading. Not surprisingly, most of the employees with whom I talked were either confused or alienated. The big, thick books did not rally them together or inspire change. In fact, they probably had just the opposite effect.

In a few of the less successful cases that I have seen, management had a sense of direction, but it was too complicated or blurry to be useful. Recently, I asked an executive in a midsize company to describe his vision and received in return a barely comprehensible 30-

If you can't communicate the vision to someone in five minutes or less and get a reaction that signifies both understanding and interest, you are not done.

minute lecture. Buried in his answer were the basic elements of a sound vision. But they were buried—deeply.

A useful rule of thumb: If you can't communicate the vision to someone in five minutes or less and get a reaction that signifies both understanding and interest, you are not yet done with this phase of the transformation process.

Error 4: Undercommunicating the Vision by a Factor of Ten

I've seen three patterns with respect to communication, all very common. In the first, a group actually does develop a pretty good transformation vision and then proceeds to communicate it by holding a single meeting or sending out a single communication. Having used about 0.0001% of the yearly intracompany communication, the group is startled when few people seem to understand the new approach. In the second pattern, the head of the organization spends a considerable amount of time making speeches to employee groups, but most people still don't get it (not surprising, since vision captures only 0.0005% of the total yearly communication). In the third pattern, much more effort goes into newsletters and speeches, but some very visible senior executives still behave in ways that are antithetical to the vision. The net result is that cynicism among the troops goes up, while belief in the communication goes down.

Transformation is impossible unless hundreds or thousands of people are willing to help, often to the point of making short-term sacrifices. Employees will not make sacrifices, even if they are unhappy with the status quo, unless they believe that useful change is possible. Without credible communication, and a lot of it, the hearts and minds of the troops are never captured.

This fourth phase is particularly challenging if the short-term sacrifices include job losses. Gaining understanding and support is tough when downsizing is a part of the vision. For this reason, successful visions usually include new growth possibilities and the commitment to treat fairly anyone who is laid off.

Executives who communicate well incorporate messages into their hour-by-hour activities. In a routine discussion about a business problem, they talk about how proposed solutions fit (or don't fit) into the bigger picture. In a regular performance appraisal, they talk about how the employee's behavior helps or undermines the vision. In a review of a division's quarterly performance, they talk not only about the numbers but also about how the division's executives are contributing to the transformation. In a routine Q&A with employees at a company facility, they tie their answers back to renewal goals.

In more successful transformation efforts, executives use all existing communication channels to broadcast the vision. They turn boring, unread company newsletters into lively articles about the vision. They take ritualistic, tedious quarterly management meetings and turn them into exciting discussions of the transformation. They throw out much of the company's generic management education and replace it with courses that focus on business problems and the new vision. The guiding principle is simple: Use every possible channel, especially those that are being wasted on nonessential information.

Perhaps even more important, most of the executives I have known in successful cases of major change learn to "walk the talk." They consciously attempt to become a living symbol of the new corporate culture. This is often not easy. A 60-year-old plant manager who has spent precious little time over 40 years thinking about customers will not suddenly behave in a customer-oriented way. But I have witnessed just such a person change, and change a great deal. In that case, a high level of urgency helped. The fact that the man was a part of the guiding coalition and the vision-creation team also helped. So did all the communication, which kept reminding him of the desired behavior, and all the feedback from his peers and subordinates, which helped him see when he was not engaging in that behavior.

Communication comes in both words and deeds, and the latter are often the most powerful form. Nothing undermines change more than behavior by important individuals that is inconsistent with their words.

Error 5: Not Removing Obstacles to the New Vision

Successful transformations begin to involve large numbers of people as the process progresses. Employees are emboldened to try new approaches, to develop new ideas, and to provide leadership. The only constraint is that the actions fit within the broad parameters of the overall vision. The more people involved, the better the outcome.

To some degree, a guiding coalition empowers others to take action simply by successfully communicating the new direction. But communication is never sufficient by itself. Renewal also requires the removal of obstacles. Too often, an employee understands the new vision and wants to help make it happen, but an elephant appears to be blocking the path. In some cases, the elephant is in the person's head, and the challenge is to convince the individual that no external obstacle exists. But in most cases, the blockers are very real.

Sometimes the obstacle is the organizational structure: Narrow job categories can seriously undermine efforts to increase productivity or make it very difficult even to think about customers. Sometimes compensation or performance-appraisal systems make people choose between the new vision and their own self-interest. Perhaps worst of all are bosses who refuse to change and who make demands that are inconsistent with the overall effort.

One company began its transformation process with much publicity and actually made good progress through the fourth phase. Then the change effort ground to a halt because the officer in charge of the company's largest division was allowed to undermine most of the new initiatives. He paid lip service to the process but did not change his behavior or encourage his managers to change. He did not reward the unconventional ideas called for in the vision. He allowed human resource systems to remain intact even when they were clearly inconsistent with the new ideals. I think the officer's motives were complex. To some degree, he did not believe the company needed major change. To some degree, he felt personally threatened by all the change. To some degree, he was afraid that he could not produce both change and the expected operating profit. But despite the fact that they backed the renewal effort, the other officers did virtually nothing to stop the one blocker. Again, the reasons were complex. The company had no history of confronting problems like this. Some people were afraid of the officer. The CEO was concerned that he might lose a talented executive. The net result was disastrous. Lower-level managers concluded that senior management had lied to them about their commitment to renewal, cynicism grew, and the whole effort collapsed.

In the first half of a transformation, no organization has the momentum, power, or time to get rid of all obstacles. But the big ones must be confronted and removed. If the blocker is a person, it is important that he or she be treated fairly and in a way that is consistent with the new vision. Action is essential, both to empower others and to maintain the credibility of the change effort as a whole.

Error 6: Not Systematically Planning for, and Creating, Short-Term Wins

Real transformation takes time, and a renewal effort risks losing momentum if there are no short-term goals to meet and celebrate. Most people won't go on the long march unless they see compelling evidence in 12 to 24 months that the journey is producing expected results. Without short-term wins, too many people give up or actively join the ranks of those people who have been resisting change.

One to two years into a successful transformation effort, you find quality beginning to go up on certain indices or the decline in net income stopping. You find some successful new product introductions or an upward shift in market share. You find an impressive productivity improvement or a statistically higher customer satisfaction rating. But whatever the case, the win is unambiguous. The result is not just a judgment call that can be discounted by those opposing change.

Creating short-term wins is different from hoping for short-term wins. The latter is passive, the former active. In a successful transformation, managers actively look for ways to obtain clear performance improvements, establish goals in the yearly planning system, achieve the objectives, and reward the people involved with recognition, promotions, and even money. For example, the guiding coalition at a U.S. manufacturing company produced a highly visible and successful new product introduction about 20 months after the start of its renewal effort. The new product was selected about six months into the effort because it met multiple criteria: It could be designed and launched in a relatively short period, it could be handled by a small team of people who were devoted to the new vision, it had upside potential, and the new product-development team could operate outside the established departmental structure without practical problems. Little was left to chance, and the win boosted the credibility of the renewal process.

Managers often complain about being forced to produce short-term wins, but I've found that pressure can be a useful element in a change effort. When it becomes clear to people that major change will take a long time, urgency levels can drop. Commitments to produce short-term wins help keep the urgency level up and force detailed analytical thinking that can clarify or revise visions.

Error 7: Declaring Victory Too Soon

After a few years of hard work, managers may be tempted to declare victory with the first clear performance improvement. While celebrating a win is fine, declaring the war won can be catastrophic. Until changes sink deeply into a company's culture, a process that can take five to ten years, new approaches are fragile and subject to regression.

In the recent past, I have watched a dozen change efforts operate under the reengineering theme. In all but two cases, victory was declared and the expensive consultants were paid and thanked when the first major project was completed after two to three years. Within two more years, the useful changes that had been introduced slowly disappeared. In two of the ten cases, it's hard to find any trace of the reengineering work today.

Over the past 20 years, I've seen the same sort of thing happen to huge quality projects, organizational development efforts, and more. Typically, the problems start early in the process: The urgency level is not intense enough, the guiding coalition is not powerful enough, and the vision is not clear enough. But it is the premature victory celebration that kills momentum. And then the powerful forces associated with tradition take over.

Ironically, it is often a combination of change initiators and change resistors that creates the premature victory celebration. In their enthusiasm over a clear sign of progress, the initiators go overboard. They are then joined by resistors, who are quick to spot any opportunity to stop change. After the celebration is over, the resistors point to the victory as a sign that the war has been won and the troops should be sent home. Weary troops allow themselves to be convinced that they won. Once home, the foot soldiers are reluctant to climb back on the ships. Soon thereafter, change comes to a halt, and tradition creeps back in.

Instead of declaring victory, leaders of successful efforts use the credibility afforded by short-term wins to tackle even bigger problems. They go after systems and structures that are not consistent with the transformation vision and have not been confronted before. They pay great attention to who is promoted, who is hired, and how people are developed. They include new reengineering projects that are even bigger in scope than the initial ones. They understand that renewal efforts take not months but years. In fact, in one of the most successful transformations that I have ever seen, we quantified the amount of change that occurred each year over a seven-year period. On a scale of one (low) to ten (high), year one received a two, year two a four, year three a three, year four a seven, year five an eight, year six a four, and year seven a two. The peak came in year five, fully 36 months after the first set of visible wins.

Error 8: Not Anchoring Changes in the Corporation's Culture

In the final analysis, change sticks when it becomes "the way we do things around here," when it seeps into the bloodstream of the corporate body. Until new behaviors are rooted in social norms and shared values, they are subject to degradation as soon as the pressure for change is removed.

Two factors are particularly important in institutionalizing change in corporate culture. The first is a conscious attempt to show people how the new approaches, behaviors, and attitudes have helped improve performance. When people are left on their own to make the connections, they sometimes create very inaccurate links. For example, because results improved while charismatic Harry was boss, the troops link his mostly idiosyncratic style with those results instead of seeing how their own improved customer service and productivity were instrumental. Helping people see the right connections requires communication. Indeed, one company was relentless, and it paid off enormously. Time was spent at every major management meeting to discuss why performance was increasing. The company newspaper ran article after article showing how changes had boosted earnings.

The second factor is taking sufficient time to make sure that the next generation of top management really does personify the new

After a few years of hard work, managers may be tempted to declare victory with the first clear performance improvement. While celebrating a win is fine, declaring the war won can be catastrophic.

approach. If the requirements for promotion don't change, renewal rarely lasts. One bad succession decision at the top of an organization can undermine a decade of hard work. Poor succession decisions are possible when boards of directors are not an integral part of the renewal effort. In at least three instances I have seen, the champion for change was the retiring executive, and although his successor was not a resistor, he was not a change champion. Because the boards did not understand the transformations in any detail, they could not see that their choices were not good fits. The retiring executive in one case tried unsuccessfully to talk his board into a less seasoned candidate who better personified the transformation. In the other two cases, the CEOs did not resist the boards' choices, because they felt the transformation could not be undone by their successors. They were wrong. Within two years, signs of renewal began to disappear at both companies.

• • •

There are still more mistakes that people make, but these eight are the big ones. I realize that in a short article everything is made to sound a bit too simplistic. In reality, even successful change efforts are messy and full of surprises. But just as a relatively simple vision is needed to guide people through a major change, so a vision of the change process can reduce the error rate. And fewer errors can spell the difference between success and failure.

Reprint R0701J
Harvard Business Review OnPoint 1710
To order, see the next page
or call 800-988-0886 or 617-783-7500
or go to www.hbr.org

Further Reading

Leading Change is also part of the *Harvard Business Review* OnPoint collection **Lead Change Successfully, 3rd Edition,** Product no. 1908, which includes these additional articles:

Cracking the Code of Change
Michael Beer and Nitin Nohria
Harvard Business Review
April 2001
Product no. 651X

Managing Change: The Art of Balancing
Jeanie Daniel Duck
Harvard Business Review
November–December 2000
Product no. 5416

The Hard Side of Change Management
Harold L. Sirkin, Perry Keenan, and
Alan Jackson
Harvard Business Review
October 2005
Product no. 1916

Part VI

Taken from *Greener Management International*

EMS and Sustainable Development

A Model and Comparative Studies of Integration

Ulku Oktem
The Wharton School, University of Pennsylvania, USA

Phil Lewis
Rohm and Haas Corporation, USA

Deborah Donovan
Sunoco, USA

James R. Hagan
GlaxoSmithKline, UK

Thomas Pace
Burlington Northern and Santa Fe Railway Co., USA

With the renewed drive for competitive advantage and improved effectiveness, organisations are integrating environmental, health, safety (EHS) and sustainable development (SD) initiatives into business systems in new ways. In this paper we present a sustainable management system (SMS) model for EHS and SD integration along with four case studies, illustrating variations. Our model is grounded in the environmental management system (EMS) principles. While managers looking to present a business case for SMS frequently find it difficult to develop a complete financial cost–benefit analysis, it is noteworthy that these successful cases took a different approach. In each case, first and foremost management recognised the strategic value of having an SMS, and did not rely explicitly on cost–benefit analysis for justification. As demonstrated by the case studies, organisations will find a variety of viable approaches to achieve the successful implementation of a strategically important SMS.

- Environmental management system (EMS)
- Sustainable development
- Environmental, health and safety (EHS)
- Sustainable management system (SMS)
- Rohm and Haas
- GlaxoSmithKline
- Sunoco
- Burlington Northern and Santa Fe Railway Co. (BNSF)

Dr **Ulku Oktem** is a Senior Research Fellow at the Risk Management and Decision Processes Center and Adjunct Professor at Operations and Decision Processes Department of the Wharton School of the University of Pennsylvania. She has a PhD in chemical engineering and worked as a manager in R&D and Corporate EH&S departments of Rohm and Haas Company.

The Wharton School, University of Pennsylvania, 558 Jon M. Huntsman Hall, 3730 Walnut Street, Philadelphia, PA 19104.6340, USA

oktem@wharton.upenn.edu

Philip G. Lewis, Vice President of EHS and SD, is also an adjunct faculty in occupational medicine both at the University of Pennsylvania and at the Johns Hopkins University. He was a Clinton Presidential appointee to the Board of Directors of the Mickey Leland Urban Air Toxics Research Center, and is a Fellow of both the American College of Preventive Medicine and the American College of Occupational and Environmental Medicine.

Rohm and Haas Corporation, 100 Independence Mall West, 9th Floor, Philadelphia, PA 19106-2399, USA

PLewis@RohmHaas.com

Deborah Donovan holds a BS in chemical engineering from Northeastern University and an MBA from the California State University. Ms Donovan worked for Texas Instruments, Asland Chemical and Sunoco in manufacturing, engineering, management, product stewardship and health/safety prior to assuming her current position. As Director HES Performance, she is responsible for Sunoco's HES services groups and improving processes through management systems.

Sunoco, Ten Penn Center, 1801 Market Street, Philadelphia, PA 19103, USA

donovan@amgen.com

Dr **James R. Hagan** is responsible for worldwide EHS programmes including the setting of the direction for the company and the provision of environment, health and safety scientific and engineering support. Before working for GlaxoSmithKline, Dr Hagan worked for the US Environmental Protection Agency and in the chemical industry. He is a Registered Professional Engineer, a Diplomat of Environmental Engineering and a Certified Quality Manager.

GlaxoSmithKline, 2200 Renaissance Blvd Ste. 105, King of Prussia, PA 19406-2755, USA

James.R.Hagan@gsk.com

Thomas J. Pace, Assistant Vice President of Medical Environmental Health, BNSF Railway Co., is an adjunct faculty member at the University of North Texas Health Science Center. Dr Pace is Board Certified by the American Board of Preventive Medicine in Occupational and Environmental Medicine and is a member of the American College of Occupational and Environmental Medicine and the American College of Preventive Medicine.

Burlington Northern and Santa Fe Railway Co., 2500 Lou Menk Drive, Fort Worth, TX 76131, USA

Thomas.Pace@BNSF.com

N THIS PAPER WE PRESENT A STATE-OF-THE-ART MODEL FOR A 'SUSTAINABLE management system' (SMS), which integrates corporate environmental, health, safety and sustainable development. This model is developed and based on the collective experience of the authors, and enhanced by information presented in the literature.

The presentation of the model is followed by four case studies: Rohm and Haas (R&H), GlaxoSmithKline (GSK), Sunoco, Inc. and Burlington Northern and Santa Fe Railway Co. (BNSF).

Our model is rooted in the principles of an environmental management system (EMS), which has been shown to have a positive impact on overall corporate performance (Klassen and McLanghlin 1996; Bansal 1999; Corbett and Kirsch 2000; PricewaterhouseCoopers 2002; Andrews *et al.* 2003; Melnyk *et al.* 2003). As demonstrated by Responsible Care® and OHSAS (Occupational Health and Safety Assessment Specifications), ISO 14000 can be extrapolated to safety and health standards as well (Corbett and Kirsch 2001). Our model also incorporates sustainable development (SD) practices into this all-encompassing management system.

The approach of incorporating sustainable development into the environmental, health and safety (EHS) management system reflects both the origins and the evolution of SD. EHS management systems, developed in response to the need to address adverse consequences of industrial activities, ensure compliance by addressing business issues with an insider's knowledge of operations and provide a sustainable level of protection of employees, the public and the environment.

By contrast, sustainable development is focused on the core of the business itself. It looks to long-term future impacts of the business with respect to the utilisation of resources and the provision of goods and services. Once the company has identified its vision in terms of SD, the use of management systems allows the company to take the initial phases of its plan in a comprehensive fashion. Whether the focus is on company mission, improved utilisation of natural resources, or greater reliance on renewable resources, the future effort looks to ensure that future generations benefit from a standard of living that is at least equal to today's.

A single management system would help comply with the requirements imposed by an ever-increasing number of regulations (Dowell 2001; Oktem 2003). We hypothesise that, by combining the management of EHS and SD, firms would not only comply with current regulatory expectations more effectively, but also could improve their overall performance and productivity without a substantial increase in resources. This concept may also influence public policy instruments (Green and New 2000; Coglianese 2003; Nill and Petschow 2003).

We argue that SD's integration would not only enhance EMS's positive impact on corporate performance, but also would influence the corporate structure. European and US agencies and voluntary organisations have developed different management guidelines, but currently there is no single guideline or certification for SMS. Each of the case studies covered in this paper has chosen a different and valid pathway to establish its practices.

Rationale for a new model

The most important aspect of SMS is to understand that, although each of its elements originates from the same Deming[1] view of organisation that underlies the rest of enter-

---

1 Doctor W. Edwards Deming is the legendary management/quality guru who helped American industry to improve its product and process quality in the second half of the 20th century.

prise management, they are usually not viewed as essential to the business of enterprise. While nothing could be further from the truth, this means that the first organisational challenge is to have EHS and SD properly represented in the senior management ranks of the enterprise and the board. While few managers have difficulty understanding the wisdom of having legal, human resources and financial management systems in place, there is little if anything in their education or experience to prepare them for the obvious need for an effective SMS.[2]

Therefore, we developed an empirical model based on the following three principles:

1. The idea of seamless and effective integration of SMS principles into corporate governance. Several organisations issued guidelines for implementing SD either as a stand-alone programme or as part of ISO 14001 (GEMI 2002; Gilding *et al.* 2002; Timberlake 2002; Rittenhouse 2003). Various operational aspects of EMS have been addressed in the literature (Green and New 2000; Hall 2001; Sroufe 2003) with fewer references on the organisational structure (O'Brien 2001).

2. A corporate structure that would nurture an SMS operation. A complex set of variables, including corporate structure, individuals' skills, corporate culture and resources, play an important role in the success of any structural reorganisation (Burke and Litwin 1992). We identified certain elements as core components for successful implementation.

3. Provision of a framework for future enterprise resource planning (ERP) designs by identifying key elements, practices and crucial links of a corporate practice where EMS and SD are fully integrated. Current ERP systems have been generated either from the perspective of accounting (SAP) or human resource management (People Soft). The advantages they provide to enterprises are legion (Buckingham 2003). That said, none of the currently available ERPs is fully developed to allow immediate installation and maintenance of an SMS.

A model of a fully integrated corporate EMS and SD system

We developed a management model for a corporation to practise total integration of EMS and SD. In envisioning and describing this model we have used the term 'EMS' in an all-encompassing manner, including environment, health and safety (EHS). Potential variations of this model, where corporate structure as well as practices are modified without compromising the total integration, are also discussed.

The model comprises best practice observed in the industry and modified by the authors' vision of the 'ideal state'. Although this model is developed based on practices in the chemical, pharmaceutical, petrochemical and transportation industries, we expect the basic principles to apply to all other businesses.

The model has five components:

▶ Business case

▶ Organisational component

▶ Operational component

▶ ERP/IT (information technology)

▶ Monitoring and audits

---

2 The top ten MBA schools' curriculum does not include any required EHS and SD courses.

In the following sections each component is articulated, and its relationship to others and to corporate governance is discussed.

Building a business case

Type of cost and/or benefit	Details
Direct cost of EHS and SD system	Salaries of part-time and full-time employees dedicated to EHS and SD activities
Direct benefits of EHS and SD	Expected savings in waste disposal, lost work days, workers' compensation
Indirect costs	Costs associated with monitoring, reporting and other activities related to regulatory requirements
Potential savings in future and contingent liability	Savings that would materialise due to reduced fines, penalties and future liabilities (e.g. non-compliance, remediation, personal injury, property damage, industrial accidents)
Intangible savings: internal	Savings from costs that would be borne by the company (e.g. customer acceptance, worker morale, union relations, community relations)
Intangible savings: external	Savings in costs borne by society (e.g. impact of operations on housing costs, degradation of habitat)
Business opportunities: new business or modified operations	Identifying new businesses (e.g. providing EHS and SD services, creating a new product line to help low-income society) Savings in resource consumption (e.g. energy, water, raw material) due to modified processes and products

Table 1 FACTORS TO BE CONSIDERED IN BUILDING A BUSINESS CASE FOR EHS/SD

Building a business case for a SMS is not straightforward. In Table 1 we have listed a number of items and their contribution to business case development. Most of the time environmental initiatives are influenced by external stakeholders (Angell 2001; Delmas 2001), and it is difficult to judge financially the value of simply being a good corporate citizen (Holliday *et al.* 2002; Melnyk *et al.* 2003).

The American Institute of Chemical Engineers (AIChE 1999) has developed a 'total cost and benefit assessment methodology' (TCA). This method can be reverse-engineered to identify some of the factors and their contributions to building a business case. Table 1 includes terminology used in TCA. Since good business practices already include sustainable development initiatives as an integral part of the decision-making process, we recommend a broader look into factors for building a business case.

Organisational component

The importance of management buy-in for an effective SMS, while increasingly recognised (Angell 2001; O'Brien 2001), continues to be absent. Once management arrives at an understanding of the need for an SMS and there is an appropriate seat at the senior levels of management for the head of the function, the other components of the system easily follow.

The organisation must designate who is responsible for achieving objectives and targets at each relevant function and level of the enterprise and ensure the means and time by which they may be achieved. When needed, programmes must be amended to ensure that SMS management is also an integral part of projects.

Once a plan has been developed, there must be a clear structure for implementing it. Management must provide essential resources, including human resources and specialised skills, and technology and financial resources. The organisation's senior management must appoint specific management representative(s) who have defined SMS roles, responsibilities and authority, with accountability to the governing board of the enterprise.

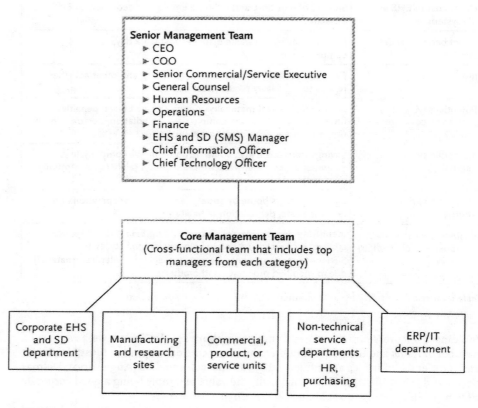

Figure 1 CORPORATE STRUCTURE

In Figure 1 an example of a management system design is shown which would enable the firm to implement the above principles. Having a core management team, which reports to the senior SMS manager, and which is facilitated by business or facility EHS and SD manager(s) would make timely consideration of issues possible. The core team would have the main EHS and SD performance responsibility for the corporation.

Although recent literature (Angell 2001; Delmas 2001) suggests that EMS and quality management systems do not have precisely the same drivers, success factors or challenges, we think for successful SMS performance establishing a link to the quality management systems can provide rewarding synergies.

Operational component

SMS processes have to be linked to the overall enterprise strategic plan, which addresses the needs of several different groups of stakeholders: the owner (whether private or public), the customer, the community, and employees or volunteers. The senior management must define the organisation's SMS policy and ensure: a commitment to continual improvement and to prevention of pollution and work-related injuries/illnesses; a commitment to comply with relevant EHS and SD regulations, laws and voluntary codes of practice; a framework for setting and reviewing SMS objectives and targets; integration into business objectives and corporate strategy, including product discovery and development; inclusion of the supply chain and customers; documentation, implementation and maintenance, communication to all employees; openness in dealing with the public; and incorporation of continual knowledge transfer and process improvement principles (Lundberg 1989; Berry 1991; Simonin 1999).

The organisation must establish and maintain a documented procedure to identify and access legal and other requirements to which the organisation is subject. There must be established, maintained and communicated written SMS objectives and targets for each relevant function and level within the organisation.

When establishing and reviewing its objectives, an organisation must consider the legal and other requirements, significant EHS and SD aspects, technological options, financial, operational and business requirements, and concerns of interested parties.

The organisation must identify training needs. It must require that all personnel whose work may create a significant impact on the workplace, community and environment receive appropriate training. It must ensure that employees and contractors at all relevant levels are aware of the importance of conformance with the SMS policy and procedures, the significant impacts of their work activities, the benefits of improved personal SMS-related performance, and the potential consequences of departure from specific operating procedures.

The organisation must establish and maintain information, in paper or electronic form, to describe the core elements of SMS. There must be directions to related documentation. The organisation must establish and maintain procedures for controlling all documents required by the SMS plan to ensure that they can be located, periodically reviewed, revised as necessary and approved for adequacy by authorised personnel.

The organisation must establish and maintain procedures for internal communication and dialogue between the levels and functions of the organisation, and external communications with the interested parties regarding the enterprise's EHS and SD aspects.

Records must be maintained to demonstrate conformance to the requirements of this SMS. These records must be readily retrievable and traceable to the activity, products or service involved.

SMS must extend its sphere of influence to the firm's suppliers (Hall 2001) since suppliers' performance can expose companies to higher risks and large firms are usually under pressure from their stakeholders to address their suppliers' EHS and SD performance. External stakeholders may also play an important role in environmental performance of a company (Delmas 2001; Angell 2001) and can help firms to gain competitive advantage.

There are many significant relationships between a formal or certified EMS (Melnyk *et al.* 2003) and improved corporate performance. Although there is no single certification that indicates top performance in the combined areas of EHS and SD, EMAS (Eco-Management and Audit Scheme), CERES, ISO 14000 certifications and GRI (Global Reporting Initiative) are important steps.

ERP/IT

Recent developments in ERP on IT platforms are facilitating business operations not only within a firm's internal operation but also extending to supply chain management. In a fully integrated system it can be difficult to distinguish whether an action or a decision was made with an additional consideration of EHS and SD, or as a good business decision alone. A smart ERP system can be very helpful for establishing and revising an SMS business case.

Complying with applicable laws, collecting EHS- and SD-related data and mining it to obtain meaningful results, such as performance values for the overall corporation as well as individual sites and businesses, can be greatly facilitated by a well-designed ERP system on an IT platform. Although there are programs developed for this purpose, they are far from being fully satisfactory in terms of meeting the current corporate requirements listed above.

Monitoring and audits

The organisation's senior management and governing board must, at regular intervals, review the SMS to ensure continuing suitability, adequacy and effectiveness. The management review process must make certain that the necessary information is collected to allow management and outside observers to carry out such an evaluation. The management review must address the possible need for changes to policy, objectives and other elements of the SMS in light of the audit results, changing circumstances and the commitment to continual improvement.

Special attention must be directed towards identifying the potential for accidents and emergency situations that adversely affect employees, environment and surrounding communities, and for preventing and mitigating the EHS and SD impacts that may be associated with them (Phimister et al. 2003).

The organisation must have an audit system to periodically evaluate compliance with relevant EHS and SD legislation, regulations and company standards. The organisation must establish and maintain procedures, and define responsibility and authority, for handling and investigating non-conformance, and must take action to mitigate the impacts caused by non-conformance and initiate corrective and preventative action.

Any corrective or preventative action taken to eliminate the causes of actual and potential non-conformance must be appropriate to the magnitude of problems and commensurate with the EHS and SD impact encountered.

In Table 2 we propose sample cells of a universal maturity matrix to provide guidance for assessing a corporation's SMS performance. This matrix must be supplemented with industry- and company-specific criteria and must be revised periodically.

Case studies

In this section we present four case studies to demonstrate the variations in implementing the above model. After reviewing all cases, the reader will be able to identify and appreciate the differences between corporate practices to achieve the same purpose of establishing an effective SMS.

Criteria	Early in development	Middle of the road	Well established
Establishing and communicating to the employees the EHS and SD structure and responsibilities	Upper management identified the structure and selected team members	Managers understand responsibilities and issue commitment letters Management structure communicated to employees	A performance matrix for managers is established and used in calculating compensation
EHS and SD policy defined and put in action	Specific objectives defined Data collection system developed Customer communication established	Pollution prevention measurements established Targets are in place for waste reduction, safety records, energy consumption, etc.	Policy revised and improved periodically All registrations completed Initial targets met Established EHS and SD systems at all suppliers

Note: A firm can be at different stages with respect to various criteria

Table 2 SAMPLE MATURITY MATRIX

Case study 1:
EHS and SD management system (SMS) at the Rohm and Haas Company

Building a business case
The history of Rohm and Haas Company, emanating from the original partners, Otto Rohm and Otto Haas, allowed for a deep concern for both employees and the environment in which the company operated. From the founding of the company in 1909, through the groundbreaking memo issued by F.O. Haas, chairman of the company in the 1960s, noting the company's responsibility to attend to environmental concerns, there has been a general acceptance that managing environmental, health and safety concerns was an important part of achieving business success. The sense of the fuller nature of business continued with the development of water-based acrylic paints and the company's decision to become one of the initial signatories to the International Chamber of Commerce's Business Charter for Sustainable Development. The general understanding of the increasing importance of environment, health, safety and sustainable development to consumers and governments was sufficient to prompt the company to establish the Board Committee on Sustainable Development in December 2002.

Organisational component
Environment, health, safety and sustainable development cascade in the company from the board committee to the executive council which consists of the CEO (chief executive officer), COO (chief operating officer), the general counsel, vice president for human resources, the chief financial officer and two senior business vice presidents. At the level below the executive council, in a group known as the leadership council, which includes all the company vice presidents and above, sit the chief information officer, the vice president for manufacturing, the chief technology officer and the vice president for environmental, health, safety and sustainable development. Within each one of the busi-

nesses, manufacturing and regional units are senior EHS and SD managers, who are responsible for ensuring profitable top-line growth through the SMS.

Operational component

For more than a decade the company has been managed through the use of the Five Voices concept, which requires all managers to conduct business in a manner that meets the needs of the customers, the owners, communities, the employees and the underlying processes that generate the products and services. Rooted in a Deming approach to quality, the Five Voices approach as a management system requires constant improvement of performance. In 1997, in order to ensure appropriate training of transitioning professionals and documentation of the EHS and SD system, separate standards for management systems around processes and products were issued. Developed to ensure the ongoing operations around EHS and SD, Rohm and Haas Company met the expectations of ISO 14001, EMAS and Responsible Care®. The SMS standards require that all the components of these externally determined management systems are in place globally, with the exception of the particular administrative requirements for registration or certification under the various schemes. The decision to include the latter is left to the business or enterprise manager. Implementation of the current standards is in progress.

ERP/IT

Throughout the 1990s, the IT backbone for the EHS and other corporate systems was a diverse lot of hardware and software that supported the individual business or enterprise view of how best to implement the individual SMS functions. With the agreement to install an enterprise resource planning (ERP) system, the company also realised the importance of implementing the EHS and SD module to the system. That process is ongoing, though complicated by the fact that none of the currently available ERP systems was built from the perspective of EHS and SD or with a need for general management attention to the area in mind. That said, the standardisation of work processes that is required of a fully integrated ERP results in an approach to business that enhances SMS performance.

Monitoring and audits

In the 1970s and beginning with the environmental area, Rohm and Haas Company started auditing against internal standards. Over the years the system has continued to improve and develop from the best practices of the financial auditing world. In the past decade, the audits have expanded to include protocols with specific questions on compliance with local law and regulations along with the other areas of EHS and SD. The audits are conducted worldwide and all sites are held to the same performance expectations. While the capability exists to carry out purely systems audits, there continues to be a preference for compliance-centred audits.

Case study 2: EHS and SD management system (SMS) at GlaxoSmithKline

Building a business case

In the late 1970s and early 1980s, a great awareness of the need to provide a greater level of protection than was required by simple legal compliance led to the development and adoption of internal global EHS standards by all the heritage companies that merged to form GlaxoSmithKline (GSK). These standards defined the ways of working that met or exceeded legal and regulatory requirements in all countries in which heritage GSK companies did business. Compliance with both legal requirements and internal standards were tracked through routine audits of all manufacturing and R&D operations.

However, the results from these audits were found to vary with time and with root-cause reviews, demonstrating job changes of key individuals or external stresses which drew attention elsewhere.

As a result, environment, health and safety management systems were adopted by heritage GSK organisations in the 1990s. This occurred primarily because there was common global experience of attempts at putting EHS compliance systems in without the necessary processes and procedures. Invariably, at most of the GSK operations, there was a concerted effort to install a response to the need to comply with certain laws, regulations or company standards. The difficulty was that compliance could not be sustained without a reliance on systems. The approach to the EHS management systems came about primarily to ensure that it was an integral part of the organisational procedure of each and every GSK heritage site and not based on the strength of individuals' activities.

The benefit of the use of management systems has recently been demonstrated by the ability of the company to maintain its levels of compliance and environment, health and safety performance during the last merger of companies to form GSK.

The company is now embarking on a programme to embed sustainable development into the fabric of the operations. The initial phase is to look at natural resource utilisation, both to improve efficiencies and to examine the possibility of a greater reliance on renewable resources. The emphasis at present is to develop and implement processes in R&D, procurement, capital expenditures and other related areas. These areas will be controlled through the use of management systems and then tracked by audits.

Governance

GSK has several groups that identify governance and ethical issues, recommend ways to manage them and periodically review the management of the issues. EHS issues are among those reviewed and addressed by these groups.

The Risk Oversight and Compliance Council (ROCC) is responsible for co-ordinating the internal control and risk management activities of the company. EHS is identified as one of the areas of the business that has the potential for serious adverse consequences if not managed properly. The vice president of corporate environment, health and safety (CEHS) is a member of the ROCC. The ROCC reports its evaluation of EHS risk management to the corporate executive team (CET).

The CET actively manages EHS issues. The chief executive officer (CEO) is the identified champion of EHS issues for both the CET and the board. The CEO ensures that EHS issues are regularly debated to verify that GSK is pursuing responsible programmes for all operations.

The board of directors has two committees that evaluate the management and effectiveness of the EHS programme. These review and oversight mechanisms provide opportunities for EHS issues to be considered at the highest level of the organisation.

The Audit Committee of the board reviews EHS performance to confirm that issues are properly managed and controlled. The vice president of CEHS makes regular presentations to the Audit Committee so that they can review measures of EHS performance. They also review the results of the EHS audits of GSK operations, contract manufacturers and key suppliers.

The Corporate Social Responsibility Committee (CSRC) of the board reviews social, ethical and environmental issues that have the potential to seriously affect GSK's business and reputation. The VP of CEHS provides reports to the CSRC on those aspects of EHS performance that have social implications with a focus on sustainable development.

ISO certification

In reviewing the costs and benefits of ISO certification, GSK is considering the adoption of ISO 14001 and OHSAS 18001 because certification would provide:

- ► An external certification of GSK's management systems that gives the company's internal systems greater credibility with the public

- ► A heightened awareness of the criticality of maintaining management systems

- ► A reward to all the operations who were implementing the management systems approach

- ► A cost-effective approach compared with individual site ISO certifications

This certification is being conducted by the consulting firm SGS from Zurich, Switzerland. While GSK is currently in the evaluation phase of ISO certification, the value of EHS management systems was made abundantly clear in the transition of the merger. While mergers generally have a disrupting effect on operations, with an EHS management system in place, GSK was able to maintain and improve its EHS performance from both heritage organisations.

Organisational component

Corporate support

It was understood that, to implement EHS management systems on a global basis, a template or a model for sites would ease the implementation hurdle. Therefore, the GSK heritage companies developed prototype management systems that could be adopted by the sites. These model or prototype management systems were developed by the corporate group and distributed on a global basis.

Implementation at sites

Implementation at sites occurred in a variety of ways depending on the culture that existed in that operation. The recommended approach was to ensure that the site manager took ownership of the responsibility of implementing this management system, and then, with the assistance of the EHS manager, delegated responsibilities for various activities to different organisations dependent on their involvement in the issue at hand.

Operational components

Within GSK, the revisions that occurred with the new standards were to make management systems an implementation activity throughout the entire system requirements, and not only for manufacturing and R&D but for commercial and office buildings as well. GSK also further expanded responsibilities into key suppliers and their contract manufacturers.

The new audit system provides a scored response in order to ease comparison and tracking, and provides a more comprehensive view of various activities beyond just strict EHS compliance. GSK now looks at business continuity, loss prevention, emergency response, employee health and sustainability. The CEO and the heads of the various operations that support implementation have approved this approach.

ERP/IT

GSK was fortunate in its merger in that there were heritage EHS information management systems that needed to be revised. Based on this revision, GSK adopted a commercial system developed by Entropy of Lancaster, UK, to assist them in this regard. Entropy's Internet-ready system is being implemented in modules and not only provides an underpinning for the implementation of management systems but is also aligned with ISO certification.

Monitoring and audits
The audit system was modified to incorporate both the review of compliance with laws and corporate standards, and the implementation of management systems. This combined approach was critical since early efforts in the 1980s were not successful due to a disconnect between audit results and the implementation of the recommendations. Therefore, it evolved into a paper exercise. The audit programme was scored so that the sites would have an appreciation of how well they were progressing during each visit, and they could also gauge how well they were doing compared with others in the organisation.

Case Study 3: Sunoco's Operations Excellence Management System (OEMS)

Building a business case
In 2000, Sunoco began exploring development and implementation of a management system. At the time, there were already a number of developments in the management systems arena. There was a push by the automakers to move towards the ISO 14001 environmental management system. The National Enforcement Investigative Center (NEIC) had developed a 12-step compliance focused environmental management system that was being used in consent order settlements, and many companies were looking to integrate EHS performance with reliability and mechanical integrity systems.

The company wanted to implement an integrated management system that would improve its performance and help achieve its strategic objective of having a safe, reliable, environmentally sound operation.

Hence, the company realised early on that excellent EHS performance goes hand in hand with excellent reliability and operations integrity. The resulting Operations Excellence Management System (OEMS) is an integrated approach that will provide the framework for managing the EHS and operations integrity elements of Sunoco's business.

In order to avoid the pitfalls with 'the programme of the month' approach, Sunoco encompassed several other systems and programmes into OEMS to reinforce that the management system is the way to accomplish all necessary work. The basis for the design of OEMS includes the following systems:

► ISO 14001 Environmental Management System

► NEIC compliance-focused environmental management system

► Responsible Care management system

► OSHA (Occupational Health and Safety Assessment) Voluntary Protection Program

► ISO 9001 Quality Management System

► Occupational Health and Safety Assessment Series 18001 Health and Safety Management System

In addition, the OEMS incorporates energy conservation and plant security programme requirements adopted in 2001 by the American Chemistry Council.

Organisational component
A cross-functional team of professionals was assembled to build the OEMS for Sunoco. The team was co-led by a senior EHS professional and a senior operations professional. The members of the team included maintenance management and hourly (union)

positions, operations management and hourly (union) positions, a senior environmental professional and a senior health and safety professional. An outside consultant with management systems expertise facilitated the team. It was important for Sunoco to have the effort driven jointly by EHS and operations since the operations departments control the resources and are responsible for the daily operations of the facilities. The EHS department provides support to operations, but is not accountable for compliance with EHS laws and regulations. The sponsor of the team is the senior vice president of the refining and supply (R&S) business unit who provides support and leadership. By implementing OEMS, Sunoco is changing the culture of the business, which, in its view, is not something that happens from the bottom up. The top-down leadership and commitment is the catalyst that got the entire effort in motion.

R&S has developed a three-year implementation plan that identified key tasks. Each facility participating in the implementation appointed a management systems representative whose function is to facilitate the implementation at each plant, not to do all the work him or herself. The management systems representatives are high-level operations personnel who have a high degree of credibility with the line organisation. They are recognised high-potential employees, which sends the message to others that this effort is important enough to put the organisation's best people on it.

The management systems representatives have performed gap analyses of the processes they currently have in place against the OEMS. The gaps have been prioritised and teams are assembled to address the gaps.

The OEMS management systems representatives get together quarterly to ensure consistency in implementation and to discuss issues and opportunities that could benefit all locations.

Operational component

The OEMS focuses resources on attaining and sustaining compliance with the firm's legal and other requirements, managing EHS and operations integrity aspects and improving the reliability of its operations to minimise impacts on employees, contractors, the community and the environment. OEMS also fosters a culture of continuous performance improvement.

The management system is viewed as a process for getting work completed efficiently, not as a project. The basis of the OEMS is the plan–do–check–act cycle. This continuous process starts with management commitment and leadership. The senior management in the organisation shows their commitment and leadership by articulating a policy and setting out expectations for the organisation.

Implementation

Sunoco is a company composed of autonomous business units and a shared services organisation which houses functions that provide services to each business unit (examples are legal, EHS, human resources, finance). In 2003, the refining and supply (R&S) business unit decided to roll out the OEMS as a pilot for the rest of the company. Other business units will evaluate their operations and determine the benefit and timing of the implementation of OEMS.

ERP/IT

There are several tools and processes that are the foundation of building a management system and they are being developed from a corporate or business unit (versus plant) perspective. They include document control procedures and supporting information technology tools. It was very important to Sunoco not to leave the OEMS in a binder on a shelf, but to make it available to all employees whenever and wherever needed. The company intranet has provided the facility for this vision to become reality.

Sunoco is also evaluating information technology tools for developing compliance matrices, compliance task management, and air, water and waste management modules. Having these tools will facilitate the tracking of legal and other requirements and EHS performance, deliver and track training requirements, and track management programme progress.

Monitoring and audits

To monitor implementation, Sunoco is performing management systems assessments at each participating facility. This assessment is evaluating progress with implementation of the management system, not compliance with laws and regulations. Sunoco has an existing compliance-auditing programme for that purpose. The assessments are being added to the auditing function and will not replace the traditional compliance audits.

Certification

As a member of the American Chemistry Council, Sunoco has an obligation to certify its management system under the Responsible Care programme. The Responsible Care Management System offers the opportunity to be certified to ISO 14001 as well as the Responsible Care Management System (RCMS) standards. Sunoco has not yet decided on certification strategy, as there are pros and cons for each. Certifying to ISO 14001 provides credibility with the public and customers but not necessarily with the regulating community. ISO 14001 is about continuous improvement in environmental management, not compliance with laws and regulations. However, it should be noted that many environmental regulators are requiring ISO 14001 certification as part of compliance agreements. The Responsible Care programme is much more comprehensive than ISO 14001 and has credibility with the public who live near the plants, but not with the regulators or customers. To certify to the RCMS may bring community credibility, but does not carry the same weight as an ISO 14001 certificate.

Case study 4: SMS at Burlington Northern and Santa Fe Railway

Building a business case

The railroad industry is extremely mature and, like other commodity product businesses, must compete aggressively in terms of cost. The railroad metric is unit cost per gross ton-mile moved. Because of high fixed costs related to infrastructure, much attention is given to fuel costs, which account for 10–12% of operating expense. Environmentally, approximately 1 tonne of CO_2 and 160 kg of NO_x are generated by burning 3,800 litres of diesel fuel. Therefore SD concerns dominate the SMS agenda.

In the railroad industry environmental issues are mainly dominated by fuel conservation, the very centre of the sustainability debate. In 2002, The Burlington Northern Santa Fe (BNSF) burned approximately 4.5 billion litres of diesel fuel. Since 1995, BNSF has experienced a 9% decrease in fuel consumption (greater than 380 million litres savings). The enterprise opportunity of further decreasing operational cost by improving fuel efficiency with the concomitant decrease in environmental pollution is not trivial.

Operational component

Efficiency gains are an integral part of railroad viability. BNSF has achieved a leadership role in applying technology to achieve efficiency gains in many operational areas. With respect to fuel use reductions, environmental improvement is completely consistent with organisational operational efficiency objectives. The BNSF business model drives the development and implementation of technological advances in fuel use conservation. The environmental management system benefit and opportunity to promote sustainability is a welcomed secondary gain.

Organisational component
Currently at BNSF, EHS and associated functions are organisationally located in the operations and human resources spheres, with a strong interdisciplinary approach to decision-making and goal setting. More specifically, environmental and safety functions report through a senior VP (vice president) in operations; and medical, health services, industrial hygiene, vocational rehab, drug and alcohol, and employee assistance report through a senior VP in human resources. Moving to an integrated model for EHS and SD, more fully able to leverage financial and technical organisational resources, is currently a process in evolution.

Fuel efficiency goals at BNSF are established annually by the COO based on the state of technology surrounding efficiency advances and the state of the corporate financial plan. Co-ordination of the fuel reduction plan is the responsibility of a senior VP in operations. Resources for R&D, new equipment, equipment retrofitting, etc. are drawn from capital and operating budgets as appropriate, with the input of several functional groups including environmental, mechanical, IT, engineering and finance. Projects are approved using cost–benefit analysis modelling with external risk–reward variables, such as environmental or safety impact, entered into the calculus. The internal functional unit collaboration in project approval constitutes a multifunctional EMS. The level of project integration between the line and the traditional environmental functional group is significant.

Actual projects may be accomplished in-house or in co-development with external entities such as industry associations including Association of American railroads, academic groups such as the University of Illinois, and governmental agencies such as the Department of Energy and Federal Railroad Administration (FRA). In addition, there is significant collaboration with equipment vendors such as General Electric and General Motors.

ERP/IT
Currently, several advanced IT systems are in place in the BNSF health services, safety, environmental and human resource areas. These are in addition to the complex systems developed to efficiently operate a railroad, which encompasses over 53,000 km of track, many thousands of locomotives, and rolling stock. An effort to identify potential system platform and database synergies to allow for the cross-sharing of relational and other data pertaining to employee health, safety and environment, is presently in process.

Monitoring and audits
BNSF conducts comprehensive periodic audits for compliance in areas related to customary EHS components in addition to regulations unique to the railroad industry including FRA mandates in operational and drug and alcohol programme compliance. The audits primarily reflect US regulatory parameters although additional audit components are included to reflect local requirements for its operations outside the US.

Current BNSF fuel conservation initiatives

Fuel conservation initiatives include both administrative and technical elements. Administrative efforts include regulating locomotive speed, idling times and train configurations. Current technological projects under way at BNSF to conserve fuel include:

▶ Hybrid locomotives, which harness energy from the process of dynamic braking, store the energy, then re-apply the energy to train locomotion. This project has the potential to create a 20% gain in fuel efficiency.

- Train wheel lubrication (either biodegradable petroleum products or lubricants made from soy or vegetable products)

- Idling reduction technology

- Ultra-low-friction bearings for rolling stock

- Aerodynamic improvements to locomotives and rolling stock

- Fuel cell integration for motive power

Conclusions and future studies

We presented a model for a combined environment, health, safety and sustainable development management system. This SMS model is primarily based on EMS principles that are already recognised as good business practice, and is implemented under various names in different firms. We view the idea of SMS as a natural evolution of the systems approach that has evolved over the last two decades. This concept is beginning to surface in the literature and is already captured in the Responsible Care code of the chemical industry. We hypothesise that an integrated SMS would increase the efficiency, productivity and compliance of overall corporate performance—a hypothesis that is yet to be proven on a large scale. It is our belief that a large number of firms are either considering implementing or are implementing similar systems. The benefits and problems of integrated management systems need further study as increasing numbers of corporations start utilising them.

A well-developed maturity matrix, with cells similar to that presented in Table 2, can serve as a useful guideline for a corporation to plan and establish an integrated system. A detailed study of various performance components used by different organisations and their value in developing an effective system needs to be studied further.

We also hypothesise that having suppliers with a widely recognised high performance in SMS can improve a corporation's image, which could translate into more business. This, again, is an area that needs to be further researched.

The model we present in this article highlights the key practice points. Although we did not specifically identify any gaps in the available ERP/IT tools, the principles provided in this paper can be used as guidelines to improve existing systems or develop new ones.

We also demonstrated, through the four case studies, that corporations are moving towards integrated EHS and SD management systems, each following a slightly different path. Diverse business drivers and implementation schemes can achieve similar results as long as they include the basic principles highlighted in our model. Clearly, improving the efficiency of managing EHS and SD, anticipating the potential of cost savings, having smoother merger and acquisition activities, and being a good corporate citizen are in the core of each plan. Although currently it is difficult to fully quantify the benefits of an integrated SMS, with the emerging tools—such as TCA developed by a consortium for AIChE—and anticipated modifications in ERP/IT programmes, we feel that in the future organisations will have a much better ability to analyse SMS costs versus benefits.

References

AIChE (American Institute of Chemical Engineers) (1999) *Total Cost Assessment Methodology (TCA)* (AIChE; www.aiche.org/cwrt/pdf/tca.pdf).

American Chemistry Council (2005) *Responsible Care® Code* (American Chemistry Council; www.responsiblecare-us.com/about.asp).

Andrews, R.N.L., and D. Amaral (2003) 'Environmental Management Systems: Do They Improve Performance?', *Project Final Report: Executive Summary* (Chapel Hill, NC: University of North Carolina at Chapel Hill).

Angell, L.C. (2001) 'Comparing the Initiatives of Baldrige Award Winners', *Production and Operations Management* 10: 3.

Bansal, P. (1999) *Taking Stock of ISO 14001 Certifications: Final Report* (Washington, DC: Environmental Protection Agency).

Berry, T.H. (1991) *Managing the Total Quality Transformation* (New York: McGraw-Hill): 39-53.

Buckingham, L. (2003) 'Making a Case for Implementing an EMIS', *Chemistry Business*, February 2003.

Burke, W.W., and G.H. Litwin (1992) 'A Causal Model of Organizational Performance and Change', *Journal of Management* 18.3: 523-45.

Coglianese, C. (2003) *Management-Based Regulation: Prescribing Private Sector Management to Achieve Public Goals* (Harvard University Working Paper; Cambridge, MA: Harvard University Press).

Corbett, C.J., and D.A. Kirsch (2000) 'ISO 14001: An Agnostic's Report from the Front Line', *ISO 9000 + ISO 14000 News*, March/April 2000: 2.

—— and —— (2001) 'International Diffusion of ISO 14001 Certification', *Production and Operations Management* 10: 3.

Delmas, M. (2001) 'Stakeholders and Competitive Advantage: The Case of ISO 14001', *Production and Operation Management* 10: 3.

Dowell, A.M. (2001) 'Regulations: Build a System or Add Layers?', *Process Safety Progress* 20.4: 247-52.

GEMI (Global Environmental Management Initiative) (2002) 'Exploring Pathways to a Sustainable Enterprise', *SD Planner User Guide* (Global Environmental Management Initiative [GEMI]; www.gemi.org/docs/PubTools.htm).

Gilding, P., M. Holgarth and D. Reed (2002) *Single Bottom Line Sustainability: How a Value Centered Approach to Corporate Sustainability Can Pay Off for Shareholders and Society* (Falls Church, VA: Ecos Corporation USA).

Green, K., B. Morton and S. New (2000) 'Greening Organizations', *Organization and Environment* 13.2: 206-25.

Hall, J. (2001) 'Environmental Supply-Chain Innovation', *Greener Management International* 35 (Autumn 2001): 105-19.

Holliday, C.O. Jr, S. Schmidheiny and P. Watts (2002) *Walking the Talk: The Business Case for Sustainable Development* (Sheffield, UK: Greenleaf Publishing): 28-38.

ISO (International Organisation for Standardisation) (2002) *ISO 14000 Family of International Standards and Environmental Management* (Geneva: ISO).

Klassen, R.D., and C.P. McLanghlin (1996) 'The Impact of Environmental Management on Firm Performance', *Management Science* 42: 8.

Lundberg, C.C. (1989) 'On Organizational Learning: Implications and Opportunities for Expanding Organizational Development', *Research in Organizational Change and Development* V3: 61-82.

Melnyk, S.A., R.P. Sroufe and R. Calantone (2003) 'Assessing the Impact of Environmental Management Systems on Corporate and Environmental Performance', *Journal of Operations Management* 21.3: 329-51.

Nill, J., and U. Petschow (2003) 'Obstacles and Opportunities for a "Green" Industrial Policy', in D. Bourg and S. Erkman (eds.), *Perspectives on Industrial Ecology* (Sheffield, UK: Greenleaf Publishing): 223-32.

O'Brien, T. (2001) *Ford and ISO 14001* (New York: McGraw-Hill).

Oktem, U.G. (2003) 'Near-Miss: A Tool to Integrate Safety, Health and Environmental and Security Management', *AIChE Proceedings of the 37th Annual Loss Prevention Symposium*, New Orleans, LA, Spring 2003: 226-42.

Phimister, J.R., U.G. Oktem, P.R. Kleindorfer and H. Kunreuther (2003) 'Near-Miss Management Systems in the Chemical Process Industry', accepted for publication in *Risk Analysis*.

PricewaterhouseCoopers LLP (2002) *2002 Sustainability Survey Report* (PricewaterhouseCoopers LLP; www.pwc.com/fr/pwc_pdf/pwc_sustainability.pdf).

Rittenhouse, D.G. (2003) 'Piecing together a Sustainable Development Strategy', *CEP*, March 2003: 32-38.

Simonin, B.L. (1999) 'Ambiguity and the Process of Knowledge Transfer in Strategic Alliances', *Strategic Management Journal* 20: 595-623.

Sroufe, R. (2003) 'Effects of Environmental Management Systems on Environmental Management Practices and Operations', *The Production and Operations Management Society*, Fall 2003: 416-31.

Timberlake, L. (ed.) (2002) *The Business Case for Sustainable Development* (Geneva: World Business Council for Sustainable Development).

Current Operational Practices of U.S. Small and Medium-Sized Enterprises in Europe

by Edmund Prater and Soumen Ghosh

This article presents the results of a survey of all U.S.-owned small and medium-sized enterprises (SMEs) with physical facilities in Europe. It is a snapshot of the role of key strategic, tactical, and operational elements of U.S. SME globalization in Europe. It presents descriptive results regarding drivers of expansion, barriers to entry, entry strategies and current operating strategies, growth strategies, operational barriers, and the use of strategic alliances by SMEs in Europe. The findings are also compared with the literature on large firms. This allows the reader to see the distinct differences between small and large U.S. firms operating in Europe.

Introduction

The global market has traditionally been the battlefield of large, multinational corporations (MNCs). However, the past 20 years has witnessed the evolution of a new global manufacturing environment, with firms of all sizes now competing globally in order to obtain new competitive advantages. Unfortunately, most global operational research has focused on the practices of MNCs and neglected the fact that small and medium sized enterprises (SMEs) and MNCs do not operate in similar ways. This paper helps fill that gap by presenting the results of a survey of all U.S.-owned SMEs in Europe and detailing their key strategic, tactical, and operational elements.

The literature's neglect of smaller firms is ironic because, in developing countries, SMEs account for more than 90 percent of all jobs, sales, and value added. In developed countries, SMEs account for over 50 percent of these measures (UN 1992). In fact, firms with fewer than 500 employees employ almost half of the U.S. workforce, and over 88 percent of U.S. firms have fewer than 20 employees (Fiegenbaum and Karnani 1989). In addition, U.S.-based SMEs are increasingly active in global markets. A

Dr. Prater is assistant professor in the Department of Information Systems and Operations Management at the University of Texas at Arlington. His current research interests include international supply chains, small and medium-sized enterprises, and logistics outsourcing.

Dr. Ghosh is professor of operations management and director of the Center for Quality and Change Leadership in the DuPree College of Management at the Georgia Institute of Technology.

survey of over 400 winners of the Entrepreneur of the Year (EOY) Award found that 56 percent of the respondents were active in the global arena and that another 39 percent plan to expand into new global markets (Ernst & Young 1995).

The objective of this paper is to further investigate the salient features related to some of the strategic, tactical, and operational elements of SMEs as they globalize. Although some research has looked at general SME issues and foreign direct investment, most studies have focused on large multinational corporations or small firms that export directly (Czinkota and Johnston 1983). This neglects the operational needs of those firms that have moved beyond exporting to establish a physical presence in markets abroad. For those SMEs that have moved beyond direct exporting and actually placed facilities overseas, research on understanding the strategic and operational aspects of the globalization process is virtually missing in the current literature. This is of concern as there are differences with respect to both general and specific operational issues (Cagliano, Blackmon, and Voss 2001).

This paper presents the results of an investigation of the role of key strategic, tactical, and operational elements of U.S. SME globalization in Europe. It presents descriptive results regarding drivers of expansion, barriers to entry, entry strategies and current operating strategies, growth strategies, operational barriers, and the use of strategic alliances by SMEs in Europe. The findings are also compared with the literature on large firms. This allows the reader to see the typical differences among these factors between small and large firms operating in Europe.

There are several reasons to focus on Europe. First, for U.S. SMEs, Europe has been the most popular location for over-seas expansion because of the relative similarities in markets, language, and culture in comparison with other areas of the world. Second, we feel that the overall globalization process of U.S. SMEs in the world can be effectively studied by focusing on U.S. SME globalization in Europe because of the longer history of U.S. firms in Europe compared to other regions of the world. Third, focusing on Europe also helps to keep the study tractable and manageable as gathering data on a worldwide basis for U.S. SMEs is extremely difficult. The data collection for this study was conducted with the collaboration of the Lorraine (France) Development Agency, the Euro Information Center, and the Center for International Business Education and Research (CIBER) at Georgia Tech.

International Expansion: Theory versus Practice

There are several models that have been used to describe how firms expand into the international arena. The product life cycle model (Vernon 1966) focuses on product innovation and scale economies within an individual firm. The Uppsala model (Johanson and Vahlne 1977), also known as the Stage Theory, focuses on a logical and gradual process of internationalization by companies. The Monopolistic Advantage Theory (Hymer 1976) is based on an economic view of optimal costs and revenues. It posits that firms will internationalize after consolidating an economic advantage (for example, low cost or increased market share and revenues) in their domestic market. On the other hand, the core of the Oligopolistic Theory (Knickerbocker 1973) is risk reduction. Specifically, the internationalization of a business is prone to risk. Firms wish to reduce this risk as much as possible. In order to do so, they will imitate the actions of other members of their oligopoly. The goal is that by imitating other firms' actions, they reduce the risk of being different (Oviat and McDougall 1995, 1994; McDougall, Shane, and Oviatt 1994). However, the Network Theory (Jarillo 1988; Thorelli 1986) argues that markets are basically relationships between customers, suppliers, competitors, manufacturers, and others.

These models are applied regularly to large MNCs. However, researchers have argued that these models cannot be applied directly to smaller firms in most cases. For example, Dodge, Fullerton, and Robbins (1994) specifically mention that "there is a need to modify the paradigm which characterizes the stages of growth progression and the resulting sets of problems encountered . . . It is readily apparent that competition, and not the stages of the organizational life cycle, is the dominant dimension in bringing about change in the relative importance of identified problems for small business . . . small businesses with a short-term perspective do not fit into the hypothesized model of the organizational life cycle." Recently, research has begun to address this issue. For example, a six-stage model of small business internationalization has also been developed (Dollinger 1995). This model moves from passive to active exporting and then to developing physical facilities abroad. In addition, Gankema, Snuf, and Zwart (2000) argue that stage theory can be adapted (within certain limits) to SMEs. However, the key question is still left unanswered: if the stages and growth progression of small firms differ from larger firms, then how do the operational decisions and choices differ?

As an example of specific differences, let us look at a firm's global supply chain structure, which has an important bearing on its global competitiveness. A firm's global supply chain structure deals with the management and strategic positioning of the different elements of its supply chain [research and development (R&D), manufacturing plants, distribution centers, suppliers, and sales centers] around the globe. Traditionally, MNCs have used self-contained logistical structures. However, MNCs have now begun to look at their global supply chain as an integrated unit. This has evolved to where special product lines are transported using optimized logistics centers. A logistics center is an integrated system that uses fewer carriers, and outsources or joint ventures many of its functions to third-party providers (Goldsborough 1992). Contrary to the current practices of large MNCs, a pilot study conducted by the authors found distinct differences for smaller firms. Of those firms that were either expanding into Europe or were expanding current operations within Europe, very few considered outsourcing or joint/venturing agreements. Similarly, Roth (1992) found that medium-sized firms opted for "selective globalization" where they focused on a subset of the supply chain. This behavior is provoked by the cost of configuring and coordinating integrated logistics systems to support the entire global supply chain, even though the best SMEs do focus on their entire supply chains (Anderson and Fagerhaug 1999). This is just one specific example of how SME operations overseas differ from larger firms. The goal of this research is to help identify other operational differences between SMEs and MNCs in the international arena and lay the groundwork for further research.

Research Design
Data Collection

The initial step of the research was the construction of a mailing database of all U.S.-owned SMEs with physical operations in Europe. These operations included manufacturing, R&D, or warehousing/distribution facilities. This step is a key hurdle that has possibly limited research on SMEs in the past as SMEs frequently change status. For example, 71 percent of all start-up firms in the U.S. fail within their first eight years of existence (Small Business Administration, U.S. 1995). Of those that initially succeed in foreign markets, many are acquired by locally owned firms, whose ownership and management change fairly often. Larger firms, on the other hand, are relatively stable, thus easing the process of developing a mailing database. In this case Dun and Bradstreet succeeded in combining several sources to develop the needed mailing database of *all* U.S.-owned SMEs with physical operations in Europe.

The survey instrument was mailed to every U.S.-owned firm with some type of manufacturing operation in Europe, thus eliminating issues of sample selection bias. After removing surveys that were not complete or undeliverable, we had the following mailing and response statistics, as shown in Table 1.

The overall response rate was 8.0 percent. Although this response rate is not as high as one might wish, this survey is the only one to the authors' knowledge that surveys the entire sample of U.S. SMEs with manufacturing operations in Europe. The problem of somewhat low response rates in international data collection efforts has also been noted by other empirical studies of this nature (Klassen and Whybark 1994), which found that achieving high survey

response rates in studies addressing an international environment is difficult. Another contributing factor may have been that the survey did not go out under a specific group letterhead. Instead, the survey was sent out under a joint letterhead of the European Union (EU) Information Directorate and the CIBER office of Georgia Tech. Although confidentiality was assured, there is a possibility that U.S. firms may have been reluctant to disclose any information to an official EU body for fear of it being turned over to their European competitors.

For the usable surveys returned, Table 2 shows the percentage responses by industry type. The Mann–Whitney nonparametric test was run to test the difference between mean response rates for firm sizes in each group of Standard Industry Classification (SIC in Table 2) codes. None of the differences were found to be statistically significant at the 0.10 significance level, thereby indicating the absence of any specific industry bias in the response rates.

The responses were also checked for country bias. Although the majority of responses came from Western European firms, this is also where the majority of U.S.-owned firms in Europe are located. Thus, no statistical country specific bias was found among the sample responses.

To determine the possibility of nonresponse bias in the survey data, we fol-

Table 1
Survey Statistics

Total Survey Population	Usable Surveys Returned	Undeliverable[a]	Nominal Response Rate
1,394	104	98	8.0 percent

[a]This includes surveys that were undeliverable because the firms are no longer in business and those that are no longer U.S. owned.

**Table 2
Survey Response
Percentages by Industry
Type**

SIC Codes	Small Firms (percent)
10–19	3.2
20–29	6.5
30–39	32.3
40–49	3.2
50–59	54.8

lowed the method recommended in Armstrong and Overton (1977) and Lambert and Harrington (1990), where statistically significant differences were tested for in the responses of early and late waves of the returned surveys. The last ten survey items in the analysis were considered to be representative of the nonrespondents. The sample of 104 usable surveys was split into two groups based on early (94) and late (10) returns. T-tests were performed on these two groups. The results of these tests indicated no significant differences among the two groups, thus suggesting that nonresponse bias is not a problem in this study.

Survey Validity Issues

During the design of the survey instrument, several validity measures were addressed. These are content, face, and criterion validity (Fink 1995). In this study, content validity was established by a pilot survey and on-site interviews conducted by the authors, as well as the findings from the EOY survey (Ernst & Young 1995). In addition, the survey was pretested with several global logistics and operations managers.[1] The logistics and operations managers also provided

content and face validity. The criterion validity of the survey was established by using the EOY study (Ernst & Young 1995) with U.S. results from 1990–1995 and the Canadian results from 1995. Also, all aspects of the survey were reviewed and tested through on-site interviews of U.S.- and locally owned firms throughout Europe. These interviews were conducted by using the case study guidelines given in Chetty (1996).

Empirical Results

As mentioned earlier, the intent of this study is to perform an exploratory analysis in order to identify the key factors critically impacting the European entry and operations issues faced by U.S. SMEs with physical operations in Europe. These factors are compared to those previously identified in the literature for large firms so that comparative differences can be observed. The key issues influencing the internationalization of SMEs that are addressed in this study are as follows:

- country location,
- drivers for European expansion,
- barriers to entry,
- current operations strategies,
- growth strategies,
- key issues in European operations, and
- use of strategic alliances.

In the remainder of this section, findings and analysis of the survey data are presented to shed light on the above factors that are important determinants of the SME globalization process.

Country Location in Europe

As shown in Figure 1, the preferred location for U.S. SME entry into Europe is the United Kingdom. This is followed

[1]These included consultants from Salomon Brothers and the Georgia Tech Logistics Institute as well as executives from Consolidated Traffic Management Services and Shell Oil.

Figure 1
Preferred Investment (Entry) Locations for U.S. SMEs in Europe

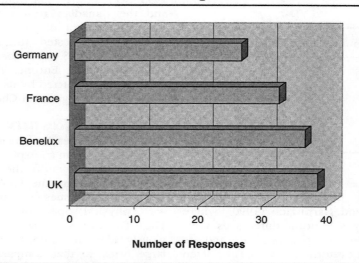

by the Benelux region, France, and Germany (multiple choices were allowed from each respondent). Most practitioners seem to agree that the reason for expansion into the United Kingdom is based on the historical ties between the United Kingdom and United States. This is also supported by the "psychic distance" aspect of the Uppsala model (Johanson and Vahlne 1977). The key issue is the "psychic distance" to these foreign markets, that is, the differences between two countries in language, culture, business practice, and so on. Smaller firms feel comfortable moving to a country with a similar culture and language. French firms expanding into the North American market work similarly by first moving into French Quebec. The Benelux region (the combination of Belgium, the Netherlands, and Luxembourg) is another popular area for U.S. SMEs because of its logistics expertise and history of international trading practices. France and Germany are popular because of their centralized location and access to other European areas.

Drivers for European Expansion

In trying to develop a "snapshot" of SME globalization practices, it is interesting to identify the drivers influencing initial entry. The key drivers that smaller firms considered when entering the European market are shown in Table 3. The responses were based on a five-point Likert scale with 1 = not at all important and 5 = very important. The bars on the right side represent the results of the Fisher multiple comparison test for differences in means (each bar represents groupings within which the differences in means are not statistically significant). Duncan's and Tukey's multiple range tests were also performed. However, the Fisher test was slightly more discriminatory and provided more distinct groups.

Of course, the most important driver of entry to European markets is access to

Table 3
Entry Drivers for European Expansion

Entry Driver	Mean Score		
• Access to New Markets and Potential Market Growth	4.74		
• Follow Clients	3.40		
• Availability of Resources	2.87		
• Product Maturation	2.74		
• Access to Technology	2.67		
• Cost of Resources	2.64		
• Increased Domestic Competition	2.46		
• Decline of Demand in U.S. Market	2.05		
• U.S. Regulations, Taxes, and Laws	2.02		
• Response to Foreign Firm Entering the U.S. Market	1.82		

new markets. However, there are distinct differences between the drivers for SMEs found here and those found for MNCs previously in the literature. Specifically, one key difference from MNC drivers is that of the need to follow clients. Our on-site interviews with small firm owners have borne out that this is a key issue that is overlooked by most research. Many firms end up overseas not because of some strategy or long-term plan. Instead, they are forced there to keep a business presence with a current client. In some cases, small firms have no choice in the matter. A larger firm determines to move to a particular overseas location and the smaller supplier is simply expected to follow. Thus, in many cases, small firms have far less control over their international plans and strategies than larger MNCs. As an example, recent research (Meyer and Skak 2002) found that an SME's business network and plain serendipity were major drivers in entering Eastern Europe.

Entry Barriers

It is expected that expanding into a new overseas market entails overcoming several barriers. The main entry barriers experienced by U.S. SMEs expanding into Europe are listed below in Table 4, along with the Fisher multiple comparison results.

Some of the issues on this list come as no surprise. For example, it is well established in the literature that knowledge of foreign languages and cultures is an important factor for firms expanding overseas (Barkema, Bell, and Pennings 1996). In addition, management's working knowledge of international markets and related issues is important to export success (Moini 1995). Similar research has been carried out for larger firms. For example, Klassen and Whybark (1994) show the following as the key issues (in order of importance) for MNCs:

- lack of a global view,
- manufacturing strategy,
- culture/language differences,
- managing global logistics,
- managing factory networks,
- organizational structure,
- transfer of management skills,
- performance measurement,
- material sourcing,
- international communication, and
- foreign exchange management.

Table 4
Entry Barriers

Entry Barrier	Mean Score
• Dealing with Culture/Language Differences of the Target Markets/Countries	3.92
• International Communication between Facilities	3.56
• Management's Lack of a Working Knowledge about International Markets, Practices, Sources, Destinations, and Politics	3.38
• Foreign Exchange Rates	3.33
• Developing an Effective Organizational Structure in Your Facilities in Europe	3.26
• Managing Global Logistics	3.20
• Transfer of Management Skills from the U.S. to Europe	2.59
• Developing Adequate Performance Measurements for Operations in Europe	2.59
• Developing a Long-Term Manufacturing Strategy and Applying It to Day-to-Day Operations	2.53
• Continuing Material Sourcing from the U.S. or Developing New Material Sources in Europe	2.53
• Managing Factory (Production) Networks	2.28

However, there are specific differences between Klassen and Whybark's issues and those for SMEs. First, managing foreign exchange risk ranked last for MNCs, while it is among the second tier of concerns for SMEs. This may be attributed to the fact that managing short-term cash flow is a critical issue for smaller firms. In fact, cash flow problems are often the primary cause for the failure of SMEs (Small Business Administration, U.S. 1994). In an international market, the fluctuations of exchange rates can be weathered by larger firms but have a much more negative impact on the financial resources of SMEs. This has direct implications on the ability of an SME to export and physically expand into international markets (Westhead and Wright 2001).

International communications was ranked very low for MNCs, but among SMEs it is second in overall importance. This probably reflects the ability of larger firms to set up corporate communication networks via satellite or microwave. Larger firms can also rotate teams of individuals between the home office and foreign divisions, thus keeping lines of communication open between organizational units. These resources are usually not available to SMEs, although the advent of the World Wide Web has provided greater communications resources to SMEs.

Finally, the need to develop a manufacturing strategy ranked high for MNCs but low for SMEs. This reflects issues addressed in the next section, namely that SMEs often tend to ignore long-term strategic planning, and focus more on short-term operational issues.

European Entry and Current Operating Strategies

Once a firm has made the strategic decision to locate facilities overseas, it must then determine its entry strategy (Hill, Hwang, and Chan 1990). We were interested in identifying not only the SME's entry strategies, but also the operations strategies that were currently being used for operations and competitive advantage. The responses to those questions were evaluated and are shown in Tables 5 and 6, respectively. Note that the mean score reflects a binary value of 1 (the strategy was used) or 0 (the strategy was not used). Each firm could list multiple strategies.

In comparing the entry strategies with the current operations strategies, there seems to be very little difference. There is a growing use of more capital intensive strategies, such as establishing overseas subsidiaries and manufacturing facilities, following an SME's entry into Europe. However, as indicated by the Fisher test, this does not appear to be statistically significant.

In terms of initial strategies that SMEs use to expand into Europe, the key issue seems to be cost. It is not surprising that entry strategies with the least investment and capital intensity were the most preferred by SMEs. Operational strategies for SMEs tend to focus on low-cost options such as using local management or exporting. Of course, this can have negative long-term as well as short-term effects (Bernstein 2001). However, MNCs have the financial capital to use joint ventures or buyouts as options in their international expansion.

These findings are interesting in that they seem to indicate that there is no strong connection between entry strategies and current operations strategies. This lends support to previous research on SME strategy. Specifically, Bantel and Osborn (1995) found that smaller firms were more likely to have no identifiable strategy. They also found that SMEs tend to concentrate on means rather than the end in their operations. This may be due to the amount of competition and uncer-

Table 5
Initial Entry Strategies

Entry Strategy	Mean Score
• Using Locally Hired Management	0.46
• Alliances with Foreign Distributors	0.44
• Exporting	0.28
• Overseas Sales Office	0.28
• Overseas Subsidiaries	0.28
• Licensing Programs	0.13
• Joint Ventures	0.13
• Overseas Manufacturing Facility	0.13
• Foreign Acquisition	0.10
• Technology Alliances with Foreign Companies	0.02
• Alliances with Foreign Suppliers	0.02

Table 6
Current Operations Strategies

Current Operating Strategy	Mean Score		
• Using Locally Hired Management	0.59		
• Overseas Subsidiaries	0.54		
• Overseas Sales Office	0.51		
• Alliances with Foreign Distributors	0.38		
• Exporting	0.26		
• Overseas Manufacturing Facility	0.18		
• Licensing Programs	0.12		
• Foreign Acquisitions	0.12		
• Alliances with Foreign Suppliers	0.08		
• Joint Ventures	0.08		
• Technology Alliances with Foreign Companies	0.05		

Table 7
Growth Strategies

Growth Strategy	Mean Score		
• Introduce New Products/Services	3.64		
• Expand into New International Markets	3.33		
• Expand into New European Markets	3.28		
• Upgrade Financial Systems and Information	3.79		
• Upgrade Operations Technology	2.77		
• Acquire Another Company	2.08		
• Merge with Another Company	1.18		

tainty that a firm has to deal with. In addition, Matthews and Scott (1995) have found that formal planning among SMEs is inversely proportional to the uncertainty in their business environment. Thus, when uncertainty is high, SMEs tend to rely on "gut instinct" rather than a formal planning process. Other research has viewed this lack of a planned strategy as "serendipity on a firm's growth path" (Meyer and Skak 2002). One other issue to note is the lack of use of joint ventures (JVs). While U.S. firms do not use joint ventures, this does not mean that JVs are not used in other global areas. In China, for example, when *guanxi* (personal relationships) are vital to business, it has been shown (Worldsources 2000) that SMEs do make use of JVs to a large extent.

Growth Strategies

Once a firm has established a presence in Europe, its next goal is usually to establish a growth strategy in the short to medium term. The growth strategies that were identified by the respondents are shown in Table 7 and seem to match very well with the data gathered on the EOY Award winners (Ernst & Young 1995).

The top three strategies are in the same statistical grouping and are not surprising. Introducing new products and expanding into new markets are fairly well established growth strategies for firms. However, it is interesting to note that upgrading operations technology is not used as a frequent growth strategy by SMEs. This differs from larger firms operating in the international arena. For example, Bowersox et al. (1989) found that leading edge MNCs emphasize their operational and logistics capabilities. They provide extra support for these areas to obtain a strategic advantage (Bowersox 1987).

Operational Challenges

In addition to entry, operational, and growth strategies, there are also several operational challenges that SMEs must deal with. These operational challenges can be quite different than those encountered by the firm in its home market. Table 8 lists the key operational challenges identified by the SME respondents.

Obtaining good financial data was a major operational issue identified by SMEs. As mentioned in the previous section, this is probably attributable to the fact that managing cash flow is a critical issue for SMEs. In contrast, MNCs not only have larger cash reserves than SMEs, but financial institutions are more willing to advance credit to MNCs. While this issue is frequently challenging in an SME's home country, it can be particularly exasperating in foreign countries (U.S. Small Business Administration 1994).

Another key operational challenge is achieving the desired attributes of quality, given its critical importance for attaining market success. In this case, it seems that SMEs have heeded the market pressure for greater emphasis on quality issues as previous research has argued for (Azzone and Cainarca 1993). Dealing with environmental issues did not score that highly. While it has been argued that environmental issues are important (Daugherty, Autry, and Ellinger 2001; Bartlett and Ghoshal 1991), our on-site interviews showed a wait-and-see attitude among SMES. Specifically, only SMEs with operations in Germany tend to place a great deal of emphasis on environmental issues. This is because German law has historically stipulated that firms deal with reverse logistics

Table 8
Operational Challenges

Operational Challenges	Mean Score						
• Obtaining Good Financial Data	3.80						
• Improving Quality	3.69						
• Improving Automation/Technology	3.38						
• Managing Inventory	3.12						
• Dealing with Environmental Issues	3.10						
• Having Reliable Suppliers	2.92						
• Improving Turnaround Time	2.79						
• Outsourcing Business Functions	2.15						

requirements. Although similar laws have been passed for the entire EU, these are being phased in. Most SMEs seem to be waiting until the last moment to address any detrimental environmental impacts of their daily operations. Of course, this neglect of environmental issues is not a new phenomenon for SMEs (Biondi, Frey, and Iraldo 2000).

Another issue is that of outsourcing business functions. There is a wealth of literature that argues for the benefit of outsourcing business functions for large firms in order to reduce overhead, focus on core competencies, and manage the supply chain (Goldsborough 1992; Wyatt 1992). While one would expect that the same issues would hold true for SMEs, we find that outsourcing ranked last (statistically significant) among operational challenges. It is possible that this result for SMEs is attributable to the issue of control and coordination. Outsourcing business functions often increase the dissemination risk of proprietary knowledge and know-how, and SMEs therefore tend to be more careful about this. However, our on-site interviews indicate that SMEs with higher information technology capabilities are more likely to outsource some of their business functions. This is due to their increased ability to track, control, and coordinate these activities. However, as has been shown before (Rishel and Burns 1997), not all SMEs integrate their technical capabilities in order to support their operations.

Strategic Alliances

Data were also gathered on 30 different business operations that could be outsourced or collaborated via joint venture agreements. These data include information on the typical contract lengths for each of these 30 business areas if they were outsourced. No SME had any contractual agreement that was over 12 months long. This supports the idea that SMEs generally do not tend to make use of strategic alliances for collaborative operations. Research has found that while formal cooperation such as strategic alliances and joint ventures are common for large firms (Wyatt 1992; Bowersox 1990), SMEs in general prefer flexible and informal relationships (Malecki and Tootle 1996). However, it should be noted that this particular aspect of SME behavior may not be applicable to other regions. As mentioned previously, recent research on SMEs in China (Worldsources 2000) found the use of joint ventures and strategic alliances to be very useful. This is supported by the small-business stage model outlined in Rowden's (2001) article, which argues that SMEs should use joint ventures and strategic partnerships for foreign production. This points out the fact that the operational differences between SMEs in different international arenas may be just as great as those differences between SMEs and MNCs.

Conclusions

This research provides a "snapshot" of the globalization practices of U.S. SMEs in Europe. This was carried out by using empirical data collected from a survey of all U.S. SMEs that have moved beyond exporting to setting up physical operations in Europe. While differences between SMEs and MNCs have been noted before, research has tended to focus on differences in overall structure and responses to different economic environments. This paper not only provides information on some strategic aspects of operations but also shows distinct differences of a daily operational nature. It also points out specific areas for further research. These include:

- Regarding entry drivers for European expansion, it was found that many times SMEs are pulled overseas by being required to follow

Current Operational Practices of U.S. Small and Medium-Sized Enterprises in Europe **33**

their clients. Thus, SMEs may need to be proactive in determining what the long-term plans are of the firms they supply. This would provide them with some degree of "heads up" planning about the possibility of expanding overseas. It would be interesting to determine the percentage of SMEs (if any) provided with this type of long-term planning information.

- Regarding entry barriers, international communications between overseas facilities is the second biggest barrier that SMEs face, whereas MNCs list this very low on their problem list. Thus, it would be helpful to conduct research into what structural and organizational systems can aid SMEs in coordinating international operations.

- U.S. SMEs did not take advantage of outsourcing of operational functions such as logistics even though it has been argued for years that this is an efficient operations strategy. Research has been carried out on the factors that influence logistics outsourcing by large MNCs (Rao and Young 1994). However, it is necessary to determine what barriers SMEs face in logistics outsourcing and what factors help support its use.

- Another major difference between SMEs and MNCs was found in strategic alliances. While these tend to be used in many categories by MNCs, we found no examples of small firms making use of any type of long-term alliance in Europe. This is probably due to the need of SMEs to keep relationships flexible in order to respond quickly to changing business conditions. However, it has been shown that strategic alliances are used by SMEs in China (Worldsources 2000). Thus, it would be helpful to under-

stand what specific regional factors facilitate the use of JVs and strategic alliances.

- SMEs in Germany have begun to deal with environmental issues such as reverse logistics. Yet other SMEs throughout the EU delay resolving these issues until required by law. As reverse logistics is "fast becoming a competitive necessity" (Daugherty, Autry, and Ellinger 2001), there is a need to determine if there are other governmental policies or business inducements that can facilitate SMEs in embracing environmental issues.

References

Anderson, B., and T. Fagerhaug (1999). "Benchmarking Supply Chain Management: Finding the Best Practices," *Journal of Business & Industrial Marketing*, 14(5/6), 378–390.

Armstrong, J. S., and T. S. Overton (1977). "Estimating Non-Response Bias in Mail Surveys," *Journal of Marketing Research*, 14, 396–402.

Azzone, G., and G. C. Cainarca (1993). "The Strategic Role of Quality in Small-Sized Firms," *Small Business Economics*, 1.

Bantel, K. A., and R. N. Osborn (1995). "The Influence of Performance, Environment and Size on the Identifiably of Firm Strategy," *British Journal of Management*, 6, 235–248.

Barkema, H., J. Bell, and J. M. Pennings (1996). "Foreign Entry, Cultural Barriers and Learning," *Strategic Management Journal*, 17, 151–166.

Bartlett, C., and S. Ghoshal (1991). *Managing across Borders: The Transnational Solution*. Boston, MA: Harvard Business School Press.

Bernstein, M. (2001). "Small Firms Ill-Prepared for Euro," *Financial Management* (July–August), 8.

Biondi, V., M. Frey, and F. Iraldo (2000). "Environmental Management Systems and SMEs," *Greener Management International*, Spring (29), 55–70.

Bowersox, D. (1987). *Integrated Logistics: A Competitive Weapon*. Oak Brook, IL: Council of Logistics Management.

———— (1990). "The Strategic Benefit of Logistics Alliances," *Harvard Business Review* (July–August), 36–45.

Bowersox, D., P. Daugherty, D. Cornelia, D. Rogers, and D. Wardlow (1989). *Leading Edge Logistics: Competitive Positioning for the 1990s*. Oak Brook, IL: Council of Logistics Management.

Cagliano, R., K. Blackmon, and Voss (2001). "Small Firms under MICRO-SCOPE: International Differences in Production/Operations Management Practices and Performance," *Integrated Manufacturing Systems*, 12(7), 469–482.

Chetty, Sylvie (1996). "The Case Study Method for Research in Small and Medium Sized Firms," *International Small Business Journal*, 15(1), 73–86.

Czinkota, M. R., and W. J. Johnston (1983). "Exporting: Does Sales Volume Make a Difference?" *Journal of International Business Studies*, 14(Spring), 147–153.

Daugherty, P. J., C. W. Autry, and A. E. Ellinger (2001). "Reverse Logistics: The Relationship between Resource Commitment and Program Performance," *Journal of Business Logistics*, 22(1), 107–123.

Dodge, H. R., S. Fullerton, and J. E. Robbins (1994). "Stage of the Organizational Life Cycle and Competition as Mediators of Problem Perception for Small Businesses," *Strategic Management Journal*, 15, 121–134.

Dollinger, M. (1995). *Entrepreneurship*. Burr Ridge, IL: Irwin.

Ernst & Young (1995). 1995 Membership Survey Findings, Entrepreneur of the Year Institute.

Fiegenbaum, A., and A. Karnani (1989). "Output Flexibility—a Competitive Advantage for Small Firms," *Strategic Management Journal*, 12(July), 101–114.

Fink, A. (1995). *The Survey Handbook*. Thousand Oaks, CA: Sage Publications.

Gankema, H. G., H. R. Snuf, and P.S. Zwart (2000). "The Internationalization Process of Small and Medium-Sized Enterprises: An Evaluation of Stage Theory," *Journal of Small Business Management*, 38(4), 15–28.

Goldsborough, W. (1992). *Global Logistics Management*. Menlo Park, CA: SRI International.

Hill, C. W., L. P. Hwang, and K. W. Chan (1990). "An Eclectic Theory of the Choice of International Entry Mode," *Strategic Management Journal*, 11, 117–128.

Hymer, S. H. (1976). *The International Operations of National Firms: A Study of Direct Foreign Investment*. Cambridge, MA: MIT Press.

Jarillo, J. C. (1988). "On Strategic Networks," *Strategic Management Journal*, 9(1), 31–40.

Johanson, J., and J. Vahlne (1977). "The Internationalization Process of the Firm: A Model of Knowledge Development on Increasing Foreign Commitments," *Journal of International Business Studies* 8(Spring–Summer), 23–32.

Klassen, R., and C. Whybark (1994). "Barriers to the Management of International Operations," *Journal of Operations Management*, 11(March), 385–397.

Knickerbocker, F. T. (1973). "Oligopolistic Reaction and Multinational Enterprise," *International Executive*, 15(2), 7–10.

Lambert, D. M., and T. C. Harrington (1990). "Measuring Nonresponse Bias in Customer Service Mail Surveys," *Journal of Business Logistics*, 11(2), 5–26.

Malecki, E. J., and D. M. Tootle (1996). "The Role of Networks in Small Firm Competitiveness," *International*

Journal of Technology Management, 11(3/4), 42–56.

Matthews, C. H., and S. G. Scott (1995). "Uncertainty and Planning in Small and Entrepreneurial Firms: An Empirical Assessment," *Journal of Small Business Management*, 33(4), 34–52.

McDougall, P. P., S. Shane, and B. M. Oviatt (1994). "Explaining the Formation of International New Ventures: The Limits of Theories from International Business Research," *Journal of Business Venturing*, 9(6), 469–487.

Meyer, K., and A. Skak (2002). "Networks, Serendipity and SME Entry into Eastern Europe," *European Management Journal*, 20(2), 179–189.

Moini, A. H. (1995). "An Inquiry into Successful Exporting: An Empirical Investigation Using a Three-Stage Model," *Journal of Small Business Management*, 33(3), 9–25.

Oviatt, B. M., and P. P. McDougall (1995). "Global Start-Ups: Entrepreneurs on a Worldwide Stage," *Academy of Management Executive*, 9(2), 30–44.

——— (1994). "Toward a Theory of International New Ventures," *Journal of International Business Studies*, 24(1), 45–64.

Rao, K., and R. R. Young (1994). "Global Supply Chains: Factors Influencing Outsourcing of Logistics Functions," *International Journal of Physical Distribution & Logistics Management*, 24(6), 11–19.

Rishel, T. D., and O. M. Burns (1997). "The Impact of Technology on Small Manufacturing Firms," *Journal of Small Business Management* 35(January), 2–10.

Roth, K. (1992). "International Configuration and Coordination Archetypes for Medium-Sized Firms in Global Industries," *Journal of International Business Studies* 23(3), 533–549.

Rowden, R. W. (2001). "Research Note: How a Small Business Enters the International Market," *Thunderbird International Business Review*, 43(2), 257–268.

Small Business Administration, U. S. (1994). *Handbook of Small Business Data*. Washington, D.C.: U.S. Government Printing Office.

——— (1995). *Small Business Economic Indicators*. Springfield VA: National Technical Information Service.

Thorelli, H. B. (1986). "Networks: Between Markets and Hierarchies," *Strategic Management Journal*, 7(1), 37–52.

United Nations (UN) (1992). *The United Nations Conference on Trade and Development (Unctad) Programme on Transnational Corporations*. United Nations.

Vernon, R. (1966). "International Investment and International Trade in the Product Life Cycle," *Quarterly Journal of Economics* 80(May), 190–207.

Westhead, P., and M. Wright (2001). "The Internationalization of New and Small Firms: A Resource-Based View," *Journal of Business Venturing*, 16(4), 333–359.

Worldsources (2000). "Survey on SMEs Gives Thumbs Up to Joint Ventures," *Hong Kong Imail*, September 22.

Wyatt, L. (1992). "Effective Supplier Alliances and Partnerships," *International Journal of Physical Distribution & Logistics Management*, 22(6), 28–30.

Lean Accounting and Finance

Cash flow tells the tale.

Orest (Orry) Fiume

A whole industry has developed around helping companies become "Lean." Books and articles have been written, seminars have been presented, and consulting firms have started Lean practices. In spite of this, most companies that attempt to transform themselves to Lean either fail or attain only a portion of the benefits possible. Why is this?

Certainly the principles of Lean are easy to agree with. No one argues that the benefits are not worth pursuing. But as easy as it is to agree with, the reality is that Lean is hard to do. Most people look at Lean as some "manufacturing thing" and only implement elements of it such as cells and Kanban. Very few companies understand that Lean is a business strategy, not a manufacturing tactic, and are unable, or unwilling, to address changing the other aspects of the business.

Like any strategy, in order to successfully implement Lean, everything the company does has to support it, and whatever doesn't has to be changed. Thus, product development processes, sales terms and marketing programs, human resource policies and procedures, and accounting systems have to be examined in order to insure that they do not contain elements that contradict the Lean strategy. In most companies the accounting systems, and the accountants, tend to be the most significant barrier to successfully implementing Lean.

Incompatible Accounting

In 1987 H. Thomas Johnson and Robert Kaplan in their book *Relevance Lost: The Rise and Fall of Management Accounting* clearly stated that traditional management accounting was inadequate for today's environment. If that was true then, it is certainly truer now as companies attempt to account for the Lean enterprise with tools that were developed in the early part of the 20th century.

In its simplest form accounting and the information it produces, such as financial statements, are nothing more than a mirror, which when held up to the operations of the company gives the reflection of those operations valued in dollars. Today we still use accounting systems based on principles such as absorption, standard costs, and variance analysis which where developed to deal with operations that were based on large batches, long leadtimes and lots of inventory at every stage of production. When these systems are used to account for operations based on flow, short leadtimes, and very little inventory, the results that are being reported are distorted, just as a trick mirror at the carnival fun house distorts our image when we stand in front of it. Even worse, it's not mere distortion, but for companies successful in reducing inventory these systems report the results as negative! In effect, management is being lied to by the traditional accounting systems. More about this problem later. First, let's look at accounting in support of the Lean enterprise in its broadest sense.

The Four Dimensions of Lean Accounting

There are four dimensions of transforming accounting to support the Lean environment:

1) Transactions appropriate for the manufacturing practices employed
2) Performance metrics that measure the right thing and motivate the right behavior
3) Accounting processes, cost management techniques, and financial reporting that adhere to Lean principles
4) Recognition that investment management decision making is defferent.

Appropriate Transactions

The first dimension is relatively straightforward. It recognizes the fact that planning and control of flow/pull scheduling processes is simpler than that for batch/push scheduling processes. Flow/pull processes are set up to produce to actual customer demand whereas batch/push processes are set up to produce to a forecast. From an operational standpoint many of the mechanics of MRP systems are replaced with systems, such as Kanban, that are much more visual. Many of the transactions that support MRP, such as labor tickets and move tickets, can be eliminated. A simple principle to keep in mind is that transactions that exist in the factory should serve an operational purpose. They should not exist just for accounting.

The Right Performance Measures

In the second dimension, most of the performance measures that exist in traditional batch and queue operations should not be used in a Lean operation. Measures such as direct to indirect labor ratios, labor efficiency, machine utilization, and earned labor dollars can lead one to make poor decisions in the Lean environment. For example, one of the fundamental principles in Lean is to manufacture product to takt time, which is the rate at which customers buy products measured in time. For example, if we operate one shift with 450 minutes available each day and customers buy 900 units per day on average, the takt time is 30 seconds. If we can produce one unit every 30 seconds we will satisfy the customers' demand. If we can't, we have unhappy customers.

On the other hand, machine utilization is geared to "reducing" the piece part cost by producing as much as possible. The behavior this generates is to overproduce, resulting in excess inventory.

Another fundamental principle of Lean is the total elimination of waste. This principle recognizes the fact that:

PRODUCTIVITY = WEALTH

If our focus is to eliminate waste, such as increase productivity, then many of our metrics should measure this. A working definition of productivity is the relationship between the quantity of output and the quantity of resources (input) consumed in creating that output. If we get more output with the same level of input we have a productivity gain. Therefore, measuring productivity gains focuses on quantities, not dollars.

In our education and experience we are trained to focus on measuring things in dollars, but productivity cannot improve through financial engineering. Only physical change can influence the relationship between quantities of output and quantities of input. Therefore, these metrics should be quantity-based and maintained where work is done.

In most companies the accounting systems, and the accountants, tend to be the most significant barrier to successfully implementing Lean.

Unlike the traditional metrics that are focused on results, most metrics in the Lean environment should focus on the process. If we focus on the process and remove non-valued activities such as unnecessary movement, excess wait time, rework, and the other "Seven Sins of Waste," the results — improved productivity — will come.

Once we recognize that many of the traditional performance measures are inappropriate for the Lean enterprise, the question arises, "what should we measure?" In this environment, some metrics are close to being universal — customer service, productivity, defect reduction, takt time, and cycle time. Others depend on the specific business. However, it is possible to identify some of the attributes of a good performance measurement system, as shown in Figure 1.

Attributes of a Good Lean Performance Measurement System

Supports the Lean strategy

Motivates the right behavior (such as, eliminate waste)

Number of metrics not excessive, so as to maintain focus

Mostly non-financial

Simple and easy for people doing the work to understand; the connection between their actions and each measure is clear

Measures the process, not the people

Measures compare actual versus goals

Avoids indices, as they are not actionable

Must be timely: hourly, daily, weekly as appropriate

Displays trend lines to mark continuous improvement

Make them visual and post where everyone can see them.

Figure 1.

Walker Systems, Inc., a Wiremold company, is a good example of measuring the process and not the people. There, when we started measuring the reasons that we did not meet takt time, cell by cell, we discovered that two reasons represented more than 50 percent of the occurrences, material unavailability, and unplanned downtime. The third most recurring reason was people-related, but was due to inadequate training, not inadequate effort. Thus it too was really a management problem, not a people problem.

Lean Accounting

Accounting processes, cost management, and financial reporting are the heart of what the accounting function is involved in day-to-day. Whenever we get involved in discussions regarding the implementation of Lean in other companies we hear all kinds of excuses why it doesn't apply to them: They make different products, they are bigger and more complex, they are smaller and can't devote the resources to improvement. In some way they are different, so it won't work there.

However, the reality is that from business to business there are more similarities than differences. Whether in manufacturing or in service, each company has to take an order from a customer, deliver a product or service, send an invoice, and collect. Each has to purchase things, receive them, and pay for them. Each has to produce that product or render that service. Each wants to develop new products or services. Each has to hire and pay people. These generic business processes may differ in detail from one business to another, but they are similar in attempting to do the same basic functions. And each is similar in containing huge amounts of waste.

From an accounting perspective the work content of most of these processes has a high degree of clerical activities and a low degree of analytical content. And each is similar in that the same principles of process improvement that make the factory Lean can and should be applied to them. In doing so the work content can be changed so that less time is spent on non-value added clerical content and more time is devoted to value added analytical content. This is just one of the ways the accounting function can contribute to the Lean transformation.

The traditional manufacturing environment devotes significant resources to "cost accounting," which emphasizes determining the cost of each product made and trying to control costs by adhering to budgets. In the Lean company, accountants must take a broader view ... one of cost management. As the company tries to deliver products and services that are more competitive in terms of functionality, cost, quality, and delivery, cost management focuses on providing information regarding the profitable use of resources in providing these things. This broader view of cost must include cost planning in addition to cost control and cost accounting.

Cost Planning: Target Costing

Several studies have estimated the amount of a product's life cycle cost that is committed during the product design process. Results vary, but range between 85-95 percent of the total life cycle costs. In other words, everything we do day-to-day, short of redesigning the product, affects only 5-15 percent of life cycle costs. And yet most product developers focus only on fit, form, and function and are blind to costs until near the end of the product development cycle when the accountants figure out the "cost," add a profit to determine the selling price, and marketing decides if they can sell it at that price. If they can't (that is, the market price is lower) the only alternative is to redesign the product (which itself is waste) or accept a lower profit.

However, incorporating target costing into the product development process can avoid this no-win cycle. Michiharu Sakuri has described target costing as "a cost-planning tool used for controlling design specifications and production techniques. Therefore it is oriented much more towards management and engineering rather than accounting."

Target costing recognizes the reality that the old cost-plus method of pricing died many decades ago. The market sets the price. Instead of Cost + Profit = Selling Price, the current reality is Selling Price - Cost = Profit. In target costing the marketing group must identify the selling price during the product conception stage and then apply the formula: Selling Price - Profit = Target Cost. The target profit is established by management and can only be changed by management.

The target cost becomes part of the product specification. At every tollgate of the development process that cost is estimated. If it is above the target cost by an amount that cannot be corrected in the future stages of the development process, the project cannot move forward. Thus, even at the product concept stage, the cost can be estimated, and if it is not acceptable, the concept can be changed before significant resources are committed to a concept that will not yield an acceptable profit. In addition to target costing, if the company applies the principle of designing the manufacturing process concurrent with designing the product, life cycle costs can be significantly reduced.

Cost Control: Lean Style

In addition to cost planning, the concept of cost management includes cost control and cost accounting. Cost control has become a euphemism for cost reduction, and in the Lean environment the principal method of cost reduction is by the kaizen process. This is a team-based approach of studying a problem and implementing improvements ... all within a three- to five-day period. It has a bias for action because it doesn't look for the perfect solution, but allows for partial solutions. As long as some improvement is made, that's all right. Another kaizen event will look at that same area again and additional improvements will be made in the future.

The other major tool to reduce costs in the Lean environment is a system of performance metrics, most of which are non-financial. The cost of waste is the mathematical product of the frequency of defects times the severity of them. Non-financial measures are aimed at reducing the frequency of defects. If defects can be eliminated then severity becomes a non-issue.

Cost Accounting

In the traditional batch and queue environment the typical method of looking at cost is through standard cost accounting, absorption, and variance analysis. Figure 2 represents a "text book" standard cost P&L

Standard Cost Comparison: Traditional Case

	This Year	Last Year
Net Sales		
	100,000	90,000
Cost of Sales:		
Standard Costs	48,000	45,000
Purchase Price Variance	(3,000)	10,000
Material Usage Variance	(2,000)	5,000
Labor Efficiency Variance	7,000	(8,000)
Labor Rate Variance	(2,000)	9,000
OH Volume Variance	2,000	2,000
OH Spending Variance	(2,000)	8,000
OH Efficiency Variance	16,000	(17,000)
Total Cost of Sales	64,000	54,000
Gross Profit	36,000	36,000
Gross Profit as a Percent of Sales	36%	40%

Figure 2.

for a company that had an increase in sales but no increase in gross profit. In this author's experience, most people do not understand a standard cost P&L so that this presentation of the information is virtually useless. It gives virtually no meaningful information as to why sales increased but profit didn't. Worse still, if this company's VP of operations had convinced the CEO that they should start implementing Lean and these were the reported results, he would most like get an order like, "I don't know what you are doing, but stop it, it's killing us." In addition to the inability of this presentation format to provide meaningful information, the mechanics of absorption accounting underlying it motivates the wrong behavior.

In standard cost, absorption accounting overhead rates are set based on an overhead spending budget and the number of labor or machine hours expected to be incurred. Then on a month-by-month bases overhead is "absorbed" based on the actual hours "earned." If the number of hours earned is less that the budgeted hours, an unfavorable overhead volume variance is created.

Although most first-line supervisors may not understand the ins and outs of standard cost accounting, they quickly learn that unfavorable variances are bad and that unfavorable volume variances can be avoided by creating enough hours. Thus at the end of the month they search around to see what parts can be made that will create the largest number of hours, regardless of what MRP or any other schedule calls for. The problem is that there is no connection between hours and what the customer wants. The result — avoiding the unfavorable variance creates excess inventory.

The other significant problem with standard cost accounting is that it attempts to calculate individual product costs by allocating overhead costs based on hours. At a time when overhead was a fraction of direct labor cost, this was appropriate. However, because of the changing profile of costs, overhead has become a multiple of direct labor cost. Overhead rates between 200 percent and 400 percent of labor are not unusual. As an accountant I know that the amount of overhead allocated to various departments, and therefore to products, is dependant on the allocation methods I choose.

Choosing one method over another can make an individual product's cost vary significantly. And yet most companies believe they "know" their product costs — out to four decimal places — a classic case of confusing precision with accuracy. How many companies make decisions to discontinue a product because the accounting system makes it appear to be unprofitable? Or how many companies run end of quarter specials of those products that the accounting system reports as very profitable? If I were to choose different allocation methods, would the decisions be different?

If the standard cost P&L is not a useful management tool, can we create something that is? At Wiremold, we addressed this issue in the early 1990s and decided to use the following principles to guide us:

-Must be usable by non-accountants
-Must eliminate complexity in presentation
-Must have a higher degree of assignable costs and a lower degree of allocated costs
-Must include both financial and non-financial data
-Must motivate the right decisions.

Figure 3 shows an alternate presentation for the same company displaying information about the prime costs incurred. From this presentation we can see that the manufacturing group has actually done a pretty good job. Labor costs are down, as are services, supplies and scrap. Benefit costs clearly showed up as a problem in Figure 2, so I know that I have to address this.

The "bottom line" as to why gross profit did not increase as sales did, is that in our Lean implementation we have successfully reduced inventories. This has a negative impact on profits in the periods that we do this. Inventory turns have improved, as

Lean Manufacturing Cost Summary

	This Year	Last Year	+(-)%
Net Sales	100,000	90,000	11.1
Cost of Sales:			
Purchases	25,300	34,900	(25.7)
Inventory (Inc)/Dec: Mat'l Content	6000	(6000)	
Total Materials	31,300	28,900	8.3
Processing Costs:			
Factory Wages	11,000	11,500	(4.3)
Factory Salaries	2,100	2,000	5.0
Factory Benefits	7,000	5,000	40.0
Services & Support	2,200	2,500	(12.0)
Equipment Depreciation	2,000	1,900	5.3
Scrap	2,000	4,000	(50.0)
Total Processing Costs	26,300	26,900	(2.2)
Occupancy Costs:			
Building Depreciation	200	200	0.0
Building Services	2,200	2,000	10.0
Total Occupancy Costs	2,400	2,200	9.1
Total Manufacturing Costs	60,000	58,000	3.4
Inv, Inc/(Dec): Labor & OH Content	4,000	(4,000)	
Cost of Sales	64,000	54,000	18.5
Gross Profit	36,000	36,000	0.0
Gross Profit as a Percent of Sales	36.0%	40.0%	

(This example corresponds with that in Figure 2.)

Figure 3.

has cash flow, but the traditional standard cost statements lied to us. They told us something bad was happening.

Why is that? The item called "inventory" on the balance sheet is comprised of two things. The first is the material content of the entire inventory. This is what's physically there. The second element is deferred labor and overhead. This represents the cost incurred to produce inventory that we have not sold yet. When we do sell it these costs become a non-cash charge to profits in the period it is sold.

The alternate format P&L clearly shows this. The change in inventory has been displayed separately in its two elements. The material portion is netted against purchases, because as we consume the inventory we can reduce our purchases. The labor and overhead element is added to the total manufacturing costs and there is little, if any, offset. During the transition period there is little opportunity to temporarily reduce overhead until we normalize the inventory levels since most overhead is fixed.

Some would say that since we are not replenishing inventory at the rate it was sold during this period, we don't need all of the labor force. However, we must also insure that our human resource policies support the Lean strategy. Companies that successfully implement Lean quickly learn that most of the good ideas for productivity improvements come from the people doing the work. They know where the problems

are and in most cases have good ideas as to how to correct them.

But people will not work themselves out of a job, so in order to get significant productivity gains over the long haul the workforce must be given a qualified employment guarantee. This generally takes the form of a statement such as "No one will lose employment as a result of productivity gains." Therefore through this inventory transition period the only "relief" that can be obtained regarding labor costs is through reduced overtime and natural attrition. What do you do with the "excess" labor? Training, kaizens, aggressive implementation of the 5 Ss, insourcing from suppliers ...

Cash Flow Tells the Tale

Almost anyone in accounting and finance can follow an argument based on cash flow, and as previously mentioned; even though this company did not report increased profits it improved its cash position. Figure 4 shows cash generated from manufacturing for the last two years. Because of the improvement in inventory turns in this example, cash generated from manufacturing improved in excess of 23 percent. In order to estimate in advance the amount of cash that can be freed up from inventory we believe that companies that successfully implement Lean should be able to double their inventory turns in two years and quadruple them in four years.

Investment Management

The last dimension in transforming accounting to support the Lean enterprise is rethinking investment management. In most companies "investment management" makes people think of capital expenditures. In the Lean environment it takes on a broader definition. For example, most companies don't "plan" working capital. In the Lean business you should, month-by-month. Improving inventory turns is not something that should happen at the end of the year so as to make the metrics look good. It needs to happen continuously throughout the year, because in addition to

Comparison of Cash Flow from Manufacturing

	This Year	Last Year
Gross Profit	36,000	36,000
Equipment Depreciation	2,000	1,900
Building Depreciation	200	200
Change: Labor & OH in Inventory	4000	(4000)
Total Cash Flow from Manufacturing	42,000	34,100

Figure 4.

freeing up cash, it frees up lots of space, which accelerates the Lean transformation.

In addition to working capital, the investment plan should consider the number of people employed. We have been conditioned to think of people as expense, since that's how we account for them. But if we think of them as investments we change our behavior.

In the current economic environment most companies certainly have placed severe restrictions on hiring. But in good times it is relatively easy to "justify" an additional staffing position. If that position becomes a permanent addition to the company's infrastructure then we have made an investment.

Suppose the wage and benefit cost of that new position is $50,000. Then over a 30-year career, using an 8% discount rate, that position has a present value of $563,000. In your company, what type of justification do you have to go through to buy a half-million dollar machine?

We look at people as part of our infrastructure. When we consider the lifetime cost of each person, it becomes apparent that as we implement Lean and attrition takes place, we have to be very reluctant to replace that attrition. That's how the productivity gains that we achieve become actualized.

Becoming Lean also changes the way we look at capital spending. The first principle is "creativity before capital." For example, in the traditional environment when we talked about reducing machine setup time the engineers started talking about how much they would have to spend to achieve it. In the kaizen environment we learned that we could reduce setup times by 90 to 95 percent with a five-day kaizen event with no capital spending.

We also learned that full automation is expensive and tends to create a production environment with little flexibility. However, semi-automation (letting the machine do machine work and people do people work) costs a tiny fraction of full automation, plus it creates much more flexibility. The payoff from flexibility is great because operating conditions, customer demand, and products are always changing.

Therefore, in the capital justification process we have to consider factors that may not be easily quantified. These include improvements in flexibility, quality, throughput, delivery, etc. In addition, in the justification process we should allow a direct offset for a permanent reduction in inventory. After all, if a particular capital expenditure can lead to a permanent reduction in inventory we are just trading one asset for another. Which is better ... inventory that can become obsolete or damaged, or plant capacity that is flexible enough to respond to changing customer demand on a timely basis?

Communicating the Change

We may all agree that transforming the value delivery process to Lean will yield significant benefits and recognize that it is a business strategy and not just some manufacturing tactic. However we have an unavoidable earnings problem to explain. As we bring inventories down, we create a negative charge to current income. How do we deal with that?

The answer is communication, and lots of it. We need to communicate with each of the stakeholders in the enterprise to insure that each one understands the benefits, and effect, on them. This includes employees, unions, suppliers, and eventually customers.

We need to communicate the purposes and logic of the accounting changes with auditors, banks, the board of directors, and shareholders. We need to communicate with the auditors because changing the business and accounting systems will have an effect on their audit plan. Waiting until they arrive on the scene to commence the audit can only cause confusion, and extra audit hours. That can be avoided if auditors are included in the discussions along the way.

If we have financial covenants that are stated in conventional terms (such as working capital ratio of 2 to 1) we may need to start a dialogue with our banks to modify them. Boards of directors and shareholders need to be educated about the benefits of Lean and also of the short-term effect of reducing inventories on reported profits. If the short-term positive cash flow is shown side by side with the negative profit effects, the complete picture can be seen. It's possible to do; I've done it.

If the company is publicly traded, communicating with shareholders at this level of detail may be difficult so the target audience should be the analysts that follow the company's stock. They need to be educated in Lean and helped to understand all of its implications. And having them participate in a kaizen event probably wouldn't hurt.

Get Your Accounting Team on Board

What are the first steps to take to prevent the accounting team from becoming a barrier to the Lean transformation? The first steps are education and participation. The accounting team must be included in all of the Lean education offered to operating employees. And they must participate in shop floor kaizens. They cannot be allowed to opt out. Only by doing so will they gain a full appreciation of the implications of Lean on the economics of the business and on the accounting systems. In this way they can become a full partner in the transformation process and not just bystanders throwing hand grenades of misinformation.

Orry Fiume recently retired as vice president finance and administration from The Wiremold Company.

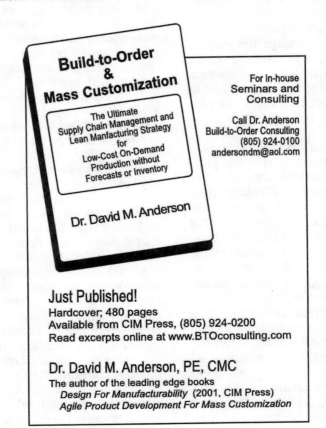